Fodor's 98

California

The complete guide, thoroughly up-to-date

Packed with details that will make your trip

The must-see sights, off and on the beaten path

What to see, what to skip

Mix-and-match vacation itineraries

City strolls, countryside adventures

Smart lodging and dining options

Essential local do's and taboos

Transportation tips, distances and directions

Key contacts, savvy travel tips

When to go, what to pack

Clear, accurate, easy-to-use maps

Fodor's Travel Publications, Inc.
New York • Toronto • London • Sydney • Auckland
www.fodors.com/

Fodor's California

EDITOR: Daniel Mangin

Editorial Contributors: Dianne Aaronson, Colleen Dunn Bates, Vince Bielski, Julie Bourland, David Brown, Deke Castleman, Lori Chamberlain, Shane Christensen, Kate Deely, Jeanne Fay, Claudia Gioseffi, Therese Iknoian, Edie Jarolim, Christina Knight, Stacey Kulig, Kristina Malsberger, Amy McConnell, Ellen Melinkoff, Maribeth Mellin, Rebecca Miller, Andy Moore, Clark Norton, Marty Olmstead, Tracy Patruno, Cynthia Queen, Tina Rubin, Heidi Sarna, Helayne Schiff, M. T. Schwartzman (Gold Guide editor), Kathryn Shevelow, Sharon Silva, Julene Snyder, Dinah A. Spritzer, Sharron Wood, Bobbi Zane

Editorial Production: Janet Foley

Maps: David Lindroth, *cartographer*; Steven K. Amsterdam, *map editor*

Design: Fabrizio La Rocca, *creative director*; Guido Caroti, *associate art director*; Jolie Novak, *photo editor*

Production/Manufacturing: Robert B. Shields

Cover Photograph: Catherine Karnow/Woodfin Camp

Copyright

Special Sales

CONTENTS

Contents

Maps

ON THE ROAD WITH FODOR'S

WE'RE ALWAYS THRILLED to get letters from readers, especially one like this:

It took us an hour to decide what book to buy and we now know we picked the best one. Your book was wonderful, easy to follow, very accurate, and good on pointing out eating places, informal as well as formal. When we saw other people using your book, we would look at each other and smile.

Our editors and writers are deeply committed to making every Fodor's guide "the best one"—not only accurate but always charming, brimming with sound recommendations and solid ideas, right on the mark in describing restaurants and hotels, and full of fascinating facts that make you view what you've traveled to see in a rich new light.

About Our Writers

Our success in achieving our goals—and in helping to make your trip the best of all possible vacations—is a credit to the hard work of our contributors.

Dianne Aaronson moved to Singapore after filing her final revision of the Mojave Desert and Death Valley chapter. Dianne, who has written health and fitness articles for San Francisco Bay Area and other publications, has contributed to other Fodor's guides, including *San Francisco '96* and *'97* and *California's Best Bed & Breakfasts*. **Julie Bourland,** an avid hiker who updated the Sierra National Parks chapter, is an associate editor at *Parenting* magazine. **Deke Castleman,** who updated the Lake Tahoe chapter, grew up in New York and Boston but fled the East Coast for the wide-open spaces of the American West. He discovered the region's many wonders while engaged in a variety of occupations—door-to-door vacuum-cleaner salesman in central California, tour guide at Alaska's Denali National Park, and locksmith on Lake Tahoe's north shore.

Claudia Gioseffi, who updated the Wine Country and Monterey Bay chapters, brings an art, food, and wine background to *California '98*. The author of an ongoing series of artist profiles for Caldwell Snyder Galleries of New York and San Francisco, Claudia has contributed to *Country Bed & Breakfast Inns,* the *Epicurean Rendezvous* guides, and other publications. **Andy Moore** was born across the street from Disney Studios near beautiful downtown Burbank. His childhood included many family vacations throughout the Golden State, including gold panning expeditions with his grandfather, memories he relived while updating the Sacramento and the Gold Country chapter. **Clark Norton,** author of Fodor's *Where Do We Take the Kids? California* guide, wrote a new San Joaquin Valley chapter for *California '98*. The recipient of several major travel-writing awards, Clark has written about traveling with children for *Parenting, Family Fun, California Travel Ideas, Baby Talk,* and the *San Francisco Examiner.*

Marty Olmstead, who revised the North Coast and Far North chapters, is the former travel editor of *San Francisco Focus* magazine, for which she crisscrossed the state many times. Accounts of her voyages around the globe have appeared in *Travel and Leisure,* the *Los Angeles Times, Geo, Glamour,* and the *San Francisco Chronicle.* Since 1989 she has lived in Sonoma County, which she "appreciates for its role in California's history and its proximity to grapes—the North Coast's most famous (legal) crop." **Bobbi Zane,** who revised the Palm Springs chapter and wrote the Sacramento and the Gold Country chapter, has been visiting the state's southern desert region since her grandfather, a Hollywood producer, took her on weekend getaways to La Quinta Resort. She returns to the area yearly. She has contributed to *California's Best Bed & Breakfasts* and *San Diego '98* among many other Fodor's titles. With her husband, Gregg, she publishes *Yellow Brick Road,* a monthly newsletter about bed-and-breakfast inns.

Daniel Mangin, the editor of *California '98,* moved to New York to work as a senior editor at Fodor's after spending 20 years in the Golden State, most of them in San Francisco. He first traversed California as the stage manager and lighting director of two '70s punk rock bands, one of which, he reminisces, "hit just short of the big time. One year we stayed at low-budget motels, the next year it was four-star hotels with private butlers and antique furniture (we were well-behaved rockers). The experience taught me what travelers of all budgets need and expect." Daniel co-authored *Fodor's Sunday in San Francisco*. Fodor's guides he has edited include *California's Best Bed & Breakfasts, San Diego '98, Seattle & Vancouver '98, Turkey,* and three West Coast–oriented gay guides—to Los Angeles, the Bay Area, and the Pacific Northwest.

New This Year

Clark Norton drove up and down Highway 99 to research *California '98*'s new San Joaquin Valley chapter, inspecting restaurants, motels, and small inns and visiting what some readers may find to be a surprising number of attractions in the agricultural heartland of California. One of Clark's favorites was the Colonel Allensworth State Historic Park 40 mi southwest of Visalia. The park is on the site of the only California town settled, governed, and financed by African-Americans.

Also new this year are revised walking and driving tours of San Francisco, Los Angeles, and San Diego; additional coverage of San Jose, and new dining and lodging selections in Palm Springs.

And this year, Fodor's joins Rand McNally, the world's largest commercial mapmaker, to bring you a detailed color map of California. Just detach it along the perforation and carry it along on your travels.

We're also proud to announce that the American Society of Travel Agents has endorsed Fodor's as its guidebook of choice. ASTA is the world's largest and most influential travel trade association, operating in more than 170 countries, with 27,000 members pledged to adhere to a strict code of ethics reflecting the Society's motto, "Integrity in Travel." ASTA shares Fodor's devotion to providing smart, honest travel information and advice to travelers, and we've long recommended that our readers consult ASTA member agents for the experience and professionalism they bring to the table.

On the Web, check out Fodor's site (www.fodors.com/) for information on major destinations around the world and travel-savvy interactive features. The Web site also lists the 80-plus radio stations nationwide that carry the Fodor's Travel Show, a live call-in program that airs every weekend. Tune in to hear guests discuss their adventures—or call in to get answers for your most pressing travel questions.

How to Use This Book

Organization

Up front is the **Gold Guide,** an easy-to-use section divided alphabetically by topic. Under each listing you'll find tips and information that will help you move through California. You'll also find addresses and telephone numbers of organizations and companies that offer destination-related services and detailed information and publications.

The first chapter in the guide, Destination: California, helps get you in the mood for your trip. New and Noteworthy cues you in on trends and happenings, What's Where gets you oriented, Pleasures and Pastimes describes the activities and sights that make California unique, Fodor's Choice showcases our top picks, and Festivals and Seasonal Events alerts you to special events.

Each city chapter in *California '98* begins with an Exploring section, which is subdivided by neighborhood; each subsection recommends a walking or driving tour and lists sights in alphabetical order. Dining, lodging, nightlife and the arts, outdoor activities and sports, and shopping sections follow the exploring tours.

Each regional chapter is divided by geographical area; within each area, towns are covered in logical geographical order, and attractive stretches of road and minor points of interest between them are indicated by the designation *En Route*. And within town sections, all restaurants and lodgings are grouped together.

To help you decide what to visit in the time you have, all chapters begin with recommended itineraries; you can mix and match those from several chapters to create a complete vacation. The A-to-Z section that ends all chapters covers getting there and getting around. It also provides helpful contacts and resources.

Icons and Symbols

★   Our special recommendations
✕   Restaurant
🏠   Lodging establishment
✕🏠   Lodging establishment whose restaurant warrants a special trip
⚠   Campgrounds
☕   Good for kids (rubber duckie)
☞   Sends you to another section of the guide for more information
✉   Address
☎   Telephone number
🕐   Opening and closing times
💰   Admission prices (those we give apply to adults; substantially reduced fees are almost always available for children, students, and senior citizens)

Numbers in white and black circles that appear on the maps, in the margins, and within the tours correspond to one another.

Dining and Lodging

The restaurants and lodgings we list are the cream of the crop in each price range. In the city chapters, price charts appear before the first restaurant listing. In regional chapters, you'll find the charts in the Pleasures and Pastimes section that follows the chapter introduction. Assume that the restaurants listed serve lunch and dinner daily unless otherwise noted.

Hotel Facilities

We always list the facilities that are available—but we don't specify whether they cost extra: When pricing accommodations, always ask what's included. Unless otherwise noted, assume that all rooms have private baths and that rates do not include any meals.

Restaurant Reservations and Dress Codes

Reservations are always a good idea; we note only when they're essential or when they are not accepted. Book as far ahead as you can, and reconfirm when you get to town. Unless otherwise noted, the restaurants listed are open daily for lunch and dinner. We mention dress only when men are required to wear a jacket or a jacket and tie.

Credit Cards

The following abbreviations are used: **AE,** American Express; **D,** Discover; **DC,** Diners Club; **MC,** MasterCard; and **V,** Visa.

Please Write to Us

You can use this book in the confidence that all prices and opening times are based on information supplied to us at press time; Fodor's cannot accept responsibility for any errors. Time inevitably brings changes, so always confirm information when it matters—especially if you're making a detour to visit a specific place. In addition, when making reservations be sure to mention if you have a disability or are traveling with children, if you prefer a private bath or a certain type of bed, or if you have specific dietary needs or other concerns.

Were the restaurants we recommended as described? Did our hotel picks exceed your expectations? Did you find a museum we recommended a waste of time? If you have complaints, we'll look into them and revise our entries when the facts warrant it. If you've discovered a special place that we haven't included, we'll pass the information along to our correspondents and have them check it out. So send us your feedback, positive and negative: email us at editors@fodors.com (specifying the name of the book on the subject line) or write the California editor at Fodor's, 201 East 50th Street, New York, New York 10022. Have a wonderful trip!

Karen Cure

Karen Cure
Editorial Director

Northern California

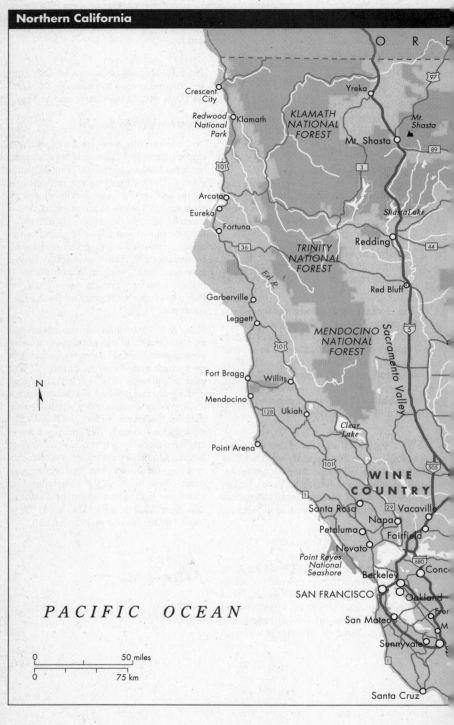

PACIFIC OCEAN

Crescent
City

Redwood
National
Park

Klamath

Arcata

Eureka

Fortuna

Garberville

Leggett

Fort Bragg

Mendocino

Point Arena

Willits

Ukiah

KLAMATH
NATIONAL
FOREST

Yreka

Mt.
Shasta

Mt. Shasta

Shasta Lake

Redding

TRINITY
NATIONAL
FOREST

Eel R.

MENDOCINO
NATIONAL
FOREST

Red Bluff

Sacramento Valley

Clear
Lake

Santa Rosa

Petaluma

Novato

Point Reyes
National
Seashore

SAN FRANCISCO

San Mateo

Berkeley

Oakland

Sunnyvale

Santa Cruz

Napa

Fairfield

Vacaville

WINE
COUNTRY

Conc

Frer

M

O R E

97

89

3

44

5

101

36

101

128

1

101

505

29

680

1

N

0   50 miles
0   75 km

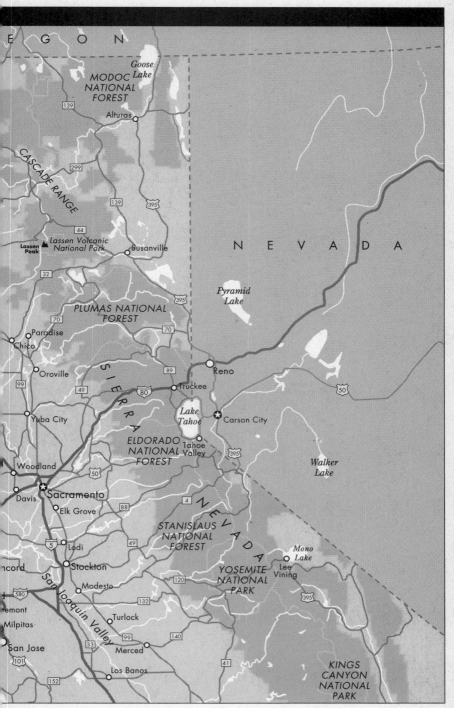

OREGON

Goose Lake

MODOC NATIONAL FOREST

[139] Alturas

CASCADE RANGE

[299]

[139] [395]

[44]

Lassen Peak ▲ Lassen Volcanic National Park

Susanville

NEVADA

[32]

PLUMAS NATIONAL FOREST

[70]

Paradise

Chico

[395]

Pyramid Lake

[70]

S I E R R A

[89]

Reno

Truckee

Oroville

[99] [49] [80]

[50]

Yuba City

Lake Tahoe

Carson City

ELDORADO NATIONAL FOREST

Tahoe Valley

[395]

Woodland

[50]

Walker Lake

Davis

Sacramento

[4]

N E V A D A

Elk Grove

[88]

[5] Lodi

STANISLAUS NATIONAL FOREST

[49]

Mono Lake

ncord

Stockton

Lee Vining

Modesto

[120]

YOSEMITE NATIONAL PARK

[395]

[580]

[132]

emont

Turlock

Milpitas

[33] [99]

[140]

San Jose

Merced

San Joaquin Valley

[101]

Los Banos

[41]

[152]

KINGS CANYON NATIONAL PARK

Southern California

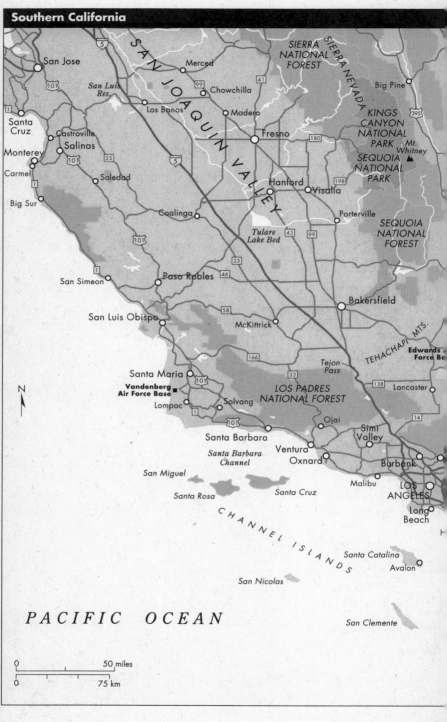

PACIFIC OCEAN

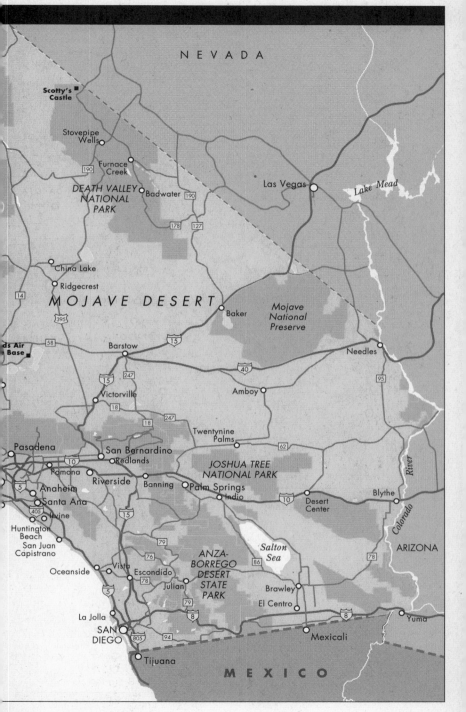

NEVADA

Scotty's Castle ■

Stovepipe Wells

[190] Furnace Creek

DEATH VALLEY NATIONAL PARK

Badwater [190]

Las Vegas

Lake Mead

[178] [127]

China Lake

Ridgecrest

MOJAVE DESERT

[14]

[395]

Baker

Mojave National Preserve

ds Air ■ Base

[58]

Barstow

[15]

[40]

Needles

[95]

[15] [247]

Victorville

Amboy

[18]

[18] [247]

Twentynine Palms

Pasadena

San Bernardino

[62]

Colorado River

[10]

Redlands

JOSHUA TREE NATIONAL PARK

Pomona

Riverside

Banning

Palm Springs

[10]

Desert Center

Blythe

Anaheim

Santa Ana

Indio

[405]

Irvine

[15]

Huntington Beach

San Juan Capistrano

[79]

ANZA-BORREGO DESERT STATE PARK

Salton Sea

ARIZONA

[78]

Oceanside

Vista

[76]

Escondido

[78]

Julian

[86]

Brawley

[5]

Vista

La Jolla

[79]

El Centro

[8]

[8]

Yuma

SAN DIEGO

[805]

[94]

Mexicali

Tijuana

MEXICO

The United States

CANADA

BRITISH COLUMBIA
ALBERTA
SASKATCHEWAN
MANITOBA

Vancouver
Victoria
Calgary
Regina
Winnipeg

Seattle
Olympia
WASHINGTON
Spokane
Trans-Canada Hwy.

Portland
Salem
Columbia R.
Great Falls
Missouri R.
NORTH DAKOTA
Fargo
Bismarck

OREGON
IDAHO
MONTANA
Helena
Billings
SOUTH DAKOTA
Pierre
Missouri R.

Boise
Snake R.
WYOMING

Carson City
Sacramento
San Francisco
Fresno
NEVADA
Salt Lake City
UTAH
Cheyenne
NEBRASKA
Lincoln

Las Vegas
Colorado R.
Denver
Colorado Springs
COLORADO
KANSAS

Santa Barbara
Los Angeles
San Diego
CALIFORNIA
Flagstaff
Santa Fe
Albuquerque
Amarillo
OKLAHOMA
Oklahoma City

PACIFIC OCEAN
BAJA CALIFORNIA
SONORA
ARIZONA
Phoenix
Tucson
NEW MEXICO
El Paso
Rio Grande
DALLAS

CHIHUAHUA
TEXAS
Austin
San Antonio

MEXICO
COAHUILA
NUEVO LEON
TAM-AULIPAS

RUSSIA
ARCTIC OCEAN
Bering Strait
Bering Sea
Nome
ALASKA
Fairbanks
CANADA

ALEUTIAN ISLANDS
Anchorage
Juneau

PACIFIC OCEAN

0   400 miles
0   400 km
N

Honolulu
Oahu
Maui
HAWAII
Hawaii
PACIFIC OCEAN

World Time Zones

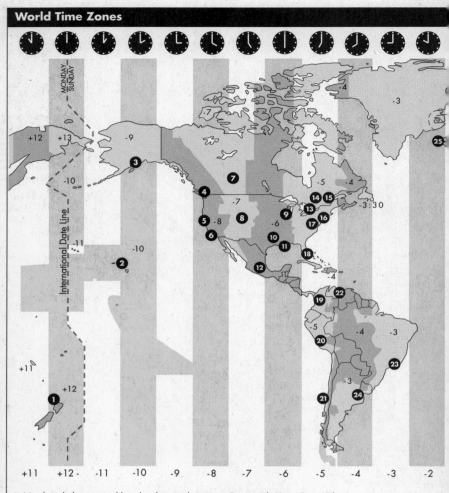

Numbers below vertical bands relate each zone to Greenwich Mean Time (0 hrs.).
Local times frequently differ from these general indications,
as indicated by light-face numbers on map.

Algiers, **29**
Anchorage, **3**
Athens, **41**
Auckland, **1**
Baghdad, **46**
Bangkok, **50**
Beijing, **54**

Berlin, **34**
Bogotá, **19**
Budapest, **37**
Buenos Aires, **24**
Caracas, **22**
Chicago, **9**
Copenhagen, **33**
Dallas, **10**

Delhi, **48**
Denver, **8**
Djakarta, **53**
Dublin, **26**
Edmonton, **7**
Hong Kong, **56**
Honolulu, **2**

Istanbul, **40**
Jerusalem, **42**
Johannesburg, **44**
Lima, **20**
Lisbon, **28**
London
(Greenwich), **27**
Los Angeles, **6**
Madrid, **38**
Manila, **57**

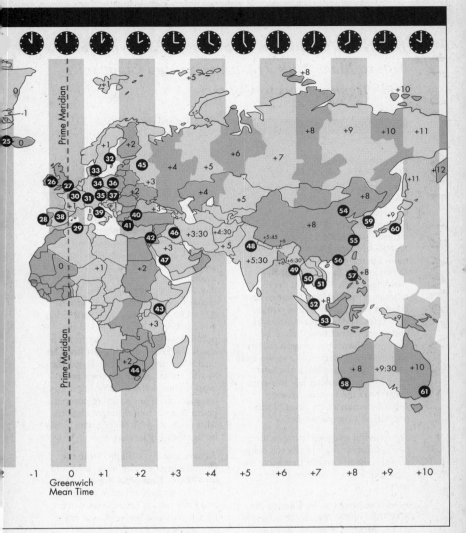

Mecca, **47**
Mexico City, **12**
Miami, **18**
Montréal, **15**
Moscow, **45**
Nairobi, **43**
New Orleans, **11**
New York City, **16**

Ottawa, **14**
Paris, **30**
Perth, **58**
Reykjavík, **25**
Rio de Janeiro, **23**
Rome, **39**
Saigon (Ho Chi Minh City), **51**

San Francisco, **5**
Santiago, **21**
Seoul, **59**
Shanghai, **55**
Singapore, **52**
Stockholm, **32**
Sydney, **61**
Tokyo, **60**

Toronto, **13**
Vancouver, **4**
Vienna, **35**
Warsaw, **36**
Washington, D.C., **17**
Yangon, **49**
Zürich, **31**

SMART TRAVEL TIPS

THE GOLD GUIDE / SMART TRAVEL TIPS

SMART TRAVEL TIPS A TO Z

Basic Information on Traveling in California, Savvy Tips to Make Your Trip a Breeze, and Companies and Organizations to Contact

A
AIR TRAVEL

MAJOR AIRLINE OR LOW-COST CARRIER?

Most people choose a flight based on price. Yet there are other issues to consider. Major airlines offer the greatest number of departures; smaller airlines—including regional, low-cost and no-frill airlines—usually have a more limited number of flights daily. Major airlines have frequent-flyer partners, which allow you to credit mileage earned on one airline to your account with another. Low-cost airlines offer a definite price advantage and fewer restrictions, such as advance-purchase requirements. Safety-wise, low-cost carriers as a group have a good history, but check the safety record before booking any low-cost carrier; call the Federal Aviation Administration's Consumer Hotline (☞ Airline Complaints, *below*).

See Arriving and Departing *in* the A to Z section at the end of each chapter for a list of carriers that serve the region or regions covered in the chapter.

➤ MAJOR AIRLINES: **Air Canada** (☎ 800/776–3000). **Alaska** (☎ 800/426–0333). **America West** (☎ 800/235–9292). **American** (☎ 800/433–7300). **British Airways** (☎ 800/247–9297). **Continental** (☎ 800/231–0856). **Delta** (☎ 800/241–4141). **Japan Air Lines** (☎ 800/525–3663). **Northwest** (☎ 800/225–2525). **TWA** (☎ 800/892–4141). **United** (☎ 800/241–6522). **US Airways** (☎ 800/428–4322).

➤ SMALLER AIRLINES: **Carnival Air Lines** (☎ 800/824–7386). **Midwest Express** (☎ 800/452–2022). **Reno Air** (☎ 800/736–6247). **Skywest** (☎ 800/453–9417). **Southwest** (☎ 800/435–9792).

➤ FROM THE U.K.: **American** (☎ 0345/789–789). **British Airways** (☎ 0345/222–111). **Delta** (☎ 0800/414–767). **United** (☎ 0800/888–555). **Virgin Atlantic** (☎ 01293/747–747).

GET THE LOWEST FARE

The least-expensive airfares to California are priced for round-trip travel. Major airlines usually require that you **book in advance and buy the ticket within 24 hours**, and you may have to **stay over a Saturday night.** It's smart to **call a number of airlines, and when you are quoted a good price, book it on the spot**—the same fare may not be available on the same flight the next day. Airlines generally allow you to change your return date for a fee of $25–$50. If you don't use your ticket you can apply the cost toward the purchase of a new ticket, again for a small charge. However, most low-fare tickets are nonrefundable. To get the lowest airfare, **check different routings.** If your destination or home city has more than one gateway, compare prices to and from different airports. Also price off-peak flights, which may be significantly less expensive.

To save money on flights from the United Kingdom and back, **look into an APEX or Super-PEX ticket.** APEX tickets must be booked in advance and have certain restrictions. Super-PEX tickets can be purchased at the airport on the day of departure—subject to availability.

DON'T STOP UNLESS YOU MUST

When you book, **look for nonstop flights** and **remember that "direct" flights stop at least once.** Try to **avoid connecting flights,** which require a change of plane. Two airlines may jointly operate a connecting flight, so ask if your airline operates every segment—you may find that your preferred carrier flies you only part of the way.

USE AN AGENT

Travel agents, especially those who specialize in finding the lowest fares (☞ Discounts & Deals, *below*), can be especially helpful when booking a plane ticket. When you're quoted a price, **ask your agent if the price is likely to get any lower.** Good agents know the seasonal fluctuations of airfares and can usually anticipate a sale or fare war. However, waiting can be risky: The fare could go *up* as seats become scarce, and you may wait so long that your preferred flight sells out. A wait-and-see strategy works best if your plans are flexible, but if you must arrive and depart on certain dates, don't delay.

AVOID GETTING BUMPED

Airlines routinely overbook planes, knowing that not everyone with a ticket will show up, but sometimes everyone does. When that happens, airlines ask for volunteers to give up their seats. In return these volunteers usually get a certificate for a free flight and are rebooked on the next flight out. If there are not enough volunteers the airline must choose who will be denied boarding. The first to get bumped are passengers who checked in late and those flying on discounted tickets, **so get to the gate and check in as early as possible,** especially during peak periods.

Always **bring a photo ID to the airport.** You may be asked to show it before you are allowed to check in.

ENJOY THE FLIGHT

For better service, **fly smaller or regional carriers,** which often have higher passenger-satisfaction ratings. Sometimes you'll find leather seats, more legroom, and better food.

For more legroom, **request an emergency-aisle seat;** don't however, sit in the row in front of the emergency aisle or in front of a bulkhead, where seats may not recline.

If you don't like airline food, **ask for special meals when booking.** These can be vegetarian, low-cholesterol, or kosher, for example.

To avoid jet lag try to maintain a normal routine while traveling. **Eat light meals, drink water (not alcohol), and move about the cabin** to stretch your legs.

COMPLAIN IF NECESSARY

If your baggage goes astray or your flight goes awry, complain right away.

Most carriers require that you file a claim immediately.

➤ AIRLINE COMPLAINTS: U.S. Department of Transportation **Aviation Consumer Protection Division** (✉ C-75, Washington, DC 20590, ☎ 202/366–2220). Federal Aviation Administration **(FAA) Consumer Hotline** (☎ 800/322–7873).

AIRPORTS

Major gateways to California are Los Angeles International Airport, San Francisco International Airport, and San Diego International Airport Lindbergh Field. Flying time is roughly five hours from New York and four hours from Chicago. Flying between San Francisco and Los Angeles takes one hour.

➤ AIRPORT INFORMATION: **Los Angeles International Airport** (☎ 310/646–5252). **San Diego International Airport Lindbergh Field** (☎ 619/231–2100). **San Francisco International Airport** (☎ 650/761–0800).

B

BUS TRAVEL

Greyhound (☎ 800/231–2222).

C

CAMERAS, CAMCORDERS, & COMPUTERS

Always **keep your film, tape, or computer disks out of the sun.** Carry an extra supply of batteries, and **be prepared to turn on your camera, camcorder, or laptop** to prove to security personnel that the device is real. Always **ask for hand inspection of film,** which becomes clouded after successive exposure to airport x-ray machines, and **keep videotapes and computer disks away from metal detectors.**

➤ PHOTO HELP: Kodak Information Center (☎ 800/242–2424). *Kodak Guide to Shooting Great Travel Pictures,* available in bookstores or from Fodor's Travel Publications (☎ 800/533–6478); $16.50 plus $4 shipping.

CAR RENTAL

Rates in Los Angeles begin at around $28 a day and $140 a week. This does not include tax on car rentals, which is 8¾%. In San Diego, rates for an economy car with unlimited mileage begin around $23 a day and $137 a week. This does not include tax on car rentals, which is 7¾%. In San Francisco, rates begin around $38 a day and $138 a week. This does not include tax on car rentals, which is 8¼%.

➤ MAJOR AGENCIES: **Alamo** (☎ 800/ 327–9633; 0800/272–2000 in the U.K.). **Avis** (☎ 800/331–1212; 800/ 879–2847 in Canada). **Budget** (☎ 800/527–0700; 0800/181181 in the U.K.). **Dollar** (☎ 800/800–4000; 0990/565656 in the U.K., where it is known as Eurodollar). **Hertz** (☎ 800/654–3131; 800/263–0600 in Canada; 0345/555888 in the U.K.). **National InterRent** (☎ 800/227– 7368; 0345/222525 in the U.K., where it is known as Europcar Inter-Rent).

CUT COSTS

To get the best deal, **book through a travel agent who is willing to shop around.** When pricing cars, **ask about the location of the rental lot.** Some off-airport locations offer lower rates, and their lots are only minutes from the terminal via complimentary shuttle. You also may want to **price local car-rental companies,** whose rates may be lower still, although their service and maintenance may not be as good as those of a name-brand agency. Remember to ask about required deposits, cancellation penalties, and drop-off charges if you're planning to pick up the car in one city and leave it in another.

Also **ask your travel agent about a company's customer-service record.** How has it responded to late plane arrivals and vehicle mishaps? Are there often lines at the rental counter, and, if you're traveling during a holiday period, does a confirmed reservation guarantee you a car?

Be sure to **look into wholesalers,** companies that do not own fleets but rent in bulk from those that do and often offer better rates than traditional car-rental operations. Prices are best during off-peak periods.

➤ RENTAL WHOLESALERS: **Auto Europe** (☎ 207/842–2000 or 800/223–5555, FAX 800/235–6321). The **Kemwel**

Group (☎ 914/835–5555 or 800/ 678–0678, FAX 914/835–5126).

NEED INSURANCE?

When driving a rented car you are generally responsible for any damage to or loss of the vehicle. You also are liable for any property damage or personal injury that you may cause while driving. Before you rent, **see what coverage you already have** under the terms of your personal auto-insurance policy and credit cards.

For about $14 a day, rental companies sell protection, known as a collision- or loss-damage waiver (CDW or LDW) that eliminates your liability for damage to the car; it's always optional and should never be automatically added to your bill. Some states, including California, have capped the price of CDW and LDW.

In most states you don't need CDW if you have personal auto insurance or other liability insurance. However, **make sure you have enough coverage to pay for the car.** If you do not have auto insurance or an umbrella policy that covers damage to third parties, purchasing CDW or LDW is highly recommended.

BEWARE SURCHARGES

Before you pick up a car in one city and leave it in another, **ask about drop-off charges or one-way service fees,** which can be substantial. Note, too, that some rental agencies charge extra if you return the car before the time specified on your contract. To avoid a hefty refueling fee, **fill the tank just before you turn in the car,** but be aware that gas stations near the rental outlet may overcharge.

MEET THE REQUIREMENTS

In the United States you must be 21 to rent a car, and rates may be higher if you're under 25. You'll pay extra for child seats (about $3 per day), which are compulsory for children under five, and for additional drivers (about $2 per day). Residents of the United Kingdom will need a reservation voucher, a passport, a U.K. driver's license, and a travel policy that covers each driver in order to pick up a car.

CHILDREN & TRAVEL

CHILDREN IN CALIFORNIA

In many ways California is made to order for traveling with children: Kids love Disneyland, the San Diego Zoo, the Monterey Aquarium, the San Francisco cable cars, the city-owned gold mine in Placerville, and the caverns at Lake Shasta.

Be sure to plan ahead and **involve your youngsters** as you outline your trip. When packing, include things to keep them busy en route. On sightseeing days try to schedule activities of special interest to your children. If you are renting a car don't forget to **arrange for a car seat** when you reserve. Most hotels in California allow children under a certain age to stay in their parents' room at no extra charge, but others charge them as extra adults; be sure to **ask about the cutoff age for children's discounts.**

LOCAL INFORMATION

Consult Fodor's lively by-parents, for-parents **Where Should We Take the Kids? California** (available in bookstores, or ☎ 800/533–6478); $17.

FLYING

As a general rule, infants under two not occupying a seat fly free. If your children are two or older **ask about children's airfares.**

In general the adult baggage allowance applies to children paying half or more of the adult fare.

According to the FAA it's a good idea to use safety seats aloft for children weighing less than 40 pounds. Airlines, however, can set their own policies: U.S. carriers allow FAA-approved models but usually require that you buy a ticket, even if your child would otherwise ride free, since the seats must be strapped into regular seats. Airline rules vary regarding their use, so it's important to **check your airline's policy about using safety seats during takeoff and landing.** Safety seats cannot obstruct any of the other passengers in the row, so get an appropriate seat assignment as early as possible.

When making your reservation, **request children's meals or a free-standing bassinet** if you need them; the latter are available only to those seated at the bulkhead, where there's enough legroom. Remember, however, that bulkhead seats may not have their own overhead bins, and there's no storage space in front of you—a major inconvenience.

GROUP TRAVEL

If you're planning to take your kids on a tour, look for companies that specialize in family travel.

➤ FAMILY-FRIENDLY TOUR OPERATORS: **Rascals in Paradise** (✉ 650 5th St., Suite 505, San Francisco, CA 94107, ☎ 415/978–9800 or 800/872–7225, FAX 415/442–0289).

CONSUMER PROTECTION

Whenever possible, **pay with a major credit card** so you can cancel payment if there's a problem, provided that you can provide documentation. This is a good practice whether you're buying travel arrangements before your trip or shopping at your destination.

If you're doing business with a particular company for the first time, **contact your local Better Business Bureau and the attorney general's offices** in your state and the company's home state, as well. Have any complaints been filed?

Finally, if you're buying a package or tour, always **consider travel insurance** that includes default coverage (☞ Insurance, *below*).

➤ LOCAL BBBS: **Council of Better Business Bureaus** (✉ 4200 Wilson Blvd., Suite 800, Arlington, VA 22203, ☎ 703/276–0100, FAX 703/525–8277).

CUSTOMS & DUTIES

ENTERING THE U.S.

Visitors age 21 and over may import the following into the United States: 200 cigarettes or 50 cigars or 2 kilograms of tobacco, 1 liter of alcohol, and gifts worth $100. Prohibited items include meat products, seeds, plants, and fruits.

ENTERING CANADA

If you've been out of Canada for at least seven days you may bring in C$500 worth of goods duty-free. If you've been away for fewer than seven days but more than 48 hours, the duty-free allowance drops to

C$200; if your trip lasts 24–48 hours, the allowance is C$50. You may not pool allowances with family members. Goods claimed under the C$500 exemption may follow you by mail; those claimed under the lesser exemptions must accompany you.

Alcohol and tobacco products may be included in the seven-day and 48-hour exemptions but not in the 24-hour exemption. If you meet the age requirements of the province or territory through which you reenter Canada you may bring in, duty-free, 1.14 liters (40 imperial ounces) of wine or liquor or 24 12-ounce cans or bottles of beer or ale. If you are 16 or older you may bring in, duty-free, 200 cigarettes and 50 cigars; these items must accompany you.

You may send an unlimited number of gifts worth up to C$60 each duty-free to Canada. Label the package UNSOLICITED GIFT—VALUE UNDER $60. Alcohol and tobacco are excluded.

➤ INFORMATION: **Revenue Canada** (⊠ 2265 St. Laurent Blvd. S, Ottawa, Ontario K1G 4K3, ☎ 613/993–0534; 800/461–9999 in Canada).

ENTERING THE U.K.

From countries outside the European Union, including the United States, you may import, duty-free, 200 cigarettes or 50 cigars; 1 liter of spirits or 2 liters of fortified or sparkling wine or liqueurs; 2 liters of still table wine; 60 milliliters of perfume; 250 milliliters of toilet water; plus £136 worth of other goods, including gifts and souvenirs.

➤ INFORMATION: **HM Customs and Excise** (⊠ Dorset House, Stamford St., London SE1 9NG, ☎ 0171/202–4227).

D

DISABILITIES & ACCESSIBILITY

ACCESS IN CALIFORNIA

California is a national leader in making attractions and facilities accessible to people with disabilities. Since 1982 the state building code has required that all areas for public use be made accessible. State laws more than a decade old provide special privileges, such as license plates allowing special parking spaces, unlimited parking in time-limited spaces, and free parking in metered spaces. Insignia from states other than California are honored.

TIPS & HINTS

When discussing accessibility with an operator or reservationist, **ask hard questions.** Are there any stairs, inside or out? Are there grab bars next to the toilet and in the shower/tub? How wide is the doorway to the room? To the bathroom? For the most extensive facilities meeting the latest legal specifications, **opt for newer accommodations,** which are more likely to have been designed with access in mind. Older buildings or ships may offer more limited facilities. Be sure to **discuss your needs before booking.**

➤ COMPLAINTS: **Disability Rights Section** (⊠ U.S. Dept. of Justice, Box 66738, Washington, DC 20035-6738, ☎ 202/514–0301 or 800/514–0301, FAX 202/307–1198, TTY 202/514–0383 or 800/514–0383) for general complaints. **Aviation Consumer Protection Division** (☞ Air Travel, above) for airline-related problems. **Civil Rights Office** (⊠ U.S. Dept. of Transportation, Departmental Office of Civil Rights, S-30, 400 7th St. SW, Room 10215, Washington, DC 20590, ☎ 202/366–4648) for problems with surface transportation.

TRAVEL AGENCIES & TOUR OPERATORS

The Americans with Disabilities Act requires that travel firms serve the needs of all travelers, but some agencies and operators specialize in making travel arrangements for individuals and groups with disabilities.

➤ TRAVELERS WITH MOBILITY PROBLEMS: **Access Adventures** (⊠ 206 Chestnut Ridge Rd., Rochester, NY 14624, ☎ 716/889–9096), run by a former physical-rehabilitation counselor. **Hinsdale Travel Service** (⊠ 201 E. Ogden Ave., Suite 100, Hinsdale, IL 60521, ☎ 630/325–1335), a travel agency that benefits from the advice of wheelchair traveler Janice Perkins. **Wheelchair Journeys** (⊠ 16979 Redmond Way, Redmond, WA 98052, ☎ 425/885–2210 or 800/313–4751), for general travel arrangements.

➤ TRAVELERS WITH DEVELOPMENTAL DISABILITIES: **New Directions** (⊠ 5276 Hollister Ave., Suite 207, Santa Barbara, CA 93111, ☎ 805/967–2841, FAX 805/964–7344). **Sprout** (✉ 893 Amsterdam Ave., New York, NY 10025, ☎ 212/222–9575 or 888/222–9575, FAX 212/222–9768).

Be a smart shopper and **compare all your options before making a choice.** A plane ticket bought with a promotional coupon may not be cheaper than the least expensive fare from a discount ticket agency. For high-price travel purchases, such as packages or tours, keep in mind that what you get is just as important as what you save. Just because something is cheap doesn't mean it's a bargain.

LOOK IN YOUR WALLET

When you use your credit card to make travel purchases you may get free travel-accident insurance, collision-damage insurance, and medical or legal assistance, depending on the card and the bank that issued it. American Express, MasterCard, and Visa provide one or more of these services, so **get a copy of your credit card's travel-benefits policy.** If you are a member of the American Automobile Association (AAA) or an oil-company-sponsored road-assistance plan, always **ask hotel or car-rental reservationists about auto-club discounts.** Some clubs offer additional discounts on tours, cruises, or admission to attractions. And don't forget that auto-club membership entitles you to free maps and trip-planning services.

DIAL FOR DOLLARS

To save money, **look into "1-800" discount reservations services,** which use their buying power to get a better price on hotels, airline tickets, even car rentals. When booking a room, always **call the hotel's local toll-free number** (if one is available) rather than the central reservations number—you'll often get a better price. Always ask about special packages or corporate rates.

➤ AIRLINE TICKETS: ☎ 800/FLY–4–LESS. ☎ 800/FLY–ASAP.

➤ HOTEL ROOMS: **Accommodations Express** (☎ 800/444–7666). **Central Reservation Service (CRS)** (☎ 800/548–3311). **Hotel Reservations Network (HRN)** (☎ 800/964–6835).

Players Express Vacations (☎ 800/458–6161). **Quickbook** (☎ 800/789–9887). **RMC Travel** (☎ 800/245–5738). **Steigenberger Reservation Service** (☎ 800/223–5652).

SAVE ON COMBOS

Packages and guided tours can both save you money, but don't confuse the two. When you buy a package your travel remains independent, just as though you had planned and booked the trip yourself. Fly/drive packages, which combine airfare and car rental, are often a good deal.

JOIN A CLUB?

Many companies sell discounts in the form of travel clubs and coupon books, but these cost money. You must use participating advertisers to get a deal, and only after you recoup the initial membership cost or book price do you begin to save. If you plan to use the club or coupons frequently you may save considerably. Before signing up, find out what discounts you get for free.

➤ DISCOUNT CLUBS: **Entertainment Travel Editions** (✉ Box 1068, Trumbull, CT 06611, ☎ 800/445–4137); $28–$53, depending on destination. **Great American Traveler** (✉ Box 27965, Salt Lake City, UT 84127, ☎ 800/548–2812); $49.95 per year. **Moment's Notice Discount Travel Club** (✉ 7301 New Utrecht Ave., Brooklyn, NY 11204, ☎ 718/234–6295); $25 per year, single or family. **Privilege Card International** (✉ 201 E. Commerce St., Suite 198, Youngstown, OH 44503, ☎ 330/746–5211 or 800/236–9732); $74.95 per year. **Sears's Mature Outlook** (✉ Box 9390, Des Moines, IA 50306, ☎ 800/336–6330); $14.95 per year. **Travelers Advantage** (✉ CUC Travel Service, 3033 S. Parker Rd., Suite 1000, Aurora, CO 80014, ☎ 800/548–1116 or 800/648–4037); $49 per year, single or family. **Worldwide Discount Travel Club** (✉ 1674 Meridian Ave., Miami Beach, FL 33139, ☎ 305/534–2082); $50 per year family, $40 single.

G

San Francisco, Los Angeles, West Hollywood, San Diego, and Palm Springs are among the California cities with visible lesbian and gay communities.

LOCAL INFORMATION

Many California cities large and small have lesbian and gay publications available in sidewalk racks and at bars and other social spaces; most have extensive events and information listings.

➤ LOCAL PAPERS: **Bay Area Reporter** (✉ 395 9th St., San Francisco 94103, ☎ 415/861–5019). **Bottom Line** (✉ 1243 N. Gene Autry Trail, Suite 121, Palm Springs 92262, ☎ 619/323–0552). **Edge** (✉ 6434 Santa Monica Blvd., Los Angeles 90038, ☎ 213/962–6994). **Gay & Lesbian Times** (✉ 3911 Normal St., San Diego, 92103, ☎ 619/299–6397). **Mom Guess What Newspaper** (✉ 1725 L St., Sacramento 95814, ☎ 916/441–6397).

➤ SWITCHBOARDS AND HOT LINES: **Gay and Lesbian Community Services Center** (✉ 1625 N. Schrader Blvd., Los Angeles 90028, ☎ 213/993–7400). **Lambda Community Center** (✉ 919 20th St., Sacramento 95814, ☎ 916/442–0185). **Lesbian and Gay Men's Community Center** (✉ 3916 Normal St., San Diego 92103, ☎ 619/692–4297). **Pacific Center Lesbian, Gay and Bisexual Switchboard** (☎ 510/841–6224).

➤ GAY- AND LESBIAN-FRIENDLY TRAVEL AGENCIES: **Advance Damron** (✉ 1 Greenway Plaza, Suite 800, Houston, TX 77046, ☎ 713/682–2002 or 800/695–0880, FAX 713/888–1010). **Club Travel** (✉ 8739 Santa Monica Blvd., West Hollywood, CA 90069, ☎ 310/358–2200 or 800/429–8747, FAX 310/358–2222). **Islanders/Kennedy Travel** (✉ 183 W. 10th St., New York, NY 10014, ☎ 212/242–3222 or 800/988–1181, FAX 212/929–8530). **Now Voyager** (✉ 4406 18th St., San Francisco, CA 94114, ☎ 415/626–1169 or 800/255–6951, FAX 415/626–8626). **Yellowbrick Road** (✉ 1500 W. Balmoral Ave., Chicago, IL 60640, ☎ 773/561–1800 or 800/642–2488, FAX 773/561–4497). **Skylink Women's Travel** (✉ 3577 Moorland Ave., Santa Rosa, CA 95407, ☎ 707/585–8355 or 800/225–5759, FAX 707/584–5637), serving lesbian travelers.

H

HEALTH

DIVERS' ALERT

Do not fly within 24 hours of scuba diving.

I

INSURANCE

Travel insurance is the best way to **protect yourself against financial loss.** The most useful policies are trip-cancellation-and-interruption, default, medical, and comprehensive insurance.

Without insurance you will lose all or most of your money if you cancel your trip, regardless of the reason. It's essential that you **buy trip-cancellation-and-interruption insurance,** particularly if your airline ticket, cruise, or package tour is nonrefundable and cannot be changed. When considering how much coverage you need, look for a policy that will cover the cost of your trip plus the nondiscounted price of a one-way airline ticket, should you need to return home early. Also **consider default or bankruptcy insurance,** which protects you against a supplier's failure to deliver.

Citizens of the United Kingdom can buy an annual travel-insurance policy valid for most vacations during the year in which it's purchased. If you are pregnant or have a preexisting medical condition, make sure you're covered. According to the Association of British Insurers, a trade association representing 450 insurance companies, it's wise to buy extra medical coverage when you visit the United States.

If you have purchased an expensive vacation, comprehensive insurance is a must. **Look for comprehensive policies that include trip-delay insurance,** which will protect you in the event that weather problems cause you to miss your flight, tour, or cruise. A few insurers sell waivers for preexisting medical conditions. Companies that offer both features include Access America, Carefree Travel, Travel Insured International, and Travel Guard (☞ *below*).

Always **buy travel insurance directly from the insurance company;** if you buy it from a travel agency or tour operator that goes out of business you probably will not be covered for the agency or operator's default, a major risk. Before you make any purchase, **review your existing health and home-owner's policies** to find out whether they cover expenses incurred while traveling.

➤ TRAVEL INSURERS: In the United States, **Access America** (✉ 6600 W. Broad St., Richmond, VA 23230, ☎ 804/285–3300 or 800/284–8300), **Carefree Travel Insurance** (✉ Box 9366, 100 Garden City Plaza, Garden City, NY 11530, ☎ 516/294–0220 or 800/323–3149), **Near Travel Services** (✉ Box 1339, Calumet City, IL 60409, ☎ 708/868–6700 or 800/654–6700), **Travel Guard International** (✉ 1145 Clark St., Stevens Point, WI 54481, ☎ 715/345–0505 or 800/826–1300), **Travel Insured International** (✉ Box 280568, East Hartford, CT 06128-0568, ☎ 860/528–7663 or 800/243–3174), **Travelex Insurance Services** (✉ 11717 Burt St., Suite 202, Omaha, NE 68154-1500, ☎ 402/445–8637 or 800/228–9792, FAX 800/867–9531), **Wallach & Company** (✉ 107 W. Federal St., Box 480, Middleburg, VA 20118, ☎ 540/687–3166 or 800/237–6615). In Canada, **Mutual of Omaha** (✉ Travel Division, 500 University Ave., Toronto, Ontario M5G 1V8, ☎ 416/598–4083; 800/268–8825 in Canada). In the United Kingdom, **Association of British Insurers** (✉ 51 Gresham St., London EC2V 7HQ, ☎ 0171/600–3333).

L

LODGING

Hotels in cities may or may not provide parking facilities, and there is usually a charge if they do. Motels, which are more common along the highways and outside cities, have parking space but may not have some of the amenities that hotels typically have—on-site restaurants, lounges, and room service.

Bed-and-breakfasts and inns are extremely popular in California. These are not usually economy lodgings—their prices are often at the top of the scale. Most typically they are large, older homes, renovated and decorated with antiques, with a half-dozen guest rooms. Sometimes the inn is a renovated hotel from the last century with a dozen or more rooms. The price usually includes breakfast, which may be a Continental breakfast—juice, coffee, and some simple pastries—or a four-course feast. Baths may be private or shared. Few B&Bs allow smoking; virtually none take pets.

APARTMENT & VILLA RENTALS

If you want a home base that's roomy enough for a family and comes with cooking facilities, **consider a furnished rental.** These can save you money, however some rentals are luxury properties, economical only when your party is large. Home-exchange directories list rentals (often second homes owned by prospective house swappers), and some services search for a house or apartment for you (even a castle if that's your fancy) and handle the paperwork. Some send an illustrated catalog; others send photographs only of specific properties, sometimes at a charge. Up-front registration fees may apply.

➤ RENTAL AGENTS: **Europa-Let/Tropical Inn-Let** (✉ 92 N. Main St., Ashland, OR 97520, ☎ 541/482–5806 or 800/462–4486, FAX 541/482–0660). **Hometours International** (✉ Box 11503, Knoxville, TN 37939, ☎ 423/690–8484 or 800/367–4668). **Property Rentals International** (✉ 1008 Mansfield Crossing Rd., Richmond, VA 23236, ☎ 804/378–6054 or 800/220–3332, FAX 804/379–2073). **Rent-a-Home International** (✉ 7200 34th Ave. NW, Seattle, WA 98117, ☎ 206/789–9377 or 800/488–7368, FAX 206/789–9379). **Hideaways International** (✉ 767 Islington St., Portsmouth, NH 03801, ☎ 603/430–4433 or 800/843–4433, FAX 603/430–4444) is a travel club whose members arrange rentals among themselves; yearly membership is $99.

CAMPING

➤ INFORMATION: **California Travel Parks Association** (✉ Box 5648, Auburn, CA 95604, ☎ 530/823–1076, FAX 916/823–6331).

➤ RESERVATIONS: **Destinet** (✉ 9450 Carroll Park Dr., San Diego, CA 92121, for California's national (☎ 800/365–2267) and state (☎ 800/444–7275) parks.

HOME EXCHANGES

If you would like to exchange your home for someone else's, **join a home-exchange organization,** which will send you its updated listings of available exchanges for a year and will include your own listing in at least one of them. Making the arrangements is up to you.

➤ EXCHANGE CLUBS: **HomeLink International** (✉ Box 650, Key West, FL 33041, ☎ 305/294–7766 or 800/638–3841, FAX 305/294–1148) charges $83 per year.

M
MONEY

ATMS

Before leaving home, **make sure that your credit cards have been programmed for ATM use.**

➤ ATM LOCATIONS: **Cirrus** (☎ 800/424–7787). **Plus** (☎ 800/843–7587).

P
PACKING FOR CALIFORNIA

The most important single rule to bear in mind in packing for a California vacation is to **prepare for changes in temperature.** An hour's drive can take you up or down many degrees, and the variation from daytime to nighttime in a single location is often marked. Take along sweaters, jackets, and clothes for layering as your best insurance for coping with variations in temperature. Include shorts or cool cottons unless you are packing for a midwinter ski trip. Always tuck in a bathing suit; most lodgings have a pool, spa, and sauna.

While casual dressing is a hallmark of the California lifestyle, in the evening men will need a jacket and tie for many good restaurants, and women will be more comfortable in something dressier than regulation sightseeing garb.

Considerations of formality aside, bear in mind that **San Francisco and other coastal towns can be chilly** at any time of the year, especially in summer, when the fog is apt to descend and stay.

Bring an extra pair of eyeglasses or contact lenses in your carry-on luggage, and if you have a health prob-

lem, **pack enough medication** to last the entire trip. It's important that you **don't put prescription drugs or valuables in luggage to be checked:** It might go astray.

LUGGAGE

In general you are entitled to check two bags on flights within the United States. Airline liability for baggage is limited to $1,250 per person on flights within the United States. On international flights it amounts to $9.07 per pound or $20 per kilogram for checked baggage (roughly $640 per 70-pound bag) and $400 per passenger for unchecked baggage. Insurance for losses exceeding these amounts can be bought from the airline at check-in for about $10 per $1,000 of coverage; note that this coverage excludes a rather extensive list of items, which is shown on your airline ticket.

Before departure, **itemize your bags' contents** and their worth, and label the bags with your name, address, and phone number. (If you use your home address, cover it so that potential thieves can't see it readily.) Inside each bag, **pack a copy of your itinerary.** At check-in, **make sure that each bag is correctly tagged** with the destination airport's three-letter code. If your bags arrive damaged or fail to arrive at all, file a written report with the airline before leaving the airport.

PARKS

NATIONAL PARKS

You may be able to **save money on park entrance fees** by getting a discount pass. The Golden Eagle Pass ($25) gets you and your companions free admission to all parks for one year. (Camping and parking are extra.) Both the Golden Age Passport, for U.S. citizens or permanent residents age 62 and older, and the Golden Access Passport, for travelers with disabilities, entitle holders to free entry to all national parks plus 50% off fees for the use of many park facilities and services. Both passports are free; you must show proof of age and U.S. citizenship or permanent residency (such as a U.S. passport, driver's license, or birth certificate) or proof of disability. All three passes are available at all national park entrances. Golden Eagle and Golden

Access passes are also available by mail.

➤ PASSES BY MAIL: **National Park Service** (✉ Dept. of the Interior, Washington, DC 20240).

STATE PARKS

➤ INFORMATION: **California State Park System** (✉ Dept. of Parks and Recreation, Box 942896, Sacramento 94296, ☎ 916/653–6995).

PASSPORTS & VISAS

CANADIANS

A passport is not required to enter the United States.

U.K. CITIZENS

British citizens need a valid passport to enter the United States. If you are staying for fewer than 90 days on vacation, with a return or onward ticket, you probably will not need a visa. However, you will need to fill out the Visa Waiver Form, 1-94W, supplied by the airline.

➤ INFORMATION: **London Passport Office** (☎ 0990/21010) for fees and documentation requirements and to request an emergency passport. **U.S. Embassy Visa Information Line** (☎ 01891/200–290) for U.S. visa information; calls cost 49p per min or 39p per min cheap rate. **U.S. Embassy Visa Branch** (✉ 5 Upper Grosvenor St., London W1A 2JB) for U.S. visa information; send a self-addressed, stamped envelope. Write the **U.S. Consulate General** (✉ Queen's House, Queen St., Belfast BTI 6EO) if you live in Northern Ireland.

S

SENIOR-CITIZEN TRAVEL

To qualify for age-related discounts, **mention your senior-citizen status up front** when booking hotel reservations (not when checking out) and before you're seated in restaurants (not when paying the bill). Note that discounts may be limited to certain menus, days, or hours. When renting a car, **ask about promotional car-rental discounts,** which can be cheaper than senior-citizen rates.

➤ EDUCATIONAL TRAVEL PROGRAMS: **Elderhostel** (✉ 75 Federal St., 3rd floor, Boston, MA 02110, ☎ 617/426–7788).

SPORTS

FISHING

California has abundant fishing options: deep-sea fishing expeditions, surf fishing from the shore, and freshwater fishing in streams, rivers, lakes, and reservoirs. You'll need a California fishing license. State residents pay $25.25 ($4.25 for senior citizens and those on limited income), but nonresidents must fork over $68.50 for a one-year license. Both residents and nonresidents can purchase a one-day license for $9.

➤ INFORMATION: **Department of Fish and Game** (✉ 3211 S St., Sacramento 95816, ☎ 916/227–2244).

STUDENTS

➤ STUDENT IDS AND SERVICES: **Council on International Educational Exchange** (✉ CIEE, 205 E. 42nd St., 14th floor, New York, NY 10017, ☎ 212/822–2600 or 888/268–6245, FAX 212/822–2699), for mail orders only, in the United States. **Travel Cuts** (✉ 187 College St., Toronto, Ontario M5T 1P7, ☎ 416/979–2406 or 800/667–2887) in Canada.

➤ HOSTELING: **Hostelling International—American Youth Hostels** (✉ 733 15th St. NW, Suite 840, Washington, DC 20005, ☎ 202/783–6161, FAX 202/783–6171). **Hostelling International—Canada** (✉ 400-205 Catherine St., Ottawa, Ontario K2P 1C3, ☎ 613/237–7884, FAX 613/237–7868). **Youth Hostel Association of England and Wales** (✉ Trevelyan House, 8 St. Stephen's Hill, St. Albans, Hertfordshire AL1 2DY, ☎ 01727/855215 or 01727/845047, FAX 01727/844126). Membership in the United States, $25; in Canada, C$26.75; in the United Kingdom, £9.30.

➤ STUDENT TOURS: **Contiki Holidays** (✉ 300 Plaza Alicante, Suite 900, Garden Grove, CA 92840, ☎ 714/740–0808 or 800/266–8454, FAX 714/740–0818).

T

TELEPHONES

AREA CODES

Several new area codes have recently been introduced in California, and more changes are planned in the near future. In some (but not all) cases, the telephone companies will provide a grace period that allows callers to dial the old area code for a few months. Within this book we have listed the area codes that were scheduled to be in use by November 1, 1997. The following are some recent area-code changes or ones that at press time were scheduled to occur in 1998:

➤ NORTHERN AND CENTRAL CALIFORNIA: Before the end of 1997, most of northeastern California except for Sacramento and some nearby towns and counties will begin to use 530 instead of 916.

The area south of San Francisco began using 650 instead of 415 in summer 1997.

In March 1998, parts of Alameda and Contra Costa counties and small portions of Solano and San Joaquin counties will begin to use 925 instead of 510.

During summer 1998, towns along the Central Coast—in Monterey and San Benito counties and most of Santa Cruz County—will switch to 831 from 408.

➤ SOUTHERN CALIFORNIA: In summer 1998, the areas surrounding downtown Los Angeles will begin to use 323 instead of 213.

Certain portions of southeastern Los Angeles and some places in Orange County switched from 562 from 310 in early 1997.

San Gabriel Valley began using 626 rather than 818 in mid-1997.

The southern portion of Orange County will begin using 949 rather than 714 in mid-1998.

In March 1997, portions of San Diego, Imperial Riverside, San Bernadino, Mono, Kern, and Inyo counties began using 760 instead of 619.

The 209 area code for the Central Valley, Yosemite National Park, and surrounding regions was scheduled to split in late 1998; at press time it was still unclear which areas will use the new code, whose number had not been determined.

CALLING HOME

➤ TO OBTAIN ACCESS CODES: AT&T USADirect (☎ 800/874–4000). MCI Call USA (☎ 800/444–4444). Sprint Express (☎ 800/793–1153).

TIPPING

At restaurants, a 15% tip is standard for waiters; up to 20% may be expected at more expensive establishments. The same goes for taxi drivers, bartenders, and hairdressers. Coat-check operators usually expect $1; bellhops and porters should get 50¢ to $1 per bag; hotel maids in upscale hotels should get about $1 per day of your stay. On package tours, conductors and drivers usually get $10 per day from the group as a whole; check whether this has already been figured into your cost. For local sightseeing tours, you may individually tip the driver-guide $1 if he or she has been helpful or informative. Ushers in theaters do not expect tips.

TOUR OPERATORS

Buying a prepackaged tour or independent vacation can make your trip to California less expensive and more hassle-free. Because everything is prearranged you'll spend less time planning.

Operators that handle several hundred thousand travelers per year can use their purchasing power to give you a good price. Their high volume may also indicate financial stability. But some small companies provide more personalized service; because they tend to specialize, they may also be more knowledgeable about a given area.

A GOOD DEAL?

The more your package or tour includes, the better you can predict the ultimate cost of your vacation. Make sure you know exactly what is covered, and beware of hidden costs. Are taxes, tips, and service charges included? Transfers and baggage handling? Entertainment and excursions? These can add up.

If the package or tour you are considering is priced lower than in your wildest dreams, be skeptical. Also, make sure your travel agent knows the accommodations and other services. Ask about the hotel's location, room size, beds, and whether it has a pool, room service, or programs for children, if you care about these. Has your agent been there in person or sent others you can contact?

BUYER BEWARE

Each year consumers are stranded or lose their money when tour operators—even very large ones with excellent reputations—go out of business. So **check out the operator.** Find out how long the company has been in business, and ask several agents about its reputation. **Don't book unless the firm has a consumer-protection program.**

Members of the National Tour Association and United States Tour Operators Association are required to set aside funds to cover your payments and travel arrangements in case the company defaults. Nonmembers may carry insurance instead. Look for the details, and for the name of an underwriter with a solid reputation, in the operator's brochure. Note: When it comes to tour operators, **don't trust escrow accounts.** Although there are laws governing charter-flight operators, no governmental body prevents tour operators from raiding the till. For more information, *see* Consumer Protection, *above.*

➤ TOUR-OPERATOR RECOMMENDATIONS: **National Tour Association** (✉ NTA, 546 E. Main St., Lexington, KY 40508, ☎ 606/226–4444 or 800/755–8687). **United States Tour Operators Association** (✉ USTOA, 342 Madison Ave., Suite 1522, New York, NY 10173, ☎ 212/599–6599, FAX 212/599–6744).

USING AN AGENT

Travel agents are excellent resources. When shopping for an agent, however, you should **collect brochures from several sources**; some agents' suggestions may be skewed by promotional relationships with tour and package firms that reward them for volume sales. If you have a special interest, **find an agent with expertise in that area** (☞ Travel Agencies, *below*). Don't rely solely on your agent, who may be unaware of small-niche operators. Note that some special-interest travel companies only sell directly to the public and that some large operators only accept bookings made through travel agents.

SINGLE TRAVELERS

Prices for packages and tours are usually quoted per person, based on two sharing a room. If traveling solo, you may be required to pay the full double-occupancy rate. Some operators eliminate this surcharge if you agree to be matched with a roommate of the same sex, even if one is not found by departure time.

GROUP TOURS

Among companies that sell tours to California, the following are nationally known, have a proven reputation, and offer plenty of options. The classifications used below represent different price categories, and you'll probably encounter these terms when talking to a travel agent or tour operator. The key difference is usually in accommodations, which run from budget to better, and better-yet to best.

➤ DELUXE: **Globus** (✉ 5301 S. Federal Circle, Littleton, CO 80123-2980, ☎ 303/797–2800 or 800/221–0090, FAX 303/347–2080). **Maupintour** (✉ 1515 St. Andrews Dr., Lawrence, KS 66047, ☎ 913/843–1211 or 800/255–4266, FAX 913/843–8351). **Tauck Tours** (✉ Box 5027, 276 Post Rd. W, Westport, CT 06881-5027, ☎ 203/226–6911 or 800/468–2825, FAX 203/221–6828).

➤ FIRST CLASS: **Brendan Tours** (✉ 15137 Califa St., Van Nuys, CA 91411, ☎ 818/785–9696 or 800/421–8446, FAX 818/902–9876). **Caravan Tours** (✉ 401 N. Michigan Ave., Chicago, IL 60611, ☎ 312/321–9800 or 800/227–2826, FAX 312/321–9845). **Collette Tours** (✉ 162 Middle St., Pawtucket, RI 02860, ☎ 401/728–3805 or 800/832–4656, FAX 401/728–1380). **Gadabout Tours** (✉ 700 E. Tahquitz Canyon Way, Palm Springs, CA 92262–6767, ☎ 619/325–5556 or 800/952–5068). **Mayflower Tours** (✉ Box 490, 1225 Warren Ave., Downers Grove, IL 60515, ☎ 708/960–3430 or 800/323–7064).

➤ BUDGET: **Cosmos** (☞ Globus, *above*).

PACKAGES

Like group tours, independent vacation packages are available from major tour operators and airlines. The companies listed below offer vacation packages in a broad price range.

➤ AIR/HOTEL: **American Airlines Fly AAway Vacations** (☎ 800/321–

2121). **Continental Vacations** (☎ 800/634–5555). **Delta Dream Vacations** (☎ 800/872–7786, FAX 954/ 357–4687). **United Vacations** (☎ 800/328–6877). **US Airways Vacations** (☎ 800/455–0123).

➤ CUSTOM PACKAGES: **Amtrak's Great American Vacations** (☎ 800/321–8684).

➤ FLY/DRIVE: **American Airlines Fly AAway Vacations** (☞ Air/Hotel, *above*). **Continental Vacations** (☞ Air/Hotel, *above*). **United Vacations** (☞ Air/Hotel, *above*).

➤ HOTEL ONLY: **SuperCities** (✉ 139 Main St., Cambridge, MA 02142, ☎ 800/333–1234).

➤ FROM THE U.K.: **British Airways Holidays** (✉ Astral Towers, Betts Way, London Rd., Crawley, West Sussex RH10 2XA, ☎ 01293/723–121). **Jetsave** (✉ Sussex House, London Rd., East Grinstead, West Sussex RH19 1LD, ☎ 01342/312–033). **Key to America** (✉ 1–3 Station Rd., Ashford, Middlesex TW15 2UW, ☎ 01784/248–777). **Kuoni Travel Ltd.** (✉ Kuoni House, Dorking, Surrey RH5 4AZ, ☎ 01306/742–222). **Premier Holidays** (✉ Premier Travel Center, Westbrook, Milton Rd., Cambridge CB4 1YG, ☎ 01223/516–688).

THEME TRIPS

➤ ADVENTURE: **Access to Adventure** (✉ Box 92520 Hwy. 96, Somes Bar, CA 95568, ☎ 530/469–3322 or 800/552–6284, FAX 530/469–3357). **American Wilderness Experience** (✉ 2820-A Wilderness Pl., Boulder, CO 80301-5454, ☎ 303/444–2622 or 800/444–0099, FAX 303/444–3999). **Tahoe Trips & Trails** (✉ Box 6952, Tahoe City, CA 96145, ☎ 530/583–4506 or 800/581–4453, FAX 530/ 583–1861). **Trek America** (✉ Box 189, Rockaway, NJ 07866, ☎ 201/ 983–1144 or 800/221-0596, FAX 201/ 983–8551).

➤ ARCHAEOLOGY: **Crow Canyon Archaeological Center** (✉ 23390 Country Rd. K, Cortez, CO 81321, ☎ 970/565–8975 or 800/422–8975, FAX 970/565–4859).

➤ BICYCLING: **Backroads** (✉ 801 Cedar St., Berkeley, CA 94710-1800, ☎ 510/527–1555 or 800/462–2848, FAX 510/527–1444). **Bicycle Adven-** tures (✉ Box 11219, Olympia, WA 98508, ☎ 360/786–0989 or 800/ 443–6060, FAX 360/786–9661). **Cycle America** (✉ Box 485, Cannon Falls, MN 55009, ☎ 507/263–2665 or 800/245–3263). **Imagine Tours** (✉ Box 475, Davis, CA 95617, ☎ 530/ 758–8782). **Timberline** (✉ 7975 E. Harvard, #J, Denver, CO 80231, ☎ 303/759–3804 or 800/417–2453, FAX 303/368–1651).

➤ CROSS-COUNTRY SKIING: **Backroads** (☞ Bicycling, *above*).

➤ FISHING: **Anglers Travel** (✉ 3100 Mill St., #206, Reno, NV 89502, ☎ FAX 702/853–9132). **Fishing International** (✉ Box 2132, Santa Rosa, CA 95405, ☎ 707/539–3366 or 800/ 950–4242, FAX 707/539–1320). **Rod and Reel Adventures** (✉ 3507 Tully Rd., #B6, Modesto, CA 95356-1052, ☎ 209/524–7775 or 800/356–6982, FAX 209/524–1220).

➤ GOLF: **Stine's Golftrips** (✉ Box 2314, Winter Haven, FL 33883-2314, ☎ 813/324–1300 or 800/428–1940, FAX 941/325–0384).

➤ HORSEBACK RIDING: **American Wilderness Experience** (☞ Adventure, *above*). **Equitour FITS Equestrian** (✉ Box 807, Dubois, WY 82513, ☎ 307/455–3363 or 800/545–0019, FAX 307/455–2354).

➤ LEARNING: **Earthwatch** (✉ Box 9104, 680 Mount Auburn St., Watertown, MA 02272, ☎ 617/926–8200 or 800/776–0188, FAX 617/926–8532) for research expeditions. **National Audubon Society** (✉ 700 Broadway, New York, NY 10003, ☎ 212/979–3066, FAX 212/353–0190). **Oceanic Society Expeditions** (✉ Fort Mason Center, Bldg. E, San Francisco, CA 94123-1394, ☎ 415/441–1106 or 800/326–7491, FAX 415/474–3395). **Smithsonian Study Tours and Seminars** (✉ 1100 Jefferson Dr. SW, Room 3045, MRC 702, Washington, DC 20560, ☎ 202/357–4700, FAX 202/ 633–9250).

➤ MUSIC: **Dailey-Thorp Travel** (✉ 330 W. 58th St., #610, New York, NY 10019-1817, ☎ 212/307–1555 or 800/998–4677, FAX 212/974–1420).

➤ RIVER RAFTING: **Access to Adventure** (☞ Adventure, *above*). **Action Whitewater Adventures** (✉ Box

1634, Provo UT 84603, ☎ 800/453–1482, 𝔽𝔸𝕏 801/375–4175). **OARS** (✉ Box 67, Angels Camp, CA 95222, ☎ 209/736–4677 or 800/346–6277, 𝔽𝔸𝕏 209/736–2902). **Whitewater Voyages** (✉ 5225 San Pablo Dam Rd., El Sobrante, CA 94803, ☎ 510/222–5994 or 800/488–7238, 𝔽𝔸𝕏 510/758–7238).

➤ SAILING: **Five Star Charters** (✉ 85 Liberty Ship Way, Ste. 112, Sausalito, CA 94965, ☎ 415/332–7187 or 800/762–6287, 𝔽𝔸𝕏 415/332–6811).

➤ SPAS: **Spa-Finders** (✉ 91 5th Ave., #301, New York, NY 10003-3039, ☎ 212/924–6800 or 800/255–7727).

➤ SPORTS: **Championship Tennis Tours** (✉ 7350 E. Stetson Dr., #106, Scottsdale, AZ 85251, ☎ 602/990–8760 or 800/468–3664, 𝔽𝔸𝕏 602/990–8744). **Dan Chavez's Sports Empire** (✉ Box 6169, Lakewood, CA 90714-6169, ☎ 562/920–2350 or 800/255–5258). **Spectacular Sport Specials** (✉ 5813 Citrus Blvd., New Orleans, LA 70123-5810, ☎ 504/734–9511 or 800/451–5772, 𝔽𝔸𝕏 504/734–7075).

➤ TRAIL RUNNING: **Backroads** (☞ Bicycling, *above*).

➤ WALKING/HIKING: **American Wilderness Experience** (☞ Adventure, *above*). **Backroads** (☞ Bicycling, *above*).

TRAIN TRAVEL

Amtrak's *Zephyr* train from Chicago via Denver stops in Oakland, California. The Amtrak *Coast Starlight* train travels between Los Angeles and Seattle.

➤ INFORMATION: **Amtrak** (☎ 800/872–7245).

TRAVEL AGENCIES

A good travel agent puts your needs first. **Look for an agency that specializes in your destination, has been in business at least five years, and emphasizes customer service.** If you're looking for an agency-organized package or tour, your best bet is to choose an agency that's a member of the National Tour Association or the United States Tour Operator's Association (☞ Tour Operators, *above*).

➤ LOCAL AGENT REFERRALS: **American Society of Travel Agents** (✉ ASTA, 1101 King St., Suite 200, Alexandria, VA 22314, ☎ 703/739–2782, 𝔽𝔸𝕏 703/684–8319). **Alliance of Canadian Travel Associations** (✉ 1729 Bank St., Suite 201, Ottawa, Ontario K1V 7Z5, ☎ 613/521–0474, 𝔽𝔸𝕏 613/521–0805). **Association of British Travel Agents** (✉ 55–57 Newman St., London W1P 4AH, ☎ 0171/637–2444, 𝔽𝔸𝕏 0171/637–0713).

TRAVEL GEAR

Travel catalogs specialize in useful items, such as compact alarm clocks and travel irons, that can **save space when packing.**

➤ MAIL-ORDER CATALOGS: **Magellan's** (☎ 800/962–4943, 𝔽𝔸𝕏 805/568–5406). **Orvis Travel** (☎ 800/541–3541, 𝔽𝔸𝕏 540/343–7053). **TravelSmith** (☎ 800/950–1600, 𝔽𝔸𝕏 800/950–1656).

U

U.S. GOVERNMENT

The U.S. government can be an excellent source of inexpensive travel information. When planning your trip, **find out what government materials are available.**

➤ ADVISORIES: **U.S. Department of State American Citizens Services Office** (✉ Room 4811, Washington, DC 20520); enclose a self-addressed, stamped envelope. **Interactive hot line** (☎ 202/647–5225, 𝔽𝔸𝕏 202/647–3000). **Computer bulletin board** (☎ 202/647–9225).

➤ PAMPHLETS: **Consumer Information Center** (✉ Consumer Information Catalogue, Pueblo, CO 81009, ☎ 719/948–3334) for a free catalog that includes travel titles.

V

VISITOR INFORMATION

For general information about California, contact the state tourism office; to contact visitors bureaus and chambers of commerce for regional and local information, see individual chapters.

➤ STATEWIDE INFORMATION : **California Division of Tourism** (✉ 801 K St., Suite 103, Sacramento, CA 95814, ☎ 916/322–2881 or 800/862–2543, 𝔽𝔸𝕏 916/322–3402).

➤ IN THE U.K.: **California Tourist Office** (✉ ABC California, Box 35, Abingdon, Oxfordshire OX14 4TB, ☎ 0891/200–278, ℻ 0171/242–2838). Calls cost 50p per minute peak rate or 45p per minute cheap rate. Brochures can be obtained by sending to the above address a cheque for £3 made to ABC California.

W
WHEN TO GO

Any time of the year is the right time to go to California. There won't be skiable snow in the mountains between Easter and Thanksgiving; there will usually be rain in December, January, and February in the lowlands, if that bothers you; it will be much too hot to enjoy Palm Springs or Death Valley in the summer. But San Francisco, Los Angeles, and San Diego are delightful year-round; the Wine Country's seasonal variables are enticing; and the coastal areas are almost always cool.

The climate varies amazingly in California, not only over distances of several hundred miles but occasionally within an hour's drive. A foggy, cool August day in San Francisco makes you grateful for a sweater, tweed jacket, or light wool coat.

Head north 50 mi to the Napa Valley to check out the Wine Country, and you'll probably wear shirt sleeves and thin cottons.

Daytime and nighttime temperatures may also swing widely apart. Take Sacramento, a city that is at sea level but in California's Central Valley. In the summer, afternoons can be very warm indeed, in the 90s and occasionally over 100°. But the nights cool down, often dropping 40°.

It's hard to generalize much about the weather in this varied state. Rain comes in the winter, with snow at higher elevations. Summers are dry everywhere. As a rule, compared to the coastal areas, which are cool year-round, inland regions are warmer in summer and cooler in winter. As you climb into the mountains, there are more distinct variations with the seasons: Winter brings snow, autumn is crisp, spring is variable, and summer is clear and warm.

➤ FORECASTS: **Weather Channel Connection** (☎ 900/932–8437), 95¢ per minute from a Touch-Tone phone.

CLIMATE

The following are average daily maximum and minimum temperatures for the major California cities.

Climate in California

LOS ANGELES

Jan.	64F	18C	May	72F	22C	Sept.	81F	27C
	44	7		53	12		60	16
Feb.	64F	18C	June	76F	24C	Oct.	76F	24C
	46	8		57	14		55	13
Mar.	66F	19C	July	81F	27C	Nov.	71F	22C
	48	9		60	16		48	9
Apr.	70F	21C	Aug.	82F	28C	Dec.	66F	19C
	51	11		62	17		46	8

SAN DIEGO

Jan.	62F	17C	May	66F	19C	Sept.	73F	23C
	46	8		55	13		62	17
Feb.	62F	17C	June	69F	21C	Oct.	71F	22C
	48	9		59	15		57	14
Mar.	64F	18C	July	73F	23C	Nov.	69F	21C
	50	10		62	17		51	11
Apr.	66F	19C	Aug.	73F	23C	Dec.	64F	18C
	53	12		64	18		48	9

SAN FRANCISCO

Jan.	55F	13C	May	66F	19C	Sept.	73F	23C
	41	5		48	9		51	11
Feb.	59F	15C	June	69F	21C	Oct.	69F	21C
	42	6		51	11		50	10
Mar.	60F	16C	July	69F	21C	Nov.	64F	18C
	44	7		51	11		44	7
Apr.	62F	17C	Aug.	69F	21C	Dec.	57F	14C
	46	8		53	12		42	6

THE GOLD GUIDE / SMART TRAVEL TIPS

1 Destination: California

RESTLESS NIRVANA

COASTAL CALIFORNIA began its migration from somewhere far to the south millions of years ago. It's still moving north along the San Andreas Fault, but you have plenty of time for a visit before Santa Monica hits the Arctic Circle. If you've heard predictions that some of the state may fall into the Pacific, take the long view and consider that much of California has been in and out of the ocean throughout its history. The forces that raised its mountains and formed the Central Valley are still at work.

Upheaval has always been a fact of life in California—below ground and above. Floods, earthquakes, racial strife, immigration woes, high unemployment, and Orange County's scandal-ridden bankruptcy are but a few of the high-profile traumas—not to mention the O.J. Simpson murder case—that have tarnished California's image in recent years. Things got so bad in the early 1990s that U-Haul declared a shortage of trucks because so many residents were abandoning the Golden State. This was just fine with the many natives whose "Welcome to California: Now Go Home" bumper stickers had greeted several decades of arrivals—few states have grown as rapidly as California, which had a population of approximately 7 million as World War II came to a close and now is home to about 32 million.

From the outside looking in, it may have seemed that, along with its AAA bond rating, California had lost its appeal as a travel destination. But even before its stunning mid-1990s economic turnaround, the Golden State had too many "positives" to be written off: dramatic coastline; rugged desert and mountain regions; Hollywood glitz and Palm Springs glamour; a potpourri of Pacific Rim, European, and Latin American influences; and a fabled history as a conduit for fame and fortune, hope and renewal.

California has always been a place where initiative—as opposed to class, family, or other connections—is honored above all

else. The state has lured assertive types who metaphorically or otherwise have come seeking "gold"—in the Sacramento foothills, in Hollywood, and, more recently, in the Silicon Valley. To be sure, not everyone achieves the mythical California dream, but neither is it totally an illusion. The sense of infinite possibility, as much a by-product of the state's varied and striking land forms as media hype, is what most tourists notice on their first trip. It's why so many return—sometimes forever.

More so than most of its residents are willing to admit, California is a land of contradiction, where "reality" is a matter of opinion—which is why the cinema, an enterprise based wholly on the manipulation of reality, is the perfect signature industry for the state. Take for instance two volumes in many local libraries about the historic chain of 21 California missions established by Spanish Catholic priests, most notably Father Junípero Serra. One book is titled *California's Missions: Their Romance and Beauty*. Its author details Serra's strategy "to convert and civilize the Indians" who resided in late-18th-century California. The other tome, *The Missions of California: A Legacy of Genocide,* disputes the contentions of "mission apologists" and illustrates how on levels physical and spiritual the mission system "was the first disaster for the Indian population of California."

The truth? It's likely somewhere in between (though recent scholarship has tended to show Serra and other missionaries in a less than favorable light). The treatment of other groups over the years has been equally problematic, and the scapegoating of "foreigners"—often by first-generation Californians with no sense of the irony of their protestations—is a cyclical blot on the state's conscience. California's move to the forefront of the controversy over affirmative action gave many across the nation the impression that its residents wish only to roll back the clock. But the circumstances here are more complex than they appear on the surface because the state has a more diverse population than most others in the Union. In any case, as with the debate over immigration and the previous "taxpayer revolts" of the 1970s and 1980s, the state's residents have forced discussion of an issue that citizens elsewhere have brooded over but not confronted.

California is a restless nirvana. The sun shines and all is beautiful; then the earth shakes and all is shattered. It's time to rebuild. And the state bounces back—San Francisco from the 1906 and 1989 quakes, Los Angeles from ones in 1971 and 1994, much of the state from incredible flooding in 1997. Billions are made during the Cold War defense boom; then communism collapses, bases close, and unemployment skyrockets. It's time to diversify. And the state does, making new overtures to Asia and Latin America.

And to tourists, who find that although California isn't perfect—what place is?—it's a source of endless diversion, natural and man-made. "Wow!" is a word one hears often here—at Half Dome in Yosemite, during the "Backdraft: 10,000 Degrees of Excitement" experience at Universal Studios, driving through the Mojave Desert, or walking among the redwoods of Humboldt County. If Texans like things "big" and New Yorkers like a little style, what delights Californians most is drama—indoors or out.

There is no way to take in this "show" in one trip, so don't try. Seventy-five percent of California's visitors return at least once, an impressive quotient of satisfied customers. As you travel through California's various regions you will get a sense of the great diversity of cultures, the ongoing pull between preservation and development, and the state's unique place in the landscapes of geography and the imagination.

NEW AND NOTEWORTHY

San Francisco

The renaissance South of Market Street (SoMa) continues, as new shops, galleries, and museums join the area's flagship cultural institutions, the **San Francisco Mu-** seum of Modern Art and the **Yerba Buena Gardens** complex. The nearby **Moscone Convention Center** is slated for expansion over the next few years; the roof of Moscone South will be the foundation of a Children's Center, scheduled to open in 1998. The mix of public buildings and open space will include a studio for technology and the arts, an ice skating rink, a day-care center, children's gardens, and a 1903 Charles I. D. Looff carousel that once entertained visitors to Playland at the Beach.

At Ocean Beach near the former site of Playland, the Willis Polk–designed **Beach Chalet** reopened in 1997 after being closed since the 1970s. The ground floor, which has a wraparound mural depicting San Francisco life in the 1930s, contains the Golden Gate Park visitor center. Upstairs is a very popular brew pub–restaurant.

Performing-arts organizations began to return in 1997 to their seismically upgraded homes, among them the **War Memorial Opera House,** home to San Francisco's opera and ballet companies.

Seventeen historic F-line streetcars chug up and down the length of **Market Street,** harkening back to another time. The cars, gathered from across the world, are painted in the livery of their cities of origin: many hail from the United States, but there are also cars from Blackpool, England, and Milan, Italy. Designed in the 1920s and '30s, the cars are a pleasure to ride—their large comfortable seats and pristine interiors match their colorful, carefully painted exteriors. The fare is the same as the more modern buses, making this a real bargain.

Los Angeles

After a decade's fling with Italian cuisine, Angelenos are falling in love with French bistro cooking. New spots like **Mimosa, Pastis,** and **Le Petit Bistro** are wowing crowds with such classics as cassoulet and bouillabaisse.

Skeptics doubted Wolfgang Puck could succeed with a serious, grown-up restaurant after his forays into frozen food and mall cafés, but they were proven wrong with the opening of the **Spago Beverly Hills,** on the site of the former Bistro Garden in Beverly Hills.

You can now try out the **Century Plaza Hotel's Cyber Suite** complete with a digitized butler, a brass console in the entryway that will draw your bath, adjust the room temperature, and dim the lights—think Mr. Belvedere meets Kit, the talking car from *Knight Rider.* There's cable TV, a laser disk, a Windows desktop, Internet access, and more. What will all this multimedia frenzy cost you? About $2,000 a night.

Bergamot Station, a stop on the now defunct Red Car trolley line, has morphed into an arts showcase with nearly three dozen galleries on its 5½ acres. Los Angeles eagerly awaits the opening of the **J. Paul Getty Center** on a hillside above Brentwood; the opening date has been delayed several times, but it should open by late 1997.

Nickelodeon has come to **Universal Studios Hollywood.** "Totally Nickelodeon" involves audiences in the same games and stunts shown on Nick's most popular TV shows—and yes, the Sliminator *is* there, dispensing gallons of the green goo on guest volunteers.

Family fun takes a new twist at the **Club Disney** playland in Thousand Oaks, where parents and kids (10 and up) can enjoy everything from computer games and other challenges to a 30-ft climbing ladder. And in Valencia, near Hollywood, **Six Flags Hurricane Harbor**—a pirate's paradise of water slides and lagoons—hoisted its sails in 1997 for summer family entertainment.

San Diego

With its biotechnology companies luring business from around the world, San Diego is angling for a leadership role as the new millennium approaches. Several future-oriented projects have already come to fruition.

Those who arrive by air will notice dramatic upgrades to **San Diego International Airport Lindbergh Field,** the most eye-catching improvement being the addition of a $1.5 million public-art project. A new commuter terminal, scheduled for completion in November 1997, will service Alaska Commuter, American Eagle, Continental Connection, Delta Connection, Northwest Airlink, and US Airways Express. The airport's main terminals have been dressed up with a brighter color scheme.

As part of the continuing effort to make San Diego easier to get around, the **San Diego Trolley,** a light-rail transit system, laid more track. The Mission Valley Line, with access to shopping and entertainment, was scheduled to open in late 1997. The Mission Valley Line starts at the Old Town Transit Center and connects with the trolley's North Line, the Coaster commuter rail line, and major bus routes. It serves six stations east of Mission Valley. Sports fans and shoppers will cheer for the stops at Fashion Valley and Jack Murphy Stadium. The **Fashion Valley** stop is part of an extensive overhaul at this Mission Valley shopping mall. A new upper level and the addition of 100 shops and a theater complex have increased Fashion Valley's size from 1.4 million to 1.6 million square ft.

On the wilder side, the Zoological Society of San Diego's **Wild Animal Park** in the San Pasqual Valley installed a new walking exhibit in summer 1997. The sprawling park, which visitors usually view on a monorail ride through four huge field areas inhabited by a mix of exotic hoofstock, now welcomes visitors to walk through the heart of its East Africa exhibit. Following a stream to an African waterhole, a path winds past Okapi, giraffes, and cheetahs. A floating walkway leads to a working research station. Discount passes can be purchased for those who would like to see both the Wild Animal Park and the **San Diego Zoo,** where, after a two-year delay, two pandas on an extended loan from China have finally arrived. The zoo is in **Balboa Park,** which also holds the **Reuben H. Fleet Theater and Science Center.** A multimillion-dollar expansion scheduled for completion by May 1998, in time for the center's 25th anniversary, will double the facility's size. Among the new exhibits will be one that allows visitors to participate in simulated scientific missions.

A new mile-long bicycle, skating, and pedestrian path in **Mission Bay Park** has made walking in the city even more pleasurable. The path hugs Bahia Point, in front of the Bahia Hotel, and connects to many other bike paths in the coastal area.

WHAT'S WHERE

Keep in mind the very long distances. If you drive between San Francisco and Los Angeles on Highway 1, remember that it is not only more than 400 mi but also a difficult road to drive. Scenic routes, such as Highway 1 along the coast, Highway 49 in the Gold Country, and Highways 50 and 120 across the Sierra Nevada, require attention to driving and enough time for frequent stops.

The Central Coast

Highway 1 between Big Sur and Santa Barbara is a spectacular stretch of terrain. The curving road demands an unhurried pace, but even if it didn't, you'd find yourself stopping often to take in the scenery. Don't expect much in the way of dining, lodging, or even history until you arrive at Hearst Castle, publisher William Randolph Hearst's testament to his own fabulousness. Sunny, well-scrubbed Santa Barbara's Spanish-Mexican heritage is reflected in the architectural style of its courthouse and mission.

The Far North

Soaring mountain peaks, wild rivers brimming with fish, and almost infinite recreational possibilities make the Far North a sports-lover's paradise. Hot nightspots and cultural enclaves do not abound, but you will find some of the best hiking, fishing, and hunting in the state. Some Bay Area families return to this region year after year. Many enjoy the outdoors from their own piece of paradise—a private houseboat. Keep in mind that much of the Far North can be very hot in summer.

Lake Tahoe

The largest alpine lake in North America is famous for its clarity, deep blue water, and snowcapped peaks. Though Lake Tahoe possesses abundant natural beauty and accessible wilderness, nearby towns are highly developed and the roads around it often congested. Summertime is generally cooler here than in the Sierra Nevada foothills, and the clean mountain air bracingly crisp. When it gets hot, beaches and brisk water are only minutes away.

Los Angeles

In certain lights Los Angeles displays its Spanish heritage, but much more evident is its participation in the Pacific Rim cultural and economic boom. Hollywood, the beaches, and Disneyland are all within an hour's drive. Also here are freeways (lots of them), important examples of 20th-century domestic architecture, and Beverly Hills, noted for its shops and mansions. Despite the city's reputation for a laid-back lifestyle, a visit here can be fairly overwhelming because of the size and variety of the region. Careful planning will help.

The Mojave Desert and Death Valley

When most people assemble their "must-see" list of California attractions, the desert isn't often among the top contenders. What with its heat and vast, sparsely populated tracts of land, the desert is no Disneyland. But that's precisely why it deserves a closer look. The natural riches here stagger: rolling waves of sand dunes, black cinder cones thrusting up hundreds of feet into the air from a blistered desert floor, riotous sheets of wildflowers, bizarrely shaped Joshua trees basking in an orange glow at sunset, and an abundant silence that is both dramatic and startling.

Monterey Bay

The Monterey Peninsula is steeped in history. The town of Monterey was California's first capital, the Carmel Mission headquarters for California's entire 18th-century mission system. The peninsula also has a rich literary past. John Steinbeck's novels immortalize the area, and Robert Louis Stevenson strolled its streets for inspiration for *Treasure Island*. The present is equally illustrious. Blessed with a natural splendor undiminished by time or commerce, the peninsula is home to visionary marine habitats and luxurious resorts and golf courses.

The North Coast

The North Coast can only be summed up in superlatives. Migrating whales and other sea mammals swim past the dramatic bluffs that make the 400 mi of shoreline north of San Francisco to the Oregon border among the most photographed landscapes in the country. Along cypress- and redwood-studded Highway 1 you will find many small inns, uncrowded state beaches and parks, art galleries, and restaurants serving imaginative dishes that showcase locally produced ingredients.

Palm Springs Desert Resorts

Palm Springs and its neighbors—Palm Desert, Rancho Mirage, Indian Wells—are among the fastest-growing and wealthiest communities in the nation. The desert lures visitors and residents for the same reasons: striking scenery and the therapeutic benefits of a warm, arid climate. Resort hotel complexes contain championship golf courses, tennis stadiums, and sparkling swimming pools—lushly landscaped oases, towering palms, natural waterfalls, and hot mineral springs round out the picture.

Sacramento and the Gold Country

The gold-mining region of the Sierra Nevada foothills is a less expensive, if also less sophisticated, region of California but not without its pleasures, natural and man-made. Spring brings wildflowers, and in fall the hills are colored by bright-red berries and changing leaves. The hills are golden in the summer—and hot. The Gold Country has a mix of indoor and outdoor activities, one of the many reasons it's a great place to take the kids.

San Diego

To visitors, the city and county of San Diego may seem like a conglomeration of theme parks: Old Town and the Gaslamp Quarter historically oriented ones, the wharf area a maritime-heritage playground, La Jolla a genteel throwback to southern California elegance, Balboa Park a convergence of the town's cerebral and action-oriented personae. There are, of course, real theme parks—Sea World and the zoo and Wild Animal Park—but the great outdoors, in the form of forests, landscaped urban areas, and a string of sandy beaches, forms the biggest of them all.

San Francisco

San Francisco is a sophisticated city with world-class hotels and the greatest concentration of excellent restaurants in the state. The town has an undeserved reputation as the kook capital of the United States, yet it's the country's number one tourist destination. Why? To use the vernacular, the vibe here is cool, from North Beach coffeehouses to Chinatown tea emporiums, Golden Gate Park, and Haight Street's head shops (yes, they're still around). People in San Francisco know how to have a good time; the high spirits can't help but rub off on visitors.

The San Joaquin Valley

The San Joaquin Valley, one of the world's most fertile agricultural zones, is California's heartland. This sunbaked region contains a wealth of rivers, lakes, and waterways; the water, in turn, nurtures vineyards, dairy farms, orchards, fields, and pastures that stretch to the horizon. And while you're never far from cities, mountains, or national parks here, you'll find that the area possesses attractions of its own, beginning with the warmth of its land and people.

The Sierra National Parks

The highlight for many California travelers is a visit to one of the national parks in the Sierra Nevada range. Yosemite is the state's most famous park and every bit as sublime as one expects. Its Yosemite-type or U-shape valleys were formed by the action of glaciers during recent ice ages. Other examples are found in Kings Canyon and Sequoia national parks, which are adjacent to each other and usually visited together. All the Sierra National Parks contain fine, tall groves of *Sequoiadendron giganteum* trees.

The Wine Country

The Wine Country is one of California's most popular tourist regions. Many Sonoma and Napa Valley wineries are perfect sites for meals, picnics, or tastings, and there are top-notch bed-and-breakfasts and restaurants in the area. There are many ways to explore the region: hiking and bicycling for the active set and going on balloon, train, and glider rides for those seeking a less strenuous overview. People here know how to pamper themselves: in Calistoga and other towns are resorts and health spas with mud baths, massages, sulfur whirlpool baths, and other rejuvenating treatments.

PLEASURES AND PASTIMES

Beaches

With 1,264 mi of coastline, California is well supplied with beaches. You can walk on them, lie and sun on them, watch seabirds and hunt for shells, dig clams, or spot seals and sea otters at play. From December through March you can witness the migrations of the gray whales. What you can't always do at these beaches is swim. From San Francisco northward, the water is too cold for all but extremely hardy souls. Even along the southern half of the coast, some beaches are too dangerous for swimming because of the undertow. Look for signs and postings and take them seriously.

Access to beaches in California is generally excellent. The state park system includes many fine beaches, and oceanside communities have their own public beaches. Through the work of the California Coastal Commission, many stretches of private property that would otherwise seal off a beach from outsiders have public-access paths and trails.

Dining

California's name has come to signify a certain type of modern, healthful, sophisticated cuisine, using local ingredients, creatively combined and served in often stunning presentations. San Francisco and Los Angeles have scores of top-notch restaurants—an expensive meal at one of these gourmet shrines is often the high point of a trip to California. The Wine Country just north of San Francisco is also known for superb restaurants, as is the city of Santa Barbara. In coastal areas, most restaurants' menus usually include some seafood, fresh off the boat. Don't neglect the culinary bounty of California's mixed ethnic population—notably Mexican and Chinese, but also Japanese, Scandinavian, Italian, French, Belgian, English, Thai, and German restaurants.

Fishing

California has abundant fishing options: deep-sea, surf, and freshwater. *See* Sports *in* the Gold Guide to learn how to obtain the necessary license.

Golf

Golf is a year-round sport in California. Pebble Beach and the Palm Springs desert resorts have the most famous links, but there are championship courses all over the state. *See* Outdoor Activities and Sports in each chapter for listings of area courses.

Hot-Air Ballooning

Large, colorful balloons drift across the valleys of the Wine Country, where the air drafts are particularly friendly to this pastime, as well as in San Diego, the Palm Springs area, and the Gold Country. Hot-air ballooning is not cheap, however: a ride costs in excess of $100. *See* Tour Operators *in* the Gold Guide and the Outdoor Activities and Sports sections of each chapter for listings of companies that operate in the state.

Parks

NATIONAL PARKS➤ There are eight national parks in California: Death Valley, Joshua Tree, Lassen Volcanic, Redwood, Sequoia, Kings Canyon, Yosemite, and the Channel Islands. National monuments include Cabrillo, in San Diego, and Muir Woods, north of San Francisco.

California has three national recreation areas: Golden Gate, with 87,000 acres both north and south of the Golden Gate Bridge in San Francisco; the Santa Monica Mountains, with 150,000 acres from Griffith Park in Los Angeles to Point Mugu in Ventura County; and Whiskeytown-Shasta-Trinity, with 240,000 acres, including four major lakes, in the Far North. The Point Reyes National Seashore is on a peninsula north of San Francisco.

STATE PARKS➤ California's state-park system includes more than 200 sites; many are recreational and scenic, others historic or scientific. Among the most popular are Angel Island in San Francisco Bay, reached by ferry from San Francisco or Tiburon; Anza-Borrego Desert, 600,000 acres of the Colorado Desert northeast of San Diego; Humboldt Redwoods, with its tall trees; Empire Mine, one of the richest mines in the Mother Lode, in Grass Valley; Hearst Castle at San Simeon; and Leo Carrillo Beach, north of Malibu, with lively tidal pools and numerous secret coves. Most state parks are open year-round.

Skiing

Snow skiing in the Lake Tahoe area and elsewhere is generally limited to the period between Thanksgiving and late April, though in years of heavy snowfall skiers can still hit some trails as late as July. Other ski options include Mt. Shasta and Lassen Volcanic National Park in the Far North; Mammoth Lake and the San

Bernardino Mountains in southern California; and Badger Pass in Yosemite National Park.

Water Sports

Swimming and surfing, scuba diving, and skin diving in the Pacific Ocean are year-round pleasures in the southern part of the state, although these become seasonal sports on the coast from San Francisco northward. Sailboats are available for rent in many places along the coast and inland. River rafting—white-water and otherwise—canoeing, and kayaking are popular, especially in the northern part of the state, where there are many rivers.

Wine Tasting

You can visit wineries in many parts of the state, not only in the Wine Country of the Sonoma and Napa valleys. Vintners associations in the Gold Country, Santa Barbara, Santa Cruz, and other wine-growing areas provide brochures (see individual chapters for details) with lists of wineries that open for tastings. Wineries and good wine stores will package your purchases for safe travel or shipping.

FODOR'S CHOICE

No two people will agree on what makes a perfect vacation, but it can be helpful to know what others think. Below is a list of Fodor's Choices. We hope you'll have a chance to experience some of them yourself while visiting California. We have tried to include something for everyone and from every price category. For more detailed information about each entry, refer to the appropriate chapters within this guidebook.

Lodging

⭐ **Château du Sureau, Oakhurst.** The romantic château is a fairy-tale castle. With Erna's Elderberry House restaurant, one of California's best, right on the premises, you may find it hard to tear yourself away to visit nearby Yosemite National Park. $$$$

⭐ **Hotel Bel-Air, Los Angeles.** This secluded celebrity mecca's exotic gardens and creek (complete with swans) make for a resortlike ambience right in the city. $$$$

⭐ **Post Ranch Inn, Big Sur.** This luxurious retreat is the ultimate in environmentally conscious architecture. Each unit has its own hot tub, stereo system, private deck, and massage table. $$$$

⭐ **Ritz-Carlton Hotel, Laguna Niguel.** The classiest hotel along the coast, the Ritz draws guests from around the world with its ocean views, gleaming marble, and stunning antiques. $$$$

⭐ **Sherman House, San Francisco.** The words "crème de la crème" best describe this French-Italianate mansion in Pacific Heights with a sumptuous Old World feel. $$$$

⭐ **Hotel Monaco, San Francisco.** Hip and hot, with an impish postmodern design, the Monaco has snappy-looking public areas and comfortable rooms. $$$

⭐ **The Lodge at Torrey Pines, La Jolla.** This inn commands a view of miles and miles of coastline. It's adjacent to a public golf course, a state beach, and a nature reserve. $$

⭐ **San Simeon Pines Motel, Cambria.** Set amid 9 acres of pines and cypresses, this motel-style resort near Hearst Castle has its own golf course and is directly across from Leffingwell's Landing, a state picnic area on the rocky beach. $–$$

Scenic Drives

⭐ **17-Mile Drive, Carmel.** The wonders are both man-made and natural as this road winds its way through Carmel and Pebble Beach.

⭐ **Highway 1 from Big Sur to San Simeon.** The twisting section of coastal highway affords some breathtaking ocean vistas before arriving at Hearst Castle.

⭐ **Highway 49, the Gold Country.** California's pioneer past comes to life in the many towns along this 325-mi highway at the base of the Sierra foothills.

⭐ **Kings Canyon Highway.** During the summer, the stretch of Highway 180 in Kings Canyon National Park from Grant Grove to Cedar Grove is spectacular.

⭐ **Mulholland Drive, Los Angeles.** One of the most famous thoroughfares in Los Angeles winds through the Hollywood Hills and across the spine of the Santa Monica Mountains, stopping just short of the Pacific Ocean.

Historic Buildings

★ **Coit Tower, San Francisco.** The 1930s murals at this monument to its city's volunteer firefighters are as striking as the view.

★ **Lachryma Montis (General Vallejo's Home), Sonoma.** The last Mexican governor of California built this large Victorian Gothic house with a white marble fireplace in every room.

★ **Griffith Park Observatory and Planetarium, Los Angeles.** One of the largest telescopes in the world is open to the public for free viewing every clear night. In the planetarium—immortalized in *Rebel Without a Cause*—dazzling daily shows duplicate the starry sky.

★ **Hearst Castle, San Simeon.** The renowned attraction, formerly a playground for the rich and famous, sits in solitary splendor on the 127 acres that were the heart of newspaper magnate William Randolph Hearst's 250,000-acre ranch.

★ **Hotel Del Coronado, San Diego.** Coronado Island's most prominent landmark was the world's first electrically lighted hotel.

★ **Mann's Chinese Theater, Hollywood.** The architecture of the former "Grauman's Chinese" is a fantasy of pagodas and temples. Its courtyard is open for browsing of celebrity cement hand- and footprints.

★ **Mission Santa Barbara.** The "queen" of the chain of 21 Spanish missions established in California is still active as a Catholic church.

★ **California State Capitol, Sacramento.** The lacy plasterwork of the rotunda of this 1869 structure has all the complexity and color of a Fabergé egg. Outside, the 40-acre Capitol Park is one of the oldest gardens in the state.

Breathtaking Sights

★ **El Capitan and Half Dome, Yosemite National Park.** Yosemite's two most famous peaks are also its most photographed.

★ **View from Emerald Bay Lookout, Lake Tahoe.** This aquatic cul-de-sac is famed for its jewel-like shape and colors.

★ **Golden Gate Bridge Vista Point and Marin Headlands, Marin County.** On a clear day, San Francisco glistens from this vantage point at the bridge's north end.

★ **Huntington Library, Art Gallery, and Gardens, Pasadena.** The botanical splendors here include the 12-acre Desert Garden and 1,500 varieties of camellias.

★ **La Jolla Cove at sunset.** It's beautiful any time of day, but as the sun goes down over the cove and its towering palms, the view is a postcard come to life.

Restaurants with Fabulous Atmosphere

★ **Stars, San Francisco.** Jeremiah Tower's eatery is a must on every traveling gourmet's itinerary. The dining room has a clublike ambience, and the food ranges from grills to ragouts to sautés. *$$$*

★ **George's at the Cove, La Jolla.** A wall-length window in the elegant main dining room, renowned for its fresh seafood specials, overlooks the cove. *$$–$$$*

★ **Granita, Malibu.** Wolfgang Puck's coastal outpost has striking interior details and a menu that favors seafood, along with the chef's signature California-inspired dishes. *$$–$$$*

★ **Greens at Fort Mason, San Francisco.** The expansive bay views alone would be worth a visit to this airy restaurant. The bonus: a wide, eclectic, and creative spectrum of meatless cooking. *$$–$$$*

★ **Café Beaujolais, Mendocino.** All the rustic charm of peaceful, backwoods Mendocino is here, with great country cooking to boot. *$$*

★ **Montrio, Monterey.** *Esquire* named this Restaurant of the Year in 1995, declaring that it "sums up in every way what is best about California restaurants." The magazine's right. *$$*

★ **Samoa Cookhouse, Samoa (near Eureka).** Get a feel for dining during the heyday of the North Coast logging industry at this lumberman's hangout, which dates back to the late 19th century. *$*

BOOKS AND VIDEOS

San Francisco

BOOKS> Many novels are set in San Francisco, but none come better than *The*

Maltese Falcon, by Dashiell Hammett, the founder of the hard-boiled school of detective fiction. *The Barbary Coast: An Informal History of the San Francisco Underworld,* published in 1933 and still in print, is Herbert Asbury's searing look at life in what really was a wicked city before the turn of the century. Another standout is Vikram Seth's *Golden Gate,* a novel in verse about life in San Francisco and Marin County in the early '80s. Others are John Gregory Dunne's recent *The Red White and Blue* and Alice Adams's *Rich Rewards.*

Two books that are filled with interesting background information on the city are Richard H. Dillon's *San Francisco: Adventurers and Visionaries* and *San Francisco: As It Is, As It Was,* by Paul C. Johnson and Richard Reinhardt.

Armistead Maupin's soap-opera-style *Tales of the City* stories are set in San Francisco; they were made into a successful 1993 PBS series.

VIDEOS➤ *San Francisco,* starring Clark Gable and Jeanette MacDonald, re-creates the 1906 earthquake with outstanding special effects. In *Escape from Alcatraz,* Clint Eastwood plays the prisoner who allegedly escaped from the famous jail on a rock in the San Francisco Bay. *The Times of Harvey Milk,* about San Francisco's first openly gay elected official, won the Academy Award for best documentary feature in 1984. Alfred Hitchcock immortalized Mission Dolores and the Golden Gate Bridge in *Vertigo,* the eerie story of a detective with a fear of heights, starring Jimmy Stewart and Kim Novak. A few other noteworthy films shot in San Francisco are *Dark Passage,* with Humphrey Bogart; the 1978 remake of *Invasion of the Body Snatchers*; and the 1993 comedy *Mrs. Doubtfire,* starring Robin Williams.

Los Angeles

BOOKS➤ *Los Angeles: The Enormous Village, 1781–1981,* by John D. Weaver, and *Los Angeles: Biography of a City,* by John and LaRee Caughey, will give you a fine background in how it came to be the city it is today. The unique social and cultural life of the whole southern California area is explored in *Southern California: An Island on the Land,* by Carey McWilliams.

One of the most outstanding features of Los Angeles is its architecture. *Los Angeles: The Architecture of Four Ecologies,* by Reyner Banham, relates the physical environment to the architecture. *Architecture in Los Angeles: A Compleat Guide,* by David Gebhard and Robert Winter, is exactly what the title promises and is very useful.

Many novels have been written with Los Angeles as the setting. One of the very best, Nathanael West's *Day of the Locust,* was first published in 1939 but still rings true. Budd Schulberg's *What Makes Sammy Run?,* Evelyn Waugh's *The Loved One,* and Joan Didion's *Play It As It Lays* are unforgettable. Other novels that give a sense of contemporary life in Los Angeles are *Sex and Rage,* by Eve Babitz, and *Less Than Zero,* by Bret Easton Ellis. Raymond Chandler and Ross Macdonald have written many suspense novels with a Los Angeles background.

VIDEOS AND TV➤ *Day of the Locust* and *Play It As It Lays* were made into two of the grimmer cinematic portraits of life in Los Angeles. Billy Wilder's *Sunset Boulevard* is a classic portrait of a faded star and her attempt to recapture past glory. Roman Polanski's *Chinatown,* arguably one of the best American films ever made, is a fictional account of the wheeling and dealing that helped make L.A. what it is today. Southern California's varied urban and rural landscapes are used to great effect (as is an all-star cast that includes Ethel Merman and Spencer Tracy) in Stanley Kramer's manic *It's a Mad, Mad, Mad, Mad World.*

San Diego

BOOKS➤ There is no better way to establish the mood for your visit to Old Town San Diego than by reading Helen Hunt Jackson's 105-year-old romantic novel, *Ramona,* a best-seller for more than 50 years and still in print. The Casa de Estudillo in Old Town has been known for many years as Ramona's Marriage Place because of its close resemblance to the house described in the novel. Richard Henry Dana Jr.'s *Two Years Before the Mast* (1869), based on the author's experiences as a merchant sailor, provides a masculine perspective on early San Diego history.

Other novels with a San Diego setting include Raymond Chandler's mystery about the waterfront, *Playback;* Wade Miller's mystery, *On Easy Street;* Eric Higgs's gothic thriller, *A Happy Man;* Tom Wolfe's satire of the La Jolla surfing scene, *The Pump House Gang;* and David Zielinski's modern-day story, *A Genuine Monster.*

VIDEOS AND TV➤ Filmmakers have taken advantage of San Diego's diverse and amiable climate since the dawn of cinema. Westerns, comedy-westerns, and tales of the sea were early staples: *Cupid in Chaps, The Sagebrush Phrenologist* (how's that for a title?), the 1914 version of *The Virginian,* and Lon Chaney's *Tell It to the Marines* were among the silent films shot in the area. Easy-to-capture outdoor locales have lured many productions south from Hollywood over the years, including the following military-oriented talkies, all or part of which were shot in San Diego: James Cagney's *Here Comes the Navy* (1934), Errol Flynn's *Dive Bomber* (1941), John Wayne's *The Sands of Iwo Jima* (1949), Ronald Reagan's *Hellcats of the Navy* (1956, costarring Nancy Davis, the future First Lady), Rock Hudson's *Ice Station Zebra* (1967), Tom Cruise's *Top Gun* (1986), Sean Connery's *Hunt for Red October,* Charlie Sheen's *Navy Seals* (1990), and Danny Glover's *Flight of the Intruder* (1991). Rob Lowe did not make his infamous home videos here, but he did shoot some of *Desert Shield* (1991).

In a lighter military vein, the famous talking mule hit the high seas in *Francis Joins the Navy* (1955), in which a very young Clint Eastwood has a bit part. The Tom Hanks–Darryl Hannah hit *Splash* (1984), *Spaceballs* (1987), *Hot Shots* (1991), *Wayne's World II* (1993), and Ellen Degeneres's *Mr. Wrong* (1996) are more recent comedies with scenes filmed here. The city has a cameo role in the minihit *Flirting with Disaster* (1996), and one of the best comedies ever made, director Billy Wilder's *Some Like It Hot*—starring Marilyn Monroe, Jack Lemmon, and Tony Curtis—takes place at the famous Hotel Del Coronado (standing in for a Miami resort).

The amusingly low-budget *Attack of the Killer Tomatoes* (1976) makes good use of local scenery—and the infamous San Diego Chicken. The producers must have liked what they found in town as they returned for three sequels: *Return of the Killer Tomatoes* (1988), *Killer Tomatoes Strike Back* (1990), and—proving just how versatile the region is as a film location—*Killer Tomatoes Go to France* (1991). Unlike many films in which San Diego itself doesn't figure in the plot, the screen version of Helen Hunt Jackson's novel *Ramona* (1936) starring Loretta Young as the title character, incorporated historical settings (or replicas).

Television producers zip south for series and made-for-TV movies all the time. The alteration of San Diego's skyline in the 1980s was partially documented on the hit show *Simon & Simon.* San Diego is virtually awash in syndicated productions: *Silk Stalkings, Baywatch, High Tide,* and *Renegade* all shoot here. Reality and cop shows love the area, too: *Unsolved Mysteries, Rescue 911, America's Missing Children, Totally Hidden Video, America's Most Wanted,* and *America's Funniest People* have all taped in San Diego, making it one of the most-seen—yet often uncredited—locales in movie- and videoland.

Around the State

BOOKS➤ John Steinbeck immortalized the Monterey-Salinas area in numerous books, including *Cannery Row* and *East of Eden.* Joan Didion captured the heat—solar, political, and otherwise—of the Sacramento Delta area in *Run River.* Mark Twain's *Roughing It* and Bret Harte's *The Luck of Roaring Camp* evoke life during the gold rush. For a window on the past and present of the Central Valley, see *Highway 99: A Literary Journey Through California's Great Central Valley,* edited by Stan Yogi.

VIDEOS AND TV➤ Steinbeck's *East of Eden* was a hit film starring James Dean and later a television movie; both are on video now. Buster Keaton's masterpiece *Steamboat Bill, Jr.* was shot in Sacramento. The cult favorite *Harold and Maude* takes place in the San Francisco Bay Area. The exteriors in Alfred Hitchcock's *Shadow of a Doubt* were shot in Santa Rosa, and his ultracreepy *The Birds* was shot in Bodega Bay, along the North Coast. *Shack Out on 101* is a loopy 1950s beware-the-Commies caper also set on the California coast.

Erich von Stroheim used a number of northern California locations for his films: *Greed* takes place in San Francisco but includes excursions to Oakland and other points in the East Bay. Carmel is one of the locations for his *Foolish Wives*. The various *Star Trek* movies and Michelangelo Antonioni's *Zabriskie Point* are among the features that have made use of the eastern desert region. Initial footage of Sam Peckinpah's western *Ride the High Country* was shot in the Sierra Nevada mountains before his studio yanked him back to southern California, where he blended the original shots with ones of the Santa Monica Mountains and the Hollywood Hills.

FESTIVALS AND SEASONAL EVENTS

WINTER

➤ JANUARY: Palo Alto's annual **East-West Shrine All-Star Football Classic** (☎ 415/661–0291) is America's oldest all-star sports event. In Pasadena, the annual **Tournament of Roses Parade and Football Game** (☎ 626/449–7673) takes place on New Year's Day, with lavish flower-decked floats, marching bands, and equestrian teams, followed by the Rose Bowl game.

➤ FEBRUARY: The legendary **AT&T Pebble Beach National Pro-Am** golf tournament (☎ 408/649–1533) begins in late January and ends in early February. San Francisco's Chinatown is the scene of parades and noisy fireworks, all part of a several-day **Chinese New Year Celebration** (☎ 415/982–3000). Los Angeles also has a Chinese New Year Parade (☎ 213/617–0396). Indio's **Riverside County Fair and National Date Festival** (☎ 800/811–3247) is an exotic event with an Arabian Nights theme; camel and ostrich races, date exhibits, and tastings are among the draws.

SPRING

➤ MARCH: **Snowfest** in North Lake Tahoe (☎ 530/583–7625) is the largest winter carnival in the West, with skiing, food, fireworks, parades, and live music. The finest female golfers in the world compete for the richest purse on the LPGA circuit at the **Nabisco Dinah Shore Golf Tournament** in Rancho Mirage (☎ 760/324–4546). The **Mendocino/Fort Bragg Whale Festival** (☎ 800/726–2780) includes whale-watching excursions, marine art exhibits, wine and beer tastings, crafts displays, and a chowder contest.

➤ APRIL: A large cast presents the **Ramona Pageant,** a love story based on the novel by Helen Hunt Jackson, on weekends in late April and early May on a mountainside outdoor stage (☎ 800/645–4465).

➤ MAY: Inspired by Mark Twain's story "The Notorious Jumping Frog of Calaveras County," the **Jumping Frog Jubilee** in Angels Camp (☎ 209/736–2561) is for frogs and trainers who take their competition seriously. Sacramento hosts the four-day **Dixieland Jazz Jubilee** (☎ 916/372–5277); the late-May event is the world's largest Dixieland festival, with 125 bands from around the world. In Monterey, the squirmy squid is the main attraction for the Memorial Day weekend **Great Monterey Squid Festival** (☎ 408/649–6544). You'll see squid cleaning and cooking demonstrations, taste treats, and enjoy the usual festival fare: entertainment, arts and crafts, and educational exhibits.

SUMMER

➤ JUNE: Starting in late May and running into early June is a national ceramics competition and exhibition called **Feats of Clay** in the Gold Country (☎ 916/645–9713). The **Summer Solstice Ride & Arts Celebration** (☎ 209/223–5145) boosts spirits with bicycle rides, walks, and hands-on arts and crafts workshops for adults and children in Plymouth. During the first weekend in June, Pasadena City Hall Plaza hosts the **Chalk It Up Festival.** Artists use the pavement as their canvas to create masterpieces that wash away when festivities have come to a close. There are also musical performances and exotic dining kiosks. The proceeds benefit arts and homeless organizations of the Light-Bringer Project (☎ 626/449–3689). The **Napa Valley Wine Auction** in St. Helena features open houses, a wine tasting, and an auction. Preregistration by April 1 is required (☎ 707/942–9775).

➤ JULY: During the **Carmel Bach Festival,** the works of Johann Sebastian Bach and 18th-century contemporaries are performed for three weeks; events include concerts, recitals, and seminars (✉ Box 575, Carmel 93921, ☎ 408/624–1521). During the last full weekend in July, Gilroy, the self-styled Garlic Capital of the World, celebrates its smelly but delicious product with the **Gilroy Garlic Festival** (☎ 408/842–1625), featuring such unusual concoctions as garlic ice cream.

➤ AUGUST: The **California State Fair** (☎ 916/263–3000) showcases the state's agricultural side, with high-tech exhibits, a rodeo, horse racing, a carnival, and big-name entertainment. It runs 18 days from August to Labor Day in Sacramento. Santa Barbara's **Old Spanish Days' Fiesta** (☎ 805/962–8101) is the nation's largest all-equestrian parade. The citywide celebration includes two parades, two Mexican marketplaces, free variety shows with costumed dancers and singers, a carnival, and a rodeo.

AUTUMN

➤ SEPTEMBER: In Guerneville, jazz fans and musicians jam at John-

son's Beach for the **Russian River Jazz Festival** (☎ 707/869–3940). The **San Francisco Blues Festival** (☎ 415/826–6837) is held at Fort Mason in late September. The **Los Angeles County Fair** in Pomona (☎ 909/623–3111) is the largest county fair in the world. It hosts entertainment, exhibits, livestock, horse racing, food, and more.

➤ OCTOBER: The **Grand National Rodeo, Horse, and Stock Show** (☎ 415/469–6057) at San Francisco's Cow Palace is a 10-day, world-class competition, with 3,000 top livestock and horses. In Carmel, speakers and poets gather for readings on the beach, seminars, a banquet, and a book signing at the **Tor House Poetry Festival** (☎ 408/624–1813), which honors the late poet Robinson Jeffers, an area resident for many years.

➤ NOVEMBER: The **Death Valley '49er Encampment,** at Furnace Creek, commemorates the historic crossing of Death Valley

in 1849, with a fiddlers' contest and an art show (☎ 760/786–2331). Pasadena's **Doo Dah Parade,** a fun-filled spoof of the annual Rose Parade, features the Lounge Lizards, who dress as reptiles and lip-sync to Frank Sinatra favorites, and West Hollywood cheerleaders in drag (☎ 626/449–3689).

➤ DECEMBER: For the **Newport Harbor Christmas Boat Parade** in Newport Beach (☎ 714/729–4400), more than 200 festooned boats glide through the harbor nightly December 17–23. In Columbia in early December, the **Miner's Christmas Celebration** features costumed carolers and children's piñatas. Related events include a Victorian Christmas feast at the City Hotel, lamplight tours, and Las Posados Nativity Procession (☎ 209/536–1672). The internationally acclaimed El Teatro Campesino (☎ 408/623–2444) annually stages its nativity play *La Virgen Del Tepeyac* in the Mission San Juan Bautista.

2 The North Coast

From Muir Beach to Crescent City

The North Coast can only be summed up in superlatives. Migrating whales and other sea mammals swim past the dramatic bluffs that make the 400 miles of shoreline north of San Francisco to the Oregon border among the most photographed landscapes in the country. Along cypress- and redwood-studded Highway 1 you will find many small inns, uncrowded state beaches and parks, art galleries, and restaurants serving imaginative dishes that showcase locally produced ingredients.

BETWEEN SAN FRANCISCO BAY and the Oregon border lies the aptly named Redwood Empire, where national, state, and local parks welcome visitors year-round. The shoreline's natural attributes are self-evident, but the area is also rich in human history, having been the successive domain of Native American Miwoks and Pomos, Russian traders, Hispanic settlers, and more contemporary fishing folk and loggers. All have left visible legacies. This region is sparsely populated, with only a handful of towns with more than 1,000 inhabitants.

By Marty
Olmstead

Pleasures and Pastimes

Beaches
The waters of the Pacific along the North Coast are fine for seals, but most humans find the temperatures downright arctic. When it comes to spectacular cliffs and seascapes, though, the North Coast beaches are second to none. Explore tidal pools, watch for sea life, or dive for abalone. Don't worry about crowds: On many of these beaches you will have the sands largely to yourself.

Bicycling
Hardy riders take to Highway 1 year-round to experience the full beauty of the North Coast by mountain or racing bike. If you've trained sufficiently, biking all or a portion of the coast can be exhilarating. Bike-rental facilities are included in the Outdoor Activities and Sports listings for some of the towns covered in this chapter.

Dining
Despite its small population, the North Coast lays claim to several well-regarded restaurants. Seafood is abundant, of course, as are locally grown vegetables and herbs. In general, dining options are more varied near the coast than inland. Dress is usually informal, though dressy casual is the norm at some of the pricier establishments listed below.

CATEGORY	COST*
$$$$	over $50
$$$	$30–$50
$$	$20–$30
$	under $20

*per person for a three-course meal, excluding drinks, service, and 7¼% tax

Fishing
Depending on the season (and whether it's a good year in general for fishing), you can fish for rockfish, salmon, and steelhead in the rivers. Charters leave from Fort Bragg, Eureka, and elsewhere for ocean fishing. There's particularly good abalone diving around Jenner, Fort Ross, Point Arena, Westport, and Trinidad.

Lodging
Restored Victorians, rustic lodges, country inns, small hotels, and chic new structures are among the accommodations available along the North Coast. In several cases there are only one or two places to spend the night in a particular town; some of these are destinations in themselves. The best bed-and-breakfasts along the coast are often sold out on weekends months in advance, so reserve early.

CATEGORY	COST*
$$$$	over $175
$$$	$120–$175
$$	$80–$120
$	under $80

All prices are for a standard double room, excluding 8%–10% tax.

Nightlife and the Arts

Eureka, Ferndale, and Mendocino have long-standing repertory theater companies that perform contemporary and classic American plays. As for nightlife, if you're after a swinging, raucous time, the North Coast may not be the place for you, though almost every town of any size has a watering hole, often with good live music.

Whale-Watching

From any number of excellent observation points along the coast, you can watch gray whales during their annual winter migration season or, in the summer and fall, blue or humpback whales. Another option is a whale-watching cruise (☞ Contacts and Resources *in* the North Coast A to Z, *below*).

Exploring the North Coast

Exploring the northern California coast is easiest by car. Highway 1 is a beautiful, if sometimes slow and nerve-racking, drive. You'll want to stop frequently to appreciate the views, and there are many portions of the highway along which you won't drive faster than 20–40 mph. You can still have a fine trip even if you don't have much time, but be realistic and don't plan to drive too far in one day. The itineraries below proceed north from San Francisco.

Numbers in the text correspond to numbers in the margin and on the North Coast maps.

Great Itineraries

IF YOU HAVE 3 DAYS

Some of the finest redwoods in California reside less than 20 mi north of San Francisco in **Muir Woods National Monument** ①. After walking through the woods, stop for an early lunch in **Inverness** or continue on to **Fort Ross State Historic Park** ⑦, a reconstructed 19th-century Russian settlement. If you haven't eaten lunch, a deli-grocery store nearby sells picnic ingredients. Catch the sunset at quiet ⊞ **Gualala.** On the morning of day two, drive to ⊞ **Mendocino** ⑨. Spend the rest of your time in the North Coast browsing the many galleries, shops, historic sites, and beaches and parks of this cliffside enclave. Return to San Francisco via Highway 1, or the quicker route of Highway 128 east (from Highway 1 at the Navarro River, 10 mi south of Mendocino) to U.S. 101 south.

IF YOU HAVE 7 DAYS

Early on your first day, walk through **Muir Woods** ①. Then visit windswept **Stinson Beach** ② for a walk on the shore and lunch. In springtime and early summer, head north on Highway 1 to Bolinas Lagoon, where you can see bird nestings at **Audubon Canyon Ranch** ③, a 1,000-acre wildlife sanctuary. At other times of the year, continue north on Highway 1. One-third of a mile beyond **Olema,** look for a sign marking the turnoff for the **Bear Valley Visitor Center** ⑤, the gateway to the **Point Reyes National Seashore.** Tour a reconstructed Miwok Indian Village that's just a short walk from the visitor center. Spend the night in nearby ⊞ **Inverness** or one of the other coastal Marin towns. The next day, stop at **Goat Rock State Beach** and **Fort Ross State Historic Park** ⑦ on the way to ⊞ **Mendocino** ⑨. Explore the town the rest of the day. On your third morning head to **Fort Bragg** for a visit to the **Mendocino Coast Botanical Gardens**

18

The North Coast

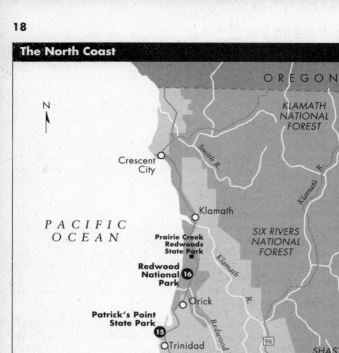
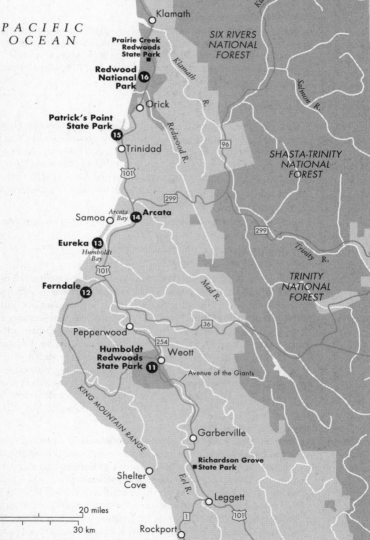

O R E G O N

KLAMATH NATIONAL FOREST

Crescent City

Klamath

Smith R.

Klamath R.

PACIFIC OCEAN

SIX RIVERS NATIONAL FOREST

Prairie Creek Redwoods State Park

Redwood National Park 16

Klamath R.

Salmon R.

Orick

Patrick's Point State Park 15

Trinidad

Redwood R.

96

SHASTA-TRINITY NATIONAL FOREST

101

299

Samoa

Arcata Bay

14 Arcata

299

Eureka 13

Humboldt Bay

Trinity R.

Ferndale 12

101

Mad R.

TRINITY NATIONAL FOREST

Pepperwood

36

254

Weott

Humboldt Redwoods State Park 11

Avenue of the Giants

KING MOUNTAIN RANGE

Garberville

Richardson Grove State Park

Shelter Cove

Eel R.

Leggett

1

101

0   20 miles

0   30 km

Rockport

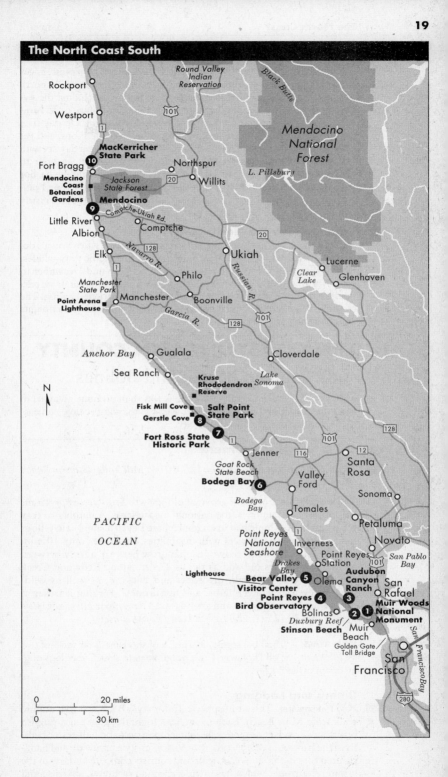

The North Coast South

Rockport

Westport

Round Valley Indian Reservation

Black Butte

MacKerricher State Park

Fort Bragg ⑩ Northspur

Mendocino Coast Botanical Gardens

Jackson State Forest

Willits

Mendocino National Forest

L. Pillsbury

⑨ **Mendocino**

Little River

Comptche-Ukiah Rd.

Albion

Comptche

Navarro R.

Elk

[128]

Philo

Ukiah

Russian R.

Lucerne

Clear Lake

Glenhaven

Manchester State Park

Manchester

Boonville

[20]

Point Arena Lighthouse

Garcia R.

[128] [101]

Anchor Bay

Gualala

Cloverdale

Sea Ranch

Kruse Rhododendron Reserve

Lake Sonoma

N

Fisk Mill Cove

Salt Point State Park

Gerstle Cove ⑧

⑦

Fort Ross State Historic Park

[1]

Jenner

[116]

Santa Rosa

[12]

[128]

Goat Rock State Beach

Valley Ford

[101]

Bodega Bay ⑥

Sonoma

Bodega Bay

Tomales

Petaluma

PACIFIC

OCEAN

Point Reyes National Seashore

[1]

Inverness

Novato

Drakes Bay

Point Reyes Station

San Pablo Bay

Lighthouse

Bear Valley Visitor Center

⑤ Olema

Audubon Canyon Ranch

[101]

San Rafael

Point Reyes Bird Observatory

④

③

Muir Woods National Monument

Bolinas

② ①

Stinson Beach

Duxbury Reef

Muir Beach

Golden Gate Toll Bridge

San Francisco Bay

San Francisco

[280]

0 ___ 20 miles

0 ___ 30 km

and possibly a trip on the *Skunk Train.* If you're in the mood to splurge, late on your third afternoon drive inland on Highway 1 to U.S. 101 north and spend the night at the Benbow Inn in ⚇ **Garberville.** Otherwise, linger in the Mendocino area. Either way, on your fourth day continue north through parts of **Humboldt Redwoods State Park** ⑪, including the **Avenue of the Giants.** Stop for the night in the Victorian village of ⚇ **Ferndale** ⑫ and visit the cemetery and the **Ferndale Museum.** On day five, drive to ⚇ **Eureka** ⑬. Have lunch in **Old Town,** visit the shops, and get a feel for local marine life on a Humboldt Bay cruise. Begin day six with breakfast at the **Samoa Cookhouse** before driving about an hour to **Patrick's Point State Park** ⑮. Have a late lunch overlooking the harbor in **Trinidad** before returning to Eureka for the night. Return to San Francisco on day seven. The drive back takes six hours on U.S. 101; it's nearly twice as long if you take Highway 1.

When to Tour the North Coast

The North Coast is a year-round destination, though when you go determines what you will see. The migration of the Pacific gray whales, for instance, is a wintertime phenomenon, roughly mid-December to early April. Winter days are usually more clear than summer days, particularly July and August, when views are often obstructed by fog. The coastal climate is quite similar to San Francisco's, although winter nights are colder than in the city.

SOUTHERN COASTAL MARIN COUNTY
Muir Woods, Stinson Beach, and Bolinas

Much of the Marin County coastline is less than an hour away from San Francisco, but the pace is slower. Most of the sights below can easily be done as day trips from the city.

Muir Woods National Monument

❶ *17 mi north of San Francisco on U.S. 101 to Mill Valley/Stinson Beach exit (Hwy. 1).*

The world's most popular grove of old-growth *Sequoia sempervirens* was one of the country's first national monuments. A number of easy hikes can be accomplished in an hour; there's even a short valley-floor trek, accessible to travelers with disabilities, that takes only 10 minutes to walk. The coast redwoods that grow here are mostly between 500 and 800 years old and as tall as 236 ft. Along Redwood Creek are other trees—live oak, madrone, and buckeye, as well as wildflowers (even in winter), ferns, and mushrooms. Parking is easier at Muir Woods before 10 AM and after 4 PM. ⊠ *Panoramic Hwy., off Hwy. 1,* ☎ *415/388–2595.* ⌷ *Free.* ☉ *Daily 8 AM–sunset.*

OFF THE BEATEN PATH   **MUIR BEACH** – Small but scenic, this patch of shoreline 3 mi south of Muir Woods just off Highway 1 is a good place to stretch your legs and gaze out at the Pacific.

Dining and Lodging

$$$–$$$$ ⚁⚇ **Pelican Inn.** This atmospheric Tudor-style B&B is a five-minute ★   walk from Muir Beach. Each room has Oriental scatter rugs, English prints, heavy velvet draperies, hanging tapestries, and half-tester beds. Even the bathrooms are special, with Victorian-style hardware and hand-painted tiles in the shower. Locals and tourists compete at darts in the ground-floor pub, which has a wide selection of brews, sherries, and ports. The Pelican's restaurant (closed Monday; $$–$$$) serves sturdy

English fare, from fish-and-chips to prime rib and Yorkshire pudding. Room rates include a full English breakfast. ⊠ *10 Pacific Way, at Hwy. 1, 94965,* ☎ *415/383–6000. 7 rooms. Restaurant. MC, V.*

Stinson Beach

❷ *8 mi from Muir Woods via Panoramic Hwy., 25 mi from San Francisco, U.S. 101 to Hwy. 1.*

Stinson Beach has the most expansive sands (4,500 ft) in Marin County; it's as close (when the fog hasn't rolled in) as you'll get to the stereotypical feel of a southern California beach. On any hot summer weekend, every road to Stinson Beach is jam-packed, so factor this into your plans.

Dining and Lodging

$–$$$ ✗ **Stinson Beach Grill.** A great selection of beer and wine, art on the
★   walls, and outdoor seating on a heated deck are among the draws here, but the food is memorable, too. Seafood and several types of oysters are served at lunch and dinner; the evening menu includes pasta, lamb, chicken, seafood, and southwestern specialties. ⊠ *3465 Hwy. 1,* ☎ *415/868–2002. AE, MC, V.*

$–$$ ✗ **Sand Dollar.** This pleasant pub serves hamburgers and other sandwiches for lunch and decent seafood for dinner; there's an outdoor dining deck. ⊠ *Hwy. 1,* ☎ *415/868–0434. MC, V.*

$$$–$$$$ 🏨 **Casa del Mar.** One of the few places to hang your hat in Stinson, this Mediterranean-style inn has extensive landscaping and an exceptional collection of paintings and sculptures by local artists. Accommodations are on the small side, but light colors and lots of windows create a feeling of spaciousness. ⊠ *37 Belvedere Ave., 94970,* ☎ *415/ 868–2124. 5 rooms. AE, MC, V.*

Bolinas

❸ The **Audubon Canyon Ranch,** a 1,000-acre wildlife sanctuary along the Bolinas Lagoon, is open for courting and mating season, mid-March through mid-July. Great blue herons and egrets are among the 60 species that call this home. The egrets nest in the redwood trees in Schwarz Grove. Telescopes and bird-hide observation posts allow for easier viewing. A small museum surveys the geology and natural history of the region. ⊠ *4900 Hwy. 1, along Bolinas Lagoon,* ☎ *415/868–9244.* 🎫 *Donation requested.* ☯ *Mid-Mar.–mid-July, weekends 10–4.*

If you're looking for abuse, at the northern edge of Bolinas Lagoon, 2 mi beyond the Audubon Canyon Ranch, take the unmarked road running west from Highway 1. It leads to the sleepy town of **Bolinas.** Don't expect a warm welcome: Some residents of Bolinas are so wary of tourism that whenever the state tries to post signs, they tear them down.

Nightlife

Smiley's Schooner Saloon. Virtually the *only* nightlife in Bolinas, this congenial bar hosts live music on Friday and Saturday nights. ⊠ *41 Wharf Rd.,* ☎ *415/868–1311.*

POINT REYES NATIONAL SEASHORE
Duxbury Reef, Olema, and Inverness

The Point Reyes National Seashore, which borders the northern reaches of the Golden Gate National Recreation Area (☞ Chapter 5), is a great place for hiking to secluded beaches, viewing wildlife, and driving through rugged, rolling grasslands. Highlights here include the ½-mi Earthquake Trail, which passes by what is believed to be the epicenter of the 1906 quake that destroyed much of San Francisco, and the late-19th-century Point Reyes Lighthouse, a good spot to watch for whales. Horses and mountain bikes are permitted on some trails. The towns of Olema, Point Reyes Station, Inverness, and Tomales, all in or near the national seashore area, have dining, lodging, and recreational facilities.

Duxbury Reef Area

2 mi northwest of Bolinas off Mesa Rd.

❹ Birders love the **Point Reyes Bird Observatory,** a sanctuary and research center within the Point Reyes National Seashore but more easily accessible from Bolinas. The area harbors nearly 225 species of bird life; banding occurs daily May through November as well as weekends and Wednesdays December through April, weather permitting. ⊠ *West on Mesa Rd., off Olema–Bolinas Rd.,* ☎ *415/868–0655.* ▣ *Free.* ☉ *Visitor center daily 8–6.*

Mile-long **Duxbury Reef,** a nature preserve, is the largest shale intertidal reef in North America. Check a tide table if you plan to explore the reef, which is accessible only at low tide. Look for starfish, barnacles, sea anemones, purple urchins, limpets, sea mussels, and the occasional red and black abalone. ⊠ *From Bolinas, take Mesa Rd. off Olema–Bolinas Rd.; make left on Overlook Dr. and right on Elm Ave. to beach parking lot.*

Olema

9 mi from Bolinas on Hwy. 1.

★ ❺ The Point Reyes National Seashore's **Bear Valley Visitor Center** has exhibits of park wildlife. The rangers here dispense advice about beaches, the Point Reyes Lighthouse, whale-watching, hiking trails, and camping. A reconstructed Miwok Indian Village that is only a short walk from the visitor center provides insight into the daily lives of the first human inhabitants of this region. ⊠ *Bear Valley Rd. west of Hwy. 1,* ☎ *415/663–1092.* ▣ *Free.* ☉ *Weekdays 9–5, weekends 8–5.*

Outdoor Activities and Sports

Many of the beaches in Point Reyes National Seashore are accessible off Bear Valley Road. **Limantour Beach** (⊠ End of Limantour Beach Rd.) is one of the most beautiful of Point Reyes sands; trails lead to other beaches north and south of here. **Trailhead Rentals** (⊠ 88 Bear Valley Rd., at Hwy. 1, ☎ 415/663–1958) supplies bicycles and binoculars. **Five Brooks Stables** (⊠ 8001 Hwy. 1, ☎ 415/663–1570) rents horses and equipment; from the stables, horseback trails wind through the Point Reyes woods and along the beaches.

Point Reyes Station

2 mi north of Olema on Hwy. 1.

Point Reyes Station, a stop on the North Pacific Coast Narrow-Gauge Railroad until 1933, has a number of false-front buildings, including the popular Western Saloon. The busiest place in town is Toby's Feed Barn, which sells offbeat gifts (many festooned with cows) as well as serious feed and grain to local farmers. There's a market on Main Street for picking up picnic supplies en route to Point Reyes.

Lodging

$ 🏠 **Point Reyes Hostel.** These dorm-style lodgings in an old clapboard ranch house are a good deal for budget travelers. The family room is limited to families with children five and under and must be reserved well in advance. ⊠ *Off Limantour Rd., Box 247, 94956,* ☎ *415/663–8811. Send $12 per adult per night, $6 per child with parent, with reservation request; state your gender. Shared kitchen. MC, V.*

Shopping
Gallery Route One (⊠ 11101 Hwy. 1, ☎ 415/663–1347), a nonprofit cooperative, exhibits area artists in all media.

Inverness

4 mi from Point Reyes Station on Sir Francis Drake Blvd., northwest from Hwy. 1.

Inverness boomed after the 1906 earthquake when wealthy San Franciscans built summer homes in its hills. Today, many of the structures serve as full-time residences or small B&B inns. A deli, a grocery store, restaurants, and shops are all located along Sir Francis Drake Boulevard.

★ The **Point Reyes Lighthouse Visitors Center** is a 45-minute drive from Inverness, across rolling hills that resemble Scottish heath. On busy weekends during the season, parking near the lighthouse is difficult. The view alone persuades most people to make the effort of walking down—and then back up—the hundreds of steps from the clifftops to the lighthouse below. If you choose to skip the descent, you can still see the whales from the cliff. ⊠ *Western end of Sir Francis Drake Blvd.,* ☎ *415/669–1534.* ☉ *Thurs.–Sun. 10–5 (steps close at 4:30).*

Dining and Lodging
$ ✕ **Grey Whale.** This casual place is a good stop for pizza, salad, pastries, and espresso. ⊠ *12781 Sir Francis Drake Blvd.,* ☎ *415/669–1244. MC, V.*

$$$ ✕🔲 **Manka's.** Three intimate wood-paneled dining rooms, glowing with candlelight and piano music, provide the setting for creative American-regional cuisine. Specialties include line-caught fish, unusual game such as caribou and pheasant that are grilled in the fireplace, and homemade desserts. Two of the four smallish guest rooms above the restaurant (closed Tuesday and Wednesday year-round, Sunday–Thursday in January; no lunch) have private decks that look onto Tomales Bay. Rooms in the Redwood Annex and two cabins are also available. ⊠ *30 Calendar Way, 94937,* ☎ *415/669–1034. 14 rooms. Restaurant. AE, MC, V.*

$$–$$$$ 🔲 **Blackthorne Inn.** An adult-size fantasy tree house, this imaginative structure is highlighted by a 3,500-square-ft deck with stairways to higher decks. The solarium was made with timbers from San Francisco wharves; the outer walls are salvaged doors from a railway station. A glass-sheathed, octagonal tower called the Eagle's Nest crowns the inn. Room rates include a buffet breakfast. ⊠ *266 Vallejo Ave., Box 712, Inverness Park 94937,* ☎ *415/663–8621. 5 rooms, 2 with shared bath. Hot tub. MC, V.*

$$$ 🔲 **Ten Inverness Way.** The comfortable living room of this low-key inn has a classic stone fireplace and a player piano; cozy rooms are highlighted by such homespun touches as patchwork quilts, lived-in-looking antiques, and dormer ceilings with skylights. The rates include a full breakfast. ⊠ *Inverness Way, Box 63, 94937,* ☎ *415/669–1648. 5 rooms. Hot tub. MC, V.*

Shopping
Shaker Shops West (⊠ 5 Inverness Way, ☎ 415/669–7256) carries fine reproduction Shaker furniture and gift items.

Valley Ford

23 mi north of Point Reyes Station on Hwy. 1.

Lodging

$$$–$$$$ 🏠 **Sonoma Coast Villa.** This secluded oasis in the coastal hills between Valley Ford and Bodega Bay is a most unusual inn. Founded as an Arabian horse ranch in 1976, the 60-acre property has a single-story row of accommodations beside a swimming pool. Red-tile roofs, a stucco exterior, Mediterranean-style landscaping, and two courtyards create a European ambience. Rooms are decorated individually, but all have slate floors, French doors, beamed ceilings, and wood-burning fireplaces. Nine new guest rooms are scheduled for completion before the end of 1997. The restaurant is closed November–March. ⊠ *16702 Hwy. 1, Bodega 94922,* ☎ *707/876–9818 or 888/404–2255,* 🖷 *707/876–9856. 6 rooms. Restaurant, pool, hot tub. AE, MC, V.*

$$ 🏠 **Inn at Valley Ford.** The rooms at this small B&B, a Victorian farmhouse built in the late 1860s, are named after literary figures, characters, or periods. Books commemorating each chamber's theme grace its bookshelves. Bird-watching is a favorite pastime here: blue herons, egrets, hawks, and owls make Valley Ford their home. Room rates include a full gourmet breakfast, which comes with the inn's specialty, old-fashioned cream scones. ⊠ *14395 Hwy. 1, Box 439, 94972,* ☎ *707/876–3182. 4 rooms with 2 shared baths, 1 cottage suite with private bath. DC, MC, V.*

OFF THE
BEATEN PATH   **OSMOSIS ENZYME BATHS –** The tiny town of Freestone, 4 mi north of Tomales, has a few good shops, such as Pastorale, a women's clothing boutique, but the real reason to detour inland from Highway 1 is Osmosis Enzyme Baths. This spa, in a two-story clapboard house on extensive grounds, specializes in several treatments, including a detoxifying "dry" bath in a blend of enzymes and fragrant wood shavings. After 20 minutes in the tub, opt for a 75-minute massage in one of the freestanding Japanese-style pagodas near the creek that runs through the property. ⊠ *209 Bohemian Hwy., Freestone,* ☎ *707/823–8231.*

SONOMA AND MENDOCINO

Bodega Bay to Fort Bragg

The gently rolling countryside of coastal Marin gives way to more dramatic scenery north of Bodega Bay. Cattle cling for their lives (or so it seems) to steep inclines alongside the increasingly curvy highway, now traveling right along the coast. Past Jenner, the road twists and turns; by the time it reaches Sea Ranch, hairpin curves and stunning vistas compete for drivers' attention.

Bodega Bay

❻   *8 mi from Valley Ford on Hwy. 1, 65 mi north of San Francisco via U.S. 101 and Hwy. 1.*

Bodega Bay is one of the busiest harbors on the Sonoma County coast. Commercial boats pursue ocean fish as well as the famed Dungeness crabs. Galleries and T-shirt shops line both sides of Highway 1; a short drive around the harbor leads to the Pacific. This is the last stop, townwise, before Gualala, and a good spot for stretching your legs and taking in the salt air. For a closer look, visit the **Bodega Marine Laboratory** (☎ 707/875–2211 for directions), on a 326-acre reserve on nearby Bodega Head. The lab gives free one-hour tours and peeks at intertidal invertebrates, such as sea stars and sea anemones, on Friday from 2 to 3:45 PM.

Dining and Lodging

$$$ ✕⊠ **Inn at the Tides.** This complex of condominium-style buildings has spacious rooms with high ceilings and uncluttered decor. All rooms have a view of the harbor, and some have fireplaces. Room rates include a Continental breakfast. The inn's two restaurants serve both old-style and more adventurous seafood dishes; in season, you can buy a slab of salmon or live or cooked crab at a seafood stand on the premises. ⊠ *800 Hwy. 1, Box 640, 94923,* ☎ *707/875–2751 or 800/541–7788,* ℻ *707/875–2669. 86 rooms. 2 restaurants, refrigerators, room service, pool, hot tub, sauna, coin laundry. AE, MC, V.*

Outdoor Activities and Sports

Bodega Bay Sportfishing (⊠ Bay Flat Rd., ☎ 707/875–3344) charters ocean-fishing boats and rents equipment. The operators of the 700-acre **Chanslor Guest Ranch** (⊠ 2660 Hwy. 1, ☎ 707/875–2721) lead guided horseback rides along the coastal wetlands, the beach, and into Salmon Creek canyon.

Shopping

The **Ren Brown Gallery** (⊠ 1781 Hwy. 1, ☎ 707/875–2922) on the north end of town is renowned for its selection of Asian arts, crafts, furnishings, and design books. This two-floor gallery also represents a number of local artists worth checking out.

Jenner

10 mi north of Bodega Bay on Hwy. 1.

The Russian River empties into the Pacific Ocean at Jenner. The town has a couple of good restaurants and some shops. Just south of the river is windy **Goat Rock State Beach,** where a colony of sea lions (walk north from the parking lot) resides most of the year. The beach is open daily from 8 AM to sunset; there's no day-use fee.

Dining

$$–$$$ ✕ **River's End.** At the right time of year, diners at this rustic restaurant
★ can view sea lions lazing on the beach below. The creative fare is eclectic/German—seafood, venison, and duck dishes. Brunches here are exceptional. ⊠ *Hwy. 1, north end of Jenner,* ☎ *707/865–2484. MC, V. Closed Jan.–Feb. 13.*

Fort Ross State Historic Park

 9 mi north of Jenner on Hwy. 1.

Fort Ross, completed in 1821, became Russia's major fur-trading outpost in California. The Russians brought Aleut sea-otter hunters down from their Alaskan bailiwicks to hunt pelts for the czar. In 1841, the area depleted of seal and otter, the Russians sold their post to John Sutter, later of gold-rush fame. After a local Anglo rebellion against the Mexicans, the land fell under U.S. domain, becoming part of California in 1850. The state park service has reconstructed Fort Ross, including its Russian Orthodox chapel, a redwood stockade, the officers' barracks, and a blockhouse. The excellent museum here documents the fort's history and some of the North Coast's. ⊠ *Hwy. 1,* ☎ *707/847–3286.* ⊒ *$6 per vehicle (day use).* ☉ *Daily 10–4:30. No dogs allowed past parking lot.*

Lodging

$$$$ ⊡ **Timberhill Ranch.** The winding country road just south of Fort Ross
★ that leads east from Highway 1 to the Timberhill Ranch gives visitors

just enough time to ease into the restful pace of this secluded resort. Simple and serene, Timberhill has 15 cabins decorated with quilts and fresh flowers. Each has a fireplace and private patio where guests can enjoy the breakfast brought to them on a golf cart—perhaps sharing croissants with the resident ducks and geese that waddle up from the ranch's huge pond. Timberhill's inspired six-course dinners (included, with breakfast, in the room rates) take place by candlelight. ⊠ *35755 Hauser Bridge Rd. (Timber Cove Post Office), 95421,* ☎ *707/847– 3258,* FAX *707/847–3342. 15 cottages. Minibars, refrigerators, pool, outdoor hot tub, tennis courts, hiking. AE, MC, V.*

$$–$$$$ 🏨 **Fort Ross Lodge.** The lodge, about 1½ mi north of the same-named Russian fort, is somewhat dated and wind-bitten, but all but four of its rooms have fireplaces and views of the Sonoma shoreline; some have a private hot tub on a back patio. Seven hill units have sauna, hot tub, and fireplace. ⊠ *20705 Hwy. 1, 95450,* ☎ *707/847–3333. 22 rooms. Refrigerators. AE, MC, V.*

Salt Point State Park

⑧   *11 mi north of Jenner on Hwy. 1.*

Salt Point State Park yields a glimpse of nature virtually untouched by humans. At the 6,000-acre park's **Gerstle Cove** you'll probably catch sight of seals sunning themselves on the beach's rocks and deer roaming in the meadowlands. The unusual formations in the sandstone are called tafoni and are the product of hundreds of years of erosion. A very short drive leads to Fisk Mill Cove. A five-minute walk uphill brings you to a bench from which there is a dramatic overview of Sentinel Rock and the pounding surf below. ⊠ *Hwy. 1,* ☎ *707/847–3221.* 💰 *$5 per vehicle (day use). Camping $14 peak season, $12 off-season (*☎ *800/444–7275).* ☉ *Daily sunrise–sunset.*

Kruse Rhododendron Reserve, a peaceful, 317-acre forested park, has thousands of rhododendrons that bloom in light shade in the late spring. ⊠ *Hwy. 1, north of Fisk Mill Cove.* 💰 *Free.*

Lodging

$ 🏨 **Stillwater Cove Ranch.** Seventeen miles north of Jenner, this former boys' school that overlooks Stillwater Cove has been transformed into a pleasant, if spartan, place to lodge. ⊠ *22555 Hwy. 1, 95450,* ☎ *707/ 847–3227. 6 rooms. No credit cards.*

Sea Ranch

18 mi from Fort Ross on Hwy. 1.

Sea Ranch is a development of stylish second homes on 5,000 acres overlooking the Pacific. To appease critics, Sea Ranch built public beach-access trails off Highway 1 south of Gualala. Even some militant environmentalists deem the structures designed by architects William Turnbull and Charles Moore to be reasonably congruent with the surroundings; others find the weathered wood buildings beautiful.

Dining and Lodging

$$$–$$$$ ✕🏨 **Sea Ranch Lodge.** Set high on a bluff with ocean views, the lodge is close to beaches, trails, and golf. Some rooms have fireplaces, and some have hot tubs. Handcrafted wood furnishings and quilts create an earthy, contemporary look. The restaurant, which overlooks the Pacific, serves good seafood and homemade desserts. Guests receive a complimentary Continental breakfast. ⊠ *60 Sea Walk Dr., Box 44, 95497,* ☎ *707/785–2371 or 800/732–7262,* FAX *707/785–2243. 20 rooms. Restaurant. AE, MC, V.*

$$–$$$$ ⊞ **Sea Ranch Escape.** The Sea Ranch houses, sparsely scattered on a grass meadow fronting a stretch of ocean, are a striking sight from Highway 1. Groups or families can rent fully furnished houses for two nights (minimum) or more. Linen, housekeeping, and catering services are available for a fee. You can dine at superb nearby restaurants or stock up on provisions from one of the markets in Gualala and make use of the full kitchens. All houses have TVs and VCRs; some have hot tubs and some take pets. Rates are most expensive next to the surf; prices recede with distance from the beach. ⊠ *60 Sea Walk Dr., Box 238, 95497,* ☎ *707/ 785–2426 or 800/732–7262,* ℻ *707/785–2124. 55 houses. MC, V.*

Gualala

11 mi north of Sea Ranch on Hwy. 1.

This former lumber port remains a sleepy drive-through except for the several ocean-view motels that serve as headquarters for visitors exploring the coast. It lies just north of the Gualala River (a good place for fishing), which serves as the county line for Mendocino. On the river's Sonoma side, **Gualala Point Regional Park** (⊠ Hwy. 1, ☎ 707/ 785–2377), open daily from 8 AM until sunset, is an excellent whale-watching spot. The park has picnicking—the day-use fee is $3—and camping for $14 per night; campsites are available on a first-come, first-served basis during winter, but reservations are required from May through October.

Dining and Lodging

$$–$$$$ ✕⊞ **St. Orres.** One of the North Coast's most eye-catching inns, St. Orres reflects the area's Russian influence. The main house is crowned by two onion-domed towers. The exterior is further accented by balconies, stained-glass windows, and wood-inlaid towers. Two rooms overlook the sea, and the other six are set over the garden or forest; all the rooms in the main house share baths. The tranquil woods behind the house hold 11 rustic cottages; eight have woodstoves or fireplaces. Those traveling with children are placed in the cottages. Room rates include a full breakfast. The inn's restaurant (closed Wednesday in winter) serves dinner only, a fixed-price meal ($$$–$$$$) with a choice of five entrées (meat or fish) plus soup and salad. ⊠ *Hwy. 1, 2 mi north of Gualala, Box 523, 95445,* ☎ *707/884–3303,* ℻ *707/884–3903. 8 rooms with shared baths, 11 cottages. Restaurant, hot tub, sauna, beach. MC, V.*

$$$–$$$$ ⊞ **Whale Watch Inn.** This fine inn lives up to its name—most rooms here have views (through cypress trees) down the coast, where whales often come close to shore on their northern migration in early spring. Year-round, the scent of pine and salt-sea air fills the rooms, all of which have fireplaces and small decks; some have whirlpool baths or kitchens. A 132-step stairway leads down to a small, virtually private beach. Set amid 2½ acres, the Whale Watch maintains well-kept gardens that bloom even in winter. A full breakfast is brought to guests in their rooms. ⊠ *35100 Hwy. 1, 95445,* ☎ *707/884–3667 or 800/942–5342,* ℻ *707/ 884–4815. 12 rooms, 6 suites. AE, MC, V.*

$$–$$$ ⊞ **Old Milano Hotel.** Overlooking the spectacular coast just north of
★ Gualala and set amid English gardens, the Old Milano is one of California's premier B&Bs. The 1905 mansion is listed on the National Register of Historic Places. Rooms are appointed with exceptional antiques; five of the upstairs rooms have ocean views, and another overlooks the gardens. All upstairs rooms share bathrooms. The downstairs master suite has a private sitting room and a picture window framing the sea. Those in search of something different might consider the caboose with a wood-burning stove. The rates include breakfast. Din-

ner, not included in the rates, is usually offered Wednesday through Sunday. ⊠ *38300 Hwy. 1, 95445,* ☎ *707/884–3256. 9 rooms. Hot tub. MC, V. No smoking.*

$ ⊡ **Gualala Hotel.** Gualala's oldest hotel, which once housed timber mill workers, has small, no-nonsense rooms furnished with down-home-looking antiques. Most rooms share baths. Rooms in the front have ocean views (and some street noise). The intensely atmospheric first-floor saloon was an old Jack London haunt. ⊠ *39301 Hwy. 1,* ☎ *707/884– 3441. 19 rooms, 5 with private bath. Restaurant, bar. AE, D, MC, V.*

En Route   For a dramatic view of the surf, take the marked road off Highway 1 north of the fishing village of Point Arena to the **Point Arena Lighthouse** (☎ *707/882–2777*). First constructed in 1870, the lighthouse was destroyed by the 1906 earthquake that also devastated San Francisco. Rebuilt in 1907, it towers 115 ft from its base, 50 ft above the sea. The lighthouse is open for tours daily from 11 until 2:30, one hour later in summer and on some holidays; admission is $2.50. As you continue north on Highway 1 toward Mendocino there are several beaches, most notably the one at **Manchester State Park,** 3 mi north of Point Arena. If you're driving directly to Mendocino from points south and just want to grab a quick lunch or a good cup of coffee, visit the café at the **Greenwood Pier Inn** (⊠ 5928 Hwy. 1, ☎ 707/877–9997) in Elk.

Elk

39 mi north of Gualala on Hwy. 1.

Dining and Lodging

$$$–$$$$ ✕⊡ **Harbor House.** Constructed in 1916 by a timber company to entertain its guests, this redwood ranch-style house has a dining room with a view of the Pacific. Five of the six rooms in the main house have fireplaces, and some are furnished with antiques original to the house. There are also four smallish cottages with fireplaces and decks. Room rates include breakfast and dinner. The restaurant (reservations essential), which serves California cuisine, is highly recommended; there's limited seating for those not spending the night. ⊠ *5600 S. Hwy. 1, 95432,* ☎ *707/877–3203. 10 rooms. Restaurant. No credit cards.*

$$–$$$$ ⊡ **Elk Cove Inn.** Private and very romantic rooms and suites are perched
★   on a bluff above the pounding surf. Accommodations range from a petite but smartly furnished room without a view to a huge ocean-view suite with a stereo system, a whirlpool tub, and a wet bar. All rooms have coffee and hand-embroidered cloths; some rooms have wood-burning stoves. Rates include a full gourmet breakfast. Ask about off-season discount packages. ⊠ *6300 S. Hwy. 1, Box 367, 95432,* ☎ *707/ 877–3321,* ℻ *707/877–1808. 11 rooms, 4 suites. Beach. AE, MC, V.*

Albion

4 mi north of Elk on Hwy. 1.

Dining and Lodging

$$$ ✕ **Ledford House.** The menu at this restaurant on a bluff is divided into hearty bistro dishes—mainly stews and pastas—and equally large-portioned examples of California cuisine: ahi tuna, grilled meats, and the like. ⊠ *3000 N. Hwy. 1,* ☎ *707/937–0282. AE, MC, V. Closed Mon. in summer, Mon.–Tues. in winter. No lunch.*

$$$–$$$$ ✕⊡ **Albion River Inn.** Modern two-room cottages at this inn overlook the dramatic bridge and seascape where the Albion River empties into the Pacific. All but two have decks facing the ocean. Six have hot tubs

for two, and eight have double bathtubs. The decor ranges from antique furnishings to wide-back willow chairs. A full breakfast is included. In the glassed-in dining room, which serves grilled dishes and fresh seafood, the views are as captivating as the food. ⊠ *3790 N. Hwy. 1, Box 100, 95410,* ☎ *707/937–1919; 800/479–7944 from northern CA;* FAX *707/937–2604. 20 rooms. Restaurant. AE, MC, V.*

Little River

3 mi north of Albion on Hwy. 1.

Little River is home to **Van Damme State Park,** one of the coast's best spots for abalone diving. The visitor center here has interesting displays on ocean life and Native American history. ⊠ *Hwy. 1,* ☎ *707/937–5804 for park, 707/937–4016 for visitor center.*

The nearby **Pygmy Forest** contains wizened trees, some more than a century old, that stand only 3 to 4 ft tall. Highly acidic soil and poor drainage combine to stunt the trees' growth. To reach the forest by car, turn left on Little River Airport Road, ½ mi south of Van Damme State Park, and continue 3½ mi to the clearly marked parking area.

Dining and Lodging

$$ ✕ **Little River Restaurant.** Despite its modest appearance, this tiny place across from the Little River Inn serves some of the best dinners in the Mendocino area. Steak and fresh seafood are the specialties. ⊠ *Hwy. 1,* ☎ *707/937–4945. No credit cards. Closed Tues.–Thurs. year-round, Mon.–Thurs. in Dec. No lunch.*

$$$$ ✕🏠 **Heritage House.** The cottages at this resort have stunning ocean views. The dining room, also with a Pacific panorama, serves breakfast and dinner, which are included with the room rate for guests; others should make reservations in advance. Each room's decor is unique, but all are appointed with plush furnishings, and many have private decks, fireplaces, and whirlpool tubs. ⊠ *Hwy. 1, 95456,* ☎ *707/937–5885,* FAX *707/937–0318. 72 rooms. Restaurant. MC, V. Closed Jan.–mid-Feb.*

$$–$$$$ 🏠 **Glendeven Inn.** The New England–style main house of this tran-
★ quil inn has five rooms, all with private baths, three with fireplaces. A converted barn holds a two-bedroom suite with kitchen and an art gallery. The 1986 Stevenscroft building has a high-peaked, gabled roof and weathered barnlike siding. The four rooms within all have fireplaces. The owners, both designers, have decorated the guest rooms with antiques, contemporary art, and ceramics. Room rates include breakfast. ⊠ *8221 N. Hwy. 1, 95456,* ☎ *707/937–0083,* FAX *707/937–6108. 9 rooms, 1 suite. AE, MC, V.*

Mendocino

❾ *2 mi north of Little River on Hwy. 1, 153 mi from San Francisco, north on U.S. 101, west on Hwy. 128, and north on Hwy. 1.*

This 19th-century town may look familiar to fans of the television series *Murder, She Wrote.* Mendocino played the role of Cabot Cove, Maine. The subterfuge worked because so many of the original settlers here came from the Northeast and built houses in the New England style. The Blair House at 45110 Little Lake Street was the home of Jessica Fletcher (Angela Lansbury's character) in the series. Mendocino has also played the part of a California town, most notably in the Elia Kazan production of John Steinbeck's novel *East of Eden,* starring James Dean. The building on Main Street (at Kasten Street) that houses the astronomy-oriented Out of This World store was the Bay City Bank in the film.

By the 1950s, artists and craftspeople began flocking here, finding the setting inspirational and less suburban than places like Sausalito. In their wake came other adventuresome souls, several of whom opened small inns in large older homes. Others established restaurants and cafés. There is still a bit of the old town to be seen in dives like Dick's Place, a bar near the Mendocino Hotel. The rest of the small downtown area is devoted almost exclusively to restaurants and shops.

The area arts scene is flourishing. The **Mendocino Art Center** (⊠ 45200 Little Lake St., ☎ 707/937–5818) has exhibits, art classes, a gallery, and a theater. The **Kelley House Museum** (⊠ 45007 Albion St., ☎ 707/ 937–5791) is a refurbished 1861 structure displaying historical photographs of Mendocino's logging days, antique cameras, Victorian-era clothing, furniture, and artifacts. Admission is $1; the museum is open June to September, daily 1 to 4, and October to May, Friday to Monday 1 to 4. The tiny green and red **Temple of Quan Ti** (⊠ Albion St., west of Kasten St., ☎ 707/937–5123), the oldest Chinese temple on the North Coast, dates to 1852. It's only open weekends by appointment, but you can peer in the window and see everything there is to see.

The restored **Ford House,** built in 1854, serves as the visitor center for Mendocino Headlands State Park. The house has a scale model of Mendocino as it looked in 1890, when the town had 34 water towers and a 12-seat outhouse. History walks leave from the house Saturdays at 1 PM. The park itself consists of the cliffs that border the town; access is free. ⊠ *Ford House, Main St., west of Lansing St.,* ☎ *707/937–5397.* ⊡ *Free.* ☉ *Daily 11–4, with possible midweek closings in winter.*

★ The **Mendocino Coast Botanical Gardens** were established as a private preserve in 1962, with additional acreage added over the years. Along 2 mi of coastal trails, with ocean views and observation points for whale-watching, is a splendid array of flowers; the rhododendrons are at their peak from April to June, and fuchsias, heather, and azaleas are resplendent. You can have lunch or dinner at the on-site Gardens Grill (☞ Dining and Lodging *in* Fort Bragg, *below*). ⊠ *18220 N. Hwy. 1, between Mendocino and Fort Bragg,* ☎ *707/964–4352.* ⊡ *$5.* Apr.–Oct., daily 9–5; Nov.–Mar., daily 9–4.

Side Trip to the Anderson Valley

Mendocino's ocean breezes might seem too cool for grape growing, but summer days can be quite warm just over the hills in the Anderson Valley and the cooler nights there permit a longer ripening period. Chardonnays and pinot noirs find the valley's climate particularly hospitable. Tasting here is a decidedly more laid-back affair than in the Napa and Sonoma valleys. Most tasting rooms are open from 11 to 5 daily and charge a nominal fee (usually deducted if you purchase any wines) to sample a few vintages. To get to the Anderson Valley from Mendocino take Highway 1 south to Highway 128 east.

Husch (⊠ 4400 Hwy. 128, Philo, ☎ 707/895–3216), one of the valley's oldest wineries, sells a superb gewürztraminer. At the elegant tasting room at **Roederer Estate** (⊠ 4501 Hwy. 128, Philo, ☎ 707/ 895–2288), you can taste sparkling wines produced by the American affiliate of the famous French champagne maker. **Scharffenberger Cellars** (⊠ 8501 Hwy. 128, Philo, ☎ 800/824–7754) was the first Anderson Valley winery to produce award-winning sparkling wines. If you're not up for a trip to the valley, **Fetzer Vineyards** (⊠ Main St. between Lansing and Kasten Sts., Mendocino, ☎ 707/937–6191) has a tasting room next to the Mendocino Hotel.

Dining and Lodging

$$ ✗ **Cafe Beaujolais.** All the rustic charm of peaceful, backwoods Men-
★ docino is here, with great country cooking to boot. The ever-evolving
dinner menu is cross-cultural and includes such delicacies as Yucate-
can Thai crab cakes and a barbecued rock-shrimp-filled corn crepe with
avocado and blood-orange pico de gallo. Owner Margaret Fox runs
the mail-order Cafe Beaujolais bakery—be sure to take home a pack-
age or two of her irresistible *panforte,* a dense cake made with almonds,
hazelnuts, or macadamia nuts. ⊠ *961 Ukiah St.,* ☎ *707/937–5614.*
No credit cards.

$$ ✗ **955 Ukiah St.** The interior of this smart restaurant beside Cafe
Beaujolais is woodsy and the California cuisine creative. Specialties in-
clude pastas topped with original sauces and fresh fish. Pacific red snap-
per is wrapped in phyllo dough and topped with pesto and lemon sauce.
⊠ *955 Ukiah St.,* ☎ *707/937–1955. MC, V. Closed Mon.–Tues.*
July–Nov., Mon.–Wed. Dec.–June. No lunch.

$$–$$$$ ✗⌂ **MacCallum House.** With the most meticulously restored Victorian
exterior in Mendocino, this 1882 inn, complete with gingerbread trim,
transports patrons back to another era. Comfortable furnishings and
antiques enhance the period feel. In addition to the main house, there
are individual cottages and barn suites around a garden with a gazebo.
The menu at the firelit, redwood-paneled restaurant (reservations es-
sential) changes quarterly. The focus is on fresh local seafood. ⊠
45020 Albion St., Box 206, 95460, ☎ *707/937–0289 or 800/609–*
0492. 19 rooms. Restaurant, bar. MC, V.

$$–$$$$ ✗⌂ **Mendocino Hotel.** From the outside, this hotel looks like something out of the Wild West, with a period facade and balcony that over-
hangs the raised sidewalk. Inside, an elegant atmosphere is achieved
by stained-glass lamps, Remington paintings, polished wood, and Persian carpets. All but 14 of the rooms have private baths, and the 19th-
century decor is appealing. Deluxe garden rooms have fireplaces and
TVs. The wood-paneled dining room, fronted by a glassed-in solarium, serves fine fish dishes and the best deep-dish ollalieberry pies in
California. ⊠ *45080 Main St., Box 587, 95460,* ☎ *707/937–0511 or*
800/548–0513, ℻ *707/937–0513. 51 rooms. Restaurant, bar, room*
service. AE, MC, V.

$$$–$$$$ ⌂ **Headlands Inn.** All rooms at this magnificently restored 1868 Cape
★ Cod–style building have private baths, feather beds, and fireplaces; some
overlook a garden and the pounding surf, and others have village
views. There is also a private cottage on the premises. Gourmet break-
fast is served in your room, and afternoon tea is served in an upstairs
sitting room. ⊠ *Howard and Albion Sts., Box 132, 95460,* ☎ *707/*
937–4431. 5 rooms. AE, MC, V.

$$$–$$$$ ⌂ **Stanford Inn by the Sea.** Set back from the highway, this two-story
★ lodge expanded in 1996 with new suites that are even more elegant than
the original wood-paneled rooms. All accommodations have decks
with ocean views, four-poster or sleigh beds, fireplaces or woodstoves,
and paintings by local artists. The inn, the only one on the North Coast
with an organic garden *and* resident llamas, has a huge reception lounge
where guests can read by the fire or enjoy the ocean view over a cooked-
to-order breakfast or afternoon wine and hors d'oeuvres, all included
in the rates. ⊠ *South of Mendocino, east on Comptche–Ukiah Rd. (off*
Hwy. 1), Box 487, 95460, ☎ *707/937–5615 or 800/331–8884,* ℻ *707/*
937–0305. 24 rooms. Refrigerators, indoor pool, hot tub, sauna, bi-
cycles. AE, D, DC, MC, V.

$$–$$$$ ⛪ **Agate Cove Inn.** Facing the Mendocino Headlands across a rocky cove, this inn is ideally situated for watching whales migrating during the winter. Adirondack chairs are set on a small deck for just that purpose; guests may borrow the inn's binoculars for a closer look. Each blue-and-white cottage unit is individually decorated, mostly in quilts, floral wallpaper, and canopy or four-poster beds. There are four single and four duplex cottages; another two rooms are in the 1860s farmhouse, where country breakfasts are prepared on an antique woodstove in full view of the Pacific. ✉ *11201 N. Lansing St., 95460,* ☎ *707/937–0551. 10 rooms. MC, V.*

$$–$$$ ⛪ **Blackberry Inn.** Kids are bound to go wild for the Wild West theme of this hilltop complex. Each single-story unit has a false front, creating the image of a frontier town—there's a bank, a saloon, Belle's Place (of hospitality), and "offices" for doctors and sheriffs, as well as other themed accommodations. The owners were inspired to build this place in the late 1970s by the old James Garner movie *Support Your Local Sheriff.* Rooms are cheery and spacious, most have wood-burning stoves or fireplaces, and all but one have at least a partial ocean view. The inn is a short drive east of town down a quiet side street. Two rooms have kitchenettes. ✉ *44951 Larkin Rd., 95460,* ☎ *707/937–5281 or 800/950–7806. 16 rooms. MC, V.*

$$–$$$ ⛪ **Joshua Grindle Inn.** The original farmhouse of this B&B on a 2-acre hilltop has five guest rooms, a parlor, and a dining room. Two outbuildings, the Watertower (an upper room has windows on all four sides) and the Cottage hold five additional rooms. Furnishings throughout the inn are simple but comfortable American antiques: Salem rockers, wing chairs, steamer-trunk tables, painted pine beds. Room rates include a full breakfast. ✉ *44800 Little Lake Rd., 95460,* ☎ *707/937–4143. 10 rooms. MC, V.*

Nightlife and the Arts

Mendocino Theatre Company (✉ Mendocino Art Center, 45200 Little Lake St., ☎ 707/937–4477) has been around for more than two decades. The community theater's repertoire ranges from classics like *Uncle Vanya* to more recent works like *Other People's Money.*

Patterson's Pub (✉ 10485 Lansing St., ☎ 707/937–4782), an Irish-style watering hole, is a friendly gathering place day or night, though it does become boisterous as the evening wears on. Live bands entertain on Friday nights.

Outdoor Activities and Sports

Catch-a-Canoe and Bicycles Too (✉ Stanford Inn by the Sea, Mendocino, ☎ 707/937–0273) has daily and hourly rentals of regular and outrigger canoes and mountain and suspension bicycles.

Shopping

Many fine artists exhibit their wares in Mendocino, and the streets of this compact town are so easily walkable that you're sure to find a gallery with something that strikes your fancy. You might start at the **Mendocino Art Center** (☞ *above*). **Old Gold** is a good place to look for locally designed and crafted jewelry.

Fort Bragg

10 mi north of Mendocino on Hwy. 1.

Fort Bragg has changed more than any other coastal town in the last few years. The decline in what was the top industry, timber, is being offset in part by a boom in charter-boat excursions and other tourist pursuits. The city is also attracting many artists—even luring some from nearby Mendocino, where the cost of living is higher. This basically blue-collar town is the commercial center of Mendocino County.

The **Skunk Train,** a remnant of the region's logging days, dates from 1885 and travels a route, through redwood forests inaccessible to automobiles, from Fort Bragg to the town of Willits, 40 mi inland. A fume-spewing, self-propelled train car that shuttled passengers along the railroad got nicknamed the *Skunk Train,* and the entire line has been called that ever since. Excursions are now given on historic trains and replicas of the *Skunk Train* motorcar that are more aromatic than the original. In summer you have a choice of going partway to Northspur, a three-hour round-trip, or making the full seven-hour journey to Willits and back. ⊠ *Foot of Laurel St., Fort Bragg,* ☎ *707/964–6371. Fort Bragg–Willits: departs daily 9:20 AM.* ⌧ *$26. Fort Bragg–Northspur: departs mid-June–early Sept., daily 9:20 AM and 1:40 PM; early Sept.–mid-June 10 AM and 2 PM.* ⌧ *$21.*

★ ❿ **MacKerricher State Park** includes 10 mi of sandy beach and several square miles of dunes. Fishing (at two freshwater lakes, one stocked with trout), canoeing, hiking, jogging, bicycling, camping (143 sites available), and harbor-seal watching at Laguna Point are among the popular activities, many of which are accessible to travelers with disabilities. Whales can often be spotted December through mid-April from the nearby headland. Rangers lead nature hikes throughout the year. ⊠ *Hwy. 1, 3 mi north of Fort Bragg,* ☎ *707/937–5804.* ⌧ *Free.*

Dining and Lodging

$$–$$$ ✕ **Gardens Grill.** The restaurant at the Mendocino Coast Botanical Gardens (☞ *above*) specializes in applewood-grilled steak, seafood, and vegetarian dishes. The preparations are tasty and inventive, and the view of the gardens from the outdoor deck is splendid. ⊠ *18218 N. Hwy. 1, at the south end of Fort Bragg,* ☎ *707/964–7474. MC, V. No dinner Tues.–Wed.*

$$ ✕ **The Restaurant.** The name may be generic, but this place isn't. California cuisine is served in a dining room that doubles as an art gallery. There is a jazz brunch on Sunday. ⊠ *418 N. Main St.,* ☎ *707/964–9800. MC, V. Closed Wed. No lunch Sat., Mon., Tues.*

$ ✕ **Headlands Coffee House.** The coffeehouse acts as a cultural center and local gathering place. There's live music most nights. ⊠ *120 E. Laurel St.,* ☎ *707/964–1987. No credit cards.*

$–$$$ ▥ **Surf and Sand Lodge.** You have to go north of Fort Bragg to find lodgings with unimpeded ocean views, and they're just what you'll get at this souped-up motel. As its name implies, it's practically on the beach—right out the door are pathways down to the rock-strewn shore. The six cheaper rooms don't have views, but all the bright and fresh accommodations come with enough amenities (including coffeemakers, hair dryers, and binoculars) to make you feel that you're staying somewhere grander than a motel. The fancier of the second-story rooms have hot tubs and fireplaces. ⊠ *1131 N. Main St., 95437,* ☎ *707/964–9383 or 800/964–0184. 30 rooms. Refrigerators, in-room VCRs. MC, V.*

Nightlife

North Coast Brewing Company (⊠ 444 N. Main St., ☎ 707/964–3400) has live jazz on Saturday night and home-brewed beer and pub grub Tuesday through Saturday.

Outdoor Activities and Sports

Ricochet Ridge Ranch (⊠ 24201 N. Hwy. 1, ☎ 707/964–7669) conducts guided trail rides to the Mendocino–Fort Bragg beaches. **Matlick's** *Tally*

Ho II (✉ 11845 N. Main St., ☎ 707/964–2079) operates whale-watching trips between December and April, as well as fishing excursions.

En Route   North on Highway 1 from Fort Bragg past the mill town of Westport, the road cuts inland around the **King Range,** a stretch of mountain so rugged that it was impossible to build the intended major highway through it. Highway 1 joins the larger U.S. 101 at the town of Leggett. **Richardson Grove State Park,** north of Leggett along U.S. 101, marks your first encounter with the truly giant redwoods, but there are even more magnificent stands farther north in Humboldt and Del Norte counties.

REDWOOD COUNTRY
Garberville to Crescent City

The majestic redwoods that grace California's coast become more plentiful as you head north. Their towering ancient presence defines the landscape.

Garberville

70 mi from Fort Bragg on Hwy. 1 to U.S. 101, 197 mi north of San Francisco on U.S. 101.

Although it's the largest town in the vicinity of Humboldt Redwoods State Park, Garberville hasn't changed a whole lot since timber was king. There's still no traffic light, and only a couple of stop signs, along its six-block main drag, but the town is a pleasant place to stop for lunch, pick up picnic provisions, or poke through arts-and-crafts stores. A few miles below Garberville, perched along Eel River, is an elegant Tudor resort, the **Benbow Inn** (☞ *below*), which is listed on the National Register of Historic Places. Even if you are not staying here, stop in for a drink or a meal and a look at the architecture and gardens.

Dining and Lodging

$ ✕ **Woodrose Cafe.** This unpretentious eatery, a local favorite, serves basic breakfast items and healthy lunches. Dishes include chicken, pasta, and vegetarian specials. ✉ *911 Redwood Dr.,* ☎ *707/923–3191. No credit cards. No dinner. No lunch weekends.*

$$$$ ✕⌂ **Benbow Inn.** Set alongside the Eel River one highway exit south
★   of Garberville, this three-story Tudor-style manor resort is the equal of any in the region. The most luxurious of the antiques-filled rooms are on the terrace, with fine views of the Eel River; some have fireplaces, and 18 have TVs with VCRs. Guests have canoeing, tennis, golf, and pool privileges at an adjacent property. The wood-paneled dining room ($$–$$$) serves American cuisine, with the focus on fresh salmon and trout dishes. ✉ *445 Lake Benbow Dr., 95442,* ☎ *707/923–2124 or 800/355–3301. 55 rooms. Restaurant, lobby lounge, refrigerators, lake. AE, D, MC, V. Closed early Jan.–mid-Mar.*

Humboldt Redwoods State Park

⑪ *15 mi north of Garberville on U.S. 101.*

The **Avenue of the Giants** (Highway 254) begins about 7 mi north of Garberville and winds north to Pepperwood. Along this stretch of two-lane blacktop you will find yourself enveloped by some of the tallest trees on the planet. The road cuts through part of the Humboldt Redwoods State Park, 51,222 acres of redwoods and waterways, and follows the south fork of the Eel River. The visitor center (☎ 707/

946–2263) near Weott is open in the spring and summer and can provide information on the region's recreational opportunities and flora and fauna. Founders Grove contains some of the tallest trees in the park.

Ferndale

⑫ *30 mi north of Weott via U.S. 101 to Hwy. 211.*

The residents of the stately town of Ferndale maintain some of the most sumptuous Victorian homes in California, many of them built by 19th-century timber barons and Scandinavian dairy farmers. The queen of them all is the **Gingerbread Mansion**, a B&B (☞ *below*). A beautiful sloped graveyard sits on Ocean Avenue west of Main Street. Numerous shops carry a map for self-guided tours of this lovingly preserved town.

The **Ferndale Museum** is a storehouse of antiques from the turn of the century. ⊠ *515 Shaw Ave.,* ☎ *707/786–4466.* ⬚ *$1.* ☉ *Oct.–June 1, Wed.–Sat. 11–4, Sun. 1–4; also Tues. 11–4 in summer.*

Lodging

$$$–$$$$ ⊞ **Gingerbread Mansion.** The exterior of this classic Victorian B&B has the most playful paint job on the North Coast. The mansion's carved friezes set off its gables, and turrets dazzle the eye. Inside, comfortable parlors and spacious bedrooms are laid out in flowery Victorian splendor. Some rooms have views of the mansion's elegant English garden, and one has side-by-side bathtubs. Innkeeper Ken Tolbert transformed the top floor into a suite that is so deluxe it would be suitable for a top San Francisco hotel—a vision in marble, with black and gold accents, it holds a claw-foot tub and a shower that could fit six. Ask about off-season discounts. Room rates include a full breakfast. ⊠ *400 Berding St., off Brown St., Box 40, 95536,* ☎ *707/786–4000. 10 rooms. AE, MC, V.*

$$–$$$ ⊞ **Victorian Inn.** This hostelry occupies the second floor of a renovated Victorian building on Ferndale's perfectly preserved Main Street. Rooms are decorated in muted colors and have antique armoires, feather comforters, original moldings, and some claw-foot tubs. Downstairs are the inn's casual bar and restaurant, where a complimentary Continental breakfast is served. ⊠ *400 Ocean Ave., at Main St.,* ☎ *707/786–4949 or 800/576–5949,* FAX *707/786–4648. 12 rooms. AE, D, DC, MC, V.*

Outdoor Activities and Sports

Eel River Delta Tours (⊠ 285 Morgan Slough Rd., 95536, ☎ 707/786–4187) conducts a two-hour boat trip that emphasizes the wildlife and history of the Eel River's estuary and salt marsh.

Shopping

Ferndale's shops are all lined up along Main Street. **Golden Gait Mercantile** (⊠ 421 Main St., ☎ 707/786–4891) seems to be lost in a time warp, what with Burma Shave products and old-fashioned long johns as well as penny candy. For gifts, you can't do better than **Withywindle** (⊠ 358 Main St., ☎ 707/786–4763) which sells local stoneware, porcelain, jewelry, and wearable art. The shopkeepers also specialize in gift baskets crammed with gourmet products.

Eureka

⑬ *10 mi north of Ferndale, 269 mi north of San Francisco on U.S. 101.*

Eureka, population 28,500, is the North Coast's largest city. It has gone through cycles of boom and bust, first with mining and later with timber and fishing. There are nearly 100 Victorian buildings here, many of them well preserved. The most splendid is the **Carson Mansion** (✉ M and 2nd Sts.), built in 1885 by the Newsom brothers for timber baron William Carson. The house is now occupied by a private men's club. Across the street is another Newsom extravaganza popularly known as the **Pink Lady.**

For proof that contemporary architects still have the skills to design lovely Victoriana, have a look at the **Carter House** B&B inn (✉ 3rd and L Sts.; ☞ *below*) and keep in mind that it was built in the 1980s, not the 1880s.

The **Chamber of Commerce** has maps for self-guided driving tours of Eureka's architecture, and information on how to join organized tours. ✉ *2112 Broadway,* ☎ *707/442–3738 or 800/356–6381.* ☉ *Weekdays 9–5.*

The **Clarke Memorial Museum** has an extraordinary collection of northwestern California Native American basketry and artifacts of Eureka's Victorian, logging, and maritime eras. ✉ *240 E St.,* ☎ *707/443–1947.* ▧ *Donations accepted.* ☉ *Feb.–Dec., Tues.–Sat. and July 4 noon–4.*

The structure that gave **Fort Humboldt State Historic Park** its name once guarded white settlers against the Indians. Ulysses S. Grant was posted here in 1854. The old fort is no longer around, but on its grounds are re-creations of the logging industry's early days, including a museum, some ancient steam engines (they rev them up the third Saturday of the month), and a logger's cabin. The park is a good place for a picnic. ✉ *3431 Fort Ave.,* ☎ *707/445–6567.* ▧ *Free.* ☉ *Daily 9–5.*

To explore the waters around Eureka, take a **Humboldt Bay Harbor Cruise.** You can observe some of the region's bird life while sailing past fishing boats, oyster beds, and decaying timber mills. ✉ *Pier at C St.,* ☎ *707/445–1910 or 707/444–9440.* ▧ *$9.50. Departs Mar.–Nov., daily 1, 2:30, and 4. Cocktail-cruise fare $7.50. Departs daily 5:30.*

Dining and Lodging

$$$–$$$$ ✕ **Chemin de Fer.** This is the kind of restaurant to keep in mind for special occasions. The food is fresh and elaborate: grilled duck, prawns with curry and pears, pork tenderloin, salmon in parchment, and nearly a dozen first courses. The dessert list is even longer. ✉ *518 F St.,* ☎ *707/441–9292. AE, MC, V. Closed Mon. No lunch weekends.*

$$$ ✕ **Restaurant 301.** Mark and Christi Carter, owners of Eureka's fanciest hotels, also run one of the town's best restaurants. Most of the vegetables and herbs used in the food are grown at the hotel's greenhouse and nearby ranch. Try the superbly presented fish or duck, and don't skip the appetizers—especially the warm goat cheese and pâté. ✉ *301 L St.,* ☎ *707/444–8062. AE, D, DC, MC, V. No lunch.*

$ ✕ **Cafe Waterfront.** This small eatery across from the marina has a long bar with a TV. Sandwiches and affordable seafood dishes are the menu mainstays. ✉ *102 F St.,* ☎ *707/443–9190. MC, V.*

$ ✕ **Ramone's.** The casual bakery café also serves light sandwiches. It's been voted Eureka's best place to grab a cup of coffee. ✉ *2223 Harrison Ave.,* ☎ *707/442–6082. No credit cards. No dinner.*

$ ✕ **Samoa Cookhouse.** The recommendation here is more for atmosphere, ★ of which there is plenty: this is a longtime loggers' hangout. The Samoa's cooks serve three substantial meals family-style at long wooden tables. Meat dishes dominate the menu. Save room (if possible) for dessert. ✉ *Cookhouse Rd. (from U.S. 101, cross Samoa Bridge, turn left onto Samoa Rd., then left 1 block later onto Cookhouse),* ☎ *707/ 442–1659. AE, D, MC, V.*

$$$–$$$$
★   **☷ Carter House, Hotel Carter, and Cottage.** The Carter family runs three
properties in downtown Eureka. The Carter House, built in 1982 fol-
lowing the floor plan of a San Francisco mansion, has an antiques-laden
sitting area and gorgeous rooms with heirloom furniture. Two doors
down, the Cottage, an original Victorian, contains three rooms and a
big sitting area with contemporary southwestern decorations. The
hotel, catercorner to the Carter House, has an elegant lobby and suites.
Handsome brocaded spreads cover the beds; some rooms have fireplaces
and whirlpool tubs. A large breakfast, served in the hotel's sunny din-
ing room, is included with a night's stay in any of the three buildings.
⊠ *Hotel: 301 L St., 95501,* ☎ ＦＡＸ *707/444–8062; 23 rooms. Carter
House:* ⊠ *1033 3rd St.,* ☎ *707/445–1390; 5 rooms. Cottage:* ⊠ *3rd
St.,* ☎ *707/445–1390; 3 rooms. AE, D, DC, MC, V.*

$$–$$$$
  ☷ An Elegant Victorian Mansion. This restored Eastlake mansion in a
residential neighborhood east of the Old Town lives up to its name.
Each room is decked out in period furnishings and wall coverings, down
to the carved-wood beds, fringed lamp shades, and pull-chain commodes.
The innkeepers may even greet you in vintage clothing and surprise
you with old-fashioned ice-cream sodas in the afternoon. They'll lure
you further into their time warp with silent movies on tape, old records
played on the windup Victrola, croquet on the rose-encircled lawn, and
guided tours of local Victoriana in their antique automobile. The Victorian flower garden holds more than 100 rosebushes. Room rates include a full gourmet breakfast. ⊠ *14th and C Sts., 95501,* ☎ *707/
444–3144,* ＦＡＸ *707/442–5594. 4 rooms with 4 shared baths. Massage,
sauna, croquet, bicycles, laundry service. MC, V.*

Nightlife
Lost Coast Brewery & Cafe (⊠ 617 4th St., ☎ 707/445–4480), a
bustling microbrewery, is the best place in town to relax with a pint
of strong ale or porter. It serves soups, salads, and light meals for lunch
and dinner.

Outdoor Activities and Sports
Hum-Boats (⊠ 2 F St., ☎ 707/443–5157) provides sailing rides, sail-
boat rentals, guided kayak tours, and sea kayak rentals and lessons.
The company also runs a water-taxi service on Humboldt Bay.

Shopping
Eureka has several art galleries in the district running from C to I streets
between 2nd and 3rd streets. Specialty shops in Old Town include the
original **Restoration Hardware** (⊠ 417 2nd St., ☎ 707/443–3152), a
good place to find stylish yet functional home and garden accessories
and clever polishing and cleaning products. The **Irish Shop** (⊠ 334 2nd
St., ☎ 707/443–8343) carries imports from the Emerald Isle, mostly
fine woolens.

Arcata

⑭ *9 mi north of Eureka on U.S. 101.*

The home of Humboldt State University is one of the few California
burgs to retain a town square. A farmers' market takes place in the
square on Saturday morning May through November. For a self-guided
tour of Arcata that includes some of its restored Victorian buildings,
pick up a map from the **Chamber of Commerce** (⊠ 1062 G St., ☎ 707/
822–3619). It's open weekdays from 10 to 4.

Dining and Lodging
$$
  ✕ Abruzzi. Salads and hefty pasta dishes take up most of the menu at
this upscale Italian restaurant just off the town square. Abruzzi serves
panini (Italian sandwiches) at lunch and pastas (such as linguine

pescara, with a spicy seafood-and-tomato sauce) for lunch and dinner. ⊠ *791 8th St., at corner of H St. (entrance on H St.),* ☎ *707/826–2345. AE, D, MC, V. No lunch weekends.*

$ ✕ **Crosswinds.** This restaurant serves Continental cuisine in a sunny Victorian setting, to the tune of live classical music. ⊠ *10th and I Sts.,* ☎ *707/826–2133. MC, V. Closed Mon. No dinner.*

$–$$ 🏨 **Hotel Arcata.** Flowered bedspreads and claw-foot bathtubs lend character to the rooms of this historic landmark overlooking the town square. Rates include use of a nearby health club as well as (on weekdays) Continental breakfast. ⊠ *708 9th St., 95521,* ☎ *707/826–0217 or 800/344–1221,* FAX *707/826–1737. 32 rooms. Restaurant. AE, D, DC, MC, V.*

Shopping
For its size, Arcata has an impressive selection of book, housewares, clothing, fabric, and other shops, especially near its town square. **Plaza Design** (⊠ 808 G St., ☎ 707/822–7732) specializes in gifts, papers, and innovative furnishings.

Trinidad

14 mi north of Arcata on U.S. 101.

Visited by a Portuguese expedition in 1595, the waters here are now sailed by fishing boats trolling for salmon. Picturesque Trinidad Bay's harbor cove and rock formations look both raw and tranquil.

Dining and Lodging
$$–$$$ ✕ **Larrupin' Cafe.** This restaurant has earned widespread fame for its
★ Cajun ribs and fresh fish dishes, served in a bright-yellow two-story house on a quiet country road 2 mi north of Trinidad. ⊠ *1658 Patrick's Point Dr.,* ☎ *707/677–0230. Reservations essential. No credit cards. Closed Mon.–Wed. in winter, Tues. in summer. No lunch.*

$–$$ ✕ **Merryman's Dinner House.** Fresh fish and a romantic oceanfront setting make this a perfect spot for hungry lovers. ⊠ *100 Moonstone Beach,* ☎ *707/677–3111. No credit cards. No lunch, no dinner weekdays Oct.–Mar.*

$–$$ ✕ **Seascape.** With its glassed-in main room and a deck for alfresco dining, this is an ideal place to take in the splendor of Trinidad Bay. The breakfasts are great, the lunches are substantial, and the dinners showcase local seafood. ⊠ *At pier,* ☎ *707/677–3762. MC, V.*

$$$ 🏨 **Trinidad Bay Bed and Breakfast.** Overlooking Trinidad Bay, this Cape Cod–style shingle house has an unforgettable ocean view. The innkeepers provide a wealth of information about the nearby wilderness, beach, and fishing habitats. The living room is warmed by a crackling fireplace. Room rates include breakfast. ⊠ *560 Edwards St., Box 849, 95570,* ☎ *707/677–0840. 2 rooms and 2 suites (1 with fireplace). Reservations essential. D, MC, V. Closed Dec.–Jan.*

Patrick's Point State Park

⑮ *5 mi north of Trinidad, 25 mi north of Eureka on U.S. 101.*

This park is a "sleeper" that relatively few people know about, but those who do return again and again. On a forested plateau almost 200 ft above the surf, it has stunning views of the Pacific (good for whale and sea-lion watching), picnic areas, bike trails, and hiking trails through old-growth forest. There are also tidal pools at Agate Beach and a small museum with natural-history exhibits. ☎ *707/677–3570.* 🎫 *$5 per vehicle (day use). Camping $14 per vehicle.*

Redwood National Park

16 *22 mi north (Orick entrance) of Trinidad on U.S. 101.*

After 115 years of intensive logging, this 113,200-acre parcel of tall trees came under government protection in 1968, marking the California environmentalists' greatest victory over the timber industry. The park encompasses three state parks (Prairie Creek Redwoods, Del Norte Coast Redwoods, and Jedediah Smith Redwoods) and is more than 40 mi long.

For detailed information about Redwood National Park, stop at the **Redwood Information Center** (☎ 707/488–3461) between the park entrance and the town of Orick. There you can also get a free permit to drive up the steep, 17-mi road (the last 6 mi are gravel) to reach the Tall Trees Grove, where a 3-mi round-trip hiking trail leads to the world's first-, third-, and fifth-tallest redwoods. Whale-watchers will find the deck of the visitor center an excellent observation point, and birders will enjoy the nearby Freshwater Lagoon, a popular layover for migrating waterfowl.

Within Lady Bird Johnson Grove, just off Bald Hill Road, is a short circular trail to resplendent redwoods. This section of the park was dedicated by, and named for, the former first lady. For additional spectacular scenery, take Davison Road to Fern Canyon. This gravel road winds through 4 mi of second-growth redwoods, then hugs a bluff 100 ft above the pounding Pacific surf for another 4 mi.

To reach the entrance to Redwood's Prairie Creek Redwoods State Park, take the Elk Prairie Parkway exit off the U.S. 101 bypass. Extra space has been paved alongside the parklands, providing fine vantage points from which to observe an imposing herd of Roosevelt elk grazing in the adjoining meadow. Revelation Trail in Prairie Creek is fully accessible to visitors with disabilities.

Lodging

$ **Hostelling International—Redwood National Park.** This turn-of-the-century inn is a stone's throw from the ocean; hiking begins just beyond its doors. Lodging is dormitory style. ⊠ *14480 U.S. 101, at Wilson Creek Rd. (20 mi north of Orick), Klamath, 95548,* ☎ FAX *707/482–8265. No credit cards.*

Crescent City

40 mi north of Orick on U.S. 101.

Del Norte County's largest town is named for the shape of its harbor; during the 1800s this was an important steamship stop. At the bottom of B Street at **Popeye's Landing** you can rent a crab pot, buy some bait, and try your luck at crabbing. At low tide from April to September, you can walk from the pier across the ocean floor to the oldest lighthouse on the North Coast (1856), **Battery Point Lighthouse** (☎ 707/464–3089), and take a $2 tour Wednesday through Sunday from 10 to 4.

Dining and Lodging

$ ✕ **Harbor View Grotto.** This glassed-in dining hall overlooking the Pacific prides itself on its fresh fish entrées. ⊠ *155 Citizen's Dock Rd.,* ☎ *707/464–3815. MC, V.*

$ ▦ **Curly Redwood Lodge.** This lodge was built from a single redwood tree, which produced 57,000 board ft of lumber. The room decor makes the most of that tree, with paneling, platform beds, and dressers built into the walls. ⊠ *701 Redwood Hwy. S, 95531,* ☎ *707/464–2137,* FAX *707/464–1655. 36 rooms. AE, DC, MC, V.*

En Route   Travelers continuing north to the Smith River near the Oregon border will find fine trout and salmon fishing as well as a profusion of flowers. Ninety percent of America's lily bulbs are grown in this area.

THE NORTH COAST A TO Z

Arriving and Departing

By Car

Highway 1 and U.S. 101 are the main north–south coastal routes. Highway 1 is often curvy and difficult all along the coast. Driving directly to Mendocino from San Francisco is quicker by taking U.S. 101 north to Highway 128 west (from Cloverdale) to Highway 1 north instead of driving up the coast on Highway 1. Once it gets into Humboldt County, U.S. 101 itself becomes as twisting as Highway 1 as it continues on to the northernmost corner of the state. **Hertz** (☎ 800/654–3131) rents cars at the Eureka-Arcata airport (no phone) in McKinleyville.

By Plane

United Express (☎ 800/241–6522) has regular nonstop flights from San Francisco to Eureka/Arcata. This is the fastest and most direct way to reach the redwood country.

Getting Around

By Car

Although there are excellent services along Highway 1 and U.S. 101, gas stations and mechanics are few and far between on the smaller roads.

Contacts and Resources

Emergencies

Ambulance (☎ 911). **Police** (☎ 911).

Guided Tours

Oceanic Society Expeditions (✉ Fort Mason, San Francisco, ☎ 415/474–3385) conducts whale-watching and other nature cruises north and west of San Francisco throughout much of the year. **New Sea Angler and Jaws** (✉ Bodega Bay, ☎ 707/875–3495) runs cruises on weekends December–April.

Visitor Information

Eureka/Humboldt County Convention and Visitors Bureau (✉ 1034 2nd St., Eureka 95501, ☎ 800/346–3482; 800/338–7352 in CA). **Fort Bragg–Mendocino Coast Chamber of Commerce** (✉ Box 1141, Fort Bragg 95437, ☎ 800/726–2780). **Redwood Empire Association** (✉ Cannery, 2801 Leavenworth St., 2nd floor, San Francisco 94133, ☎ 415/543–8334, FAX 415/543–8337). **Sonoma County Visitors and Convention Bureau** (✉ 10 4th St., Santa Rosa 95401, ☎ 707/575–1191). **West Marin Chamber of Commerce** (✉ Box 1045, Point Reyes Station 94956, ☎ 415/663–9232).

3 The Far North

Including Mt. Shasta, Lake Shasta, and Lassen Volcanic National Park

Soaring mountain peaks, wild rivers brimming with fish, and almost infinite recreational possibilities make the Far North a sports-lover's paradise. Hot nightspots and cultural enclaves do not abound, but you will find some of the best hiking, fishing, and hunting in the state. Some Bay Area families return to this region year after year. Many enjoy the outdoors from their own piece of paradise—a private houseboat. Keep in mind that much of the Far North can be very hot in summer.

THE FAR NORTH LANDSCAPE has been writ large by ancient volcanic activity. The scenery is best symbolized
by Mt. Shasta, a 14,162-ft-high mountain that can be
seen for miles around. Less dramatic but more extensive is Lassen Volcanic National Park at the southern end of the Cascade Range. The
geology here is interesting, not merely for evidence of past but also current geothermal activity. The 10,457-ft Mt. Lassen and 50 wilderness
lakes are the park's centerpieces. The Far North's natural and artifi-
cially created wonders include immense Shasta Dam and the sulfur vents
and bubbling mud pots of Lassen Volcanic National Park. Plentiful access to the wilderness, without crowding, is the Far North's hallmark.
There are few towns and fewer cities. Natural history dwarfs the foot-
steps of mankind in this grand gymnasium for body and soul.

By Marty
Olmstead

Pleasures and Pastimes

Camping

You'll find everything from the well-outfitted campgrounds in McArthur-
Burney Falls Memorial State Park, which have hot water, showers, and
flush toilets, to isolated campsites on Lake Shasta that can be reached
only by boat. There are seven campgrounds within Lassen Volcanic
National Park. Reservations are not accepted; it's first come, first
served. For campground and other information, contact Lassen Volcanic National Park or the Shasta Cascade Wonderland Association
(☞ Contacts and Resources *in* the Far North A to Z, *below*).

Dining

Redding, the urban center of the Far North, has the greatest selection
of restaurants. In the smaller towns, cafés and simple restaurants are
the rule, though there is the occasional culinary surprise. Dress is always informal in the Far North.

CATEGORY	COST*
$$$$	over $50
$$$	$30–$50
$$	$20–$30
$	under $20

per person for a three-course meal, excluding drinks, service, and 7¼% tax

Lodging

Beyond the large chain hotels and motels in the Redding area, accommodations are a blend of rusticity, simplicity, and coziness. Most
visitors to rural areas spend much of their time in the outdoors and
prefer informal camps and motels. Wilderness resorts close in fall and
reopen only after the snow season ends in May.

CATEGORY	COST*
$$$$	over $175
$$$	$120–$175
$$	$80–$120
$	under $80

All prices are for a standard double room, excluding 8% tax.

Outdoor Activities and Sports

Fishing, houseboating, and animal-pack trips are popular Far North
diversions. Cascading rivers, mammoth lakes, and bountiful streams
draw sportfishers. Hikers, backpackers, hunters, skiers, and other outdoor enthusiasts enjoy idyllic conditions for most of the year. Castle
Crags State Park and Lassen Volcanic National Park have abundant

hiking and walking trails. In winter, the uncrowded slopes of Mt. Shasta contain challenging ski runs.

Exploring the Far North

The Far North encompasses three vast counties (Tehama, Shasta, and Trinity), land that stretches from the valleys east of the Coast Range to the Nevada border and from the almond and olive orchards north of Sacramento to the Oregon border.

Numbers in the text correspond to numbers in the margin and on the Far North map.

Great Itineraries

The tri-county area's most scenic parts lie along the two-lane roads that crisscross the region, which is bisected by I–5. East of I–5 are dramatic mountain peaks, to the west heavily forested areas and interesting small towns.

IF YOU HAVE 3 DAYS

From I–5 above Redding, head northeast on Highways 299 and 89 to **McArthur-Burney Falls Memorial State Park** ⑥. To appreciate the falls, take the short stroll to an overlook or hike down for an even closer view. Continue north on Highway 89. Long before you arrive in the town of ⊡ **Mt. Shasta** ⑦ you will spy the conical peak for which it is named. This is a great photographic opportunity, particularly late in the day, when low-lying clouds often cast a pink glow on the mountain. The central Mt. Shasta exit east leads out of town along the **Everett Memorial Highway.** Take this scenic drive, which climbs to almost 8,000 ft. The views of the mountain and the valley below are extraordinary. Stay overnight in town. On the second day, head south on I–5 toward the **Lake Shasta Caverns** ⑧ and the **Shasta Dam** ⑨. **Lake Shasta** is visible on both sides of the highway as it crosses the water near the dam, which is on the west side of I–5. Overnight either in ⊡ **Redding** ⑪ or ⊡ **Weaverville** ⑩. Near Redding, Highway 299 leads west toward the **Whiskeytown-Shasta-Trinity National Recreation Area.** Visit Weaverville on your third day—take the **Joss House** tour—and have lunch in town before returning to Redding.

IF YOU HAVE 5 OR 6 DAYS

Get a glimpse of the Far North's heritage in **Red Bluff** ① at the **Kelly-Griggs House Museum** and **William B. Ide Adobe State Historic Park** ②. Head north on I–5 and settle in for the night in the town of ⊡ **Mt. Shasta.** The next day, check on trail conditions on **Mt. Shasta** ⑦ and pick up maps at the Forest Service Ranger Station. Pack a picnic lunch before taking the **Everett Memorial Highway** up the mountain and hiking around. Spend the night a few miles south in ⊡ **Dunsmuir** at the **Railroad Car Resort,** where all the accommodations are old cabooses. On your third day, take an early morning hike in nearby **Castle Crags State Park,** whose 225-million-year-old crags tower over the Sacramento River at heights of up to 6,000 ft. Continue south on I–5 and tour **Shasta Dam** ⑨. Spend the night camping in the area or in ⊡ **Redding** ⑪. On your fourth morning, head west on Highway 299 to **Shasta,** a gold-mining town that's a shadow of its former, prosperous self. Continue west on 299 to ⊡ **Weaverville** ⑩ and stay the night there or back in Redding. If you will be leaving the area on your fifth day but have a little time, zip north and visit **Lake Shasta Caverns** ⑧. If you're remaining and it's between late May and early October, spend the next day and a half exploring **Lassen Volcanic National Park.** Highway 44 heads east from Redding into the park, entering near **Chaos Jumbles** ⑤, created by a rock avalanche. Also on Lassen Park Road are **Hot Rock** ④, a huge

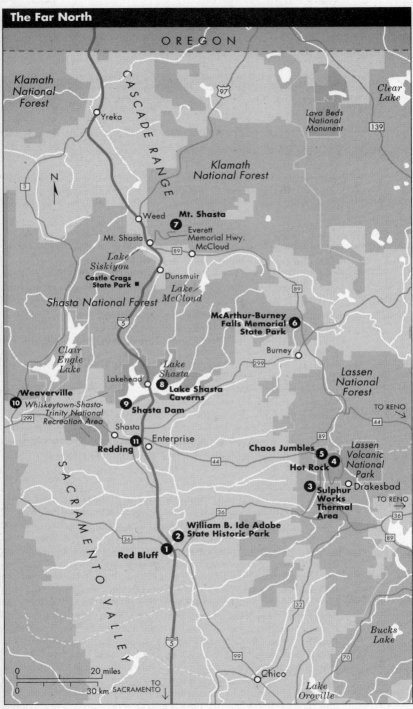

The Far North

OREGON

Klamath National Forest

Yreka

97

Clear Lake

CASCADE RANGE

Lava Beds National Monument

139

Klamath National Forest

N

3

Weed

Mt. Shasta

7

Everett Memorial Hwy.

Mt. Shasta

McCloud

89

Lake Siskiyou

Castle Crags State Park

Dunsmuir

Lake McCloud

Shasta National Forest

89

I-5

McArthur-Burney Falls Memorial State Park **6**

Clair Engle Lake

Burney

299

Lake Shasta

Lakehead

8 **Lake Shasta Caverns**

Lassen National Forest

Weaverville

10

Whiskeytown-Shasta-Trinity National Recreation Area

9 **Shasta Dam**

TO RENO

299

Shasta

44

Enterprise

89

Redding

11

Chaos Jumbles **5**

4

Lassen Volcanic National Park

44

Hot Rock

Drakesbad

3 **Sulphur Works Thermal Area**

TO RENO

36

89

S A C R A M E N T O

William B. Ide Adobe State Historic Park

36

2

1

Red Bluff

V A L L E Y

32

Bucks Lake

I-5

99

70

0 20 miles

0 30 km

Chico

TO SACRAMENTO

Lake Oroville

boulder that tumbled onto its current site during volcanic activity earlier this century, and the **Sulphur Works Thermal Area** ③, where you can have a stinky good time viewing the steam vents.

When to Tour the Far North

This region attracts the greatest number of tourists during the summer, when the fishing is easy and the camping is comfortable. Summers can be dry and scorching; families flock to the lakes for swimming and motorboating. The valley around Redding is mild in the winter, but cooler temperatures prevail at the higher elevations to the east and north. In winter, Mt. Shasta is a good downhill ski area. Otherwise, much of the area is too cold for outdoor pleasures, and roads to the region's most awesome sights, including much of Lassen Volcanic National Park, are closed from October until late May because of hazardous driving conditions. Be aware that many restaurants and museums here have limited hours and sometimes close for stretches of the off-season.

FROM RED BLUFF TO MT. SHASTA

Lassen, Mt. Shasta, Weaverville, and Redding

The sights below are arranged in a loop that begins in the south at I–5 in Red Bluff and swings around to the northeast on state highways, through Lassen Volcanic National Park and then north to Mt. Shasta. The remaining attractions are off I–5 heading south toward Redding, with a jog to the west to the towns of Shasta and Weaverville.

Red Bluff

❶ *179 mi north of San Francisco, I–80 to I–505 to I–5.*

Named for the color of its soil and its location above the Sacramento River, Red Bluff was established in the mid-19th century, just before Victorian architecture became the style of choice. Historic structures of two types remain: Restored Victorians line the streets west of Main Street; downtown looks like a stage set for a western movie.

The **Kelly-Griggs House Museum,** a restored 1880s Victorian home, holds an impressive collection of antique furniture, housewares, and clothing arranged as though a refined Victorian family were still in residence: An engraved silver tea server waits at the end table; a "Self Instructor in Penmanship" sits on a desk; and costumed mannequins seem frozen in conversation in the upstairs parlor. The museum's collection includes carved china cabinets and Native American basketry. In the Ishi Room is an exhibit about the "last wild Indian." *Persephone,* the painting over the fireplace, is by Sarah Brown, daughter of abolitionist John Brown, whose family settled in Red Bluff after his execution. The Brown home is part of the self-guided tour of Red Bluff Victoriana; maps are available here. ⊠ *311 Washington St.,* ☎ *530/527–1129.* ☞ *Donation suggested.* ☉ *Thurs.–Sun. 1–4.*

❷ The **William B. Ide Adobe State Historic Park** is a memorial to the first and only president of the short-lived California Republic of 1846. The Bear Flag Party proclaimed California a sovereign nation, no longer under the dominion of Mexico, and the republic existed for 25 days before it was occupied by the United States. The flag concocted for the republic has survived, with only minor refinements, as California's state flag. This adobe, thought to have been Ide's adobe, was built in the 1850s and now displays period furnishings and artifacts of the era. ⊠ *21659 Adobe Rd.,* ☎ *530/529–8599.* ☞ *$3 donation requested per* *vehicle.* ⊙ *Park and picnic facilities 8 AM–sunset year-round; home 11–4 in summer (in winter, look for ranger to unlock house).*

Dining

$$ ✕ **Snack Box.** A renovated Victorian cottage is cheerfully decorated with unabashedly corny pictures and knickknacks, all rural and many featuring cattle and sheep. The food need make no apologies, however. Soups, omelets, blue-plate specials, and even simple items such as grilled-cheese sandwiches are perfectly executed. ⊠ *257 Main St., 1 block from Kelly-Griggs Museum,* ☎ *530/529–0227. MC, V. No dinner.*

Lassen Volcanic National Park

45 mi east of Redding on Hwy. 44, 48 mi east of Red Bluff on Hwy. 36.

Lassen Volcanic National Park provides a look at three sides of the world's largest plug volcano. Except for the Nordic ski area, the park is largely inaccessible from late October to late May because of snow. The Lassen Park Road (the continuation of Highway 89 within the park) is closed to cars in winter but open to intrepid cross-country skiers, conditions permitting. Even in the best of weather, services are sparse. In the southwest corner of the park, a café and a gift shop are open during the summer. At the Manzanita Lake campground, another store, also open only in summer, has gas and fast food. The *Lassen Park Guide,* available for a nominal fee at the visitor center and park entrance, details these and other facilities. ⊠ *Headquarters and visitor center: 38050 Hwy. 36 E, Mineral 96063,* ☎ *530/595–4444.* ⊑ *$5 per vehicle in summer, free in winter.* ⊙ *Visitor center weekdays 8–4:30 year-round, summer weekends 8–4:30; hrs sometimes vary.*

In 1914 the 10,457-ft Mt. Lassen began a series of 300 eruptions that continued for seven years. Molten rock overflowed the crater, and the mountain emitted clouds of smoke and hailstorms of rocks and volcanic cinders. Proof of the volcano's volatility becomes evident shortly
❸ after you enter the park at the **Sulphur Works Thermal Area.** Boardwalks take you over bubbling mud and hot springs and through the nauseating sulfur stink of steam vents. ⊠ *Lassen Park Rd., south end of park.*

Bumpass Hell Trail, a 3-mi round-trip hike to the park's most interesting thermal-spring area, allows visitors to view hot and boiling springs, steam vents, and mud pots up close. The trail climbs and descends several hundred feet. Stay on trails and boardwalks near the thermal areas. What may appear to be firm ground may be only a thin crust over scalding mud. ⊠ *Off Lassen Park Rd., 5 mi north of Sulphur Works Thermal Area.*

❹ **Hot Rock,** a 400-ton boulder, tumbled down from the summit during the volcano's active period and was still hot to the touch when locals found it. Although cool now, it's still an impressive sight. ⊠ *Lassen Park Rd., north end of park.*

❺ **Chaos Jumbles** was created 300 years ago when an avalanche from the Chaos Crags lava domes spread hundreds of thousands of rocks 2 to 3 ft in diameter over a couple of square miles. ⊠ *Lassen Park Rd., north end of park.*

Dining and Lodging

$$$$ ✕▦ **Drakesbad Guest Ranch.** The 100-year-old guest ranch at Drakesbad, at elevation 5,700 ft near Lassen Volcanic National Park's southern border on Lake Almanor, is isolated from most of the rest of the park. Rooms in the lodge, bungalows, and cabins don't have electricity; they're lighted by kerosene lamps. But the accommodations are clean and comfortable and include furnace heat and either half or full bath. Reservations should be made well in advance (the waiting list can be up to two years long); all meals are included. ⊠ *Chester–Warner Valley Rd., north from Hwy. 36 (booking office: 2150 N. Main St., Suite 5, Red Bluff 96080),* ☎ *530/529–1512,* FAX *530/529–4511. 19 rooms. Dining room, pool, badminton, horseback riding, horseshoes, Ping-Pong, volleyball, fishing. MC, V. Closed early Oct.–early June.*

$ ╳⚑ **Lassen Mineral Lodge.** Reserve rooms at this motel-style property as far in advance as possible. You can rent cross-country skis at the lodge's ski shop; there's also a general store. ⊠ *Hwy. 36, Mineral 96063,* ☎ *530/595–4422. 20 rooms. Restaurant, bar, pool, tennis courts. MC, V.*

Outdoor Activities and Sports

SNOWSHOE TOURS

National Park Service rangers conduct snowshoe tours at **Mt. Lassen Ski Park.** Various natural history topics are covered. ☎ *530/595–4444 for directions. No reservations.* ✆ *$1.* ☉ *Jan.–Apr., Sat. 1:30* PM.

McArthur-Burney Falls Memorial State Park

❻ *30 mi north of Lassen Volcanic National Park on Hwy. 89.*

Just inside the southern boundary of this state park, Burney Creek wells up from the ground and divides into two cascades that fall over a 129-ft cliff and into a pool below. The thundering water creates a mist at the base of the falls, often highlighted by a rainbow. Countless ribbonlike falls stream from hidden moss-covered crevices—an ethereal backdrop to the main cascades. Each day, 100 million gallons of water rush over these falls; Theodore Roosevelt proclaimed them "the eighth wonder of the world." A self-guided nature trail descends to the foot of the falls. There is a lake and beach for swimming. A campground, picnic sites, trails, and other facilities are available. The camp store is open Memorial Day–Labor Day. ⊠ *24898 Hwy. 89, Burney 96013,* ☎ *530/335–2777.* ✆ *$5 per vehicle (day use). Camping: May–Sept., $14 per night; Oct.–Apr., $12 per night. Campground reservations (necessary in summer) are made through Destinet,* ☎ *800/444–7275.*

Mt. Shasta

❼ *52 mi from McArthur-Burney Falls Memorial State Park on Hwy. 89, 61 mi north of Redding on I–5.*

Mt. Shasta—the mountain and the town—made headlines in 1987, when participants in the worldwide Harmonic Convergence converged on the region because they believed the mountain held special powers. They weren't the first: Legends of eerie phenomena and mythical animals have been part of mountain lore for decades.

The crowning jewel of the 2.5-million-acre Shasta–Trinity National Forest, Mt. Shasta is popular with day hikers, especially in spring, when flowers like the fragrant Shasta lily adorn the rocky slopes. But few people make it to the perennially ice-packed summit of this 16-million-year-old dormant volcano. An automobile road travels only as high as the timberland, and the final 6,000 ft are a tough climb of rubble, ice, and snow.

As for the town of Mt. Shasta, it is not so much a destination as a place to eat and sleep: Even on the main thoroughfare there isn't much to do or see.

Dining and Lodging

$$–$$$ ✕ **Michael's Restaurant.** Wood paneling, candlelight, and wildlife prints by local artists create an unpretentious setting for Italian specialties like stuffed calamari, filet mignon scaloppine, linguine pesto, and other Continental dishes. ✉ *313 N. Mt. Shasta Blvd.,* ☏ *530/926–5288. AE, D, MC, V. Closed Sun.–Mon.*

$$ ✕ **Acacia Restaurant, Bar and Grill.** The menu at this relatively recent addition to the Far North dining scene is a mélange of classic and trendy dishes—veal piccata, vegetable curry, prime rib, rack of lamb, and several seafood options. Acacia serves breakfast on Saturday and Sunday mornings. ✉ *1136 S. Mt. Shasta Blvd.,* ☏ *530/926–0250. AE, D, MC, V.*

$$ ✕ **Lily's.** This restaurant in a white clapboard home—complete with picket fence—serves several fine pastas, including one with sun-dried tomatoes and artichoke hearts. Among the unusual salads are a spicy shrimp-and-chicken dish and the Jalisco—steak and greens with tomatoes. ✉ *1013 S. Mt. Shasta Blvd.,* ☏ *530/926–3372. AE, D, MC, V.*

$–$$ 🏨 **Tree House Best Western.** The clean, standard rooms at this motel less than a mile from downtown Mt. Shasta are decorated with natural-wood furnishings. ✉ *111 Morgan Way, at I–5 and Lake St., Box 236, 96067,* ☏ *530/926–3101 or 800/528–1234,* 📠 *530/926–3542. 95 rooms. Restaurant, lounge, indoor pool. AE, D, DC, MC, V.*

Outdoor Activities and Sports

HIKING

The **Forest Service Ranger Station** (☏ 530/926–4511) provides constantly updated information on trail conditions. The **Fifth Season Mountaineering Shop** (☏ 530/926–3606) operates a recorded 24-hour climber-skier report (☏ 530/926–5555).

MOUNTAIN CLIMBING

Shasta Mountain Guides (☏ 530/926–3117) leads hiking, climbing, and ski-touring groups to the summit of Mt. Shasta.

SKIING

Mt. Shasta Ski Park. On the southeast flank of Mt. Shasta are three lifts on 300 skiable acres. The terrain is 20% beginner, 60% intermediate, 20% advanced. Top elevation is 6,600 ft; its base, 5,500 ft; its vertical drop, 1,100 ft. The longest run is 1²⁄₁₀ mi. Night skiing goes until 10 PM Wednesday through Saturday. There is a ski school with a beginner's special: lifts, rentals, lessons. The "Powder Pups" program is for children age four to seven. Lodge facilities include food and beverages, ski shop, and rentals. ✉ *Hwy. 89 exit east from I–5, south of Mt. Shasta,* ☏ *530/926–8610; 530/926–8686 for snow information.*

Dunsmuir

10 mi south of Mt. Shasta on I–5.

This tiny town fell on hard times with the disappearance of the railroad and the decline of logging. Named for a 19th-century coal baron, Dunsmuir is surrounded by Crags Creek State Park. The town's other major attraction, especially for kids, is the nearby **Railroad Park Resort,** whose patrons spend the night in restored rail cars.

Crags Creek State Park is a hiker's paradise. Granite spires created millions of years ago still poke the skies at altitudes of more than 4,000 ft. There are excellent trails at lower altitudes in this 6,000-acre park, which also has picnic areas, rest rooms, showers, and, for $12 a night, plenty of campsites. ✉ *Off I–5, 6 mi south of Dunsmuir,* ☏ *530/235–2684.* 🚗 *$5 per vehicle (day use).*

Lodging

$–$$ 🏨 **Railroad Park Resort.** The antique cabooses at this railroad buff's delight have been converted into cozy, wood-paneled motel rooms in honor of Dunsmuir's railroad legacy. The resort has a modestly *Orient Express*–style dining room and a lounge fashioned from vintage rail cars. The landscaped grounds contain a huge logging steam engine and a restored water tower. ✉ *100 Railroad Park Rd., 96025,* ☎ *530/235–4440 or 800/974–7245,* FAX *530/235–4470. 24 cabooses, 4 cabins. Restaurant (no lunch), pool, hot tub, camping, mountain bikes. AE, D, MC, V.*

$ 🏨 **Dunsmuir Inn Bed and Breakfast.** It's not fancy, but this homey inn— a good deal considering that room rates include a made-to-order breakfast—is comfortable and within easy walking distance of the historic downtown area. Another plus: The innkeeper runs a little ice cream parlor in an enclosed porch area. Rooms are decorated with simple residential furniture. ✉ *5432 Dunsmuir Ave., 96025,* ☎ *530/235–4543. 5 rooms. AE, D, DC, MC, V.*

Lake Shasta Area

34 mi south of Mt. Shasta (to town of Lakehead) on I–5, 12 mi north of Redding on I–5.

The many Shastas—mountain, lake, river, town, dam, and forest—derive from the name of the Indians who inhabited parts of the region in the 19th century (variously, Shatasla and Sastise). The Indian pronunciation for the river was *tschasta,* which evolved into modern-day speech.

8 Stalagmites, stalactites, odd flowstone deposits, and crystals entice visitors of all ages to the **Lake Shasta Caverns.** A two-hour tour includes a catamaran ride across the McCloud arm of Lake Shasta and a bus ride up Grey Rock Mountain to the cavern entrance. The caverns are a constant 58°F year-round, making them an appealingly cool retreat on a hot summer day. All cavern rooms are well lit, and the crowning jewel is the awe-inspiring cathedral room. The guides are friendly, enthusiastic, and informative. ✉ *Shasta Caverns Rd. exit from I–5,* ☎ *530/238–2341 or 800/795–2283.* 💵 *$12.* ⊙ *Daily 9–4; tours May–Sept. on the hr, Oct.–Apr. at 10, noon, and 2.*

★ **Lake Shasta** has 370 mi of shoreline and 21 varieties of fish. You can rent fishing boats, ski boats, sailboats, canoes, paddleboats, Jet Skis, and Windsurfer boards at one of the many marinas and resorts along the shore. Lake Shasta is known as the houseboat capital of the world. *See* Outdoor Activities and Sports, *below,* for information about rentals.

★ **9** **Shasta Dam** is the second-largest and the fourth-tallest concrete dam in the United States. At twilight the sight is magical, with Mt. Shasta gleaming above the not-quite-dark water and deer frolicking on the hillside beside the dam. The dam is lit after dark, but there is no access from 10 PM to 6 AM. The visitor center has fact sheets and photographic and historic displays. ✉ *Shasta Dam Blvd.,* ☎ *530/275–4463.* ⊙ *Dam 6 AM–10 PM; visitor center weekdays 8–5 (tours at 10, noon, 2 year-round, more often in summer), weekends 9–5 (tours 10, noon, 2 year-round, on the hr 9–4 in summer).*

Dining

$$ ✕ **Tail O' the Whale.** This restaurant overlooking Lake Shasta is distinguished by its nautical decor. Seafood, prime rib, poultry, and Cajun pepper shrimp are the specialties. ✉ *10300 Bridge Bay Rd., Bridge Bay exit from I–5,* ☎ *530/275–3021. D, MC, V.*

Outdoor Activities and Sports

FISHING

The Fishin' Hole (✉ 3844 Shasta Dam Blvd., Central Valley 96019, ☎ 530/275–4123) carries supplies and provides information about conditions, licenses, and fishing packages.

HOUSEBOATING

Houseboats come in all sizes except small. As a rule these moving homes come with cooking utensils, dishes, and most of the equipment you'll need—you supply food and linens. Renters are given a short course in how to maneuver the boats before they set out on cruises; it's not difficult, as the houseboats are slow moving. You can fish, swim, sunbathe on the flat roof, or just sit on the deck and watch the world go by. The shoreline of Lake Shasta is beautifully ragged, with countless inlets; it's not hard to find privacy. Expect to spend a minimum of $200 a day for a craft that sleeps six. There is usually a three-night minimum in peak season. **Shasta Cascade Wonderland Association** (☞ Contacts and Resources *in* the Far North A to Z, *below*) has more information.

Shasta

7 mi west of Redding on Hwy. 299.

The ruins of the once-prosperous gold-mining town of Shasta, now a 13-acre **state historic park** with a few restored buildings, afford the opportunity to see how prospectors lived a century ago. A museum in the old courthouse has an eclectic array of California paintings, memorabilia, and a *Prairie Traveler* guidebook with advice on encounters with Indians. Continue down to the basement to see the iron-bar jail cells, and step outside for a look at the scaffold where murderers were hanged. ✉ *Hwy. 299*, ☎ *530/243–8194.* ☜ *$2.* ☉ *Wed.–Sun. 10–5.*

Weaverville

🔟 *40 mi west of Shasta on Hwy. 299 (called Main St. in town).*

This old mountain town of nearly 5,000 is one of the Far North's most charming. Although the city includes rows of car dealers and the like, its downtown blocks maintain their gold-rush ambience. Weaverville is a popular headquarters for family vacations and biking, hiking, fishing, hunting, and gold-panning excursions.

John Weaver was one of three men who built the first cabin, in 1850, in the town that would later be named for him. By 1851, Weaverville was the Trinity County seat and included neighboring communities such as Frenchtown, Englishtown, Germantown, Irishtown, and a sizable Chinatown.

The most visible legacy of the Chinese presence is the **Weaverville Joss House,** a Taoist temple built in 1874. Called Won Lim Miao, the "Temple Amongst the Forest Beneath the Clouds," by Chinese miners, it attracts worshipers from around the world. With its golden altar, carved wooden canopies, and intriguing artifacts, the Joss House is a piece of California history that can best be appreciated in the company of a guide. The original temple building and many of its furnishings—some of which had come from China—were burned in 1873, but members of the local Chinese community soon rebuilt it. An ornate wooden gate leads to the porch of this bright-blue building. ✉ *Oregon and Main Sts.,* ☎ *530/623–5284.* ☜ *Nominal charge for 40-min guided tours, on the hr 10–4.* ☉ *Summer daily 10–5, rest of yr Thurs.–Mon. 10–5.*

Fires destroyed many parts of Weaverville; surviving buildings are mostly brick. Since the upper floor of many old downtown buildings was often owned by a different person than the lower floor, outdoor spiral staircases were constructed to permit each owner a private entrance. Three such buildings remain visible in the downtown Historic District.

The **Trinity County Courthouse** (✉ Court and Main Sts.), built in 1857 as a store, office building, and hotel, was converted to county use in 1865. The Apollo Saloon in the basement became the county jail.

Trinity County Historical Park is home to the Jake Jackson Memorial Museum, which has a blacksmith shop, a replica stamp mill, and the original jail cells of the Trinity County Courthouse. ✉ *408 Main St.,* ☎ *530/623–5211.* ☉ *May–Oct., daily 10–5; Nov.–Apr., Tues.–Sat. noon–4.*

Dining and Lodging

$$ ✕ **La Grange.** This eatery is one of the few places in Weaverville open for lunch and dinner six days a week. Stick to basics like chicken and pasta; the kitchen is not as dependable when it comes to dishes like trout. On the plus side, La Grange serves plenty of vegetables and sells beer and wine. ✉ *315 N. Main St.,* ☎ *530/623–5325. AE, D, MC, V.*

$ ✕ **La Casita.** Weaverville's only real Mexican restaurant serves the standard regimen—all the quesadillas (including one with roasted chili peppers), tostadas, enchiladas, tacos, and tamales you could want, many of them available in a vegetarian version. This casual spot is open from late morning through early evening, so it's great for a mid-afternoon snack. ✉ *254 Main St.,* ☎ *530/623–5797. No credit cards.*

$ ⊡ **Red Hill Motel.** Housekeeping cabins make this the best choice among Weaverville motels. A two-bedroom cabin with a full kitchen is popular with families. ✉ *Box 234, Red Hill Rd., 96093,* ☎ *530/623–4331. 14 rooms, 10 of them cabins with carports. D, DC, MC, V.*

Outdoor Activities and Sports

FISHING
Just below the Lewiston Dam, east of Weaverville on Highway 299, is the **Fly Stretch** of the Trinity River, a world-class flyfishing area. The **Pine Cove Boat Ramp** provides quality fishing access for visitors with disabilities—decks here are built over prime trout-fishing water. Open all year, Pine Cove is best for fishing from April through October.

HIKING
Several trails offer different levels of day hikes close to Weaverville as well as multiday hikes within the Trinity Alps Wilderness. Contact the **Weaverville Ranger Station** (☎ 530/623–2121) for maps and information.

Shopping
All the good shopping is right downtown. To dress the part of the Wild West explorer, check out the **Western Shop** (✉ 226 Main St., ☎ 530/623–6494) for outdoor gear, bolo ties, cowboy hats, and much more. To get your bearings, try the extraordinary selection of books on the natural history, attractions, and interesting sights of the Far North at **Hays Bookstore** (✉ 106 Main St., ☎ 530/623–2516).

OFF THE BEATEN PATH

TRINITY HERITAGE SCENIC BYWAY – This road, on maps as Highway 3, runs north from Weaverville for 120 mi up to its intersection with I–5, just before Yreka in the town of Edgewood. Natural attractions are visible all along this beautiful, forest-lined road, which is often closed during the winter months. A major portion of the route follows the path established by early miners and settlers as it climbs from 2,000 to 6,500 ft.

Redding

⑪ *218 mi from San Francisco on I–80 to I–505 to I–5 north, 12 mi south of Lake Shasta on I–5.*

With a population of approximately 70,000, Redding is by far the largest city in the Far North. Though not of much interest, it serves as a useful headquarters for exploring the surrounding countryside.

Dining and Lodging

$$ ✕ **Hatch Cover.** This establishment's dark-wood paneling and views of the adjacent Sacramento River give diners a shipboard feel. The menu emphasizes seafood, but you can also get steaks and combination plates. The appetizer menu is extensive, a good excuse for enjoying the outside deck in nice weather. Check out the exotic after-dinner drinks. ⊠ *202 Hemsted Dr. (from Cypress Ave. exit off I–5, turn left, then right on Bechelli La., and left on Hemsted Dr.),* ☎ *530/223–5606. AE, D, MC, V. No lunch weekends.*

$$ ✕ **Jack's Grill.** Although it looks like a dive from the outside, this steak house and bar is immensely popular with residents throughout the territory who come in for 16-ounce steaks. The place is usually jam-packed and noisy. ⊠ *1743 California St.,* ☎ *530/241–9705. AE, MC, V. Closed Sun. No lunch.*

$$–$$$ ☷ **Brigadoon Castle Bed & Breakfast.** Fifteen winding miles from I–5, this 83-acre estate is crowned with an Elizabethan-style castle that opened as a B&B in 1996. Marble baths, antiques, and luxurious fabrics make this an elegant retreat. A separate cottage has a kitchen and a hot tub. Room rates include breakfast and, on Friday through Sunday, dinner. ⊠ *9036 Zogg Mine Rd., Igo 96047,* ☎ *530/396–2785 or 888/343–2836. Hot tub, mountain bikes. AE, D, MC, V.*

$$–$$$ ☷ **Red Lion Motor Inn.** Landscaped grounds and a large patio area with outdoor food service are the highlights here. Rooms are spacious and comfortable. Misty's, the lobby's fancy restaurant ($$$), is popular among locals for its steak Diane. Pets are allowed with advance notice. ⊠ *1830 Hilltop Dr. (Hwy. 44/299 exit east from I–5), 96002,* ☎ *530/221–8700 or 800/547–8010,* 𝖥𝖠𝖷 *530/221–0324. 194 rooms. Restaurant, bar, coffee shop, room service, pool, wading pool, hot tub, putting green. AE, D, MC, V.*

$ ☷ **Colony Inn.** Here's a budget option—doubles with queen-size beds go for around $40—off I–5's Cypress exit. ⊠ *2731 Bechelli La.,* ☎ *530/223–1935 or 800/354–5222,* 𝖥𝖠𝖷 *530/223–1176. 75 rooms. Pool. AE, D, DC, MC, V.*

Outdoor Activities and Sports

The **Fly Shop** (⊠ 4140 Churn Creek Rd., ☎ 530/222–3555) has information about licenses, current fishing conditions, guides, and special fishing packages.

Park Marina Watersports (⊠ 2515 Park Marina Dr., ☎ 530/246–8388) rents rafts and canoes from May to September.

THE FAR NORTH A TO Z

Arriving and Departing

By Bus

Greyhound Lines (☎ 800/231–2222) buses travel I–5, serving Red Bluff, Redding, Dunsmuir, and Mt. Shasta City.

By Car
I–5, an excellent four-lane divided highway, runs up the center of California through Red Bluff and Redding and continues north to Oregon. Lassen Park can be reached by Highway 36 from Red Bluff or (except in winter) Highway 44 from Redding; Highway 299 leads from Redding to McArthur-Burney Falls Memorial State Park. Highways 36 and 299 are good two-lane roads that are kept open year-round. If you are traveling through this area in winter, however, always carry snow chains in your car.

By Plane
Redding Municipal Airport (⊠ Airport Rd., ☎ 530/224–4321) is served by United Express (☎ 800/241–6522).

By Train
Amtrak (☎ 800/872–7245) has stations in Redding (⊠ 1620 Yuba St.) and Dunsmuir (⊠ 5750 Sacramento Ave.).

Getting Around

By Bus
In Redding, a city bus system, **"The Ride"** (☎ 530/241–2877), serves the local area daily except Sunday.

By Car
An automobile is virtually essential to tour the Far North unless you arrive by bus, plane, or train and intend to travel the region entirely by foot or bicycle.

Contacts and Resources

Area Code
The area code in the Far North was scheduled to change from 916 to 530 on November 1, 1997.

Car Rental
Avis (⊠ Redding Municipal Airport, ☎ 530/221–2855 or 800/331–1212). **Enterprise** (⊠ 361 E. Cypress Ave., Redding, ☎ 530/223–0700 or 800/325–8007). **Enterprise** (⊠ 570 Antelope Blvd., Red Bluff, ☎ 530/529–0177 or 800/325–8007). **Hertz** (⊠ Redding Municipal Airport, ☎ 530/221–4620 or 800/654–3131).

Emergencies
Ambulance (☎ 911). **Police** (☎ 911).

Visitor Information
Lassen Volcanic National Park (⊠ 38050 Hwy. 36 E, Mineral 96063, ☎ 530/595–4444). **Mt. Shasta Convention and Visitors Bureau** (⊠ 300 Pine St., Mt. Shasta 96067, ☎ 530/926–4865 or 800/926–4865). **Northern Buttes District Office, State of California Department of Parks and Recreation** (⊠ 400 Glen Dr., Oroville 95966, ☎ 530/538–2200). **Red Bluff–Tehama County Chamber of Commerce** (⊠ 100 Main St., Red Bluff 96080, ☎ 530/527–6220 or 800/655–6225). **Redding Convention and Visitors Bureau** (⊠ 777 Auditorium Dr., Redding 96001, ☎ 530/225–4100 or 800/874–7562). **Shasta Cascade Wonderland Association** (⊠ 14250 Holiday Rd., Redding 96003, ☎ 530/275–5555 or 800/326–6944). **Siskiyou County Visitors Bureau** (⊠ 808 W. Lennox St., Yreka 96097, ☎ 530/842–7857 or 800/446–7475). **Trinity County Chamber of Commerce** (⊠ 210 Main St., Weaverville 96093, ☎ 530/623–6101).

4 The Wine Country

You don't have to be a wine enthusiast to appreciate the mellow beauty of Napa and Sonoma counties, whose rolling hills and verdant vineyards resemble those of Tuscany and Provence. Here, among state-of-the-art wineries, award-winning restaurants, and luxury hotels where mud baths and massage are daily rituals, you just might discover that life need have no nobler purpose than enjoying the fruits of the earth.

By Claudia
Gioseffi

IN 1862, AFTER AN EXTENSIVE TOUR of the wine-producing areas of Europe, Count Agoston Haraszthy de Mokcsa reported a promising prognosis about his adopted California: "Of all the countries through which I passed, not one possessed the same advantages that are to be found in California. . . . California can produce as noble and generous a wine as any in Europe; more in quantity to the acre, and without repeated failures through frosts, summer rains, hailstorms, or other causes."

The "dormant resources" that the father of California's viticulture saw in the balmy days and cool nights of the temperate Napa and Sonoma valleys are in full fruition today. Although the wines produced here are praised and savored by connoisseurs throughout the world, the area continues to be a proving ground for the latest techniques of grape growing and wine making.

For many, wine making is a second career. Making wine is said to be a good way to turn a large fortune into a small one, but that hasn't deterred the doctors, former college professors, publishing tycoons, art dealers, and others who come here to try their hands at it.

In 1975 Napa Valley had no more than 20 wineries; today there are more than 240. In Sonoma County, where the web of vineyards is looser, there are well over 100 wineries, and development is now claiming the cool Carneros region, at the head of the San Francisco Bay, deemed ideal for growing the chardonnay grape.

In addition to great food and wine, you'll find a window into California history in the Wine Country. The town of Sonoma is filled with remnants of Mexican California and the solid, ivy-covered, brick wineries built by Haraszthy and his disciples. Calistoga is a virtual museum of Steamboat Gothic architecture, replete with the fretwork and clapboard beloved of gold rush prospectors and 19th-century spa goers. St. Helena is home to a later architectural fantasy, the beautiful art nouveau mansion of the Beringer brothers.

The area's natural beauty draws a continuous flow of tourists—from the spring, when the vineyards bloom yellow with wild mustard, to the fall, when the grapes are ripe. Haraszthy was right: This is a chosen place.

Pleasures and Pastimes

Dining
Many star chefs from urban areas throughout the United States have migrated to the Wine Country, drawn by the area's renowned produce and world-class wines—the products of fertile soil and near-perpetual sun. As a result of this marriage of imported talent and indigenous bounty, food now rivals wine as the principal attraction of the region—a reality underscored by the establishment of the Culinary Institute of America's West Coast headquarters in St. Helena.

Higher quality has, of course, meant higher prices. However, those on a budget will also find appealing inexpensive eateries. Gourmet delis offer superb picnic fare, and brunch is a cost-effective strategy at high-end restaurants.

With few exceptions (which are noted in individual restaurant listings), dress is informal. Where reservations are indicated as essential, you may need to reserve a week or more ahead; during the summer and early fall harvest seasons you may need to book several months ahead.

56

The Wine Country

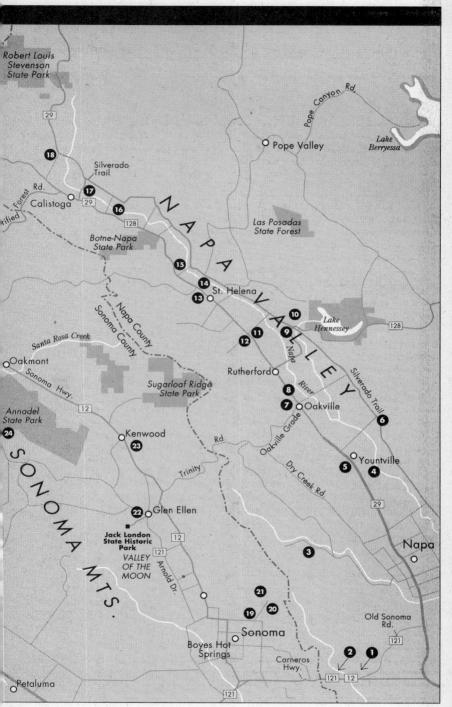

CATEGORY	COST*
$$$$	over $50
$$$	$30–$50
$$	$20–$30
$	under $20

per person for a three-course meal, excluding drinks, service, and 7½% sales tax

Hot-Air Ballooning

Balloon flights take place soon after sunrise, when the calmest, coolest time of day offers maximum lift and soft landings. Prices depend on the duration of the flight, number of passengers, and services (some companies provide extras such as pickup at your lodging or a champagne brunch after the flight). Expect to spend about $165 per person.

Lodging

The area's many inns, hotels, and spas are usually exquisitely appointed. Most local bed-and-breakfasts have historic Victorian and Spanish architecture and serve a full country breakfast. Not surprisingly, a stay in the Wine Country is expensive. Santa Rosa, the largest population center in the area, has the largest selection of rooms, many at moderate rates. Try there if you've failed to reserve far enough in advance or have a limited budget.

CATEGORY	COST*
$$$$	over $175
$$$	$120–$175
$$	$80–$120
$	under $80

All prices are for a standard double room, excluding 14% tax.

Spas and Mud Baths

Mineral soaks, mud baths, and massage are rejuvenating local traditions. Calistoga is known worldwide for its spring water–fed mineral tubs and mud baths full of volcanic ash. Sonoma, St. Helena, and other towns also have full-service spas.

Wine Tasting

Learning about the origin of the grapes, the terraces on which they're grown, the weather that produced them, and the methods by which they're transformed into wine will give you a new understanding and appreciation of wine—and a great afternoon (or all-day) diversion. For those new to the wine tasting game, Mondavi and Korbel Champagne Cellars both give general tours geared toward teaching novices the basics on how wine and champagne are made and what to look for when you taste. Unless otherwise noted, the wineries in this chapter are open daily year-round and charge no fee for admission, tours, or tastings.

Exploring the Wine Country

Numbers in the text correspond to numbers in the margin and on the Wine Country map.

Great Itineraries

The Wine Country is comprised of two main areas: the Napa Valley and the Sonoma Valley. Five major paths cut through both valleys: U.S. 101 and Highways 12 and 121 through Sonoma County, and Highway 29 north from Napa. The 25-mi Silverado Trail, which runs parallel to Highway 29 north from Napa to Calistoga, is a more scenic, less crowded route with several distinguished wineries.

IF YOU HAVE 2 DAYS

Start at the circa-1857 **Buena Vista Carneros Winery** ⑳. From there, take the Oakville Grade to stylish, historic 🔶 **St. Helena,** taking time to admire the views of Sonoma and Napa valleys from the Sonoma Mountains. After lunch in St. Helena, take the 30-minute tour of **Beringer Vineyards** ⑬. The next day drive to **Calistoga** for an early morning balloon ride, an afternoon trip to the mud baths, and a visit to **Clos Pegase** ⑰ before heading back to St. Helena for dinner at Greystone— the Culinary Institute of America's beautiful West Coast campus.

IF YOU HAVE 5 OR 6 DAYS

Begin in the town of **Sonoma,** whose colorful plaza and mission evoke early California's Spanish past. Afterward, head north to 🔶 **Glen Ellen** and the Valley of the Moon. Picnic and explore the grounds at Jack London State Historic Park. The next morning visit **Kenwood Vineyards** ㉓ before heading north to **Healdsburg** in Dry Creek Valley via Santa Rosa and U.S. 101. In this less trafficked haven of northern Sonoma County, a host of "hidden" wineries—including **Dry Creek Vineyard** ㉕ and **Quivera** ㉖—lie nestled in the woods. Spend the night in 🔶 **Healdsburg.** On the third day cross over into Napa Valley—take Mark Springs Road east off U.S. 101's River Road exit and follow the signs on Porter Creek Road to Petrified Forest Road to Highway 29. Spend the day (and the night) in the quaint town of 🔶 **Calistoga,** noted for its mud baths and mineral springs. Wake up early on the fourth day for a balloon ride. If you're feeling energetic, take to the **Silverado Trail** for a bike ride with stops on the north side of town at **Chateau Montelena** ⑱ and the south side of town at **Clos Pegase** ⑰. On day five, visit the galleries, shops, and eateries of St. Helena before heading to **Yountville,** stopping for lunch at one of its many acclaimed restaurants before heading up the hill to the **Hess Collection Winery and Vineyards** ③.

When to Tour the Wine Country

"Crush," the term used to indicate the season when grapes are picked and crushed, usually takes place in September or October, depending on the weather. From September until December the entire Wine Country celebrates its bounty with street fairs and festivals. The Napa Valley Wine Festival takes place the first weekend in November; the Sonoma County Harvest Fair, with its famous grape stomp, is held the first weekend in October. Golf tournaments, wine auctions, and art and food fairs dot the calendar throughout the fall.

In season (April–October) the Napa Valley draws crowds of tourists, and traffic along Highway 29 from St. Helena to Calistoga is often backed up on weekends. The Sonoma Valley, Santa Rosa, and especially Healdsburg are less crowded. It's best to book lodging, restaurant, and winery reservations well in advance. Many wineries give tours at specified times and require appointments.

To avoid crowds, visit the Wine Country during the week and get an early start in the morning (most wineries open around 10). Pack a sun hat, since summer is usually very hot and dry, and autumn can be even hotter.

Although winter in the Wine Country lacks the bright yellows and greens of spring and the brilliant golds and reds of autumn, the season's quiet, stark beauty is appealing in its own way. A destination for many on Thanksgiving, the region is full of cozy B&Bs that prepare elaborate holiday dinners. Yountville's Festival of Lights in December celebrates the holidays with ongoing entertainment all month long.

THE NAPA VALLEY

The Napa Valley is the undisputed capital of American wine production, with more than 240 wineries. Famed for its unrivaled climate and neat rows of vineyards, the area is nonetheless made up of small, quirky towns whose Victorian Gothic architecture, with its narrow, gingerbread facades and pointed arches, is reminiscent of a distant world. Calistoga feels like an Old West frontier town, with wooden-plank storefronts and people in cowboy hats; St. Helena is posh, with tony shops and elegant restaurants; Yountville is small, concentrated, and redolent of American history, yet fast becoming a culinary hub.

With the Napa River twisting through the region and long, winding country roads, boating and bicycling are two popular pastimes. For professionally arranged riverboat excursions, contact the **Napa Valley Riverboat Company** (⊠ 402 Riverside Rd., Napa, ☎ 707/226–2628). For bicycle rentals, try **Napa Valley Cyclery** (⊠ 4080 Byway East, Napa, ☎ 707/255–3377, FAX 707/255–3380).

Napa

47 mi from San Francisco, north on U.S. 101, west on Hwy. 37, north and east on Hwy. 121/12 to Hwy. 29; 46 mi from San Francisco, east and north on I–80 to Hwy. 37 west to Hwy. 29 north.

Although the town of Napa doesn't offer much in the way of attractions, it is the largest town in the Carneros grape-growing region that straddles southern Napa and Sonoma counties. The area has a long, cool growing season tempered by maritime breezes and lingering fogs off the San Pablo Bay—optimum slow-growing conditions for pinot noir and chardonnay grapes.

Most destinations in the Napa and Sonoma valleys are easily accessible from Napa. For those seeking an affordable alternative to the hotels and B&Bs in the heart of the Wine Country, Napa's chain lodgings (most of the major companies are represented) are a good option—but stay on the north side of town near Yountville; some of the sections to the south are downright seedy.

❶ Domaine Carneros occupies a 138-acre estate dominated by a classic château inspired by Champagne Taittinger's historic Château de la Marquetterie in France. Carved into the hillside beneath the winery, Domaine Carneros's cellars produce sparkling wines reminiscent of the Taittinger style. At night the château is a glowing beacon rising above the dark vineyards. By day activity buzzes throughout the visitor center, the touring and tasting rooms, and the kitchen and dining room, where private luncheons and dinners emphasize food and wine pairings. ⊠ *1240 Duhig Rd.,* ☎ *707/257–0101.* ☉ *Daily 10:30–6. Tours hourly in summer; at 11, 1, and 3 in winter.*

Learn the history and folklore of the rare alambic brandy at the **❷ Carneros Alambic Distillery.** Tours include an explanation of the double-distillation process, which eliminates all but the finest spirits for aging; a view of the French-built alambic pot stills that resemble Aladdin's lamp; a trip to the atmospheric oak barrel house, where taped angels' chants create an otherworldly mood; and a sensory evaluation of vintage brandies (no tasting allowed, by law). ⊠ *1250 Cuttings Wharf Rd. (from Domaine Carneros, head 1 mi east on Carneros Hwy.),* ☎ *707/253–9055.* ☉ *Apr.–Dec., daily 10–5; Jan.–Mar., daily 10:30–4:30. Tours on the hr.*

★ ❸ The **Hess Collection Winery and Vineyards** is an unexpected discovery on a hilltop 9 mi northwest of Napa (don't give up; the road leading to the winery is long and winding). The simple, rustic limestone structure, circa 1903, holds Swiss owner Donald Hess's personal art collection, including works by contemporary European and American artists such as Robert Motherwell, Francis Bacon, and Frank Stella. Cabernet sauvignon is the real strength here, though Hess also produces some fine chardonnays. Visitors are free to tour the property unchaperoned. ⊠ *4411 Redwood Rd., west off Hwy. 29,* ☎ *707/255–1144.* ⊙ *Daily 10–4.*

❹ The winery at **Trefethen Vineyards** was built in 1886; today it's the only wooden, gravity-powered winery in Napa. Trefethen is known for its reserve cabernet as well as its 1993 merlot, available only on the premises. ⊠ *1160 Oak Knoll Ave., off Hwy. 29,* ☎ *707/255–7700.* ⊙ *Daily 10–4:30. Tours by appointment.*

Dining and Lodging

$$–$$$ ✕ **La Boucane.** Chef-owner Jacques Mokrani has created a gorgeous little gem of a restaurant in a restored 1885 Victorian decorated with period antiques. Classic French cuisine (rack of lamb, champagne crisp duck) is delivered with style in a candlelit dining room with silver settings and fine linen. ⊠ *1778 2nd St., at Jefferson St., downtown Napa,* ☎ *707/253–1177. MC, V. Closed Sun. and Jan. No lunch.*

$$ ✕ **Bistro Don Giovanni.** Giovanni and Donna Scala, the culinary couple behind the success of Ristorante Piatti, have created a wine list that's as locally representative as their menu is eclectic. The ambience is casual Mediterranean, with terra-cotta tile floors and high ceilings; there's also a spacious outdoor patio with an expansive view of the valley. Don't miss the individual pizzas cooked in a wood-burning oven and topped with ingredients such as pesto, goat cheese, and shrimp. ⊠ *4110 St. Helena Hwy. (Hwy. 29),* ☎ *707/224–3300. AE, DC, MC, V.*

$$ ✕ **Brown Street Grill.** This downtown grill serves home-style fare in a casual setting. Simple salads and classic plates of roast chicken and grilled steak are masterfully handled, and the thick, tasty sandwiches, stuffed with valley-grown tomatoes, are trenchermen's treats at lunchtime. ⊠ *1300 Brown St.,* ☎ *707/255–6395. MC, V. Closed Sun.*

$$$$ ✕🏨 **Silverado Country Club.** This luxurious 1,200-acre property in the hills east of the town of Napa has cottages, kitchen apartments, and one- to three-bedroom efficiencies, many with fireplaces. With two golf courses (greens fee: $110, which includes cart), eight pools, and 22 tennis courts, it's a place for serious sports enthusiasts and anyone who enjoys the conveniences of a full-scale resort. The elegant Vintner's Court (closed Sunday through Tuesday; reservations essential), with California–Pacific Rim cuisine, serves dinner only; there is a seafood buffet on Friday night and a champagne brunch on Sunday. ⊠ *1600 Atlas Peak Rd. (6 mi east of Napa via Hwy. 121), 94558,* ☎ *707/257–0200 or 800/532–0500,* ℻ *707/257–2867. 277 condo units (300 sleeping rooms). 3 restaurants, bar, 8 pools, 2 18-hole golf courses, 22 tennis courts, bicycles. D, DC, MC, V.*

Outdoor Activities and Sports

GOLF

The 18-hole **Chardonnay Club** course (⊠ 2555 Jameson Canyon Rd., ☎ 707/257–8950) is a favorite among Bay Area golfers. The greens fee, $60 weekdays and $80 weekends, includes a cart. *See also* **Silverado Country Club,** *above.*

TENNIS

Vintage High School (⊠ 1375 Trower Ave.) maintains eight public tennis courts. **Napa High School** (⊠ 2474 Jefferson St.) maintains six tennis courts with coin-operated night lights. Call the Napa Valley School District (☎ 707/253–3715) for information.

Yountville

13 mi north of the town of Napa on Hwy. 29.

Yountville at first glance looks like a slightly backwater town because of its small size and bungalow-style houses. Despite its modest appearance, however, the town is home to three of the Wine Country's finest restaurants and two of its most renowned wineries. Another attraction is **Vintage 1870** (⊠ 6525 Washington St., ☎ 707/944–2451), a 26-acre complex of boutiques, restaurants, and gourmet stores. The vine-covered brick buildings were built in 1870 and housed a winery, livery stable, and distillery.

⑤ Luggage-meister Louis Vuitton and French champagne producer Moet-Hennessy own **Domaine Chandon.** Tours of the sleek, modern facilities on the beautifully maintained property include sample flutes of the méthode champenoise sparkling wine. Champagne is $3–$4 per glass, hors d'oeuvres are complimentary, and an elegant restaurant beckons gourmets. ⊠ *California Dr., west of Hwy. 29,* ☎ *707/944–2280.* ⊙ *May–Oct., daily 9–5; Nov.–Apr., Wed.–Sun. 9–5. Tours throughout the day.*

⑥ In 1993 the World Wine Championships gave **Stag's Leap Wine Cellars** a platinum award for their 1990 reserve chardonnay, designating it the highest-ranked premium chardonnay in the world. The winery's red table wine, Cask 23, consistently earns accolades as well. ⊠ *5766 Silverado Trail,* ☎ *707/944–2020.* ⊠ *$3 tasting fee.* ⊙ *Daily 10–4. Tours by appointment.*

Dining and Lodging

$$$$ ✕ **Domaine Chandon.** Part of the world-renowned winery, this large, formal dining room caters to food and wine aficionados with a daily changing menu of French-inspired California cuisine. Sonoma duck breast is served with polenta and green-olive sage juice; plump mussels float in a delicate Thai broth. The cavernous room looks out over miles of vineyards and native oaks. There is also a tree-shaded patio. ⊠ *California Dr. (take Yountville exit off Hwy. 29 toward Veterans' Home),* ☎ *707/944–2892. Reservations essential. AE, D, DC, MC, V. No dinner Mon.–Tues. Apr.–Oct.*

$$$$ ✕ **French Laundry.** Gardens, fresh flowers, and gentle lighting make
★   patrons of the French Laundry feel like well-tended houseguests being treated to an exquisite meal. The prix fixe menus include entrées such as pan-roasted Virginia striped bass with sweet peppers and black olives; and for dessert, coffee and doughnuts—cinnamon-sugar doughnuts with cappuccino ice cream. ⊠ *6640 Washington St.,* ☎ *707/944–2380. Reservations essential. AE, MC, V. Closed Mon. and 1st 2 wks in Jan. No lunch Sun., Tues.*

$$ ✕ **Mustards Grill.** Grilled fish, steak, local fresh produce, and an im-
★   pressive wine list are the trademarks of this boisterous bistro with a black-and-white marble floor and upbeat artwork. The thin, crisp, golden onion rings are addictive. ⊠ *7399 St. Helena Hwy., 1 mi north of Yountville,* ☎ *707/944–2424. Reservations essential. D, DC, MC, V.*

$$ ✕ **Ristorante Piatti.** This stylish trattoria with a pizza oven and an open kitchen is known for regional Italian cooking—the perfect cure for a jaded appetite. Homemade pastas are the best bet. ⊠ *6480 Washington St.,* ☎ *707/944–2070. AE, MC, V.*

$ ✕ **The Diner.** One of the best-known stopovers in the Napa Valley, this breakfast-centric eatery has local sausages and house potatoes that are not to be missed. Healthful versions of Mexican and American classics are served for dinner. ⊠ *6476 Washington St.,* ☎ *707/944–2626. No credit cards. Closed Mon.*

$$$$ 🏨 **La Residence.** Even though it's within feet of the St. Helena Highway, "La Res," as it's known, is secluded and romantic enough to make you feel as if you've flown to France, or at least New Orleans. The hotel is housed in two buildings: the Mansion, a renovated 1870s Gothic Revival manor house built by a riverboat captain from New Orleans; and Cabernet Hall, a newer French-style barn. Guest rooms have period antiques, fireplaces, and double French doors opening onto verandas or patios. ⊠ *4066 St. Helena Hwy. (Hwy. 29), 4 mi south of Yountville,* ☎ *707/253–0337,* FAX *707/253–0382. 20 rooms. Dining room, pool, hot tub, business services. D, DC, MC, V.*

$$$$ 🏨 **Napa Valley Lodge.** Spacious rooms overlook the vineyards and the valley at this hacienda-style lodge; a tile roof, covered walkways, balconies, patios, and colorful gardens add to the Mediterranean mood. Coffee, a Continental breakfast, and the morning paper are complimentary. ⊠ *2230 Madison St., at Hwy. 29,* ☎ *707/944–2468 or 800/ 368–2468,* FAX *707/944–9362. 55 rooms. Refrigerators, pool, hot tub, sauna, exercise room. D, DC, MC, V.*

$$$$ 🏨 **Vintage Inn.** All the rooms at this luxurious inn have fireplaces, whirlpool baths, private verandas or patios, hand-painted fabrics, window seats, and shuttered windows. Guests are treated to a welcome bottle of wine, Continental breakfast with champagne, and afternoon tea. ⊠ *6541 Washington St., 94599,* ☎ *707/944–1112 or 800/351–1133,* FAX *707/944–1617. 80 rooms. Refrigerators, pool, spa, tennis court, bicycles. D, DC, MC, V.*

Hot-Air Ballooning

Balloons Above the Valley (⊠ Box 3838, Napa 94558, ☎ 707/253–2222; 800/464–6824 in CA) is a reliable organization. Another hot-air ballooning company is **Napa Valley Balloons** (⊠ Box 2860, Yountville 94599, ☎ 707/944–0228; 800/253–2224 in CA).

Oakville

2 mi west of Yountville on Hwy. 29.

There are three reasons to visit the town of Oakville: its grocery store, its scenic mountain grade, and its magnificent, highly exclusive winery. The **Oakville Grocery** (⊠ 7856 St. Helena Hwy.), built in the late 1880s to serve as a grocery store and Wells Fargo Pony Express stop, carries gourmet foods and difficult-to-find wines. Custom-packed picnic baskets are a specialty. Along the mountain range that divides the Napa and Sonoma valleys, the **Oakville Grade** is a twisting half-hour route with breathtaking views of both valleys. Though the surface of the road is good, it can be difficult to negotiate at night, and trucks are advised not to attempt it at any time.

 At **Robert Mondavi,** the winery that created fumé blanc, tasters are encouraged to take the 60-minute production tour with complimentary tasting before trying the reserve reds ($1–$5 per glass). In-depth three- to four-hour tours and gourmet lunch tours are also popular. ⊠ *7801 St. Helena Hwy.,* ☎ *707/259–9463.* ☉ *May–Oct., daily 9–5:30; Nov.–Apr., daily 9:30–4:30. Tours by appointment.*

❽ **Opus One,** the combined venture of famed California wine maker Robert Mondavi and French baron Philippe Rothschild, is famed for its vast (1,000 barrels side by side on a single floor) semicircular barrel cellar modeled on the Château Mouton Rothschild winery in France. The futuristic building is the work of the same architects who built the Transamerica Pyramid in San Francisco. The state-of-the-art facilities produce about 20,000 cases (a relatively small quantity) of ultra-premium, Bordeaux-style red wine from grapes grown in the estate's own vineyards and in the surrounding area. ⊠ *7900 St. Helena Hwy. (Hwy. 29),* ☎ *707/963–1979.* ☜ *Tasting fees vary.* ☉ *Daily 10–4:30. Tours by appointment.*

Rutherford

1 mi northwest of Oakville on Hwy. 29.

From a fast-moving car, Rutherford is a quick blur of dark forest, a rustic barn or two, and maybe a country store. Then it's gone. But don't speed by this tiny hamlet; with its singular microclimate and soil, this is an important viticultural center.

❾ The tour at **Mumm Napa Valley** is particularly educational and entertaining. A joint venture of Mumm—the French champagne house—and Seagram, the winery is considered one of California's premier sparkling-wine producers. Its Napa Brut Prestige and ultrapremium Vintage Reserve are the best known. An art gallery contains a permanent exhibit of photographs by Ansel Adams that record the wine-making process. ⊠ *8445 Silverado Trail,* ☎ *707/942–3434.* ☉ *Daily 10:30– 6. Tours 11–3.*

❿ The wine at **Rutherford Hill Winery** is aged in French oak barrels stacked in more than 30,000 sq ft of caves—the largest such facilities in the nation. Tours of the caves can be followed by a picnic in oak, olive, or madrona orchards. ⊠ *200 Rutherford Hill Rd., off the Silverado Trail,* ☎ *707/963–7194.* ☉ *Weekdays 10–4:30, weekends 10–5. Tour times vary seasonally, call ahead.*

⑪ **Beaulieu Vineyard** utilizes the same wine-making process, from crush to bottle, as it did the day it opened at the turn of the last century. The winery's cabernet is a benchmark of the Napa Valley, and its Georges du Latour Private Reserve remains a collector's favorite. ⊠ *1960 St. Helena Hwy. (Hwy. 29),* ☎ *707/963–2411.* ☉ *Daily 10–5. Tours daily 11–3:30.*

⑫ **Niebaum-Coppola Estate** has consistently received high ratings for its Rubicon and other wines. When touring film director Francis Ford Coppola's winery, visit the museum of movie memorabilia, which includes Don Corleone's desk and chair from *The Godfather,* costumes from *Dracula,* and a café. ⊠ *1991 St. Helena Hwy. (Hwy. 29),* ☎ *707/963– 9099.* ☉ *Daily 10–5. Tours daily, times vary.*

Dining and Lodging

$$–$$$$ ✕▥ **Auberge du Soleil.** Here you can sit on a wisteria-draped deck
★ sipping a late-afternoon glass of wine, with acres of terraced olive groves and rolling vineyards at your feet. Inside, Santa Fe accents create an atmosphere of irresistible indolence. The hotel's restaurant is a symphony of earth tones and wood beams, with a frequently changing menu that emphasizes local produce and also includes unusual specialties such as roasted lobster sausage and rosemary-roasted rack of lamb. ⊠ *180 Rutherford Hill Rd. (off Silverado Trail north of Rte. 128), 94573,* ☎ *707/963–1211 or 800/348–5406,* 𝔽𝔸𝕏 *707/963– 8764. 50 rooms. Pool, hot tub, massage, steam room, 3 tennis courts, exercise room. D, MC, V.*

$$$$ 🏨 **Rancho Caymus Inn.** California-Spanish in style, this inn has well-maintained gardens and large suites with kitchens and whirlpool baths. Well-chosen details include decorative handicrafts, beehive fireplaces, tile murals, stoneware basins, and llama-hair blankets. ⊠ *1140 Rutherford Rd. (junction of Hwys. 29 and 128), 94573,* ☎ *707/963–1777 or 800/845–1777,* FAX *707/963–5387. 26 rooms. DC, MC, V. 2-night minimum Apr.–Nov.*

St. Helena

2 mi northwest of Oakville on Hwy. 29.

By the time Charles Krug planted grapes in St. Helena around 1860, quite a few vineyards already existed. Today the town beckons visitors with its abundant selection of wineries—many of which lie along the route from Yountville to St. Helena—and restaurants, including Greystone on the West Coast campus of the Culinary Institute of America. Arching sycamore trees bow across Main Street (Highway 29) to create a pleasant, shady drive.

⑬ Established in 1876, **Beringer Vineyards** is the oldest continuously operating winery in the Napa Valley. In 1883 the Beringer brothers, Frederick and Jacob, built the Rhine House Mansion, where tastings are now held among Belgian art nouveau hand-carved oak and walnut furniture and stained-glass windows. Tours, given every 30 minutes, include a visit to underground wine tunnels made of volcanic ash that were dug by Chinese laborers in the 19th century. ⊠ *2000 Main St.,* ☎ *707/963–4812.* ☉ *Daily 9:30–4; summer hrs sometimes extended to 5. Tours daily every 30 mins.*

⑭ **Charles Krug Winery** opened in 1861 when Count Haraszthy loaned Krug a small cider press. The oldest winery in the Napa Valley, it is run by the Peter Mondavi family. The gift shop stocks everything from gourmet food baskets with grape-shape pasta to books about the region and its wines. ⊠ *2800 N. Main St.,* ☎ *707/963–5057.* ☉ *Daily 10:30–5:30. Tours 11:30, 1:30, and 3:30.*

⑮ **Freemark Abbey Winery** was originally called the Tychson Winery—it was built in 1886 by Josephine Tychson, the first woman to establish a winery in California. It has long been known for its cabernets, whose grapes come from the fertile Rutherford Bench; all other wines are estate grown, including a much-touted late-harvest riesling. ⊠ *3022 St. Helena Hwy. N,* ☎ *707/963–9694.* ☉ *Mar.–Dec., daily 10–4:30; Jan.–Feb., Thurs.–Sun. 10–4:30. Tour daily at 2.*

For some nonalcoholic sightseeing, visit the **Silverado Museum,** in a pristine Victorian building. Its Robert Louis Stevenson memorabilia consists of more than 8,000 artifacts, including first editions, manuscripts, and photographs. ⊠ *1490 Library La., at Adams St.,* ☎ *707/963–3757.* ☑ *Free.* ☉ *Tues.–Sun. noon–4.*

The **Culinary Institute of America,** the country's leading school for chefs, set up its West Coast headquarters in the century-old Greystone Winery, the former site of the Christian Brothers Winery and a national historic landmark. The CIA campus has 30 acres of herb and vegetable gardens, a 15-acre merlot vineyard, and a Mediterranean-inspired restaurant (☞ Wine Spectator Greystone Restaurant, *below*) that's open to the public. Also on the property are a well-stocked culinary store, a quirky corkscrew and winepress museum, and a culinary library. ⊠ *2555 Main St.,* ☎ *800/333–9242.* ☑ *Free.*

Dining and Lodging

$$$$ ✕ **Terra.** Hiro Stone and Lissa Doumani, the chef-owners of this unpretentious restaurant in a century-old stone foundry, honed their culinary skills at the side of chef Wolfgang Puck. Southern French and northern Italian favorites here include a pear and goat cheese salad with warm pancetta and sherry vinaigrette, and duck breast in an intriguing cherry sauce. ⊠ *1345 Railroad Ave.,* ☎ *707/963–8931. Reservations essential. MC, V. Closed Tues. No lunch.*

$$$ ✕ **Trilogy.** Chef-owner Diane Pariseau pairs one of the best and most extensive contemporary wine lists in the valley with superb renditions of California-French cuisine on a daily changing prix fixe menu. Her grilled chicken breast on a nest of sautéed apples and green peppercorns, and grilled tuna steak with olive oil and sweet red pepper puree are artfully presented. With a mere 10 tables, the secluded dining room feels like a country home. ⊠ *1234 Main St.,* ☎ *707/963–5507. Reservations essential. MC, V. Closed Mon. and 3 wks in Dec. No lunch weekends.*

$$$ ✕ **Wine Spectator Greystone Restaurant.** The restaurant of the Culinary Institute of America draws part of its staff from the institute, although professional chefs command the kitchen. The menu has a Mediterranean spirit and emphasizes small plates such as roasted peppers and eggplant and chicken terrine with aioli. ⊠ *2555 Main St.,* ☎ *707/967–1010. AE, DC, MC, V. Closed Tues.*

$$–$$$ ✕ **Showley's.** Garlic chicken and roasted monkfish with garlic mashed potatoes are among the recommended items on the changing menu here. Starters are equally well prepared, especially the chili *en nogada,* made with pork, pine nuts, and chutney and served with a walnut–crème fraîche sauce. ⊠ *1327 Railroad Ave.,* ☎ *707/963–1200. AE, D, MC, V. Closed Mon.*

$$ ✕ **Brava Terrace.** Vegetables plucked straight from the restaurant's garden enliven chef Fred Halpert's trademark pasta, risotto, and cassoulet dishes; chocolate-chip crème brûlée provides a grand finale. Brava has a comfortably casual ambience with a full bar, a large stone fireplace, a romantic outdoor terrace overlooking a shady brook, and a heated deck with views of the valley floor and Howell Mountain. ⊠ *3010 St. Helena Hwy. (Hwy. 29), ½ mi north of downtown St. Helena,* ☎ *707/963–9300. Reservations essential. AE, D, DC, MC, V. Closed Wed. Nov.–Apr. and last 2 wks of Jan.*

$$ ✕ **Tra Vigne.** This Napa Valley fieldstone building has been transformed
★ into a striking trattoria with a huge wood bar, high ceilings, and plush banquettes. Homemade mozzarella, olive oil and vinegar, and house-cured pancetta and prosciutto contribute to a one-of-a-kind tour of Tuscan cuisine. Although getting a table without a reservation is sometimes difficult, drops-ins can sit at the bar. The outdoor courtyard in summer is a sun-splashed Mediterranean vision of striped umbrellas and awnings, crowded café tables, and rustic pots overflowing with flowers. ⊠ *1050 Charter Oak Ave., off Hwy. 29,* ☎ *707/963–4444. Reservations essential in dining room. D, DC, MC, V.*

$$$–$$$$ ✕▥ **Meadowood Resort.** Manicured croquet lawns, a golf course, and gorgeous hiking trails add to the glamour of this sprawling 256-acre resort with a rambling country lodge and 79 bungalow suites. For the popular weekend brunch (nonguests welcome), refined French cuisine with a California twist is served as part of a prix fixe menu in either a dining room with a cathedral ceiling, a fireplace, and greenery or outdoors on a terrace overlooking the golf course. Reservations are essential at the restaurants. ⊠ *900 Meadowood La., 94574,* ☎ *707/963–3646 or 800/458–8080,* ☏ *707/963–3532. 85 rooms. 2 restaurants, bar, room service, 2 pools, hot tub, massage, sauna, steam room, 9-hole golf course, 7 tennis courts, croquet, health club. D, DC, MC, V.*

$$$$ ⊞ **Harvest Inn.** This Tudor-style inn with 47 fireplaces overlooks a 14-acre vineyard and the hills beyond. Although the property is close to a highway, the lush landscaping and award-winning brick and stonework create an illusion of remoteness. Most rooms have wet bars, refrigerators, antique furnishings, and fireplaces. Pets are allowed in certain rooms for a $20 fee. Complimentary breakfast is served in the breakfast room and on the patio overlooking the vineyards. ⊠ *1 Main St., 94574,* ☎ *707/963–9463 or 800/950–8466,* ℻ *707/963–4402. 55 rooms. Refrigerators, 2 pools, hot tub. D, MC, V.*

$$$$ ⊞ **Wine Country Inn.** Surrounded by a pastoral landscape of vineyards and hills dotted with old barns and stone bridges, this is a peaceful New England–style retreat. Rural antiques fill all the rooms, most of which overlook the vineyards with either a balcony, patio, or deck. Most rooms have fireplaces, and some have private hot tubs. A hearty complimentary country breakfast is served buffet style in the sun-splashed common room, and wine tastings are scheduled in the afternoons. ⊠ *1152 Lodi La., off Hwy. 29, 94574,* ☎ *707/963–7077,* ℻ *707/963–9018. 24 rooms. Pool, hot tubs. MC, V.*

Shopping

Handcrafted candles made on the premises are for sale at the **Hurd Beeswax Candle Factory,** next door to the Freemark Abbey Winery (⊠ 3020 St. Helena Hwy. N, ☎ 707/963–7211). Bargain hunters will delight in the many designer labels for sale at the **Village Outlet Stores** complex on St. Helena Highway, across the street from Freemark Abbey Winery. **On the Vine** (⊠ 1234 Main St., ☎ 707/963–2209) carries wearable art and unique jewelry inspired by food and wine themes.

Calistoga

3 mi northwest of St. Helena on Hwy. 29.

In addition to its wineries, Calistoga is noted for its mineral water, hot mineral springs, mud baths, steam baths, and massages. The Calistoga Hot Springs Resort was founded in 1859 by maverick entrepreneur Sam Brannan, whose ambition was to found "the Saratoga of California." He tripped up the pronunciation of the phrase at a formal banquet—it came out "Calistoga"—and the name stuck.

The **Sharpsteen Museum** has a magnificent diorama of the Calistoga Hot Springs Resort in its heyday. Other exhibits document Robert Louis Stevenson's time in the area and the career of museum founder Ben Sharpsteen, an animator at the Walt Disney studio. ⊠ *1311 Washington St.,* ☎ *707/942–5911.* ⊡ *Free.* ☉ *May–Oct., daily 10–4; Nov.–Apr., daily noon–4.*

At **Indian Springs,** $90 entitles enthusiasts to a mud bath, mineral-water shower, and mineral-water bath, plus time in the steam room, a blanket wrap, and a 25-minute massage. The cost without massage is $55. The spa has 16 cottages with studio or one-bedroom units and a larger structure with three bedrooms. ⊠ *1712 Lincoln Ave.,* ☎ *707/942–4913.* ☉ *Daily 9–7. Reservations recommended for spa treatments.*

16 For the ultimate sybaritic splurge, treat yourself to a post-mud-bath glass of wine. A good place to start is **Sterling Vineyards,** which sits on a hilltop to the east of Calistoga, its pristine white Mediterranean-style buildings reached by an enclosed gondola from the valley floor. The view from the tasting room is superb, and the gift shop is one of the best in the valley. ⊠ *1111 Dunaweal La.,* ☎ *707/942–3300.* ⊡ *Tram $6.* ☉ *Daily 10:30–4:30. Tours by appointment.*

★ ⑰ Designed by postmodern architect Michael Graves, **Clos Pegase** is a one-of-a-kind structure packed with unusual art objects from the collection of art-book publisher and owner Jan Shrem. Works of art even appear in the underground wine tunnels. ⊠ *1060 Dunaweal La.,* ☎ *707/942–4981.* ⊘ *Daily 10:30–5. Tours by appointment.*

⑱ **Chateau Montelena** is a vine-covered stone French château constructed circa 1882 and set amid Chinese-inspired gardens, complete with a man-made lake with gliding swans and islands crowned by Chinese pavilions. The pavilions are available for picnics on a first-come, first-served basis for wine purchasers. Château Montelena produces award-winning chardonnays and cabernet sauvignons. ⊠ *1429 Tubbs La.,* ☎ *707/942–5105; 800/222–7288 outside Bay Area.* ⊘ *Daily 10–4. Tours by reservation at 11 and 2.*

☺ Many families bring children to Calistoga to see **Old Faithful Geyser of California** blast its 60-ft tower of steam and vapor about every 40 minutes (the pattern is disrupted if there's an earthquake in the offing). One of just three regularly erupting geysers in the world, it is fed by an underground river that heats to 350°F. The spout lasts three minutes. ⊠ *1299 Tubbs La., 1 mi north of Calistoga,* ☎ *707/942–6463.* ⊡ *$5.* ⊘ *During daylight savings time, daily 9–6; winter, daily 9–5.*

☺ The **Petrified Forest** contains the remains of the volcanic eruptions of Mount St. Helena 3.4 million years ago. The force of the explosion uprooted the gigantic redwoods, covered them with volcanic ash, and infiltrated the trees with silica and minerals, causing petrifaction. Explore the museum, then picnic on the grounds. ⊠ *4100 Petrified Forest Rd., 5 mi west of Calistoga,* ☎ *707/942–6667.* ⊡ *$3.* ⊘ *Summer, daily 10–6; winter, daily 10–4:30.*

☺ **Robert Louis Stevenson State Park,** on Highway 29 about 3 mi northeast of Calistoga, encompasses the summit of Mount St. Helena. It was here, in the summer of 1880, in an abandoned bunkhouse of the Silverado Mine, that Stevenson and his bride, Fanny Osbourne, spent their honeymoon. The stay inspired Stevenson's "The Silverado Squatters," and Spyglass Hill in *Treasure Island* is thought to be a portrait of Mount St. Helena.

Dining and Lodging

$$–$$$ ✕ **All Seasons Café.** Bistro cuisine has a California spin in this sun-filled setting with marble tables and a black-and-white checkerboard floor. The seasonal menu includes organic greens, wild mushrooms, local game birds, and house-smoked beef, chicken, and salmon, as well as homemade breads, desserts, and ice cream from an on-site ice cream plant. The café's owners also run the Hydro Bar brew pub across the street. ⊠ *1400 Lincoln Ave.,* ☎ *707/942–9111. MC, V. Closed Wed.*

$$–$$$ ✕ **Calistoga Inn.** Grilled meat and fish for dinner and soups, salads, and sandwiches for lunch are prepared with flair at this microbrewery with a tree-shaded outdoor patio. ⊠ *1250 Lincoln Ave.,* ☎ *707/942–4101. AE, MC, V.*

$$–$$$ ✕ **Catahoula Restaurant and Saloon.** Using a large wood-burning oven,
★   chef Jan Birnbaum churns out California-Cajun dishes such as spicy gumbo with andouille sausage and for dessert, wood-fire-cooked chocolate s'mores. Sit at the counter and watch the chef cook—it's the best entertainment in town. ⊠ *Mount View Hotel, 1457 Lincoln Ave.,* ☎ *707/942–2275. Reservations essential. MC, V. Closed Tues. and Jan.*

$–$$ ✕ **Checkers.** You'll find unusual pizzas and pastas plus a few surprises—a Thai pizza with peanuts and a noodle dish that resembles chow mein—at this whimsically decorated Italian restaurant. ⊠ *1414 Lincoln Ave.,* ☎ *707/942–9300. MC, V.*

$–$$ ✕ **Pacifico.** Technicolor ceramics and subtropical plants adorn this Mexican restaurant that serves Oaxacan and other fare. ✉ *1237 Lincoln Ave.,* ☎ *707/942–4400. MC, V.*

$$$$ ▦ **Cottage Grove Inn.** Moss-covered elm trees shade 16 cottages with various themes—botanical, nautical, musical, and floral among them. Rooms have skylights, pastel colors, and plush furnishings; fireplaces, CD players, VCRs, two-person hot tubs, and front porches with wicker rocking chairs add to the coziness. Spas and restaurants are within walking distance. Rates include Continental breakfast and afternoon wine and cheese. ✉ *1711 Lincoln Ave., 94515,* ☎ *707/942–8400 or 800/ 799–2284,* ℻ *707/942–2653. 16 rooms. Breakfast room, refrigerators, in-room VCRs. AE, D, DC, MC, V.*

$$$–$$$$ ▦ **Brannan Cottage Inn.** This exquisite Victorian cottage with lacy white fretwork, large windows, and a shady porch is the only one of Sam Brannan's 1860 resort cottages still standing on its original site. Rooms have their own private entrances, and elegant stenciled friezes of stylized wildflowers cover the walls. A full breakfast is included. ✉ *109 Wapoo Ave., 94515,* ☎ *707/942–4200. 6 rooms. Breakfast room. MC, V.*

$$$–$$$$ ▦ **Mount View Hotel.** The Mount View is one of the valley's most elegant resorts. A full-service European spa offers state-of-the-art pampering, and three cottages are each equipped with private redwood deck, Jacuzzi, and wet bar. ✉ *1457 Lincoln Ave., 94515,* ☎ *707/942–6877,* ℻ *707/942–6904. 33 rooms. Restaurant, pool, spa. MC, V.*

$$$ ▦ **Meadowlark Country House.** The ambience is decidedly laid-back (particularly for the Wine Country) at this inn surrounded by 20 hillside acres just north of downtown Calistoga. The main house, built in 1886, and a newer building down a gravel path hold unfussy but country-stylish rooms. Rates include a full breakfast. ✉ *601 Petrified Forest Rd.,* ☎ *707/942–5651 or 800/942–5651,* ℻ *707/942–5023. 7 rooms. Breakfast room, pool. MC, V.*

$–$$ ▦ **Calistoga Spa Hot Springs.** The spa's no-nonsense motel-style rooms all have kitchenettes stocked with utensils and coffeemakers, which makes them popular with families and travelers on a budget (there's a supermarket a block away). The on-premises spa includes mineral baths, mud baths, three pools, and a hot tub. There's a two-night minimum on weekends (three nights on holiday weekends). ✉ *1006 Washington St., 94515,* ☎ *707/942–6269. 57 rooms. Snack bar, kitchenettes, 2 pools, wading pool, hot tub, spa, meeting room. MC, V.*

Outdoor Activities and Sports

Calistoga Balloon Company (☎ 707/942–6546, 707/944–8177, or 800/ 333–4359) charters flights out of Calistoga or, depending on weather conditions, out of St. Helena, Oakville, or Rutherford. **Calistoga Gliders** (✉ 1546 Lincoln Ave., ☎ 707/942–5000) glider and biplane rides provide a bird's-eye view of the entire valley. On clear days visibility extends to the San Francisco skyline, the snowcapped Sierra peaks, and the Pacific Ocean. Fees vary from $69 to $150 depending on the length of the flight and whether one or two passengers have boarded. **Getaway Adventures and Bike Shop** (✉ 1117 Lincoln Ave., ☎ 707/942– 0332) rents bikes and conducts winery and other bike tours.

THE SONOMA VALLEY

While the Napa Valley is upscale and elegant, Sonoma Valley is rustic and unpretentious. Its name is Miwok Indian for *many moons.* Farther north, other Sonoma County valleys, such as Alexander, Dry Creek, and Russian River, are equally haunting in their beauty and just as prolific in their production of quality wines.

Sonoma

14 mi west of the town of Napa on Hwy. 12; 45 mi from San Francisco, north on U.S. 101, east on Hwy. 37, and north on Hwy. 121/12.

Sonoma is the oldest town in the Wine Country; its historic town plaza is the site of the last and the northernmost of the 21 missions established by the Franciscan order of Father Junípero Serra. The central plaza also includes the largest group of old adobes north of Monterey. The **Mission San Francisco Solano,** whose chapel and school were used to bring Christianity to the Native Americans, is now a museum with a fine collection of 19th-century watercolors. ⊠ *114 Spain St. E,* ☎ *707/938–1519.* ▧ *$2, includes the Sonoma Barracks on the central plaza and General Vallejo's home, Lachryma Montis (☞ below).* ☉ *Daily 10–5.*

⑲ Originally planted by Franciscans of the Sonoma Mission in 1825, the **Sebastiani Vineyards** were bought by Samuele Sebastiani in 1904. Red wines are king here; to complement them, Sylvia Sebastiani has recorded her good Italian home cooking in a family recipe book, *Mangiamo.* Tours include a look at a collection of impressive carved-oak casks. ⊠ *389 4th St. E,* ☎ *707/938–5532.* ☉ *Daily 10–5. Tours 10–4:30.*

⑳ It was at the landmark **Buena Vista Carneros Winery** (follow signs from the plaza), set among towering trees and fountains, that Count Agoston Haraszthy de Mokcsa laid the basis for modern California wine making, bucking the conventional wisdom that vines should be planted on well-watered ground by instead planting on well-drained hillsides. Chinese laborers dug tunnels 100 ft into the hillside, and the limestone they extracted was used to build the main house. ⊠ *18000 Old Winery Rd., off Napa Rd.,* ☎ *707/938–1266.* ☉ *Daily 10:30–4:30. Tour daily at 2.*

㉑ **Ravenswood** is literally dug into the mountains like a bunker and famous for its legendary zinfandel, although the merlot should be tasted as well. From May through Labor Day the winery serves barbecued chicken and ribs in the vineyards to complement its hearty wines. ⊠ *18701 Gehricke Rd., off Spain St.,* ☎ *707/938–1960.* ☉ *Daily 10–4. Tours by appointment, 11–4.*

A tree-lined approach leads to **Lachryma Montis,** which General Mariano Vallejo, the last Mexican governor of California, built for his large family in 1851; the state purchased the home in 1933. The Victorian Gothic house is secluded in the midst of beautiful gardens; opulent Victorian furnishings, including a white-marble fireplace in every room, are particularly noteworthy. ⊠ *W. Spain St. and 3rd St.,* ☎ *707/938–1519.* ▧ *$2.* ☉ *Daily 10–5. Tours by appointment.*

Dining and Lodging

$$ ✕ **Ristorante Piatti.** Pizza from the wood-burning oven and northern Italian specials (spit-roasted chicken, ravioli with lemon cream) are served in a rustic Italian setting with an open kitchen and bright wall murals or on the outdoor terrace. ⊠ *El Dorado Hotel, 405 1st St. W,* ☎ *707/ 996–2351. AE, MC, V.*

$ ✕ **The Café.** The atmosphere is informal at this bistro with overstuffed booths, ceiling fans, and an open kitchen. Country breakfasts, pizza from the wood-burning oven, and tasty Californian renditions of northern Italian cuisine are the specialties. There's also a great weekday brunch. ⊠ *Sonoma Mission Inn, 18140 Sonoma Hwy. (2 mi north of Sonoma on Hwy. 12 at Boyes Blvd.),* ☎ *707/938–9000. AE, DC, MC, V.*

$ ✕ **La Casa.** Whitewashed stucco, red tile, and serapes adorn this restaurant just around the corner from Sonoma's plaza. There's bar seating, a patio out back, and an extensive menu of traditional Mexican food: chimichangas and snapper Veracruz for entrées, sangria to drink, and flan for dessert. The food is not the world's best, but locals love the casual atmosphere. ⊠ *121 E. Spain St.,* ☎ *707/996–3406. AE, DC, MC, V.*

$$$–$$$$ ✕▥ **Sonoma Mission Inn & Spa.** Despite its unlikely location off the main street of tiny, down-home Boyes Hot Springs, guests come from afar to use the hotel's extensive spa facilities and treatments—including a pool that's heated by warm mineral water pumped from underground wells—and also for the classic spa food served at the Grille and at the less formal Café (☞ *above*). In the main lodge, the Historic Inn rooms have modern comforts such as sleek bathrooms with pedestal sinks. Thirty newer suites in a secluded, tree-shaded area have verandas or patios, Jacuzzis, and fireplaces. ⊠ *18140 Hwy. 12 (2 mi north of Sonoma at Boyes Blvd.), Box 1447, 95476,* ☎ *707/938–9000 or 800/358–9022; 800/862–4945 in CA;* FAX *707/996–5358. 200 rooms. 2 restaurants, 2 bars, coffee shop, 2 pools, hot tub, spa, 2 tennis courts. AE, DC, MC, V.*

$$$–$$$$ ▥ **Thistle Dew Inn.** A half block from Sonoma Plaza, this turn-of-the-century Victorian home is filled with collector's-quality Arts and Crafts furnishings. Owners Larry and Norma Barnett live on the premises, and Larry prepares creative, sumptuous breakfasts and hors d'oeuvres in the evenings. Four of the six rooms have private entrances and decks, and all have queen-size beds with antique quilts, private baths, and air-conditioning. Some rooms have fireplaces; some have Jacuzzis. Welcome bonuses include a hot tub and free use of the inn's bicycles. ⊠ *171 W. Spain St., 95476,* ☎ *707/938–2909; 800/382–7895 in CA. 6 rooms. AE, MC, V.*

$$–$$$ ▥ **El Dorado Hotel.** Claude Rouas, owner of Napa Valley's acclaimed
★ Auberge du Soleil, opened this small hotel. Rooms reflect Sonoma's Mission era, with Mexican-tile floors and white walls. The best rooms are Numbers 3 and 4, which have big balconies overlooking Sonoma Plaza. ⊠ *405 1st St. W, 95476,* ☎ *707/996–3030 or 800/289–3031,* FAX *707/996–3148. 26 rooms. Restaurant, pool. AE, MC, V.*

$$–$$$ ▥ **Vineyard Inn.** Built as a roadside motor court in 1941, this inn with red-tile roofs brings a touch of Mexican village charm to an otherwise lackluster location—at the junction of two main highways. Set in the heart of Sonoma's Carneros region, across from two vineyards, it's the closest lodging to Sears Point Raceway. Rooms have queen-size beds. Continental breakfast is included. ⊠ *23000 Arnold Dr., at Hwys. 116 and 121, 95476,* ☎ *707/938–2350 or 800/359–4667. 9 rooms, 4 suites. Breakfast room. AE, MC, V.*

Shopping

Several shops in the four-block **Sonoma Plaza** attract gourmets from miles around. Within the plaza, serious picnickers stop at the **Sonoma French Bakery** (⊠ 466 1st St. E, ☎ 707/996–2691), famous for its sourdough bread and cream puffs. The **Sonoma Cheese Factory** (⊠ 2 Spain St., ☎ 707/996–1000), run by the same family for four generations, makes Sonoma jack cheese and the tangy Sonoma Teleme. Great swirling baths of milk and curds are visible through the windows, along with flat-pressed wheels of cheese.

Glen Ellen

7 mi north of Sonoma on Hwy. 12.

Writer Jack London lived in the Sonoma Valley for many years; the craggy, quirky, and creek-bisected town of Glen Ellen commemorates him with place names and nostalgic establishments. A bookstore in **Jack London Village** (✉ 14301 Arnold Dr., ☎ 707/935–1240) is filled with some of London's harder-to-find titles. Century-old **Jack London Saloon** (✉ Arnold Dr., ☎ 707/996–3100) has a brooding, nostalgic appeal.

In the hills above Glen Ellen—known as the Valley of the Moon—lies **Jack London State Historic Park.** London's collection of South Seas artifacts can be seen at the House of Happy Walls, a museum of London's effects. The ruins of Wolf House, which London designed and which mysteriously burned down just before he was to move in, are close to the House of Happy Walls. London is buried on the property. ✉ *2400 London Ranch Rd.,* ☎ *707/938–5216.* ⚐ *Parking $5 per car.* ☉ *Park daily 9:30–sunset, museum daily 10–5.*

㉒ **Benziger Family Winery** specializes in premium estate and Sonoma County wines. The company's Imagery Series is a low-volume release of unusual red and white wines distributed in bottles with art labels by well-known artists from all over the world. Free tram tours through the vineyards depart several times a day, weather permitting. ✉ *1883 London Ranch Rd.,* ☎ *707/935–3000.* ⚐ *Varying tasting fees (for premium estate wines only).* ☉ *Daily 10–4:30. Tours every ½ hr, Mar.–Sept. 9:30–5, Oct.–Feb. 9:30–4.*

Lodging

$$$$ 🏨 **Gaige House Inn.** Ardath Rouas, one of the originators of Auberge du Soleil in the Napa Valley, owns and runs this charming inn, which was built in the 19th century as a personal residence. A large pool surrounded by a green lawn, striped awnings, white umbrellas, and magnolias conjures a manicured Hamptons-like glamour right in the middle of rustic Glen Ellen. Inside, abstract art contrasts nicely with the inn's antiques and traditional furnishings. The chef's first-rate gourmet country breakfast is served in a bright dining room downstairs or outside on the terrace. ✉ *13540 Arnold Dr., 95442,* ☎ *707/935–0237 or 800/935–0237,* ⮯ *707/935–6411. 9 rooms. Breakfast room, pool, jogging. AE, D, MC, V.*

$$$–$$$$ 🏨 **Beltane Ranch.** Part of a working cattle and grape-growing ranch— the nearby Kenwood Winery sells a chardonnay made from the ranch's grapes—the Beltane is surrounded by miles of trails through oak-studded hills. Innkeeper Rosemary Woods and her family, who have lived here for 50 years, have stocked the comfortable living room with dozens of books on the area. The rooms, all with private baths and antique furniture, open onto the building's wraparound porch. ✉ *11775 Sonoma Hwy. (Hwy. 12), 95442,* ☎ *707/996–6501. 4 rooms. Tennis court, hiking, horseshoes. No credit cards.*

$$$–$$$$ 🏨 **Glenelly Inn.** This sunny little establishment offers all the comforts of home—including a hot tub in the garden. Mother and daughter innkeepers Ingrid and Kristi Hallamore serve breakfast in front of the common room's cobblestone fireplace and also provide local delicacies in the afternoon. On sunny mornings guests may eat outside under the shady oak trees. ✉ *5131 Warm Springs Rd., 95442,* ☎ *707/996–6720. 8 rooms. Breakfast room, outdoor hot tub. MC, V.*

Kenwood

3 mi north of Glen Ellen on Hwy. 12.

Kenwood has a historic train depot and several restaurants and shops that specialize in locally produced gourmet products. Its inns, restaurants, and winding roads nestle in soothing bucolic landscapes.

㉓ The beautifully rustic grounds at **Kenwood Vineyards** complement the attractive tasting room and artistic bottle labels. Although Kenwood produces all premium varietals, the winery is best known for its signature Jack London Vineyard reds—pinot noir, zinfandel, merlot, and a unique Artist Series cabernet. ⊠ *9592 Sonoma Hwy. (Hwy. 12),* ☎ *707/833–5891.* ◌ *Daily 10–4:30. No tours.*

Dining

$$ ✕ **Kenwood Restaurant & Bar.** This is where Napa and Sonoma chefs eat on their nights off. Indulge in California country cuisine in the sunny South of France–style dining room or head through the French doors to the patio for a memorable view of the vineyards. ⊠ *9900 Hwy. 12,* ☎ *707/833–6326. MC, V. Closed Mon.*

Santa Rosa

8 mi northwest of Kenwood on Hwy. 12.

Santa Rosa is the Wine Country's largest city and a good bet for moderately priced hotel rooms, especially for those who have not reserved in advance.

The **Luther Burbank Home and Gardens** commemorates the great botanist who lived and worked on these grounds for 50 years, single-handedly developing the modern techniques of hybridization. Arriving as a young man from New England, he wrote: "I firmly believe. . . that this is the chosen spot of all the earth, as far as nature is concerned." The Santa Rosa plum, Shasta daisy, and lily of the Nile agapanthus are among the 800 or so plants he developed or improved. ⊠ *Santa Rosa and Sonoma Aves.,* ☎ *707/524–5445.* ▨ *Gardens free; guided tours of house and greenhouse $2.* ◌ *Gardens Nov.–Mar., daily 8–5; Apr.–Oct., daily 8–7. Tours Apr.–Oct., Wed.–Sun. 10–4.*

★ **㉔** **Matanzas Creek Winery** specializes in three varietals—sauvignon blanc, merlot, and chardonnay; all three have won glowing reviews from various magazines. Huge windows in the visitor center overlook a field of 3,100 tiered and fragrant lavender plants. After you taste the wines, ask for the self-guided garden tour book ($1) and take a walk. ⊠ *6097 Bennett Valley Rd.,* ☎ *707/528–6464.* ◌ *Daily 10–4:30. Tours by appointment.*

Dining and Lodging

$$$ ✕ **Cafe Lolo.** Co-owner Michael Quigley, the former chef at Meadowood, prepares fresh seafood, pasta, free-range chicken, and lots of goat cheese and local produce. Don't pass up the chocolate kiss, an individual cake with a wonderfully soft, rich center. ⊠ *620 5th St.,* ☎ *707/ 576–7822. AE, D, DC, MC, V. Closed Sun. No lunch Sat.*

$$$ ✕ **John Ash & Co.** The thoroughly regional cuisine relies on ingredients grown in Sonoma County and in the restaurant's organic garden. In spring local lamb might be roasted with hazelnuts and honey; in fall farm pork could be paired with fresh figs and Gravenstein apples. With patio seating outside and a cozy fireplace indoors, the slightly formal restaurant looks like a Spanish villa amid the vineyards. A café menu offers bites between meals. ⊠ *4330 Barnes Rd. (River Rd. exit west*

from Hwy. 101), ☎ 707/527–7687. *Weekend reservations essential. AE, MC, V. No lunch Mon.*

$–$$ ✕ **Lisa Hemenway's.** A shopping center on the outskirts of town seems an unlikely location for a restaurant find, but chef Hemenway has created a light and airy eatery with soft colors and a garden view from the patio. There is a fresh fish special each day, often prepared with Asian spices. The adjacent café, Tote Cuisine, has a vast selection of tempting take-out selections for picnickers. ⊠ *714 Village Ct. Mall (east from U.S. 101 on Hwy. 12), at Farmer's La. and Sonoma Ave.,* ☎ *707/ 526–5111. AE, MC, V.*

$ ✕ **Mixx.** Housemade ravioli, grilled Cajun prawns, and lamb curry are among the favorites at this restaurant known for its great service and eclectic cuisine. All the dishes are based on locally grown ingredients and served with Napa Valley wine. ⊠ *135 4th St., at Davis St. (behind the mall on Railroad Sq.),* ☎ *707/573–1344. AE, MC, V. No lunch weekends.*

$$$$ ▦ **Vintner's Inn.** Set on 50 acres of vineyards, this French provincial inn has large rooms, many with wood-burning fireplaces, and a trellised sundeck. Breakfast is complimentary, and the John Ash & Co. restaurant tempts guests to other meals. Guests are entitled to discount passes to an affiliated health club nearby, and VCRs can be rented for a small fee. ⊠ *4350 Barnes Rd. (River Rd. exit west from U.S. 101), 95403,* ☎ *707/575–7350 or 800/421–2584,* ℻ *707/575–1426. 44 rooms. Restaurant, hot tub. AE, DC, MC, V.*

$$$ ▦ **Fountaingrove Inn.** All rooms at this elegant, comfortable inn have
★   work spaces. Buffet breakfast is complimentary, and there's also an elegant restaurant with a piano player and a stellar menu. Guests have access to a nearby 18-hole golf course, a tennis court, and a health club, all for an additional fee. Golf packages are available, as are discounts for senior citizens. ⊠ *101 Fountaingrove Pkwy. (near U.S. 101), 95403,* ☎ *707/578–6101 or 800/222–6101,* ℻ *707/544–3126. 82 rooms. Restaurant, in-room modem lines, room service, pool, hot tub, meeting rooms. AE, D, DC, MC, V.*

$$–$$$ ▦ **Los Robles Lodge.** This pleasant, relaxed motel overlooks a pool that's
★   set into a grassy landscape. Pets are allowed, except in executive rooms. Some rooms have whirlpools. ⊠ *1985 Cleveland Ave. (Steele La. exit west from U.S. 101), 95401,* ☎ *707/545–6330 or 800/255–6330,* ℻ *707/575–5826. 104 rooms. Restaurant, coffee shop, pool, outdoor hot tub, nightclub, coin laundry. AE, D, DC, MC, V.*

Nightlife and the Arts

The **Luther Burbank Performing Arts Center** offers a full calendar of concerts, plays, and other performances by locally and internationally known artists. Send away for the calendar in advance if you're planning a trip. ⊠ *50 Mark West Springs Rd.,* ☎ *707/546–3600.* ☉ *Box office Mon.–Sat. noon–6 and approximately 1 hr before most events.*

Outdoor Activities and Sports

GOLF

The **Fountaingrove Country Club** (⊠ 1525 Fountaingrove Pkwy., ☎ 707/579–4653) has an 18-hole course. The greens fee, which includes a mandatory cart, runs $35–$70 depending on the time of day and the day of week.

HOT-AIR BALLOONING

Sonoma Thunder Wine Country Balloon Safaris (☎ 707/538–7359 or 800/759–5638) operates out of Santa Rosa, although many flights originate outside Healdsburg.

Healdsburg

17 mi north of Santa Rosa on U.S. 101.

Healdsburg is centered by a fragrant plaza surrounded by shade trees, appealing antiques shops, and restaurants. A whitewashed bandstand is the venue for free summer concerts of jazz, bluegrass, and other music.

㉕ **Dry Creek Vineyard** is well known for its fumé blanc. The winery's reds, especially zinfandels and cabernets, have also begun to earn notice. Flowering magnolia and redwood trees provide an ideal setting for picnics. ⌧ *3770 Lambert Bridge Rd.,* ☎ *707/433–1000.* ☉ *Daily 10:30–4:30. Tours by appointment.*

㉖ An unassuming winery in a wood and cinder-block barn, **Quivera** produces some of the most interesting wines in Dry Creek Valley. Though it is known for its exquisitely balanced and fruity zinfandel, it also makes a superb blend of red varietals called Dry Creek Cuvée. ⌧ *4900 W. Dry Creek Rd.,* ☎ *707/431–8333.* ☉ *Daily 10–4:30. Tours daily; weekends by appointment if time permits.*

OFF THE
BEATEN PATH

CLOS DU BOIS – Ten miles north of Healdsburg on Highway 116, these vineyards produce the fine estate chardonnays of the Alexander and Dry Creek valleys that have been mistaken for great French wines. ⌧ *19410 Geyserville Ave., Geyserville,* ☎ *707/857-3100 or 800/222-3189.* ☉ *Daily 10–4:30. No tours.*

Dining and Lodging

$–$$ ✕ **Bistro Ralph.** Ralph Tingle has created a culinary hit with his California home-style cuisine. The small menu changes weekly and may include Szechuan pepper calamari as a first course. The stark industrial setting is tempered by a couple of trees perched incongruously on the bar and a friendly waitstaff. ⌧ *109 Plaza St., off Healdsburg Ave.,* ☎ *707/433–1380. Reservations essential. MC, V. No lunch weekends.*

$$$–$$$$ ✕▥ **Madrona Manor.** This 1881 Victorian mansion, surrounded by 8 acres of wooded and landscaped grounds, provides a storybook setting for a candlelight dinner or brunch on the outdoor deck. Those who stay the night can sleep either in the splendid three-story mansion, the carriage house, or one of two separate cottages. Mansion rooms are recommended: All nine have fireplaces, and five contain the antique furniture of the original owner. Though breakfast is served to guests only, others can sample great seasonal dishes in the evening. ⌧ *1001 Westside Rd. (central Healdsburg exit from U.S. 101, left on Mill St.), Box 818, 95448,* ☎ *707/433–4231 or 800/258–4003,* FAX *707/433–0703. 21 rooms. Restaurant, pool. AE, D, DC, MC, V.*

$$$$ ▥ **Healdsburg Inn on the Plaza.** This 1900 brick building has a bright solarium and a roof garden. The rooms, most with fireplaces, are spacious, with quilts and pillows piled high on antique beds. In the bathrooms claw-foot tubs are outfitted with rubber ducks. Full breakfast, afternoon coffee and cookies, and early evening wine and popcorn are included. ⌧ *110 Matheson St., Box 1196, 95448,* ☎ *707/433–6991. 10 rooms. Breakfast room. MC, V.*

$$ ▥ **Best Western Dry Creek Inn.** Continental breakfast and a bottle of wine are complimentary at this three-story Spanish Mission–style motel, and there's also a coffee shop next door. Midweek discounts are available, and direct bus service from San Francisco's airport can be arranged. ⌧ *198 Dry Creek Rd., 95448,* ☎ *707/433–0300 or 800/528–1234; 800/222–5784 in CA;* FAX *707/433–1129. 102 rooms. Pool, hot tub, coin laundry. AE, D, DC, MC, V.*

OFF THE   **KORBEL CHAMPAGNE CELLARS** – The tour at Korbel clearly explains the
BEATEN PATH   process of making sparkling wine, and a display of old photographs
provides a historical overview of the Russian River area. The winery's
19th-century buildings and gorgeous rose gardens are a delight in their
own right. ✉ *13250 River Rd., Guerneville,* ☎ *707/887–2294.* ✪
Oct.–Apr., daily 9–4:30; May–Sept., daily 9–5. Tours on the hr 10–3.

THE WINE COUNTRY A TO Z

Arriving and Departing

By Bus
Greyhound (☎ 800/231–2222) runs buses from the Transbay Termi-
nal at 1st and Mission streets in San Francisco to Sonoma and Santa
Rosa.

By Car
From San Francisco cross the Golden Gate Bridge, go north on U.S.
101, east on Highway 37, and north and east on Highway 121. For
Sonoma wineries, head north at Highway 12; for Napa's, continue east
on Highway 121, and turn left (to the northwest) when Highway 121
runs into Highway 29.

From Berkeley and other East Bay towns, take I–80 north to Highway 37 west to Highway 29 north. From points north of the Wine Country, take U.S. 101 south to Geyserville and follow Highway 128
southeast into the Napa Valley.

By Plane
The closest major airports are in San Francisco and Oakland. *See* San
Francisco A to Z *in* Chapter 5 for airport and airline information.

Getting Around

By Bus
Sonoma County Area Transit (☎ 707/585–7516) and **Napa Valley Transit** (☎ 707/255–7631) both provide transportation between towns in
the Wine Country.

By Car
Although traffic on the two-lane country roads can be heavy, the best
way to get around the sprawling Wine Country is by private car.
Rentals are available at the airports and in San Francisco, Oakland,
Santa Rosa, and Napa.

Contacts and Resources

B&B Reservation Agencies
Bed & Breakfast Exchange (✉ 1407 Main St., Suite 102, St. Helena
94574, ☎ 707/942–5900) arranges reservations for resorts, country
clubs, and B&Bs.

The Wine Country Bed & Breakfast Inns of Sonoma County (✉ Box
51, Geyserville 95441, ☎ 707/433–4667) is a rotating B&B referral
service representing 14 of the best inns of northern Sonoma County.
A free inn map and brochure may be requested by mail or toll-free by
phone, 800/354–4743.

Wine Country Reservations (✉ Box 5059, Napa 94581, ☎ 707/257–
7757, FAX 707/257–7844) provides service to the entire Wine Country
and is especially resourceful during the busy summer months, when
finding a B&B on short notice can be difficult.

Emergencies
Ambulance (☎ 911). **Police** (☎ 911).

Guided Tours
Full-day guided tours of the Wine Country usually include lunch and cost about $50. The guides, some of whom are winery owners themselves, know the area well and may show you some lesser-known cellars. Reservations are usually required.

California Wine Adventures (✉ 1258 Arroyo Sarco, Napa 94558, ☎ 707/257–0353), a family-owned operation, has been custom designing private tours for groups since 1974. Cost includes a gourmet picnic lunch or dinner.

Gray Line (✉ 350 8th St., San Francisco 94103, ☎ 415/558–9400) has bright red double-decker buses that tour the Wine Country.

Great Pacific Tour Co. (✉ 518 Octavia St., San Francisco 94102, ☎ 415/626–4499) operates full-day tours of Napa and Sonoma, including a summer picnic lunch and a winter restaurant lunch, in passenger vans that seat 14.

HMS Tours (✉ 707 4th St., Santa Rosa 95404, ☎ 707/526–2922 or 800/367–5348) offers customized tours of the Wine Country for six or more people, by appointment only.

Napa Valley Wine Train (✉ 1275 McKinstry St., Napa 94559, ☎ 707/253–2111 or 800/427–4124) allows you to enjoy lunch, dinner, or weekend brunch on one of several restored 1915 Pullman railroad cars that run between Napa and St. Helena. Dinner costs $69.50, lunch $63, brunch $56.50; per-person prices include train fare, meals, tax, and service. On weekend brunch trips and weekday lunch trips you can ride a special "Deli" car for $25. In winter, service is sometimes limited to Thursday through Sunday; call ahead.

Wine Country Wagons (✉ Box 1069, Kenwood 95452, ☎ 707/833–2724, FAX 707/833–1041) conducts four-hour horse-drawn wagon tours that include three wineries and end at a private ranch, where a lavish buffet lunch is served. Tours depart daily at 10 from May through October; advance reservations are required.

Visitor Information
Calistoga Chamber of Commerce (✉ 1458 Lincoln Ave., Calistoga 94515, ☎ 707/942–6333). **Calistoga Resort Council** (✉ Box 442, Calistoga 94515, ☎ 707/942–2255). **Healdsburg Chamber of Commerce** (✉ 217 Healdsburg Ave., Healdsburg 95448, ☎ 707/433–6935; 800/648–9922 in CA). **Napa Valley Conference and Visitors Bureau** (✉ 1310 Napa Town Center, Napa 94559, ☎ 707/226–7459). **Redwood Empire Association** (✉ The Cannery, 2801 Leavenworth St., 2nd floor, San Francisco 94133, ☎ 415/543–8334). **St. Helena Chamber of Commerce** (✉ 1080 Main St., St. Helena 94574, ☎ 707/963–4456 or 800/799–6456). **Sonoma County Convention and Visitors Bureau** (✉ 5000 Roberts Lake Rd., Rohnert Park 94928, ☎ 707/586–8100 or 800/326–7666). **Sonoma Valley Visitors Bureau** (✉ 453 1st St. E, Sonoma 95476, ☎ 707/996–1090).

5 San Francisco

*With Side Trips to Marin County,
the East Bay, and the Peninsula*

San Francisco is a sophisticated city
with world-class hotels and the greatest
concentration of excellent restaurants
in the state. The town has an
undeserved reputation as the kook
capital of the United States, yet it's the
country's number one tourist
destination. Why? To use the
vernacular, the vibe here is cool, from
North Beach coffeehouses to
Chinatown tea emporiums, Golden
Gate Park, and Haight Street's head
shops (yes, they're still around). People
in San Francisco know how to have a
good time; the high spirits can't help
but rub off on visitors.

I N ITS FIRST LIFE, SAN FRANCISCO was little more than a small, well-situated settlement. Founded by Spaniards in 1776, it was prized for its natural harbor, so commodious that "all the navies of the world might fit inside it," as one visitor wrote. The 1848 discovery of gold at John Sutter's sawmill in the nearby Sierra foothills transformed the sleepy village into a city of 30,000. As millions of dollars' worth of gold was panned and blasted out of the hills, a "western Wall Street" sprang up. Just as gold production began to taper off, prospectors turned up a rich vein of silver in and around Virginia City, Nevada. San Francisco, the nearest financial center, prospered again. The city remains a financial hub, though nowadays its attentions are as much transoceanic as transcontinental. San Francisco prides itself on its role as a Pacific Rim capital, and overseas investment has become a vital part of its economic life. In terms of both geography and culture, San Francisco is about as close as you can get to Asia in the United States.

Loose, tolerant, and even licentious are words that are used to describe San Francisco; bohemian communities thrive here. As early as the 1860s, the "Barbary Coast"—a collection of taverns, whorehouses, and gambling joints on or near Pacific Avenue close to the waterfront— was famous, or infamous. North Beach, the city's Little Italy, became the home of the Beat Movement in the 1950s. The Haight-Ashbury district became synonymous with hippiedom, giving rise to such legendary bands as Jefferson Airplane, Big Brother and the Holding Company (fronted by Janis Joplin), and the Grateful Dead in the 1960s. And, as most of the world knows, lesbians and gay men have found the town hospitable.

The Gay and Lesbian Freedom Day Parade, each June, vies with the Chinese New Year Parade, in February, as the city's most elaborate. They both get competition from Japantown's Cherry Blossom Festival, in April; the Columbus Day and St. Patrick's Day parades; Carnaval in the Hispanic Mission District in late May; and the May Day march, a labor celebration in a labor town. The mix of ethnic, economic, social, and sexual groups can be bewildering, but the city's residents—whatever their origin—face it with aplomb and even gratitude. Everybody in San Francisco has an opinion about where to get the best burrito or the hottest Szechuan eggplant or the strongest cappuccino, and even the most staid citizens have learned how to appreciate good camp.

Technically speaking, San Francisco is only California's fourth-largest city, behind Los Angeles, San Diego, and nearby San Jose. But that statistic is misleading: The Bay Area, which stretches from the bedroom communities north of Oakland and Berkeley south through Silicon Valley (the Peninsula cities that have become the center of America's computer industry) and San Jose, is really one continuous megacity, with San Francisco as its heart.

EXPLORING SAN FRANCISCO

Updated by
Chris Borris

San Francisco is a relatively small city, with just over 750,000 residents nested on a 46½-square-mile tip of land between San Francisco Bay and the Pacific Ocean. San Franciscans cherish the city's colorful past, and many older buildings have been spared from demolition and nostalgically converted into modern offices and shops. Bernard Maybeck, Julia Morgan, Willis Polk, and Arthur Brown Jr. are among the noted architects whose designs still grace the city's downtown and neighborhoods.

Exploring San Francisco (*Boxes Refer to Detail Maps*)

PACIFIC OCEAN

Golden Gate Bridge

Fort Point

101

The Presidio

Baker Beach

Land's End

Palace of the Legion of Honor

China Beach

Northern Waterfront/ Marina and the Presidio

Lincoln Park

SEACLIFF

Clement St.

8th Ave.

Arguello

Point Lobos

Geary Blvd.

25th

19th

Balboa St.

Blvd.

Turk

Cliff House

43rd

34th

Ave.

Ave.

Golden Gate Park

Ave.

RICHMOND

Fulton St.

Stanyan St.

Kennedy Dr.

Golden Gate Park

Middle Dr.

Lincoln Way

Great

28th Ave.

Judah St.

Funston Ave.

7th Ave.

Lawton St.

1

Noriega St.

Ortega St.

19th Ave.

Clarendon Ave.

Hwy.

41st Ave.

Sunset Blvd.

SUNSET

Quintara St.

14th Ave.

Dewey Blvd.

McCoppin Square

Taraval St.

Dr.

Mt. Davidson

Larsen Park

Portola

Yerba Buena Ave.

Vicente St.

Stern Grove

Monterey

Blvd.

Miramar Ave.

N

San Francisco Zoo

Sloat Blvd.

STONESTOWN

Junipero Serra Blvd.

Ocean Ave.

Plymouth Ave.

Harding Park

San Francisco State Univ.

Holloway Ave.

Skyline Blvd.

Lake Merced

Lake Merced Blvd.

Font Blvd.

Garfield St.

0   1 mile
0   1 km

Brotherhood Way

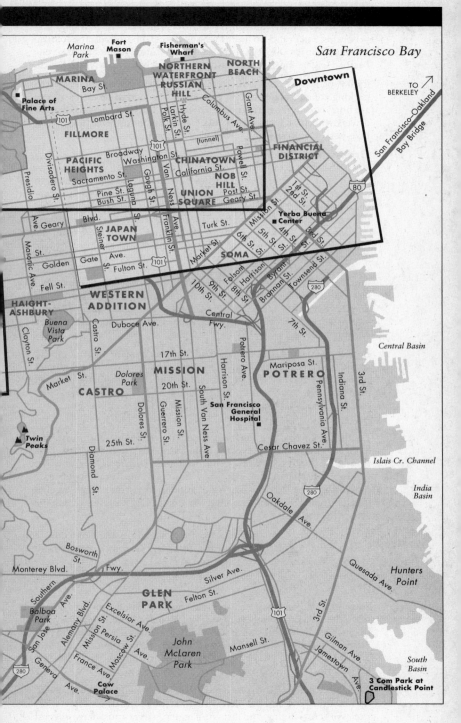

San Francisco Bay

TO BERKELEY

Downtown

San Francisco-Oakland Bay Bridge

Marina Park

Fort Mason

Fisherman's Wharf

NORTHERN WATERFRONT

NORTH BEACH

MARINA

Bay St.

RUSSIAN HILL

Columbus Ave.

Grant Ave.

Palace of Fine Arts

Lombard St.

Hyde St.

Larkin St.

Polk St.

FINANCIAL DISTRICT

FILLMORE

Broadway

Washington St.

CHINATOWN

Powell St.

1st St.

2nd St.

(tunnel)

PACIFIC HEIGHTS

Divisadero St.

Sacramento St.

California St.

NOB HILL

UNION SQUARE

Post St.

Geary St.

3rd St.

Pine St.

Bush St.

Presidio

Gough St.

Van Ness Ave.

Franklin St.

Laguna St.

Yerba Buena Center

Mission St.

5th St.

4th St.

Geary Blvd.

JAPAN TOWN

Turk St.

6th St.

St.

Masonic Ave.

Steiner St.

Ave.

Market St.

SOMA

7th St.

Golden Gate Ave.

Fulton St.

Fell St.

Folsom St.

Harrison St.

Bryant St.

Brannan St.

Townsend St.

HAIGHT-ASHBURY

WESTERN ADDITION

9th St.

10th St.

8th St.

Central Fwy.

Buena Vista Park

Duboce Ave.

Castro St.

Clayton St.

17th St.

Central Basin

Market St.

Dolores Park

MISSION

20th St.

Potrero Ave.

Harrison St.

Mariposa St.

POTRERO

Indiana St.

3rd St.

CASTRO

South Van Ness Ave.

Mission St.

Guerrero St.

San Francisco General Hospital

Pennsylvania Ave.

Dolores St.

25th St.

Islais Cr. Channel

Twin Peaks

Diamond St.

Cesar Chavez St.

India Basin

Oakdale Ave.

Bosworth St.

Monterey Blvd.

Fwy.

Silver Ave.

Hunters Point

Southern Ave.

Balboa Park

Alemany Blvd.

GLEN PARK

Felton St.

Quesada Ave.

San Jose Ave.

Excelsior Ave.

Mission St.

Persia Ave.

Moscow St.

John McLaren Park

Mansell St.

3rd St.

Gilman Ave.

South Basin

Geneva Ave.

France Ave.

Cow Palace

Jamestown Ave.

3 Com Park at Candlestick Point

San Francisco neighborhoods retain strong cultural, political, and ethnic identities. Locals know this pluralism is the real life of the city. Experiencing San Francisco means visiting the neighborhoods: the colorful Mission District, the gay Castro, countercultural Haight Street, serene Pacific Heights, bustling Chinatown, and still bohemian North Beach.

Exploring involves navigating a maze of one-way streets and restricted parking zones. Public parking garages or lots tend to be expensive, as are hotel parking spaces. The famed 40-plus hills can be a problem for drivers who are new to the terrain. Cable cars, buses, and trolleys can take you to or near many of the area's attractions.

Great Itineraries

IF YOU HAVE 3 DAYS

Spend your first morning exploring Chinatown and North Beach. In the afternoon visit the South of Market area—don't miss the San Francisco Museum of Modern Art or Yerba Buena Gardens. Get up early the next morning for a boat ride to Alcatraz (make your reservations at least a week in advance during the summer; boats leave from the Fisherman's Wharf area). On your return, have lunch at any of Pier 39's many eateries. Check out the sea lions lounging on the docks (have your camera ready) or visit the Underwater World at Pier 39 aquarium. Stroll the Embarcadero Promenade toward the Ferry Building, and ride up Market Street on one of the F-line antique trolleys to Union Square. End your day on Nob Hill, where you can watch a tropical storm in dry comfort in the Polynesian-themed Tonga Room bar at the Fairmont Hotel.

Begin your third day in Golden Gate Park. In the late afternoon head to the famed corner of Haight and Ashbury, where you'll find hippies both vintage and newly minted crowding the sidewalks. In the evening, take in a performance of the long-running revue *Beach Blanket Babylon,* a hilarious send-up of San Francisco's idiosyncratic ways.

IF YOU HAVE 5 DAYS

Follow the three-day itinerary outlined above. Begin your fourth day along the Marina Green. Nearby is the rococo Palace of Fine Arts. Pass through the Presidio, exiting in the Richmond District for a visit to the California Palace of the Legion of Honor. The museum's stylish café has views of the Golden Gate—and good food, if you haven't yet had lunch. From the Legion, continue west to the Cliff House to catch the sunset (or the fog).

Start your fifth morning with a bracing walk across the Golden Gate Bridge. Continue on to Sausalito and Tiburon in Marin County, or head south to Filoli estate on the Peninsula.

Union Square

Since 1850 Union Square has been the heart of San Francisco's downtown. Its name derives from a series of violent pro-union demonstrations staged here just prior to the Civil War. This is where you will find the city's finest department stores and its most exclusive boutiques. There are 40 hotels within three blocks of the square, and the city's leading art galleries and downtown theater district are nearby.

The square itself is a 2.6-acre oasis planted with palms, boxwood, and seasonal flowers, and peopled with a kaleidoscope of characters: office workers sunning and brown-bagging, street musicians, several very vocal preachers, and a fair share of homeless people. Events throughout the year include fashion shows, free noontime concerts, ethnic celebrations, and noisy demonstrations. Auto and bus traffic is often gridlocked on the four bordering streets. Post, Stockton, and Geary are one-way. Powell runs in both directions until it crosses Geary, where it becomes one-way south to Market Street. Union Square covers a convenient but costly four-story underground garage; close to 3,000 cars use it on busy holiday shopping and strolling days. For cheaper parking try the nearby Sutter-Stockton Garage.

A Good Walk

Numbers in the text correspond to numbers in the margin and on the Downtown San Francisco map.

The **San Francisco Visitors Information Center** ① is on the lower level of Hallidie Plaza at Powell and Market streets. For a true San Francisco treat, head up the stairs to the **cable car terminus** ②. Heading north from the cable car terminus along Powell Street, it's three blocks to **Union Square** ③. The stately and historic **Westin St. Francis Hotel** ④ dominates the corner of Geary and Powell streets. Directly across the square from the St. Francis is the **TIX Bay Area** ⑤ discount booth. Due east of the booth is **Maiden Lane** ⑥, a two-block alley lined with boutiques, sidewalk cafés, and San Francisco's only Frank Lloyd Wright building. At Kearny Street, turn right and walk to O'Farrell, then right again to return to Stockton Street. Union Square is something of a shopper's theme park, something you can experience vividly at either the **F.A.O. Schwarz** ⑦ toy store at Stockton and O'Farrell or two blocks north on Stockton (at Post) at the entertaining, if relentlessly commercial, **Niketown** athletic clothing and goods complex. A block farther is Sutter Street; go right one block on Sutter to view the beaux arts–style **Hammersmith Building** ⑧ or left one block and check out the art deco building at **450 Sutter Street** ⑨. One and a half blocks east of the Hammersmith Building you'll find the **Hallidie Building** ⑩, on the north side of Sutter; notice its graceful all-glass facade and Venetian detailing.

TIMING

Allow about two hours to roam the Union Square area. Stepping into the Macy's store on Union Square or browsing the other boutiques in the vicinity can eat up countless hours; if you're a shopper give yourself extra time here. The cable car ride from Powell and Market down to Fisherman's Wharf only takes about 20 minutes—but waiting in line can take twice as long.

Sights to See

② **Cable car terminus.** This is the starting point for two of the three operating lines. The Powell-Mason line climbs up Nob Hill, then winds through North Beach to Fisherman's Wharf. The Powell-Hyde car also crosses Nob Hill but then continues up Russian Hill and down Hyde Street to Victorian Park, across from the Buena Vista Cafe and near Ghirardelli Square. The cable car system dates from 1873, when Andrew Hallidie demonstrated his first car on Clay Street; in 1964 the tramlike vehicles were designated national historic landmarks. In summertime there are often long lines to board any of the three systems; if possible, plan your cablecar ride for mid-morning or mid-afternoon during the week to avoid crowds. Buy your ticket ($2 one way) on board, at nearby hotels, or at the police/information booth near the turnaround. *See* Getting Around *in* San Francisco A to Z for more details about the system. ⊠ *Powell and Market Sts.*

⑦ **F.A.O. Schwarz.** The prices are not Toys 'R' Us, but it's worth stopping by this three-floor playland just to look at the 6-ft-tall stuffed animals and elaborate fairy tale sculptures. Among the wares are a large Barbie section, an astounding supply of lush and expensive stuffed an-

84

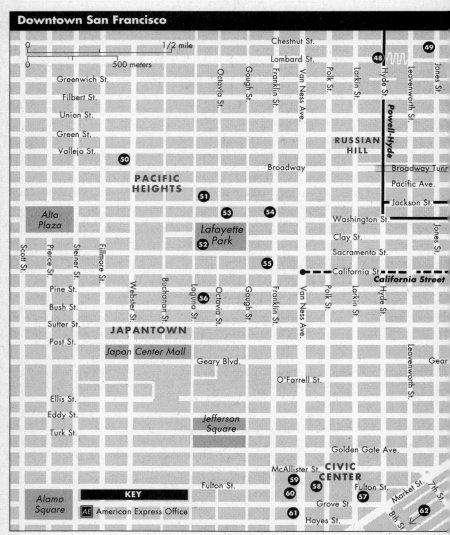

Downtown San Francisco

RUSSIAN HILL

PACIFIC HEIGHTS

Alta Plaza

Lafayette Park

JAPANTOWN

Japan Center Mall

Jefferson Square

CIVIC CENTER

Alamo Square

KEY

AE American Express Office

Powell–Hyde

California Street

Chestnut St.
Lombard St.
Greenwich St.
Filbert St.
Union St.
Green St.
Vallejo St.
Broadway
Broadway Tunl
Pacific Ave.
Jackson St.
Washington St.
Clay St.
Sacramento St.
California St.
Pine St.
Bush St.
Sutter St.
Post St.
Geary Blvd.
O'Farrell St.
Ellis St.
Eddy St.
Turk St.
Golden Gate Ave.
McAllister St.
Fulton St.
Grove St.
Hayes St.

Scott St.
Pierce St.
Steiner St.
Fillmore St.
Webster St.
Buchanan St.
Laguna St.
Octavia St.
Gough St.
Franklin St.
Van Ness Ave.
Polk St.
Larkin St.
Hyde St.
Leavenworth St.
Jones St.
Market St.
7th St.
8th St.

0   1/2 mile
0   500 meters

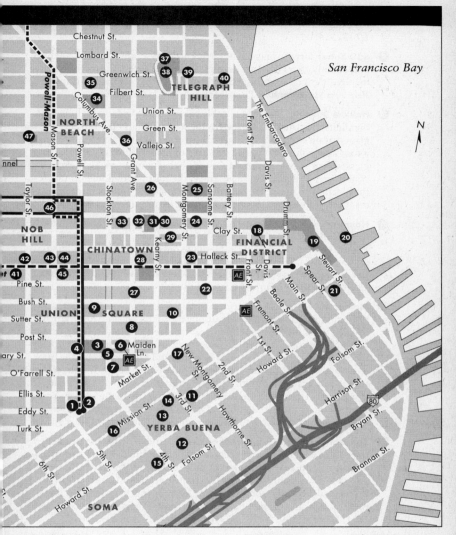

San Francisco Bay

imals (the priciest is a whopping $15,000), and just about every other toy imaginable. ⊠ *48 Stockton St.,* ☎ *415/394–8700.* ⊘ *Mon.–Sat. 10–7, Sun. 11–6.*

❾ 450 Sutter Street. This 1928 terra-cotta skyscraper (now a medical and dental office) is an art deco masterpiece, with handsome Mayan-inspired designs covering both the exterior and interior surfaces. ⊠ *Between Stockton and Powell Sts.*

❿ Hallidie Building. Named for cable car inventor Andrew Hallidie, this building is best viewed from across the street. Willis Polk's revolutionary glass-curtain wall—believed to be the world's first such creation—hangs a foot beyond the reinforced concrete of the frame. With its reflecting glass, decorative exterior fire escapes that appear to be metal balconies, and Venetian Gothic cornice, the unusual building dominates the block. Also notice the horizontal ornamental bands of birds at feeders. ⊠ *130 Sutter St., between Kearny and Montgomery Sts.*

❽ Hammersmith Building. Glass walls and a playful design distinguish this small, colorful beaux arts–style structure, built in 1907. The Foundation for Architectural Heritage once described the building as a "commercial jewel box"; appropriately, it was originally designed for use as a jewelry store. Buy breakfast downstairs at **Franciscan Croissants.** ⊠ *301 Sutter St.*

❻ Maiden Lane. Known as Morton Street in the Barbary Coast era, this red-light district reported at least one murder a week. After the 1906 fire destroyed the brothels, the street emerged as Maiden Lane, and it has since become a daytime pedestrian mall, with a patchwork of umbrella-shaded tables, between Stockton and Kearny streets. The brick structure at 140 Maiden Lane is the only Frank Lloyd Wright structure in San Francisco. With its circular interior ramp and skylights, it is said to have been a model for the Guggenheim Museum in New York. It now houses the Circle Gallery, which shows the limited-edition art jewelry (worth a look) of Erté. ⊠ *Between Stockton and Kearny Sts.*

❶ San Francisco Visitors Information Center. Conveniently located below the cable car terminus, the center has a multilingual staff and maps, brochures, and information on daily events. Visitors can pick up coupons for substantial savings on tourist attractions, as well as pamphlets (and, depending on the season, discount vouchers) for most downtown hotels. ⊠ *Hallidie Plaza, lower level, Powell and Market Sts.,* ☎ *415/391–2000.* ⊘ *Weekdays 9–5:30, Sat. 9–3, Sun. 10–2.*

❺ TIX Bay Area. This service provides half-price day-of-performance tickets (cash or traveler's checks only) to performing arts events, as well as regular full-price box office services. Telephone reservations are not accepted for half-price tickets. Also available are Explorer Passes, which provide entry to Golden Gate Park's museums at a discount rate, and Muni Passports, short-term tourist passes for all city buses and cable cars. ⊠ *Stockton St. at Union Square,* ☎ *415/433–7827.* ⊘ *Tues.–Thurs. 11–6, Fri.–Sat. 11–7.*

❸ Union Square. At center stage, the Victory Monument, by Robert Ingersoll Aitken, commemorates Commodore George Dewey's victory over the Spanish fleet at Manila in 1898. The 97-ft Corinthian column, topped by a bronze figure symbolizing naval conquest, was dedicated by Theodore Roosevelt in 1903 and withstood the 1906 earthquake. After the earthquake and fire of 1906, the square was dubbed "Little St. Francis" because of the temporary shelter erected for residents of the St. Francis Hotel.

❹ Westin St. Francis Hotel. The second-oldest hotel in the city, originally built in 1904, was conceived by Charles Crocker and his associates as an elegant hostelry for their millionaire friends. The hotel's Turkish baths once had ocean water piped in. After the 1906 quake gutted the hotel, a larger, more luxurious residence was opened in 1907. The hotel has had its share of notoriety. Silent-film comedian Fatty Arbuckle's career plummeted—faster than one of the St. Francis tower's glass-walled elevators—after a wild 1921 party in one of the suites in the older wing went awry. In 1975 Sara Jane Moore, standing among a crowd outside the hotel, attempted to shoot then-president Gerald Ford. As might be imagined, no plaques commemorate these events in the establishment's lobby. The ever-helpful staff will, however, gladly direct you to the traditional teatime ritual—or if you prefer, to champagne and caviar—in the dramatic art deco **Compass Rose** lounge (☎ 415/774–0167). Elaborate Chinese screens, secluded seating alcoves, and soothing background music make this an ideal rest stop after frantic shopping or sightseeing. ⊠ *335 Powell St., at Geary St.,* ☎ *415/397-7000.*

South of Market (SoMa) and the Embarcadero

The vast tract of downtown land south of Market Street along the waterfront and west to the Mission District—also known by the acronym SoMa—is the center of a burgeoning arts scene.

Numbers in the text correspond to numbers in the margin and on the Downtown San Francisco map.

A Good Walk

The showpiece of the South of Market area is the **San Francisco Museum of Modern Art** ⑪, housed in a modernist brick building and dominating a half block of 3rd Street between Howard and Mission streets. Across from the museum is the cluster of buildings known as Yerba Buena Center, between Folsom and Mission streets and 3rd and 4th streets. Within the complex is the **Moscone Convention Center** ⑫, and **Yerba Buena Gardens** ⑬, a green expanse adjacent to the performance and gallery space known as **Center for the Arts** ⑭. Across 4th Street from Moscone Center is the **Ansel Adams Center for Photography** ⑮. From Ansel Adams, head north up 4th Street and cross Mission; walk a half block west to the **Cartoon Art Museum** ⑯.

Take 4th Street north to Market Street to where 3rd, Market, Kearny, and Geary streets converge. Walk east on Market Street past **Lotta's Fountain** to New Montgomery and the **Palace Hotel** ⑰. Continue east on Market Street, taking note of several "flatiron" buildings (including an older one at No. 540–548 and a newer one at No. 388) angling into the thoroughfare. Toward the end of Market is the **Embarcadero Center** ⑱, a five-block complex that holds retail stores, offices, and the Hyatt Regency Hotel. On the waterfront side of the hotel is outdoor **Justin Herman Plaza** ⑲.

Across the Embarcadero roadway from Justin Herman Plaza stands the **Ferry Building** ⑳. North of the Ferry Building at Pier 5 is the initial section of the 5-ft-wide, 2½-mi-long glass-and-concrete **Promenade Ribbon,** billed by the city as the "longest art form in the nation." At Embarcadero and Mission, you can't miss the ornate **Audiffred Building,** built in 1889 by a homesick gentleman as a reminder of his native France, and now housing the Boulevard restaurant. Heading west down Mission turn south on Steuart Street; halfway down the block is the entrance to the **Rincon Center** ㉑, which houses some famous murals depicting California history. Across from the Rincon Center on

Steuart is the small but worthwhile **Jewish Museum,** housed in the Jewish Community Federation Building.

TIMING

Because this walk contains several museums, set aside an entire afternoon. Plan on spending a couple of hours at SFMOMA. The Center for the Arts, Yerba Buena Gardens, and the Ansel Adams Center each merit an hour or more as well. For the walk down Market Street and along the waterfront, an hour should be sufficient unless you plan to browse in the Embarcadero Center's many shops.

Sights to See

⓯ Ansel Adams Center for Photography. Ansel Adams himself created this center in Carmel in 1967. In 1989 it moved to SoMa. The center presents historical and contemporary photography and changing exhibitions of Adams's work. ✉ *250 4th St.,* ☎ *415/495–7000.* ⌨ *$5.* ☉ *Tues.–Sun. 11–5, 1st Thurs. of month 11–8.*

California Historical Society. This vast repository of Californiana includes 500,000 photographs, 150,000 manuscripts, thousands of books, periodicals, prints, and paintings as well as gold-rush paraphernalia. ✉ *678 Mission St.,* ☎ *415/357–1848.* ⌨ *$3.* ☉ *Tues.–Sat. 11–5.*

⓰ Cartoon Art Museum. Krazy Kat, Zippy the Pinhead, Batman, and a whole crew of other colorful cartoon icons greet you at the entrance to the Cartoon Art Museum. Changing and permanent exhibits survey everything from the impact of underground comics and the "Peanuts" strip to the contributions of women and African-American cartoonists. ✉ *814 Mission St., Suite 200,* ☎ *415/546–3922.* ⌨ *$4.* ☉ *Wed.–Fri. 11–5, Sat. 10–5, Sun. 1–5.*

⓮ Center for the Arts. The center presents dance, music, performance, theater, visual arts, film, video, and installations—from the community-based to the international—with an emphasis on the cultural diversity of San Francisco. The complex includes a theater and a forum, three visual arts galleries, a film and video screening room, a gift shop, a café, and an outdoor performance stage where there's midday music daily from April through October. ✉ *701 Mission St.,* ☎ *415/978–2787.* ⌨ *Galleries $5; free 1st Thurs. of month 6–8 PM.* ☉ *Galleries and box office Tues.–Sun. 11–6.*

⓲ Embarcadero Center. John Portman designed this complex of shops, restaurants, cinemas, hotels, and office space. Louise Nevelson's 54-ft-high black-steel sculpture, *Sky Tree,* stands guard over Building 3 and is among the 20-plus works of art throughout the center. The **Hyatt Regency Hotel** has a spectacular lobby—it had a featured role in the 1970s disaster epic *The Towering Inferno*—with a 20-story hanging garden and glass elevators that are fun to ride (unless you're susceptible to vertigo). ✉ *Clay St. between Battery St. and the Embarcadero.* ☉ *Weekdays 10–7, Sat. 10–6, Sun. noon–6.*

⓴ Ferry Building. The beacon of the port area is the Embarcadero's quaint Ferry Building; its 230-ft clock tower was modeled after the campanile of Seville's cathedral. The building has held its post since 1896 and is now the headquarters of the Port Commission and the World Trade Center's office. A waterfront promenade that extends from the piers north of here to the San Francisco–Oakland Bay Bridge is great for jogging, in-line skating, watching sailboats on the bay, or enjoying a picnic. Ferries from behind the Ferry Building sail to Sausalito, Larkspur, Tiburon, and the East Bay. ✉ *The Embarcadero, at the foot of Market St.*

The Jewish Museum. This small museum hosts exhibits on Jewish art, history, and culture. The curators here don't shy away from controversial programs, hosting exhibits such as *Art and the Rosenberg Era,* an in-depth look at freedom of expression, and *Bridges & Boundaries: African Americans and American Jews.* ⊠ *121 Steuart St.,* ☎ *415/543– 8880.* ⊑ *$5; free 1st Mon. of month.* ⊙ *Mon.–Wed. noon–6, Thurs. noon–8, Sun. 11–6.*

⑲ **Justin Herman Plaza.** The plaza on the waterfront side of the Hyatt Regency plays host to arts-and-crafts shows, street musicians, skateboarders, and mimes on weekends year-round. On sunny days it's a good spot to enjoy a snack from one of Embarcadero Center's dozen or so take-out shops. During the winter holidays an ice rink is set up here. ⊠ *The Embarcadero north of Market St.*

Lotta's Fountain. This quirky monument, now largely unnoticed by local passersby, was a gift to the city from singer Lotta Crabtree, a Mae West prototype. The fountain itself is unspectacular, but Crabtree's history is interesting. Her "brash music-hall exploits" so enthralled San Francisco's early population of miners that they were known to shower her with gold nuggets and silver dollars after her performances. The buxom Ms. Crabtree is depicted in one of the Anton Refregier murals in Rincon Center (☞ *below*). ⊠ *Intersection of 3rd, Market, Kearny, and Geary Sts.*

⑫ **Moscone Convention Center.** The site of the 1984 Democratic convention is distinguished by a contemporary glass-and-girder lobby at street level (all convention exhibit space is underground) and a monolithic, column-free interior. ⊠ *Howard St. between 3rd and 4th Sts.*

⑰ **Palace Hotel.** The Palace, a Sheraton property, opened in 1875. The hotel has a storied past—President Warren Harding died here while still in office in 1923—some of which is recounted in the glass cases off the main lobby. The original Palace was destroyed by fire following the 1906 earthquake, despite a 28,000-gallon reservoir fed by four artesian wells. The current building dates from 1909; late-1980s renovations included the restoration of the glass-dome Garden Court restaurant and the installation of original mosaic-tile floors in Oriental-rug designs. Maxfield Parrish's wall-size painting, *The Pied Piper,* dominates the hotel's Pied Piper Bar. There are guided tours of the hotel's grand interior (☎ 415/546–5026) Tuesday, Wednesday, and Saturday at 10:30 AM and Thursday at 2 PM. ⊠ *2 New Montgomery St.,* ☎ *415/392–8600.*

㉑ **Rincon Center.** A five-story water column resembling a ministorm dominates the center's street-level mall area. In addition to the mall, there are two modern towers of offices and apartments. In front of all this is a former post office built in the Streamline Moderne style. In the post office's historic lobby is a series of murals by Anton Refregier that depict California life from the days when Native Americans were the state's sole inhabitants through World War I. Completion of this significant work was interrupted by World War II and political infighting; the latter led to some alteration in Refregier's "radical" historical interpretations. A permanent exhibit below the murals contains interesting photographs and artifacts of life in the Rincon area in the 1800s.

★ ⑪ **San Francisco Museum of Modern Art.** SFMOMA took center stage in the SoMa arts scene in January 1995, winning acclaim for its adventurous programming, which includes traveling exhibits and multimedia installations. Works by Henri Matisse, Pablo Picasso, Georgia O'Keeffe, Frida Kahlo, Jackson Pollock, and Andy Warhol are among the highlights of the permanent collection. Post–World War II holdings in photography are particularly strong. The striking modernist structure, designed by Swiss architect Mario Botta, consists of a stepped-back, burnt-sienna brick facade and a central tower constructed of alternating bands of black and white stone. Inside, natural light from the tower floods the central atrium and some of the museum's galleries. SFMOMA's café, accessible from the street, provides a comfortable, reasonably priced refuge for drinks and light meals. ⊠ *151 3rd St.,* ☎ *415/357–4000.* ⌦ *$7; free 1st Tues. of month.* ⊙ *Mon.–Tues. and Fri.–Sun. 11–6, Thurs. 11–9 (½-price entry 6–9).*

★ ⓭   **Yerba Buena Gardens.** A large expanse of green is surrounded by a circular walkway lined with benches and sculptures. The waterfall memorial to Martin Luther King Jr. is the focal point of the gardens: Powerful streams of water surge over large, jagged stone columns, mirroring the enduring force of King's words that are carved on the stone walls and on glass blocks behind the waterfall. Above the memorial are two restaurants and an overhead walkway to the Moscone Center's main entrance. ⊠ *Between 3rd, 4th, Mission, and Howard Sts.* ⊙ *Sunrise–10 PM.*

The Heart of the Barbary Coast

When San Francisco was a brawling, boozing, extravagant upstart of a town in the latter half of the 19th century, Jackson Square and the Financial District were at the heart of the action. It was on Montgomery Street, in the heart of the Financial District, that Sam Brannan proclaimed the historic gold discovery on the American River in 1848. The gold rush brought streams of people from across America and Europe, transforming the onetime frontier town into a cosmopolitan city almost overnight. Along with the prospectors came many other fortune seekers: Saloon keepers, gamblers, and prostitutes all flocked to the so-called Barbary Coast (now Jackson Square and the Financial District). Underground dance halls, casinos, bordellos, and palatial homes sprung up as the city grew to 250,000 in only a quarter of a century. Along with the quick money came a wave of violence: Diarists commented that hardly a day would pass without bloodshed in the gambling dens or on the streets, and "houses of ill-repute" proliferated. As one Frenchman noted: "There are also some honest women in San Francisco, but not very many."

By 1917 the excesses of the Barbary Coast had fallen victim to the Red-Light Abatement Act and the ire of church leaders—the wild era was over, and the young city was forced to grow up. Jackson Square is now a sedate district of refurbished brick buildings housing high-end antiques shops and architecture firms. The Financial District has grown into a congested canyon of soaring skyscrapers, gridlocked traffic, and bustling pedestrians. Only one remnant of the gold-rush era remains: Along the former wharf-dominated streets below Montgomery between California and Broadway, and underlying many building foundations, lay at least 100 ships that were abandoned by frantic crews and passengers caught up in gold fever. Balance Alley, a short alley between Jackson and Gold streets, is said to have been named after the ship that's buried there.

Numbers in the text correspond to numbers in the margin and on the Downtown San Francisco map.

A Good Walk

In October 1996 the city designated 50 sites as stops along an official, 3.8-mi-long Barbary Coast Trail. Marked with bronze sidewalk plaques on every street corner, the trail begins at the Old Mint, at 5th and Mission streets, and runs north through downtown, Chinatown, Portsmouth

Square, Jackson Square, North Beach, and Fisherman's Wharf, ending at Aquatic Park. For information about the sites on the trail, pick up a brochure at the San Francisco Visitors Information Center (☞ Union Square, *above*). To catch its most interesting highlights, start at Montgomery and Market streets (the Montgomery BART lets out here), and walk two blocks east on Market (toward the Ferry Building clock tower) to Sansome Street. Go north two blocks to Pine Street, where you will find the **Pacific Stock Exchange** ㉒, built in 1915; just around the corner on Sansome is the art deco Stock Exchange Tower. Head west on Pine Street to Montgomery and turn north to find the **Wells Fargo Bank History Museum** ㉓, between California and Sacramento streets; its collection provides a good introduction to gold rush history.

Two blocks up from the Wells Fargo Museum is the landmark **Transamerica Pyramid** ㉔, on Montgomery Street between Clay and Washington streets. Walking through Transamerica's small park, on the east side of the building, you'll exit on Washington Street; just to your left is Hotaling Place, a historic alley that is your entrée to **Jackson Square** ㉕, the heart of the Barbary Coast. The quaint 19th-century brick buildings lining the alley, Jackson Street, and the surrounding blocks convey a flicker of the past. Of particular note here is the former **A. P. Hotaling whisky distillery,** on the corner of Hotaling Place and Jackson Street. Head west to Montgomery and north up Columbus Avenue to visit the **San Francisco Brewing Company** ㉖, the last standing saloon of the Barbary Coast era and a place overflowing with freshly brewed beers and history.

TIMING

Two hours should be enough time to see everything in this town, unless you plan on trying all the homemade beers at the San Francisco Brewing Company. The Wells Fargo Museum deserves a half hour. If you're interested in antiques, leave extra time for the shops in Jackson Square. Evenings and weekends are peaceful times to admire the distinctive architecture, though the museums in corporate headquarters are closed at those times. If you want to see activity, go on a weekday around lunchtime.

Sights to See

㉕ **Jackson Square.** Though most of the red-light district was destroyed in the 1906 fire, the old brick buildings and narrow alleys recall the romance and rowdiness of the early days. Some of the city's earliest business buildings, survivors of the 1906 quake, still stand in Jackson Square, between Montgomery and Sansome streets. The tiny alley connecting Washington and Jackson streets is named for the head of the **A. P. Hotaling Company whiskey distillery,** which was at 451 Jackson. The distillery was the largest liquor repository on the West Coast. The alley is lined with restored 19th-century brick buildings, so take your time wandering through. The old Hotaling building has unfortunately been painted a dull green and reveals little of its infamous past. But a plaque on the side of the building repeats a famous query about its surviving the quake: IF, AS THEY SAY, GOD SPANKED THE TOWN FOR BEING OVER FRISKY, WHY DID HE BURN THE CHURCHES DOWN AND SAVE HOTALING'S WHISKY? The **Ghirardelli Chocolate Factory** was once housed at 415 Jackson, though nothing marks the spot as such; it's now an art gallery. ⊠ *Between Washington, Broadway, Montgomery, and Sansome Sts.*

㉒ **Pacific Stock Exchange.** Ralph Stackpole's monumental 1930 granite sculptural groups, *Earth's Fruitfulness* and *Man's Inventive Genius,* flank this imposing structure, which dates from 1915. The Stock Exchange Tower, around the corner at 155 Sansome Street, is a 1930 modern classic by architects Miller and Pfleuger, with an art deco gold ceiling and a black marble wall entry. ⊠ *301 Pine St. (tower around corner at 155 Sansome St.).*

㉖ San Francisco Brewing Company. Built in 1907, this pub looks like a museum piece from the Barbary Coast days. An old upright piano dating from the early part of the century sits in the corner under the original stained-glass windows. Take a seat at the beautiful old mahogany bar and look down at the white-tile spittoon. In an adjacent room look for the handmade copper brewing kettle, now used to produce a dozen beers—with names like Pony Express—using old-fashioned gravity-flow methods. ⊠ *155 Columbus Ave.,* ☎ *415/434–3344.*

㉔ Transamerica Pyramid. The city's most photographed high-rise is the 853-ft Transamerica Pyramid. Designed by William Pereira and Associates in 1972, the controversial symbol has become more acceptable to local purists over time. A fragrant redwood grove along the east side of the building, replete with benches and a cheerful fountain, is a nice place to unwind. ⊠ *600 Montgomery St.*

㉓ Wells Fargo Bank History Museum. There were no formal banks in San Francisco during the early years of the gold rush, and miners often entrusted their gold dust to saloon keepers. In 1852 Wells Fargo opened its first bank in the city, and the company established banking offices in the mother lode camps, using stagecoaches and pony express riders to service the burgeoning state. (California's population boomed from 15,000 to 200,000 between 1848 and 1852.) The museum displays samples of nuggets and gold dust from mines and has a mural-size map of the Mother Lode. The showpiece is the century-old Concord stagecoach that in the mid-1850s carried 18 passengers from St. Joseph, Missouri, to San Francisco in three weeks. ⊠ *420 Montgomery St.,* ☎ *415/396–2619.* ▣ *Free.* ☉ *Weekdays 9–5.*

Chinatown

Chinatown, bordered roughly by Bush, Kearny, Powell, and Broadway, is home to one of the largest Chinese communities outside Asia. Recent immigrants from Southeast Asian countries are also making their mark on the neighborhood. The two main drags are Grant Avenue, where most of the tourist shops reside, and Stockton Street, where many locals do business. Merely strolling through Chinatown and its many bazaars, restaurants, and curio shops yields endless pleasures, but you'll have a better chance of experiencing an authentic bit of one of the world's oldest cultures by venturing off the beaten track.

Numbers in the text correspond to numbers in the margin and on the Downtown San Francisco map.

A Good Walk

Visitors usually enter Chinatown through the green-tiled **Chinatown Gate** ㉗, at Bush Street and Grant Avenue. A block and a half north at California is **Old St. Mary's Church** ㉘. Continue north on Grant Avenue and take a right on Commercial to the tiny but fascinating **Chinese Historical Society** ㉙ a block and a half down. Head back west to Kearny Street, and go north to the Holiday Inn. On the third floor is the **Chinese Culture Center** ㉚. Take the suspended walkway over Kearny from the Holiday Inn to **Portsmouth Square** ㉛. West on Washington is the **Old Chinese Telephone Exchange** ㉜. Continue west past Grant Avenue to Waverly Place and the **Tien Hou Temple** ㉝. Head south a block and turn right on Clay Street; a half block up is the redbrick **Chinatown YWCA.** Return to Stockton and head south a half block to the **Kong Chow Temple.** Next door is the elaborate **Chinese Six Companies** building.

Allow at least two hours to see Chinatown. The museums and temples deserve a half hour each.

Sights to See

㉗ Chinatown Gate. This pagoda-topped, green-tile gate, flanked on both sides of Grant Avenue by stone dragons, is an exotic introduction to one of San Francisco's most interesting and culturally cohesive neighborhoods. ✉ *Bush St. and Grant Ave.*

Chinatown YWCA. This handsome redbrick building was originally established as a meeting place and residence for Chinese women in need of social services. A large Chinese lantern welcomes those who enter through its arched doorway; inside, the lobby evokes early 20th-century Chinatown, with heavy, filigreed wood furniture and mirrors etched with delicate calligraphy. Julia Morgan, the architect of Hearst Castle, designed the building. ✉ *965 Clay St.*

㉚ Chinese Culture Center. This community organization displays the work of Chinese and Chinese-American artists and presents traveling exhibits relating to Chinese culture. Weekend afternoon (2 PM) walking tours ($15) of historic points in Chinatown can be arranged. ✉ *Holiday Inn, 750 Kearny St., 3rd floor,* ☎ *415/986–1822.* 🎫 *Free.* ⏰ *Tues.–Sun. 10–4.*

㉙ Chinese Historical Society. This careworn but important museum documents the history of Chinese immigrants and their descendants from the early 1800s to the present. ✉ *650 Commercial St., at Clay and Kearny Sts.,* ☎ *415/391–1188 (move to 965 Clay St. scheduled for fall 1998).* 🎫 *Free.* ⏰ *Tues.–Fri. 10–4, Sat. 11–2.*

Chinese Six Companies. Many fine examples of Chinese architecture line Stockton Street, but this is perhaps the most noteworthy. With its curved roof tiles and elaborate cornices, the imposing structure's oversize pagoda cheerfully dominates the block. ✉ *843 Stockton St.*

Kong Chow Temple. Amid the statuary, flowers, orange offerings, and richly colored altars (red signifies "virility," green "longevity," and gold "majesty") are a couple of plaques announcing that MRS. HARRY S. TRUMAN CAME TO THIS TEMPLE IN JUNE 1948 FOR A PREDICTION ON THE OUTCOME OF THE ELECTION. . . . THIS FORTUNE CAME TRUE. Place a dollar bill in the donation box as you enter. The air at Kong Chow Temple is often thick with incense, a bit ironic, what with the Chinese Community Smoke-Free Project two floors below. ✉ *855 Stockton St.*

㉜ Old Chinese Telephone Exchange. The original Chinatown burned down after the 1906 earthquake, and this was the first building to set the style for the new Chinatown. The three-tier pagoda, now the Bank of Canton, was built in 1909. The exchange's operators were renowned for their "tenacious memories"—they knew all their callers by name rather than number. ✉ *743 Washington St.*

NEED A BREAK?
Dim sum, a variety of pastries filled with meat, fish, and vegetables, is the Chinese version of a smorgasbord, delivered on stacked food-service carts from which customers make selections. At **New Asia** (✉ 772 Pacific Ave., ☎ 415/391–6666), dim sum is available daily from 8:30 AM to 9 PM.

㉘ Old St. Mary's Church. This brick and granite building was dedicated in 1854 and served as the city's Catholic cathedral until 1891. (The current seat of the Catholic church in San Francisco, which replaced the successor to Old St. Mary's, is the ultramodern St. Mary's Cathedral at 1111 Gough Street.) Old St. Mary's hosts a Noontime Concert series every Tuesday and Thursday at 12:30. Across California Street is **St. Mary's Park,** a tranquil setting for local sculptor Beniamino (Benny) Bufano's *Sun Yat-sen.* The 12-ft statue of the founder of the Republic of China was installed on the site of the leader's favorite reading spot during his years of exile in San Francisco.

③ **Portsmouth Square.** This former potato patch that became the plaza for Yerba Buena (the Mexican settlement that was later renamed San Francisco) is where Captain John B. Montgomery raised the American flag in 1846 to claim the territory for the United States. Note the bronze galleon atop a 9-ft granite shaft; designed by Bruce Porter, the sculpture was erected in 1919 in memory of Robert Louis Stevenson, who often visited the site during his 1879–80 residence. Now dotted with pagoda-shaped structures, the park is a favorite spot for morning t'ai chi. By noon, dozens of men play a Chinese version of chess, engaged in not always legal competition that the police occasionally interrupt. A sand-covered children's playground sits below the main level of the square. ⊠ *Kearny St. between Washington and Clay Sts.*

③ **Tien Hou Temple.** Day Ju, one of the first three Chinese to arrive in San Francisco, dedicated the temple to the Queen of the Heavens and the Goddess of the Seven Seas in 1852. Climb three flights of stairs past two mah-jongg parlors whose patrons hope the spirits above will favor them. In the entryway, elderly ladies can often be seen preparing "money" to be burned as offerings to various Buddhist gods. A (real) dollar placed in the donation box on their table will bring a smile (and is expected). Red-and-gold lanterns adorn the ceiling. Notice the wood carving suspended from the ceiling, depicting a number of gods at play. ⊠ *125 Waverly Pl.* ⊙ *Daily 10–4.*

North Beach and Telegraph Hill

Novelist and resident Herbert Gold calls North Beach "the longest-running, most glorious American bohemian operetta outside Greenwich Village." Indeed, to anyone who's spent some time in its eccentric old bars and cafés or wandered its charming side streets and steep alleys, North Beach evokes everything from the wild Barbary Coast days to the no less sedate beatnik era. You can still find family operettas performed at Caffè Trieste, Italian bakeries that appear frozen in time, and homages to Jack Kerouac and Allen Ginsberg. Like neighboring Chinatown, this is a section of the city where eating is unavoidable: The streets are packed with Italian delicatessens, bakeries, Chinese markets, coffeehouses, and ethnic restaurants.

Numbers in the text correspond to numbers in the margin and on the Downtown San Francisco map.

A Good Walk

Washington Square ㉞ is at the intersection of Union Street and Columbus Avenue. Just north of the square is the double-turreted cathedral of **Saints Peter and Paul** ㉟. Head south on Columbus to the corner of Vallejo and the **St. Francis of Assisi Church** ㊱, a Victorian-era structure. From here you can slip down Columbus to a Beat-era landmark, the **City Lights** bookstore at No. 261, or walk east on Vallejo and north on **Grant Avenue,** which is filled with eclectic shops and old-time bars and cafés. When you reach Union Street, you're just a block and a half north of Washington Square.

Head up steep **Telegraph Hill** ㊲ to **Coit Tower** ㊳. Coit Tower can be reached by car (though parking is limited) or public transportation—board the No. 39-Coit at Columbus Avenue and Union Street. To walk up to the tower, head east up Filbert Street; turn north (left) at

Grant, go one block to Greenwich, and ascend the steps on your right. Cross the street at the top of the first set of stairs and continue up the curving stone steps to Coit Tower.

Steps take you down the east side of Telegraph Hill. At Montgomery Street, perched on the side of the hill, is **Julius' Castle** ㊱, all royal spires and breathtaking views. A block to the right at 1360 Montgomery, where the Filbert steps intersect, is a distinguished-looking art deco apartment building. Descend the Filbert steps amid roses, fuchsias, irises, and trumpet flowers—courtesy of Grace Marchant, who labored for nearly 30 years to transform a dump into a treasure. The serene **Levi Strauss headquarters** ㊵ is at the foot of the hill.

TIMING

To visit Coit Tower, hike Telegraph Hill, and visit the sights mentioned here, set aside two to three hours. By its nature, though, North Beach is a place to linger—a visit here can easily fill an entire afternoon.

Sights to See

★ ㊳ **Coit Tower.** The 180-ft-tall Coit Tower stands as a monument to the city's volunteer firefighters. Early during the gold rush, Lillie Hitchcock Coit ("Miss Lil") was said to have deserted a wedding party and chased down the street after her favorite engine, the Knickerbocker Number 5, clad in her bridesmaid finery. She was soon made an honorary member of the Knickerbocker Company, and after that always signed herself "Lillie Coit 5" in honor of her favorite engine. When Lillie died in 1929, she left the city the $125,000 that was spent to build Coit Tower. Inside the tower are 19 Work Projects Administration–era murals depicting labor union workers. Ride the elevator to the top to enjoy the panoramic view. ⊠ *On top of Telegraph Hill.* 🖃 *$3.* 🕙 *Daily 10–6.*

Grant Avenue. Originally called Calle de la Fundación, Grant Avenue is the oldest street in the city. In the section between Columbus Avenue and Filbert Street, you'll find atmospheric cafés, authentic Italian delis, odd curio shops and unusual import stores, and dusty bars—like The Saloon and Grant & Green Blues Club. A Saturday afternoon must is Caffè Trieste (⊠ 601 Vallejo St., at Grant Ave., ☎ 415/392–6739), where the Giotta family presents a weekly musical (patrons are encouraged to participate). Beginning at 1:30, the program ranges from Italian pop and folk music to operas. ⊠ *Between Columbus Ave. and Filbert Sts.*

㊱ **Julius' Castle.** The dark-paneled interior of this official historic landmark (founder Julius Roz had his craftsmen use materials left over from the 1915 Panama–Pacific International Exposition) is almost as dazzling as the view. The contemporary Italian food is worth the splurge—if you dine here, ask for a table on the upper floor's outside terrace for the best vista. Reservations are essential. ⊠ *1541 Montgomery St.,* ☎ *415/392–2222.* 🕙 *Daily 5–10 PM.*

㊵ **Levi Strauss headquarters.** This carefully landscaped complex appears so collegiate it is affectionately known as LSU (Levi Strauss University). Fountains and grassy knolls complement the redbrick buildings, providing a perfect environment for brown-bag and picnic lunches. Delis and other take-out shops are nearby. ⊠ *Levi's Plaza, 1155 Battery St.*

㊱ **St. Francis of Assisi Church.** An 1860 Victorian Gothic building with a terra-cotta facade stands on the site of the frame parish church that served the gold-rush Catholic community. ⊠ *610 Vallejo St.*

㊳ **Saints Peter and Paul.** The twin turrets of this Romanesque cathedral that was completed in 1924 are local landmarks. On the first Sunday of October a mass and a parade to Fisherman's Wharf are part of the annual Blessing of the Fleet. ⊠ *666 Filbert St., at Washington Square Park.*

③⑦ **Telegraph Hill.** Telegraph Hill residents command some of the best views in the city, as well as the most difficult ascents to their aeries (the flower-lined steps flanking the hill make the climb more than tolerable for them and visitors, though). The Hill is capped by Coit Tower (☞ *above*). ⊠ *Between Lombard, Filbert, Kearny, and Sansome Sts.*

③④ **Washington Square.** This may well be the daytime social heart of what was once considered "Little Italy"—though in the early morning the dominating sight is of a hundred or more elderly Asians engaged in t'ai chi. By mid-morning groups of conservatively dressed elderly Italian men arrive. Nearby, kids toss Frisbees, jugglers juggle, and Chinese matrons stare impassively at the passing parade. ⊠ *Between Columbus Ave., Stockton, Filbert, and Union Sts.*

Nob Hill and Russian Hill

Once called the Hill of Golden Promise, the slope above Union Square was officially dubbed Nob Hill during the 1870s, when San Francisco's "the Big Four" financiers—Charles Crocker, Leland Stanford, Mark Hopkins, and Collis Huntington—built their hilltop estates. Nob Hill is still home to many of the city's elite, as well as several of San Francisco's finest hotels. During the 1890s, a group of bohemian artists and writers that included Charles Norris, George Sterling, and Maynard Dixon lived on Russian Hill.

Numbers in the text correspond to numbers in the margin and on the Downtown San Francisco map.

A Good Walk

Begin at California and Taylor streets at the **Masonic Auditorium** ④①, an enormous high-columned structure—the lobby mural is the highlight of a visit. Across California Street is **Grace Cathedral** ④②. East on California one block (toward Mason Street) is the **Pacific Union Club** ④③, a brownstone whose shell survived the '06 quake. Across Mason from the club is the **Fairmont Hotel** ④④. Across California from the Fairmont is the **Mark Hopkins Inter-Continental Hotel** ④⑤, famed for its Top of the Mark lounge. Head north three blocks on Mason Street to the **Cable Car Museum** ④⑥, the "brain" of the cable-car network.

From the Cable Car Museum continue four blocks north on Mason Street to Vallejo Street. Steep stairs lead to the multilevel **Ina Coolbrith Park** ④⑦. From here you can meander north on Mason Street to Union. Head west on Union and north on Hyde to the top of **Lombard Street** ④⑧, a.k.a. the "crookedest street in the world." Take the steps down to Leavenworth Street. A block north and east (on Chestnut Street) is the **San Francisco Art Institute** ④⑨.

TIMING
This tour covers a lot of ground, much of it steep. To do it all, including brief stops at Grace Cathedral and the Cable Car Museum, a person in reasonable shape will want to set aside about 3 hours.

Sights to See

④⑥ **Cable Car Museum.** On exhibit are photographs, old cable cars, signposts, ticketing machines, and other memorabilia dating from 1873. The four sets of massive powerhouse wheels that move the entire cable car system steal the show: The design is so simple it seems almost unreal. You can also go downstairs and check out the innards of the system. ⊠ *1201 Mason St., at Washington St.,* ☎ *415/474–1887.* ☞ *Free.* ☉ *Oct.–Mar., daily 10–5; Apr.–Sept., daily 10–6.*

④④ **Fairmont Hotel.** The Fairmont's dazzling opening was delayed a year by the 1906 quake, but since then the marble palace has hosted presidents, royalty, movie stars (Valentino, Dietrich), and local nabobs. Things have changed since its early days: On the eve of World War I you could get a room for as low as $2.50 per night, meals included. Nowadays, prices run in the thousands—this being for a night in the eight-room penthouse suite. The lobby is a warm blend of flamboyant rose-floral carpeting, lush red-velvet chairs, gold faux-marble columns, and gilt ceilings. The hotel's kitschy **Tonga Room** (☞ Nightlife and the Arts, *below*) is a hoot. ⊠ *950 Mason St.,* ☎ *415/772–5000.*

㊷ Grace Cathedral. This soaring Gothic structure erected on the site of Charles Crocker's mansion took 53 years to build. The gilded bronze doors at the east entrance were taken from casts of Ghiberti's Gates of Paradise on the baptistery in Florence. Perhaps the most unique feature of Grace, the local seat of the Episcopal church, is its 35-ft-wide meditation Labyrinth, a large, purplish rug that's a replica of the 13th-century stone labyrinth on the floor of the Charters Cathedral. Outdoors is a terrazzo meditation labyrinth. Also noteworthy is an AIDS Memorial Chapel with a sculpture by the late artist Keith Haring. ⊠ *1051 Taylor St.,* ☎ *415/749–6300.* ⊙ *Daily 7–6; gift shop Mon.– Sat. 10–5, Sun. 9:30–11 and 12:30–3:30.*

㊿ Ina Coolbrith Park. This attractive park is composed of a series of terraces on the side of a hill. An Oakland librarian and poet, Ina Coolbrith introduced both Jack London and Isadora Duncan to the world of books. In 1915 she was named poet laureate of California. The climb to the park is steep, so make use of the benches at various levels. ⊠ *Vallejo St. between Mason and Taylor Sts.*

★ **㊽ Lombard Street.** San Francisco's "crookedest" street drops down the east face of Russian Hill in eight switchbacks. Few tourists with cars can resist the lure of the steep descent, but it's made less than scary by the very slow speed at which you must proceed. Pedestrians can make a quicker descent by taking the steps on either side of the street. ⊠ *Lombard St. between Hyde and Leavenworth Sts.*

㊺ Mark Hopkins Inter-Continental Hotel. A combination of French château and Spanish Renaissance architecture (with terra-cotta detailing), this hotel has hosted statesmen, royalty, and Hollywood celebrities. The **Top of the Mark** cocktail lounge is remembered fondly by thousands of World War II veterans who jammed the lounge before leaving for overseas duty; wives and sweethearts watching the ships depart gave the room's northwest nook its name—Weepers' Corner. ⊠ *1 Nob Hill, at California and Mason Sts.,* ☎ *415/392–3434.*

㊶ Masonic Auditorium. Formally called the California Masonic Memorial Temple, this building was erected by Freemasons in 1957. The impressive lobby mosaic depicts the Masonic fraternity's role in California history and industry. There's also an intricate model of King Solomon's Temple in the lobby. ⊠ *1111 California St.,* ☎ *415/776–4917.* ⊙ *Lobby weekdays 8–5.*

㊸ Pacific Union Club. The quake and fire of 1906 knocked down all of Nob Hill's palatial mansions save one: the shell of James Flood's brownstone. This broad-beam structure was built by the Comstock silver baron in 1886. In 1909 the property was purchased by the Pacific Union Club, a bastion of the wealthy and powerful. Adjacent is a small park that hosts frequent art shows. ⊠ *1000 California St.*

㊾ San Francisco Art Institute. A Moorish-tiled fountain in a tree-shaded courtyard greets you as you enter the institute. The Spanish colonial-style building was erected on Russian Hill in 1926. Don't miss the impressive seven-section fresco painted in 1931 by Mexican master Diego

Rivera in the student gallery to the left as you enter the institute: It's one of only three Bay Area murals painted by Rivera. ✉ *800 Chestnut St.,* ☎ *415/771–7020.* ✆ *Gallery free.* ☼ *McBean Gallery Tues.– Sat. 10–5 (Thurs. until 8), Sun. noon–5; student gallery daily 9–9.*

Pacific Heights

Some of the city's most expensive and dramatic real estate—including mansions and town houses priced at $1 million and up—is in Pacific Heights. Grand old Victorians line the streets, and from almost any point in this neighborhood you get a magnificent view.

Numbers in the text correspond to numbers in the margin and on the Downtown San Francisco map.

A Good Walk

At Webster Street and Broadway are three notable **Broadway estates** ⑩. South on Webster Street is **Bourn Mansion.** Head east on Jackson Street to the red-sandstone **Whittier Mansion** ⑪, at the corner of Laguna Street. One block south on Laguna is **Lafayette Park** ⑫. Walking east on Washington along the edge of Lafayette Park, the most imposing residence is the formal French **Spreckels Mansion** ⑬ at the corner of Octavia Street. Continue east to Franklin Street and turn left (north). Halfway down the block is the **Haas-Lilienthal House** ⑭. Heading back south on Franklin, stop to see several **Franklin Street buildings** ⑮ and several more **noteworthy Victorians** ⑯ nearby.

TIMING
Set aside about two hours to see the sights mentioned here. Most of the attractions are walk-bys, but you'll be covering a good bit of pavement, some of it steep. Tours of the Haas-Lilienthal House, which is only open on Wednesday and Sunday afternoons, take about one hour. The guided tours of Pacific Heights from the house take two hours.

Sights to See

Bourn Mansion. This Georgian brick mansion was built in 1896 for William B. Bourn, who had inherited a Mother Lode gold mine. Architect Willis Polk, who designed this structure, also designed Bourn's palatial Peninsula estate, Filoli (☞ Side Trips from San Francisco, *below*). ✉ *2550 Webster St.*

⑩ **Broadway estates.** Broadway uptown is home to several classic showplaces. The three-story Italian Renaissance palace at **2222 Broadway** (notice the intricately filigreed doorway) was built by Comstock mine heir James Flood and later donated to a religious order. The Convent of the Sacred Heart purchased the baroque brick Grant House at **2220 Broadway.** These two buildings, along with a Flood property at **2120 Broadway** are all used as school quarters. ✉ *Broadway between Fillmore and Buchanan Sts.*

⑮ **Franklin Street buildings.** Don't be fooled by the neoclassical **Golden Gate Church** (✉ 1901 Franklin St.) building—what at first looks like a stone facade is actually redwood painted white. At **1735 Franklin** you'll find a stately brick Georgian built in the early 1900s for a coffee merchant. On the northeast corner of Franklin and California streets is the tapestry brick **Christian Science church**; the Tuscan Revival building has noteworthy terra-cotta detailing. The **Coleman House** (✉ 1701 Franklin St.) is a twin-turreted Queen Anne mansion built for a gold-rush mining and lumber baron. Don't miss the large stained-glass window on the house's north side. ✉ *Franklin St. between Washington and California Sts.*

54 **Haas-Lilienthal House.** This 1886 Queen Anne survived the 1906 earth-quake and fire and is the only fully furnished Victorian open to the public. The carefully kept rooms provide an intriguing glimpse of turn-of-the-century taste and lifestyle. A small display of photographs on the bottom floor proves this elaborate house was modest compared with some of the giants that fell to the fire. Volunteers conduct tours two days a week, as well as an informative two-hour tour of the east-ern portion of Pacific Heights on Sunday afternoon. ⌧ *2007 Franklin St., near Washington St.,* ☎ *415/441–3004.* ⬚ *$5.* ☉ *Wed. noon–4 (last tour at 3), Sun. 11–5 (last tour at 4). Pacific Heights tours ($5) leave the house Sun. at 12:30.*

52 **Lafayette Park.** Clusters of trees dot this oasis for sunbathers, dog-lovers, and Frisbee throwers. During the 1860s, a tenacious squatter, Sam Hol-laday, built himself a big wooden house in the center of the park. Hol-laday even instructed city gardeners as if the land were his own and defied all orders to leave. The house was finally torn down in 1936.

56 **Noteworthy Victorians.** Two stunning **Italianate Victorians** (⌧ 1818 and 1834 California St.) stand out on the 1800 block of California. A block farther is the Victorian-era **Atherton House** (⌧ 1990 California St.), which combines Queen Anne, Stick-Eastlake, and other architec-tural elements. The Victorians on the east side of the 1800 block of Laguna Street cost only $2,000–$2,600 when they were built in the 1870s. ⌧ *California St. between Franklin and Octavia Sts.; Laguna St. between Pine and Bush Sts.*

53 **Spreckels Mansion.** This formal French estate was built for sugar heir Adolph Spreckels and his wife, Alma. Mrs. Spreckels was so pleased with her house that she commissioned architect George Applegarth to design a similarly classical structure: the California Palace of the Le-gion of Honor in Lincoln Park. One of the city's great iconoclasts, Alma Spreckels is the model for the bronze figure atop the Victory Monu-ment in Union Square. ⌧ *2080 Washington St., at Octavia St.*

51 **Whittier Mansion.** This red-sandstone structure was one of the most elegant 19th-century houses in the state. It has a Spanish-tiled roof and enormous scrolled bay windows on all four sides. The Whittier Man-sion was built so solidly that only a chimney toppled over during the 1906 quake. ⌧ *2090 Jackson St., at Laguna St.*

OFF THE
BEATEN PATH
JAPANTOWN – Around 1860, a wave of Japanese-Americans arrived in San Francisco, which they named "Soko." After the 1906 fire destroyed wooden homes in other parts of the stricken city, many of these recent im-migrants settled in the Western Addition. By the 1930s they had opened shops, markets, meeting halls, and restaurants and established Shinto and Buddhist temples. Japantown was virtually disbanded during World War II when many of its residents, including second- and third-generation Ameri-cans, were "relocated" in camps. Today Japantown, or "Nihonmachi," is centered on the slopes of Pacific Heights, north of Geary Boulevard, be-tween Fillmore and Laguna streets; the Nihonmachi Cherry Blossom Festi-val is celebrated two weekends every April. The three-block-long Japan Center (⌧ Post St. between Fillmore and Laguna Sts.) contains shops, restaurants, a cineplex, and the very fine Kabuki Hot Springs spa.

Civic Center and Mission Dolores

City Hall and the cluster of handsome adjoining cultural institutions that make up San Francisco's Civic Center stand as one of the coun-try's great governmental building complexes—a seeming realization of the visions put forth by turn-of-the-century proponents of the City Beautiful. But illusion soon gives way to reality: On the streets and plazas of the Civic Center live many of the city's most destitute residents, and much of the area is undergoing seismic retrofitting in the wake of the 1989 Loma Prieta earthquake. Things will likely look better by the end of the century. From the Civic Center, it's a quick ride on the underground or a manageable walk to historic Mission Dolores.

Numbers in the text correspond to numbers in the margin and on the Downtown San Francisco map.

A Good Tour

Start your walk at the **San Francisco Public Library** ⑰ at Fulton and Larkin streets. Across from the library to the west are Civic Center Plaza and **City Hall** ⑱. Across Van Ness Avenue from City Hall are—from north to south, each taking up most of a block—the **Veterans Building** ⑲, the **War Memorial Opera House** ⑳, and **Louise M. Davies Symphony Hall** ㉑. The Hayes Valley strip of galleries, shops, and restaurants is a block south of Grove on Hayes Street between Franklin and Laguna streets. After you've explored Hayes Valley, backtrack to Gough and head south to Market. To visit **Mission Dolores** ㉒, you have two options. The Van Ness Avenue Muni light-rail station is two blocks east; catch a J car, get off at 16th and Church streets, and walk one block east on 16th to Dolores Street. Or you can walk up Market Street to treelined Dolores Street (which runs into Market across from Safeway) and walk south to 16th Street. From the mission, you can easily proceed either to the **Mission District** or the **Castro** (☞ *below*).

TIMING
Walking the Civic Center area takes about 45 minutes, not counting tours of the library or Davies Hall, or shopping in Hayes Valley. Add 20 to 30 minutes to walk or train up to Mission Dolores, which can be explored in a half hour.

Sights to See

⑱ **City Hall.** This French Renaissance Revival masterpiece of granite and marble was modeled after the Capitol in Washington. Its dome, which is even higher than the Washington version, dominates the area. The building is scheduled to reopen in late 1998 after a three-year seismic upgrade is completed. ⊠ *Between Van Ness Ave., Polk, Grove, and McAllister Sts.*

㉑ **Louise M. Davies Symphony Hall.** The 2,750-seat hall is the home of the San Francisco Symphony, which is led by Michael Tilson-Thomas. It took several years to sort out the modern structure's acoustical problems, the solutions to which are discussed on docent-led tours. ⊠ *201 Van Ness Ave.,* ☎ *415/552–8338.* ☞ *Tours $3.* ☉ *Tours of Davies Hall Wed. and Sat. by appointment, tours of Davies and the Performing Arts Center Mon. hourly 10–2.*

Mission District. Home to lively Italian and Irish communities earlier in the century—you'll still find Italian restaurants and Irish pubs here, as well as Arabic bookstores, Vietnamese markets, and Filipino eateries—the Mission District has been heavily Latino since the late 1960s, when immigrants from Mexico and Central America began arriving. From Mission Dolores, you can head east on 16th Street to a "new bohemia" section of cafés and funky shops around 16th and Valencia streets, and then on into the commercial heart of the Mission District—Valencia and Mission streets between 16th and 24th streets.

㉒ **Mission Dolores.** The mission comprises two churches standing side by side. Completed in 1791, the small adobe building known as Mission San Francisco de Asis is the oldest standing structure in San Francisco and the sixth of the 21 California missions founded by Father Junípero Serra. Its ceiling depicts original Ohlone Indian basket designs, executed in vegetable dyes. Services are held in both the Mission San Francisco de Asis and next door in the handsome multidomed Basilica. ✉ *Dolores and 16th Sts.,* ☎ *415/621–8203.* ☜ *$2.* ☉ *Daily 9–4.*

㊄ San Francisco Public Library. The city's main library, which opened in April 1996, is a modernized version of the old beaux arts library that sits just across Fulton Street (that building will become the new site of the Asian Art Museum within a few years). The new structure contains centers for the hearing and visually impaired, a gay-and-lesbian history center, African-American and Asian centers, and a rooftop garden and terrace. The San Francisco History Room and Archives holds a wealth of historic photographs, maps, and other memorabilia. At the library's center is a five-story atrium with a skylight, a grand staircase, and murals painted by local artists. Across Hyde Street behind the library is brick-lined United Nations Plaza. ✉ *Larkin St. between Grove and Fulton Sts.,* ☎ *415/557–4440 or 415/557–4567 for archives hrs.* ☉ *Mon. 10–6, Tues.–Thurs. 9–8, Fri. 11–5, Sat. 9–5, Sun. noon–5.*

㊹ Veterans Building. The United Nations charter was signed in 1945 in the **Herbst Theatre** (☎ 415/392–4400) here. Today Herbst is a popular venue for lectures and readings, classical ensembles, and dance performances. The street-level **San Francisco Arts Commission Gallery** (☎ 415/554–6080) exhibits the work of local artists. The mayor's office and other city departments temporarily located here are scheduled to move back into the City Hall in late 1998. ✉ *401 Van Ness Ave.*

㊿ War Memorial Opera House. The opera house is modeled after its European counterparts, with a vaulted and coffered ceiling, a marble foyer, two balconies, and an unusual art deco chandelier that resembles a huge silver sunburst. The San Francisco Opera and Ballet companies perform here. ✉ *301 Van Ness Ave.,* ☎ *415/621–6600.*

OFF THE
BEATEN PATH

THE CASTRO – Historians are still trying to discover what turned a sleepy working-class neighborhood west of the Civic Center into a mecca for lesbians and gay men. Some point to the San Francisco's libertarian traditions, and others note that as a huge military embarkation point during World War II, the city provided an anonymous haven. Whatever the cause, the area surrounding the intersection of Castro and Market streets became a social, cultural, and political center for gays. Especially on weekends, the streets of the Castro teem with a wide assortment of folks out shopping, pushing political causes, heading to art films, and lingering in bars and cafés. Cutting-edge clothing stores and unique gift shops predominate, as do pairs of pretty young things of all genders and sexual persuasions (even heterosexual) holding hands. The 1,500-seat Castro Theatre (✉ 429 Castro St.), which opened in 1922, is the neighborhood's landmark. The birthplace and workshop of the Names Project (✉ 2362 Market St.), which manages the AIDS Memorial Quilt, is around the corner. Nurse a cappuccino at the Café Flore (✉ 16th and Market Sts.) to overhear the latest Castro dish. To get to the Castro from the Civic Center, take one of Market Street's above-ground antique trolleys.

The Northern Waterfront

For the sight, sound, and smell of the sea, hop the Powell-Hyde cable car from Union Square and take it to the end of the line. The views as you descend Hyde Street down to the bay are nothing short of breathtaking—tiny sailboats bob in the whitecaps, Alcatraz hovers ominously in the distance, and the Marin Headlands form a rugged backdrop to the often fog-shrouded Golden Gate Bridge. Be sure to bring good walking shoes and a jacket or sweater.

Numbers in the text correspond to numbers in the margin and on the Northern Waterfront/Marina and the Presidio map.

A Good Walk

Begin at the **National Maritime Museum** ① and, two blocks east, the **Hyde Street Pier** ②. Across from the museum is redbrick **Ghirardelli Square** ③. A half block east of the Hyde Street Pier on Beach Street lies the three-story **Cannery** ④, another attractive brick complex whose restaurants and shops overlook an open-air courtyard. North of the Cannery on Jefferson Street is **Fisherman's Wharf** ⑤. Continue east for a couple more blocks and join the crowds at **Pier 39** ⑥, a playland and shopper's extravaganza. Backtrack a few hundred feet to Pier 41 to catch the boat to **Alcatraz Island.**

TIMING

For the entire Northern Waterfront circuit, set aside a half day, not including shopping or dining. Boat tours take from one to three hours.

Sights to See

★ **Alcatraz Island.** The boat ride to the island is brief (15 minutes) but affords beautiful views of the city, Marin County, and the East Bay. The audio tour, highly recommended, includes the observations of guards and prisoners about life in one of America's most notorious penal colonies. A ranger-led tour surveys the island's ecology. Plan to spend at least three hours for the visit and boat rides combined. Reservations, which can be made up to two weeks in advance, are strongly recommended, even in the off-season. ✉ *Boats to the island leave from Pier 41,* ☎ *415/773–1188 for information or 415/705–5555 for tickets.* 🎫 *$11 ($7.75 without audio); add $2 per ticket to charge by phone at 415/546–2700.* ☉ *Ferry departures Sept.–late May, daily 9:30–2:30; late May–Aug., daily 9:30–4:15.*

Angel Island. For an outdoorsy adventure, consider a day at Angel Island, just northwest of Alcatraz. Discovered by Spaniards in 1775 and declared a U.S. military reserve 75 years later, the island was used from 1910 until 1940 as a screening ground for Asian immigrants, who were often held for months, even years, before being granted entry. In 1963 Angel Island was made a state park. A scenic path winds around the island's perimeter. ✉ *Boats to island leave from Pier 43½,* ☎ *415/546–2628 or 415/435–1915.* 🎫 *$10.* ☉ *Ferry departures late Nov.–early Mar., weekends only; early Mar.–late Nov., weekends 10–2, weekdays at 10 AM.*

❹ **The Cannery.** This three-story repository of shops and restaurants was built in 1894 to house what became the Del Monte Fruit and Vegetable Cannery. The **Museum of the City of San Francisco** (☎ 415/928–0289) on the third floor is worth a brief stop. ✉ *2801 Leavenworth St.,* ☎ *415/771–3112.* ☉ *Mon.–Sat. 10–6, Sun. 11–6; until 8:30 Thurs.–Sat. in summer (restaurants open later).*

Ferries. Cruises are an exhilarating way to see the bay. Among the cruises offered by the **Red and White Fleet** (✉ Pier 43½, ☎ 415/546–2628) are frequent one-hour swings under the Golden Gate Bridge and along the Northern Waterfront. More interesting—and just as scenic—are the tours to Sausalito, Angel Island, Alcatraz, Tiburon, Muir Woods, and the Napa Valley Wine Country. The **Blue and Gold Fleet** (✉ Pier 39, ☎ 415/705–5555) conducts daily 1¼-hour tours under both the Bay and Golden Gate bridges, as well as Friday- and Saturday-night dinner-dance cruises (reservations required) from late April until mid-

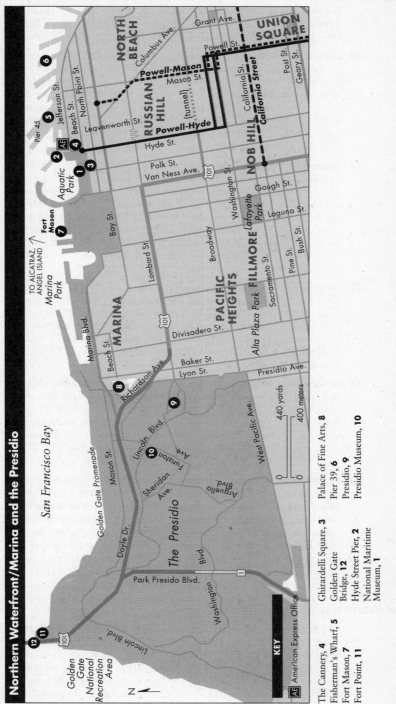

Northern Waterfront/Marina and the Presidio

San Francisco Bay

UNION SQUARE

NORTH BEACH

Grant Ave.

Columbus Ave.

Powell St.

Powell-Mason

Mason St.

RUSSIAN HILL (tunnel)

Powell-Hyde

Leavenworth St.

Jefferson St.

Beach St.

North Point St.

Pier 45

Hyde St.

California St.

California Street

Post St.

Geary St.

NOB HILL

Aquatic Park

Polk St.

Van Ness Ave.

Washington St.

Gough St.

Lafayette Park

Laguna St.

TO ALCATRAZ, ANGEL ISLAND

Fort Mason

Marina Park

Bay St.

Broadway

FILLMORE

Pine St.

Bush St.

Sacramento St.

Lombard St.

PACIFIC HEIGHTS

Marina Blvd.

Beach St.

MARINA

Divisadero St.

Alta Plaza Park

Baker St.

Lyon St.

Presidio Ave.

Richardson Ave.

West Pacific Ave.

Lincoln Blvd.

Funston Ave.

440 yards

400 meters

Mason St.

Golden Gate Promenade

Sheridan Ave.

Arguello Blvd.

The Presidio

Doyle Dr.

Blvd.

Park Presidio Blvd.

Washington

Golden Gate National Recreation Area

Lincoln Blvd.

N

KEY

AE American Express Office

The Cannery, **4**
Fisherman's Wharf, **5**
Fort Mason, **7**
Fort Point, **11**

Ghirardelli Square, **3**
Golden Gate
 Bridge, **12**
Hyde Street Pier, **2**
National Maritime
 Museum, **1**

Palace of Fine Arts, **8**
Pier 39, **6**
Presidio, **9**
Presidio Museum, **10**

December. Blue and Gold also runs ferries to Oakland, Alameda, and Vallejo (the latter includes trips on the Wine Train and to Marine World Africa USA). ⊠ *Fisherman's Wharf between Piers 43½ and 39.*

⑤ Fisherman's Wharf. The chaotic streets of the wharf hold numerous seafood restaurants—including sidewalk crab pots and counters where take-out shrimp and crab cocktails are sold. T-shirts and sweats, gold chains galore, redwood furniture, and acres of artwork (some original) beckon visitors. The World War II submarine USS *Pampanito* (☎ 415/441–5819) at Pier 45 provides a fascinating (if claustrophobic) look at life down under during wartime. ⊠ *Jefferson St. between Leavenworth St. and Pier 39.*

③ Ghirardelli Square. This complex of 19th-century redbrick factory buildings—once the home of the aromatic Ghirardelli Chocolate Company—has been transformed into a network of specialty shops, cafés, restaurants, and galleries. Two unusual shops in the Cocoa Building are the **Xanadu Gallery** (☎ 415/441–5211) and **Folk Art International** (☎ 415/928–3340): Both display museum-quality tribal art from Asia, Africa, Oceania, and the Americas. ⊠ *900 North Point St.,* ☎ *415/775–5500.* ☉ *Jan.–Mar., Sun.–Thurs. 10–6, Fri.–Sat. 10–9; Apr.–Dec., daily 10–9.*

② Hyde Street Pier. The pier, one of the wharf area's best bargains, always bustles with activity. The highlight is the collection of historic ships: the *Balclutha,* an 1886 full-rigged, three-mast sailing vessel that sailed around Cape Horn 17 times; the *Eureka,* a side-wheel ferry; the *C. A. Thayer,* a three-masted schooner; and the *Hercules,* a tugboat. ⊠ *Hyde St., north of Jefferson St.,* ☎ *415/929–0202.* ☞ *$3.* ☉ *Fall–spring, daily 9:30–5; summer, daily 10–6.*

① National Maritime Museum. You'll feel as if you're out to sea when you step inside this sturdy, rounded structure. Part of the San Francisco Maritime National Historical Park, which includes the Hyde Street Pier, the museum exhibits ship models, photographs, maps, and other artifacts chronicling the development of San Francisco and the West Coast through maritime history. ⊠ *Aquatic Park at the foot of Polk St.,* ☎ *415/556–3002 or 415/929–0202.* ☞ *Donation suggested.* ☉ *Daily 10–5.*

⑥ Pier 39. This shopping and entertainment complex is the most popular of San Francisco's waterfront attractions. Children enjoy the brilliantly colored double-decker **Venetian Carousel.** At **Underwater World** (☎ 415/623–5300), moving walkways transport visitors through a space surrounded on three sides by water filled with indigenous San Francisco Bay marine life. Above water, don't miss the sea lions that bask and play on the docks on the pier's northwest side. Start your visit at the newly opened **Welcome Center,** inside the Citybank Cinemax Theater, open 9–5:30 daily. ⊠ *Pier 39 off Jefferson St.*

The Marina and the Presidio

The Marina district was a coveted place to live until the 1989 earthquake, when the area's homes suffered the worst damage in the city because the Marina is built on landfill. Though many homeowners and renters left in search of more solid ground, the Marina is still popular with young professionals. Especially on weekends, Chestnut Street, the neighborhood's main drag, is filled with a well-to-do crowd. Fort Mason is on the eastern edge of the Marina district, the Presidio on its western side.

Numbers in the text correspond to numbers in the margin and on the Northern Waterfront/Marina and the Presidio map.

A Good Tour

You can reach the Marina easily by public transportation. Muni Bus 38 from Union Square heads west to Fillmore Street (where you can transfer to Bus 22; Chestnut Street is one block north of Lombard Street and Fort Mason is three blocks east of the 22's terminus) and to Park Presidio Boulevard (transfer to Bus 28 to go through the Presidio). But this is the place to use your car if you have one; you might even consider renting one for a day to cover the area, as well as Lincoln Park, Golden Gate Park, and the western shoreline.

Begin with a visit to **Fort Mason** ⑦. To get to the **Palace of Fine Arts** ⑧ by car, take Lombard Street west and stay in the right lane as it curves toward Golden Gate Bridge (watch carefully for signs or you'll wind up on the bridge). Inside the Palace is the **Exploratorium,** a hands-on science museum. The least confusing way to get to the **Presidio** ⑨ from the Palace is to exit from the south end of the Lyon Street parking lot and head east (left) on Bay Street. Turn right (north) onto Baker Street, right on Francisco and take it across Richardson Avenue to Lyon Street. Make a left onto Lyon, a right at Lombard Street, and proceed through the main gate to Presidio Boulevard. Turn right onto Presidio, which becomes Lincoln Boulevard after a block or so. Turn left on Funston Avenue to reach the **Presidio Museum** ⑩, a 19th-century former hospital with exhibits on the history of the military in San Francisco. From here it's four blocks west on Lincoln to the Presidio Visitors Information Center on the corner of Lincoln and Montgomery Street.

Just before the visitor center, a turnoff on the right leads to **Fort Point** ⑪, a collection of military buildings sitting in the shadow of the Golden Gate Bridge; the highlight is the redbrick fortress directly underneath the bridge. To get to Fort Point, follow Lincoln Boulevard for a couple of miles, curving past a large cemetery. Just before the bridge you'll see a parking lot marked FORT POINT on the right. Park and follow the signs leading to Fort Point, walking downhill through a lightly wooded area; to the right is the old mine depot and to the left is the Fort Point defense fortification, which is open for tours. To walk the short distance to the **Golden Gate Bridge** ⑫, follow the signs from the Fort Point parking lot; to drive across the bridge, continue past the parking lot and watch for the turnoff on the right. If you're going to walk across the bridge, park in the Fort Point lot.

TIMING

If you drive, plan to spend at least three hours, not including a walk across the Golden Gate Bridge or hikes along the shoreline—each of which will take a few hours. If you're coming with kids, you'll probably want to budget extra time for the Exploratorium.

Sights to See

★ ♺ **Exploratorium.** The curious of all ages flock to this hands-on museum to enjoy and learn from some of the 600 exhibits. The dark, touchy-feely Tactile Dome is immensely popular. Regular science demonstrations (lasers, dissection of a cow's eye, and the like) begin around 10:30 each day. ✉ *Baker and Beach Sts.,* ☎ *415/561–0360 for general information or 415/561–0362 for required reservations for Tactile Dome.* 🎟 *$9; free 1st Wed. of month.* ☉ *Tues.–Sun. 10–5, Wed. until 9:30; official Mon. holidays 10–5.*

❼ **Fort Mason.** Originally a depot for the shipment of supplies to the Pacific during World War II, Fort Mason was converted into a cultural center in 1977. It now houses nonprofit museums (including the Mexican, Italian-American, Craft and Folk Art, and African-American), theaters, galleries, and some unusual shops. Most of the museums are closed on Monday and some also aren't open on Tuesday. ⊠ *Buchanan St. and Marina Blvd.,* ☎ *415/979–3010 for event information.*

⓫ Fort Point. Anticipating the Civil War, the U.S. Army constructed Fort Point between 1853 and 1861 to protect San Francisco from sea attack by Confederate forces. It was never used for that purpose, but was employed as a coastal defense fortification post during World War II. The national historic site is now a museum filled with military memorabilia. Guided group tours and cannon drills are offered daily by National Park rangers. The top floor affords a superb view of the bay. ⊠ *Lincoln Blvd. near Golden Gate Bridge,* ☎ *415/556–1693.* ▣ *Free.* ☼ *Wed.–Sun. 10–5.*

★ ⓬ Golden Gate Bridge. San Francisco's connection to Marin County has long wowed sightseers with its unique rust-color beauty and simple but powerful art deco design. Nearly 2 mi across, it is one of the longest bridges in the world—and also one of the strongest, made to withstand winds of more than 100 mi per hour. A vista point on the Marin side affords a spectacular view of the city. To get to the bridge from the Marina district, head north on Doyle Drive from Richardson Avenue or Marina Boulevard.

★ ❽ Palace of Fine Arts. San Francisco's rosy rococo Palace of Fine Arts is at the very end of the Marina. The palace is the sole survivor of the many tinted plaster buildings (a temporary classical city of sorts) built for the 1915 Panama-Pacific International Exposition. Bernard Maybeck designed the classic beauty, which was reconstructed in concrete and reopened in 1967, thanks to legions of sentimental citizens and a huge private donation. The massive columns, great rotunda (dedicated to the glory of Greek culture), and swan-filled lagoon have been used in countless fashion layouts and films. ⊠ *Baker and Beach Sts.,* ☎ *415/563–7337 for palace tours.*

❾ Presidio. Currently part of the Golden Gate National Recreation Area, the Presidio was a military post for more than 200 years. Don Juan Bautista de Anza and a band of Spanish settlers first claimed the area in 1776. It became a Mexican garrison in 1822 when Mexico gained its independence from Spain, until U.S. troops forcibly occupied it in 1846. The U.S. Sixth Army was stationed here until October 1994. The more than 1,400 acres of rolling hills, majestic woods, and redbrick army barracks present an air of serenity in the middle of the city. There are two beaches, a golf course, and picnic sites, and the views of the bay, the Golden Gate Bridge, and Marin County are sublime. The **Presidio Visitors Information Center** (⊠ Lincoln Blvd. and Montgomery St., ☎ 415/561–4323) has maps, brochures, and schedules for guided walking and bicycle tours. It's open daily from 10 to 5. ⊠ *Between Marina and Lincoln Park.*

❿ Presidio Museum. This museum in a former military hospital built in 1863 focuses on the role played by the military in San Francisco's development. Behind it are two cabins that housed refugees from the 1906 earthquake and fire. Photos on the wall of one cabin depict rows and rows of temporary shelters at the Presidio and in Golden Gate Park following the disaster. ⊠ *Lincoln Blvd. and Funston Ave.,* ☎ *415/561–4331.* ▣ *Free.* ☼ *Wed.–Sun. 10–4.*

Golden Gate Park

In 1887 Scotsman John McLaren transformed this desolate brush- and sand-covered expanse in the central-western part of San Francisco into a rolling, beautifully landscaped 1,000-acre oasis that stretches more than 2 mi and ends dramatically at the ocean. Because it is so large, the best way for many visitors to get from one end to the other is by car (though you'll want to do a lot of walking in between). On weekends you can park all day for $3 at the University of California at San Francisco garage (enter at Irving Street and 2nd Avenue); from there a shuttle leaves every 10 minutes for the park's museums. Muni also services the park. The No. 5 Fulton bus stops along its northern edge, and the N-Judah light-rail car stops one to two blocks south of the park. Much of the park east of Park Presidio Boulevard is closed to traffic on Sunday.

From May through October, free guided walking tours are offered every weekend by the Friends of Recreation and Parks (☎ 415/263–0991). If you plan to visit more than one attraction, consider purchasing a Golden Gate Explorer Pass ($12), which grants admission to the de Young and Asian Art museums, plus the California Academy of Sciences, the Japanese Tea Garden, and (when it reopens) the Conservatory. The passes are good for up to six months (the length depends on what time of year you buy the pass), so you can visit the attractions at your leisure. The passes can be purchased at any of the above sights or at TIX Bay Area in Union Square. Be forewarned: The fog can sweep into the park with amazing speed; always bring a sweatshirt or jacket.

Numbers in the text correspond to numbers in the margin and on the Golden Gate Park map.

A Good Walk
If you're coming from downtown, take a westbound Bus 5-Fulton or Bus 21-Hayes to Arguello Boulevard and Fulton Street, then walk south about 500 ft into the park to John F. Kennedy Drive. You can also take the N-Judah streetcar (underground part of the way) to many stops parallel to the park; from any stop past Arguello, walk north a couple of blocks.

A good place to start your Golden Gate Park tour is at the **Conservatory** ① and surrounding gardens, on Conservatory Drive near Fulton Street. Walk west on Conservatory Drive to the **M. H. de Young Memorial Museum** ② and the **Asian Art Museum** ③. Next to the Asian museum is the **Japanese Tea Garden** ④.

Coming out of the tea garden, cut across the Music Concourse, where outdoor concerts are sometimes held, to the **California Academy of Sciences** ⑤. To the west of the academy is a small but charming **Shakespeare Garden.** From here walk west to the main road, turn left, and follow its curves to **Strybing Arboretum & Botanical Gardens** ⑥. From Strybing walk west to peaceful **Stow Lake** ⑦. If you opt to walk the rest of the way to the ocean, you'll pass by several meadows, a stadium, a buffalo paddock, and a few small lakes. Just past the golf course and nearly at the ocean, you'll find the beautifully restored **Dutch Windmill** ⑧, an adjoining garden, and the restored **Beach Chalet.**

TIMING
You can easily spend a whole day in Golden Gate Park, especially if you walk the whole distance. Set aside an hour each for the Academy of Sciences, the Asian Art Museum, and the de Young Museum. Even if you plan to explore only the eastern end of the park (up to Stow Lake), allot at least four hours.

Sights to See
❸ **Asian Art Museum.** A world-famous collection of more than 12,000 sculptures, paintings, and ceramics from 40 countries, illustrating major periods of Asian art, is housed here. One standout permanent exhibit is the Leventritt Collection of blue-and-white porcelains. On the second floor are treasures from Iran, Turkey, Syria, India, Tibet, Nepal, Pakistan, Korea, Japan, Afghanistan, and Southeast Asia. There

Golden Gate Park

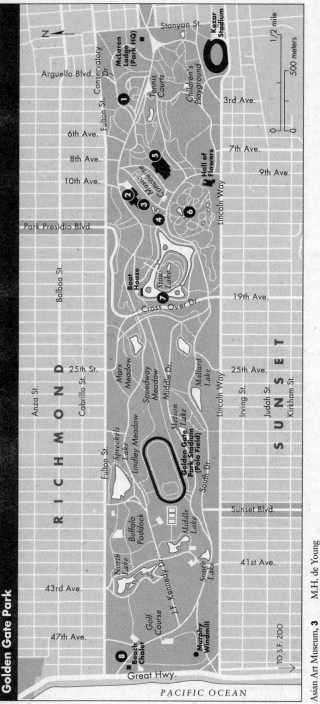

Asian Art Museum, **3**
California Academy of
Sciences, **5**
Conservatory, **1**
Dutch Windmill, **8**
Japanese Tea
Garden, **4**

M.H. de Young
Memorial Museum, **2**
Stow Lake, **7**
Strybing Arboretum &
Botanical Gardens, **6**

are daily guided tours. ⊠ *Tea Garden Dr. off John F. Kennedy Dr., near 10th Ave. and Fulton St.,* ☎ *415/668–8921.* 🎫 *$6 for both the Asian and de Young museums (additional $1 for same-day admission to Legion of Honor Museum in Lincoln Park).* ☉ *Wed.–Sun. 9:30–5, 1st Wed. of month until 8:45.*

★ **Beach Chalet.** This 1925 structure that overlooks Ocean Beach is one of architect Willis Polk's simpler designs, yet it still impresses. The chalet, which had been closed since the 1970s for renovations and lack of a suitable tenant, reopened to great fanfare in early 1997. A wraparound Work Projects Administration mural depicts San Francisco in the 1930s; the labels describing the various panels add up to a minihistory of Depression-era life in the city. A three-dimensional model of the park, artifacts from the 1894 Mid-Winter Exposition and other park events, and a visitor center are all here as well. On a clear day, the brew pub–restaurant upstairs (notice the carved bannister on the way up) has views of the Farralon Islands three dozen miles away. ⊠ *On the Great Hwy., south of Fulton St.*

👆 ❺ **California Academy of Sciences.** One of the country's top natural history museums houses an aquarium and a planetarium, plus numerous exhibits. The **Steinhart Aquarium,** with its dramatic 100,000-gallon Fish Roundabout, contains 14,000 creatures, including a living coral reef with colorful fish, tropical sharks, and a rainbow of hard and soft corals. The "Touch Tide Pool" allows kids to cozy up to starfish, hermit crabs, and other sea creatures. Other exhibits include a floor that simulates various-level earthquakes, life-size elephant-seal models, and the **African Hall,** depicting animals (real but stuffed) specific to Africa in their native vegetation.

There is an additional charge (up to $2.50) for **Morrison Planetarium** shows (☎ 415/750–7145 for daily schedule). The Laserium presents evening laser light shows (☎ 415/750–7138 for schedule and fees) at Morrison Planetarium, accompanied by rock, classical, and other types of music; educational shows outline laser technology. Around the southeast corner of the building is the **Shakespeare Garden,** with 200 flowers mentioned by the Bard, as well as engraved bronze panels with floral quotations. ⊠ *Music Concourse Dr. off South Dr., across from Asian Art and de Young museums,* ☎ *415/750–7145.* 🎫 *$7; $1 discount with Muni transfer; free 1st Wed. of month.* ☉ *Memorial Day–Labor Day, daily 9–6; Labor Day–Memorial Day, daily 10–5.*

❶ **Conservatory.** The oldest building in the park (built in 1876) and the last remaining wood-frame Victorian conservatory in the country, the Conservatory is a copy of London's famous Kew Gardens. Because of damage from a 1995 storm, the Conservatory is closed indefinitely, but its outdoor gardens are still being maintained. ⊠ *Conservatory Dr. near Fulton St.,* ☎ *415/362–0808.*

❽ **Dutch Windmill.** At the very western end of the park is a restored 1902 windmill with a wood-shingled upper section and a heavy cement bottom. The windmill overlooks the curvy, photogenic **Queen Wilhelmina Tulip Garden,** which blooms in early spring and late summer. ⊠ *Off Fulton St. between 47th Ave. and the Great Hwy.*

❹ **Japanese Tea Garden.** This serene 4-acre landscape of small ponds, streams, waterfalls, stone bridges, Japanese sculptures, bonsai trees, miniature pagodas, and some nearly vertical wooden "humpback" bridges was created for the 1894 Mid-Winter Exposition. The Tea House is a popular spot for relaxing. Go in the spring if you can, when the cherry blossoms bloom. ⊠ *Tea Garden Dr. off John F. Kennedy Dr.,* ☎ *415/752–4227.* 🎫 *$2.50.* ☉ *Daily 8:30–6:30 (closes earlier in winter).*

❷ M. H. de Young Memorial Museum. The de Young contains the best collection of American art on the West Coast, including paintings, sculpture, textiles, and decorative arts from colonial times through the 20th century. The John D. Rockefeller III Collection of American Paintings is especially noteworthy, with more than 200 paintings of American masters such as Copley, Eakins, Bingham, and Sargent. The de Young also exhibits African, Native American, and Meso-American art, including sculpture, baskets, textiles, and ceramics. The **Café de Young** has outdoor seating in the Oakes Garden. ⊠ *Tea Garden Dr. off John F. Kennedy Dr., near 10th Ave. and Fulton St.,* ☎ *415/863–3330 for 24-hr information.* ☞ *$6 for both the de Young and Asian museums (additional $1 for same-day admission to Legion of Honor Museum in Lincoln Park); free 1st Wed. of month until 5.* ☉ *Wed.–Sun. 9:30– 5, 1st Wed. of month until 8:45.*

❼ Stow Lake. This small body of water surrounds Strawberry Hill; a couple of bridges allow visitors to cross over and ascend the hill. A waterfall cascades down from the top of the hill; panoramic views make it worth the short hike up here. Down below, rent a boat or a bicycle (☎ 415/752–0347) or stroll around the perimeter. ⊠ *Off John F. Kennedy Dr. east of Crossover Dr.*

❻ Strybing Arboretum & Botanical Gardens. The 70-acre arboretum specializes in plants from areas with climates similar to that of the Bay Area, such as South Africa, the Mediterranean, and the west coast of Australia; more than 8,000 plants and tree varieties bloom in gardens throughout the grounds. Group walks or children's walks can be arranged (☎ 415/661–3584), and Strybing regularly hosts classes, lectures, and plant sales. ⊠ *9th Ave. at Lincoln Way,* ☎ *415/661–1316.* ☞ *Free.* ☉ *Weekdays 8–4:30, weekends 10–5. Tours leave bookstore weekdays at 1:30, weekends at 10:30.*

OFF THE BEATEN PATH

THE HAIGHT – East of Golden Gate Park is the neighborhood known as "the Haight." Despite the presence of a Gap store (on the legendary Haight-Ashbury corner, no less) and a growing number of upscale galleries and shops, this is still home to anarchist book collectives and shops selling incense and tie-dye T-shirts. Even a few "smoke shops" remain from the area's 1960s flower-power heyday. The Haight's famous political spirit—it was the first neighborhood in the United States to lead a revolt against freeways, and it continues to host regular (sometimes successful) boycotts against chain stores—exists alongside some of the finest Victorian-lined streets in the city; more than 1,000 such houses occupy Golden Gate Park's "Panhandle" and the streets of Ashbury Heights. Haight Street itself is known for its vintage merchandise, including clothes, records, books, and a host of miscellany such as crystals, jewelry, and candles. The house at 710 Ashbury Street, just past Waller Street, was the '60s crash pad of Jerry Garcia and his Grateful Dead bandmates.

Lincoln Park and the Western Shoreline

From Land's End in Lincoln Park are some of the best views of the Golden Gate (the name was originally given to the opening of San Francisco Bay long before the bridge was built) and the Marin Headlands. Ocean Beach and the Great Highway run along the western edge of the city from just below the historic Cliff House to the San Francisco Zoo.

A Good Drive

A car is useful for exploring this stretch. There are plenty of hiking trails, and buses service most of the sights, but the distances between some are fairly great. Start at **Lincoln Park,** at 34th Avenue (the extension into the park is sometimes called Legion of Honor Drive) and Clement Street; those without a car can take Bus 38-Geary to get here. Within Lincoln Park is the **California Palace of the Legion of Honor.** From the museum, head back out on Legion of Honor Drive to Geary Boulevard, one block south of Clement, and follow Geary west until it forks to the right (past 39th Avenue) and becomes Point Lobos Avenue. Just past 48th Avenue is parking for the **Cliff House.** Three-mile-long **Ocean Beach** begins just south of the Cliff House, flanked by the Great Highway. A couple of miles down, at the intersection of the Great Highway and Sloat Boulevard, is the **San Francisco Zoo.** If you're coming to the zoo from downtown, you can take the L-Taraval Muni streetcar directly.

TIMING
This tour requires about three hours—more if you don't have a car. Plan on spending an hour at the Palace of the Legion of Honor or the zoo.

Sights to See
California Palace of the Legion of Honor. This ¾-scale adaptation of the 18th-century French original sits on a cliff overlooking the ocean, the Golden Gate Bridge, and the Marin Headlands. The 20-plus galleries on the upper level are devoted to the permanent collection of European art (paintings, sculpture, decorative arts, tapestries) from the 14th through the 20th centuries. The Rodin collection is noteworthy—an original cast of Rodin's *The Thinker* welcomes you as you walk through the Legion's courtyard. The lower level showcases prints and drawings, English and European porcelain, and ancient Assyrian, Greek, Roman, and Egyptian art; it also contains galleries for special exhibitions.

The **Legion Café** on the lower level has a garden terrace and a view of the Golden Gate Bridge. North of the museum (across Camino del Mar) is George Segal's *The Holocaust,* a sobering monument whose white-plaster figures lie sprawled and twisted on the ground, while one lone figure peers out from behind barbed wire. ⊠ *34th Ave. at Clement St.,* ☎ *415/863–3330 for 24-hr information.* 🖾 *$7, free 2nd Wed. of month.* ☉ *Tues.–Sun. 9:30–5, 1st Sat. of month until 8:45.*

Cliff House. This San Francisco landmark has had three incarnations. The original, built in 1863, hosted several U.S. presidents and wealthy locals who would drive their carriages out to Ocean Beach; it was destroyed by fire on Christmas Day 1894. The second and most beloved Cliff House was built in 1896; it rose eight stories with an observation tower 200 ft above sea level. It also succumbed to fire, a year after surviving the 1906 quake. The present building, erected in 1909, has restaurants, a pub, and a gift shop. The dining areas overlook Seal Rock (the barking marine mammals sunning themselves are actually sea lions).

Just below the Cliff House is the **Musée Mécanique** (☎ 415/386–1170), a time-warped arcade with a collection of antique mechanical contrivances, including peep shows and nickelodeons. Some of the favorites are the giant, rather creepy "Laughing Sal," an arm-wrestling machine, and mechanical fortune-telling figures who speak from their curtained boxes. An especially disturbing display is the "Opium-Den," a tiny diorama with Chinese figures clearly depicting the effects of heavy drug use. The museum is open daily; admission is free, but you may want to bring a few quarters or singles to play the many games.

The Musée Mécanique looks out on a fine observation deck and the **Golden Gate National Recreation Area Visitors' Center** (☎ 415/556–8642), which contains historic photographs of the Cliff House and the glass-roof **Sutro Baths** complex, which covered 3 acres just north of the

Cliff House. The baths were closed in 1952 and burned down in 1966. You can explore the ruins on your own or take ranger-led walks on weekends. ⊠ *1090 Point Lobos Ave.,* ☎ *415/386–3330.* ⊙ *Weekdays 8 AM–10:30 PM, weekends 8 AM–11 PM; cocktails served nightly until 2 AM.*

Lincoln Park. At one time all the city's cemeteries were here, segregated by nationality. In their place is an 18-hole golf course with large and well-formed Monterey cypresses lining the fairways. There are scenic walks throughout the 275-acre park, with postcard-perfect views from many spots, especially **Land's End** (the trail starts outside the Palace of the Legion of Honor, at the end of El Camino del Mar). The trails out to Land's End, however, are for skilled hikers only: Landslides are frequent, and danger lurks along the steep cliffs. ⊠ *Entrance at 34th Ave. at Clement St.*

Ocean Beach. Stretching 3 mi along the western (Pacific) side of the city, this is a beautiful beach for walking, running, or lying in the sun—but not for swimming. Surfers here wear wet suits year-round; the water is extremely cold. Paths on both sides of the Great Highway lead from Lincoln Avenue to Sloat Boulevard (near the zoo); the beachside path winds through landscaped sand dunes, while the paved path across the highway is good for biking and rollerblading. ⊠ *Along the Great Hwy. from the Cliff House to Sloat Blvd. and beyond.*

ⓒ **San Francisco Zoo.** First established in 1889 in Golden Gate Park, the zoo is home to more than 1,000 species of birds and animals, 130 of which are designated as endangered. Among the protected are the snow leopard, the Sumatran tiger, the jaguar, and the Asian elephant. A favorite attraction is the greater one-horned rhinoceros, next to the African elephants. **Gorilla World** is one of the largest and most natural gorilla habitats of any zoo in the world. The **Primate Discovery Center** houses 14 endangered species in atriumlike enclosures. The **Feline Conservation Center,** a large naturalistic setting for rare cats, is designed to encourage breeding among endangered felines. Don't miss the big cat feeding—they love their horse meat—Tuesday through Sunday at 2. The 7-acre **South American Gateway** exhibit re-creates habitats replete with howler monkeys, tapirs, and a cloud forest. The children's zoo has a minipopulation of about 300 mammals, birds, and reptiles, plus an insect zoo, a baby-animal nursery, and a beautifully restored 1921 Dentzel Carousel. A ride astride one of the 52 hand-carved animals costs $1. ⊠ *Sloat Blvd. and the Great Hwy.,* ☎ *415/753–7083.* ⊡ *$7; free 1st Wed. of month; children's zoo $1.* ⊙ *Daily 10–5; children's zoo weekdays 11–4, weekends 10:30–4:30.*

DINING

By Sharon Silva

San Francisco probably has more restaurants per capita than any other city in the United States, including New York. Practically every ethnic cuisine is represented. Most upper-end restaurants offer valet parking—worth considering in crowded neighborhoods such as North Beach, Union Square, Nob Hill, the Richmond District, and the Civic Center. There is often a nominal charge and a time-length restriction on validated parking.

CATEGORY	COST*
$$$$	over $50
$$$	$30–$50
$$	$20–$30
$	under $20

per person for a three-course meal, excluding drinks, service, and 8½% sales tax

American

Castro

$$ ✕ **2223.** Dishes at John Cunin's restaurant (also known as the No-Name) include thin-crust pizza topped with pancetta and Teleme cheese, earthy seasonal soups, chicken with garlic mashed potatoes, and Thai shrimp salad with sesame. For Sunday brunch there might be French toast or eggs Benedict on a tasty herb scone. ✉ *2223 Market St.,* ☎ *415/431–0692. MC, V. No lunch Sat.*

Civic Center

$$$ ✕ **Stars.** Jeremiah Tower's dining room has a clublike ambience, and
★ the food ranges from grills to ragouts to sautés—some daringly creative and some classical. Dinners here are pricey, but those on a budget can order a hot dog, pizza, or stylish chicken tacos at the bar. ✉ *150 Redwood Alley, off Van Ness Ave.,* ☎ *415/861–7827. Reservations essential. AE, DC, MC, V. No lunch weekends.*

$$ ✕ **Carta.** Each month Carta's talented chefs concoct a menu from a different country or region—Oaxaca, Turkey, Russia, Provence, Morocco, and New England are among the places represented to date. There are usually about 10 small plates, three main courses, and perhaps three desserts. ✉ *1772 Market St.,* ☎ *415/863–3516. AE, MC, V. Closed Mon. No lunch weekends.*

Cow Hollow/Marina

$$ ✕ **Perry's.** This watering hole and meeting place for the button-down singles set serves good, honest saloon food—London broil, corned beef hash, one of the best hamburgers in town, and a great breakfast. Brunch is served on weekends. A second Perry's is located downtown. ✉ *1944 Union St.,* ☎ *415/922–9022;* ✉ *185 Sutter St.,* ☎ *415/989–6895. AE, MC, V.*

$ ✕ **World Wrapps.** This hip eatery serves what are essentially global burritos: Fillings range from Peking duck to Thai chicken, from roasted vegetables to couscous and cucumber. A wide selection of healthful smoothies—papaya, blackberry, and the like—matches up surprisingly well with the hearty wrapps. ✉ *2257 Chestnut St.,* ☎ *415/563–9727;* ✉ *2227 Polk St.,* ☎ *415/931–9727. No credit cards.*

Embarcadero North

$$ ✕ **Fog City Diner.** The long, narrow dining room emulates a luxurious railroad car. The menu is innovative, drawing its inspiration from regional cooking throughout the United States. Try the pork chop with plum "ketchup," the barbecued rabbit with cheddar grits and warm greens, or the shrimp and scallop fisherman's pie. ✉ *1300 Battery St.,* ☎ *415/982–2000. D, DC, MC, V.*

$$ ✕ **MacArthur Park.** Year after year San Franciscans pronounce this handsomely renovated pre-earthquake warehouse their favorite spot for ribs, but the oak-wood smoker and mesquite grill also turn out a wide variety of all-American fare, from steaks and hamburgers to seafood. ✉ *607 Front St.,* ☎ *415/398–5700. AE, DC, MC, V. No lunch weekends.*

Embarcadero South

$$–$$$ ✕ **Boulevard.** Nationally acclaimed chef Nancy Oakes's menu is seasonally in flux, but you will always find her signature juxtaposition of aristocratic fare—foie gras is a favorite—with homey comfort foods like maple-cured pork loin. The weekday afternoon bistro service is less formal and expensive than regular dining. ✉ *1 Mission St.,* ☎ *415/543–6084. Reservations essential. AE, D, DC, MC, V. No lunch weekends.*

$$–$$$ ✕ **One Market.** The bustling bilevel brasserie of Bradley Ogden and Michael Dellar seats 170, and a large bar-café serves snacks from noon on. Soft-shell crabs and locally caught fish are among the spe-

114

Downtown San Francisco Dining

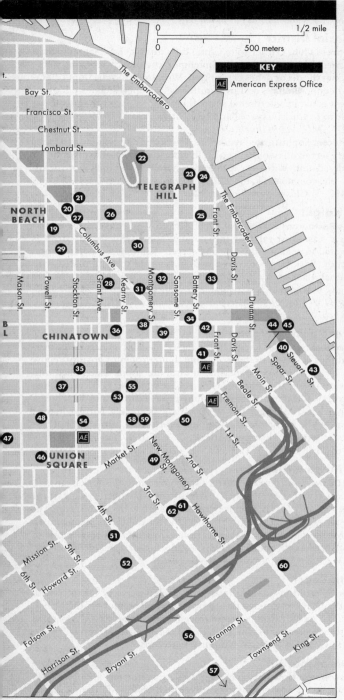

cialties. ⊠ *1 Market St.,* ☎ *415/777–5577. Reservations essential. AE, DC, MC, V. Closed Sun. No lunch Sat.*

Financial District

$$$ ✕ **Cypress Club.** Owner John Cunin calls this place a "San Francisco brasserie." This categorizes the contemporary American cooking somewhat, but the decor defies description. With stone mosaic floors, hammered copper arches, and overstuffed velvet upholstery, the look of Cypress could be interpreted as anything from a parody of an ancient temple to a futuristic space bar. ⊠ *500 Jackson St.,* ☎ *415/296–8555. AE, DC, MC, V. No lunch.*

$$$ ✕ **Rubicon.** Sophisticated renditions of seafood and poultry and other fare are served on two floors to Hollywood big shots—the investor list includes Robin Williams, Robert De Niro, and Francis Ford Coppola—and common folk, too. ⊠ *558 Sacramento St.,* ☎ *415/434–4100. AE, MC, V. Closed Sun. No lunch Sat.*

The Haight

$$ ✕ **Eos Restaurant & Wine Bar.** Chef Arnold Wong has created an impressive East-West table at this popular spot. Grilled skirt steak is marinated in a Thai red curry and served with mashed potatoes and bok choy. Pork loin is flavored with ginger and soy and paired with Southeast Asian sticky rice. The wine bar next door shelves some 400 vintages, any of which is available at your dining table. ⊠ *901 Cole St.,* ☎ *415/566–3063. Reservations essential. AE, MC, V. Closed Sun. No lunch.*

Lower Pacific Heights

$$ ✕ **The Meetinghouse.** A regularly changing menu of modernized American dishes is served in this appealing dining room of creamy yellow walls, broad plank floors, and Shaker furniture. Johnnycakes filled with rock shrimp and accompanied with a colorful pepper relish are among the most popular first courses. Hominy-crusted catfish and duck breast with cornmeal crisps are among the satisfying entrées. Partner Joanna Karlinsky, the house bread baker and pastry chef, turns out hot biscuits and wonderful berry shortcakes. ⊠ *1701 Octavia St.,* ☎ *415/ 922–6733. AE, MC, V. Closed Mon.–Tues. No lunch.*

The Mission District

$$ ✕ **42 Degrees.** Just next door to the Esprit outlet store, this sleek industrial-style space with a curving metal staircase and a seductive view of the bay is a magnet for the younger crowd with a few bucks to spend. The name refers to the latitude of Provence, and the California menu infused with Mediterranean touches ranges from calves' liver with grilled onions to duck breast with fiddlehead ferns. ⊠ *235 16th St.,* ☎ *415/777–5559. MC, V. Closed Sun. No dinner Mon.–Tues.*

North Beach

$$ ✕ **Bix.** This old-fashioned supper club is reminiscent of a theater, with a bustling bar and dining tables downstairs and banquettes on the balcony. The menu offers contemporary renditions of classic American fare; there's piano music in the evenings. ⊠ *56 Gold St.,* ☎ *415/433– 6300. AE, D, DC, MC, V. No lunch weekends.*

South of Market

$$$ ✕ **Hawthorne Lane.** The large high-ceiling bar at this popular SoMa eatery serves a selection of irresistible small plates—Thai-style squid, tempura-battered green beans with mustard sauce, stylish pizzas. Patrons in the light-flooded dining room engage in more serious eating, from foie gras to grilled quail. ⊠ *22 Hawthorne St.,* ☎ *415/777–9779. Reservations essential. D, DC, MC, V. No lunch weekends.*

$$ ✕ **Infusion Bar and Restaurant.** "Infusion" refers to the bevy of glass decanters lined up like foot soldiers behind the sleek wood bar of this up-to-the-minute SoMa destination. They hold flavored vodkas— mango, chili, anise, coconut. Many folks sip one of the enhanced spirits while dipping into a tasty appetizer such as an iron skillet of roasted mussels or a hillock of batter-fried calamari. Entrées range from meats to pastas. The live music starts up at 9, so eat early if you are looking for a tranquil repast. ⊠ *555 2nd St.,* ☎ *415/543–2282. AE, DC, MC, V.*

Sunset District

$$ ✕ **Beach Chalet.** In a historic colonnaded building with handsome murals depicting San Francisco in the mid-1930s, this San Francisco newcomer is *the* place to watch the sun set over the Pacific while indulging in fine microbrews and eclectic American fare—steamed mussels and pizzette, house-made chorizo and seafood gumbo, and the like. ⊠ *1000 Great Hwy.,* ☎ *415/386–8439. Reservations essential. MC, V.*

Union Square

$$$–$$$$ ✕ **Postrio.** Superchef Wolfgang Puck periodically commutes from Los Angeles to make an appearance in his restaurant's open kitchen. A three-
★ level bar and dining area is highlighted by palm trees and museum-quality contemporary paintings. Attire is formal; food is Puckish Californian with Mediterranean and Asian overtones, emphasizing pastas, grilled seafood, and house-baked breads. Substantial breakfast and bar menus (with great pizza) can be found here as well. ⊠ *545 Post St.,* ☎ *415/776–7825. Reservations essential. AE, D, DC, MC, V.*

$$$ ✕ **Campton Place.** Chef Todd Humphries carries on the innovative traditions of opening chef Bradley Ogden with great aplomb and has added
★ his own touches, embellishing traditional American dishes with ethnic flavors. Those who wish to sample a fuller range of Humphries's culinary accomplishments can order the six-course tasting menu, which stretches from caviar to squab. His delightfully crumbly cornbread can be addictive. Breakfast and brunch are major events. A bar menu offers samplings of some appetizers plus a caviar extravaganza. ⊠ *340 Stockton St.,* ☎ *415/955–5555. Reservations essential. AE, D, DC, MC, V.*

$$ ✕ **Grand Café.** This beaux arts establishment draws crowds from early morning until late at night. The dramatic dining room, formerly a hotel ballroom, is decorated with cabaret-style murals, striking chandeliers, and large booths. The more casual bar area has dozens of pen-and-ink cartoon sketches. The café's menu is French-California, with an emphasis on seasonal local ingredients. ⊠ *Hotel Monaco, 501 Geary St.,* ☎ *415/292–0101. AE, D, DC, MC, V.*

Chinese

Chinatown

$–$$ ✕ **Great Eastern.** Large tanks in the busy Great Eastern dining room contain Dungeness crabs, black bass, abalone, catfish, shrimp, rock cod, and other creatures of the sea; a wall-hung menu in both Chinese and English specifies their cost. Sea conch stir-fried with yellow chives, crab with vermicelli in a clay pot, and steamed fresh scallops with garlic sauce are among the many specialties. In the wee hours Chinese night owls often drop in for a plate of noodles or a bowl of *congee* (rice gruel). ⊠ *649 Jackson St.,* ☎ *415/986–2550. AE, MC, V.*

$–$$ ✕ **R&G Lounge.** Downstairs (entrance on Kearny Street) is a usually packed no-tablecloth dining room; the classier upstairs space (entrance on Commercial Street) serves exceptional Cantonese banquet fare. A menu with photographs helps diners decide among the many exotic dishes, from dried scallops with seasonal vegetables to steamed bean curd with shrimp meat. ⊠ *631 Kearny St.,* ☎ *415/982–7877 or 415/982–3811. AE, DC, MC, V.*

Embarcadero North

$$ ✕ **Harbor Village.** Classic Cantonese cooking, dim sum lunches, and fresh seafood from the restaurant's tanks are the hallmarks of this 400-seat branch of a Hong Kong establishment. The setting is opulent, with Chinese antiques and teak furnishings. There's validated parking at the Embarcadero Center Garage. ⊠ *4 Embarcadero Center,* ☎ *415/781–8833. AE, DC, MC, V.*

Financial District

$ ✕ **Yank Sing.** The city's oldest teahouse remains among the best purveyors of the bite-size Chinese specialties—fried dumplings, steamed shrimp in rice noodles, parchment chicken, and the like—known as dim sum. ⊠ *427 Battery St.,* ☎ *415/362–1640;* ⊠ *49 Stevenson St.,* ☎ *415/541–4949. AE, DC, MC, V. Stevenson branch closed weekends. No dinner.*

Richmond District

$$ ✕ **Hong Kong Flower Lounge.** This outpost of a famous Asian restaurant is known in particular for its seafood—crabs, shrimp, catfish, lobsters, scallops—which is plucked straight from tanks and prepared in a variety of ways, from classic to contemporary. Dim sum is offered at midday. ⊠ *5322 Geary Blvd.,* ☎ *415/668–8998. AE, D, DC, MC, V.*

$–$$ ✕ **Ton Kiang.** Regional Hakka specialties served here include salt-baked chicken, braised stuffed bean curd, wine-flavored dishes, delicate fish and beef balls, and casseroles of meat and seafood cooked in clay pots. Of the two branches on Geary Boulevard, the one at 5821 is more stylish and serves excellent dim sum. ⊠ *3148 Geary Blvd.,* ☎ *415/752–4440;* ⊠ *5821 Geary Blvd.,* ☎ *415/387–8273. MC, V.*

French

Civic Center

$$–$$$ ✕ **California Culinary Academy.** Patrons watch student chefs at work on a double-tier stage while dining on classic French cooking offered as a prix fixe meal or a bountiful buffet. On the lower level is an informal à la carte grill. ⊠ *625 Polk St.,* ☎ *415/771–3500. Reservations essential for Fri.-night buffet. AE, DC, MC, V. Closed weekends; hrs vary slightly with school programs.*

Cow Hollow/Marina

$$ ✕ **Bistro Aix.** Named for the southern French town of Aix-en-Provence, this lively bistro with light wood banquettes, a heated patio, and friendly service attracts diners from the surrounding neighborhood and beyond. On weekdays a two-course prix fixe dinner includes a choice of soup or salad followed by roast chicken, top sirloin, or seafood pasta—for not much more than the price of a movie ticket. Addictive cracker-crust pizzas, superb steamed mussels, and house-baked breads are additional draws. ⊠ *3340 Steiner St.,* ☎ *415/202–0100. MC, V. No lunch.*

$–$$ ✕ **Cassis Bistro.** This sunny yellow operation recalls small bistros tucked away on side streets in French seaside towns. The food—onion tart, sautéed chicken breast, veal ragout, braised rabbit—is comfortingly home style. ⊠ *2120 Greenwich St.,* ☎ *415/292–0770. No credit cards. Closed Sun.–Mon. No lunch.*

Embarcadero North

$$ ✕ **Pastis.** At lunchtime the sunny cement bar and sleek wooden banquettes of chef-owner Gerald Hirigoyen's restaurant are crowded with workers from surrounding offices; they come to fuel up on steamed salmon with celery root or grilled prawns marinated in *pastis* (anise-

flavored French liqueur). The evening menu might include seared scallops, braised oxtails, or duck confit. ⊠ *1015 Battery St.,* ☎ *415/391–2555. AE, MC, V. Closed Sun. No lunch Sat.*

$$ ✕ **Plouf.** This sleek spot, whose catchy name means "splash," serves mussels in seven generously portioned, reasonably priced preparations, among them *marinière* (garlic and parsley), apple cider, leeks and cream, and crayfish and tomato. Main courses run the gamut from steak *frites* (with matchstick fries) to steamed sea bass. French vintages are well represented on the carefully selected wine list. ⊠ *40 Belden Pl.,* ☎ *415/986–6491. MC, V. Closed Sun. No lunch Sat.*

$ ✕ **Café Claude.** With a zinc bar, old-fashioned banquettes, and cinema posters, this is one of the most atmospheric French cafés downtown. Order a croque monsieur, salade niçoise, or simple daube and you'll soon be whistling the "Marseillaise." ⊠ *7 Claude La.,* ☎ *415/392–3505. AE, DC, MC, V. Closed Sun.*

Midtown

$$$ ✕ **La Folie.** This pretty storefront café showcases the nouvelle cuisine of
★ Roland Passot. Much of the food is edible art—whimsical presentations in the form of savory terrines, *galettes* (flat, round cakes), and napoleons—or elegant accompaniments such as bone-marrow flan. ⊠ *2316 Polk St.,* ☎ *415/776–5577. AE, D, DC, MC, V. Closed Sun. No lunch.*

Nob Hill

$$$–$$$$ ✕ **Ritz-Carlton Dining Room and Terrace.** There are two distinctly dif-
★ ferent places to eat in this neoclassical Nob Hill showplace. The formal Dining Room has a harpist playing; it serves only three- to five-course French dinners with Bay Area touches. The executive chef is Sylvain Portay, formerly of New York's Le Cirque. Chef Paul Murphy oversees the more casual French-California menu at the cheerful Terrace, which has a large garden patio for outdoor dining. The Terrace serves breakfast, lunch, dinner, and a Sunday jazz brunch, with piano music at lunchtime and a jazz trio at weekend dinners. ⊠ *600 Stockton St.,* ☎ *415/296–7465. AE, D, DC, MC, V. Closed Sun. No lunch.*

North Beach

$ ✕ **Des Alpes.** Basque dinners at rock-bottom prices are the big draw here: Soup, salad, *two* entrées—sweetbreads on puff pastry and rare roast beef are a typical pair—ice cream, and coffee are all included in the price. Service is family style. ⊠ *732 Broadway,* ☎ *415/788–9900. D, DC, MC, V. Closed Mon. No lunch.*

Richmond District

$$–$$$ ✕ **Alain Rondelli.** Chef Rondelli adapts his background in classic yet
★ contemporary French cooking to the agricultural abundance and Asian-Hispanic influences of California: a zap of jalapeño chili here, a bit of star anise there. Two-part entrées are a Rondelli signature: a breast of chicken followed with a confit of the leg in a custard tart, for example. ⊠ *126 Clement St.,* ☎ *415/387–0408. MC, V. Closed Mon.–Tues.*

South of Market

$$ ✕ **Fringale.** The bright yellow paint on this dazzling bistro stands out
★ like a beacon on an otherwise bleak industrial street. Biarritz-born chef Gerald Hirigoyen serves French Basque–inspired creations; his *frisée aux lardons* (grilled scallops) and crème brûlée are classics. ⊠ *570 4th St.,* ☎ *415/543–0573. Reservations essential. AE, MC, V. Closed Sun. No lunch Sat.*

Union Square

$$$$ ✕ **Fleur de Lys.** The menu changes constantly at this award-winning restaurant; lobster bisque, Maryland crab cakes, seared venison medallions, and veal on a bed of wild mushrooms bear witness to chef-partner Hu-

bert Keller's international scope. The intimate dining room, like a sheikh's tent, is encased with hundreds of yards of paisley. ⊠ *777 Sutter St.,* ☎ *415/673–7779. Reservations essential. Jacket required. AE, DC, MC, V. Closed Sun.*

$$$$ ✕ **Masa's.** Presentation is as important as the food itself in this pretty,
★ flower-filled dining spot in the Vintage Court Hotel. Decadent ingredients such as foie gras and black truffles are incorporated into chef Julian Serrano's recipes. Try the napoleon of alternating slices of potato and lobster doused in a saffron dressing or any of the savory first-course tarts. ⊠ *648 Bush St.,* ☎ *415/989–7154. Reservations essential. Jacket and tie. AE, D, DC, MC, V. Closed Sun.–Mon. and 1st 2 wks of Jan. No lunch.*

Greek and Middle Eastern

Financial District

$$ ✕ **Faz.** Creamy *baba ghanoush* (eggplant spread), beef-and-rice-filled dolmas, and a Persian-inspired platter of feta cheese, pungent olives, and garden-fresh herbs are all great choices here. The signature smoked-fish platter includes salmon, trout, and sometimes sturgeon. ⊠ *161 Sutter St.,* ☎ *415/362–0404. AE, DC, MC, V. Closed Sun. No lunch Sat.*

North Beach

$$ ✕ **Maykadeh.** Lamb dishes with rice are the specialties of this authentic Persian restaurant, whose setting is so elegant that the modest check comes as a great surprise. The kabobs and pilafs are particularly good. ⊠ *470 Green St.,* ☎ *415/362–8286. MC, V.*

$ ✕ **Helmand.** Authentic Afghani cooking, elegant surroundings with white napery and rich Afghan carpets, and amazingly low prices make Helmand worth a visit. Don't miss the *aushak* (leek-filled ravioli served with yogurt and ground beef). The lamb dishes are also exceptional. There's free nighttime validated parking at Helmand Parking at 468 Broadway. ⊠ *430 Broadway,* ☎ *415/362–0641. AE, MC, V. No lunch weekends.*

Indian

The Haight

$$ ✕ **Indian Oven.** The tandoori chef at this handsome storefront restaurant has mastered the intricacies of northern Indian clay-oven cooking, consistently turning out flavorful meats and breads. There's an excellent roasted eggplant dish; the chicken curries and crisp vegetable *pakoras* (fritters), served with a sprightly tamarind chutney, are another good bet. ⊠ *223 Fillmore St.,* ☎ *415/626–1628. MC, V. No lunch.*

Northern Waterfront and Embarcadero

$$ ✕ **Gaylord's.** Mildly spiced northern Indian food is served here, along with meats and breads from the tandoori ovens and several vegetarian dishes. The dining rooms are elegantly appointed, complete with Indian paintings and gleaming silver service. The Ghirardelli Square location has bay views. Both locations offer validated parking. ⊠ *Ghirardelli Sq.,* ☎ *415/771–8822;* ⊠ *Embarcadero 1,* ☎ *415/397–7775. AE, D, DC, MC, V. No lunch Sun. at Embarcadero.*

Italian

Civic Center

$$$ ✕ **Vivande Ristorante.** Owner-chef Carlo Middione's spacious restaurant features the rustic fare of southern Italy, from focaccia with grilled radicchio and fennel to pasta tossed with a tangle of mushrooms to grilled lamb chops. A late-supper menu attracts the Performing Arts Center crowd. ⊠ *670 Golden Gate Ave.,* ☎ *415/673–9245. AE, DC, MC, V.*

Cow Hollow/Marina

$$ ✕ **Pane e Vino.** The Italian-born owner-chef of Pane e Vino concentrates
★ on specialties from Tuscany and the North. Roasted whole sea bass, creamy
risotto, and pastas with tomato sauces are among the dishes regulars can't
resist. ⊠ *3011 Steiner St.,* ☎ *415/346–2111. MC, V. No lunch Sun.*

$$ ✕ **Zinzino.** Thin pizzas at this animated restaurant are topped with
prosciutto and arugula or fennel sausage and caramelized onions. A
mound of lump-free mashed potatoes imaginatively flavored with Chi-
anti accompanies a thick beef tenderloin. A moist roast half chicken
is paired with a salad of frisée, warm potatoes, and goat cheese. For
dessert, try the roasted apple with vanilla-bean ice cream and caramel
sauce. ⊠ *2355 Chestnut St.,* ☎ *415/346–6623. MC, V. No lunch.*

Embarcadero North

$$ ✕ **Il Fornaio.** This handsome tile-floored, wood-paneled complex com-
bines a café, bakery, and upscale trattoria with outdoor seating. The
Tuscan cooking features pizzas from a wood-burning oven, superb pas-
tas and gnocchi, and grilled poultry and seafood. ⊠ *Levi's Plaza,
1265 Battery St.,* ☎ *415/986–0100. AE, DC, MC, V.*

$$ ✕ **Oritalia.** The name says it all—the Orient and Italy. Chef Bruce Hill's
fusion cuisine is delightful: Korean beef with sesame seeds, and crispy
shrimp and pork dumplings with cilantro-mint sauce are among the
offerings. ⊠ *1915 Fillmore St.,* ☎ *415/346–1333. AE, DC, MC, V.
No lunch.*

North Beach

$$$ ✕ **Julius' Castle.** The view from this legendary Telegraph Hill restau-
rant is arguably the best in the city: You can see both bridges, Trea-
sure Island, Alcatraz, sailboats skimming along the water, and the
East Bay hills. The grilled salmon fillet with fava beans and caramelized
onions is a good choice, as is the pheasant with seared polenta. ⊠ *1541
Montgomery St.,* ☎ *415/392–2222. Reservations essential. AE, DC,
MC, V. No lunch.*

$$ ✕ **Rose Pistola.** The food at chef-owner Reed Hearon's eatery celebrates
★ the neighborhood's Ligurian roots. A wide assortment of small antipasti
plates—roasted peppers, house-cured fish, fava beans and pecorino
cheese—and pizzas from a wood-burning oven are favorites, as are
the classic San Francisco seafood stew called cioppino, and roasted rabbit with polenta. A large and inviting bar area opens onto the sidewalk.
⊠ *532 Columbus Ave.,* ☎ *415/399–0499. Reservations essential.
AE, MC, V.*

$ ✕ **Capp's Corner.** Diners at this family-style trattoria sit elbow to elbow
★ at long oilcloth-covered tables to feast on bountiful, well-prepared five-
course dinners. For calorie counters or the budget-minded, a simpler
option includes a bowl of minestrone, a salad, and pasta. ⊠ *1600
Powell St.,* ☎ *415/989–2589. AE, D, DC, MC, V. No lunch weekends.*

$ ✕ **L'Osteria del Forno.** The northern Italian proprietors of this unpre-
★ tentious restaurant prepare small plates of simply cooked vegetables,
a few robust pastas, a roast of the day, creamy polenta, and wonderful thin-crust pizzas. ⊠ *519 Columbus Ave.,* ☎ *415/982–1124. Reservations not accepted. No credit cards. Closed Tues.*

Russian Hill

$$ ✕ **Hyde Street Bistro.** The ambience says quintessential neighborhood
★ bistro, but the food is part tavern, part trattoria, and closely in line
with the Austro-Italian tradition of Italy's northeastern Friuli region.
Strudels and spaetzles are served alongside pastas and polentas, potato
dumplings are paired with Gorgonzola sauce, and the pastries belie the
chef-owner's Austrian roots. ⊠ *1521 Hyde St.,* ☎ *415/441–7778. AE,
MC, V. No lunch.*

Union Square

$$ × **Kuleto's.** The contemporary cooking of northern Italy, the atmo-
★ sphere of old San Francisco, and a terrific bar menu showcasing con-
temporary and traditional antipasti have made this spot off Union Square
a hit. Grilled seafood dishes are among the specialties. Breakfast is also
served. ⊠ *221 Powell St.,* ☎ *415/397–7720. AE, D, DC, MC, V.*

$$ × **Scala's Bistro.** A large open kitchen stands at the rear of a fashionable dining room that serves breakfast, lunch, and dinner. Grilled Porto-
bello mushrooms and a tower of fried calamari are among the favorite
antipasti; the pastas and grilled meats satisfy most main-course appetites.
⊠ *432 Powell St.,* ☎ *415/395–8555. AE, DC, MC, V.*

Japanese

Financial District

$$–$$$ × **Kyo-ya.** Tempuras, one-pot dishes, deep-fried and grilled meats, and
★ a choice of three dozen sushi selections are among the spectacular offerings at this authentic Japanese restaurant. The lunch menu is more
limited than dinner, but does include a sampler of four classic dishes
encased in a handsome lacquered lunch box. ⊠ *Palace Hotel, 2 New
Montgomery St., at Market St.,* ☎ *415/546–5000. AE, D, DC, MC,
V. Closed Sun. No lunch Mon. and Sat.*

Japantown

$ × **Mifune.** Thin, brown *soba* (buckwheat) and thick, white *udon* (wheat)
noodles are the specialties at this North American outpost of an Osaka-
based noodle empire that prepares such traditional Japanese combinations as fish cake–crowned udon and *tenzaru* (cold noodles and hot
tempura with a gingery dipping sauce). Validated parking is available
at the Japan Center garage. ⊠ *Japan Center, Kintetsu Bldg., 1737 Post
St.,* ☎ *415/922–0337. Reservations not accepted. AE, D, DC, MC, V.*

$ × **Sanppo.** This small place has an enormous selection of almost every
type of Japanese food: yakis, nabemono dishes, donburi, udon, and
soba, not to mention feather-light tempura, interesting side dishes, and
sushi. Validated parking is available at the Japan Center garage. ⊠ *1702
Post St.,* ☎ *415/346–3486. Reservations not accepted. MC, V. Closed
Mon. No lunch Sun.*

Richmond District

$$ × **Kabuto Sushi.** Behind a black-lacquered counter, master chef Sachio
Kojima flashes his knives with the grace of a samurai warrior. In ad-
dition to exceptional sushi and sashimi, traditional Japanese dinners
are served. ⊠ *5116 Geary Blvd.,* ☎ *415/752–5652. MC, V. Closed
Sun.–Mon. No lunch.*

Mediterranean

Civic Center

$$–$$$ × **Zuni Café & Grill.** A window-filled balcony dining area overlooks
★ Zuni's large bar, where shellfish (the oyster selection here is one of the
best in town) and drinks are dispensed. A whole roast chicken and Tus-
can bread salad for two is a popular order, as are the grilled meats and
vegetables. ⊠ *1658 Market St.,* ☎ *415/552–2522. Reservations es-
sential. AE, MC, V. Closed Mon.*

Cow Hollow/Marina

$$–$$$ × **PlumpJack Café.** The regularly changing menu at this clubby dining
★ room spans the Mediterranean, with an herbed chicken flanked by po-
lenta and crispy duck confit among the possibilities. The racks that line
the dining room hold reasonably priced vintages from California and
beyond. ⊠ *3201 Fillmore St.,* ☎ *415/463–4755. AE, MC, V. Closed
Sun. No lunch Sat.*

Financial District

$$$ ✕ **Vertigo.** Chefs at this three-level dining room ~~in~~ Pyramid prepare French and Italian cuisine with stro~~ng~~ A grilled pork chop arrives with curry-dusted beans, and ~~i~~ vored with lime. Seafood is especially fresh here—and like eve~~ry~~ else on the menu, it's creatively prepared. A bar menu offers afterno~~on~~ snacks. ✉ *600 Montgomery St.,* ☎ *415/433–7250. AE, D, DC, MC, V. Closed Sun. No lunch Sat.*

The Mission District

$$ ✕ **Bruno's.** The menu at this smart, retro-'50s eatery changes regularly but often includes a satisfying warm quail salad, steamed mussels in orange-saffron broth, and salmon with quinoa pilaf. Two adjoining rooms book some of the hottest music entertainment in town. ✉ *2389 Mission St.,* ☎ *415/550–7455. Reservations essential. MC, V. Closed Mon. No lunch.*

North Beach

$$ ✕ **Moose's.** National luminaries head for Moose's when they're in town. A Mediterranean-inspired menu includes innovative appetizers, pastas, seafood, and grills. The surroundings are classic and comfortable, with views of Washington Square and Russian Hill from a front café area; counter seats have a view of the open kitchen. There's live music at night and a fine Sunday brunch. ✉ *1652 Stockton St.,* ☎ *415/989–7800. Reservations essential. AE, DC, MC, V.*

South of Market

$$ ✕ **LuLu.** Under the high barrel-vaulted ceiling, beside a large open ★ kitchen, diners feast on sizzling mussels roasted in an iron skillet, plus pizzas, pastas, and wood-roasted poultry, meats, and shellfish; sharing dishes is the custom here. A smaller, quieter room off to one side makes conversation easier. ✉ *816 Folsom St.,* ☎ *415/495–5775. Reservations essential. AE, DC, MC, V.*

Mexican/Latin American/Spanish

Cow Hollow/Marina

$$ ✕ **Café Marimba.** Fanciful folk art adorns the walls of this colorful Mexican café, where an open kitchen turns out contemporary renditions of regional specialties: silken mole *negro* (sauce of chilies and chocolate) from Oaxaca, served in tamales and other dishes; shrimp prepared with roasted onions and tomatoes in the style of Zihuatanejo; and chicken with a marinade from Yucatán stuffed into an excellent taco. ✉ *2317 Chestnut St.,* ☎ *415/776–1506. MC, V. No lunch Mon.*

Russian Hill

$$ ✕ **Zarzuela.** This small, crowded storefront serves nearly 40 different hot and cold tapas, plus a dozen main courses. There is a tapa to suit every palate, from poached octopus atop new potatoes and hot garlic-flecked shrimp to slabs of Manchego cheese with paper-thin slices of serrano ham. The paella of saffron-scented rice weighed down with prawns, mussels, and clams is guaranteed to make the most unsentimental Madrileño homesick. ✉ *2000 Hyde St.,* ☎ *415/346–0800. MC, V. Reservations not accepted. Closed Sun.*

South of Market

$$ ✕ **Thirstybear.** The cavernous interior of concrete floors, rustic brick walls, and shiny tanks holding 7,000 homemade brews is cool and utilitarian, but the small plates of garlic-and-sherry-infused fish cheeks, steamed mussels, grilled garlic-studded shrimp, and white beans with sausage and aioli will warm you right up. Bigger appetites can dig into paella Valenciana. ✉ *661 Howard St.,* ☎ *415/974–0905. MC, V. No lunch weekends.*

$ ✕ **Chevys.** This branch of a popular Mexican minichain is decked with funky neon signs. Of note are the fajitas and the grilled quail and seafood. Another Chevys is in the Embarcadero Center. ✉ *4th and Howard Sts.,* ☎ *415/543–8060;* ✉ *Embarcadero 2,* ☎ *415/391–2323. AE, MC, V.*

Russian

Richmond District

$–$$ ✕ **Katia's.** Come here for live Russian music (most evenings) and lively Russian food. Small plates of smoked salmon and blini, marinated mushrooms, and meat- or vegetable-filled piroshki are wonderful ways to start a meal. Light chicken or potato cutlets or delicate *pelmeni* (small meat-filled dumplings in broth) are fine main courses. Save room for a meringue drizzled with berry sauce or a flaky napoleon. ✉ *600 5th Ave.,* ☎ *415/668–9292. AE, DC, MC, V. Closed Mon.*

Seafood

Civic Center

$$ ✕ **Hayes Street Grill.** Up to 15 kinds of seafood are chalked on the blackboard each night at this extremely popular restaurant. The fish is simply grilled, accompanied by a choice of sauces ranging from tomato salsa to a spicy Szechuan peanut concoction to beurre blanc. Appetizers are unusual, and desserts are lavish. ✉ *320 Hayes St.,* ☎ *415/863–5545. Reservations essential. AE, D, DC, MC, V. No lunch weekends.*

Financial District

$$$ ✕ **Aqua.** Chef-owner Michael Mina has a talent for creating contemporary versions of French, Italian, and American classics: Expect mussel, crab, or lobster soufflés; chunks of lobster alongside lobster-stuffed ravioli; and rare *ahi* tuna paired with foie gras. Desserts are miniature museum pieces—try the warm chocolate tart—and the wine list is comprehensive. ✉ *252 California St.,* ☎ *415/956–9662. Reservations essential. AE, DC, MC, V. Closed Sun. No lunch Sat.*

Northern Waterfront

$$ ✕ **McCormick & Kuleto's.** This seafood emporium in Ghirardelli Square has a fabulous view of the bay from every seat in the house, an Old San Francisco atmosphere, and dozens of varieties of fish and shellfish. The food has its ups and downs, but even on foggy days you can count on the view. Validated parking is available in the Ghirardelli Square garage. ✉ *Ghirardelli Sq., Beach and Larkin Sts.,* ☎ *415/929–1730. AE, D, DC, MC, V.*

Southeast Asian

Cow Hollow

$–$$ ✕ **Betelnut.** Pan-Asian offerings and an adventurous drinks menu draw a steady stream of diners for cuisine that is not always successful (but don't pass up a plate of the tasty stir-fried dried anchovies, chilies, peanuts, garlic, and green onions), but always intriguing. ✉ *2030 Union St.,* ☎ *415/929–8855. D, DC, MC, V.*

The Mission District

$–$$ ✕ **Slanted Door.** Behind the canted facade of this trendy new north Mission restaurant, you'll find what owner Charles Phan describes as "real Vietnamese home cooking." There are fresh spring rolls packed with rice noodles, pork, shrimp, and pungent mint leaves, and fried vegetarian imperial rolls concealing bean thread noodles, cabbage, and taro. Catfish arrives in a clay pot, and fried game hen is nicely sparked by a tamarind dipping sauce. ✉ *584 Valencia St.,* ☎ *415/861–8032. MC, V. Closed Sun.*

Richmond District

$–$$ ✕ La Vie. Chefs at this Vietnamese restaurant prepare traditional dishes such as *nep chien* (deep-fried balls of sticky rice stuffed with a mixture of finely cut pork, shrimp, and mushrooms). One fun-to-eat entrée consists of small cakes made from shrimp, rice flour, and yellow mung beans: You wrap up the cakes in crisp lettuce leaves and dip them in a spicy fish sauce. ⊠ *5380 Geary Blvd.,* ☎ *415/668–8080. AE, MC, V.*

$–$$ ✕ Le Soleil. The food of Vietnam is the specialty of this pastel, light-filled restaurant. Try the excellent raw-beef salad; crisp, flavorful spring rolls; a simple stir-fry of chicken and aromatic fresh basil leaves; or large prawns simmered in a clay pot. ⊠ *133 Clement St.,* ☎ *415/ 668–4848. MC, V.*

South of Market

$ ✕ Manora. On the extensive menu here, the fried soft-shell crabs with a tamarind dipping sauce and the whitefish steamed in banana leaves are recommended, as are the traditional Thai curries featuring meats, poultry, or seafood. ⊠ *1600 Folsom St.,* ☎ *415/861–6224. MC, V. No lunch weekends.*

Steak Houses

Marina

$$ ✕ Izzy's Steak & Chop House. Terrific steaks, chops, and seafood plus all the trimmings—such as cheesy scalloped potatoes and creamed spinach—are served here. There's validated parking at the Lombard garage. ⊠ *3345 Steiner St.,* ☎ *415/563–0487. AE, DC, MC, V. No lunch.*

Midtown

$$$ ✕ Harris'. Ann Harris serves some of the best dry-aged steaks in town,
★ but don't overlook the starter of smoked salmon or entrées of grilled salmon or calves' liver with onions and bacon. There is also an extensive bar menu and a first-rate pecan pie. ⊠ *2100 Van Ness Ave.,* ☎ *415/ 673–1888. AE, DC, MC, V. No lunch.*

Vegetarian

Civic Center

$$ ✕ Millennium. The kitchen looks to the Mediterranean, with pastas, polenta, and grilled vegetables among its most successful dishes. For true believers, there is *seitan* (a whole-wheat meat substitute) steak in Marsala sauce, a chocolate mousse cake made from tofu, and organic wines and beers. ⊠ *246 McAllister St.,* ☎ *415/487–9800. MC, V. No lunch.*

Marina

$$ ✕ Greens. Dinners at this restaurant with expansive bay views are à
★ la carte on weeknights, but only a five-course prix fixe dinner is served on Saturday. Sunday brunch is a good time to watch local sailboat owners take out their crafts. There's public parking at Fort Mason Center. ⊠ *Fort Mason Bldg. A (fort entrance: Laguna St. and Marina Blvd.),* ☎ *415/771–6222. MC, V. No lunch Mon., no dinner Sun.*

LODGING

Updated by Sharron Wood

The hotels listed below are on or close to public transportation lines. Some properties on Lombard Street and in the Civic Center area have free parking, but daily parking fees at downtown and Fisherman's Wharf lodgings can be $20 or even higher. Reservations for all accommodations are advised, especially during the peak season, May through October.

For those in search of budget accommodations (under $50), try the Adelaide Inn (☞ Union Square/Downtown, *below*) or the YMCA Central Branch (✉ 220 Golden Gate Ave., ☎ 415/885–0460).

An alternative to hotels and motels is staying in private homes and apartments, available through **American Family Inn/Bed & Breakfast San Francisco** (☎ 415/931–3083, FAX 415/921–2273), **Bed & Breakfast International–San Francisco** (☎ 415/696–1690 or 800/872–4500, FAX 415/696–1699), and **American Property Exchange** (☎ 415/863–8484 or 800/747–7784, FAX 415/440–1008).

CATEGORY	COST*
$$$$	over $175
$$$	$120–$175
$$	$80–$120
$	under $80

All prices are for a standard double room, excluding 14% tax.

Union Square/Downtown

$$$$ ⊡ **Campton Place.** Behind a simple brownstone facade, quiet reigns.
★   Highly attentive personal service begins the moment uniformed doormen greet guests outside the marble-floor lobby. Rooms, small but well appointed, have double-pane windows, Chinese armoires, and good-size writing desks. The Campton Place Restaurant is famed for its breakfast. Wednesday martini nights (5:30–8:30) in the lounge have become a favorite midweek cruising ground for the downtown crowd. ✉ *340 Stockton St., 94108,* ☎ *415/781–5555 or 800/235–4300,* FAX *415/ 955–5536. 117 rooms. Restaurant, bar, in-room safes, minibars, no-smoking rooms, room service, laundry service and dry cleaning, concierge, meeting rooms, parking (fee). AE, DC, MC, V.*

$$$$ ⊡ **The Clift.** This Grand Heritage hotel towers over San Francisco's theater district; its crisp, forest green awnings and formal door service provide subtle hints of the elegance within. Rooms, some rich with dark woods and burgundies, others refreshingly pastel, all have large writing desks, plants, and flowers. Be sure to sample a cocktail in the art deco Redwood Room lounge, complete with chandeliers and a sweeping redwood bar. ✉ *495 Geary St., 94102,* ☎ *415/775–4700 or 800/ 652–5438,* FAX *415/441–4621. 329 rooms. Restaurant, bar, in-room modem lines, minibars, no-smoking floor, room service, exercise room, laundry service and dry cleaning, concierge, meeting rooms, parking (fee). AE, DC, MC, V.*

$$$$ ⊡ **Pan Pacific Hotel.** Exotic flower arrangements and elegant Asian touches set this business hotel apart from others. Bathrooms lined with terra-cotta Portuguese marble are the highlight of the guest rooms, which are decorated primarily in pale green or mauve and beige tones. In-room fax machines and three phones in each room are a few of the excellent business amenities. The hotel's restaurant, Pacific, is well regarded for its California cuisine. ✉ *500 Post St., 94102,* ☎ *415/771– 8600 or 800/327–8585,* FAX *415/398–0267. 330 rooms. Restaurant, bar, lobby lounge, in-room modem lines, minibars, no-smoking floors, room service, exercise room, piano, laundry service and dry cleaning, concierge, business services, meeting rooms, parking (fee). AE, D, DC, MC, V.*

$$$$ ⊡ **Prescott Hotel.** The Prescott's rooms, which vary only in size and
★   shape, are traditional in style and decorated in a rich hunter green. Each bed is backed by a partially-mirrored wall and has a boldly-patterned spread; bathrooms have marble-top sinks and gold fixtures. Guests can

order room service from the on-site Postrio and have access to the health club next door. ⊠ *545 Post St., 94102,* ☎ *415/563–0303 or 800/283– 7322,* FAX *415/563–6831. 165 rooms. Restaurant, bar, lobby lounge, in-room modem lines, no-smoking floors, room service, concierge, business services, meeting rooms, parking (fee). AE, D, DC, MC, V.*

$$$$ ☷ **Westin St. Francis.** The St. Francis, with its imposing facade, black marble lobby, and gold-top columns, looks more like a great public building than a hotel. The effect is softened by the columns and exquisite woodwork of the Compass Rose bar and restaurant. Many rooms in the original building are small by modern standards, but all retain their original Victorian-style moldings and are decorated with Empire-style furnishings. Rooms in the modern tower are larger, with Oriental-style lacquered furniture; ask for a room above the 15th floor for a spectacular view of the city. ⊠ *335 Powell St., 94102,* ☎ *415/397–7000 or 800/ 228–3000,* FAX *415/774–0124. 1,192 rooms. 3 restaurants, 2 bars, in-room modem lines, in-room safes, no-smoking floors, room service, exercise room, nightclub, concierge, business services, meeting rooms, travel services, parking (fee). AE, D, DC, MC, V.*

$$$ ☷ **Chancellor Hotel.** This family-owned hotel is one of the best buys on Union Square. The moderate-size Edwardian-style rooms have high ceilings and peach, green, and rose color schemes; ceiling fans and deep bathtubs are a treat. Connecting rooms are available. ⊠ *433 Powell St., 94102,* ☎ *415/362–2004 or 800/428–4748,* FAX *415/362–1403. 137 rooms. Restaurant, bar, no-smoking floors, room service, concierge, parking (fee). AE, D, DC, MC, V.*

$$$ ☷ **Galleria Park.** The comfortable rooms at this hotel a few blocks
★ east of Union Square have floral bedspreads, stylish striped wall-paper, and white furniture that includes a writing desk. Four floors are no-smoking. ⊠ *191 Sutter St., 94104,* ☎ *415/781–3060 or 800/ 792–9639,* FAX *415/433–4409. 177 rooms. 2 restaurants, in-room modem lines, minibars, no-smoking floors, room service, exercise room, jogging, concierge, business services, meeting rooms. AE, D, DC, MC, V.*

$$$ ☷ **Hotel Diva.** Although the Diva's proximity to the theater district attracts visitors of an artistic bent, the hotel is also popular with tourists and business travelers. The black-and-silver color scheme with touches of gray extends to the nightclub-esque lobby and to the rooms, which vary in size and are comfortable but not fussy. Black-lacquer armoires, writing desks, and headboards complete the effect. ⊠ *440 Geary St., 94102,* ☎ *415/885–0200 or 800/553–1900,* FAX *415/346–6613. 110 rooms. Restaurant, in-room modem lines, in-room safes, no-smoking floors, exercise room, business services, meeting room. AE, D, DC, MC, V.*

$$$ ☷ **Hotel Monaco.** With its yellow beaux arts facade, the Monaco
★ stands in stark contrast to its more stately neighbor, the Clift. Inside, a faux steamer trunk serves as a front desk, a dramatic staircase has bronze filigree and gray-and-black marble steps, and a French inglenook fireplace climbs two stories above the lobby. Rooms contain an inviting blend of Chinese-inspired armoires, bamboo writing desks, and high-back upholstered chairs. ⊠ *501 Geary St., 94102,* ☎ *415/292– 0100 or 800/214–4220,* FAX *415/292–0111. 201 rooms. Restaurant, bar, no-smoking rooms, in-room modem lines, room service, spa, laundry service and dry cleaning, business services, parking (fee). AE, D, DC, MC, V.*

$$$ ☷ **Hotel Rex.** Literary and artistic creativity are celebrated at the stylish Hotel Rex. Original artwork adorns the walls, and the proprietors even host book readings and roundtable discussions in the common areas, which are decorated in warm, rich tones. Rooms have writing desks and lamps with whimsically hand-painted shades. ⊠ *562 Sutter St., 94102,* ☎ *415/433–4434,* FAX *415/433–3695. 94 rooms. Bar, lobby*

Downtown San Francisco Lodging

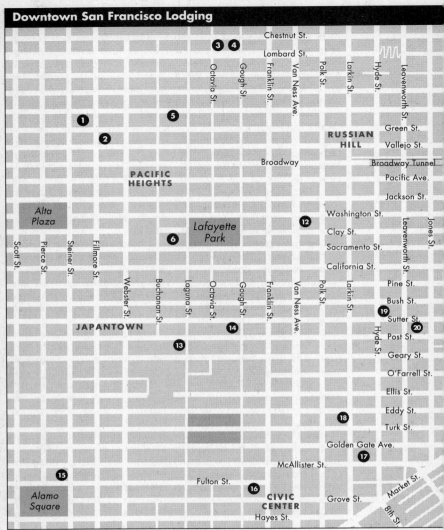

The Abigail, **17**
Adelaide Inn, **21**
The Andrews, **20**
The Archbishops Mansion, **15**
Bed and Breakfast Inn, **5**
Campton Place, **41**
Chancellor Hotel, **39**
The Clarion, **57**

The Clift, **34**
Commodore International, **22**
Embassy Suites San Francisco Airport—Burlingame, **53**
The Fairmont, **27**
Galleria Park, **44**
Grant Plaza, **48**
Harbor Court, **51**

Holiday Lodge and Garden Hotel, **12**
Hotel Bohème, **49**
Hotel Diva, **33**
Hotel Majestic, **14**
Hotel Monaco, **35**
Hotel Rex, **30**
Hotel Sofitel–San Francisco Bay, **54**
Hotel Triton, **45**

The Huntington, **25**
Hyatt at Fisherman's Wharf, **8**
Hyatt Regency, **47**
Inn at the Opera, **16**
Inn at Union Square, **38**
King George, **37**
La Quinta Motor Inn, **52**
Mandarin Oriental, **50**

KEY

AE American Express Office

San Francisco Bay

The Mansions, **6**
Marina Inn, **3**
Mark Hopkins
Inter–Continental, **26**
Marriott at
Fisherman's Wharf, **7**
The Maxwell, **36**
Nob Hill
Lambourne, **46**
The Palace Hotel, **43**
Pan Pacific Hotel, **32**

Petite Auberge, **23**
Phoenix Hotel, **18**
Prescott Hotel, **31**
Radisson Miyako
Hotel, **13**
Red Roof Inn, **58**
Ritz–Carlton, San
Francisco, **28**
San Francisco Airport
Hilton, **55**

San Remo, **11**
Sherman House, **2**
Sir Francis Drake, **40**
Town House Motel, **4**
Travelodge Hotel at
Fisherman's Wharf, **10**
Tuscan Inn, **9**
Union Street Inn, **1**

Vintage Court, **29**
The Westin, **56**
Westin St. Francis, **42**
White Swan Inn, **24**
York Hotel, **19**

lounge, in-room modem lines, minibars, no-smoking rooms, laundry service and dry cleaning, concierge, parking (fee). AE, D, DC, MC, V.

$$$ ⊡ **Hotel Triton.** The Triton caters to fashion, entertainment, music, and film-industry types, who appreciate the iridescent pink-and-gold-painted rooms with S-curve dervish chairs, curly-neck lamps, and odd-ball light fixtures. Attached to the hotel is the trendy newsstand, coffeehouse, and dining room, the Café de la Presse, which serves as a gathering place for foreign visitors. ⊠ *342 Grant Ave., 94108,* ☎ *415/394–0500 or 800/433–6611,* FAX *415/394–0555. 140 rooms. In-room modem lines, no-smoking floors, exercise room, laundry service, business services, meeting rooms, parking (fee). AE, D, MC, V.*

$$$ ⊡ **Inn at Union Square.** With its tiny but captivating lobby with trompe l'oeil bookshelves painted on the walls, this inn feels like someone's home. Comfortable Georgian-style rooms with sumptuous goose-down pillows promote indolence. Complimentary Continental breakfast, afternoon tea, and evening wine and hors d'oeuvres are served in front of a fireplace in a sitting area on each floor. Tipping is not permitted. ⊠ *440 Post St., 94102,* ☎ *415/397–3510 or 800/288–4346,* FAX *415/989–0529. 30 rooms. No-smoking floors, parking (fee). AE, DC, MC, V.*

$$$ ⊡ **King George.** Behind the George's white-and-green Victorian facade, rooms are compact but nicely furnished in classic English style, with walnut furniture and a muted rose color scheme. British and Japanese tourists and suburban couples seeking a weekend getaway frequent this adult-oriented hotel. ⊠ *334 Mason St., 94102,* ☎ *415/ 781–5050 or 800/288–6005,* FAX *415/391–6976. 143 rooms. Tea shop, no-smoking floors, meeting rooms, parking (fee). AE, D, DC, MC, V.*

$$$ ⊡ **Sir Francis Drake.** The Drake's opulent lobby has wrought-iron balustrades, chandeliers, and Italian marble, but the guest rooms have the flavor of a B&B, with California colonial–style furnishings and floral-print fabrics. The decor appeals to pleasure travelers, but business travelers will appreciate the modem hookups and voice mail. Local party-giver Harry Denton runs the Starlight Room on the top floor. ⊠ *450 Powell St., 94102,* ☎ *415/392–7755 or 800/227–5480,* FAX *415/395–8599. 417 rooms. 2 restaurants, in-room modem lines, no-smoking rooms, nightclub, concierge, meeting rooms, parking (fee). AE, D, DC, MC, V.*

$$$ ⊡ **Vintage Court.** This bit of the Napa Valley just off Union Square has lavish rooms decorated on a Wine Country theme. Every afternoon complimentary wine is served in front of a crackling fire in the lobby. A Continental breakfast is served each morning, and for fine food, guests need go no farther than the lobby to get to Masa's, the celebrated French restaurant. Guests have access to an affiliated health club one block away. ⊠ *650 Bush St., 94108,* ☎ *415/392–4666 or 800/654–1100,* FAX *415/ 433–4065. 107 rooms. Restaurant, bar, minibars, no-smoking floors, refrigerators, parking (fee). AE, D, DC, MC, V.*

$$$ ⊡ **White Swan Inn.** The White Swan has all the comforts of home—personal front-door keys, complimentary soft drinks and bottled water, free copies of the *San Francisco Chronicle*. Rooms are large, with dark wood furniture and an English country theme. Afternoon tea is served in the lounge, where comfortable chairs and sofas invite lingering. ⊠ *845 Bush St.,* ☎ *415/775–1755 or 800/999–9570,* FAX *415/775–5717. 26 rooms. Breakfast room, meeting rooms, parking (fee). AE, MC, V.*

$$$ ⊡ **York Hotel.** Hitchcock fans may recognize the exterior of this reasonably priced, family-owned hotel four blocks west of Union Square; Kim Novak hid out here in *Vertigo*. The moderate-size rooms are a tasteful mix of Mediterranean styles. All have huge closets. This is perhaps the most gay-friendly of San Francisco's more elegant hotels. Room rates include a Continental breakfast. ⊠ *940 Sutter St., 94109,* ☎ *415/*

885–6800 or 800/808–9675, ℻ 415/885–2115. *96 rooms. Bar, no-smoking floors, exercise room, nightclub, concierge, parking (fee). AE, D, DC, MC, V.*

$$–$$$ 🏨 **Petite Auberge.** This inn's lobby, festooned with bears of all shapes, sizes, and costumes, sets the tone; the country kitchen and side garden create a pastoral atmosphere in the midst of downtown. The rooms are small, but each has an old-fashioned writing desk and a much-needed armoire—there's little or no closet space. ⊠ *863 Bush St., 94108,* ☎ *415/928–6000 or 800/365–3004,* ℻ *415/775–5717. 26 rooms. Breakfast room, no-smoking floors, parking (fee). AE, DC, MC, V.*

$$ 🏨 **The Andrews.** Two blocks west of Union Square, this Queen Anne–style abode with a dark-gray-and-white facade began its life as the Sultan Turkish Baths in 1905. Today Victorian antique reproductions, old-fashioned flower curtains with lace sheers, iron bedsteads, and good-size closets more than make up for the diminutive guest rooms and baths. A buffet-style Continental breakfast is served daily on every floor. ⊠ *624 Post St., 94109,* ☎ *415/563–6877 or 800/926–3739,* ℻ *415/928–6919. 48 rooms. Restaurant, no-smoking rooms, concierge, parking (fee). AE, MC, V.*

$$ 🏨 **Commodore International.** Entering the Commodore's lobby is like stepping onto the main deck of an ocean liner of yore: Neodeco chairs look like the backdrop for a film about transatlantic crossings; and steps away is the Titanic Cafe, where goldfish bowls and bathysphere-inspired lights add to the sea-cruise mood. The fairly large rooms with monster closets are painted in soft yellows and golds. ⊠ *825 Sutter St., 94109,* ☎ *415/923–6800 or 800/338–6848,* ℻ *415/923–6804. 113 rooms. Restaurant, no-smoking rooms, nightclub, laundry service and dry cleaning, parking (fee). AE, D, MC, V.*

$$ 🏨 **The Maxwell.** Formerly known as the Raphael, the Maxwell is a simple but stylish hotel just a few blocks from Union Square. Behind the dramatic black and red curtains, the Victorian-style lobby welcomes you with a green velvet sofa and boldly patterned chairs. Rooms have a clubby, retro feel and deep jewel tones. ⊠ *386 Geary St., 94102,* ☎ *415/986–2000 or 888/734–6299,* ℻ *415/397–2447. 153 rooms. Restaurant, bar, in-room modem lines, no-smoking floors, room service, laundry service, concierge, parking (fee). AE, D, DC, MC, V.*

$ 🏨 **Adelaide Inn.** The bedspreads at this quiet retreat may not match the drapes or carpets, and the floors may creak, but the rooms are sunny, clean, and cheap: $42 to $48 for a double, each with shared bath. Tucked away in an alley, this funky European-style pension hosts many guests from Germany, France, and Italy. ⊠ *5 Isadora Duncan Ct., at Taylor St. between Geary and Post Sts., 94102,* ☎ *415/441–2474 or 415/441–2261,* ℻ *415/441–0161. 18 rooms. Breakfast room, refrigerators. AE, MC, V.*

$
★ 🏨 **Grant Plaza.** This bargain hotel in the shadow of the Chinatown Gate has small but clean rooms starting at $57. Rooms on the top floor are newer, slightly fancier, and more expensive; for a quieter stay ask for one in the back. ⊠ *465 Grant Ave., 94108,* ☎ *415/434–3883 or 800/472–6899,* ℻ *415/434–3886. 72 rooms. Parking (fee). AE, MC, V.*

Financial District

$$$$ 🏨 **Hyatt Regency.** The concrete exterior of the Hyatt Regency is an unlikely introduction to the spectacular 17-story atrium lobby within. Rooms, some with bay-view balconies, are decorated in two styles: Both have cherry-wood furniture, but one strikes a decidedly more masculine tone with a black-and-brown color scheme, while the other has soft rose-and-plum combinations. ⊠ *5 Embarcadero Center, 94111,* ☎ *415/788–1234 or 800/233–1234,* ℻ *415/398–2567. 805 rooms.*

2 *restaurants, bar, lobby lounge, no-smoking floors, room service, exercise room, concierge, concierge floor, parking (fee). AE, D, DC, MC, V.*

$$$$ 🏨 **Mandarin Oriental.** The Mandarin comprises the top 11 floors (38
★   to 48) of San Francisco's third-tallest building—the First Interstate Center—so all rooms have panoramic vistas of the city and beyond. Rooms are decorated in a light creamy yellow with black accents; bathtubs are flanked by large windows. ⊠ *222 Sansome St., 94104,* ☎ *415/885–0999 or 800/622–0404,* ℻ *415/433–0289. 158 rooms. Lobby lounge, in-room modem lines, minibars, no-smoking floors, room service, laundry service and dry cleaning, concierge, business services, meeting rooms, parking (fee). AE, D, DC, MC, V.*

$$$$ 🏨 **Palace Hotel.** One of the city's grand hotels—with a guest list that has included Enrico Caruso, Herbert Hoover, and Amelia Earhart—the Palace has an indoor lap pool with a skylight, a health club, and a business center. With their 14-ft ceilings, rooms are splendid on a smaller scale. Modern amenities are carefully integrated into the classic decor, from the TV inside the mahogany armoire to the telephone in the marble bathroom. ⊠ *2 New Montgomery St., 94105,* ☎ *415/392–8600 or 800/325–3535,* ℻ *415/543–0671. 550 rooms. 3 restaurants, bar, room service, health club, laundry service, parking (fee). AE, D, DC, MC, V.*

$$$ 🏨 **Harbor Court.** This cozy hotel, formerly a YMCA, is noted for ex-
★   emplary service. The small rooms, some with bay views, have partial canopy beds resting on wood casements. The adult-oriented Harbor Court attracts corporate types (especially on weekdays) as well as the average traveler. Guests have free access to YMCA facilities (including a 150-ft heated indoor pool). ⊠ *165 Steuart St., 94105* ☎ *415/882–1300 or 800/346–0555,* ℻ *415/882–1313. 131 rooms. In-room modem lines, minibars, no-smoking floors, room service, business services, parking (fee). AE, D, DC, MC, V.*

Nob Hill

$$$$ 🏨 **The Fairmont.** Perched atop Nob Hill, the Fairmont has the most awe-inspiring lobby in the city, with a soaring vaulted ceiling; towering, hand-painted faux-marble columns; gilt mirrors; red-velvet upholstered chairs; and a grand wraparound staircase. The tower rooms, which have spectacular city and bay views, reflect a more modern style than their smaller Victorian counterparts in the older building. The kitschy Tonga Room, site of San Francisco's busiest happy hour, is a must-see. ⊠ *950 Mason St., 94108,* ☎ *415/772–5000 or 800/527–4727,* ℻ *415/837–0587. 596 rooms. 4 restaurants, 5 bars, room service, barbershop, beauty salon, health club, spa, laundry service and dry cleaning, concierge, business services, car rental. AE, D, DC, MC, V.*

$$$$ 🏨 **The Huntington.** Attentive personal service is the hallmark of this hotel. Rooms and suites reflect the Huntington's traditional style, albeit with a '90s bent. Opulent materials such as raw silks and velvets are mixed and matched in a rich color scheme of cocoa, gold, and burgundy. ⊠ *1075 California St., 94108,* ☎ *415/474–5400 or 800/227–4683; 800/652–1539 in CA;* ℻ *415/474–6227. 140 rooms. Restaurant, bar, in-room modem lines, no-smoking rooms, room service, laundry service and dry cleaning, concierge, meeting rooms. AE, D, DC, MC, V.*

$$$$ 🏨 **Mark Hopkins Inter-Continental.** Rooms at this San Francisco landmark have dramatic furnishings of gray, silver, and khaki. Italian marble lines the bathrooms. Even-number rooms on high floors have views of the Golden Gate Bridge. No visit would be complete without partaking of the panoramic views from the Top of the Mark, *the* rooftop lounge in San Francisco since 1939. ⊠ *999 California St., 94108,* ☎ *415/392–3434 or 800/662–4455,* ℻ *415/421–3302. 392 rooms. 2 restaurants,*

2 lounges, room service, exercise room, laundry service and dry cleaning, concierge, business services, car rental. AE, D, DC, MC, V.

$$$$ ☐ **Ritz-Carlton, San Francisco.** Consistently rated one of the top hotels
★ in the world by *Condé Nast Traveler,* the Ritz-Carlton is a stunning tribute to beauty, splendor, and warm, sincere service. Crystal chandeliers and museum-quality 18th- and 19th-century oil paintings adorn an opulent lobby. Rooms are elegant and spacious, and every bath is appointed with double sinks, hair dryers, and vanity tables. A maid service cleans twice a day, and guests staying on the butler level enjoy the added luxury of their own butler. ⊠ *600 Stockton St., at California St., 94108,* ☎ *415/296–7465 or 800/241–3333,* FAX *415/296–8261. 336 rooms. 2 restaurants, bar, lobby lounge, laundry service and dry cleaning, concierge, business services, meeting rooms, parking (fee). AE, D, DC, MC, V.*

$$$ ☐ **Nob Hill Lambourne.** This urban retreat designed with the travel-
★ ing executive in mind takes pride in taking care of business while offering stress-reducing pleasures. Personal computers, fax machines, personalized voice mail, laser printers, and a fully equipped boardroom help guests maintain their edge, while the on-site spa, with massages, body scrubs, manicures, and pedicures, helps them take it off. Rooms have queen-size beds with double-padded, hand-sewn mattresses and contemporary furnishings in Mediterranean colors. A deluxe Continental breakfast and evening wine service are complimentary. ⊠ *725 Pine St., at Stockton St., 94108,* ☎ *415/433–2287 or 800/274–8466,* FAX *415/433–0975. 20 rooms. Lobby lounge, in-room modem lines, kitchenettes, no-smoking floors, in-room VCRs, spa, business services, parking (fee). AE, D, DC, MC, V.*

Fisherman's Wharf/North Beach

$$$$ ☐ **Hyatt at Fisherman's Wharf.** Location is the key to this hotel's popularity with business travelers and families. The moderate-size guest rooms, a medley of greens and burgundies with dark woods and brass fixtures, have double-pane windows to keep out the often considerable street noise. Each floor has a laundry room. ⊠ *555 North Point St., 94133,* ☎ *415/563–1234 or 800/233–1234,* FAX *415/563–2218. 313 rooms. Restaurant, sports bar, no-smoking floors, pool, outdoor hot tub, health club, coin laundry, meeting rooms, parking (fee). AE, D, DC, MC, V.*

$$$ ☐ **Marriott at Fisherman's Wharf.** Behind an unremarkable sand-color facade, the Marriott strikes a grand note in its lavish, low-ceiling lobby, with marble floors and English club–style furniture. Rooms, all with turquoise, blue, and white color schemes, have dark wood and Asian-art touches. ⊠ *1250 Columbus Ave., 94133,* ☎ *415/775–7555 or 800/228–9290,* FAX *415/474–2099. 255 rooms. Restaurant, bar, no-smoking floors, health club, meeting rooms, parking (fee). AE, D, DC, MC, V.*

$$$ ☐ **Tuscan Inn.** The condolike exterior of the inn—reddish brick with white concrete—gives little indication of the charm of the relatively small, Italian-influenced guest rooms with white-pine furniture and floral bedspreads and curtains. Room service is provided by Cafe Pescatore, the Italian seafood restaurant off the lobby. Morning coffee, tea, and biscotti are complimentary, and wine is served in the early evening. ⊠ *425 North Point St., 94133,* ☎ *415/561–1100 or 800/648–4626,* FAX *415/561–1199. 220 rooms. Restaurant, room service, meeting rooms. AE, D, DC, MC, V.*

$$ ☐ **Hotel Bohème.** In the middle of historic North Beach, this little bargain gives guests a taste of the past. The small rooms, decorated with European armoires, bistro tables, and memorabilia from the '50s and '60s, recall the beat generation. Coral-color walls and handmade lamp-

shades complete the nostalgic mood. ☒ *444 Columbus Ave., 94133,* ☎ *415/433–9111,* FAX *415/362–6292. 16 rooms. AE, D, MC, V.*

$$ 🏨 **Travelodge Hotel at Fisherman's Wharf.** Taking up an entire city block, the Travelodge is the only bay-front hotel at Fisherman's Wharf and is known for its reasonable rates. The higher-price rooms on the third and fourth floors have balconies that provide unobstructed views of Alcatraz and overlook a landscaped courtyard and pool. ☒ *250 Beach St., 94133,* ☎ *415/392–6700 or 800/578–7878,* FAX *415/986–7853. 250 rooms. 3 restaurants, no-smoking rooms, pool, free parking. AE, D, DC, MC, V.*

$ 🏨 **San Remo.** This three-story blue-and-white Italianate Victorian has
★ a down-home ambience. The somewhat cramped rooms are crowded with furniture: vanities, rag rugs, pedestal sinks, ceiling fans, antique armoires, and brass, iron, or wooden beds. Guests share six shower rooms, one bathtub chamber, and six scrupulously clean toilets with brass pull chains and oak tanks. Special rates are available for longer stays. ☒ *2237 Mason St., 94133,* ☎ *415/776–8688 or 800/352–7366,* FAX *415/776– 2811. 62 rooms. No-smoking rooms, parking (fee). AE, DC, MC, V.*

Pacific Heights, Cow Hollow, and the Marina

$$$$ 🏨 **Sherman House.** This landmark mansion on a low hill in residen-
★ tial Pacific Heights is San Francisco's most luxurious small hotel. Rooms are individually decorated with Biedermeier, English Jacobean, or French Second Empire antiques. Tapestry-like canopies over four-poster featherbeds, wood-burning fireplaces with marble mantels, and black-granite bathrooms—some with whirlpool baths—complete the picture. ☒ *2160 Green St., 94123,* ☎ *415/563–3600 or 800/424–5777,* FAX *415/563–1882. 14 rooms. Dining room, room service, in-room VCRs, piano, concierge, airport shuttle. AE, DC, MC, V.*

$$$ 🏨 **Union Street Inn.** This ivy-draped Edwardian 1902 home affords a
★ cozy intimacy that has made it popular with honeymooners and other romantics. Of the six rooms, one standout is the Wildrose, with a garden view, a whirlpool tub, and a king-size brass bed. An elaborate complimentary breakfast is served to guests in the parlor, in the garden, or in their rooms. ☒ *2229 Union St., 94123,* ☎ *415/346–0424,* FAX *415/ 922–8046. 6 rooms. Breakfast room, no-smoking rooms, parking (fee). AE, MC, V.*

$$–$$$ 🏨 **Bed and Breakfast Inn.** Pierre Deux and Laura Ashley are the inspirations for the English country–style rooms at San Francisco's first B&B. Though the rooms with shared bath are quite small, the Mayfair, a private apartment above the main house, and the Garden Suite, an even more deluxe apartment, are spacious alternatives for families or larger parties. ☒ *4 Charlton Ct., at Union St., 94123,* ☎ *415/921– 9784. 6 rooms, 1 with bath, 2 apartments. Breakfast room, parking (fee). No credit cards.*

$$ 🏨 **Holiday Lodge and Garden Hotel.** This three-story, split-level hotel with a redwood-and-stone facade has a laid-back, West Coast mood. Rooms either overlook or open onto landscaped grounds with palm trees and a heated swimming pool. White beamed ceilings, beige wood paneling, and floral bedspreads give the rooms a vaguely '50s look. The hotel is quiet, even though it's on one of the city's busiest streets. ☒ *1901 Van Ness Ave., 94109,* ☎ *415/776–4469 or 800/367–8504,* FAX *415/474– 7046. 76 rooms. Kitchenettes, free parking. AE, D, DC, MC, V.*

$ 🏨 **Marina Inn.** This inn five blocks from the Marina offers B&B-style accommodations at motel prices. English country–style rooms are sparsely appointed, with queen-size two-poster beds, small pine-wood writing desks, nightstands, and armoires; the wallpaper and bedspreads are aggressively floral. Complimentary Continental breakfast and afternoon sherry are served in the central sitting room. ⊠ *3110 Octavia St., at Lombard St., 94123,* ☎ *415/928–1000 or 800/274–1420,* FAX *415/928–5909. 40 rooms. Lobby lounge, no-smoking floor, barbershop, beauty salon. AE, MC, V.*

$ ⊞ **Town House Motel.** What this recently renovated, family-oriented motel lacks in luxury it makes up for in value. The modest medium-size rooms have a southwestern pastel color scheme, lacquered-wood furnishings, and either a king-size bed or two doubles. Continental breakfast is complimentary. ⊠ *1650 Lombard St., 94123,* ☎ *415/885–5163 or 800/ 255–1516,* FAX *415/771–9889. 24 rooms. Airport shuttle, free parking. AE, D, DC, MC, V.*

Civic Center/Van Ness

$$$ ⊞ **The Archbishops Mansion.** The hotel's 15 guest rooms, each named
★   for a famous opera, are individually decorated with intricately carved antiques; many have Jacuzzi tubs or fireplaces. Though not within easy walking distance of many restaurants or tourist attractions, its perch on the corner of Alamo Square near the Painted Ladies—San Francisco's famous Victorian homes—makes for a scenic, relaxed stay. Enjoy the complimentary Continental breakfast in the ornate dining room or in the privacy of your own suite; there's also an afternoon wine service. ⊠ *1000 Fulton St., 94117,* ☎ *415/563–7872 or 800/543–5820,* FAX *415/885–3193. 15 rooms. Breakfast room, lobby lounge, no-smoking rooms, in-room VCRs, piano, meeting room, free parking. AE, MC, V.*

$$$ ⊞ **Hotel Majestic.** One of San Francisco's original grand hotels, this five-story yellow-and-white Edwardian with gingerbread and scrollwork looks like a wedding cake. Most rooms have fireplaces and either a hand-painted, four-poster canopied bed or two-poster bonnet twin beds, and most have a mix of French Empire and English antiques and custom furniture. The hotel's romantic Café Majestic evokes turn-of-the-century San Francisco. ⊠ *1500 Sutter St., 94109,* ☎ *415/441– 1100 or 800/869–8966,* FAX *415/673–7331. 57 rooms. Restaurant, bar, laundry service and dry cleaning, parking (fee). AE, DC, MC, V.*

$$$ ⊞ **Inn at the Opera.** Behind the marble-floor lobby of this seven-story
★   hotel are rooms of various sizes, decorated with creamy pastels and dark wood furnishings. Even the smallest singles have queen-size beds. The bureau drawers are lined with sheet music, and every room is outfitted with terry-cloth robes, a microwave oven, a minibar, fresh flowers, and a basket of apples. Those in the know say the back rooms are the quietest. ⊠ *333 Fulton St., 94102,* ☎ *415/863–8400 or 800/325–2708; 800/423–9610 in CA;* FAX *415/861–0821. 48 rooms. Restaurant, lobby lounge, room service, concierge, parking (fee). AE, DC, MC, V.*

$$$ ⊞ **The Mansions.** This twin-turreted Queen Anne was built in 1887 and today houses one of the most unusual hotels in the city. Rooms, which contain an odd collection of furnishings, vary in theme from the tiny Tom Thumb room to the opulent Josephine suite. Owner Bob Pritikin's pig painting and other "porkabilia" are scattered throughout the hotel. Other nice touches are the sculpture and flower gardens and the nightly concerts. Full breakfast is included. ⊠ *2220 Sacramento St., 94115,* ☎ *415/929–9444,* FAX *415/567–9391. 26 rooms. Breakfast room, dining room, billiards, laundry service, parking (fee). AE, DC, MC, V.*

$$$ ⊞ **Radisson Miyako Hotel.** Near the Japantown complex and Fillmore Street, this pagoda-style hotel is frequented by Asian travelers and others with a taste for the East. Some guest rooms are in the tower building; others are in the garden wing, which has traditional seasonal gardens. Japanese-style rooms have futon beds with tatami mats. Western rooms have traditional beds with mattresses. Both types of rooms feature Japanese touches such as shojis; most have their own soaking rooms with

a bucket and stool and a Japanese tub (1 ft deeper than Western tubs). ⊠ *1625 Post St., at Laguna St., 94115,* ☎ *415/922–3200 or 800/533– 4567,* FAX *415/921–0417. 218 rooms. Restaurant, bar, exercise room, laundry service and dry cleaning, business services. AE, D, DC, MC, V.*

$$ 🛏 **The Abigail.** Faux-stone walls, a faux-marble front desk, and an old-fashioned telephone booth in the lobby make for an eclectic decor at this smallish hotel in a marginal neighborhood. Hissing steam radiators, sleigh beds, and antiques complete the mood. ⊠ *246 McAllister St., 94102,* ☎ *415/861–9728 or 800/243–6510,* FAX *415/861–5848. 60 rooms. Restaurant, laundry service. AE, D, DC, MC, V.*

$$ 🛏 **Phoenix Hotel.** This hideaway on the edge of the Tenderloin district is a little bit south-of-the-equator and a little bit Gilligan's Island. Its bungalow style rooms, decorated with handmade bamboo furniture and original art by San Francisco artists, have white-beamed ceilings, white wooden walls, and vivid tropical-print bedspreads. All rooms face a pool (with a mural by Francis Forlenza on its bottom) and sculpture garden. An in-house cable channel plays films made in San Francisco and films about bands on the road. ⊠ *601 Eddy St., 94109,* ☎ *415/776–1380 or 800/248–9466,* FAX *415/885–3109. 44 rooms. Restaurant, bar, room service, pool, massage, nightclub, laundry service, free parking. AE, D, DC, MC, V.*

The Airport

Because they cater primarily to midweek business travelers, airport hotels often cut weekend prices drastically; be sure to inquire. Airport shuttle buses and a full complement of services are provided by all the following hotels.

$$$$ 🛏 **Embassy Suites San Francisco Airport–Burlingame** (⊠ 150 Anza Blvd., Burlingame 94010, ☎ 650/342–4600 or 800/362–2779, FAX 650/ 343–8137). 🛏 **Hotel Sofitel–San Francisco Bay** (⊠ 223 Twin Dolphin Dr., Redwood City 94065, ☎ 650/598–9000 or 800/763–4835, FAX 650/598–0459). 🛏 **The Westin** (⊠ 1 Old Bayshore Hwy., Millbrae 94030, ☎ 650/692–3500 or 800/228–3000, FAX 650/872–8111).

$$$ 🛏 **San Francisco Airport Hilton** (⊠ San Francisco International Airport, Box 8355, 94128, ☎ 650/589–0770 or 800/445–8667, FAX 650/589– 4696).

$$ 🛏 **The Clarion** (⊠ 401 E. Millbrae Ave., Millbrae 94030, ☎ 650/ 692–6363 or 800/223–7111, FAX 650/697–8735). 🛏 **La Quinta Motor Inn** (⊠ 20 Airport Blvd., South San Francisco 94080, ☎ 650/583–2223 or 800/531–5900).

$ 🛏 **Red Roof Inn.** (⊠ 777 Airport Blvd., Burlingame 94010, ☎ 650/ 342–7772 or 800/843–7663).

NIGHTLIFE AND THE ARTS

Updated by
Julene Snyder

A spirit of playfulness has pervaded San Francisco's arts, entertainment, and nightlife scenes ever since its days as a rowdy sailors' port. Perhaps nothing is more purely San Franciscan than *Beach Blanket Babylon,* a raucous cabaret act at Club Fugazi. The San Francisco Opera, the San Francisco Symphony, and the San Francisco Ballet are all nationally renowned, and dozens of alternative groups represent everything from gay and lesbian performance art to family circus and mime.

Nightlife

Although San Francisco is a compact city, with the prevailing influences of some neighborhoods spilling into others, the following generalizations should help you find the kind of entertainment you're looking for. **Nob Hill** is noted for its plush piano bars and panoramic skyline lounges. **North Beach** maintains a sense of its beatnik past in atmospheric bars and coffeehouses. Touristy **Fisherman's Wharf** is great for people-watching and attracts plenty of street performers. **Union Street** is home away from home for singles in search of company. South of Market—**SoMa,** for short—contains highly popular nightclubs, bars, and lounges. Gay men hang out in the **Castro District** and on **Polk Street,** lesbians in the **Mission District** (and sometimes the **Castro**). Twentysomethings and alternative types should check out the ever funky **Mission District** and **Haight Street** scenes.

Rock, Pop, Folk, and Blues

The Blue Lamp (✉ 561 Geary St., ☎ 415/885–1464), a downtown hole in the wall showcasing blues performers, has an aura of faded opulence.
Bottom of the Hill (✉ 1233 17th St., at Texas St., ☎ 415/626–4455), in the Potrero Hill District, showcases some of the city's best local alternative rock and blues.
DNA Lounge (✉ 375 11th St., near Harrison St., ☎ 415/626–1409), a two-floor SoMa haunt, hosts independent rock, funk, and rap on most weekends and DJ dancing on weeknights.
The Fillmore (✉ 1805 Geary Blvd., at Fillmore St., ☎ 415/346–6000), one of San Francisco's most famous rock music halls, serves up a varied menu of national and local acts: rock, reggae, grunge, jazz, comedy, folk, acid house, and more.
Freight and Salvage Coffee House (✉ 1111 Addison St., Berkeley, ☎ 510/548–1761), one of the finest folk houses in the country, is worth a trip across the bay. Blues, Cajun, and bluegrass artists also perform in this smoke- and alcohol-free space.
Great American Music Hall (✉ 859 O'Farrell St., at Polk St., ☎ 415/885–0750) hosts top-drawer entertainment—blues, folk, jazz, alternative rock, and occasionally comedy.
Kilowatt (✉ 3160 16th St., ☎ 415/861–2595) attracts adventurous indie-rock fans, with an emphasis on loud, cutting-edge local and national acts.
Last Day Saloon (✉ 406 Clement St., between 5th and 6th Aves., ☎ 415/387–6343) presents blues, Cajun, rock, and jazz artists.
Slim's (✉ 333 11th St., at Harrison St., ☎ 415/522–0333) specializes in what it labels "American roots music"—blues, jazz, and classic rock, and also presents alternative rock "spoken word" concerts.
Trocadero Transfer (✉ 520 4th St., at Bryant St., ☎ 415/495–6620), a cavernous SoMa space full of nooks and crannies, is a magnet for young alternative rock fans; Monday, Wednesday, and Friday are dance nights. Other nights of the week find touring and local bands that lean toward the louder side of the musical spectrum.

Jazz

Bruno's (✉ 2389 Mission St., at 19th St., ☎ 415/550–7455) is a slice of retro heaven in the Mission District. Drink swanky cocktails while listening to jazz, swing, and other bands.
Cafe du Nord (✉ 2170 Market St., at Sanchez St., ☎ 415/979–6545) hosts some of the liveliest jam sessions in town.
Elbo Room (✉ 647 Valencia St., at Sycamore St., ☎ 415/552–7788) is a convivial spot to hear up-and-coming jazz acts upstairs or relax in the hopping environs downstairs.
Enrico's (✉ 504 Broadway, at Kearny St., ☎ 415/982–6223), a beat-era tradition, is hip once again—the indoor/outdoor café has a high-life ambience, a fine menu (tapas and Italian), and mellow nightly jazz combos.

Jazz at Pearl's (✉ 256 Columbus Ave., near Broadway, ☎ 415/291–8255) is a good bet—the talent level is remarkably high, especially considering that there is rarely a cover.

Julie Ring's Heart and Soul (✉ 1695 Polk St., at Clay St., ☎ 415/673–7100), a sleek, plush 1940s retro room, captures the ambience of another era with just a hint of lounge-revival irony. The kitchen serves excellent appetizers and meals while local and national combos and vocalists perform jazz from the '40s through the '60s.

Kimball's East (✉ 5800 Shellmound St., Emeryville, ☎ 510/658–2555), in a shopping complex just off I–80 near Oakland, hosts such talents as El DeBarge, Jeffrey Osborne, and Mose Allison. With an elegant interior and fine food, it's one of the Bay Area's most luxurious supper clubs.

Orocco East-West Supper Club (✉ 3565 Geary St., at Arguello Blvd., ☎ 415/387–8788) is a newish addition to S.F.'s wave of retro supper clubs. Malaysian chef Alexander Ong oversees sensational East-West hybrid dishes; the two-story room presents live mellow jazz Wednesday from 8:30 PM and weekends from 6:30 PM.

Up and Down Club (✉ 1151 Folsom St., ☎ 415/626–2388), a hip restaurant and club whose owners include supermodel Christy Turlington, books up-and-coming jazz artists downstairs, as well as dancing to a DJ upstairs, Monday through Saturday.

Yoshi's (✉ 510 Embarcadero St., near Jack London Sq., Oakland, ☎ 510/238–9200) continues to be one of the Bay Area's best jazz venues. Jazz greats including Betty Carter, local favorite Kenny Burrell, Joshua Redman, and Cecil Taylor have played here, along with blues and Latin performers.

Cabarets

Club Fugazi (✉ 678 Green St., ☎ 415/421–4222) presents the long-running (two decades plus) *Beach Blanket Babylon,* a wacky musical send-up of San Francisco moods and mores. While the choreography is colorful, the singers brassy, and the songs witty, the real stars are the comically exotic costumes and famous ceiling-high "hats." Order tickets as far in advance as possible; the show has been sold out up to a month in advance. Those under 21 are admitted only to the Sunday matinee.

Coconut Grove (✉ 1415 Van Ness Ave., ☎ 415/776–1616) has a '40s supper-club ambience, superb (if pricey) cocktails, and nouvelle cuisine. Depending on the night you'll find swing, ragtime jazz, R&B, Latin salsa, or big-band music.

Finocchio's (✉ 506 Broadway, near Columbus Ave., ☎ 415/982–9388) hosts a drag revue that's decidedly retro—it's been running since 1936—which for the most part only adds to its charm.

Josie's Cabaret and Juice Joint (✉ 3583 16th St., at Market St., ☎ 415/861–7933), a small café and cabaret in the Castro District, books performers who reflect the countercultural feel of the neighborhood—from stand-up comedians to musicians to drag queens to monologuists.

New Orleans Room (✉ Mason and California Sts., ☎ 415/772–5259), in the Fairmont hotel, has a somewhat tacky 1960s hotel-bar ambience. Still, the talent on display is first-rate: Recent guests have included Cybill Shepherd and Frank Sinatra Jr.

Comedy Clubs

Cobb's Comedy Club (✉ The Cannery, 2801 Leavenworth St., at Beach St., ☎ 415/928–4320) books super stand-up comics such as Jake Johannsen, Rick Overton, and Janeane Garofalo.

Punch Line (✉ 444 Battery St., between Clay and Washington Sts., ☎ 415/397–7573), a launching pad for the likes of Jay Leno and Whoopi

Goldberg, features some of the area's top talents. Buy tickets in advance at BASS outlets (☎ 510/762–2277) or from the club's charge line (☎ 415/397–4337).

Dancing Emporiums

El Rio (✉ 3158 Mission St., ☎ 415/282–3325) is a casual Mission District spot with salsa dancing on Sunday (from 4 PM), '70s soul and funk on Wednesday, a global dance party on Friday, and live rock Saturday and Sunday.

Metronome Ballroom (✉ 1830 17th St., ☎ 415/252–9000) is at its most lively on weekend nights, when ballroom dancers come for lessons and revelry at this smoke- and alcohol-free spot.

Oz (✉ 335 Powell St., between Geary and Post Sts., ☎ 415/774–0116), on the top floor of the St. Francis Hotel—accessible via a glass elevator—has marble floors, plush chairs, a splendid panorama of the city, and dancing to a variety of sounds.

Voodoo (✉ 601 Eddy St., ☎ 415/921–3845), adjacent to Miss Pearl's Jam House, offers DJ dancing six nights a week, with genres ranging from funk to jazz to soul to street.

Piano Bars

Redwood Room (✉ Taylor and Geary Sts., ☎ 415/775–4700), in the Clift Hotel, is a classy art deco lounge with a low-key but sensuous ambience. Klimt reproductions cover the walls, and mellow sounds fill the air.

Ritz-Carlton Hotel (✉ 600 Stockton St., ☎ 415/296–7465) has a tastefully appointed lobby lounge where a harpist plays during afternoon high tea (weekdays 2:30–4:30, weekends 1–4:30). The lounge shifts to piano (with occasional vocal accompaniment) for cocktails until 11:30 weeknights and 1:30 AM weekends.

Washington Square Bar and Grill (✉ 1707 Powell St., on Washington Sq., ☎ 415/982–8123), affectionately known as the "Washbag" among San Francisco politicians and newspaper folk, hosts pianists performing jazz and popular standards.

Skyline Bars

Carnelian Room (✉ 555 California St., ☎ 415/433–7500), on the 52nd floor of the Bank of America Building, offers what is perhaps the loftiest view of San Francisco's magnificent skyline. The dress code requires jackets; ties are optional.

Crown Room (✉ California and Mason Sts., ☎ 415/772–5131), the aptly named lounge on the 24th floor of the Fairmont Hotel, is one of the most luxurious of the city's skyline bars. Just riding the glass-enclosed Skylift elevator is an experience in itself.

Harry Denton's Starlight Room (✉ 450 Powell St., ☎ 415/395–8595) has rose-velvet booths, romantic lighting, a small dance floor, and staff clad in tuxes or full-length gowns. Whenever live combos aren't playing, taped Sinatra rules.

Top of the Mark (✉ California and Mason Sts., ☎ 415/392–3434) hosts live music Wednesday through Saturday nights and dancing to standards from the '20s, '30s, and '40s on Friday and Saturday. The view is superb seven nights a week.

Singles Bars

Harry Denton's (✉ 161 Steuart St., ☎ 415/882–1333), one of San Francisco's liveliest, most upscale saloons, is packed with well-dressed young professionals.

Holding Company (⊠ 2 Embarcadero Center, ☎ 415/986–0797), one of the most popular weeknight Financial District watering holes, is where scores of office workers gather to enjoy friendly libations. The kitchen and bar are open weekdays.

Johnny Love's (⊠ 1500 Broadway, at Polk St., ☎ 415/931–8021) live-music offerings range from ska to swing to rockabilly to reggae. Late-night dancing to DJ-spun modern rock is also an option.

Perry's (⊠ 1944 Union St., at Buchanan St., ☎ 415/922–9022), the most famous of San Francisco's singles bars, is usually jam-packed. You can dine here on great hamburgers as well as more substantial fare.

Wine Bars

EOS Restaurant & Wine Bar. (☞ Dining, *above*.)

Hayes and Vine (⊠ 377 Hayes St., ☎ 415/626–5301) provides a warm haven, replete with earth tones and dominated by a white-onyx bar that's lit from underneath. Patrons select from 550 wines available by the bottle or 40 by the glass. Cheeses, pâtés, and caviar are among the culinary offerings.

London Wine Bar (⊠ 415 Sansome St., ☎ 415/788–4811), a warm Financial District spot (open weekdays only), serves 40 wines by the glass from a cellar of 8,000 bottles. Monthly dinners with wine makers are popular.

Longtime Favorites

Buena Vista (⊠ 2765 Hyde St., ☎ 415/474–5044), the Fisherman's Wharf area's most popular bar, introduced Irish coffee to the New World—or so they say. Because it has a fine view of the waterfront, it's usually packed with tourists.

Cypress Club (⊠ 500 Jackson St., at Columbus Ave., ☎ 415/296–8555) is an eccentric restaurant-bar where sensual, '20s-style opulence clashes with Fellini/Dalí frivolity.

Tonga Room (⊠ 950 Mason St., at California St., ☎ 415/772–5278) is San Francisco's house of high kitsch. Fake palm trees and "grass huts," a "lake" (combos play pop standards on a floating barge), and sprinkler system "rain" (complete with simulated thunder and lightning) create a tropical atmosphere that only grows more surreal as you quaff the selection of very fruity and very potent novelty cocktails.

Vesuvio Cafe (⊠ 255 Columbus Ave., between Broadway and Pacific Ave., ☎ 415/362–3370), near the legendary City Lights Bookstore, is little altered since its heyday as a haven for the beat poets.

Gay and Lesbian Nightlife

Gay Male Bars

Alta Plaza Restaurant & Bar (⊠ 2301 Fillmore St., at Washington St., ☎ 415/922–1444) is an upper Fillmore restaurant-bar that caters to nattily dressed guppies (gay yuppies) and their admirers. Live jazz is offered Sunday through Thursday nights; a DJ takes over on weekends.

Detour (⊠ 2348 Market St., at Noe St., ☎ 415/861–6053) draws a crowd that's youngish and a bit surly. The music is loud but well selected; go-go dancers hold court on Saturday night.

The Metro (⊠ 3600 16th St., at Market St., ☎ 415/703–9750), more upscale than the nearby Detour, has a balcony that overlooks the intersection of Noe, 16th, and Market streets.

Midnight Sun (⊠ 4067 18th St., at Castro St., ☎ 415/861–4186), one of the Castro's longest-standing and most popular bars, has riotously programmed giant video screens. Don't expect to hear yourself think.

N Touch (⌧ 1548 Polk St., at Sacramento St., ☎ 415/441–8413), a tiny dance bar, has long been popular with Asian–Pacific Islander gay men. In addition to videos, there's karaoke Tuesday and Sunday nights, and go-go boys perform Thursday night.

Pleasuredome (⌧ Club Townsend, 177 Townsend St., at 3rd St., ☎ 415/985–5256), a long-running, Sunday-only, gay-male-oriented dance event, shows no signs of slowing down.

Lesbian Bars

Club Q (⌧ 177 Townsend St., at 3rd St., ☎ 415/647–8258), a monthly (first Friday of every month) dance party from Page Hodel's One Groove Productions, is geared to "women and their friends" and is always packed.

CoCo Club (139 8th St., at Howard St., ☎ 415/626–2337), home to DJ Downtown Donna's Faster Pussycat on Sunday night, offers a variety of theme nights, including a drag cabaret, a coed erotic cabaret, and a woman's speakeasy. Saturday is women's night.

Girl Spot (⌧ 401 6th St., at Harrison St., ☎ 415/337–4962), affectionately nicknamed the G-Spot, recently moved to SoMa's End Up. Every Saturday night from 9, dance to Top 40, house, and R&B; several top San Francisco DJs keep the mix lively.

The Lexington Club (⌧ 3464 19th St., at Mission St., ☎ 415/863–2052), which has a hip and groovy jukebox, attracts a frisky young crowd.

Luna Sea (⌧ 2940 16th St., No. 216C, at S. Van Ness Ave., ☎ 415/863–2989) is a woman's gallery and theater space featuring an ever-changing lineup of visual arts displays, performance art, and readings. Some events are for women only. The space is smoke- and alcohol-free.

Red Dora's Bearded Lady Café and Cabaret (⌧ 485 14th St., at Guerrero St., ☎ 415/626–2805), a neighborhood venue, serves a predominantly lesbian and gay clientele. It's also a gallery with mostly women's work, with occasional music and spoken word.

The Arts

Updated by
Julene Snyder

Half-price, same-day tickets to many local and touring stage shows go on sale (cash only) at 11 AM, Tuesday through Saturday, at the **TIX Bay Area** booth, on the Stockton Street side of Union Square between Geary and Post streets. TIX is also a full-service ticket agency for theater and music events around the Bay Area (open until 6 Tuesday through Thursday and 7 Friday and Saturday). For recorded information about TIX tickets, call 415/433–7827. The city's charge-by-phone ticket service is **BASS** (☎ 510/762–2277 or 415/776–1999). **City Box Office** (⌧ 153 Kearny St., Suite 402, ☎ 415/392–4400) has a downtown charge-by-phone service.

Dance

The **San Francisco Ballet** (⌧ 301 Van Ness Ave., ☎ 415/865–2000), under the direction of Helgi Tomasson, has a primary season of classic and contemporary works that runs from February through May. The company's annual December presentation of the *Nutcracker* is spectacular.

Music

San Francisco Symphony (⌧ Davies Symphony Hall, Van Ness Ave. at Grove St., ☎ 415/864–6000) performs September through May under the direction of Michael Tilson Thomas.

Cal Performances (⌧ Zellerbach Hall, Bancroft and Telegraph Aves., Berkeley, ☎ 510/642–9988) presents acclaimed artists in all disciplines, from classical soloists to the latest jazz, world music, theatre, and dance ensembles.

Old First Concerts (✉ Old First Presbyterian Church, Van Ness Ave. at Sacramento St., ☎ 415/474–1608) is a well-respected Friday evening and Sunday afternoon series that offers chamber music, vocal soloists, new music, and jazz.

Stern Grove (✉ Sloat Blvd. at 19th Ave., ☎ 415/252–6252) is the location of the nation's oldest continual free summer music festival, 10 Sunday afternoon performances of symphony, opera, jazz, pop music, and dance. The amphitheater is in a eucalyptus grove below street level; dress for cool weather.

Opera

San Francisco Opera (✉ 301 Van Ness Ave., ☎ 415/864–3330) returned in fall 1997 to the War Memorial Opera House. The company performs a season of 10 operas from September to December and also schedules occasional summer festivals.

Theater

Three major commercial theaters, operated by the Shorenstein-Nederlander organization, are the **Curran** (✉ 445 Geary St., ☎ 415/474–3800), the **Golden Gate** (✉ Golden Gate Ave. and Taylor St., ☎ 415/474–3800), and the **Orpheum** (✉ 1192 Market St., near the Civic Center, ☎ 415/474–3800). **Marines Memorial Theatre** (✉ Sutter and Mason Sts., ☎ 415/441–7444) presents touring shows plus some local performances. **Theatre on the Square** (✉ 450 Post St., ☎ 415/433–9500) is a popular smaller venue.

The city's major nonprofit theater company is the **American Conservatory Theater (ACT),** which presents plays, from classics to contemporary works, often in rotating repertory. ACT performs at the **Geary Theater** (✉ 415 Geary St., ☎ 415/749–2228).

The leading producer of new plays is the **Magic Theatre** (✉ Bldg. D, Fort Mason Center, Laguna St. and Marina Blvd., ☎ 415/441–8822), which presents works by Octavio Solis, Jon Robin Baitz, Claire Chafee, and others. The **San Francisco Shakespeare Festival** offers free performances on summer weekends in Golden Gate Park (☎ 415/422–2222). The major avant-garde presenting organization is **Theater Artaud** (✉ 450 Florida St., in the Mission District, ☎ 415/621–7797). Some contemporary theater events, in addition to dance and music, are scheduled at the theater in the **Center for the Arts at Yerba Buena Gardens** (✉ 3rd and Howard Sts., ☎ 415/978–2787).

The **Lorraine Hansberry Theatre** (✉ 620 Sutter St., ☎ 415/474–8800) specializes in plays by black writers. **Theatre Rhinoceros** (✉ 2926 16th St., ☎ 415/861–5079) showcases gay and lesbian performers. **BRAVA!** (✉ 2789 24th St., ☎ 415/647–2822) fosters work by women playwrights and directors.

Berkeley Repertory Theatre (☎ 510/845–4700) performs an adventurous mix of classics and new plays. **California Shakespeare Festival** (☎ 510/548–9666), the Bay Area's largest outdoor summer theater event, performs in an amphitheater east of Oakland on Gateway Boulevard, just off state Highway 24.

OUTDOOR ACTIVITIES AND SPORTS

Beaches

Updated by
Tara Duggan

Baker Beach

Baker Beach is a local favorite, with gorgeous views of the Golden Gate Bridge, the Marin Headlands, and the bay. Its strong, dangerous waves make swimming a dangerous prospect, but the mile-long shoreline is ideal for fishing, building sand castles, or watching sea lions play in the surf. On warm days the entire beach is packed with bodies taking in the sun. Look for Baker Beach in the southwest corner of the Presidio, beginning at the end of Gibson Road, which turns off Bowley Street. The beach has picnic tables, grills, and trails that lead all the way to Golden Gate Bridge.

China Beach

Named for the poor Chinese fishermen who once camped here, China Beach, south of Baker Beach, has gentle waters April through October. It's sometimes marked on maps as Phelan Beach.

Ocean Beach

South of the Cliff House, Ocean Beach stretches along the western (ocean) side of San Francisco. Though certainly not the city's cleanest beach, it's wide and sandy, stretching for miles and perfect for a long walk or jog. It's popular with surfers, but swimming is not recommended.

Participant Sports

For information on participant sports, check the monthly issues of *City Sports* magazine, available free at sporting goods stores, tennis centers, and other recreational sites. The most important running event of the year is the *Examiner* Bay-to-Breakers race on the third Sunday in May. For information on this race, call 415/512–5000, ext. 2222.

Bicycling

With its legendary hills, San Francisco offers countless cycling challenges—but also plenty of level ground. To avoid the former, look for a copy of the *San Francisco Biking/Walking Guide* ($3): Sold in select bookstores, the guide indicates street grades and delineates biking routes that avoid major hills and heavy traffic. A completely flat route, the **Embarcadero** gives you a clear view of open waters and the Bay Bridge on the pier side, and sleek high-rises on the other. **Golden Gate Park** has paths throughout. Bike shops are strategically placed near favorite routes.

Boating and Sailing

Sailors take to San Francisco Bay year-round, but tricky currents and strong winds make the bay hazardous for inexperienced navigators. Boat rentals and charters are available throughout the Bay Area and are listed under "Boat Renting" in the Yellow Pages. **A Day on the Bay** (☎ 415/922–0227) is in San Francisco's small-craft marina, just minutes from the Golden Gate Bridge and open waters. **Cass' Marina** (✉ 1702 Bridgeway, at Napa St., ☎ 415/332–6789), in Sausalito, has a variety of sailboats that can be rented as long as you have a qualified sailor in the group.

Stow Lake (☎ 415/752–0347), in Golden Gate Park, has rowboat, pedal boat, and electric boat rentals. The lake is open daily for boating, but call for seasonal hours.

Fishing

Fishing boats leave from San Francisco, Sausalito, Berkeley, Emeryville, and Point San Pablo. They go for salmon and halibut outside the bay or striped bass and giant sturgeon within the bay (though heavy pollution in the bay may lower the quality of your catch). In San Francisco lines can be cast from San Francisco Municipal Pier, Fisherman's Wharf, Baker Beach, or Aquatic Park. Trout fishing is possible at Lake Merced; you can rent rods and boats and buy bait at the **Lake Merced Boating and Fishing Company** (✉ 1 Harding Rd., ☎ 415/753–1101). One-day licenses, good for ocean fishing only, are available for $5.75 on the charters; sporting goods stores sell full-year state licenses. Most charters depart daily from Fisherman's Wharf during the salmon-fishing season.

Lovely Martha's Sportfishing (⊠ Fisherman's Wharf, Berth 3, ☎ 415/871–1691) operates salmon-fishing excursions as well as bay tours. **Wacky Jacky** (⊠ Fisherman's Wharf, Pier 45, ☎ 415/586–9800) will take you salmon fishing in a sleek, fast, and comfortable 50-ft boat.

Fitness

The drop-in fee at the various branches of the **24-Hour Fitness** center (⊠ 1200 Van Ness St., ☎ 415/776–2200; ⊠ 350 Bay St., ☎ 415/395–9595; ⊠ 100 California St., ☎ 415/434–5080; ⊠ 2nd St. at Folsom, ☎ 415/543–7808) is $15. The **Embarcadero YMCA** (⊠ 169 Steuart St., ☎ 415/957–9622) has racquetball, a 25-meter swimming pool, and aerobics classes for $12. Those who prefer a women-only atmosphere can work out at the **Women's Training Center** (⊠ 2164 Market St., ☎ 415/864–6835) for a $10 day fee, which includes use of the sauna.

Golf

Call the golf information line (☎ 415/750–4653) to get detailed directions to the city's golf courses and reserve tee times. The **Presidio Golf Course** (⊠ W. Pacific Ave. and Arguello Blvd., ☎ 415/561–4653), an 18-holer managed by Arnold Palmer's company, is by most accounts the city's best course. **Harding** and **Fleming parks** (⊠ Harding Rd. and Skyline Blvd., ☎ 415/664–4690) have an 18-hole, par-72 course and a 9-hole executive course, respectively. **Lincoln Park** (⊠ 34th and Clement Sts., ☎ 415/221–9911) is an 18-hole, par-68 course. **Golden Gate** (⊠ 47th Ave. between Fulton St. and John F. Kennedy Dr., ☎ 415/751–8987) is a 9-holer in Golden Gate Park just above Ocean Beach.

Tennis

The San Francisco Recreation and Park Department maintains 132 public tennis courts throughout the city; all courts are free except those in Golden Gate Park. At **Mission Dolores Park** (⊠ 18th and Dolores Sts.), six courts are available on a first-come, first-served basis. There are 16 public courts in **Golden Gate Park** (☎ 415/753–7101), the only facility that allows you to make advance reservations.

Spectator Sports

3Com Park at Candlestick Point is the name of the stadium formerly known as Candlestick Park. Though it has a new name, the stadium is just as windy as ever—take along extra layers of clothing for day or night games. City shuttles marked Ballpark Special leave from numerous stops (☎ 415/673–6864). The best way get to the **Oakland Coliseum** and **Oakland Coliseum–Arena** is on a BART train (☎ 800/817–1717) to the Coliseum stop. To drive from San Francisco, take I–80 to I–580 to I–980 to I–880.

Baseball

The **San Francisco Giants** (☎ 415/467–8000) play at 3Com Park. Games rarely sell out. The **Oakland A's** play at the Oakland Coliseum (☎ 510/638–0500). Game-day tickets are usually available.

Basketball

The **Golden State Warriors** play NBA basketball at the Oakland Coliseum Arena. Tickets are available through BASS (☎ 510/762–2277).

Football

The **San Francisco 49ers** (☎ 415/468–2249) play at 3Com Park, but the games are almost always sold out far in advance. The brawling (on-field and off) **Oakland Raiders** play at the Oakland Coliseum. Except for high-profile games, tickets (☎ 510/639–7700 or 510/762–2277) are usually available.

Hockey
See San Jose Sharks *in* Side Trip to San Jose, *below.*

Soccer
The **San Jose Clash** (☎ 408/985–4625) brought major league soccer to the Bay Area in 1996. Look for the team from April through September in San Jose's Spartan Stadium; at other times of year they host qualifying games for international soccer competitions.

SHOPPING

From fringe fashions in the Haight to leather chaps in the Castro, San Francisco's many distinctive neighborhoods offer consumers a bit of everything. There are ginseng health potions in Chinatown, fine antiques and art in Jackson Square, handmade kites and kimonos in Japantown, and bookstores specializing in everything from beat poetry to ecology throughout the city. For those who prefer the mainstream, there are high-end boutiques on Union Street and fine department stores in Union Square.

Major Shopping Districts

The Castro/Noe Valley
Revised by
Julene Snyder

Often called the gay capital of the world, the Castro is filled with clothing boutiques, home accessory stores, and various specialty stores. **A Different Light Bookstore** doubles as an unofficial community center. **Under One Roof** (⌧ 2362-B Market St., ☎ 415/252–9430) donates the profits from its home and garden items, gourmet foods, bath products, books, frames, and cards to northern California AIDS organizations.

Just south of Castro on 24th Street, the largely residential Noe Valley is an enclave of gourmet food stores, used record shops, clothing boutiques, and specialty gift stores. Much of Armistead Maupin's *Tales of the City* was filmed in the villagelike neighborhood, whose small shops and relaxed street life evoke a '70s mood. At **Panetti's** (⌧ 3927 24th St., ☎ 415/648–2414) you'll find whimsical picture frames, journals, costume jewelry, and more.

Chinatown
Racks of Chinese silks, toy trinkets, colorful pottery, baskets, and carved figurines are displayed in racks on the sidewalks, alongside herb stores that specialize in ginseng and roots. Dominating the neighborhood are the sights and smells of food: crates of bok choy, tanks of live crabs, and hanging whole chickens.

Embarcadero Center
Five modern towers of shops, restaurants, and offices plus the Hyatt Regency Hotel make up the Embarcadero Center, downtown at the end of Market Street.

Fisherman's Wharf
Pier 39 is one of the world's most visited sites, though the shops at Ghirardelli Square and the Cannery are more interesting. All three also have restaurants plus musicians, mimes, magicians, and other entertainment.

The Haight
Haight Street is always an attraction for visitors, if only to see the sign at Haight and Ashbury streets. These days, in addition to tie-dyed shirts, you'll find high-quality vintage clothing, funky jewelry, art from around the world, and reproductions of art deco accessories.

Hayes Valley
Hayes Valley, just west of the Civic Center, is an up-and-coming shopping district. The area is packed with art galleries and unusual stores such

as **Worldware** (⊠ 336 Hayes St., ☎ 415/487–9030), where everything from clothing to furniture to candles is made of organic materials.

Japantown

The three-block **Japan Center** (⊠ Between Laguna and Fillmore Sts. and Geary Blvd. and Post St.) includes an 800-car public garage and three shop-filled buildings. Especially worthwhile are the Kintetsu and Kinokuniya buildings, where shops and showrooms sell cameras, tapes and records, new and old porcelains, pearls, antique kimonos, tansu chests (Japanese chests used mainly for storage), paintings, and more.

The Marina District

Chestnut Street, one block north of Lombard Street and stretching from Fillmore to Broderick streets, caters to the shopping whims of Marina District residents. Among the district's standouts, **Lucca Delicatessen** is famous for its handmade ravioli and its huge selection of Italian gourmet goods.

The Mission

Known as one of the city's sunniest neighborhoods, the Mission is also one of its most ethnically diverse, with a large Latino population and a growing contingent of young artists, musicians, and new bohemians. In addition to those with a hunger for inexpensive Mexican food, the area draws bargain shoppers with its many used clothing, furniture, and alternative book stores. The main shopping streets are Mission and Valencia between 16th and 24th streets.

North Beach

Shopping here is clustered tightly around Washington Square and Columbus Avenue. Businesses include clothing boutiques and antiques and vintage wares shops. Once the center of the beat movement, North Beach still has a bohemian spirit that's especially apparent at **City Lights,** where the beat poets live on.

Pacific Heights

Pacific Heights residents head for Fillmore Street between Post Street and Pacific Avenue, and Sacramento Street between Lyon and Maple streets, where private residences alternate with good bookstores, fine clothing and gift shops, thrift stores, and art galleries. A local favorite is the **Sue Fisher King Company,** whose quality home accessories fit right into this upscale neighborhood.

South of Market

Dozens of discount outlets, most open daily, have sprung up along the streets and alleyways bordered by 2nd, Townsend, Howard, and 10th streets. At the other end of the spectrum are the gift shops of the Museum of Modern Art (⊠ 151 3rd St.) and the Center for the Arts at Yerba Buena Gardens (⊠ 3rd and Mission Sts.); both sell handmade jewelry and various other great gift items.

Union Square

Serious shoppers head straight to Union Square, San Francisco's main shopping artery and the site of most department stores, including Macy's, Neiman Marcus, and Saks Fifth Avenue. Also here are the Disney Store, F.A.O. Schwarz, and the Virgin Megastore, along with the boutiques of Hermès of Paris, Gucci, Celine of Paris, Alfred Dunhill, Louis Vuitton, and Cartier. Across from the cable car turntable at Powell and Market streets is the San Francisco Shopping Centre (⊠ 865 Market St.), with the Nordstrom department store and three dozen other businesses, including a two-floor Warner Bros. store (☎ 415/974–5254), with mementos of the studio's past and present.

Union Street

Out-of-towners sometimes confuse Union Street with Union Square. Nestled at the foot of a hill between Pacific Heights and the Marina District, the street is lined with contemporary fashion and custom jewelry shops, along with a few antiques shops and art galleries.

SIDE TRIPS FROM SAN FRANCISCO

Sausalito and Tiburon

Sausalito

Updated by
Kristina
Malsberger
and Sharron
Wood

Like much of San Francisco, Sausalito had a raffish reputation before it went upscale. Discovered in 1775 by Spanish explorers and named Saucelito (Little Willow) for the trees growing around its springs, the town served as a port for whaling ships during the 19th century. By the mid-1800s wealthy San Franciscans were making Sausalito their getaway across the bay; they built lavish Victorian summer homes in the hills, many of which still stand today. Sausalito developed its bohemian flair in the '50s and '60s, but even before that its many bordellos at the turn of the century attracted a somewhat resolute crowd—mainly sailors and dock workers. The town remains friendly and casual, although summer traffic jams can fray nerves. If possible, visit on a weekday—and take the ferry.

Bridgeway is Sausalito's main thoroughfare and prime destination, with the bay, yacht harbor, and waterfront restaurants on one side, and more restaurants, shops, and hillside homes on the other. Stairs along the west side of Bridgeway climb the hill to Sausalito's wooded neighborhoods.

The **Village Fair** (⊠ 777 Bridgeway, ☎ 415/332–1902) is a four-story former warehouse that's been converted into a warren of clothing, crafts, and gift boutiques.

The U.S. Army Corps of Engineers uses the **Bay Model,** a 400-square-ft replica of the entire San Francisco Bay and the San Joaquin–Sacramento River delta, to reproduce the rise and fall of tides, the flow of currents, and the other physical forces at work on the bay. The model is housed in a former World War II shipyard building, along with a display on shipbuilding history. At the same site is the *Wapama,* a hulking World War I–era steam freighter being restored by volunteers. ⊠ *2100 Bridgeway, at Marinship Way,* ☎ *415/332–3871.* ⊡ *Free.* ⊙ *Labor Day–Memorial Day, Tues.–Sat. 9–4; Memorial Day–Labor Day, Tues.–Fri. 9–4, weekends 10–6.*

Some of the 400 **houseboats** that make up Sausalito's "floating homes community" line the shore of Richardson Bay. The sight of these colorful, quirky abodes is one of Marin County's most famous views—they range from rustic to eccentric to flamboyant. For a close-up view of the houseboats, head north on Bridgeway from downtown, turn right on Gate 6 Road, and park where it dead-ends at the public shore.

The **Bay Area Discovery Museum** fills five former military buildings with entertaining and enlightening hands-on exhibits. Youngsters and their families can fish from a boat at the indoor wharf, explore the skeleton of a house, and make multitrack recordings. From San Francisco take the Alexander Avenue exit from U.S. 101 and follow signs to East Fort Baker. ⊠ *557 McReynolds Rd., at East Fort Baker,* ☎ *415/487–4398.* ⊡ *$7.* ⊙ *Summer, Tues.–Sun. 10–5; fall–spring, Tues.–Thurs. 9–4 and Fri.–Sun. 10–5.*

The Bay Area

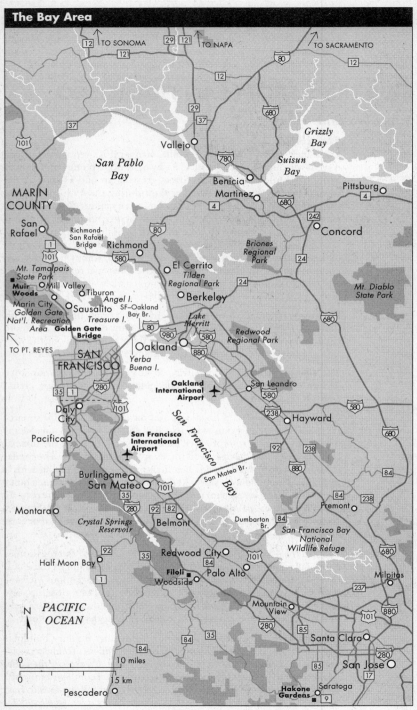

TO SONOMA
TO NAPA
TO SACRAMENTO

San Pablo Bay

Grizzly Bay

Suisun Bay

Vallejo

Benicia

Martinez

Pittsburg

Concord

MARIN COUNTY

San Rafael

Richmond-San Rafael Bridge

Richmond

Briones Regional Park

Mt. Diablo State Park

El Cerrito

Tilden Regional Park

Berkeley

Mt. Tamalpais State Park

Mill Valley

Muir Woods

Tiburon

Angel I.

Marin City

Sausalito

Treasure I.

SF–Oakland Bay Br.

Golden Gate Nat'l. Recreation Area

Golden Gate Bridge

Lake Merritt

Redwood Regional Park

TO PT. REYES

SAN FRANCISCO

Oakland

Yerba Buena I.

San Leandro

Daly City

Oakland International Airport

Pacifica

Hayward

San Francisco International Airport

San Francisco Bay

Burlingame

San Mateo

Montara

San Mateo Br.

Crystal Springs Reservoir

Belmont

Dumbarton Br.

Fremont

San Francisco Bay National Wildlife Refuge

Half Moon Bay

Redwood City

Filoli

Woodside

Palo Alto

Milpitas

PACIFIC OCEAN

N

Mountain View

Santa Clara

San Jose

0   10 miles
0   15 km

Pescadero

Hakone Gardens

Saratoga

DINING

$$$ ✕ **Mikayla at Casa Madrona.** Although the food at this longtime Sausalito hilltop dining room has followed a rocky course, the view has never been less than superb. The California menu, based on grilled fish and meats, is built around fresh local foods. Sunday brunch is popular. ⊠ *801 Bridgeway,* ☎ *415/331–5888. Reservations essential weekends. AE, D, DC, MC, V. No lunch.*

$$ ✕ **Alta Mira.** This Sausalito landmark, in a Spanish-style hotel a block above Bridgeway, has spectacular views of the bay from a heated front terrace and a windowed dining room. It's a favored Bay location for Sunday brunch (try the famed eggs Benedict and Ramos Fizz), alfresco lunch, or cocktails at sunset. Though the California-Continental cuisine is inconsistent, the view never fails. ⊠ *125 Bulkley Ave.,* ☎ *415/ 332–1350. AE, DC, MC, V.*

$$ ✕ **Spinnaker.** Spectacular bay views, homemade pastas, and seafood specialties are the prime attractions in this contemporary building beyond the harbor near the yacht club. You might find a stately pelican perched on one of the pilings just outside. ⊠ *100 Spinnaker Dr.,* ☎ *415/332–1500. AE, DC, MC, V.*

$–$$ ✕ **Christophe.** The early-bird dinners at this charming French dining room are a penny pincher's delight. A four-course meal costs no more than two admissions to a first-run movie, and the choices include such irresistible plates as duck confit, lamb fillet with port wine sauce, and chocolate profiteroles. Prices rise reasonably as the night goes on. ⊠ *1919 Bridgeway,* ☎ *415/332–9244. MC, V. Closed Mon. No lunch.*

$ ✕ **Lighthouse Café.** This inexpensive coffee shop serves breakfast and lunch—omelets, sandwiches, and burgers—every day from 6:30 (7 on weekends). Most find the down-to-earth atmosphere and simple fare— including Danish meatballs, herring, and salmon open-face sandwiches—a welcome break from tourist traps and seafood extravaganzas. ⊠ *1311 Bridgeway,* ☎ *415/331–3034. Reservations not accepted. No credit cards.*

Tiburon

On a peninsula called Punta de Tiburon (Shark Point) by the Spanish explorers, this beautiful Marin County community maintains a villagelike atmosphere despite the encroachment of commercial establishments in the downtown area. The harbor faces Angel Island across Raccoon Strait. San Francisco is directly south, 6 mi across the bay, which makes the view from the decks of restaurants on the harbor a major attraction. More low-key than Sausalito, life in Tiburon has centered around the waterfront ever since the town's incarnation in 1884, when ferryboats from San Francisco connected here with a railroad to San Rafael. Whenever the weather is pleasant, and particularly during the summer, the ferry is the most relaxing way to visit and avoid traffic and parking problems.

Tiburon's **Main Street** is lined on the bay side with restaurants with outdoor decks that jut out over the harbor, giving diners a bird's-eye view of San Francisco. On the other side of the narrow street are shops and galleries that sell casual clothing, gifts, jewelry, posters, and paintings.

At the end of the block, Main Street turns into **Ark Row,** a tree-shaded walk lined with antiques and specialty stores. Look closely, and you'll see that some of the buildings are actually old houseboats that once floated in Belvedere Cove before being beached and transformed into stores. **Windsor Vineyards** (⊠ 72 Main St., ☎ 415/435–3113) has free tastings in a converted 19th-century rooming house.

The stark-white **Old St. Hilary's Historic Preserve,** a Victorian-era Carpenter Gothic church, stands like a puritanical matriarch overlooking the town from her hillside perch. Operated by the Landmarks Society as a historical and botanical museum, the church is surrounded by a wildflower preserve that is spectacular in May and June, when the rare black jewel flower is in bloom. ✉ *Esperanza St. off Mar West St.,* ☎ *415/435–2567.* ☞ *Free.* ☉ *Apr.–Oct., Wed. and Sun. 1–4.*

In a wildlife sanctuary on the route into Tiburon is the 1876 **Lyford House,** a Victorian fantasy that serves as headquarters for the Richardson Bay Audubon Society. ✉ *376 Greenwood Beach Rd., off Tiburon Blvd.,* ☎ *415/388–2524.* ☞ *Free.* ☉ *Nov.–Apr., Sun. 1–4.*

DINING

$$ ✕ **Guaymas.** Come here for authentic Mexican dishes such as seviche, *carnitas ropa* (slowly roasted pork with salsa and black beans), mesquite-grilled fish, tamales, and *pollo en mole* (chicken with chocolate sauce, chilies, and countless spices). The heated terrace bar has views of the bay. Sunday brunch is popular, so reserve in advance. ✉ *5 Main St., at ferry terminal,* ☎ *415/435–6300. DC, MC, V.*

$$ ✕ **Tutto Mare Ristorante.** A wood-burning oven here ensures crisp-crust pizzas, while upstairs an exhibition kitchen turns out pastas and grilled fish, meats, and fowl. The floor-to-ceiling windows on the second floor look out on a heated outdoor deck that is crowded with diners on mild days and evenings. ✉ *9 Main St.,* ☎ *415/435–4747. AE, DC, MC, V.*

$ ✕ **Sam's Anchor Cafe.** Sam's is a major draw for tourists and old salts, who flock to its outside deck for bay views and beer. The informal restaurant has mahogany wainscoting and old photos on the walls. Crayons and a color-in menu cater to kids. Burgers, fresh seafood, sandwiches, soups, and salads are standards, but food pales next to the atmosphere. ✉ *27 Main St.,* ☎ *415/435–4527. AE, D, DC, MC, V.*

Sausalito and Tiburon Essentials

ARRIVING AND DEPARTING

By Bus: Golden Gate Transit (☎ 415/332–6600) buses travel to Sausalito and Tiburon from 1st and Mission streets and other points in the city. The trip takes 45 minutes one-way.

By Car: To get to Sausalito from San Francisco, cross the Golden Gate Bridge and head north on U.S. 101 to the Sausalito exit. Go south on Bridgeway to the municipal parking lot (bring plenty of change for the meters) near the center of town. The trip takes 20 to 45 minutes one-way. To get to Tiburon, take U.S. 101 to the Tiburon Boulevard exit.

By Ferry: The **Golden Gate Ferry** (☎ 415/332–6600) crosses the bay to Sausalito from the south wing of the Ferry Building at Market Street and the Embarcadero; the trip takes 30 minutes. **Red & White Fleet** ferries (☎ 415/546–2896) depart daily for Sausalito and Tiburon from Pier 43½ at Fisherman's Wharf. Ferries also depart to Tiburon weekdays only from the Ferry Building. Catamaran boats travel to Tiburon in 20 minutes, but the slower ferries can take up to an hour.

The East Bay

Oakland

Oakland's allure lies in its amazing diversity: Only here can you find a Nigerian clothing store, a beautifully renovated Victorian home, a Buddhist meditation center, and a salsa club, all in the same block. Oakland's multifaceted nature reflects its colorful and often tumultuous history. Once a cluster of Mediterranean-style homes and gardens that served as a bedroom community for San Francisco, the city became a hub of shipbuilding and industry almost overnight when the United States entered World War II. In the '60s and '70s, an intense community pride gave rise to militant groups like the Black Panther Party and the Symbionese Liberation Army, but the groups were no match for the economic hardships and racial tensions that plagued Oakland in the post-war era. In many neighborhoods the reality was widespread poverty and gang violence—subjects that dominated the songs of myriad Oakland rappers.

Oakland is a mosaic of its past: Affluent types have once again flocked to the city's hillside homes as a warmer and more spacious alternative to San Francisco, while a constant flow of new residents—many from Central America and Asia—ensures continued diversity, vitality, and growing pains. Many neighborhoods to the west and south of downtown remain run-down and unsafe, but a renovated downtown area and the thriving Jack London Square have injected new life into the city. Some areas, like Piedmont and Rockridge, are perfect places for browsing, eating, or just relaxing between sightseeing trips to Oakland's architectural gems, rejuvenated waterfront, and numerous green spaces.

Numbers in the margin correspond to points of interest on the Oakland map.

❶ The **Oakland Museum of California** is housed in landscaped buildings that display the state's art, history, and natural science. The Gallery of Natural Sciences surveys a typical stretch of California from the Pacific Ocean to the Nevada border, including plants and wildlife. A breathtaking film, *Fast Flight,* condenses the trip into five minutes. The museum's sprawling Cowell Hall of California History includes everything from Spanish-era artifacts to a gleaming fire engine that battled the flames in San Francisco in 1906. The museum's Gallery of California Art has an eclectic collection of modern works and early landscapes; of particular interest are paintings by Richard Diebenkorn, Joan Brown, Elmer Bischoff, and David Park, all members of the Bay Area Figurative School, which flourished here after World War II. ⊠ *1000 Oak St., at 10th St.,* ☎ *510/238–3401.* ⊠ *$5.* ⊙ *Wed.–Sat. 10–5, Sun. noon–7.*

❷ A proud reminder of the days when Oakland was a wealthy bedroom community, the **Camron-Stanford House** exudes dignity from its foundation up to its ornate widow's walk. Built in 1876, the Victorian served as the home of the Oakland Museum from 1910 to 1967. Six painstakingly redecorated period rooms occupy the upper floor—a tribute to the craftsmanship and dedication that went into the 1978 restoration. ⊠ *1418 Lakeside Dr.,* ☎ *510/836–1976.* ⊠ *$4.* ⊙ *Wed. 11–4, Sun. 1–5.*

❸ **Lake Merritt** is a 155-acre oasis surrounded by parks, with several out-
❹ door attractions on the north side. The **Rotary Nature Center and Waterfowl Refuge** (☎ 510/238–3739) at the foot of Perkins Street is the nesting site of herons, egrets, geese, and ducks in the spring and summer. It's open daily from 10 to 5.

❺ The **Paramount Theater** (⊠ 2025 Broadway, ☎ 510/465–6400) is perhaps the city's best example of the art deco style. It is a venue for concerts and performances of all kinds. For $1 you can take a two-hour tour of the building at 10 AM on the first and third Saturday of each month.

❻ **Preservation Park** is an idyllic little street lined with 14 restored Victorian homes and tidy, bright green lawns. Wooden benches surrounding a bubbling fountain provide an excellent place to enjoy the architecture and take a brief respite from the busy city center.

❼ A former resident of Oakland, writer Jack London spent many a day boozing and brawling in the waterfront area now called **Jack London Square,** home to a collection of shops, restaurants, small museums, and

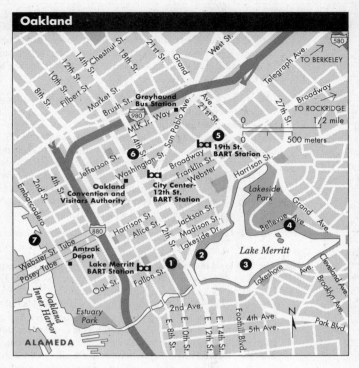

historic sites. A bronze bust in the square commemorates London, author of *The Call of the Wild, The Sea Wolf, Martin Eden,* and *The Cruise of the Snark,* among others. **Heinold's First and Last Chance Saloon** (⊠ 56 Jack London Sq., ☎ 510/839–6761) was one of London's old haunts.

The upscale neighborhood of **Rockridge,** northeast of downtown on Broadway, is one of Oakland's most desirable places to live. For a look at California bungalow architecture at its finest, explore the tree-lined streets that radiate out from College Avenue just north and south of the BART station. **College Avenue** is the main shopping strip here. At **Market Hall** (⊠ 5655 College Ave., ☎ 510/547–4005), an airy European-style marketplace, eight gourmet specialty shops offer everything from Napa Valley wines to garlic goat cheese to organic produce.

Berkeley

Although the University of California dominates Berkeley's heritage and contemporary life, the two are not synonymous: The city of 100,000 facing San Francisco across the bay has other interesting attributes. Surrounding the campus are several dozen cafés, without which the city might very well collapse. Students, faculty, and other Berkeley residents spend hours nursing coffee concoctions of various persuasions while they read, discuss, and debate—or eavesdrop on others doing the same.

The **Phoebe Hearst Museum of Anthropology** has a collection of more than 4,000 artifacts, only a small fraction of which are on display at any time. Exhibits might survey the archaeology of ancient America or the crafts of Pacific Islanders. The museum also houses artifacts made by Ishi, the lone survivor of a California Indian tribe. ⊠ *U.C. Berkeley, Kroeber Hall,* ☎ *510/642–3681.* ➥ *$2.* ⊙ *Wed.–Sun. 10–4:30, Thurs. until 9.*

The **Berkeley Art Museum** houses an interesting collection of works spanning five centuries, though the emphasis is on contemporary art. Changing exhibits—everything from life-size altarpieces to *Wizard of Oz*–inspired installations—line the spiral ramps and balcony galleries. Don't miss the vibrant paintings by the abstract expressionist Hans Hofmann. On the ground floor is the **Pacific Film Archive**, which programs historic and contemporary films. ⊠ *2626 Bancroft Way,* ☎ *510/642–0808 for museum or 510/642–1124 for film-program information.* ▭ *$6.* ⊘ *Wed. and Fri.–Sun. 11–5, Thurs. 11–9.*

More than 13,500 species of plants from all over the world flourish in the 34-acre **U.C. Botanical Garden**—all made possible by Berkeley's temperate climate. Informative tours of the garden are given weekends at 1:30. Benches and shady picnic tables make this a relaxing alternative to the busy main campus. ⊠ *Centennial Dr.,* ☎ *510/642–3343.* ▭ *Free.* ⊘ *Daily 9–4:45.*

☾ The fortresslike **Lawrence Hall of Science** is a dazzling science education center with hands-on displays for children. On weekends there are special lectures, demonstrations, and planetarium shows, and on clear Saturday nights from 8 to 11, the museum sets up telescopes on its outdoor plaza for the popular Saturday Night Stargazing. ⊠ *Centennial Dr.,* ☎ *510/642–5132.* ▭ *$6.* ⊘ *Daily 10–5.*

The 2,000-acre **Tilden Park** (☎ 510/562–7275) is an oasis in the midst of the city, with a botanical garden, an 18-hole golf course, an environmental education center, and 2,000 acres crisscrossed by paths and sprinkled with picnic sites. Among the children's attractions are miniature steam trains, pony rides, and the vintage menagerie-style carousel.

DINING

$$–$$$$ ✕ **Chez Panisse Café & Restaurant.** Alice Waters remains the mastermind behind this legendary eatery. In the downstairs restaurant, where redwood paneling, a fireplace, lavish floral arrangements, and personal service create the ambience of a private club, dinners are prix fixe and pricey, although the cost is lower on weekdays. The daily changing menu might include salmon wrapped in grape leaves with spinach gratin and chanterelles, or beef fillet with fried zucchini flowers. Upstairs in the café the atmosphere is informal, the crowd livelier, the prices lower, and the menu simpler. ⊠ *1517 Shattuck Ave., north of University Ave.,* ☎ *510/548–5525 for restaurant, 510/548–5049 for café. Reservations essential for restaurant. AE, D, DC, MC, V. Closed Sun.*

$$ ✕ **Café Rouge.** The short seasonal menu at this Mediterranean-style bistro runs the gamut from the sophisticated—salmon with fennel-and-olive compote—to the everyday—a hamburger topped with cheddar and flanked by a pile of fries. ⊠ *1782 4th St.,* ☎ *510/525–1440. MC, V. No dinner Mon.*

$ ✕ **Bette's Oceanview Diner.** Buttermilk pancakes that you'll never forget are just one of the specialties at this 1930s-inspired diner, complete with checkered floors and burgundy booths. There are also *huevos rancheros* (Mexican-style scrambled eggs) and lox and eggs for breakfast, and kosher East Coast franks, Chinese chicken salad, and a slew of sandwiches for lunch. The wait for a seat can be long; if you're starving, Bette's To Go, right next door, will press food into your hands in a hurry. ⊠ *1807 4th St.,* ☎ *510/644–3230. No credit cards. No dinner.*

$ ✕ **Picante Cocina Mexicana.** A no-nonsense, barnlike place, Picante is a find for anyone in search of good Mexican food for a song. The flour is freshly ground for the tortillas and tamales, the salsas are complex, and the combinations are inventive: Try tamales filled with butternut squash and chilies or a simple taco of roasted *poblanos* (peppers) and sautéed onions. ⊠ *1328 6th St.,* ☎ *510/525–3121. MC, V.*

East Bay Essentials

ARRIVING AND DEPARTING

By Car: Take I–80 east across the Bay Bridge. To go to Oakland, take I–580 off the Bay Bridge to the Grand Avenue exit for Lake Merritt. To reach downtown and the waterfront, take I–980 from I–580 and exit at 12th Street. To get to Berkeley, stay on I–80 and take the University Avenue exit through downtown Berkeley to the campus, or take the Ashby Avenue exit and turn left on Telegraph Avenue to the traditional campus entrance; there is a parking garage on Channing Way. Both trips take about 30 minutes, longer during rush hour.

By Light Rail: BART trains (☎ 800/817–1717) make stops in downtown Berkeley and in several parts of Oakland, including Rockridge. Use the Lake Merritt station for the Oakland Museum and southern Lake Merritt, the Oakland City Center–12th Street station for downtown, and the 19th Street station for the Paramount Theater and the north side of Lake Merritt. From the Berkeley station it's a five-minute walk on Center Street to the western edge of campus. Both trips take from 45 minutes to one hour one-way.

VISITOR INFORMATION

Oakland Convention and Visitors Authority (✉ 550 10th St., Suite 214, ☎ 510/839–9000). **Berkeley Visitor Information Center** (✉ University Hall, Room 101, University Ave. and Oxford St., ☎ 510/642–5215).

The Peninsula

Depending on where you enter the peninsula area south of San Francisco, you'll experience one of three faces. Along U.S. 101, on the eastern side of the peninsula, you'll see office complex after shopping center after tower. A few miles west, I–280 takes you past lakes, reservoirs, and rolling hills. Highway 1 travels along the coast.

Half Moon Bay

Although the San Mateo County coast is only a few miles from the inland peninsula and San Francisco, its undeveloped hills, rugged coastline, and quaint towns and inns are worlds away from urban sprawl, strip shopping centers, and traffic congestion. Set out from San Francisco down scenic Highway 1, hugging the twists and turns of the coast, or venture 11 mi west from I–280 near San Mateo, over hilly Highway 92. Main Street in Half Moon Bay, the coast's most populated community (10,000 people) is lined with five blocks of small crafts shops, art galleries, and outdoor cafés, many housed in renovated 19th-century structures. Half Moon Bay comes to life on the third weekend in October, when 300,000 people gather for the **Half Moon Bay Art and Pumpkin Festival** (☎ 650/726–9652).

The 4-mi stretch of **Half Moon Bay State Beach** (✉ Hwy. 1, west of Main St., ☎ 650/726–8819) is perfect for long walks, kite flying, and picnic lunches, though the 50°F water and dangerous currents prevent most visitors from swimming.

The **Bicyclery** (✉ 432 Main St., ☎ 650/726–6000) has bike rentals and will provide information on organized rides up and down the coast. If you prefer to go it alone, try the 3-mi bike trail that leads from Kelly Avenue in Half Moon Bay to Mirada Road in Miramar.

Built in 1928 after two horrible shipwrecks on the point, the **Point Montara Lighthouse** still has its original light keeper's quarters from the late 1800s. Gray whales pass this point during their migration from November through April, so bring your binoculars. The lighthouse is also a youth hostel known for its outdoor hot tub at ocean's edge. (✉

16th St. at Hwy. 1, Montara, ☎ *650/728–7177.* ⊙ *Call for hrs, tours, and lodging rates.*

DINING AND LODGING

$–$$ ✕ **San Benito House.** Tucked inside a historic inn in the heart of Half Moon Bay, this homey operation prepares memorable sandwiches with bread baked in the restaurant's oven. Candlelight dinners feature fresh fish and house-made pastas. ⊠ *356 Main St.,* ☎ *650/726–3425. MC, V. No dinner Mon.–Wed.*

$–$$ ✕ **Two Fools.** The kitchen tosses together big organic salads and packs contemporary burritos with a healthy mix of ingredients. A slice of old-fashioned American meat loaf topped with caramelized onions is sandwiched in a house-made bun at lunchtime. Locals stop here regularly for takeout at lunch and dinnertime. ⊠ *408 Main St.,* ☎ *650/712–1222. MC, V. No dinner Mon.–Tues.*

$$$$ ⊞ **Mill Rose Inn.** Perhaps the most decadent B&B in the entire Bay Area, the Mill Rose Inn pampers guests with in-room fireplaces, antique beds stacked high with down comforters, decanters of sherry and brandy on the tables, in-room coffee and cocoa, and baskets of fruit and candies. Room rates include a lavish champagne breakfast and afternoon snacks. ⊠ *615 Mill St., 94019,* ☎ *650/726–8750,* ℻ *650/726–3031. 4 rooms, 2 suites. No-smoking rooms, refrigerators, in-room VCRs. AE, D, DC, MC, V.*

$$ ⊞ **The Goose and Turrets.** Knickknacks from the international travels of innkeepers Raymond and Emily Hoche-Mong fill the shelves here, and the common area with a wood-burning stove is like an art and history museum. A full breakfast, afternoon goodies, and homemade chocolate truffles are sure to make anyone feel at home. ⊠ *835 George St., 94037,* ☎ *650/728–5451. 5 rooms. Breakfast room, no-smoking rooms, boccie. AE, D, DC, MC, V.*

OFF THE BEATEN PATH   **PESCADERO** – Walking down Stage Road, Pescadero's main street, it's hard to believe you're only 30 minutes from the high-tech Silicon Valley. The few short blocks that make up the downtown area could almost serve as the backdrop for a western movie, with Duarte's Tavern (⊠ 202 Stage Rd., ☎ 650/879-0464) serving as the centerpiece. November through April you can look for mussels at Pescadero State Beach, where sandy expanses, tidal pools, and outcroppings form one of the coast's more scenic beaches. At the Pescadero Marsh Natural Preserve, hikers can spy on birds and other wildlife by following any of the trails that crisscross 500 acres of marshland. Early spring and fall are the best times to visit. ⊠ Pescadero State Beach, Hwy. 1, ☎ 650/879-2170. ⊠ Free; parking $5. ⊙ 8–sunset.

Palo Alto and Woodside

Palo Alto's main attraction is the campus of **Stanford University,** whose 8,200 acres of grass-covered hills were once part of Leland Stanford's farm. (Stanford, a railroad baron, was governor of California in the 1800s; the university is named for his son.) Surrounding the campus are residential neighborhoods lined with cafés, bookstores, and music shops.

The main campus entrance, **Palm Drive,** is an extension of University Avenue from Palo Alto. Lined with majestic palm trees and leading directly to the main quadrangle, this entrance will give you a full perspective of Stanford's unique California mission–Romanesque architecture and its western Ivy League ambience. Free one-hour **walking tours** of Stanford University leave daily at 11 and 3:15 from the Visitor Information Booth (☎ 650/723–2560 or 650/723–2053) at the front of the quadrangle.

The **Stanford Art Gallery** is home to visiting shows, some student works, and a selection of the university's historical artifacts. Through 1998 the gallery will display works from the Stanford Museum of Art, which is closed for renovations until at least early 1999. ⊠ *Next to Hoover Tower,* ☎ *650/723–2842 or 650/723–4177 for a recording of current exhibits.* 🖭 *Donation requested.* 𝕆 *Tues.–Fri. 10–5, weekends 1–5. Guided gallery tours Thurs. at 12:15 and Sun. at 2.*

For a look at some less traditional art, seek out the inconspicuous **Papua New Guinea Sculpture Garden,** tucked into a small, heavily treed plot of land. The garden is filled with tall, ornately carved wooden poles, drums, and carved stones—all created on location by 10 artists from Papua New Guinea who spent six months there in 1994. Detailed plaques explain the concept and the works. ⊠ *Santa Teresa St. and Lomita Dr.,* ☎ *650/723–3421.* 🖭 *Free.*

One of the few great country houses in California that remains intact in its original setting is **Filoli,** in Woodside. Built between 1915 and 1917 for wealthy San Franciscan William B. Bourn II, it was designed by Willis Polk in a Georgian Revival style, with redbrick walls and a tile roof. The name is not Italian but Bourn's acronym for "fight, love, live." As interesting to visitors as the house—whose exterior was shot as the Carrington mansion in the television series *Dynasty*—are the 16 acres of formal gardens. These were planned and developed over a period of more than 50 years and preserved for the public when the last private owner, Mrs. William P. Roth, deeded Filoli to the National Trust for Historic Preservation.

The gardens take advantage of the natural surroundings of the 700-acre estate and its vistas. Among the designs are a sunken garden, a yew alley, and a rose garden developed by Mrs. Roth. In the middle of it all is a charming teahouse designed in the Italian Renaissance style. From May to early fall Filoli hosts a monthly series of Sunday afternoon jazz concerts: You bring a picnic or buy a box lunch; Filoli provides tables, sodas, wine, fruit, and popcorn. In December a crafts boutique, an annual Christmas brunch, and afternoon holiday teas take place in the festively decorated mansion. ⊠ *Cañada Rd. (from San Francisco, take I–280, turn right at Edgewood Rd. exit, and right onto Cañada),* ☎ *650/364–2880.* 🖭 *$10.* 𝕆 *Mid-Feb.–mid-Nov., Tues.–Thurs. for guided tours (reservations essential), Fri.–Sat. for self-guided tours.*

One peninsula oddity unknown even to most residents is the **Pulgas Water Temple,** where exquisitely groomed grounds surround a Romanesque temple and a reflecting pool. The temple commemorates the massive underground pipeline project of the early 1930s that channeled water from Hetch Hetchy near Yosemite to the Crystal Springs Reservoir on the peninsula—a task for which the thirsty area residents were grateful enough to dedicate a temple. ⊠ *Cañada Rd., 1½ mi north of Edgewood Rd., Woodside,* ☎ *650/872–5900.* 🖭 *Free.* 𝕆 *Weekdays 9–4.*

DINING AND LODGING

$$–$$$ ✕ **Stars Palo Alto.** The glass walls of celebrity chef Jeremiah Tower's dining room are removed to create alfresco seating on sunny days. The menu emphasizes the same fresh local ingredients, light cooking hand, and Mediterranean accents found at other Tower enterprises. ⊠ *365 Lytton Ave.,* ☎ *650/321–4466. Reservations essential. AE, DC, MC, V.*

$$ ✕ **Evvia.** Oak floors, ceiling beams, a large fireplace, and hand-painted pottery create a stunning interior for this California-influenced Greek restaurant. Start your meal with fried calamari and smelt or white beans baked with tomato sauce and topped with feta; follow with grilled striped bass with a sprightly vinaigrette or lemony roast chicken. ✉ *420 Emerson St.,* ☎ *650/326–0983. AE, DC, MC, V. No lunch weekends.*

$$ ✕ **Flea Street Café.** Sunday brunch at this intimate country inn is a local institution, with warm buttermilk biscuits, homemade jams, and seductive pancake, egg, and omelet creations as the star offerings. Young diners have access to a fully stocked toy chest. ✉ *Alameda de las Pulgas (take Sand Hill Rd. west from the Stanford Shopping Center or east from I–280; turn right on Alameda),* ☎ *650/854–1226. MC, V. Closed Mon.*

$$ ✕ **Village Pub.** Patrons at this restaurant near Filoli elbow up to a carved oak bar to sample the ale or relax in the stylishly simple modern dining room to savor creative California rustic fare. Steamed mussels, crab cakes, roast duck, and delectable pastas are regular offerings on the menu, which changes daily. ✉ *2967 Woodside Rd., ¼ mi east of I–280,* ☎ *650/851–1294. AE, DC, MC, V. No lunch weekends.*

$ ✕ **Bok Choy.** This pan-Asian noodle house next to Bloomingdale's draws spending-weary shoppers who are happy to sit down to a plate of reasonably priced fresh noodles tossed with seafood, meat, or poultry. Try the house-made ginger ale. ✉ *2-A Stanford Shopping Center (from I–280, head east on Sand Hill Rd. and turn right at El Camino Real),* ☎ *650/325–6588. MC, V.*

$$$ ▦ **The Victorian on Lytton.** Only a block from downtown Palo Alto, this inn caters to business travelers who want comfort and amenities without teddy bears and lace. Spacious rooms have canopy beds. Complimentary breakfast is ordered the night before and brought to your room in the morning. ✉ *555 Lytton Ave., 94301,* ☎ *650/322–8555,* ℻ *415/ 322–7141. 10 rooms. No-smoking rooms. AE, D, DC, MC, V.*

The Peninsula Essentials

ARRIVING AND DEPARTING

By Car: The most pleasant direct route down the peninsula is I–280, the Junipero Serra Freeway, which passes by the Crystal Springs Reservoir. To get to Half Moon Bay, exit I–280 at Highway 92 and head west toward the coast. For Stanford University, exit at Sand Hill Road and drive east. Turn right on Arboretum, then right again on Palm Drive, which leads to the center of campus. U.S. 101, also known as the Bayshore Freeway, is more direct but also more congested; from there take University Avenue or Embarcadero Road west to Stanford. For Woodside take the Woodside Road exit of I–280 or U.S. 101 and drive west.

By Train: CalTrain (☎ 800/660–4287) runs from 4th and Townsend streets in San Francisco to Palo Alto; from there take the free Marguerite shuttle bus (☎ 650/723–9362) to the Stanford campus and the Palo Alto area. Buses run about every 15 minutes from 6 AM to 8 PM and are timed to connect with trains and public transit buses.

VISITOR INFORMATION

Half Moon Bay Chamber of Commerce (✉ 520 Kelly Ave., ☎ 650/726–8380). **Palo Alto Chamber of Commerce** (✉ 325 Forest Ave., ☎ 650/ 324–3121).

THE SOUTH BAY

Revised by Therese Iknoian and Sharon Silva

Once seen merely as a far-flung, nondescript suburb of San Francisco, San Jose and its environs have grown up and blossomed into a metropolis. Not only is San Jose's population larger than that of its older sister to the north, it now has its own ballet, symphony, repertory theater, nationally recognized museums, downtown nightlife, and exclusive hotels. In 1996 the area was voted the 11th-most-desirable place to live in

Greater San Jose

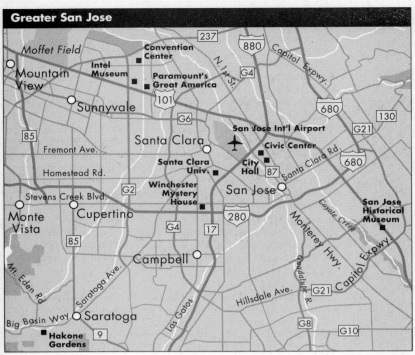

North America, rising from 49th place three years earlier and topping San Francisco's 17th-place ranking. Factors in that vote were the South Bay's strong job market, low crime rate, and warm, sunny climate.

San Jose

In the last few years San Jose's downtown has become a major destination for entertainment, arts, nightlife, and sports at the 17,400-seat San Jose Arena; at the same time, IBM, Adobe Systems, and other businesses have set up their headquarters here. Strikingly modern architecture now coexists with finely restored 19th-century and mission-style buildings. Downtown can be easily explored by foot, with side trips by light-rail, but visitors still need a car to get to outlying communities and sights such as the Egyptian Museum and the Winchester Mystery House.

Numbers in the text correspond to numbers in the margin and on the Downtown San Jose map.

① In collaboration with New York's Whitney Museum, the **San Jose Museum of Art** is exploring the development of 20th-century American art with exhibits of pieces from the permanent collections of both. The series will run through the year 2000. ⊠ *110 S. Market St.,* ☎ *408/294–2787.* ☞ *$6, free 1st Thurs. of month.* ☉ *Tues.–Wed. and Fri.–Sun. 10–5, Thurs. 10–8.*

② ② The **Children's Discovery Museum,** an angular purple building near the convention center, exhibits interactive installations on space, technology, the humanities, and the arts. Children can dress up in period costumes, create jewelry from recycled materials, or play on a real fire truck. ⊠ *180 Woz Way, at Auzerais St.,* ☎ *408/298–5437.* ☞ *$6.* ☉ *Tues.– Sat. 10–5, Sun. noon–5.*

Children's Discovery Museum, **2**

Egyptian Museum and Planetarium, **7**

Fallon House, **5**

Guadalupe Gardens, **9**

Municipal Rose Garden, **8**

Peralta Adobe, **4**

San Jose Museum of Art, **1**

St. Joseph's Cathedral, **6**

Tech Museum of Innovation, **3**

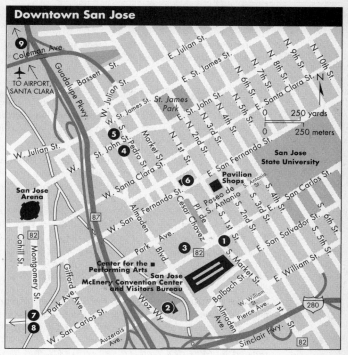

Downtown San Jose

❸ The nationally recognized **Tech Museum of Innovation,** across from the convention center, presents high-tech information through hands-on lab exhibits that are fun and accessible, allowing visitors to discover and demystify disciplines such as interactive media, biotechnology, robotics, and space exploration. In late 1998 the museum is expected to move into a new building, Future Tech at Park Avenue and Market Street, which is six times larger than its current headquarters. ✉ *145 W. San Carlos St.,* ☎ *408/279–7150.* ✐ *$6.* ☾ *Tues.–Sun. 10–5.*

❹ The circa-1797 **Peralta Adobe** is the last remaining structure from the pueblo that was once San Jose. The two-room home has been furnished to interpret life in the first Spanish civil settlement in California and during the Mexican rancho era. Across the street from the Peralta Adobe is **❺** the **Fallon House,** built in 1855 by San Jose's seventh mayor, Thomas Fallon. The Victorian mansion's 15 rooms were renovated to period style. One admission fee gains you access to both buildings. ✉ *175 W. St. John St.,* ☎ *408/993–8182.* ✐ *$6.* ☾ *Guided tours Wed.–Sun. 11–4:30.*

❻ The 15th-century Renaissance-style **St. Joseph's Cathedral,** built in 1877, has extraordinary stained-glass windows and murals. The multidomed cathedral occupies the site where a small adobe church served the first residents of the Pueblo of San Jose in 1803. ✉ *90 S. Market St.,* ☎ *408/283–8100.*

❼ The **Egyptian Museum and Planetarium,** owned by the Rosicrucian Order, exhibits the West Coast's largest collection of Egyptian and Babylonian antiquities, including mummies and an underground replica of a pharaoh's tomb. The complex is surrounded by a garden filled with palms, papyrus, and other plants recalling ancient Egypt. The planetarium offers programs like the popular "Celestial Nile," which describes the significant role astrology played in ancient Egyptian myths and religions.

⊠ *1600 Park Ave., at Naglee Ave.,* ☎ *408/947–3636.* ⊒ *$6.75 museum, $4 planetarium.* ☉ *Daily 9–5, planetarium weekdays only.*

Several outstanding gardens add green space to downtown San Jose.
❽ The **Municipal Rose Garden** (⊠ Naglee and Dana Aves., ☎ 408/277–4191) has 5 acres of roses with 3,500 shrubs and trees in 189 beds.

The new **Heritage Rose Garden** (⊠ Taylor and Spring Sts., ☎ 408/277–4191) has won national acclaim for its 5,000 rose bushes and trees on
❾ 4 acres. The Heritage garden is part of **Guadalupe Gardens,** 150 acres of planned open space, gardens, and recreational areas in the airport's periphery.

A couple of miles west of downtown lies the **Winchester Mystery House.** Convinced that spirits would harm her if construction ever stopped, firearms heiress Sarah Winchester constantly added to her house. For 38 years, beginning in 1884, she kept hundreds of carpenters working around the clock, creating a bizarre 160-room Victorian labyrinth with stairs going nowhere and doors that open into walls. The brightly painted house and well-tended gardens are a favorite family attraction. ⊠ *525 S. Winchester Blvd., between Stevens Creek Blvd. and I–280,* ☎ *408/247–2101.* ⊒ *$12.50.* ☉ *Guided tours Nov.–Feb., daily 9:30–4; Mar.–Oct., hrs vary, call ahead.*

OFF THE   **HAKONE GARDENS** – Designed in 1918 by a man who had been an im-
BEATEN PATH   perial gardener in Japan, these gardens in Saratoga, 10 mi west of San
                 Jose, have been carefully maintained, with koi (carp) ponds and sculp-
                 tured shrubs. ⊠ *21000 Big Basin Way,* ☎ *408/741–4994.* ⊒ *Free;
                 parking $3 Mon. and Wed.–Fri., $5 weekends, free Tues.* ☉ *Weekdays
                 10–5, weekends 11–5.*

Dining and Lodging

$$$ ✕ **Emile's.** Swiss chef and owner Emile Mooser's specialties include
★   house-cured gravlax, osso buco, rack of lamb, and a Grand Marnier soufflé. The interior of his restaurant is distinguished by romantic lighting, stunning floral displays, and an unusual leaf sculpture on the ceiling. ⊠ *545 S. 2nd St.,* ☎ *408/289–1960. AE, MC, V. Closed Sun.–Mon. No lunch Tues.–Thurs. and Sat.*

$$$ ✕ **Paolo's.** Rabbit stuffed with salsa verde and radicchio and delicate handmade pastas are among the appealing, up-to-the-moment offerings here. At lunchtime the dining room is a sea of suits, with bankers and brokers entertaining clients. At night well-dressed families and couples turn up. ⊠ *333 W. San Carlos St.,* ☎ *408/294–2558. AE, D, DC, MC, V. Closed Sun. No lunch Sat.*

$$ ✕ **Gordon Biersch Brewery Restaurant.** The scene at this brew pub is so busy on Friday night that the waitstaff hands out beepers to would-be diners so they can be signaled when their table is ready. Twenty- and thirtysomethings make up most of the crowd; they happily feast on glazed chicken wings, blue-cheese burgers, and garlic fries. ⊠ *33 E. San Fernando St.,* ☎ *408/294–6785. AE, MC, V.*

$ ✕ **Chez Sovan.** The original San Jose branch of this Cambodian restaurant, which serves only lunch, stands in a rather homely stretch of town, but the newer Campbell location offers a pleasant setting in addition to its satisfying fare. The spring rolls are delectable at both addresses, as are the noodle dishes, grilled meats, and flavorful curries. ⊠ *923 N. 13th St.,* ☎ *408/287–7619;* ⊠ *2425 S. Bascom Ave., Campbell* ☎ *408/371–7711. AE, MC, V. Closed Sat. No lunch Sun. at San Jose location.*

$$$$ ☷ **Fairmont Hotel.** Rooms at this affiliate of the same-named San Francisco hotel have every imaginable comfort, from down pillows and cus-

tom-designed comforters to oversize bath towels changed twice a day. ⊠ *170 S. Market St., at Fairmont Pl., 95113,* ☎ *408/998–1900 or 800/527–4727,* FAX *408/287–1648. 500 rooms, 41 suites. 4 restaurants, bar, no-smoking floors, room service, pool, health club, business services. AE, D, DC, MC, V.*

$$$ 🎏 **Hotel De Anza.** Business travelers will appreciate the many amenities at this lushly appointed art deco hotel, including computers, cellular phones, and personal voice-mail services. ⊠ *233 W. Santa Clara St., 95113,* ☎ *408/286–1000 or 800/843–3700,* FAX *408/286–0500. 91 rooms, 9 suites. Restaurant, in-room modem lines, minibars, in-room VCRs, exercise room, nightclub. AE, DC, MC, V.*

$$ 🎏 **Sundowner Inn.** Just off U.S. 101 north of San Jose, this contemporary hotel offers full services for business travelers. A library stocks 500 complimentary videotapes; there's also a library full of best-sellers you can borrow. A complimentary breakfast buffet is served poolside. ⊠ *504 Ross Dr., Sunnyvale 94089,* ☎ *408/734–9900 or 800/223–9901,* FAX *408/747–0580. 93 rooms, 12 suites. Restaurant, no-smoking rooms, pool, sauna, exercise room, laundry service, meeting room. AE, D, DC, MC, V.*

Nightlife and the Arts

NIGHTLIFE

Try **Big Lil's Barbary Coast Dinner Theater** (⊠ 157 W. San Fernando St., ☎ 408/295–7469) for a fresh take on the Old West; it serves up comedy, melodrama, and ribs. Just west of downtown, the **Garden City Lounge** (⊠ 360 S. Saratoga Ave., ☎ 408/244–3333) has free jazz seven nights a week. **San Jose Live!** at the Pavilion (⊠ 150 S. 1st St., ☎ 408/294–5483) consists of a restaurant, a sports bar, a sing-along piano bar, and a dance club—all under one roof. Pick up a pool cue at trendy **South First Billiards** (⊠ 420 S. 1st St., ☎ 408/294–7800), in the SoFA—South of First (Street) Area—conglomeration of clubs.

Mirassou Vineyards (⊠ 3000 Aborn Rd., ☎ 408/274–4000) organizes elegant eight-course candlelight dinners, accenting food and wine pairings ($82 per person). Dinners are offered every spring and fall; call for a schedule.

THE ARTS

Designed by the Frank Lloyd Wright Foundation, the **Center for Performing Arts** (⊠ 255 Almaden Blvd., ☎ 408/277–3900) is the venue for performances of the American Musical Theatre of San Jose (⊠ 1717 Technology Dr., ☎ 408/453–7108), the San Jose Symphony (⊠ 495 Almaden Blvd., ☎ 408/288–2828), and the San Jose Cleveland Ballet (⊠ Almaden Blvd. and Woz Way, ☎ 408/288–2800). The **San Jose Repertory Theatre** (⊠ 101 Paseo de San Antonio, ☎ 408/291–2255), the only resident professional theater in Silicon Valley, occupies a new six-story, 581-seat theater. For schedules and tickets call the companies directly or phone BASS (☎ 408/998–2277). The season generally runs from September through June.

Sports

Home to the San Jose Sharks hockey team and known to area sports fans as the Shark Tank or, simply, the Tank, the 17,400-seat **San Jose Arena** (⊠ Santa Clara St. at Autumn St., ☎ 408/287–9200 or 408/998–2277 for tickets) looks like a giant hothouse, with its glass entrance, shining metal armor, and skylight ceiling. Besides hockey, the arena also hosts tennis matches, basketball games, indoor soccer, national-name music concerts, ice-skating shows, and other events.

Santa Clara

Santa Clara University, founded in 1851 by Jesuits, was California's first college. The campus's **de Saisset Art Gallery and Museum** has a permanent collection that includes California mission artifacts and a full calendar of temporary exhibits. ⊠ *500 El Camino Real,* ☎ *408/554–4528.* ☜ *Free.* ⊙ *Tues.–Sun. 11–4.*

In the center of Santa Clara University's campus is the **Mission Santa Clara de Asis,** the eighth of 21 California missions founded under the direction of Father Junípero Serra and the first to honor a woman. A spectacular garden here has 4,500 roses, many classified as antiques. ⊠ *500 El Camino Real,* ☎ *408/554–4023.* ☜ *Free.* ⊙ *Weekdays 8–6, Sat. noon–3:30 for self-guided tours.*

Visitors to the **Intel Museum** can learn how computer chips are made and follow the development of the Intel Corporation's microprocessor, memory, and systems product lines. Guided tours are available by reservation. ⊠ *Robert Noyce Bldg., 2200 Mission College Blvd. (off Montague Expressway, just north of U.S. 101),* ☎ *408/765–0503.* ☜ *Free.* ⊙ *Weekdays 8–5.*

Skylights cast natural light for viewing the exhibitions in the **Triton Museum of Art.** A permanent collection of 19th- and 20th-century sculpture by artists from the Bay Area is displayed in the garden, which you can see through a curved-glass wall at the rear of the building. Inside there are rotating exhibits of contemporary works in a variety of media and a permanent collection of 19th- and 20-century American artists, many from California. ⊠ *1505 Warburton Ave. (take Scott Blvd. north off El Camino Real),* ☎ *408/247–3754.* ☜ *$5 suggested donation.* ⊙ *Tues. 10–9, Wed.–Sun. 10–5.*

Dining and Lodging

$$ ✕ **Birk's.** Silicon Valley's businesspeople come to this sophisticated American grill to unwind after a hard day of paving the way to the future. The menu is traditional, strong on steaks and chops. Try the smoked prime rib, served with garlic mashed potatoes and creamed spinach, or the rotisserie-grilled chicken or ribs. ⊠ *3955 Freedom Circle, at U.S. 101 and Great America Pkwy.,* ☎ *408/980–6400. AE, DC, MC, V. No lunch weekends.*

$$ ⌸ **Biltmore Hotel & Suites.** This hotel's central Silicon Valley location makes it a popular choice for business travelers. In the past several years, the atrium lobby has been enclosed and the ballroom expanded. Other attractions are a brew pub, an espresso bar, and 16 meeting rooms. ⊠ *2151 Laurelwood Rd., 95054,* ☎ *408/988–8411 or 800/255–9925,* ℻ *408/988–0225. 128 rooms, 134 suites. Restaurant, lounge, in-room modem lines, no-smoking rooms, pool, hot tub, health club, meeting rooms, airport shuttle, free parking. AE, D, DC, MC, V.*

$$ ⌸ **Madison Street Inn.** At this refurbished Queen Anne Victorian, a complimentary full breakfast and afternoon refreshments are served on a brick garden patio with a bougainvillea-draped trellis. The inn has the feel of a private home. ⊠ *1390 Madison St., 95050,* ☎ *408/249–5541,* ℻ *408/249–6676. 5 rooms, 3 with bath. No-smoking rooms, pool, hot tub, meeting rooms. AE, D, DC, MC, V.*

South Bay Essentials

ARRIVING AND DEPARTING

By Car: The quickest route to San Jose from San Francisco is I–280. From there take the Guadalupe Parkway (also known as Highway 87) north, then the Santa Clara Street exit east to downtown. For Saratoga, take Highway 85 south to Saratoga/Sunnyvale Road and drive south.

To reach Santa Clara, take U.S. 101 and exit south on the San Tomas Expressway; turn left on El Camino Real (also known as Highway 82). To avoid the often heavy commuter traffic on U.S. 101, use Highway 280 during rush hours. Just before the San Jose exit, take I–880 north to the Alameda, which becomes El Camino Real (82); turn left off the exit ramp and follow the signs to Santa Clara.

By Train and Bus: CalTrain (☎ 800/660–4287) runs from 4th and Townsend streets in San Francisco to Santa Clara's Railroad and Franklin streets stop (near the university) and to San Jose's Rod Diridon station. The trip to Santa Clara takes approximately 1¼ hours; the trip to San Jose takes about 1½ hours. A shuttle links downtown San Jose to the CalTrain station, across from the Arena, every 20 minutes during morning and evening commute hours (☎ 408/321–2300). From the Santa Clara station, use Greyhound (☎ 800/231–2222).

GETTING AROUND

By Light Rail and Trolley: In San Jose, light-rail trains serve most major attractions, shopping malls, historic sites, and downtown. Service on weekdays is every 10–15 minutes between 4:30 AM and 1:30 AM, on weekends every 15–30 minutes between 5:45 AM and 1:30 AM. Tickets are valid for two hours; they cost $1.10 one-way or $2.20 for a day pass. Historic trolleys operate in downtown San Jose from 11 to 7 during the summer and on some holidays throughout the year. The fare is 50¢ for all ages. Buy tickets for the light-rail and the trolleys at vending machines in any transit station. For more information call or visit the **Transit Information Center** (✉ 4 N. 2nd St., San Jose, ☎ 408/321–2300).

VISITOR INFORMATION

Santa Clara Chamber of Commerce and Convention and Visitors Bureau (✉ 1850 Warburton Ave., Santa Clara 95052, ☎ 408/244–8244). **San Jose Convention and Visitors Bureau** (✉ 150 W. San Carlos St., 95110, ☎ 408/977–0900; ✉ 333 W. San Carlos St., Suite 1000, San Jose 95110, ☎ 408/295–9600). **San Jose Tourist Bureau's FYI Hotline** (☎ 408/295–2265).

SAN FRANCISCO A TO Z

Arriving and Departing

By Bus
Greyhound (☎ 800/231–2222) serves San Francisco from the Transbay Terminal at 1st and Mission streets.

By Car
Interstate 80 finishes its westward journey from New York's George Washington Bridge at the San Francisco–Oakland Bay Bridge. U.S. 101, running north–south through the entire state, enters the city across the Golden Gate Bridge and continues south down the peninsula, along the west side of the San Francisco Bay.

By Plane
The major gateway to San Francisco is the **San Francisco International Airport** (✉ U.S. 101, south of San Francisco, ☎ 650/761–0800). **Oakland Airport** (✉ 1 Airport Dr., off I–880, ☎ 510/577–4000) is across the bay but not much farther away from downtown San Francisco (take I–880 to I–980 to I–580 to I–80), although traffic on the Bay Bridge may at times make travel time longer. **San Jose International Airport** (☎ 408/277–4759) is 3 mi from downtown San Jose.

Carriers serving San Francisco include **Alaska, American, Continental, Delta, Southwest, TWA, United,** and **US Airways.** Carriers flying into Oakland include **American, Delta, Southwest,** and **United.** Carriers serving San Jose include **Alaska, American, America West, Continental, Delta, Northwest, TWA,** and **United.** *See* Air Travel *in* the Gold Guide for airline phone numbers.

BETWEEN THE AIRPORT AND DOWNTOWN

SFO Airporter (☎ 415/495–8404) serves downtown hotels. **SuperShuttle** (☎ 415/558–8500) will take you from the airport to anywhere within the city limits of San Francisco. SuperShuttle also serves the Oakland airport. At the San Jose airport, call **South & East Bay Airport Shuttle** (☎ 408/559–9477).

By Train

Amtrak (☎ 800/872–7245) trains—the *Zephyr,* from Chicago via Denver, and the *Coast Starlight,* traveling between Los Angeles and Seattle—stop in Emeryville (✉ 5885 Landregan St.) and Oakland (✉ 245 2nd St., in Jack London Sq.). Shuttle buses connect the Emeryville station and San Francisco's Ferry Building (✉ 30 Embarcadero, at the foot of Market St.).

Getting Around

By Bus and Light Rail

San Francisco Municipal Railway System, or **Muni** (☎ 415/673–6864), includes buses, light-rail vehicles, and antique trolleys. There is 24-hour service, the fare is $1. The exact fare is always required; dollar bills or change are accepted. Transfers are issued free upon request at the time the fare is paid. They are valid for 90 minutes to two hours for two boardings of a bus or streetcar in any direction.

A $6 pass good for unlimited travel all day on all routes can be purchased from ticket machines at cable-car terminals and at the Visitor Information Center in Hallidie Plaza.

You can use **Bay Area Rapid Transit** (**BART**) (☎ 800/817–1717) trains to reach Oakland, Berkeley, Concord, Richmond, Fremont, Colma, and Martinez; extensions are expected to open southeast to Castro Valley and Dublin. Trains also travel south from San Francisco as far as Daly City. Fares run from $1.10 to $4.70, and a $3 excursion ticket buys a three-county tour.

By Cable Cars

Cable cars are popular, crowded, and an experience to ride: Move toward one quickly as it pauses, wedge yourself into any available space, and hold on! The sensation of moving up and down some of San Francisco's steepest hills in a small, open-air, clanging conveyance is not to be missed.

The fare (for one direction) is $2. Exact change is preferred, but operators will make change up to $20. There are self-service ticket machines (which do make change) at a few major stops and at all the terminals. The one exception is the busy cable car terminal at Powell and Market streets; purchase tickets at the kiosk there. Be wary of street people attempting to "help" you buy a ticket.

The Powell-Mason line (No. 59) and the Powell-Hyde line (No. 60) begin at Powell and Market streets near Union Square and terminate at Fisherman's Wharf. The California Street line (No. 61) runs east and west from Market Street near the Embarcadero to Van Ness Avenue.

By Car

Driving in San Francisco can be a challenge because of the hills, the one-way streets, and the traffic. Take it easy, remember to curb your wheels when parking on hills, and use public transportation whenever possible. This is a great city for walking and a terrible city for parking. On certain streets, parking is forbidden during rush hours. Look for the warning signs; illegally parked cars are towed. Downtown parking lots are often full and always expensive. Finding a spot in North Beach at night, for instance, may be impossible.

Contacts and Resources

Doctors

Two hospitals with 24-hour emergency rooms are **San Francisco General Hospital** (⊠ 1001 Potrero Ave., ☎ 415/206–8000) and the **Medical Center at the University of California, San Francisco** (⊠ 500 Parnassus Ave., ☎ 415/476–1000).

Physician Access Medical Center (⊠ 26 California St., ☎ 415/397–2881) is a drop-in clinic in the Financial District, open weekdays 7:30 AM–5 PM. **Access Health Care** (☎ 415/565–6600) provides drop-in medical care at Davies Medical Center, Castro Street at Duboce Avenue, daily 8 to 8.

Emergencies

Ambulance (☎ 911). **Police** (☎ 911).

Guided Tours

ORIENTATION TOURS

Golden Gate Tours (☎ 415/788–5775) uses both vans and buses for its 3½-hour city tour ($25), offered mornings and afternoons. You can combine the tour with a bay cruise ($34). Customers are picked up at hotels and motels. Senior-citizen and group rates are available. Tours are daily; reserve a day ahead.

Gray Line (☎ 415/558–9400) operates tours of the city, the Bay Area, and northern California. The city tour ($28), on double-decker buses, lasts 3½ hours and departs from the Transbay Terminal at 1st and Mission streets five to six times daily. Gray Line picks up at centrally located hotels. Make reservations a day in advance.

Gray Line–Cable Car Tours sends motorized cable cars on a one-hour loop from Union Square to Fisherman's Wharf ($15) and on two-hour tours that include the Presidio, Japantown, and the Golden Gate Bridge ($22). No reservations are necessary.

The **Great Pacific Tour** (☎ 415/626–4499) uses 13-passenger vans for its daily 3½-hour city tour ($27). Tours are available to Monterey, the Wine Country, and Muir Woods.

Tower Tours (☎ 415/434–8687) uses 20-passenger vans for city tours and 25-passenger buses for trips outside San Francisco to Muir Woods and Sausalito, the Wine Country, Monterey and Carmel, and Yosemite. The city tour takes 3½ hours ($25). Tours are daily; make reservations one day in advance.

WALKING TOURS

Castro District: Trevor Hailey (☎ 415/550–8110) leads a 3¾-hour tour, focusing on the history and development of the city's gay and lesbian community, that takes in the Castro Theatre, shops and cafés, and the NAMES Project, home of the AIDS memorial quilt. Tours depart at 10 AM Tuesday through Saturday from Castro and Market streets. The cost is $35, which includes brunch. Reservations are required.

Chinatown with the "Wok Wiz": Cookbook author Shirley Fong-Torres (☎ 415/981–8989) and her staff offer 3½-hour tours of Chinese markets, other businesses, and a fortune-cookie factory. The $37 fee includes lunch; the cost is $25 without lunch. Shorter group tours start at $15 per person.

Chinese Cultural Heritage Foundation (☎ 415/986–1822) conducts two walking tours of Chinatown. The Heritage Walk leaves Saturday at 2 PM and lasts about two hours; the cost is $15. The Culinary Walk, a three-hour stroll through the markets and food shops, plus a dim sum lunch, is offered Tuesday through Friday at 10:30 AM; the fee is $30.

City Guides (☎ 415/557–4266), a free service sponsored by the Friends of the Library, tours Chinatown, North Beach, Coit Tower, Pacific Heights mansions, Japantown, the Haight-Ashbury, historic Market Street, the Palace Hotel, and downtown roof gardens and atriums. Schedules are available at the San Francisco Visitors Center at Powell and Market streets and at library branches.

Late-Night Pharmacies

Several **Walgreen Drug Stores** have 24-hour pharmacies, including stores at 135 Powell Street, near Market Street (☎ 415/391–7222) and 3201 Divisadero Street, at Lombard Street (☎ 415/931–6417).

Visitor Information

Redwood Empire Association Visitor Information Center (✉ The Cannery, 2801 Leavenworth St., 2nd floor, 94133, ☎ 415/394–5991 or 888/678–8507). **San Francisco Convention and Visitors Bureau** (✉ 900 Market St., at Powell St., 94102, ☎ 415/391–2000).

6 Sacramento and the Gold Country

Including Highway 49 from Nevada City to Mariposa

The gold-mining region of the Sierra Nevada foothills is a less expensive, if also less sophisticated, region of California but not without its pleasures, natural and man-made. Spring brings wildflowers, and in fall the hills are colored by bright-red berries and changing leaves. The hills are golden in the summer—and hot. The Gold Country has a mix of indoor and outdoor activities, one of the many reasons it's a great place to take the kids.

By Bobbi Zane

Updated by
Andy Moore

JAMES MARSHALL TURNED UP a gold nugget in the tailrace of a sawmill he was constructing along the American River and ushered in a whole new era for California. Before January 24, 1848, what became the Golden State had been a beautiful but sparsely populated land over which Mexico and the United States were still wrestling. With Marshall's discovery and its subsequent confirmation by President James Polk in his State of the Union speech on December 5, 1848, prospectors came to seek their fortunes in the Mother Lode.

As gold fever seized the nation, California's population of 15,000 swelled to 265,000 within three years—44,000 newcomers arrived by ship in San Francisco in the first 10 months alone, the majority of them men under 40, either unattached or with families back east. Most spent about two years in California before returning home, usually with empty pockets or having barely broken even. Historians have noted that the consequences of the gold rush were more than monetary: '49ers who remained in the state contributed to a freer culture that eschewed many of the constricting conventions and values of the eastern states.

Originally, the term Mother Lode denoted a gold-bearing quartz vein 120 mi long between Mariposa to the south and Auburn to the north. It ranged in width from 2 mi to only a few yards. By 1865 it had yielded more than $750 million in gold. As prospectors headed farther afield, the entire gold-rush region came to be known as the Mother Lode. Ironically, neither Marshall, nor John Sutter, on whose property Marshall discovered gold, got rich from the discovery.

The boom brought on by the gold rush lasted scarcely 20 years, but it changed California forever. It produced 546 mining towns, of which fewer than 250 remain. The hills were alive, not only with prospecting and mining but also with business, the arts, plenty of gambling, and a fair share of crime. Opera houses went up alongside brothels, and the California State Capitol in Sacramento was built with the gold dug out of the hills. Some of the nation's most treasured writers—Mark Twain and Bret Harte among them—began their careers writing about the mining camps. Gold-rush lore immortalized notorious bandits: Legend has it that Joaquin Murieta's crime spree—he robbed miners by day, then partied by night at local saloons—followed an assault on him and his family by Yankee prospectors. When the law finally caught up with the debonair Black Bart, who targeted Wells Fargo stagecoaches and left behind poems (signed "Black Bart—PO-8") at his crime scenes, he turned out to be a well-known San Franciscan.

The northern California cities of Sacramento, San Francisco, and Stockton grew quickly to meet the needs of the surrounding gold fields. Saloon keepers and canny merchants recognized that the real gold was to be made from the '49ers. Potatoes and onions sold for as much as $1 apiece, making entrepreneurs like storekeeper Samuel Brannan millionaires. Much important history was made in Sacramento, the key center of commerce during this period. Pony Express riders ended their nearly 2,000-mi journeys in the city in the 1860s. The Transcontinental Railroad, conceived here by the Big Four (Leland Stanford, Mark Hopkins, Collis P. Huntington, and Charles Clocker), was completed in 1869.

By the 1960s, the scars left on the Gold Country landscape by mining had largely healed. To promote tourism, townspeople began restoring vintage structures, historians developed museums, and the state established parks and recreation areas that preserved this extraordinary episode in American history. Today, visitors flock to Nevada City, Auburn, Coloma, Sutter Creek, and Columbia, not only to relive the past but also to explore museums and art galleries, experience traditional celebrations, and stay over at bed-and-breakfast inns.

Pleasures and Pastimes

Adventuring

Scenic and challenging Gold Country rivers, particularly the American and Tuolumne, lure white-water enthusiasts each spring and summer. Early-morning balloon excursions take aeronauts above treetops in deep canyons of the American River. Throughout the region weekend prospectors pan for gold, turning up big nuggets frequently enough to inspire others to participate.

Dining

American, Italian, and Mexican fare is common in the Gold Country, but chefs here also prepare ambitious Continental, French, and California cuisine. Away from Sacramento or the interstate highways, national fast-food chains are few and far between. It's not difficult, though, to find the makings for a good picnic in most Gold Country towns.

CATEGORY	COST*
$$$$	over $50
$$$	$30–$50
$$	$20–$30
$	under $20

per person for a three-course meal, excluding drinks, service, and 7¼% tax

Lodging

Full-service hotels, budget motels, small inns, and even a fine hostel can all be found in Sacramento. The main accommodations in the larger towns along Highway 49—among them Placerville, Nevada City, Auburn, and Mariposa—are chain motels and bed-and-breakfast inns. Many Gold Country B&Bs occupy former mansions, miners' cabins, and other historic buildings.

CATEGORY	COST*
$$$$	over $175
$$$	$120–$175
$$	$80–$120
$	under $80

All prices are for a standard double room, excluding 7¼% tax (12% in Sacramento).

Shopping

Shoppers visit the Gold Country in search of antiques, collectibles, art, quilts, toys, tools, decorative items, and furnishings. Handmade quilts and crafts can be found in Sutter Creek, Jackson, and Amador City; Auburn and Nevada City support a number of gift boutiques.

Exploring Sacramento and the Gold Country

Visiting Old Sacramento's museums is a good way to steep yourself in gold-rush history, but the Gold Country's heart lies along Highway 49, which winds the 325-mi north–south length of the historic mining area. The highway, often a twisting, hilly, two-lane road, begs for a convertible with the top down.

Numbers in the text correspond to numbers in the margin and on the Gold Country and Sacramento maps.

Great Itineraries

IF YOU HAVE 1 DAY

Drive east from Sacramento on I–80 to **Auburn** ⑯ for a tour of the landmark **Placer County Courthouse** and its museum. Travel south on Highway 49 to the **Marshall Gold Discovery State Historic Park** ⑰ at Coloma. Head back to Sacramento for a cocktail or a soda at the bar on the *Delta King* and an evening stroll and dinner along the waterfront in **Old Sacramento.** The historical attractions will be closed, but you'll still get a feel for life here in the last half of the 19th century.

IF YOU HAVE 3 DAYS

In three days, you can make a larger loop from Sacramento. Begin your tour on Highway 49 north of I–80. Walk deep into the recesses of the **Empire Mine** ⑮ near **Grass Valley,** and then drive 4 mi north on Highway 49 for a visit to the historic **Miners Foundry** in **Nevada City** ⑭. After lunch, travel south to ⊞ **Auburn** ⑯, where you can take in the **Placer County Courthouse** and museum, have dinner, and spend the night. Early the next morning, head south to tour **Marshall Gold Discovery State Historic Park** ⑰ in Coloma. Continue south to ⊞ **Sutter Creek** ⑲, where you can spend the afternoon exploring the boutiques and antiques stores. If exploring a good vintage is more your game, take a detour to the **Shenandoah Valley,** southeast of **Placerville,** and taste some wine before continuing on to Sutter Creek. Either way, spend the night in one of Sutter Creek's historic B&Bs. Return early to **Sacramento** the next day to visit the **California State Railroad Museum** ① and **Sutter's Fort** ⑫.

IF YOU HAVE 5 DAYS

Visit the **Empire Mine** ⑮, **Nevada City** ⑭, and ⊞ **Auburn** ⑯ on day one. See Coloma's **Marshall Gold Discovery State Historic Park** ⑰ on the second day, and then continue on to ⊞ **Sutter Creek** ⑲. On your third morning, visit the **Amador County Museum** in **Jackson** ⑳ before heading south on Highway 49 and east on Highway 4 for lunch in **Murphys** ㉒. Back on Highway 49 still southward is ⊞ **Columbia State Historic Park** ㉓. You can live a bit of history by dining and spending the night at the City Hotel. If you've been itching to pan for gold, do that in the morning in the state park, and then head back to ⊞ **Sacramento** (Highway 49 north to Highway 16 west) for a riverboat cruise. Visit the **California State Railroad Museum** ① and **Sutter's Fort** ⑫ on day five.

When to Tour the Gold Country

The Gold Country is the most pleasant in the spring, when the wildflowers are in bloom, and in the fall. Summers are beautiful, too, but also hot: Temperatures in the 90s and even the 100s are common all summer long. Sacramento winters tend to be cold and foggy. Throughout the year Gold Country towns stage community and ethnic celebrations. In December, many towns deck themselves out for the Christmas holidays. Sacramento hosts the annual Jazz Jubilee in May and the California State Fair in August. Flowers bloom on Daffodil Hill in March. Nevada City hosts Music in the Mountains concerts in June and July.

SACRAMENTO

The gateway to the Gold Country, the seat of California state government, and an agricultural hub, the city of Sacramento plays many important contemporary roles. One and a half million people live in the metropolitan area, and the continuing influx of newcomers seeking opportunity, sunshine, and lower housing costs than in coastal California have made it one of the nation's fastest-growing regions. The

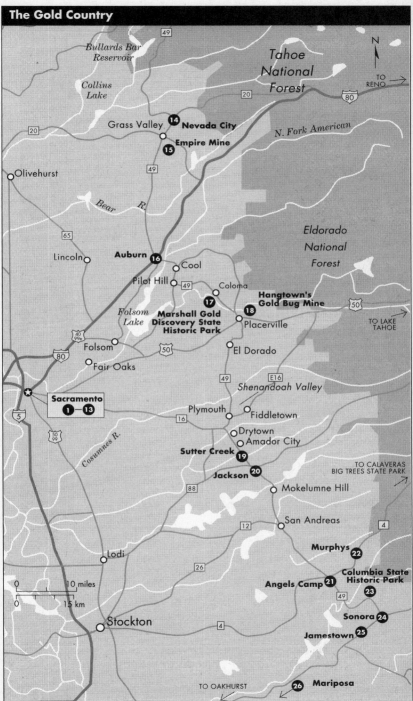

The Gold Country

Sacramento

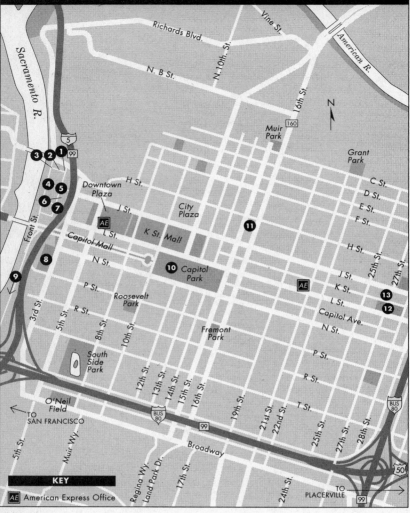

Sacramento R.

Richards Blvd.

Vine St.

American R.

N. 10th St.

N. B St.

16th St.

5

99

Muir
Park

160

N

Grant
Park

C St.

D St.

H St.

E St.

Downtown
Plaza

City
Plaza

F St.

Front St.

I St.

AE

L St.

K St. Mall

H St.

25th St.

27th St.

Capitol Mall

N St.

J St.

AE

K St.

Capitol
Park

Capitol Ave.

L St.

13

12

P St.

Roosevelt
Park

N St.

3rd St.

5th St.

8th St.

10th St.

R St.

Fremont
Park

P St.

R St.

South
Side
Park

12th St.

13th St.

14th St.

15th St.

16th St.

19th St.

21st St.

22nd St.

T St.

BUS
80

O'Neil
Field

TO
SAN FRANCISCO

Muir Wy.

BUS
80

99

25th St.

27th St.

28th St.

5th St.

Regina Wy.

Land Park Dr.

17th St.

Broadway

24th St.

TO
PLACERVILLE

99

50

KEY

AE American Express Office

B.F. Hastings
Building, **5**
California Military
Museum, **7**
California State
Capitol, **10**
California State
Railroad Museum, **1**
Crocker Art
Museum, **8**
Discovery Museum, **3**
Eagle Theater, **4**
Governor's
Mansion, **11**
Huntington, Hopkins
& Co. Store, **2**

State Indian
Museum, **13**
Sutter's Fort, **12**
Towe Ford
Museum of
Automotive
History, **9**
Visitor Information
Center, **6**

city is home to professional symphony, ballet, opera, and theater companies. Nightclubs range from quiet piano bars to country-western and rock-and-roll venues. Midtown's many new cafés and downtown's revived K Street Mall are testaments to Sacramento's growing sophistication.

Sacramento has more than 2,000 acres of both natural and developed parkland. This "city of a million trees" is planted with grand old evergreens, deciduous and fruit-bearing trees (the streets are virtually littered with oranges in springtime), and even giant palms, giving it a shady, lush quality. Genteel Victorian edifices sit side-by-side with art deco and postmodern skyscrapers.

The greater Sacramento area hosts many cultural events. A sampling includes the Martin Luther King Jr. Community Celebration in January, the Mardi Gras Parade in February, the Camellia Show and St. Patrick's Day Parade in March, April's Festival de la Familia, the Waterfront Art Festival and the Pacific Rim Street Fest in May, the California Railroad Festival in June, Shakespeare in the Park in July, the Original Midtown Fair in August, the Rice Festival in September, the Harvest Fest and Oktoberfest in October, and the Native American Film Festival & Arts and Crafts Fair in November.

Old Sacramento and Downtown

87 mi northeast of San Francisco, I–80 to Hwy. 99.

Wood sidewalks and horse-drawn carriages on cobblestone streets lend a 19th-century feel to Old Sacramento, a 28-acre area along the Sacramento River waterfront. The museums at the north end of this district hold artifacts of state and national significance. Historic buildings house shops and restaurants. River cruises and train rides bring gold-rush history to life. Call the Old Sacramento Events Hotline (☎ 916/558–3912) for information on living-history re-creations and merchant hours.

A Good Tour

Old Sacramento, the State Capitol and park surrounding it, and Sutter's Fort lie on an east–west axis that begins at the Sacramento River. The walk from Old Sacramento to the State Capitol is easy, passing through the Downtown Plaza shopping mall and pedestrians-only K Street. This area takes on a festive atmosphere during a market held on Thursday evening. A free shuttle links the Convention Center, the K Street Mall, downtown, and Old Sacramento. The shuttle runs every 15 minutes, Monday through Saturday from 11 to 7:30, and Sunday from 11 to 6. Stops are marked by orange and purple "Free Shuttle" signs.

Park your car in the municipal parking garage under I–5 at 2nd Street (enter on I Street between 2nd and 3rd streets), and head to the superb **California State Railroad Museum** ①, then browse through the hardware and household items at the **Huntington, Hopkins & Co. Store** ②. Next door are the hands-on exhibits of the kids-oriented **Discovery Museum** ③.

To learn more about Sacramento's role in rail history, walk a few paces south to the **Central Pacific Passenger Depot.** Across Front Street is the **Eagle Theater** ④, the first building constructed as a theater in California. The **Central Pacific Freight Depot,** next to the **Passenger Depot,** houses a new **Public Market** (closed Monday), where you'll find merchant stalls with food and gift items. The foot of K Street (at Front Street) is a great spot for viewing the Sacramento River wharf area and the restored sternwheeler the *Delta King*. One can almost visualize the bustle of shipping activity during the gold rush and in the years following. If your timing is lucky you'll witness a modern commotion when the golden **Tower Bridge** (a 1935 single-span lift bridge) sounds bells and sirens, and then elevates for ships to sail under.

Now walk to the corner of 2nd and J streets to see the **B. F. Hastings Building** ⑤, which houses a reconstruction of the first chambers of the California State Supreme Court. The **Visitor Information Center** ⑥ is on 2nd Street. The collection of the **California Military Museum** ⑦ next door spans the period from before statehood to modern times.

A must-see a few blocks south of Old Sacramento is the **Crocker Art Museum** ⑧, the oldest art museum in the American West. From here, car buffs (and kids) will want to walk south on Front Street to the **Towe Ford Museum of Automotive History** ⑨. If you'd rather skip the automotive museum, walk up 3rd Street to the Capitol Mall, which leads to the **California State Capitol** ⑩.

If you're still going strong, walk up to H Street to **Governor's Mansion** ⑪. Otherwise, walk back to your car via J Street, stopping in the K Street Mall if you're in the mood for shopping.

Though it requires a drive, **Sutter's Fort** ⑫ is not to be missed: It was Sacramento's earliest settlement; evocative exhibits bring that era back to life. Just north of the fort is the **State Indian Museum** ⑬, which displays arts and crafts made by California's earliest inhabitants.

TIMING

This tour makes for a leisurely day, less if you only visit Old Sacramento. Most of the attractions are open daily, except for the Military Museum, Discovery Museum, B. F. Hastings Building, and the Crocker Art Museum, which are all closed Monday. At press time (summer 1997) there were rumblings that budget cuts might lead to reduced hours in the state-run sights below; call ahead to be sure they're open.

Sights to See

❺ **B. F. Hastings Building.** A reconstruction of the first chambers of the California State Supreme Court occupies the second floor of this 1853 building; on the first floor there's a Wells Fargo Bank and a small display of Wells Fargo memorabilia. ✉ *1000 2nd St.* ⊘ *Tues.–Sun. 10–5.*

❼ **California Military Museum.** A storefront entrance leads to three floors containing more than 30,000 artifacts—uniforms, weapons, photographs, documents, medals, and flags of all kinds—that trace Californians' roles in military and militia activities throughout U.S. history. An interesting display outlines the African-American experience. Another includes Civil War–era medical equipment. ✉ *1119 2nd St.,* ☎ *916/442–2883.* ⊡ *$3.* ⊘ *Tues.–Sun. 10–4:30.*

❿ **California State Capitol.** The Golden State's capitol was built in 1869 and underwent extensive restoration in the late 1970s and early 1980s. The lacy plasterwork of the 120-ft-high rotunda has the complexity and color of a Fabergé Easter egg. Underneath the gilded dome are marble floors, glittering chandeliers, monumental staircases, original artwork, replicas of 19th-century state offices, and legislative chambers decorated in the style of the 1890s. Hallway displays for each of California's counties reflect the state's diversity. Guides conduct tours of the building and the 40-acre Capitol Park, which contains a rose garden, an impressive display of camellias (Sacramento's city flower), and the California Vietnam Veterans Memorial. ✉ *Capitol Mall and 10th St.,* ☎ *916/324–0333.* ⊡ *Free.* ⊘ *Daily 9–4; tours hourly.*

★ ☙ **❶** **California State Railroad Museum.** Near what was once the terminus of the Transcontinental and Sacramento Valley railroads (the actual terminus was at Front and K streets), this 100,000-square-ft museum is the largest of its kind in North America, with 21 locomotives and railroad cars on display and 46 exhibits. You can walk through a post-office car and peer into cubbyholes and canvas bags of mail, enter a sleeping car that simulates the swaying on the roadbed and the flashing lights of a passing town at night, or glimpse the elegance of the first-class dining car on the *Super Chief.* Allow at least a couple of hours to experience the museum fully. ⊠ *125 I St.,* ☎ *916/448–4466.* ☞ *$6.* ☉ *Daily 10–5.*

☙ **Central Pacific Passenger Depot.** At this reconstructed 1876 station there's rolling stock to admire, a typical waiting room, and a little café. Rides on a steam-powered train depart from the freight depot, just south of the passenger depot. The train makes a 40-minute loop along the Sacramento riverfront. ⊠ *930 Front St.,* ☞ *$6 (free with same-day ticket from California State Railroad Museum); train ride $5 additional, operates every weekend Apr.–Sept., 1st weekend of month Oct.–Dec.* ☉ *Depot daily 10–5.*

★ **❽** **Crocker Art Museum.** The oldest art museum in the American West has a collection of European, Asian, and California art, including *Sunday Morning in the Mines,* a large canvas depicting the mining industry of the 1850s, and a magnificent Yosemite landscape by Thomas Hill. The museum's lobby and ballroom retain the original 1870s woodwork, plaster moldings, and imported English tiles. ⊠ *216 O St.,* ☎ *916/264–5423.* ☞ *$4.50.* ☉ *Tues.–Wed. and Fri.–Sun. 10–5, Thurs. 10–9.*

☙ **❸** **Discovery Museum.** The building that holds this museum is a replica of the 1854 City Hall and Waterworks. The emphasis here is on interactive exhibits that combine history, science, and technology. Visitors can sift for gold, walk into an Indian thatched hut, or experience the goings-on in the print shop of the old *Sacramento Bee* newspaper. A replica of a turn-of-the-century store holds colorfully labeled cans and fruit crates. A giant old windmill turns overhead while almond cans snake through the space on a modern conveyor belt. The Gold Gallery includes a fine collection of nuggets and veins. Child-oriented, hands-on science and computer exhibits rotate on a regular basis. ⊠ *101 I St.,* ☎ *916/264–7057.* ☞ *$3.50.* ☉ *Summer, Tues.–Sun. 10–5; winter, Tues.–Fri. noon–5, weekends 10–5.*

❹ **Eagle Theater.** When the Eagle opened in 1849, audiences of 300 to 400 people paid $3 and $5 in gold coin or dust to sit on rough boards and watch professional actors. This replica still features the tent-like canvas and ship's-timber walls of olden times, though now there's insulation and the bench seats are cushioned. The theater hosts programs that range from a 13-minute slide show to puppet, minstrel, and juggling acts. ⊠ *925 Front St.,* ☎ *916/323–6343.*

⓫ **Governor's Mansion.** This 15-room house was built in 1877 and used by the state's chief executives from the early 1900s until 1967, when then-governor Ronald Reagan vacated it in favor of a newly built home in the suburbs. Many of the Italianate mansion's interior decorative details were ordered through the Huntington Hopkins hardware store, one of whose partners, Albert Gallatin, was the original occupant. Persian carpets and scratch ceilings commingle with wall-to-wall carpeting and modern fixtures in this often-redecorated house. Each of the seven marble fireplaces has a petticoat mirror that ladies strolled past to see if their slips were showing. The mansion is said to be one of the first homes in California to have an indoor bathroom. ✉ *1526 H St.,* ☎ *916/323–3047.* 🎫 *$3.* ⊙ *Daily 10–4; tours hourly.*

❷ Huntington, Hopkins & Co. Store. This is a replica of the 1850 hardware store opened by Collis Huntington and Mark Hopkins, two of the Big Four businessmen who formed the Central Pacific Railroad. Displays show the picks, shovels, gold pans, and other paraphernalia miners used during the gold rush, as well as household hardware and appliances used by later settlers. ✉ *113 I St.,* ☎ *916/323–9280.* ⊙ *Usually daily 10–4, but call ahead, as volunteer staffing is inconsistent.*

★ ᕙ ⓭ State Indian Museum. One of several interesting displays at this well-organized museum is devoted to Ishi, the last Yahi Indian to emerge from the mountains (in 1911), who provided insight into the existence of this group of Native Americans. The exhibits of arts and crafts here invite lengthy exploration; an evocative 10-minute historical video plays continuously. ✉ *2601 K St.,* ☎ *916/324–0971.* 🎫 *$3.* ⊙ *Daily 10–5.*

★ ᕙ ⓬ Sutter's Fort. Sacramento's earliest settlement was founded by German-born Swiss immigrant John Augustus Sutter in 1839. Visitors walk a self-guided tour, with audio speakers at each stop explaining exhibits that include a blacksmith's shop, a bakery, a prison, living quarters, and livestock areas. Costumed docents sometimes reenact fort life, demonstrating crafts, food preparation, and firearm maintenance. ✉ *2701 L St.,* ☎ *916/445–4422.* 🎫 *$5 Memorial Day–Labor Day; $3 rest of yr.* ⊙ *Daily 10–5.*

❾ Towe Ford Museum of Automotive History. The museum's collection of vintage cars and trucks emphasizes Ford models through the years. Car clubs congregate here, and occasionally owners can be seen working on vehicles. Docents are usually available to talk about specific models, including 1923 and 1931 fire trucks, a snazzy 1903 red Cadillac Model A right-hand-drive runabout, several "woody" station wagons, and Ford Phaetons from the 1930s that collector Edward Towe drove from Uruguay and Argentina to Colorado (home of a sister museum). The California State Automobile Association funded a 1920s roadside café and garage exhibit. A gift shop sells vintage-car magazines, model kits, old license plates, and many other car-related items. ✉ *2200 Front St., at V St.,* ☎ *916/442–6802.* 🎫 *$5.* ⊙ *Daily 10–6.*

❻ Visitor Information Center. The models for this center that opened in 1996 were similarly helpful havens in Europe. Here one can obtain brochures about nearby attractions, arrange lodgings, check local restaurant menus, rent strollers or wheelchairs, avail themselves of the fully functioning post office, and receive directions in five languages. ✉ *1101 2nd St., at K St.,* ☎ *916/442–7644.* ⊙ *Daily 9–4:30.*

Dining

CALIFORNIA

$$$ ✕ Rio City Café. Eclectic lunch and dinner menus and huge floor-to-ceiling windows with views of an Old Sacramento Wharf are the dual attractions of this bright restaurant. When the weather is good you can enjoy your meals at water's edge. Rio City serves both light and hearty fare: calamari salad, duck enchiladas with tomatillo sauce, venison stew in pinot-noir sauce over spaetzle, fettuccine with sun-dried tomato pesto. ✉ *1110 Front St.,* ☎ *916/442–8226. AE, D, DC, MC, V.*

$$ ✕ Capitol Grill. This busy restaurant has a political theme, with campaign posters and other memorabilia tacked all over the walls. The moderate prices and casual atmosphere appeal to a young after-work crowd. Contemporary California dishes on the menu often have Asian or Italian accents—sesame-crusted ahi, black-pepper fettuccine, Chinese noodle salad. ✉ *2730 N St.,* ☎ *916/736–0744. AE, DC, MC, V. No lunch weekends.*

$$ ✕ **Paragary's Bar and Oven.** Pizza is the specialty at this casual, noisy restaurant, which is popular with the downtown state-worker crowd for lunch or dinner. You won't go hungry here—pasta, dessert, and even appetizer portions are enormous. ✉ *1401 28th St.,* ☎ *916/457–5737. AE, D, DC, MC, V. No lunch weekends.*

CALIFORNIA- ITALIAN

$$ ✕ **Harlow's.** The popular Harlow's has extraordinary seafood specials and a downright succulent cheesecake. Dining can be noisy and crowded, but the service is excellent and people-watching is fun, especially at the bar. Upstairs, there's a cigar room. ✉ *2708 J St.,* ☎ *916/441–4693. AE, D, DC, MC, V. Closed Sun.–Mon. No lunch weekends.*

CALIFORNIA–PACIFIC RIM

$$–$$$ ✕ **California Fats.** This is the better of two Old Sacramento restaurants carrying the Fats name. The extensive Pacific Rim–influenced menu combines intriguing flavors: seared ahi and glazed duck from a wood-fired oven, pastas with overtones of ginger and coriander, and venison in a cashew crust, in addition to steaks and seafood. The restaurant's vibrant decor portrays the history of Chinese immigrants. ✉ *1015 Front St.,* ☎ *916/441–7966. AE, MC, V.*

CHINESE

$$–$$$ ✕ **Frank Fat's.** Known as the "third house" of the California legislature, where lawmakers and lobbyists have been making deals for more than 50 years, Frank Fat's is renowned more for its watering-hole atmosphere than its so-so Chinese food. The menu emphasizes Cantonese cuisine, but there are items from other regions of China. Signature dishes include brandy-fried chicken, stir-fried clams in black bean sauce, plus a couple of items from the American menu: New York steak and banana cream pie. ✉ *806 L St.,* ☎ *916/442–7092. AE, MC, V. No lunch weekends.*

ITALIAN

$$$ ✕ **Biba.** Owner Biba Caggiano is an authority on Italian cuisine, the
★ author of several cookbooks, and the star of a national TV show on cooking. The capitol crowd flocks here for her delicate pasta dishes, baked spinach lasagna, and homemade tortelloni. Caggiano also offers a great osso buco, rabbit tenderloin, and grilled pork loin, as well as regional specialties. ✉ *2801 Capitol Ave.,* ☎ *916/455–2422. AE, MC, V. Closed Sun. No lunch Sat.*

MEXICAN

$–$$ ✕ **Centro.** Its cuisine may not be as authentic as claimed, but Centro, one of the most popular restaurants in town, deserves credit for conceiving dishes well outside the taco-burrito realm. Unusual items include adobo marinated pork and black-bean and chipotle chili tamales. ✉ *2730 J St.,* ☎ *916/442–2552. AE, DC, MC, V. No lunch weekends.*

Lodging

$$$–$$$$ 🏨 **Delta King.** This grand old riverboat, now permanently moored at Old Sacramento's waterfront, once transported passengers between Sacramento and San Francisco. Among many design elements of note are its main staircase, mahogany paneling, and brass fittings. The best of the 44 staterooms are on the river side toward the back of the boat. Room rates include a Continental breakfast. ✉ *1000 Front St., 95814,* ☎ *916/444–5464 or 800/825–5464,* FAX *916/444–5314. 44 rooms.*

Restaurant, bar, air-conditioning, meeting rooms, parking (fee). AE, D, DC, MC, V.

$$$–$$$$ ⊞ **Hyatt Regency at Capitol Park.** With its dramatic marble-and-glass
★   lobby and luxuriously appointed rooms, this hotel across the street from
the capitol and adjacent to the convention center is arguably Sacra-
mento's finest. The service here is outstanding. The best rooms have
Capitol Park views. ⊠ *1209 L St., 95814,* ☎ *916/443–1234 or 800/
233–1234,* FAX *916/321–6699. 500 rooms. 2 restaurants, bar, air-con-
ditioning, pool, hot tub, exercise room, nightclub, meeting rooms, car
rental. AE, D, DC, MC, V.*

$$$–$$$$ ⊞ **Radisson Hotel Sacramento.** Mediterranean-style two-story build-
ings clustered around a large artificial lake on an 18-acre landscaped
site contain fairly large rooms, with art deco appointments and fur-
nishings. Many have patios or balconies. More a resort than other Sacra-
mento-area hotels, the Radisson presents summer jazz concerts in a
lakeside amphitheater and holds barbecues on warm evenings. ⊠ *500
Leisure La., 95815,* ☎ *916/922–2020 or 800/333–3333,* FAX *916/649–
9463. 314 rooms. 2 restaurants, air-conditioning, pool, exercise room,
boating, bicycles, meeting rooms. AE, D, DC, MC, V.*

$$–$$$$ ⊞ **Amber House Bed & Breakfast Inn.** Three separate homes compose
★   this B&B in a historic district near the capitol. The original house, the
Poet's Refuge, is a Craftsman-style home with five bedrooms named
after famous poets. Next door, a 1913 Mediterranean-style home has
a French Impressionist motif. The third, an 1897 Dutch Colonial Revival home, has gardens where weddings occasionally take place. All
rooms have private baths tiled with Italian marble; several rooms have
bathrooms with two-person hot tubs, fireplaces, and skylights. Service
is excellent. Room rates include breakfast. ⊠ *1315 22nd St., 95816,*
☎ *916/444–8085 or 800/755–6526,* FAX *916/552–6529. 14 rooms.
Air-conditioning, bicycles. AE, D, DC, MC, V.*

$$–$$$ ⊞ **Abigail's Bed and Breakfast Inn.** This 1912 Colonial Revival man-
sion sits on a tree-shaded street near the capitol. Two parlors flank a
grand staircase leading to bedrooms with pencil-post or canopied beds.
One room has a Jaccuzi. Room rates include full breakfast and evening
refreshments. ⊠ *2120 G St., 95816,* ☎ *916/441–5007 or 800/858–
1568,* FAX *916/441–0621. 5 rooms. Air-conditioning, outdoor hot tub.
AE, D, DC, MC, V.*

$$–$$$ ⊞ **Holiday Inn Capitol Plaza.** Despite its decided lack of charm, this
hotel has the best location for visiting Old Sacramento and the Downtown Plaza. It's also within walking distance of the capitol. ⊠ *300 J
St., 95814,* ☎ *916/446–0100 or 800/465–4329,* FAX *916/446–0117.
364 rooms. Restaurant, bar, air-conditioning, pool, 2 saunas, convention center, free parking. AE, DC, MC, V.*

$$ ⊞ **Best Western Sutter House.** Many consider this family-owned prop-
erty (formerly the Best Western Ponderosa) to be the best value down-
town. Many of the rooms open onto a courtyard surrounding a pool.
Room rates include a Continental breakfast. ⊠ *1100 H St., 95814,* ☎
916/441–1314; 800/830–1314 in CA; FAX *916/441–5961. 98 rooms.
Restaurant, air-conditioning, lounge, pool, laundry service, free park-
ing. AE, D, DC, MC, V.*

$ ⊞ **Sacramento International Hostel.** This renovated landmark 1885
Victorian mansion has a grand mahogany staircase, a stained-glass
atrium, frescoed ceilings, and several carved and tiled fireplaces. Dor-
mitory rooms and bedrooms suitable for singles, couples, and fami-
lies are available, as is a shared kitchen. The hostel is within walking
distance of most area attractions and the Amtrak and Greyhound sta-
tions. ⊠ *900 H St., 95814,* ☎ *916/443–1691 or 800/909–4776, ext.
40. 70 beds. MC, V.*

Nightlife and the Arts

BARS AND NIGHTCLUBS

Busby Berkeley's (⊠ Hyatt Regency at Capitol Park, 1209 L St., ☎ 916/443–1234) has views of the capitol. DJs play music Tuesday through Saturday.

Fox and Goose (⊠ 1001 R St., ☎ 916/443–8825), a casual pub with live music (including open-mike some evenings), has been rated the "best morning-after" spot by the *Sacramento Bee* for its breakfasts. Traditional pub food (fish and chips, Cornish pasties) is served weekday evenings from 5:30 to 9:30.

Harlow's (⊠ 1708 J St., ☎ 916/441–4693) draws a young crowd to its art deco bar–nightclub for DJ music after 9.

CULTURAL EVENTS

Sacramento Community Center Theater (⊠ 13th and L Sts., ☎ 916/264–5291) is the home of the symphony, opera, ballet, and Music Circus, which presents professional musical theater in summer.

SACTIX (⊠ 701 K St., near 7th St., ☎ 916/442–2500), open daily from 10 to 6, has half-price, cash-only, day-of-the-event tickets for area arts and entertainment.

Outdoor Activities and Sports

BASKETBALL

The **Sacramento Kings** of the National Basketball Association play at the Arco Arena (⊠ 1 Sports Pkwy., ☎ 916/928–6900).

BICYCLING

Jedediah Smith Memorial Bicycle Trail runs for 23 mi from Old Sacramento to Beals Point in Folsom, mostly along the American River.

FITNESS

Capitol Health Club (⊠ 1515 8th St., ☎ 916/442–3927) has a workout area, a lap pool, aerobics and yoga classes, racquetball, handball, and basketball. The drop-in fee for nonmembers is $10.

Shopping

MALLS

Downtown Plaza, comprising the K Street Mall along with many neighboring shops and restaurants, has shopping and entertainment; there's a Thursday-night market, and in winter an outdoor ice-skating rink is set up. **Arden Fair Mall,** northeast of downtown off I–80 in the North Area, is Sacramento's largest shopping center. **Pavilions Mall** (⊠ Fair Oaks Blvd. and Howe Ave.) has many boutiques.

SPECIALTY SHOPS

Among the T-shirt and yogurt emporiums in Old Sacramento are some interesting art galleries and bookstores. The **Artists' Collaborative Gallery** (⊠ 1007 2nd St., ☎ 916/444–3764) has ever-changing exhibits by top local artists and craftspeople. **Bookmine** (⊠ 1015 2nd St., ☎ 916/441–4609) sells used and rare books. The **Elder Craftsman** (⊠ 130 J St., ☎ 916/264–7762) specializes in items made by local senior citizens.

THE GOLD COUNTRY

Highway 49 from Nevada City to Mariposa

Highway 49 winds the length of the historic gold-mining area, linking the towns of Nevada City, Grass Valley, Auburn, Placerville, Sutter Creek, Sonora, and Mariposa. Most are gentrified versions of once rowdy mining camps, vestiges of which remain in roadside museums, old mining structures, and historic inns.

Nevada City

⑭ *62 mi north of Sacramento, I–80 to Hwy. 49.*

Nevada City, once known as the Queen City of the Northern Mines, is the most appealing of the northern Mother Lode towns. The iron-shuttered brick buildings that line the narrow, winding downtown streets contain antiques shops, galleries, a winery, bookstores, boutiques, B&Bs, and many restaurants. Horse-drawn carriage tours add to the romance, as do gas-powered streetlights. At one point in the 1850s Nevada City had a population of nearly 10,000, enough to support much cultural activity, a tradition that continues to this day. The **Nevada City Chamber of Commerce** (⊠ 132 Main St., ☎ 530/265–2692) has books about the area and a free walking-tour map of the most interesting old buildings.

With its gingerbread-trimmed bell tower, **Firehouse No. 1** is one of the Gold Country's most photographed buildings. Now a museum, it houses relics of the fateful Donner Party (victims of a severe Sierra Nevada snowstorm), gold-rush artifacts, and a Chinese Joss House. ⊠ *214 Main St.,* ☎ *530/265–5468.* ☉ *Daily 11–4.*

The redbrick **Nevada Theatre,** constructed in 1865, is California's oldest theater building in continuous use. Mark Twain, Emma Nevada, and many other superstars of bygone times appeared on its stage. The present-day home of the Foothill Theater Company (☎ 916/265–8587), the Nevada also screens films weekly and hosts theatrical and musical events as diverse as Duke Ellington and Grateful Dead tributes. ⊠ *401 Broad St.,* ☎ *530/265–6161.*

The **Miners Foundry,** erected in 1856, produced machines for gold mining and logging. The Pelton Water Wheel, a source of power for the mines (the wheel also jump-started the hydroelectric power industry), was invented here. A cavernous building, the foundry now serves as a cultural center that presents plays, concerts, a Victorian Christmas fair, a teddy-bear convention, antiques show, themed period parties, and other events. ⊠ *325 Spring St.,* ☎ *530/265–5040.*

You can watch while you sip at the **Nevada City Winery,** where the tasting room overlooks the production area. ⊠ *Miners Foundry Garage, 321 Spring St.,* ☎ *530/265–9463.* ☉ *Tasting daily noon–5.*

Dining and Lodging

$$–$$$$ ✕ **Country Rose Café.** The lengthy country-French menu at this antiques-laden café includes seafood, beef, lamb, chicken, and ratatouille. In the summer, there is outdoor service on a verdant patio. ⊠ *300 Commercial St.,* ☎ *530/265–6248. AE, DC, MC, V.*

$$ ✕ **Friar Tuck's.** A guitar player performs nightly at this vaguely 1960s-retro, wine cellarlike gathering spot; sometimes patrons sing along. Hearty offerings include large portions of rack of lamb, roast duck, fondue, Iowa beef, Hawaiian fish specials, and Tuck's bouillabaisse. There's an extensive wine and beer list as well as a full bar. ⊠ *111 N. Pine St.,* ☎ *530/265–9093. AE, MC, V. No lunch.*

$$ ✕ **Potager at Seleya's.** Fish, fowl, meat, and pasta dishes all come cre-
★ atively prepared at this sophisticated restaurant. Appetizers include wild mushrooms gratin and *potager* (soup). Beef Wellington, salmon roulade, and loin of lamb are signature entrées. Caesar salads are mixed at your table; breads and desserts are baked on the premises. Much of the produce and herbs are grown in the chef-owner's garden. The adjacent

Potager to Go (☎ 530/265–0558) sells gourmet deli items weekdays from 11 to 3. ✉ *320 Broad St.,* ☎ *530/265–5697. AE, MC, V. Closed Mon. No lunch.*

$ ✕ **Cirino's.** American-Italian dishes—seafood, pasta, and veal—are served at this informal bar and grill. The restaurant's handsome Brunswick bar is of gold-rush vintage. ✉ *309 Broad St.,* ☎ *530/265–2246. AE, D, MC, V.*

$–$$$ ⊡ **Flume's End.** This inn was built at the end of a historic flume that once brought water into Nevada City's mines. Rooms are on several levels, most with creek views. Two have hot tubs. The decor is eclectic Victorian, but with wall-to-wall carpeting. Homey and casual, the inn has several romantic nooks. Room rates include a full breakfast. ✉ *317 S. Pine St., 95959,* ☎ *530/265–9665 or 800/991–8118. 6 rooms. MC, V.*

$–$$$ ⊡ **Red Castle Inn.** A state landmark, this 1860 Gothic Revival man-
★ sion stands on a forested hillside overlooking Nevada City. Its brick exterior is trimmed with white icicle woodwork; verandas and terraced gardens add to the charm. A steep private pathway leads down through the gardens into town. Elaborately decorated rooms have handsome antique furnishings and Oriental rugs, and though they don't have phones or TVs a portable phone is available for guest use. The knowledgeable innkeepers are well-versed in local history and present-day lore (including rumors about ghost sightings), and their breakfast gatherings (room rates include a full gourmet meal) in the parlor are interesting and convivial. ✉ *109 Prospect St., 95959,* ☎ *530/265–5135. 7 rooms. MC, V.*

$–$$ ⊡ **Northern Queen Inn.** Most of the accommodations at this bright, creekside inn are typical motel units, but there are eight two-story chalets and eight rustic cottages with efficiency kitchens in a secluded, wooded area. ✉ *400 Railroad Ave. (Sacramento St. exit off Hwy. 49), 95959,* ☎ *530/265–5824,* ℻ *530/265–3720. 85 rooms. Restaurant, refrigerators, pool, spa, convention center. AE, DC, MC, V.*

Grass Valley

4 mi south of Nevada City on Hwy. 49.

More than half of California's total gold production was extracted from mines around Grass Valley. Unlike in neighboring Nevada City, urban sprawl surrounds Grass Valley's historic downtown, but the Empire Mine and the North Star Power House and Pelton Wheel Exhibit are among the Gold Country's most fascinating exhibits.

The **Grass Valley/Nevada County Chamber of Commerce** is housed in a reproduction of the home on this site owned by notorious dancer Lola Montez, who moved to Grass Valley in the early 1850s. Lola was no great talent—her popularity among miners derived from her suggestive "Spider Dance"—but her loves, which reportedly included composer Franz Liszt, were legendary. She had arrived in California not too long after, according to one account, being "permanently retired from her job as Bavarian king Ludwig's mistress," literary muse, and political adviser. Seems she pushed too hard for democracy, which contributed to his overthrow and her banishment as a witch. Or so the story went. The memory of licentious Lola lingers on in Grass Valley, as does her bathtub. ✉ *248 Mill St.,* ☎ *916/273–4667.*

The landmark **Holbrooke Hotel,** built in 1851, hosted Lola Montez, Mark Twain, Ulysses S. Grant, and a stream of other U.S. presidents. Its restaurant/saloon is one of the oldest still operating west of the Mississippi. ✉ *212 W. Main St., 95945,* ☎ *530/273–1353 or 800/933–7077,* ℻ *530/273–0434.*

★ ⓘ The hard-rock gold mine at **Empire Mine State Historic Park,** worked from 1850 right up to 1956, was one of California's richest—an estimated 5.8 million ounces were extracted from its 367 mi of underground passages. Fifty-minute tours allow visitors to walk into a mine shaft, peer into the mine's deeper recesses, and also view the owner's "cottage," with its exquisite woodwork. The visitor center has mining exhibits, and a picnic area is nearby. ⌧ *10791 E. Empire St. (Empire St. exit south from Hwy. 49),* ☎ *530/273–8522.* ⌨ *$3.* ⊙ *Summer, daily 9–6; winter, daily 10–5. Tours in summer on the hr 11–4; winter weekends only at 1 (cottage only) and 2 (mine yard only).*

☀ The **North Star Power House and Pelton Wheel Exhibit** stars a 32-ft-high Pelton enclosed waterwheel said to be the largest ever built. It was used to power mining operations and was a forerunner of the modern water turbines that generate hydroelectricity. There are hands-on displays for children and a picnic area. ⌧ *Empire and McCourtney Sts. (Empire St. exit north from Hwy. 49),* ☎ *530/273–4255.* ⌨ *Donation requested.* ⊙ *May–Oct., daily 10–5.*

Auburn

ⓖ *24 mi south of Grass Valley on Hwy. 49, 34 mi northeast of Sacramento on I–80.*

Auburn is the Gold Country town most accessible to travelers on the interstate. An important transportation center during the gold rush, Auburn has a small old town with narrow climbing streets, cobblestones, wooden sidewalks, and many original buildings. A $1 trolley operated by the **Placer County Visitor Information Center** (☎ 530/887–2111 or 800/427–6463) loops through downtown and Old Town, with stops at some local hotels and inns. Old Town has a Saturday farmers' market (8 AM–noon) where fresh local produce, flowers, baked goods, and gifts are for sale.

Auburn's standout structure is the **Placer County Courthouse.** The classic gold-domed building houses the Placer County Museum, which documents the area's history—Native American, railroad, agricultural, and mining—from the early 1700s to 1900. ⌧ *101 Maple St.,* ☎ *530/889–6500.* ⌨ *Free.* ⊙ *Tues.–Sun. 10–4.*

The **Bernhard Museum Complex,** whose centerpiece is the former Traveler's Rest Hotel, was built in 1851 and occupied by the Bernhard family from 1868 to 1957. The Bernhard Residence and adjacent winery buildings reflect family life in the late Victorian era; a carriage house displays several period conveyances. ⌧ *291 Auburn-Folsom Rd.,* ☎ *530/889–6500.* ⌨ *$1 (includes entry to Gold Country Museum).* ⊙ *Tues.–Fri. 11–3, weekends noon–4.*

The **Gold Country Museum,** worth peeking into, surveys life in the mines. Exhibits include a walk-through mine tunnel, a gold-panning stream, and a replica saloon. ⌧ *1273 High St., off Auburn-Folsom Rd.,* ☎ *530/889–6500.* ⌨ *$1 (includes entry to Bernhard Museum Complex).* ⊙ *Tues.–Fri. 10–3:30, weekends 11–4.*

Dining and Lodging

$$–$$$ ✕ **Latitudes.** An 1870 Victorian is the setting for delicious multicul-
★   tural cuisine with interesting combinations of fresh ingredients. The menu (with monthly specials from specific geographic regions) includes seafood, chicken, and turkey entrées prepared with Mexican spices, curries, cheese, or teriyaki sauce. The beer and wine list is as extensive and eclectic as the menu. Sunday brunch here is deservedly

popular. Local artwork adorns the walls. ✉ *130 Maple St.,* ☎ *530/885–9535. AE, MC, V. No lunch Sat., no dinner Mon.–Tues.*

$ ✕ **Awful Annie's.** Big patio umbrellas (and outdoor heaters when necessary) allow patrons to sit inside or outside and take in the view of old-town Auburn at this popular spot for breakfast (a specialty: omelets with chili) or lunch. ✉ *160 Sacramento St.,* ☎ *530/888–9857. AE, MC, V. No dinner.*

$–$$$ ⊞ **Powers Mansion Inn.** This inn hints at the opulence the gold-rush gentry enjoyed. Two light-filled parlors have gleaming oak floors, Asian antiques, and ornate Victorian chairs and settees. Photos on the walls relate the story of the gold fortune that built the mansion. A second-floor maze of narrow corridors leads to the guest rooms, which have brass and pencil-post beds with handmade quilts. Breakfast is included in the room rate. ✉ *164 Cleveland Ave., 95603,* ☎ *530/885–1166,* ℻ *530/885–1386. 11 rooms. AE, MC, V.*

$$ ⊞ **Holiday Inn.** Perched on a hill above the freeway across from Old Auburn, the hotel has an imposing columned entrance but a welcoming lobby. Rooms are chain-standard but attractively furnished; all have work areas and coffeemakers. Rooms nearest the parking lot can be noisy. ✉ *120 Grass Valley Hwy., 95603,* ☎ *530/887–8787 or 800/814–8787,* ℻ *530/887–9824. 96 rooms. Restaurant, bar, in-room modem lines, pool, spa, business services, convention center. AE, D, DC, MC, V.*

$ ⊞ **Auburn Inn.** The decor at this well-maintained inn is contemporary, in teal and pastel colors. Some rooms are designed for wheelchair users. Though a short distance from the freeway, the inn is fairly quiet. Rates include a Continental breakfast. ✉ *1875 Auburn Ravine Rd., Foresthill exit north from I–80, 95603,* ☎ *530/885–1800 or 800/272–1444,* ℻ *530/888–6424. 81 rooms. No-smoking rooms, pool, spa, coin laundry. AE, D, DC, MC, V.*

Coloma

18 mi south of Auburn on Hwy. 49.

The California gold rush started in Coloma. "My eye was caught with the glimpse of something shining in the bottom of the ditch," James Marshall recalled later. Marshall himself never found any more "color," as gold came to be called.

★ ⑰ Most of Coloma lies within **Marshall Gold Discovery State Historic Park.** Though it is often crowded with tourists in summer, Coloma hardly resembles the mob scene it was in 1849, when 2,000 prospectors had staked out claims along the streambed. The town's population grew to 4,000, supporting seven hotels, three banks, and many stores and businesses. But when reserves of the precious metal dwindled, prospectors left as quickly as they had come. The park contains a number of buildings dating back to the gold rush, a working replica of John Sutter's mill near where John Marshall first saw gold, and a self-guided trail that leads to a monument marking his discovery. The museum here is not as interesting as the outdoor exhibits, which often include a blacksmith working red-hot metal with a hammer. ✉ *Hwy. 49,* ☎ *530/622–3470.* ⌖ *$5 per vehicle (day use).* ☉ *Park daily 8 AM–sunset. Museum summer, daily 10–5; Labor Day–Memorial Day, daily 10–4:30.*

Lodging

$$–$$$ ⊞ **Coloma Country Inn.** A restored 1852 Victorian set on 5 private acres of state parkland is now a fine B&B. Five rooms are in the main house, with two suites in a carriage house. Appointments include antique double and queen-size beds, private sitting areas, handmade quilts, sten-

ciled friezes, and fresh flowers. Balloon and white-water-rafting packages are available. Room rates include a full country breakfast. ⊠ *345 High St., 95613,* ☎ *530/622–6919. 7 rooms, 2 with shared bath. No credit cards.*

Placerville

10 mi south of Coloma on Hwy. 49, 44 mi east of Sacramento on U.S. 50.

It's hard to imagine now, but in 1849 about 4,000 miners had staked out every gully and hillside in Placerville, turning the town into a rip-roaring camp of log cabins, tents, and clapboard houses. The area was then known as Hangtown, a graphic allusion to the summary nature of frontier justice. It took on the name Placerville in 1854 and became an important supply center. Several American industrialists—Mark Hopkins, Philip Armour, and John Studebaker—got their starts here.

★ ⑱ **Hangtown's Gold Bug Mine,** owned by the city of Placerville, has a fully lighted shaft and is open for self-guided touring. A shaded stream runs through the park, and there are picnic facilities. ⊠ *1 mi off U.S. 50, north on Bedford Ave.,* ☎ *530/642–5238.* ⊡ *$2.* ☉ *May 6–Oct., daily 10–4; Nov.–Mar. 1 and Apr. 6–May 5, weekends 10–4.*

OFF THE BEATEN PATH

APPLE HILL – Roadside stands sell fresh produce from more than 50 family farms in this area. During the fall harvest season (September–December) members of the Apple Hill Growers Association (☎ 530/644-7692) open their orchards and vineyards for apple and berry picking, picnicking, and wine and cider tasting. Many sell baked items and picnic food. ⊠ *About 5 mi east of Hwy. 49; take Camino exit from U.S. 50.*

Dining and Lodging

$$$ ✕ **Zachary Jacques.** It's not easy to locate, but call for directions—
★ this country-French restaurant is worth the effort. A seasonally changing menu focuses on fresh fish and vegetables. Appetizers might include escargots or mushrooms prepared in several ways, roasted garlic with olive oil served on tapenade toast, or spicy lamb sausage. Entrées such as roast rack of lamb, *daube Provençale* (beef stew), and scallops and prawns in lime butter receive traditional preparation. ⊠ *1821 Pleasant Valley Rd. (3 mi east of Diamond Springs),* ☎ *530/626–8045. AE, MC, V. Closed Mon.–Tues. No lunch.*

$$ ✕ **Café Luna.** Tucked into the back of the Creekside Place shopping complex is a small restaurant with about 30 seats indoors, plus outdoor tables overlooking a creek. An extensive wine selection complements healthful entrées such as grilled chicken breast with blueberry and pasilla salsa. ⊠ *451 Main St.,* ☎ *530/642–8669. AE, MC, V. Closed Sun. No dinner Mon.–Tues.*

$ ✕ **Lil' Mama D. Carlo's Italian Kitchen.** This comfortable Italian restaurant with a pleasant wait staff serves enormous portions of pasta, chicken, and some vegetarian dishes, heavy on the garlic, often in a red sauce. The wine list features local vintages. ⊠ *482 Main St.,* ☎ *530/626–1612. MC, V. No lunch.*

$$ ▥ **Best Western Placerville Inn.** This motel's serviceable rooms are done in the chain's trademark pastels; the pool comes in handy during the hot summer months. There is a coffee shop–restaurant on the premises. ⊠ *6850 Greenleaf Dr., near U.S. 50's Missouri Flats exit, 95667,* ☎ *530/622–9100 or 800/854–9100,* ⅎₐₓ *530/622–9376. 105 rooms. Restaurant, pool, hot tub. AE, D, DC, MC, V.*

Shenandoah Valley

16 mi south of Placerville on Shenandoah Rd., east of Hwy. 49.

The most concentrated Gold Country wine-touring area lies in the rolling hills of the Shenandoah Valley, just east of Plymouth. This section of Amador County contains 17 mostly family-run wineries on scenic back roads. Robust zinfandel is the primary grape grown here, but vineyards also produce chardonnay and cabernet sauvignon. Most are open weekend afternoons; several have shady picnic areas, gift shops, and galleries or museums. Maps are available from the **Amador County Chamber of Commerce** (☞ Contacts and Resources *in* Sacramento and the Gold Country A to Z, *below*).

Sobon Estate (✉ 14430 Shenandoah Rd., ☎ 209/245–6554) operates the Shenandoah Valley Museum, illustrating pioneer life and wine making in the valley. It's open daily 10 to 5. **Charles Spinetta Winery** (✉ 12557 Steiner Rd., ☎ 209/245–3384), which has a wildlife gallery, is open Tuesday to Sunday 10 to 5. The gallery at **Shenandoah Vineyards** (✉ 12300 Steiner Rd., ☎ 209/245–4455), open daily 10–5, features the work of contemporary Bay Area artists.

Lodging

$$ 🛏 **Amador Harvest Inn.** This B&B adjacent to Deaver Vineyards occupies a bucolic lakeside spot in the Shenandoah Valley. A contemporary Cape Cod–style structure has homey guest rooms with private baths. Public areas include a spacious living room with fireplace and a music room with a view of the lake. Room rates include a full breakfast. ✉ *12455 Steiner Rd., 95669,* ☎ *209/245–5512. 4 rooms. MC, V.*

Amador City

6 mi south of Plymouth on Hwy. 49.

The history of tiny Amador City mirrors the boom-to-bust-to-boom cycle of many Gold Country towns. With an output of $42 million in gold, its Keystone Mine was one of the most productive in the Mother Lode. After all the gold was extracted, the miners cleared out and the area suffered, but Amador City now derives its wealth from tourists, who come to browse through its antiques and specialty shops and see historic landmarks.

Dining and Lodging

$$–$$$ ✕🛏 **Imperial Hotel.** The whimsically decorated rooms at this 1879 hotel
★   mock Victorian excesses in a 20th-century way. Antique furnishings include iron and brass beds, gingerbread flourishes, and, in one room, art deco appointments. The two front rooms, which can be noisy, have balconies. The hotel's fine restaurant serves meals in a bright dining room and on the patio outdoors. The menu changes quarterly; the cuisine ranges from vegetarian to country-hearty to trendy. Room rates include breakfast; there is a two-night minimum weekends. ✉ *Hwy. 49, 95601,* ☎ *209/267–9172 or 800/242–5594,* FAX *209/267–9249. 6 rooms. Restaurant, bar. AE, D, DC, MC, V.*

Sutter Creek

★ ⑲ *2 mi south of Amador City on Hwy. 49.*

Sutter Creek is a charming conglomeration of balconied buildings, Victorian homes, and neo–New England structures. The stores along Highway 49 (called Main Street in the town proper) are worth visiting to hunt for works by the many local artists and craftspeople.

Dining and Lodging

$–$$ ✕ **Ron and Nancy's Palace.** This unpretentious restaurant serves Continental cuisine, with daily specials such as chicken Marsala and veal piccata. The hearty lunch menu has a varied sandwich selection and some of the entrées available for dinner. ⊠ *76 Main St.,* ☎ *209/267–1355. AE, D, DC, MC, V.*

$ ✕ **Somewhere in Time.** Sip a cup of tea, sample a sinful dessert, or lunch on sandwiches and salad before or after browsing through the antiques shops in this very Victorian boutique–dining complex. The building, erected in 1860, was originally a miners' saloon run by Chinese immigrants. ⊠ *34 Main St.,* ☎ *209/267–5789. D, MC, V. No dinner.*

$$–$$$ 🛏 **Foxes Bed & Breakfast.** The rooms in this white 1857 clapboard
★   house are handsome, with high ceilings, antique beds, and lofty armoires. All rooms have queen-size beds; four have wood-burning fireplaces or cable TV. A full breakfast (included in the room rate) is cooked to order and delivered on a silver service to guests' rooms or to the gazebo in the garden. ⊠ *77 Main St., 95685,* ☎ *209/267–5882,* FAX *209/267–0712. 7 rooms. D, MC, V.*

$$–$$$ 🛏 **Gold Quartz Inn.** Floral wallpaper, ruffled curtains, quilts, lace, and period furnishings decorate the spacious rooms at this Queen Anne–style inn at the edge of Sutter Creek. All have king-size beds, many have additional beds and large porches, and two are equipped for people with disabilities. Breakfast is served in the dining room and afternoon tea in the butler's pantry; both are included in the room rate. ⊠ *15 Bryson Dr., 95685,* ☎ *209/267–9155; 800/752–8738 in CA;* FAX *209/267–9170. 24 rooms. Air-conditioning, meeting rooms. AE, D, MC, V.*

$$ 🛏 **Picture Rock Inn.** Original redwood paneling, wainscoting, beams, and cabinets lend the Picture Rock a cozy feel, as do leaded- and stained-glass windows. Eclectic furnishings span several eras from Victorian to art deco—a 1920s carousel horse is suspended mid-leap in the front room. Most rooms have views and gas-log fireplaces; all have private baths. Room rates include a full breakfast. ⊠ *55 Eureka St., 95685,* ☎ *209/267–5500 or 800/399–2389. 6 rooms. Air-conditioning. AE, D, MC, V.*

$ 🛏 **Aparicio's Hotel.** Budget-minded travelers will appreciate this clean hotel. Large rooms contain two queen beds; they're decorated with antique reproductions. ⊠ *271 Hanford St., 95685,* ☎ *209/267–9177,* FAX *209/267–5303. 52 rooms. Restaurant, lounge, meeting rooms. AE, D, MC, V.*

OFF THE   **DAFFODIL HILL –** Each spring a 4-acre hillside east of Sutter Creek erupts
BEATEN PATH   in a riot of yellow and gold as 300,000 daffodils emerge and burst into bloom. The garden is the work of members of the McLaughlin family, which has owned this site since 1887. Daffodil plantings began in the 1930s and continue each winter. The timing of the display depends upon weather but usually takes place between mid-March and mid-April. ⊠ *Shake Ridge Rd., about 13 mi east of Sutter Creek,* ☎ *209/223–0350.* 🎟 *Free.* ☉ *Daily in season 9–5.*

Jackson

20 *8 mi south of Sutter Creek on Hwy. 49.*

Jackson once had the world's deepest and richest mines, the Kennedy and Argonaut, which together produced $70 million in gold. These were deep rock mines, tunnels for which extended as much as a mile underground. Most of the miners who worked the lode here were of Serbian or Italian origin; they gave the town a European character that persists to this day. Churches, cemeteries, and festivals carry Serbian or Italian names. Jackson has a number of aboveground pioneer cemeteries in which the headstones tell the stories of local Serbian and Italian families. The terraced cemetery on the grounds of the handsome **St. Sava Serbian Orthodox Church** (⊠ 724 N. Main St.) is the most impressive.

Jackson wasn't the Gold Country's rowdiest town, but the party lasted longer here than most anywhere else: "Girls' dormitories" and nickel slots flourished until the mid-1950s. Now the heart of Jackson's historic section is the **National Hotel** (⊠ 2 Water St.), which operates an old-time saloon in the lobby; the hotel is especially active on weekends, when people come from miles around to participate in the Saturday-night sing-alongs.

The **Amador County Museum,** built in the late 1850s as a private home, provides a colorful take on gold-rush life. Displays include a kitchen with a woodstove, the Amador County bicentennial quilt, many original furnishings, and a classroom. A time line recounts the county's checkered past. The museum also conducts hourly tours of large-scale working models of the nearby Kennedy Mine. ⊠ 225 Church St., ☎ 209/223–6386. ⊞ Museum free, building with mine $1. ☉ Wed.–Sun. 10–4.

Dining and Lodging

$–$$ ✕ **Upstairs Restaurant.** Chef Layne McCollum takes a creative approach to contemporary American cuisine—gourmet fowl, fresh seafood, and meat—in this intimate (12 tables) restaurant with fresh flowers, white table linens, and soft music. The baked-brie and roast-garlic appetizer and homemade soups are specialties; local wines are reasonably priced. Downstairs there's a streetside bistro and wine bar for lunch and lounging. ⊠ 164 Main St., ☎ 209/223–3342. D, DC, MC, V. Closed Mon.

$ ✕ **Rosebud's Classic Cafe.** Art deco decor and music from the 1930s and 1940s set the mood at this homey café. Among the classic American menu items are hot roast beef, turkey, and meat loaf with mashed potatoes smothered in gravy. Charbroiled burgers, freshly baked pies, and espresso or gourmet coffees round out the lunch menu. Omelets, hotcakes, and many other items are served for breakfast. ⊠ 26 Main St., ☎ 209/223–1035. MC, V. No dinner.

$$–$$$ ▦ **Court Street Inn.** This Victorian has tin ceilings and a redwood staircase. The cozy first-floor Muldoon Room has a fireplace; Blair Room has a large whirlpool and a Wedgwood stove. The Indian House, a two-bedroom guest cottage, has a large bathroom. Room rates include a full breakfast and evening refreshments. ⊠ 215 Court St., 95642, ☎ 209/223–0416 or 800/200–0416. 7 rooms. Air-conditioning, outdoor hot tub. AE, D, MC, V.

$ ▦ **Best Western Amador Inn.** Convenience and price are the main attractions of this sprawling two-story motel right on the highway. Rooms are nicely decorated; many have fireplaces. ⊠ 200 S. Hwy. 49, 95642, ☎ 209/223–0211 or 800/543–5221, FAX 209/223–4836. 118 rooms. Restaurant, pool, laundry service. AE, D, DC, MC, V.

Angels Camp

㉑ *20 mi south of Jackson on Hwy. 49.*

Angels Camp is famed chiefly for its May jumping-frog contest, based on Mark Twain's "The Jumping Frog of Calaveras County." The writer reputedly heard the story of the jumping frog from Ross Coon, proprietor of Angels Hotel, which has been operating since 1856.

Angels Camp Museum holds a granny's attic of gold-rush relics—historic photos, rocks, petrified wood, and old mining equipment. The huge Pelton Water Wheel exhibit explains how the apparatus was used to supply water power to the mines. ⊠ *753 S. Main St.,* ☎ *209/736–0049.* ☞ *$1.* ☾ *Jan.–Feb., weekends 10–3; Mar.–Nov., daily 10–3.*

<table>
<tr><td>OFF THE
BEATEN PATH</td><td>THE CALIFORNIA CAVERNS AND MOANING CAVERN – A ½-mi subterranean trail at the California Caverns winds through several large chambers and past underground streams and lakes. There aren't many steps to climb but it's a fairly hefty walk, with some narrow passageways and steep spots. Wearing the hard hat that's provided is a must so you don't bump your head. The caverns, at a constant 53°F, contain crystalline formations not found elsewhere; the 80-minute guided tour includes fascinating history and geology. A 235-step spiral staircase leads into the vast (big enough to hold the Statue of Liberty) Moaning Cavern. More adventurous sorts can rappel into the chamber—ropes and instruction are provided. Once inside, you'll see giant (and still growing) stalactites and stalagmites and an archaeological site that holds some of the oldest human remains yet found in America (unlucky people fell into the cavern an average of once every 130 years starting back 13,000 years ago). ⊠ California Caverns: 8 mi east of San Andreas, off Mountain Ranch Rd., ☎ 209/736-2708. ☞ $7.50. ☾ Usually May–mid-Dec., but call ahead. ⊠ Moaning Cavern: Parrots Ferry Rd., 2 mi south of town of Vallecito, off Hwy. 4 east of Angels Camp, ☎ 209/736-2708. ☞ $6.75. ☾ Summer, daily 9–6; winter, daily 10–5.</td></tr>
</table>

Murphys

㉒ *10 mi east of Angels Camp on Hwy. 4.*

Murphys is a well-preserved town of white picket fences, Victorian houses, and interesting shops. The guest register at the **Murphys Historic Hotel and Lodge** records the visits of Horatio Alger and Ulysses S. Grant, who joined the 19th-century swarms visiting the giant sequoia groves in nearby Calaveras Big Trees State Park, on Highway 4, 15 mi east of town.

The **Kautz Ironstone Winery and Caverns** is worth a visit even if you don't like wine; tours take visitors into aging underground tunnels cooled by a waterfall from a natural spring. The winery schedules entertainment, concerts, art shows, and other events on weekends. ⊠ *1894 Six Mile Rd.,* ☎ *209/728–1251.* ☾ *Daily 11–5.*

Dining and Lodging

$–$$ ✕ **Grounds.** Light Italian entrées, grilled fresh vegetables, chicken breast, seafood, and steak are the specialties at this bistro and coffee shop. Sandwiches, salads, and homemade soups are served for lunch. The atmosphere here is friendly and the service attentive. ⊠ *402 Main St.,* ☎ *209/728–8663. MC, V. Closed Tues. No dinner Wed.*

$$–$$$$ 🏠 **Dunbar House 1880.** The oversize rooms in this elaborate Italianate-style home, decorated with an eclectic selection of antiques, have brass beds, down comforters, wood-burning stoves, and claw-foot tubs. Broad wraparound verandas encourage lounging, as do colorful gardens and shady elm trees. The Cedar room's sunporch has a two-person whirlpool tub and a view of a white-flowering almond tree; in Sequoia you can gaze at the garden while soaking in a bubble bath. Breakfast (included) is an elegant affair. ⊠ *271 Jones St., 95247,* ☎ *209/728–2897 or 800/692–6006, ext. 321;* ⅲ *209/728–1451. 4 rooms. Refrigerators, in-room VCRs. AE, MC, V.*

$–$$ 🏨 **Murphys Historic Hotel and Lodge.** This 1855 stone hotel figured in Bret Harte's short story "A Night at Wingdam." The register contains signatures of Mark Twain and bandit Black Bart. Accommodations are in the historic hotel and a modern motel-style addition. The older rooms are furnished with antiques, many of them large, heavy, and hand-carved. The hotel has a friendly old-time saloon. Continental breakfast is included in the room rate. ✉ *457 Main St., 95247,* ☎ *209/728–3444 or 800/532–7684,* FAX *209/728–1590. 29 rooms (9 historic rooms share baths). Restaurant, bar, meeting rooms. AE, D, DC, MC, V.*

OFF THE
BEATEN PATH
CALAVERAS BIG TREES STATE PARK – This state park is home to 150 of the largest and rarest living things on the planet—magnificent giant sequoia redwood trees. Some are almost 3,000 years old, 90 ft around at the base, and about 250 ft tall. The park's self-guided trails range from a 200-yard trail to 1-mi and 5-mi loops through the groves. Overnight campgrounds and picnic areas are available; swimming, wading, and sunbathing on the Stanislaus River are popular in summer. ✉ *Off Hwy. 4, 15 mi northeast of Murphys (4 mi northeast of Arnold),* ☎ *209/795–2334.* 💲 *$5 per car.* ☉ *Park daily sunrise–sunset; visitor center May–Oct., daily 10–4, Nov.–Apr., weekends 11–3.*

Columbia State Historic Park

★ ㉓ *14 mi south of Angels Camp, Hwy. 49 to Parrots Ferry Rd.*

🐣 Columbia State Historic Park, known as the Gem of the Southern Mines, comes as close to a gold-rush town in its heyday as you can get. Visitors ride stagecoaches, pan for gold, or watch a blacksmith working at his anvil. Street musicians give lively performances in summer. Restored or reconstructed buildings include a Wells Fargo Express office, a Masonic temple, stores, saloons, two hotels, a firehouse, churches, a school, and a newspaper office. All are staffed to simulate a working 1850s town. ☎ *209/532–4301.* 💲 *Free.* ☉ *Park daily 8:30–5, museum daily 9–4:30.*

Dining and Lodging

$–$$ ✕🏨 **City Hotel.** The rooms in this restored 1856 hostelry are furnished with period antiques. Two have balconies overlooking Main Street, and six parlor rooms open onto a second-floor sitting room. All the accommodations have private half baths with showers nearby; robes and slippers are provided. The restaurant (closed Monday), one of the Gold Country's best, serves French-accented California cuisine complemented by a huge selection of California wines. The What Cheer Saloon is right out of a western movie. Room rates include breakfast. ✉ *Main St., Columbia 95310,* ☎ *209/532–1479,* FAX *209/532–7027. 10 rooms with ½ bath. Restaurant, bar. AE, D, MC, V.*

$–$$ 🏨 **Fallon Hotel.** The state of California restored this 1857 hotel. All rooms have antiques and a private half bath; there are separate men's and women's showers. Continental breakfast (included in the room rates) is served; if you occupy one of the five balcony rooms, you can sit outside with your coffee and watch the town wake up. ✉ *Washington St., Columbia 95310,* ☎ *209/532–1470,* FAX *209/532–7027. 14 rooms with ½ bath. AE, D, MC, V.*

Nightlife and the Arts

Columbia Actors' Repertory (☎ 209/532–4644), a local professional company, presents a full season of plays, comedies, and musicals at the Historic Fallon House Theater. The City Hotel (☞ *above*) offers combined lodging, dinner, and theater packages.

Sonora

㉔ *4 mi south of Columbia, Parrots Ferry Rd. to Hwy. 49.*

Miners from Mexico founded Sonora and made it the biggest town in the Mother Lode. Following a period of racial and ethnic strife, the Mexicans moved on, leaving Americans to build the city based on commerce that is visible today. Sonora's downtown historic section sits atop the Big Bonanza Mine, one of the richest in the state. Another mine, on the site of nearby Sonora High School, yielded a 28-pound nugget and produced 990 pounds of gold in a single week in 1879. Reminders of the gold rush are everywhere in Sonora, in prim Victorian houses, typical Sierra stone storefronts, and awning-shaded sidewalks. Reality intrudes beyond the town's historic heart with strip malls, shopping centers, and modern motels. If the countryside surrounding Sonora seems familiar, that's because much of it has appeared in western and other movies over the years. Scenes from *High Noon, For Whom the Bell Tolls, The Virginian, Back to the Future III,* and *Unforgiven* were filmed here.

The **Tuolumne County Museum and History Center** occupies a building that served as a jail until 1951. It's been restored to an earlier period and houses a jail museum, historic exhibits, a case with gold nuggets, an extensive collection of vintage firearms and paraphernalia, and the libraries of a historical society and a genealogical society. ⊠ *158 W. Bradford St.,* ☏ *209/532–1317.* ☞ *Free.* ☉ *Sun., Mon., Wed. 9–4; Tues., Thurs., Fri. 10–4; Sat. 10–3:30.*

Dining and Lodging

$$ ✕ **Josephine's California Trattoria.** This restaurant with indoor and outdoor dining serves contemporary California and traditional Tuscan cuisine. Seared ahi, roasted red peppers, duckling with polenta, Delta crayfish risotto, and angel hair pasta with fresh seafood are among the seasonal dishes one might find on the menu. Single-portion pizzas are a staple. The extensive, reasonably priced wine list showcases Sierra foothill and Italian vintages. There is live music several nights a week, either in the bar or in the dining room. ⊠ *Gunn House Hotel, 286 S. Washington St.,* ☏ *209/533–4111. Restaurant, bar. AE, D, MC, V. No lunch.*

$–$$ ✕ **Banny's Cafe.** Its pleasant environment and hearty yet refined dishes make Banny's a quiet alternative to Sonora's eateries with live music. Appetizers such as the wilted goat cheese with roasted whole garlic, herb croutons, and a sun-dried tomato vinaigrette or the spicy pork sticks with peanut sauce can be followed by a grilled salmon fillet entrée with spinach red-pepper aioli, a chicken breast grilled on a bed of black beans with chili-corn salsa, or eggplant grilled with shiitake mushrooms, leeks, roasted tomato pesto, and mozzarella. Salads include vegetable ragout, spinach with smoked apple-wood bacon, and traditional Caesar. ⊠ *83 S. Stewart St.,* ☏ *209/533–4709. D, DC, MC, V.*

$ ✕ **Coyote Creek Cafe & Grill.** The fare here is multinational: Lunch might include pasta Castroville (with artichoke-hearts marinara), a Zuni black-bean plate, and Szechuan chicken. Spanish tapas and grilled steak are among the dinner entrées. The low-key café heats up each night with live music and dancing that draw a youngish crowd. ⊠ *177 S. Washington St.,* ☏ *209/532–9115. Reservations not accepted. D, MC, V.*

$$–$$$ 🛏 **Ryan House Bed and Breakfast Inn.** Attentive innkeepers make this 1850s farmhouse a fine place to stay, but there's more privacy than might be expected at such a small inn. Guest rooms are furnished with antiques. A garden suite in the attic has a large sitting area set into the gables, a pink and burgundy bathroom with double soaking tub, and a brass-and-iron bed. Everyone has access to the three parlors and the sunny kitchen, where complimentary snacks and beverages are always available. In springtime the garden blooms with colorful flowers of all kinds, including some antique roses as old as the house itself. Room rates include a full breakfast (with some of the best scones in California). Lodging-and-theater packages are available. ⊠ *153 S. Shepherd St., 95370,* ☎ *209/533–3445 or 800/831–4897. 4 rooms. Air-conditioning. AE, MC, V.*

$–$$$ 🏠 **Sonora Oaks Motor Hotel.** Standard motel-issue rooms at this East Sonora establishment are clean and fairly spacious. Larger ones have outside sitting areas; four have fireplaces, whirlpool tubs, and tranquil hillside views. Because the motel is right off Highway 108, the front rooms can sometimes be noisy. ⊠ *19551 Hess Ave., 95370,* ☎ *209/533–4400 or 800/532–1944,* FAX *209/532–1964. 100 rooms. Restaurant, lounge, pool, meeting rooms. AE, D, DC, MC, V.*

Jamestown

㉕ *4 mi south of Sonora on Hwy. 49.*

Compact Jamestown supplies a touristy, superficial view of gold-rush era life. Shops filling brightly colored buildings along Main Street sell antiques and gift items.

The California State Railroad Museum operates **Railtown 1897** at what were the headquarters and general shops of the Sierra Railway from 1897 to 1955. The railroad has appeared in more than 200 movies and television productions, including *Petticoat Junction, The Virginian, High Noon,* and, more recently, *Unforgiven.* Visitors can view old locomotives and coaches, the roundhouse, an air-operated 60-ft turntable, and shop rooms. Six-mile, 40-minute steam train rides through the countryside are available weekends during part of the year. ⊠ *5th Ave. and Reservoir Rd., off Hwy. 49,* ☎ *209/984–3953.* 🖭 *$2 roundhouse tour, $6 train ride.* ☾ *Daily 9:30–4:30; train rides May–Sept. weekends 11–3, Oct.–Nov. Sat. only.*

Dining and Lodging

$ ✕🏠 **National Hotel.** The decor at this hotel that has been in business since 1859 is authentic—brass beds, patchwork quilts, and lace curtains—but not overly embellished. All rooms have private baths, some rooms have no phone. The saloon, which still has its original 19th-century redwood bar, is a great place to linger. The popular restaurant serves big lunches: hamburgers and fries, salads, and Italian entrées. More upscale Continental cuisine is prepared for dinner (reservations essential). Room rates include breakfast. ⊠ *77 Main St., 95327,* ☎ *209/984–3446; 800/894–3446 in CA;* FAX *209/984–5620. 9 rooms. Restaurant, air-conditioning. AE, D, DC, MC, V.*

Mariposa

㉖ *31 mi south of Jamestown on Hwy. 49.*

Mariposa marks the southern end of the Mother Lode. Much of the land in this area was part of a 44,000-acre land grant Col. John C. Fremont acquired from Mexico before gold was discovered and California became a state.

At the **California State Mining and Mineral Museum,** a glittering, 13-pound chunk of ore makes it clear what the gold rush was about. Displays include a replica of a typical tunnel dug by hard-rock miners, a miniature stamp mill, and a panning and sluicing exhibit. ⊠ *Mariposa*

County Fairgrounds, Hwy. 49, ☎ 209/742–7625. ⌷ $3.50. ☉ May–Sept., Wed.–Mon. 10–9; Oct.–Apr., Wed.–Sun. 10–4.

Dining and Lodging

$ ✕ **Castillo's Mexican Food.** Tasty tacos, enchiladas, chili rellenos, and burrito combinations, plus chimichangas, fajitas, steak, and seafood, are served in a casual storefront setting. Garden seating is available in the spring and summer. ⊠ *4995 5th St., ☎ 209/742–4413. MC, V.*

$$ ⌷ **Little Valley Inn.** Pine paneling, historical photos, and old mining tools recall Mariposa's heritage at this modern B&B with three rooms in a building separate from the main house. A suite that sleeps five people includes a full kitchen. The large grounds include a creek where guests can pan for gold (a helpful dog stirs the creekbed). Room rates include a full breakfast. ⊠ *3483 Brooks Rd., off Hwy. 49, ☎ 209/742–6204 or 800/889–5444, FAX 209/742–5099. 3 rooms. Air-conditioning, refrigerators, in-room VCRs, horseshoes. AE, MC, V.*

$–$$ ⌷ **Comfort Inn of Yosemite.** This white three-story building with a broad veranda sits on a hill above Mariposa. Some of the comfortable rooms have sitting areas. Room rates include a Continental breakfast. ⊠ *4994 Bouillon St., 95338, ☎ 209/966–4344 or 800/321–5261, FAX 209/966–4655. 62 rooms. Air-conditioning, pool, outdoor hot tub. AE, D, DC, MC, V.*

SACRAMENTO AND THE GOLD COUNTRY A TO Z

Arriving and Departing

By Bus
Greyhound (☎ 800/231–2222) serves Sacramento, Auburn, and Placerville. It's a two-hour trip from San Francisco's Transbay Terminal at 1st and Mission streets to the Sacramento station at 7th and L streets.

By Car
Sacramento lies at the junction of I–5 and I–80, just under 90 mi northeast of San Francisco. It's about an eight-hour drive north on I–5 from Los Angeles. I–80 continues northeast through the Gold Country toward Reno, about three hours from Sacramento. Lake Tahoe is two hours east of Sacramento via U.S. 50 or I–80.

By Plane
Sacramento Metro Airport (☎ 916/648–0700), 12 mi northwest of downtown Sacramento on I–5, is served by Alaska, America West, American, Delta, Northwest, Southwest, and United airlines. *See* Air Travel *in* the Gold Guide for airline phone numbers.

San Francisco International Airport and **Oakland International Airport** are about two hours from Sacramento (☞ Chapter 5).

By Train
Amtrak (☎ 800/872–7245) runs trains to Sacramento frequently from Oakland's Jack London Square station (⊠ 245 2nd St.). Trains making this 2½-hour trip stop in Emeryville, Richmond, Martinez, and Davis; some stop at Berkeley and Suisin-Fairfield as well. Shuttle buses connect the Emeryville station (⊠ 5885 Landregan St.) and San Francisco's Ferry Building (⊠ 30 Embarcadero, at the foot of Market St.); other San Francisco pickup points are at the main entrance to Pier 39 and the corner of 4th and Market streets near Union Square.

Getting Around

By Bus

Sacramento Regional Transit (☎ 916/321–2877) buses and light-rail vehicles transport passengers in Sacramento. Buses run 6 AM to 9 PM, trains 5 AM to 12:30 AM.

By Car

Traveling by car is the most convenient way to see the Gold Country, since most of the area's towns are too small to provide a base for public transportation. From Sacramento, three highways fan out toward the east, all intersecting with Highway 49: I–80 heads 30 mi northeast to Auburn; U.S. 50 goes east 40 mi to Placerville; and Highway 16 angles southeast 45 mi to Plymouth. Highway 49 is an excellent two-lane road that winds and climbs through the foothills and valleys, linking the principal Gold Country towns.

Contacts and Resources

Emergencies

Ambulance (☎ 911). **Fire** (☎ 911). **Police** (☎ 911).

Mercy Hospital of Sacramento Promptcare (✉ 4001 J St., ☎ 916/453–4424). **Sutter General Hospital** (✉ 2801 L St., ☎ 916/733–8900). **Sutter Memorial Hospital** (✉ 52nd and F Sts., ☎ 916/733–1000).

Guided Tours

Channel Star Excursions (✉ 110 L St., Sacramento 95814, ☎ 916/552–2933 or 800/433–0263) operates the *Spirit of Sacramento,* a paddle-wheel riverboat, which takes passengers on happy-hour, dinner, luncheon, and champagne brunch cruises in addition to one-hour narrated river tours. The **Coloma Country Inn** (✉ Box 502, Coloma 95613, ☎ 530/622–6919) operates ballooning and rafting packages on the American River in conjunction with B&B accommodations. **Gold Prospecting Expeditions** (✉ 18170 Main St., Jamestown 95327, ☎ 209/984–4653 or 800/596–0009, FAX 209/984–0711) arranges one-hour to two-week excursions.

SHOPPING

Hop Around (✉ 2600 North Ave., Sacramento 95838, ☎ 916/927–2877 or 800/356–9838), a $12 shopping and narrated sightseeing shuttle operated by Gray Line/Frontier Tours, covers most downtown tourist attractions. Reservations must be made at least 24 hours in advance.

Visitor Information

Amador County Chamber of Commerce (✉ 125 Peek St., Jackson 95642, ☎ 209/223–0350). **El Dorado County Chamber of Commerce** (✉ 542 Main St., Placerville 95667, ☎ 530/621–5885 or 800/457–6279). **Grass Valley/Nevada County Chamber of Commerce** (✉ 248 Mill St., Grass Valley 95945, ☎ 530/273–4667 or 800/655–4667). **Mariposa County Visitors Bureau** (✉ 5158 Hwy. 140, Mariposa 95338, ☎ 209/966–2456 or 800/208–2434). **Placer County Tourism Authority** (✉ 13464 Lincoln Way, Auburn 95603, ☎ 530/887–2111 or 800/427–6463). **Sacramento Convention and Visitors Bureau** (✉ 1421 K St., Sacramento 95814, ☎ 916/264–7777). **Tuolumne County Visitors Bureau** (✉ Box 4020, 55 W. Stockton St., Sonora 95370, ☎ 209/533–4420 or 800/446–1333).

7 Lake Tahoe

*The California and
Nevada Shores*

The largest alpine lake in North
America is famous for its clarity, deep
blue water, and snowcapped peaks.
Though Lake Tahoe possesses
abundant natural beauty and accessible
wilderness, nearby towns are highly
developed and the roads around it
often congested. Summertime is
generally cooler here than in the Sierra
Nevada foothills, and the clean
mountain air bracingly crisp. When it
gets hot, the plentiful beaches and brisk
water are only minutes away.

Updated by
Deke
Castleman

LAKE TAHOE lies 6,225 ft above sea level in the Sierra Nevada range, straddling the state line between California and Nevada. The border gives this popular resort region a split personality. About half the visitors here arrive intent on low-key sightseeing, hiking, fishing, camping, and boating. The rest head directly for the Nevada side of the lake, where bargain dining, big-name entertainment, and the lure of a jackpot draw customers into the glittering casinos. Tahoe is also a popular wedding and honeymoon destination: Couples can get married with no waiting period or blood tests at chapels all around the lake. On Valentine's Day the chapels become veritable assembly lines—four times as many ceremonies take place on that day than on any other. Incidentally, the legal marrying age in California and Nevada is 18 years, but one must be 21 to gamble or drink.

Summer's cool temperatures provide respite from the heat in the surrounding deserts and valleys. Although swimming in Lake Tahoe is always brisk—68°F is about as warm as it gets—the lake's beaches are generally crowded at this time of year. Those who prefer solitude can escape to the many state parks, national forests, and protected tracts of wilderness that ring the 22-mi-long, 12-mi-wide lake. From midautumn to late spring, multitudes of skiers and winter-sports enthusiasts are attracted to Tahoe's 15 downhill skiing resorts and 11 cross-country centers—North America's largest concentration of skiing facilities. Ski resorts try to open by Thanksgiving, if only with machine-made snow, and can operate through May or even later. Most accommodations, restaurants, and some parks are open year-round.

The first white man to find this spectacular region was Captain John C. Fremont in 1844, guided by famous scout Kit Carson. Not long afterward, silver was discovered in Nevada's Comstock Lode at Virginia City, and as the bonanza hit, the Tahoe Basin's forests were leveled to provide lumber for mine-tunnel supports. By the turn of the century, wealthy Californians were building lakeside estates here, some of which survive. Improved roads brought the less affluent in the 1920s and 1930s, when modest bungalows began to fill the shoreline, where the woods had grown back. The first casinos opened in the 1940s. Ski resorts brought another development boom and turned the lake into a year-round destination.

Lake Tahoe's water is 99.7% pure, cleaner than drinking water in most U.S. cities. The water is so clear that you can see as deep as 75 ft. Over the last few decades, however, road construction and other building projects have washed soil and minerals into the lake, leading to a growth of algae that threatens its fabled clarity. After the environmental movement gained strength in the 1970s, a moratorium on new shoreline construction was declared and a master plan was instituted to control development.

During some summer weekends it seems that absolutely every tourist—100,000 at peak periods—is in a car on the main road that circles the 72-mi shoreline. The crowds and congestion increase as the day wears on. But at a vantage point overlooking Emerald Bay early in the morning, on a trail in the national forests that ring the basin, or on a sunset cruise on the lake itself, one can forget the ubiquitous hordes and the commercial development and absorb the grandeur.

Pleasures and Pastimes

Camping

Campgrounds abound in the Tahoe area, run by the state park service, the U.S. Forest Service, city utility districts, and private operators. Sites range from primitive and rustic to upscale and luxurious. Make summer reservations far in advance, as spaces are almost always in high demand (☞ Contacts and Resources *in* Lake Tahoe A to Z, *below*).

Dining

Restaurants at Lake Tahoe range from rock-and-wood decor to elegant French, with stops along the way for Swiss chalet and spare modern. The food, too, is varied and may include delicate Continental or nouvelle-Californian sauces, mesquite- and olive-wood-grilled specialties, and wild game in season. On weekends and in high season, expect a long wait to be seated in the more popular restaurants. During slower periods, some places may close temporarily or limit their hours, so call ahead to verify.

Casinos use their restaurants to attract gaming customers. Their marquees often tout "$5.99 prime rib dinners" or "$1.39 breakfast specials." Some of these meal deals may not be top quality; they're usually found in the coffee shops and buffets. But the finer restaurants in casinos generally deliver good food, service, and atmosphere.

Unless otherwise noted, even the most expensive Tahoe eating places welcome customers in casual clothes—not surprising in this year-round vacation mecca—but don't expect to be served in most restaurants if you're barefoot, shirtless, or wearing a skimpy bathing suit.

CATEGORY	COST*
$$$$	over $50
$$$	$30–$50
$$	$20–$30
$	under $20

per person for a three-course meal, excluding drinks, service, and 7%–7¼% tax

Gambling

Nevada's major casinos are also full-service hotels and resorts. They make discounted lodging packages available throughout the year. The casinos share an atmosphere of garish neon and noise, but conditioned air and no-smoking areas eliminate the hazy pall of the past. Six are clustered on a strip of U.S. 50 in Stateline—Caesars, Harrah's, Harvey's, Horizon, and Lakeside, plus Bill's, a lower-stakes "junior" casino (no lodging) that appeals to less-experienced players. Four others stand on the north shore: the Hyatt Regency, Cal-Neva, Tahoe Biltmore, and Crystal Bay Club. Open 24 hours a day, 365 days a year, these casinos have table games (craps, blackjack, roulette, baccarat, poker, keno, pai gow poker, bingo, and big six), race and sports books, and thousands of slot machines—1,750, for instance, at Harrah's. There is no charge to enter and there is no dress code.

The hotels attract potential players into their high-profit casinos with shows, celebrity entertainers, and restaurants and lounges that are open around the clock. All gamblers are offered complimentary beverages; higher-stakes players can qualify for complimentary meals, rooms, room service, golf, even private yacht parties. Parking is plentiful in enclosed garages and open lots; valet parking is technically free, but a $1 or $2 tip is customary.

Golf

The Tahoe area is nearly as popular with golfers as it is with skiers. Half a dozen superb courses dot the mountains around the lake, with magnificent views, thick pines, fresh cool air, and lush fairways and greens. Encountering wildlife is not uncommon if you have to search for your ball out-of-bounds.

Hiking

There are five U.S. National Forests in the Tahoe Basin and a half-dozen state parks. The main areas for hiking include the Tahoe Rim Trail, a 150-mi trail along the ridgelines above the lake; Desolation Wilderness, a vast 63,473-acre preserve of granite peaks, glacial valleys, subalpine forests, the Rubicon River, and more than 50 lakes; and the trail systems near Lake Tahoe Visitor Center and D. L. Bliss, Emerald Bay, Sugar Pine Point, and Lake Tahoe-Nevada state parks.

Lodging

Quiet inns on the water, motel rooms in the heart of the casino area, rooms at the casinos themselves, and lodges close to ski runs are among the Tahoe options. During summer and ski season the lake is crowded; reserve space as far ahead as possible. Spring and fall give you a little more leeway and lower—sometimes significantly lower—rates. Price categories listed below reflect high-season rates.

CATEGORY	COST*
$$$$	over $175
$$$	$120–$175
$$	$80–$120
$	under $80

All prices are for a standard double room, excluding 9%–10% tax.

Skiing

Lake Tahoe area is a Nordic skier's paradise. You can even cross-country ski on fresh snow right on the lakeshore beaches. Skinny skiing (slang for cross-country) at the resorts can be costly, but you get the benefits of machine grooming and trail preparation. If it's bargain Nordic you're after, take advantage of thousands of acres of public forest and parkland trails.

The mountains around Lake Tahoe are bombarded by blizzards throughout the winter (and sometimes the fall and spring); 10- to 12-ft bases are not uncommon. The profusion of downhill resorts guarantees a nearly infinite variety of terrains, conditions, and challenges. To save money, look for packages offered by lodges and resorts; some include interchangeable lift tickets that allow you to try different slopes. Midweek packages are usually lower in price, and most resorts offer family discounts. Free shuttle-bus service is available between most ski resorts and lodgings.

Sno-Park Areas

There are five public Sno-Park areas in the vicinity, some for snowmobiling and cross-country skiing, as well as sledding. All are maintained by the Department of Parks and Recreation (☞ Contacts and Resources *in* Lake Tahoe A to Z, *below*). To use them you need to obtain a permit in advance.

Swimming

Thirty-six public beaches line Lake Tahoe. Lifeguards stand duty at some of the swimming beaches, and yellow buoys mark safe areas where motorboats are not permitted. Opening and closing dates for beaches vary with the climate and available park-service personnel.

Exploring Lake Tahoe

The most common way to explore the Lake Tahoe area is to drive the 72-mi road that follows the shore through wooded flatlands and past beaches, climbing to vistas on the rugged west side of the lake and descending to the busiest commercial developments and casinos on its eastern edge. Undeveloped Lake Tahoe–Nevada State Park occupies well more than half of the Nevada side of Lake Tahoe, stretching north from the glitzy border town of Stateline to the upscale master-planned community of Incline Village. The California side, particularly South Lake Tahoe, is more fully developed, though much wilderness remains. At press time (summer 1997), plans to switch the area code on the California side of Lake Tahoe from 916 to 530 were proceeding on schedule.

Great Itineraries

Although, or perhaps because, the distance around Lake Tahoe is relatively short, the desire to experience the whole area can be overwhelming. It takes only one day "to see it"—drive around the lake, stretch your legs at a few overlooks, take a nature walk, and wander among the casinos at Stateline. If you have more time, you can laze on a beach and swim, venture onto the lake or into the mountains, and sample Tahoe's finer restaurants. If you have five days, you can write a guidebook. But be careful—you may become so attached to Tahoe that you begin visiting realtors and researching the job market.

Numbers in the text correspond to numbers in the margin and on the Lake Tahoe map.

IF YOU HAVE 3 DAYS

On your first day, stop in **South Lake Tahoe** ① and pick up provisions for a picnic lunch. Start with some morning beach fun at the **Pope-Baldwin Recreation Area** ③ and check out the area's **Tallac Historic Site.** Head west on Highway 89, stopping at the **Lake Tahoe Visitor Center** ④ and the **Emerald Bay** ⑤ lookout. Have lunch at the lookout, or hike down—be forewarned: The hike back up is steep—to **Vikingsholm,** a Viking castle replica. In the late afternoon, explore the trails and mansions at **Sugar Pine Point State Park** ⑦, then backtrack on Highway 89 and U.S. 50 for dinner in South Lake Tahoe. On your second day, cruise on the *Tahoe Queen* glass-bottom sternwheeler out of South Lake Tahoe or the MS *Dixie II* sternwheeler out of **Zephyr Cove** ⑰ in the morning, and then ride the **Heavenly Tram** ② at Heavenly Ski Resort. Have lunch high above the lake and (except in snow season) take a walk on one of Heavenly's nature trails. If you're itching to try your luck at the casinos, **Stateline** ⑱ is only moments away from the tram base; visit one before having dinner in the area. Start your third day by heading north on U.S. 50, stopping at **Cave Rock** ⑯ and (after turning north on Highway 28) at **Sand Harbor Beach** ⑮. If *Bonanza* looms large in your memory, drop by **Ponderosa Ranch** ⑭, or continue on to **Crystal Bay** ⑫ to hike the Stateline Lookout Trail above Crystal Bay. If you have the time, drive to **Tahoe City** ⑧ to see its Gatekeeper's Log Cabin Museum.

IF YOU HAVE 5 DAYS

Pick up a picnic on your first day and visit **Pope-Baldwin Recreation Area** ③. Then head west to **Lake Tahoe Visitor Center** ④ and the **Emerald Bay** ⑤ lookout. Hike to **Vikingsholm** or, if that seems too strenuous, proceed directly to **Sugar Pine Point State Park** ⑦. Have dinner in **Tahoe City** ⑧ or South Lake Tahoe. On your second day, cruise on the *Tahoe Queen* or MS *Dixie II* in the morning, then ride the **Heavenly Tram** ② and have lunch and possibly a hike. Spend the late afternoon or early

Lake Tahoe

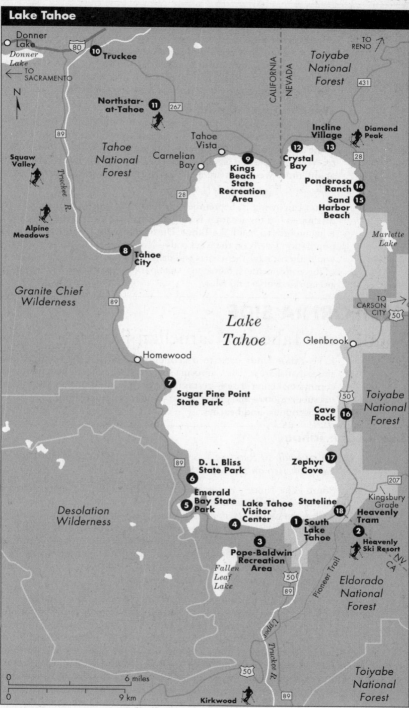

Donner Lake

Donner Lake

TO SACRAMENTO

10 Truckee

80

89

Toiyabe National Forest

TO RENO

431

CALIFORNIA NEVADA

Northstar-at-Tahoe 11

267

Tahoe National Forest

Tahoe Vista

Carnelian Bay

28

9 Kings Beach State Recreation Area

12 Crystal Bay

Incline Village 13

Diamond Peak

28

Ponderosa Ranch 14

Sand Harbor Beach 15

Squaw Valley

Truckee R.

Alpine Meadows

8 Tahoe City

Granite Chief Wilderness

89

Marlette Lake

TO CARSON CITY

50

Lake Tahoe

Homewood

Glenbrook

7
Sugar Pine Point State Park

50

Toiyabe National Forest

Cave Rock 16

Desolation Wilderness

89

6 D. L. Bliss State Park

Zephyr Cove 17

5 Emerald Bay State Park

4 Lake Tahoe Visitor Center

Stateline

18

207

Kingsbury Grade

Heavenly Tram

1 South Lake Tahoe

2 Heavenly Ski Resort

3 Pope-Baldwin Recreation Area

Fallen Leaf Lake

50

Eldorado National Forest

Pioneer Trail

89

Upper Truckee R.

0   6 miles
0   9 km

50

Kirkwood

89

Toiyabe National Forest

NV CA

evening at one of the **Stateline** ⑱ casinos. On the third day, visit **Cave Rock** ⑯ and the **Ponderosa Ranch** ⑭, and hike the Stateline Lookout Trail above **Crystal Bay** ⑫. Have lunch in Crystal Bay and spend the afternoon at the nearby **Kings Beach State Recreation Area** ⑨. On the fourth day, hang out at **Sand Harbor Beach** ⑮ or, if it's winter, on the ski slopes. On day five, rent a bike and ride from **D. L. Bliss State Park** ⑥ to **Tahoe City** ⑧ and explore the Gatekeeper's Log Cabin Museum.

When to Tour Lake Tahoe

Except to ski bunnies, Tahoe is the most fun during the summer. The best strategy for avoiding crowds is to do as much as you can as early in the day as you can. The parking lots for the Lake Tahoe Visitor Center, Vikingsholm, and Gatekeeper's Log Cabin Museum can be jammed at any time. Weekends are most congested, but weekdays are busy as well.

If you can swing it, September and October, when the throngs have dissipated but the weather is still pleasant, are among the most satisfying months to visit Lake Tahoe. During the winter ski season, Tahoe's population swells on the weekends—if you're able to come mid-week you'll almost have the resorts and neighboring towns to yourself. Most of the visitor centers, mansions, state parks, and beaches are closed between November and May.

CALIFORNIA SIDE

South Lake Tahoe to Carnelian Bay

Lake Tahoe lends itself to a geopolitical division between the two states that share it. The California side is the more developed, both with commercial enterprises—restaurants, motels, lodges, resorts, residential subdivisions—and public-access facilities, such as historic sites, parks, campgrounds, and beaches.

South Lake Tahoe

❶ *50 mi south of Reno on U.S. 395 and U.S. 50, 198 mi northeast of San Francisco on I–80 to U.S. 50.*

South Lake Tahoe's raison d'être is tourism: The lake region's largest community feeds the casinos at Stateline; the ski slopes at Heavenly Valley; the swimmers, boaters, cyclists, and campers of the south shore; and the hikers and backpackers of Eldorado National Forest and Desolation Wilderness. U.S. 50 heading northeast into town is lined with motels, lodges, and restaurants, but as you head northwest away from town on Highway 89, which straddles the lakefront, commercial development gives way to national-forest lands.

★ ☜ ❷ Whether you're a skier or not, you'll want to ride 2,000 ft up the slopes of Heavenly Ski Resort on the 50-passenger **Heavenly Tram,** which runs part way up the mountain, to 8,200 ft. There you'll find a memorable view of Lake Tahoe and the Nevada desert. When the weather's fine you can take one of three (successively more difficult) hikes around the mountaintop. Monument Peak Restaurant, open daily during tram hours, serves basic American food cafeteria style—lunch, dinner, and Sunday brunch in summer, and lunch only in winter. ⊠ *Head north on Ski Run Blvd. off U.S. 50 and follow signs to parking lot,* ☎ *702/ 586–7000.* ⌑ *Tram $12.* ☉ *Tram runs June–Oct., daily 10–9; Nov.– May, daily 8:30–4.*

The 500-passenger **Tahoe Queen** (⊠ Ski Run Marina, off U.S. 50, ☎ 530/541–3364 or 800/238–2463), a glass-bottom paddlewheeler, makes 2¼-hour lake cruises year-round during the day from South Lake Tahoe and operates sunset and dinner cruises. Fares are $14 to $18. In winter, the boat shuttles skiers to north-shore ski areas on weekdays for $18 round-trip.

A year-round professional-size ice-skating facility, **South Lake Tahoe Ice Center,** opened in December 1996. The million-dollar rink caters to skaters of all levels, from first-timers to figure skaters and hockey leaguers. ✉ *1176 Rufus Allen Blvd.,* ☎ *530/542–4700.* ⌧ *Prices vary.* ⊙ *Mon.–Thurs. 10–8, Fri.–Sat. 10–10, Sun. 10–6.*

Dining and Lodging

$$–$$$ ✗ **Nepheles.** A rough-pine chalet on the road to Heavenly Ski Resort houses this cozy restaurant that serves creative California cuisine. Entrées range from aged-beef-and-prawns stir-fry and pecan-encrusted chicken breast to broiled elk with black-currant merlot sauce and ahi tuna in a pineapple vinaigrette. Appetizers include a Thai-chicken-and-smoked-ham taco, escargots, and swordfish egg rolls. ✉ *1169 Ski Run Blvd.,* ☎ *530/544–8130. AE, D, DC, MC, V. No lunch.*

$$–$$$ ✗ **Swiss Chalet.** Swiss decor is carried out with great consistency at this Tahoe institution. The Continental menu includes schnitzel, sauerbraten, fondue, steaks, fresh seafood, and homemade pastries. ✉ *2544 U.S. 50,* ☎ *530/544–3304. AE, MC, V. Closed Nov. 25–Dec. 5. No lunch.*

$$ ✗ **Scusa!** This intimate Italian restaurant on the road to the Heavenly Ski Resort has a smart, modern decor. Cappelini, linguine, fettuccine, penne, ravioli, and lasagna are on the menu, along with hearty calzones, exotic pizzas, steak, chicken, and fresh fish entrées. The panfried calamari with red peppers and capers are a treat. And don't pass up the rosemary-flavored flat bread, baked fresh daily. ✉ *1142 Ski Run Blvd.,* ☎ *530/542–0100. AE, MC, V. No lunch.*

$ ✗ **Red Hut Waffle Shop.** A vintage Tahoe diner, all chrome and red plastic, the Red Hut is a tiny place with a dozen counter stools and a dozen booths. It's a traditional breakfast spot for locals and visitors in the know, who appreciate the huge omelets, the banana, pecan, and coconut waffles, and other good food. ✉ *2749 U.S. 50,* ☎ *530/541–9024. Reservations not accepted. No credit cards. No dinner.*

$$–$$$ ✗⊡ **Christiania Inn.** An antiques-filled bed-and-breakfast across the street from the base of the Heavenly Tram, the Christiania is a local favorite. The American-Continental menu emphasizes fresh seafood, prime beef, and veal. Midday buffets are served on holidays, and appetizers, soups, and salads are available in the lounge daily after 2, winter only. Upstairs at the inn ($$–$$$$), two rooms and four suites come with king- or queen-size beds and private baths. Three of the suites are two-story affairs with wood-burning fireplaces and wet bars; two have saunas and one has a whirlpool tub. A complimentary Continental breakfast is delivered to guests' doors each morning. ✉ *3819 Saddle Rd., 96151,* ☎ *530/544–7337 or 530/541–5210,* ℻ *530/541–5342. 6 rooms. Restaurant, bar. MC, V.*

$$$–$$$$ ⊡ **Embassy Suites.** In this opulent all-suites hotel, decorated Sierra-★ lodge style, fountains and waterwheels splash in the nine-story atriums, where complimentary full breakfasts and evening cocktails are served daily. Glass elevators rise to guest suites, each with a living room, dining area, and separate bedroom. ✉ *4130 Lake Tahoe Blvd., 96150,* ☎ *530/544–5400 or 800/362–2779,* ℻ *530/544–4900. 400 suites. 3 restaurants, indoor pool, hot tub, sauna, exercise room, nightclub. AE, D, DC, MC, V.*

$$$–$$$$ 🏨 **Forest Inn Suites.** The location is excellent—5½ acres bordering a pine forest, a half block from Harrah's and Harvey's, and adjacent to a supermarket, cinema, and shops. Rooms are modern and pleasant. Ski rentals are available, and a free shuttle to Heavenly Valley ski area is provided. ⊠ *1101 Park Ave., 96150,* ☎ *530/541–6655 or 800/822–5950,* FAX *530/544–3135. 124 units. Kitchens, 2 pools, 2 hot tubs, sauna, putting green, health club, volleyball, bicycles, coin laundry. AE, D, DC, MC, V.*

$$–$$$ 🏨 **Best Western Station House Inn.** This inn has won design awards
★ for its exterior and interior. The rooms have king- and queen-size beds and double-vanity bathrooms. The location is good, near a private beach yet close to the casinos. American breakfast is complimentary from October to May. ⊠ *901 Park Ave., 96150,* ☎ *530/542–1101 or 800/822–5953,* FAX *530/542–1714. 102 rooms. Restaurant, lounge, pool, hot tub. AE, D, DC, MC, V.*

$$–$$$ 🏨 **Inn by the Lake.** Across the road from a beach, this luxury motel
★ has spacious and comfortable rooms furnished in contemporary style (blond oak and pale peach). All have balconies; some have lake views, wet bars, and in-room kitchens. Room rates include Continental breakfast, and the inn provides a free shuttle bus to the casinos. ⊠ *3300 Lake Tahoe Blvd., 96150,* ☎ *530/542–0330 or 800/877–1466,* FAX *530/541–6596. 99 rooms. Pool, sauna, hot tub, bicycles, coin laundry. AE, D, DC, MC, V.*

$–$$$ 🏨 **Royal Valhalla Motor Lodge.** Two- and three-bedroom suites with complete kitchens make this motel at Stateline Avenue attractive to families. Some of the simple, modern rooms have private balconies. Continental breakfast is complimentary. ⊠ *4104 Lakeshore Blvd., 96157,* ☎ *530/544–2233 or 800/999–4104,* FAX *530/544–1436. 100 rooms. Pool, hot tub, coin laundry. AE, DC, MC, V.*

$$ 🏨 **Lakeland Village Beach and Ski Resort.** This complex on 1,000 ft of private beach has a range of accommodations: studios, suites, and town houses, all with kitchens, fireplaces, and private decks or balconies. Ask about ski packages. ⊠ *3535 Lake Tahoe Blvd., 96150,* ☎ *530/544–1685 or 800/822–5969,* FAX *530/544–0193. 208 units. Kitchens, 2 pools, wading pool, hot tub, 2 saunas, 2 tennis courts, beach, boating, fishing, coin laundry. AE, D, MC, V.*

$$ 🏨 **Tahoe Seasons Resort.** Most rooms at this resort, which is set among pine trees on a mountain across from the Heavenly Ski Resort, are outfitted with fireplaces. Every room has a whirlpool and minikitchen. The decor is contemporary, heavy on the teal. ⊠ *3901 Saddle Rd., 96157,* ☎ *530/541–6700, 530/541–6010, or 800/540–4874,* FAX *530/541–0653. 183 suites. Restaurant, lounge, refrigerators, pool, hot tub, 2 tennis courts, volleyball, airport shuttle. AE, DC, MC, V.*

$–$$ 🏨 **Best Western Lake Tahoe Inn.** Near Harrah's on 6 acres, with gardens and the Heavenly Ski Resort directly behind, this large motel has modern rooms decorated in soothing colors. The rates include a full breakfast. ⊠ *4110 Lake Tahoe Blvd., 96150,* ☎ *530/541–2010 or 800/528–1234,* FAX *530/542–1428. 400 rooms. Restaurant, lounge, 2 pools, hot tub. AE, D, DC, MC, V.*

$–$$ 🏨 **Travelodge.** There are two members of the national chain in South Lake Tahoe; both are convenient to casinos, shopping, and recreation and have some no-smoking rooms. Free local calls, HBO, and in-room coffee add to the budget appeal. ⊠ *3489 U.S. 50 at Bijou Center, 96150,* ☎ *530/544–5266 or 800/982–1466,* FAX *530/544–6985; 59 rooms.* ⊠ *4003 U.S. 50, 96150,* ☎ *530/541–5000 or 800/982–2466,* FAX *530/544–6910; 66 rooms. Pool at each; Bijou Center has a restaurant. AE, D, DC, MC, V.*

$ ⬚ **Best Tahoe West Inn.** A long-established motel proud of its repeat business, the Tahoe West is three blocks from the beach and downtown casinos. The exterior is rustic, rooms are neatly furnished, and beds are queen size. Twelve rooms have kitchenettes. A free shuttle to casinos and ski areas is provided. ⊠ *4107 Pine Blvd., 96150,* ☎ *530/ 544–6455, 800/522–1021, or 800/700–8246,* FAX *530/544–0508. 60 rooms. Pool, hot tub, sauna, beach. AE, D, DC, MC, V.*

Outdoor Activities and Sports

CROSS-COUNTRY SKIING

For the ultimate in groomed conditions, head to America's largest cross-country ski resort, **Royal Gorge** (⊠ Box 1100, Soda Springs 95728, ☎ 530/426–3871), which has 197 mi of 18-ft-wide track for all abilities, 88 trails on 9,172 acres, two ski schools, and 10 warming huts. Four cafés, two hotels, and a hot tub and sauna are also on-site. **Kirkwood Ski Resort** (☞ *below*) has 50 mi of groomed-track skiing, with skating lanes, instruction, and rentals.

DOWNHILL SKIING

Heavenly Ski Resort gives skiers plenty of choices. Go up the Heavenly Tram on the California side to ski the imposing face of Gunbarrel or the gentler runs at the top, or ride the Sky Express high-speed quad chair to the summit and choose wide cruising runs or steep tree skiing. Or drive over the Kingsbury Grade to the Boulder or Stagecoach lodges and stay on the Nevada-side runs, which are usually less crowded. Snowmaking covers both sides, top to bottom, for generally good conditions. The ski school, like everything else at Heavenly, is large and has a program for everyone, from beginner to expert. ⊠ *Ski Run Blvd., Box 2180, Stateline, NV 89449,* ☎ *530/541–1330 or 800/243–2836; 530/541–7544 for snow information;* FAX *530/541– 2643. 4,800 acres, rated 20% beginner, 45% intermediate, 35% expert. Longest run 5½ mi, base 6,540', summit 10,040'. Lifts: 25 total, including 3 high-speed quads.*

Kirkwood Ski Resort lies 36 mi south of Lake Tahoe in an alpine-village setting. Most of the runs off the top are rated expert only, but intermediate and beginning skiers have their own vast bowl, where they can ski through trees or wide-open spaces. This is a destination resort, with 120 condominiums, several shops and restaurants in the base village, overnight RV parking, and a shuttle bus to Lake Tahoe. There is snowboarding on all runs, and lessons, rentals, and sales are available. For Nordic skiing, *see* Cross-Country Skiing, *above.* ⊠ *Hwy. 88, Box 1, Kirkwood 95646,* ☎ *209/258–6000; 209/258–7000 lodging information; 209/258–3000 snow information;* FAX *209/258–8899. 2,000 acres, rated 15% beginner, 50% intermediate, 35% advanced. Longest run 2½ mi, base 7,800', summit 9,800'. Lifts: 12 chairs, 1 surface.*

Shopping

There's some good shopping south of town at the **Factory Outlet Stores** (⊠ U.S. 50 and Hwy. 89).

Pope-Baldwin Recreation Area

❸ *5 mi west of South Lake Tahoe on Hwy. 89.*

At the Pope-Baldwin Recreation Area's **Tallac Historic Site,** a museum and three magnificently restored estates provide a glimpse of the lifestyles of the 1920s wealthy. Cultural events take place from June to September. The Valhalla Renaissance Festival (☎ 530/542–4166), which re-creates the arts, culture, and entertainments of the 15th and 16th centuries, is held at Camp Richardson in June. Guided tours of the Pope House and a museum at the Baldwin Estate are conducted in summer. ✉ *Tallac Historic Site free, Pope House tour $2 (hrs vary, reservations necessary),* ☎ *530/541–5227.* ◷ *Tallac Historic Site year-round dawn–dusk. Recreation Area late May–Oct., dawn–dusk. Museum June–Labor Day, daily 10–4; Labor Day–Sept., daily 10–3.*

❹ The U.S. Forest Service operates the **Lake Tahoe Visitor Center** on Taylor Creek. You can visit the site of a Washoe Indian settlement; walk self-guided trails through meadow, marsh, and forest; and inspect the Stream Profile Chamber, an underground, underwater display with windows letting visitors look right into Taylor Creek (in the fall you may see spawning salmon digging their nests). In summer, forest-service naturalists organize discovery walks and nighttime campfires, with singing and marshmallow roasts. The center has a free cassette player and a self-guided audio tour of the lake. ✉ *Hwy. 89,* ☎ *530/573–2674 (in season only).* ◷ *June–Sept., daily 8–5:30; Oct., weekends 8–5:30.*

Emerald Bay State Park

★ ❺ *4 mi west of Pope-Baldwin Recreation Area on Hwy. 89.*

Emerald Bay, a 3-mi-long and 1-mi-wide fjord-like bay, was carved by massive glaciers millions of years ago. Famed for its jewel-like shape and colors, it surrounds Fannette, Tahoe's only island. Highway 89 is high above the lake at the centerpiece of Emerald Bay State Park; from the **Emerald Bay lookout** you can survey the whole scene.

A steep, 1-mi trail from the lookout leads down to **Vikingsholm,** a 38-room estate completed in 1929. The owner, Lora Knight, had this precise replica of a 1,200-year-old Viking castle built out of materials native to the area, without disturbing the existing trees. She furnished it with Scandinavian antiques and hired artisans to custom-build period reproductions. The sod roof sprouts wildflowers each spring. There are picnic tables nearby and a gray-sand beach for strolling. The hike back up is a major huff (especially for those not used to the elevation), but there are benches and stone culverts to rest on. At the 150-ft-high peak of Fannette Island are the remnants of a stone structure known as the Tea House, built in 1928 so that guests of Lora Knight could have a place to enjoy afternoon refreshments after a motorboat ride out to Fannette. The island is off-limits February through June to protect nesting Canada geese; the rest of the year, it's open for day use only. ☎ *530/525–7277.* ✉ *$2.* ◷ *Memorial Day–Labor Day, daily 10–4.*

D. L. Bliss State Park

❻ *3 mi north of Emerald Bay State Park on Hwy. 89.*

D. L. Bliss State Park takes its name from Duane LeRoy Bliss, a 19th-century lumber magnate. At one time Bliss owned nearly 75% of Tahoe's lakefront, along with local steamboats, railroads, and banks. The Bliss family donated these 1,200 acres to the state in the 1930s; the park now shares 6 mi of shoreline with Emerald Bay State Park. At the north end of Bliss is **Rubicon Point,** which overlooks one of the lake's deepest spots. Short trails lead to an old lighthouse and Balancing Rock, which weighs in at 250,000 pounds and balances on a fist of granite. Hikes also take you to remote beaches and all the way to Vikingsholm in Emerald Bay State Park. ☎ *530/525–7277.* ✉ *$5 per vehicle (day use).* ◷ *Spring–fall.*

Camping

⚠ **D. L. Bliss State Park Campground.** A wooded, hilly, quiet setting makes for blissful family camping near the lake. Reserve sites as far in advance as possible. ✉ *Off Hwy. 89,* ☎ *800/444–7275 for reservations. 168 sites.* 🗺 *$16–$20.* ☉ *Memorial Day–late Sept.*

Sugar Pine Point State Park

★ ❼ *8 mi north of D. L. Bliss State Park on Hwy. 89.*

The main attraction at Sugar Pine Point State Park is **Ehrman Mansion,** a stone-and-shingle 1903 summer home, furnished in period style, that manifests the rustic aspirations of the era's wealthy residents. Also in the park are a log trapper's cabin from the mid-19th century, a nature preserve with wildlife exhibits, a lighthouse, the start of the 10-mi-long biking trail to Tahoe City, and an extensive system of hiking and cross-country trails. ☎ *530/525–7232 year-round; 530/525–7982 in season.* 🗺 *Free; state park $5 per vehicle (day use).* ☉ *Memorial Day–Labor Day, daily 11–4.*

Camping

🏕 **General Creek Campground.** This homey campground on the mountain side of Highway 89 is one of the few public ones to remain open in winter, primarily for cross-country skiers. ✉ *Hwy. 89,* ☎ *800/444–7275 for reservations. 175 sites.* 🗺 *$14.* ☉ *Year-round.*

Tahoe City

❽ *10 mi north of Sugar Pine Point State Park on Hwy. 89, 14 mi south of Truckee on Hwy. 89.*

Tahoe City holds many stores and restaurants within a compact area. Here, Highway 89 turns north from the lake to Squaw Valley, Donner Lake, and Truckee, while Highway 28 continues northeast around the lake toward Kings Beach and Nevada. The Outlet Gates control the surface level of Lake Tahoe and the amount of water spilled into the Truckee River, the lake's only outlet. Giant trout, common before the severe drought of the late 1980s and early 1990s, have returned; look down and see them from Fanny Bridge, so called for the rows of visitors' backsides leaning over the railing.

★ The **Gatekeeper's Log Cabin Museum** in Tahoe City preserves the area's past, displaying Washoe and Paiute artifacts as well as late-19th- to early 20th-century settlers' memorabilia. ✉ *130 W. Lake Blvd.,* ☎ *530/583–1762.* 🗺 *Free.* ☉ *May 15–Oct. 1, daily 11–5.*

The **Watson Cabin Living Museum,** a 1909 log cabin built by Robert M. Watson and his son and filled with turn-of-the-century furnishings, is in the middle of Tahoe City. Costumed docents act out the daily life of a typical pioneer family. ✉ *560 N. Lake Blvd.,* ☎ *530/583–8717 or 530/583–1762.* 🗺 *Free.* ☉ *June 15–Labor Day, daily noon–4.*

Dining and Lodging

$$$ ✕ **Christy Hill.** Panoramic lake views and fireside dining distinguish this restaurant, which serves California cuisine—fresh seafood (such as mahi with a ginger and pepper crust in a cabernet demi-glace) and game (including broiled New Zealand venison)—prepared by the owner-chef. ✉ *Lakehouse Mall, 115 Grove St.,* ☎ *530/583–8551. AE, MC, V. Closed Mon. (spring and fall). No lunch.*

$$–$$$ ✕ **Grazie! Ristorante & Bar.** The smell of garlic warms you as soon as you enter this northern Italian restaurant, as does the wide, double-sided fireplace. There are a half-dozen hearty pasta dishes and six pizza choices, but the stars are the antipasti and pasta salads. Chicken is cooked on a wood-burning rotisserie and rack of lamb on the grill; both are served with homemade sauces. ✉ *Roundhouse Mall, 700 N. Lake Blvd.,* ☎ *530/583–0233. AE, D, DC, MC, V.*

$$-$$$ ✕ **Wolfdale's.** An intimate restaurant occupying a remodeled 100-
   ★   year-old house, Wolfdale's serves a popular mix of Japanese-Califor-
          nia cuisine. The menu, which changes weekly, showcases several
          imaginative entrées, such as grilled Southwest-style chicken with cel-
          ery-root potatoes and brazed lamb shank with tomatoes, rosemary, and
          parsnip puree. ⊠ *640 N. Lake Blvd.,* ☎ *530/583–5700. MC, V. No
          lunch.*

$-$$$ ✕ **Jake's on the Lake.** Handsome rooms of oak and glass provide a
   ★   suitably classy setting for Continental food on the water. The seafood
          bar here is extensive; a varied dinner menu includes meat and poultry
          but emphasizes fresh fish. ⊠ *Boatworks Mall, 780 N. Lake Blvd.,* ☎
          *530/583–0188. AE, MC, V. No lunch in winter, except during holi-
          day season.*

$$$$ ✕🏨 **Resort at Squaw Creek.** Nearly half the guest rooms are suites at
          this complex, composed of a main lodge, an outdoor arcade of shops
          and boutiques, and a 405-room hotel. Some units have fireplaces and
          full kitchens, and all have original art, custom furnishings, and good
          views. Just outside the hotel entrance you can board a triple chairlift
          to Squaw Valley's slopes. Dining options range from haute cuisine to
          pastries and coffee. ⊠ *400 Squaw Creek Rd., 96146,* ☎ *530/583–6300,*
          ℻ *530/581–6632. 405 rooms. 4 restaurants, bar, 3 pools, 4 hot tubs,
          sauna, spa, 18-hole golf course, 2 tennis courts, health club, ice-skat-
          ing. AE, D, DC, MC, V.*

$$-$$$$ ✕🏨 **Sunnyside Restaurant and Lodge.** Only the river-rock fireplace and
   ★   a mounted buffalo head remain from the early 1900s lodge that orig-
          inally stood on this site. Its impressive, sunny replacement, built in the
          mid-1980s, has a marina and an expansive lakefront deck with steps
          down to a narrow gravel beach. Rooms are decorated in a crisp nau-
          tical style, with prints of boats hanging on the pinstripe wall coverings
          and sea chests as coffee tables. Each room has its own deck, with lake
          and mountain views. Continental breakfast is included in the rate, but
          this is not a full-service hotel. Seafood is the specialty of the very fine
          Continental restaurant ($$–$$$). ⊠ *1850 W. Lake Blvd.,* ☎ *530/583–
          7200,* ℻ *530/583–2551. 23 rooms. Restaurant, lounge, beach. AE,
          MC, V.*

$$$-$$$$ 🏨 **Chinquapin Resort.** A deluxe development on 95 acres of forested
   ★   land 3 mi northeast of Tahoe City contains roomy one- to four-bed-
          room town houses and condos with great views of the lake and the
          mountains. Each unit has a fireplace, a fully equipped kitchen, and laun-
          dry facilities. A minimum one-week stay is required July and August.
          In winter the minimum is two nights. ⊠ *3600 N. Lake Blvd., 96145,*
          ☎ *530/583–6991 or 800/732–6721,* ℻ *530/583–0937. 172 town
          houses and condos. Pool, saunas, 7 tennis courts, hiking, horseshoes.
          MC, V.*

$-$$ 🏨 **Rodeway Inn.** This skinny seven-story tower is within easy walk-
          ing distance of the beaches, marina, shops, and restaurants of Tahoe
          City. Rooms are clean and comfortable, if not luxurious, and have great
          lake views. ⊠ *645 N. Lake Blvd., 96145,* ☎ *530/583–3711 or 800/
          228–2000,* ℻ *530/583–6938. 51 rooms. Pool, hot tub. AE, D, DC,
          MC, V.*

Outdoor Activities and Sports

DOWNHILL SKIING

Alpine Meadows Ski Area is a ski-cruiser's paradise, with skiing from
two peaks—Ward, a great open bowl, and Scott, for tree-lined runs.
Alpine has some of Tahoe's most reliable conditions and a fine snowmaking system; it's usually the first in the area to open each Novem-

ber and the last to close, in May or even June. The base lodge has rentals, a cafeteria, a restaurant-lounge, a bar, a bakery, a sports shop, and ski schools for adults and children of all skill levels and for skiers with disabilities. There's also an area for overnight RV parking. Ski from every lift; there are no "transportation" lifts and snowboarding is prohibited. ⊠ *6 mi northwest of Tahoe City off Hwy. 89, 13 mi south of I–80, Box 5279, Tahoe City 96145, ☎ 530/583–4232; 530/581–8374 snow phone; 800/441–4423 information; FAX 530/583–0963. 2,000 acres, rated 25% easier, 40% more difficult, 35% most difficult. Longest run 2½ mi, base 6,835', summit 8,637'. Lifts: 2 high-speed quads, 2 triples, 7 doubles, 1 surface.*

Squaw Valley USA was the site of the 1960 Olympics. The immense resort has changed significantly since then, but the skiing is still world-class, with steep chutes and cornices on six Sierra peaks. Beginners delight in riding the tram to the top, where there is a huge plateau of gentle runs. At the top of the tram, you'll find the High Camp Bath and Tennis Club in the lodge, which has impressive views from its restaurants, bars, and outdoor ice-skating pavilion. Base facilities are clustered around the Village Mall, with shops, dining, condos, hotels, and lodges. The valley golf course doubles as a cross-country ski facility. On the other side of the golf course is the Resort at Squaw Creek, with its own run and quad chairlift that runs to Squaw's ski terrain. ⊠ *Hwy. 89, 5 mi northwest of Tahoe City, Squaw Valley USA 96146, ☎ 530/583–6985; 800/545–4350 reservations; 530/583–6955 snow information; FAX 530/581–7106. 4,000 acres, rated 25% beginner, 45% intermediate, 30% advanced. Longest run 3 mi, base 6,200', summit 9,050'. Lifts: 6-passenger gondola, cable car, 3 quads, 8 triples, 14 doubles, 5 surface.*

GOLF

Resort at Squaw Creek Golf Course (⊠ 400 Squaw Creek Rd., Olympic Valley, ☎ 530/583–6300), an 18-hole championship course, was designed by Robert Trent Jones Jr. The $110 greens fee includes a cart. Golfers use pull carts at the nine-hole **Tahoe City Golf Course** (⊠ Hwy. 28, Tahoe City, ☎ 530/583–1516). The greens fee is $18, cart $12 additional.

Carnelian Bay to Kings Beach

5 to 10 mi northeast of Tahoe City on Hwy. 28.

The small lakeside commercial districts of Carnelian Bay and Tahoe Vista service the thousand or so locals who live in the area year-round and the thousands more who have summer residences or launch their boats here. Kings Beach, the last town heading east on Highway 28 before the Nevada border, is to Crystal Bay what South Lake Tahoe is to Stateline: a bustling California village full of motels and rental condos, restaurants and shops, used by the hordes of hopefuls who pass through on their way to the "luck" machines and gaming tables in Nevada.

 The 28-acre **Kings Beach State Recreation Area,** one of the largest such areas on the lake, is open year-round. Its long beach becomes crowded with people swimming, sunbathing, jet skiing, riding in paddle boats, and playing volleyball and Frisbee. There's a good playground for kids here. ⊠ *North Lake Blvd., Kings Beach, ☎ 530/546–7248. ☞ Free day use, parking $4.*

Dining

$$–$$$ ✕ **Captain Jon's.** The dining room is small and cozy, with linen cloths and fresh flowers on the tables. On chilly evenings a fireplace with a raised brick hearth warms diners. The lengthy dinner menu is old-style country French, with two dozen daily specials; the emphasis is on fish and hearty salads. The restaurant's lounge, which serves light meals, is on the water in a separate building with a pier where guests can tie up their boats. ✉ 7220 N. Lake Blvd., Tahoe Vista, ☎ 530/546–4819. AE, DC, MC, V. No lunch in winter (usually Nov.–June).

$–$$$ ✕ **Gar Woods Grill and Pier.** This stylish but casual lakeside restaurant recalls the area's past, with light-pine paneling, floor-to-ceiling picture windows overlooking the lake, a river-rock fireplace, and boating photographs. The menu includes such eclectic dishes as Thai chicken salad, grilled-salmon salad, a seafood sauté, and pastas. There's an extensive wine list, and Sunday brunch is served. ✉ 5000 N. Lake Blvd., Carnelian Bay, ☎ 530/546–3366. AE, MC, V.

$ ✕ **Log Cabin Caffe.** Almost always hopping, this Kings Beach eatery specializes in healthful, hearty breakfast and lunch entrées—pancakes, waffles, freshly baked pastries, health-food sandwiches, and ice cream. It's a good place on the north shore for an espresso or cappuccino. Get here early on weekends; this is a popular spot for brunch. ✉ 8692 N. Lake Blvd., ☎ 530/546–7109. MC, V.

Outdoor Activities and Sports

GOLF

Old Brockway Golf Course (✉ Hwys. 267 and 28, Kings Beach, ☎ 530/546–9909) is a nine-hole, par-36 course. The greens fee is $25 for nine holes, plus $16 cart rental; $45 for 18 holes plus $25 cart rental.

SNOWMOBILING

Snowmobiling Unlimited (✉ Box 460, Carnelian Bay 96140, ☎ 530/583–5858) conducts guided tours, rents equipment, and operates a track to zoom around on.

SWIMMING

The **North Tahoe Beach Center** has a 26-ft hot tub and a beach with an enclosed swimming area and four sand volleyball courts. The popular spot has a barbecue and picnic area, a fitness center, windsurfing and nonmotorized boat rentals, a snack bar, and a clubhouse with games. ✉ 7860 N. Lake Blvd., Kings Beach, ☎ 530/546–2566. ✎ $7.

Truckee

⑩ 13 mi northwest of Kings Beach on Hwy. 267, 14 mi north of Tahoe City on Hwy. 89.

Old West facades line the main street of Truckee, a favorite stopover for people traveling from the Bay Area to the north shore of Lake Tahoe. Galleries and boutiques are plentiful, but you will also find low-key diners, discount skiwear, and an old-fashioned five-and-dime store. Stop by the information booth in the Amtrak depot (✉ Railroad St. at Commercial Rd.) for a walking-tour map of historic Truckee.

Donner Memorial State Park commemorates the Donner Party, a group of 89 westward-bound pioneers who were trapped in the Sierra in the winter of 1846–47 in snow 22 ft deep. Only 47 survived, some by cannibalism and others by eating animal hides. The Immigrant Museum's hourly slide show details the Donner Party's plight. Other displays relate the history of other settlers and of railroad development through the Sierra. ✉ Off I–80, 2 mi west of Truckee, ☎ 530/582–7892. ✎ $2. ☉ Sept.–May, daily 10–4; June–Aug., daily 10–5.

Northstar-at-Tahoe

⓫ *6 mi south of Truckee on Hwy. 267, 15 mi north of Tahoe City on Hwy. 28 to Hwy. 267.*

Dining and Lodging

$$$–$$$$ ✕🏨 **Northstar-at-Tahoe Resort.** This is the area's most complete destination resort. The center of action is the Village Mall, a concentration of restaurants, shops, recreation facilities, and accommodations—hotel rooms, condos, and private houses. The resort is popular with families because of its many sports activities. Summer rates are lower than winter rates. ✉ *Off Hwy. 267, Box 129, 96160,* ☎ *530/562–1010 or 800/ 466–6784,* FAX *530/562–2215. 230 units. 3 restaurants, deli, 18-hole golf course, 10 tennis courts, horseback riding, bicycles, skiing, sleigh rides, snowmobiling, recreation room, baby-sitting. AE, D, MC, V.*

Outdoor Activities and Sports

CROSS-COUNTRY AND DOWNHILL SKIING

Northstar-at-Tahoe Resort. Two northeast-facing, wind-protected bowls provide some of the best powder skiing in the Lake Tahoe area, including steep chutes and long cruising runs. Top-to-bottom snowmaking and intense grooming assure good conditions. Northstar-at-Tahoe also gives cross-country skiers access to alpine ski slopes for telemarking and provides 40 mi of groomed, tracked trails with a wide skating lane. There's a ski shop, rentals, and instruction. ✉ *Hwy. 267 between Truckee and Kings Beach, Box 129, Truckee 96160,* ☎ *530/562–1330 snow information,* FAX *530/562–2215. 1,800 acres, rated 25% beginner, 50% intermediate, 25% advanced. Longest run 2.9 mi, base 6,400', summit 8,600'. Lifts: 6-passenger express gondola, 3 doubles, 3 triples, 2 tows, 4 high-speed quads.*

NEVADA SIDE

From Crystal Bay to Stateline

You don't need a roadside marker to know when you've crossed from California into Nevada. The lake's water and the pine trees may be identical on the other side, but the flashing lights and elaborate marquees of casinos announce legal gambling in garish hues.

Crystal Bay

⓬ *1 mi east of Kings Beach on Hwy. 28., 30 mi north of South Lake Tahoe on U.S. 50 to Hwy. 28.*

Right at the Nevada border, Crystal Bay holds a cluster of casinos; one, the **Cal-Neva Lodge** (☞ Dining and Lodging, *below*), is bisected by the state line. This joint opened in 1927 and has weathered nearly as many scandals—the largest involving Frank Sinatra—as it has blizzards. The **Tahoe Biltmore** has a popular $1.39 breakfast special served 24 hours a day. **Jim Kelley's Nugget** closes during the winter months.

Dining and Lodging

$–$$ ✕ **Soule Domain.** A romantic 1927 pine-log cabin with a stone fire-
★ place is the setting for some of Lake Tahoe's most creative and delicious dinners. Chef-owner Charles Edward Soule IV's specialties include grilled tuna with papaya-mango salsa, and filet mignon with shiitake mushrooms, Gorgonzola, and brandy. ✉ *Cove St. across from Tahoe Biltmore,* ☎ *530/546–7529. Reservations essential on weekends. AE, DC, MC, V. No lunch.*

$$–$$$ ✕🖭 **Cal-Neva Lodge.** All the rooms in this hotel on Highway 28 at Crystal Bay have views of Lake Tahoe and the mountains. There is an arcade with video games for children, cabaret entertainment, and, in addition to rooms in the main hotel, 12 cabins with living rooms and seven two-bedroom chalets. ✉ *2 Stateline Rd., Box 368, 89402, ☎ 702/832–4000 or 800/225–6382, ⅋ 702/831–9007. 220 rooms. Restaurant, coffee shop, pool, hot tub, sauna, tennis courts, casino, 3 chapels. AE, D, DC, MC, V.*

Incline Village

⓭ *3 mi east of Crystal Bay on Hwy. 28.*

Incline Village, one of Nevada's few master-planned communities, dates back to the early 1960s; it's still privately owned. Check out **Lakeshore Drive** to see some of the most expensive real estate in Nevada. Incline is the only town on Lake Tahoe without a central commercial district, planned this way to prevent congestion and to preserve a natural feel.

There are plenty of recreational diversions—hiking and biking trails, the area's greatest concentration of tennis courts, and a **Recreation Center** (✉ 980 Incline Way, ☎ 702/832–1300) with an eight-lane swimming pool, a cardiovascular-fitness area, a basketball court, a game room, and a snack bar.

OFF THE BEATEN PATH
MT. ROSE – If you want to ski the absolute highest slopes in the Lake Tahoe region, Highway 431 leads north out of Incline Village to Mt. Rose. Reno is another 30 mi farther.

⓮ The popular 1960s television western *Bonanza* inspired the **Ponderosa Ranch** theme park. Attractions include the Cartwrights' ranch house, a western town, and a saloon. There's also a self-guided nature trail, free pony rides for children, and, if you're here from 8 to 9:30 in the morning, a breakfast hayride. During the winter, you can tour the ranch house (10 to 3:30, $6.50) and visit the gift shop. ✉ *Hwy. 28, 2 mi south of Incline Village, ☎ 702/831–0691. ▨ $8.50, hayride $2. ☉ Mid-Apr.–Oct., daily 9:30–5.*

Dining and Lodging

$$ ✕ **Stanley's Restaurant and Lounge.** With its intimate bar and pleasant dining room, this local favorite is a good bet any time for straightforward American fare on the hearty side (barbecued pork ribs, beef Stroganoff). Lighter bites, such as seafood Cobb salad, are also available, along with ample breakfasts; try the eggs Benedict or a chili-cheese omelet. There's a deck for outdoor dining in summer. ✉ *941 Tahoe Blvd., ☎ 702/831–9944. Reservations not accepted. AE, MC, V.*

$ ✕ **Azzara's.** A typical Italian trattoria with light, inviting decor, Azzara's serves a dozen pasta dishes and many pizzas, as well as chicken, lamb, veal, shrimp, and beef. Dinners include soup or salad, a vegetable, a pasta, and garlic bread. This is a no-smoking restaurant. ✉ *Incline Center Mall, 930 Tahoe Blvd., ☎ 702/831–0346. MC, V. Closed Mon.*

$$$–$$$$ ✕🖭 **Hyatt Lake Tahoe Resort Hotel/Casino.** Some of the rooms in this luxurious hotel on the lake have fireplaces, but all the accommodations here are top-notch. A children's program and rental bicycles are available. The restaurants are the Lone Eagle Grille (fairly good Continental, with steak, seafood, pasta, and rotisserie dishes), the Ciao Mein Trattoria (Asian-Italian), and the Sierra Cafe (open 24 hours; Sunday brunch and dinner buffets). ✉ *Lakeshore and Country Club*

Drs., 89450, ☎ *702/831–1111 or 800/233–1234,* FAX *702/831–7508. 460 rooms. 2 restaurants, coffee shop, lounge, room service, pool, 2 saunas, spa, 2 tennis courts, health club, casino, laundry service. AE, D, DC, MC, V.*

Outdoor Activities and Sports

BOAT CRUISE

The **Sierra Cloud** (☎ 702/831–1111), a trimaran with a big trampoline lounging surface, cruises the north-shore area mornings and afternoons from the Hyatt Regency Hotel in Incline Village May to October. Fares run $30 to $40.

CROSS-COUNTRY AND DOWNHILL SKIING

Diamond Peak has a fun, family atmosphere with many special programs and affordable rates. A learn-to-ski package that includes rentals, a lesson, and a lift ticket, is $35; a parent-child ski package is $42, with each additional child's lift ticket $6. There is a half-pipe run just for snowboarding. Snowmaking covers 80% of the mountain, and runs are well groomed nightly. The ride up the 1-mi Crystal chair rewards you with the best views of the lake from any ski area. Diamond Peak is less crowded than some of the larger areas, and has free shuttles to lodging in nearby Incline Village. Diamond Peak Cross-Country (✉ off Hwy. 431, ☎ 702/832–1177) has 22 mi of groomed track with skating lanes. The trail system goes from 7,400 ft to 9,100 ft with endless wilderness to explore. ✉ *1210 Ski Way, Incline Village, NV 89450, off Hwy. 28 to Country Club Dr.,* ☎ *702/832–1177 or 800/468–2463,* FAX *702/832–1281. 655 acres, rated 18% beginner, 46% intermediate, 36% advanced. Longest run 2½ mi, base 6,700', summit 8,540'. Lifts: 6 doubles, 1 quad.*

GOLF

Incline Championship (✉ 955 Fairway Blvd., ☎ 702/832–1144) is an 18-hole, par-72 course with a driving range. The $115 greens fee includes the cart. **Incline Mountain** (✉ 690 Wilson Way, ☎ 702/832–1150) is an easy 18-holer; par is 58. The $50 greens fee includes the cart.

OFF THE BEATEN PATH

CARSON CITY AND VIRGINIA CITY – Nevada's capital, Carson City, is less than an hour away from Lake Tahoe. At Spooner Junction, where Highway 28 meets U.S. 50, head east on U.S. 50, away from the lake. In 10 mi you reach U.S. 395, where you turn left and go 1 mi north to Carson City. Most of its historic buildings and other attractions are along U.S. 395, the main street through town. At the south end of town is the Carson City Chamber of Commerce (✉ 1900 S. Carson St., ☎ 702/882–1565), which has visitor information. About a 30-minute drive northeast of Carson City, on Highway 342 off U.S. 50 East, is the fabled mining town of Virginia City, which has sights and activities of historical interest amid touristy diversions.

Sand Harbor Beach

★ ⓯ *4 mi south of Incline Village on Hwy. 28, 22 mi north of South Lake Tahoe on U.S. 50 to Hwy. 28.*

Sand Harbor Beach, within the Lake Tahoe–Nevada State Park, has a popular beach that is sometimes filled to capacity by 11 AM on summer weekends. A pop-music festival (☎ 702/832–1606 or 800/468–2463) is held here in July and a Shakespeare festival every August.

U.S. 50 from Spooner Junction to Zephyr Cove

13 mi south of Sand Harbor Beach (to Cave Rock) on Hwy. 28 to U.S. 50.

★ ⑯ **Cave Rock,** 25 yards of solid stone at the southern end of Lake Tahoe–Nevada State Park, is sacred to the Washoe Indians, who used it as a burial site. Tahoe Tessie, the lake's version of the Loch Ness monster, is reputed to live in a cavern below the impressive outcrop, which is the throat of an extinct volcano. Cave Rock towers over a parking lot, a lakefront picnic ground, and a boat launch; the rest area provides the best vantage point of this cliff. ✉ *U.S. 50, 3 mi south of Glenbrook.*

⑰ The largest settlement between Incline Village and Stateline is **Zephyr Cove,** which is still only a tiny resort. It has a beach, a marina, a campground, a picnic area, a coffee shop in a historic log lodge, rustic cabins for rent, and nearby riding stables. The 550-passenger **MS Dixie II** (☎ 702/588–3508), a sternwheeler, sails year-round from Zephyr Cove Marina to Emerald Bay on lunch and dinner cruises. Fares are $14 to $36. The ***Woodwind*** (☎ 702/588–3000), a glass-bottom trimaran, sails on regular and champagne April to October cruises from Zephyr Cove Resort. Fares are $14 to $20.

OFF THE **KINGSBURY GRADE** – This road, also known as Route 207, is one of
BEATEN PATH three roads that access Tahoe from the east. Originally a toll road used by wagon trains to get over the Sierras' crest, it has sweeping views of the Carson Valley. Off Route 206, which intersects 207, is Genoa, the oldest settlement in Nevada. Along Main Street are small but interesting museums and the state's longest-standing saloon.

Stateline

⑱ *5 mi south of Zephyr Cove on U.S. 50.*

Stateline is a great border town in the Nevada tradition. Its four high-rise casinos are as vertical and contained as the commercial district of South Lake Tahoe on the California side is horizontal and sprawling. And Stateline is as relentlessly indoors-oriented as the rest of the lake is undeniably focused on the outdoors. This strip is where you'll find the most concentrated action at Lake Tahoe: restaurants (including the typically Nevada buffets), showrooms with famous headliners and razzle-dazzle revues, luxury rooms and suites, and 24-hour casino gambling.

Dining and Lodging

$$–$$$$ ✕ **Llewellyn's Restaurant.** Elegantly decorated in blond wood and
★ pastels, the restaurant atop Harvey's casino merits special mention. Almost every table has superb views of Lake Tahoe. Dinner entrées—seafood, meat, and poultry—are served with unusual accompaniments, such as sturgeon in potato crust with saffron sauce or veal with polenta, herbs, and pancetta. Lunches are reasonably priced, with gourmet selections as well as hamburgers. The adjacent bar is a classy, quiet place to have a drink. ✉ *Harvey's Resort, U.S. 50,* ☎ *702/588–2411 or 800/ 553–1022. AE, D, DC, MC, V.*

$$–$$$ ✕ **Chart House.** It's worth the drive up the steep grade to see the view from here—try to arrive for sunset. The American menu of steak and seafood is complemented by an abundant salad bar. The restaurant has a children's menu. ✉ *329 Kingsbury Grade,* ☎ *702/588–6276. AE, D, DC, MC, V. No lunch.*

$$$–$$$$ ✕⌂ **Harrah's Tahoe Hotel/Casino.** Luxurious guest rooms here have private bars and two full bathrooms, each with a television and telephone. All rooms have views of the lake and the mountains, but the least-obstructed views are from the higher floors. Top-name entertainment is presented in the South Shore Room. Among the restaurants, the romantic 16th-floor Summit is a standout. The menu changes nightly and includes creatively presented salads; lamb, venison, or seafood entrées with delicate sauces; and sensuous desserts. Other restaurants serve Italian, deli, and traditional meat-and-potatoes cuisine. There's also a 24-hour café, a buffet with a view, and a candy store. ⊠ *U.S. 50, Box 8, 89449,* ☎ *702/588–6611 or 800/648–3773,* FAX *702/788–3274. 534 rooms. 5 restaurants, café, room service, indoor pool, barbershop, beauty salon, hot tubs, health club, casino, video games, laundry service, kennel. AE, D, DC, MC, V.*

$$–$$$$ ✕⌂ **Harvey's Resort Hotel/Casino.** Owner Harvey Gross played an im-
★ portant role in persuading the state to keep U.S. 50 open year-round, making Tahoe accessible in winter. His namesake hotel, which started as a cabin in 1944, is now the largest resort in Tahoe. Any description of the place runs to superlatives, from the 40-ft-tall crystal chandelier in the lobby to the 88,000-square-ft casino. Rooms have custom furnishings, oversize marble baths, and minibars. The health club, spa, and pool are free to guests, a rarity for this area. Among its restaurants, Llewellyn's (☞ *above*) is outstanding. Also noteworthy is the Sage Room Steak House, which serves prime beef, veal, and seafood, as well as Continental dishes such as braised pheasant and escargots. ⊠ *U.S. 50, Box 128, 89449,* ☎ *702/588–2411 or 800/648–3361,* FAX *702/782–4889. 741 rooms. 8 restaurants, pool, barbershop, beauty salon, hot tub, spa, health club, casino, chapel. AE, D, DC, MC, V.*

$$–$$$$ ⌂ **Caesars Tahoe.** Most of the rooms and suites at this 16-story hotel-casino have oversize Roman tubs, king-size beds, two telephones, and a view of Lake Tahoe or the encircling mountains. The opulent casino encompasses 40,000 square ft. Top-name entertainers perform in the 1,600-seat Circus Maximus. The local Planet Hollywood is here, plus Chinese, Italian, and American restaurants, a 24-hour coffee shop, and a yogurt emporium. ⊠ *55 U.S. 50, Box 5800, 89449,* ☎ *702/588–3515; 800/648–3353 reservations and show information;* FAX *702/586–2068. 440 rooms. 5 restaurants, coffee shop, indoor pool, hot tub, saunas, spa, 4 tennis courts, health club. AE, D, DC, MC, V.*

$$–$$$ ⌂ **Horizon Casino Resort.** Many of the guest rooms at this smaller hotel-casino have lake views. The casino has a beaux arts decor, brightened by pale molded wood and mirrors. The Grande Lake Theatre, Golden Cabaret, and Aspen Lounge present shows, as well as up-and-coming and name entertainers. Le Grande Buffet has a nightly prime-rib special. ⊠ *U.S. 50, Box C, 89449,* ☎ *702/588–6211 or 800/322–7723,* FAX *702/588–1344. 539 rooms. 3 restaurants, pool, 3 hot tubs, exercise room, meeting rooms. AE, D, DC, MC, V.*

$$–$$$ ⌂ **Lakeside Inn and Casino.** The smallest of the Stateline casinos, and not nearly as glitzy as the big four, Lakeside has a rustic look. Guest rooms are in lodges, away from the casino area. ⊠ *U.S. 50 at Kingsbury Grade, Box 5640, 89449,* ☎ *702/588–7777 or 800/624–7980,* FAX *702/588–4092. 123 rooms. Restaurant, pool. AE, D, DC, MC, V.*

Nightlife

Major entertainment is found at the larger casinos. The top venues are the Circus Maximus at Caesars Tahoe, the Emerald Theater at Harvey's, the South Shore Room at Harrah's, and Horizon's Grand Lake Theatre. Each theater is as large as a Broadway house. Typical headliners are Jay Leno, David Copperfield, Kenny Rogers, and Johnny

Mathis. For Las Vegas–style production shows—fast-paced dancing, singing, and novelty acts—try Harrah's or the Horizon. The big showrooms also occasionally present performances of Broadway musicals by touring Broadway companies or casts assembled for the casino. Reservations are almost always required for superstar shows. Depending on the act, cocktail shows usually cost from $12 to $40. Smaller casino cabarets sometimes have a cover charge or drink minimum.

Bars around the lake present pop- and country-music singers and musicians, and in winter the ski resorts do the same. Summer alternatives are outdoor music events, from chamber quartets to jazz bands and rock performers, at Sand Harbor and the Lake Tahoe Visitors Center amphitheater.

Outdoor Activities and Sports

GOLF

Edgewood Tahoe (⊠ U.S. 50 and Lake Pkwy., behind Horizon Casino, Stateline, ☎ 702/588–3566) is an 18-hole, par-72 course with a driving range. The $150 greens fee includes a cart (though you can walk if you wish); the course is open from 7 AM to 3 PM. The 18-hole, par 70 **Lake Tahoe Golf Course** (⊠ U.S. 50, between Lake Tahoe Airport and Meyers, ☎ 530/577–0788) has a driving range. The greens fee is $42, cart $18 additional (carts are required Friday, Saturday, and Sunday). The greens fee at the 18-hole, par 66 **Tahoe Paradise Golf Course** (⊠ U.S. 50, near Meyers, South Lake Tahoe, ☎ 530/577–2121) is $29. A cart is $12 additional.

SCUBA DIVING

Sun Sports (⊠ 1018 Herbert Ave., No. 4, South Lake Tahoe, ☎ 530/541–6000) is a full-service PADI dive center with rentals and instruction.

LAKE TAHOE A TO Z

Arriving and Departing

By Bus
Greyhound Lines (☎ 800/231–2222) stops in Sacramento; Truckee; and Reno, Nevada.

By Car
Lake Tahoe is 198 mi northeast of San Francisco, a drive of just under four hours when traffic and the weather cooperate. Avoid the heavy traffic leaving the San Francisco area for Tahoe on Friday afternoon and returning on Sunday afternoon. The major route is I–80, which cuts through the Sierra Nevada about 14 mi north of the lake; from there state highways 89 and 267 reach the north shore. U.S. 50 is the more direct highway to the south shore, taking about 2½ hours from Sacramento. From Reno, you can get to the north shore by heading west on Highway 431 off U.S. 395, 8 mi south of town (a total of 35 mi). For the south shore, continue south on U.S. 395 through Carson City, and then head west on U.S. 50 (55 mi total).

By Plane
Reno–Tahoe International Airport (☎ 702/328–6400), 35 mi northeast of the closest point on the lake, is served by airlines that include American, America West, Continental, Delta, Northwest, Reno Air, Skywest, Southwest, and United. *See* Air Travel *in* the Gold Guide for airline phone numbers. **Tahoe Casino Express** (☎ 702/785–2424 or 800/446–6128) has daily scheduled transportation from Reno to South Lake Tahoe from 6:15 AM until 12:30 AM.

Lake Tahoe Airport (☎ 530/542–6180) on U.S. 50 is 3 mi south of the lake's shore. **Mountain Air Express** (☎ 800/788–4247) provides service on 19-seaters Thursday to Monday from Long Beach and Oakland, CA.

Getting Around

By Bus
South Tahoe Area Ground Express (STAGE, ☎ 530/573–2080) runs 24 hours along U.S. 50 and through the neighborhoods of South Lake Tahoe. **Tahoe Area Regional Transit** (TART, ☎ 530/581–6365 or 800/736–6365) operates buses along Lake Tahoe's northern and western shores between Tahoma (from Meeks Bay in summer) and Incline Village daily from 6:30 AM to 6:30 PM. Free shuttle buses run among the casinos, major ski resorts, and motels of South Lake Tahoe.

By Car
The scenic 72-mi highway around the lake is marked Highway 89 on the southwest and west, Highway 28 on the north and northeast shores, and U.S. 50 on the east and southeast. It takes about three hours to drive, but allow plenty of extra time—heavy traffic on busy holiday weekends can prolong the trip, and there are frequent road repairs in summer. During winter, sections of Highway 89 may be closed, making it impossible to complete the circular drive—in California, call 800/427–7623 to check road conditions. I–80, U.S. 50, and U.S. 395 are all-weather highways, but there may be delays as snow is cleared during major storms. Carry tire chains from October to May (car-rental agencies provide them with their vehicles).

By Taxi
Yellow Cab (☎ 530/542–1234) serves all of Tahoe Basin. **Sierra Taxi** (☎ 530/577–8888) serves Tahoe's south shore. On the north shore, try **Tahoe-Truckee Taxi** (☎ 530/582–8294).

Contacts and Resources

Area Code
The area code on the California side of the Tahoe Basin was scheduled to change from 916 to 530 on November 1, 1997.

Emergencies
Ambulance (☎ 911). **California Highway Patrol** (☎ 530/587–3510). **Nevada Highway Patrol** (☎ 702/687–5300). **Police** (☎ 911).

Guided Tours
BY BOAT

The *Tahoe Queen* (☞ South Lake Tahoe *in* California Side, *above*), the *Sierra Cloud* (☞ Incline Village *in* Nevada Side, *above*), and MS *Dixie II* and *Woodwind* (☞ U.S. 50 from Spooner Junction to Zephyr Cove *in* Nevada Side, *above*) all provide guided boat tours.

BY BUS OR CAR

Gray Line (☎ 702/331–1147 or 800/822–6009) runs daily tours to South Lake Tahoe, Carson City, and Virginia City. **Luxury Limousines of Tahoe** (☎ 530/542–2277 or 800/458–9743) also provides around-the-lake tours.

Lake Tahoe Adventures (✉ 2286 Utah Ave., South Lake Tahoe 96150, ☎ 530/541–5875) operates a trek skirting the Desolation Wilderness in four-wheel-drive all-terrain vehicles.

BY HOT-AIR BALLOON
Lake Tahoe Balloons (☎ 530/544–1221) conducts year-round excursions (champagne brunch included) over the lake or over the Carson Valley for $165 per person.

BY PLANE
CalVada Seaplanes Inc. (☎ 530/546–3984) provides rides over the lake for $50 to $85 per person, depending on the length of the trip. **High Country Soaring** (☎ 702/782–4944) glider rides over the lake and valley depart from the Douglas County Airport, Gardnerville.

Reservations Agencies
Destinet (☎ 800/444–7275 for campgrounds in California state parks). **Lake Tahoe Visitors Authority** (☎ 800/288–2463 for south-shore lodging). **Resort Association Visitors and Convention Bureau** (☎ 800/824–6348 for north-shore lodging).

Road Conditions
California roads in Tahoe area (☎ 530/445–7623). **California roads approaching Tahoe** (☎ 800/427–7623). **Nevada roads** (☎ 702/793–1313).

Visitor Information
California State Department of Parks and Recreation (☎ 530/653–8569). **Lake Tahoe Hotline** (☎ 530/542–4636 for south-shore events; 530/546–5253 for north-shore events; 702/831–6677 for Nevada events). **Lake Tahoe Visitors Authority** (✉ 1156 Ski Run Blvd., South Lake Tahoe, CA 96150, ☎ 530/544–5050 or 800/288–2463). **Resort Association Visitors and Convention Bureau** (✉ Box 5578, Tahoe City, CA 96145, ☎ 530/583–3494 or 800/824–6348, FAX 530/581–4081). **Ski Report Hotline** (☎ 415/864–6440). **U.S. Forest Service** backcountry recording (☎ 530/587–2158).

8 The Sierra National Parks

*Yosemite, Kings Canyon,
and Sequoia*

*The highlight for many California
travelers is a visit to one of the national
parks in the Sierra Nevada range.
Yosemite is the state's most famous
park and every bit as sublime as one
expects. Its Yosemite-type or U-shape
valleys were formed by the action of
glaciers during recent ice ages. Other
examples are found about 150 miles
southeast in Kings Canyon and Sequoia
national parks, which are adjacent to
each other and usually visited together.
All the Sierra National Parks contain
fine, tall groves of Sequoiadendron
giganteum trees.*

YOSEMITE, KINGS CANYON, AND SEQUOIA national parks are famous throughout the world for their unique sights and experiences. Yosemite, especially, should be on your "don't miss" list. Unfortunately, it's on everyone else's as well (the park hosts 4 million visitors annually), so advance lodging reservations are essential. During a week's stay, you can exit and reenter the parks as frequently as you wish by showing your pass.

Updated by
Julie Bourland

Pleasures and Pastimes

Camping

One highlight of a camping trip to the Sierra national parks is opening your eyes in the morning to nearby meadows and streams, and then suddenly seeing the unforgettable landscape of giant granite in the distance, as if for the first time. Another is looking up at an awe-inspiring number of stars and spying one falling quickly through the night sky.

Destinet (☞ Contacts and Resources *in* the Sierra National Parks A to Z, *below*) handles reservations for the parks' campgrounds that require them. You can reserve campsites up to five months in advance, depending upon availability. It's possible to get a campsite upon arrival by stopping at the Campground Reservations Office in Yosemite Valley, but this is a chancy strategy. The campgrounds outside the valley that are not on the reservation system are first-come, first-served.

Campgrounds near each of the major tourist centers in Kings Canyon and Sequoia parks are equipped with tables, grills, garbage cans, and either flush or pit toilets. Depending on the site, you may need to bring your own drinking water. The one campground that takes reservations, which can be made through Destinet from one day up to five months in advance, is Lodgepole in Sequoia. All others assign sites on a first-come, first-served basis; on weekends in July and August they are often filled by Friday afternoon.

Dining

Snack bars, coffee shops, and cafeterias in the parks are not expensive, but you may not want to waste precious time hunting for food, especially during the day; instead, stop at a grocery store and fill your ice chest with the makings of a picnic to enjoy under giant trees. The three fanciest accommodations within Yosemite National Park are also the prime dining spots. Especially in the off-season it's easy to zip out of the park to dine at the restaurants in the border towns (☞ Outside Yosemite National Park, *below*). With few exceptions (all noted), dress is casual at the restaurants listed below.

CATEGORY	COST*
$$$$	over $50
$$$	$30–$50
$$	$20–$30
$	under $20

per person for a three-course meal, excluding drinks, service, and 7¼% tax

Hiking

Hiking is the primary outdoor sport in the Sierra national parks. Two of the most popular are the ones to Bridalveil Fall and Glacier Point. The trails to upper and lower Yosemite Falls and Mirror Lake are favorites because of their beauty, moderate duration, and reasonable difficulty. The parks' visitor centers have trail maps.

Lodging

Most accommodations inside Yosemite, Kings Canyon, and Sequoia can best be described as "no frills." Some have no electricity or indoor plumbing. Other than the Ahwahnee and Wawona hotels in Yosemite, lodging is geared toward those who prefer basic motels, rustic cabins, and campgrounds in natural settings to full service and luxury. Except during the off-peak season, November to March, rates in Yosemite are pricey given the general quality of the lodging. Reservations (☞ Contacts and Resources for each park *in* the Sierra National Parks A to Z, *below*) should be made well in advance, especially in summer.

Reservations are recommended for visits to Kings Canyon and Sequoia at any time of the year because it's a long way out if the lodgings there are full. All the parks' lodges and cabins are open during the summer months, but in winter only some in Grant Grove remain open. Lodging rates are consistent throughout the year. The park's concessionaire has plans to build a 30-room hotel in Grant Grove, which administrators hope will be up and running by mid-1998. The town of Three Rivers on Highway 198 southwest of Sequoia has a few more lodges and restaurants from which to choose.

CATEGORY	COST*
$$$$	over $175
$$$	$120–$175
$$	$80–$120
$	under $80

All prices are for a standard double room, excluding 9%–10% tax.

Nature Lore

In Yosemite from early May to late September and during some holiday periods, actor Lee Stetson portrays noted naturalist John Muir, bringing to life Muir's wit, wisdom, and storytelling skill. Stetson's programs—"Conversation with a Tramp" and "The Spirit of John Muir"—are two of the park's best-loved shows. Locations and times are listed in the *Yosemite Guide,* the newspaper handed to visitors upon entering the park. Stetson, as John Muir, also leads free interpretive walks twice a week during the summer; the walks start at the visitor center.

Exploring the Sierra National Parks

The Sierra national parks encompass two basic geographical regions. The most famous is Yosemite Valley. Its granite peaks and domes, such as El Capitan and Half Dome, rise more than 3,000 ft above the valley floor. Two of the five waterfalls that cascade over the valley's rim are among the world's 10 highest. And the Merced River, placid here, runs through the valley. Such extravagant praise has been written of this valley (John Muir described it as "a revelation in landscape affairs that enriches one's life forever") and so many beautiful photographs taken (by Ansel Adams and others) that you may wonder if the reality can possibly measure up. For almost everyone, it does; Yosemite is a reminder of what "breathtaking" and "marvelous" really mean.

Kings Canyon and Sequoia national parks share their administration and a main highway. Although you may want to concentrate on either Kings Canyon or Sequoia, most people visit both parks in one trip.

Numbers in the text correspond to numbers in the margin and on the Yosemite and Kings Canyon and Sequoia National Parks maps.

Great Itineraries

We recommend allowing several days to explore the parks, but if your time is limited, a one-day guided tour of one of the parks will at least allow you a glimpse of their wonders. We also recommend that you make your plans far enough in advance so you can stay in the parks themselves, not in one of the "gateway cities" in the foothills or Central Valley. You'll probably be adjusting to a higher altitude, dealing with traffic, and exercising a fair amount. Save your energy for exploring, not driving to and from the parks.

Yosemite Valley is the primary destination for many visitors, especially those who won't be making backpack or pack-animal trips. Because the valley is only 7 mi long and averages less than 1 mi in width, you can visit sites in whatever order you choose and return to your favorites at different times of the day. Famous for their hiking trails and giant sequoia trees, Kings Canyon and Sequoia provide a true wilderness experience, less interrupted by civilization and crowds.

IF YOU HAVE 3 DAYS

Exploring only Yosemite National Park is the best strategy for those whose time is limited. Enter the park via the Big Oak Flat Entrance, and head east on Big Oak Flat Road. As you enter the valley, traffic is diverted onto a one-way road. Continue east, following the signs to Yosemite Valley's **visitor center** ①, which has information and a store with picnic supplies. Loop back west for a short hike and picnic near **Yosemite Falls** ②, the highest waterfall in North America. Continue west for a valley view of famous **El Capitan** ⑦ peak. You can also picnic at this spot. As you exit the valley, take Wawona Road south, stopping at misty **Bridalveil Fall** ③ before making a left onto Glacier Point Road. From **Glacier Point** ⑨ you'll get a phenomenal bird's-eye view of the entire valley, including **Half Dome** ⑧, **Vernal Fall** ⑤, and **Nevada Fall** ⑥. If you want to avoid the busloads at Glacier Point, stop at **Sentinel Dome** ⑩ instead—after a mildly strenuous 1-mi hike you get a view similar to the one from the Glacier Point except for the peek into the valley. Sunsets from either spot are dazzling. Continue south on Highway 41 to the Wawona Hotel, where you can have a relaxing drink on the veranda or in the cozy lobby bar.

On day two, spend the morning and early afternoon walking through the **Mariposa Grove of Big Trees** ⑫ (take the Big Trees Tram if you don't want to walk as much). Return to Wawona and visit the **Pioneer Yosemite History Center** ⑪. Head back to Yosemite Valley on Wawona Road for an early-evening beverage at the Ahwahnee Hotel's bar (enjoy the patio view in good weather), and explore the hotel's lobby and other public areas. Have dinner at the Ahwahnee or one of the other valley eateries. On the third morning, have breakfast near the visitor center before hiking to **Vernal Fall** ⑤ or **Nevada Fall** ⑥.

IF YOU HAVE 5 DAYS

Spend your first day exploring the ▦ **Yosemite Valley area** ①–⑩. On the second day, pack plenty of food and drive to **Hetch Hetchy Reservoir** ⑬ via Big Oak Flat Road and Highway 120. Then continue east on Tioga Pass Road—also called Highway 120, it's open only until the first big snow—to **Tuolumne Meadows** ⑭, the largest subalpine meadow in the Sierra. Time permitting, head east to Mono Lake. In the fall, golden aspen trees along the way make for a memorable drive. (If Tioga Pass Road is closed, on day two you can take a hike to **Vernal Fall** ⑤ or **Nevada Fall** ⑥ instead, and in the afternoon, head south to Wawona, stopping at **Pioneer Yosemite History Center** ⑪.) Wake up early on day three and spend the morning wandering beneath the giant sequoias at Wawona's **Mariposa Grove of Big Trees** ⑫. Then head southward to ▦ **Kings Canyon National Park** (about a three- to four-hour drive), entering on Highway 180 at the Big Stump Entrance. Stop at **Grant Grove** ⑮; walk along the 1-mi Big Stump Trail and visit the famous

General Grant tree. If you're camping you'll need to get situated before sunset; if you're staying at one of the park's lodges, check in and then have dinner. On the fifth day, pass briefly through **Lodgepole** ⑳ in **Sequoia National Park** and pick up tickets to the Crystal Cave. Visit the **Giant Forest** ㉒ before stopping at the **Crystal Cave** ㉓.

When to Tour the Sierra National Parks

Summer is the most crowded season for all the parks, though the population density at Kings Canyon and Sequoia is much less than at Yosemite. During extremely busy periods—when snow closes high country roads in late spring or on crowded summer weekends—Yosemite Valley may be closed to all vehicles unless their drivers have overnight reservations. Because the parks are accessible year-round, it is possible to avoid these conditions. From mid-April to Memorial Day and from Labor Day to mid-October, the weather is usually hospitable and the parks less bustling.

The falls at Yosemite are at their most spectacular in May and June. By the end of the summer, however, some may have dried up. They begin flowing again in late fall with the first storms, and during the winter they may be dramatically hung with ice. Because the Yosemite valley floor is only 4,000 ft high, snow there is never very deep, and it is possible to camp even in the winter (January highs are in the mid-40s, lows in the mid-20s). Tioga Pass Road is closed in winter (roughly late October to May), so you can't see Tuolumne Meadows then. The road to Glacier Point beyond the turnoff for Badger Pass is also not cleared in winter, but it is groomed for cross-country skiing. In parts of Kings Canyon and Sequoia snow may remain on the ground into June; the flowers in the Giant Forest meadows hit their peak in July.

YOSEMITE NATIONAL PARK

Yosemite Valley, Wawona, Tuolumne Meadows, and Mono Lake

Yosemite, with 1,170 square mi of parkland, is 94½% undeveloped wilderness, most of it accessible only to backpackers and horseback riders. The western boundary dips as low as 2,000 ft in the chaparral-covered foothills; the eastern boundary rises to 13,000 ft at points along the Sierra crest.

Yosemite is so large that it functions as five parks. **Yosemite Valley** and **Wawona** are open all year. **Hetch Hetchy** closes after the first main snow and reopens in May or June. The high country, **Tuolumne Meadows**, is open for summer hiking. **Badger Pass Ski Area** is open in winter only. Christmas is a very busy time, with lodging reservations best made up to a year in advance.

The fee to visit Yosemite National Park is $20 per car, $10 per person if you don't arrive in a car, good for seven days.

Yosemite Valley Area

214 mi southeast of San Francisco on I–80 to I–580 to I–205 to Hwy. 120, 330 mi northeast of Los Angeles on I–5 to Hwy. 99 to Hwy. 41.

 Yosemite National Park's headquarters is near the east end of the Yosemite Valley, where there are also restaurants, stores, a gas station, the Ahwahnee Hotel, Yosemite Lodge, a medical clinic, and a **visitor center** where park rangers dispense information and wilderness permits (necessary for overnight backpacking). There are exhibits on natural and human history as well as an adjacent Indian Cultural Museum and a re-created Ahwahneechee village. ⊠ *Off Northside Dr.,* ☎ *209/372–0200.* ☉ *Daily 9–5; extended hrs in summer.*

★ ❷ **Yosemite Falls** is the highest waterfall in North America and the fifth-highest in the world. The upper falls (1,430 ft), the middle cascades (675 ft), and the lower falls (320 ft) combine for a total of 2,425 ft and, when viewed from the valley, appear as a single waterfall. A ¼-mi trail leads from the parking lot to the base of the falls. The Yosemite Falls Trail is a strenuous 3½-mi climb rising 2,700 ft, taking you above the top of the falls. It starts at Sunnyside Campground.

★ ❸ **Bridalveil Fall,** a filmy fall of 620 ft that is often diverted as much as 20 ft one way or the other by the breeze, is the first view of Yosemite Valley for those who arrive via the Wawona Road. Native Americans called the fall Pohono ("puffing wind"). There is a very short (¼-mi) trail from a parking lot on the Wawona Road to its base.

❹ At 1,612 ft, **Ribbon Fall** is the highest single fall in the valley but also the first one to dry up in the summer because the snow and rain that fall upon the rock's flat surface evaporate quickly at this height.

❺ **Vernal Fall** (317 ft) is bordered by fern-covered black rocks, and rainbows play in the spray at the base. The hike on a paved trail from the Happy Isles nature area to the bridge at the base of Vernal Fall is only moderately strenuous and less than 1 mi long. It's another steep ¾ mi along Yosemite's Mist Trail, open only in the warmer months, up to the top of Vernal Fall.

❻ **Nevada Fall** (594 ft) in Yosemite Valley is the first major fall as the Merced River comes out of the high country. It's an additional, not very strenuous 2 mi along the Mist Trail from Vernal Fall (☞ *above*) to the top of Nevada Fall.

Vernal and Nevada falls are on the Merced River at the east end of Yosemite Valley. The roads here are closed to private cars, but a free shuttle bus runs frequently from the village. Both falls can also be viewed from Glacier Point (☞ *below*). From May through October, the Happy Isles nature area is open daily 9 to 5 and has exhibits on ecology.

★ ❼ **El Capitan** is the largest exposed granite monolith in the world, almost twice the height of the Rock of Gibraltar. It rises 3,593 ft above the valley.

★ ❽ **Half Dome** is the most distinctive rock in Yosemite: The west side of the dome is fractured vertically and cut away to form a 2,000-ft cliff. Its top, which rises 4,733 ft from the valley floor, is 8,842 ft above sea level.

★ ❾ **Glacier Point** yields what may be the most spectacular view of the valley and the High Sierra—especially at sunset—that you can get without hiking. The Glacier Point Road leaves Wawona Road (Highway 41) about 23 mi southwest of the valley; then it's a 16-mi drive, with fine views into higher country. From the parking area, walk a few hundred yards and you'll be able to see Nevada, Vernal, and Yosemite falls as well as Half Dome and other peaks. This road is closed beyond the turnoff for Badger Pass Ski Area in the winter.

❿ The view from **Sentinel Dome** is almost the same as the one from Glacier Point, minus the peek into the floor of Yosemite Valley. A 1.1-mi path begins at a parking lot on Glacier Point Road a few miles below the Glacier Point. The trail is just long and strenuous enough to keep the crowds and tour buses away, but it's by no means rugged (though the last few hundred feet on the rock itself are a bit steep).

Dining and Lodging

$$-$$$ ✕ **Mountain Room Broiler.** The food becomes secondary when you see Yosemite Falls through this dining room's window-wall. Best bets are steaks, chops, roast duck, and a fresh herb-basted roast chicken. ✉ *Yosemite Lodge, off Northside Dr.,* ☎ *209/372–1281. D, DC, MC, V. No lunch.*

$$$$ ✕🏠 **Ahwahnee Hotel & Restaurant.** This grand 1920s-style mountain
★ lodge is constructed of rocks and sugar-pine logs, with exposed timbers. The decorative style of the Grand Lounge and Solarium is a tribute to the local Miwoks and Paiutes; the motifs continue in the room decor. The Ahwahnee Restaurant ($$$–$$$$) with its 34-ft-tall trestle-beam ceiling, full-length windows, and twinkling chandeliers, is the most impressive and romantic in Yosemite. Classic American specialties include steak, trout, and prime rib, all competently prepared. Generations of Californians have made a ritual of spending Christmas and New Year's here, so make plans one year in advance; reservation lotteries are conducted for both periods. Another busy season is during January and February, when the Ahwahnee hosts its annual Chef's Holiday, featuring cooking lessons and banquets by leading chefs from all over the United States. ✉ *Ahwahnee Rd. north of Northside Dr.,* ☎ *209/252–4848 for lodging reservations, 209/372–1489 for restaurant. 123 rooms. Restaurant, lounge, pool, tennis. D, DC, MC, V.*

$-$$ ✕🏠 **Yosemite Lodge.** The rooms in this lodge near Yosemite Falls vary from functional motel-style units with two double beds to downright spartan cabins with or without baths. The lodge's restaurant has high-finish natural wood tables and many potted representatives of the local greenery and flora. Breakfast is hearty and all-American. The buffet-style dinner menu covers the full beef, chicken, and fish spectrum, but also includes vegetarian fare. ✉ *Off Northside Dr.,* ☎ *209/252–4848 for lodging reservations, 209/372–1269 for restaurant. 246 rooms. Restaurant, lounge, pool. D, DC, MC, V.*

$-$$ 🏠 **Curry Village.** These are plain accommodations: cabins with bath and without, and tent cabins with rough wood frames and canvas walls and roofs. It's a step up from camping (linens, blankets, and maid service are provided), but food and cooking are not allowed because of the animals. If you stay in a cabin without bath, showers and toilets are centrally located, as they would be in a campground. ✉ *South side of Southside Dr.,* ☎ *209/252–4848. Cafeteria, pool, ice-skating. D, DC, MC, V. 180 cabins, 426 tent cabins, 18 motel rooms. Cafeteria, pool, ice-skating. D, DC, MC, V.*

$ ⛺ **Housekeeping Camp.** These rustic three-walled cabins with canvas roofs, set along the Merced River, may be rented up to seven nights, but are difficult to get; reserving at least 366 days in advance is advised. You can cook here on gas stoves rented from the front desk. ✉ *North side of Southside Dr., between Curry Village and chapel,* ☎ *209/ 252–4848. 266 units, with no bath (maximum 4 per cabin). Toilet and shower in central shower house. D, DC, MC, V.*

Outdoor Activities and Sports

BICYCLING

Yosemite Lodge and **Curry Village** have bicycle rentals (☎ 209/372– 1208) for $5.25 per hour or $20 per day, from April through October.

CAMPING

Thousands enjoy camping in Yosemite every year, but there are a few things to remember. Use the metal food-storage boxes found at every site. Park regulations mandate that visitors store food properly to pre-

Yosemite National Park

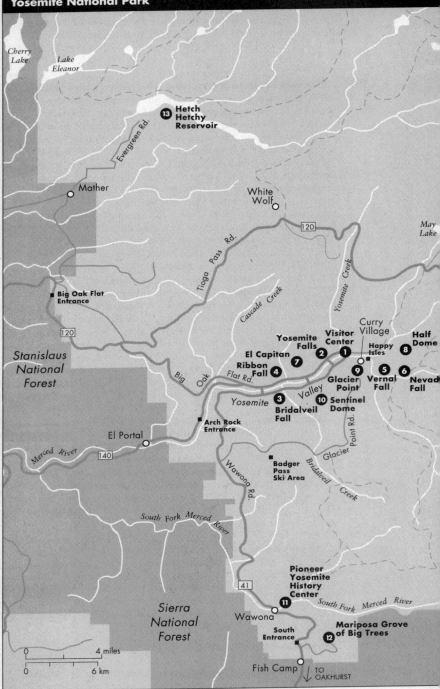

Cherry Lake

Lake Eleanor

13 Hetch Hetchy Reservoir

Mather

White Wolf

May Lake

120

Evergreen Rd.

Tioga Pass Rd.

Big Oak Flat Entrance

120

Cascade Creek

Yosemite Creek

Stanislaus National Forest

Big Oak

Flat Rd.

Curry Village

Visitor Center

Yosemite Falls

El Capitan

Ribbon Fall

7

2

1

Happy Isles

Half Dome

8

9

5

6

4

Glacier Point

Vernal Fall

Nevada Fall

3

Bridalveil Fall

10

Sentinel Dome

Yosemite

Valley

Point Rd.

Arch Rock Entrance

El Portal

140

Merced River

Glacier

Badger Pass Ski Area

Wawona Rd.

Bridalveil

Creek

South Fork Merced River

Pioneer Yosemite History Center

41

South Fork Merced River

11

Wawona

Mariposa Grove of Big Trees

12

South Entrance

Sierra National Forest

0   4 miles

0   6 km

Fish Camp

↓ TO OAKHURST

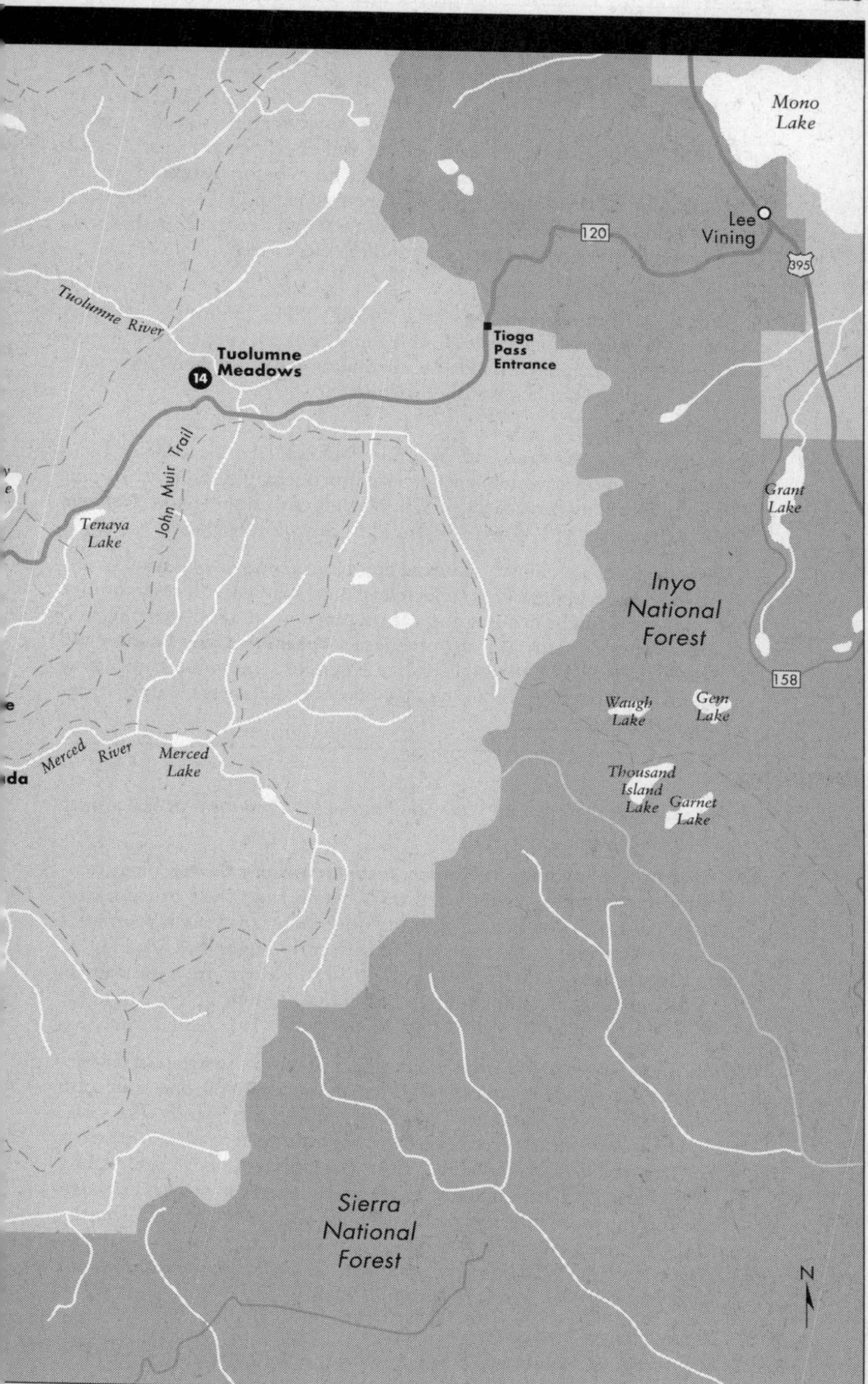

Mono
Lake

120

Lee
Vining

395

Tuolumne River

**Tuolumne
Meadows**

14

Tioga
Pass
Entrance

Grant
Lake

John Muir Trail

Tenaya
Lake

Inyo
National
Forest

158

Merced River

Merced
Lake

Waugh
Lake

Gem
Lake

Thousand
Island
Lake

Garnet
Lake

Sierra
National
Forest

N

vent bears from getting it. Move all food, coolers, and items with a scent (including toiletries) from your car to the storage box. Canisters for backpackers may be rented for $3 per day in most park stores. Keep an eye peeled for rattlesnakes below 7,000 ft. Though rarely fatal, bites require a doctor's attention. Marmots, small members of the squirrel family, enjoy getting under a vehicle and chewing on radiator hoses and car wiring. Always check under the hood before driving away. Finally, don't drink water directly from streams and lakes, as intestinal disorders may result. Destinet (☞ Contacts and Resources *in* the Sierra National Parks A to Z, *below*) handles reservations.

ROCK CLIMBING

Yosemite Mountaineering (☎ 209/372–8344) conducts beginner through intermediate rock-climbing and backpacking classes. A one-day session includes a hands-on introduction to climbing. Classes are held April to October, weather permitting.

WINTER SPORTS

Badger Pass Ski Area, off Yosemite National Park's Glacier Point Road, has nine downhill runs serviced by one triple and three double chairlifts, and two excellent ski schools. Its gentle slopes make **Yosemite Ski School** (☎ 209/372–1330) an ideal downhill beginners' area.

Yosemite's cross-country skiing center has a groomed and tracked 21-mi loop from Badger Pass to Glacier Point, where, with reservations, you can overnight in a hut and eat prepared meals. Snowshoeing and snow-camping trips are also available. **Yosemite Cross-Country Ski School** (☎ 209/372–8444) is run by Yosemite Mountaineering. Curry Village in Yosemite Valley has an outdoor skating rink open from Thanksgiving to April.

Wawona

25 mi south of Yosemite Valley on Hwy. 41, 16 mi north of Fish Camp on Hwy. 41.

⑪ The historic buildings in **Pioneer Yosemite History Center,** open year-round for viewing, were moved to Wawona from their original sites in the park. A living-history program in summer re-creates Yosemite's past. The program runs from late June to early September, Wednesday through Sunday 9 AM to 1 PM and 2 to 5 PM. Nearby are a post office, a gift shop and a small store, and a service station. ⊠ *On Hwy. 41, Wawona,* ☎ *209/375–6514 (gift shop).* ⊘ *Hrs vary; call ahead.*

⑫ **Mariposa Grove of Big Trees,** a fine grove of naturally fire-resistant *Sequoiadendron giganteum* can be visited on foot or on the one-hour tram rides for $7 in the summer. The grove is open daily 9 to 6. The Grizzly Giant is the oldest tree here; its age is estimated to be 2,700 years. The tree's base diameter is 30.7 ft, its circumference is 96½ ft, and its height is 210 ft. The road to the grove closes when Yosemite is crowded and during the winter; park in Wawona and take the free shuttle, which operates late spring through early fall, 9 to 5. It picks up passengers near the Wawona service station. ⊠ *Off Hwy. 41 near the Fish Camp entrance to Yosemite National Park.*

Dining and Lodging

$–$$ ✕🏨 **Wawona Hotel and Dining Room.** The Wawona Hotel, an 1879 National Historic Landmark, sits at the southern end of Yosemite National Park, near the Mariposa Grove of Big Trees. It's an old-fashioned Victorian estate of whitewashed buildings with wraparound verandas. Most rooms are small but pleasant; half do not have private bath. You can watch deer graze on the meadow while dining in the

Wawona's romantic, candlelit dining room ($–$$$; reservations not accepted), which dates from the late 1800s. The menu emphasizes California ingredients, such as grilled trout coated with corn meal, braised pork chops stuffed with apples and roasted almonds on a bed of wild rice, and rib-eye steak with onions and red potatoes. A traditional Sunday brunch is served from 7:30 to 1:30. ✉ *Hwy. 41, Wawona 95389,* ☎ *209/375–6556 (front desk), 209/375–1425 (dining room). 104 rooms. Restaurant, lounge, outdoor pool, 9-hole golf course, tennis, horseback riding. D, DC, MC, V.*

Hetch Hetchy, Tuolumne, and Mono Lake

⑬ The **Hetch Hetchy Reservoir** is about 40 mi from Yosemite Valley, via Big Oak Flat Road and Highway 120. The reservoir supplies water and power to San Francisco. Some say John Muir died of heartbreak when this beautiful valley was dammed and buried beneath 300 ft of water in 1913.

Tioga Pass Road (Highway 120), open only in summer, is a scenic route ⑭ to **Tuolumne Meadows,** the largest subalpine meadow in the Sierra. It's 55 mi from Yosemite Valley. There are campgrounds, a gas station, a store (with a very limited and expensive choice of provisions), stables, a lodge, and a visitor center that is open from late June until Labor Day from 8 AM to 7:30 PM. This area is the trailhead for many backpack trips into the High Sierra. It will take about that amount of time to get acclimated to the altitude: 8,575 ft.

Highway 120 meets U.S. 395 at the town of Lee Vining. North on U.S. 395 is impressive **Mono Lake,** renowned for its striking "tufa towers"– calcium carbonate formations—and nesting grounds for migratory birds. The tufa's visibility comes "courtesy" of the City of Los Angeles, which since the '40s (and not without great controversy) has been diverting water from streams that feed the lake, lowering its water level and exposing the tufa.

Rangers and naturalists lead tours of Mono Lake's tufa and other wildlife, daily in the summer, weekends only (sometimes on cross-country skis) in winter. The **Mono Basin Visitors Center** (✉ Hwy. 395, Lee Vining, ☎ 760/647–3044) has brochures and information.

OUTSIDE YOSEMITE NATIONAL PARK
Bass Lake, El Portal, Fish Camp, and Oakhurst

Several towns surrounding Yosemite National Park, all within an hour's drive of Yosemite Village, provide additional dining and lodging options.

Bass Lake

18 mi south of Yosemite National Park's South Entrance, Hwy. 41 to Bass Valley Rd.

Dining

$–$$$ ✕ **Ducey's on the Lake.** The lodge-style restaurant at the Ducey's Suites resort attracts boaters, locals, and tourists with lamb, steak, lobster, and pasta dishes. Burgers, sandwiches, and salads are served at the upstairs Bar & Grill. ✉ *54432 Rd. 432, Bass Lake,* ☎ *209/642–3131. Reservations essential for Sun. brunch. D, DC, MC, V.*

Outdoor Activities and Sports

Pines Marina (✉ Bass Lake Reservoir, ☎ 209/642–3565), open April
to October and at other times as the weather permits, rents ski boats,
house- and fishing boats, and Jet Skis.

El Portal

*8 mi west of Yosemite National Park's Arch Rock Entrance on Hwy.
140.*

Dining and Lodging

$$–$$$ 🏨 **Yosemite View Lodge.** The back building at Yosemite View has
rooms with balconies overlooking the bolder-strewn Merced River, majestic pines, and a picnic patio with hot tubs and heated pools. Large
rooms have king-size beds, and most have fireplaces and kitchenettes.
The lodge is on the public bus route to Yosemite National Park and
near fishing and river rafting. The fare at the on-site Parkline restaurant ($–$$) includes burgers, steak, and chicken. ✉ 11136 Hwy. 140,
95318, ☎ 209/379–2681 or 800/321–5261, FAX 209/379–2704. 158
rooms. Restaurant, bar, 2 pools, 3 hot tubs. MC, V.

$$ 🏨 **Cedar Lodge.** The lobby of this complex in the pines is heavy on
plaids and teddy bears. Rooms range from suites with kitchenettes to
family units to more romantic accommodations with spa tubs for two.
The uncomplicated menu at the restaurant ($–$$) includes steaks, burgers, chicken Marsala, and calamari. ✉ 9966 Hwy. 140, 95318, ☎ 209/
379–2612 or 800/321–5261, FAX 209/379–2712. 206 rooms. 2 restaurants, pools, hot tubs, business services. AE, MC, V.

Fish Camp

*37 mi south of Yosemite Valley floor, 4 mi south of Yosemite National
Park's South Entrance on Hwy. 41.*

The small town of Fish Camp has one service station, a post office, a
general store, and the **Yosemite Mountain Sugar Pine Railroad,** a 4-mi
steam-train ride through the forest. A Saturday-evening Moonlight Special excursion includes dinner and old-fashioned entertainment. ✉
56001 Hwy. 41, ☎ 209/683–7273. 🎫 $9.75. ☉ Mar.–Oct., daily; on
limited basis in winter.

Dining and Lodging

$$$ 🏨 **Tenaya Lodge.** One of the region's largest hotels is perfect for peo-
ple who enjoy hiking in the wilderness but prefer coming home to lux-
ury. A southwestern motif prevails in the ample rooms, which are
decorated in mauve, green, and rust. Guests may dine by a cozy fire-
place at the Sierra Restaurant ($–$$), which serves California-style Italian dishes, fish, and steak. ✉ 1122 Hwy. 41, Box 159, 93623, ☎ 209/
683–6555; 800/635–5807 for lodging reservations and restaurant; FAX
209/683–8684. 242 rooms. 2 restaurants, 2 lounges, room service, indoor-outdoor pools, health club, laundry service and dry cleaning, meeting room. AE, D, DC, MC, V.

$$–$$$ 🏨 **Narrow Gauge Inn.** This motel-style property is comfortably furnished,
with old-fashioned decor and railroad memorabilia. The inn's lodge-like
restaurant ($–$$), which serves straightforward California and ranchero-
inspired cuisine, is festooned with moose, bison, and other wildlife trophies. ✉ 48571 Hwy. 41, 93623, ☎ 209/683–7720, FAX 209/683–2139.
26 rooms. Restaurant, bar, pool, hot tub. D, MC, V. Closed Nov.–Feb.

Oakhurst

*50 mi south of Yosemite Valley, 23 mi south of Yosemite National Park's
South Entrance on Hwy. 41.*

Motels and restaurants line both sides of Highway 41 as it cuts through the formerly sleepy town of Oakhurst. A theater in the Oakhurst mall shows current movies, and you can stock up on major provisions at local grocery and general stores.

Dining and Lodging

$$$$ ✕ **Erna's Elderberry House.** The restaurant operated by Vienna-born
★ Erna Kubin, owner of Château du Sureau (☞ *below*), is another expression of her passion for beauty, charm, and impeccable service. White walls and dark beams accent the dining room's high ceilings, and arched windows reflect the glow of many candles. A six-course, prix-fixe dinner in rhythm with the seasons is elegantly paced and accompanied by superb wines. This is a dining experience to remember. Sunday brunch is also served. ⊠ *48688 Victoria La.,* ☎ *209/683–6800. AE, MC, V. Closed 1st 3 wks of Jan. No lunch Sat.–Tues.*

$$$$ 🏨 **Château du Sureau.** This romantic, beautiful inn is a fairy tale. From
★ the moment regal gates magically open and you step out of your car (think mice-driven coach), and a lady in waiting takes your coat and bags, you will not lift a finger. A winding staircase seems to carry you up to your room; you'll fall asleep in the glow of a crackling fire amid goosedown pillows and a comforter that rivals Cloud Nine. Château du Sureau is enveloped in an alluring serenity that greets you when you raise the curtains next morning and breathe in the fragrant gardens and cool air from the mist-shrouded pines. Eat a hearty European breakfast in the dining room downstairs and plan your Sierra stay in the piano room, which has an exquisite ceiling mural. ⊠ *48688 Victoria La., Box 577, 93644,* ☎ *209/683–6860,* FAX *209/683–0800. 9 rooms. Restaurant, outdoor pool. AE, MC, V.*

$$–$$$ 🏨 **Shilo Inn.** Spacious, sunny, pine-furnished rooms here have kitchenettes and wet bars. Popcorn and coffee are at your fingertips 24 hours a day in the lobby. Room rates include a Continental breakfast. ⊠ *40644 Hwy. 41, 93644,* ☎ *209/683–3555,* FAX *209/683–3386. 80 rooms. Pool, hot tub, sauna, steam room, exercise room, coin laundry. AE, D, DC, MC, V.*

KINGS CANYON AND SEQUOIA NATIONAL PARKS

Grant Grove, Cedar Grove, and Lodgepole

General Grant and Sequoia national parks were established in 1890, along with Yosemite. Additions to General Grant National Park over the years included the Redwood Canyon area and the drainages of the south and middle forks of the Kings River. The whole region was eventually renamed Kings Canyon National Park.

The major attractions of the parks are the big trees (*Sequoiadendron giganteum*—the most extensive groves and the most impressive specimens are found here) and the stunning alpine scenery. They are not as tall as the coast redwoods (*Sequoia sempervirens*), but they are older and more massive. The exhibits at the visitor centers explain the special relationship between these trees and fire (their thick, fibrous bark helps protect them from fire and insects) and their ability to live so long and grow so big.

The parks encompass land from only 1,700 ft above sea level to more than 14,000 ft. Mt. Whitney, on the eastern side of Sequoia, is the highest mountain (14,494 ft) in the contiguous United States. Most of both parks is accessible only on foot or with a pack animal. The Gen-

Kings Canyon and Sequoia National Parks

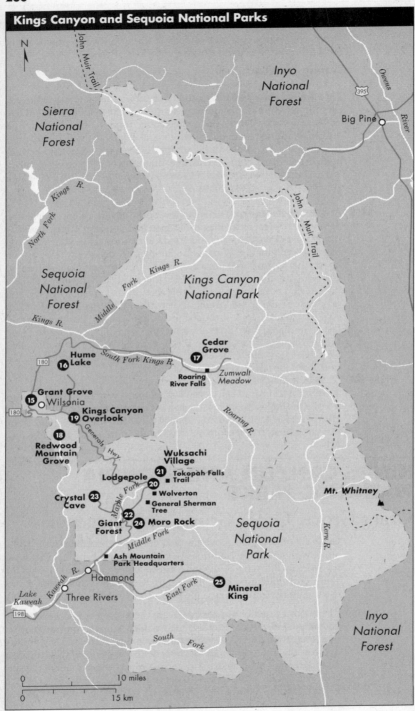

N

Sierra National Forest

Inyo National Forest

John Muir Trail

395

Owens River

Big Pine

Kings R.

North Fork

Sequoia National Forest

Middle Fork Kings R.

Kings R.

Kings Canyon National Park

John Muir Trail

Kings R.

South Fork Kings R.

Cedar Grove

180

Hume Lake 16

17

Roaring River Falls

Zumwalt Meadow

Grant Grove 15
Wilsonia

180

Kings Canyon Overlook 19

Generals Hwy.

Roaring R.

18

Redwood Mountain Grove

Wuksachi Village

Lodgepole 21
20

Tokopah Falls Trail

Marble Fork

Wolverton

Crystal Cave 23

General Sherman Tree

Mt. Whitney

Giant Forest
22
24 **Moro Rock**

Middle Fork

Kaweah R.

Ash Mountain Park Headquarters

Hammond

Three Rivers

Lake Kaweah

198

East Fork

25 **Mineral King**

Sequoia National Park

Kern R.

Inyo National Forest

South Fork

| 0 | 10 miles |
| 0 | 15 km |

erals Highway (46 mi from Highway 180 in Kings Canyon National Park to the Ash Mountain Entrance in Sequoia National Park) links the parks' major groves and is open year-round except during severe weather.

The two parks possess sublime camping areas, though some may lack running water and power hookups. Potwisha, Grant Grove, Lodgepole, Dorst, and Cedar Grove campgrounds are the only areas where trailers and RVs are permitted (and space for them even here is scarce). The length limit for RVs is 40 ft, for trailers 35 ft, but the park service recommends that trailers be no longer than 22 ft. Disposal stations are available in most of the main camping areas. Lodgepole, Potwisha, and Azalea campsites stay open all year, but Lodgepole is not plowed and camping is limited to recreational vehicles in plowed parking lots or snow tenting. Other campgrounds are open from whenever the snow melts until late September or early October. Campers should be aware that the nights, and even the days, can be chilly into June.

Horseback riding is available at Grant Grove, Cedar Grove, Wolverton (between Lodgepole and Giant Forest), and Mineral King. Ask at the visitor centers for the specifics. In the winter there is cross-country skiing and snowshoeing. Networks of marked trails are found at Grant Grove and Giant Forest. Rangers sometimes lead snowshoe walks through Grant Grove and Giant Forest on winter weekends. Check with the visitor center for details.

The entrance fee to Kings Canyon and Sequoia is $10 per vehicle, $5 for those who don't arrive by car.

Grant Grove and Cedar Grove

100 mi southeast of Oakhurst, Hwy. 41 to Hwy. 180.

⑮ **Grant Grove** is the grove (or what remains of a larger grove decimated by logging) that was designated as General Grant National Park in 1890. It is now Kings Canyon's most highly developed area. Like entering a ghost town, a walk along the 1-mi Big Stump Trail, starting near the park entrance, graphically demonstrates the effects of heavy logging on these groves. An alternate ⅓-mi trail is fairly accessible to travelers with disabilities. The most famous tree in this area is the approximately 2,000-year-old General Grant. The Gamlin Cabin is a pioneer cabin. The Centennial Stump, the remains of a large sequoia cut for display at the 1876 Philadelphia Centennial Exhibition, can also be viewed here. ⊠ *Kings Canyon Hwy. (Hwy. 180), 1 mi from Big Stump Entrance.*

Grant Grove Village has a visitor center, a gas station, a grocery store, campgrounds, a coffee shop, overnight lodging, trail maps, and horse rentals. The visitor center has exhibits on the *Sequoiadendron giganteum* and the area. ⊠ *Kings Canyon Hwy.*

⑯ **Hume Lake,** a reservoir built early this century by loggers, is now the site of many Christian camps and a public campground. This small lake, just outside Kings Canyon's borders, has views of high mountains in the distance. ⊠ *Hwy. 180 northeast 8 mi from Grant Grove, off Hume Lake Rd. (also accessible off side road from Generals Hwy.).*

★ ⑰ The **Cedar Grove** area is a valley that snakes along the south fork of the Kings River. A spectacular drive along Kings Canyon Highway takes one hour from Grant Grove to the end of the road, where you can hike, camp, or turn right around for the ride back. Built by convict labor in the 1930s, the road (usually closed November through April) clings to some dramatic cliffs along the way: Watch out for falling rocks. The highway passes the scars where large groves of big trees were logged at the beginning of the century. It runs along the south fork and through dry foothills covered with yuccas that bloom in the summer. There are amazing views into the deepest gorge in the United States, at the confluence of the two forks, and up the canyons to the High Sierra.

Cedar Grove was named for the incense cedars that grow in the area. Horses can be rented here, a good way to continue your explorations; there are also campgrounds, lodgings, a small ranger station, a snack bar, a convenience market, and a gas station. Short trails circle Zumwalt Meadow and lead to the base of Roaring River Falls; Cedar Grove is the trailhead for many backpackers.

Dining and Lodging

$ ✗⌷ **Cedar Grove Lodge.** Although accommodations are close to the road and there is quite a bit of traffic through here, Cedar Grove manages to retain a quiet atmosphere. Book way in advance—the motel-lodge has only 18 rooms. Each room is air-conditioned and carpeted and has a private shower and two queen-size beds. A self-serve restaurant has top sirloin, hamburgers, hot dogs, and sandwiches for lunch and dinner. Breakfast is eggs, bacon, and toast. You can take food from the restaurant to picnic tables along the river's edge. ☏ *209/335–5500. AE, MC, V. Closed mid-Oct.–mid-May.*

$ ✗⌷ **Grant Grove Village.** The nicest accommodations here are the carpeted cabins with private baths, electric wall heaters, and double beds. Simpler cabins, heated by woodstoves and lit by kerosene lamps, are near a central rest room and shower facility. A family-style coffee shop serves American standards for breakfast, lunch, and dinner: eggs, burgers, and steak. There are also chef's salads, fruit platters, and seasonal fish specials. A 30-room, somewhat more upscale hotel is scheduled to be up and running in Grant Grove by summer 1998. ☏ *209/335–2354 or 209/335–5500. AE, MC, V.*

Outdoor Activities and Sports

WINTER SPORTS

Rentals (including snowshoes), lessons, and tours are offered at Grant Gove and at Wolverton (☏ 209/565–5500).

YEAR-ROUND SPORTS

Montecito-Sequoia Lodge provides year-round family-oriented recreation. Depending on the season, lodging rates include all meals or just breakfast and dinner. Winter activities include cross-country skiing and lessons. Among the summer activities offered in a six-night Club Med–like package are canoeing, sailing, and waterskiing on the resort's private lake, horseback riding, a preschool program, volleyball, horseshoes, tennis, archery, and nature hikes. In spring and fall, some of the summer activities occur, but guests are able to book shorter stays. ⌂ *Generals Hwy., 11 mi south of Grant Grove, ☏ 800/227–9900 for brochures and information.*

Along the Generals Highway

The **Generals Highway** begins south of Grant Grove, continuing through the lower portion of Kings Canyon National Park and through a grand section of the Sequoia National Forest before entering Sequoia National Park.

★ ⑱ The **Redwood Mountain Grove** is the largest grove of big trees in the world. As you exit Kings Canyon on the Generals Highway, there are several paved turnouts from which you can look out over the grove (and into the smog of the Central Valley). The grove itself is accessible only on foot or horseback.

⑲ **Kings Canyon Overlook,** a large turnout on the north side of the Generals Highway less than 2 mi from Redwood Mountain Grove, has views across the canyon of mountain peaks and the backcountry. If you drive east on Highway 180 to Cedar Grove along the south fork, you will see these canyons at much closer range.

Lodgepole

⑳ *26 mi south of Grant Grove on the Generals Hwy.*

Lodgepole sits in a canyon on the Marble Fork of the Kaweah River. Lodgepole pines, rather than sequoias, grow here because the U-shape canyon conducts air down from the high country that is too cold for the big trees but is just right for lodgepoles. This developed area has a campground, a gas station, a store, a public laundry, a gift shop, and a post office. An ice cream parlor and public showers are open in the summer only. ☎ 209/335–5500; 800/365–2267 *for campground reservations.*

★ ☙ The **Lodgepole Visitor Center** has the best exhibits in Sequoia or Kings Canyon, a small theater that shows films about the parks, and the Walter Fry Nature Center (open July through Labor Day), which has hands-on exhibits and activities that are geared toward children. You can buy tickets for the Crystal Cave (☞ *below*) at the visitor center. A very short marked nature trail leads from behind the visitor center down to the river. Except when the river is flowing fast, this is a good place to rinse one's feet in cool water, because the trail runs past a "beach" of small rocks along the river. ☎ 209/565–3782. ☼ *Hrs vary; call ahead.*

The **Tokopah Falls Trail** is an easy and rewarding 2-mi hike up the river from the Lodgepole Campground. It is the closest you can get to the high country without taking a long hike. Trail maps are available at the Lodgepole Visitor Center. Remember to bring insect repellent during the summer, when the mosquitoes can be ferocious.

㉑ The current park concessionaire has tentative plans to develop **Wuksachi Village** to replace the dining, lodging, and other facilities that have been housed for years in Giant Forest Village. At press time (summer 1997) precise plans for Wuksachi had not been finalized. Call the park service (☎ 209/335–5500) for an update.

Giant Forest

㉒ *4 mi south of Lodgepole on the Generals Hwy.*

The Giant Forest is known for its numerous and varied trails through a series of sequoia groves. Well-constructed paths range in length from ⅓ mi to as far as one cares to walk. They are not paved, crowded, or lined with barricades, so one quickly gets the feeling of being alone in the woods, surrounded by rows of impressive trees.

Be sure to visit one of the meadows here. You can get the best views of the big trees from them, and in July the flowers are in full bloom. Round Meadow is the most easily accessible, with its ⅓-mi, wheelchair-accessible "Trail for All People." Crescent and Log meadows are accessible but slightly longer trails than Round Meadow. Tharp's Log, at Log Meadow, is a pioneer cabin built in a fallen sequoia. There is also a log cabin near Huckleberry Meadow that children will enjoy exploring.

The most famous tree in the area is the **General Sherman Tree,** off the Generals Highway between Giant Forest and Lodgepole. In summer there is usually a ranger nearby to answer questions, and there are benches so you can sit and contemplate the tree's immensity: It is 274.9 ft tall and 102.6 ft around at its base, but what's also extraordinary is that it is so wide for such a long way up—the first major branch is 130 ft above the ground.

The Congress Trail starts at the General Sherman Tree and travels past a series of large trees and younger sequoias. This is probably the most popular hike in the area, and it also has the most detailed booklet, so it is a good way to learn about the ecology of the groves. The booklet costs $1 and is available in summer at information stands near the General Sherman Tree.

The 2½-mi Crescent Meadow Moro Rock Road takes off from the Generals Highway and leads to other points of interest in the Giant Forest area as well as to the trails to Crescent and Log meadows. The road actually goes through the Tunnel Log (there is a bypass for RVs that are too tall—7 ft, 9 inches and more—to fit). Auto Log is a fallen tree onto which you can drive your car for a photograph.

★ ㉓ **Crystal Cave** is the best known of Sequoia's many caves. Its interior was formed from limestone that metamorphosed into marble and is decorated with stalactites and stalagmites. To visit the cave, you must first stop at the Lodgepole Visitor Center (☞ *above*) or the Foothills Visitor Center at Ash Mountain (on the Generals Highway, 1 mi inside Sequoia National Park) to buy a ticket—they're not sold at the cave. With ticket in hand, drive to the end of a narrow, twisting, 7-mi road off the Generals Highway, 2.2 mi south of Giant Forest Village. From the parking area it is a 15-minute hike down a steep path to the cave's entrance. There are 45-minute guided tours daily on the half hour between 10 AM and 3 PM from mid-June through Labor Day and hourly Friday through Monday from mid-May to mid-June and after Labor Day through September. ☎ *209/565–3759.* ⬛ *$4.*

★ ㉔ **Moro Rock,** a granite monolith 6,725 ft high, rises from the edge of the Giant Forest. During the Depression, the Civilian Conservation Corps built a staircase to the top. There are 400 steps, and the trail often climbs along narrow ledges over steep drops. The view from the top is striking. To the southwest you look down the Kaweah River to Three Rivers, Lake Kaweah, and—on clear days—the Central Valley and the Coast Range. To the northeast you look up into the High Sierra. Below, you look thousands of feet to the middle fork of the Kaweah River.

Mineral King

㉕ *52 mi south of Lodgepole, on the Generals Hwy. and Mineral King Rd.*

The Mineral King area was incorporated into Sequoia National Park in 1978 after residents and conservationists in the 1960s derailed plans for a winter-sports resort. It is accessible in summer only by a narrow, twisting, and steep road (trailers and RVs not recommended) off Highway 198 several miles outside the park entrance. This is a tough but exciting 25-mi drive (budget 90 minutes each way) to a beautiful alpine valley. There are two campgrounds and a ranger station here; facilities are very limited, but some supplies are available. Many backpackers use this as a trailhead; fine day-hiking trails lead from here as well.

THE SIERRA NATIONAL PARKS A TO Z

Yosemite National Park

Arriving and Departing

BY BUS

Yosemite VIA (⊠ 710 W. 16th St., Merced, ☎ 800/369–7275) runs three daily buses from Merced to Yosemite Valley. There are Greyhound (☎ 800/231–2222) and Amtrak (☎ 800/872–7245) connections with Yosemite VIA in Merced. The 2½-hour trip costs $38 per person, round-trip, which includes admission to the park.

BY CAR

Yosemite is a four- to five-hour drive from San Francisco (take I–80 to I–580 to I–205 to Highway 120) and a six-hour drive from Los Angeles (take I–5 north to Highway 99 to Fresno, and Highway 41 north to Yosemite). Highways 41, 120, and 140 all intersect with Highway 99, which runs north–south through the Central Valley.

Via Highway 41: If you're coming from the south, Highway 41, which passes through Fresno, is the most direct path to Yosemite. Highway 41 (called Wawona Road inside the park) provides the most dramatic entrance, via the Wawona Tunnel, into Yosemite Valley. One hundred and five miles from Fresno (or 60 from Madera on Highway 145 to Highway 41), Highway 41 leaves the San Joaquin Valley floor to climb through oak-studded hills before descending to the town of Oakhurst, the southern terminus of Highway 49, which links the Gold Country towns for 300-plus mi to the north. Highway 41 continues to the north past the Bass Lake turnoff into Fish Camp and on through the park's South Entrance.

Via Highway 140: Arch Rock Entrance is 75 mi northeast of Merced via Highway 140, the least mountainous road.

Via Highway 120: Highway 120 is the northernmost route—the one that travels farthest and slowest through the foothills. You'll arrive at the park's Big Oak Flat Entrance, 88 mi east of Manteca. If you are coming from the east, you could cross the Sierra from Lee Vining on Highway 120 (Tioga Pass). This route takes you over the Sierra crest and past Tuolumne Meadows. It's scenic, but the mountain driving may be stressful for some, and it's open only in the summer.

BY PLANE

Fresno Air Terminal (⊠ 5175 Clinton Way, ☎ 209/498–4095) is the nearest major airport. It is served by Delta, American, United Express, US Airways, and several regional carriers. United Express also serves Merced Airport (⊠ 20 Macready Dr., ☎ 209/385–6873). *See* Air Travel *in* the Gold Guide for airline phone numbers.

Getting Around

BY BUS

Thanks to the free shuttle bus that runs around the eastern end of Yosemite Valley (7:30 AM to 10 PM in the summer and early fall, 10 AM to 10 PM the rest of the year), it is possible to tour the area without a car. From 9 to 5 in the summer, a free shuttle runs from Wawona to the Mariposa Grove of Big Trees. Bus tours (☞ Guided Tours, *below*) are another option.

BY CAR

Auto traffic in Yosemite National Park is sometimes restricted during peak periods. Check conditions before driving in. Large RVs and trailers are not allowed on some roads. You should have tire chains when you drive in these mountains from November through April; the eastern entrance to the park at Tioga Pass is at nearly 10,000 ft.

BY FOOT

If you are hiking up any of the steep trails, remember to stay on the trail. Also consider the effect of the altitude on your endurance. Talk to the rangers at the visitor centers about which trails they recommend to get you acclimated to the altitude before you can exert yourself fully. If you plan to backpack overnight, you'll need a wilderness permit (free), available at visitor centers or ranger stations.

Contacts and Resources

EMERGENCIES

Ambulance (☎ 911). **Fire** (☎ 911). **Police** (☎ 911).

GUIDED TOURS

California Parlor Car Tours (✉ Cathedral Hill Hotel, 1101 Van Ness Ave., San Francisco 94109, ☎ 415/474–7500 or 800/227–4250) runs several California tours that include Yosemite. Lodging and some meals are included; you can choose to stay in either Yosemite Lodge or the Ahwahnee (there's a difference in price, of course).

Yosemite Concession Services (☎ 209/252–4848 for reservations) conducts daily guided bus tours of Glacier Point, the Yosemite Valley floor, and the Mariposa Grove of Big Trees. The Grand Tour, which costs about $42, covers the park highlights. Reservations can also be made for trips on horseback. Fees run from $45 for a one-way Glacier Point excursion to $67 for a full-day horseback ride.

RESERVATIONS

Camping: Destinet (✉ 9450 Carroll Park Dr., San Diego 92121, ☎ 619/452–8787; 800/436–7275 in the U.S.; TDD 800/274–7275).

Lodging: Yosemite Concession Services Corporation (✉ Central Reservations, 5410 E. Home, Fresno 93727, ☎ 209/252–4848).

ROAD CONDITIONS

Yosemite Area Road and Weather Conditions (☎ 209/372–0200).

VISITOR INFORMATION

Southern Yosemite Visitors Bureau (✉ 49074 Civic Circle, Oakhurst 93644, ☎ 209/683–4636). **Yosemite National Park** (✉ National Park Service, Information Office, Box 577, Yosemite National Park 95389, ☎ 209/372–0200 for 24-hr information or 209/372–0264).

Kings Canyon and Sequoia National Parks

Arriving and Departing

BY BUS

Greyhound (☎ 800/231–2222) serves Fresno and Visalia. **Amtrak** (☎ 800/872–7245) serves Fresno.

BY CAR

Under average conditions, it takes about six hours to reach Kings Canyon and Sequoia national parks from San Francisco and about five hours to do so from Los Angeles. Two major routes, Highways 180 and 198, intersect with Highway 99, which runs north–south through the Central Valley.

From the north, enter Kings Canyon National Park via Highway 180, 53 mi east of Fresno. From the south, enter Sequoia National Park via Highway 198, 36 mi from Visalia. If you are coming from Los Angeles, take Highway 65 north from Bakersfield to Highway 198 east of Visalia.

Fresno Air Terminal (⊠ 5175 Clinton Way, ☎ 209/498–4095) is the nearest major airport to Kings Canyon and Sequoia national parks. *See* Arriving and Departing *in* Yosemite National Park *in* the Sierra National Parks A to Z, *above,* for more information.

Getting Around

BY BUS

Sequoia–Kings Canyon Park Services Company (☎ 209/335–5500) runs a shuttle bus between major points in the Giant Forest and Lodgepole. All-day passes are available, or you can pay by the ride.

BY CAR

Most people take Highway 180 to Kings Canyon–Sequoia, coming into Kings Canyon National Park at the Big Stump Entrance. Highways 180 and 198 are connected through the parks by the Generals Highway, a paved two-lane road that is open year-round, though portions between Lodgepole and Grant Grove may be closed for weeks at a time during heavy snowstorms (carry chains in winter). Drivers of RVs and drivers who are not comfortable on mountain roads should probably avoid the southern stretch between the Potwisha Campground and Giant Forest Village. These very twisty 16 mi of narrow road rise almost 5,000 ft and are not advised for vehicles over 22 ft long. The rest of the Generals Highway is a well-graded two-lane road and a pleasure to drive.

Highway 180 (called Kings Canyon Highway inside the park) beyond Grant Grove to Cedar Grove is open only in summer, as is the road to Mineral King. Both roads may present a challenge to inexperienced drivers. Large vehicles are discouraged. Campers and RVs are not advised on the Mineral King road. Trailers are not allowed in Mineral King campgrounds.

Contacts and Resources

EMERGENCIES
Ambulance (☎ 911). **Fire** (☎ 911). **Police** (☎ 911).

GUIDED TOURS
Sequoia–Kings Canyon Park Services Company (☎ 209/335–5500) conducts an all-day van tour of Kings Canyon mid-May through mid-October. The fare is $22.

RESERVATIONS
Camping: Destinet (⊠ 9450 Carroll Park Dr., San Diego 92121, ☎ 619/452–8787; 800/436–7275 in the U.S.; TDD 800/274–7275).

Lodging: Sequoia–Kings Canyon Park Services Company (☎ 209/335–5500, FAX 209/335–5502).

ROAD CONDITIONS
Sequoia–Kings Canyon Road and Weather Information (☎ 209/565–3351).

Northern California Road Conditions (☎ 800/427–7623).

VISITOR INFORMATION
National Park Service (⊠ Fort Mason, Bldg. 201, San Francisco 94123, ☎ 415/556–0560). **Sequoia and Kings Canyon National Parks** (⊠ Three Rivers 93271, ☎ 209/565–3134).

9 The San Joaquin Valley

From Stockton to Bakersfield

The San Joaquin Valley, one of the world's most fertile agricultural zones, is California's heartland. This sunbaked region contains a wealth of rivers, lakes, and waterways; the water, in turn, nurtures vineyards, dairy farms, orchards, fields, and pastures that stretch to the horizon. And while you're never far from cities, mountains, or national parks here, you'll find that the area possesses attractions of its own, beginning with the warmth of its land and people.

By Clark
Norton

UNTIL THE MID-19TH CENTURY, the San Joaquin Valley was a phenomenon waiting to happen. Millions of acres of flat, often parched land lay in wait for workers and water. When settlers and irrigation techniques did arrive, the region was transformed into a miracle of cultivation. Gold discoveries, starting in the 1850s, sparked the birth of some towns; the coming of the railroads in the next few decades spurred the development of others. Over the last century and a half, the Valley's open lands and untapped resources have attracted a polyglot of pioneers, adventurers, farmers, ranchers, developers, railroad tycoons, gold prospectors, oil riggers, dairymen, sheepherders, and war refugees—including immigrants from places as diverse as Oklahoma and Portugal, China and Mexico, Armenia and Laos, many of whom have laid the rails and picked the crops.

The mix has produced sometimes volatile labor relations—most prominently in Cesar Chavez's United Farm Workers Union's controversial grape boycotts of the 1960s and '70s—and social strife: early battles between railroad men and farmers, long-standing discrimination against Chinese and other Asians. But the region's diversity has also created a vibrant social fabric—often celebrated at the Valley's many cultural festivals and chronicled by some of the country's finest writers. Fresno native and Pulitzer Prize winner William Saroyan, Stockton native Maxine Hong Kingston, 19th-century novelist Frank Norris, and *Grapes of Wrath* author John Steinbeck have all contributed to the Valley's literary heritage.

Though the Valley's agricultural riches remain, potential changes whirl like dust devils in the fields. Prime farmland is being plowed under to make room for new housing. Modesto, Fresno, and Bakersfield are among the fastest growing cities in the country, as big-city "refugees" flee in search of cheaper real estate and more space. With development has come unsightly sprawl, traffic jams, air pollution, and pressure on crucial water supplies, all of which threatens to overwhelm the Valley's traditional charms.

For most travelers the San Joaquin Valley is primarily a place to pass through en route to Yosemite, Sequoia, and Kings Canyon national parks or while driving between San Francisco and Los Angeles. But if you spend a few hours or days here, you'll discover historic mansions, abundant outdoor recreation, and friendly people proud to show off their local treasures.

Pleasures and Pastimes

Dining
Fast-food places and chain restaurants dominate Valley highways and major intersections, but off the main drag the possibilities increase. Armenian, Basque, and Vietnamese restaurants—along with more common Mexican, Chinese, and Italian eateries—reflect the Valley's ethnic mix. A few cutting-edge bistros serve the type of California cuisine found in San Francisco and Los Angeles. And why not? The Valley produces many of those ingredients.

CATEGORY	COST*
$$$$	over $50
$$$	$30–$50
$$	$20–$30
$	under $20

*per person for a three-course meal, excluding drinks, service, and 7¼% tax

Festivals, Tours, and Tastings

Anyone who likes to eat can enjoy an agricultural "theme" trip through the San Joaquin Valley. Apple ranches and almond, cheese, and chocolate factories are among the many options. Also, watch for seasonal farmers' markets; some towns block off entire streets and turn the weekly markets into minifestivals. Official Valley festivals celebrate everything from the asparagus and raisin crops to residents' Chinese, Greek, Swedish, and Tahitian roots. If you know you'll be visiting a particular town, especially in the fall, call the local chamber of commerce (☞ Visitor Information *in* the San Joaquin Valley A to Z, *below*) for festival information.

Lodging

Chain motels and hotels are the norm in the San Joaquin Valley. Most are utilitarian but perfectly clean and comfortable, and prices tend to be considerably lower than in more popular tourist destinations. A few Victorian-style bed-and-breakfasts, some of them great values, are also available.

CATEGORY	COST*
$$$$	over $175
$$$	$120–$175
$$	$80–$120
$	under $80

All prices are for a standard double room, excluding 8% tax.

Outdoor Activities and Sports

Several cities and towns serve as convenient starting-off points for whitewater rafting trips on the Stanislaus, Merced, Kings, and Kern rivers. Fishing is another favored activity in the rivers and lakes; the lakes are also prime spots for boating and windsurfing. Stockton is a popular rental area for houseboating on the Sacramento Delta, and Bakersfield is a center for stock-car racing. Wildlife refuges provide opportunities for bird- and animal-watching.

Exploring the San Joaquin Valley

The 225-mi San Joaquin Valley cuts through San Joaquin, Stanislaus, Merced, Madera, Fresno, Kings, Tulare, and Kern counties, and is bounded by the mighty Sierra Nevada to the east and the smaller coastal ranges to the west. Besides the San Joaquin, other major rivers include the Stanislaus, Tuolomne, Fresno, and Kern; an elaborate system of sloughs and canals also provides water to the countryside. Interstate 5 runs north–south through the Valley, as does California state Highway 99.

Numbers in the text correspond to numbers in the margin and on the San Joaquin Valley and Fresno Area maps.

Great Itineraries

IF YOU HAVE 1 DAY

Touring the Fresno area is a good strategy for those with only one day to explore the Valley. The **Chaffee Zoological Gardens** in **Roeding Park** ⑦ contain a striking tropical rainforest. If you have kids in tow, proceed to nearby **Playland** and **Storyland.** The **Forestiere Underground Gardens** ⑥ on Shaw Avenue is not to be missed if it's open. In springtime take the self-guided **Blossom Trail** driving tour through orchards, vineyards, and fields. Along the trail in **Reedley** is the **Mennonite Quilt Center.** Depending on your mood and the weather, you can spend part of the afternoon at **Wild Water Adventures** or visit the **Fresno Metropolitan Museum,** whose highlights include an exhibit on author William Saroyan.

The San Joaquin Valley

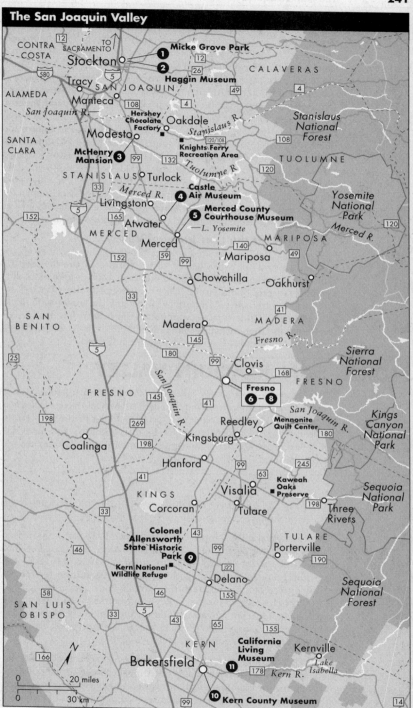

IF YOU HAVE 3 DAYS

On your first morning, visit the ⛫ **Stockton** area. Start at the **Micke Grove Park** ①, 10 mi north of the city off Highway 99. The **Haggin Museum** ② in Stockton's Victory Park is one of the Valley's top art museums, and the **World Wildlife Museum** contains remarkable mounted-animal displays. The next morning, stop off at the **Castle Air Museum** ④ just north of Merced in Atwater or proceed directly to ⛫ **Fresno** ⑥–⑧. In the evening, take in a show at **Roger Rocka's** or the **Tower Theatre**, both in Fresno's Tower District. On the third morning, drive to **Hanford** via Highways 99 and 43 and stroll around **Courthouse Square** and **China Alley**. After lunch, continue south on Highway 43 to **Colonel Allensworth State Historic Park** ⑨, which is on the site of a now deserted town founded by African Americans in 1908. Continue south on Highway 43 and east on Highway 46 to return to Highway 99, which continues south to ⛫ **Bakersfield.** If you arrive before it closes, stop in for a quick visit to the **Kern County Museum** ⑩. Have dinner and take in the country-western music at **Buck Owens' Crystal Palace.**

When to Visit the San Joaquin Valley

Spring, when wildflowers are in bloom and the scent of fruit blossoms is in the air, and fall, when leaves turn red and gold, are the prettiest times of year to visit. Many of the Valley's top festivals take place during these seasons. Summertime, when temperatures often top 100 degrees, can be oppressive. Wintertime can get cold and raw—with thick, ground-hugging tule fog a common driving hazard—and some attractions close. But during December a number of the Valley's historic homes and museums get gussied up for the holidays.

NORTH SAN JOAQUIN VALLEY

The northern section of the Valley cuts through San Joaquin, Stanislaus, and Merced counties, from the edges of the Sacramento Delta and the fringes of the Gold Country to the flat, almost featureless terrain between Modesto and Merced. If you're heading to Yosemite National Park from northern California, chances are you'll pass through (or very near) at least one of these gateway cities.

Stockton

80 mi from San Francisco; east on I–80 to I–580 to I–205, north on I–5; 45 mi south of Sacramento on I–5 or Hwy. 99.

California's first inland port—connected since 1933 to San Francisco via a 60-mi-long deepwater channel—is wedged between I–5 and Highway 99, on the eastern end of the great Sacramento River Delta. Stockton, founded during the gold rush as a way station for miners traveling from San Francisco to the Mother Lode and now a city of 228,000, helps distribute the Valley's agricultural products to the world. Its best-known natives include author Maxine Hong Kingston and rock singer Chris Isaak. If you're here in late April, don't miss the **Stockton Asparagus Festival** (☎ 209/943–1987).

About 10 mi north of town (halfway between Stockton and Lodi), oak-shaded **Micke Grove Park** contains the compact **Micke Grove Zoo.** The zoo's noteworthy Island Lost in Time displays endangered primates found only on the African island of Madagascar. Paseo Pantera is a showcase for mountain lions. The **San Joaquin County Historical Museum,** the state's only accredited agricultural museum, is another of the park's big draws. Other attractions include **Funderwoods,** a family amusement park with rides geared to ages 2 to 10, and a **Japanese garden.** ✉ *11793 N. Micke Grove Rd., Lodi; take Eight Mile Rd. off Hwy.*

99, 8 mi north of Stockton, then ½ mi west to Micke Grove Rd., ☎
209/331–7400; 209/331–7270 zoo; 209/331–2055 museum; 209/
369–5437 Funderwoods. ☒ *Park entry fee $2 weekdays, $4 week-*
ends and holidays. Zoo: $1.50. Museum: $2. ☉ *Park: daily 8 AM–dusk.*
Zoo: May–Aug., Mon.–Fri. 10–5, Sat.–Sun. 10–7; Sept.–Apr., daily
10–5. Museum: Wed.–Sun., 1–4:45 PM. Funderwoods: schedule varies.

★ ❷ The **Haggin Museum** in pretty Victory Park has one of the San Joaquin
Valley's finest art collections. Late-19th-century American and French
paintings—Bierstadt and Moran landscapes, a Gauguin still life—are
among the highlights, supplemented by small antiquities collections (including an Egyptian mummy). You can bone up on local history here,
too. ☒ *1201 N. Pershing Ave.,* ☎ *209/462–4116.* ☒ *Free; suggested
donation $2.* ☉ *Tues.–Sun. 1:30–5.*

☾ The **World Wildlife Museum,** which claims to have the largest collection of mounted zoological specimens—more than 2,000—is aimed primarily at school groups but is open to the public. Two cavernous rooms
are a testament to taxidermy: Displays include Alaska Yukon moose,
Indian black bears, Russian wild boars, African bongos, and South American jaguars. At the impressive Sheep Mountain Bighorns, you'll find
ibexes, mountain goats, and rare argalis and golden takins. ☒ *1245 W.
Weber Ave.,* ☎ *209/465–2834.* ☒ *$4.* ☉ *Wed.–Sun. 9–5.*

Dining and Lodging

$$$ ✕ **Le Bistro.** The dishes at one of the Valley's most upscale restaurants
are fairly standard Continental fare—lamb loin, filet of sole, sautéed
prawns, soufflé Grand Marnier—but you can count on high-quality
ingredients and presentation with a flourish. ☒ *Marina Center Mall,
3121 W. Benjamin Holt Dr. (off I–5; behind Lyon's),* ☎ *209/951–0885.
AE, D, MC, V.*

$ ✕ **On Lock Sam.** Run by the same family since 1898, this Stockton land-
mark is now in a modern pagoda-style building, with framed Chinese
prints on the walls, a garden outside one window, and a sparkling bar
area in front of the entrance. One touch of old-time Chinatown remains:
A few booths have curtains that can be drawn for complete privacy.
The Cantonese food would be ho-hum in San Francisco, but it's among
the Valley's best. ☒ *333 S. Sutter St.,* ☎ *209/466–4561. AE, MC, V.*

$ ▦ **Best Western Stockton Inn.** Four mi from downtown, this good-size
motel has a convenient location just off Highway 99. A big plus here
on hot days is the large central courtyard with a pool and lounge chairs.
Most rooms are also spacious; free in-room movies are provided by
satellite. The attached Sutter Street Bar & Grill is open for three meals
a day. ☒ *4219 Waterloo Rd., 95215,* ☎ *209/931–3131.* FAX *209/931–
0423. 141 rooms. Restaurant, bar, no-smoking rooms, pool, wading
pool, hot tub, laundry service, meeting rooms. AE, D, DC, MC, V.*

$ ▦ **City Center Days Inn.** If you want to stay near Stockton's waterfront,
this is a good budget choice—double rooms usually fall below $50.
Rooms are decent size, the rates include free HBO movies and Conti-
nental breakfast, and the waffle house next door is open for breakfast
and lunch. The motel is at a busy intersection; the smallish outdoor
pool area can get noisy. ☒ *33 N. Center St., 95202,* ☎ *209/948–6151.*
FAX *209/948–1220. 95 rooms. No-smoking rooms, pool, meeting
rooms. AE, D, DC, MC, V.*

Outdoor Activities and Sports

Several companies rent houseboats (usually for three, four, or seven days
in a variety of sizes) on the Delta waterways near Stockton, among them
Paradise Point Marina (☒ 8095 Rio Blanco Rd., ☎ 209/952–1000),
King Island Resort (☒ 11530 W. Eight Mile Rd., ☎ 209/951–2188),

and **Herman & Helen's** (✉ Venice Island Ferry, ☎ 209/951–4634). Or call the **Delta Rental Houseboat Hotline** (☎ 209/477–1840).

En Route Manteca, population 45,000, is the largest town between Stockton and Modesto. The top attraction is the **Manteca Waterslides at Oakwood Lake** (✉ 874 E. Woodward Ave., between I–5 and Hwy. 99, ☎ 209/ 239–2500). The park has a children's area, and the attached resort has a lake, a campground, and picnic grounds. The water park is open May to September (daily Memorial Day to Labor Day, weekends the rest of May and September); call for hours. The campground is open all year.

Modesto

29 mi south of Stockton on Hwy. 99.

Modesto, a gateway to Yosemite and the southern reaches of the Gold Country, was founded in 1870 to serve the Central Pacific Railroad. The frontier town was originally named Ralston, after a railroad baron, but as the story goes he modestly declined—thus "Modesto." Today, the Stanislaus County seat is a tree-lined city of 190,000. The town is perhaps best known as the site of the annual Modesto Invitational Track Meet and Relays and birthplace of film producer-director George Lucas, creator of *Star Wars* and *American Graffiti*. (Cruise 10th Street between G and K streets to relive the *Graffiti* days.) The city's most famous landmark, the **Modesto Arch** (✉ 9th and I Sts.), bears its motto: "Water, Wealth, Contentment, Health."

Modesto holds a well-attended **International Festival** (☎ 209/521–3852) in early October that celebrates the cultures, crafts, and cuisines of many nationalities. The **Blue Diamond Growers Store** (✉ 4800 Sisk Rd., Salidas, ☎ 209/545–3222) shows a film about almond-growing and sells nuts in many flavors.

★ ❸ Modesto's 1883 **McHenry Mansion,** built by a pioneer wheat farmer-banker, is the city's sole surviving original Victorian home. The Italianate-style mansion has been lovingly restored and redecorated to reflect Modesto life in the late 19th century. Docents lead half-hour guided tours except during December, when the mansion is decked out in holiday finery. The grounds are shaded by oaks, elms, magnolias, redwoods, and palms. ✉ *15th and I Sts.,* ☎ *209/577–5341.* 🎟 *Free.* ☉ *Tues.– Thurs. and Sun. 1–4, Fri. noon–3.*

The **McHenry Museum** is a jumbled repository of early Modesto and Stanislaus County memorabilia, including re-creations of an old-time barber shop, a kitchen, a schoolroom, a doctor's office, a blacksmith's shop, and a general store—the latter stocked with goods from hair crimpers to corsets. ✉ *1402 I St.,* ☎ *209/577–5366.* 🎟 *Free.* ☉ *Tues.–Sun. noon–4.*

Dining and Lodging

$$ ✕ **Early Dawn Cattlemen's Steakhouse and Saloon.** The parking lots overflow at this popular local hangout, and so do the plates bearing barbecued steaks that run up to two pounds and more. The whiskey-marinated saloon steak is a house specialty; chicken and seafood are lighter choices. ✉ *1000 Kansas Ave.,* ☎ *209/577–5833. AE, D, MC, V. No lunch Sat.*

$–$$ ✕ **Modesto Stanislaus Firehouse Pub & Grille.** Just down the block from the McHenry Mansion, this casual restaurant serves up good soups, sandwiches, and salads, along with more hearty fare like baby back ribs and beef kebabs. Gutsy starters—garlic fries, buffalo wings, onion rings—make good pub food (the bar serves 117 different beers). ✉ *924 15th St.,* ☎ *209/575–3473. AE, MC, V. Closed Sun.*

$$–$$$ ⊠ **Doubletree Hotel.** Modesto's largest lodging towers 15 stories over downtown; the Modesto Convention Center is adjacent, and a good brew pub, St. Stan's, is across the street. The rooms have coffeemakers, irons, desks, and three phones. ⊠ *1150 9th St., 95354,* ☎ *209/526–6000,* FAX *209/526–6096. 258 rooms. Restaurant, café, bar, no-smoking rooms, room service, pool, hot tub, sauna, exercise room, nightclub, laundry service, meeting rooms, airport shuttle. AE, D, DC, MC, V.*

$$ ⊡ **Best Western Mallard's Inn.** The duck decor is, thankfully, unobtrusive at this nicely landscaped motel just off Highway 99. The comfortably furnished rooms are large and all have coffeemakers; some rooms have microwaves and refrigerators stocked with milk and cookies. Mallard's Grill, off the lobby, serves breakfast and dinner daily. ⊠ *1720 Sisk Rd., 95350,* ☎ *209/577–3825 or 800/294–4040,* FAX *209/577–1717. 126 rooms and suites. Restaurant, no-smoking rooms, room service, pool, hot tub, laundry service, business services, meeting rooms. AE, D, DC, MC, V.*

Oakdale

15 mi east of Modesto on Hwy. 108.

Oakdale, a bit off the beaten path from Modesto, has two year-round attractions of great interest to children. And if you're here in mid-May, check out the **Oakdale Chocolate Festival** (☎ 209/847–2244).

☺ The only **Hershey Chocolate Factory** in the country that allows the public to tour its production facilities plays Willie Wonka to a host of chocolate lovers. After the half-hour guided walking tours—which cover the chocolate-making process from cocoa bean to candy bar—everyone gets a sample. ⊠ *120 S. Sierra Ave.,* ☎ *209/848–8126.* ⊡ *Free.* ☉ *Weekday tours 8:30–3, visitor center weekdays 8:30–5.*

☺ The featured attraction at the **Knights Ferry Recreation Area** is the 355-ft-long Knights Ferry covered bridge, the longest in California. Built in 1864, the bridge (closed to motor vehicles) crosses the Stanislaus River near the ruins of an old grist mill. The park has picnic and barbecue areas along the river banks, as well as fishing, hiking, rafting, and canoeing. ⊠ *18020 Sonora Rd., Knights Ferry; 12 mi east of Oakdale via Hwy. 108,* ☎ *209/881–3517.* ⊡ *Free.* ☉ *Mon.–Fri., 8–noon and 1–4; Sat.–Sun. 10–2.*

You can sample the wares at **Bloomingcamp Apple Ranch** (⊠ 10528 Hwy. 120, ☎ 209/847–1412). **Oakdale Cheese & Specialties** (⊠ 10040 Hwy. 120, ☎ 209/848–3139) has tastings as well.

Merced and Atwater

38 mi south of Modesto (to Merced) on Hwy. 99; 53 mi from Oakdale west and then south on Hwy. 108 and south on Hwy. 99.

Merced, population 56,000, is a common stopover en route to Yosemite National Park. The town of Atwater is 6 mi north of Merced on Highway 99. The **Kiki Raina Tahiti Fete** (☎ 209/383–1435) takes place in Merced in late March.

☺ ❹ At the outdoor **Castle Air Museum,** adjacent to Castle Air Force Base in Atwater, you can stroll among fighter planes and other historic military aircraft. The 44 restored vintage warbirds include the B-25 Mitchell medium-range bomber (best known for the "Jimmy Doolittle raid" on Tokyo following the attack on Pearl Harbor) and the speedy SR-71 Blackbird, used for reconnaissance over Vietnam and Libya. ⊠ *Santa Fe Dr. and Buhach Rd., Atwater; take the Buhach Rd. exit off Hwy. 99 in At-*

water and follow signs, ☎ *209/723–2178.* 🖼 *$5.* ⊘ *Memorial Day–Oct. 1, daily 9–5; Oct. 2–Memorial Day, daily 10–4.*

❺ Even if you don't go inside, be sure to swing by the **Merced County Courthouse Museum.** The three-story former courthouse, built in 1875, is a striking example of the Victorian Italianate style. The upper two floors are now a museum of early Merced history. Highlights include an 1870 Chinese temple with carved redwood altars, and an ornate restored courtroom. ✉ *21st and N Sts.,* ☎ *209/723–2401.* 🖼 *Free.* ⊘ *Wed.–Sun. 1–4.*

The **Merced Multicultural Arts Center,** opened in late 1996, displays rotating exhibits of paintings, sculpture, and photography. The annual festival Threads: A Tapestry of Cultures, which celebrates the area's ethnic diversity, is held here on a mid-October weekend. ✉ *645 W. Main St.,* ☎ *209/388–1090.* 🖼 *Free.* ⊘ *Weekdays 9–5.*

Dining and Lodging

$$ ✕ **Sir James.** Merced's most earnestly upscale restaurant—low lighting, rose-colored linens, complimentary sorbet between courses—is still casual enough to attract a local jeans-and-flannel crowd. Prime rib, steak, and filet mignon are the staples here, but the seafood (including a fine mix grill) is fresh and well prepared. ✉ *1111 Motel Dr.,* ☎ *209/723–5551. AE, D, DC, MC, V. Closed Sun.–Mon. No lunch.*

$ ✕ **Main Street Cafe.** This bright downtown café dishes up soups, salads, sandwiches, pastries, ice cream, and espresso. Sandwiches (try the chicken breast with pesto mayonnaise on Francesi bread) are served with tasty side salads. ✉ *460 W. Main St.,* ☎ *209/725–1702. Closed Sun. No dinner.*

$–$$ 🏨 **Days Inn.** The compact rooms here manage to pack in an impressive array of amenities: a writing table, a refrigerator, a microwave, an AM/FM radio, a coffeemaker, a bathroom phone, a safe, and a 26-inch TV with HBO and VCR (tapes are for rent in lobby). ✉ *1199 Motel Dr., 95340, near the intersection of Hwys. 99 and 140,* ☎ *209/722–2726,* FAX *209/722–7083. 24 rooms. No-smoking rooms, refrigerators, in-room VCRs, pool. AE, D, DC, MC, V.*

Outdoor Activities and Sports

At **Lake Yosemite Regional Park** (✉ N. Lake Rd., off Yosemite Ave., 5 mi northeast of Merced, ☎ 209/385–7426), you can boat, swim, windsurf, waterski, and fish on a 387-acre reservoir. Boat rentals and picnic areas are available.

MID–SAN JOAQUIN VALLEY

Fresno, Hanford, and Visalia

The mid–San Joaquin Valley extends over three counties—Fresno, Kings, and Tulare. From Fresno, Highway 41 leads north 95 mi to Yosemite and Highway 180 snakes east 55 mi to Kings Canyon (Sequoia National Park is 30 mi farther). From Visalia, Highway 198 winds east 35 mi to the Generals Highway, which leads into Sequoia and Kings Canyon. Historic Hanford, about 16 mi west of Visalia along Highway 198, is an often overlooked gem.

Fresno

50 mi south of Merced, 117 mi south of Stockton, 110 mi north of Bakersfield on Hwy. 99.

Sprawling Fresno, with nearly 400,000 people, is the center of the richest agricultural county in America; grapes, cotton, oranges, and turkeys are among the major products. The city's most famous native, Pulitzer Prize–winning playwright and novelist William Saroyan (*The Time of Your Life, The Human Comedy*), was born here in 1908. You can see one of his boyhood homes at 3204 East El Monte Way, and his home at the time of his death in 1981 at 2729 West Griffith Way. The seemingly endless parade of strip malls and fast-food joints can be depressing, but local character does lurk beneath the commercialization. The city is home to 75 ethnic communities (from Armenian to Vietnamese), a burgeoning arts scene, and several public parks.

Woodward Park, 300 acres of jogging trails, picnic areas, and playgrounds in the northern reaches of the city, is especially pretty in the spring—when plum and cherry trees, magnolias, and camellias bloom—and the fall, when leaves lend a riot of color. Don't miss the **Shin Zen Japanese Friendship Garden** with a teahouse, a koi pond, arched bridges, a waterfall, and lakes. ✉ *Audubon Dr. and Friant Rd.,* ☎ *209/498–1551.* ➤ *Park $2 per car, Japanese Garden $1.* ☉ *Mar.–Oct., daily 7 AM–10 PM; Nov.–Feb., daily 7–7.*

★ ♻ ❻ Sicilian immigrant Baldasare Forestiere spent 40 years carving out the remarkable **Forestiere Underground Gardens,** a subterranean realm of rooms, tunnels, grottoes, alcoves, and arched passageways that extends for more than 10 acres beneath what is now busy, mall-pocked Shaw Avenue. Just a fraction of Forestiere's prodigious output is on view, but you can tour his underground living quarters, including bedrooms (one with a fireplace), the kitchen, the living room, the bath, a fish pond, and an aquarium. Skylights allow exotic, full-grown fruit trees—one bearing seven different kinds of citrus—to flourish as far as 22 ft below ground. ✉ *5021 W. Shaw Ave.,* ☎ *209/271–0734.* ➤ *$6.* ☉ *Memorial Day–Labor Day, Wed.–Sun. 10–4; Easter–Memorial Day and Labor Day–Thanksgiving (weather permitting), weekends noon–3.*

★ ♻ ❼ Tree-shaded **Roeding Park,** Fresno's largest, has picnic areas, playgrounds, tennis courts, and the **Chaffee Zoological Gardens.** The most striking exhibit is the tropical rainforest, where exotic birds often greet visitors along the paths and bridges. Elsewhere you'll find tigers, grizzly bears, sea lions, tule elk, camels, elephants, and hooting siamangs. There's also a computerized reptile house and a petting zoo. **Playland,** for kids, has a minitrain, a Ferris wheel, a small roller coaster, and a merry-go-round. Kids have more to explore at **Storyland.** ✉ *Olive and Belmont Aves.,* ☎ *209/498–4239; 209/498–2671 zoo; 209/486–2124 Playland; 209/264–2235 Storyland.* ➤ *Parking $1 (Feb.–Oct.), zoo $4.50, Storyland $2.75.* ☉ *Park: Mar.–Oct., daily 7 AM–10 PM; Oct.–Mar., daily 7–7. Zoo: Mar.–Oct., daily 9–5; Nov.–Feb., daily 10–4. Playland and Storyland: schedules vary (closed Dec.–Jan.).*

The drive along fan-palm-lined Kearney Boulevard is one of the best reasons to visit the **Kearney Mansion Museum,** which stands in shaded 225-acre **Kearney Park** 7 mi west of town. Guided 45-minute tours take you through the recently renovated turn-of-the-century home of Fresno's onetime "Raisin King." ✉ *7160 W. Kearney Blvd.,* ☎ *209/441–0862.* ➤ *$4 (park entrance $3, waived for museum visitors).* ☉ *Museum Fri.–Sun., tours at 1, 2, and 3 PM.*

♻ ❽ The **Fresno Metropolitan Museum** presents often innovative art, history, and hands-on science exhibits. The permanent William Saroyan History Gallery presents a riveting introduction in words and pictures to the author's life and times. ✉ *1555 Van Ness Ave.,* ☎ *209/441–1444.* ➤ *$4.* ☉ *Tues.–Sun. 11–5.*

Fresno Area

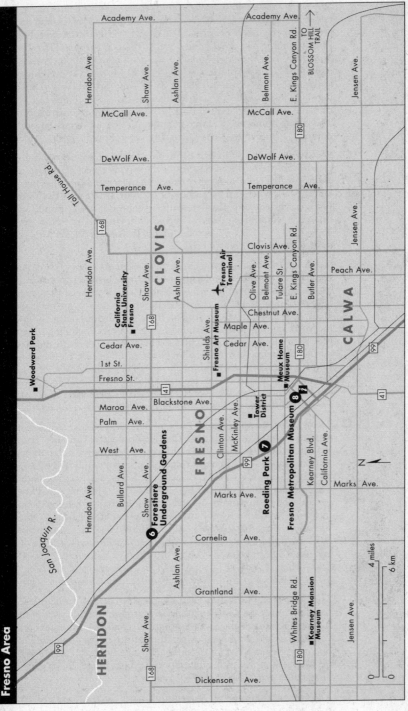

Academy Ave.
Academy Ave.
Herndon Ave.
Shaw Ave.
Ashlan Ave.
Belmont Ave.
E. Kings Canyon Rd.
TO BLOSSOM HILL TRAIL
Jensen Ave.

McCall Ave.
McCall Ave.
180

DeWolf Ave.
DeWolf Ave.

Temperance Ave.
Temperance Ave.

168
CLOVIS
Clovis Ave.
Jensen Ave.

Herndon Ave.
Shaw Ave.
Ashlan Ave.
Fresno Air Terminal
Olive Ave.
Belmont Ave.
Tulare St.
E. Kings Canyon Rd.
Peach Ave.
Butler Ave.

California State University Fresno
168
Chestnut Ave.
Maple Ave.
CALWA

Shields Ave.
Fresno Art Museum
Cedar Ave.
Cedar Ave.
180
99

Woodward Park
1st St.
Fresno St.
Meux Home Museum
41
41

Maroa Ave.
Blackstone Ave.
Tower District
8 i

Palm Ave.
McKinley Ave.
Clinton Ave.
Fresno Metropolitan Museum

West Ave.
99
Roeding Park 7
Kearney Blvd.
California Ave.
N

Bullard Ave.
Shaw Ave.
Forestiere Underground Gardens
FRESNO
Marks Ave.

Herndon Ave.
6
Marks Ave.

San Joaquin R.
Cornelia Ave.

Ashlan Ave.
Grantland Ave.
Whites Bridge Rd.
Kearney Mansion Museum
Jensen Ave.

99
Shaw Ave.
180
4 miles
6 km

168
HERNDON
Dickenson Ave.
0   0

The **Fresno Art Museum** in small Radio Park has seven galleries that exhibit American, Mexican, and French art. ⊠ *2233 N. 1st St.,* ☎ *209/ 441–4220.* ☞ *$2; free Tues.* ☉ *Tues.–Fri. 10–5, weekends noon–5; closed last 2 wks of Aug.*

The **Meux Home Museum,** inside a restored 1888 Victorian, displays furnishings and decor typical of early Fresno. Guided tours lead from the front parlor to the backyard carriage house. ⊠ *Tulare and R Sts.,* ☎ *209/233–8007.* ☞ *$4.* ☉ *Feb.–Dec., Fri.–Sun. noon–4 (last tour 3:30 PM).*

OFF THE BEATEN PATH

BLOSSOM TRAIL – This 62-mi self-guided driving tour takes in Fresno's surrounding orchards, citrus groves, and vineyards at the height of spring blossom season. Almond, plum, apple, orange, lemon, apricot, and peach blossoms shower the landscape with shades of white, pink, and red. (The most colorful and aromatic time to go is from late February through March.) The route passes through several small towns and past rivers, lakes, and canals. The Fresno Convention & Visitors Bureau (⊠ 808 M St., 93721; ☎ 209/233–0836 or 800/788–0836) has route maps; directional and crop identification signs also mark the trail. Allow at least two to three hours for the tour.

Dining and Lodging

$$$ ✕ **Giulia's Italian Trattoria.** The look here is light and airy, but the southern Italian food is rustic, hearty, and intensely flavored. Bruschetta, steamed mussels, and polenta with grilled sausage are top choices, but also look for seasonal specials. ⊠ *Winepress Shopping Center, 3050 W. Shaw Ave.,* ☎ *209/276–3573. AE, D, DC, MC, V. No lunch Sun.*

$ ✕ **Armenian Cuisine.** This small restaurant is a magnet for local Sarkisians and Krikorians, who flock here for the tasty lamb, beef, and chicken kebabs, accompanied by Armenian peda bread, eggplant salad, and yalanchi (cold stuffed grape leaves). ⊠ *742 W. Bullard St.,* ☎ *209/435– 4892. AE, DC, MC, V. Closed Sun.*

$ ✕ **Kim's Vietnamese Restaurant.** You'll find good food at bargain prices here: Specialties include hot beef salad, sizzling chicken, and sautéed seafood with ginger. Multicourse lunches or dinners—from soup to dessert and tea, with salad, entrée, and rice in between—are well under $10. ⊠ *5048 N. Maroa St.,* ☎ *209/225–0406. MC, V. Closed Sun.*

$–$$ 🏨 **Piccadilly Inn Shaw.** This two-story property is attractively landscaped, with a big central swimming pool and a restaurant with an outdoor patio. The sizable rooms have king- and queen-size beds; along with coffeemakers, some have refrigerators, microwaves, and fireplaces. ⊠ *2305 W. Shaw Ave., 93711,* ☎ *209/226–3850,* FAX *209/226–2448. 194 rooms and suites. Restaurant, no-smoking rooms, pool, hot tub, exercise room, coin laundry, laundry service, business services, meeting rooms. AE, D, DC, MC, V.*

$ 🏨 **La Quinta Inn.** Rooms are good-size at this three-story motel near downtown. Some have king-size beds, microwaves, and refrigerators. The rates include a Continental breakfast. ⊠ *2926 Tulare St., 93721,* ☎ *209/442–1110,* FAX *209/237–0415. 130 rooms. No-smoking rooms, room service, pool, coin laundry, meeting rooms. AE, D, DC, MC, V.*

Nightlife and the Arts

The **Tower Theatre for the Performing Arts** (⊠ 815 E. Olive Ave., ☎ 209/485–9050), a onetime movie house that's given its name to the trendy Tower District of theaters, clubs, restaurants, and cafés, presents theatrical, ballet, classical, jazz, and other live performances from spring through fall. **Roger Rocka's Music Hall** (⊠ 1226 N. Wishon Ave., ☎ 209/266–9494 or 800/371–4747), a dinner theater in the Tower District, stages six Broadway-style musicals or comedies a year. The **Fresno Philharmonic Orchestra** (☎ 209/261–0600) performs classical concerts (sometimes pops) on weekends, usually at the William Saroyan Theatre (✉ 700 M St.), from September to June.

Outdoor Activities and Sports

Wild Water Adventures (✉ 11413 E. Shaw Ave., Clovis, ☎ 209/299–9453 or 800/564–9453), a 50-acre water theme park east of Fresno, is open from late May to early September.

Shopping

Old Town Clovis (✉ 5th and Pollasky Sts., Clovis) is an area of restored brick buildings and brick sidewalks, with numerous antiques shops and art galleries (along with restaurants and saloons). Head east on Fresno's Shaw Avenue to get to Clovis.

OFF THE
BEATEN PATH

MENNONITE QUILT CENTER – The colorful handiwork of local Mennonite quilters is on display here. Try to visit on Monday (except holidays), when two dozen or so quilters come in to stitch, patch, and chat over coffee. Prime viewing time—with the largest number of quilts—is in February and March, just before the center holds its annual early April auction. Ask a docent to take you to the locked upstairs room, where most of the quilts are hung; she'll explain the fine points of patterns such as the Log Cabin Romance, the Dahlia, and the Snowball-Star. ✉ *1012 G St., Reedley; take Manning Ave. exit off Hwy. 99 and go 12 mi east;* ☎ *209/638-3560.* ☞ *Free.* ⊙ *Weekdays 9:30-4:30, Sat. 10-2.*

Hanford

★ *35 mi from Fresno, south on Hwy. 99 and Hwy. 43.*

Founded in 1877 as a Southern Pacific Railroad stop, Hanford once had one of California's largest Chinatowns—the Chinese came to help build the railroads, and stayed to farm and open restaurants. You can take a self-guided walking tour or sign up in advance for guided walking tours ($2.50 per adult) arranged by the **Hanford Visitor Agency** (☎ 209/582–5024). One tour explores the restored historic buildings of Courthouse Square. Another heads to narrow China Alley, with stops at the town's Taoist Temple and other sights.

The **Hanford Carnegie Museum,** now occupying the onetime Carnegie Library, a Romanesque building dating from 1905, displays fashions, furnishings, toys, and military exhibits from Kings County's yesteryears. ✉ *109 E. 8th St.,* ☎ *209/584–1367.* ☞ *$1.* ⊙ *Tues.–Fri. noon–3, Sat. noon–4.*

In the 1893 **Taoist Temple,** a first-floor museum displays photos, furnishings, and kitchenware from Hanford's once-bustling Chinatown. The second-floor temple, largely unchanged for a century, contains altars, carvings, and ceremonial staves. You can visit as part of a guided walking tour (☞ *above*) or by calling the temple directly and making an appointment two weeks in advance. ✉ *12 China Alley,* ☎ *209/582-4508.* ☞ *Free; donations welcome.* ⊙ *By appointment only.*

Dining and Lodging

$$–$$$ ✕ **Imperial Dynasty.** Despite its name and elegant teak-and-porcelains Chinese decor, Imperial Dynasty serves primarily French cuisine. For a memorable meal, start with the garlicky escargots and continue with the veal sweetbreads or rack of lamb. Avoid the overcooked, over-sauced seafood. The extensive wine list contains many prized vintages. ✉ *China Alley (corner of 7th and Green Sts.),* ☎ *209/582–0196. AE, MC, V. Closed Mon. No lunch.*

$ ✕ **Justo's.** With a late 1880s decor (it's set in Hanford's old Opera House), a sometimes rowdy bar, and family-style Basque cuisine, Justo's is one of the liveliest restaurants in town. Entrées include calamari steak and a Basque variation on fried chicken. The side dishes—soup, salads, beef tongue, stew, rice and beans—could make an entire meal. ⊠ *129 W. 7th St.,* ☎ *209/583–7713. MC, V. No lunch Sun.*

$–$$ 🏠 **Irwin Street Inn.** This bed-and-breakfast inn is one of the few lodgings in the Valley that warrants a detour. Four tree-shaded, restored Victorian homes have been converted into spacious, comfortable rooms and suites. Most have antique armoires, dark wood detailing, leaded-glass windows, and four-poster beds; bathrooms come with old-fashioned tubs, brass fixtures, and marble basins. The inn's restaurant serves lunch daily and dinner every night except Sunday (Thursday to Saturday only in January). Room rates include a Continental breakfast. ⊠ *522 N. Irwin St., 93230,* ☎ *209/583–8000 or 888/583–8080,* FAX *209/583–8793. 30 rooms. Restaurant, pool. AE, MC, V.*

Nightlife and the Arts

The 1,000-seat, restored Moorish-Castillian–style **Hanford Fox Theater** (⊠ 326 N. Irwin St., ☎ 209/584–4423), built as a movie palace in 1929, now periodically hosts country-western bands and other live performances.

Visalia

16 mi from Hanford, east on Hwy. 198; 40 mi from Fresno, south on Hwy. 99 and east on Hwy. 198.

Founded in 1852 by a native of Visalia, Kentucky, Visalia (population 75,000) is the Tulare County seat and center of one of the world's top milk-producing regions (it's also a major exporter of oranges, grapes, plums, peaches, and cotton). The town contains a number of historic homes; ask the **visitor center** (⊠ 301 E. Acequia, 93921, ☎ 209/738–3435 or 800/524–0303) for a free guide detailing them. On a clear day, the views of the often snow-capped Sierra Nevada peaks to the east are stunning.

The **Chinese Cultural Center,** housed in a pagoda-style building, mounts exhibits on Chinese art and culture. ⊠ *500 Akers Rd., at Hwy. 198,* ☎ *209/625–4545.* 🎫 *Free; donations welcome.* ⊙ *Wed.–Sun. 11–6.*

In oak-shaded **Mooney Grove Park,** you can picnic alongside duck ponds, rent a boat in a lagoon, view a replica of the famous **End of the Trail Statue** (the original, once here, is now in the Cowboy Hall of Fame in Oklahoma), and visit the **Tulare County Museum.** The indoor-outdoor museum has several turn-of-the-century re-created environments and displays Yokuts tribal artifacts (basketry, arrowheads, clamshell-necklace currency), collections of saddles and guns, Victorian-era dolls, and quilts and gowns. ⊠ *27000 S. Mooney Blvd., 5 mi south of downtown,* ☎ *209/733–6616 for park and museum.* 🎫 *Park $3 per car, museum $2.* ⊙ *Park: daily from 8* AM; *closing hrs. vary seasonally. Museum: Memorial Day weekend–Labor Day, Mon. and Wed.–Fri. 10–4, weekends noon–6; Mar.–Memorial Day weekend and Labor Day–Sept., Mon. and Thurs.–Sun. 10–4; Oct.–Feb., Mon. and Thurs.–Fri. 10–4, weekends 1–4.*

Self-guided nature trails at the 300-acre **Kaweah Oaks Preserve**—a wildlife sanctuary off the main road to Sequoia National Park and accessible only to hikers—lead past oak, sycamore, cottonwood, and willow trees, and provide chances to spot hawks, hummingbirds, and great blue herons (among 125 species of birds), along with lizards, coyotes, and cottontails. ✉ *Follow Hwy. 198 7 mi east of Visalia, turn north on Rd. 182, and go ½ mi to gate on left-hand side of road,* ☎ *209/738–0211.* 🎫 *Free.* ☻ *Daily, daylight hrs.*

Dining and Lodging

$–$$ ✕ **Michael's on Main.** With its open kitchen, wood-fired grill, ceiling fans, and white floor tiles, Michael's adds contemporary sophistication to Visalia's downtown dining. Dishes are prepared with an Italian accent, with pastas a mainstay. ✉ *123 W. Main St.,* ☎ *209/635–2686. AE, D, DC, MC, V. Closed Sun.*

$ ✕ **Caliente.** This sparkling clean taco and burrito place en route to Mooney Grove Park makes good use of char-broiled, fresh ingredients. Try the innovative "Gourmet Wraps"—wood-fired shrimp in a chipotle tortilla or grilled vegetables in a spinach tortilla. You'd have to be ravenous to spend $10 a person here. ✉ *2250 S. Mooney Blvd.,* ☎ *209/733–8226. MC, V.*

$$ ▥ **The Spalding House.** Built in 1901, this restored Colonial-Revival B&B—decked out with antiques, Oriental rugs, hand-crafted woodwork, and glass doors—is one of several historic homes in the vicinity. Guests have use of a 1,500-volume library and music room with grand piano. The three guest suites each have a sitting room, a bedroom, and a private bath—but no phones or TVs. Room rates include a full breakfast. ✉ *631 N. Encina St., 93291,* ☎ *209/739–7877,* 🅵🅰🆇 *209/625–0902. 3 suites. No-smoking rooms. MC, V.*

$–$$ ▥ **The Lamp Liter Inn.** Rooms here are decent-size, and some have refrigerators. Rates include free TV movies. A large partially tree-shaded pool beckons on hot summer days. ✉ *3300 W. Mineral King Ave., off Hwy. 198, 93291,* ☎ *209/732–4511,* 🅵🅰🆇 *209/732–1840. 100 rooms. Restaurant, coffee shop, lounge, pool, meeting rooms. AE, D, DC, MC, V.*

Colonel Allensworth State Historic Park

★ ⊙ *40 mi from Visalia, south on Hwy. 99, west on J22 at Earlimart and south on Hwy. 43.*

An ex-slave who rose to become the country's highest-ranking black officer founded Allensworth—the only California town settled, governed, and financed by African-Americans—in 1908. After enjoying early prosperity, Allensworth became a ghost town; its buildings have been rebuilt or restored to reflect the era when it thrived. Each October, three days of festivities mark the town's rededication. ✉ *4129 Palmer Ave.,* ☎ *805/849–3433.* 🎫 *$3 per car.* ☻ *Daily 10–4:30.*

OFF THE **KERN NATIONAL WILDLIFE REFUGE** – Ducks, snowy egrets, peregrine fal-
BEATEN PATH cons, warblers, and other birds inhabit the marshes and wetlands here from November to April. Follow the 3½-mi radius tour route (pick up maps at the entrance), which has several good viewing spots. ✉ *Corcoran Rd., 19 mi west of Delano on Hwy. 155 (Garces Hwy.); from Allensworth take Hwy. 43 south to Hwy. 155 west,* ☎ *805/725–2767.* 🎫 *Free.* ☻ *Daily sunrise–sunset.*

SOUTHERN SAN JOAQUIN VALLEY

Bakersfield and Kernville

When gold was discovered in Kern County in the 1860s, settlers flocked to the southern end of the San Joaquin Valley. Today black gold—oil—has become the area's most valuable commodity, but Kern is also the country's third-largest agricultural-producing county. From the flat plains around Bakersfield, the landscape graduates to rolling hills and then mountains as it climbs east to Kernville, which lies in the Kern River Valley.

Bakersfield

80 mi from Visalia, west on Hwy. 198, south on Hwy. 99; 288 mi from San Francisco, east on I–80 and I–580, south on I–5.

Bakersfield's founder, Colonel Thomas Baker, arrived with the discovery of gold in the nearby Kern River Valley in 1851. Now Kern County's largest city (population 212,000), Bakersfield probably is best known as "Nashville West," a country-music haven and hometown of performers Buck Owens and Merle Haggard. It's also home to a symphony orchestra and two good museums.

★ ☺ ❿ The **Kern County Museum/Lori Brock Children's Discovery Center** form one of the San Joaquin Valley's top museum complexes. The indoor-outdoor Kern County Museum—highlighted by an open-air, walk-through historic village with more than 50 restored or re-created buildings—pays homage to the era of the 1860s to 1940s. The indoor museum holds exhibits about Native Americans and the "Bakersfield Sound" in country music. The adjacent Children's Discovery Center has permanent and changing hands-on displays and activities. ✉ 3801 Chester Ave., ☎ 805/861–2132. ⊡ $5. ☉ Weekdays 8–5, Sat. 10–5, Sun. noon–5.

★ ☺ ⓫ At the **California Living Museum** (CALM), a combination zoo, botanical garden, and natural-history museum—with an emphasis on zoo—all animal and plant species displayed are native to the state. Within CALM's reptile house lives every species of rattlesnake found in California. The landscaped grounds—nestled among the rolling hills about a 20-minute drive northeast of Bakersfield—also shelter bald eagles, tortoises, coyotes, mountain lions, and foxes. ✉ 14000 Alfred Harrell Hwy. (Hwy. 178 east, then 3½ mi northwest on Alfred Harrell Hwy.), ☎ 805/872–2256. ⊡ $3.50. ☉ Wed.–Sun. 9–4.

Dining and Lodging

$–$$ ✕ **Uricchio's Trattoria.** This smartly designed downtown restaurant draws everyone from office workers to oil millionaires—all attracted by the tasty food, trendy open kitchen, and indoor and outdoor seating. Panini—Italian sandwiches served at lunch only—pasta, and Italian-style chicken dishes dominate the menu; the chicken piccata outsells all other offerings. ✉ 1400 17th St., ☎ 805/326–8870. AE, D, DC, MC, V. Closed Sun. No lunch Sat.

$ ✕ **Chalet Basque.** Trencherman-size dinners here include soup, pink beans, hors d'oeuvres, vegetables, and potatoes, all served family style. Leave room for main courses like roast leg of lamb or beef bourguignonne, or Basque-style specials such as ox-tail stew or lamb shanks. ✉ 200 Oak St., ☎ 805/327–2915. AE, MC, V. Closed Sun.–Mon.

$$ ▥ **Doubletree Hotel.** The location is convenient, just off Highways 99, 58, and 178. Spacious rooms have coffeemakers (some have refrigerators) and a balcony or patio. ✉ 3100 Camino Del Rio Ct., 93308, ☎ 805/323–7111, ℻ 805/323–0331. 246 rooms and 14 suites. Restaurant, bar, coffee shop, no-smoking rooms, room service, pool, hot tub, laundry service, business services, meeting rooms, airport shuttle. AE, D, DC, MC, V.

$ ▥ **Quality Inn.** Near downtown, but in a relatively quiet location just off Highway 99, this two-story motel offers good value. Most rooms have king- or queen-size beds, and all have free in-room movies. Some have refrigerators and a patio or a balcony looking out on the heated pool. Complimentary coffee and donuts are served. ⊠ *1011 Oak St., 93304,* ☎ *805/325–0772,* ⅎ⅍ *805/325–4646. 90 rooms. Pool, indoor hot tub, sauna, exercise room, coin laundry, meeting rooms. AE, D, DC, MC, V.*

Nightlife and the Arts

The **Bakersfield Symphony Orchestra** (☎ 805/323–7928) performs classical music concerts at the Convention Center (⊠ 1001 Truxton Ave.) on Sunday from October through May.

Buck Owens' Crystal Palace (⊠ 2800 Pierce Rd., ☎ 805/328–7560) is a combination nightclub, restaurant, and showcase of country-music memorabilia. Country-western singers—owner Buck Owens among them—perform. A dance floor beckons customers who can still twirl after sampling the menu of steaks, burgers, nachos, and gooey desserts. Entertainment is free most weeknights, Friday and Saturday nights bring a $3 cover charge, and some big-name acts require tickets.

Outdoor Activities and Sports

CAR RACING

At **Bakersfield Speedway** (⊠ 304 Egret Ct., ☎ 805/393–3373), stock and sprint cars race around a ⅓-mi clay oval track. **Mesa Marin Raceway** (⊠ 11000 Kern Canyon Rd., ☎ 805/366–5711) presents high-speed stock-car, super-truck, and NASCAR racing on a ½-mi paved oval course.

Shopping

18th and 19th streets between H and R streets, and H Street between Brundage Lane and California Avenue, contain one of the greatest concentrations of antiques shops in the country. **Goodies from the Past** (⊠ 1610 19th St., ☎ 805/636–0368), **Central Park Antique Mall** (⊠ 701 19th St., ☎ 805/633–1143), and the **Great American Antique Mall** (⊠ 625 19th St., ☎ 805/322–1776) all have huge selections.

Kernville

50 mi from Bakersfield, northeast on Hwy. 178, north on Hwy. 155.

The wild and scenic Kern River, which flows through Kernville en route from Mt. Whitney to Bakersfield, delivers some of the most exciting white-water rafting in the state. Kernville (population 1,200) rests in a mountain valley on both banks of the river, and also at the northern tip of Lake Isabella (a dammed portion of the river used as a reservoir and for recreation). A center for rafting outfitters, Kernville has lodgings, eating places, and antiques shops. The main streets are lined with Old West–style buildings, reflecting Kernville's heritage as a rough-and-tumble gold mining town known as Whiskey Flat (the current town dates from the 1950s, when it was moved upriver to make room for Lake Isabella). The scenic road from Bakersfield winds between the rushing river on one side and sheer granite cliffs on the other.

Dining and Lodging

$$–$$$ ✕ **Ewing's on the Kern.** The views outshine the food at this well-known restaurant, but there are few prettier spots to eat than high above the Kern, either at one of the outdoor tables—come early to get a seat for Sunday brunch—or at one of the indoor window tables. The menu is strictly old standards: prime rib, steaks, seafood, pastas, and chicken. ⊠ *125 Buena Vista Dr.,* ☎ *760/376–2411. AE, D, DC, MC, V. No lunch Mon.–Sat.*

$ ✕ **Debbie Du's Diner.** This down-home diner ("Where Everyone Is Family") serves up some of the least expensive food in town—ask for the Strugglers Specials, all under $10—along with colorful talk from the locals, who drop in for biscuits and gravy, burgers, or meat loaf. ✉ *13423 Sierra Way,* ☎ *760/376–4663. No credit cards.*

$$–$$$ ⊡ **Whispering Pines Lodge.** You can choose a cottage or a river-view bungalow here. Some rooms have full kitchens, fireplaces, and whirlpool tubs; all have refrigerators, coffeemakers, and free HBO. Room rates include a full breakfast. ✉ *13745 Sierra Way, 93238,* ☎ *760/376–3733,* FAX *760/376–3735. 17 rooms. Pool, hot tub, meeting rooms. AE, MC, V.*

$ ⊡ **River View Lodge.** This rustic motel has knotty pine walls and compact but clean rooms, some with microwaves and VCRs. And yes, many units do have river views. Picnic and barbecue facilities are in the tree-shaded yard. Winter rates fall below $50 a night on some rooms. The rates include a Continental breakfast. ✉ *2 Sirretta St., just off Kernville Rd., 93238,* ☎ *760/376–6019,* FAX *760/376–4147. 10 rooms. No-smoking rooms, refrigerators. AE, DC, MC, V.*

Outdoor Activities and Sports

WHITE-WATER RAFTING

The three sections of the Kern River—known as the Lower Kern, Upper Kern, and the Forks—add up to nearly 50 mi of white water, ranging from Class I–V (easy to expert). The Lower and Upper Kern are the most popular and accessible sections. Organized trips range from one hour (with prices as low as $15) to two days and more. Rafting season generally runs from late spring through summer, though that can vary by the section of the river and the water levels. Outfitters include **Chuck Richards Whitewater** (☎ 760/379–4444), **Kern River Tours** (☎ 760/379–4616), **Mountain & River Adventures** (☎ 760/376–6553 or 800/861–6553), and **Sierra South** (☎ 760/376–3745).

BOATING, FISHING, AND WINDSURFING

The Lower Kern River, which extends from Lake Isabella to Bakersfield and beyond, is open for fishing year-round. Catches include rainbow trout, catfish, smallmouth bass, crappie, and bluegill. Lake Isabella is popular with anglers, water skiers, sailors, and windsurfers. Its shoreline marinas—**French Gulch Marina** (☎ 760/379–8774), **Red's Kern Valley Marina** (☎ 760/379–1634 or 800/553–7337), and **Dean's North Fork Marina** (☎ 760/376–1812)—have boats for rent, bait and tackle, and moorings year-round.

THE SAN JOAQUIN VALLEY A TO Z

Arriving and Departing

By Bus

From San Francisco, Sacramento, or Los Angeles, **Greyhound Lines** (☎ 800/231–2222) makes stops in Stockton, Modesto, Merced, Fresno, Visalia, and Bakersfield.

By Car

To drive to the San Joaquin Valley from San Francisco, take I–80 east to I–580, and I–580 east to I–5, which leads south to the Valley (several roads then lead east to Highway 99); or continue east on I–580 to I–205, which leads to I–5 north to Stockton or (via Highway 120) east to Highway 99 at Manteca. You can then head south on Highway 99. To reach the Valley from Los Angeles, follow I–5 north;

Highway 99 veers north about 15 mi after entering the Valley, north of Lebec.

By Plane

Fresno Air Terminal (✉ 5175 E. Clinton Ave., ☎ 209/498–4095) is serviced by American and American Eagle, Delta, United Express, and US Airways Express. **Kern County Airport at Meadows Field** (✉ 1401 Skyway Dr., Bakersfield, ☎ 805/393–7990) is serviced by American and American Eagle, Skywest-Delta, and United Express. United Express flies from San Francisco to **Modesto City Airport** (✉ 617 Airport Way, ☎ 209/577–5318) and **Visalia Municipal Airport** (✉ 9500 Airport Dr., ☎ 209/738–3201). *See* Air Travel *in* the Gold Guide for airline phone numbers.

By Train

Amtrak's (☎ 800/872–7245) San Joaquin Line travels between Oakland and Bakersfield, stopping in Stockton, Riverbank (near Modesto), Merced, Fresno, and Hanford.

Getting Around

By Bus

Greyhound (☎ 800/231–2222) provides service between major Valley cities. **Orange Belt Stages** (☎ 800/266–7433) provides bus service, including Amtrak connections, to many Valley locations, including Stockton, Merced, Madera, Fresno, Hanford, and Bakersfield.

By Car

Highway 99 is the main route between the Valley's major cities and towns. I–5 runs roughly parallel to it to the west, but misses the major population centers; its main use is for quick access from San Francisco or Los Angeles. Major roads that connect I–5 with Highway 99 are Highways 120 (to Manteca), 132 (to Modesto), 140 (to Merced), 152 (to Chowchilla, via Los Banos), 198 (to Hanford and Visalia), and 58 (to Bakersfield).

Contacts and Resources

Car Rentals

At least some major car rental agencies are represented in Stockton, Modesto, Fresno, Visalia, and Bakersfield. *See* Car Rental *in* the Gold Guide for phone numbers.

Emergencies

Ambulance (☎ 911). **Police** (☎ 911).

Guided Tours

Central Valley Tours (✉ 1869 E. Everglade, Fresno 93720, ☎ 209/323–5552) provides general and customized tours of the Fresno area and the Valley. **Kings River Expeditions** (✉ 211 N. Van Ness, Fresno, ☎ 209/233–4881 or 800/846–3674) arranges white-water rafting trips on the Kings River. Contact **River Journey** (✉ 14842 Orange Blossom Rd., Oakdale, ☎ 209/847–4671 or 800/292–2938) and **Sunshine River Adventures** (✉ Box 1445, Oakdale 95361, ☎ 209/848–4800 or 800/829–7238) to raft the Stanislaus River.

Visitor Information

Fresno City & County Convention and Visitors Bureau (✉ 808 M St., 93721, ☎ 209/233–0836 or 800/788–0836. **Greater Bakersfield Convention & Visitors Bureau** (✉ 1033 Truxton Ave., 93301, ☎ 805/325–5051 or 800/325–6001). **Hanford Visitor Agency** (✉ 200 Santa Fe Ave., Suite D, 93230, ☎ 209/582–5024). **Kern County Board of Trade** (✉

In case you want to see the world.
At American Express, we're here to make your journey a smooth one. So we have over 1,700 travel service locations in over 120 countries ready to help. What else would you expect from the world's largest travel agency?
do more®
AMERICAN EXPRESS
Travel
http://www.americanexpress.com/travel

In case you want to be welcomed there.

We're here to see that you're always welcomed at establishments everywhere. That's why millions of people carry the American Express® Card – for peace of mind, confidence, and security, around the world or just around the corner.

do more®

AMERICAN EXPRESS

Cards

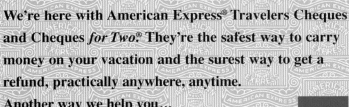

2101 Oak St., Bakersfield 93302, ☎ 805/861–2367 or 800/500–5376). **Merced Conference and Visitors Bureau** (✉ 690 W. 16th St., 95340, ☎ 209/384–3333 or 800/446–5353). **Modesto Convention and Visitors Bureau** (✉ 1114 J St., 95353, ☎ 209/571–6480). **Stockton/San Joaquin Convention and Visitors Bureau** (✉ 46 W. Fremont St., Stockton 95202, ☎ 209/943–1987 or 800/350–1987). **Visalia Convention and Visitors Bureau** (✉ 301 E. Acequia, 93291, ☎ 209/738–3435 or 800/524–0303).

10 Monterey Bay

From Santa Cruz to Carmel Valley

The Monterey Peninsula is steeped in history. The town of Monterey was California's first capital, the Carmel Mission headquarters for California's entire 18th-century mission system. The peninsula also has a rich literary past. John Steinbeck's novels immortalize the area, and Robert Louis Stevenson strolled its streets for inspiration for Treasure Island. *The present is equally illustrious. Blessed with a natural splendor undiminished by time or commerce, the peninsula is home to visionary marine habitats and luxurious resorts and golf courses.*

By Claudia
Gioseffi

IN 1542, MONTEREY BAY'S WHITE SAND BEACHES, pine forests, and rugged coastline captivated explorer Juan Rodríguez Cabrillo, who claimed it for Spain. Spanish missionaries, Mexican rulers, and land developers would come and go, all of them instinctively knowing not to destroy the peninsula's God-given assets or historical sites. The area has never relied solely on its looks, however. Certainly you can't ignore its deep green forests of Monterey cypress—oddly gnarled trees that grow nowhere else—its aquamarine waters, or the dance of cloud shadows upon its rolling emerald hills and winsome meadows. Yet there are industrial, a bit messy, claims to fame—whaling for one, sardines for another. And its meticulously preserved adobe houses and missions, layers of a Spanish and Mexican past left remarkably undisturbed, create a terra-cotta skyline that testifies to the Monterey Peninsula's singular place in California history.

With the arrival of Father Junípero Serra and Commander Don Gaspar de Portola from Spain in 1770, Monterey became both the military and ecclesiastical capital of Alta California. Portola established the first of California's four Spanish presidios; Serra founded the second of 21 Franciscan missions, later moving it from Monterey to its current site in Carmel.

When Mexico revolted against Spain in 1822, Monterey remained the capital of California under Mexican rule. The town grew into a lively seaport, drawing Yankee sea traders who added their own cultural and political influence. Then, on July 7, 1846, Commodore John Sloat arrived in Monterey and raised the American flag over the Custom House, claiming California for the United States.

Although Monterey's whaling industry boomed at this time, and would continue to thrive until the early 1900s, the city's political importance in the new territory was short-lived. The state constitution was framed in Colton Hall, but Monterey was all but forgotten once gold was discovered at Sutter's Mill near Sacramento. After the gold rush, the state capital moved from Monterey and the town became a sleepy backwater.

At the turn of the century, the Monterey Peninsula began to draw tourists with the opening of the Del Monte Hotel, the most palatial resort the West Coast had ever seen. It was then that writers and artists such as John Steinbeck, Henry Miller, Robinson Jeffers, Francis McComas, and Ansel Adams also discovered the peninsula, adding their legacy to the region while capturing its magic on canvas, paper, and film. In the 1920s and 1930s, Cannery Row's sardine industry took off, but by the late 1940s and early 1950s the fish had simply disappeared. The cause of this is still in dispute, though overfishing, water contamination, and a change in ocean currents that lowered the area's water temperature are the likely contenders. In 1995 in nearby Salinas, sardines were packed again for the first time since the 1950s. Visitors can buy them in Cannery Row, where activity has returned in the form of renovated buildings that house specialty shops, boutiques, and restaurants.

All aspects of the peninsula's diverse cultural and maritime heritage can be felt today, from Monterey's Path of History to its busy harbor and wharf. Modern-day attractions include the Monterey Jazz Festival and the Monterey Bay National Marine Sanctuary—the nation's largest undersea canyon, larger and deeper than the Grand Canyon. The sanctuary supports a rich brew of marine life, from fat, barking sea lions to tiny plantlike anemones. Carmel Valley, the "Sunbelt" of the Monterey Peninsula, averages 283 sunny days a year and, seemingly, that many resorts; the fertile Salinas Valley has become the "Salad Bowl of the Nation." Pacific Grove's century-old Victorians have redefined the bed-and-breakfast trade for the 1990s, and Pebble Beach's championship golf courses are the scene of many a prestigious tournament. Special annual events pay tribute to old traditions, and ethnic and religious festivities, such as Pacific Grove's Butterfly Parade, the Carmel Shakespeare Festival, and the Santa Rosalia Festival, link the past with the present.

Pleasures and Pastimes

Dining

Monterey is the richest area for dining along the coast between San Francisco and Los Angeles. The surrounding waters abound with fish, wild game roams the foothills, and the inland valleys are the vegetable basket of California; nearby Castroville dubs itself the Artichoke Capital of the World. Except at beachside stands and the inexpensive eateries listed below, casual but attractive resort wear is the norm. The few places where more formal attire is required are noted.

CATEGORY	COST*
$$$$	over $50
$$$	$30–$50
$$	$20–$30
$	under $20

*per person for a three-course meal, excluding drinks, service, and 6½%–8¼% tax

Golf

Since the opening of the Del Monte Golf Course in 1897, golf has been an integral part of the Monterey Peninsula's social and recreational scene. The greens fee for 18 holes runs from $15 to $225, depending on the time and course. Many hotels will help with golf reservations or have golf packages; inquire when you make your reservation.

Lodging

Monterey-area accommodations range from no-frills motels and historic hotels to upscale establishments that are a bit impersonal and clearly designed for conventions. Others pamper the individual traveler in grand style, especially some of the small inns and B&Bs in Carmel. Pacific Grove has quietly turned itself into the region's B&B capital. Carmel and Carmel Valley also have fine B&Bs; other lodgings vary from beachside motels to luxury complexes. Even more luxurious are the resorts in exclusive Pebble Beach. The rates below are for two people in the high season, April to October. Rates during winter, especially at the larger hotels, drop by as much as 50%, and B&Bs often offer midweek specials at this time of year. Lodgings booked through Monterey's 800/555–9283 number include an informational brochure and discount coupons good at restaurants, attractions, and shops.

CATEGORY	COST*
$$$$	over $175
$$$	$120–$175
$$	$80–$120
$	under $80

*All prices are for a standard double room, excluding 10½% tax.

Surfing

Santa Cruz is the surf capital of northern California. Steamer's Lane, between the boardwalk and the lighthouse, always has a decent break and plays host to several competitions in the summer.

Whale-Watching

On their annual migration between the Bering Sea and Baja California, 45-ft gray whales can be spotted not far off the Monterey coast.

They sometimes can be seen with binoculars from shore, but a whale-watching cruise is the best way to view these magnificent mammals up close. The migration south takes place between December and March—late January is prime viewing time. The migration north is from March to June. Two thousand blue whales and 600 humpbacks come north from Mexico to spend the summer feeding; they're easily spotted late summer and early fall. Rarer minke whales, orcas, sperm whales, and fin whales have been sighted in mid-August. Even if no whales surface, bay cruises almost always encounter some unforgettable marine life.

Exploring Monterey Bay

The population centers here are towns, not cities, and their individual charms complement Monterey Bay's natural beauty. Santa Cruz sits at the top of the curve, and the Monterey Peninsula, including Monterey, Pacific Grove, and Carmel, occupies the lower end. In between, Highway 1 cruises along the coastline, passing windswept beaches piled high with sand dunes. Along the route are fields of artichoke plants and the towns of Watsonville and Castroville. Different times of day and season bring out the various moods: walking at the edge of the ocean on a stark winter morning, seabirds in loud commotion overhead; spotting a rainbow on the horizon after an afternoon squall; sipping a cool chardonnay in the warm glow of an outdoor fireplace as the sun slips into the Pacific.

Numbers in the text correspond to numbers in the margin and on the Monterey Bay, Monterey and Pacific Grove, and Carmel and 17-Mile Drive maps.

Great Itineraries

Despite its compact size, the Monterey Peninsula is packed with diversions—it would take more than a weekend to get beyond the surface. If you have an interest in California history and historic preservation, the place to start is Monterey, with its adobe buildings along the downtown Path of History. Fans of Victorian architecture will want to explore the many fine examples in Pacific Grove. In Carmel you can shop till you drop, and when summer and weekend hordes overwhelm the town's clothing boutiques, art galleries, housewares outlets, and gift shops, you can slip off to enjoy the coast.

IF YOU HAVE 3 DAYS

Visit 🔀 **Monterey** ②–⑲, a seaside town with a vibrant history. Walk along the streets of Cannery Row and stop at **Steinbeck's Spirit of Monterey Wax Museum** ⑯ or the **Old General Store** ⑰, and then have lunch before heading to the **Monterey Bay Aquarium** ⑲, at the south end of the Row, for the rest of the afternoon. After your aquarium visit, head on foot via the oceanfront recreation trail to **Fisherman's Wharf** ⑬ to enjoy the sights and catch the sunset. If you're not up to the hubbub along the wharf, slip into the serene bar at the Monterey Plaza Hotel. The following day, visit the **Larkin House** ⑥, **Cooper-Molera Adobe** ⑦, and (Robert Louis) **Stevenson House** ⑧, stopping for lunch when the need hits. Then pick up some juice and late-afternoon snacks to take on **17-Mile Drive** ㉕–㉙. Catch the sunset along 17-Mile Drive or at nearby **Point Lobos State Reserve** ㉞. On the third day, drive a short distance south to **Carmel** ㉚–㉞. Visit the **Carmel Mission** ㉛ and have lunch while browsing through the **Ocean Avenue** shopping area before stopping at **Tor House** ㉜, the residence of the late poet Robinson Jeffers. No matter what time of year you're visiting Monterey Bay, stroll over to Scenic Road and spend time on Carmel Beach before leaving the area.

IF YOU HAVE 5 DAYS
On your first three days, visit **Monterey** ②–⑲, stopping at the **Custom House** ②, **Larkin House** ⑥, **Cooper-Molera Adobe** ⑦, **Stevenson House** ⑧, and **Colton Hall** ⑨ on day one. On your second morning, get a visceral feel for Monterey Bay marine life with a **whale-watching or other cruise,** have lunch upon your return to dry land, and then visit **Steinbeck's Spirit of Monterey Wax Museum** ⑯, the **Old General Store** ⑰, and **Fisherman's Wharf** ⑬. On the morning of day three, head to **Monterey Bay Aquarium** ⑲, have lunch along Cannery Row upon exiting, and then spend the rest of the afternoon either tasting wine at **Ventana Vineyards** on the Monterey–Salinas Highway or enjoying the Monterey waterfront. On your fourth day, visit **Carmel Mission** ㉛ and **Tor House** ㉜ and have lunch while exploring the shops along **Ocean Avenue** in Carmel. Pick up some juice and late-afternoon snacks for a spin on **17-Mile Drive** ㉕–㉙. Catch the sunset along 17-Mile Drive or at nearby **Point Lobos State Reserve** ㉞. On day five explore the shoreline and Victorian houses of **Pacific Grove** ⑳–㉔ in the morning and lunch there. If you have time, visit **San Juan Bautista** ㊲, a classic mission village, before departing.

IF YOU HAVE 7 DAYS
On days one through three, explore 🏙 **Monterey** ②–⑲. Spend day four in **Carmel** ㉚–㉞ and along **17-Mile Drive** ㉕–㉙. On day five, stop in **Pacific Grove** ⑳–㉔, including the oldest continuously operating lighthouse on the West Coast, **Point Piños Light Station** ㉒. Visit **Asilomar State Beach,** a sanctuary of dunes, tidal pools, and pocket-size beaches on day six. On your last day in the area, drive inland to **San Juan Bautista** ㊲.

When to Tour Monterey Bay

Summer is peak season, with crowds everywhere and generally mild weather. A sweater or windbreaker is nearly always necessary along the coast, where a cool breeze usually blows and fog is on the way in or out. Inland, temperatures in Salinas or Carmel Valley can be a good 15 or 20 degrees warmer than those in Carmel and Monterey. Off-season, from November to April, fewer people visit and the mood is more introspective. The rains come in January and February. Most of the historic sights in Monterey are open daily, though hours vary between peak and nonpeak season; call ahead to be sure.

MONTEREY BAY

Santa Cruz to Carmel Valley

Set along 90 mi of arc-shaped coastline, like jewels in a tiara, the towns of Monterey Bay combine the somewhat funky, beachcomber aspects of California's culture with the state's more glamorous, refined tendencies. Past and present merge gracefully here. As the city of Monterey's first mayor, Carmel Martin, described it early in this century: "Monterey Bay is the one place where people can live without being disturbed by manufacturing and big factories. I am certain that the day is coming when this will be the most desirable place in the whole state of California."

Santa Cruz

❶ *74 mi south of San Francisco, I–280 to Hwy. 17 to Hwy. 1; 48 mi north of Monterey on Hwy. 1.*

The beach town of Santa Cruz is sheltered by the surrounding mountains from the coastal fog to the north and south and from the smoggy skies of the San Francisco Bay area. The climate here is mild, and it is

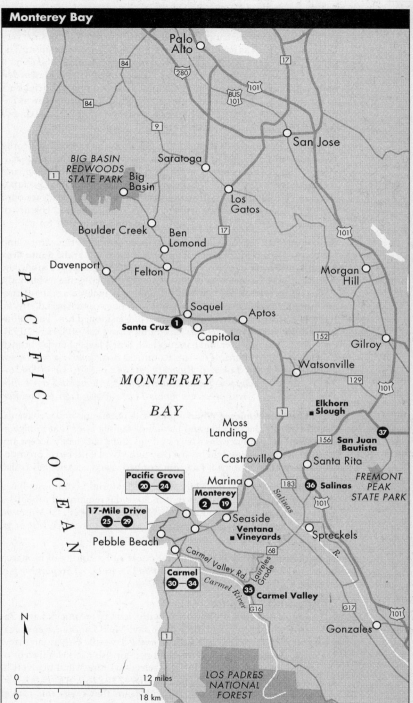

84

280

84

17

BUS
101

US
101

9

Palo
Alto

San Jose

*BIG BASIN
REDWOODS
STATE PARK*

1

Saratoga

Big
Basin

Los
Gatos

17

Boulder Creek

Ben
Lomond

Davenport

Felton

Morgan
Hill

Soquel

Aptos

101

Santa Cruz ❶

Capitola

152

Gilroy

Watsonville

129

101

PACIFIC

MONTEREY

BAY

Moss
Landing

1

**Elkhorn
Slough** ■

**San Juan
Bautista** ㊲

Castroville

156

Santa Rita

*FREMONT
PEAK
STATE PARK*

OCEAN

Pacific Grove
⑳—㉔

Marina

Salinas

183

㊱ **Salinas**

Monterey
❷—⑲

101

17-Mile Drive
㉕—㉙

Seaside

**Ventana
Vineyards** ■

Spreckels

Pebble Beach

Carmel Valley Rd

68

Laureles Grade

Carmel
㉚—㉞

Carmel River

㉟ **Carmel Valley**

R.

N

G16

G17

101

Gonzales

1

0 ——————— 12 miles

0 ——————— 18 km

*LOS PADRES
NATIONAL
FOREST*

usually warmer and sunnier than elsewhere along the coast this far north. A haven for those opting out of the rat race and a bastion of '60s-style counterculture values, Santa Cruz has been at the forefront of such very Californian trends as health food, recycling, and environmentalism. The historic heart of the downtown area is along Pacific Avenue, where you'll find the shops, restaurants, and other establishments in **Pacific Garden Mall.** Although it remains less manicured than its upmarket neighbors to the south, Santa Cruz is more urban than the agricultural towns between it and the Monterey Peninsula. Nearby Capitola, Soquel, and Aptos are home to some quality restaurants and small inns.

The town gets some of its youthful and unflagging spirit from the nearby **University of California at Santa Cruz.** The school's harmonious redwood buildings are perched on the forested hills above the town, and the campus is tailor-made for the contemplative life, with a juxtaposition of sylvan settings and sweeping vistas over open meadows onto the bay. The humanities department offers a major in the "History of Consciousness," and this does seem to be the perfect spot for it.

★ ☕ Santa Cruz has been a seaside resort since the mid-19th century, and the merry-go-round and Giant Dipper roller coaster at the **Santa Cruz Beach Boardwalk** date back to the early 1900s. Elsewhere along the boardwalk the Casino Arcade has its share of video-game technology, as does Neptune's Kingdom, whose highlights include a state-of-the-art miniature golf course with robotic and fiber-optic special effects. But this is still primarily a place of good old-fashioned fun. The colonnades of the turn-of-the-century Cocoanut Grove (☎ 408/423–2053), now a convention center and banquet hall, host a lavish Sunday brunch beneath the glass dome of its Sun Room. ⊠ *Boardwalk: along Beach St. west from San Lorenzo River,* ☎ *408/423–5590 or 408/426–7433.* 🎟 *$17.95 (day pass for unlimited rides).* ☉ *Memorial Day–Labor Day 11 AM–9 PM; rest of yr, weekends 11 AM–9 PM, later in summer.*

The **Santa Cruz Municipal Wharf** is lined with restaurants and is enlivened from below by the barking and baying of the sea lions that lounge in communal heaps under the wharf's pilings and shamelessly accept any seafood offerings tossed their way. Down the West Cliff Drive promontory at **Seal Rock,** pinnipeds hang out, sunbathe, and occasionally frolic.

The **Lighthouse** (a.k.a. the Mark Abbott Memorial Lighthouse) has a surfing museum with artifacts that include the remains of a board a shark munched on. ⊠ *W. Cliff Dr.,* ☎ *408/429–3429.* ☉ *Museum: summer, Mon. and Wed.–Fri. noon–4, weekends noon–5; rest of yr, Mon., Thurs., and Fri. noon–4, weekends noon–5.*

☕ **Natural Bridges State Park** has tidal pools and a colony of monarch butterflies. ⊠ *2531 W. Cliff Dr.,* ☎ *408/423–4609.* 🎟 *$6 parking fee.* ☉ *Park 8 AM–sunset, visitor center 10–4.*

Dining and Lodging

$$$ ✕ **Stagnaro Brothers.** On the ocean with views of Steamer's Lane, Pacific Grove, Monterey, and (on a clear day) Moss Landing, this casual eatery serves 20 types of fresh seafood every day—the Fisherman's stew is a great sampler. The Stagnaro-run open-air fish market adjacent to the restaurant stocks an equally large selection of fresh and frozen fish. ⊠ *Outer end of Municipal Wharf,* ☎ *408/423–2180. AE, D, MC, V.*

$$ ✕ **Chez Renee.** The husband-and-wife team that owns this retreat
★   serves French-inspired cuisine. Specialties include sweetbreads with two sauces (Madeira and mustard), duck and home-preserved brandied cherries, and deep-sea scallops garnished with smoked salmon and dill. Save room for the excellent dessert soufflés. ⊠ *9051 Soquel Dr., Aptos,* ☎ *408/688–5566. MC, V. No lunch Sat.*

$$ ✕ **Clouds Downtown.** Modern, bright, and trendy, with an emphasis on local produce such as artichokes from Castroville, this establishment serves vegetarian dishes that please the town's large "vegan" population. But with an unbeatable pot roast, Clouds is decidedly *not* a vegetarian restaurant. ✉ *110 Church St.,* ☎ *408/429–2000. AE, MC, V.*

$$ ✕ **El Palomar.** The restaurant of the Palomar Hotel has vaulted ceilings and wood beams. Among the best Californian-Mexican dishes are homemade tamales, seviche, and chili verde. Seafood is a major emphasis here. ✉ *1336 Pacific Ave.,* ☎ *408/425–7575. Reservations not accepted. AE, D, MC, V.*

$$ ✕ **India Joze.** You'll find an eclectic mix of Southeast Asian, Indian, and Persian specialties at this downtown favorite that's been open since the early '70s. Try chicken or snapper with *java* sauce—a delicious concoction of fresh basil, ginger, and tamarind—or any of the grilled dishes with *pangang*, a ginger, garlic, and lime marinade. Chutney (known as "chut" here) and the curries are also worth ordering. ✉ *1001 Center St.,* ☎ *408/427–3554. AE, DC, MC, V.*

$–$$ ✕ **O Mei Sichuan Chinese Restaurant.** Not your run-of-the-mill chop-suey joint, this sophisticated place serves some unusual dishes: *gan pung* (boneless fried chicken served with a spicy garlic sauce), *gan bian* (dried sautéed beef with hot pepper and ginger on crispy rice noodles), and rock cod prepared Taiwan style (filleted and breaded, with chili-vinegar sauce). ✉ *2316 Mission St. (Hwy. 1),* ☎ *408/425–8458. AE, MC, V. No lunch weekends.*

$–$$ ✕ **Positively Front Street.** This eatery serves fresh seafood—or bring in your own and the chef will cook it to order. Burgers and pizza cater to the beach-and-boardwalk crowd, who dine comfortably with those who prefer salmon. Up a hill from a break in Front Street, the restaurant is named to clear up any confusion about its address. ✉ *44 Front St.,* ☎ *408/426–1944. MC, V.*

$ ✕ **Caffè Pergolesi.** You can read the newspaper and enjoy a pastry at one of the veranda tables at this coffeehouse inside a Victorian residence. Or have a light meal inside, surrounded by local artists' works. ✉ *418 Cedar St.,* ☎ *408/426–1775. No credit cards.*

$ ✕ **Scontriano's Dolphin Restaurant.** Occupying a scenic site at the end of the Municipal Wharf, this casual restaurant serves up standard breakfasts—hotcakes, French toast, omelets, cereals—plus seafood lunches and dinners. ✉ *At the end of Santa Cruz Municipal Wharf,* ☎ *408/426–5830. MC, V.*

$$$–$$$$ 🏨 **Dream Inn.** Within a short stroll of the Beach Boardwalk and wharf, this beachfront resort opens right onto Cowell Beach. If it's too cold to swim in the ocean, you can head for the heated swimming pool and tub. Rooms have VCRs and balconies or patios. Children under 12 stay free with parents. ✉ *175 W. Cliff Dr., 95060,* ☎ *408/426–4330 or 800/662–3838,* FAX *408/427–2025. 164 rooms. 2 restaurants, refrigerators, pool, sauna, hot tub. AE, D, DC, MC, V.*

$$$–$$$$ 🏨 **Inn at Depot Hill.** This inventively designed hotel in a former rail depot has taken the *Orient Express* as its theme. Each double room or suite, complete with fireplace and feather beds, is inspired by a different European destination—Delft, the Netherlands; Portofino, Italy; Sissinghurst, England; the Côte d'Azur, France. One is decorated like a Pullman car for a railroad baron. Some accommodations have balconies with private hot tubs. Room rates include a full breakfast and late-afternoon wine and hors d'oeuvres. ✉ *250 Monterey Ave., Capitola-by-the-Sea 95010,* ☎ *408/462–3376 or 800/572–2632,* FAX *408/462–3697. 8 rooms. In-room modem lines, no-smoking rooms, in-room VCRs. AE, MC, V.*

$$ 🏠 **Harbor Inn.** Lived-in furniture and wooden beds make a stay at this quiet inn reminiscent of a visit to grandma's. The antithesis of a chain motel, the inn is clean, comfortable, and a great bargain. Many rooms have kitchenettes, and groups of four can get a suite. Harbor Inn is southeast of town yet close to the beach and yacht harbor. ⊠ *645 7th Ave.,* ☎ *408/479–9731. 19 rooms, 14 with bath. MC, V.*

Nightlife and the Arts

The **Cabrillo Music Festival** in Santa Cruz (☎ 408/426–6966 or 408/429–3444), one of the longest-running new-music festivals, brings in American and other composers for two weeks in early August.

Shakespeare Santa Cruz (⊠ Performing Arts Complex, University of California at Santa Cruz, ☎ 408/459–2121) puts on a six-week Shakespeare festival in July and August that also includes 20th-century works. Some performances are outdoors in the striking Redwood Glen.

Outdoor Activities and Sports

BEACHES

Surfers in Santa Cruz gather for the spectacular waves and sunsets at **Pleasure Point** (⊠ East Cliff and Pleasure Point Drs.). Steamer's Lane, between the boardwalk and the lighthouse, is another favored spot. The surf at **New Brighton State Beach** (⊠ 1500 State Park Dr., Capitola) is challenging; campsites are available. South of Santa Cruz, **Manresa State Beach** (⊠ Manresa Dr., La Selva Beach, ☎ 408/761–1795) has premium surfing conditions, but the water here is treacherous, so the beach is recommended only for sunbathing. **Beach 'n' Bikini Surf Shop** (⊠ Beach and Front Sts., ☎ 408/427–2355) rents surfboards and wet suits by the day.

BICYCLING

Bikes can be rented from **Surf City Rentals** (⊠ 46 Front St., ☎ 408/426–6450).

BOATS AND CHARTERS

Original Stagnaro Fishing Trips (⊠ Center of Santa Cruz Municipal Wharf, ☎ 408/427–2334) operates salmon and rock-cod fishing expeditions; the $39 fee includes bait. The company also operates $18 whale-watching cruises December through April.

Monterey

48 mi south of Santa Cruz on Hwy. 1; 122 mi south of San Francisco on I–280 to Hwy. 17 to Hwy. 1; 334 mi north of Los Angeles on U.S. 101 to Hwy. 68 west from Salinas.

Monterey was California's first capital. A good deal of the city's early history can be gleaned from the well-preserved adobe buildings of

★ **Monterey State Historic Park** (☎ 408/649–7118). Far from being a hermetic period museum, the park facilities are an integral part of the day-to-day business life of the town—some of the buildings still serve as government offices and include a store and a restaurant. A 2-mi self-guided walking tour of the park is outlined in the brochure "Path of History," available at many of the landmark buildings in the park. A $5 ticket offered by the park gains visitors entrance to Casa Soberanes, the Cooper-Molera Adobe, the Larkin House, and the Stevenson House (☞ *below*) and includes a guided walking tour of the area.

❷   The **Custom House,** built by the Mexican government in 1827, was the first stop for sea traders whose goods were subject to duty. An upper story was later added to the adobe structure. At the beginning of the Mexican-American War in 1846, Commodore John Sloat raised the American flag over the building and claimed California for the United

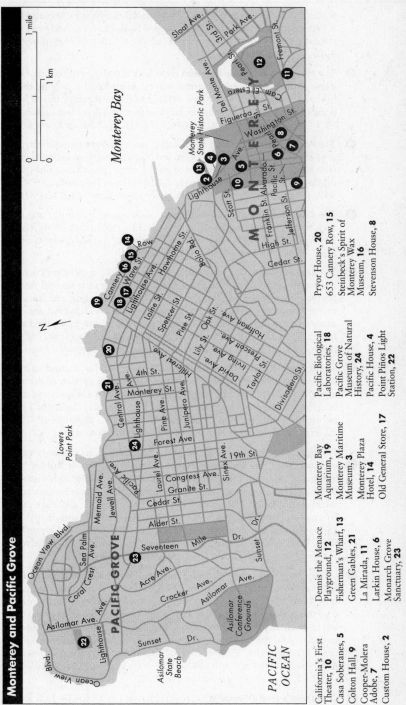

Monterey and Pacific Grove

California's First Theater, **10**
Casa Soberanes, **5**
Colton Hall, **9**
Cooper-Molera Adobe, **7**
Custom House, **2**

Dennis the Menace Playground, **12**
Fisherman's Wharf, **13**
Green Gables, **21**
La Mirada, **11**
Larkin House, **6**
Monarch Grove Sanctuary, **23**

Monterey Bay Aquarium, **19**
Monterey Maritime Museum, **3**
Monterey Plaza Hotel, **14**
Old General Store, **17**

Pacific Biological Laboratories, **18**
Pacific Grove Museum of Natural History, **24**
Pacific House, **4**
Point Piños Light Station, **22**

Pryor House, **20**
653 Cannery Row, **15**
Steinbeck's Spirit of Monterey Wax Museum, **16**
Stevenson House, **8**

States. Now the lower floor displays examples of a typical cargo from a 19th-century trading ship. ✉ *1 Custom House Plaza across from Fisherman's Wharf,* ☎ *408/649–2909.* 🎟 *Free.* ◷ *Sept.–May, daily 10–4; June–Aug., daily 10–5.*

❸ The **Monterey Maritime Museum** includes the private collection of maritime artifacts of a former Carmel mayor, Allen Knight. Among the exhibits of ship models, scrimshaw items, and nautical prints, the highlight is the enormous multifaceted Fresnel lens from the Point Sur Lighthouse. ✉ *5 Custom House Plaza,* ☎ *408/375–2553.* 🎟 *$5.* ◷ *Daily 10–5.*

❹ The **Pacific House,** a former hotel and saloon, is now a museum that surveys life in early California. There are Native American artifacts, gold-rush relics, historic photographs of old Monterey, and a costume gallery displaying various period fashions. ✉ *10 Custom House Plaza,* ☎ *408/649–2907.* 🎟 *Free.* ◷ *Sept.–May, daily 10–4; June–Aug., daily 10–5.*

❺ The **Casa Soberanes,** a low-ceiling classic adobe structure, was once a Custom House guard's residence. ✉ *336 Pacific St.,* ☎ *408/649–7118.* 🎟 *$2.* ◷ *Varied hrs; call for schedule of guided tours. Gardens Sept.–May, daily 10–4; June–Aug., daily 10–5.*

❻ The **Larkin House,** one of the most architecturally significant homes in California, was built in 1835. A veranda encircles the second floor of the two-story adobe, reflecting the Mexican and New England influences on the Monterey style. The rooms are furnished with period antiques, many of them brought from New Hampshire to Monterey by the Larkin family. ✉ *510 Calle Principal, between Jefferson and Pacific Sts.,* ☎ *408/649–7118.* 🎟 *$2.* ◷ *Varied hrs; call for schedule of guided tours.*

❼ The restored **Cooper-Molera Adobe,** a 2-acre complex, includes a house dating from the 1820s, a visitor center, and a large garden enclosed by a high adobe wall. The tile-roof house is filled with antiques and memorabilia, mostly from the Victorian era, that illustrate the life of a prosperous pioneer family. ✉ *Polk and Munras Sts.,* ☎ *408/649–7118.* 🎟 *$2.* ◷ *Varied hrs; call for schedule of guided tours.*

❽ For literary and history buffs, one of the Monterey Path of History's greatest treasures is the **Stevenson House,** named in honor of Robert Louis Stevenson, author of *Treasure Island* and other classics, who boarded there briefly in a tiny upstairs room. In addition to Stevenson's room, which is furnished with items from his family's estate, there are period rooms—one is a children's nursery stocked with Victorian toys and games—and a gallery of the author's memorabilia. ✉ *530 Houston St.,* ☎ *408/649–7118.* 🎟 *$2.* ◷ *Varied hrs; call for schedule of guided tours. Gardens Sept.–May, daily 10–6; June–Aug., daily 10–5.*

❾ California's equivalent of Independence Hall is **Colton Hall,** where a convention of delegates met in 1849 to draft the first state constitution. Now the historic white building, which has served as a school, a courthouse, and the county seat, is a museum furnished as it was during the constitutional convention. The extensive grounds outside the hall surround the Old Monterey Jail, where inmates languished behind thick granite walls. ✉ *500 block of Pacific St., between Madison and Jefferson Sts.,* ☎ *408/646–5640.* 🎟 *Free.* ◷ *Mar.–Oct., daily 10–noon and 1–5; Nov.–Feb., 10–noon and 1–4.*

❿ **California's First Theater** was constructed in the 1840s by Jack Swan, an English sailor who settled in Monterey, as a saloon with adjoining apartments. Soldiers from the New York Volunteers who were on assignment in Monterey put on plays in the building. Performances are still given here (☞ Nightlife and the Arts, *below*). ✉ *Scott and Pacific Sts.,* ☎ *408/649–7118 or 408/375–4916; docent schedule varies.*

The **Monterey Peninsula Museum of Art** contains the works of distinguished artists who have worked in the area, among them photographers Ansel Adams and Edward Weston. Another focus is international folk art; the collection ranges from Kentucky hearth brooms to Tibetan prayer wheels. ⊠ *559 Pacific St., across the street from Colton Hall,* ☎ *408/372–7591.* ⊠ *$3.* ☉ *Tues.–Sat. 10–5, Sun. 1–5.*

⑪ At **La Mirada,** Asian and European antiques fill a 19th-century adobe house. A newer 10,000-square-ft gallery space, designed by architect Charles Moore, houses Asian and Californian regional art. The permanent collection includes works by Armin Carl Hansen, as well as a large netsuke collection. Outdoors are magnificent rose and rhododendron gardens. ⊠ *720 Via Mirada, at Fremont St.,* ☎ *408/372–3689.* ⊠ *$3.* ☉ *Tues.–Sat. 10–4, Sun. 1–4.*

★ ☙ ⑫ **Dennis the Menace Playground** (⊠ Fremont St. and Camino El Estero), in Lake El Estero Park, is an imaginative play area whose name pays tribute to the cartoon creation of local resident Hank Ketcham. The equipment is on a grand scale and made for daredevils; there's a dizzyingly high rotating platform, a clanking suspension bridge, and a real Southern Pacific steam locomotive. Rowboats and paddleboats can be rented on U-shape Lake El Estero, home to a varied assortment of ducks, mud hens, and geese.

Inevitably, visitors are drawn to Monterey's waterfront, if only because the mournful barking of sea lions makes its presence impossible to ignore. The whiskered marine mammals are best enjoyed while
☙ ⑬ walking along **Fisherman's Wharf,** an aging pier crowded with souvenir shops, fish markets, seafood restaurants, and popcorn stands. Although tacky and touristy to the utmost, the wharf is a good place to visit with children.

Cannery Row has undergone several transformations since it was immortalized in John Steinbeck's 1945 novel of the same name. The street that Steinbeck described was crowded with sardine canneries processing, at their peak, nearly 200,000 tons of the smelly silver fish a year. During the mid-1940s, however, the sardines mysteriously disappeared from the bay, eventually causing the canneries to close. Over the years the old tin-roof canneries have been converted to restaurants, art galleries, and minimalls with shops selling T-shirts, fudge, and plastic otters. Recent tourist development along the row has been more tasteful, however, including several stylish inns and hotels.

⑭ The historic **Monterey Plaza Hotel** (⊠ 400 Cannery Row) sits on the site of an estate built by Hugh Tevis for his bride, who died on their honeymoon. It's a good place to relax over a drink and watch for otters.

Although John Steinbeck would have trouble recognizing Cannery Row today, there are still some historical and architectural features from
⑮ its colorful past. One building to notice is **653 Cannery Row.** Its tiled Chinese dragon roof dates from 1929.

⑯ Characters from the novel *Cannery Row* are depicted in wax at **Steinbeck's Spirit of Monterey Wax Museum,** which also presents a 25-minute description of the history of the area over the past 400 years, with a recorded narration by Steinbeck himself. ⊠ *700 Cannery Row,* ☎ *408/375–3770.* ⊠ *$4.95.* ☉ *Daily 9–9.*

⑰ The building now called the **Old General Store** (⊠ 835 Cannery Row) is the former Wing Chong Market that Steinbeck called Lee Chong's Heavenly Flower Grocery in *Cannery Row.* A weathered wooden
⑱ building at 800 Cannery Row was the **Pacific Biological Laboratories**

where Edward F. Ricketts, the inspiration for Doc in *Cannery Row,* did much of his marine research.

★ ☚ ⑲ Science, conservationism, and theater merge with great success at the **Monterey Bay Aquarium.** The Outer Bay wing, which opened in March 1996, is devoted to the mysteries of the open ocean and completes the aquarium's picture of Monterey Bay, the nation's largest marine sanctuary. Its million-gallon indoor ocean—highlighted by the largest window on earth—re-creates the sunlit blue water where Monterey Bay meets the open sea. In this habitat, blue and soupfin sharks, barracuda, pelagic stingrays, ocean sunfish (which can weigh a ton or more), green sea turtles, and schools of fast-moving tuna swim together. Some of these sea creatures are on exhibit for the first time. The Outer Bay wing also houses the country's largest collection of jellyfish. Expect long lines and sizable crowds at the aquarium on weekends, especially during the summer. Braving the crowds is worth it, however, especially to see the original wing's three-story Kelp Forest exhibit, the only one of its kind in the world, and another display of the sea creatures and vegetation found in the inner Monterey Bay. Among other standouts are a bat-ray petting pool, where the flat velvetlike creatures can be touched as they swim by; a 55,000-gallon sea-otter tank; and an enormous outdoor artificial tidal pool that supports anemones, crabs, sea stars, and other colorful creatures. ⊠ *886 Cannery Row,* ☎ *408/648–4888; 800/756–3737 in CA for advance tickets.* 🎟 *$14.75.* ☉ *Daily 10–6 (9–6 in summer); box office closes at 5:30.*

A five-minute drive from downtown Monterey leads to the highly regarded **Ventana Vineyards,** known for its chardonnays and Johannisberg Rieslings. Ventana's knowledgeable and hospitable owners, Doug and LuAnn Meador, invite guests to bring lunch to eat while tasting wines on a patio and deck. ⊠ *2999 Monterey–Salinas Hwy. (Hwy. 68),* ☎ *408/372–7415.* ☉ *Daily 11–5.*

OFF THE
BEATEN PATH
ELKHORN SLOUGH – A few miles north of Monterey, east of the tiny harbor town of Moss Landing, is one of only two federal research reserves in California, the Elkhorn Slough at the National Estuarine Research Reserve. Its 1,400 acres of tidal flats and salt marshes form a complex environment supporting more than 200 species of birds. A walk along the meandering waterways and wetlands can reveal hawks, white-tailed kites, owls, herons, and egrets. Sharks may be observed in the summer months. You can wander at leisure or, on weekends, take a guided walk (10 AM and 1 PM) to the heron rookery. ⊠ *1700 Elkhorn Rd., Watsonville,* ☎ *408/728–2822 for directions.* 🎟 *$2.50; free with any California hunting or fishing license.* ☉ *Wed.–Sun. 9–5.*

Dining and Lodging

$$$ ✕ **Duck Club.** The elegant and romantic dining room of the Monterey Plaza Hotel (☞ *below*) is built over the waterfront on Cannery Row, overlooking the bay. The menu strongly emphasizes duck but also includes seafood, meat, and pasta. ⊠ *400 Cannery Row,* ☎ *408/646–1700. AE, D, DC, MC, V.*

$$$ ✕ **Fresh Cream.** Local residents recommend this outstanding restaurant in Heritage Harbor that has superb views over the bay. The cuisine is French, with light, imaginative Californian accents. Some favorites on the seasonal menu are the rack of lamb Dijonnaise and the roast boned duck in black-currant sauce. Fresh Cream presents live chamber music on Wednesday nights. ⊠ *99 Pacific St., Suite 100C,* ☎ *408/375–9798. AE, D, DC, MC, V. No lunch.*

$$–$$$ ✕ **Whaling Station Inn.** A pleasing mixture of rough-hewn wood and
★ sparkling white linen makes this restaurant a festive yet comfortable
place to enjoy mesquite-grilled fish and meats. There are excellent artichoke appetizers and fresh salads. ✉ *763 Wave St.*, ☎ *408/373–3778.
AE, D, DC, MC, V. No lunch.*

$$ ✕ **Bradley's Harbor Front Restaurant.** This restaurant—with possibly
the best location on the harbor—is so far out on a pier that it's almost
seaworthy. Though the exterior is salty, windblown, and surrounded
by dry-docked boats, the atmosphere inside recalls a 1920s European
bistro. Regional American fare with various ethnic influences includes
avocado pancakes with salsa and fresh fish specials. The desserts are
rich and delicious. ✉ *32 Cannery Row, at Coast Guard Pier*, ☎ *408/
655–6799. Reservations essential on weekends. AE, D, DC, MC, V.*

$$ ✕ **Cafe Fina.** Italian seafood dishes are the specialty of this understated
wharf restaurant. Highlights include mesquite-grilled fish dishes and
linguine in clam sauce with baby shrimp and tomatoes. The wine list
is extensive. ✉ *47 Fisherman's Wharf*, ☎ *408/372–5200. AE, D,
DC, MC, V.*

$$ ✕ **Domenico's.** Under the same ownership as the Whaling Station Inn
and nearby Abalonetti, Domenico's serves Italian seafood preparations,
mesquite-grilled meats, and homemade pastas. The blue-and-white
nautical decor keeps the place comfortably casual; white drapery lends
an air of elegance lacking in most restaurants on the wharf. ✉ *50 Fish-
erman's Wharf*, ☎ *408/372–3655. AE, D, DC, MC, V.*

$$ ✕ **Ferrante's.** Gorgeous views of both the town and the bay can be
had from this restaurant atop the 10-story Monterey Marriott. The
chicken cashew fettuccine with sun-dried tomatoes is especially good.
Brunch is served Sunday. ✉ *350 Calle Principal*, ☎ *408/649–4234.
AE, D, DC, MC, V. No lunch.*

$$ ✕ **Montrio.** In November 1995 *Esquire* named the then eight-month-
★ old Montrio its Restaurant of the Year, declaring that it "sums up in
every way what is best about California restaurants." The publication
also singled out Montrio's chef, Brian Whitmer, as one of America's finest.
If your appetite for hearty cooking and clean, strong flavors has been
stimulated by a day of bracing Monterey Bay breezes, this European-
inspired American bistro is the place to go. Grilled Portobello mush-
room "steak" with ragout of vegetables—the most requested dish—and
risotto with artichokes are just two of the menu highlights. Housed in
a landmark building that served as Monterey's firehouse from 1890 to
1910, the restaurant has an interior that is a montage of brick, rawhide,
and wrought iron. Whimsical paintings, crayons on every table, and un-
usual-looking sound mufflers on the ceiling (they're supposed to be clouds)
keep the mood lighthearted. ✉ *414 Calle Principal*, ☎ *408/648–8880.
Reservations essential on weekends. AE, D, MC, V.*

$–$$ ✕ **Abalonetti.** From a squid lover's point of view, wharfside Abalonetti
is the best place in town, serving all kinds of squid dishes: deep-fried,
sautéed with wine and garlic, or baked with eggplant. Abalone is another specialty, and the fresh fish is broiled or blackened and served
with beurre blanc or pesto. Seafood pasta and wood-fired pizza are
also on the menu. ✉ *57 Fisherman's Wharf*, ☎ *408/373–1851. AE,
D, DC, MC, V.*

$–$$ ✕ **Paradiso Trattoria.** Follow the aroma of marinating olives, roasted
garlic, and platters of focaccia to this bright Cannery Row establishment where California and Mediterranean specialties and pizzas from
a wood-burning oven are the luncheon fare. Seafood is a good choice
for dinner, which is served in a formal dining room that overlooks a
lighted beachfront and lapping surf. Every table has an ocean view. ✉
654 Cannery Row, ☎ *408/375–4155. AE, D, DC, MC, V.*

$–$$ ✕ **Tarpy's Roadhouse.** Fun, dressed-down roadhouse lunch and din-
ner are served in a renovated farmhouse built in the early 1900s. The
kitchen cooks everything Mom used to make, only better. ⊠ *2999 Monterey–Salinas Hwy. (Hwy. 68), at Canyon Del Rey Rd.,* ☎ *408/647–
1444. AE, D, MC, V.*

$ ✕ **Old Monterey Cafe.** Breakfast here, which is served until early af-
ternoon, can include fresh-baked muffins and eggs Benedict. This is
also a good place to relax with a cappuccino or coffee made from freshly
ground beans. ⊠ *489 Alvarado St.,* ☎ *408/646–1021. Reservations
not accepted. DC, MC, V.*

$$$$ ⌂ **Old Monterey Inn.** Perhaps no other inn conjures up the past and
★   beauty of the Monterey Peninsula or provides such a complete escape
so close to everything the area has to offer. The three-story English Tudor
country manor that has become the Old Monterey Inn was completed
in 1929, replete with hand-carved window frames, balustrades, Gothic
archways, and ceiling panels. Loving restoration by proprietors Gene
and Ann Swett included a rose garden now surrounded by giant holly
trees, 100-year-old gnarled oaks, fragrant eucalyptus, and majestic
redwoods. The couple's thoroughness and thoughtfulness extend to their
hospitality—a well-stocked medicine cabinet, the book placed on your
bed at night, a sumptuous featherbed and down comforter. ⊠ *500 Martin St., 93940,* ☎ *408/375–8284 or 800/350–2344,* FAX *408/375–6730.
10 rooms. Concierge. MC, V.*

$$$$ ⌂ **Spindrift Inn.** This small hotel on Cannery Row has the street's only
★   private beach; a rooftop garden overlooks Monterey Bay. Spacious rooms
with sitting areas, hardwood floors, fireplaces, and down comforters
are among the indoor pleasures. The rates include a Continental breakfast, brought to the room on a silver tray, and afternoon wine and cheese.
⊠ *652 Cannery Row, 93940,* ☎ *408/646–8900 or 800/841–1879,*
FAX *408/646–5342. 42 rooms. Refrigerators. AE, D, DC, MC, V.*

$$$–$$$$ ⌂ **Hotel Pacific.** All the rooms at the modern, adobe-style Hotel Pa-
cific are suites, handsomely appointed with four-poster featherbeds,
hardwood floors, Indian rugs, fireplaces, honor bars, and balconies or
patios. Room rates a include Continental breakfast and afternoon tea.
⊠ *300 Pacific St., 93940,* ☎ *408/373–5700; 800/554–5542 in CA;*
FAX *408/373–6921. 105 rooms. Refrigerators, 2 hot tubs, laundry ser-
vice. AE, D, DC, MC, V.*

$$$–$$$$ ⌂ **Hyatt Regency Monterey.** Although its rooms and atmosphere are
less glamorous than at some other resorts in the region, the facilities
here are excellent. ⊠ *1 Old Golf Course Rd., 93940,* ☎ *408/372–1234
or 800/233–1234; 800/824–2196 in CA;* FAX *408/375–3960. 575
rooms. Restaurant, café, 2 bars, 2 pools, 2 hot tubs, massage, 18-hole
golf course, putting green, 6 tennis courts, exercise room, bicycles, chil-
dren's programs. AE, D, DC, MC, V.*

$$$–$$$$ ⌂ **Monterey Bay Inn.** This hotel on Cannery Row is under the same own-
ership as the Spindrift Inn. Rooms, decorated in peach and green tones,
have private balconies, VCRs, honor bars, terry-cloth robes, and binoc-
ulars for viewing marine life; most rooms have breathtaking bay views.
In-room Continental breakfast is included. ⊠ *242 Cannery Row, 93940,*
☎ *408/373–6242 or 800/424–6242,* FAX *408/373–7603. 47 rooms.
Refrigerators, 2 hot tubs, sauna, exercise room. AE, D, DC, MC, V.*

$$$–$$$$ ⌂ **Monterey Plaza Hotel.** This sophisticated full-service hotel commands
★   a superb waterfront location on Cannery Row, where frolicking sea
otters can be observed from the wide outdoor patio and from many
of the room balconies. The architecture and decor blend early Cali-
fornian and Mediterranean styles and retain a little of the old cannery
design. ⊠ *400 Cannery Row, 93940,* ☎ *408/646–1700 or 800/631–*

1339; 800/334–3999 in CA; FAX *408/646–0285. 285 rooms. 2 restaurants, exercise room, laundry service. AE, D, DC, MC, V.*

$$–$$$$ 🏨 **Best Western Monterey Beach Hotel.** Rooms here may be nondescript, but this hotel has a great waterfront location about 2 mi north of town, with panoramic views of the bay and the Monterey skyline. Grounds are pleasantly landscaped, and the hotel has a large pool with a sunbathing area. ⊠ *2600 Sand Dunes Dr., 93940,* ☎ *408/394–3321 or 800/242–8627,* FAX *408/393–1912. 196 rooms. Restaurant, lounge, pool, hot tub, exercise room. AE, D, DC, MC, V.*

$$–$$$$ 🏨 **Cannery Row Inn.** Gas fireplaces and complimentary Continental breakfast are among the amenities at this small hotel on a street above Cannery Row. Some rooms have private balconies with bay views. ⊠ *200 Foam St., 93940,* ☎ *408/649–8580 or 800/876–8580,* FAX *408/ 649–2566. 32 rooms. Refrigerators, hot tub. AE, D, MC, V.*

$$–$$$ 🏨 **Monterey Hotel.** Standard rooms in this 1904 structure, which was restored in the late 1980s, are small but well appointed with reproduction antique furniture; master suites have fireplaces and sunken baths. Room rates include a Continental breakfast and evening refreshments. ⊠ *406 Alvarado St., 93940,* ☎ *408/375–3184 or 800/727–0960,* FAX *408/373–2894. 45 rooms. Parking (fee). AE, D, DC, MC, V.*

$$ 🏨 **Del Monte Beach Inn.** A small B&B, the Del Monte contains reasonably priced rooms decorated à la Martha Stewart. Be sure to check in before 9 PM, when the office closes. ⊠ *1110 Del Monte Ave., 93940,* ☎ *408/649–4410,* FAX *408/375–3818. 18 rooms. AE, D, MC, V.*

$$ 🏨 **Paramount Motel.** In the town of Marina 8 mi north of Monterey, this motel appears a bit shabby on the outside, but the proprietor is friendly and the rooms are clean, comfortable, and reasonably priced. No reservations are accepted; arrive early. ⊠ *3298 Del Monte Blvd., Marina, 93933,* ☎ *408/384–8674. 6 rooms. No credit cards.*

$–$$ 🏨 **Arbor Inn.** This stylish motel has a friendly, country-inn atmosphere. Continental breakfast is served in a pine-paneled lobby with a tile fireplace; in-room coffee is also complimentary. Rooms are light and airy, some with fireplaces and some with accessibility for visitors with disabilities. ⊠ *1058 Munras Ave., 93940,* ☎ *408/372–3381,* FAX *408/372–4687. 55 rooms. Hot tub. AE, D, DC, MC, V.*

$–$$ 🏨 **Monterey Bay Lodge.** A pleasant location on the edge of Mon-
★ terey's El Estero Park gives this motel an edge over its many competitors along Munras Avenue. Indoor plants and a secluded courtyard with a pool are other pluses. ⊠ *55 Aguajito Rd., 93940,* ☎ *408/372–8057 or 800/558–1900,* FAX *408/655–2933. 45 rooms. Restaurant, pool. AE, D, DC, MC, V.*

Nightlife and the Arts

BARS, CLUBS

Doc Ricketts' Lab (⊠ 95 Prescott St., ☎ 408/649–4241), one block above Cannery Row, hosts live bands—rock, blues, jazz, reggae, and folk.

Planet Gemini (⊠ 625 Cannery Row, ☎ 408/373–1449) presents comedy shows most nights, followed by dancing to DJ or live music. Country-and-western music and dancing happens Wednesday nights.

Safari Club (⊠ Bay Park Hotel, 1425 Munras Ave., ☎ 408/649–1020) has karaoke on Saturday nights.

Sly McFlys (⊠ 700 Cannery Row, ☎ 408/649–8050), a popular watering hole, has a publike atmosphere.

MUSIC FESTIVALS

Dixieland Monterey (⊠ 177 Webster St., Suite A-206, 93940, ☎ 408/ 443–5260), held on the first full weekend of March, presents Dixieland jazz bands in cabarets, restaurants, and hotel lounges on the Monterey waterfront.

Monterey Jazz Festival (☎ 408/373–3366 *for information, 800/307–3378 for tickets*) attracts jazz and blues greats to the Monterey Fairgrounds on the third full weekend of September.

Monterey Bay Blues Festival (✉ Box 1400, Seaside 93955, ☎ 408/394–2652) brings out blues fans in June to the Monterey Fairgrounds.

THEATER

California's First Theater (✉ Scott and Pacific Sts., ☎ 408/375–4916) is home to the Troupers of the Gold Coast, who perform 19th-century melodramas.

Monterey Bay Theatrefest (☎ 408/622–0700) presents free outdoor performances at Custom House Plaza on weekend afternoons and evenings during most of the summer.

Wharf Theater (✉ Fisherman's Wharf, ☎ 408/649–2332) focuses on the American musical past and present.

Outdoor Activities and Sports

BEACHES

The local waters around Monterey are generally too cold and turbulent for swimming. **Monterey Municipal Beach,** east of Wharf No. 2, has shallow waters that are warm and calm enough for wading.

BICYCLING

For bicycle rentals try **Bay Bikes** (✉ 640 Wave St., ☎ 408/646–9090). **Adventures by the Sea Inc.** (✉ 299 Cannery Row, ☎ 408/372–1807) rents bikes, kayaks, and Rollerblades. Mopeds, motorcycles, and bikes can be rented from **Monterey Moped Adventures** (✉ 1250 Del Monte Ave., ☎ 408/373–2696); a driver's license is required.

CAR RACING

Four major races take place each year on the 2.2-mi, 11-turn **Laguna Seca Raceway** (✉ 1021 Monterey–Salinas Hwy., ☎ 408/648–5100). They range from Indianapolis 500–style races to one with more than 300 restored models from earlier eras.

FISHING

Half- and full-day fishing trips can be arranged by **Monterey Sport Fishing** (✉ 96 Fisherman's Wharf, ☎ 408/372–2203 or 800/200–2203), **Randy's Fishing Trips** (✉ 66 Fisherman's Wharf, ☎ 408/372–7440), and **Sam's Fishing Fleet** (✉ 84 Fisherman's Wharf, ☎ 408/372–0577).

GOLF

Laguna Seca Golf Club (✉ 10520 York Rd., off Hwy. 68, ☎ 408/373–3701), a course with an 18-hole layout updated by Robert Trent Jones Jr., has a $55 greens fee (cart rental $25) for nonmembers.

Old Del Monte Golf Course (✉ 1300 Sylvan Rd., ☎ 408/373–2700) has the most reasonable greens fee in the area: $50 per player plus $15 cart rental, with an $18 twilight special after 2:30 in winter and 4:30 in summer.

KAYAKING

Monterey Bay Kayaks (✉ 693 Del Monte Ave., ☎ 408/373–5357; 800/649–5357 in CA) has rentals, classes, and guided natural-history tours.

ROLLER SKATING

Del Monte Gardens (✉ 2020 Del Monte Ave., ☎ 408/375–3202), an old-fashioned rink, rents skates.

SCUBA DIVING

Aquarius Dive Shops (✉ 2040 Del Monte Ave., ☎ 408/375–1933) gives diving lessons, rents equipment, and operates guided dive tours. Call ☎ 408/657–1020 for local scuba-diving conditions.

TENNIS

Monterey Tennis Center (☎ 408/372–0172) has details about area facilities.

WHALE-WATCHING

Monterey Sport Fishing (⊠ 96 Fisherman's Wharf, ☎ 408/372–2203 or 800/200–2203), **Randy's Fishing Trips** (⊠ 66 Fisherman's Wharf, ☎ 408/372–7440), and **Sam's Fishing Fleet** (⊠ 84 Fisherman's Wharf, ☎ 408/372–0577) operate whale-watching expeditions.

Shopping

John Riley Golf (⊠ 601 Wave St., ☎ 408/373–8855) carries custom-made golf clubs. **Loes Hinse** (⊠ 542 Lighthouse Ave., ☎ 408/373–7553) is the well-kept secret of locals who prefer to wear original designs. **Old Monterey Book Co.** (⊠ 136 Bonifacio Pl., off Alvarado St., ☎ 408/372–3111) specializes in rare old books and prints. **Sea Fantasies** (⊠ 400 Cannery Row, ☎ 408/375–5033) owner Lee Austin collects rare pearls, precious coral, and ancient marine fossils on adventures to Fiji, India, and West Africa. He designs furniture, sculpture, and jewelry with his finds.

Pacific Grove

3 mi south of Monterey on Hwy. 1 to Hwy. 68; from Cannery Row, Wave St. becomes Ocean View Blvd. at Monterey–Pacific Grove border.

If not for the dramatic strip of coastline in its backyard, Pacific Grove could easily pass for a typical small town in the Heartland. Beginning as a summer retreat for church groups more than a century ago, the town recalls its prim and proper Victorian heritage in the host of tiny board-and-batten cottages and stately mansions lining its streets.

Even before the church groups migrated here, Pacific Grove had been receiving thousands of annual guests in the form of bright orange-and-black monarch butterflies. Known as Butterfly Town USA, Pacific Grove is the winter home of monarchs that migrate south from Canada and the Pacific Northwest to take residence in the pine and eucalyptus groves between October and March. The sight of a mass of butterflies hanging from the branches like a long, fluttering veil is unforgettable.

A prime way to enjoy Pacific Grove is to walk or bicycle along its 3 mi of city-owned shoreline, a clifftop area following Ocean View Boulevard that is landscaped with succulents and native plants and has benches on which to sit and gaze at the sea. Marine and bird life can be spotted here, including colonies of cormorants drawn to the massive rocks rising out of the surf.

20 Among the Victorians of note is the **Pryor House** (⊠ 429 Ocean View Blvd.), a massive shingled structure with a leaded- and beveled-glass **21** doorway. **Green Gables** (⊠ 5th St. and Ocean View Blvd.), a romantic Swiss Gothic–style mansion with steeply peaked gables and stained-glass windows, is now a B&B.

🔄 **Lovers Point Park,** on Ocean View Boulevard midway along the waterfront, has a grassy area with a gorgeous coastal view. A sheltered beach there has a children's pool and picnic area. Glass-bottom boat rides, which permit viewing of the plant and sea life below, are available in summer.

★ 🔄 **22** At **Point Piños Light Station,** the oldest continuously operating lighthouse on the West Coast, visitors can learn about the lighting and foghorn operations and wander through a small museum containing historical memorabilia from the U.S. Coast Guard. ⊠ *Asilomar Ave. between*

Ocean View Blvd. and Lighthouse Ave., ☎ *408/648–3116.* ✉ *Free.* ⊙ *Weekends 1–4.*

㉓ Although many of their original nesting grounds have vanished, the **Monarch Grove Sanctuary** (✉ 1073 Lighthouse Ave.) is still a good spot for viewing butterflies. It is adjacent to the Butterfly Grove Inn.

✆ **㉔** If you are in Pacific Grove when the monarch butterflies aren't, an approximation of this annual miracle is on exhibit at the **Pacific Grove Museum of Natural History.** In addition to a finely crafted butterfly tree exhibit, the museum displays a collection of 400 mounted birds native to Monterey County and screens a film about the monarch butterfly. ✉ *165 Forest Ave.,* ☎ *408/648–3116.* ✉ *Free.* ⊙ *Tues.–Sun. 10–5.*

★ A beautiful coastal area in Pacific Grove is **Asilomar State Beach,** on Sunset Drive between Point Piños and the Del Monte Forest. The 100 acres of dunes, tidal pools, and pocket-size beaches form one of the region's richest areas for marine life.

Dining and Lodging

$$$ ✕ **Melac's.** Complementing Pacific Grove's quiet charm, this country restaurant is as friendly as its food is delicious. French-born Jacques Melac greets his guests personally and enjoys helping them pair wines with wife Janet's menu. The couple met in Paris when she attended the Cordon Bleu School, where she graduated first in her class. At Melac's she cooks each generously portioned dish to order, optimizing on seasonal local ingredients. Request the grilled quail with roasted garlic and Oregon chanterelles, the seafood cassoulet, or the roasted duckling with port and fresh figs if they're on the menu, and settle in for the evening. ✉ *663 Lighthouse Ave.,* ☎ *408/375–1743. AE, DC, MC, V. Closed Sun.–Mon. No lunch Sat.*

$$$ ✕ **Old Bath House.** A romantic, nostalgic atmosphere permeates this
★ converted bathhouse overlooking the water at Lovers Point. The classic regional menu here makes the most of local seafood and produce. When they're available, the salmon and Monterey Bay prawns are particularly worth ordering. The restaurant has a less expensive menu for late-afternoon diners. ✉ *620 Ocean View Blvd.,* ☎ *408/375–5195. AE, D, DC, MC, V. No lunch.*

$$ ✕ **Fandango.** With its stone walls and country furniture, this restaurant has the earthy feel of a southern European farmhouse. Complementing the ambience are the robust flavors of the cuisine, which ranges from southern France, Italy, Spain, and Greece to North Africa, from paella and cannelloni to couscous. ✉ *223 17th St.,* ☎ *408/372– 3456. AE, D, DC, MC, V.*

$$ ✕ **The Tinnery.** This family-oriented restaurant serves pancakes and omelets for breakfast, burgers and other sandwiches for lunch. Broiled salmon with fresh Hollandaise sauce, mesquite-grilled meats, and English fish-and-chips are dinner-menu highlights. ✉ *631 Ocean View Blvd., at 17th St.,* ☎ *408/646–1040. Reservations not accepted. AE, D, DC, MC, V.*

$–$$ ✕ **Consuelo's.** Meals here start with complimentary quesadillas, presented on a huge platter, then move into fare such as fajitas, tostadas, enchiladas, marinated chicken, and flautas. There's a children's menu as well. If the weather's nice you can sit outside in the shade of a huge Indian pine tree. ✉ *361 Lighthouse Ave.,* ☎ *408/372–8111. AE, D, MC, V.*

$–$$ ✕ **Crocodile Grill.** Wooden crocodiles, ant eaters, and toucans go hand in hand with the adventurous New American concoctions of the Crocodile. Amazon catfish and bayou brochette are especially tasty, as are the *pupusas* (fancy quesadillas) and *tostaditas* (tortillas topped with green cashew salsa). If you can't decide what to order, try the Jamaican curry shrimp cakes. ⊠ *701 Lighthouse Ave.,* ☎ *408/655–3311. AE, D, MC, V. Closed Tues. No lunch.*

$–$$ ✕ **Gernot's.** The ornate Victorian-era Hart Mansion is a delightful setting in which to dine on seafood and game served with light sauces. Continental specialties include wild boar bourguignonne, roast venison, and veal medallions. ⊠ *649 Lighthouse Ave.,* ☎ *408/646–1477. AE, MC, V. Closed Mon. No lunch.*

$ ✕ **Fishwife.** Good fresh fish with a Mexican twist makes this the locals' choice for lunch or a casual dinner. ⊠ *Sunset Ave. and Asilomar Blvd., at end of Hwy. 68,* ☎ *408/375–7107. Reservations essential on weekends. AE, D, DC, MC, V.*

$ ✕ **Peppers.** This cheerful white-walled café serves fresh seafood and traditional dishes from Mexico and Latin America. The red and green salsas are excellent. ⊠ *170 Forest Ave.,* ☎ *408/373–6892. AE, D, DC, MC, V. Closed Tues. No lunch Sun.*

$$$–$$$$ 🏠 **Green Gables Inn.** Stained-glass windows framing an ornate fire-
★ place and other interior detail work compete with the spectacular bay views at this century-old house built by a sea captain to house his mistress. Rooms in a carriage house perched on a hill out back are larger, have ocean views and more modern amenities, and afford more privacy than rooms in the main house, which have more charm. The room rates include a breakfast buffet (breakfast in bed is also an option) and afternoon hors d'oeuvres and wine. ⊠ *104 5th St., 93950,* ☎ *408/375–2095 or 800/722–1774,* ℻ *408/375–5437. 11 rooms, 4 with shared bath. AE, MC, V.*

$$$–$$$$ 🏠 **Martine Inn.** Most B&Bs in Pacific Grove are Victorian houses; this
★ one is a pink stucco Mediterranean-style villa overlooking the water. The many antiques here include a mahogany suite exhibited at the 1893 Chicago World's Fair, movie costume designer Edith Head's bedroom suite, and an 1860 Chippendale Revival four-poster bed. A glassed-in parlor has a stunning ocean view. Room rates include a full breakfast and afternoon wine and hors d'oeuvres. ⊠ *255 Ocean View Blvd., 93950,* ☎ *408/373–3388 or 800/852–5588,* ℻ *408/373–3896. 23 rooms. AE, D, MC, V.*

$$$–$$$$ 🏠 **Seven Gables Inn.** Four yellow-gabled clapboard buildings share a corner lot and a great view of the ocean. The main house was built in 1886, the other three between 1910 and 1940. European antiques of various periods—gold-leaf mirrors, crystal chandeliers, and marble statues—create a formal atmosphere. The gracious innkeeper, Susan Flatley, grew up in the house and shares her knowledge about it and the area. Room rates include a full breakfast and afternoon tea. ⊠ *555 Ocean View Blvd., 93950,* ☎ *408/372–4341. 14 rooms. Refrigerators. MC, V. No smoking indoors. 2-night minimum weekends, 3-night minimum holiday weekends.*

$$–$$$$ 🏠 **The Centrella.** This handsome century-old Victorian mansion and
★ garden cottages two blocks from Lovers Point Beach has an attractive garden, claw-foot bathtubs, and wicker and brass furnishings. Depending on the time of day, a sideboard in the large parlor is laden with breakfast treats, cookies and fruit, sherry and wine, or hors d'oeuvres. ⊠ *612 Central Ave., 93950,* ☎ *408/372–3372 or 800/233–3372,* ℻ *408/ 372–2036. 21 rooms, 5 cottages. AE, MC, V.*

$$–$$$ 🏠 **Gosby House Inn.** Most of the rooms in this yellow Victorian B&B in the town center have a private bath, and some have fireplaces. The inn has an informal, country air; its innkeepers are knowledgeable and

can supply sightseeing or restaurant suggestions. Room rates include a full breakfast, plus afternoon hors d'oeuvres served in a sunny parlor or by the fireplace in the living room. ⊠ *643 Lighthouse Ave., 93950,* ☎ *408/375–1287 or 800/527–8828,* FAX *408/655–9621. 22 rooms, 2 with shared bath. AE, MC, V.*

$$ ⛺ **Asilomar Conference Center.** A summer camp–like atmosphere pervades this assortment of 28 rustic but comfortable lodges in the middle of a 105-acre state park across from the beach. Room rates include breakfast. ⊠ *800 Asilomar Blvd., 93950,* ☎ *408/372–8016,* FAX *408/ 372–7227. 314 rooms. Cafeteria, pool. MC, V.*

Outdoor Activities and Sports

GOLF

Pacific Grove Municipal Golf Course (⊠ 77 Asilomar Blvd., ☎ 408/648–3177) has a greens fee—$24 to $28; cart rental $23—that is only a fraction of those in nearby Pebble Beach. The course has spectacular ocean views on its back nine—and ice-plant-covered sand dunes that make keeping on the fairway a must. Tee times may be reserved up to seven days in advance.

TENNIS

Pacific Grove Municipal Courts (☎ 408/648–3129) has information about the town's public tennis courts.

Shopping

American Tin Cannery Outlet Center (⊠ 125 Ocean View Blvd., ☎ 408/ 372–1442) carries designer clothing, jewelry, accessories, and home decorating items at 25%–65% discounts. **Wooden Nickel** (⊠ Central and Fountain Aves., ☎ 408/646–8050) sells country-French accent pieces for the home.

17-Mile Drive and Pebble Beach

Off Sunset Dr. in Pacific Grove, or Hwy. 1 at N. San Antonio Rd. in Carmel.

★   Some sightseers balk at the $6.50-per-car fee, but most agree that it is well worth the price to explore **17-Mile Drive,** an 8,400-acre microcosm of the Monterey coastal landscape. Once inside, you see primordial nature preserved in quiet harmony with palatial estates. All along 17-Mile Drive are rare Monterey cypress, trees so gnarled and twisted that Robert Louis Stevenson once described them as "ghosts fleeing before the wind."

㉕   **Bird Rock,** the largest of several islands at the southern end of the Monterey Country Club's golf course, teems with harbor seals, sea lions, cormorants, and pelicans. Sea creatures and birds also make use of **Seal Rock,**
㉖   the larger of a group of islands just south of Bird Rock. The most pho-
㉗   tographed tree is the weather-sculpted **Lone Cypress** that grows out of a precipitous outcrop above the waves. A parking area makes it possible to stop for a view of the Lone Cypress, but walking out to it is not allowed.

Many of the stately homes along 17-Mile Drive reflect the classic Monterey or Spanish Mission style typical of the region. A standout
㉘   is the **Crocker Marble Palace,** a waterfront estate inspired by a Byzantine castle. This baroque mansion is easily identifiable by its dozens of marble arches. Underground pipes heat water in the estate's beach.

Perhaps no more famous concentration of celebrated golf courses ex-
㉙   ists anywhere in the world. Most notable is the **Pebble Beach Golf Links,** with its famous 18th hole, around which the ocean plays a major role. Even if you're not a golfer, views of the impeccable greens can be en-

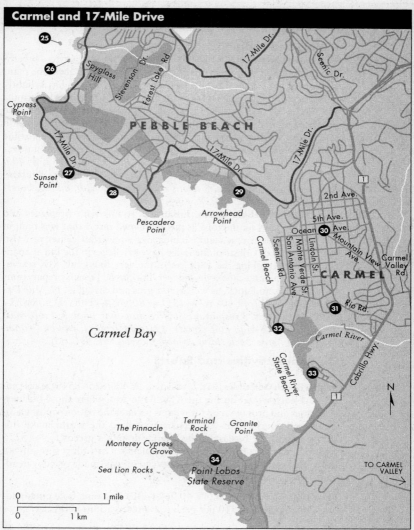

Carmel and 17-Mile Drive

25
26
Spyglass Hill
Stevenson Dr.
Forest Lake Rd.
17-Mile Dr.
Scenic Dr.
Cypress Point
17-Mile Dr.
27
Sunset Point
28
Pescadero Point
17-Mile Dr.
29
Arrowhead Point
17-Mile Dr.
PEBBLE BEACH
2nd Ave.
5th Ave.
Ocean Ave.
30
Lincoln St.
Monte Verde St.
San Antonio Ave.
Mountain View Ave.
CARMEL
Carmel Valley Rd.
Carmel Beach
Scenic Rd.
31
Rio Rd.
32
Carmel River
Cabrillo Hwy.
Carmel Bay
Carmel River State Beach
33
1
N
The Pinnacle
Terminal Rock
Granite Point
Monterey Cypress Grove
Sea Lion Rocks
34
Point Lobos State Reserve
TO CARMEL VALLEY

0 ___ 1 mile
0 ___ 1 km

Bird Rock, **25**
Carmel Mission, **31**
Carmel Plaza, **30**
Carmel River State Park, **33**
Crocker Marble Palace, **28**
Lone Cypress, **27**

Pebble Beach Golf Links, **29**
Point Lobos State Reserve, **34**
Seal Rock, **26**
Tor House, **32**

joyed over a drink or lunch at the Lodge at Pebble Beach or the Inn at Spanish Bay, the two resorts located along the drive.

Dining and Lodging

$$$$ ✕🖬 **Inn at Spanish Bay.** This 270-room resort sprawls across a breathtaking stretch of shoreline along 17-Mile Drive. Under the same management as the Lodge at Pebble Beach (☞ *below*), the inn has a slightly more casual feel, though its 600-square-ft rooms are no less luxurious. The inn has its own tennis courts and golf course, but guests also have privileges at all the Lodge facilities. For dinner, the excellent Bay Club restaurant, which serves haute Italian cuisine, overlooks the coastline and the golf links. Try Roy's Restaurant for more casual and innovative Euro-Asian fare. ✉ *2700 17-Mile Dr., Box 1589, 93953, ☎ 408/647–7500 or 800/654–9300, ℻ 408/647–7443. 270 rooms. 3 restaurants, bar, pool, massage, 8 tennis courts, health club, hiking, horseback riding. AE, DC, MC, V.*

$$$$ ✕🖬 **Lodge at Pebble Beach.** Luxurious rooms with fireplaces and
★ wonderful views set the tone at this renowned resort that was built in 1919. The golf course, tennis club, and equestrian center are also highly regarded. Guests of the lodge have privileges at the Inn at Spanish Bay. Overlooking the 18th green, the very fine Club XIX restaurant is an intimate, café-style spot serving classic French preparations of veal, lamb, and duck, as well as foie gras and caviar. ✉ *17-Mile Dr., Box 1418, 93953, ☎ 408/624–3811 or 800/654–9300, ℻ 408/625–8598. 161 rooms. 3 restaurants, coffee shop, bar, pool, hot tub, massage, sauna, 18-hole golf course, 12 tennis courts, exercise room, health club, horseback riding, beach, bicycles. AE, DC, MC, V.*

Outdoor Activities and Sports

GOLF

Pebble Beach Golf Links (✉ 17-Mile Dr., ☎ 408/625–8518) takes center stage each winter during the AT&T Pro-Am, where show-business celebrities and pros team up for what is perhaps the nation's most glamorous golf tournament. Golfers from around the world make this course one of the busiest in the region, despite a greens fee of $275 plus $20 for a cart ($225 and a complimentary cart for resort guests). Individual reservations for nonguests can only be made one day in advance on a space-available basis.

Peter Hay (✉ 17-Mile Dr., ☎ 408/624–3811), a nine-hole pitch-and-putt course, charges $10 per person, no reservations necessary.

Poppy Hills (✉ 17-Mile Dr., ☎ 408/625–2035), designed in 1986 by Robert Trent Jones Jr., was named by *Golf Digest* as one of the world's top 20 courses. The greens fee for the general public is $130, with a cart $30 additional. Individuals may reserve up to one month in advance, groups up to a year.

Spanish Bay Golf Links (✉ 17-Mile Dr., north end, ☎ 408/624–3811), which hugs a choice stretch of shoreline, is designed in the rugged manner of a traditional Scottish course, with sand dunes and coastal marshes interspersed among the greens. The greens fee is $165 plus $20 cart rental ($150 for resort guests); individuals are advised to make reservations up to two months in advance.

Spyglass Hill (✉ Spyglass Hill Rd., ☎ 408/624–3811), where the holes are long and unforgiving, is a famous Pebble Beach course. With the first five holes bordering on the Pacific, and the rest reaching deep into the Del Monte Forest, the views offer some consolation. The greens fee is $200, plus $20 for a cart and $40 more for a caddy (the fee is $175 with complimentary cart for resort guests). Reservations are essential and may be made up to one month in advance.

HORSEBACK RIDING

Pebble Beach Equestrian Center (✉ Portola Rd. and Alva La., ☎ 408/ 624–2756) rents horses, a great way to enjoy the Del Monte Forest, which has 26 mi of bridle trails.

Carmel

5 mi south of Monterey on Hwy. 1 (or via 17-Mile Drive's Carmel Gate).

Although the community has grown quickly over the years and its population quadruples with tourists on weekends and during the summer, Carmel retains its identity as a quaint village; buildings still have no street numbers, and live music is banned in the local watering holes. You can wander the side streets at your own pace, poking into hidden courtyards and stopping at Hansel-and-Gretel-like cafés for tea and crumpets.

㉚ Downtown Carmel's chief lure is shopping. Its main street, **Ocean Avenue,** is a charming (except to architectural purists) mishmash of ersatz English Tudor, Mediterranean, and other styles. **Carmel Plaza** in the east end of the village proper at Ocean and Junipero avenues, is one of several newer malls. It has more than 50 shops, restaurants, and small branches of major department stores.

★ **㉛** Before it became an art colony in the early 20th century and long before it became a shopping and browsing mecca, Carmel was an important religious center during the establishment of Spanish California. That heritage is preserved in the Mission San Carlos Borromeo del Rio Carmelo, more commonly known as the **Carmel Mission.** Founded in 1770, it served as headquarters for the mission system in California under Father Junípero Serra. Adjoining the stone church are a tranquil garden planted with California poppies and museum rooms that include an early kitchen, Father Serra's spartan sleeping quarters, and the oldest college library in California. ✉ *Rio Rd. and Lasuen Dr.,* ☎ *408/624–3600.* ☞ *$2.* ☉ *Sept.–May, Mon.–Sat. 9:30–4:30, Sun. 10:30–4:30; June–Aug., Mon.–Sat. 9:30–7:30, Sun. 10:30–7:30.*

㉜ Scattered throughout the pines in Carmel are the houses and cottages that were built for writers, artists, and photographers who discovered the area decades ago. Among the most impressive dwellings is **Tor House,** a stone cottage built by the poet Robinson Jeffers in 1919 on a craggy knoll overlooking the sea. The low-ceiling rooms are filled with portraits, books, and unusual art objects, including a white stone from the Great Pyramid in Egypt. The highlight of the small estate is Hawk Tower, a detached edifice set with stones from the Carmel coastline, as well as one from the Great Wall of China. Within the tower is a Gothic-style room, which served as a retreat for the poet's wife, Una, an accomplished musician. The docents who lead tours are well informed about the poet's work and life. ✉ *26304 Ocean View Ave.,* ☎ *408/624–1813 or 408/ 624–1840.* ☞ *$5. No children under 12.* ☉ *Tours Fri. and Sat. 10–3; reservations suggested.*

㉝ Carmel's greatest beauty is its rugged coastline, with pine and cypress forests and countless inlets. **Carmel River State Park** stretches for 106 acres along Carmel Bay. On sunny days the waters appear nearly as turquoise as those of the Caribbean. The park has a sugar-white beach with high dunes and a nature preserve that provides excellent bird-watching for pelicans, kingfishers, hawks, and sandpipers. ✉ *Off Scenic Rd., south of Carmel Beach,* ☎ *408/626–4909.* ☉ *Daily 9 AM–sunset.*

㉞ **Point Lobos State Reserve,** a 456-acre headland, lies just south of Carmel. There are few roads, and the best way to explore is to walk along one of the many hiking trails. The Cypress Grove Trail leads through a forest of rare Monterey cypress (one of only two natural groves remaining), clinging to the rocks above an emerald-green cove. Sea Lion Point Trail is a good place to observe sea lions. From the other trails you can spot otters, harbor seals, and (during winter and spring) migrating whales. Part of the reserve is an undersea marine park open to qualified scuba divers. If you have a dog, note that state law prohibits dogs within the reserve. ⊠ *Hwy. 1,* ☎ *408/624–4909; 800/444–7275 to reserve for scuba diving.* ⌑ *$6 per vehicle.* ☉ *May–Sept., daily 9– 6:30; Oct.–Apr., daily 9–4:30.*

Dining and Lodging

$$$ ✕ **Anton and Michel.** Superb European cuisine is served at this elegant restaurant in Carmel's shopping district. The tender lamb dishes are fantastic and well complemented by the extensive wine list. The real treats, however, are the flaming desserts. Outdoor dining is available in the courtyard. ⊠ *Mission St. and 7th Ave.,* ☎ *408/624–2406. AE, D, DC, MC, V.*

$$$ ✕ **Cafe Gringo.** Maybe it's not 100% Mexican, but Gringo has its own style—something the chef calls New Wave Mexican cuisine. It means dishes such as fresh tamales with artichokes and mushrooms tossed in for a more exotic taste, or a quesadilla with Monterey Jack and manchego cheeses, bacon, and roasted *pasilla* chili, topped with a mango salsa. The full bar serves margaritas, Mexican beers, and South American, Chilean, and local wines. Service is first class. ⊠ *Paseo San Carlos Courtyard, San Carlos St. between Ocean and 7th Aves.,* ☎ *408/ 626–8226. AE, MC, V.*

$$$ ✕ **Crème Carmel.** This bright and airy small restaurant has a California-French menu that changes according to the season. Try the charbroiled Muscovy duck with celery-root puree and green peppercorn or the beef tenderloin prepared with cabernet. ⊠ *San Carlos St. near 7th Ave.,* ☎ *408/624–0444. AE, DC, MC, V. No lunch.*

$$$ ✕ **French Poodle.** Specialties on the traditional French menu at this intimate restaurant include duck breast in port and an excellent abalone; for dessert, the "floating island" is delicious. ⊠ *Junipero and 5th Aves.,* ☎ *408/624–8643. AE, DC, MC, V. Closed Sun. No lunch.*

$$–$$$ ✕ **Casanova.** Southern French and northern Italian cuisine come together in one of the most romantic restaurants in Carmel. A heated outdoor garden and extensive list of more than 1,000 domestic and imported wines enhance the dining experience. Highlights include housemade pasta and desserts. ⊠ *5th Ave. between San Carlos and Mission Sts.,* ☎ *408/625–0501. MC, V.*

$$ ✕ **Flaherty's Seafood Grill & Oyster Bar.** This bright blue-and-white-tile fish house cranks out steaming bowls of mussels, clams, cioppino, and crab chowder. Seafood pastas and daily fresh fish selections are also available. ⊠ *6th Ave. and San Carlos St.,* ☎ *408/624–0311. AE, MC, V.*

$$ ✕ **Hog's Breath Inn.** Although it is resting somewhat on its Hollywood laurels, the eatery co-owned by actor and former Carmel mayor Clint Eastwood has a convivial publike atmosphere, with roaring fireplaces and rustic decor. The food is no-nonsense: meat and seafood entrées with sautéed vegetables. Many items—Dirty Harry Burger, Sudden Impact (Polish sausage) sandwich, etcetera—are named after Eastwood movies. ⊠ *San Carlos St. and 5th Ave.,* ☎ *408/625–1044. Reservations not accepted. AE, DC, MC, V.*

$$ ✕ **Kincaid's Bistro on the Boulevard.** Robert Kincaid's namesake bistro
★ reflects his culinary roots at Monterey's ever-popular Fresh Cream. With Kincaid's, he takes French bistro cuisine farther into the country. Cassoulet made with white beans, duck confit, rabbit sausage, and garlic

prawns is always on the stove and best enjoyed with a rustic red wine. Dried sage and lavender hanging from exposed ceiling beams, rag-painted floors, and ochre-washed walls make you feel as if you've stepped into an old farmhouse in Provence. Be sure to leave room for dessert, particularly the soufflé with lemon and orange zest or the chocolate bag with chocolate shake. ⊠ *Crossroads Center, 217 Crossroads Blvd.,* ☎ *408/624–9626. AE, D, MC, V. Closed Sun. No lunch Sat.*

$$ ✕ **La Bohème.** This campy, offbeat restaurant offers a one-selection, fixed-price menu, which includes soup and salad. You may be bumping elbows with your neighbor in the faux-European-village courtyard, but the predominantly French cuisine is delicious, and the atmosphere is friendly. ⊠ *Dolores St. and 7th Ave.,* ☎ *408/624–7500. Reservations not accepted. MC, V. No lunch.*

$$ ✕ **Lugano Swiss Bistro.** Geography is destiny, and good Swiss cooking derives its singular character from a blend of French, Italian, and German cuisines. At Lugano, fondue is the centerpiece. The house specialty is an original version made with Gruyère, Emmentaler, and Appenzeller—custom has it that if a lady loses her dipping cube in the fondue she pays with a kiss; if a man loses one, he buys a bottle of wine. Rosemary chicken, plum-basted duck, and fennel pork loin rotate on the rotisserie to the sound of accordion music. Call ahead for a table in the back room, with its hand-painted street scene of the chef's native Lugano. ⊠ *The Barnyard, Hwy. 1 and Carmel Valley Rd.,* ☎ *408/626–3779. AE, MC, V.*

$$ ✕ **Pine Inn.** An old favorite of locals, this Victorian-style restaurant serves traditional American fare. Outdoor dining is also available at tables set up around the gazebo. ⊠ *Ocean Ave. and Monte Verde St.,* ☎ *408/624–3851. AE, D, DC, MC, V.*

$$ ✕ **Raffaello.** Sparkling Raffaello serves excellent northern Italian cuisine, superb pasta, Monterey Bay prawns with garlic butter, local sole poached in champagne, and the specialty of the house, veal Piemontese. ⊠ *Mission St. between Ocean and 7th Aves.,* ☎ *408/624–1541. AE, DC, MC, V. Closed Tues. and 1st wk in Jan. No lunch.*

$$ ✕ **Simpson's.** Not the newest or most creative place in town, this dependable restaurant has warm service and a good wine list. Family run— a daughter brings you to your table, one son is in the kitchen, another tends bar, and Mom manages the room—it maintains a comforting, old-fashioned American ambience. An open dining room and tables with flowers and white tablecloths set the mood for steak and potatoes, rice and seafood. ⊠ *San Carlos St. and 5th Ave.,* ☎ *408/624– 5755. AE, MC, V. No lunch. Closed Sun.*

$–$$ ✕ **Rio Grill.** The best bets in this Santa Fe–style setting are the meat
★ and seafood (such as fresh tuna or salmon) cooked over an oakwood grill. ⊠ *101 Crossroads Blvd., Hwy. 1 and Rio Rd.,* ☎ *408/625–5436. AE, MC, V.*

$ ✕ **Friar Tuck's.** This busy wood-paneled coffee shop serves huge omelets at breakfast and at lunch dishes up 16 different hamburgers. ⊠ *5th Ave. and Dolores St.,* ☎ *408/624–4274. Reservations not accepted. DC, MC, V. No dinner Sept.–June.*

$ ✕ **Thunderbird Bookstore and Restaurant.** At this well-stocked bookstore, you can also enjoy a light lunch or dinner—or order a cappuccino and a pastry and browse among the books. A hearty beef soup, sandwiches, popovers, and cheesecake are the best-sellers. ⊠ *3600 The Barnyard, Hwy. 1 and Carmel Valley Rd.,* ☎ *408/624–9414. AE, MC, V.*

$$$$ ✕🏨 **Highlands Inn.** An unparalleled location on high cliffs above the
★ Pacific just south of Carmel gives the Highlands views that stand out even in a region famous for them. Accommodations are in plush spa suites and condominium-style units with wood-burning fireplaces and

ocean-view decks; some rooms have full kitchens. The contemporary French menu at the inn's Pacific's Edge restaurant includes fillet of beef with blue-cheese potato gratin, roasted shallots, and a Portobello mushroom sauce; grilled Atlantic salmon wrapped in pancetta with local baby artichokes; and a succulent honey-roasted breast of duck. ⊠ *Hwy. 1, Box 1700, 93923,* ☎ *408/624–3801 or 800/538–9525; 800/682– 4811 in CA; 408/624–0471 restaurant;* FAX *408/626–1574. 105 suites, 37 king rooms. 2 restaurants, lounge, refrigerators, pool, 3 hot tubs, bicycles, baby-sitting. AE, D, DC, MC, V.*

$$$$ 🖫 **Carriage House Inn.** This small inn with a wood-shingled exterior has rooms with open-beam ceilings, fireplaces, down comforters, and sunken baths. Continental breakfast, wine, and hors d'oeuvres are included in the room rates. ⊠ *Junipero Ave. between 7th and 8th Aves., Box 1900, 93921,* ☎ *408/625–2585 or 800/422–4732,* FAX *408/624– 2967. 13 rooms. In-room safes, refrigerators. AE, D, DC, MC, V.*

$$$–$$$$ 🖫 **La Playa Hotel.** The hotel was built in 1902 by Norwegian artist Christopher Jorgensen for his bride, a member of the famous Ghirardelli chocolate clan. The Terrace Grill and central garden, riotous with color, provide wonderful views of Carmel's magnificent coastline. All rooms are done in pale terra-cotta with green and blue accents and contain hand-carved furniture. Some accommodations have ocean views. You can also opt for a cottage; all have full kitchens and a patio or a terrace, and some have wood-burning fireplaces. ⊠ *Camino Real at 8th Ave., Box 900, 93921,* ☎ *408/624–6476 or 800/582–8900,* FAX *408/624–7966. 75 rooms, 5 cottages. Restaurant, bar, pool, laundry service. AE, DC, MC, V.*

$$$–$$$$ 🖫 **Tickle Pink Motor Inn.** Perched on a towering cliff, this inn has spec-
★ tacular vistas of the Big Sur coastline, which you can contemplate from your private balcony. Fall asleep to the sound of surf crashing below and wake up to Continental breakfast and the morning paper in bed. If you prefer the company of fellow travelers, breakfast is also served buffet-style in the lounge, as are complimentary wine and cheese in the afternoon. Many rooms have wood-burning fireplaces, and there are four luxurious spa suites. The staff is friendly and ready to please. ⊠ *155 Highlands Dr., 93923,* ☎ *408/624–1244 or 800/635–4774,* FAX *408/626– 9516. 34 rooms. Bar, outdoor hot tub, refrigerators. AE, MC, V.*

$$–$$$$ 🖫 **Lobos Lodge.** The white stucco units here are set amid cypresses, oaks, and pines on the edge of the business district. All accommodations have fireplaces and some private brick patios. The rates include a Continental breakfast. ⊠ *Monte Verde St. and Ocean Ave., Box L–1, 93921,* ☎ *408/624–3874,* FAX *408/624–0135. 30 rooms. Refrigerators. AE, MC, V.*

$$–$$$$ 🖫 **Mission Ranch.** Clint Eastwood rescued this inn that was built in the 1850s. The main farmhouse, set in pastureland next to the ocean, where sheep still graze, has six rooms around a Victorian parlor; other options include cottages, a hayloft, and a bunkhouse. Handmade quilts, princess-and-the-pea stuffed mattresses, and carved wooden beds round out the country ambience. ⊠ *26270 Dolores St., 93923,* ☎ *408/624–6436 or 800/538–8221,* FAX *408/626–4163. 31 rooms. Restaurant, piano bar, 6 tennis courts, exercise room, pro shop. AE, D, DC, MC, V.*

$$–$$$$ 🖫 **Pine Inn.** A traditional favorite of generations of Carmel visitors has
★ Victorian-style decor complete with grandfather clock, padded fabric panels, antique tapestries, and marble-topped furnishings. Only four blocks from the beach, the inn has its own brick courtyard of specialty shops and an Il Forniao restaurant. ⊠ *Ocean Ave. and Lincoln St., Box 250, 93921,* ☎ *408/624–3851 or 800/228–3851,* FAX *408/624– 3030. 49 rooms. Restaurant, bar, coffee shop. AE, D, DC, MC, V.*

$$$
★
Cobblestone Inn. Quilts and country antiques, stone fireplaces in guest rooms and the sitting-room area, and a complimentary gourmet breakfast buffet and afternoon tea contribute to the homey feel at this English-style inn. ⊠ *8th and Junipero Aves., Box 3185, 93921,* ☎ *408/625–5222,* FAX *408/625–0478. 24 rooms. No-smoking rooms, refrigerators. AE, DC, MC, V.*

$$$
Tally Ho Inn. This is one of the few inns in Carmel's center with good views of the ocean. There are penthouse units with fireplaces and an English garden courtyard. Continental breakfast and after-dinner brandy are included in the rates. ⊠ *Monte Verde St. and 6th Ave., Box 3726, 93921,* ☎ *408/624–2232 or 800/624–2290,* FAX *408/624–2661. 14 rooms. AE, D, MC, V.*

$$–$$$
Best Western Carmel Mission Inn. This modern inn on the edge of Carmel Valley has a lushly landscaped pool and hot tub area and is close to the Barnyard and Crossroads shopping centers. Rooms are large, some with spacious decks. ⊠ *3665 Rio Rd., at Hwy. 1, 92923,* ☎ *408/624–1841 or 800/348–9090,* FAX *408/624–8684. 165 rooms. Restaurant, bar, refrigerators, pool, 2 hot tubs. AE, D, DC, MC, V.*

$$–$$$
Cypress Inn. For more than 60 years, this inn has been known for its bright white Moorish-Mediterranean facade and Spanish-tile roof. When Doris Day became part owner in 1988, she added her own touches. Posters from her many movies and gold albums grace the walls of the cocktail lounge; photo albums of her favorite canines top the coffee table in the lobby. A generous breakfast is served in a sunny room, or you can enjoy your morning meal in a garden courtyard surrounded by bougainvillea. ⊠ *Lincoln St. and 7th Ave., 93921,* ☎ *408/624–3871 or 800/443–7443,* FAX *408/624–8216. 34 rooms. Refrigerators. AE, MC, V.*

$–$$
Carmel River Inn. Besides attracting those on a budget, the almost-50-year-old inn appeals to travelers who enjoy a bit of distance from the madding crowd—downtown Carmel in July, for instance. Yet the area's beaches are only 1½ mi away. The blue and white motel at the front of the property contains units with king-size beds, cable TV, small refrigerators, and coffeemakers. Cabins out back sleep up to six; some have fireplaces and kitchens. Clean, safe, and across the street from a supermarket, the inn may be upscale Carmel's only true lodging bargain. ⊠ *Hwy. 1 at Carmel River Bridge, Box 221609, 93922,* ☎ *408/624–1575 or 800/882–8142,* FAX *408/624–0290. 43 rooms. MC, V.*

Nightlife and the Arts

MUSIC

Carmel Bach Festival (☎ 408/624–2046) has presented the work of Johann Sebastian Bach and his contemporaries in concerts and recitals for more than 60 years.

Chamber Music Society of the Monterey Peninsula (☎ 408/625–2212) presents well-known chamber groups in concert and holds an annual chamber-music contest for young musicians.

Monterey County Symphony (☎ 408/624–8511) performs a series of classical to pop concerts October through May in Salinas and Carmel.

THEATER

Contemporary Carmel Theatre Festival (☎ 408/655–3200) presents the works of modern playwrights and boundary-breaking performance ensembles.

Pacific Repertory Theater (☎ 408/622–0700) specializes in contemporary comedy and drama.

Sunset Community Cultural Center (⊠ San Carlos St. between 8th and 10th Aves., ☎ 408/624–3996), which presents concerts, lectures, and headline performers throughout the year, is the Monterey Bay area's top venue for the performing arts.

Shopping

ART GALLERIES

Carmel Art Association (✉ Dolores St. between 5th and 6th Aves., ☎ 408/624–6176) exhibits the paintings, sculpture, and prints of local artists.

Cottage Gallery (✉ Mission St. and 6th Ave., ☎ 408/624–7888) focuses on traditional impressionism and classical realism.

Highlands Sculpture Gallery (✉ Dolores St. between 5th and 6th Aves., ☎ 408/624–0535) is devoted to indoor and outdoor sculpture, primarily work done in stone, bronze, wood, and metal.

Masterpiece Gallery (✉ Dolores St. and 6th Ave., ☎ 408/624–2163) exhibits early California impressionists and Bay Area figurative art.

Photography West Gallery (✉ Ocean Ave. and Dolores St., ☎ 408/625–1587) exhibits photography by Ansel Adams and other 20th-century artists.

CHILDREN

Mischievous Rabbit (✉ Lincoln Ave. between 7th and Ocean Aves., ☎ 408/624–6854) sells toys, nursery bedding, books, music boxes, party supplies, china, and hand-painted and handmade clothing embellished with characters from *Winnie the Pooh* tales.

CLOTHING AND ACCESSORIES

Madrigal (✉ Carmel Plaza and San Carlos Ave., ☎ 408/624–3477) carries sportswear, sweaters, and accessories for women and men.

Pat Areias (✉ Lincoln Ave., south of Ocean Ave., ☎ 408/626–8668) puts a respectfully modern spin on the Mexican tradition of great silversmithing—one that acknowledges the trade's Spanish and Indian roots—with a line of sterling silver buckles, belts, and jewelry.

GARDEN

Shop in the Garden (✉ Lincoln Ave., near Ocean Ave., ☎ 408/624–6047) is a secret garden, hidden in a courtyard behind shops. You'll hear the babble of its outdoor fountains and tinkle of its wind chimes before you see it.

MEMORABILIA

Golf Arts and Imports (✉ Dolores St. and 6th Ave., ☎ 408/625–4488) carries antique golf prints and clubs, rare golf books, and other golfing memorabilia.

Carmel Valley

35 *5–10 mi east of Carmel, Hwy. 1 to Carmel Valley Rd.*

Carmel Valley Road, which turns inland at Highway 1 just south of Carmel, is the main thoroughfare through the town of Carmel Valley, a secluded enclave of horse ranchers and other well-heeled residents who prefer the area's perpetually dry, sunny climate to the fog and wind on the coast. In tiny Carmel Valley village are several crafts shops and art galleries. **Garland Ranch Regional Park** (✉ Carmel Valley Rd., 10 mi east of Carmel, ☎ 408/659–4488) has hiking trails and picnic facilities.

The beautiful **Château Julien** winery, recognized internationally for its chardonnay and merlot, gives tours weekdays at 10:30 AM and 2:30 PM by appointment. The tasting room is open daily. ✉ *8940 Carmel Valley Rd.,* ☎ *408/624–2600.* ☉ *Weekdays 8–5, weekends 11–5.*

Dining and Lodging

$$$$ ✕🏠 **Quail Lodge.** Guests at this highly regarded resort on the grounds of a private country club have access to golf, tennis, and 853 acres of wildlife preserve frequented by deer and migratory fowl. Modern rooms with European decor are clustered in several low-rise buildings; pets are welcome. The Covey at Quail Lodge (jacket required; no lunch) serves European cuisine—rack of lamb, mustard-crested salmon with shrimp capellini, abalone, and mousseline of sole—in a romantic lakeside setting. ✉ *8205 Valley Greens Dr., 93923,* ☎ *408/624–1581 or 800/538–9516,* FAX *408/624–3726. 100 rooms. 2 restaurants, 2 bars, 2 pools, hot tub, 18-hole golf course, putting green, 4 tennis courts. AE, DC, MC, V.*

$$$$
★ 🏠 **Carmel Valley Ranch Resort.** This all-suites resort, well off Carmel Valley Road on a hill overlooking the valley, is a stunning piece of contemporary California architecture. Down-home touches include handmade quilts, wood-burning fireplaces, and watercolors by local artists. Rooms have cathedral ceilings, oversize decks, and fully stocked wet bars. ✉ *1 Old Ranch Rd., 93923,* ☎ *408/625–9500 or 800/422–7635,* FAX *408/624–2858. 100 suites. 2 restaurants, 2 pools, hot tubs, saunas, 18-hole golf course, 13 tennis courts. AE, DC, MC, V.*

$$$$ 🏠 **Stonepine Estate Resort.** The former estate of the Crocker banking family has been converted to an ultradeluxe (and ultraexpensive) inn nestled in 330 pastoral acres. This is where Brooke Shields and Andre Agassi were married in 1997. The main house, richly paneled and furnished with antiques, holds eight individually decorated suites and a private dining room for guests only. Less formal but still luxurious rooms are also available in the ranch-style Paddock House. The property's romantic cottages include one that is straight out of *Hansel and Gretel.* ✉ *150 E. Carmel Valley Rd., Box 1543, 93924,* ☎ *408/659–2245,* FAX *408/659–5160. 18 rooms and cottages. Dining room, 2 pools, 2 tennis courts, archery, exercise room, horseback riding, mountain bikes. AE, MC, V.*

$$–$$$$ 🏠 **Valley Lodge.** In this small, pleasant inn, there are rooms surrounding a garden patio and separate one- and two-bedroom cottages with fireplaces and full kitchens. Room rates include Continental breakfast and the morning paper. ✉ *Carmel Valley Rd. at Ford Rd., Box 93, 93924,* ☎ *408/659–2261 or 800/641–4646,* FAX *408/659–4558. 31 rooms. Pool, hot tub, sauna, exercise room. AE, MC, V.*

Outdoor Activities and Sports

GOLF

Carmel Valley Ranch Resort (✉ 1 Old Ranch Rd., ☎ 408/626–2510), designed by Pete Dye, has a front nine that runs along the Carmel River and back nine that reaches well up into the mountains. Guests at the resort have access to the course; the $97 greens fee includes cart rental.

Golf Club at Quail Lodge (✉ 8000 Valley Greens Dr., ☎ 408/624–2770) incorporates several lakes into its course. Although private, the course is open to guests at the adjoining Quail Lodge and by reciprocation with other private clubs. The $95 greens fee ($125 for nonguests) includes cart rental.

Rancho Cañada Golf Club (✉ Carmel Valley Rd., ☎ 408/624–0111) has 36 holes, some of them overlooking the Carmel River. Fees range from $15 to $70, plus $25 cart rental, depending on course and tee time selected.

TENNIS

Carmel Valley Inn Swim and Tennis Club (✉ Carmel Valley Rd. and Laureles Grade, ☎ 408/659–3131) allows nonmembers to play on its courts for a small fee.

Shopping

Bighorn Gallery (✉ 26390 Carmel Rancho La., ☎ 408/625–2288) exhibits artworks on western, wildlife, marine, aviation, and African themes.

Tancredi & Morgen (✉ Valley Hills Center, Carmel Valley Rd., ☎ 408/625–4477), a country store, sells ornate birdcages, sweet-smelling herbal garlands, antique toys, and hand-embroidered children's clothing.

Maison Val du Soleil (✉ 8 El Caminito Rd., ☎ 408/659–5757) contains two floors of country-French antiques and contemporary paintings. Southwest landscapes by American artists and street scenes by French watercolorist Jack Lestrade are noteworthy.

Salinas

36 *17 mi east of the Monterey Peninsula on Hwy. 68; from Carmel Valley Rd, take Laureles Grade north to Hwy. 68.*

Salinas is the population center of a rich agricultural valley where fertile soil, an ideal climate, and a good underground water supply produce optimum growing conditions for crops such as lettuce, broccoli, tomatoes, strawberries, flowers, and wine grapes. This unpretentious town may lack the sophistication and scenic splendors of the coast, but it will interest literary and architectural buffs. Turn-of-the-century buildings have been the focus of ongoing renovation, much of it centered on the original downtown area of South Main Street, with its handsome stone storefronts. The memory and literary legacy of Salinas native (and winner of the Pulitzer and Nobel prizes) John Steinbeck are well honored here.

The **Steinbeck Center Foundation** has information about John Steinbeck exhibits, tours of area landmarks mentioned in his novels, and the schedule of events for the annual Steinbeck festival. ✉ *371 Main St.,* ☎ *408/753–6411.* ◷ *Weekdays 9–4 and Sat. (May–Sept.) 10–2.*

John Steinbeck did much of his research for *East of Eden,* a novel partially drawn from his Salinas boyhood, at what is now called the
★ **Steinbeck Library.** The library contains tapes of interviews with people who knew Steinbeck and a display of photos, first editions, letters, original manuscripts, and other items pertaining to the novelist. Entrance to the archives, which contain original manuscripts and first editions, is by appointment only. ✉ *350 Lincoln Ave.,* ☎ *408/758–7311.* ▨ *Free.* ◷ *Mon.–Wed. 10–9, Thurs.–Sat. 10–6.*

The **Harvey-Baker House,** a preserved redwood home built in 1868 for Salinas's first mayor, is one of the finest private residences built in the town during the 19th century. ✉ *238 E. Romie La.,* ☎ *408/757–8085.* ▨ *Free.* ◷ *1st Sun. of month 1–4, weekdays by appointment.*

The meadows above the Alisal Slough hold the **Jose Eusebio Boronda Adobe,** the last unaltered adobe home from Mexican California. The house contains furniture and period artifacts. ✉ *333 Boronda Rd.,* ☎ *408/757–8085.* ▨ *Free.* ◷ *Weekdays 10–2, Sun. 1–4, Sat. by appointment.*

Dining

$ ✕ **Steinbeck House.** John Steinbeck's birthplace, a Victorian frame house, has been converted into a lunch-only eatery, run by the volunteer Valley Guild. The restaurant contains some Steinbeck memorabilia and serves fare that incorporates locally grown produce. ✉ *132 Central Ave.,* ☎ *408/424–2735.* ◷ *Weekdays for 2 sittings at 11:45 AM and 1:15 PM.*

Pick up the phone.
Pick up the miles.

1-800-FLY-FREE

Now when you sign up with MCI you can receive up to 8,000 bonus frequent flyer miles on one of seven major airlines.

Then earn another 5 miles for every dollar you spend on a variety of MCI services, including MCI Card® calls from virtually anywhere in the world.*

You're going to use these services anyway. Why not rack up the miles while you're doing it?

Is this a great time, or what? :-)

Urban planning.

CITYPACKS

The ultimate guide to the city—a complete pocket guide plus a full-size color map.

www.fodors.com

Outdoor Activities and Sports

One of the oldest and most famous rodeos in the West is the annual **California Rodeo** (☎ 408/757–2951) in Salinas, which takes place in mid-July.

San Juan Bautista

③⑦ *18 mi north of Salinas on U.S. 101.*

★ Sleepy San Juan Bautista, protected from development since 1933, when much of it became **San Juan Bautista State Historic Park,** is about as close to early 19th-century California as you can get. On the first Saturday of each month, on Living History Day, costumed volunteers entertain visitors with period events—quilting bees, tortilla making, and butter churning. ⊠ *Hwy. 156,* ☎ *408/623–4881.* ⊡ *$2.* ☉ *Daily 10–4:30.*

The centerpiece for the village is a wide green plaza ringed by historic buildings: a restored blacksmith shop, a stable, a pioneer cabin, and a jailhouse. Running along one side of the square is **Mission San Juan Bautista,** a long, low, colonnaded structure founded by Father Fermin Lasuen in 1797. A poignant spot adjoining it is Mission Cemetery, where more than 4,300 Native Americans who converted to Christianity are buried in unmarked graves. ⊠ *408 S. 2nd St.,* ☎ *408/623–2127.* ⊡ *$1.* ☉ *Mar.–Oct., daily 9:30–5:30; Nov.–Feb., daily 9:30–4:30.*

After the mission era, San Juan Bautista became an important crossroads for stagecoach travel. The principal stop in town was the **Plaza Hotel,** a collection of adobe buildings with furnishings from the 1860s. The **Castro-Breen Adobe,** furnished with Spanish colonial antiques, presents a view of domestic life in the village. It is next door to the Plaza Hotel.

Shopping

Small antiques shops and art galleries line San Juan Bautista's side streets.

MONTEREY BAY A TO Z

Arriving and Departing

By Bus

Greyhound Lines (☎ 800/231–2222) serves Monterey from San Francisco three times daily; the trip takes from three to five hours, depending on the number of stops.

By Car

The drive south from San Francisco to Monterey can be made comfortably in three hours or less. The most scenic way is to follow Highway 1 down the coast past flower, pumpkin, and artichoke fields and the seaside communities of Pacifica, Half Moon Bay, and Santa Cruz. Unless the drive is made on sunny weekends when locals are heading for the beach, the two-lane coast highway takes no longer than the freeway.

Of the freeways from San Francisco, a fast but enjoyable route is I–280 south to Highway 17, just south of San Jose. Highway 17 crosses the redwood-filled Santa Cruz mountains between San Jose and Santa Cruz, where it intersects with Highway 1. Another option is to follow U.S. 101 south through San Jose to Salinas and then take Highway 68 west to Monterey.

From Los Angeles, the drive to Monterey can be made in less than a day by heading north on U.S. 101 to Salinas and then heading west on Highway 68. The spectacular but slow alternative is to take U.S. 101 to San Luis Obispo and then follow the hairpin turns of Highway 1 up the coast. Allow at least three extra hours if you do.

By Plane
Monterey Peninsula Airport (✉ 200 Fred Kane Dr., ☎ 408/648–7000) is 3 mi from downtown Monterey—on Highway 68 to Olmsted Road—and is served by American Eagle, United, United Express, and US Airways Express. *See* Air Travel *in* the Gold Guide for airline phone numbers.

By Train
Amtrak (☎ 800/872–7245) runs the *Coast Starlight* between Los Angeles and Seattle, making a stop in Salinas (✉ 11 Station Pl.).

Getting Around

By Bus
Monterey–Salinas Transit (☎ 408/424–7695) provides frequent service between towns and many major sightseeing spots and shopping areas for $1.25 per ride, with an additional $1.25 for each zone you travel into, or $3.75 to $7.50 for a day pass, according to zone.

By Car
Highway 1 runs north–south, linking the towns of Santa Cruz, Monterey, and Carmel. Highway 68 runs northeast from Pacific Grove toward Salinas, which U.S. 101 bisects. North of Salinas, U.S. 101 links up with Highway 156 to San Juan Bautista. Parking is especially difficult in Carmel and in the vicinity of the Monterey Bay Aquarium.

Contacts and Resources

Doctors
Community Hospital of Monterey Peninsula (✉ 23625 Holman Hwy., Monterey, ☎ 408/624–5311). **Monterey County Medical Society** (☎ 408/373–4197).

Emergencies
Ambulance (☎ 911). **Police** (☎ 911).

Guided Tours
California Parlor Car Tours (☎ 415/474–7500 or 800/227–4250) operates motor-coach tours of northern California departing from San Francisco that include the Monterey Peninsula.

Chardonnay II (☎ 408/423–1213) accommodates 49 passengers for cruises on Monterey Bay, leaving from the yacht harbor in Santa Cruz.

Rider's Guide (✉ 484 Lake Park Ave., Suite 255, Oakland 94610, ☎ 510/653–2553) produces a self-guided audiotape tour detailing the history, landmarks, and attractions of the Monterey peninsula and Big Sur for $13.95, or $16.95 in vinyl binder, plus $2 postage.

Pharmacies
Surf 'n' Sand (✉ 6th and Junipero Sts., Carmel, ☎ 408/624–1543) has a pharmacy open weekdays 9 to 6, Saturday and holidays 9 to 2.

Visitor Information
Monterey Peninsula Visitors and Convention Bureau (✉ 380 Alvarado St., Monterey 93942, ☎ 408/649–1770). **Monterey Wine Country Associates** (☎ 408/375–9400). **Salinas Chamber of Commerce** (✉ 119 E. Alisal St., Salinas 93902, ☎ 408/424–7611). **Santa Cruz County Conference and Visitors Council** (✉ 701 Front St., Santa Cruz 95060, ☎ 408/425–1234 or 800/833–3494). **Santa Cruz Mountain Winegrowers Association** (☎ 408/479–9463).

11 The Central Coast

From Big Sur to Santa Barbara

Highway 1 between Big Sur and Santa Barbara is a spectacular stretch of terrain. The curving road demands an unhurried pace, but even if it didn't, you'd find yourself stopping often to take in the scenery. Don't expect much in the way of dining, lodging, or even history until you arrive at Hearst Castle, publisher William Randolph Hearst's testament to his own fabulousness. Sunny, well-scrubbed Santa Barbara's Spanish-Mexican heritage is reflected in the architectural style of its courthouse and mission.

THE COASTLINE BETWEEN CARMEL and Santa Barbara, a distance of just over 200 mi, is one of the most popular drives in California. Except for a few smallish cities—Ventura and Santa Barbara in the south and San Luis Obispo in the north—the area is sparsely populated. Between settlements, whose inhabitants relish their isolation at the sharp edge of land and sea, grazing cattle dot the landscape, and in the springtime wildflowers cover the hillsides. Around Big Sur, the Santa Lucia mountains drop down to the Pacific with dizzying grandeur, but as you move south, the shoreline gradually flattens into the long, sandy beaches of Santa Barbara and Ventura.

Updated by
Edie Jarolim

Throughout the region are pleasant little towns, such as Cambria and Ojai, where resident artists create and sell their work. The wineries of the Santa Ynez Valley are steadily building reputations for their quality vintages. The Danish town of Solvang is an amusing stopover for hearty Scandinavian fare and an architectural change of pace.

Santa Barbara is your introduction to the unhurried hospitality and easy living of southern California. Only 95 mi north of Los Angeles, Santa Barbara works hard to maintain its relaxed atmosphere and cozy scale. Wedged between the Pacific and the Santa Ynez Mountains, it's never had much room for expansion. The city's setting, climate, and architecture combine to produce a Mediterranean feel that permeates not only its look but its pace.

Pleasures and Pastimes

Dining
The Central Coast from Big Sur to Solvang is far enough off the interstate to ensure that nearly every restaurant or café has its own personality—from chic to down-home and funky. There aren't many restaurants from Big Sur until you reach Hearst Castle. Cambria's cooks, true to the town's British-Welsh origins, serve up English fare complete with peas and Yorkshire pudding but also California and Continental cuisine.

The dishes of Santa Barbara's chefs rival those of their counterparts in the state's larger centers. Fresh seafood is plentiful, prepared old-style American in longtime wharfside hangouts or with more trendy accents at newer eateries. If you're after good, cheap food with an international flavor, follow the locals to Milpas Avenue on the east edge of Santa Barbara's downtown. Dining attire on the Central Coast is generally casual, though slightly dressy casual wear is the custom at the expensive to very expensive restaurants listed below.

CATEGORY	COST*
$$$$	over $50
$$$	$30–$50
$$	$20–$30
$	under $20

*per person for a three-course meal, excluding drinks, service, and 7¼%–7¼% sales tax

Lodging
Big Sur has only a few places to stay, but even its budget accommodations have character. From San Simeon to San Luis Obispo there are many moderately priced hotels and motels—some nicer than others, but mostly just basic lodgings. Wherever you stay, make your reser-

vations well ahead of time in the summer, particularly in Santa Barbara.

CATEGORY	COST*
$$$$	over $175
$$$	$120–$175
$$	$80–$120
$	under $80

All prices are for a standard double room, excluding 9%–10% tax.

Missions

Three important California missions established by Franciscan friars are within the Central Coast region. La Purisima is the most fully restored, Santa Barbara's is perhaps the most beautiful of the state's 21 missions, and Mission San Luis Obispo de Tolosa has a fine museum with many Chumash Indian artifacts.

Wineries

Centered in the Solvang area and spreading north toward San Luis Obispo and south toward Santa Barbara is a winemaking region with much of the variety but none of the glitz or crowds of northern California's Napa Valley. Many wineries are in the rolling hills of the Santa Maria or Santa Ynez valleys. They tend to be fairly small, but most have tasting rooms (some have tours) and you'll often meet the winemakers themselves. There are maps and brochures at visitor centers in Solvang, San Luis Obispo, and Santa Barbara, or you can contact the wine associations of Paso Robles and Santa Barbara (☞ Contacts and Resources *in* the Central Coast A to Z, *below*).

Exploring the Central Coast

Driving is the easiest way to experience the Central Coast. The entire distance from Big Sur to Santa Barbara could be tackled in one long day, but that would defeat the purpose of taking the scenic coastal highway. Even a brief trip would allow the luxury of winding down Highway 1 to take in the rugged coastline from Monterey through Big Sur to San Luis Obispo. A better option is to take several days, allowing time to savor Big Sur, Hearst Castle, the beaches, and Santa Barbara.

Numbers in the text correspond to numbers in the margin and on the Central Coast and Santa Barbara maps.

Great Itineraries

The three-day itinerary below is arranged as a loop from either San Francisco or Los Angeles. The seven-day trip is organized from north to south.

IF YOU HAVE 3 DAYS

Especially in the summertime, make reservations for a visit to Hearst Castle well before you depart for the coast. Maximize your time by taking U.S. 101 from San Francisco or Los Angeles directly to **San Luis Obispo** ⑩. Just north of town, stop by the kitschy **Madonna Inn.** Continue on to **Mission San Luis Obispo de Tolosa,** overlooking the San Luis Creek. Drive west on Highway 46 and north on Highway 1 and stay overnight in 🏨 **Cambria.** Take a morning tour of **Hearst Castle** ⑦, spend some time viewing the exhibits at the visitor center, and then head south on U.S. 101 to 🏨 **Santa Barbara** ⑭–㉗. Spend the late afternoon at **Stearns Wharf** ⑯ or along **Cabrillo Boulevard.** In the morning, visit the **Santa Barbara County Courthouse** ㉑ and **Mission Santa Barbara** ㉕ before continuing to your next destination.

The Central Coast

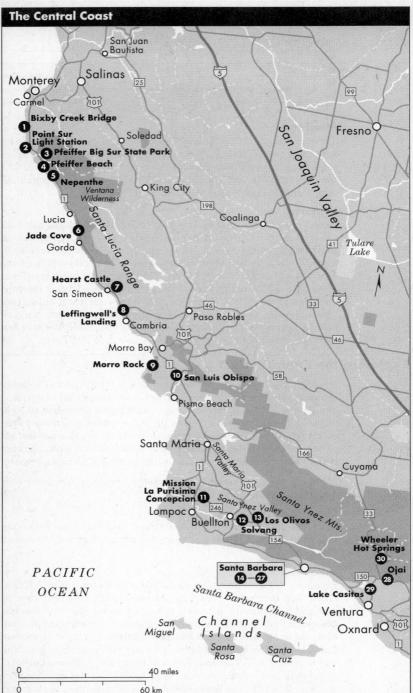

San Juan
Bautista

Monterey Salinas

Carmel

Bixby Creek Bridge

1

**Point Sur
Light Station**

2

3 **Pfeiffer Big Sur State Park**

Soledad

4 **Pfeiffer Beach**

5

Nepenthe

*Ventana
Wilderness*

King City

Lucia

Jade Cove **6**

Gorda

Santa Lucia Range

Coalinga

*Tulare
Lake*

N

Hearst Castle **7**

San Simeon

**Leffingwell's
Landing** **8**

Cambria

Paso Robles

Morro Bay

Morro Rock **9**

10 **San Luis Obispo**

Pismo Beach

Santa Maria

*Santa
Maria
Valley*

Cuyama

**Mission
La Purisima
Concepcion** **11**

Santa Ynez Valley

Lompoc

Buellton

12 **13** **Los Olivos**

Solvang

Santa Ynez Mts.

**Wheeler
Hot Springs**

30

Santa Barbara

14 — **27**

Ojai

28

Lake Casitas

29

Ventura

PACIFIC
OCEAN

Santa Barbara Channel

San
Miguel

*Channel
Islands*

Oxnard

*Santa
Rosa*

*Santa
Cruz*

0   40 miles

0   60 km

Make ☒ **Big Sur** your destination for the first day and most of the second. If you're in the area on a weekend, take a tour of **Point Sur Light Station** ②, which has stood for a century on its sandstone cliff. Watch the waves break on **Pfeiffer Beach** ④, one of the few places where you can actually set foot on the shore. Observe the glories of **Los Padres National Forest** up close by hiking one of the many trails in the **Ventana Wilderness,** or stay along the shore and hunt for jade at **Jade Cove** ⑥. Plan to reach ☒ **Cambria** by the evening of day two. Have dinner and explore the town's shops.

On day three, take a morning tour of **Hearst Castle** ⑦, have lunch, and take the quicker of two possible routes—U.S. 101 south to Highway 246 east—to **Mission La Purisima Concepcion** ⑪, the most fully restored mission in the state. Loop back on 246 to U.S. 101 heading south to ☒ **Santa Barbara** ⑭–㉗. On day four, visit **Stearns Wharf** ⑯ and walk or bike to sandy **East Beach** ⑱ and the **Andree Clark Bird Refuge** ⑲. Have dinner on **State Street** and check out the area's shops and clubs. On your fifth day, get a feel for the city's architecture and history at the **Santa Barbara County Courthouse** ㉑ and **Mission Santa Barbara** ㉕. North of the mission, the paths along the 65-acre **Santa Barbara Botanic Garden** ㉗ wind through an impressive cross-section of local vegetation. Have dinner in **Montecito** and explore the Coast Village Road shopping district. It's a short walk from here to the shore to catch the sunset before or after you eat. On your sixth day, experience the area's marine life on a half-day cruise of the **Channel Islands.** On day seven, drive east along the coast on U.S. 101 and then on Highway 150 inland to ☒ **Ojai** ㉘, which is set in a jewel-like valley. Sample the therapeutic services at the spa at **Wheeler Hot Springs** ㉚ and, reinvigorated, wander through Ojai.

When to Tour the Central Coast

The Central Coast is hospitable most of the year. Fog often rolls in north of Pismo Beach during the summer; you'll need a jacket, especially after sunset, close to the shore. The rains usually come December through March. Santa Barbara is pleasant year-round. Hotel rooms fill up in the summer, but from April to early June and in the early fall the weather is almost as fine and it's less hectic. Most of the Central Coast's major sights are open daily. One exception is the Point Sur Light Station, which is available for touring only on weekends and, April to October, also on Wednesdays.

HIGHWAY 1 TO SOLVANG

Big Sur, San Simeon, Cambria, and San Luis Obispo

Big Sur

152 mi from San Francisco, south on I–280 and U.S. 101, west on Hwy. 68 and south on Hwy. 1; 27 mi south of Monterey on Hwy. 1.

Startling views and hairpin turns alternate in quick succession on Highway 1 along the Central Coast. Long a retreat of artists and writers, Big Sur has managed to preserve its ancient forests and rugged coast from the onslaught of development, serving as a reminder of California's impressive geological history. Much of the area lies within several state parks and the more than 165,000-acre **Ventana Wilderness,** itself part of the Los Padres National Forest. The counterculture spirit of Big Sur is evident today in tie-dyed clothing upon some locals and the presence of the Esalen Institute, a mecca of the human growth-potential movement. Originally established as a home to curative baths in 1910, Esalen exploded in the 1960s as a place to explore consciousness, environmental issues, and nude bathing.

1 The graceful arc of **Bixby Creek Bridge** is a photographer's dream. There is a small parking area on the north side from which to take a photo or begin a walk across the 550-ft span. ⊠ *Hwy. 1, 13 mi south of Carmel.*

★ **2** **Point Sur Light Station,** a century-old beacon, stands watch from atop a sandstone cliff. Four lighthouse keepers lived here with their families. Their homes and working spaces are open to the public on 2½- to 3-hour, ranger-led tours. Considerable walking is involved. ⊠ *Point Sur State Historical Park, Hwy. 1, 19 mi south of Carmel,* ☎ *408/625– 4419.* ⊡ *$5.* ⊙ *Tours generally Sat. 10 AM and 2 PM, Sun. 10 AM, plus Apr.–Oct., Wed. 10 and 2; call ahead to check.*

3 A short hiking trail at **Pfeiffer Big Sur State Park** leads up a redwood-filled valley to a waterfall. You can go back the same (easier) way or continue on the trail and take a loop that leads you along the valley wall, with views of the tops of the redwood trees you were just walking among. Stop in at the **Big Sur Ranger Station,** just west of the park entrance, for information on the entire Big Sur area. ⊠ *Hwy. 1, 8½ mi south of Point Sur Light Station,* ☎ *408/667–2315.*

4 Through a hole in one of the big rocks at **Pfeiffer Beach** you can watch the waves break first on the sea side and then again on the beach side. ⊠ *Off Hwy. 1; the 2-mi road to beach is immediately past Big Sur Ranger Station.* ⊡ *$5 per vehicle.*

5 **Nepenthe** overlooks lush meadows to the ocean below. The house was once owned by Orson Welles and Rita Hayworth, though his biographer says they spent little time there. Downstairs from the on-site restaurant and café is a crafts and gift shop, displaying, among other items, the work of the acclaimed fabric designer Kaffe Fassett, who grew up at Nepenthe. ⊠ *Hwy. 1, 2½ mi south of Big Sur Ranger Station.*

6 **Jade Cove** is a well-known jade-hunting spot along the coast. Rock hunting is allowed on the beach, but you may not remove anything from the walls of the cliffs. ⊠ *Hwy. 1, 10 mi south of Lucia.*

Dining and Lodging

$$–$$$ ✕ **Nepenthe.** You'll not find a grander coastal view between San Francisco and Los Angeles than the one from here. The standard American fare—burgers, sandwiches, and salads at lunchtime—is overpriced, so it is the location that is the draw (don't bother coming after dark). Nepenthe serves lunch and dinner; the outdoor Café Kevah serves breakfast and lunch. ⊠ *Hwy. 1, south end of town,* ☎ *408/667–2345. AE, MC, V.*

$$$$ ✕ **Post Ranch Inn.** This luxurious retreat is the ultimate in environ-
★ mentally conscious architecture. The redwood guest houses, all with dizzyingly splendid views of either the Pacific or the mountains, blend unobtrusively into a wooded cliff 1,200 ft above the ocean. Each unit, done in a beautifully spare, almost Japanese style, has its own spa tub, fireplace, stereo system, private deck, massage table, and a refrigerator with free snacks. On-site activities include everything from guided hikes to tarot-card readings. The inn's restaurant, which serves cutting-edge American fare, is the best in the area. Rates include a Continental breakfast buffet. ⊠ *Hwy. 1, Box 219, 93920,* ☎ *408/667–2200 or 800/527–2200,* ℻ *408/667–2512. 30 units. Restaurant, bar, 2 pools, spa, exercise room, shop, library. AE, MC, V.*

$$$$ ✕⊡ **Ventana Inn.** The activities at this quintessential California get-
★   away are purposely limited to sunning at poolside—there is a cloth-
      ing-optional deck—and walks in the hills nearby. Buildings that are
      scattered in clusters on a hillside above the Pacific hold rooms with
      natural-wood walls and cool tile floors. The hotel's stone and wood
      Ventana Restaurant serves California cuisine with Continental influ-
      ences. For a real event, come here for weekend brunch on the terrace,
      with spectacular views over golden hills down to the ocean. Room rates
      include a justly renowned Continental breakfast and complimentary
      afternoon wine and cheese buffet. ⊠ *Hwy. 1, 93920,* ☏ *408/667–2331
      or 800/628–6500,* ℻ *408/667–2419. 62 rooms. Restaurant, 2 pools,
      2 Japanese baths, sauna, exercise room. AE, D, DC, MC, V. 2-night
      minimum stay on weekends and holidays.*

$–$$$ ✕⊡ **Deetjen's Big Sur Inn.** This inn has a certain rustic charm, at least
      for travelers not too attached to creature comforts. There are no locks
      on the doors (except from the inside), the heating is by wood-burning
      stove in half of the rooms, and your neighbor can often be heard
      through the walls. Still, it's a special place, set among redwood trees.
      Each room is individually decorated and given a name like Château
      Fiasco. The restaurant (reservations essential) in the main house serves
      stylish fare that includes roasted half duck, ribeye steak, and lamb sir-
      loin for dinner, wonderfully light and flavorful pancakes for breakfast.
      There is no lunch. ⊠ *Hwy. 1, south end of town, 93920,* ☏ *408/667–
      2377 for inn, 408/667–2378 for restaurant. 20 rooms, 15 with bath.
      Restaurant. MC, V.*

$$–$$$ ⊡ **Big Sur Lodge.** The motel-style cottages of this Pfeiffer Big Sur State
      Park property make it a good choice for families. The lodging area sits
      in a meadow surrounded by redwood and oak trees. Some accommo-
      dations have fireplaces, some kitchens. None have a TV or a phone.
      ⊠ *Hwy. 1, Box 190, 93920,* ☏ *408/667–2171 or 800/424–4787,*
      ℻ *408/667–3110. 61 rooms. Restaurant, grocery, pool, shop. AE,
      MC, V.*

Outdoor Activities and Sports

CAMPING

There are many campsites along Highway 1, but they can fill up early
anytime but winter. In Big Sur, campsites are at Pfeiffer Big Sur and
Julia Pfeiffer Burns state parks. Near Hearst Castle, camping is avail-
able at several smaller state parks (San Simeon, Atascadero, Morro Bay,
Montana de Oro, Avila Beach, and Pismo Beach). Most sites require
reservations from Destinet (☏ 800/444–7275).

San Simeon

57 mi south of Big Sur on Hwy. 1.

Whalers founded San Simeon in the 1850s but had virtually abandoned
the town by the time Senator George Hearst reestablished it 20 years
later. Hearst bought up most of the surrounding ranch land, built a
1,000-ft wharf, and turned San Simeon into a bustling port. His son,
William Randolph, further developed the area during the construction
of Hearst Castle. Today, the town, which is 3 mi east of the road lead-
ing to the castle, is basically a row of gift shops, restaurants, and mo-
tels along Highway 1.

★ ❼ **Hearst Castle,** known officially as the Hearst San Simeon State His-
      torical Monument, sits in solitary splendor atop La Cuesta Encantada
      (the Enchanted Hill). Its buildings and gardens are spread over the 127
      acres that were the heart of newspaper magnate William Randolph
      Hearst's 250,000-acre ranch.

Buses from the visitor center at the bottom of the hill take visitors to the neoclassical extravaganza above. Hearst devoted nearly 30 years and some $10 million to building this elaborate estate. He commissioned renowned architect Julia Morgan—who was also responsible for buildings at U.C. Berkeley—but was very much involved with the final product, a pastiche of Italian, Spanish, Moorish, and French styles. The art-filled main building and three guest "cottages" are connected by terraces and staircases and surrounded by reflecting pools, gardens, and statuary. In its heyday, the castle was a playground for Hearst, Hollywood celebrities, and the rich and powerful from around the world.

Although construction began in 1919, the project was never officially completed. Work was halted in 1947 when Hearst had to leave San Simeon due to failing health. The Hearst family presented the property to the state of California in 1958.

Guides conduct four different daytime tours and (part of the year) one evening tour of various parts of the main house and grounds; if this is your first visit, Tour No. 1, the most basic, is recommended. Daytime tours take just under two hours. Docents dress in period costume as Hearst's guests and staff for the slightly longer evening tour, which begins at sunset. All tours include a ½-mi walk and 150–400 stairs. A 40-minute film shown at a giant-screen theater gives a rather sanitized version of Hearst's life and of the construction of the castle, but the shots of the scenery are dazzling. Reservations for the tours, which can be made up to eight weeks in advance, are a virtual necessity. ⊠ *San Simeon State Park, 750 Hearst Castle Rd.,* ☎ *805/927–2020 or 800/ 444–4445.* 🖭 *Day tour $14, evening tour (spring and fall) $25, film $6.* ☉ *Tours daily 8:20 AM–3:20 PM (later in summer); additional tours take place most Fri. and Sat. evenings Mar.–May and Sept.–Dec. MC, V.*

Dining and Lodging

$$ ✕ **Europa.** The menu here includes dishes from Germany, Hungary, and Italy—goulash with spätzle, stuffed pork roast with kielbasa, and homemade pasta. Steaks and fresh fish are also served. Crisp linen tablecloths brighten the small dining room. ⊠ *9240 Castillo Dr. (Hwy. 1),* ☎ *805/927–3087. MC, V. Closed Sun. No lunch.*

$$ 🏨 **Best Western Cavalier.** Reasonable rates, a prime oceanfront loca-
★ tion, and well-equipped rooms—all with a TV with VCR, and some with wood-burning fireplaces and private patios—make this a good choice in the Hearst Castle area. ⊠ *9415 Hearst Dr., 93452,* ☎ *805/ 927–4688 or 800/826–8168,* 𝖥𝖠𝖷 *805/927–6472. 90 rooms. 2 restaurants, refrigerators, 2 outdoor pools, hot tub, exercise room, coin laundry. AE, D, DC, MC, V.*

Cambria

9 mi south of San Simeon on Hwy. 1.

Cambria, an artists' colony full of turn-of-the-century homes, is divided into the newer West Village and the original East Village. Each has its own personality and bed-and-breakfasts, restaurants, art galleries, and shops. You can still detect traces of the Welsh miners who settled here in the 1890s. Moonstone Beach Drive, which runs along the coast, is lined with motels. **Leffingwell's Landing,** a state picnic ground at its northern end, is a good place for examining tidal pools and watching otters as they frolic in the surf. Walkers will love the maze of footpaths along the beach side of Moonstone Beach Drive.

Dining and Lodging

$–$$ ✕ **Hamlet at Moonstone Gardens.** In the middle of 3 acres of luxuri-
★ ant gardens, this restaurant has an enchanting patio that's perfect for
lunch. The upstairs dining room looks out onto the Pacific or the gardens. The fish of the day comes poached in white wine; other entrées
range from hamburgers to rack of lamb. Downstairs at the Pacific Wine
Works, you can taste wines from more than 50 wineries. A fine-arts
gallery and a woodcarving gallery share the grounds. ✉ *Hwy. 1 at Moonstone Beach Dr.,* ☎ 805/927–3535. MC, V.

$–$$ ✕ **Robin's.** "Multiethnic" only begins to describe the dining possibil-
ities at this antiques-filled restaurant nestled among Monterey pines.
Tandoori prawns, quesadillas, a Thai red curry, an array of salads (more
for lunch than dinner), quite a few vegetarian entrées, hamburgers for
the kids, and some truly fine desserts (house specialty: French apple
pie with fresh whipped cream) are all on Robin's menu. ✉ *4095 Burton Dr.,* ☎ 805/927–5007. MC, V. No lunch Sun.

$$–$$$ 🏠 **Best Western Fireside Inn.** This modern motel has spacious rooms
with sofas, upholstered lounge chairs, refrigerators, and coffeemakers.
Some rooms have whirlpools or ocean views, and all have fireplaces.
Continental breakfast is served in a room adjacent to the pool. The
inn is just across from the beach, with fishing nearby. ✉ *6700 Moonstone Beach Dr., 93428,* ☎ 805/927–8661; 800/528–1234 *central reservations;* FAX *805/927–8584. 46 rooms. Pool, hot tub. AE, D, DC,
MC, V.*

$$–$$$ 🏠 **Fog Catcher Inn.** Its landscaped gardens and 10 thatched-roof build-
ings lend the Fog Catcher the feel of an English country village. Most
rooms (among them 10 minisuites) have ocean views. All have fireplaces
and are done in floral chintz with light wood furniture. Room rates
include breakfast. ✉ *6400 Moonstone Dr., 93428,* ☎ 805/927–1400
or 800/425–4121, FAX *805/927–0204. 60 rooms. Pool, hot tub. AE,
D, DC, MC, V.*

$$–$$$ 🏠 **Squibb House.** Owner Bruce Black restored this Gothic Revival
Italianate structure and his craftsmen built many of the pine furnishings. Room rates include a Continental breakfast. ✉ *4063 Burton Dr.,
93428,* ☎ 805/927–9600. 5 rooms. MC, V.

$–$$$ 🏠 **Bluebird Motel.** Rooms at this garden motel near Cambria's East
Village range from simply furnished doubles to nicer creekside suites
with fireplaces, VCRs, refrigerators, and patios. ✉ *1880 Main St., 93428,*
☎ 805/927–4634 *or* 800/552–5434, FAX *805/927–5215. 37 rooms.
AE, D, DC, MC, V.*

$$ 🏠 **San Simeon Pines Resort.** Set amid 9 acres of pines and cypresses,
★ this motel-style resort has its own golf course and is directly across from
Leffingwell's Landing, a state picnic area on the rocky beach. The accommodations include cottages with their own landscaped backyards.
Rooms in some parts of the complex are for adults only, and others
are reserved for families. ✉ *7200 Moonstone Beach Dr. (mailing address: Box 117, San Simeon 93452),* ☎ 805/927–4648. 58 rooms. Pool,
9-hole golf course, croquet, shuffleboard, playground. AE, MC, V.

Morro Bay

20 mi south of Cambria on Hwy. 1.

★ ❾ Morro Bay is separated from the ocean by a 4½-mi sand barrier and
a causeway that leads to the huge monolith of **Morro Rock.** A short
walk around the base of the rock—one of nine such mini volcanic peaks,
or "morros," in the area—leads to a breakwater, with the sheltered harbor (home of a large fishing fleet) on one side and the crashing waves
of the Pacific on the other. Morro Bay is also a wildlife preserve, pro-

tecting the nesting areas of endangered falcons; one doesn't need to get too close to divine that the rock is alive with birds. The tall smokestacks of the PG&E plant just behind the waterfront can be seen from anywhere in the bay. Also in town is a chessboard with human-size pieces.

Dining and Lodging

$–$$ X **Dorn's.** This seafood café that overlooks the harbor resembles a Cape Cod cottage. It's open for breakfast, lunch, and dinner. Excellent fish and native abalone are on the dinner menu. ⊠ *801 Market Ave.,* ☎ *805/772–4415. AE, MC, V.*

$$–$$$$ 🛏 **The Inn at Morro Bay.** Set a bit away from town, inside the state park and across from a heron rookery, this upscale hotel complex has romantic country French–style rooms. Some have a fireplace, a Jacuzzi, and a bay view; others look out at extensive gardens. There's a golf course across the road and mountain bikes are free for guests. Even if you're a bird lover, it's best not to book a room near the rookery; otherwise, you'll be in for a morning din. ⊠ *60 State Park Rd., 93442,* ☎ *805/772–5651 or 800/321–9566,* ℻ *805/772–4779. 96 rooms. Restaurant, bar, pool. AE, D, DC, MC, V.*

$–$$ 🛏 **Adventure Inn.** Colorful nautical murals decorate this small motel on the harbor and facing Morro Rock. Rooms are plain but comfortable; amenities include coffeemakers and free HBO and local calls. Complimentary Continental breakfast is served by the pool on weekends. ⊠ *1150 Embarcadero, 93442,* ☎ ℻ *805/772–5607;* ☎ *800/799–5607 in CA. 16 rooms. Restaurant, refrigerators, pool, spa. AE, MC, V.*

Outdoor Activities and Sports

FISHING

There is access to salt- and fresh-water fishing spots all along the coast. **Virg's Sport Fishing** (⊠ Morro Bay embarcadero, ☎ 805/772–1222 or 800/762–5263) and **Bob's Sportfishing** (⊠ Morro Bay embarcadero, ☎ 805/772–3340) operate deep-sea trips.

KAYAKING

You can rent canoes as well as kayaks at **Kayaks of Morro Bay** (⊠ 699 Embarcadero, ☎ 805/772–1119).

San Luis Obispo

🔟 *14 mi south of Morro Bay on Hwy. 1, 230 mi south of San Francisco on I–280 to U.S. 101, 112 mi north of Santa Barbara on U.S. 101.*

About halfway between San Francisco and Los Angeles, San Luis Obispo is an appealing little urban center set among rolling hills and extinct volcanos. It is home to two decidedly different institutions: California Polytechnic State University, known as Cal Poly, and the exuberantly garish Madonna Inn. The town has restored its old railroad depot as well as several Victorian-era homes; the Chamber of Commerce (☞ Contacts and Resources *in* the Central Coast A to Z, *below*) has a list of self-guided historic walks. On Thursday from 6 to 9 PM, a four-block-long evening farmers' market takes place on Higuera Street.

★ **Mission San Luis Obispo de Tolosa,** established in 1772, overlooks San Luis Obispo Creek. The mission's museum exhibits artifacts of the Chumash Indians and early Spanish settlers. ⊠ *751 Palm St.,* ☎ *805/543–6850.* 🎟 *$2.* ☉ *Memorial Day weekend–Dec., daily 9–5; Jan.–late May, daily 9–4.*

Dining and Lodging

$$–$$$ ✕ **Cafe Roma.** Authentic northern Italian cuisine is the specialty of this warm, elegant restaurant on Railroad Square. Under a large mural of sunny Tuscany, you can dine on squash-filled ravioli with sage and butter sauce or filet mignon glistening with port and Gorgonzola. ⊠ *1819 Osos St.,* ☎ *805/541–6800. AE, D, DC, MC, V. Closed Mon. No lunch weekends.*

$$ ✕ **Buona Tavola.** Locals favor this northern Italian restaurant, whose menu highlights include homemade agnolotti filled with scampi in a creamy saffron sauce and braised lamb shank with grilled polenta. Outdoor dining is available on a flower-filled patio. ⊠ *1037 Monterey St.,* ☎ *805/545–8000. D, MC, V.*

$ ✕ **Big Sky.** Charles Myers, owner of this comfortable restaurant, aims
★   to provide what he calls "world beat" cuisine, using local ingredients: organic fruits and vegetables, hormone-free chicken, and pork and chicken sausages produced in San Luis Obispo. This results in an eclectic menu that encompasses dishes from the Mediterranean, the Sun Belt, North Africa, and the Southwest. Big Sky is *the* hip local gathering spot for breakfast, lunch, and dinner. ⊠ *1121 Broad St.,* ☎ *805/545–5401. MC, V.*

$$–$$$$ ✕▥ **Apple Farm.** Decorated to the hilt with floral bedspreads and wall-
★   paper, and with watercolors by local artists, each room in this country-style hotel has a gas fireplace; some have canopy beds and cozy window seats. There's a working grist mill in the garden-filled courtyard. The adjoining restaurant serves such hearty country fare as chicken with dumplings and smoked ribs. ⊠ *2015 Monterey St., 93401,* ☎ *805/544–2040; 800/374–3705 in CA;* 🅵🅰🆇 *805/546–9495. 103 rooms. Restaurant, pool, hot tub. AE, D, MC, V.*

$$–$$$$ ▥ **Madonna Inn.** A designer's imagination run amok, this place is as much a tourist attraction as a place to stay. It is the ultimate in kitsch, from its rococo bathrooms to its pink-on-pink, froufrou dining areas. Each room is unique, to say the least: Rock Bottom is all stone, even the bathroom; the Safari Room is decked out in animal skins; Old Mill features a waterwheel that powers cuckoo-clock-like figurines. Humor value aside, the Madonna is pretty much a duded-up motel, so don't expect much in the way of luxury. ⊠ *100 Madonna Rd., 93405,* ☎ *805/543–3000 or 800/543–9666,* 🅵🅰🆇 *805/543–1800. 109 rooms. Bar, coffee shop, dining room, shops. MC, V.*

$–$$ ▥ **Adobe Inn.** This clean, well-run establishment of cheerful motel-style rooms done in Southwest colors, serves excellent full breakfasts. The friendly owners will help you plan your stay in the area, even if you don't choose one of their reasonably priced packages—a bicycle tour, say, or a wine-tasting itinerary. ⊠ *1473 Monterey St., 93401,* ☎ *805/ 549–0321 or 800/676–1588,* 🅵🅰🆇 *805/549–0383. 15 rooms. Kitchenettes. AE, D, MC, V.*

Nightlife and the Arts

MUSIC

The **San Luis Obispo Mozart Festival** (☎ 805/781–3008) takes place in late July and early August. Settings include the Mission San Luis Obispo de Tolosa and the new, $25 million performing arts center on the Cal Poly campus. Not all the music is Mozart; you'll hear Haydn and other composers. The Festival Fringe presents free concerts outdoors.

En Route   Highway 1 and U.S. 101 become one road for a short stretch just south of San Luis Obispo. San Luis Bay Drive loops off the highway to Avila Beach, a usually quiet town that comes alive on weekends, when Cal

Poly students take over. As you continue south, 20 mi of sandy, southern California–style shoreline begins at the town of Pismo Beach, where the action centers on the shops and arcades near the pier. From here there are **two routes to Solvang.** The direct route is U.S. 101, past Arroyo Grande, Santa Maria, and rural countryside that is becoming increasingly less rural. At Buellton, head east on Highway 246 to Solvang. The other option is to take Highway 1, which twists along the coast (and inland a bit at times) past Guadalupe, Vandenberg Air Force Base, and Lompoc. Along the roads near Lompoc, also known as the Flower-Seed Capital of the World, vast fields of brightly colored flowers bloom from May through August. At Lompoc, Highway 246 travels east from Highway 1, past Mission La Purisima Concepcion through Buellton to Solvang. Highway 1 continues south and east until it rejoins U.S. 101 at Las Cruces, 9 mi below Buellton.

La Purisima Mission State Historic Park

★ ⓫ *58 mi south of San Luis Obispo, Hwy. 1 to Hwy. 246 east or U.S. 101 to Hwy. 246 west.*

Mission La Purisima Concepcion, the most fully restored mission in the state, was founded in 1787. Its stark and still-remote setting powerfully evokes the life of the early Spanish settlers in California. Once a month from March through September, costumed docents demonstrate crafts; every day, displays illustrate the secular as well as religious life of the mission. A corral near the parking area holds several farm animals, including sheep that are descendants of the original mission stock. ✉ *2295 Purisima Rd., off Mission Gate Rd.,* ☎ *805/ 733–3713 or 805/733–1303 to schedule a tour.* 🚗 *$5 per vehicle.* 🕐 *Daily 9–5.*

Solvang

⓬ *23 mi east of Mission La Purisima Concepcion, 3 mi east of U.S. 101, on Hwy. 246.*

You'll know when you've reached the Danish town of Solvang: The architecture suddenly turns to half-timbered buildings and windmills, with flags galore. Although it's aimed squarely at tourists, there is a genuine Danish heritage here—more than two-thirds of the town is of Danish descent. The 300 or so shops that sell Danish goods and knick-knacks and specialty gift items are all within easy walking distance; many are along Copenhagen Drive and Alisal Road. Solvang Bakery, at 460 Alisal Road, is one of a half-dozen aroma-filled bakeries in town. If Solvang seems too serene and orderly to be true, find a copy of William Castle's 1961 film *Homicidal,* which used the town as the backdrop for gender-bending murder and mayhem.

Dining and Lodging

$$–$$$ ✕ **The Hitching Post.** You'll find everything from grilled artichokes to ostrich at this casual eatery in nearby Buellton, but most people come here for what is claimed to be the best Santa Maria–style barbecue in the state. The oak used in the barbecue imparts a wonderfully smokey taste. ✉ *406 E. Hwy 246, Buellton,* ☎ *805/688–0676. AE, MC, V. No lunch.*

$ ✕ **Restaurant Molle-Kroen.** Locals come to this cheerful upstairs dining room when they want a good Danish meal at a good price. ✉ *435 Alisal Rd.,* ☎ *805/688–4555. AE, D, DC, MC, V.*

$$$$ ✕🏨 **Alisal Guest Ranch and Resort.** Sixteen hundred or so head of cattle still graze the huge (10,000-acre) grounds of Alisal Ranch, which

first opened to guests in 1946 and soon attracted the likes of Clark Gable and Doris Day. Rooms are plain, with appealing western touches; all have refrigerators and wood-burning fireplaces. Activities here include golf, tennis, horseback riding, and nature-watching, and sailing, windsurfing, pedal boating, and fishing on a 90-acre lake. Hearty meals are served home-style in the rustic yet elegant Ranch Room if the weather isn't warm enough for an outdoor barbecue. Breakfast and dinner are included in the room rates, but many of the activities are extra. ⊠ *1054 Alisal Rd., 93463,* ☎ *805/688–6411 or 800/425–4725,* FAX *805/688–2510. 73 rooms and suites. Restaurant, bar, pool, 2 18-hole golf courses, 7 tennis courts, croquet, Ping-Pong, shuffleboard, volleyball, billiards, library. AE, DC, MC, V.*

$$–$$$$ 🏨 **Chimney Sweep Inn.** The larger (and more expensive) cottages here, built in a half-timbered style, were inspired by the C. S. Lewis children's books, *The Chronicles of Narnia.* The six cottages have kitchens and fireplaces; five also have hot tubs. Room rates include a Continental breakfast. ⊠ *1554 Copenhagen Dr., 93463,* ☎ *805/688–2111 or 800/ 824–6444,* FAX *805/688–8824. 28 rooms. Hot tub. AE, D, MC, V.*

$–$$ 🏨 **Best Western Kronborg Inn.** Rooms at this comfortable motel three blocks from the center of town are spacious; most have balconies overlooking the pool. Room rates include a Continental breakfast. ⊠ *1440 Mission Dr., 93463,* ☎ *805/688–2383,* FAX *805/688–1821. 39 rooms. Pool, hot tub. AE, D, DC, MC, V.*

Nightlife and the Arts

Pacific Conservatory of the Performing Arts (☎ 805/922–8313; 800/ 549–7272 in CA) presents a full spectrum of theatrical events, from classical to contemporary, along with a few musicals, in different theaters in Solvang and Santa Maria. Summer events in Solvang are held in the open-air Festival Theatre, on 2nd Street off Copenhagen Drive.

Outdoor Activities and Sports

Cachuma Lake (⊠ Hwy. 154, ☎ 805/688–4658), a jewel of an artificial lake 12 mi east of Solvang, has hiking, fishing, horseback riding, boating, and interpretive nature programs.

BICYCLING

Quadricycles, four-wheel carriages, and bicycles are available at **Surrey Cycle Rental** (⊠ 475 1st St.) and **Breezy's Carriages** (⊠ 414 1st St.), both in Solvang at ☎ 805/688–0091.

GLIDER RIDES

Windhaven Glider (⊠ Santa Ynez Airport, Hwy. 246 east of Solvang, ☎ 805/688–2517) takes passengers on scenic rides of up to 40 minutes.

Los Olivos

⑬ *1 mi north of Solvang on Alamo Pintado Rd.*

This pretty village in the Santa Ynez Valley was once on El Camino Real and later on major stage and rail routes. It's so sleepy today, however, that it was selected as the site for TV's *Return to Mayberry.* Known for its row of art galleries, antiques stores, and country markets, this is a relaxing point of departure for touring the many wineries in the region. **Los Olivos Tasting Room & Wine Shop** (⊠ 2905 Grand Ave., ☎ 805/688–7406) is a good place to sample the wares of a number of local producers. You can also get information here on area winery tours.

Dining and Lodging

$$$–$$$$ ✕🏨 **Los Olivos Grand Hotel.** The individually decorated rooms in this luxury inn—the only place to overnight in Los Olivos—are in a lawn-fronted house that contains the lobby and restaurant and an equally attractive residence across the street with a pool and a hot tub. All the spacious accommodations have a fireplace, a seating area, and a wet bar; six also have a hot tub. Entrées such as oven-roasted salmon or grilled lamb T-bone are complemented by a fine selection of local bottles at Remington's, the hotel's well-respected dining room. Rates include breakfast, served in the main building or in your room. ✉ 2860 Grand Ave., 93441, ☎ 805/688–7788 or 800/446–2455, ℻ 805/688–1942. 21 rooms. Pool, hot tub. AE, MC, V.

OFF THE   **SAN MARCOS PASS** – Highway 154 winds its spectacular way south
BEATEN PATH   from Solvang (drive east on Highway 246 to 154) through the Los
              Padres National Forest. This former stagecoach route rejoins U.S. 101
              just north of Santa Barbara. The lively Cold Spring Tavern (☞ Santa Bar-
              bara Dining and Lodging, *below*) has been serving travelers since the
              stagecoach days.

SANTA BARBARA

45 mi south of Solvang on U.S. 101.

Santa Barbara has long been an oasis for Los Angeles residents in need of rest and recuperation, but combining as it does the best attributes of a resort town and a sophisticated city, it is no outpost. The attractions in Santa Barbara begin with the ocean and end in the foothills of the Santa Ynez Mountains. In the few miles between the beaches and the hills are downtown, then the old mission, and, a little higher up, the botanic gardens. A few miles farther up the coast, but still very much a part of Santa Barbara, is the exclusive residential district of Hope Ranch. To the east is the district called Montecito, whose informal but classy Coast Village Road has shops and restaurants.

Santa Barbara is on a jog in the coastline, so the ocean is actually to the south. Directions can be confusing. "Up" the coast is west, "down" toward Los Angeles is actually east, and the mountains are north. A car is handy, but not essential, if you're planning on staying pretty much in town. The beaches and downtown are easily explored by bicycle or on foot, and the Santa Barbara Trolley (☞ Contacts and Resources *in* the Central Coast A to Z, *below*) takes visitors to most major hotels and sights, which can also be reached on the local buses.

The **Tourist Information Center** (✉ 1 Santa Barbara St., at Cabrillo Blvd., ☎ 805/965–3021) distributes a free guide to a scenic drive that circles the town with a detour into the downtown. It passes the harbor, beaches, Hope Ranch, and the old mission, yields fine views on the way to Montecito, and then returns you to the beaches. You can pick up the drive, marked with blue SCENIC DRIVE signs, anywhere along the loop. A free guide to the downtown area, the "Red Tile Walking Tour," is also available at the visitor center. It hits historical spots in a 12-block area.

The Waterfront

You'll hear locals refer to the waterfront as "the ocean," but by any name it's a beautiful area, with palm-studded promenades and plenty of sand.

A Good Tour

Start your tour at the **Santa Barbara Yacht Harbor** ⑭. Walk east on Cabrillo Boulevard, the main harborfront drag, and head a few blocks inland to view the huge **Moreton Bay Fig Tree** ⑮. It's back to the coast again for **Stearns Wharf** ⑯, where the **Sea Center** ⑰ is a major attraction. Unless you're an inveterate walker, you'll probably want to get into your car at this point and drive east along Cabrillo Boulevard to reach **East Beach** ⑱ and the nearby **Andree Clark Bird Refuge** ⑲. Want to see more creatures? Adjoining the lagoon is the **Santa Barbara Zoo** ⑳.

TIMING

You could make this an all-day excursion or devote just two or three hours to it if you drive and only stop briefly at the various attractions; you'll likely want to spend at least an hour at the zoo. The waterfront is lovely as evening approaches, but don't hang around to see a sunset over the ocean: Remember, this stretch of shore faces south, not west.

Sights to See

⑲ **Andree Clark Bird Refuge.** This peaceful lagoon and gardens sits just north of East Beach. Bike trails and footpaths, punctuated by signs identifying both native and migratory birds, skirt the lagoon. ⊠ *1400 E. Cabrillo Blvd.* ⊠ *Free.*

OFF THE BEATEN PATH

CHANNEL ISLANDS NATIONAL PARK AND NATIONAL MARINE SANCTUARY Hearty travelers should consider a day visit or an overnight camping trip to one of the five Channel Islands that often appear in a haze on the Santa Barbara horizon. The most popular is Anacapa Island, 11 mi off the coast. The islands' remoteness and unpredictable seas protected them from development and now provide a nature enthusiast's paradise. On a good day, you'll be able to view seals, sea lions, and much bird life. From December through March, migrating whales can be seen close up. On land, tide pools are often accessible. Underwater, divers can view fish, giant squid, and coral. Frenchy's Cove, on the west end of the island, has a swimming beach and fine snorkeling. The waters of the channel are often rough and can make for a rugged boat ride out to the islands (*see* Boats and Charters *in* Outdoor Activities and Sports, *below*, for information about group outings).

⑱ **East Beach.** The wide swath of sand at the east end of Cabrillo Boulevard is a great spot for people-watching. An inordinate number of sunbathers here look as if they ought to be fashion models. Sand volleyball courts, summertime lifeguard and sports competitions, and arts-and-crafts shows on Sundays and holidays make for an often lively experience. Showers (no towels), lockers, and beach rentals—also a weight room—are provided at the Cabrillo Pavilion Bathhouse (⊠ 1118 Cabrillo Blvd., ☎ 805/965–0509). Next to the boathouse, there's an elaborate jungle-gym play area for children.

⑮ **Moreton Bay Fig Tree.** Planted in 1877, this tree is so huge it reputedly can provide shade for 10,000 people. In recent years it has become a gathering place for homeless people. ⊠ *Chapala St. between U.S. 101 and Cabrillo Blvd.*

⑭ **Santa Barbara Yacht Harbor.** A paved man-made breakwater protects this harbor. You can take a ½-mi walk along the breakwater, check out the tackle and bait shops, or hire a boat. ⊠ *West end of Cabrillo Blvd.*

 ⑳ **Santa Barbara Zoo.** The natural settings of the zoo shelter elephants, gorillas, exotic birds, and big-game cats, such as the rare amur leop-

Santa Barbara

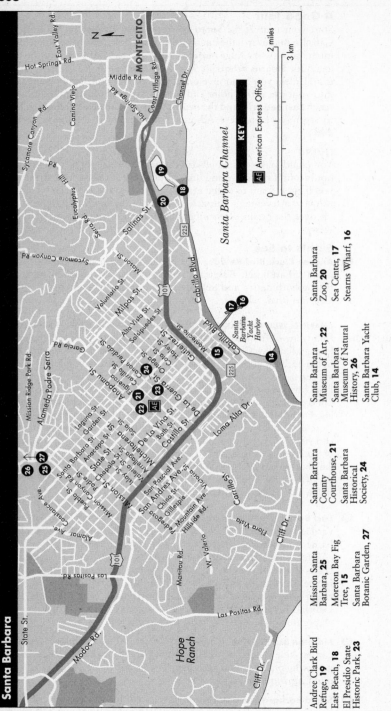

KEY

AE American Express Office

0 2 miles

0 3 km

Santa Barbara Channel

Andree Clark Bird
Refuge, **19**
East Beach, **18**
El Presidio State
Historic Park, **23**

Mission Santa
Barbara, **25**
Moreton Bay Fig
Tree, **15**
Santa Barbara
Botanic Garden, **27**

Santa Barbara
County
Courthouse, **21**
Santa Barbara
Historical
Society, **24**

Santa Barbara
Museum of Art, **22**
Santa Barbara
Museum of Natural
History, **26**
Santa Barbara Yacht
Club, **14**

Santa Barbara
Zoo, **20**
Sea Center, **17**
Stearns Wharf, **16**

ard, a thick-furred, high-altitude dweller from Asia. Youngsters enjoy the scenic railroad and barnyard petting zoo. ☒ *500 Niños Dr.,* ☎ *805/ 962–6310.* 🎫 *$5.* ⊙ *Daily 10–5.*

🐾 ⑰ **Sea Center.** This branch of the Santa Barbara Museum of Natural History that specializes in exhibits of marine life is a major attraction on Stearns Wharf. Aquariums, life-size models of whales and dolphins, undersea dioramas, interactive computer-video displays, and the remains of shipwrecks depict marine life from the Santa Barbara coastline to the Channel Islands. Visitors to the Touch Tank handle marine invertebrates, fish, and marine plants collected from nearby waters. ☒ *211 Stearns Wharf,* ☎ *805/962–0885.* 🎫 *$2.* ⊙ *Sea Center Sat.–Mon. and Wed. 10–5, Tues., Thurs., Fri. noon–5 (call weekday mornings Oct.– May to make sure school field trips haven't closed center to public); Touch Tank daily noon–4.*

⑯ **Stearns Wharf.** Extending the length of three city blocks into the Pacific, the wharf has a view back toward Santa Barbara that gives visitors a good sense of its size and general layout. Although it's a nice walk from the Cabrillo Boulevard parking areas, you can also drive out and park (for a fee) on the pier and then wander through the shops or stop for a meal at one of the wharf's restaurants or the snack bar. ☒ *Cabrillo Blvd. at the foot of State St.,* ☎ *805/966–6624.*

Downtown and the Foothills

A Good Tour

Start your downtown walk at the **Santa Barbara County Courthouse** ㉑ at the corner of Anacapa and Anapamu streets. One block west on Anapamu Street, beyond the Spanish-style public library, is the **Santa Barbara Museum of Art** ㉒. Walking south from the courthouse, you'll pass **El Paseo,** a shopping arcade built around an old adobe home. There are several such arcades in the area, as well as many small art galleries. If you make a right at Anacapa and East Cañon Perdido streets, you'll soon reach **El Presidio State Historic Park** ㉓. From the park, head south one block to De La Guerra Street and the turn left (east) to reach the museum of the **Santa Barbara Historical Society** ㉔.

Hop in your car and take State Street north (away from the water) to Los Olivos Street. Turn right (east) and you'll soon see **Mission Santa Barbara** ㉕. From the mission you can walk the block north to the **Santa Barbara Museum of Natural History** ㉖. You'll probably want to drive the 1½ mi north to the **Santa Barbara Botanic Garden** ㉗.

TIMING

Some of Santa Barbara's most interesting attractions are on this tour: Set aside an hour each for the art and natural-history museums and for the botanic gardens. Of course, you might be drawn into the shops and galleries on State Street and never make it to any of the other places at all.

Sights to See

㉓ **El Presidio State Historic Park.** Founded in 1782, the Presidio was one of four military strongholds established by the Spanish along the coast of California. The guardhouse, El Cuartel, one of the two original adobe buildings that remain of the complex, is the oldest building owned by the state. ☒ *123 E. Cañon Perdido St.,* ☎ *805/966–9719.* 🎫 *Free.* ⊙ *Daily 10:30–4:30.*

🐾 **Kids' World public playground.** Children and adults enjoy the complex maze of fantasy climbing structures, turrets, slides, and tunnels built by Santa Barbara parents. ☒ *Santa Barbara St. near Micheltorena St.*

OFF THE
BEATEN PATH

LOTUSLAND – Only a limited number of people are permitted to visit the 37-acre estate that once belonged to Polish opera singer Ganna Walska; the hours and time of year that Lotusland is open are limited, too, and one must take part in a 1½- to 2-hour guided group tour. That said, it's worth trying to get a reservation to see the celebrated gardens. Many of the exotic trees and other subtropical flora were planted in 1882 by horticulturist R. Kinton Stevens; Madame Walksa, who purchased the estate in 1941, further developed the grounds. Among the highlights are an outdoor theater, a topiary garden, a horticultural clock, a huge collection of rare bromeliads, and a lotus pond. ⊠ *Ganna Walska Lotusland, 695 Ashley Rd., Montecito,* ☎ *805/969-9990,* ⅢⅩ *805/969-4423.* ⌦ *$10.* ☉ *Tours mid-Feb.–mid-Nov., Wed.–Sun.*

★ ㉕ **Mission Santa Barbara.** The architecture and layout of this mission, which was established in 1786, evolved from adobe-brick buildings with thatched roofs to more permanent edifices as the mission's population burgeoned during its early years. An earthquake in 1812 destroyed the third church built on the site; its replacement, the present structure, is still used as a Catholic church, though during the post-Mission era it also served as a boys school and a seminary. Cacti, palm trees, and other succulents grow in the pleasant garden beside the mission. ⊠ *2201 Laguna St.,* ☎ *805/682–4149.* ⌦ *$3.* ☉ *Daily 9–5.*

★ ㉗ **Santa Barbara Botanic Garden.** Five-plus miles of trails meander through the garden's 65 acres of native plants. The Mission Dam, built in 1806, stands just beyond the redwood grove and above the partially uncovered aqueduct that once carried water to Mission Santa Barbara. An ethnobotanical display contains replicas of the plants used by the Chumash Indians. ⊠ *1212 Mission Canyon Rd.,* ☎ *805/682–4726.* ⌦ *$3.* ☉ *Mar.–Oct., weekdays 9–5, weekends 9–6; Nov.–Feb., weekdays 9–4, weekends 9–5. Guided tours daily at 2; additional tour at 10:30 AM Thurs., Sat., and Sun.*

★ ㉑ **Santa Barbara County Courthouse.** With its hand-painted tiles and spiral staircase, the courthouse has all the grandeur of a Moorish palace. This magnificent building was completed in 1929, part of a rebuilding process after a 1925 earthquake destroyed many downtown structures. At the time Santa Barbara was also in the midst of a cultural awakening, and the trend was toward an architecture appropriate to the area's climate and history. The result is the harmonious Mediterranean-Spanish look of much of the downtown area, especially municipal buildings. An elevator takes visitors to an arched observation area in the courthouse tower that has a panoramic view of the city. The murals in the supervisors' ceremonial chambers on the courthouse's second floor were painted by an artist who did backdrops for some of Cecil B. DeMille's silent films. ⊠ *1100 block of Anacapa St.,* ☎ *805/962–6464.* ☉ *Weekdays 8:30–4:30, weekends 10–5. Free 1-hr guided tours Mon.–Sat. 2 PM.*

㉔ **Santa Barbara Historical Society.** The society's museum exhibits decorative and fine arts, furniture, costumes, and documents from the town's past. Adjacent is the Gledhill Library, a collection of books, photographs, maps, and manuscripts about the area. ⊠ *136 E. De La Guerra St.,* ☎ *805/966–1601.* ⌦ *Museum $3, library $2 per hr up to $5.* ☉ *Museum Tues.–Sat. 10–5, Sun. noon–5; library Tues.–Fri. 10–4, 1st Sat. of month 1–4.*

㉒ **Santa Barbara Museum of Art.** The museum houses a fine permanent collection of ancient sculpture, Asian art, French Impressionist paintings, and a sampling of American artists, such as Grandma Moses. ⊠ *1130 State St.,* ☎ *805/963–4364.* ⌦ *$4; free Thurs. and 1st Sun. of*

month. ◷ *Tues.–Sat. 11–5 (until 9 Thurs.), Sun. noon–5. Guided tours
Tues.–Sun. 1* PM.

❀ ㉖ **Santa Barbara Museum of Natural History.** A full-size skeleton of a blue
whale at the entrance serves as a landmark for the museum complex.
Highlights include the planetarium and E. L. Wiegand Space Lab; a
room of dioramas illustrating Chumash Indian history and culture; and
the bird diversity room, filled with startlingly lifelike taxidermized specimens, complete with nests and eggs. Many of the exhibits have interactive components. ✉ *2559 Puesta del Sol Rd.,* ☎ *805/682–4711.*
💳 *$5.* ◷ *Mon.–Sat. 9–5, Sun. 10–5.*

Dining and Lodging

$$$–$$$$ ✕ **The Stonehouse.** This atmospheric restaurant in a turn-of-the-cen-
tury granite farmhouse is part of the San Ysidro Ranch resort. The con-
temporary southern American menu offers such treats as dry-aged
New York steak with smoked tomato-horseradish sauce and clam
hash, seared rare *ahi* tuna in an herb crust with sun-dried-tomato
couscous, and an excellent four-course vegetarian menu. Even better
than the generally wonderful food is the pastoral setting. Be sure to
have lunch—salads, pastas, and sandwiches—on the tree-house-like out-
door patio. At night, the candlelit interior becomes seriously roman-
tic. ✉ *900 San Ysidro La., Montecito,* ☎ *805/969–4100. Reservations
essential. AE, MC, V.*

$$$ ✕ **Citronelle.** The offspring of Michel Richard's famed Citrus in Los
★ Angeles has brought Santa Barbarans some of the best California-
French cuisine they've ever had this close to home. The accent is on
Riviera-style dishes: light and delicate but loaded with intriguing good
tastes. The desserts are unmatched anywhere in southern California.
There are splendid, sweeping views of the harbor from the dining
room's picture windows—try to arrive before sunset. ✉ *901 E. Cabrillo
Blvd.,* ☎ *805/963–0111. Reservations essential. AE, D, DC, MC, V.*

$$–$$$ ✕ **Café Buenos Aires.** The always busy Buenos Aires serves salads, sand-
wiches, pastas, and traditional Argentine empanadas (small turnovers
filled with chicken, beef, or vegetables) for lunch. Dinner can be fashioned out of potato omelets, Spanish red sausage in beer sauce, octopus stewed with tomato and onion, and other tapas. Pastas and
Argentine specialties—larger empanadas, grilled short ribs, or grilled
rib-eye steak sautéed in sweet butter, both served with homemade
french fries (with or without garlic and parsley)—are among the main
entrées. ✉ *1316 State St.,* ☎ *805/963–0242. Reservations essential
for dinner. AE, DC, MC, V.*

$$–$$$ ✕ **Harbor Restaurant.** This sparkling spot on the pier is where locals
like to take out-of-town guests for great views and somewhat overpriced
average American food. The casual nautical-theme bar and grill upstairs serves sandwiches, large salads, and a huge variety of appetizers; the outdoor terrace is a glorious spot for a sandwich or a beer on
a sunny day. Downstairs you'll find good-size portions of fresh seafood,
prime rib, and steaks. Every seat has a harbor view. ✉ *210 Stearns Wharf,*
☎ *805/963–3311. AE, MC, V.*

$$–$$$ ✕ **Palace Café.** The Palace has won acclaim for its Cajun and Creole
dishes, such as blackened redfish and jambalaya with dirty rice.
Caribbean fare here includes delicious coconut shrimp. Just in case the
dishes aren't spicy enough for you, each table has a bottle of hot sauce.
Be prepared for a wait of up to 45 minutes on weekends. ✉ *8 E. Cota
St.,* ☎ *805/966–3133. AE, MC, V. No lunch.*

$$ ✕ **Andria's Harborside.** The seafood entrées are decent at this sprawl-
ing, nautical-style eatery, but most people come here for the creamy
clam chowder or the fresh oysters—and for the harbor views. Nightly

entertainment at the piano bar adds to the bustling atmosphere. ✉ *336 W. Cabrillo Blvd.,* ☎ *805/966–3000. AE, D, DC, MC, V.*

\$\$ ✕ **Cold Spring Tavern.** Well worth the drive out of town, this century-old roadhouse is on the former stagecoach route through the San Marcos Pass. It's part Harley-biker hangout and part romantic country hideaway, a mix that works surprisingly well. Game dishes—rabbit, venison, quail—are the specialty, along with American standards like ribs, steak, and a great chili. It's a one-of-a-kind spot. ✉ *5995 Stagecoach Rd., San Marcos Pass,* ☎ *805/967–0066. AE, MC, V.*

\$\$ ✕ **Emilio's.** A harborside location and innovative northern Italian fare make this intimate place popular with locals and tourists. Starters on the seasonal menu might include crispy roast duck on a risotto cake. The ravioli stuffed with butternut squash or potato gnocchi with rock shrimp are standouts. During the week a three-course vegetarian tasting menu is available, as are two prix-fixe wine-tasting menus. ✉ *324 W. Cabrillo Blvd.,* ☎ *805/966–4426. AE, D, MC, V. No lunch.*

\$\$ ✕ **Montecito Café.** The ambience is upscale yet casual at this pleasant restaurant serving contemporary California-American cuisine—fresh fish, grilled chicken, steak, and pasta. The salads and lamb dishes are particularly inventive. ✉ *1295 Coast Village Rd.,* ☎ *805/969–3392. AE, MC, V.*

\$\$ ✕ **Pane & Vino.** This tiny trattoria with an equally small sidewalk dining terrace sits in a tree-shaded, flower-decked shopping center. The cold antipasto is very good, as are grilled meats and fish, pastas, and salads. ✉ *1482 E. Valley Rd., Montecito,* ☎ *805/969–9274. Reservations essential. MC, V. No lunch Sun.*

\$–\$\$ ✕ **Arigato Sushi.** Sushi fans will appreciate the fresh seafood served in this atmospheric Japanese restaurant and sushi bar. Innovation reigns here, with creations such as sushi pizza on seaweed and Hawaiian sashimi salad. ✉ *11 W. Victoria St.,* ☎ *805/965–6074. Reservations not accepted. AE, MC, V. No lunch.*

\$–\$\$ ✕ **Brigitte's.** This lively State Street café serves California cuisine and local wines at relatively low prices. The individual pizzas are always worth trying, as are the pastas (such as basil fettuccine with prawns and roasted peppers in pesto), grilled fresh fish, and roast lamb. ✉ *1327 State St.,* ☎ *805/966–9676. Reservations not accepted. MC, V. No lunch Sun.*

\$ ✕ **D'Angelo.** The bread served by many of the town's best restaurants comes from the ovens of this popular bakery, which has recently added a few indoor and outdoor tables. Come for breakfast—the brioches are awesome—or for a sandwich or pastry break from shopping on nearby State Street. D'Angelo is open Monday through Saturday from 7 AM to 6 PM, Sunday from 8 to 4. ✉ *25 W. Gutierrez St.,* ☎ *805/962–5466. MC, V. No dinner.*

\$ ✕ **La Super-Rica.** A favorite of Julia Child's, this food stand with a patio
★   serves the best and hottest Mexican dishes between Los Angeles and San Francisco. Fans drive for miles to fill up on the soft tacos and incredible beans. ✉ *622 N. Milpas St., at Alphonse St.,* ☎ *805/963–4940. No credit cards.*

\$ ✕ **Roy.** This downtown storefront is a real bargain. Owner-chef Leroy Gandy serves a \$12.50 fixed-price dinner that includes a small salad, fresh soup, and a tempting roster of Cal-Mediterranean main courses: shrimp ravioli, marinated leg of lamb with eggplant ratatouille, grilled salmon with pineapple-orange-mango chutney and a mint-butter sauce. Expect a wait on weekends. ✉ *7 W. Carrillo St.,* ☎ *805/966–5636. Reservations not accepted. AE, MC, V. Closed Mon.*

\$ ✕ **Your Place.** Tasty seafood, curries, and vegetarian dishes keep this small restaurant packed for lunch and dinner. The sea scallops garnished with crispy basil are alone worth a trip. Your Place has consistently been named best Thai restaurant by local periodicals. ⊠ *22 N. Milpas St.,* ☎ *805/966–5151. AE, MC, V. Closed Mon.*

$$$$ ✕▦ **Four Seasons Biltmore Hotel.** Santa Barbara's grande dame has
★   long been the favored spot for the town's high society and the visiting
rich and famous to indulge in quiet California-style luxury. Muted pastels and bleached woods give the cabanas behind the main building an
airy feel without sacrificing the hotel's reputation for understated elegance. Surrounded by lush (but always perfectly manicured) gardens
and palm trees, the Biltmore is a bit more formal than other properties in town. Dining is indoors and formal at the hotel's La Marina
Restaurant—the California-Continental menu changes monthly—and
outdoors and more casual at The Patio. ⊠ *1260 Channel Dr., Montecito 93108,* ☎ *805/969–2261 or 800/332–3442,* ℻ *805/969–5715.
234 rooms. 2 restaurants, bar, pool, hot tub, spa, putting green, 3 tennis courts, croquet, health club, shuffleboard. AE, DC, MC, V.*

$$$$ ✕▦ **San Ysidro Ranch.** At this luxury "ranch" you can feel at home
★   in jeans and cowboy boots, but be prepared to dress for dinner. A hideout for the Hollywood set, this romantic place hosted John and Jackie
Kennedy on their honeymoon. Guest cottages, all with down comforters
and wood-burning stoves or fireplaces, are scattered among 14 acres
of orange trees and flower beds; hiking trails crisscross 500 acres of
open space surrounding the property. The Stonehouse Restaurant (☞
above) is a Santa Barbara institution. The hotel, which welcomes children and pets, provides personal beauty services and 24-hour room service. ⊠ *900 San Ysidro La., Montecito 93108,* ☎ *805/969–5046 or
800/368–6788,* ℻ *805/565–1995. 43 rooms. Restaurant, pool, massage, spa, tennis courts, boccie, exercise room, horseback riding, horseshoes. AE, MC, V. 2-day minimum stay on weekends, 3 days on
holidays.*

$$$–$$$$ ▦ **Simpson House Inn.** Traditional B&B fans will enjoy the beautifully
★   appointed Victorian main house of this inn on a quiet acre in the heart
of town. Those seeking total privacy and sybaritic comfort should choose
one of the exceptional new cottages or century-old barn suites, each
complete with wood-burning fireplace, luxurious bedding, state-of-the-art electronics, and a whirlpool bath. In-room spa services such as massage and body wraps are available. Room rates include a full breakfast.
⊠ *121 E. Arrellaga St., 93101,* ☎ *805/963–7067 or 800/676–1280,*
℻ *805/564–4811. 14 rooms. AE, D, MC, V. 2-night minimum stay
on weekends.*

$$$ ▦ **The Upham.** This handsomely restored Victorian hotel amid an acre
of gardens in the historic downtown area was established in 1871. Period furnishings and antiques adorn the rooms and cottages, some of
which have fireplaces and private patios. Room size varies from small
to quite spacious. Continental breakfast, afternoon wine and cheese,
and bedtime Oreos and milk are served in the lobby. The on-site restaurant, Louie's (☎ *805/963–7003*), serves good California cuisine. ⊠
1404 De La Vina St., 93101, ☎ *805/962–0058 or 800/727–0876,* ℻
805/963–2825. 50 rooms. AE, D, DC, MC, V.

$$–$$$$ ▦ **Ambassador by the Sea.** The wrought-iron trim and mosaic tiling
on this Spanish-style building near the harbor and Stearns Wharf give
it the feel of a typical California beach motel. The rooms have verandas, and sundecks overlook the ocean and a bike path. ⊠ *202 W. Cabrillo
Blvd., 93101,* ☎ *805/965–4577,* ℻ *805/965–9937. 32 rooms. Pool.
AE, D, DC, MC, V.*

$$–$$$$ ▦ **Old Yacht Club Inn.** Built in 1912 as a private home in the California Craftsman style, this inn near the beach was one of Santa Barbara's
first B&Bs. The rooms have turn-of-the-century furnishings and Ori-

ental rugs. The adjacent Hitchcock House holds five rooms with private entrances, including a luxury suite. Guests receive a complimentary full breakfast and evening wine and have the use of bikes and beach chairs. There is no smoking. ⊠ *431 Corona del Mar Dr., 93103,* ☎ *805/962–1277 or 800/676–1676; 800/549–1676 in CA;* FAX *805/962–3989. 10 rooms. Dining room. AE, D, DC, MC, V.*

$$–$$$$ 🏨 **Villa Rosa.** The rooms and intimate lobby of this Spanish-style stucco-and-wood hotel one block from the beach are decorated in an informal southwestern style. Rates include a Continental breakfast, wine and cheese in the afternoon, and port and sherry in the evening. ⊠ *15 Chapala St., 93101,* ☎ *805/966–0851,* FAX *805/962–7159. 18 rooms. Pool, hot tub. AE, MC, V.*

$ 🏨 **Motel 6.** The low price and location near the beach are the pluses for this no-frills place. Reserve well in advance all year. ⊠ *443 Corona del Mar Dr., 93103,* ☎ *805/564–1392,* FAX *805/963–4687. 51 rooms. Pool. AE, D, DC, MC, V.*

Nightlife and the Arts

Most major hotels present nightly entertainment during the summer season and live weekend entertainment all year. State Street has a good jazz scene. Santa Barbara supports a professional symphony and a chamber orchestra. The proximity to the University of California at Santa Barbara assures an endless stream of visiting artists and performers. To see what's scheduled around town pick up a copy of the free weekly *Santa Barbara Independent* newspaper.

BARS AND CLUBS

Blue Agave (⊠ 20 E. Cota St., ☎ 805/899–4694) draws a chic Gen-X crowd with its designer martinis, rich leather couches, crackling fireplace, pool tables, cigar balcony, and good food.

Joe's Cafe (⊠ 536 State St., ☎ 805/966–4638), where steins of beer accompany hearty bar food, is a fun, if occasionally rowdy, collegiate hangout.

Left at Albuquerque (⊠ 803 State St., ☎ 805/564–5040), offering 141 types of tequila in a Southwest setting, isn't one of your more sedate nightspots.

Plow & Angel (⊠ San Ysidro Ranch, 900 San Ysidro La., Montecito, ☎ 805/969–5046) has live jazz on Thursday and Friday; then and at other times it's perfect for those seeking quieter conversation, an early-California ambience, perhaps even romance.

Soho (⊠ 1221 State St., ☎ 805/962–7776), a hip restaurant and hangout, presents weeknight jazz music; on weekends, the mood livens with good blues and rock.

PERFORMING ARTS

Arlington Theater (⊠ 1317 State St., ☎ 805/963–4408), a spectacular Moorish-style former movie palace, is home to the Santa Barbara Symphony.

Center Stage Theatre (⊠ Paseo Nuevo, 700 block of State St., 2nd floor, ☎ 805/963–0408) presents plays and readings.

Granada Theatre (⊠ 1216 State St., ☎ 805/966–2324), a restored movie palace, is the headquarters of the Santa Barbara Civic Light Opera.

Lobero Theatre (⊠ 33 E. Cañon Perdido St., ☎ 805/963–0761), a state landmark, hosts community theater groups and touring professionals.

Outdoor Activities and Sports

BEACHES

Santa Barbara's beaches don't have the big surf of the shoreline farther south, but they also don't have the crowds. A short walk from
the parking lot can usually find you a solitary spot. Be aware that fog
often hugs the coast until about noon in June and July.

The usually gentle surf at **Arroyo Burro County Beach** (✉ Cliff Dr. at
Las Positas Rd.) makes it ideal for families with young children. **Go-
leta Beach Park** (✉ Ward Memorial Hwy.) is a favorite with college
students from the nearby University of California campus. Succes-
sively west of Santa Barbara off U.S. 101 are **El Capitan, Refugio,** and
Gaviota state beaches, each with campsites, picnic tables, and fire pits.
East of the city is the sheltered, sunny, often crowded **Carpinteria State
Beach.**

BICYCLING

The level, two-lane, 3-mi Cabrillo Bike Lane passes the Santa Barbara
Zoo, Andree Clark Bird Refuge, beaches, and the harbor. There are
restaurants along the way, or you can stop for a picnic along the palm-
lined path looking out on the Pacific. **Beach Rentals** (✉ 22 State St.,
☎ 805/966–6733) has bikes, quadricycles, and skates. **Cycles 4 Rent**
(✉ Fess Parker's Red Lion Resort, 633 E. Cabrillo Blvd., ☎ 805/564–
4333, ext. 444) has bikes and quadricycles.

BOATS AND CHARTERS

Island Packers (✉ 1867 Spinnaker Dr., Ventura, ☎ 805/642–1393)
conducts day trips and camping excursions to the five Channel Islands.
Boats link up with national-park naturalists for hikes and nature programs. Unpredictable weather can limit island landings. Reservations
are essential in the summer.

Santa Barbara Sailing Association (✉ Santa Barbara Yacht Harbor
launching ramp, ☎ 805/962–2826 or 800/350–9090) provides sailing instruction, rents and charters sailboats, and organizes dinner and
sunset champagne cruises, island excursions, and whale-watching expeditions.

Sea Landing Sportfishing (✉ Cabrillo Blvd. at Bath St. and breakwater, ☎ 805/963–3564) operates fully equipped surface and deep-sea
fishing charters year-round, plus dinner cruises and island and whale-
watching excursions.

GOLF

Sandpiper Golf Course (✉ 7925 Hollister Ave., Goleta, ☎ 805/968–
1541) is a challenging 18-hole course. **Santa Barbara Golf Club** (✉ Las
Positas Rd. and McCaw Ave., ☎ 805/687–7087) has an 18-hole
course.

HORSEBACK RIDING

The Circle Bar B Guest Ranch (✉ 1800 Refugio Rd., Goleta, ☎ 805/
968–3901) operates trail rides—minimum 1½ hours—for parties of 1
to 26; one four-hour excursion includes a picnic lunch.

POLO

Santa Barbara Polo & Racquet Club (✉ Via Real off Santa Claus La.,
Carpinteria, ☎ 805/684–8667) invites the public to watch Sunday
matches April through October. Admission is $5.

TENNIS

Many Santa Barbara hotels have their own courts, but there are also
excellent public facilities. Day permits, for $3, are available at these
courts (☎ 805/564–5517): **Las Positas Municipal Courts** (✉ 1002 Las

Positas Rd.), **Municipal Courts** (⊠ Near Salinas St. and U.S. 101), and **Pershing Park** (⊠ Castillo St. and Cabrillo Blvd.).

The east end of Santa Barbara's East Beach has more than a dozen sand-lots. There are some casual pickup games, but if you get into one, be prepared—these folks play for keeps.

Shopping

State Street, the commercial hub of Santa Barbara, is a joy to shop. Thrift shops, elegant women's wear, bookstores, sporting goods, shopping centers, quirky storefronts—it's all here, and it's all accessible on foot or on the 25¢ battery-powered trolley that runs between the waterfront and the 1300 block. Swank boutiques line Montecito's **Coast Village Road,** where members of the landed gentry pick up truffle oil, picture frames, and designer sweats.

SHOPPING AREAS

In all, 32 shops, art galleries, and studios share the courtyard and gardens of **El Paseo** (⊠ Cañon Perdido St. between State and Anacapa Sts.), a shopping arcade rich in history. Lunch on the outdoor patio is a nice break during a downtown tour. Open-air **Paseo Nuevo** (⊠ 700 and 800 blocks of State St.) is home to chains such as the Eddie Bauer Home Store, Nordstrom, Macy's, and the California Pizza Kitchen, but is more notable for cherished local institutions like Stampa Barbara (rubber-stamp paradise) and the children's clothier This Little Piggy.

In Santa Barbara a dozen **antiques and gift shops** are clustered in restored Victorian buildings on Brinkerhoff Avenue, two blocks west of State Street at West Cota Street. Serious antiques hunters head a few miles south of Santa Barbara to the beach town of Summerland, which is rife with shops and markets. Wanda Livernois publishes a map and guide to Santa Barbara antiques dealers, available at 533 Brinkerhoff Avenue (or call ☎ 805/962–4247 to have one mailed).

BOOKS

Chaucer's Bookstore (⊠ Loreto Plaza, 3321 State St., ☎ 805/682–6787) is the city's best-stocked independent. **Earthling Book Shop and Café** (⊠ 1137 State St., ☎ 805/965–0926) is arguably Santa Barbara's cultural and intellectual center. Rambling yet homey, the Earthling holds book signings, poetry readings, a children's story time, and many other events. The book and magazine selection is terrific.

CLOTHING

Big Dog Sportswear (⊠ 6 E. Yanonali St., ☎ 805/963–8728), a Santa Barbara–based company, has gone national, so you may have spotted the sweats and surf wear with the St. Bernard logo in other parts of the country.

Pacific Leisure (⊠ 929 State St., ☎ 805/962–8828) stocks the latest in casual and beach wear, shoes, and beach towels.

Territory Ahead (⊠ 515 State St., ☎ 805/962–5558), a high-quality outdoorsy catalog company whose only showroom is in Santa Barbara, sells fashionably rugged clothing for men and women.

Wendy Foster–Pierre LaFond (⊠ 833 State St., ☎ 805/966–2276), an upscale local clothier, captures the fluid California style of women's wear. There are two even tonier branches in Montecito (⊠ 516 San Ysidro Rd., ☎ 805/565–1502; ⊠ 1221 Coast Village Rd., ☎ 805/565–1599). The store on Coast Village Road goes by the name Angel.

KITCHEN
Jordano's (✉ 3025 De La Vina St., ☎ 805/965–3031) attracts cooks and kitchen junkies from Los Angeles and beyond. Part professional restaurant supply house, part gourmet store, and part cooking school, this sprawling shop stocks everything from seafood forks to espresso machines, flavored oils to herb pots.

OJAI

㉘ *40 mi southeast of Santa Barbara, U.S. 101 to Hwy. 150 to Hwy. 33.*

In and around rural Ojai acres of orange and avocado groves look like the postcard images of agricultural southern California from decades ago. Recent years have seen an influx of artists, showbiz types, and other Angelenos who have opted for a life out of the fast lane. Moviemaker Frank Capra used the Ojai Valley as a backdrop for his 1936 classic, *Lost Horizon.* The compact town can be easily explored on foot, or hop on **The Ojai Valley Trolley,** which takes riders on a one-hour loop (7:40 to 5:40 weekdays, 9 to 5 weekends). If you tell the driver you're a visitor, you'll get an informal guided tour. If you want to walk, the **Ojai Visitor Center** (✉ 150 W. Ojai Ave.) has information about the sights around town. The valley sizzles in the summer, when temperatures routinely reach 90°F.

The works of local artists can be seen in the Spanish-style shopping arcade along the main street. **The Art Center** (✉ 113 S. Montgomery, ☎ 805/646–0117) exhibits artworks and presents theater and dance. **The Ojai Valley Museum** (✉ 130 W. Ojai Ave., ☎ 805/640–1390) documents the valley's history and displays Native American artifacts.

A stroll around town should include a stop at **Bart's Books** (✉ 302 W. Matilija, ☎ 805/646–3755), an outdoor store sheltered by native oaks and overflowing with used books. **Local Hero** (✉ 254 E. Ojai Ave., ☎ 805/646–3165) sells books and hosts music, readings, and book-signings on weekend evenings. There's also a café here. On Sunday, local organic and specialty growers sell their produce from 10 to 2 (9 to 1 in summer) at the **Farmers Market** on the plaza behind the arcade. On Wednesday evenings in summer, the free all-American music played by the Ojai Band draws crowds to **Libbey Park** in the heart of town.

A hiker's paradise, Ojai is home of the 9-mi **Ojai Valley Trail** and many more paths in the surrounding hills. The Ojai Chamber of Commerce (☞ Contacts and Resources *in* the Central Coast A to Z, *below*) pub-
㉙ lishes a regional trail map. Nearby **Lake Casitas** on Highway 150, which has boating, fishing, and camping, was the venue for the 1984 Summer Olympic rowing events.

㉚ One of the attractions in Ojai is a hot spring that makes use of natural mineral water from nearby hills. The spa at **Wheeler Hot Springs** emerges like an oasis 7 mi north of town on Highway 33. Its tall palms and herb gardens are fed by an adjacent stream, and natural mineral waters fill the four redwood hot tubs and a large pool. Massage and skin-care services are also available. The restaurant here, which serves California-Mediterranean cuisine that incorporates herbs grown in the spa's garden, is open Thursday to Sunday. Reservations are essential. Weekend brunch packages that include massage and use of the hot tub are a sybarite's dream. ✉ *16825 Maricopa Hwy.,* ☎ *805/646–8131 or 800/994–3353.* ◷ *Mon.–Thurs. 9–9, Fri.–Sun. 9 AM–10 PM. Reservations advised at least a wk in advance for weekends, especially for spa.*

Dining and Lodging

$$$ ✕ **L'Auberge.** Tasty country-French–Belgian food is paired with a terrific country setting here. When the weather's fine, those in the know reserve an early table on the patio so they can accompany their rack of lamb with a glorious sunset. ✉ *314 El Paseo Rd.,* ☎ *805/646–2288. AE, MC, V. No lunch weekdays.*

$$–$$$ ✕ **Suzanne's Cuisine.** Fine contemporary European fare is served in a homey room with a fireplace and on an adjoining covered patio. Fresh seafood is a specialty here—swordfish with ginger-lime sauce or salmon with sauerkraut in a dill beurre blanc are two possibilities—but pastas and meat dishes are also well prepared. Salads and soups star at lunchtime. Most of the bread and all the desserts, including a warm chocolate tart with a white coffee sauce, are made on the premises. ✉ *502 W. Ojai Ave.,* ☎ *805/640–1961. MC, V. Closed Tues and 1st 2 wks in Jan.*

$$$$ ✕⚏ **Oaks at Ojai.** This well-known, comfortable but not luxurious health spa has a fitness package that includes lodging; three nutritionally balanced, surprisingly good low-calorie meals; complete use of spa facilities; and 16 optional fitness classes. ✉ *122 E. Ojai Ave., 93023,* ☎ *805/646–5573 or 800/753–6257,* FAX *805/640–1504. 46 rooms. Dining room, pool, hot tubs, sauna, exercise room. D, MC, V. 2-day minimum stay.*

$$$$ ✕⚏ **Ojai Valley Inn & Spa.** This outdoorsy golf-oriented resort is set
★ on landscaped grounds lush with flowers. The peaceful setting comes with hillside views in nearly all directions; nearby is the inn's 800-acre ranch, where guests can hike, mountain bike, ride horses, and birdwatch. Some of the nicer rooms are in the original adobe building. Families make use of popular Camp Ojai, held in summer and on holidays for kids age 4 to 12, and the remarkable collection of miniature animals in the petting farm. By the time you read this, a new spa with 28 massage and treatment rooms, a cardiovascular floor, a beauty salon, quiet rooms, and three penthouse guest rooms should be completed. The two restaurants tout "Ojai regional cuisine" that incorporates locally grown produce and locally made foods. ✉ *Country Club Rd., 93023,* ☎ *805/646–5511 or 800/422–6524,* FAX *805/646–7969. 207 units. 2 restaurants, bar, 2 pools, spa, 18-hole golf course, 8 tennis courts, hiking, horseback riding, mountain bikes. AE, D, DC, MC, V.*

$–$$ ⚏ **Best Western Casa Ojai.** This modern hotel sits on Ojai's main street, across from Soule Park Golf Course. Rooms are simple and clean. Room rates include a Continental breakfast. ✉ *1302 E. Ojai Ave., 93023,* ☎ *805/646–8175 or 800/255–8175,* FAX *805/640–8247. 45 rooms. Pool, hot tub. AE, D, DC, MC, V.*

The Arts

For more than five decades, the **Ojai Festival** (☎ 805/646–2094) has attracted internationally known progressive and traditional musicians for concerts the weekend after Memorial Day.

THE CENTRAL COAST A TO Z

Arriving and Departing

By Bus

Greyhound Lines (☎ 800/231–2222) provides service from San Francisco and Los Angeles to San Luis Obispo and Santa Barbara.

By Car

U.S. 101 and Highway 1 are the main routes into the Central Coast from Los Angeles and San Francisco. Once within the region, connecting roads heading west to the coast from inland California are few and far between. Once you start south from Carmel, for instance, there is no route off until Highway 46 heads inland from Cambria to connect with U.S. 101. I–280 from San Francisco linking to U.S. 101 to San Luis Obispo is the quicker, easier alternative, but it misses the coast entirely.

By Plane

America West Express, American/American Eagle, Skywest/Delta, United/United Express, and US Airways Express fly into **Santa Barbara Municipal Airport** (✉ 500 Fowler Rd., ☎ 805/683–4011), 8 mi from downtown. *See* Air Travel *in* the Gold Guide for airline phone numbers.

Roadrunner Shuttle Service (☎ 800/247–7919) runs vans from LAX to Ojai and Santa Barbara. **Santa Barbara Airbus** (☎ 805/964–7759 or 800/733–6354) shuttles travelers between Santa Barbara and Los Angeles. The **Santa Barbara Metropolitan Transit District** (☎ 805/683–3702) Bus 11 runs from the airport to the downtown transit center.

By Train

Amtrak (☎ 800/872–7245) runs the *Coast Starlight* from Los Angeles along the coast from Santa Barbara to San Luis Obispo. From there it heads inland for the rest of the route to the San Francisco Bay Area and Seattle. Local numbers are, in Santa Barbara, ☎ 805/963–1015; in San Luis Obispo, ☎ 805/541–0505.

Getting Around

By Bus

From Monterey and Carmel, **Monterey–Salinas Transit** (☎ 408/899–2555) operates buses to Big Sur May–September. From San Luis Obispo, **Central Coast Transit** (☎ 805/541–2228) runs buses around the town and out to the coast. **Santa Barbara Metropolitan Transit District** (☎ 805/683–3702) provides local service. The **State Street** and **Waterfront shuttles** cover their respective territories during the day.

By Car

The best way to see the most dramatic section of the Central Coast, the 70 mi between Big Sur and San Simeon, is by car. Heading south on Highway 1, you'll be on the ocean side of the road and will get the best views. Don't expect to make good time along here. The road is narrow and twisting with a single lane in each direction, making it difficult to pass slower traffic or the many lumbering RVs. In fog or rain, the drive can be downright nerve-racking.

Highway 1 and U.S. 101 run north–south more or less parallel, with Highway 1 hugging the coast and 101 remaining a few to a few-dozen miles inland. Along some stretches the two roads join and run together for a while. At Morro Bay, Highway 1 moves inland for 13 mi and connects with U.S. 101 at San Luis Obispo. From here, south to Pismo Beach, the two highways run concurrently. U.S. 101 is the quicker route to Santa Barbara; Highway 1 rejoins it just north of town at Las Cruces.

Contacts and Resources

Doctors
Cottage Hospital (✉ Pueblo St. at Bath St., Santa Barbara, ☎ 805/682–7111; 805/569–7210 for emergency).

Emergencies
Ambulance (☎ 911). **Police** (☎ 911).

Guided Tours
Eagle- and wildlife-watching excursions are offered on the *Osprey,* a 48-ft cruiser that plies Cachuma Lake, a 20-minute drive from Solvang, and a 40-minute one from Santa Barbara. For additional information, contact the **Cachuma Lake Recreation Area,** Santa Barbara County Park Department (✉ Star Route, Santa Barbara 93105, ☎ 805/568–2460).

Santa Barbara Trolley Co. (☎ 805/965–0353) has five daily, regularly scheduled 90-minute runs from 10 AM to 4 PM. A motorized San Francisco–style cable car delivers visitors to major hotels, shopping areas, and attractions. Stop or not, as you wish, and pick up a later trolley when you're ready to move on. The trolley departs from and returns to Stearns Wharf. The fare is $5.

Road Conditions
Caltrans (☎ 800/427–7623 in CA).

Visitor Information
Big Sur Chamber of Commerce (✉ Box 87, 93920, ☎ 408/667–2100). **California Dept. of Parks and Recreation (Big Sur)** (☎ 408/667–2315). **Cambria Chamber of Commerce** (✉ 767 Main St., 93428, ☎ 805/927–3624). **Morro Bay Chamber of Commerce** (✉ 880 Main St., 93442, ☎ 805/772–4467 or 800/231–0592). **Ojai Chamber of Commerce** (✉ Box 1134, 150 W. Ojai Ave., 93024, ☎ 805/646–8126). **Paso Robles Vintners and Growers Association** (1940 Spring St., Paso Robles 93446, ☎ 805/239–8463). **San Luis Obispo Chamber of Commerce** (✉ 1039 Chorro St., 93401, ☎ 805/781–2777). **San Simeon Chamber of Commerce** (✉ 9255 Hearst Dr., 93452, ☎ 805/927–3500 or 800/342–5613). **Santa Barbara Conference and Visitors Bureau** (✉ 12 E. Carrillo St., 93101, ☎ 805/966–9222 or 800/927–4688). **Santa Barbara County Vintners' Association** (✉ Box 1558, Santa Ynez 93460, ☎ 805/688–0881 or 800/218–0881). **Santa Barbara Tourist Information Center** (✉ 1 Santa Barbara St., at Cabrillo Blvd., 93101, ☎ 805/965–3021). **Solvang Conference and Visitors Bureau** (✉ 1511A Mission Dr., 93464, ☎ 805/688–6144 or 800/468–6765).

12 Los Angeles

In certain lights Los Angeles displays its Spanish heritage, but much more evident is its cultural vibrancy as a cultural and economic center on the Pacific Rim. Hollywood, the beaches, and the valleys are all within an hour's drive. Also here are important examples of 20th-century domestic architecture, miles of freeways, and famous Beverly Hills. Everything about Los Angeles is grand—even overdone—which is part of the city's charm: It's all for show, but the show's usually a good one.

Updated by
Jeanne Fay

YOU'RE PREPARING FOR YOUR TRIP to Los Angeles. You're psyching up with Beach Boys CDs and Hollywood epics. You've pulled out your Hawaiian shirts and tennis shorts. You've even labored on a Stairmaster and gone to a tanning salon, just so you won't look too much like a tourist when you hit the Coast.

Well, relax. *Everybody's* a tourist in LaLa Land. Even the stars are starstruck (just look at all the celebrities watching other celebrities at Eclipse or the new Spago Beverly Hills). Los Angeles is a city of ephemerals, transience, and above all, illusion. Nothing here is quite real, and that's the reality of it all. That air of anything-can-happen is what motivates thousands to move to and millions to visit this promised land each year.

None of this was imagined when Spanish settlers founded Pueblo de la Reina de Los Angeles in 1781. In fact, no one predicted a golden future for desert-dry southern California until well after San Francisco and northern California had a head start with their own gold rush. The dusty outpost of Los Angeles eventually had oil and orange groves, but the key to its success came on the silver screen: the movies. The same sunshine that draws today's visitors beckoned Cecil B. DeMille and Jesse Lasky in 1913; the two show-biz pioneers were the first to shoot a feature-length movie here. It took another 14 years to break through the cinematic sound barrier, but meanwhile the silent-film era made Hollywood synonymous with fantasy and glamour.

Outrageous partying, extravagant homes, eccentric clothing, and money, money, money have been symbols of life in Los Angeles ever since. Even the more conservative oil, aerospace, computer, banking, and import/export industries on the booming Pacific Rim have enjoyed the prosperity that inevitably leads to fun living.

For some, this place is built on personal enhancements—the body beautiful, a big fat bank account, and the hottest hot rod—while others try to right global wrongs through the arts, politics, or spiritual exploration. For some it is enough just to surf and sun. Set off from the rest of the continent by mountains and desert, and from the rest of the world by an ocean, this corner of creation has evolved a unique identity that engenders envy, fascination, ridicule, and scorn—often all at once. Don't count on observing and absorbing it all in a day, a week, or even two. Indeed, this second largest American city gives you too many choices between its canyons and its coast; odds are you'll be exhausted far faster than you can anticipate in this far-flung, far-out metropolis.

EXPLORING LOS ANGELES

Because Los Angeles is so spread out, seeing the sights—from the Huntington Library in San Marino to the *Queen Mary* in Long Beach—requires an organized itinerary. Don't jump willy-nilly from place to place, as you'll just become lost, confused, and frustrated with this multifaceted metropolis. We've divided the major sightseeing areas of Los Angeles into eight driving and walking tours:

Downtown contains varied architecture and the lively neighborhoods of Chinatown and Little Tokyo.

Hollywood has lost the glamour of its heyday, but you'll still find famous sights, museums, and historic buildings.

Wilshire Boulevard reveals an eye-opening cross section of the city as it meanders west from downtown.

Westside neighborhoods are posh and trendy, with plenty of shopping and sightseeing opportunities.

Santa Monica, Venice, Pacific Palisades, and **Malibu** are seaside towns along Los Angeles's Pacific coast.

Palos Verdes, San Pedro, and Long Beach are farther south, also edging the Pacific.

Highland Park, Pasadena, and **San Marino** are well-to-do inland suburbs.

The San Fernando Valley gave birth to that special breed of teenager known as the Valley Girl ("like, gag me with a spoon"); the Valley holds Universal Studios and other attractions.

Great Itineraries

IF YOU HAVE 3 DAYS

Spend your first day exploring Hollywood and West Hollywood. If you have time, visit Beverly Hills. Start the second day downtown (after the morning rush), and then drive west on the Hollywood Freeway (U.S. 101), south on the Harbor Freeway (I–110), and west on the Santa Monica Freeway (I–10). Have lunch and spend the rest of the day and early evening touring Santa Monica and Malibu. Be sure to catch the Pacific sunset at either of these two coastal towns. On your third day, take either the Universal Studios Hollywood or the Warner Bros. Studios tour. (The Universal tour will take most of the day; if you opt for Warner's, you'll have time to visit other San Fernando Valley sights.)

IF YOU HAVE 5 DAYS

Follow the three-day itinerary above. Begin day four (after it opens in late 1997) at the Getty Center—or if you're in a less highbrow mood, the Museum of Television & Radio. Have lunch at the ocean-view Getty Center restaurant or on the way—via the San Diego Freeway (I–405) north to the Ventura Freeway (U.S. 101/Highway 134) east to the Golden State Freeway (I–5) south—to your next stop, Griffith Park. Spend the rest of the afternoon here before heading to Los Feliz for dinner. Start early on your last day with a visit to the *Queen Mary* in Long Beach. After lunch, head north on the Long Beach Freeway (I–710), east on the San Bernardino Freeway (I–10), north on Rosemead Boulevard (Highway 19), and west on Huntington Drive to the Huntington Library, Art Collections, and Botanical Gardens. Have dinner in Pasadena and explore a little of Old Town.

Downtown Los Angeles

All those jokes about Los Angeles being a city without a center simply aren't true anymore. Though Angelenos ruthlessly turned their backs on downtown a few decades ago and hightailed it to the suburbs, there was and still is a downtown. Now the city core is enjoying an ongoing resurgence of attention from urban planners, real-estate developers, and downtown office workers who have discovered the advantages of living close to work.

Downtown Los Angeles can be explored by car or by DASH—Downtown Area Short Hop. This minibus service has several routes that travel past most of the attractions listed below, stopping every two blocks or so. If you hop on and off to see attractions, it will cost you every time, but the 25¢ is worth it because you can travel quickly and be assured of finding your way. Call DASH (☎ 213/808–2273) for routes and hours of operation.

A Good Tour

Numbers in the text correspond to numbers in the margin and on the Downtown Los Angeles map.

You can tour much of downtown from your car, but you'll want to get out occasionally to soak up the atmosphere. After parking at a meter on Spring or 9th street, head north on **Broadway** ①, pausing at the old movie palaces that line the avenue and the **Bradbury Building** ②. Walk through the thoroughfare's markets if the mood hits you. Drive northeast on Broadway to reach **Chinatown** ③. On the west side of North Broadway you'll see the entrance—pagoda-facade structures in an outdoor arcade. Drive back south a few blocks to Cesar E. Chavez Avenue and turn left to get to **Olvera Street** ④ and **El Pueblo de Los Angeles Historical Monument,** which honor the original settlement of the area in 1781. Park in the lot; it's expensive, but metered spots are few and far between in this part of downtown.

From the monument area, walk across Alameda Street to tour **Union Station** ⑤. From Union Station, walk or drive south on North Main Street toward Temple Street, the northern border of downtown. Just before Temple on the left is the **Los Angeles Children's Museum** ⑥. To the right on the next block is the back of **Los Angeles City Hall** ⑦, downtown's original skyscraper. Walk south on Main Street and turn left on 2nd Street. About two blocks down you'll hit **Little Tokyo** ⑧, where sushi bars and noodle stands line San Pedro Street. Head back north along San Pedro to 1st Street. The **Geffen Contemporary** ⑨ art museum is one block to the east. To the west, at the northwest corner of Grand Avenue, you'll see two large square buildings on either side of a round structure surrounded by a moat, and an outdoor public area with a fountain that pops up unexpectedly from the sidewalk—geyserlike. This is the **Music Center** ⑩, Los Angeles's theater hub. Head south from here on Grand Avenue, and two blocks down on your left you'll see the imposing **Museum of Contemporary Art** ⑪ (MOCA), a modern red sandstone building tipped with a pyramidal skylight. While you're in the area, walk across California Plaza to **Angel's Flight Railway** ⑫. This small Victorian way station is the shortest railway in the world, L.A.'s petite answer to San Francisco's cable cars.

Back on Grand, walk into the shadowing skyscrapers that gather around 5th Street. To the left is the historic **Regal Biltmore Hotel** ⑬. Walk through the hotel's public areas to **Pershing Square,** where trees shade the business crowd during an afternoon respite and concrete walls tantalize graffiti artists. A little south of the square, on Olive Street, stands the art deco **Oviatt Building** ⑭. Across the street from the Biltmore on Grand Street is the back of the **Central Library** ⑮; walk around to the front and relax in the 1½-acre garden. Head two blocks west along 5th Street to Figueroa Street, and turn right to another hotel, the **Westin Bonaventure** ⑯, easily recognized by its quintet of mirrored cylindrical towers. You may experience a touch of vertigo if you ascend in the outdoor glass elevator to the revolving 35th floor of the Bonaventure. Head south on Flower Street and turn left on Olympic Boulevard to reach the **Museum of Neon Art** ⑰, on the corner of Hope Street.

You can end your tour at the Museum of Neon Art or backtrack a few blocks west to Figueroa and head south to reach **Exposition Park,** home of the 1932 and 1984 Olympics and two fascinating museums: the **California Science Center** ⑱ and the **Natural History Museum of Los**

Angeles County ⑲. Adjacent to Exposition Park is the **University of Southern California** ⑳, the oldest major private university on the West Coast.

TIMING

A downtown visit involves several parking stops, so be prepared with plenty of quarters for meters—and make sure you read the restrictions on street signs; not abiding by them can mean heavy fines and even towing. Seeing downtown can be accomplished in a very full day—or two more leisurely days. The area is less crowded on weekends; if you can only visit midweek, start your visit after the morning rush hour. Strolling up Broadway can take half an hour. Chinatown and neighboring Olvera Street are easily seen in less than two hours. The Museum of Contemporary Art and the museums in Exposition Park can be seen in an hour or so each, perhaps a little more for MOCA.

Sights to See

⑫ **Angel's Flight Railway.** The turn-of-the-century funicular dubbed "the shortest in the world" began operating again in 1996 after having been closed for nearly 30 years. Two original orange-and-black wooden cable railway cars take riders on a 70-second ride up a steep incline from Hill Street (between 3rd and 4th streets) to the fountain-filled California Plaza. ▨ *25¢ one-way.* ⊙ *Daily 6:45 AM–10 PM.*

★ ❷ **Bradbury Building.** A novice architect drew his inspiration for this 1893 structure from a conversation with his dead brother via a Ouija board. The classy office building, which once housed sweatshops, is a marvelous specimen of Victorian-era commercial architecture. The interior atrium courtyard, with its glass skylight and open balconies and elevator, is a popular movie locale (parts of *Blade Runner* were filmed here). The building is only open weekdays 9 to 5 (although the doors are often unlocked on Saturday); its owners prefer that you not wander too far past the lobby. ✉ *304 S. Broadway, at 3rd St.,* ☎ *213/626–1893.*

❶ **Broadway.** One of Los Angeles's busiest streets has dozens of shops and sidewalk vendors between 1st and 9th streets. This can be an exhilarating slice-of-life walk as you pass old movie theaters like the **Orpheum** (✉ 842 S. Broadway) and the **Million Dollar** (✉ 307 S. Broadway), but keep on the alert for pickpockets. **Grand Central Market** (✉ 317 S. Broadway, ☎ 213/624–2378), the city's largest and most active food market, is open Monday through Saturday from 9 to 6, and Sunday from 10 to 5:30.

⊛ ⑱ **California Science Center.** Children love the many "hands-on" exhibits at the former California Museum of Science and Industry. The Aerospace Hall features a DC-3, DC-8, rockets, and satellites; the Kinsey Hall of Health reveals the inner workings of the body; the Our Urban Environment exhibit examines recycling, reusing, and reducing waste; and EGGciting Beginnings shows how chicks, frogs, and humans develop from eggs. ✉ *Exposition Park, 700 State Dr.,* ☎ *213/744–7400.* ▨ *Free; parking $5.* ⊙ *Daily 10–5.*

★ ⑮ **Central Library.** Major fires in the 1980s closed the library for six years. Today, at twice its former size, it's the third-largest public library in the nation. The original Goodhue building still stands, completely restored to its 1926 condition, with shimmering Egyptian-style bas-reliefs around its roofline. Enter through wooden doors that recall an old Spanish-era mission to see Dean Cornwell's murals depicting the history of California. A 1½-acre outdoor garden within the library complex has a restaurant. ✉ *630 W. 5th St., at Flower St.,* ☎ *213/228–7000.* ▨ *Free.* ⊙ *Mon. and Thurs.–Sat. 10–5:30, Tues.–Wed. noon–8, Sun. 1–5; docent tours weekdays at 12:30, Sat. at 11 and 2, Sun. at 2.*

Exploring Los Angeles *(Boxes Refer to Detail Maps)*

PACIFIC OCEAN

0   5 miles

0   5 km

SAN GABRIEL MOUNTAINS

Angeles Crest Hwy. ②

LA CAÑADA
FLINTRIDGE

▲ Mt. Wilson

**Highland Park,
Pasadena, and
San Marino**

Foothill Fwy.
②⑩

Pasadena Fwy.

②

⑪⓪

ALHAM-
BRA

SAN
GABRIEL

EL
MONTE

③⑨

Dodger
Stadium

San Bernardino Fwy.
⑩

MONTEREY
PARK

...town

⑥⓪

Pomona Fwy.

Santa Ana Fwy.

Rosemead Blvd.

Fwy.

WHITTIER

⑦②

HUNTINGTON
PARK

⑦⑩

San Gabriel River

DOWNEY

⑲

④②

③⑨

COMPTON

⑤

Riverside Fwy.

Long Beach Fwy.

Fwy.

⑥⓪⑤

LAKEWOOD

ANAHEIM

⑨⑪

Fwy.

⑦⑩

⑲

Pacific Coast Hwy.

GARDEN
GROVE

**LONG
BEACH**

San Diego Fwy.
③⑨

⑤⑤

...ng Beach

①

Downtown Los Angeles

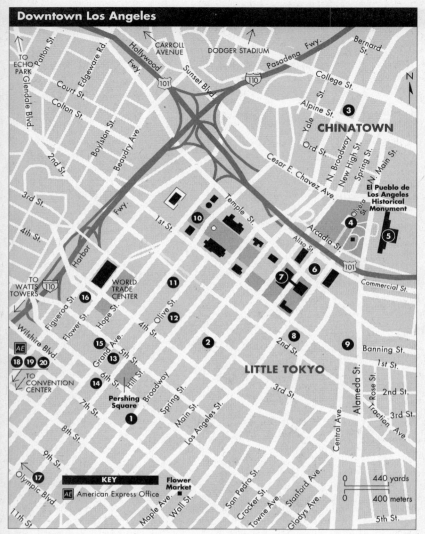

To Echo Park
TO ECHO PARK
Glendale Blvd.
Patton St.
Court St.
Colton St.
Edgeware Rd.
Boylston St.
Beaudry Ave.
2nd St.
3rd St.
4th St.
Harbor Fwy.
Figueroa St.
Flower St.
Hope St.
Grand Ave.
5th St.
6th St.
Hill St.
7th St.
8th St.
9th St.
Olympic Blvd.
11th St.
Maple Ave.
Wall St.
Hollywood Fwy.
CARROLL AVENUE
Sunset Blvd.
DODGER STADIUM
Pasadena Fwy.
Bernard St.
College St.
Alpine St.
Yale St.
Ord St.
N. Broadway
New High St.
Spring St.
N. Main St.
CHINATOWN
Cesar E. Chavez Ave.
El Pueblo de Los Angeles Historical Monument
Olvera St.
Arcadia St.
Aliso St.
Commercial St.
Banning St.
1st St.
2nd St.
3rd St.
Alameda St.
Rose St.
Traction Ave.
Central Ave.
Temple St.
1st St.
2nd St.
3rd St.
Broadway
Spring St.
Main St.
Los Angeles St.
San Pedro St.
Crocker St.
Towne Ave.
Stanford Ave.
Gladys Ave.
5th St.
WORLD TRADE CENTER
Olive St.
4th St.
LITTLE TOKYO
Pershing Square
TO WATTS TOWERS
Wilshire Blvd.
TO CONVENTION CENTER
Flower Market

KEY

AE American Express Office

Flower Market ■

0 ——— 440 yards
0 ——— 400 meters

N

---

❸ **Chinatown.** More than 15,000 Chinese, along with people from other Asian nations, live in the Chinatown area, but many thousands more regularly frequent dim sum and other restaurants and markets filled with exotic fruits and vegetables. ✉ *Bordered by Yale, Bernard, Ord, and Alameda Sts.*

El Pueblo de Los Angeles Historical Monument. This site that commemorates Los Angeles's heritage encompasses many significant buildings, a park, and festive **Olvera Street** (☞ *below*). ✉ *Olvera and Temple Sts.*

Exposition Park. Originally developed in 1880 as an open-air farmers' market, this 114-acre public space hosted Olympic festivities in 1932 and 1984 in conjunction with the adjacent Memorial Coliseum and Sports Arena. The park is home to the **California Science Center** (☞ *above*) and the **Natural History Museum of Los Angeles County** (☞ *below*). ✉ *Between Exposition and Martin Luther King Jr. Blvds.*

❾ **Geffen Contemporary at MOCA.** The warehouse-like building of the former Temporary Contemporary museum, part of the Museum of Contemporary Art (☞ *below*), exhibits part of MOCA's permanent collection and usually one fairly cutting-edge temporary installation. The permanent collection, which spans the years between World War II and the 1970s, uses time lines and a chronological layout to place the art in its appropriate historical context. ✉ *152 N. Central Ave.,* ☎ *213/ 626–6222.* 🎫 *$6; free with MOCA admission on same day and free Thurs. after 5.* ⊙ *Tues.–Wed. and Fri.–Sun. 11–5, Thurs. 11–8.*

❽ **Little Tokyo.** The original neighborhood of Los Angeles's Japanese community remains a cultural focal point though many of its settlers' descendants have long since departed. Nisei Week ("Nisei" is the name for second-generation Japanese) is celebrated here every August with traditional drums, dancing, a carnival, and a huge parade. Little Tokyo has dozens of sushi bars, tempura restaurants, trinket shops, and even a restaurant that serves nothing but eel. **The Japanese American Cultural and Community Center** (✉ *244 S. San Pedro St.,* ☎ *213/628– 2725*) presents such events as Kabuki theater straight from Japan. ✉ *Bordered by 1st, San Pedro, 3rd, and Los Angeles Sts.*

☙ ❻ **Los Angeles Children's Museum.** The many hands-on exhibits here include Sticky City (where kids get to pillow fight with abandon in a huge pillow-filled room), a TV studio (where they can produce their own videos), and the Cave (where hologram dinosaurs lurk, seeming almost real). ✉ *310 N. Main St.,* ☎ *213/687–8800.* 🎫 *$5.* ⊙ *Sat.–Mon. 10– 5, daily 10–5 during summer vacation.*

❼ **Los Angeles City Hall.** This often photographed building has made numerous appearances on *Superman, Dragnet,* and other popular television shows. Erected in the late 1920s, the 28-story art deco treasure remained until 1957 the only structure to break the city's height limit of 13 stories. All the floors above the fifth have been evacuated since the 1994 Northridge earthquake. ✉ *200 N. Spring St.*

★ ⓫ **Museum of Contemporary Art at California Plaza.** The 3,000-piece permanent collection of MOCA is split between Geffen Contemporary (☞ *above*) and the nine galleries within this red sandstone building designed by renowned Japanese architect Arata Isozaki. The collection represents art from 1940 to the present, including works by Mark Rothko, Franz Kline, and Susan Rothenberg. ✉ *250 S. Grand Ave.,* ☎ *213/ 626–6222.* 🎫 *$6; free Thurs. 5–8.* ⊙ *Tues.–Wed. and Fri.–Sun. 11– 5, Thurs. 11–8.*

⓱ Museum of Neon Art. This museum pays tribute to the art of neon—a form of lighting that evolved from advertising status to fine art in less than half a century. Installations range from traditional signs to elaborate seascapes. ⊠ *501 W. Olympic Blvd.,* ☎ *213/489–9918.* ⊠ *$5; free 2nd Thurs. of month.* ⊙ *Tues.–Wed. and Fri.–Sat. 11–6, Thurs. 11–8, Sun. noon–6.*

⓾ Music Center. The cultural center for Los Angeles since its opening in 1969, this multi-use venue trades off with the Moorish Shrine Auditorium as the site of the Academy Awards. Limousines arrive for the big-screen event at the Hope Street drive-through, and celebrities are whisked through the crowds to the largest and grandest of the three theaters, the **Dorothy Chandler Pavilion,** named after the wife of former *Los Angeles Times* publisher Norman Chandler. Mrs. Chandler was instrumental in raising the money to build the complex. The round building in the middle, the **Mark Taper Forum,** is a smaller theater that often presents works of an experimental nature. The **Ahmanson,** at the north end, hosts many musical comedies. The vast complex's cement plaza has a fountain and Jacques Lipchitz sculpture. ⊠ *1st St. and Grand Ave.,* ☎ *213/972–7211; 213/972–7483 tour reservations.* ⊠ *Tour free.* ⊙ *75-min tour Tues.–Sat. 10–1:30; schedule subject to change.*

★ ☺ **⓳ Natural History Museum of Los Angeles County.** The museum has a rich collection of prehistoric fossils and extensive bird, insect, and marine-life exhibits. A brilliant display of stones can be seen in the Gem and Mineral Hall. An elaborate taxidermy exhibit shows North American and African mammals in detailed replicas of their natural habitats. ⊠ *Exposition Park, 900 Exposition Blvd.,* ☎ *213/744–3414.* ⊠ *$6; free 1st Tues. of month.* ⊙ *Tues.–Sun. 10–5; 1-hr tours at 1.*

★ ☺ **❹ Olvera Street.** One-block Olvera Street tantalizes with tile walkways, piñatas, mariachis, and authentic Mexican food. On weekends, the restaurants are packed, and there is usually music in the plaza and along the street. Two Mexican holidays, Cinco de Mayo (May 5) and Independence Day (September 16), also draw huge crowds. To see Olvera Street at its quietest, visit late on a weekday afternoon. The long shadows heighten the romantic feeling of the passageway. For information, stop in the **Olvera Street Visitors Center,** housed in the Sepulveda House (⊠ 622 N. Main St., ☎ 213/628–1274), a Victorian built in 1887 as a hotel and boardinghouse. The center is open Monday through Saturday from 10 to 3.

Avila Adobe (⊠ E–11 Olvera St.), built in 1818 and open daily from 9 to 5, is considered the oldest building still standing in Los Angeles. This simple adobe with a traditional interior courtyard is furnished in the style of the 1840s.

At the beginning of Olvera Street is **The Plaza,** a Mexican-style park that's shaded by a huge Moreton Bay fig tree. There are plenty of walkways and benches here. On weekends, mariachis and folkloric dance groups often perform.

The Old Firehouse, an 1884 building on the south side of the Plaza, contains early fire-fighting equipment and old photographs. Buildings seen on tours that start here include the Merced Theater, Masonic Hall, Pico House, and Garnier Block—all ornate examples of the late-19th-century style. Under the Merced, Masonic Hall, and Garnier Block are passageways once used by Chinese immigrants.

The dining choices on Olvera Street range from fast-food stands to sit-down restaurants. The most authentic Mexican food is at **La Luz del Dia** (⊠ 107 Paseo de la Plaza, ☎ 213/628–7495). **La Golondrina** (⊠

17 Olvera St., ☎ 213/628–4349), which is inside the historic **Pelanconi House,** has a delightful patio and an extensive menu.

⑭ Oviatt Building. Ornate Lalique glass decorates the entire lobby of this 1928 art deco building, originally designed as the business and residence of a local clothier. Call ahead to schedule a tour and take the elevator to the 13th-floor penthouse, a 4,000-square-ft masterpiece that once included such amenities as a sand beach. ⊠ *617 S. Olive St., ☎ 213/622–6096.*

⑬ Regal Biltmore Hotel. The beaux arts Biltmore opened in 1923. The hotel's lobby has the feel of a Spanish palace, and its indoor pool looks like a Roman bath. The Academy Awards were held here in the 1930s; the hotel has also appeared in many films, among them *Chinatown, The Fabulous Baker Boys, The Poseidon Adventure,* and *Independence Day.* ⊠ *506 S. Grand Ave., ☎ 213/624–1011.*

Southern California Flower Market. Stores and stalls here open up in the middle of the night to sell wholesale flowers and houseplants to the city's florists. Many stalls stay open until late morning, peddling leftovers at bargain prices to anyone who comes along. The public is welcome to enter (and purchase the leftovers) after 8 AM. ⊠ *700 block of Wall St., ☎ 213/627–2482.*

★ ⑤ Union Station. This building is among those that have defined Los Angeles to moviegoers the world over. It was built in 1939 in a style that subtly combines Streamline Moderne and Moorish design elements. The waiting room alone is worth a look, its majestic scale so evocative of movies past that you'll half expect to see Carole Lombard or Barbara Stanwyck step off a train and sashay through. ⊠ *800 N. Alameda St.*

⑳ University of Southern California. Join a free one-hour campus tour of U.S.C. on weekdays, taking in the more notable of its 191 buildings, like the Romanesque **Doheny Memorial Library; Widney Alumni Hall,** a two-story clapboard dating to 1880; and **Mudd Memorial Hall of Philosophy,** whose rare-book collection includes examples from the 13th through 15th centuries. ⊠ *3551 University Ave., adjacent to Exposition Park, ☎ 213/740–6605. ⊙ Call for tour schedule.*

OFF THE
BEATEN PATH

WATTS TOWERS – The jewel of rough South Central L.A. is the legacy of Simón Rodia, a tile setter who emigrated from Italy to California and erected what came to be one of the world's greatest folk-art structures. From 1921 until 1954, without any help, this eccentric man built three cement towers, using pipes, bed frames, and anything else he could find. He embellished them with bits of colored glass, broken pottery, and more than 70,000 seashells. The towers are now the centerpiece of a state historic park and cultural center. You don't want to linger here after dark. ⊠ *Watts Cultural Center, 1765 E. 107th St.; take I–110 to I–105 east; exit north at S. Central Ave., turn right onto 108th St., left onto Graham Ave. ☜ Free; weekend tours (10–4) $1. ⊙ Daily 9–5.*

⑯ Westin Bonaventure Hotel & Suites. Sheathed in mirrored glass, this John Portman building looks like science-fiction fantasy. Nonguests can use only one elevator, which rises through the roof of the lobby to the revolving restaurant and bar on the 35th floor. ⊠ *404 S. Figueroa St., ☎ 213/624–1000.*

Hollywood

Once a glamour center, Hollywood was where most big motion picture studios were headquartered and where movies premiered with such tremendous fanfare that they became the talk of the globe. Now Paramount is the only original major studio still physically in Hollywood, and the occasional film debut doesn't come close to its former grandeur. Today the core of the famous town is actually somewhat seedy, though plans are afoot to rectify this. So why visit? Because its legacy is forever in the air, an eternal tribute to American film's hold on the world's imagination. Most visitors are able to look past the junky shops and campy museums for a sense of the town's glittering past. Though Hollywood is no longer "Hollywood," no visit to Los Angeles would be complete without at least a brief peek.

A Good Tour
Numbers in the text correspond to numbers in the margin and on the Hollywood map.

To get a good glimpse of the heart of Hollywood, for part of your visit you'll want to go it on foot—an anomaly in this vehicle-obsessed metropolis. For safety reasons it's best to park in the pay lot next to **Mann's Chinese Theatre** ①. Join in the ritual of putting your own feet into the imprints of those of the dozens of stars cemented in immortality. Be sure to look across the street while you're there; El Capitan Theatre's exuberant art deco facade, impeccably restored by Disney, is sure to enchant.

As you walk east on Hollywood Boulevard, the main attraction is at your feet. Between Gower Street and La Brea Avenue are hundreds of star-studded sidewalk dedications that form the famous **Hollywood Walk of Fame** ②. The first block east of Highland Avenue contains the world's glitziest McDonald's and the even kitschier **Hollywood Wax Museum** ③. Back on Hollywood Boulevard, walk east a few blocks to the sedate art deco masterpiece that houses the illustrious **Frederick's of Hollywood** ④. Keep heading east to the legendary corner of **Hollywood and Vine** ⑤. From here, you can spot two major points of interest, the **Capitol Records Tower** ⑥ and the **Pantages Theater** ⑦.

Return to your car and drive north on Highland Avenue and then east on Franklin Avenue past the giant **HOLLYWOOD sign** ⑧ crowning the Hollywood Hills on the left. About 2 mi past Vine, at Hollywood Boulevard and Vermont Avenue, you'll find Frank Lloyd Wright's **Hollyhock House** ⑨, part of the Barnsdall Art Park. Then turn north up Vermont, where you'll enter the sector of East Hollywood known as Los Feliz (The Happy Ones). You'll see many upscale residences originally belonging to top silent-film stars here. Vermont leads into **Griffith Park** ⑩, a 4,000-acre nature refuge in the middle of Los Angeles that holds the **Griffith Park Observatory**, the **Autry Museum of Western Heritage,** and other attractions.

Take Hollywood Boulevard west to Highland Avenue and turn right to reach the famed **Hollywood Bowl** ⑪. Across the street in a parking lot is a converted barn called the **Hollywood Studio Museum** ⑫. The museum is inside Tinseltown's first movie studio, which later became Paramount Pictures. To visit the current version of **Paramount Studios** ⑬, take Highland Avenue south to Melrose Avenue and head east to Gower Street. From Paramount, head back north on Gower to Santa Monica Boulevard and the **Hollywood Memorial Park Cemetery** ⑭, where Rudolph Valentino and many other legends are buried in style.

TIMING
Hollywood is best visited between the morning and afternoon rush hours. Your best bet for a safe walk down Hollywood Boulevard along the Walk of Fame is during daylight hours; it's easily accomplished in an hour and a half at a leisurely pace. If you plan on making pit stops

Hollywood

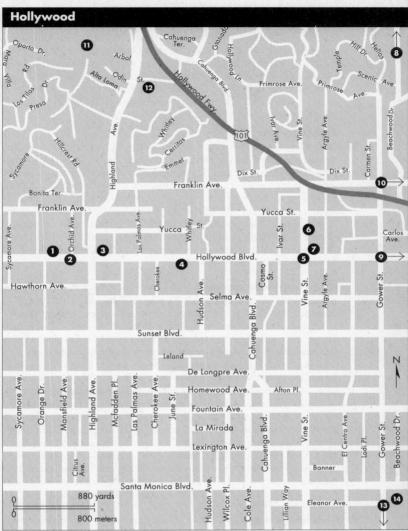

Capitol Records
Tower, **6**

Frederick's of
Hollywood, **4**

Griffith Park, **10**

Hollyhock House, **9**

Hollywood
Bowl, **11**

Hollywood
Memorial Park
Cemetery, **14**

Hollywood Sign, **8**

Hollywood Studio
Museum, **12**

Hollywood and
Vine, **5**

Hollywood Walk
of Fame, **2**

Hollywood Wax
Museum, **3**

Mann's Chinese
Theatre, **1**

Pantages
Theater, **7**

Paramount
Studios, **13**

along the way at any of the attractions, plan around half an hour for each. Motoring through Griffith Park takes half an hour, but allow extra time to visit the zoo (about two hours) and the Autry Museum (up to two hours). Arrange to see the Griffith Observatory at night for celestial viewing through its giant telescope, and keep in mind that overall, the park is overrun with locals on weekends, so get there during the week if possible. The only way to see Paramount if you're a civilian is by scheduling a weekday two-hour tour. Hollywood Memorial Park Cemetery is only open during daylight hours.

Sights to See

★ ❻ **Capitol Records Tower.** This symbol of '50s chic came into being when two big musical talents of the day, singer Nat King Cole and songwriter Johnny Mercer, suggested that the record company's headquarters be shaped to look like a stack of 45s. Although a weird concept back then, compared to much of what's gone up since in L.A., this building doesn't seem all that odd. On its south wall, look at L.A. artist Richard Wyatt's mural *Hollywood Jazz, 1945–1972,* immortalizing musical greats Duke Ellington, Billie Holiday, Ella Fitzgerald, and Miles Davis. The blinking light at the top of the tower spells out "Hollywood" in Morse code. ✉ *1750 N. Vine St.*

OFF THE
BEATEN PATH

FOREST LAWN MEMORIAL PARK – This cemetery is more than just a place where loved ones are laid to rest: It covers 300 formally landscaped acres and features a major collection of bronze statuary and art treasures, including a fascinating replica of Leonardo da Vinci's *The Last Supper* done entirely in stained glass. In the Hall of the Crucifixion-Resurrection is one of the world's largest oil paintings, *The Crucifixion* by artist Jan Styka. The picturesque grounds are perfect for a leisurely walk. Forest Lawn was the model for the setting of Evelyn Waugh's *The Loved One,* which lampooned American culture and burial practices. Many celebrities are buried here, some more flamboyantly than others. Markers for Walt Disney and Errol Flynn are near the Freedom Mausoleum. Inside the mausoleum are the wall crypts of Nat King Cole, Clara Bow, Gracie Allen, George Burns, and Alan Ladd. Clark Gable, Carole Lombard, Theda Bara, and Jean Harlow are among the luminaries buried in the Great Mausoleum. Forest Lawn does not provide information about gravesite locations. ✉ *1712 S. Glendale Ave., Glendale (east of Griffith Park),* ☎ *213/254-3131.* ⊙ *Winter, daily 9–5; summer, daily 9–6.*

❹ **Frederick's of Hollywood.** Racks of risqué and trashy lingerie have made this place famous. The bra museum displays the undergarments of living and deceased Hollywood legends—Madonna's bustier shares space with Marilyn Monroe's merry widow and Cher's kinky underwear. ✉ *6608 Hollywood Blvd.,* ☎ *213/466-8506.*

★ ❿ **Griffith Park.** Mining tycoon Griffith J. Griffith donated these 4,000 acres to the city of Los Angeles in 1896. Griffith Park has many picnic areas; hiking and horseback riding trails; **Travel Town** (✉ *5200 Zoo Dr.,* ☎ *213/662-5874*), with vintage railroad cars; two 18-hole golf courses (Harding and Wilson) and one nine-hole executive course (Roosevelt), a pro shop, and a driving range; and tennis courts.

The Los Angeles Zoo holds more than 1,200 mammals, birds, amphibians, and reptiles, grouped according to the geographic areas where they are naturally found—Africa, Australia, Eurasia, North America, and South America. There are also separate aquatic and reptile sections, as well as Adventure Island, the children's zoo. A tram stops at various points along the way. ✉ *5333 Zoo Dr., northeast corner of park,* ☎ *213/666-4090.* 🎟 *$8.25, Safari Shuttle Tour $3.* ⊙ *Daily 10–5.*

On a clear night, head for **The Griffith Observatory and Planetarium,** an art deco landmark immortalized in the James Dean film *Rebel Without a Cause*. Climb the observatory stairs to peer through the giant telescope, open to the public for free viewing every clear night. Observatory exhibits include a laserium, and dazzling daily planetarium shows whose guides point out constellations. ⊠ *Enter observatory at Vermont Ave.,* ☎ *213/664–1191.* ▭ *Hall of Science and telescope free, planetarium show $4, laserium show $7.* ⊙ *Tues.–Fri. 2–10, weekends 12:30–10; call to confirm schedule.*

The **Autry Museum of Western Heritage** is a celebration of the American West—the Hollywood and the real-life versions—with memorabilia, art, and artifacts. The collection includes Teddy Roosevelt's Colt revolver, Buffalo Bill Cody's saddle, and Annie Oakley's gold-plated Smith and Wesson guns. Video screens show clips from old Westerns. ⊠ *4700 Western Heritage Way,* ☎ *213/667–2000.* ▭ *$7.50.* ⊙ *Tues.– Sun. 10–5.*

❾ Hollyhock House. The first of several houses Frank Lloyd Wright designed in Los Angeles, this 1921 manse was commissioned by heiress Aline Barnsdall. A perfect example of the pre-Columbian style of which Wright was so fond at that time, the house features a stylized hollyhock flower, which appears in a broad band around the house's exterior and even on the dining room chairs. Hollyhock House has been restored and furnished to include original furniture designed by Wright. ⊠ *4800 Hollywood Blvd.,* ☎ *213/662–7272.* ▭ *$2.* ⊙ *Tour Wed.– Sun. at noon, 1, 2, and 3.*

⓫ Hollywood Bowl. Summer evening concerts have been a tradition since 1922 at this high-profile round arena cradled in the Hollywood Hills. Musical fare ranges from pop to jazz to classical. The 17,000-plus seating capacity ranges from boxes (where fancy alfresco preconcert meals are catered) to concrete bleachers in the rear. Come early with food and picnic in the surrounding grounds. ⊠ *2301 N. Highland Ave.,* *213/850–2000.* ⊙ *Grounds daily sunrise–sunset; call for schedule.*

⓮ Hollywood Memorial Park Cemetery. Many Hollywood stars are buried in this serene spot. Walk through the entrance to the lake area and you'll find the crypt of Cecil B. DeMille. Inside the Cathedral Mausoleum is Rudolph Valentino's crypt (the mysterious Lady in Black, who for years visited on the anniversary of his death, comes no more). Other stars interred in this section are Peter Lorre and Eleanor Powell. Norma Talmadge and Clifton Webb rest in the Abbey of Palms Mausoleum. The grave of Mel Blanc, voice of Bugs Bunny and other cartoon characters, reads, "That's all, folks!" ⊠ *6000 Santa Monica Blvd.,* ☎ *213/ 469–1181.* ⊙ *Daily 8–5.*

★ ❽ Hollywood Sign. Even on the smoggiest of days, Hollywood's trademark sign can be spotted from miles away. The sign's inimitable 50-ft-tall letters, originally spelling out "Hollywoodland," were erected in the Hollywood Hills in 1923 to promote a real-estate development scheme. In 1949, the "land" portion of the insignia was taken down.

⓬ Hollywood Studio Museum. The place where the first feature-length Hollywood film, *The Squaw Man*, was produced in 1913, this unusual landmark became Paramount Pictures, with the original company of Tinseltown moguls Jesse Lasky, Cecil B. DeMille, and Samuel Goldwyn. The entire structure was relocated in 1983 to the parking lot across from the Hollywood Bowl, and the resulting museum continues to make a lasting impression on visitors with a re-creation of DeMille's original office, early movie artifacts, and a screening room showing vintage films about Hollywood and its legends. ✉ *2100 N. Highland Ave.,* ☎ *213/874–2276.* ◻ *$4.* ◷ *Call for hrs.*

❺ Hollywood and Vine. The mere mention of this intersection inspires images of a street corner bustling with movie stars, starlets, and moguls passing by, on foot, or in snazzy Studebakers and classy Rolls-Royces. But these days, Hollywood and Vine is far from the action, and, alas, the pedestrian traffic is, well, pedestrian. No stars, no starlets, no moguls. The famed Brown Derby restaurant that once stood near the southeast corner is long gone, and the intersection these days is little more than a place for visitors to get their bearings.

★ ❷ Hollywood Walk of Fame. All along this mile-long stretch of Hollywood Boulevard sidewalk, many entertainment legends' names are embossed in brass, each at the center of a pink star embedded in dark gray terrazzo. The first eight stars were unveiled in 1960 at the northwest corner of Highland Avenue and Hollywood Boulevard: Olive Borden, Ronald Colman, Louise Fazenda, Preston Foster, Burt Lancaster, Edward Sedgwick, Ernest Torrence, and Joanne Woodward (some of these names have stood the test of time better than others). Since then, more than 2,000 others have been immortalized, though that honor doesn't come cheap—the personality in question (or more likely his or her movie studio or record company) must pay $7,500 for the privilege. To aid in the identification, celebrities are classified by one of five logos: a motion picture camera, a radio microphone, a television set, a record, and a theatrical mask. Here's a guide to a few of the more famous celebs' stars: Marlon Brando at 1765 Vine, Charlie Chaplin at 6751 Hollywood, W. C. Fields at 7004 Hollywood, Clark Gable at 1608 Vine, Marilyn Monroe at 6774 Hollywood, Rudolph Valentino at 6164 Hollywood, Michael Jackson at 6927 Hollywood, and John Wayne at 1541 Vine.

❸ Hollywood Wax Museum. Here you'll spot celebrities that real life can no longer provide (Mary Pickford, Elvis Presley, and Clark Gable) and a few that real life never did (such as the *Star Trek* cast). Other living legends on display include actors Kevin Costner and Brad Pitt. A short film on Academy Award winners is shown daily. ✉ *6767 Hollywood Blvd.,* ☎ *213/462–8860.* ◻ *$8.95.* ◷ *Sun.–Thurs. 10 AM–midnight, Fri.–Sat. 10 AM–2 AM.*

★ ❶ Mann's Chinese Theatre. You have to buy a ticket to appreciate the interior trappings of the former "Grauman's Chinese," but its courtyard, a fantasy of Chinese pagodas and temples, is open for browsing. Here you'll see those oh-so-famous cement hand- and footprints. This tradition is said to have begun at the theater's opening in 1927, with the premiere of Cecil B. DeMille's *King of Kings,* when actress Norma Talmadge accidentally stepped into the wet cement. Now more than 160 celebrities have contributed part of their appendages for posterity, along with a few other oddball imprints, like the one of Jimmy Durante's nose. ✉ *6925 Hollywood Blvd.,* ☎ *213/464–8111.*

❼ Pantages Theater. Opened in 1930 as the very pinnacle of movie-theater opulence, this legitimate venue's most prestigious claim is that from 1950 to 1959, it was the site of the Academy Awards. Today it mainly presents large-scale Broadway musicals. ✉ *6233 Hollywood Blvd.,* ☎ *213/468–1770.*

⓭ Paramount Studios. The only original major movie studio still in Hollywood has produced more than 3,000 films since its beginnings in 1912. Mae West, Mary Pickford, and John Barrymore were among the stars under contract here. The studio, including the now defunct Desilu Studios, occupies two large city blocks, and its three arched entrances are familiar landmarks from films such as the 1950 classic *Sunset Boulevard* (which showed the entrance at Bronson Avenue). You can explore the lot on two-hour guided walking tours or by joining the audience for tapings of TV shows. Children under 10 are not admitted. ⊠ *5555 Melrose Ave.,* ☎ *213/956–5575.* ⊡ *$15.* ⊙ *2-hr tour weekdays on the hr 9–2.*

Wilshire Boulevard

Wilshire Boulevard begins in the heart of downtown Los Angeles and runs west through Beverly Hills and Santa Monica, ending at the cliffs above the Pacific Ocean. Along the way, and all within a few blocks of each other, are many of Los Angeles's top architectural sites, museums, and shops.

A Good Tour

Numbers in the text correspond to numbers in the margin and on the Wilshire Boulevard map.

Start your tour at **MacArthur Park** ①, just west of downtown. Drive west, and on the left you'll spot the art deco wonder known as **Bullocks Wilshire** ②. The next area you'll pass is **Koreatown** ③. A few blocks past Vermont Avenue is **The Ambassador** ④, a once active hotel that's now closed. Farther west at Western Avenue is the fascinating art deco **Wiltern Theatre** ⑤. **Hancock Park** ⑥ is the grandiose neighborhood thriving just west of Western Avenue. The **Getty House** ⑦ on Irving Boulevard was once the estate of the wealthy oil family.

Starting at La Brea heading west on Wilshire, the **Miracle Mile** ⑧ unfolds. The few blocks just before reaching Fairfax Avenue are Los Angeles's Museum Row. Starting at Curson Avenue is a grassy park called Hancock Park (a real park, not to be confused with the residential neighborhood of the same name). Here is the **George C. Page Museum of La Brea Discoveries,** where exhibits of various prehistoric animal replicas are on display. Many fossils for these models were found next door at the **La Brea Tar Pits** ⑨, preserved in the sticky natural substance. Just beyond that, also in Hancock Park, is the **Los Angeles County Museum of Art** ⑩. Across the street is the **Craft and Folk Art Museum** ⑪. On the next block is the **Carole & Barry Kaye Museum of Miniatures** ⑫. At the next traffic light at Fairfax Avenue is the **Petersen Automotive Museum** ⑬.

On the north side of Wilshire at Fairfax is the art deco former **May Company** ⑭ department store. Take a right here and you'll come across the **Farmers Market** ⑮, one of Los Angeles's most enduring attractions.

TIMING

All the sights are on Wilshire or within a few blocks. Until you reach Museum Row, Wilshire Boulevard is best viewed through your car window. Traffic moves slowly along this main L.A. artery, so you can cruise easily without pulling over. To take in all the museums, expect to spend between two and three hours, the bulk of the time at Los Angeles County Museum of Art. Most museums on this tour are closed Monday.

Sights to See

❹ **The Ambassador.** Newcomers to Los Angeles may find it hard to believe that this hotel, now closed and surrounded by a chain-link fence, was once one of the city's grandest. The Ambassador housed the famed Coconut Grove nightclub, where everyone who was anyone went to dance in a fantasy Tahitian-island setting. The Ambassador's Fiesta Room hosted several Academy Awards presentations during the 1930s and

Wilshire Boulevard

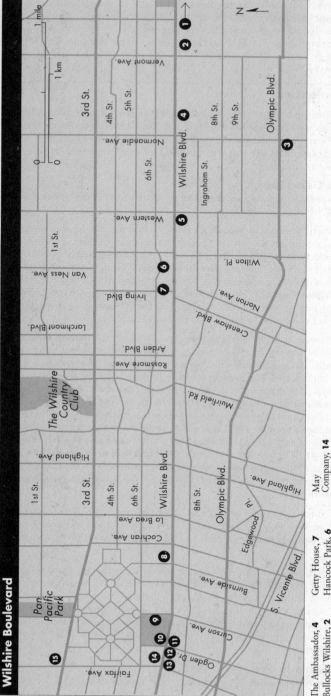

The Ambassador, **4**
Bullocks Wilshire, **2**
Carole & Barry Kaye
Museum of
Miniatures, **12**
Craft and Folk Art
Museum, **11**
Farmers Market, **15**

Getty House, **7**
Hancock Park, **6**
Koreatown, **3**
La Brea Tar Pits, **9**
Los Angeles County
Museum of Art, **10**
MacArthur Park, **1**

May
Company, **14**
Miracle Mile, **8**
The Petersen
Automotive
Museum, **13**
Wiltern Theatre, **5**

1940s. It was also used as the sets for first two film versions of *A Star Is Born*. Presidential nominee Robert F. Kennedy was shot in the ballroom on June 5, 1968. ⊠ *3400 Wilshire Blvd.*

② **Bullocks Wilshire.** The copper-trimmed Moderne exterior of this former department store (now owned by the Southwestern University of Law) has often been used as a background for films. The behind-the-store parking lot, the first facility a large Los Angeles store ever made to accommodate the automobile, was quite an innovation in 1929. On the ceiling of the porte cochere, a mural depicts the history of transportation, strangely without giving a nod to the one Los Angeles necessity—the car. ⊠ *3050 Wilshire Blvd.*

⑫ **Carole & Barry Kaye Museum of Miniatures.** This world of pint-size exhibits includes sized-down local landmarks, such as the Hollywood Bowl and the Fountainebleau Palace, as well as important L.A. architecture like an original Greene and Greene California craftsman house in ¹⁄₁₂ scale. ⊠ *5900 Wilshire Blvd.,* ☎ *213/937–6464.* ▦ *$7.50.* ⊙ *Tues.–Sat. 10–5, Sun. 11–5.*

⑪ **Craft and Folk Art Museum.** Crafts from around the world—both contemporary and folk—are displayed here on a rotating basis. Six to eight major exhibitions, covering everything from sunglasses and jewelry to architecture, are arranged each year. ⊠ *5800 Wilshire Blvd.,* ☎ *213/ 937–5544.* ▦ *$4.* ⊙ *Tues.–Sun. 11–5.*

★ **⑮** **Farmers Market.** A favorite L.A. attraction since the 1930s, what was once a farmers market only now holds over 120 stores—from antiques dealers to beauty shops—in addition to produce stalls. The market is next door to the CBS Television Studios, so you may even run into a celebrity. Thirty restaurants, many of them offering alfresco dining under umbrellas, serve international and domestic fare. **Kokomo Café** (⊠ 3rd St. side of Farmers Market, ☎ 213/933–0773) dishes up some of the best diner food anywhere in L.A. Entertaining service is almost always included in the reasonable prices. ⊠ *6333 W. 3rd St.,* ☎ *213/933– 9211.* ⊙ *Mon.–Sat. 9–6:30, Sun. 10–5 (later in summer).*

⑦ **Getty House.** In the past, the mayor of Los Angeles called this white-brick half-timber residence home. Its previous occupants, the Getty family, donated the real estate to the city. The house is not open to visitors. ⊠ *605 S. Irving Blvd.*

⑥ **Hancock Park.** This area is not an actual park, but rather one of the city's most genteel neighborhoods, remaining in vogue since its development in the 1920s. Old-money families built English Tudor houses with East Coast landscaping schemes that defy the local climate and history. ⊠ *Bordered by Highland Ave., Wilton Pl., Wilshire Blvd., and Beverly Blvd.*

③ **Koreatown.** Beginning in the 1970s, large numbers of Koreans settled in the area south of Wilshire Boulevard, along Olympic Boulevard between Vermont and Western avenues. Many street signs are in Korean only, and the typical offerings of Korean shops are available in ample supply in the large Koreatown Plaza, on the corner of Western and San Marino avenues.

★ **⑨** **La Brea Tar Pits.** *La brea* already means "tar" in Spanish (so to say "La Brea Tar Pits" is redundant), and the pits are actually of asphalt, but this name remains firm in local minds. About 40,000 years ago, deposits of oil rose to the Earth's surface, collected in shallow pools, and coagulated into sticky asphalt. In the early 20th century, geologists discovered that the sticky goo contained the largest collection of Pleistocene, or Ice Age, fossils ever found at one location: more than 600 species of birds, mammals, plants, reptiles, and insects. More than 100 tons of fossil bones have been removed in over 70 years of excavations. Statues of a family of mammoths in the big pit near the corner of Wilshire and Curson depict how many of them were entombed: Edging down to a pond of water to drink, animals were caught in the tar and unable to extricate themselves. There are several pits scattered around Hancock Park; construction in the area has often had to accommodate these oozing pits, and in nearby streets and along sidewalks, little bits of tar occasionally ooze up, unstoppable.

A satellite of the Natural History Museum of Los Angeles County, the **George C. Page Museum of La Brea Discoveries** at the La Brea Tar Pits is set, bunkerlike, half underground. A bas-relief around four sides depicts life in the Pleistocene era, and the museum has more than one million Ice Age fossils. Exhibits include reconstructed life-size skeletons of mammoths, wolves, sloths, eagles, and condors. A permanent installation shows a robotic saber-toothed cat attacking a huge ground sloth. The glass-enclosed Paleontological Laboratory permits observation of the ongoing cleaning, identification, and cataloging of fossils excavated from the nearby asphalt deposits. An interactive tar mechanism shows just how hard it would be to free oneself from the sticky mess. ✉ *5801 Wilshire Blvd.,* ☎ *213/936–2230.* ✆ *$6; free 1st Tues. of month.* ☉ *Tues.–Sun. 10–5.*

★ ⑩ **Los Angeles County Museum of Art.** The vast galleries here are in five buildings surrounding a grand central court, where, on Friday evenings, you can enjoy free jazz concerts. Highlights in the **Ahmanson Building** include an assemblage of glass from Roman times to the 19th century and an Indian and Southeast Asian art collection considered to be one of the most comprehensive in the world.

The **Hammer Building** houses special loan exhibitions. In the **Anderson Building** you'll find 20th-century painting and sculpture. The **Pavilion for Japanese Art** is a soothing world of subdued light and gently flowing water; many works, among them the internationally renowned Shin'enkan collection of screen and scroll paintings, are on view here. The Contemporary Sculpture Garden holds nine large-scale outdoor sculptures. **The B. Gerald Cantor Sculpture Garden** has bronzes by Auguste Rodin, Émile-Antoine Bourdelle, and George Kolbe. ✉ *5905 Wilshire Blvd.,* ☎ *213/857–6000; 213/857–6010 ticket information.* ✆ *$6; free 2nd Wed. of month.* ☉ *Tues.–Thurs. 10–5, Fri. 10–9, weekends 11–6.*

❶ **MacArthur Park.** A popular hangout for the elite during the 1920s and 1930s, this sanctuary of trees, lakes, and grassy knolls has seen better days. Although the riffraff comes with the territory, the grounds and historic surrounding buildings give a sense of Wilshire Boulevard's status as *the* main drag before suburbia set in. ✉ *2230 W. 6th St.*

⑭ **May Company.** The futuristic gold-tile bowed facade of this former department store exemplifies late art deco architecture. Acquired in mid-1996 by the Los Angeles County Museum of Art, the building brightens up this part of Wilshire. ✉ *Northeast corner of Wilshire Blvd. and Fairfax Ave. intersection.*

❽ **Miracle Mile.** The strip of Wilshire Boulevard between La Brea and Fairfax avenues was given this dubious title in the 1930s as a promotional gimmick to attract shoppers. The area went into a decline in the '50s and '60s, but it's now enjoying a comeback, as Los Angeles's art deco architecture has come to be appreciated, preserved, and restored. Exemplary architecture includes the **El Rey Theater** (✉ 5515 Wilshire Blvd., ☎ 213/936–6400), which is now a nightclub.

★ ⑬ **Petersen Automotive Museum.** Cars of the stars are among the popular vehicles on display here. You'll also find movie creations such as Fred's rockmobile from *The Flintstones* flick. The permanent collection, which traces the history of the automobile, includes rare French luxury cars from the '30s and '40s, as well as race cars created in southern California. The museum has an entire gallery devoted to the motorcycle, a gift shop, a research library, and an interactive Discovery Center that illustrates the mechanics of the automobile. ✉ *6060 Wilshire Blvd.,* ☎ *213/930–2277.* ✇ *$7.* ☉ *Tues.–Sun. 10–6.*

★ ❺ **Wiltern Theatre.** At the southeast corner of Wilshire and Western Avenue sits this magnificent example of all-out art deco architecture. Inside, the theater is full of opulent detail at every turn. Originally a movie theater, the Wiltern is now a multi-use arts complex. ✉ *3790 Wilshire Blvd.,* ☎ *213/380–5005.*

The Westside

The Westside of Los Angeles—which to residents means from La Brea Avenue westward to the ocean—is where the rents are the most expensive, the real-estate prices sky-high, the restaurants (and the restaurateurs) the most famous, and the shops the most chic. It's the best of the good life, southern California–style, and to really savor (and understand) the Southland, spend a few leisurely days or half days exploring this area. Short on traditional tourist attractions, the neighborhood more than makes up for this with great shopping districts, exciting walking streets, outdoor cafés, and a lively nightlife.

Once an almost forgotten parcel of county land surrounded by the city of L.A. and Beverly Hills, **West Hollywood** became an official city in 1984. The West Hollywood way—trendy, stylish, and with plenty of disposable income—spills past the official city borders.

At the abrupt Doheny Drive end of the glitzy Sunset Strip, Sunset Boulevard enters the world-famous and glamorous **Beverly Hills.** Suddenly, sidewalk street life gives way to expansive, perfectly manicured lawns and palatial homes. Incorporated as its own city early in the century, Beverly Hills has been thriving ever since. Its main thoroughfares are Sunset, Wilshire, and Santa Monica boulevards (Santa Monica is actually two parallel streets at this point: "Santa Monica" is the northern one; "Little Santa Monica," the southern).

Westwood is so busy on summer weekend evenings that many streets are closed to car traffic and visitors must park at the Federal Building at Wilshire Boulevard and Veteran Avenue and shuttle over. However you arrive, Westwood is a lively village filled with trendy restaurants, movie theaters, and colorful street life.

A Good Tour
Numbers in the text correspond to numbers in the margin and on the Westside map.

Start along **Melrose Avenue** ① between La Brea and Fairfax avenues, a few blocks south of West Hollywood proper. This 16-block stretch is a great place to people-watch. You'll notice colorful folks, many clad in way-out clothes and wild hairstyles, walking past the many one-of-a-kind shops. Heading west to San Vicente Boulevard, on the right you can't miss a large cobalt-color building with an emerald-color one behind it. This complex, known as the **Pacific Design Center** ②, houses some of L.A.'s most prestigious interior showrooms. Head south on San Vicente to Beverly Boulevard, where the colossal **Beverly Center** ③ is easily recognized by its exterior glass-enclosed escalators. After your credit cards stop sizzling, get back in the car and backtrack north on San Vicente Boulevard to Santa Monica Boulevard, the heart of West Hollywood. A few blocks farther north you'll hit the **Sunset Strip** ④. By turning right, you'll discover all the hoopla that makes this stretch of Sunset so famous: nightclubs like the House of Blues (8430 Sunset) and hotels such as the art deco Argyle (8358 Sunset).

Head back west along Sunset. Where the Strip ends, just past Doheny Drive, residential Beverly Hills begins. North of Sunset on Loma Vista Drive is the historic **Greystone Mansion** ⑤, often used as a movie locale. Farther west on Sunset at Rodeo Drive is the landmark **Beverly Hills Hotel** ⑥.

Motor south along **Rodeo Drive** ⑦ to the stretch between Santa Monica and Wilshire boulevards, and you'll be amid some of the most expensive commercial real estate in the world. A block east of Rodeo is the **Museum of Television & Radio** ⑧. Three blocks south at Wilshire Boulevard is the regal **Regent Beverly Wilshire Hotel** ⑨.

Continue south onto Pico Boulevard and turn right to the **Museum of Tolerance** ⑩. Head west on Pico to Westwood Boulevard and turn right to reach **Westwood Village Memorial Park** ⑪. After paying your respects to the Hollywood immortals buried here, drive north on Westwood Boulevard to Wilshire Boulevard and southern edge of **Westwood,** home to the **University of California at Los Angeles** ⑫ (UCLA) and the **Armand Hammer Museum of Art and Cultural Center** ⑬. Continue west on Wilshire and get on the San Diego (I–405) Freeway north, from which you can take the Getty Center Drive exit to the new **Getty Center** ⑭, and a few miles farther, the Skirball Center exit for the **Skirball Cultural Center** ⑮.

TIMING

Midday is a good time to visit the Westside. Walking Melrose can take more than an hour, depending on how much of a shopper you are and how good your parking karma is. Metered parking along Melrose is difficult to snag, and parking on side streets is sometimes limited, so read the signs carefully. One hint: Go for lunch and valet park; pick up your vehicle after you've walked around. Most sights west of Melrose can be appreciated from your car, but walk a bit of Rodeo Drive. The Museum of Television & Radio's galleries take half an hour to browse, though the library can absorb one all day. Plan to devote a few hours to the Museum of Tolerance; reserve ahead. Visiting the Armand Hammer Museum takes about an hour. The vast Getty Center is best saved for a separate trip of at least three hours; the museum at the Skirball Cultural Center will take an hour or so. Most of the museums listed below stay open late on Thursday, but the days they are closed vary.

Sights to See

⑬ **Armand Hammer Museum of Art and Cultural Center.** The eclectic permanent collection here includes thousands of works by Honoré Daumier, as well as a handful by van Gogh, Gauguin, Degas, and Mary Cassatt. There are free poetry readings Thursday evenings, art lectures and workshops during the week, and most Saturdays there are music and art events for children. ✉ *10899 Wilshire Blvd.,* ☎ *310/443–7000.* ☞ *$4.50, free Thurs. 6–9; parking $2.75.* ☉ *Tues.–Wed. and Fri.–Sat. 11–7, Thurs. 11–9, Sun. 11–5. Docent tours Sun. at 1.*

③ **Beverly Center.** The hulking monolith (nicknamed the "Brown Elephant") that dominates the corner of La Cienega and Beverly boulevards was designed as an all-in-one stop for shopping, dining, and movies. Parking is on the second through fifth floors; shops on the sixth, seventh,

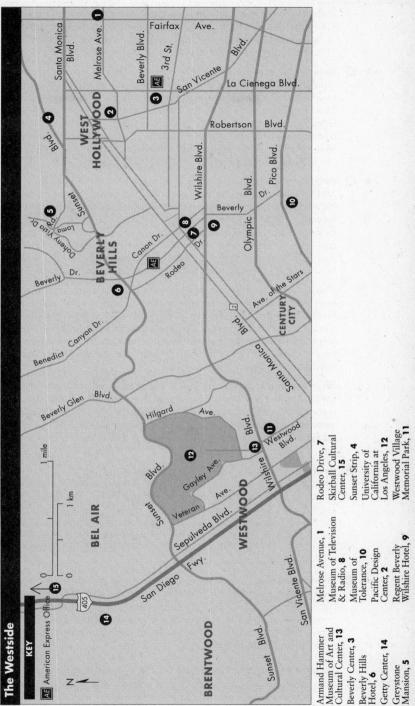

The Westside

KEY

AE American Express Office

Armand Hammer Museum of Art and Cultural Center, **13**
Beverly Center, **3**
Beverly Hills Hotel, **6**
Getty Center, **14**
Greystone Mansion, **5**

Melrose Avenue, **1**
Museum of Television & Radio, **8**
Museum of Tolerance, **10**
Pacific Design Center, **2**
Regent Beverly Wilshire Hotel, **9**

Rodeo Drive, **7**
Skirball Cultural Center, **15**
Sunset Strip, **4**
University of California at Los Angeles, **12**
Westwood Village Memorial Park, **11**

and eighth floors; and movies and restaurants on the eighth floor. You may want to avoid the movie theaters, as their screens are tiny. Don't be surprised if you see a movie star, minus makeup, out on a spree here. ✉ *8500 Beverly Blvd.,* ☎ *310/854–0070.*

★ ❻ **Beverly Hills Hotel.** Greta Garbo, Howard Hughes, and other movie-industry guests kept low profiles when staying at this pastel Spanish Colonial Revival landmark—also known as the Pink Palace—while other film luminaries, most notably Cecil B. DeMille, cut very visible deals in the Polo Lounge. The hotel, which debuted in 1912, is now owned by the Sultan of Brunei, who restored the 12-acre site to its former glory with a multimillion-dollar mid-1990s renovation. ✉ *9641 Sunset Blvd., 1 mi west of Sunset Strip,* ☎ *310/276–2251.*

★ ⓮ **Getty Center.** The Getty Center is the new home (scheduled for a late-1997 opening) of much of the art collection of the late oil billionaire J. Paul Getty. It's also a center for art scholarship, education, and conservation. Getty began collecting art in the 1930s, concentrating on three distinct areas: Greek and Roman antiquities, Baroque and Renaissance paintings, and 18th-century decorative arts. Until 1997, the collection was kept in the J. Paul Getty Museum in Malibu, which is now being renovated to house only the antiquities.

The Richard Meier–designed museum is organized as a series of pavilions around an outdoor courtyard. The decorative arts collection includes furniture, carpets, tapestries, clocks, chandeliers, and small items made for the French, German, and Italian nobility. All major schools of Western art from the late 13th century to the late 19th century are represented in the painting collection, which emphasizes Renaissance and Baroque art.

From the parking structure (reservations required), take the tram up the hill to the museum, restaurants, bookstore, and gardens. The restaurant has a beautiful view of the ocean; artist Robert Irwin designed the central garden. ✉ *1200 Getty Center Dr.,* ☎ *310/440–7300.* ▣ *Free; $5 parking fee.* ☉ *Tues.–Wed. 11–7, Thurs.–Fri. 11–9, weekends 10–6.*

❺ **Greystone Mansion.** Doheny Drive is named for oilman Edward Doheny, the original owner of this 1927 neo-Gothic mansion of over 46,000 square ft. Now owned by the city of Beverly Hills, it sits on 18½ landscaped acres and has been used in such films as *The Witches of Eastwick* and *Indecent Proposal*. The gardens are open for self-guided tours, and peeking (only) through the windows is permitted. ✉ *905 Loma Vista Dr.,* ☎ *310/550–4796.* ▣ *Free.* ☉ *Fall and winter, daily 9–5; spring and summer, daily 9–6.*

★ ❶ **Melrose Avenue.** Panache meets paparazzi and Beverly Hills chic contends with post-punk Hollywood hip along the stretch of Melrose between Fairfax and La Brea avenues. Here you'll find one-of-a-kind boutiques, some great vintage clothing and collectibles shops, and small, trendy restaurants. *See* Shopping, *below,* for descriptions of some of the avenue's stores.

OFF THE
BEATEN PATH   **MUSEUM OF JURASSIC TECHNOLOGY –** This unusual place, in a realm somewhere between a museum and an art installation, has a permanent collection of natural (and perhaps fictional) wonders such as the African stink ant and the "piercing devil" (a tiny bat that uses radar to fly through solid objects), as well as a comprehensive exhibit on the obscure figure of memory theorist Geoffrey Sonnabend. ✉ *9341 Venice Blvd., Culver City,* ☎ *310/836–6131.* ▣ *$4.* ☉ *Thurs. 2–8, Fri.–Sun. noon–6.*

⑧ Museum of Television & Radio. Revisit the great "Where's the beef?" commercial at this sleek stone-and-glass building, which opened in 1996 as a companion to the Museum of Television & Radio in New York, entirely duplicating its collection of 75,000 programs spanning 75 years. Search for your favorite commercials and television and radio shows on easy-to-use computers, and then watch or listen to them in an adjacent room. The museum also presents special exhibits of television-related art and costumes, and schedules screenings and listening series daily. ☒ 465 N. Beverly Dr., ☏ 310/786–1025. ☚ $6. ☽ Wed. and Fri.–Sun. noon–5, Thurs. noon–9.

★ ⑩ **Museum of Tolerance.** Using state-of-the-art interactive technology, this important museum adjacent to the Simon Wiesenthal Center challenges visitors to confront bigotry and racism. One of the most affecting sections covers the Holocaust—each visitor is issued a "passport" bearing the name of a child whose life was dramatically changed by the German Nazi rule and by World War II. Later, the museum goer learns the fate of that child. Anne Frank artifacts are part of the museum's permanent collection. Expect to spend at least three hours to see the whole museum. Reservations are advised; you will be allowed to enter only at specified admission times. ☒ 9786 W. Pico Blvd., ☏ 310/553–8403. ☚ $8. ☽ Sun. 10:30–5, Mon.–Thurs. 10–4, Fri. 10–1.

❷ Pacific Design Center. At the center of Los Angeles's thriving to-the-trade interior decorating business, these two buildings are known as the "Blue Whale" and the "Green Whale." Cesar Pelli designed the blue structure in the mid-1970s; the center added the green one, also by Pelli, in 1988. You can browse in many of the more than 200 showrooms weekdays from 9 to 5. Purchases can be made only through design professionals (a referral system is available). ☒ 8687 Melrose Ave., ☏ 310/657–0800.

★ ❾ **Regent Beverly Wilshire Hotel.** Anchoring the south end of Rodeo Drive at Wilshire since opening in 1928, the hotel is often home to visiting royalty and celebrities; it's where the millionaire businessman played by Richard Gere ensconced himself with the hooker played by Julia Roberts in the movie *Pretty Woman.* The lobby is small for a hotel of this size and offers little opportunity to meander; you might stop for a drink or meal in one of the hotel's restaurants. ☒ 9500 Wilshire Blvd., ☏ 310/275–5200.

★ ❼ **Rodeo Drive.** Along the fabulous shopping avenue of the rich and famous you'll find stores that sell such necessities as $200 pairs of socks wrapped in gold leaf and that take customers by appointment only. Fortunately the browsing is free. You'll find all the major names are here, Gucci, Armani, and Chanel. A fun way to spend an afternoon is to stroll the section of Rodeo (pronounced ro-*day*-o) between Santa Monica and Wilshire boulevards. At the southern end of Rodeo Drive is Via Rodeo, a curvy cobblestone street that somewhat emulates the picture-perfect layout of Disneyland's main drag, though the boutiques that thrive here are definitely for adults—with money.

⑮ Skirball Cultural Center. This pink-and-green building rising out of the Santa Monica Mountains opened in 1996. The complex, designed by Moshe Safdie, contains conference and educational centers, but the big draw is the museum, where the core exhibition is "Visions and Values: Jewish Life from Antiquity to America." Twelve galleries use artifacts, building reconstructions, and multimedia installations to tell the story of the Jewish people. ☒ 2701 N. Sepulveda Blvd., ☏ 310/440–4500. ☚ $6. ☽ Tues.–Wed. and Fri. 10–4, Thurs. 10–9, weekends noon–5.

★ ❹ **Sunset Strip.** The 1950s TV show *77 Sunset Strip* made the Strip famous, but it was popular as far back as the 1930s, when nightclubs like Ciro's and Mocambo were in their heyday and movie stars frequented the area as an after-work gathering spot. This winding, hilly stretch is enjoyable both by car (a convertible would be perfect) or on foot. The Sunset Plaza area, with its dazzling shops, is especially nice for walking; a stretch of outdoor cafés is packed for lunch and on warm evenings.

⓬ **University of California at Los Angeles.** With spectacular buildings such as the Romanesque library, the parklike UCLA campus makes for a fine stroll. In the heart of the north campus, the Franklin Murphy Sculpture Garden contains works by Henry Moore and Gaston Lachaise. The Mildred Mathias Botanic Garden is in the southeast section of the campus and is accessible from Tiverton Avenue. Maps and information are available at drive-by kiosks at major entrances, and free 90-minute walking tours of the campus are given on weekdays at 10:30 and 1:30. The tour begins at the West Alumni Center, next to Pauley Pavilion; call 310/206–0616 for reservations, which are required at least one day in advance. ⊠ *Le Conte Ave., Sunset Blvd., and Hilgard Ave. border the campus.*

⓫ **Westwood Village Memorial Park.** The Westwood stretch of Wilshire Boulevard is a corridor of cheek-by-jowl office buildings and condominiums of varying, often jarring architectural styles. Tucked behind one of these behemoths is **1218 Glendon Avenue.** In this very unlikely place for a cemetery is one of the most famous graves in the city. Marilyn Monroe is buried in a simply marked crypt on the north wall. Also buried here are Truman Capote and Natalie Wood.

Santa Monica, Venice, Pacific Palisades, and Malibu

Santa Monica is a tidy little city, about 8.3 mi square, where expatriate Brits tend to settle (there's an English music hall and several pubs here), attracted perhaps by the cool, foggy climate.

Venice was a turn-of-the-century fantasy that never quite came true. Abbot Kinney, a wealthy Los Angeles businessman, envisioned this little piece of real estate as a romantic replica of Venice, Italy. He developed 16 mi of canals, floated gondolas on them, and built scaled-down versions of the Doge's Palace and other Venetian landmarks. The canals were by and large an engineering disaster. Rebuilt in 1996, they still don't reflect the Old World connection quite as well as they might. Venice's locals are a grudgingly thrown-together mix of artistes, aging hippies, yuppies with the disposable income to spend on inflated rents, senior citizens who have lived here for decades, and the homeless.

North of Santa Monica, **Malibu** has a worldwide reputation for its swank beach houses, television- and film-star residents, and brush fires and mud slides. **Pacific Palisades** connects Santa Monica and Malibu. The narrow but expensive beachfront houses were home to movie stars back in the 1930s and are preferred by many modern-day celebrities who enjoy the get-away-from-it-all feeling this coastline area of Los Angeles provides.

A Good Drive
Numbers in the text correspond to numbers in the margin and on the Santa Monica and Venice map.

Look for the arched neon sign at the entrance to the **Santa Monica Pier** ①, to which **Pacific Park** ②, a state-of-the-art amusement park, was added in 1996. The first street east of Pacific Coast Highway is Ocean Avenue, where **Palisades Park** ③, above the cliffs, provides panoramic ocean views. Head inland a few blocks to the **Third Street Promenade** ④, an active outdoor shopping-dining-entertainment mall. From here, take 4th Street south to Pico and head east about a mile to Cloverfield. Take Cloverfield north to Michigan and take a right to find **Bergamot Station** ⑤, a complex of galleries and the home of the Santa Monica Museum of Art. Then backtrack south on Cloverfield to Ocean Park Boulevard; turn right and head almost all the way to the beach. Turn left on Main Street, on which you'll find the **California Heritage Museum** ⑥. Next stop: Venice. Skip the canals. Instead, stay on Main Street through the trendy shopping district until you hit Rose Avenue. Ahead on the left you'll spot an enormous pair of binoculars, the front of the Frank Gehry–designed Chiat-Day Mojo building. Turn right toward the sea. The main attraction of this dead end is the **Venice Boardwalk** ⑦, where the classic California beach scene is in progress. Loop back north past Santa Monica on Highway 1 to Pacific Palisades, where the grounds of the famed humorist and cowboy's estate, **Will Rogers State Historic Park** ⑧, are a great picnicking and hiking spot. Two miles north, you'll spot an enormous rendition of an Italian villa high on the cliffs to your right. That's the **J. Paul Getty Museum.** Closed now for renovations, it will reopen in a few years as America's only museum devoted to Greek and Roman antiquities. Farther down on the beach side of the highway, the Moorish-Spanish **Adamson House** ⑨ is a tiled beauty with a great Pacific view. Next door, **Malibu Lagoon State Beach** ⑩ has extensive paths that take you through a magical reserve stocked full of native birds.

TIMING

You would do well to visit the area in two excursions: Santa Monica to Venice in one day and Pacific Palisades to Malibu in another. So expect to spend a couple of days cruising the coast, unless you insist on rushing from sight to sight, not a very L.A. thing to do. If you visit during rush hour, expect to proceed at a snail's pace. Try to be outdoors come sunset: Watching the sun dip into the blue Pacific is an experience not to be missed.

Sights to See

⑨ **Adamson House.** The Rindge family, which owned much of the Malibu area in the early part of the 20th century, also owned this Moorish-Spanish–style structure, which was built in 1929. The house, encrusted with magnificent tile work from the defunct Malibu Potteries, is right on the beach—high chain-link fences keep out curious beachgoers. Even an outside dog shower, near the servants' door, is a tiled delight. Signs posted around the grounds outside direct you on a self-guided tour. ⊠ *23200 Pacific Coast Hwy.,* ☎ *310/456–8432.* ☜ *$2.* ☉ *Wed.–Sat. 11–3.*

⑤ **Bergamot Station.** This collection of old railroad cars behind the city recycling center houses more than 30 galleries and design studios featuring the work of some of the best local artists. The **Santa Monica Museum of Art,** which relocated here in 1997, mounts painting, sculpture, and other exhibits and presents performance and video art. The museum hosts free films, discussions, and readings on Friday evening. ⊠ *2525 Michigan Ave.,* ☎ *310/829–5854 Bergamot, 310/586–6488 museum.* ☜ *Galleries free, Santa Monica Museum suggested donation $4.* ☉ *Most galleries open Tues.–Sat. 11–6.*

⑥ **California Heritage Museum.** Three rooms at this vintage 1894 Victorian have been fully restored: the dining room in the style of 1890 to 1910; the living room, 1910 to 1920; and the kitchen, 1920 to 1930. The second-floor galleries contain photography and historical exhibits

Santa Monica and Venice

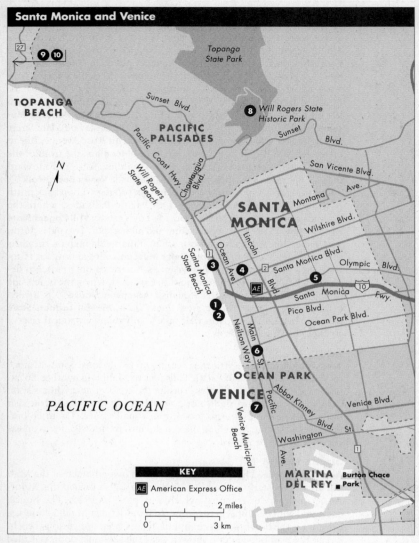

Topanga State Park

Sunset Blvd.

TOPANGA BEACH

Pacific Coast Hwy.

PACIFIC PALISADES

Will Rogers State Beach

Chautauqua Blvd.

8 Will Rogers State Historic Park

Sunset Blvd.

San Vicente Blvd.

Ave.

SANTA MONICA

Montana

Wilshire Blvd.

Ocean Ave.

Lincoln

Santa Monica State Beach

1

3

2

4

AE

Santa Monica Blvd.

Olympic Blvd.

Blvd.

5

10

Santa Monica Fwy.

Pico Blvd.

Ocean Park Blvd.

1
2

Neilson Way

Main St.

6

OCEAN PARK

VENICE

Pacific

Abbot Kinney Blvd.

Venice Blvd.

7

St.

PACIFIC OCEAN

Venice Municipal Beach

Washington Ave.

1

MARINA DEL REY

Burton Chace Park

KEY

AE American Express Office

0   2 miles

0   3 km

as well as shows by contemporary California artists. ✉ *2612 Main St.,* ☎ *310/392–8537.* ⌑ *$3.* ⊙ *Wed.–Sat. 11–4, Sun. noon–4.*

⑩ Malibu Lagoon State Beach. Visitors are asked to stay on the boardwalks at this 5-acre haven for native and migratory birds, so that the egrets, blue herons, avocets, and gulls can enjoy the marshy area. The signs that give opening and closing hours refer only to the parking lot; the lagoon itself is open 24 hours and is particularly enjoyable in the early morning and at sunset. Luckily, street-side parking is available then (but not at midday). ✉ *23200 Pacific Coast Hwy.,* ☎ *818/880–0350.*

OFF THE BEATEN PATH	**MARINA DEL REY** – Just south of Venice, the popular singles enclave of Marina del Rey is the largest man-made boat harbor in the world, with a commercial area catering to the whims of boat owners and boat groupies. The stretch between Admiralty Way and Mindinao Way has some of the area's best restaurants—expensive but worth it. From cool and breezy Burton Chace Park at the end of Mindanao Way, you can watch boats move in and out of the channel.

② Pacific Park. The 11 rides at Santa Monica Pier's 2-acre amusement facility include a roller coaster; a giant Ferris wheel; a flying submarine; and the Rock and Roll, a spinning experience including a light show and rousing music. ✉ *380 Santa Monica Pier, Santa Monica,* ☎ *310/260–8747.* ⌑ *Rides $1–$3, all-day pass $12.* ⊙ *Summer, Sun.–Thurs. 10–10, Fri.–Sat. 10 AM–midnight; winter, Fri. 2–midnight, Sat. 10 AM–midnight, Sun. 10–9.*

③ Palisades Park. The ribbon of green that runs along the top of the cliffs from Colorado Avenue to just north of San Vicente Boulevard has flat walkways usually filled with casual strollers as well as joggers who like to work out with a spectacular view of the Pacific. If you can, hang around for sunset when Palisades Park is especially enjoyable.

★ ⓒ ① Santa Monica Pier. Cafés, gift shops, a psychic adviser, arcades, and the Pacific Park amusement facility are all part of this truncated pier beneath Palisades Park. The pier's trademark 46-horse carousel, built in 1922, has appeared in many films, including *The Sting.* ✉ *Colorado Ave. and the ocean,* ☎ *310/458–8900.* ⊙ *Carousel summer, daily 11–6; winter, weekends 10–5.*

④ Third Street Promenade. Only foot traffic is allowed along a three-block stretch of 3rd Street, just a whiff away from the Pacific, that is lined with jacaranda trees and accented with ivy-topiary dinosaur fountains. Outdoor cafés, street vendors, several movie theaters, and a rich nightlife (the mix of folks down here is great, from elderly couples out for a bite to skateboarders and street musicians) make this one of Santa Monica's main gathering spots. ✉ *3rd St. between Wilshire Blvd. and Broadway.*

★ ⑦ Venice Boardwalk. This L.A. must-see—known also as Ocean Front Walk—delivers year-round action: Bicyclists zip along and bikini-clad roller and in-line skaters attract crowds as they put on impromptu demonstrations, vying for attention with magicians and street artists. A local bodybuilding club works out on the adjacent beach—it's nearly impossible not to stop and ogle the strongmen's pecs. You can rent in-line skates, roller skates, and bicycles (some with baby seats) at the south end of the boardwalk, along Washington Street, near the Venice Pier. If all the hubbub makes you hungry, stop for a bite (it's worth the wait for a patio table) at the **Sidewalk Cafe** (✉ 1401 Ocean Front Walk, ☎ 310/399–5547).

★ **⑧** **Will Rogers State Historic Park.** The late cowboy-humorist Will Rogers
lived on this site in the 1920s and 1930s. His 187-acre estate is a folksy
blend of Navajo rugs and Mission-style furniture. Rogers's only ex-
travagance was to raise the roof several feet (he waited till his wife was
in Europe to do it) so that he could practice his lasso technique indoors.
The nearby museum contains Rogers memorabilia. The park's broad
lawns are excellent for picnicking, and there's hiking on miles of
eucalyptus-lined trails. ✉ *1501 Will Rogers State Park Rd., Pacific Palisades,* ☎ *310/454–8212.* ⌑ *Free; parking $5.* ⊙ *House tours daily
10:30–4:30.*

Palos Verdes, San Pedro, and Long Beach

The hilly **Palos Verdes Peninsula** is a haven for horse lovers and other
gentrified folks, many of them executive transplants from east of the
Mississippi. The real estate in these small peninsula towns, ranging from
expensive to very expensive, is zoned for stables, and you'll often see
riders along the streets (they have the right of way).

The tidy 1920s-era white clapboard houses, and dozens of boats of all
sizes, epitomize **San Pedro** (locals steadfastly ignore the correct Spanish pronunciation—it's "San Peedro" to them), an old seaport community with a strong Mediterranean and Eastern European flavor. There
are enticing Greek and Yugoslavian markets and restaurants throughout the town.

Long Beach began as a seaside resort in the 19th century, and during
the early part of the 20th century it was a popular destination for Mid-
westerners and Dust Bowlers in search of a better life. They built street
after street of modest wood homes. To preserve transportation and shipping interests for the city of Los Angeles, Wilmington was annexed in
the late 19th century. A narrow strip of land, mostly less than ½ mi
wide, it follows the Harbor Freeway from downtown south to the port.

A Good Drive

*Numbers in the text correspond to numbers in the margin and on the
Palos Verdes, San Pedro, and Long Beach map.*

Begin at the **South Coast Botanic Garden** ①, on Crenshaw Boulevard
1 mi south of the Pacific Coast Highway. Less than a mile farther on
your right you'll see **Point Vicente Lighthouse**, a good spot to watch
for whales, and, another 2 mi away, on your left, you'll see the all-glass
Wayfarers Chapel ②. Continue south and you'll hit the western end
of the Los Angeles Harbor. Follow the signs to Cabrillo Beach and the
stark white building that houses the **Cabrillo Marine Aquarium** ③. To
reach the **Banning Residence Museum and Park** ④, take Pacific Avenue
north to the Harbor Freeway, and exit at Pacific Coast Highway.

Take Pacific Coast Highway toward Long Beach, turn south on Magnolia Avenue, and follow signs leading to the art deco ship, the **Queen
Mary** ⑤. Then take the bridge back across **Queensway Bay** to **Shoreline Drive** and **Shoreline Village** ⑥, a waterfront outdoor shopping district. Wind down in adjacent **Shoreline Aquatic Park** ⑦, for the best
view of the harbor and the Long Beach skyline. Take Ocean Boulevard
east to **Naples** ⑧, on Los Alamitos Bay, where—no surprise—the ancient art of gondola riding is all the rage.

TIMING
Plan on spending a couple of hours at the South Coast Botanic Garden. The Wayfarers Chapel is a half-hour stopover at most. If you have
kids in tow, expect to stay a couple of hours at the Cabrillo Marine
Aquarium. You'll probably want spend an hour or so at the Banning

Palos Verdes, San Pedro, and Long Beach

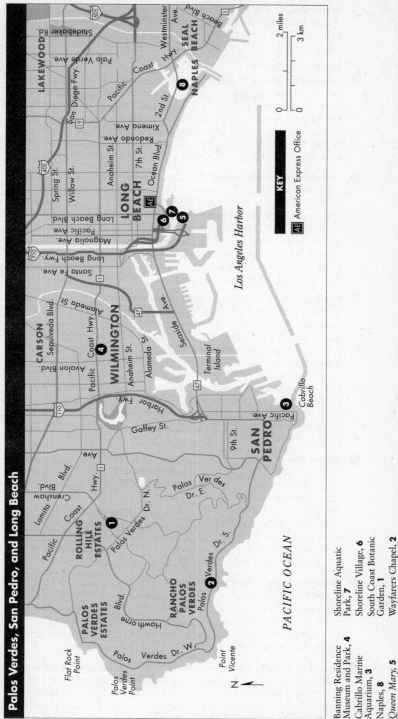

PACIFIC OCEAN

Los Angeles Harbor

KEY

AE American Express Office

2 miles

3 km

Banning Residence
Museum and Park, **4**
Cabrillo Marine
Aquarium, **3**
Naples, **8**
Queen Mary, **5**

Shoreline Aquatic
Park, **7**
Shoreline Village, **6**
South Coast Botanic
Garden, **1**
Wayfarers Chapel, **2**

Residence Museum and Park. Expect to spend a few hours at the *Queen Mary,* including stops at Shoreline Village or Shoreline Aquatic Park, and an hour or so at in Naples (more if you're going to take a gondola ride).

Sights to See

4 **Banning Residence Museum and Park.** General Phineas Banning, an early entrepreneur in Los Angeles, is credited with developing the San Pedro harbor into a viable economic entity and naming the area Wilmington (he was from Delaware). Part of his estate has been preserved in a 20-acre park. (The picnicking possibilities here are excellent.) ⊠ *401 E. M St., Wilmington,* ☎ *310/548–7777.* ☞ *House $2.* ⊙ *House tour Tues.–Thurs. 12:30–2:30, weekends 12:30–3:30 on the hr.*

3 **Cabrillo Marine Aquarium.** This gem of a small museum is dedicated to the marine life that flourishes off the southern California coast, particularly near its home in San Pedro. A modern Frank Gehry–designed building right on the beach houses 35 saltwater aquariums. There's a shark tank and a tidal tank that enables you to see the long view of a wave. On the back patio, you can reach into a shallow tank to touch starfish and sea anemones. ⊠ *3720 Stephen White Dr.,* ☎ *310/548–7562.* ☞ *Free; parking $4.50 weekdays, $5.50 weekends.* ⊙ *Weekdays noon–5, weekends 10–5.*

8 **Naples.** Actually three small islands in man-made Alamitos Bay, Naples is best experienced on foot. Park near Bay Shore Avenue and 2nd Street and walk across the bridge, where you can meander around the quaint streets with Italian names. This well-restored neighborhood has eclectic architecture: vintage Victorians, Craftsman bungalows, and Mission Revivals. You may spy a real gondola or two on the canals. You can hire them for a ride, but not on the spur of the moment. **Gondola Getaway** offers one-hour rides; the gondolas can accommodate up to six people and serve bread, salami, and cheese—you bring the wine. Reservations are essential at least one week in advance. ⊠ *5437 E. Ocean Blvd.,* ☎ *562/433–9595.* ☞ *Rides $55 per couple, $10 each additional person.* ⊙ *Cruises 11 AM–midnight.*

★ **5** **Queen Mary.** The 80,000-ton *Queen Mary* was launched in 1934, a floating treasure of art deco splendor. It took a crew of 1,100 to minister to the needs of its 1,900 demanding passengers. The former first-class passenger quarters are now a hotel. Tours of the ship are available, and guests can browse the 12 decks and witness close up the bridge, staterooms, officers' quarters, and engine rooms. There are several restaurants and shops on board. Stay late for fireworks Saturday nights in the summer. ⊠ *Pier H,* ☎ *310/435–3511.* ☞ *$11, guided 1-hr tour $7 extra.* ⊙ *Tours daily 10–4:30, later in summer.*

7 **Shoreline Aquatic Park.** Kite flyers love the winds at this park in Long Beach Harbor and casual passersby can enjoy a short walk, where the modern skyline, quaint Shoreline Village, the *Queen Mary,* and the ocean all vie for attention. The park's lagoon is off-limits for swimming, but aquacycles and kayaks can be rented during the summer months. ⊠ *Shoreline Dr. and Pine Ave.*

6 **Shoreline Village.** This setting between downtown Long Beach and the *Queen Mary* is a good place for a stroll, day or evening (when visitors can enjoy the lights of the ship twinkling in the distance). In addition to gift shops and restaurants—the best of which, **Parker's Lighthouse** (⊠ Shoreline Village, ☎ 562/432–6500), has great seafood and views of the *Queen Mary*—there's a 1906 carousel. ⊠ *Shoreline Dr. and Pine Ave.,* ☎ *562/435–2668.* ☞ *Carousel $1.* ⊙ *May–Sept., daily 10–10; Oct.–Apr., daily 10–9.*

★ **❶** **South Coast Botanic Garden.** This Rancho Palos Verdes botanical garden began life ignominiously as a garbage dump-cum-landfill. It's hard to believe that as recently as 1960, truckloads of waste (3.5 million tons) were being deposited here. With the intensive ministerings of the experts from the L.A. County Arboreta Department, the dump soon sprouted lush gardens, with all the plants eventually organized into color groups. Self-guided walking tours pass flower and herb gardens, rare cacti, and a lake with ducks. The Garden for the Senses is devoted to touching and smelling plants; the Water-Wise garden showcases alternatives to grass lawns in the parched southern California climate. Picnicking is limited to a lawn area outside the gates. ⊠ *26300 S. Crenshaw Blvd., Rancho Palos Verdes,* ☎ *310/544–6815.* ⌦ *$5.* ☉ *Daily 9–5.*

❷ **Wayfarers Chapel.** Architect Lloyd Wright, son of Frank Lloyd Wright, designed this modern glass church in 1949 to blend in with an encircling redwood forest. The redwoods are gone (they couldn't stand the rigors of urban encroachment), but another forest has taken their place, lush with ferns and azaleas, adding up to a breathtaking combination of ocean, vegetation, and an architectural wonder. This "natural church" is a popular wedding site, so avoid visiting on weekends. ⊠ *5755 Palos Verdes Dr. S, Rancho Palos Verdes,* ☎ *310/377–1650.*

Highland Park, Pasadena, and San Marino

The suburbs north of downtown Los Angeles have some of California's richest architecture as well as several fine museums. **Highland Park,** midway between downtown Los Angeles and Pasadena, was a genteel suburb in the late 1800s, whose Anglo population tried to keep an Eastern feeling alive in their architecture despite the decidedly Western landscape. Although now fully absorbed into the general Los Angeles sprawl, **Pasadena** was once a separate and distinctly defined—and very refined—city. Its varied architecture, augmented by lush landscaping, is among the most spectacular in southern California. **San Marino,** Pasadena's prestigious neighbor, is a residential retreat where each new mansion you see outdoes the previous one.

A Good Tour
Numbers in the text correspond to numbers in the margin and on the Highland Park, Pasadena, and San Marino map.

Take the Pasadena Freeway (I–110) north to the Avenue 43 exit. Be sure to slow down: the exit ramp is extremely short. Take a right, and on the east side of the freeway, you'll come across the Victorian buildings in colorful **Heritage Square** ①. On the other side of the freeway, on Avenue 43, a minute away, is **El Alisal** ②, a two-story building made out of boulders around the turn of the century. The next signal on Avenue 43 is Figueroa Avenue. Turn right and follow posted signs to the **Southwest Museum** ③, home to many Native American artifacts.

Continue on Figueroa Avenue 4 mi to Colorado Boulevard and turn right for another 2 mi to Arroyo Boulevard. Then turn left and travel about a mile up the road, where, nestled in a gully, is the famous **Rose Bowl** ④. Leave the Rose Bowl via Rosemont Avenue, driving away from the hills to the south. In less than a mile, you'll come across Orange Grove Boulevard; take a right and another right immediately and you'll come across a large, two-story shingled home, the **Gamble House** ⑤, which you may recognize from the film *Back to the Future.* Just down Orange Grove at the corner of Walnut Street, you'll discover a beaux arts estate, the Fenyes Mansion, home to the **Pasadena Historical Society** ⑥. Continue south on Orange Grove Boulevard to Colorado

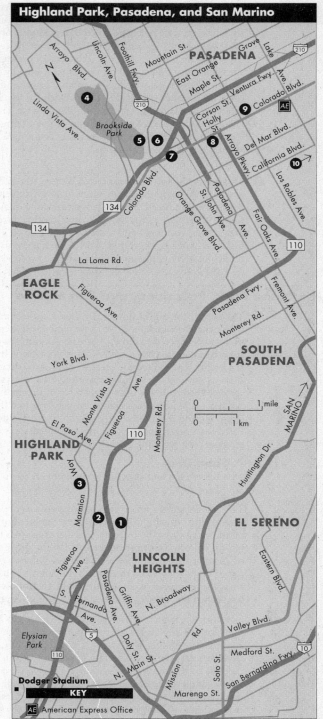

Highland Park, Pasadena, and San Marino

Boulevard, and turn left. This is Pasadena's main drag and the route for the New Year's Day Rose Parade. On the first block to your left you'll see a round contemporary building, the **Norton Simon Museum** ⑦.

Continue east down Colorado Boulevard and, after a few blocks, you'll cross the historic concrete-arched Colorado Street Bridge, built in 1913, rising 160 ft above the Arroyo Seco gorge. On the other side of the block-long overpass, you'll enter **Old Town Pasadena** ⑧, a renewed shopping and dining district. Park your car and take a stroll on Colorado Boulevard. Walking east, on your right a few blocks down, the **Pasadena Civic Center** looks like a domed Italian church in a plaza environment. The street on the far side of this city center crossing Colorado is Los Robles Avenue. Walk up one-half block north toward the hills, and you'll notice a Chinese-like building housing the **Pacific Asia Museum** ⑨. Back in your car, head east three blocks on Colorado Boulevard to El Molino Avenue. Continue south on El Molino to California Boulevard, and turn left. Soon you'll find yourself in San Marino. Follow the signs to the **Huntington Library, Art Collections, and Botanical Gardens** ⑩.

TIMING

To take advantage of the afternoon-only hours at several sites, you may want to take this tour in two separate afternoons. Pasadena could take a full day, more if you want to savor the world-class museum collections. Most of the stops before and after Pasadena are 10 minutes away or less. Set aside two hours for the Norton Simon Museum and at least a half day for the Huntington Library, Art Collections, and Botanical Gardens.

Sights to See

❷ **El Alisal.** This was once the home of eccentric Easterner-turned-Westerner Charles Lummis, who edited the magazine *The Land of Sunshine*, later *Out West*. The Harvard dropout and lifelong scholar was captivated by Native American culture (he founded the Southwest Museum), often living the lifestyle of the natives, much to the shock of his more staid Angeleno contemporaries. His house, named after a large sycamore that was once on the property, was built from 1898 to 1910 out of boulders from the arroyo itself, a romantic notion until recent earthquakes made the safety of such homes questionable. The art nouveau fireplace was designed by California artist Charles Walter Stetson. ⊠ *200 E. Ave. 43, entrance on Carlota Blvd.,* ☎ *213/222–0546.* ☞ *Free.* ☼ *Fri.–Sun. noon–4.*

❺ **Gamble House.** Built by Charles and Henry Greene in 1908, this is a spectacular example of Craftsman-style bungalow architecture. The term "bungalow" can be misleading, since the Gamble House is a huge two-story home. To wealthy Easterners such as the Gambles (as in Procter & Gamble), this type of vacation home seemed informal compared to their accustomed mansions. What makes visitors swoon here is the incredible amount of hand craftsmanship: the hand-shaped teak interiors, the Greene-designed furniture, the Emil Lange glass door. The dark exterior has broad eaves, with sleeping porches on the second floor. ⊠ *4 Westmoreland Pl.,* ☎ *626/793–3334.* ☞ *$5.* ☼ *Thurs.–Sun. noon–3, 1-hr tour every 15–20 mins.*

❶ **Heritage Square.** The square is the result of the ambitious attempt by the Cultural Heritage Foundation of Southern California to save from the wrecking ball some of the city's architectural gems of the era from 1865 to 1914. Five residences, a depot, a church, and a carriage barn have been moved to this small park from all over the city. The most breathtaking building here is **Hale House,** built in 1885. The almost garish colors of the interior and exterior are not the whim of some aging hippie painter, but rather a faithful re-creation of the palette that was, in fashion in the late 1800s. ⌧ *3800 Homer St., off Ave. 43 exit,* ☎ *626/449–0193.* 🖾 *$5; free Fri. 10–3.* ☉ *Weekends 11:30–4:30, tour every hr.*

★ ⑩ **Huntington Library, Art Collections, and Botanical Gardens.** If you only have time for one stop in the Pasadena area, it should be San Marino, where railroad tycoon Henry E. Huntington built his hilltop home in the early 1900s; since then it has established a reputation as one of the most extraordinary cultural complexes in the world, annually receiving more than a half million visitors. The library contains 4 million items, including such treasures as a Gutenberg Bible, the Ellesmere manuscript of Chaucer's *Canterbury Tales,* George Washington's genealogy in his own handwriting, and first editions by Ben Franklin and Shakespeare. The Huntington Gallery, devoted to British and French art from the 18th and 19th centuries, contains the original *Blue Boy* by Gainsborough and the monumental *Sarah Siddons as the Tragic Muse* by Reynolds.

An awesome 130-acre garden, formerly the grounds of the estate, the **Huntington Gardens** now include a 12-acre Desert Garden featuring the largest group of mature cacti and other succulents in the world, all arranged by continent. The Japanese Garden holds traditional Japanese plants, stone ornaments, a drum bridge, a Japanese house, a bonsai court, and a Zen rock garden. There are also collections of azaleas, camellias, and roses, plus herb, palm, and jungle gardens.

The Huntington Pavilion, built in 1980, has commanding views of the surrounding mountains and valleys, plus a bookstore, displays, and information kiosks. Both the east and west wings of the pavilion display paintings on public exhibition for the first time. The Ralph M. Parsons Botanical Center at the pavilion includes a botanical library, a herbarium, and a laboratory for research on plants. ⌧ *1151 Oxford Rd.,* ☎ *626/405–2100.* 🖾 *$7.50; free 1st Thurs. of month.* ☉ *Memorial Day–Labor Day, Tues.–Sun. 10:30–4:30; Labor Day–Memorial Day, Tues.–Fri. noon–4:30, weekends 10:30–4:30.*

★ ❼ **Norton Simon Museum.** The Norton Simon is a tribute to the art acumen of an extremely wealthy businessman. In 1974, Simon reorganized the failing Pasadena Art Institute and assembled one of the world's finest collections, richest in its Rembrandts, Goyas, Degas, and Picassos—and dotted with Rodin sculptures throughout. Rembrandt's development can be traced in three oils—*The Bearded Man in the Wide Brimmed Hat, Self Portrait,* and *Titus.* The most dramatic Goyas are two oils—*St. Jerome in Penitence* and the *Portrait of Dona Francisca Vicenta Chollet y Caballero.* Picasso's renowned *Woman with a Book* highlights a comprehensive collection of his paintings, drawings, and sculptures. The museum's collections of Impressionist (van Gogh, Matisse, Cézanne, Monet, Renoir, et al.) and Cubist (Braque, Gris) work is extensive. Older works include Southeast Asian artwork from 100 BC and bronze, stone, and ivory sculptures from India, Cambodia, Thailand, and Nepal. The museum also has a wealth of Early Renaissance, Baroque, and Rococo artwork. A landscaped sculpture garden with a teahouse designed by Frank Gehry opened in fall 1997. ⌧ *411 W. Colorado Blvd.,* ☎ *626/449–6840.* 🖾 *$4.* ☉ *Thurs.–Sun. noon–6.*

❽ **Old Town Pasadena.** Once the victim of decay, Pasadena's rejuvenated downtown contains bistros, elegant restaurants, and boutiques. On Raymond Street, the Hotel Green, now the Castle Apartments, is a faded Moorish fantasy of domes, turrets, and balconies. It's reminiscent of the Alhambra but with, true to its name, a greenish tint. Old Town is bisected by Colorado Boulevard, which, west of Old Town, rises onto the **Colorado Street Bridge,** a raised section of roadway on graceful arches completed in 1913 and restored in 1993. On New Year's Day throngs of people line Colorado Boulevard to watch the Rose Parade.

9 Pacific Asia Museum. Designed in the style of a northern Chinese imperial palace with a central courtyard, this gaudy building is devoted entirely to the arts and crafts of Asia and the Pacific Islands. Most objects are on loan from private collections and other museums; changing special exhibits focus on the objects of a single country. ⊠ *46 N. Los Robles Ave.,* ☎ *626/449–2742.* ⊡ *$4; free 3rd Sat. of month.* ☉ *Wed.–Sun. 10–5.*

6 Pasadena Historical Society. The 1905 **Fenyes Mansion,** the society's headquarters, still has its original furniture and paintings on the main and second floors. Basement exhibits trace Pasadena's history. There are also 4 acres of well-landscaped gardens. The mansion was the residence of Peter Sellers's simpleminded caretaker character in the film *Being There.* ⊠ *470 W. Walnut St.,* ☎ *626/577–1660.* ⊡ *$4.* ☉ *Thurs.–Sun. 1–4, 1-hr docent-led tour.*

4 Rose Bowl. Set at the bottom of a wide area of the arroyo in an older wealthy neighborhood, the facility is closed except for games and special events such as the monthly Rose Bowl Swap Meet. Held the second Sunday of the month, it is considered the granddaddy of West Coast flea markets. ⊠ *Rosemont Ave. off Arroyo Blvd.,* ☎ *626/577–3100.*

3 Southwest Museum. Readily spotted from the freeway, this huge Mission Revival building stands erect halfway up Mt. Washington. Inside is an extensive collection of Native American art and artifacts, with special emphasis on the people of the Plains, the Northwest Coast, the Southwest United States, and Northern Mexico. The basket collection is outstanding. ⊠ *234 Museum Dr., off Ave. 43 exit,* ☎ *213/221–2163.* ⊡ *$5.* ☉ *Tues.–Sun. 11–5.*

The San Fernando Valley

Although there are other valleys in the Los Angeles area, this is the one that people refer to simply as "the Valley." Sometimes there is a note of derision in their tone, since city dwellers still see it as a mere collection of bedroom communities, not worth serious thought. But the Valley has come a long way since the early 20th century when it was mainly orange groves and small ranches. Now home to more than 1 million people, this large portion of Los Angeles (with its own monthly magazine) is an area of neat bungalows and ranch-style homes situated on tidy parcels of land, with shopping centers never too far away. Fine restaurants and several major movie and television studios are an integral part of this community.

A Good Drive

Just over the hill from Hollywood Bowl via the 101 Hollywood Freeway north is **Universal City.** This mega-attraction even has its own freeway off-ramp, Universal Center Drive. **Universal Studios Hollywood** and **CityWalk** are on a large hill overlooking the San Fernando Valley, truly a city within a city. Exit the park on Barham Boulevard and turn left toward Burbank. After about a mile, the street curves around **Warner Bros. Studios,** with billboards of current films and television shows made there decorating the outside wall. After the curve, you will be on West Olive Avenue. Keep to the right and look for Gate No. 4 entrance at Hollywood Way.

Just a minute away at the second big intersection, West Olive and Alameda avenues, is the main entrance to **NBC Television Studios.** Continue east on Alameda, and on the next block to your right is **Disney Studios,** a very colorful bit of architecture. Drive south on Buena Vista and then turn left on Riverside to get a good look at the whimsical architecture. Take a left on Keystone Street and then continue east on Alameda Avenue 2 mi to the Golden State Freeway (I–5). Drive north about 12 mi to San Fernando Mission Boulevard, exit, and follow the road west ½ mi. On your right you'll spot **Mission San Fernando Rey de España.** Continue on San Fernando Mission Boulevard to Sepulveda Boulevard and turn left on Sepulveda Boulevard, looking for signs to Highway 118. Enter the on-ramp heading east, and travel about 2 mi to the Foothill Freeway (I–210) east. Follow about 14 mi along the base of the San Gabriel Mountains and take the Angeles Crest Highway exit, and then follow signs to **Descanso Gardens.**

TIMING

The major attractions of the Valley are grouped into one Exploring section to give you a sense of the place, but because the Valley is such a vast area, focus on one or two attractions and make them the destination for a half- or full-day trip. Rush-hour traffic jams on the San Diego and Hollywood freeways can be brutal, so avoid these thoroughfares at these times at all costs.

Sights to See

★ **Descanso Gardens.** Once part of the vast Spanish Rancho San Rafael that covered more than 30,000 acres, this lovely place encompasses 165 acres of native chaparral–covered slopes. A forest of California live oak trees furnishes a dramatic backdrop for thousands of camellias, azaleas, and a breathtaking new 5-acre International Rosarium, including 1,700 varieties of antique and modern roses. Descanso's Tea House contains pools, waterfalls, a Zen garden, and a gift shop and is a relaxing spot to stop for refreshments and reflection. Trams traverse the grounds, but be sure to spend some time strolling on your own to gain the full impact of this beautiful place. ⊠ *1418 Descanso Dr., La Canada,* ☎ *818/952–4400.* ✑ *$5, $2.50 3rd Tues. of month.* ⊙ *Daily 9–4:30.*

Disney Studios. Although tours are not offered inside this state-of-the-art animation studio, a visual tour from Riverside Drive shows you Disney's innovations go beyond the big and small screens to fanciful touches of architecture as well (note the little Mickey Mouse heads mounted on the surrounding fence). You can't miss this Michael Graves–designed building, erected in 1995—almost entirely made of glass, it looks like the hull of an enormous ocean liner. ⊠ *500 S. Buena Vista.*

Mission San Fernando Rey de España. An important member of a chain of 21 California missions established by Franciscan friars, Mission San Fernando was founded in 1797 and named in honor of King Ferdinand III of Spain. Fifty-six Native Americans joined the mission to make it a self-supporting community, but in the mid-1830s it began to decline after changes made under Mexican rule prompted the Native Americans to leave. The mission continued to deteriorate until 1923, when a restoration program was initiated. The church's interior is decorated with Native American designs and artifacts of Spanish craftsmanship depicting the mission's 18th-century culture. There is a small museum and gift shop. The structure has been used in countless films and television shows. ⊠ *15151 San Fernando Mission Blvd.,* ☎ *818/361–0186.* ✑ *$4.* ⊙ *Daily 9–5.*

OFF THE
BEATEN PATH

MULHOLLAND DRIVE – The dividing line between the San Fernando Valley and Los Angeles proper is one of the most famous thoroughfares in this vast metropolis. Driving the length of the hillside road is slow and can be treacherous, but the rewards are sensational views of valley and city on each side and expensive homes, many of them belonging to celebrities. Mulholland will no doubt leave a lasting impression, as you remember winding your way from the Hollywood Hills across the spine of the Santa Monica Mountains west almost to the Pacific Ocean.

NBC Television Studios. This major network's headquarters is in Burbank, as any regular viewer of *The Tonight Show* can't help knowing. For those who wish to be part of a live studio audience, free tickets are made available for tapings of the various NBC shows, and studio tours are offered weekdays. ⊠ *3000 W. Alameda Ave., Burbank,* ☎ *818/840–3537.* ☒ *$6.* ☉ *Tour weekdays 9–3.*

OFF THE
BEATEN PATH

PLACERITA CANYON NATURE CENTER – Perfect for hiking, with 4 mi of trails through 350 acres, both flat and hilly terrain take you along a streambed and through stands of oak trees. Because the park is a wildlife refuge, picnicking is limited to the designated area. The ½-mi ecology trail focuses on the flora and fauna of the area. Gold was first discovered in California in 1842 in this park (not in the Mother Lode, as most assume), at a site designated by the Oak of the Golden Dream. ⊠ *19152 W. Placerita Canyon Rd., Newhall,* ☎ *805/259–7721.* ☒ *$3 parking.* ☉ *Daily 9–5.*

★ **Universal Studios and CityWalk.** Universal City is a one-industry town, and that industry is Universal Studios. The studio has been at this site since 1915, and even then it allowed visitors to watch movies being made for 25¢. The five- to seven-hour Universal tour is an enlightening and amusing (if a bit sensational) day at the world's largest television and movie studio.

The complex stretches across more than 420 acres, many of which are traversed during the course of the tour by trams featuring usually witty running commentary by enthusiastic guides. You can experience the parting of the Red Sea, an avalanche, and a flood; meet a 30-ft-tall version of King Kong; live through an encounter with a runaway train; be attacked by the ravenous killer shark of *Jaws* fame; and endure a confrontation by aliens armed with death rays—all without ever leaving the safety of the tram. And now, thanks to the magic of Hollywood, you can also experience the perils of The Big One—an all-too-real simulation of an 8.3 earthquake, complete with collapsing earth, deafening train wrecks, floods, and other life-threatening amusements.

If you missed Kevin Costner's epic film *Waterworld*, Universal delivers a facsimile in the form of a sea war extravaganza. The newest ride is the enormous, $110 million-dollar *Jurassic Park—The Ride,* a tour through a jungle full of dinosaurs with a terrifying 84-ft water drop. There is also a New England village, an aged European town, and a replica of an archetypal New York street. Not-to-be-missed exhibits include *Back to the Future,* a $60-million flight simulator disguised as a DeLorean car that shows off state-of-the-art special effects, and *Lucy: A Tribute to Lucille Ball,* a 2,200-square-ft heart-shape museum containing a re-creation of the set from the *I Love Lucy* television show, plus other artifacts from the hit 1950s program.

At the Entertainment Center, the longest and last stop of the day, you can stroll around to enjoy various shows: In one theater animals beguile you with their tricks; in another you can pose for a photo session with the Incredible Hulk; at Castle Dracula you'll confront a variety of terrifying monsters; and at the Star Trek Theater, you can have yourself filmed and inserted as an extra in a scene from a galactic adventure already released. Bedrock is represented in the "Flintstone's Live Music Extravaganza," a stunning Stone Age revue. CityWalk opened in 1993, with a slew of lively shops and restaurants, including Spago, a copy of the star-studded Sunset Strip restaurant. ⊠ *100 Universal City Pl.,* ☎ *818/508–9600.* 🎫 *$34.* ☉ *Daily 9–7.*

Warner Bros. Studios. Two-hour tours at this major studio center in Burbank involve a lot of walking, so you should dress comfortably and casually. Somewhat technically oriented and centered more on the actual workings of filmmaking than the ones at Universal, tours here vary from day to day to take advantage of goings-on at the lot. Most tours see back-lot sets, the prop construction department, and the sound complex. A museum chronicles the studio's film and animation history. Reservations are strongly recommended one week in advance; children under 10 are not admitted. ⊠ *4000 Warner Blvd.,* ☎ *818/954–1744.* 🎫 *$29.* ☉ *Tours weekdays 9–3 on the ½ hr.*

DINING

Updated by
Colleen Dunn
Bates

Reservations are essential at the best restaurants, and at almost all restaurants on weekend evenings. As for wardrobe, you'll find that Angelenos don't always dress up to eat out, except in the very finest places. As of January 1, 1998, state law forbids smoking in any enclosed public place, including all bars and restaurants. In 1998 some establishments may allow smoking on outdoor patios, but call first to check on the policy.

Restaurants are organized first by city or neighborhood and then by cuisine.

CATEGORY	COST*
$$$$	over $50
$$$	$30–$50
$$	$20–$30
$	under $20

per person for a three-course meal, excluding drinks, service, and 8½% sales tax

Beverly Hills, Hollywood, and West Hollywood

Beverly Hills

AMERICAN

$$$ ✕ **Grill on the Alley.** The tasty, simple American fare at this fashionable spot for power lunching includes great steaks, fresh seafood, chicken potpies, and crab cakes. Repeat customers rave about the creamy Cobb salad and homemade rice pudding. ⊠ *9560 Dayton Way,* ☎ *310/276–0615. Reservations essential. AE, DC, MC, V. Closed Sun. Valet parking in evening.*

CALIFORNIA CUISINE

$$$ ✕ **Dining Room.** Murals depicting 18th-century garden scenes cover
★   the paneled walls of this elegant, European-style salon. Try the loin of Colorado lamb accompanied by eggplant and sweet-pepper lasagna. Adjoining the Dining Room is a sophisticated cocktail lounge, with romantic lighting and a pianist playing show tunes. ⊠ *Regent Beverly Wilshire, 9500 Wilshire Blvd.,* ☎ *310/275–5200. Jacket and tie. AE, D, DC, MC, V. Valet parking.*

\$\$–\$\$\$\$ ✕ **Spago Beverly Hills.** Wolfgang Puck's latest is more formal than the original Spago on Sunset Boulevard. Selections change daily, but look for the warm crawfish salad with mustard potatoes and chino beets, a splendid appetizer. For something different, try a Puck childhood favorite such as *rindsgulasch mit spatzle,* a pleasing Austrian beef stew made with sweet onions and served on a bed of Austrian pasta. Don't miss the sorbet soup for dessert. Puck's famous pizzas are also here. ⊠ *176 N. Cañon Dr.,* ☎ *310/385–0880. Reservations essential. AE, D, DC, MC, V.*

\$\$ ✕ **Jackson's Farm.** Looking more like a French farmhouse than an uptown Beverly Hills eatery, Jackson's has some of L.A.'s best down-home cooking. The comforting menu includes white corn soup, crab cakes with lemon caper tartar sauce, and rotisserie chicken with garlic mashed potatoes and spinach. ⊠ *439 N. Beverly Dr.,* ☎ *310/273–5578. AE, DC, MC, V. Parking across from restaurant.*

\$ ✕ **California Pizza Kitchen.** This is the original location of the now popular nationwide chain. The esoteric choice of pizza toppings ranges from kung-pao chicken to bacon, lettuce, and tomato. ⊠ *207 S. Beverly Dr.,* ☎ *310/275–1101. Reservations not accepted. AE, D, DC, MC, V. Free parking in lot.*

CHINESE

\$–\$\$ ✕ **The Mandarin.** The serene, traditional Mandarin serves Szechuan and Chinese country dishes. Minced chicken in lettuce-leaf tacos, Peking duck (order ahead of time), a superb beggar's chicken, scallion pancakes, and any of the noodle dishes are recommended. ⊠ *430 N. Camden Dr.,* ☎ *310/859–0926. Reservations essential. AE, DC, MC, V. No lunch weekends. Valet parking evenings.*

DELI

\$\$ ✕ **Barney Greengrass.** The delicious high-concept deli fare at the
★   eatery inside the Barneys department store includes such items as Portobello mushrooms, roasted peppers, and arugula on sourdough. Expect flawless smoked salmon, sturgeon, and cod—with or without bagels, flown in fresh from the Big Apple. ⊠ *9570 Wilshire Blvd.,* ☎ *310/ 777–5877. AE, MC, V. Valet parking.*

\$ ✕ **Nate 'n' Al's.** A famous gathering place for Hollywood comedians, gag writers, and their agents, Nate 'n' Al's serves first-rate matzo-ball soup, lox and scrambled eggs, cheese blintzes, potato pancakes, and the best deli sandwiches west of Manhattan. ⊠ *414 N. Beverly Dr.,* ☎ *310/ 274–0101. Reservations not accepted. AE, MC, V. Free parking.*

ITALIAN

\$–\$\$ ✕ **Il Fornaio Cucina Italiana.** Crispy roasted duck, herb-basted chickens, juicy rabbit, pizzas, and calzones are on the menu at this fine trattoria. The thick porterhouse steak alla Florentina at \$17.95 is the best beef buy around; another top choice is pasta stuffed with lobster, ricotta, and leeks, served with a lemon cream sauce. Sunday brunch is terrific. ⊠ *301 N. Beverly Dr.,* ☎ *310/550–8330. AE, D, DC, MC, V. Valet parking.*

KOREAN

\$\$ ✕ **Woo Lae Oak.** With the arrival of this marble-clad, high-ceilinged Beverly Hills restaurant, Korean food moved into L.A.'s culinary mainstream. Woo Lae Oak is more expensive than many other Korean places, but the food is rich and the flavors irresistible. You cook your own meats and seafood on your tabletop grill, which is great fun. ⊠ *170 N. La Cienega Blvd.,* ☎ *310/652–4187. AE, DC, MC, V. Closed Sun. Valet parking.*

Beverly Hills, Hollywood, and West Hollywood Dining and Lodging

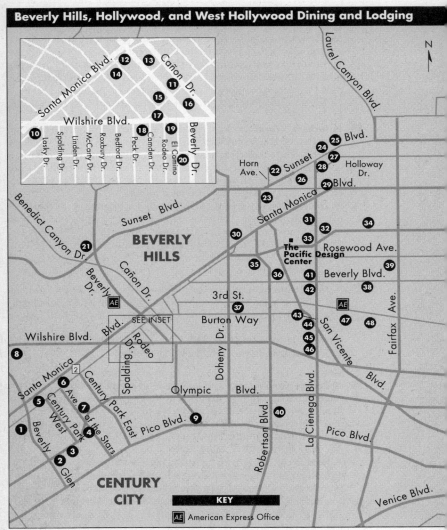

Dining

Arnie Morton's of Chicago, **44**

Authentic Cafe, **67**

Barney Greengrass, **18**

Boxer, **68**

Ca'Brea, **57**

California Pizza Kitchen, **20**

Campanile, **58**

Canter's, **39**

Cava, **47**

Cha Cha Cha, **66**

Chan Dara, **62**

Citrus, **56**

Dining Room, **19**

Dive!, **5**

Drai's **32**

Eclipse, **35**

El Cholo, **63**

Fenix, **27**

Grill on the Alley, **17**

Hard Rock Cafe, **42**

Harry's Bar & American Grill, **7**

Hollywood Canteen, **39**

Il Fornaio Cucina Italiana, **15**

Ita-Cho, **49**

Jackson's Farm, **12**

La Cachette, **1**

Le Chardonnay, **34**

Le Colonial, **36**

Le Dome, **26**

L'Orangerie, **31**

Lunaria, **6**

The Mandarin, **14**

Matsuhisa, **45**

Nate 'n' Al's, **13**

Obachine, **16**

The Palm, **30**

Patina, **59**

Pinot Hollywood, **61**

Restaurant Katsu, **64**

Roscoe's House of Chicken 'n' Waffles, **60**

Sofi, **48**

Spago, **22**

Spago Beverly Hills, **11**

Swingers, **38**

Tavola Calda, **51**

Tommy Tang's, **52**

Trattoria Farfalla, **69**

Vida, **65**

Woo Lae Oak, **46**

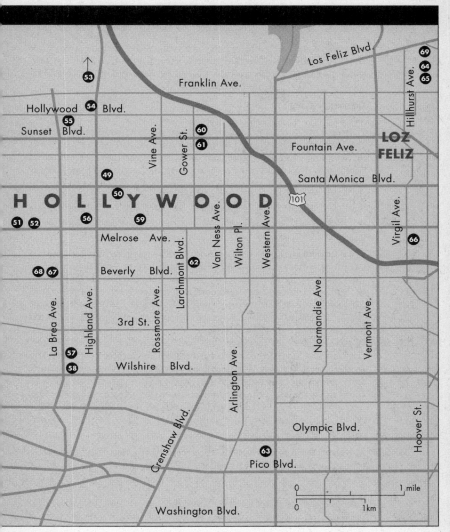

Lodging

The Argyle, **27**

Banana Bungalow Hotel and International Hostel, **53**

Beverly Hills Hotel, **21**

Beverly Hills Plaza Hotel, **8**

Beverly Prescott Hotel, **9**

Carlyle Inn, **40**

Century City Courtyard by Marriott, **3**

Chateau Marmont Hotel, **25**

Clarion Hotel Hollywood Roosevelt, **55**

Four Seasons Los Angeles, **37**

Holiday Inn Express, **2**

Hollywood Holiday Inn, **54**

Hotel Nikko, **43**

Hotel Sofitel Los Angeles, **41**

Hyatt West Hollywood on Sunset Boulevard, **24**

Le Parc Hotel, **33**

Mondrian, **28**

Park Hyatt, **4**

Peninsula Beverly Hills, **10**

Regent Beverly Wilshire, **19**

Summerfield Suites Hotel, **29**

Wyndham Bel Age Hotel, **23**

PACIFIC RIM

$$ ✗ **Obachine.** Wolfgang Puck and Barbara Lazaroff strike again, with pan-Asian food at very reasonable prices, given the high-rent neighborhood and high-profile owners. Interesting dishes include savory crab shui mai dumplings, Cambodian-style shrimp crepes, and salmon-skin salad with *daikon-ponzu* sauce. ✉ *242 N. Beverly Dr.,* ☎ *310/274–4440. AE, MC, V. Valet parking available.*

Century City

AMERICAN

$ ✗ **Dive!** This Steven Spielberg creation is as much a theme park as restaurant. Water gurgles through porthole windows, fish swim by on giant screens, and every now and then the whole place makes a simulated submarine dive. In keeping with the theme, the kitchen's specialty is submarine sandwiches. Good ones include the Parisian chicken sub and the brick oven–baked Tuscan steak sub. The desserts are rich and delicious. ✉ *10250 Santa Monica Blvd.,* ☎ *310/788–3483. Reservations not accepted. AE, D, DC, MC, V. Valet parking or free self-park.*

FRENCH

$$$ ✗ **La Cachette.** Owner-chef Jean-Francois Meteigner replaces butter-★ rich French fare with light and delicious modern French cuisine. L.A.'s fortysomething crowd dresses up (by L.A. standards) to see and be seen at this flower-filled restaurant hidden on an ugly stretch of Little Santa Monica Boulevard. It's worth the trip. ✉ *10506 Little Santa Monica Blvd.,* ☎ *310/470–4992. Reservations essential. AE, MC, V. Closed Sun. No lunch Sat. Valet parking.*

$$–$$$ ✗ **Lunaria.** Bernard Jacoupy, who made Bernard's one of the '80s best restaurants, created this bistro for food lovers and jazz listeners. The fresh Provençal food, with its sunny flavors like tomato and fennel, suits the California crowd. After 8:30 (9:30 on weekends), a wall slides open to reveal the stage and the evening's featured jazz group. There's also an oyster bar. ✉ *10351 Santa Monica Blvd.,* ☎ *310/282–8870. AE, DC, MC, V. Valet parking.*

ITALIAN

$$–$$$ ✗ **Harry's Bar & American Grill.** The decor and selection of dishes—paper-thin carpaccio, grilled fish, and excellent pastas—are acknowledged copies of Harry's Bar in Venice, but the check will be far lower than it would be in Italy. ✉ *2020 Ave. of the Stars,* ☎ *310/277–2333. Reservations essential. AE, DC, MC, V. No lunch weekends. Valet parking.*

Hollywood

AMERICAN

$–$$ ✗ **Hollywood Canteen.** This handsome diner functions as a canteen for the overpaid working stiffs in the neighborhood, including such don't-want-to-be-seen celebs as Bruce Springsteen and a host of TV actors. The food is comforting but not too heavy—try the organic field-green salad, the burger, the risotto with wild mushrooms, or the soups. ✉ *1006 Seward St.,* ☎ *213/465–0961. AE, MC, V. Closed Sun. No lunch Sat. Valet parking.*

$ ✗ **Roscoe's House of Chicken 'n' Waffles.** The name of this casual eatery may not sound appetizing, but don't be fooled: This is *the* place for down-home southern cooking—fried chicken, waffles, and grits at bargain prices. ✉ *1514 N. Gower St.,* ☎ *213/466–9329. Reservations not accepted. AE, D, DC, MC, V.*

CALIFORNIA CUISINE

$$$–$$$$ ✗ **Patina.** Superchef Joachim Splichal does wonders with game, fish, ★ and potato dishes in his much-lauded shrine to Franco-California cuisine. Standouts include Santa Barbara shrimp accompanied by fried leeks and mashed potatoes, lasagna filled with potatoes and forest mushrooms, and partridge baked to perfection. ✉ *5955 Melrose Ave.,* ☎ *213/467–1108. Reservations essential. AE, D, DC, MC, V. No lunch Wed.–Mon. Valet parking.*

$$$
★ ✕ **Citrus.** Chef Michel Richard creates superb dishes by blending French and American cuisines. Don't miss with the delectable tuna burger, the impossibly thin angel-hair pasta, or the deep-fried potatoes, sautéed foie gras, rare duck, or carpaccio salad. For an unusual taste treat, try the chicken in mushroom skin. ✉ *6703 Melrose Ave.,* ☎ *213/857–0034. Jacket required. AE, MC, V. Closed Sun. Valet parking.*

$$$ ✕ **Pinot Hollywood.** The kitchen at this Joachim Splichal eatery turns out delicious mustard chicken, John Dory cooked over an oak-wood grill, and hearty gnocchi mixed with brioche croutons and salty ham hocks. Another winner is pancetta-crowned penne with plump black olives and juicy cherry tomatoes. A more casual venue is the spacious outdoor patio, which serves simple sandwiches and salads—to take out or to eat in. ✉ *1448 N. Gower St.,* ☎ *213/461–8800. Reservations essential. AE, D, DC, MC, V. Valet parking.*

JAPANESE

$ ✕ **Ita-Cho.** Specializing in *koryori-ya,* a pub cuisine that features all sorts of dreamy little cooked dishes, this modest Japanese dining room is a must-visit on any food-lover's tour of L.A. Flawless sashimi is served, but no sushi; memorable dishes include tender pork simmered in sake and soy for two days, light fried tofu cubes in a soy-ginger-scallion sauce, and yellowtail braised with teriyaki. ✉ *6775 Santa Monica Blvd.,* ☎ *213/871–0236. Reservations essential. AE, MC, V. Self parking.*

MEXICAN

$
★ ✕ **El Cholo.** The progenitor of a chain, this landmark just south of Hollywood has been packing them in since the '20s. First-rate L.A.-Mex standards are served here—chicken enchiladas, carnitas, and, from July to October, green-corn tamales. It's friendly and fun, with large portions for a reasonable number of pesos. ✉ *1121 S. Western Ave.,* ☎ *213/734–2773. AE, DC, MC, V. Valet and metered parking.*

THAI

$–$$ ✕ **Chan Dara.** Try any of the noodle dishes, especially those with crab and shrimp, at this rambling restaurant that lures the rock-music and showbiz crowds. Also on the extensive menu are *satay* (appetizers on skewers), barbecued chicken, and catfish. Dine alfresco on the patio or just have dessert there; the mango tart is dreamy. ✉ *310 N. Larchmont Blvd.,* ☎ *213/467–1052. AE, D, DC, MC, V. No lunch weekends.*

Los Feliz

AMERICAN

$–$$ ✕ **Vida.** Heavy on bamboo, skylights, and shoji screens, the tranquil yet compelling decor transforms this 1920s bungalow into a modern 1990s space. Consider the eccentric chef's Cajun Okra Winfrey Creole gumbo or the spicy Ty Cobb salad (duck confit, spinach noodles, egg, tomatoes, and peanuts), which is so artfully made that each piece is cut into a perfect little square. ✉ *1930 N. Hillhurst Ave.,* ☎ *213/660–4446. AE, DC, MC, V. No lunch. Valet parking.*

CARIBBEAN

$–$$ ✕ **Cha Cha Cha.** Off the beaten path, this small, hip restaurant attracts a discerning, eclectic crowd. There's Jamaican jerk chicken, swordfish brochette, fried plantain chips, assorted flans, and fine Sangria. ✉ *656 N. Virgil Ave.,* ☎ *213/664–7723. AE, D, DC, MC, V. Valet parking.*

ITALIAN

$ ✕ **Trattoria Farfalla.** The daily specials at this brick-walled storefront trattoria are always good, but the regulars return for the longtime faves: Caesar salad on a pizza-crust bed; roasted free-range chicken; and pasta alla Norma, studded with rich, smoky eggplant. ✉ *1978 N. Hillhurst Ave.,* ☎ *213/661–7365. AE, DC, MC, V. Street parking.*

JAPANESE

$$$ ✕ **Restaurant Katsu.** A stark, simple, perfectly designed sushi bar with
★ a small table area serves exquisite Japanese delicacies. You can't go wrong when ordering—whether it's the seafood shabu-shabu or the *yadokari nabe* (an assortment of seafood in an abalone shell). ✉ *1972 N. Hillhurst Ave.,* ☎ *213/665–1891. Reservations essential. AE, DC, MC, V. Closed Sun. No lunch Sat. Valet parking.*

West Hollywood

AMERICAN

$$$–$$$$ ✕ **Arnie Morton's of Chicago.** In addition to a 24-ounce porterhouse, a New York strip, and a double-cut filet mignon, there are giant veal and lamb chops, thick cuts of prime rib, swordfish steaks, and imported lobsters at market price. ✉ *435 S. La Cienega Blvd.,* ☎ *310/246–1501. AE, DC, MC, V. No lunch.*

$$$–$$$$ ✕ **The Palm.** This is where you'll find the biggest and best lobsters, good steaks, prime rib, chops, great French-fried onion rings, and paper-thin potato slices. When writers sell a screenplay, they celebrate with a Palm lobster. ✉ *9001 Santa Monica Blvd.,* ☎ *310/550–8811. AE, DC, MC, V. No lunch weekends. Valet parking.*

$$$ ✕ **Campanile.** Portofino meets Hollywood head-on in this high-
★ ceilinged, stone-walled restaurant that was once Charlie Chaplin's office complex. Faves include any of the lamb dishes, like the charred version, marinated in eggplant, roasted onions, and artichokes; crisp flattened chicken with mashed potatoes and garlic confit; and perhaps the best desserts in town—try the inventive rice flan with lime caramel and brandy snaps. Dine in the enclosed courtyard for more intimacy, especially at breakfast, which is an ideal time to try out this au courant brasserie without spending a lot. ✉ *624 S. La Brea Ave.,* ☎ *213/938–1447. Reservations essential. AE, D, DC, MC, V. No lunch weekends. No dinner Sun. Valet parking.*

$–$$ ✕ **Hard Rock Cafe.** Head here for big burgers, rich milk shakes, banana splits, BLTs, and other anti-nouvelle food delights, along with loud music and rock-and-roll memorabilia. ✉ *8600 Beverly Blvd.,* ☎ *310/276–7605. Reservations not accepted. AE, DC, MC, V. Valet parking in Beverly Center.*

$ ✕ **Swingers.** Eat and schmooze at curbside tables or inside the pseudo-diner on the ground floor of a '60s no-frills hotel. A rowdy Gen-Xer crowd listens to loud alternative music while munching on top-quality hot dogs, hamburgers, ostrich burgers, and chicken breast sandwiches on fresh French bread. ✉ *8020 Beverly Blvd.,* ☎ *213/653–5858. AE, D, MC, V. Street parking.*

CALIFORNIA CUISINE

$$$–$$$$ ✕ **Fenix.** Dine in art deco splendor on chef Ken Frank's renowned rösti potatoes with golden caviar; other signature dishes include spinach soup with Maine lobster, porcini-dusted scallops with a tomato-saffron sauce, and filet mignon with red wine, shallots, and bone marrow. You may spot some Asian influences, like the honey duck salad with mango and seared foie gras, on the Franco-Californian menu. The tasting menu is recommended if you can't make up your mind. Sunday dining is restricted to poolside. ✉ *The Argyle, 8358 Sunset Blvd.,* ☎ *213/848–6677. Reservations essential. AE, D, DC, MC, V. Valet parking.*

$$–$$$ ✕ **Eclipse.** Chef Serge Falesitch injects just a hint of Provence into his
★ memorable California-Mediterranean fare in dishes like salmon in
parchment with fresh herbs. Fresh seafood is another highlight, flash
grilled or roasted in fruit-wood-burning ovens. Who wouldn't want
to savor at least one meal in this light and airy in-spot (created by Lambert Monet, Claude's grandson) with its high-beamed ceilings and
outdoor brick patio's picture-perfect garden setting? ✉ *8800 Melrose
Ave.,* ☎ *310/724–5959. Reservations essential. AE, D, DC, MC, V.
No lunch. Valet parking.*

$$–$$$ ✕ **Spago.** This is the restaurant that propelled chef-owner Wolfgang
Puck into the international culinary spotlight. Among the standouts
are his roasted cumin lamb on lentil salad with fresh coriander and
yogurt chutney, fresh oysters with green chili and black pepper
mignonette, grilled free-range chickens, and grilled Alaskan baby
salmon. ✉ *1114 Horn Ave.,* ☎ *310/652–4025. Reservations essential. D, DC, MC, V. No lunch. Valet parking.*

$$ ✕ **Boxer.** The voices of high-energy hipsters reverberate off the con-
crete floors and bare walls of this little storefront, currently a required
stop on the food-lover's map of L.A. Young chef Neil Fraser knows
what modern Angelenos want: a wonderful roasted garlic spread in-
stead of butter; rich roasted vegetable soups made with no cream or
butter; smoked salmon on a potato pancake; and caveman lamb shanks,
stained dark with slow cooking in red wine. ✉ *7615 Beverly Blvd.,*
☎ *213/932–6178. AE, MC, V. Valet parking available.*

DELI

$ ✕ **Canter's.** Ex–New Yorkers claim that this granddaddy of deli-
catessens (it opened in 1928) is the closest in atmosphere, smell, and
menu to a Big Apple corned-beef and pastrami hangout. It's open 24
hours a day. ✉ *419 N. Fairfax Ave.,* ☎ *213/651–2030. MC, V. Valet
parking.*

FRENCH

$$$$ ✕ **L'Orangerie.** For sheer elegance and classic good taste, it's hard to
★ find a lovelier restaurant in the country. The cuisine is French Mediter-
ranean—reminiscent of the menu at L'Orangerie in Versailles. Specialties
include coddled eggs served in the shell and topped with caviar, duck
with foie gras, John Dory with roasted figs, rack of lamb for two, and
an unbeatable apple tart served with a jug of double cream. ✉ *903 N.
La Cienega Blvd.,* ☎ *310/652–9770. Reservations essential. Jacket and
tie. AE, D, DC, MC, V. Closed Mon. No lunch. Valet parking.*

$$$–$$$$ ✕ **Drai's.** At Victor Drai's see-and-be-seen restaurant, the plastic
surgery on display is as skillful as chef Claude Segal's Mediterranean-
influenced French bistro fare. Consider the leg of lamb, cooked for seven
hours, or such standards as osso buco, pot-au-feu, and beef bour-
guignonne. One caveat: Expect lots of attitude from the fashionable
crowd and the waiters. ✉ *730 N. La Cienega Blvd.,* ☎ *310/358–8585.
Valet parking.*

$$$ ✕ **Le Dome.** The food here is honest, down-to-earth French: cockles
in white wine and shallots; veal ragout; veal tortellini with prosciutto,
sun-dried tomatoes, peas, and Parmesan sauce; and a genuine, stick-
to-the-ribs cassoulet. ✉ *8720 Sunset Blvd.,* ☎ *310/659–6919. Reservations essential. AE, MC, V. Closed Sun. No lunch Sat. Valet parking.*

$$–$$$ ✕ **Le Chardonnay.** Despite the high noise level, the cozy booths of this
restaurant with an art nouveau interior make it a good spot for a romantic rendezvous. Specialties include warm sweetbread salad, goat-
cheese ravioli, roast venison, grilled fish, Peking duck with a ginger and
honey sauce, and lush desserts. ✉ *8284 Melrose Ave.,* ☎ *213/655–
8880. Reservations essential. AE, D, DC, MC, V. Closed Sun.–Mon.
Valet parking.*

GREEK

$ ✗ **Sofi.** Hidden down a narrow passageway is this friendly little taverna that makes you feel like you've been transported straight to Mykonos. The food is authentic Greek cuisine: *dolmades* (stuffed grape leaves), lamb gyros, a sampling of traditional salads, phyllo pies, spanakopita, baby salmon with mushrooms, and souvlaki. ⌧ *8030¼ W. 3rd St.,* ☎ *213/651–0346. AE, D, DC, MC, V. No lunch Sun.*

ITALIAN

$$ ✗ **Ca'Brea.** The divine fare here is designed by Antonio Tommasi, for-
★ merly at Locanda Veneta. Try the roast leg of lamb with black truffle and mustard sauce, whole boneless chicken marinated and grilled with herbs, and the oh-so-popular osso buco. Starters make the meal: baked goat cheese wrapped in pancetta and served atop a Popeye-size mound of spinach. ⌧ *346 S. La Brea Ave.,* ☎ *213/938–2863. AE, D, DC, MC, V. Closed Sun. No lunch weekends.*

$ ✗ **Tavola Calda.** This low-tech Italian nirvana draws the budget-watching crowd, who are attracted to the inexpensive entrées that are all under $10. Best bets on the limited menu are the unusual gourmet pizzas, like the vegetarian pie that doesn't include cheese, and risotto that's reminiscent of Milan. ⌧ *7371 Melrose Ave.,* ☎ *213/658–6340. AE, DC, MC, V. Valet parking.*

JAPANESE

$$$–$$$$ ✗ **Matsuhisa.** Chef Nobu Matsuhisa creatively incorporates flavors
★ he discovered while journeying through Peru into his signature dishes. Consider his caviar-capped tuna stuffed with black truffles or the sea urchin wrapped in a *shiso* leaf. Tempuras are lighter than usual here, and the sushi is top-notch, very fresh and authentic. ⌧ *129 N. La Cienega Blvd.,* ☎ *310/659–9639. Reservations essential. AE, DC, MC, V. Valet parking.*

SOUTHWESTERN

$ ✗ **Authentic Cafe.** Think southwestern food has peaked? Then head to this way hip, way fun café for Santa Fe salad, wood-grilled chicken with mole, chicken casserole with corn-bread crust, and excellent vegetarian dishes. ⌧ *7605 Beverly Blvd.,* ☎ *213/939–4626. No reservations. MC, V. Self parking on street.*

SPANISH

$$–$$$ ✗ **Cava.** At this trendy establishment you can graze on tapas—tiny snacks such as baked artichoke topped with bread crumbs and tomato or a fluffy potato omelet served with crème fraîche—or feast on bigger entrées: The paella is a must, but you may also want to try *zarzuela* (lightly baked shrimp, scallops, clams, mussels, and fresh fish in a hearty tomato wine sauce) or *bistec flamenco* (aged New York steak with caramelized onions and a traditional Argentine steak sauce). ⌧ *Beverly Plaza Hotel, 8384 W. 3rd St.,* ☎ *213/658–8898. AE, D, DC, MC, V. Valet parking.*

THAI

$–$$ ✗ **Tommy Tang's.** A lot of people-watching goes on at this grazing ground for yuppies and celebs. Although portions are on the small side, they are decidedly innovative. The kitchen turns out a crisp duck marinated in ginger and plum sauce, blackened sea scallops, and a low-calorie spinach salad tossed with grilled chicken. ⌧ *7313 Melrose Ave.,* ☎ *213/937–5733. AE, DC, MC, V. Valet parking.*

VIETNAMESE

$–$$ ✗ **Le Colonial.** A bright blue neon sign beckons beautiful people to this restaurant right out of prewar Saigon. The seductive-looking dining room serves authentic dishes like chili-flavored sea bass wrapped in banana leaves, roasted chicken with lemongrass, fried spring rolls packed with pork, mushrooms, and shrimp, and shredded chicken and cabbage doused in lime juice. ⊠ *8783 Beverly Blvd.,* ☎ *310/289–0660. AE, DC, MC, V. No lunch Sun. Valet parking.*

Coastal and West Los Angeles

Bel-Air

CALIFORNIA CUISINE

$$$–$$$$ ✕ **Hotel Bel-Air.** At this most elegant of restaurants, first-rate ingredi-
★ ents are used to create fanciful French-Californian dishes. Standouts include whitefish with an onion crust, garlic potatoes, and a chardonnay-chive sauce; fillet of Angus beef with a Stilton cheese-claret sauce; and, for dessert, the chocolate "gazebo at swan lake" mousse cake. This is a great place to propose marriage or a merger. ⊠ *701 Stone Canyon Rd.,* ☎ *310/472–1211. Reservations essential. Jacket and tie. AE, DC, MC, V. Valet parking.*

Malibu

CALIFORNIA CUISINE

$$–$$$ ✕ **Granita.** At Wolfgang Puck's beachside Granita, the menu favors
★ seafood items such as grilled Atlantic salmon in lemongrass broth with seared carrots and wild mushrooms. But standard Puck favorites are also available: spicy shrimp pizza with sun-dried tomatoes and herb pesto, roasted Chinese duck with dried fruit chutney, seared foie gras with caramelized walnuts and a blood-orange port-wine glaze, and Caesar salad with oven-baked bruschetta. ⊠ *23725 W. Malibu Rd.,* ☎ *310/ 456–0488. Reservations essential. D, DC, MC, V. No lunch Mon.– Tues.*

ITALIAN

$–$$ ✕ **Tra di Noi.** Regular customers—film celebrities and nonshowbiz folk alike—love the unpretentious atmosphere of this simple restaurant that's a great place to bring kids. Nothing fancy or *nuovo* on the menu, just great lasagna, freshly made pasta, mushroom and veal dishes, and crisp fresh salads. An Italian buffet is laid out for Sunday brunch. ⊠ *3835 Cross Creek Rd.,* ☎ *310/456–0169. AE, MC, V.*

Pacific Palisades

AMERICAN

$ ✕ **Gladstone's 4 Fish.** This is the most popular restaurant along the southern California coast, serving more than a million beachgoers every year. The food is notable mostly for its Brobdingnagian portions: giant bowls of crab chowder, mounds of steamed clams, three-egg omelets, heaps of barbecued ribs, and the famous mile-high chocolate cake, which can easily feed a small regiment. The real reason to visit Gladstone's is the glorious vista of sea, sky, and beach. ⊠ *17300 Pacific Coast Hwy., at Sunset Blvd.,* ☎ *310/454–3474. AE, D, DC, MC, V. Valet parking.*

Santa Monica

AMERICAN

$$ ✕ **Ocean Avenue.** Daily specials and oyster-bar offerings are always a good choice at this restaurant across the street from the Pacific Ocean. Or try the cioppino, a fish stew made with Dungeness crab, clams, mussels, and prawns, or the kasu-marinated Chilean sea bass. ⊠ *1401 Ocean Ave.,* ☎ *310/394–5669. AE, DC, MC, V. Valet parking.*

$–$$ ✕ **Broadway Deli.** This joint venture of Michel Richard and Bruce
★ Marder is a cross between a European brasserie and an upscale diner. Whatever you feel like eating, you'll probably find it on the menu—a platter of assorted smoked fish or Caesar salad, shepherd's pie, carpac-

Dining

Bombay Cafe, **37**
Border Grill, **7**
Broadway Deli, **6**
Chinois on Main, **13**
Drago, **36**
Gilliland's, **14**
Gladstone's 4 Fish, **1**
Granita, **3**
JiRaffe, **30**
La Serenata
Gourmet, **31**
Hotel Bel-Air, **39**
Ocean Avenue, **5**
Remi, **10**
Tra di Noi, **2**
U-Zen, **38**
Valentino, **12**

Lodging

Airport
Marina Resort
Hotel & Tower, **22**
Barnabey's Hotel, **29**
Best Western Ocean
View Hotel, **4**
Best Western Royal
Palace Inn &
Suites, **32**
Century Wilshire
Hotel, **34**
Crowne Plaza
Redondo Beach &
Marina Hotel, **28**
Holiday Inn LAX, **24**
Hotel Bel-Air, **39**
Hotel Oceana, **15**
Loews Santa Monica
Beach Hotel, **8**
Marina Beach Airport
Marriott, **18**
Marina del
Rey Hotel, **21**
Marina International
Hotel and
Bungalows, **19**
Marina Pacific Hotel &
Suites, **16**
Miramar Sheraton, **9**
Pacific Shore, **17**
Red Lion Los Angeles
Airport, **26**
Ritz-Carlton, Marina
del Rey, **20**
Sheraton Gateway
Hotel at LAX, **27**
Shutters on
the Beach, **11**
Summit Hotel
Bel-Air, **35**
Westin LAX, **23**
Westwood Marquis
Hotel and Gardens, **33**
Wyndham Hotel at Los
Angeles Airport, **25**

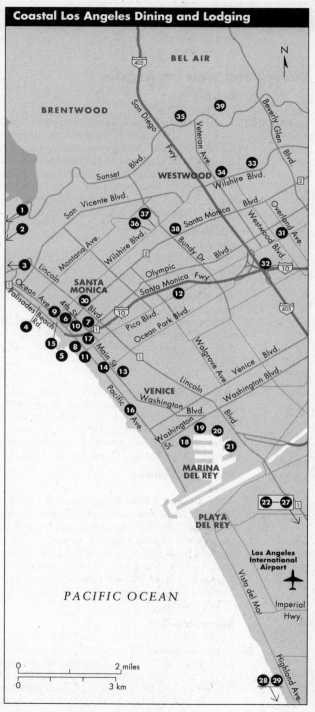

Coastal Los Angeles Dining and Lodging

cio, or broiled salmon with creamed spinach. ⊠ *1457 3rd St. Promenade,* ☎ *310/451–0616. Reservations not accepted. AE, MC, V. Valet parking weekends and evenings.*

CALIFORNIA CUISINE

$$ ✕ **Gilliland's.** Chef Gerri Gilliland prepares light, California-influenced renditions of classics from her homeland, Ireland: soda bread, Irish stew, roast stuffed pork loin, and bread pudding. In deference to the beach setting, she also makes a few good salads and spa dishes. ⊠ *2424 Main St.,* ☎ *310/392–3901. AE, D, DC, MC, V.*

$$ ✕ **JiRaffe.** The two owner-chefs may seem like young surfer dudes, but a meal here will attest to their rigorous French training and considerable skills. The flavors are pungent and sunny, plucked from the Mediterranean and right at home in Santa Monica. Try the peppery creamless carrot soup, the chopped salad of frisee, mushrooms, Parmesan, and croutons, or the sweet potato agnolotti with rock shrimp and lobster jus. For dessert, try the apple tart with a soupy caramel sauce. ⊠ *502 Santa Monica Blvd.,* ☎ *310/917–6671. Reservations essential. AE, DC, MC, V. Closed Mon. No lunch weekends. Valet parking.*

ITALIAN

$$$–$$$$ ✕ **Valentino.** Rated among the nation's best Italian restaurants, Valentino
★ is also generally considered to have the best wine list outside Western Europe. Try the superb prosciutto, fried calamari, lobster cannelloni, fresh broiled porcini mushrooms, and osso buco. For a true Valentino experience, order from the lengthy list of daily specials. ⊠ *3115 Pico Blvd.,* ☎ *310/829–4313. Reservations essential. AE, DC, MC, V. Closed Sun. Valet parking.*

$$$ ✕ **Drago.** Authentic Sicilian fare is hard to come by in the City of An-
★ gels, but affable Celestino Drago's culinary outpost makes up for this oversight. Sample his unforgettable pappardelle (wide noodles) with pheasant and morel mushroom ragout or ostrich breast with red cherry sauce. Not-to-be-missed: savory pumpkin soup accompanied by chestnut gnocchi. ⊠ *2628 Wilshire Blvd.,* ☎ *310/828–1585. AE, DC, MC, V. Valet parking.*

$$ ✕ **Remi.** A few of the best dishes at this swank Third Street Promenade trattoria include the linguine with scallops, mussels, shrimp, and fresh chopped tomatoes; the whole-wheat crepes with ricotta and spinach, topped with a tomato, carrot, and celery sauce; and the roasted pork chop stuffed with smoked mozzarella and prosciutto. ⊠ *1451 3rd St. Promenade,* ☎ *310/393–6545. Reservations essential. AE, DC, MC, V. Parking in nearby multistory mall parking lots.*

MEXICAN

$–$$ ✕ **Border Grill.** Hipsters love this loud and trendy eating hall owned
★ by the talented team of Mary Sue Milliken and Susan Feniger. The duo's menu ranges from grilled tandoori skirt steak marinated in garlic and cilantro to Yucatán seafood tacos to pepper-grilled turkey to daily seviche specials. ⊠ *1445 4th St.,* ☎ *310/451–1655. AE, D, DC, MC, V. No lunch.*

PACIFIC RIM

$$$ ✕ **Chinois on Main.** An older establishment in Wolfgang Puck's pack
★ of restaurants, this is still one of L.A.'s most crowded spots—and one of the noisiest. Both the Asian look of the place and Puck's merging of Asian and French cuisines are great fun. The seasonal menu includes dishes like grilled Mongolian lamb chops with cilantro vinaigrette and wok-fried vegetables, Shanghai lobster with spicy ginger curry sauce, and rare duck with plum sauce. ⊠ *2709 Main St., Santa Monica,* ☎ *310/392–9025. Reservations essential. AE, D, DC, MC, V. No lunch Sat.–Tues. Valet parking.*

West Los Angeles
INDIAN

$ ✕ **Bombay Cafe.** If another meal of tandoori chicken sounds dull, head
to this lively minimall café, where you'll discover the wonderful tastes
of Indian street food. Regulars return here for the chili-laden lamb
frankies (sausages), the various chutneys, the *sev puri* (little chips
topped with onions, potatoes, and chutneys), and lots of other vibrant
small dishes. ⊠ *12113 Santa Monica Blvd.,* ☎ *310/820–2070. MC,
V. Closed Mon. No lunch weekends.*

JAPANESE

$–$$ ✕ **U-Zen.** This highly regarded Japanese café offers the freshest sushi
and sashimi, a good collection of sakes, and pub food such as fried
spicy tofu and salmon-skin salad. Prices are modest, unless you get carried away with the sushi and sashimi, which is entirely possible. ⊠ *11951
Santa Monica Blvd.,* ☎ *310/477–1390. Reservations not accepted. MC,
V. No lunch weekends. Self parking.*

MEXICAN

$ ✕ **La Serenata Gourmet.** It lacks the grace and charm of its East L.A.
parent, La Serenata de Garibaldi, and the crowding can be uncom-
fortable, but this Westsider earns points for its authentic, deeply flavorful Mexican cooking. Although the moles and pork dishes are
delicious, the seafood is star here. ⊠ *10924 W. Pico Blvd.,* ☎ *310/
441–9667. Reservations not accepted. AE, D, MC, V. Closed Mon.
Street parking.*

Downtown

AMERICAN

$$$ ✕ **Nicola.** The largely American menu at this futuristic-looking restau-
rant is touched by a bit of ethnicity. Consider broiled Chilean sea bass
with caramelized orange and ginger potatoes, roasted prime rib of pork
with tomatillo sauce and corn succotash, or Mediterranean chicken with
tabbouleh and Lebanese fried potatoes. A kiosk in the courtyard op-
erated by Nicola is frequented by area workers looking for a quick and
tasty bite. ⊠ *Sanwa Bank Bldg., 601 S. Figueroa St.,* ☎ *213/485–0927.
AE, D, DC, MC, V. Closed Sun. No lunch Sat. Valet parking.*

$$–$$$ ✕ **Water Grill.** As the name suggests, seafood is the be-all and end-all
at this handsome, somewhat noisy brasserie. The oyster bar—stocked
with every cold-water variety imaginable and all sorts of other cold
shellfish—alone is worth a trip. Avoid the pastas and complicated
dishes here and stick with fresh fish and American wines. ⊠ *544 S.
Grand Ave.,* ☎ *213/891–0900. Reservations essential. AE, DC, MC,
V. No lunch weekends. Valet parking next door.*

$ ✕ **Philippe's the Original.** This downtown landmark near Union Sta-
★ tion and Chinatown has been serving its famous French dip sandwich
(four kinds of meat on a freshly baked roll) since 1908. The home cook-
ing includes potato salad, coleslaw, hearty breakfasts, and an enormous
pie selection brought in fresh daily from a nearby bakery. The best bar-
gain: a cup of java for only 10¢. ⊠ *1001 N. Alameda St.,* ☎ *213/628–
3781. Reservations not accepted. No credit cards.*

CALIFORNIA CUISINE

$$$ ✕ **Checkers.** As serene and elegant as any luxury hotel dining room
(*and* a lot less stuffy), this is a good place to talk business or romance.
Breakfasts feature such American standards as apple waffles and
smoked salmon with bagels and cream cheese. Things get a more inventive at lunch and dinner. French techniques are combined with robust Mediterranean flavors and Asian touches. Don't miss the crab cakes
with pancetta and lentil coleslaw or the buttery pork tenderloin on a

Downtown Los Angeles Dining and Lodging

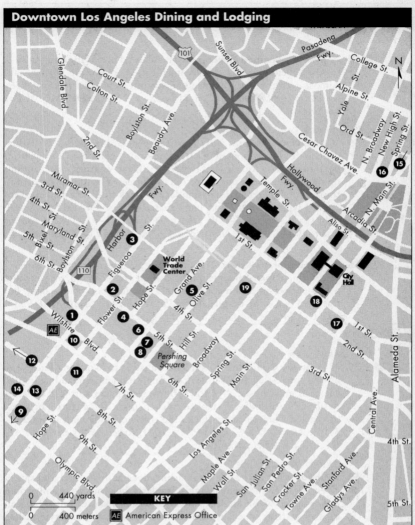

Dining

Cafe Pinot, **4**
Checkers, **6**
Mon Kee Seafood Restaurant, **16**
Nicola, **1**
Philippe's the Original, **15**
Restaurant Horikawa, **17**
Water Grill, **8**

Lodging

Figueroa Hotel and Convention Center, **14**
Holiday Inn L.A. Downtown, **12**
Hotel Inter-Continental Los Angeles, **5**
Hyatt Regency Los Angeles, **11**
Inn at 657, **9**
The InnTowne, **13**

Kawada Hotel, **19**
New Otani Hotel and Garden, **18**
Omni Los Angeles, Hotel and Centre, **10**
Regal Biltmore Hotel, **7**
Sheraton Grande Hotel, **3**
Westin Bonaventure Hotel & Suites, **2**
Wyndham Checkers Hotel, **6**

bed of white beans. ⊠ *535 S. Grand Ave.,* ☎ *213/624–0000. AE, DC, MC, V. Valet parking.*

CHINESE

$–$$ ✕ **Mon Kee Seafood Restaurant.** The seafood here is morning fresh—try the delicious garlic crab, steamed catfish, or shrimp in spicy salt. Almost everything on the menu at this often crowded place is excellent. ⊠ *679 N. Spring St.,* ☎ *213/628–6717. AE, DC, MC, V. Pay parking lot.*

FRENCH

$$ ✕ **Cafe Pinot.** Joachim and Christine Splichal, proprietors of Patina,
★ opened this eatery housed in a contemporary "glass box" on the front lawn of the Los Angeles Public Library. If the weather's fine, eat out on the terrace under one of the old olive trees. The menu is rooted in the traditional French bistro standards—steak frites, roast chicken encrusted with five mustards, lamb shank—but you'll also find superb light spa dishes. ⊠ *700 W. 5th St.,* ☎ *213/239–6500. Reservations essential. DC, MC, V. No lunch Fri.–Sat. Self and valet parking.*

JAPANESE

$$–$$$ ✕ **Restaurant Horikawa.** The menu here includes something for everyone: sushi, teppan steak, tempura, sashimi, shabu-shabu, teriyaki, and a $75-per-person seven-course dinner. All are good or excellent, but the sushi bar is the best. ⊠ *111 S. San Pedro St.,* ☎ *213/680–9355. AE, DC, MC, V. No lunch Sat. Valet parking.*

Pasadena

AMERICAN

$$–$$$ ✕ **Parkway Grill.** This is Pasadena's answer to Wolfgang Puck. The always-interesting dishes draw from many influences including Italian, Mexican, and Chinese. A typical Parkway meal might start with a roasted *pasilla* chili stuffed with smoked chicken, corn, and cilantro, progress to roasted Chinese crispy duck, and then conclude with s'mores. ⊠ *510 S. Arroyo Pkwy.,* ☎ *626/795–1001. Reservations essential. AE, DC, MC, V. Valet parking.*

CALIFORNIA CUISINE

$$ ✕ **Shiro.** What chef Hideo Yamashiro does with seafood and sauces
★ is remarkable. The menu changes regularly, but you can usually count on his famed whole sizzling catfish with *ponzu* sauce; sweet, fat scallops in saffron sauce; various sashimi salads; French-style grilled chicken with mustard sauce; and dreamy berry crème brûlées. ⊠ *1505 Mission St.,* ☎ *626/799–4774. Reservations essential. AE, DC, MC, V. Closed Mon. Self parking.*

CHINESE

$$–$$$ ✕ **Yujean Kang's Gourmet Chinese Cuisine.** Mr. Kang is one of the finest
★ nouvelle Chinese chefs in the nation. Start with tender slices of veal on a bed of enoki mushrooms topped with a tangle of quick-fried shoestring yams, or sea bass with kumquats and passion-fruit sauce. To finish, try poached plums or watermelon ice under a mantle of white chocolate. ⊠ *67 N. Raymond Ave.,* ☎ *626/585–0855. AE, D, DC, MC, V.*

FRENCH

$$$ ✕ **Bistro 45.** As stylish and sophisticated as any Westside hot spot, Bistro 45 blends rustic French comfort food—cassoulet, bouillabaisse, caramelized apple tarts—with more modern and fanciful California hybrids, like seared *ahi* with pickled vegetables and pomegranate dressing. ⊠ *45 S. Mentor Ave.,* ☎ *626/795–2478. Reservations essential. AE, MC, V. Closed Mon., except for wine-maker dinner 1st Mon. of month. Valet parking.*

$–$$ ✕ **Twin Palms.** Chef Michael Roberts's Provençal cooking keeps spir-
★ its high. His garlic-rich, feel-good food—fish soup, Portobello sandwich with pistou, succulent chicken cooked over a huge
rotisserie—perfectly suits such a profoundly Californian setting. ✉ *101
W. Green St.,* ☎ *626/577–2567. AE, DC, MC, V. Valet parking.*

THAI

$–$$ ✕ **Saladang.** Although Saladang is off the beaten track—several blocks
south of Old Pasadena—once word got out about the spinach and duck
salad, seafood soup, rice noodles with basil and bean sprouts, and beef
panang, there hasn't been an empty seat in the house. ✉ *363 S. Fair
Oaks Blvd.,* ☎ *626/793–8123. Reservations essential. AE, DC, MC,
V. Free parking in lot.*

San Fernando Valley

North Hollywood
ITALIAN

$$ ✕ **Ca'del Sole.** Start with fresh rock shrimp sautéed in a spicy garlic
★ and tomato sauce or citrus-marinated chicken wings braised with Ital-
ian bacon, rosemary, and sage. Next follow with a radicchio and
arugula salad tossed in a creamy Venetian dressing. Also recommended
is the linguine with scallops and Manila clams generously doused with
a garlic, olive oil, and white wine mixture. ✉ *4100 Cahuenga Blvd.,*
☎ *818/985–4669. Reservations essential. AE, DC, MC, V. No lunch
Sat. Valet parking.*

Sherman Oaks
CALIFORNIA CUISINE

$$ ✕ **Cafe Bizou.** If you can manage a reservation, which is not impossi-
★ ble, especially on weekdays, look forward to fine California-French bistro
fare at bargain prices. Fish dishes, such as sesame-seed-coated salmon
on potato pancake triangles, are prominent menu items. For dessert,
try the tasty caramelized tart Tatin. Wine lovers adore the mere $2 cork-
age. ✉ *14016 Ventura Blvd.,* ☎ *818/788–3536. Reservations essential. AE, MC, V. BYOB. No lunch weekends. Valet parking.*

$$ ✕ **JoeJoe's.** This is American cooking for the next century: meaty grilled
shiitakes with smoked mozzarella, roasted peppers, and a red onion salad;
smoky grilled shrimp on creamy saffron risotto with a delicate crown
of fried carrots; juicy roast beef with tangy balsamic sauce, buttery
mashed potatoes, and spinach. ✉ *13355 Ventura Blvd.,* ☎ *818/990–
8280. Reservations essential. AE, MC, V. Closed Mon. Valet available.*

ITALIAN

$$–$$$ ✕ **Posto.** Thanks to owner Piero Selvaggio, Valley residents no longer
have to drive to the Westside for good modern Italian cuisine. His chef
makes a tissue-thin pizza topped with flavorful ingredients, and the
chicken, duck, and veal sausages are made each morning, as are the
different herb breads. Other good choices include risotto with porcini
mushrooms and the veal saltimbocca with sage and prosciutto. If you
have room after all that, the desserts are delicious—try the pumpkin
cheesecake. ✉ *14928 Ventura Blvd.,* ☎ *818/784–4400. AE, D, DC,
MC, V. No lunch weekends.*

Studio City
DELI

$ ✕ **Art's Delicatessen.** One of the best Jewish-style delicatessens in the
★ city serves mammoth corned beef and pastrami sandwiches. Matzo-
ball soup and sweet-and-sour cabbage soup are specialties, and the
chopped chicken liver is delicious. ✉ *12224 Ventura Blvd.,* ☎ *818/
762–1221. Reservations not accepted. AE, D, DC, MC, V.*

FRENCH

$$–$$$ ✕ **Pinot Bistro.** Offerings at this Joachim Splichal bistro include fresh oysters, country pâtés, bouillabaisse, braised tongue and spinach, pot-au-feu, and steak with French fries. The pastry chef specializes in chocolate desserts. ⊠ *12969 Ventura Blvd.,* ☎ *818/990–0500. D, DC, MC, V. No lunch weekends. Valet parking.*

Toluca Lake

AMERICAN

$ ✕ **Paty's.** Near NBC, Warner Bros., and the Disney Studio, this homey coffee shop with eclectic decor is a good, affordable place for stargazing. Breakfasts include plump omelets and homemade biscuits served with high-quality jam. For lunch or dinner you'll find comfort in such hearty dishes as Swiss steak, roast turkey, or beef stew served in a hollowed-out loaf of home-baked bread. ⊠ *10001 Riverside Dr.,,* ☎ *818/761–9126. Weekend reservations not accepted. AE, DC, MC, V.*

LODGING

Revised and updated by Tina Rubin

Because Los Angeles is so spread out, it's good to select a hotel room not only for its ambience, amenities, and price but also for a location that is convenient to where you plan to spend most of your time. Hotels listed below are organized first by location and then by price category.

CATEGORY	COST*
$$$$	over $175
$$$	$120–$175
$$	$80–$120
$	under $80

All prices are for a standard double room, excluding 14% tax.

Beverly Hills, Century City, Hollywood, and West Hollywood

Beverly Hills and Vicinity

$$$$ 🏨 **Beverly Hills Hotel.** Many a Hollywood legend (among them Howard
★   Hughes and Elizabeth Taylor) has passed through the doors of this California landmark. In the 21 bungalows, wood-burning fireplaces, one-of-a-kind furnishings, and yards of marble create a dramatic effect. All accommodations have Ralph Lauren linens, soundproofing, stereos with CD players, and fax machines. ⊠ *9641 Sunset Blvd., 90210,* ☎ *310/ 276–2251,* FAX *310/887–2887. 203 rooms, 21 bungalows. Restaurants, bar, in-room modem lines, in-room safes, kitchenettes, no-smoking rooms, room service, pool, barbershop, beauty salon, hot tubs, massage, private cabanas, tennis court, exercise room, jogging, piano, baby-sitting, laundry service and dry cleaning, concierge, travel services, parking (fee). AE, DC, MC, V.*

$$$$ 🏨 **Beverly Prescott Hotel.** The open-air architecture of this 12-story luxury hotel is enhanced by soothing rooms decorated in warm salmon and caramel tones. Furnishings are stylish, and the rooms are spacious, with private balconies, fax machines, stereo/CD players, irons, hair dryers, and coffeemakers. The management hosts a daily wine hour in the lobby, where a fire often roars in the fireplace. ⊠ *1224 S. Beverwil Dr., 90035,* ☎ *310/277–2800 or 800/421–3212,* FAX *310/203–9537. 138 rooms, 18 suites. Restaurant, bar, minibars, no-smoking rooms, room service, in-room VCRs, pool, massage, exercise room, baby-sitting, laundry service and dry cleaning, concierge, concierge floor, business services, meeting rooms, travel services, car rental, parking (fee). AE, D, DC, MC, V.*

$$$$ 📷 **Four Seasons Los Angeles.** Formal European art and furnishings at
★ this property near Rodeo Drive are complemented by outpourings of
flora from the porte cochere to the fourth-floor pool deck. Spacious,
comfortable guest rooms are eclectic, some done in pastels, others in
black and beige. ✉ *300 S. Doheny Dr., 90048,* ☎ *310/273–2222,* FAX
*310/274–3891. 179 rooms, 106 suites. Restaurant, bar, in-room
modem lines, minibars, no-smoking rooms, room service, pool, spa,
exercise room, baby-sitting, laundry service and dry cleaning, concierge,
business services, meeting rooms, car rental, free parking and parking
(fee). AE, DC, MC, V.*

$$$$ 📷 **Hotel Nikko.** Large guest rooms at this Japanese-style hotel have fax
machines, voice mail, and executive-size desks. Traditional Japanese
soaking tubs dominate luxurious bathrooms, and a bedside remote control conveniently operates in-room lighting, temperature, TV, VCR, and
CD player. ✉ *465 S. La Cienega Blvd., 90048,* ☎ *310/247–0400,* FAX
*310/247–0315. 297 rooms, 10 suites. Restaurant, bar, in-room modem
lines, minibars, no-smoking floors, room service, pool, Japanese baths,
massage, sauna, exercise room, baby-sitting, laundry service and dry
cleaning, concierge, business services, meeting rooms, travel services,
car rental, free parking. AE, D, DC, MC, V.*

$$$$ 📷 **Hotel Sofitel Los Angeles.** This elegant French hotel's terra-cotta and
navy country-French guest rooms have pine furniture and are equipped
with voice mail and hair dryers. Rooms with southern exposure have
views of the Hollywood Hills (ask for one; the back of the property faces
a wall of the Beverly Center). ✉ *8555 Beverly Blvd., 90048,* ☎ *310/
278–5444 or 800/521–7772,* FAX *310/657–2816. 311 rooms. Restaurant, piano bar, in-room modem lines, minibars, no-smoking rooms, room
service, in-room VCRs, pool, sauna, health club, concierge, business services, travel services, car rental, parking (fee). AE, D, DC, MC, V.*

$$$$ 📷 **Peninsula Beverly Hills.** Rooms at this French Renaissance–style hotel
★ resemble luxury apartments, with antiques, rich fabrics, and marble
floors; bathrobes and hair dryers are among the many amenities. Some
suites in the two-story villas have whirlpool tubs, terraces, fireplaces,
and CD players. ✉ *9882 Little Santa Monica Blvd., 90212,* ☎ *310/
551–2888 or 800/462–7899,* FAX *310/788–2319. 195 rooms. 3 restaurants, bar, in-room modem lines, in-room safes, minibars, no-smoking floors, room service, in-room VCRs, pool, massage, sauna, spa, steam
room, health club, shops, baby-sitting, concierge, business services, travel
services, car rental, parking (fee). AE, D, DC, MC, V.*

$$$$ 📷 **Regent Beverly Wilshire.** Rooms in the older (1928) Wilshire wing
★ of this landmark Italian Renaissance–style property are especially
large; those in the Beverly wing (1971) have balconies overlooking the
pool area. ✉ *9500 Wilshire Blvd., 90212,* ☎ *310/275–5200; 800/421–
4354 in the U.S.; 800/427–4354 in CA;* FAX *310/274–2851. 275 rooms,
69 suites. 2 restaurants, bar, lobby lounge, in-room modem lines, in-
room safes, minibars, no-smoking floors, room service, in-room VCRs,
pool, beauty salon, massage, spa, health club, piano, baby-sitting,
children's program (ages 4–12), laundry service and dry cleaning,
concierge, business services, travel services, car rental, parking (fee).
AE, D, DC, MC, V.*

$$$–$$$$ **Beverly Hills Plaza Hotel.** There's a family-style feel to this all-suites
★ hotel where the friendly staff will soon know you by name. All the suites
are off the pool and have a kitchen-living room. Each accommodation
comes equipped with bathrobes, a hair dryer, in-room movies, and Nin-
tendo. ✉ *10300 Wilshire Blvd., 90024,* ☎ *310/275–5575,* FAX *310/
278–3325. 116 suites. Restaurant, bar, in-room modem lines, in-room
safes, kitchenettes, minibars, pool, massage, exercise room, video
games, laundry service and dry cleaning, concierge, business services,
parking (fee). AE, D, DC, MC, V.*

$$ 🏨 **Carlyle Inn.** The contemporary four-story Carlyle provides such extras as a complimentary buffet breakfast in the morning and a glass of wine in the late afternoon. Modern rooms with pine furniture have bathrobes, hair dryers, and turndown service. In a safe neighborhood close to Century City and Beverly Hills, this hotel is especially appealing to women. ✉ *1119 S. Robertson Blvd., 90035,* ☎ *310/275–4445 or 800/322–7595,* FAX *310/859–0496. 32 rooms. Restaurant, in-room modem lines, minibars, no-smoking rooms, room service, in-room VCRs, hot tub, exercise room, laundry service and dry cleaning, business services, travel services, parking (fee). AE, D, DC, MC, V.*

Century City

$$$$ 🏨 **Park Hyatt.** The spacious rooms here are decorated in soft beige tones with upholstered furnishings and plants. Each comes with a fax machine, a voice-mail system, and a coffeemaker. Pleasant touches abound, such as high tea in the lovely Garden Room and the complimentary limousine service within Century City and Beverly Hills. ✉ *2151 Ave. of the Stars, 90067,* ☎ *310/277–1234,* FAX *310/785–9240. 186 rooms, 181 suites. Restaurant, 2 bars, in-room modem lines, minibars, no-smoking rooms, room service, indoor and outdoor pools, hot tub, massage, sauna, steam room, spa, health club, piano, laundry service and dry cleaning, concierge, business services, convention center, meeting rooms, parking (fee). AE, D, DC, MC, V.*

$$$ 🏨 **Century City Courtyard by Marriott.** Near the Century City business complex, this comfortable hotel mixes California architecture with traditional fabrics and furnishings in light hues. Each room comes with a hair dryer, coffeemaker, iron and board, and Nintendo. ✉ *10320 W. Olympic Blvd., 90064,* ☎ *310/556–2777 or 800/321–2211,* FAX *310/ 203–0563. 134 rooms. Restaurant, bar, minibars, no-smoking rooms, room service, hot tub, exercise room, video games, baby-sitting, laundry service and dry cleaning, business services, car rental, free parking. AE, D, DC, MC, V.*

$$ 🏨 **Holiday Inn Express.** This comfortable property has large contemporary rooms. In the bathrooms, whirlpool tubs melt away the day's tensions. The executive suites, designed with lofts, have microwaves, refrigerators, and coffeemakers. A complimentary "breakfast bar" operates from 6:30 to 10:00 AM. ✉ *10330 W. Olympic Blvd., 90064,* ☎ *310/553–1000,* FAX *310/277–1633. 33 rooms, 14 suites. Breakfast room, in-room modem lines, in-room VCRs, meeting room, parking (fee). AE, D, DC, MC, V.*

Hollywood and Vicinity

$$$$ 🏨 **Chateau Marmont Hotel.** Since it opened in 1929, this very private ★ hotel with a French Normandy design has been home to reclusive entertainment industry professionals, writers, and musicians. The 1920s cottages are furnished in mission oak with Frank Lloyd Wright–inspired fabrics; the 1956 bungalows have been restored to architect Craig Ellwood's clean lines and contemporary concept. The trendy Bar Marmont, adjacent to the hotel, has its own kitchen and serves food until 1:30 AM. ✉ *8221 Sunset Blvd., 90046,* ☎ *213/656–1010 or 800/242– 8328,* FAX *213/655–5311. 10 rooms, 53 suites. Bar, dining room, in-room modem lines, in-room safes, minibars, no-smoking rooms, room service, in-room VCRs, pool, massage, exercise room, baby-sitting, laundry service and dry cleaning, concierge, business services, car rental, parking (fee). AE, DC, MC, V.*

$$ 🏨 **Clarion Hotel Hollywood Roosevelt.** The site of the first Academy Awards ceremony has an ornate art deco lobby, its original tile steps, and an elegant courtyard. In addition to the standard rooms, there are 40 Hollywood-theme suites, such as the Gable-Lombard suite or the Shirley Temple suite. ✉ *7000 Hollywood Blvd., 90028,* ☎ *213/466–*

7000 or 800/950–7667, FAX *213/466–9376. 320 rooms, 39 suites. 3 restaurants, bar, lobby lounge, no-smoking rooms, room service, pool, exercise room, nightclub, laundry service, baby-sitting, travel services, car rental, parking (fee). AE, D, DC, MC, V.*

$$ 🖼 **Hollywood Holiday Inn.** You can't miss this 23-story hotel, one of Hollywood's tallest buildings, topped by a revolving restaurant-bar that serves Sunday brunch. Rooms, decorated in standard Holiday Inn floral prints and pastels, have voice mail, hair dryers, and the other usual accoutrements. ⊠ *1755 N. Highland Ave., 90028,* ☎ *213/462–7181,* FAX *213/466–9072. 470 rooms. Restaurant, bar, coffee shop, in-room modem lines, in-room safes, kitchenettes, no-smoking floors, pool, exercise room, video games, baby-sitting, laundry service, business services, travel services, car rental, parking (fee). AE, D, DC, MC, V.*

$ 🖼 **Banana Bungalow Hotel and International Hostel.** You'll get good value for your money at this friendly hostel on 6.8 acres in the Hollywood Hills. Dorm rooms (only for travelers with international passports) are equipped with lockers, and all rooms (some of them private) have fans and are no-smoking. ⊠ *2775 Cahuenga Blvd. W, 90068,* ☎ *213/851–1129 or 800/446–7835,* FAX *213/851–1569. 45 rooms. Restaurant, fans, no-smoking rooms, pool, exercise room, billiards, recreation room, theater, coin laundry, travel services, airport shuttle, car rental, free parking. MC, V.*

West Hollywood

$$$$ 🖼 **The Argyle.** This 15-story landmark dazzles with its ornate gunmetal
★ gray, pink, and burgundy art deco facade. Inside, reproduction objets d'art and paintings grace the public spaces. Sumptuous deco detail characterizes the somewhat smallish guest rooms as well, from the design of the brass door handles to the ebony furniture. Marble bathrooms have black-and-white fixtures. ⊠ *8358 Sunset Blvd., 90069,* ☎ *213/654–7100 or 800/225–2637,* FAX *213/654–1004. 20 rooms, 42 suites, 2 penthouse suites. Restaurant, bar, in-room modem lines, in-room safes, minibars, no-smoking floors, room service, in-room VCRs, pool, sauna, exercise room, laundry service and dry cleaning, concierge, business services, convention center, meeting rooms, travel services, car rental, parking (fee). AE, D, DC, MC, V.*

$$$$ 🖼 **Le Parc Hotel.** The spacious suites at this modern low-rise hotel are decorated in shades of wine and rust, and have sunken living rooms, balconies, fireplaces, microwaves, and coffeemakers. Amenities include fax machines, dataports, hair dryers, irons and boards, stereos with CD players, and even Nintendo. ⊠ *733 N. West Knoll Dr., 90069,* ☎ *310/855–8888 or 800/578–4837,* FAX *310/659–7812. 154 suites. Restaurant, kitchenettes, minibars, no-smoking suites, in-room VCRs, pool, hot tub, sauna, tennis court, basketball, health club, video games, baby-sitting, coin laundry, concierge, business services, travel services, parking (fee). AE, DC, MC, V.*

$$$$ 🖼 **Mondrian.** Hotelmeister Ian Schrager and designer Philippe Starck
★ totally reinvented this 12-story Sunset Strip hotel in 1997. Each apartment-size accommodation has industrial-gray carpeting, floor-to-ceiling windows, slip-covered sofas, marble-top coffee tables, a kitchen with sleek Starck-designed accessories, and smallish bathrooms. Among the myriad comforts are scented candles, flowers, wool lap blankets, bathrobes, vintage movie magazines, a fax machine, and a direct private phone line. ⊠ *8440 Sunset Blvd., 90069,* ☎ *213/650–8999 or 800/525–8029,* FAX *213/650–5215. 245 rooms. Restaurant, 2 bars, outdoor café, picnic area, snack bar, tapas bar, in-room modem lines, kitchenettes, no-smoking rooms, refrigerators, room service, pool, massage, sauna, spa, steam room, health club, laundry service and dry cleaning,*

concierge, business services, meeting rooms, car rental, parking (fee). AE, D, DC, MC, V.

$$$$ ⊞ **Summerfield Suites Hotel.** This four-story all-suites property is in a
★ residential neighborhood off the Sunset Strip. The plush rooms have
private balconies, gas fireplaces, separate vanities, hair dryers, and microwaves. Most rooms have kitchens, and the hotel provides complimentary grocery shopping service. Don't cook breakfast, however;
it's gratis, and served in the café. ⊠ *1000 Westmount Dr., 90069,* ☎
310/657–7400 or 800/833–4353, 𝐅𝐀𝐗 *310/854–6744. 109 suites. Breakfast room, in-room modem lines, no-smoking suites, refrigerators, in-
room VCRs, pool, exercise room, coin laundry, laundry service and
dry cleaning, meeting room, parking (fee). AE, D, DC, MC, V.*

$$$$ ⊞ **Wyndham Bel Age Hotel.** There's a soothing, residential feel at this
★ European-style all-suites hotel that's just off the Sunset Strip. South-
facing rooms have private terraces that look out over the Los Angeles
skyline as far as the Pacific. For a little pampering, make an appointment at the famed Alex Roldan beauty salon or enjoy a meal at the
Diaghilev restaurant, where chef Tony Hodges creates Russian dishes
with French flair. ⊠ *1020 N. San Vicente Blvd., 90069,* ☎ *310/854–
1111 or 800/424–4443,* 𝐅𝐀𝐗 *310/854–0926. 200 suites. 2 restaurants,
bar, in-room modem lines, kitchenettes, no-smoking rooms, room service, pool, beauty salon, exercise room, laundry service and dry cleaning, concierge, travel services, parking (fee). AE, D, DC, MC, V.*

$$$ ⊞ **Hyatt West Hollywood on Sunset Boulevard.** Its proximity to L.A.'s
clubs of the moment (it's across the street from the House of Blues)
makes this Hyatt popular with music-industry types. Rooms, some of
them with aquariums, have a 1930s-retro feel; all have private patios
facing the boulevard. Beside the heated rooftop pool is an outdoor ex-
ercise area. The Silver Screen sports bar–restaurant is a fun spot at night,
and an espresso cart stationed in the lobby can provide your morning
jolt of caffeine. ⊠ *8401 Sunset Blvd., 90069,* ☎ *213/656–1234 or 800/
233–1234,* 𝐅𝐀𝐗 *213/650–7024. 262 rooms, 20 suites. Restaurant,
sports bar, in-room modem lines, no-smoking floors, room service, pool,
exercise room, laundry service, business services, car rental, parking
(fee). AE, D, DC, MC, V.*

Coastal and Western Los Angeles

Airport

*For additional hotels near Los Angeles International Airport (LAX),
see Manhattan Beach, Marina del Rey, and Redondo Beach.*

$$$ ⊞ **Sheraton Gateway Hotel at LAX.** There's plenty to do right in your
room here, with video games, movies, and 24-hour room service (and
coffeemakers to help wake you up if you sleep through the movies).
The hotel also has a currency exchange and a 24-hour airport shuttle.
⊠ *6101 W. Century Blvd., 90045,* ☎ *310/642–1111 or 800/325–3535,*
𝐅𝐀𝐗 *310/410–1852. 804 rooms, 92 suites. 2 restaurants, bar, sushi bar,
in-room modems, minibars, no-smoking rooms, room service, pool,
hot tub, massage, exercise room, video games, laundry service and dry
cleaning, concierge, business services, meeting rooms, travel services,
airport shuttle, car rental, parking (fee). AE, D, DC, MC, V.*

$$$ ⊞ **Westin LAX.** From its expansive, marble-columned lobby to the
★ luxurious guest rooms, the Westin is a good place to stay if you want
to be pampered but also need to be close to the airport. Rooms and
suites are decorated in muted earth tones of creams and tans to com-
plement the contemporary decor; many suites have private outdoor hot
tubs. With 42 meeting rooms, a business center, currency exchange,
and attentive service, the Westin has been recognized as a "Best of the
West" meeting facility. ⊠ *5400 W. Century Blvd., 90045,* ☎ *310/216–*

5858, 𝖥𝖠𝖷 *310/670–1948. 720 rooms, 42 suites. Restaurant, bar, in-room modem lines, minibars, no-smoking rooms, refrigerators, pool, sauna, exercise room, laundry service and dry cleaning, concierge floor, business services, meeting rooms, airport shuttle, car rental, parking (fee). AE, D, DC, MC, V.*

$$–$$$ 🏨 **Doubletree Los Angeles Airport.** A deluxe hotel, the Doubletree has oversize guest rooms with a '90s version of art deco decor and in-room movies, coffeemakers, and irons and boards. Just 3 mi north of LAX and a few minutes from Marina del Rey, the hotel is conveniently located for business travelers. ⊠ *6161 Centinela Ave., Culver City 90231,* ☎ *310/649–1776,* 𝖥𝖠𝖷 *310/649–4411. 368 rooms. Restaurant, bar, coffee shop, no-smoking floors, room service, pool, hot tub, exercise room, nightclub, baby-sitting, laundry service and dry cleaning, concierge, business services, meeting rooms, travel services, airport shuttle, car rental, free parking. AE, D, DC, MC, V.*

$$ 🏨 **Airport Marina Resort Hotel & Tower.** This contemporary hotel, in a quiet, residential area convenient to jogging paths, tennis, and golf, comprises four separate buildings. The large marble lobby is a comfortable place to relax, with writing tables, plants, and cushy sofas. ⊠ *8601 Lincoln Blvd., 90045,* ☎ *310/670–8111,* 𝖥𝖠𝖷 *310/337–1883. 760 rooms, 6 suites. Restaurant, bar, no-smoking rooms, room service, pool, hot tub, sauna, exercise room, laundry service and dry cleaning, business services, meeting rooms, airport shuttle, free parking. AE, D, DC, MC, V.*

$$ 🏨 **Holiday Inn LAX.** This 12-story international-style hotel appeals to families as well as businesspeople, with large rooms decorated in earth tones. Some accommodations are equipped with fax machines, dataports, and coffeemakers. ⊠ *9901 La Cienega Blvd., 90045,* ☎ *310/ 649–5151 or 800/624–0025,* 𝖥𝖠𝖷 *310/670–3619. 403 rooms. Restaurant, bar, pool, exercise room, video games, coin laundry, airport shuttle, parking (fee). AE, D, DC, MC, V.*

$–$$ 🏨 **Wyndham Hotel at Los Angeles Airport.** The rich brown marble in the lobby entrance and dark wood columns give a neoclassical feel to this hotel, though its guest rooms and suites are contemporary. Decorated in greens and yellows, the rooms are small (250 square ft) but have plenty of amenities, such as fax machines, voice mail, and movies. ⊠ *6225 W. Century Blvd., 90045,* ☎ *310/670–9000 or 800/996–3426,* 𝖥𝖠𝖷 *310/670–8110. 591 rooms, 12 suites. 2 restaurants, bar, in-room modem lines, in-room safes, minibars, no-smoking floors, pool, hot tub, sauna, exercise room, baby-sitting, laundry service and dry cleaning, concierge, business services, meeting rooms, car rental, parking (fee). AE, D, DC, MC, V.*

Bel-Air

$$$$ 🏨 **Hotel Bel-Air.** The bungalow-style country-French rooms of this se-
★   cluded hotel, which is tucked in a wooded canyon surrounded by estate grounds, exude the feel of a fine home with such extras as a stereo with CD player, thick terry bathrobes, and slippers. The highly regarded Dining Room features a pianist nightly. For the quietest accommodations, ask for a room near the former stable area. ⊠ *701 Stone Canyon Rd., 90077,* ☎ *310/472–1211,* 𝖥𝖠𝖷 *310/476–5890. 92 rooms. Restaurant, bar, in-room modem lines, in-room safes, minibars, no-smoking rooms, room service, in-room VCRs, pool, beauty salon, hot tubs, massage, spa, health club, baby-sitting, laundry service and dry cleaning, concierge, meeting rooms, travel services, parking (fee). AE, DC, MC, V.*

$$$$ 🏨 **Summit Hotel Bel-Air.** This low-rise hotel in the Bel-Air foothills has a southern-California feel. Rooms are decorated in muted tones of cream and gray, with furniture in sleek, modern shapes and deco-style fix-

tures. Amenities include bathrobes, coffeemakers, and hair dryers. ✉ *11461 Sunset Blvd., 90049, ☎ 310/476–6571 or 800/468–3541. 161 rooms, 8 suites. Restaurant, bar, in-room modem lines, minibars, no-smoking rooms, room service, pool, massage, spa, tennis, exercise room, baby-sitting, laundry service and dry cleaning, concierge, business services, meeting rooms, travel services, car rental, parking (fee). AE, D, DC, MC, V.*

Manhattan Beach

$$$ 🖫 **Barnabey's Hotel.** The homey rooms at this property with the feel
★   of a 19th-century English inn include lace curtains, antique European furnishings, flowered wallpaper, down comforters, and at least 50 vintage books in every room. A complimentary English buffet breakfast is served each morning. ✉ *3501 Sepulveda Blvd. (at Rosecrans), Manhattan Beach 90266, ☎ 310/545–8466 or 800/552–5285, FAX 310/545–8621. 122 rooms, 1 suite. Restaurant, pub, in-room modem lines, no-smoking rooms, pool, hot tub, bicycles, nightclub, video games, baby-sitting, laundry service and dry cleaning, concierge, business services, meeting rooms, travel services, airport shuttle, car rental, parking (fee). AE, D, DC, MC, V.*

Marina del Rey

$$$$ 🖫 **Marina Beach Airport Marriott.** Ask for upper floor rooms that face
★   the marina at this Mediterranean-style hotel. There's a gazebo on the patio if you want to relax outdoors. The on-site Stone's restaurant is known for its fresh seafood. ✉ *4100 Admiralty Way, 90292, ☎ 310/301–3000, FAX 310/448–4870. 375 rooms. Restaurant, bar, minibars, no-smoking rooms, room service, pool, laundry service and dry cleaning, business services, car rental, parking (fee). AE, D, DC, MC, V.*

$$$$ 🖫 **Ritz-Carlton, Marina del Rey.** This sumptuous European-style hotel
★   has panoramic views of the Pacific. Rooms have French doors, marble baths, honor bars, and plenty of amenities—from plush terry robes to maid service twice a day and 24-hour room service. Bistro cuisine is served in the Terrace Restaurant; Mediterranean cuisine is served in the more formal Dining Room. ✉ *4375 Admiralty Way, 90292, ☎ 310/823–1700, FAX 310/823–2403. 306 rooms. 2 restaurants, bar, lobby lounge, in-room safes, minibars, no-smoking floors, room service, pool, hot tub, massage, spa, tennis court, exercise room, boating, bicycles, baby-sitting, laundry service and dry cleaning, concierge, business services, meeting rooms, travel services, car rental, parking (fee). AE, D, DC, MC, V.*

$$$–$$$$ 🖫 **Marina International Hotel and Bungalows.** White shutters on each window and private balconies overlooking the garden or courtyard create the feel of a European village. Across from a sandy beach within the marina, the hotel is a good choice for families with children, and is close to golf and tennis facilities. ✉ *4200 Admiralty Way, 90292, ☎ 310/301–2000, FAX 310/301–6687. 110 rooms, 25 bungalows. Restaurant, bar, in-room modem lines, minibars, room service, pool, hot tub, health club, beach, boating, baby-sitting, laundry service and dry cleaning, concierge, business services, meeting rooms, travel services, airport shuttle, free parking. AE, DC, MC, V.*

$$$ 🖫 **Marina del Rey Hotel.** The rooms of this waterfront property have balconies or patios; many have harbor views. Each room is equipped with two-line voice-mail phones. ✉ *13534 Bali Way, 90292, ☎ 310/301–1000 or 800/882-4000, FAX 310/305–8513. 156 rooms, 4 suites. Restaurant, bar, in-room modem lines, no-smoking rooms, room service, pool, putting green, boating, bicycles, rollerblading, baby-sitting, laundry service and dry cleaning, concierge, business services, meeting rooms, travel services, airport shuttle, free parking. AE, DC, MC, V.*

Redondo Beach

$$$ 🏨 **Crowne Plaza Redondo Beach & Marina Hotel.** Rooms at this swank five-story hotel overlooking the Pacific are done in a tropical seaside theme with wicker furniture and soft colors; those on the fifth-floor concierge level are also equipped with two-line telephones and dataports. ⊠ *300 N. Harbor Dr., 90277,* ☎ *310/318–8888 or 800/368–9760,* FAX *310/376–1930. 339 rooms, 5 suites. Restaurant, no-smoking rooms, pool, sauna, spa, tennis court, exercise room, bicycles, nightclub, baby-sitting, coin laundry, laundry service and dry cleaning, business services, travel services, parking (fee). AE, D, DC, MC, V.*

Santa Monica

$$$$ 🏨 **Hotel Oceana.** This hotel on a bluff overlooking the ocean offers a change of pace from ultrahip downtown Santa Monica. The retro "less is more" furnishings in the living room are straight from the 1950s; bedrooms and bathrooms, luxurious and contemporary, provide every amenity. ⊠ *849 Ocean Ave., 90403,* ☎ *310/268–8344 or 800/777–0758,* FAX *310/268–7943. 63 suites. In-room modem lines, in-room safes, kitchenettes, no-smoking suites, refrigerators, room service, in-room VCRs, pool, massage, spa, exercise room, video games, coin laundry, laundry service and dry cleaning, concierge, business services, free parking. AE, D, DC, MC, V.*

$$$$ 🏨 **Loews Santa Monica Beach Hotel.** This pink, blue, and beige stucco hotel is just a few yards from the beach across a small pathway. The hotel's centerpiece is a five-story glass atrium with panoramic views of the Pacific. Accommodations are done in a casual California style with rattan and wicker furniture. ⊠ *1700 Ocean Ave., 90401,* ☎ *310/458–6700,* FAX *310/458–6761. 350 rooms, 31 suites. 2 restaurants, outdoor café, lobby bar, in-room modem lines, minibars, no-smoking floors, room service, indoor-outdoor pool, beauty salon, hot tub, massage, sauna, spa, steam room, health club, beach, windsurfing, baby-sitting, children's programs (ages 5–12), laundry service and dry cleaning, concierge, business services, meeting rooms, travel services, car rental, parking (fee). AE, D, DC, MC, V.*

$$$$ 🏨 **Miramar Sheraton.** Accommodations at the Miramar come in a 10-story tower with contemporary decor and fabulous ocean views; a six-story historical wing with oversize guest rooms and traditional furnishings; and luxurious gardenside bungalows, each with amenities that include a huge whirlpool tub and a stereo with CD and bathroom speakers. ⊠ *101 Wilshire Blvd., 90401,* ☎ *310/576–7777 or 800/325–3535,* FAX *310/458–7912. 240 rooms, 62 suites, 32 bungalows. 2 restaurants, bar, in-room modem lines, in-room safes, minibars, no-smoking floors, pool, beauty salon, massage, health club, piano, baby-sitting, laundry service and dry cleaning, concierge, business services, meeting rooms, travel services, parking (fee). AE, D, DC, MC, V.*

$$$$ 🏨 **Shutters on the Beach.** The front of Shutters opens directly onto the
★ beach promenade, just feet from the sand. The guest rooms have sliding shutter doors that open onto a tiny balcony. Amenities include Frette linens and bathrobes, clock radios, hair dryers, three telephones, and complimentary classic movies for the VCR. ⊠ *1 Pico Blvd., 90405,* ☎ *310/458–0030,* FAX *310/458–4589. 186 rooms, 12 suites. 2 restaurants, bar, lobby lounge, in-room modem lines, in-room safes, minibars, no-smoking floors, room service, in-room VCRs, pool, hot tub, massage, sauna, spa, steam room, health club, beach, windsurfing, mountain bikes, baby-sitting, laundry service and dry cleaning, concierge, business services, meeting rooms, travel services, car rental, parking (fee). AE, D, DC, MC, V.*

$$$ 🏨 **Pacific Shore.** This modern eight-story hotel is steps from the beach. Rooms are decorated with contemporary fabrics in ocean blues and

greens, and modern, light-wood furniture; some have ocean views and small balconies. Extras include hair dryers and Nintendo. A complimentary shuttle runs within 5 mi—perfect for seeing Santa Monica. ⊠ *1819 Ocean Ave., 90401,* ☎ *310/451–8711 or 800/622–8711,* ⒻⒶⓍ *310/394–3761 or 310/451–3882. 168 rooms. Restaurant, bar, in-room modem lines, in-room safes, pool, hot tub, exercise room, video games, baby-sitting, coin laundry, business services, meeting rooms, travel services, car rental, free parking. AE, D, DC, MC, V.*

$–$$ 🏨 **Best Western Ocean View Hotel.** With a coveted location in the heart of Santa Monica facing the ocean, this hotel feels fresh and clean, from its pink, sand, and aqua-trim architecture to corridors that look out on tropical greenery. Guest rooms are small but comfortable. ⊠ *1447 Ocean Ave., 90401,* ☎ *310/458–4888 or 800/452–4888,* ⒻⒶⓍ *310/458–0848. 72 rooms. In-room modem lines, no-smoking rooms, refrigerators, laundry service and dry cleaning, business services, free parking. AE, D, DC, MC, V.*

Venice

$$ 🏨 **Marina Pacific Hotel & Suites.** This hotel faces the Pacific and one of the world's most vibrant boardwalks; it's nestled among Venice's art galleries, shops, and elegant, offbeat restaurants. ⊠ *1697 Pacific Ave., 90291,* ☎ *310/399–7770 or 800/421–8151,* ⒻⒶⓍ *310/452–5479. 57 rooms, 35 suites. Restaurant, laundry service, meeting rooms, free parking. AE, D, DC, MC, V.*

Westwood

$$$$ 🏨 **Westwood Marquis Hotel and Gardens.** A favorite of corporate and entertainment types, this 15-story hotel in Westwood Village near UCLA has elegant suites and excellent amenities. Each one-, two-, or three-bedroom suite has a living room, a dining area, and a view of Bel-Air, the Pacific Ocean, or Century City. ⊠ *930 Hilgard Ave., 90024,* ☎ *310/208–8765,* ⒻⒶⓍ *310/824–0355. 258 suites. 2 restaurants, bar, outdoor café, in-room modem lines, in-room safes, minibars, no-smoking floors, refrigerators, room service, 2 pools, hot tub, massage, sauna, exercise room, video games, laundry service and dry cleaning, concierge, business services, meeting rooms, parking (fee). AE, D, DC, MC, V.*

West Los Angeles

$$–$$$ 🏨 **Century Wilshire Hotel.** The clientele of this simple hotel near UCLA and Westwood Village is largely European. Guest rooms are decorated in homey, English-style pastels and have tiled baths. Room rates include a Continental breakfast. ⊠ *10776 Wilshire Blvd., 90024,* ☎ *310/474–4506,* ⒻⒶⓍ *310/474–2535. 87 rooms, 12 suites. Breakfast room, no-smoking rooms, pool, baby-sitting, laundry service and dry cleaning, concierge, travel services, car rental, free parking. AE, DC, MC, V.*

$$ 🏨 **Best Western Royal Palace Inn & Suites.** This small hotel has a fresh "Sherwood Forest" soft green and beige color scheme. Rooms are simply but tastefully furnished and have microwaves and coffeemakers. ⊠ *2528 S. Sepulveda Blvd., 90064,* ☎ *310/477–9066 or 800/251–3888,* ⒻⒶⓍ *310/478–4133. 23 rooms, 32 suites. Refrigerators, in-room VCRs, pool, hot tub, sauna, exercise room, billiards, coin laundry, meeting room, free parking. AE, D, DC, MC, V.*

Downtown

$$$$ 🏨 **Hotel Inter-Continental Los Angeles.** Rooms at this sleek modern-art-filled high-rise have floor-to-ceiling windows with views of the Museum of Contemporary Art or the Watercourt and are decorated in contemporary style with casual California and Asian overtones. The 17th-floor business center is extensive. ⊠ *251 S. Olive St., 90012,* ☎

213/617–3300 or 800/442–5251, FAX 213/617–3399. *433 rooms, 18 suites. Restaurant, bar, minibars, no-smoking floors, room service, pool, exercise room, piano, video games, laundry service and dry cleaning, concierge, business services. AE, D, DC, MC, V.*

$$$$ 🖭 **Hyatt Regency Los Angeles.** If you're at this hotel near the Music Center to work, ask for the Business Plan, available on floors above the 18th—you'll have access to laptop computers and fax machines. Rooms, furnished with rich mahogany and cherry woods, have marble baths. ⊠ *711 S. Hope St., 90017,* ☎ *213/683–1234 or 800/233–1234,* FAX *213/629–3230. 485 rooms, 41 suites. 2 restaurants, 2 bars, in-room modem lines, no-smoking floors, room service, exercise room, children's programs, laundry service and dry cleaning, concierge, business services, meeting rooms, parking (fee). AE, D, DC, MC, V.*

$$$$ 🖭 **New Otani Hotel and Garden.** For a quintessential Japanese hotel
★ experience, visit this 21-story, ultramodern property with a ½-acre rooftop Japanese garden. In the Japanese-style suites, you'll drift into dreamland on a comfortable futon laid on a tatami mat. Western-style rooms are also available. ⊠ *120 S. Los Angeles St., 90012,* ☎ *213/629–1200; 800/273–2294 in CA; 800/421-8795 in the U.S. and Canada;* FAX *213/622–0989 or 213/622–0980. 434 rooms, 20 suites. 3 restaurants, 3 bars, in-room safes, minibars, no-smoking rooms, refrigerators, room service, Japanese baths, massage, sauna, health club, shops, piano, baby-sitting, laundry service and dry cleaning, concierge, business services, car rental, parking (fee). AE, D, DC, MC, V.*

$$$$ 🖭 **Omni Los Angeles Hotel and Centre.** The 16-story Omni is convenient to Dodger Stadium, museums, Chinatown, and the Music Center. The sparse-looking contemporary decor of the guest rooms is in shades of beige, blue, and green. ⊠ *930 Wilshire Blvd., 90017,* ☎ *213/629–4321 or 800/445–8667,* FAX *213/612–3977. 868 rooms, 35 suites. 3 restaurants, bar, in-room modem lines, minibars, no-smoking rooms, room service, pool, beauty salon, exercise room, nightclub, baby-sitting, laundry service and dry cleaning, concierge, business services, travel services, car rental, parking (fee). AE, D, DC, MC, V.*

$$$$ 🖭 **Regal Biltmore Hotel.** All 11 floors of this opulent 1923 landmark (past visitors include Mary Pickford and J. Paul Getty) were upgraded in 1997 with fresh carpeting and new lighting. Rooms are contemporary but have French-style armoires and tapestry-covered chairs. A complimentary downtown shuttle whisks guests to buildings within a 3-mi radius of the hotel. ⊠ *506 S. Grand Ave., 90071,* ☎ *213/624–1011 or 800/245–8673,* FAX *213/612–1545. 683 rooms. 2 restaurants, 2 bars, minibars, no-smoking floors, room service, in-room VCRs, indoor pool, spa, health club, baby-sitting, laundry service and dry cleaning, concierge floor, business services, travel services, car rental, parking (fee). AE, D, DC, MC, V.*

$$$$ 🖭 **Sheraton Grande Hotel.** The oversize rooms at this 14-story hotel
★ have wall-to-wall windows with city views. Accommodations come with coffeemakers and Starbucks coffee, Nintendo systems, hair dryers, irons and boards, dataports, and phones with voice mail. Complimentary limo service is provided within a 5-mi radius. ⊠ *333 S. Figueroa St., 90071,* ☎ *213/617–1133 or 800/524–7263,* FAX *213/613–0291. 469 rooms. 3 restaurants, 2 bars, in-room safes, minibars, no-smoking floors, room service, pool, 4 cinemas, piano, video games, baby-sitting, laundry service and dry cleaning, concierge, business services, travel services, car rental, parking (fee). AE, D, DC, MC, V.*

$$$$ 🖭 **Westin Bonaventure Hotel & Suites.** Architect John Portman's striking 35-story mirrored-glass high-rise received an $8 million makeover in 1997. Smallish rooms have one wall of floor-to-ceiling glass and streamlined pale furnishings. An all-suites tower is geared toward the business traveler. ⊠ *404 S. Figueroa St., 90071,* ☎ *213/624–1000* *or 800/228–3000,* FAX *213/612–4894. 1,211 rooms, 157 suites. 17 restaurants, 2 bars, minibars, no-smoking floors, room service, pool, 7 tennis courts, health club, nightclubs, baby-sitting, laundry service and dry cleaning, concierge, business services, meeting rooms, travel services, car rental, parking (fee). AE, D, DC, MC, V.*

$$$$ ⊞ **Wyndham Checkers Hotel.** Fine art and antiques fill the lobby of
★   this intimate hotel, and guest rooms have oversize beds, upholstered easy chairs, marble writing tables, and terry-cloth robes. The hotel's highly regarded restaurant serves contemporary Continental cuisine. Complimentary limo service is offered within a 2-mi radius. ⊠ *535 S. Grand Ave., 90071,* ☎ *213/624–0000,* FAX *213/626–9906. 188 rooms, 2 suites. Restaurant, bar, minibars, no-smoking floors, room service, pool, hot tub, spa, exercise room, library, baby-sitting, laundry service and dry cleaning, concierge, business services, travel services, car rental, parking (fee). AE, D, DC, MC, V.*

$$–$$$ ⊞ **Inn at 657.** The apartment-size accommodations at this property
★   near the University of Southern California have down comforters on the beds and Oriental silks on the walls. Each suite has a full kitchen with a microwave. The rate includes a hearty breakfast, homemade cookies, local telephone calls, and taxes. ⊠ *657 W. 23rd St., 90007,* ☎ *213/ 741–2200 or 800/347–7512. 6 suites. In-room modem lines, kitchenettes, no-smoking suites, refrigerators, in-room VCRs, hot tub, laundry service and dry cleaning, concierge, business services, free parking. No credit cards.*

$$ ⊞ **Figueroa Hotel and Convention Center.** The Spanish feel of this 12-story hotel built in 1926 is accented by terra-cotta-color rooms, hand-painted furniture, wrought-iron beds, and, in many, ceiling fans. The hotel's Clay Pit restaurant serves aromatic and tasty Indian food. ⊠ *939 S. Figueroa St., 90015,* ☎ *213/627–8971 or 800/421–9092,* FAX *213/689–0305. 285 rooms. 2 restaurants, 2 bars, café, in-room modem lines, room service, pool, hot tub, coin laundry, dry cleaning, concierge, travel services, car rental, free parking. AE, DC, MC, V.*

$$ ⊞ **Holiday Inn L.A. Downtown.** Spacious peach-color rooms come with coffeemakers and irons and boards. The hotel is convenient to the Museum of Contemporary Art, the convention center, and the Los Angeles Sports Arena. ⊠ *750 S. Garland Ave., 90017,* ☎ *213/628– 5242 or 800/628–5240,* FAX *213/628–1201. 205 rooms. Restaurant, bar, no-smoking rooms, room service, pool, coin laundry, laundry service and dry cleaning, meeting rooms, car rental, free parking. AE, D, DC, MC, V.*

$$ ⊞ **Kawada Hotel.** Akin to a small European hotel, this three-story red-brick property is near the Music Center and local government buildings. The immaculate guest rooms are on the small side, but come with two phones and a wet bar. ⊠ *200 S. Hill St., 90012,* ☎ *213/621–4455 or 800/752–9232,* FAX *213/687–4455. 116 rooms, 1 suite. Restaurant, bar, deli, kitchenettes, no-smoking rooms, refrigerators, room service, in-room VCRs, coin laundry, laundry service and dry cleaning, concierge, business services, meeting rooms, car rental, parking (fee). AE, DC, MC, V.*

$ ⊞ **The InnTowne.** This contemporary three-story hotel just 1½ blocks from the convention center has large rooms with beige-and-white or gray-and-white color schemes. Palm trees and a small garden surround the swimming pool. ⊠ *913 S. Figueroa St., 90015,* ☎ *213/628– 2222 or 800/457–8520,* FAX *213/687–0566. 168 rooms, 2 suites. Bar, coffee shop, room service, pool, laundry service and dry cleaning, concierge, car rental, free parking. AE, D, DC, MC, V.*

Pasadena

$$$$ 🏨 **Ritz-Carlton Huntington Hotel.** The main building of this 1906 land-
★ mark hotel is a Mediterranean-style structure that fits in perfectly with
the lavish houses of the surrounding San Marino neighborhood. Guest
rooms are traditionally furnished and handsome, although a bit small
for the price; the large marble-fitted bathrooms also look old-fashioned.
The Grill, the more formal of the two dining rooms, is a five-star restaurant. ✉ *1401 S. Oak Knoll Ave., 91106,* ☎ *626/568–3900 or 800/
241–3333,* ℻ *626/568–1842 or 626/792–6613. 383 rooms, 22 suites.
2 restaurants, bar, in-room modem lines, in-room safes, minibars, no-
smoking buildings, room service, in-room VCRs, pool, barbershop,
beauty salon, hot tub, mineral baths, spa, tennis court, health club, baby-
sitting, laundry service and dry cleaning, concierge, business services,
meeting rooms, travel services, car rental, parking (fee). AE, D, DC,
MC, V.*

San Fernando Valley

Burbank

$$$ 🏨 **Burbank Airport Hilton.** Rooms here have light oak furniture, cof-
feemakers, irons and boards, hair dryers, and in-room movies. Ask for
a room with a mountain view. ✉ *2500 Hollywood Way, 91505,* ☎
818/843–6000, ℻ *818/842–9720. 486 rooms, 77 suites. Restaurant,
bar, in-room modem lines, no-smoking floors, room service, 2 pools,
hot tub, sauna, 2 exercise rooms, coin laundry, laundry service and dry
cleaning, concierge, convention center, travel services, airport shuttle,
parking (fee). AE, D, DC, MC, V.*

$–$$ 🏨 **Safari Inn.** The common spaces at this motel-like property are comfortable, colorful, and fun, with a jungle theme. Rooms, done in tones
of muted gold and green with mahogany furnishings, have a conservative, elegant feel. All accommodations have coffeemakers, irons and
boards, and in-room movies. ✉ *1911 W. Olive, 91506,* ☎ *818/845–
8586 or 800/782–4373,* ℻ *818/845–0054. 103 rooms. Restaurant,
bar, lobby lounge, no-smoking rooms, room service, in-room VCRs, pool,
hot tub, piano, baby-sitting, laundry service and dry cleaning, business
services, travel services, car rental, free parking. AE, DC, MC, V.*

North Hollywood

$$$ 🏨 **Beverly Garland's Holiday Inn.** There's a country-club atmosphere
to this lodgelike hotel in two separate buildings. Rooms have an early
California look, with distressed furniture and muted color schemes;
balconies overlook the Sierra Madre and Santa Monica mountains. The
property is next to the Hollywood Freeway, so ask for a room facing
Vineland Avenue. ✉ *4222 Vineland Ave., 91602,* ☎ *818/980–8000
or 800/238–3759,* ℻ *818/766–5230. 258 rooms. Restaurant, bar, no-
smoking rooms, room service, pool, wading pool, sauna, tennis, laun-
dry service and dry cleaning, meeting rooms, airport shuttle, free
parking. AE, D, DC, MC, V.*

Sherman Oaks

$$$ 🏨 **Radisson Valley Center Hotel Los Angeles.** You'll find excellent ser-
vice here and amenities such as a Continental breakfast and a news-
paper. The hotel is conveniently located at I–405 and U.S. 101 in the
Sherman Oaks business district. ✉ *15433 Ventura Blvd., 91403,* ☎
818/981–5400 or 800/333–3333, ℻ *818/981–3175. 204 rooms.
Restaurant, bar, in-room modem lines, no-smoking floors, room service, pool, beauty salon, hot tub, massage, exercise room, laundry service and dry cleaning, concierge, business services, meeting rooms, travel
services, car rental, parking (fee). AE, DC, MC, V.*

Studio City

$$ ⊞ **Sportsmen's Lodge.** A low-slung, English country–style structure, this hotel is surrounded by waterfalls, a swan-filled lagoon, and a gazebo; the pool area and lush garden make you forget you're even near a city. Although the service here may not be everything you've dreamed of, the accommodations *are* comfortable and you're close to golf, tennis, and Universal Studios. ⊠ *12825 Ventura Blvd., 91604,* ☎ *818/769–4700 or 800/821–8511,* ⅋ *213/877–3898. 191 rooms. 3 restaurants, bar, no-smoking floors, room service, pool, barbershop, beauty salon, hot tub, exercise room, baby-sitting, coin laundry, laundry service and dry cleaning, travel services, airport shuttle, car rental, free parking. AE, D, DC, MC, V.*

Universal City

$$$–$$$$ ⊞ **Universal City Hilton and Towers.** Rooms at this ultramodern 24-story glass tower are done in earth tones, and the bathrooms have wall-to-wall marble. Floor-to-ceiling windows reveal breathtaking views of the San Fernando Valley and hills. The Sierra Café, decorated with splashy, cheerful art, serves good California cuisine. ⊠ *555 Universal Terrace Pkwy., 91608,* ☎ *818/506–2500,* ⅋ *818/509–2058. 471 rooms. 2 restaurants, lobby lounge, in-room modem lines, in-room safes, minibars, no-smoking floors, room service, pool, hot tub, massage, sauna, exercise room, piano, baby-sitting, laundry service and dry cleaning, business services, convention center, meeting rooms, travel services, car rental, parking (fee). AE, D, DC, MC, V.*

NIGHTLIFE AND THE ARTS

Most bars, clubs, and bistros in this go-go-go city have a shelf life shorter than the vinyl skirts at Melrose boutiques. Hollywood, the locus of L.A. nightlife, is without question the place to start your search; you can't help but stumble into a happening joint if you cruise the streets long enough. L.A. is one of the best cities in the country to catch promising rock bands or check out jazz, blues, and classical acts. As for the arts, you'll find plenty going on in L.A., from ballet to film to theater.

For the most complete listing of weekly events, check the current issue of *Los Angeles* magazine, the Calendar section of the *Los Angeles Times,* or one of the free alternative publications, the *L.A. Weekly* and *New Times Los Angeles.* For a telephone report on current music, theater, dance, film, and special events, plus a discount ticket source, call 213/688–2787. Most tickets can be purchased by phone (with a credit card) from **Ticketmaster** (☎ 213/365–3500), **TeleCharge** (☎ 800/762–7666), **Good Time Tickets** (☎ 213/464–7383), **Tickets L.A.** (☎ 213/660–8587), or **Murray's Tickets** (☎ 213/234–0123).

Nightlife

Despite the high energy level of the L.A. nightlife crowd, don't expect to be partying until dawn—this is still an early-to-bed city. Liquor laws require that bars stop serving alcohol at 2 AM, so it's safe to say that by this time, with the exception of a few after-hours clubs and coffeehouses, most jazz, rock, and disco clubs have closed for the night.

Dress codes vary. Jackets are expected at cabarets and hotels. Discos are generally casual, although some will turn away the denim-clad. It might be wise to phone ahead and check the dress code, but on the whole, Los Angeles is a casual place.

Bars

AIRPORT AND SOUTH BAY

Hennessey's Tavern (✉ 8 Pier Ave., Hermosa Beach, ☎ 310/372–5759). This newly expanded beach pub has kept its Irish motif intact while making room for the crowds of regulars.

BEVERLY HILLS, CENTURY CITY, AND VICINITY

Harper's Bar and Grill (✉ 2040 Ave. of the Stars, Century City, ☎ 310/553–1855). The drinks are generous at this great place to meet friends for cocktails before a show at the Shubert Theater.

Hotel Bel-Air (✉ 701 Stone Canyon Rd., Bel-Air, ☎ 310/472–1211). There's serene musical entertainment every night (either a pianist or a vocalist) at this secluded hotel.

La Scala (✉ 410 N. Canon, Beverly Hills, ☎ 310/275–0579). A quaint bar with an immense wine selection, La Scala is visited by celebrities nightly.

Regent Beverly Wilshire (✉ 9500 Wilshire Blvd., Beverly Hills, ☎ 310/275–5200). Plush sofas and high tables set the atmosphere for the elegant piano bar in one of L.A.'s premier hotels.

DOWNTOWN

Boyd Street (✉ 410 Boyd St., ☎ 213/617–2491). This downtown bar-restaurant with a streamlined '80s motif attracts downtown's loft-dwelling elite.

Grand Avenue Sports Bar (✉ 506 S. Grand Ave., ☎ 213/612–1595). This sleek bar in the Biltmore Hotel serves until 2 AM. Bring lots of money.

Little Joe's (✉ 900 N. Broadway, ☎ 213/489–4900). This spot is a must for sports buffs: The prices are low and the big-screen TV is always tuned to the hottest game. W. C. Fields frequented the bar in the '30s.

Rex (✉ 617 S. Olive St., ☎ 213/627–2300). This piano bar on the ground floor of the historic Oviatt Building radiates the art deco ambience of a 1930s cruise liner.

The Tower (✉ 1150 S. Olive St., ☎ 213/746–1554). This bar and restaurant atop the 32-story Transamerica Building provides a terrific view and an elegant cocktail environment.

HOLLYWOOD

Dresden Room (✉ 1760 N. Vermont Ave., ☎ 213/665–4294). Gold lamé lounge crooners perform nightly (except Sunday) at this unassuming '40s-style bar.

El Coyote (✉ 7312 Beverly Blvd., ☎ 213/939–7766). For a pick-me-up margarita, stop by this kitschy restaurant-bar and get a glass of the best—and cheapest—in town.

Formosa (✉ 7156 Santa Monica Blvd., ☎ 213/850–9050). Saved from extinction by a massive public outcry, this old Hollywood restaurant and watering hole is a favorite among hipsters and old-timers alike.

Good Luck Bar (✉ 1514 Hillhurst Ave., ☎ 213/666–3524). The Chinese motif at this trendy hot spot makes you feel like you're in a Hong Kong action movie. Check out the vintage jukebox.

Hollywood Athletic Club (✉ 6525 Sunset Blvd., ☎ 213/962–6600). A hip place to hang out, this old billiard parlor attracts a rowdy crowd.

Kibitz Room (⊠ 419 N. Fairfax Ave., ☎ 213/651–2030). This bar adjacent to Canter's Restaurant has become a trendy gathering place with live music most nights.

Lava Lounge (⊠ 1533 N. La Brea Ave., ☎ 213/876–6612). Don't be fooled by the seedy, minimall location: Inside you'll find groovy bamboo and faux-lava walls and ultra-fashionable scenesters. Weeknights there's live music.

Musso and Franks Grill (⊠ 6667 Hollywood Blvd., ☎ 213/467–5123). Film studio moguls and movie extras flock to this long-running hit, where the Rob Roys are as smooth as ever.

3 Of Clubs (⊠ 1123 N. Vine St., ☎ 213/462–1123). The unmarked, nondescript exterior hardly prepares you for this plush, dressy bar that attracts L.A.'s young and restless.

Tiki Ti (⊠ 4427 W. Sunset Blvd., ☎ 213/669–9381). This small cocktail lounge, which serves some of the city's best tropical rum drinks, is big with the singles crowd.

Yamashiro's (⊠ 1999 N. Sycamore Ave., ☎ 213/466–5125). It's an L.A. tradition to meet at this Japanese restaurant-bar at sunset for cocktails on the terrace.

MARINA DEL REY
The Warehouse (⊠ 4499 Admiralty Way, ☎ 310/823–5451). Sinfully rich piña coladas are among the lures at this popular bar.

MID-WILSHIRE
Tom Bergin's (⊠ 840 S. Fairfax Ave., ☎ 213/936–7151). One of L.A.'s most frequented Irish pubs is plastered with Day-Glo shamrocks bearing the names of regular patrons.

PASADENA
Beckham Place (⊠ 77 W. Walnut, ☎ 626/796–3399). This rather fancy "Olde English" pub is known for its huge drinks, free roast beef sandwiches at happy hour, and wing chairs placed near a roaring fire.

The Colorado Bar (⊠ 2640 E. Colorado Blvd., ☎ 626/449–3485). Art students, Gen-Xers, and aging barflies who are put off by the glitz of Old Town take refuge at this divey bar.

Q's (⊠ 99 E. Colorado Blvd., ☎ 626/405–9777). This upscale bar-pool hall in the middle of Old Town hall packs in the young collegiate crowd nightly.

Ritz-Carlton Huntington Hotel (⊠ 1401 S. Oak Knoll Ave., ☎ 626/568–3900). Entertainment is offered at The Bar, a lounge that resembles a genteel private library.

SAN FERNANDO VALLEY
Residuals (⊠ 11042 Ventura Blvd., Studio City, ☎ 818/761–8301). Actors who present a residual check for less than a dollar can trade it for a free drink here. Full of struggling thespians and wanna-bes, it's the perfect place to examine this very L.A. breed.

SANTA MONICA
The Circle (⊠ 2926 Main St., ☎ 310/392–4898). Named for its 360-degree bar, this venerable Santa Monica dive is the only neighborhood pub to survive Main Street's trendy makeover.

Gotham Hall (⊠ 1431 3rd St. Promenade, ☎ 310/394–8865). This pool hall and bar is designed like something off the set of *Batman*.

Monsoon (✉ 1212 3rd St. Promenade, ☎ 310/576–9996). Carved wooden tribal masks and other Indian and Southeast Asian deities make this one of the most elegant restaurant-bars on the always jumping Third Street Promenade.

Oar House (✉ 2941 Main St., ☎ 310/396–4725). Something old has been glued or nailed to every square inch of this popular dance bar, from motorcycles to carriages. Drinks are downright cheap.

VENICE

Hal's Bar & Grill (✉ Abbott Kinney Blvd., ☎ 310/396–3105). Abstract art decorates the walls of this bar-restaurant that's popular with local well-to-do professionals.

Rebecca's (✉ 2025 Pacific Ave., ☎ 310/306–6266). Loud and fun, this very upscale establishment with an outrageous Frank Gehry interior is a good place to rub elbows with the Venice Beach elite.

WEST HOLLYWOOD

J. Sloane's (✉ 8623 Melrose Ave., ☎ 310/659–0250). A straight bastion in an ultragay neighborhood, this is a sawdust-on-the-floor, football-on-the-tube, frat-house kind of place.

Le Dome (✉ 8720 W. Sunset Blvd., ☎ 310/659–6919). The circular bar here draws stars and lesser folk. The best time to visit is after 11 PM, when this upmarket hangout really starts to jump.

Sky Bar (✉ 8440 Sunset Blvd., ☎ 213/650–8999). You're lucky if you even get inside this poolside bar at the Hotel Mondrian packed with celebrities and other glamorous types. There's a spectacular view of the city below.

Sunset Marquis (✉ 1200 N. Alta Loma Rd., ☎ 310/657–1333). This watering hole popular with visiting celebs and their entourages is the perfect place to catch a glimpse of your favorite alternative idols.

WESTWOOD/WESTSIDE

Liquid Kitty (✉ 11780 W. Pico Blvd., ☎ 310/473–3707). This "Cocktail Nation" lounge has a neon martini glass on the outside, a hip clientele on the inside, and occasional live music that doesn't overpower conversation.

Q's (✉ 11835 Wilshire Blvd., ☎ 310/477–7550). This upscale pool hall with a dozen tables and a bar serves a yuppified clientele and neighborhood brat-packers.

Cabaret, Performance, and Variety

The Cinegrill (✉ Clarion Hotel Hollywood Roosevelt, 7000 Hollywood Blvd., Hollywood, ☎ 213/466–7000). A Hollywood landmark houses this elegant jazz club that books only top-tier performers. Hollywood artifacts line the lobby.

Glaxa Studios (✉ 3707 Sunset Blvd., Silver Lake, ☎ 213/663–5295). The emphasis is on the avant-garde and the offbeat at this bohemian café-arts venue that presents music, poetry, and performance.

Highways (✉ 1651 18th St., Santa Monica, ☎ 310/453–1755). Westside Bohemians come here to see and hear avant-garde spoken-word and performance artists. Reservations are recommended.

Luna Park (✉ 665 Robertson Blvd., West Hollywood, ☎ 310/652–0611). Locally famous drag queens strut their stuff here at this New York–style cabaret with three stages, two bars, and an eclectic mix of music.

Queen Mary (✉ 12449 Ventura Blvd., Sherman Oaks, ☎ 818/506–5619). Female impersonators vamp it up as Diana Ross, Barbra Streisand, and Bette Midler in this small club where every seat is a good one.

Comedy and Magic

Comedy and Magic Club (✉ 1018 Hermosa Ave., Hermosa Beach, ☎ 310/372–1193). This beachfront club presents many magicians and comedians seen on TV and in Las Vegas.

Comedy Store (✉ 8433 Sunset Blvd., Hollywood, ☎ 213/656–6225). Los Angeles's premier comedy showcase has been going strong for over a decade. Famous comedians occasionally make unannounced appearances.

Groundlings Theater (✉ 7307 Melrose Ave., Hollywood, ☎ 213/934–9700). The usually hilarious entertainment here consists of original skits, music, and improv. Shows are performed Thursday through Sunday.

Ice House Comedy Club and Restaurant (✉ 24 N. Mentor Ave., Pasadena, ☎ 626/577–1894). Three-act shows here, which run Wednesday through Sunday, feature comedians, celebrity impressionists, ventriloquists, and magicians.

Country Music

In Cahoots (✉ 223 N. Glendale Ave., Glendale, ☎ 818/500–1665). Learn the two-step or the West Coast swing to live music every night at this raucous dance hall—they'll teach you how for free.

Dance Clubs

Bar One (✉ 9229 Sunset Blvd., Beverly Hills, ☎ 310/271–8355). This hot spot is great for posing, staring, and dancing. Be sure to dress your best or you'll be left outside.

Checca (✉ 7323 Santa Monica Blvd., West Hollywood, ☎ 213/850–7471). Facing the old Goldwyn Studios, this lively bar-restaurant offers everything from acid jazz to standard blues to Brazilian music, often performed live.

Crush Bar (✉ 1743 Cahuenga Ave., Hollywood, ☎ 213/463–9017). If the 1960s is a decade that appeals to you, stop by this happening dance club, open Friday and Saturday evenings.

Florentine Gardens (✉ 5951 Hollywood Blvd., Hollywood, ☎ 213/464–0706). Here's one of Los Angeles's largest dance areas (with spectacular lighting), big on Latin-fusion. It's open Friday, Saturday, and Sunday.

Jewel's Catch One (✉ 4067 W. Pico Blvd., Los Angeles, ☎ 213/734–8849). This hothouse of a dance club in a dicey neighborhood mixes people of all genders, races, and sexual orientations. Its late hours—it's open until 3 AM weeknights and 4 AM weekends—and underground vibe make it a prime destination for dance fanatics.

Moonlight Tango Cafe (✉ 13730 Ventura Blvd., Sherman Oaks, ☎ 818/788–2000). This high-energy club-restaurant, big on the swing era, really gets moving in the wee hours, when a conga line inevitably takes shape on the dance floor.

The World (✉ 7070 Hollywood Blvd., Hollywood, ☎ 213/467–7070). Each night is different at this popular dance venue on the ground floor of a Hollywood office building. Catch everything from house and hip-hop to trance and techno.

Gay and Lesbian Nightlife

Axis/Love Lounge (✉ Axis: 652 N. La Peer Dr., West Hollywood, ☎ 310/659–0471; ✉ Love Lounge: 657 N. Robertson Blvd., West Hollywood, ☎ 310/659–0472). These two clubs on one site have different entrances and schedule different events. Some nights are for lesbians and some are for gay men, and there are frequent theme parties. The music runs the gamut: new wave, hi-NRG, tribal, rock, and Latin house.

Circus Disco and Arena (✉ 6655 Santa Monica Blvd., Hollywood, ☎ 213/462–1291). An ethnically mixed gay and straight crowd flocks to these two huge side-by-side discos, which feature techno and rock music.

Girl Bar (☎ 213/460–2531). L.A.'s more glamorous lesbians show up for Girl Bar parties, which are thrown at several places; call the information line for locations. In recent years, Girl Bar has been held on Friday at Axis and on Saturday at the Love Lounge (☞ *above*). Occasional parties are held at West Hollywood hotels such as the Mondrian.

The Palms (✉ 8572 Santa Monica Blvd., West Hollywood, ☎ 310/652–6188). A friendly publike lesbian bar in the heart of West Hollywood, the Palms has DJ dancing some nights, live bands and jukebox selections on others. There's a pool table. Wednesday's a hot night, as is Sunday's beer blast.

Rage (✉ 8911 Santa Monica Blvd., West Hollywood, ☎ 310/652–7055). This midsize dance club has been around for years; it remains a favorite of the "gym boy" set. There's also a video lounge.

Jazz

Atlas Bar & Grill (✉ 3760 Wilshire Blvd., Los Angeles, ☎ 213/380–8400). The eclectic entertainment at this snazzy supper club inside the historic Wiltern building includes torch singers as well as a jazz band.

Baked Potato (✉ 3787 Cahuenga Blvd. W, North Hollywood, ☎ 818/980–1615). Patrons of this tiny club are packed in like sardines to hear a powerhouse of jazz and blues. Jumbo baked potatoes are stuffed with everything from steak to vegetables.

Catalina Bar and Grill (✉ 1640 N. Cahuenga Blvd., Hollywood, ☎ 213/466–2210). Big-name acts and innovators like Latin saxophonist Paquito D. Rivera have played at this top Hollywood jazz spot. Continental cuisine is served.

Club Brasserie (✉ Hotel Bel Age, 1020 N. San Vicente Blvd., West Hollywood, ☎ 213/854–1111). You can hear exceptional jazz performers at this bar-restaurant Thursday through Saturday. The club's impressionist paintings, city views, and free admission policy are exceptional as well.

Jazz Bakery (✉ 3221 Hutchison, Culver City, ☎ 310/271–9039). Nightly and on Sunday afternoon you can have coffee and desserts while listening to world-class jazz in a smoke-free environment. The $17–$20 admission (no credit cards) includes refreshments.

Marla's Jazz Supper Club (✉ 2323 W. Martin Luther King Jr. Blvd., Los Angeles, ☎ 213/294–8430). Owned by comedy star Marla Gibbs of *The Jeffersons* and *227*, the room sizzles with blues, jazz, and easy listening.

Folk, Pop, and Rock

Al's Bar (✉ 305 S. Hewitt St., downtown, ☎ 213/625–9703). One of L.A.'s oldest rock dives, Al's is still going strong.

Blue Saloon (✉ 4657 Lankershim Blvd., North Hollywood, ☎ 818/766–4644). Come here for a shot of rock and roll, blues, country, or rockabilly.

Coconut Teaszer (✉ 8117 Sunset Blvd., ☎ 213/654–4773). Dancing to live music—raw-rock at its best—in two separate rooms, a great barbecue menu, and killer drinks make for lively fun.

The Derby (✉ 4500 Los Feliz Blvd., Los Feliz, ☎ 213/663–8979). Live music—swing, jazz, surf, and rock—fills the air nightly at this sophisticated club.

Dragonfly (✉ 6510 Santa Monica Blvd., Hollywood, ☎ 213/466–6111). Dark, cozy, mysterious—everything a rock-and-roll dive should be—this ultrahip club with a dungeonlike atmosphere presents an edgy mix of live and dance music.

Ghengis Cohen Cantina (✉ 740 N. Fairfax Ave., Hollywood, ☎ 213/653–0640). At this longtime music industry hangout, you can hear up-and-coming talent, usually in a refreshingly mellow format like MTV's "Unplugged" performances. A plus is the restaurant's updated Chinese cuisine.

House of Blues (✉ 8430 Sunset Blvd., Hollywood, ☎ 213/650–1451). Home to jazz, rock, and blues performers, this happening nightclub has an impressive following. Past performers have included Etta James, Lou Rawls, Joe Cocker, the Young Dubliners, and the Commodores.

Jabberjaw (✉ 3711 W. Pico Blvd., Mid-Wilshire, ☎ 213/732–3463). Nirvana, Beck, and many other artists played this all-ages venue long before the rest of the world heard them. Not in the best of neighborhoods (don't park on the side streets), this kitschy, alcohol-free club has a knack for booking the hottest underground bands around.

Jack's Sugar Shack (✉ 1707 N. Vine St., Hollywood, ☎ 213/466–7005). There's plenty to enjoy here, from the umbrella drinks and microbrews to the music of big-name alternative rock, surf, blues, rockabilly, Cajun, and country performers.

Kingston 12 (✉ 814 Broadway, Santa Monica, ☎ 310/451–4423). Open Thursday through Sunday, this Santa Monica club is known for its rap music, although reggae is also on tap, as is a menu of fine Jamaican food.

McCabe's Guitar Shop (✉ 3101 Pico Blvd., Santa Monica, ☎ 310/828–4497; 310/828–4403 concert information). Folk, acoustic rock, bluegrass, and soul concerts are featured in this guitar store on weekend nights.

The Palace (✉ 1735 N. Vine St., Hollywood, ☎ 213/462–3000). This plush multilevel art deco palace has a fabulous sound system, laser lights, two dance floors, four bars, a comfortable balcony, and a full bar and dining room on the top-level patio.

Pier 52 (✉ 52 Pier Ave., Hermosa Beach, ☎ 310/376–1629). Monday through Saturday nights dance bands play pure rock and roll. Sunday, however, is designated the day of blues.

The Roxy (✉ 9009 Sunset Blvd., West Hollywood, ☎ 310/276–2222). A Sunset Strip fixture, the Roxy is the club of choice for many local and touring alternative, country, blues, and rockabilly bands.

Spaceland (✉ 1717 Silverlake Blvd., Silver Lake, ☎ 213/413–4442). This tacky former disco is the place to see the hottest bands of tomorrow today.

The Troubadour (⌧ 9081 Santa Monica Blvd., West Hollywood, ☎ 310/276–6168). Once a focal point for the now-moribund L.A. heavy metal scene, the Troub has caught its second wind by booking hot alternative rock acts.

Viper Room (⌧ 8852 Sunset Blvd., West Hollywood, ☎ 310/358–1880). Part-owned by actor Johnny Depp, this is a hangout for musicians and movie stars. There's a different theme going every night from ballroom and swing to ultrahard rock.

Whiskey A Go Go (⌧ 8901 Sunset Blvd., West Hollywood, ☎ 310/535–0579). The most famous rock-and-roll club on the Sunset Strip presents up-and-coming alternative, very hard rock, and punk bands. Mondays launch L.A.'s cutting-edge acts.

The Arts

Concerts

MAJOR CONCERT HALLS

Dorothy Chandler Pavilion (⌧ 135 N. Grand Ave., ☎ 213/972–7211). Part of the Los Angeles Music Center and—with the Hollywood Bowl—the center of L.A.'s classical music scene, the 3,200-seat Pavilion is the home of the Los Angeles Philharmonic. The L.A. Opera presents classics from September through June.

Greek Theater (⌧ 2700 N. Vermont Ave., ☎ 213/665–1927). This open-air auditorium near Griffith Park has some classical performances in its mainly pop-rock-jazz schedule from June through October.

Hollywood Bowl (⌧ 2301 Highland Ave., ☎ 213/850–2000). The Bowl, one of the world's largest outdoor amphitheaters, is in a park surrounded by mountains, trees, and gardens. The Bowl's season runs early July through mid-September; the L.A. Philharmonic spends its summer season here. There are performances daily except Monday (and some Sundays); the program ranges from jazz to pop to classical. Concert goers frequently arrive early to enjoy a pre-show picnic on the park's tables. Restaurant dining is available on the grounds (☎ 213/851–3588); reserve ahead. The seats are wood—you might bring or rent a cushion. And bring a sweater because it gets chilly here in the evening. To avoid parking hassles, take one of the Park-and-Ride buses that leave from various locations around town; call the Bowl for information.

Shrine Auditorium (⌧ 665 W. Jefferson Blvd., ☎ 213/749–5123). Built in 1926 by the Al Malaikah Temple, the auditorium's decor could be called Baghdad and Beyond. Touring companies from all over the world, along with assorted gospel and choral groups, appear in this one-of-a-kind, 6,200-seat theater, as do the higher profile televised awards shows such as the American Music Awards and the Grammys.

Wilshire Ebell Theater (⌧ 4401 W. 8th St., ☎ 213/939–1128). The Los Angeles Opera Theatre comes to this Spanish-style building, erected in 1924, as do a broad spectrum of other musical performers.

Wiltern Theater (⌧ 3790 Wilshire Blvd., ☎ 213/380–5005 or 213/388–1400). The home of the Los Angeles Opera Theatre is listed in the National Register of Historic Places. The Wiltern also schedules pop, rock, and dance performances.

Dance

Bella Lewitsky Dance Co. (☎ 213/580–6338). One of L.A.'s major resident companies presents modern-dance performances regularly around town.

Shrine Auditorium (✉ 665 W. Jefferson Blvd., ☎ 213/749–5123). Touring dance companies, such as the Kirov, the Bolshoi, and the American Ballet Theater perform here.

UCLA Center for the Arts (✉ 405 N. Hilgard Ave., ☎ 310/825–2101). Visiting companies, such as Paul Taylor and the Hubbard Street Dance Company are apt to show up here.

Film

Some of the country's most historic and beautiful theaters are found in Los Angeles, hosting both first-run and revival films. **Mann's Chinese Theater** (✉ 6925 Hollywood Blvd., Hollywood, ☎ 213/464–8111) still hosts many gala premieres. The futuristic **Pacific Cinerama Dome** (✉ 6360 Sunset Blvd., Hollywood, ☎ 213/466–3401) was the first theater in the United States designed specifically for Cinerama. **Pacific's El Capitan** (✉ 6838 Hollywood Blvd., Hollywood, ☎ 213/467–7674) has been restored to its original art deco splendor; first-run movies are on the bill, as are Disney animation debuts. The **Vista Theater** (✉ 4473 Sunset, Los Feliz, ☎ 213/660–6639) has a Spanish-style facade and an ornate Egyptian interior.

TELEVISION

Audiences Unlimited (✉ 100 Universal City Plaza, Bldg. 153, Universal City 91608, ☎ 818/506–0043) helps fill seats for television programs. There's no charge, but the tickets are distributed on a first-come, first-served basis. Tickets can be picked up at Fox Television Center (✉ 5746 Sunset Blvd., Van Ness Ave. entrance), which is open weekdays 8:30 to 6. You must be 16 or older to attend a television taping. For a schedule, send a self-addressed envelope to Audiences Unlimited a few weeks prior to your visit.

Theater

MAJOR THEATERS

Geffen Playhouse (✉ 10886 Le Conte Ave., Westwood, ☎ 310/208–6500 or 310/208–5454). The 498-seat playhouse showcases new plays in the summer, primarily musicals and comedies.

James A. Doolittle Theater (✉ 1615 N. Vine St., Hollywood, ☎ 213/462–6666; 213/365–3500 Ticketmaster). This 1,038-seat house presents new plays, dramas, comedies, and musicals.

John Anson Ford Amphitheater (✉ 2580 Cahuenga Blvd. E, Hollywood, ☎ 213/974–1343 or 213/466–1767). This 1,300-seat outdoor house in the Hollywood Hills is best known for its free summer jazz, dance, and cabaret concerts.

Music Center (✉ 135 N. Grand Ave., ☎ 213/972–7211). The big downtown complex includes three theaters: the Ahmanson Theater, presenting both classics and new plays; the 3,200-seat Dorothy Chandler Pavilion, which offers a smattering of plays in between performances of the L.A. Philharmonic, L.A. Master Chorale, and L.A. Opera; and the 760-seat Mark Taper Forum (☎ 213/972–7353), which presents new works.

Pantages (✉ 6233 Hollywood Blvd., Hollywood, ☎ 213/468–1700; 213/365–3500 Ticketmaster). Large-scale Broadway musicals are usually presented here.

Wilshire Theater (✉ 8440 Wilshire Blvd., Beverly Hills, ☎ 213/468–1716 or 213/468–1799; 213/365–3500 Ticketmaster). The interior of this 1,900-seat house is art deco; musicals from Broadway are the usual fare.

SMALLER THEATERS AND COMPANIES

Actor's Gang Theater (✉ 6209 Santa Monica Blvd., Hollywood ☎ 213/ 465–0566). The founders of this theater include actor-director Tim Robbins; the fare runs from Molière to Eric Bogosian to international works by traveling companies.

Cast Theater (✉ 804 N. El Centro, Hollywood, ☎ 213/462–0265). Musicals, revivals, and avant-garde improv pieces are performed here.

Coast Playhouse (✉ 8325 Santa Monica Blvd., West Hollywood, ☎ 213/650–8507). The specialties of this 99-seat house are excellent original musicals and new dramas.

Fountain Theater (✉ 5060 Fountain Ave., Hollywood, ☎ 213/663–1525). This 80-seat theater presents original American dramas and stages flamenco dance concerts.

Japan America Theater (✉ 244 S. San Pedro St., downtown, ☎ 213/ 680–3700). This community-oriented 880-seat theater at the Japan Cultural Arts Center is home to local theater, dance troupes, and the L.A. Chamber Orchestra, plus numerous children's theater groups.

Santa Monica Playhouse (✉ 1211 4th St., Santa Monica, ☎ 310/ 394–9779). With 99 seats, this house is worth visiting for its cozy, library-like atmosphere; the good comedies, dramas, and children's programs are further incentive.

Theatre/Theater (✉ 1715 Cahuenga Blvd., Hollywood, ☎ 213/871–0210). Angelenos crowd into this 70-seat house to view original works by local authors as well as international playwrights.

OUTDOOR ACTIVITIES, BEACHES, AND SPORTS

Transplants to Los Angeles know they've become acclimated when they go to a movie on a sunny day. Although perfect weather is a constant here, visitors should still take advantage of the range of activities for every level of athlete.

Beaches

From downtown, the easiest way to hit the coast is by taking the Santa Monica Freeway (I–10) due west. Once you reach the end of the freeway, I–10 turns into Highway 1, better known as the Pacific Coast Highway, or PCH, and continues up to Oregon. Other basic routes from the downtown area include Pico, Olympic, Santa Monica, Sunset, or Wilshire boulevards. The MTA bus line runs every 20 minutes past the beaches along each of these streets.

Los Angeles County beaches (and state beaches operated by the county) have lifeguards. Public parking (for a fee) is available at most. The following beaches are listed in north–south order. Some are excellent for swimming, some for surfing (check with lifeguards for current conditions), and others for exploring. Call 310/457–9701 for beach conditions in Malibu.

El Matador State Beach. Scramble down the steps to one of Malibu's most beautiful beaches, where nude sunbathing appears to be unofficially sanctioned. The craggy boulders that make this beach private also make it somewhat dangerous: Watch the tide and don't get trapped between the boulders when it comes in. ✉ *32350 PCH, Malibu,* ☎ *310/457–1324. Parking, rest rooms.*

Leo Carrillo State Beach. This beach along a rough and mountainous stretch of coastline is the most fun at low tide, when tide pools blossom. There are hiking trails, sea caves, and tunnels; whales, dolphins, and sea lions are often seen swimming in the offshore kelp beds. The waters here are rocky and best for experienced surfers and scuba divers; the fishing is good. Campsites, set back from the beach, are $18. ⊠ *35000 block of PCH, Malibu,* ☎ *818/880–0350 or 800/444–7275. Parking, lifeguard, rest rooms, showers, fire pits.*

Zuma Beach Park. This county-run site is Malibu's largest and sandiest beach, and a favorite spot of surfers. ⊠ *30050 PCH, Malibu,* ☎ *310/457–9891. Parking, lifeguard, rest rooms, showers, food, playground, volleyball.*

Westward Beach–Point Dume. A fine spot for surfing, this ½-mi-long sandy beach has tide pools and sandstone cliffs. ⊠ *South end of Westward Beach Rd., Malibu,* ☎ *310/457–9891. Parking, lifeguard, rest rooms, food.*

Paradise Cove. With its pier and equipment rentals, this beach is a mecca for sportfishing boats. Though swimming is allowed, there are lifeguards during the summer only. ⊠ *28128 PCH, Malibu,* ☎ *310/457–9891. Parking, rest rooms, showers, food (concessions open summer only).*

Malibu Lagoon State Beach/Surfrider Beach. The steady 3- to 5-ft waves make this beach north of Malibu Pier great for long-board surfing. The International Surfing Contest is held here in September. Water runoff from Malibu Canyon forms a natural lagoon, which is a sanctuary for many birds. There are also nature trails perfect for romantic sunset strolls. ⊠ *23200 block of PCH, Malibu,* ☎ *818/880–0350. Parking, lifeguard, rest rooms, picnicking, visitor center.*

Las Tunas State Beach. Set beneath a bluff, 2-acre Las Tunas is narrow and sandy, with some rocky areas. Surf fishing is the biggest attraction here. There is a lifeguard in the summer, but swimming is not encouraged because of steel groins set offshore to prevent erosion. ⊠ *19400 block of PCH, Malibu,* ☎ *310/457–9891. Parking, rest rooms.*

Topanga County Beach. This rocky beach stretches from the mouth of the Topanga Canyon down to Coastline Drive. Dolphins sometimes come close enough to shore to startle sunbathers. The area near the canyon is a great surfing spot. ⊠ *18700 block of PCH, Malibu,* ☎ *310/394–3266. Parking, lifeguard, rest rooms, food.*

Will Rogers State Beach. Miles of sandy shoreline and consistent surf make this predominantly gay beach a popular spot for volleyball and bodysurfing. Parking is limited. ⊠ *West of PCH, Pacific Palisades,* ☎ *310/394–3266. Parking, lifeguard, rest rooms.*

Santa Monica State Beach. The widest stretch of beach on the entire Pacific coast is the second home of L.A.'s young, toned, and bronzed. The 2-mi beach has bike paths, facilities for people with disabilities, playgrounds, volleyball, and an amusement park. In summer, free rock and jazz concerts are held at the pier on Thursday nights. ⊠ *West of PCH, Santa Monica,* ☎ *310/394–3266. Parking, lifeguard, rest rooms, showers.*

Venice City Beach. The surf and sand here provide a lovely backdrop, but the real scenery at Venice Beach is on the boardwalk: Beefcake bodybuilders, crafts merchants, comedians, rappers, and street musicians all work the crowds that stroll or roll by. ⊠ *West of Pacific Ave., Venice,* ☎ *310/394–3266. Parking, rest rooms, showers, food, picnicking.*

Manhattan Beach. You can swim, dive, surf, and fish on the 2½ mi of sandy oceanfront here. Facilities include showers and rest rooms. ⊠ *West of Strand, Manhattan Beach,* ☎ *310/372–2166. Parking, lifeguard, rest rooms, showers, food, volleyball.*

Redondo Beach. This sandy beach is usually crowded in the summer, and parking is limited. The Redondo Beach Pier, which hosts a series of rock and jazz concerts in the summer, has restaurants, shops, boating launching ramps, and fishing facilities. ⊠ *Foot of Torrance Blvd., Redondo Beach,* ☎ *310/372–2166. Parking, lifeguard, rest rooms, showers, food, volleyball.*

Participant Sports

For information about tennis courts, hiking and biking trails, and anything else sports-related, call the **City of Los Angeles Recreation and Parks Department** (⊠ 200 N. Main St., Suite 1380, City Hall East, 90012, ☎ 213/485–5515) or **Los Angeles County Parks and Recreation Department** (⊠ 433 S. Vermont Ave., 90020, ☎ 213/738–2961).

Bicycling

The most beautiful bike path in Los Angeles can be found on the Pacific Ocean beach, from Temescal Canyon down to Redondo Beach. San Vicente Boulevard in Santa Monica has a wide, 5-mi cycling lane next to the sidewalk. A marked cycle path traverses Griffith Park.

Rental on the Beach has several locations in Venice (one is at ⊠ 2100 Ocean Front Walk, ☎ 310/821–9338). Bikes are $5 per hour or $18 a day. Near Griffith Park, just east of I–5, is **The Annex** (⊠ 3159 Los Feliz Blvd., ☎ 213/661–6665), which rents bicycles for $15 per day. Call the **M.T.A.** at 213/626–4455 for a map of bike trails.

Bowling

Hollywood Star Lanes (⊠ 5227 Santa Monica Blvd., Hollywood, ☎ 213/665–4111) attracts everyone from quasi-professionals to twentysomething hipsters; it's open 24 hours.

Fishing

Shore fishing and surf casting are excellent on many of the beaches, or you can fish from the Malibu, Santa Monica, and Redondo Beach piers, all of which have nearby bait-and-tackle shops.

Marina del Rey Sport Fishing (⊠ Dock 52, Fiji Way, ☎ 310/822–3625) operates boat excursions for $20 per half day. **Redondo Sport Fishing Company** (⊠ 233 N. Harbor Dr., ☎ 310/372–2111) has various excursions available. In addition to fishing charters, **L.A. Harbor Sportfishing** (☎ 310/547–9916) conducts whale-watching tours off Berth 79 at the San Pedro Harbor from late December through March.

Golf

In Griffith Park, you'll find two splendid 18-hole courses: **Harding Municipal Golf Course** and **Wilson Municipal Golf Course** (⊠ 4730 Crystal Springs Dr. for both, ☎ 213/663–2555) are about 1½ mi inside the park entrance at Riverside Drive and Los Feliz Boulevard. The ninehole **Roosevelt Municipal Golf Course** (⊠ 2650 N. Vermont Ave., ☎ 213/665–2011) can be reached through the park's Vermont Avenue entrance.

There's usually no waiting at the nine-hole pitch 'n' putt **Los Feliz Municipal Golf Course** (⊠ 3207 Los Feliz Blvd., ☎ 213/663–7758). Other pitch 'n' putt courses in Los Angeles include **Holmby Park** (⊠ 601 Club View Dr., Beverly Hills, ☎ 310/276–1604) and **Penmar** (⊠ 1233 Rose Ave., Venice, ☎ 310/396–6228).

Rancho Park Golf Course (✉ 10460 W. Pico Blvd., ☎ 310/838–7373) is a beautifully designed 18-hole course, but the towering pines will make those who slice or hook regret that they ever took up golf.

The **Balboa and Encino Golf courses** (✉ 16821 Burbank Blvd., Encino, ☎ 818/995–1170) in the San Fernando Valley are right next to each other. The **Woodley Lakes Golf Course** (✉ 6331 Woodley Ave., Van Nuys, ☎ 818/780–6886) is flat as a board and has hardly any trees. In summer, the temperature in the Valley can get high enough to fry an egg on your putter, so be sure to bring lots of sunscreen and water.

Health Clubs

There are dozens of health-club chains in the city; some sell daily or weekly memberships. Two that do are **Bodies in Motion** (✉ 10542 W. Pico Blvd., ☎ 310/836–8000), with a full range of aerobics classes including aerobic boxing and kick-boxing classes, and **24 Hour Fitness** (☎ 800/204–2400), with a dozen locations in the Los Angeles area. Both charge $10 per day.

Hiking

Will Rogers Historic State Park has a splendid nature trail. Other parks in the L.A. area that also have hiking trails include Brookside Park, Elysian Park, and Griffith Park. In the Malibu area, Leo Carrillo State Beach and the top of Corral Canyon have rock formations and caves that you can explore on foot. For further information on hiking locations and scheduled outings in Los Angeles, contact the **Sierra Club** (☎ 213/387–4287).

Horseback Riding

Bar "S" Stables (✉ 1850 Riverside Dr., Glendale, ☎ 818/242–8443) will rent you a horse for $13 an hour (plus a $10 deposit). Riders who come here can take advantage of over 50 mi of beautiful bridle trails in the Griffith Park area. **Los Angeles Equestrian Center** (✉ 480 Riverside Dr., Burbank, ☎ 818/840–8401) rents pleasure horses for riding along bridle paths throughout the Griffith Park hills. Horses rent for $15 per hour plus a $15 deposit.

In-line and Roller Skating

To rent Rollerblades, try **Boardwalk Skates** (✉ 201½ Ocean Front Walk, Venice, ☎ 310/450–6634); it charges $4 an hour or $12 for the whole day. Also try **Skatey's** (✉ 102 Washington Blvd., Venice, ☎ 310/823–7971).

If you're looking to get off the streets, there are a number of rinks in L.A. Two are **Moonlight Rollerway** (✉ 5110 San Fernando Rd., Glendale, ☎ 818/241–3630) and **Skateland** (✉ 18140 Parthenia St., Northridge, ☎ 818/885–1491).

Jogging

A scenic jogging-workout trail circles the Coliseum and Sports Arena in Exposition Park. San Vicente Boulevard in Santa Monica has a wide grassy median that splits the street for several miles. The Hollywood Reservoir, just east of Cahuenga Boulevard in the Hollywood Hills, is encircled by a 3-mi asphalt path and has a view of the Hollywood sign. Within hilly Griffith Park are thousands of acres' worth of hilly paths and challenging terrain, while Crystal Springs Drive from the main entrance at Los Feliz to the zoo is a relatively flat 5 mi. Circle Drive, around the perimeter of UCLA in Westwood, provides a 2½-mi run through academia, L.A.-style.

Tennis

Many public parks have courts that require an hourly fee. **Lincoln Park** (✉ Lincoln and Wilshire Blvds., Santa Monica), **Griffith Park** (✉ Riverside Dr. and Los Feliz Blvd.), and **Barrington Recreational Center** (✉ Barrington Ave., south of Sunset Blvd.) all have well-maintained courts with lights. For a complete list of the public tennis courts in Los Angeles, contact the **L.A. Department of Recreation and Parks** (✉ 200 N. Main St., Los Angeles, ☎ 213/485–5515) or the **Southern California Tennis Association** (✉ Box 240015, Los Angeles 90024, ☎ 310/208–3838).

Water Sports

BOATING AND KAYAKING
Action Water Sports (✉ 4144 Lincoln Blvd., Marina del Rey, ☎ 310/306–9539) rents kayaks for $35 per day.

SCUBA DIVING AND SNORKELING
Diving and snorkeling off Leo Carrillo State Beach, Catalina, and the Channel Islands is considered some of the best on the Pacific coast. Dive shops, such as **New England Divers** (✉ 4148 Viking Way, Long Beach, ☎ 562/421–8939) and **Dive 'n Surf** (✉ 504 N. Broadway, Redondo Beach, ☎ 310/372–8423), will provide you with everything you need for your voyage beneath the waves.

SURFING
See Beaches, *above.*

WINDSURFING
Malibu Ocean Sports (✉ 22935 Pacific Coast Hwy., Malibu, ☎ 310/486–6302) rents equipment through its Marina del Rey location from April through October.

Spectator Sports

The best source for tickets to all sporting events is **Ticketmaster** (☎ 213/365–3500). Among the major sports venues in the area are **Anaheim Stadium** (✉ 2000 Gene Autry Way, ☎ 714/937–7200), the **Great Western Forum** (✉ 3900 W. Manchester Blvd., Inglewood, ☎ 310/419–3100), **L.A. Memorial Coliseum** (✉ 3911 S. Figueroa St., downtown, ☎ 213/748–6131), and the **L.A. Sports Arena** (3939 S. Figueroa St., downtown, next to Coliseum, ☎ 213/748–6136).

Baseball
The **Los Angeles Dodgers** of the National League play at Dodger Stadium (✉ 1000 Elysian Park Ave., exit off I–110, Pasadena Fwy., ☎ 213/224–1448). The **Anaheim Angels** (☞ Spectator Sports *in* Chapter 13) play at Anaheim Stadium.

Basketball
COLLEGE
The **University of Southern California** (☎ 213/740–8480) plays at the L.A. Sports Arena. The Bruins of the **University of California at Los Angeles** (☎ 310/206–6831) play at Pauley Pavilion on the UCLA campus.

PROFESSIONAL
The Forum is the home court of **Los Angeles Lakers** (☎ 310/419–3182). The **Los Angeles Clippers** (213/748–8000) play at the L.A. Sports Arena.

Football
The home turf of the **USC Trojans** (☎ 213/740–8480) is the Coliseum. The **UCLA Bruins** (☎ 310/206–6831) pack 'em in at the Rose Bowl (✉ Rosemont Ave. off Arroyo Blvd.) in Pasadena.

Hockey
The **L.A. Kings** (☎ 310/673–6003) put their show on ice at the Forum. Disney's **Mighty Ducks** (☎ 714/704–2500) push the puck in Anaheim (☞ Outdoor Activities and Sports *in* Chapter 13).

Horse Racing
Santa Anita Race Track (✉ Huntington Dr. and Colorado Pl., Arcadia, ☎ 626/574–7223) is still the dominant site for Thoroughbred racing. Races take place from October to mid-November and late December to late April.

Hollywood Park (✉ Century Blvd. and Prairie Ave., Inglewood, ☎ 310/419–1500) is another favorite racing venue. It's open from mid-November to late December and from April to mid-July.

Soccer
The **Los Angeles Galaxy** team plays from April through September at the Rose Bowl in Pasadena. Stars like Andrew Shue of *Melrose Place,* who plays on the team, always draw crowds. For ticket information, call 817–5425 from any area code.

SHOPPING

Most Los Angeles shops are open from 10 to 6, although many remain open until 9 or later, particularly at the shopping centers, on Melrose Avenue, and in Westwood Village during summer. Many Melrose shops don't get moving until 11 AM but are often open Sunday, too. (In most areas, shops are open Sunday for at least a few hours.) Check the *Los Angeles Times* or the *L.A. Weekly* for sales.

Shopping Districts

Beverly Hills
Shopping in Beverly Hills centers mainly around the three-block stretch of **Rodeo Drive** between Santa Monica and Wilshire boulevards and the streets surrounding it.

Barneys New York (✉ 9570 Wilshire Blvd., ☎ 310/276–4400), the West Coast branch of the Manhattan store, is especially popular with young hipsters who come for the cutting-edge designer clothing.

Neiman-Marcus (✉ 9700 Wilshire Blvd., ☎ 310/550–5900) has been dubbed "Needless Markups" by some shoppers, but the Texas-based chain does have a superb selection of women's fashions and accessories (especially shoes).

Robinsons-May (✉ 9900 Wilshire Blvd., ☎ 310/275–5464) is a high-end department store that has many women's fashions, a few men's selections, and a good housewares department.

The **Rodeo Collection** (✉ 421 N. Rodeo Dr., ☎ 310/276–9600) is the epitome of opulence and high fashion, with many famous upscale European designers.

The buyers at **Saks Fifth Avenue** (✉ 9600 Wilshire Blvd., ☎ 310/275–4211) have good—and expensive—taste, especially in the store's extensive collection of high-end designer clothing for women.

Two Rodeo Drive (✉ Rodeo Dr. and Wilshire Blvd., ☎ 310/247–7040), a.k.a. Via Rodeo, is a collection of glossy retail shops housed on a private cobblestone street that somewhat resembles a Hollywood back lot.

FASHIONS AND HOME DECOR
Emporio Armani Boutique (✉ 9533 Brighton Way, ☎ 310/271–7790) stocks the mid-priced line of Italian designer, Giorgio Armani, as well as his accessories and perfumes.

Polo/Ralph Lauren (✉ 444 N. Rodeo Dr., ☎ 310/281–7200) serves up a complete presentation of Lauren's all-encompassing lifestyle products for home and body.

GIFTS

Hammacher Schlemmer (✉ 309 N. Rodeo Dr., ☎ 310/859–7255) is a fabulous place to unearth those hard-to-find presents for adults who never grew up, from rocking horses to "programmable hand-assembled robots."

JEWELRY

Cartier (✉ 370 N. Rodeo Dr., ☎ 310/275–4272) carries all manner of luxury gifts and jewelry with the well-known double-C insignia.

Harry Winston (✉ 371 N. Rodeo, ☎ 310/271–8554) is a favorite spot for celebrities to borrow Oscar-night jewels.

Tiffany & Co. (✉ 210 N. Rodeo Dr., ☎ 310/273–8880), the famous name in fine jewelry, silver, and more, packages each purchase in a signature blue Tiffany box.

Van Cleef & Arpels (✉ 300 N. Rodeo Dr., ☎ 310/276–1161) sells extravagant baubles and fine jewelry as delectable as you'll find anywhere.

KIDS' CLOTHES

Oilily (✉ 9520 Brighton Way, ☎ 310/859–9145) sells colorful and fun Dutch clothing and gifts for children, infants, and even their moms.

MEN'S FASHIONS

Alfred Dunhill of London (✉ 201 N. Rodeo Dr., ☎ 310/274–5351) sells British-made suits, shirts, sweaters, and slacks. Pipes, tobacco, and cigars, however, are this store's claim to fame.

Battaglia (✉ 306 N. Rodeo Dr., ☎ 310/276–7184) carries accessories, shoes, and men's apparel.

Bernini (✉ 326 N. Rodeo Dr., ☎ 310/246–1121) specializes in contemporary Italian designer fashions.

Bijan (✉ 420 N. Rodeo Dr., ☎ 310/273–6544) is a store where it helps to make an appointment. Many designs are created especially by the owner.

WOMEN'S FASHIONS

BCBG Max Azria (✉ 201C N. Rodeo Dr., ☎ 310/278–3263) carries hip, affordable clothes in great colors.

Celine (✉ 313 N. Rodeo Dr., ☎ 310/273–1243) is for luggage, shoes, and accessories as well as traditionally tailored clothing made of fine fabrics.

Chanel (✉ 400 N. Rodeo Dr., ☎ 310/278–5500), known for its fashions and cosmetics, also carries copies of the original Coco designs popular in the 1920s and '30s.

Fred Hayman Beverly Hills (✉ 273 N. Rodeo Dr., ☎ 310/271–3000) is an illustrious store that has glitzy American and European clothing, accessories, and footwear.

Harari (✉ 9646 Brighton Way, ☎ 310/859–1131) is a distinctive boutique showing off classy, forward-looking fashions.

Theodore (✉ 453 N. Rodeo Dr., ☎ 310/276–9691) carries trendy items for men and women in fabulous imported fabrics.

Downtown

The **Cooper Building** (✉ 860 S. Los Angeles St., ☎ 213/622–1139) is a bargain hunter's heaven—four floors of small clothing and shoe shops (mostly for women) with fantastic discounts.

Seventh Marketplace (✉ 735 S. Figueroa St., ☎ 213/955–7150) is an indoor-outdoor multilevel shopping center.

Melrose Avenue

Young shoppers should try their luck at the vintage shops and inexpensive boutiques along the 1½ mi of Melrose Avenue from La Brea to a few blocks west of Crescent Heights; Melrose has some other worthwhile stores both east and west of this strip, too.

Fred Segal (✉ 8118 Melrose Ave., ☎ 213/651–1935) has half a dozen interconnected shops that sell ultrahip clothing and accessories for men and women; it's a shopping mecca for trendy local teenagers.

ANTIQUES

J. F. Chen Antiques (✉ 8414 Melrose Ave., ☎ 213/655–6310) specializes in ancient Asian pieces, among them Chinese bronzes and Burmese tapestries.

Licorne (✉ 8432 Melrose Pl., ☎ 213/852–4765), which sells fine 17th-century furnishings, is one of several antiques shops on or near Melrose Place.

DESIGNER EYEWEAR

LA Eyeworks (✉ 7407 Melrose Ave., ☎ 213/653–8255) is a hip eye-fashions boutique.

HOME DECOR

Cottura (✉ 7215 Melrose Ave., ☎ 213/933–1928) stocks brightly colored Italian tableware, vases, and home accessories.

Modern Living (✉ 8125 Melrose Ave., ☎ 213/655–3898) is a 20th-century furniture gallery representing renowned international designers.

Off the Wall (✉ 7325 Melrose Ave., ☎ 213/930–1185) specializes in screwball and sublime 20th-century nostalgia items.

MEN'S AND WOMEN'S FASHIONS

Betsey Johnson (✉ 7311 Melrose Ave., ☎ 213/931–4490) has frequent—and often dramatic—sales on the American designer's vivid women's fashions.

Comme des Fous (✉ 7384 Melrose Ave., ☎ 213/653–5330) is an avant-garde clothing shop packed with innovative European designs.

Maxfield (✉ 8825 Melrose Ave., ☎ 310/274–8800) is the supplier of choice for many celebrities.

Product (✉ 7385 Beverly Blvd., ☎ 213/932–1958) carries suits and dresses for women that are decidedly on the hip side.

Todd Oldham (✉ 7386 Beverly Blvd., ☎ 213/936–6045) is the designer's shop for his expensive, brightly patterned clothes for women.

Tyler Trafficante (✉ 7290 Beverly Blvd., ☎ 213/931–9678) carries designer Richard Tyler's ultrahip, pricey women's wear.

OFFBEAT ITEMS AND VINTAGE CLOTHING

Golyester (✉ 136 S. La Brea Ave., ☎ 213/931–1339) sells funky used clothes and home furnishings.

Time After Time (✉ 7425 Melrose Ave., ☎ 213/653–8463) has time-honored garments ranging from turn-of-the-century to the 1960s, especially antique wedding dresses.

Wacko (✉ 7402 Melrose Ave., ☎ 213/651–3811) is a wild space crammed with all manner of wacky blow-up toys, cards, Elvis candles, and other semi-useless items that make good Los Angeles keepsakes.

Wasteland (✉ 7428 Melrose Ave., ☎ 213/653–3028) carries an extensive collection of retro clothing, both used and new, all reasonably priced.

Santa Monica

Third Street Promenade (☎ 310/393–8355), the strip of 3rd Street between Broadway and Wilshire Blvd., is a pedestrians-only street lined with boutiques, movie theaters, clubs, pubs, and restaurants. It's as busy at night as it is in the day, with wacky street performers to entertain as you mosey along.

Main Street leading from Santa Monica to Venice (Pico Blvd. to Rose Ave.) is another of those rare places in Los Angeles where you can indulge in a pleasant walk. While enjoying the ocean breeze, you'll pass some quite good restaurants and unusual shops and galleries. There are small chains represented here as well, like **Betsey Johnson** (✉ 2929 Main St., ☎ 310/452–7911) and **A/X Armani Exchange** (✉ 2940 Main St., ☎ 310/396–8799).

Montana Avenue, a stretch of a dozen or so blocks from 9th to 17th streets, contains boutique after boutique of high-quality goods.

Shopping Malls

The **Beverly Center** (☎ 310/854–0070), bounded by Beverly Boulevard, La Cienega Boulevard, San Vicente Boulevard, and 3rd Street, covers more than 7 acres and contains 200 stores, anchored by **Macy's** (☎ 310/854–6655) and **Bloomingdale's** (☎ 310/360–2700). Most of the stores inside are upscale but standard mall fare.

Century City Shopping Center & Marketplace (✉ 10250 Little Santa Monica Blvd., ☎ 310/277–3898), set among gleaming, tall office buildings on what used to be Twentieth Century-Fox Film Studios' back lot, is an open-air mall with an excellent roster of shops. Besides **Macy's** (☎ 310/556–1611) and **Bloomingdale's** (☎ 310/772–2100), you'll find independent boutiques and many chain stores.

The **Westside Pavilion** (☎ 310/474–6255) is a pastel-color postmodern mall with three levels of shops and restaurants. The department stores here are **Robinsons-May** (☎ 310/475–4911) and **Nordstrom** (☎ 310/470–6155).

Over "The Hill" and into the Valleys of Los Angeles, you'll be entering Mall Country. There's **Sherman Oaks Galleria** (✉ 15301 Ventura Blvd., Sherman Oaks, ☎ 818/783–7100), **The Promenade** (✉ 6100 Topanga Canyon Blvd., ☎ 818/884–7090) in Woodland Hills, **Glendale Galleria** (✉ 2148 Central Blvd., ☎ 818/240–9481), and **Encino Town Center** and **Plaza de Oro** (✉ 17200 Ventura Blvd., ☎ 818/788–6100) in Encino.

Cranberry House (✉ 12318 Ventura Blvd., Studio City, ☎ 818/506–8945) is a huge shopping arena covering half a city block, packed with 140 kiosks run by L.A.'s leading antiques dealers, who sell at very decent prices. Visit for vintage furniture, clothing, jewelry, and furnishings.

SIDE TRIPS FROM LOS ANGELES

Lake Arrowhead and Big Bear Lake

San Bernardino's mountain playground centers around the resorts of Lake Arrowhead and Big Bear, close together but distinct in appeal. Lake Arrowhead's cool mountain air is that area's lure in summertime, when people come to hike in the woods, sniff the daffodils, and play in the water. Arrowhead is more upscale than Big Bear, which comes alive in winter with skiing and snowboarding. The Rim of the World Scenic Byway, which connects with Lake Arrowhead and Big Bear Lake, is a magnificent drive. During spring and fall you can catch views of the San Bernardino Valley from an elevation of 8,000 ft.

Numbers in the margin correspond to points of interest on the Lake Arrowhead and Big Bear Lake map.

Lake Arrowhead

90 mi from Los Angeles, I–10 east to I–215 north to Hwy. 30 east (mountain resorts turnoff) to Hwy. 18 (Waterman Ave.) and then Hwy. 138 north to Hwy. 173 (Lake Arrowhead turnoff; follow signs from there).

❶ **Lake Arrowhead Village** is an alpine community with offices, shops, and eateries. You can obtain information about events, camping, and lodging from the **Lake Arrowhead Communities Chamber of Commerce** (✉ 28200 Hwy. 189, Bldg. F, Suite 290, Lake Arrowhead Village, ☎ 909/337–3715). Only residents are permitted to have boats on the lake, but you can take a scenic 50-minute cruise on the *Arrowhead Queen,* operated daily by **LeRoy Sports** (☎ 909/336–6992) from the waterfront marina. Reservations are essential. The **Lake Arrowhead Children's Museum** (☎ 909/336–1332), on the lower level of the village, has hands-on exhibits, a climbing maze, and a puppet stage.

❷ Just past the town of Rim Forest you'll come across the fire lookout tower at **Strawberry Peak.** If you brave the steep stairway to the tower, you'll be treated to a magnificent view and a lesson on fire spotting by the lookout staff. This is also a good place to have a picnic.

❸ If you're up for a barbecue in a wooded setting, visit **Baylis Park Picnic Ground,** which has plenty of spots for a good alfresco meal.

❹ **Lake Gregory,** at the ridge of Crestline, was formed by a dam constructed in 1938. Because the water temperature in summer is seldom extremely cold—as it can be in the other lakes at this altitude—this is the best swimming lake in the mountains, but it's open in summer only. There's a nominal charge to swim. Fishing is allowed, there are water slides, and you can rent rowboats at Lake Gregory Village.

Dining and Lodging

$$ ✕ **Casual Elegance.** The menu changes weekly at this casual restaurant 2 mi outside Arrowhead Village, but the steaks and seafood, as well as the service, remain first rate. ✉ *26848 Hwy. 189, Agua Fria,* ☎ *909/337–8932. AE, D, MC, V.*

$$ ✕ **Royal Oak.** This dimly lit restaurant-bar has the feel of an English pub. The best dishes include pepper steak with baked potato and creamed spinach, and halibut fillet with hollandaise sauce. ✉ *Blue Jay Village,* ☎ *909/337–6018. AE, MC, V. No lunch Sun.–Mon.*

$$$–$$$$ ▥ **Lake Arrowhead Resort.** The design and Old World graciousness of this lakeside lodge are reminiscent of the Alps. ✉ *27984 Hwy. 189, Arrowhead Village 92352,* ☎ *909/336–1511 or 800/800–6792,* ℻

Lake Arrowhead and Big Bear Lake

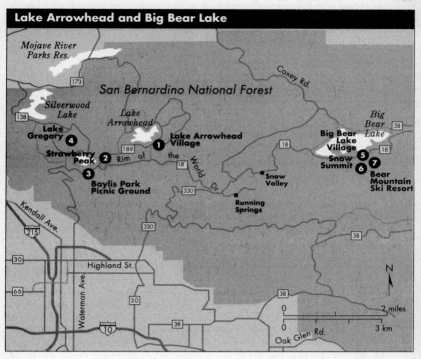

909/336–1378. 261 rooms. Restaurant, coffee shop, lounge, pool, health club, beach. AE, D, DC, MC, V.

$$–$$$ ☶ **Carriage House Bed & Breakfast.** The guest rooms of this New England–style B&B have country furnishings, down comforters, and lake views. In addition to complimentary breakfast, afternoon refreshments are served. ⊠ 472 Emerald Dr., 92352, ☎ 909/336–1400 or 800/526–5070. 3 rooms. AE, MC, V.

Big Bear Lake
110 mi from Los Angeles, I–10 east to I–215 north to Hwy. 30 east to Hwy. 330 north to Hwy. 18 east; chains are sometimes needed in winter.

❺ You'll spot an occasional chaletlike building in **Big Bear Lake Village,** an alpine- and Western-mountain-style town on the lake's south shore. The paddle wheeler ***Big Bear Queen*** (☎ 909/866–3218) departs daily, May through October, from Big Bear Marina for 90-minute scenic tours of the lake; the cost is $9.50. Fishing-boat and equipment rentals are available from several lakeside marinas, including Pine Knot Landing (☎ 909/866–2628), adjacent to Big Bear Village. For general information and lodging reservations, contact the **Big Bear Chamber of Commerce** (☎ 909/866–4607).

❻ Just southeast of Big Bear Village is **Snow Summit,** one of the area's top ski resorts. It has an 8,200-ft peak and 31 trails, along with two high-speed quads and eight other lifts. Summit has more advanced runs than nearby ski resorts and usually has the best snow. Trails are opened to mountain bikers in summer. ⊠ 880 Summit Blvd., off Big Bear Blvd., ☎ 909/866–5766.

❼ **Bear Mountain Ski Resort,** also southeast of Big Bear village, has 11 chairlifts and 35 trails. Bear Mountain caters to intermediate skiers.

On busy winter weekends and holidays, it's best to reserve tickets before heading for the mountain. ⊠ *43101 Goldmine Dr., off Moonridge Rd.,* ☎ *909/585–2519.*

Dining and Lodging

$$–$$$ ✕ **Madlon's.** Among the best dishes at this local favorite are the lamb chops with Gorgonzola butter and the cream of jalapeño soup. ⊠ *829 W. Big Bear Blvd., Big Bear City,* ☎ *909/585–3762. D, MC, V. Closed Tues.*

$$ ✕ **Iron Squirrel.** Here, in a country-French setting, you'll dine on hearty French dishes such as veal Normandie and chateaubriand. ⊠ *646 Pineknot Blvd., Big Bear Lake,* ☎ *909/866–9121. AE, MC, V.*

$ ✕ **Blue Ox Bar and Grill.** The fare at this rustic restaurant includes steaks, ribs, burgers, and chicken. The bar is great for meeting and greeting. ⊠ *441 W. Big Bear Blvd., Big Bear City,* ☎ *909/585–7886. AE, D, DC, MC, V.*

$$$–$$$$ 🏨 **Gold Mountain Manor.** A restored mansion made of logs, this structure dates back to the 1930s. Each room at the B&B within has a fireplace and an old-fashioned bed. ⊠ *1117 Anita, off North Shore Dr., Big Bear City 92314,* ☎ *909/585–6997,* ℻ *909/585–0327. 6 no-smoking rooms. D, MC, V.*

$$$ 🏨 **Apples Bed and Breakfast Inn.** This B&B surrounded by an acre of
★   pine trees feels remote and peaceful despite its location on the busy road to the ski lifts. Colorful floral wallpapers and linens adorn the rooms, which all have fireplaces. ⊠ *42430 Moonridge Rd., Big Bear Lake 92315,* ☎ *909/866–0903. 12 rooms. Outdoor hot tub. AE, D, MC, V.*

$$–$$$ 🏨 **Big Bear Inn.** Big Bear's grandest hotel resembles a mountain château in the European tradition. You may find, however, that the level of service is inconsistent. Guest rooms are furnished with brass beds and antiques. ⊠ *42200 Moonridge Rd., Big Bear Lake 92315,* ☎ *909/ 866–3471 or 800/232–7466,* ℻ *909/866–8988. 75 rooms, 3 suites. Restaurant, bar, pool. AE, MC, V.*

$$ 🏨 **Northwoods Resort.** Opened in late 1995, Northwoods is a giant log cabin with all the amenities of a resort. The rooms are large yet cozy; some have fireplaces and whirlpool tubs. Ski packages are available. ⊠ *40650 Village Dr., Big Bear Lake 92315,* ☎ *909/866–3121 or 800/866–3121,* ℻ *909/878–2122. 153 rooms and suites. Restaurant, pool, hot tub, exercise room. AE, D, DC, MC, V.*

$$ 🏨 **Robinhood Inn and Lodge.** Centrally located near Snow Summit, this family-oriented motel has affordable rooms and condos, with or without kitchenettes. Each brightly colored room is decorated with simple country furniture. Some have fireplaces or whirlpool tubs. ⊠ *40797 Lakeview Dr., Big Bear Lake 92315,* ☎ *909/866–4643 or 800/990– 9956,* ℻ *909/866–4645. 21 rooms. Restaurant, hot tub. AE, MC, V.*

Lake Arrowhead and Big Bear Lake A to Z

Contacts and Resources

LODGING

Most places require two-night weekend stays. The **Big Bear Lake Resort Association** (☎ 909/866–7000) will refer you to area innkeepers.

VISITOR INFORMATION

Lake Arrowhead Communities Chamber of Commerce (☎ 909/337–3715). **Big Bear Chamber of Commerce** (⊠ 630 Bartlett Rd., Big Bear Village, ☎ 909/866–4607).

Catalina Island

Summer, weekends, and holidays, Catalina draws thousands of L.A.-area boaters, who tie their vessels at protected moorings in Avalon and other coves. The exceptionally clear water surrounding the island attracts divers and snorkelers. Although there's not much in the way of sandy beaches, sunbathing and water sports remain popular. The main town of Avalon is a charming, old-fashioned beach community, where palm trees shade the main street and yachts bob in the crescent-shape bay. White buildings dotting the semiarid hillsides invite comparisons with the Greek isles.

Cruise ships sail into Avalon twice a week and smaller boats shuttle visitors between Avalon and Two Harbors, a small isthmus cove on the island's northwest side. The Catalina Island Company and Catalina Adventure Tours lead bus excursions beyond Avalon. If you want to explore the island other than by boat or bus, you'll have to hike (by permit only), because roads are limited and nonresident vehicles are prohibited.

Discovered by Juan Rodriguez Cabrillo in 1542, the island has sheltered many dubious characters, from Russian fur trappers (seeking sea-otter skins), slave traders, pirates, and gold miners to bootleggers, filmmakers, and movie stars. In 1919, William Wrigley Jr., the chewing gum magnate, purchased a controlling interest in the company developing the island. Wrigley had the island's most famous landmark, the Casino, built in 1929, and he made Catalina the site of spring training for his Chicago Cubs baseball team.

In 1975, the Santa Catalina Island Conservancy, a nonprofit foundation, acquired about 86% of the island to help preserve the natural resources here. Depending on which route you take, you can expect to see buffalo (whose ancestors were brought to the island for the 1925 filming of *The Vanishing American*), goats, and boar or unusual species of sea life, including such oddities as electric perch, saltwater goldfish, and flying fish.

Although Catalina can be seen in a day, there are several inviting hotels that make it worth extending your stay for one or more nights. A short itinerary might include a tour of the interior, a snorkeling excursion at Casino Point, dinner in Avalon, cocktails at one of the nightspots, and breakfast along the boardwalk. The fairly primitive Two Harbors resort area on the western side of the island is accessible by water or bus from Avalon and in summer by ferry from the mainland (☞ Arriving and Departing *in* Catalina Island Essentials, *below*).

Avalon

Take the ferry from San Pedro, Long Beach, or Newport Beach, or a catamaran from Huntington Beach. Helicopter service is offered from Long Beach and San Pedro.

Avalon, Catalina's only real town, extends from the shore of its natural harbor to the surrounding hillsides. Most of the city's activity, however, is centered along the boardwalk of Crescent Avenue, and the majority of sights are easily reached by foot. Private autos are restricted and rental cars aren't allowed, but taxis, trams, and shuttles are easily accessible. If you are determined to have a set of wheels, rent a bicycle or a golf cart. You'll find rentals along Crescent Avenue as you walk in from the dock. To hike the interior of the island, you'll need a permit (for safety reasons), available free from the Catalina Conservancy (☞ Getting Around *in* Catalina Island Essentials, *below*).

Catalina Island

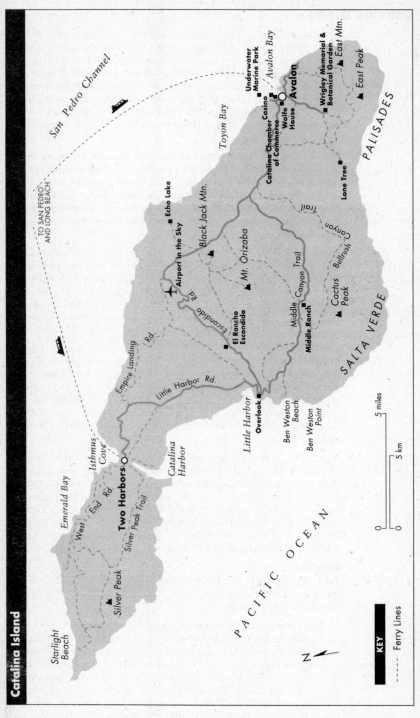

San Pedro Channel

San Pedro Channel

TO SAN PEDRO AND LONG BEACH

Starlight Beach

Emerald Bay

West End Rd.

Silver Peak Trail

Silver Peak

Isthmus Cove

Two Harbors

Catalina Harbor

Empire Landing Rd.

Little Harbor Rd.

Little Harbor
Overlook

Ben Weston Beach

Ben Weston Point

Echo Lake

Airport in the Sky

Escondido Rd.

Black Jack Mtn.

Mt. Orizaba

El Rancho Escondido

Middle Ranch

Middle Canyon Trail

Bullrush Canyon Trail

Cactus Peak

SALTA VERDE

Toyon Bay

Avalon Bay

Underwater Marine Park

Catalina Chamber of Commerce

Casino

Wolfe House

Avalon

Wrigley Memorial & Botanical Garden

East Mtn.

East Peak

Lone Tree

PALISADES

PACIFIC OCEAN

N

5 miles

5 km

KEY

----- Ferry Lines

Your first stop after you walk along the Harbor Front is **Crescent Avenue.** Look for the vivid art deco tiles that adorn the avenue's fountains and planters. The tiles, which were fired on the island by the now defunct Catalina Tile Company, are today a coveted commodity.

At the **Green Pier,** at the center of Crescent Avenue, stand with your back to the harbor and you'll be in a good position to survey Avalon. At the top of the hill on your left, is the **Inn at Mt. Ada,** now a top-of-the-line B&B, but once a getaway estate built by William Wrigley Jr. for his wife.

On the northwest point of Crescent Bay (looking to your right from Green Pier) is the **Casino.** Built in 1929, this circular white structure is considered one of the finest examples of art deco architecture anywhere. Its Spanish-inspired floors and murals show off brilliant blue and green Catalina tiles. "Casino" is the Italian word for "gathering place," and has nothing to do with gambling here. Rather, Casino life revolves around the magnificent ballroom; on holiday weekends you can attend big-band dances similar to those that made the Casino famous in the 1930s and '40s. Call 310/510–1520 for tickets. Daytime tours (☎ 310/510–8687) of the establishment, lasting about 50 minutes, cost $8. You can also visit the **Catalina Island Museum,** in the lower level of the Casino, which surveys 7,000 years of island history; or stop in at the **Casino Art Gallery,** which displays the works of local artists. In the evening, see a first-run movie at the **Avalon Theater,** noteworthy for its classic 1929 theater pipe organ. ✉ *1 Casino Way,* ☎ *310/510–2414 for museum, 310/510–0808 for art gallery, 310/510– 0179 for Avalon Theater.* 🎟 *Museum $1.50, art gallery free.* ☉ *Museum daily 10:30–4, art gallery Thurs.–Tues. 10:30–4.*

In front of the Casino, snorkelers and divers explore the crystal-clear waters of the **Underwater Marine Park at Casino Point,** where moray eels, bat rays, spiny lobsters, halibut, and other sea animals cruise around kelp forests and along the sandy bottom. The area is protected from boats and other watercraft. Snorkeling equipment can be rented on or near the pier.

Two miles south of Avalon via Avalon Canyon Road is the **Wrigley Memorial and Botanical Garden.** This garden contains plants native to southern California, including several that grow only on Catalina Island. A Spanish mausoleum that was never used by the Wrigleys is worth a look. Tram service between the memorial and Avalon is available daily between 8 AM and 5 PM. ✉ *Avalon Canyon Rd.,* ☎ *310/ 510–2288.* 🎟 *$1.50 donation.* ☉ *Daily 10–5.*

Walk through the residential hills of Avalon and you'll see interesting architecture such as the contemporary **Wolfe House** on Chimes Tower Road, built in 1928 by architect Rudolf Schindler. The house is a private residence, but you can get a good view of it from the path below and from the street. Across the street, the **Zane Grey Estate** (✉ 124 Chimes Tower Rd., ☎ 310/510–0966 or 800/378–3256) has been transformed into a rustic hotel.

Dining and Lodging

$$ ✕ **Cafe Prego.** This Italian waterfront restaurant specializes in pasta, seafood, and steak. Be prepared for a long wait if you forget to make reservations. ✉ *603 Crescent Ave.,* ☎ *310/510–1218.* AE, D, DC, MC, V.

$$ ✕ **Channel House.** Owned by a German couple, this restaurant serves
★ dishes like Catalina swordfish, duckling à l'orange, and pepper steak. There's an outdoor patio facing the harbor, as well as a dining room and a beautiful Irish bar. ✉ *205 Crescent Ave.,* ☎ *310/510–1617.* AE, D, MC, V. *Closed Jan.–Feb.*

$$$$ 🏨 **Inn on Mt. Ada.** Occupying the former Wrigley Mansion, the island's most exclusive hotel offers all the comforts of a millionaire's mansion, beginning at $340 a night during the summer season. All meals, beverages, snacks, and the use of a golf cart are included. The six bedrooms are elegantly decorated, some with canopy beds and all with traditional furniture and overstuffed chairs. The hilltop view of the Pacific is spectacular, and the service is discreet. ⊠ *398 Wrigley Rd., Avalon 90704,* ☎ *310/510–2030,* FAX *310/510–2237. 6 rooms. MC, V.*

$$–$$$ 🏨 **Hotel Metropole and Marketplace.** The romantic feel of this hotel is reminiscent of New Orleans' French Quarter hostelry. ⊠ *225 Crescent Ave., Avalon 90704,* ☎ *310/510–1884 or 800/541–8528. 48 rooms. AE, MC, V.*

$$–$$$ 🏨 **Hotel Vista del Mar.** The rooms here, most of which open onto a skylighted atrium, are surprisingly bright with contemporary rattan decor and abundant greenery. ⊠ *417 Crescent Ave., Avalon 90704,* ☎ *310/ 510–1452,* FAX *310/510–2917. 15 rooms. AE, D, MC, V.*

$$–$$$ 🏨 **Pavilion Lodge.** Across the street from the beach, this popular motel has simply furnished but spacious rooms. ⊠ *513 Crescent Ave., Avalon 90704,* ☎ *800/851–0217. 72 rooms. AE, D, DC, MC, V.*

Nightlife
El Galleon (⊠ 411 Crescent Ave., ☎ 310/510–1188) has microbrews and karaoke. At **Luau Larry's** (⊠ 509 Crescent Ave., ☎ 310/510–1919), cocktails are consumed with oyster shooters and calypso hats. The **Catalina Comedy Club** (⊠ Glenmore Plaza Hotel, Sumner St., ☎ 310/ 510–0017) books top comic acts.

Catalina Island Essentials
ARRIVING AND DEPARTING
By Boat: Catalina Cruises (☎ 800/228–2546) departs from Long Beach several times daily, taking two hours to reach Avalon before continuing to Two Harbors. The fare is $23 round-trip.

Catalina Express (☎ 310/519–1212 or 800/995–4386) makes an hour-long run from Long Beach or San Pedro to Avalon and Two Harbors; the round-trip fare from Long Beach and San Pedro is $36.

Service is also available from Newport Beach through **Catalina Passenger Service** (☎ 714/673–5245), which leaves from Balboa Pavilion at 9 AM, takes 75 minutes to reach the island, and costs $33. The return boat leaves Catalina at 4:30 PM. You can make arrangements to boat in one direction and fly in the other, but you must make reservations separately. Reservations are advised.

Sail Catalina (☎ 562/592–5790) uses a large catamaran to sail people from Avalon to Huntington Beach for $49 round-trip (the boat motors to Catalina in an hour and sails back in two to three hours). The company also offers island cruises.

By Bus: Catalina Safari Bus (☎ 310/510–7265) has regular bus service between Avalon and Two Harbors; the trip takes two hours.

By Helicopter: Island Express (☎ 310/510–2525) flies hourly from San Pedro and Long Beach. The trip takes about 15 minutes and costs $66 one-way, $121 round-trip.

GETTING AROUND
By Bicycle: Bike rentals abound in Avalon for about $6 per hour. Look for rental stands on Crescent Avenue and Pebbly Beach Road. **Brown's Bikes** (☎ 310/510–0986) is one option.

On Foot: To hike into the island's interior, you must obtain a free permit from the **Catalina Conservancy** (⊠ 3rd and Claressa, ☎ 310/510–

2595) or from **Doug Bombard Enterprises** (☎ 310/510–7265), which has a booth in the Avalon bus plaza and in Two Harbors. Permits can be obtained on the spot, daily 9 to 5.

By Golf Cart: Golf carts are the island's main form of transportation. You can rent them along Avalon's Crescent Avenue and Pebbly Beach Road for about $30 per hour. Try **Island Rentals** (⊠ 125 Pebbly Beach Rd., ☎ 310/510–1456).

GUIDED TOURS

Santa Catalina Island Company (☎ 310/510–8687) and **Catalina Adventure Tours** (☎ 310/510–2888) conduct tours of the region.

VISITOR INFORMATION

Catalina Chamber of Commerce and Visitor's Bureau (⊠ Green Pier, ☎ 310/510–1520).

LOS ANGELES A TO Z

Arriving and Departing

By Bus
Greyhound Lines (⊠ 208 E. 6th St., ☎ 800/231–2222).

By Car
Los Angeles is at the western terminus of I–10, a major interstate highway that runs all the way east to Florida. I–15, angling southwest from Las Vegas, swings through the eastern communities around San Bernardino before heading on to San Diego. I–5, which runs north–south through California, leads up to San Francisco and down to San Diego.

By Plane
The major gateway to Los Angeles is **Los Angeles International Airport,** (☎ 310/646–5252), commonly called LAX; it is serviced by several dozen major airlines, including **Air Canada, America West, American, British Airways, Continental, Delta, Japan Air Lines, Northwest, Skywest, Southwest, TWA, United,** and **US Airways.** *See* Air Travel *in* the Gold Guide for phone numbers.

Long Beach Airport (☎ 562/570–2600), at the southern tip of Los Angeles County, is served by Alaska and America West airlines.

Burbank/Glendale/Pasadena Airport (☎ 818/840–8847) serves the San Fernando Valley. Alaska, American, America West, Reno Air, Southwest, and United fly here.

Ontario International Airport (⊠ Airport Dr., south from Vineyard Ave. exit of I–10, ☎ 909/988–2700) in Riverside County is served by Alaska, America West, American, Continental, Delta, Northwest, Reno Air, Skywest, Southwest, TWA, United, and US Airways.

For information about **John Wayne Orange County Airport** (☎ 714/252–5006) *see* Orange County A to Z *in* Chapter 13.

BETWEEN THE AIRPORT AND DOWNTOWN

A taxi ride to downtown from LAX can take 30 minutes—if there is no traffic. But in Los Angeles, that's a big if. Visitors should request the flat fee ($30 at press time) to downtown or choose from the several ground transportation companies that offer set rates.

SuperShuttle (☎ 310/782–6600 or 213/775–6600) offers direct service between the airport and hotels. The trip to or from downtown hotels costs about $12. The seven-passenger vans operate 24 hours a

Los Angeles Freeways

day. In the airport, call 310/782–6600 or use the SuperShuttle courtesy phone in the luggage area; the van should arrive within 15 minutes. **Shuttle One** (☎ 310/670–6666) provides door-to-door service and low rates ($10 per person from LAX to hotels in the Disneyland/Anaheim area). **Airport Coach** (☎ 714/938–8900 or 800/772–5299) provides regular service between LAX and the Pasadena and Anaheim areas.

The following limo companies charge a flat rate for airport service, ranging from $65 to $95: **Jackson Limousine** (☎ 213/734–9955), **A-1 West Coast Limousine** (☎ 213/756–5466), and **Dav-El Livery** (☎ 310/550–0070).

Flyaway Service (☎ 818/994–5554) offers transportation between LAX and the central San Fernando Valley for $3.50. For the western San Fernando Valley and Ventura area, contact the **Great American Stage Lines** (☎ 800/287–8659). They charge from $11 to $21 one way.

MTA (☎ 213/626-4455) also offers limited airport service to all areas of greater L.A.; bus lines depart from bus docks directly across the street from airport parking lot C. Prices vary from $1.35 to $3.10; some routes require transfers. To downtown, take Bus 42 ($1.35) or the express Bus 439 ($1.85). Both take about 70 minutes.

By Train
Los Angeles can be reached by **Amtrak** (☎ 800/872–7245). The *Coast Starlight* travels from Seattle to Los Angeles. The *Sunset Limited* goes to Los Angeles from New Orleans, the *Texas Eagle* from San Antonio, and the *Southwest Chief* and the *Desert Wind* from Chicago. Trains terminate at **Union Station** (✉ 800 N. Alameda St.) in downtown Los Angeles.

Getting Around

By Bus
A ride on the **Metropolitan Transit Authority (MTA)** (☎ 213/626–4455) costs $1.35, with 25¢ for each transfer.

DASH (Downtown Area Short Hop) minibuses travel around the downtown area, stopping every two blocks or so. There are five different routes with pickups at five-minute intervals. You pay 25¢ every time you get on, no matter how far you go. DASH (☎ 213/626–4455) runs weekdays 6:30 AM to 7 PM, Saturday 10 AM to 5 PM.

By Car
In Los Angeles, it's not a question of whether wheels are a hindrance or a convenience: They're a necessity. If you plan to drive extensively, consider buying a *Thomas Guide,* which contains detailed maps of the entire county. Despite what you've heard, traffic is not always a major problem, especially if you avoid rush hours (7 to 9 AM and 3 to 7 PM). Seat belts must be worn by all passengers at all times.

More than 35 major companies and dozens of local rental companies serve a steady demand for cars at Los Angeles International Airport and various city locations. For a list of the major car-rental companies, *see* Car Rentals *in* the Gold Guide.

By Limousine
Limousines come equipped with everything from a full bar and telephone to a hot tub and a double bed. Reputable companies include **Dav-El Livery** (☎ 310/550–0070) and **First Class** (☎ 310/476–1960).

By Subway
The **Metro Red Line** runs 4½ miles through downtown, from Union Station to MacArthur Park, making five stops. The fare is $1.35.

By Taxi

You probably won't be able to hail a cab on the street in Los Angeles. Instead, you should phone one of the many taxi companies. The rate is $1.90 to start and $1.60 per mile. Two of the more reputable companies are **Independent Cab Co.** (☎ 213/385–8294) and **United Independent Taxi** (☎ 213/653–5050).

By Train

The **Metrorail Blue Line** runs daily, from 5 AM to 10 PM, from downtown Los Angeles (✉ Flower and 7th Sts.) to Long Beach (✉ 1st St. and Long Beach Ave.), with 18 stops en route, most of them in Long Beach. The fare is $1.35 one way.

Contacts and Resources

Emergencies

Ambulance (☎ 911). **Police** (☎ 911).

Most larger hospitals in Los Angeles have 24-hour emergency rooms. Two are **Cedar-Sinai Medical Center** (✉ 8700 Beverly Blvd., ☎ 310/855–5000) and **Queen of Angels Hollywood Presbyterian Medical Center** (✉ 1300 N. Vermont Ave., ☎ 213/413–3000).

Guided Tours

ORIENTATION TOURS

Los Angeles is so spread out and has such a wealth of sightseeing possibilities that an orientation bus tour may prove useful. All tours are fully narrated by a driver-guide. Reservations must be made in advance. Many hotels can book them for you.

L.A. Tours and Sightseeing (✉ 6333 W. 3rd St., at the Farmers Market, ☎ 213/937–3361 or 800/286–8752) has a $38 tour covering various parts of the city, including downtown, Hollywood, and Beverly Hills. The company also operates tours to Disneyland, Universal Studios, Magic Mountain, the beaches, and stars' homes.

Starline Tours of Hollywood (✉ 6541 Hollywood Blvd., Hollywood 90028, ☎ 800/959–3131 or 213/463–3333) picks up passengers from area hotels as well as around the corner from Mann's Chinese Theater (✉ 6925 Hollywood Blvd.). Universal Studios, Sea World, Knott's Berry Farm, stars' homes, Disneyland, and other attractions are on this company's agenda. Prices range from $26 to $68.

A more personalized look at the city can be had by planning a tour with **Casablanca Tours** (✉ Clarion Hollywood Roosevelt Hotel, 7000 Hollywood Blvd., Cabana 4, Hollywood 90028, ☎ 213/461–0156), which offers a four-hour insider's look at Hollywood and Beverly Hills. Tours are in minibuses with a maximum of 14 people, and the prices are equivalent to the large bus tours—from $35 to $68.

PERSONAL GUIDES

Elegant Tours for the Discriminating (☎ 310/472–4090) is a personalized sightseeing and shopping service for the Beverly Hills area. Joan Mansfield offers her extensive knowledge of Rodeo Drive to one, two, or three people at a time. Lunch is included.

L.A. Nighthawks (☎ 310/392–1500) will arrange your nightlife for you. For a hefty price, you'll get a limousine, a guide, and immediate entry into L.A.'s hottest nightspots.

SPECIAL-INTEREST TOURS

Advantage Tours and Charters (☎ 310/823–0321 or 213/933–1475) specializes in touring area museums, but also has beach tours.

Grave Line Tours (☏ 213/469–4149) is a clever, off-the-beaten-track tour that digs up the dirt on notorious suicides and visits the scenes of various murders, scandals, and other crimes via a luxuriously renovated hearse. Tours, which begin daily at 9:30 AM and last 2½ hours (a 12:30 tour will be scheduled if the morning one is full, and sometimes a 3:30 PM tour leaves as well), are offered Tuesday through Sunday and cost $40 per person.

Trolleywood Tours (✉ 6715 Hollywood Blvd., Suite 103, Hollywood 90028, ☏ 213/469–8184 or 800/782–7287) has daily tours that takes you through downtown Hollywood and by the "Hollywood" sign, past star's homes and through historical parts of town. The cost is $16 to $37 per person, depending on the tour.

Visitors who want something dramatically different should check with Marlene Gordon of **The Next Stage** (✉ Box 35269, Los Angeles 90035, ☏ 213/939–2688). This innovative tour company takes from 2 to 200 people, by foot, buses, or vans, in search of "the real L.A." Popular tours include Victorian L.A., Notable Women in L.A., the Insomniac's Tour, and Secret Gardens.

LA Today Custom Tours (✉ 14964 Camarosa Dr., Pacific Palisades 90272, ☏ 310/454–5730) has a wide selection of offbeat tours, some of which tie in with seasonal and cultural events, such as theater, museum exhibits, and the Rose Bowl. Groups range from 8 to 800, and prices are from $6 to $85.

WALKING TOURS

The **Los Angeles Conservancy** (☏ 213/623–2489) offers low-cost walking tours of the downtown area. Each Saturday at 10 AM one of several tours leaves from the Olive Street entrance of the Regal Biltmore Hotel. The cost is $5 per person. Make reservations because group size is limited.

Late-Night Pharmacies

The **Kaiser Bellflower Pharmacy** (✉ 9400 E. Rosecrans Ave., Bellflower, ☏ 562/461–4213) is open around the clock. Many towns have a Thrifty or Sav-On pharmacy that stays open late.

Visitor Information

California Visitor Information Center (✉ 685 S. Figueroa St., (☏ 213/689–8822). **Hollywood Visitor Information Center** (✉ 6541 Hollywood Blvd., ☏ 213/689–8822). **Los Angeles Convention and Visitors Bureau** (✉ 633 W. 5th St., Suite 6000, 90071, ☏ 213/624–7300).

13 Orange County

No place in southern California evokes the stereotype of the California good life quite the way Orange County does: Million-dollar mansions grace the coastline, golf courses meander through inland hills, and convertibles swarm Pacific Coast Highway. Buffed, tanned bodies pack the beaches— consider working out assiduously before heading to the shore, especially if you want to make a good impression on the Baywatch *recruiters.*

FEW OF THE CITRUS GROVES that gave Orange County its name remain. This region south and east of Los Angeles is now a high-tech business hub where tourism is the number one industry. Anaheim's theme parks lure hordes of visitors; numerous festivals celebrate the county's culture and relatively brief history; and the area supports fine dining, upscale shopping, and several standout visual and performing arts facilities. The stretch of coast between Seal Beach and San Clemente is often called the "American Riviera." Exclusive Newport Beach, trendy Laguna, and the up-and-coming surf town of Huntington Beach are the stars, but lesser-known gems such as Corona del Mar are also worth exploring.

Updated by
Shane
Christensen

Pleasures and Pastimes

Dining

Orange County has long been a haven for the fast-food and meat-and-potatoes crowds, but you'll also find stylish Continental fare and contemporary adaptations of European and Asian cuisine.

CATEGORY	COST*
$$$$	over $50
$$$	$30–$50
$$	$20–$30
$	under $20

per person for a three-course meal, excluding drinks, service, and 8½% sales tax

Lodging

The prices listed in this chapter are based on summer rates. Rooms often cost less in winter, especially near Disneyland (unless there's a convention in Anaheim), and weekend rates are often rock-bottom at business hotels; it's worth calling around for bargains.

CATEGORY	COST*
$$$$	over $175
$$$	$120–$175
$$	$80–$120
$	under $80

All prices are for a standard double room, excluding tax.

Outdoor Activities and Sports

Bicycles and in-line skates are popular means of transportation along the beaches. The county contains dozens of courses; we list a few public ones in this chapter; for more information contact the Southern California Golf Association (☞ Visitor Information *in* Orange County A to Z, *below*). Many hotels have tennis courts, and there are public tennis facilities throughout the county, some of which are listed below.

Joggers enjoy the Santa Ana Riverbed Trail, which hugs the Santa Ana River for 20½ mi between Pacific Coast Highway at Huntington State Beach and Imperial Highway in Yorba Linda. Surfing is permitted at most beaches year-round—check local newspapers or talk to lifeguards to learn about conditions. The best waves are usually at San Clemente, Newport Beach, and Huntington Beach. You'll find rental stands at most beaches along the coast. Never go in the water when flags with a black circle are flying, and avoid swimming near surfers. Many beaches close at night.

Exploring Orange County

Like Los Angeles, Orange County stretches over a large area, lacks a focal point, and has limited public transportation. You'll need a car and a good bit of planning to make the most of your visit. If you're headed to Disneyland, you'll probably want to stay in or near Anaheim, organize your activities around the inland-county attractions, and take excursions to the coast.

Numbers in the text correspond to numbers in the margin and on the Orange County map.

Great Itineraries

IF YOU HAVE 1 DAY

You're going to **Disneyland** ③!

IF YOU HAVE 3 DAYS

You're still going to **Disneyland** ③ (stay overnight in 🏨 **Anaheim**), but on day two, head to the coast and explore **Newport Harbor** ⑮. Have lunch at Ruby's on the pier, and then take a 90-minute harbor cruise. Spend the night in 🏨 **Newport Beach.** On day three, visit **Laguna Beach** and **Dana Point** or **Huntington Beach,** and then either hang out on the beach or head inland to **Costa Mesa,** where you can browse through **South Coast Plaza** ⑪, one of the world's largest retail, entertainment, and dining complexes.

When to Tour Orange County

The sun shines year-round in Orange County, but you can beat the crowds and the heat by visiting during spring and fall. Smart parents give kids their Disney fix during these periods (though you can still expect fairly long waits for popular rides and shows). If you're traveling with children, you could easily devote several days to the theme parks—a day or two at the Magic Kingdom, a day for Knott's Berry Farm, and perhaps a day driving to some of the area's lesser-known diversions.

INLAND ORANGE COUNTY

A 30-minute drive from downtown Los Angeles on I–5, also known as the Golden State Freeway, leads to Buena Park, home to Knott's Berry Farm and the Movieland Wax Museum. Anaheim is about five minutes farther south.

Buena Park

25 mi south of Los Angeles on I–5.

★ ☕ ❶ **Knott's Berry Farm** got its start in 1934, when Cordelia Knott began serving chicken dinners on her wedding china to supplement her family's income. Or so the story goes. The dinners and her boysenberry pies proved more profitable than husband Walter's berry farm, so the two moved first into the restaurant business and then into the entertainment business. Their park is now a 150-acre complex with 100-plus rides and attractions, 60 eating places, and 60 shops.

Many of the buildings in **Ghost Town** were relocated from their original mining-town sites. You can stroll down the street, stop and chat with the blacksmith, pan for gold, crack open a geode, ride in an authentic 1880s passenger train, or take the Gold Mine ride and descend into a replica of a working gold mine. A real treasure here is the antique Dentzel carousel.

Camp Snoopy is a kid-size High Sierra wonderland where Snoopy and his friends from the "Peanuts" comic strip hang out. Tall trees frame

Wild Water Wilderness, where you can ride white water in an inner tube in Big Foot Rapids and commune with the native peoples of the Northwest coast in the spooky Mystery Lodge. **The Boardwalk** is a water-oriented area with dolphin and sea lion shows in the Pacific Pavilion, as well as 3-D movies in the Nu Wave Theater and major productions at the Good Time Theater.

Thrill rides are placed throughout the park: the **Boomerang** roller coaster; **X-K-1,** a living version of a video game; **Kingdom of the Dinosaurs;** and **Montezooma's Revenge,** a roller coaster that goes from 0 to 55 mph in less than five seconds. **Jaguar!** simulates the motions of a cat stalking its prey, twisting, spiraling, and speeding up and slowing down as it takes guests on its stomach-dropping course. The **Wind Jammer** roller coaster, installed in 1997, races through loops, turns, and twists—even faster than all its predecessors. Shows are scheduled in Ghost Town, the Bird Cage Theater, and the Good Time Theater throughout the day. ✉ *8039 Beach Blvd.,* ☎ *714/220–5200.* 🎫 *$28.50.* ☉ *June–mid-Sept., daily 9* AM*–midnight; mid-Sept.–May, weekdays 10–6, Sat. 10–10, Sun. 10–7; park closes during inclement weather.*

➋ More than 70 years of movie magic are immortalized at the **Movieland Wax Museum,** which holds several hundred wax sculptures of Hollywood's greatest stars. You can buy a combination ticket for $16.90 that also allows you admission to the so-so Ripley's Believe It or Not, across the street. ✉ *7711 Beach Blvd.,* ☎ *714/522–1155.* 🎫 *$12.95.* ☉ *Daily 9–7.*

Dining and Lodging
$ ✕ **Mrs. Knott's Chicken Dinner Restaurant.** Mrs. Knott's fried-chicken dinners and boysenberry pies made Knott's Berry Farm famous. Her restaurant, at the park's entrance, serves breakfast, lunch, and dinner. ✉ *Knott's California MarketPlace, 8039 Beach Blvd.,* ☎ *714/220–5080. AE, D, DC, MC, V. No lunch Sun.*

$$ 🏨 **Buena Park Hotel and Convention Center.** Rooms at the Buena Park have modern light-oak furniture and are decorated in earth tones. The hotel, which is within easy walking distance of Knott's Berry Farm, provides complimentary shuttle service to Disneyland. Family Value Vacation packages, with discounted rooms and admission to one of the parks, are available. ✉ *7675 Crescent Ave., 90620,* ☎ *714/995–1111 or 800/854–8792,* 📠 *714/828–8590. 314 rooms, 36 suites. 2 restaurants, bar, pool, concierge floor. AE, D, DC, MC, V.*

Nightlife
Medieval Times Dinner and Tournament (✉ 7662 Beach Blvd., ☎ 714/521–4740 or 800/899–6600) brings back the days of yore (for $36 per person) with medieval games, fighting, and jousting. Diners eat their meals—standard chicken and ribs with plenty of sides—with their hands.

Wild Bill's Wild West Extravaganza (✉ 7600 Beach Blvd., ☎ 714/522–6414), a two-hour action-packed Old West show ($33 per person), features foot-stomping musical numbers, cancan dancers, trick-rope artists, and sing-alongs. An all-you-can-eat chicken-and-ribs dinner is served during the show.

Anaheim

26 mi east of Los Angeles on I–5.

The snowcapped Matterhorn, the centerpiece of the Magic Kingdom, dominates Anaheim's skyline, an enduring reminder of the role Dis-

420

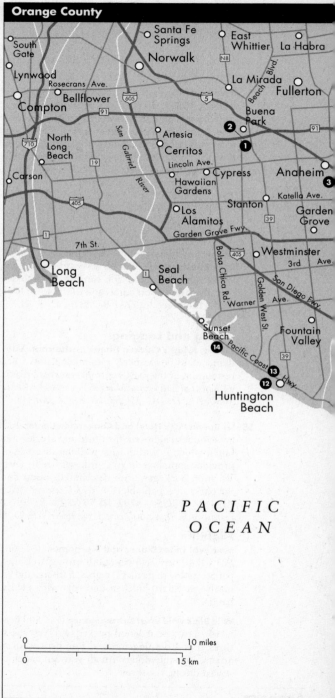

Orange County

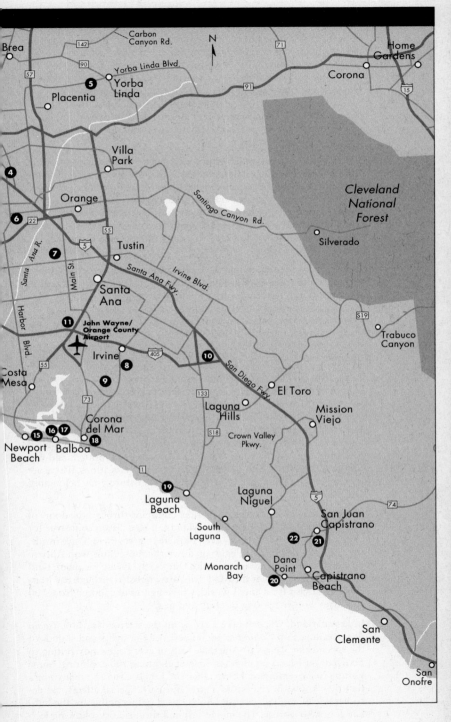

neyland has played in the urbanization and growth of Orange County. Disneyland has attracted millions of visitors and thousands of workers, and Anaheim has been their host, becoming Orange County's most populous city and accounting for more than half the county's 40,000 hotel rooms. To understand the symbiotic relationship between Disneyland and Anaheim, one need only look at the $1 billion-plus being spent to expand the park and renovate run-down areas of the city. Anaheim's vast tourism complex also includes Anaheim Stadium, home of the Anaheim Angels baseball team; the Arrowhead Pond, where the Mighty Ducks hockey team plays; and the enormous Anaheim Convention Center.

★ ⓒ ❸ When Walt Disney carved **Disneyland** out of the orange groves in 1955, it comprised four lands and fewer than 20 major attractions radiating from his idealized American Main Street. Much has changed in the intervening years, including the addition of four more lands and nearly four dozen attractions (the latest of which, a futuristic play area, should be open by fall 1998). Yet Main Street still retains its turn-of-the-century charm—it's in ever-sharper contrast with the world just outside the park gates.

Disneyland is big and, during the busy summer season, crowded. If you can, pick a rainy midweek day; surprisingly, most Disney attractions are indoors. Try to arrive early; the box office opens a half hour before the park's scheduled opening time. (On most days, guests of the Disneyland Resort and some Anaheim hotels are admitted before other visitors.) Brochures with maps, available at the entrance, list show and parade times. You can move from one area of Disneyland to another by train, monorail, or even horse-drawn carriage.

A few tips: Mickey's Toontown is usually most crowded in the mornings. Lines for rides tend to be shorter during the evening Fantasmic! show, during parades and fireworks displays (usually around 9:30), and near opening or closing time. (Even on a slow day expect to wait in line for 15 minutes or more.) Restaurants are less busy toward the beginning and end of meal periods. Expect long lines at the Blue Bayou Restaurant in New Orleans Square. Fast-food spots abound, and you can buy fruit, pasta, and frozen yogurt at various locations. There are lockers just off Main Street in which you can store your belongings and purchases.

Each of Disney's lands has theme rides. Stepping through the doors of Sleeping Beauty Castle into **Fantasyland** can be a dream come true for children. Mickey Mouse may even be there to greet them. Once inside, they can join Peter Pan's Flight; go down the rabbit hole with Alice in Wonderland; take an aerial spin with Dumbo the Flying Elephant; twirl around in giant cups at the Mad Tea Party; bobsled through the Matterhorn; or visit It's a Small World, where figures of children from 100 countries worldwide sing of unity and peace.

In **Frontierland,** you can take a cruise on the steamboat *Mark Twain* or the sailing ship *Columbia* and experience the sights and sounds of the spectacular Rivers of America. Kids of every age enjoy rafting to Tom Sawyer Island for an hour or so of climbing and exploring. Some visitors to **Adventureland** have taken the Jungle Cruise so many times that they know the operators' patter by heart. Special effects and decipherable hieroglyphics entertain guests standing in line for the Indiana Jones Adventure. The movie-inspired thrill ride, a rollicking Jeep excursion through the Temple of the Forbidden Eye, has become one of Disneyland's most popular and is well worth the wait.

The twisting streets of **New Orleans Square** offer interesting browsing and shopping, strolling Dixieland musicians, and the ever-popular Pirates of the Caribbean ride. The Haunted Mansion, populated by 999 holographic ghosts, is nearby. Theme shops sell hats, perfume, Mardi Gras merchandise, and gourmet items. The gallery here carries original Disney art.

The animated bears in **Critter Country** may charm kids of all ages, but it's **Splash Mountain,** the steepest, wettest Disney adventure, that keeps them coming back for more.

At **Mickey's Toontown** kids can climb up a rope ladder on the *Miss Daisy* (Donald Duck's boat), talk to a mailbox, and walk through Mickey's House and meet Mickey, all the while feeling that they're inside a cartoon. The Roger Rabbit Car Toon Spin, the largest and most unusual black-light ride in Disneyland history, has been packing them in since it opened here in 1994.

A stroll along **Main Street** evokes a small-town America, circa 1900, that never existed except in the popular imagination, fiction, and films. Interconnected shops and restaurants line both sides of the street. The Emporium, the largest and most comprehensive of the shops, offers a full line of Disney products, along with magic tricks, crystal, hobby and sports memorabilia, and photo supplies.

Nighttime entertainment includes Light Magic, Disneyland's newest parade down Main Street featuring performers, twinkling lights, and fireworks. Fantasmic!, a crowd-pleasing live action and special effects show, takes place on the Rivers of America and is visible from New Orleans Square. The best (albeit most expensive) way to see Fantasmic! is from the balcony of the animation gallery. Tickets for gallery seating, which include a desert buffet, cost $30 per person and sell out within minutes of the park's opening. Buy tickets on the day of the performance at the Blue Bayou Restaurant. ⊠ *1313 Harbor Blvd.,* ☎ *714/ 781–4565.* ⊠ *$34.* ☽ *June–mid-Sept., Sun.–Fri. 9 AM–midnight, Sat. 9 AM–1 AM; mid-Sept.–May, weekdays 10–6, Sat. 9–midnight, Sun. 9–10.*

❹ A 1908 Carnegie Library building houses the **Anaheim Museum,** which documents the history of Anaheim. Changing exhibits include art collections, women's history, and hobbies. A hands-on children's gallery keeps the kids entertained. ⊠ *241 S. Anaheim Blvd.,* ☎ *714/778–3301.* ⊠ *$1.50.* ☽ *Wed.–Fri. 10–4, Sat. noon–4.*

Dining and Lodging

$$–$$$ ✕ **JW's.** Part of the Anaheim Marriott complex, this upscale steak house specializes in aged beef but serves seafood—such as blackened tuna with papaya relish and swordfish Parmesan—along with lamb chops and chicken. The dining areas are quiet places where you can talk serious business or romance. ⊠ *Anaheim Marriott, 700 W. Convention Way,* ☎ *714/750–8000. AE, D, DC, MC, V. No lunch. Valet parking.*

$$–$$$ ✕ **White House.** A 1909 mansion that bears a striking resemblance to its namesake contains several small dining rooms with crisp linens, candles, and flowers. The northern Italian menu includes pasta, scallopine, and a large selection of seafood. A three-course prix-fixe lunch, served weekdays only, costs $16. ⊠ *887 S. Anaheim Blvd.,* ☎ *714/ 772–1381. AE, DC, MC, V. No lunch weekends.*

$–$$ ✕ **The Catch/Hop City Blues and Brew.** A sports-bar atmosphere on one side and California's version of the House of Blues on the other make this restaurant and nightspot across the street from Anaheim Stadium a popular destination. The Catch serves hearty portions of steak, seafood, pasta, and salads. Over at Hop City it's California Cajun cui-

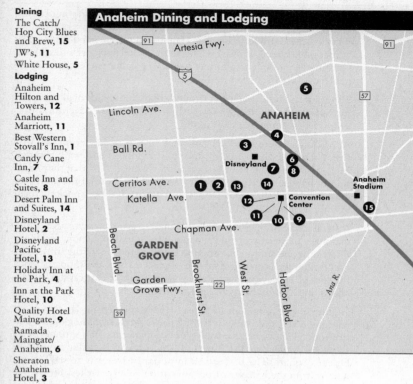

Anaheim Dining and Lodging

sine to the tune of blues from national and local acts. ✉ *1929 and 1939 S. State College Blvd.,* ☎ *714/634–1829. AE, DC, MC, V.*

$$$–$$$$ 🏨 **Disneyland Hotel.** A monorail connects this hotel to the Magic
★ Kingdom. Disney characters roam Goofy's Kitchen, Disney music fills
the courtyards, and Disney products are available for sale everywhere.
Lakes, streams, and tumbling waterfalls dot the lush grounds. Rooms
in the Bonita tower overlook the Fantasy Waters, a nighttime lighted
fountain and music display. On most days, guests staying at the hotel
are admitted to the park before the gates open to the general public.
In Goofy's Kitchen, kids can breakfast with their favorite Disney char-
acters. ✉ *1150 W. Cerritos Ave., 92802,* ☎ *714/778–6600,* 𝖥𝖠𝖷 *714/
956–6597. 1,136 rooms. 6 restaurants, 5 bars, 3 pools, hot tub, health
club, beach, concierge floor, business services. AE, D, DC, MC, V.*

$$$ 🏨 **Anaheim Hilton and Towers.** This hotel near the Anaheim Convention
Center is virtually a self-contained city—complete with its own post
office. The lobby is dominated by an airy atrium. Rooms are decorated
in pinks and greens with light-wood furniture. Because it caters to con-
ventioneers, the Hilton can be busy and noisy, with long lines at restaurants. Special children's programs are available during summer months.
✉ *777 Convention Way, 92802,* ☎ *714/750–4321 or 800/222–9923,*
𝖥𝖠𝖷 *714/740–4460. 1,576 rooms, 96 suites. 4 restaurants, 3 lounges,
pool, hot tub, health club ($10 charge), concierge, business services.
AE, D, DC, MC, V.*

$$$ 🏨 **Anaheim Marriott.** Rooms at this busy convention hotel are well
equipped for business travelers, with desks, two phones, and modem
hookups. Accommodations on the north side have good views of Dis-
neyland's summer fireworks shows. Discounted weekend and Dis-

neyland packages are available. ⊠ *700 W. Convention Way, 92802,* ☎ *714/750–8000 or 800/228–9290,* FAX *714/750–9100. 979 rooms, 54 suites. 3 restaurants, 2 lounges, 2 pools, health club, video games, concierge. AE, D, DC, MC, V.*

$$$ 🏨 **Disneyland Pacific Hotel.** Part of the 65-acre Disneyland Resort, this hotel offers many of same benefits as its sister property, the Disneyland Hotel, but in a quieter, more sophisticated setting. Rooms are spacious and modern. The Pacific has a Japanese restaurant and sushi bar and a California grill. ⊠ *1717 S. West St., 92802,* ☎ *714/956–6424,* FAX *714/956–6582. 487 rooms, 15 suites. 2 restaurants, 2 lounges, pool, hot tub, exercise room, shops, video games, concierge floor. AE, D, DC, MC, V.*

$$$ 🏨 **Sheraton Anaheim Hotel.** If you're hoping to escape the commer-
★   cial atmosphere of the hotels surrounding Disneyland, consider this replica of a Tudor-style castle. Flowers, plants, and a small pond grace the lobby, which also has a grand fireplace, a brick tower, and a spacious sitting area. Sizable rooms open onto interior gardens. A Disneyland shuttle is available. ⊠ *1015 W. Ball Rd., 92802,* ☎ *714/778–1700 or 800/325–3535,* FAX *714/535–3889. 491 rooms. Bar, deli, dining room, pool, health club. AE, D, DC, MC, V.*

$$–$$$ 🏨 **Inn at the Park Hotel.** Conventioneers love this hotel with spacious rooms, all with balconies. Rooms in the 14-story tower have good views of Disneyland's summer fireworks shows. The hotel has an attractive pool area, and its bright lobby has a tropical feel. ⊠ *1855 S. Harbor Blvd., 92802,* ☎ *714/750–1811 or 800/353–2773,* FAX *714/971–3626. 494 rooms, 6 suites. Restaurant, coffee shop, lounge, pool, hot tub, exercise room, video games. AE, D, DC, MC, V.*

$$ 🏨 **Candy Cane Inn.** This charming motel with lush landscaping and
★   spacious rooms, all with microwaves, is steps from the entrance to Disneyland's parking lot. Room rates include Continental breakfast. ⊠ *1747 S. Harbor Blvd., 92803,* ☎ *714/774–5284 or 800/345–7057,* FAX *714/772–5462. 172 rooms. Refrigerators, pool, hot tub. AE, D, DC, MC, V.*

$$ 🏨 **Holiday Inn at the Park.** The Mediterranean-style Holiday Inn was designed for families visiting the Magic Kingdom. Rooms here have a Southwest decor; some have separate sitting areas. Shuttle service is available to nearby attractions, including Knott's Berry Farm, the Movieland Wax Museum, and Medieval Times. ⊠ *1221 S. Harbor Blvd., 92805,* ☎ *714/758–0900 or 800/545–7275,* FAX *714/533–1804. 252 rooms, 2 suites. Restaurant, bar, pool, hot tub, sauna, video games. AE, D, DC, MC, V.*

$$ 🏨 **Ramada Maingate/Anaheim.** Clean and reliable, this chain hotel across the street from Disneyland provides free shuttle service and early admission to the park. Pleasant accommodations are decorated in mauve tones. McDonald's provides room service. ⊠ *1460 S. Harbor Blvd., 92802,* ☎ *714/772–6777 or 800/447–4048,* FAX *714/999–1727. 465 rooms. Restaurant, pool. AE, D, DC, MC, V.*

$–$$ 🏨 **Castle Inn and Suites.** Faux stone trim and towers create a castle-like feel at this motel across the street from Disneyland. The rooms here are big. Children under 18 stay free. ⊠ *1734 S. Harbor Blvd., 92802,* ☎ *714/774–8111 or 800/227–8530,* FAX *714/956–4736. 197 rooms. Refrigerators, pool, wading pool, hot tubs. AE, D, DC, MC, V.*

$–$$ 🏨 **Quality Hotel Maingate.** Minisuites at this property near Disneyland and the convention center include a sofa with a pull-out bed and a refrigerator; they are ideal for families on a budget. ⊠ *616 Convention Way, 92802,* ☎ *714/750–3131 or 800/231–6215,* FAX *714/750–9027. 186 rooms, 96 suites. 2 restaurants, lounge, pool. AE, D, DC, MC, V.*

$ 🏨 **Best Western Stovall's Inn.** Nice touches at this well-kept motel include a topiary garden, room decor in soft desert colors, and a friendly staff. Nintendo and movie rentals are available. Ask about discounts

if you're staying several nights. ✉ *1110 W. Katella Ave., 92802,* ☎
714/778–1880 or 800/854–8175, FAX *714/778–3805. 290 rooms.
Restaurant, bar, 2 pools, hot tub. AE, D, DC, MC, V.*

$ 🏨 **Desert Palm Inn and Suites.** This budget hotel has many things going
for it: It's midway between Disneyland and the convention center, it
has large suites (some with balconies) that can accommodate as many
as eight people, and every room has a microwave. Book well in advance, especially when large conventions are in town. ✉ *631 W. Katella
Ave., 92802,* ☎ *714/535–1133 or 800/635–5423,* FAX *714/491–7409.
103 rooms and suites. Refrigerators, pool, sauna, exercise room, laundry service. AE, D, DC, MC, V.*

INEXPENSIVE MOTELS

🏨 **Days Inn Suites** (✉ 1111 S. Harbor Blvd., ☎ 714/533–8830, FAX
714/758–0573) and 🏨 **Days Inn Maingate** (✉ 1604 S. Harbor Blvd.,
☎ 714/635–3630, FAX 714/520–3290) are two options on Disneyland's eastern boundary. 🏨 **Motel 6** (✉ 100 W. Freedman Way, ☎
714/520–9696, FAX 714/533–7539) is about three blocks from the
park. 🏨 **Travelodge** (☎ 800/826–1616) maintains four properties
in Anaheim.

Nightlife

Cowboy Boogie Co. (✉ 1721 S. Manchester, ☎ 714/956–1410), with
three dance floors and four bars, hosts live country music on Sunday
night; music is piped in the rest of the week. The place is packed
Wednesday night, when the club includes more than country music on
its playlist. Country line-dancing lessons are offered during the week.

Outdoor Activities and Sports

The **Anaheim Angels** play American League baseball at Anaheim Stadium (✉ 2000 Gene Autry Way, ☎ 714/634–2000). The **Mighty Ducks
of Anaheim** National Hockey League team plays at Arrowhead Pond
(✉ 2695 E. Katella Ave., ☎ 714/740–2000).

GOLF

Dad Miller Golf Course (✉ 430 N. Gilbert St., ☎ 714/774–8055), an
18-hole par-71 course, requires reservations seven days in advance.
Greens fee: $18–$24; optional carts $22 each.

TENNIS

Anaheim has 50 public tennis courts; phone the **Parks and Recreation
Department** (☎ 714/254–5191) for locations.

Yorba Linda and Brea

7 mi north of Anaheim, Hwy. 57 to Yorba Linda exit.

❺ The **Richard Nixon Presidential Library and Birthplace** is the final resting place of the 37th president and his wife, Pat. Exhibits illustrate the
checkered career of Nixon, the only president forced to resign from
office. Visitors can listen to the so-called smoking-gun tape from the
Watergate days, among other recorded material. Life-size sculptures
of world leaders, gifts Nixon received from international heads of
state, and a large graffiti-covered section of the Berlin Wall are on display. In contrast to some of the high-tech displays here are Pat Nixon's
tranquil rose garden and the small farmhouse where Nixon was born
in 1913. ✉ *18001 Yorba Linda Blvd.,* ☎ *714/993–3393.* 🎫 *$5.95.*
🕐 *Mon.–Sat. 10–5, Sun. 11–5.*

Dining

$$$–$$$$ ✕ **La Vie en Rose.** It's worth a detour to Brea to sample the stylishly
★   presented traditional French cuisine served inside a reproduction Nor-
man farmhouse, complete with a large turret. The fare includes seafood,

lamb, veal, and melt-in-your-mouth pastries. ⊠ *240 S. State College Blvd. (across from La Brea mall),* ☎ *714/529–8333. AE, DC, MC, V. Closed Sun.*

Garden Grove and Orange

South of Anaheim, I–5 to Hwy. 22.

❻ The **Crystal Cathedral** is the domain of television evangelist Robert Schuller. The sparkling glass structure resembles a four-pointed star, with more than 10,000 panes of glass covering a weblike steel truss to form translucent walls. Two annual pageants, "The Glory of Christmas" and "The Glory of Easter," feature live animals, flying angels, and other special effects. ⊠ *12141 Lewis St., Garden Grove,* ☎ *714/971–4013.* ⊠ *Donation requested.* ☉ *Guided tours Mon.–Sat. 9–3:30; call for schedule.*

Dining and Lodging

$$ ✕ **La Brasserie.** It doesn't *look* like a typical brasserie, but the varied French cuisine befits the name over the door. The specialty here is veal chops. There's an inviting bar-lounge. ⊠ *202 S. Main St., Orange,* ☎ *714/978–6161. AE, DC, MC, V. Closed Sun. No lunch Sat.*

$$$ 🏨 **Doubletree Hotel Anaheim.** This contemporary 20-story hotel has a dramatic lobby of marble and granite, with waterfalls cascading down the walls. Guest rooms are spacious. The hotel is near The City shopping center, Anaheim Stadium, and the Anaheim Convention Center. ⊠ *100 The City Dr., Orange 92868,* ☎ *714/634–4500 or 800/222–8733,* 𝕱𝕬𝕏 *714/978–3839. 435 rooms, 19 suites. 2 restaurants, bar, pool, 2 tennis courts, health club, concierge floor. AE, D, DC, MC, V.*

Santa Ana

12 mi south of Anaheim, I–5 to Hwy. 55.

☾ ❼ The main attraction in Santa Ana, the county seat, is the **Bowers Museum of Cultural Art.** Permanent exhibits include sculpture, costumes, and artifacts from Oceania; sculpture from west and central Africa; Pacific Northwest wood carvings; dazzling beadwork of the Plains cultures; California basketry; and still-life paintings. The 11,000-square-ft **Bowers Kidseum** adjacent to the main facility contains interactive exhibits geared toward kids ages 6–12 and offers classes, storytelling, and arts and crafts workshops. ⊠ *2002 N. Main St.,* ☎ *714/567–3600.* ⊠ *$6.* ☉ *Tues.–Sun. 10–4, Thurs. 10–9.*

Dining

$$$–$$$$ ✕ **Gustaf Anders.** Here's an unusual twist, especially for southern
★ California: a restaurant that serves Continental cuisine with a Swedish touch. The Scandinavian setting is cool, and the food takes you places you've probably never been. Try the grilled gravlax, the wild-rice pancake with golden caviar and smoked Scottish salmon, or the fillet of beef prepared with Stilton cheese, a red-wine sauce, and creamed morel mushrooms. The adjacent Gustaf Anders' Back Pocket is less expensive ($$–$$$) and more casual. ⊠ *South Coast Plaza Village, 1651 Sunflower Ave.,* ☎ *714/668–1737. AE, DC, MC, V.*

$ ✕ **National Sports Grill.** Nothing fancy here, just appetizers, burgers, pasta, and chicken, served in a casual atmosphere. After dinner, wander into the bar area to watch a game, play a round of pool, or enjoy an icy glass of domestic or imported beer on tap. ⊠ *101 Sand Pointe,* ☎ *714/979–0900. AE, D, DC, MC, V.*

Irvine

6 mi south of Santa Ana, Hwy. 55 to I–405.

8 Some of the California impressionist paintings on display at the small **Irvine Museum** depict the California landscape in the days before freeways and housing developments. ⊠ *18881 Von Karman Ave.,* ☎ *714/ 476–0294.* 🎟 *Free.* ☉ *Tues.–Sat. 11–5.*

9 The **University of California at Irvine,** best known for its biological sciences, was established on 1,000 acres of rolling ranch land donated by the Irvine family in the mid-1950s. The campus contains more than 11,000 trees from all over the world. The **Bren Events Center Fine Art Gallery** (☎ 714/824–6610) sponsors exhibitions of 20th-century art. It's free and open mid-September through mid-June, Tuesday through Saturday noon to 5. ⊠ *San Diego Fwy. (I–405) to Jamboree Rd., west to Campus Dr. S.*

10 The 32-acre **Entertainment Center at Irvine Spectrum** contains a huge cinema complex (with a six-story IMAX 3-D theater), lively restaurants and cafés, and an outdoor shopping arcade. Other highlights include Sega City's virtual-reality arcade and an Out-Takes digital photo studio. ⊠ *Exit Irvine Center Dr. at intersection of San Diego Fwy. (I– 405), Santa Ana Fwy. (I–5), and Laguna Fwy. (I–133),* ☎ *714/450– 4900 for film listings.*

Dining and Lodging

$$$ ✕ **Chanteclair.** This Franco-Italian country house is a tasteful retreat amid an island of modern high-rise office buildings. French Riviera– type cuisine is served. The chateaubriand for two and rack of lamb are recommended. ⊠ *18912 MacArthur Blvd.,* ☎ *714/752–8001. Jacket required. AE, D, DC, MC, V. No lunch Sat.*

$$–$$$ ✕ **Bistango.** A sleek, high-style, art-filled bistro, Bistango serves first-rate California cuisine: crab cakes, salads, seafood pasta, Mediterranean pizzas, and grilled ahi. Live jazz and a see-and-be-seen clientele make for a charged atmosphere. ⊠ *19100 Von Karman Ave.,* ☎ *714/752– 5222. Reservations essential. AE, D, DC, MC, V. Valet parking.*

$$ ✕ **Mitsuba.** Excellent Chinese food and sushi are served buffet-style in what resembles a formal eating hall in Taiwan. There's organization among the chaos—everyone gets served in short order. ⊠ *14110 Culver Dr.,* ☎ *714/551–1688. MC, V.*

$$ ✕ **Prego.** A much larger version of the Beverly Hills Prego, this one is
★ in an approximation of a Tuscan villa, with an outdoor patio. Try the spit-roasted meats and chicken, the charcoal-grilled fresh fish, or pizzas from the oak-burning oven. The California and Italian wines are reasonably priced. ⊠ *18420 Von Karman Ave.,* ☎ *714/553–1333. AE, DC, MC, V. No lunch weekends. Valet parking.*

$$$ 🏨 **Atrium Hotel.** Across the street from John Wayne airport and near most area offices, this garden-style hotel caters to business travelers. Rooms have large work areas, coffeemakers, two phones, and private balconies, some overlooking the pool, others the gardens. Special rates are available for weekend guests. ⊠ *18700 MacArthur Blvd., 92612,* ☎ *714/833–2770,* FAX *714/757–1228. 209 rooms. Restaurant, bar, pool, health club, car rental. AE, D, DC, MC, V.*

$$$ 🏨 **Hyatt Regency Irvine.** The modern rooms here have coffeemakers, irons, and hair dryers. Special golf packages at nearby Tustin Ranch and Pelican Hills are available and a complimentary shuttle runs to local shopping centers. Rates are lower on weekends. ⊠ *17900 Jamboree Rd., 92714,* ☎ *714/975–1234 or 800/233–1234,* FAX *714/ 852–1574. 516 rooms, 20 suites. 2 restaurants, 2 bars, pool, hot tub,*

4 tennis courts, health club, bicycles, concierge, business services. AE, D, DC, MC, V.

$$$ 🏨 **Irvine Marriott.** This contemporary hotel that towers over Koll Business Center is convenient for business travelers. Despite its size, the hotel has an intimate feel, due in part to the cozy lobby with love seats and evening entertainment (usually a jazz guitarist). Rooms, outfitted in dark woods, have large desks. ✉ *18000 Von Karman Ave., 92715,* ☎ *714/553–0100 or 800/228–9290,* FAX *714/261–7059. 489 rooms, 24 suites. 2 restaurants, sports bar, sushi bar, indoor-outdoor pool, hot tub, 4 tennis courts, health club, concierge floors, business services, airport shuttle. AE, D, DC, MC, V.*

Nightlife

Irvine Improv (✉ 4255 Campus Dr., ☎ 714/854–5455) is a comedy club open Wednesday through Sunday nights. The **Irvine Meadows Amphitheater** (✉ 8808 Irvine Center Dr., ☎ 714/855–4515 or 714/855–6111), a 15,000-seat open-air venue, presents musical events from May through October. **Metropolis** (✉ 4255 Campus Dr., ☎ 714/725–0300) has pool tables, a sushi bar, a restaurant, entertainment, dancing, and theme nights throughout the week.

Costa Mesa

10 mi southeast of Anaheim on I–5 south to Hwy. 55 south.

★ ⑪ **South Coast Plaza,** Costa Mesa's most famous landmark, is an immense retail, entertainment, and dining complex consisting of two enclosed shopping areas—Jewel Court and Crystal Court—and an open-air collection of boutiques at South Coast Village. Stores include Gucci, J. Crew, Ralph Lauren, Calvin Klein, Liz Claiborne, and F.A.O. Schwarz. A free shuttle transports the Plaza's 20 million annual visitors between sections. ✉ *3333 S. Bristol St., off I–405,* ☎ *714/435–2000.* ☺ *Weekdays 10–9, Sat. 10–7, Sun. 10–6:30.*

The **Orange County Performing Arts Center** (✉ 600 Town Center Dr.) contains a 3,000-seat facility for opera, ballet, symphony, and musicals. Richard Lippold's enormous "Firebird," a triangular-shape sculpture of polished metal surfaces that resembles a bird taking flight, extends outward from the glass-enclosed lobby. Within walking distance of the center is the **California Scenario** (✉ 611 Anton Blvd.), a 1.6-acre sculpture garden designed by Isamu Noguchi.

Dining and Lodging

$$–$$$ ✕ **Bangkok IV.** Despite its shopping-mall location—it occupies an in-
★   door patio on the third floor of the Crystal Court—this restaurant serves artistically prepared Thai cuisine. The black-and-white decor, accented with stylish flower arrangements, is dramatic. ✉ *3333 Bear St.,* ☎ *714/ 540–7661. AE, D, DC, MC, V.*

$$ ✕ **Mandarin Gourmet.** Owner Michael Chang provides what reviewers and locals consider the best Chinese cuisine in the area. His specialties include a crisp-yet-juicy Peking duck, cashew chicken, and a well-loved mu-shu pork. ✉ *1500 Adams Ave.,* ☎ *714/540–1937. AE, DC, MC, V.*

$–$$ ✕ **Planet Hollywood.** You know the routine: displays of movie memorabilia, giant TV screens showing clips of old movies, loud rock music, souvenir store, jazzed-up American fare. ✉ *1641 W. Sunflower St.,* ☎ *714/434–7827. Reservations not accepted. AE, D, DC, MC, V.*

$ ✕ **Wolfgang Puck Cafe.** The famous chef fashioned an institutional-style café, complete with high noise level, that serves Wolf's famous pastas, chicken salad, meat-loaf sandwiches, and wood-fired pizzas. The rotisserie rosemary chicken comes with scoops of garlic mashed potatoes. ⊠ *South Coast Plaza, 3333 Bristol St.,* ☎ *714/546–9653. Reservations not accepted. AE, DC, MC, V.*

$$$–$$$$ 🏨 **Westin South Coast Plaza.** Rooms at this high-rise adjoining the South Coast complex are decorated in soft colors, mostly cream and beige. The public areas are bright and pleasant. ⊠ *686 Anton Blvd., 92626,* ☎ *714/540–2500 or 800/228–3000,* FAX *714/662–6695. 373 rooms, 17 suites. Restaurant, lobby lounge, pool, 2 tennis courts, shuffleboard, volleyball. AE, D, DC, MC, V.*

$$–$$$ 🏨 **Country Side Inn and Suites.** Queen Anne–style furnishings and floral wall coverings decorate rooms that have a vaguely European feel. The reasonable room rates include breakfast and evening cocktails and hors d'oeuvres. ⊠ *325 Bristol St., 92626,* ☎ *714/549–0300 or 800/ 322–9992,* FAX *714/662–0828. 150 rooms, 150 suites. Restaurant, bar, 2 pools, exercise room. AE, D, DC, MC, V.*

$$–$$$ 🏨 **Doubletree Hotel.** Next to John Wayne airport, this modern, spacious hotel has comfortable rooms and an atrium lobby with glass elevators. Usually there's live music Saturday night in the dance club. ⊠ *3050 Bristol St., 92626,* ☎ *714/540–7000,* FAX *714/540–9176. 474 rooms, 10 suites. 2 restaurants, lounge, pool, hot tub, health club. AE, D, DC, MC, V.*

Nightlife and the Arts

Orange County Performing Arts Center (⊠ 600 Town Center Dr., ☎ 714/556–2787) presents major touring companies, among them the New York City Opera, the American Ballet Theater, and the Los Angeles Philharmonic Orchestra, along with popular musicals and other theatrical productions.

South Coast Repertory Theater (⊠ 655 Town Center Dr., ☎ 714/957–4033) presents new and traditional works on two stages.

Outdoor Activities and Sports

Costa Mesa Country Club (⊠ 1701 Golf Course Dr., ☎ 714/540–7500) has a pro shop, a driving range, and two 18-hole courses (par 70 and 72). Greens fee: $20–$24. An optional cart costs $22. Reservations are a must.

THE COAST

Scenic Pacific Coast Highway (Highway 1) runs along the Orange County coastline. Wherever you pull over, a public beach is only steps away.

Huntington Beach

Once a sleepy residential town with little more than a string of rugged surf shops, Huntington Beach has transformed itself into a shining resort area. The town's appeal arises from its broad white-sand beaches and often towering waves. The '90s have brought a new pier, a large shopping pavilion on Main Street, and a hotel resort. The family-oriented town, which hosts the Airtouch Pro Surfing Championships and the U.S. Open amateur surf competition, was voted America's safest city in a recent national survey.

⑫ **Huntington Pier** stretches 1,800 ft out to sea, well past the powerful waves that made Huntington Beach America's "Surf City." At the end of the pier sits **Ruby's diner** (☎ 714/969–7829)—part of a California chain of '40s-style eateries—along with any number of hopeful fishers and sentimental couples. The **Pierside Pavilion,** across Pacific Coast Highway from the pier, contains shops, restaurants, bars with live
 music, and a theater complex. Just up Main Street, the **International**

Surfing Museum (⊠ 411 Olive Ave., ☎ 714/960–3483), open Wednesday through Sunday noon to 5 (admission $2), pays tribute to the sport's greats in a Surfing Hall of Fame and has an impressive collection of surfboards and related memorabilia.

Huntington City Beach stretches for 3 mi from the pier area. The beach is most crowded around the pier; amateur and professional surfers brave the waves daily on its north side. Continuing north, **Huntington State Beach** (☎ 714/536–1454) parallels Pacific Coast Highway and has some barbecue pits and allows RV camping. On the state and city beaches there are changing rooms, concessions, lifeguards (except in winter), and ample parking. At the northern section of the city, **Bolsa Chica State Beach** (☎ 714/897–5911) has barbecue pits and is usually less crowded than its southern neighbors.

★ **⑭** **Bolsa Chica Ecological Reserve** beckons wildlife-lovers and bird-watchers with a restored 300-acre salt marsh that is home to 315 species of birds, plus other animals and plants. You can see many of them along a 1½-mi loop trail. In winter you're likely to see great blue herons, snowy and great egrets, common loons, and other migrating birds. At press time, the Ecological Reserve was hoping to create new trails for hiking, bird-watching, bicycling, and jogging. ⊠ *Entrance at Warner Ave. and Pacific Coast Hwy.*, ☎ *714/897–7003.* 🅿 *Free parking.* ⊘ *Daily dawn–sunset.*

OFF THE
BEATEN PATH
ALICE'S BREAKFAST IN THE PARK – Consider starting your day at this wooden brunch house tucked among Central Park's eucalyptus trees near Huntington Lake. There's seating on the outdoor patio, from which children can feed the ducks, and a small, indoor dining room with flowers and antiques. Be sure to try Alice's "outrageous cinnamon roll," freshly baked breads, and homemade muffins. ⊠ *6622 Lakeview, off Edwards St.*, ☎ *714/848-0690.* ⊘ *Daily 7–2. No credit cards.*

Lodging

$$$$ 🏨 **Waterfront Hilton.** This oceanfront hotel rises 12 stories above the surf. The Mediterranean-style resort is decorated in soft mauves, beiges, and greens. Most rooms have panoramic ocean views. ⊠ *21100 Pacific Coast Hwy., 92648,* ☎ *714/960–7873 or 800/822–7873,* ℻ *714/ 960–2642. 258 rooms, 32 suites. 2 restaurants, bar, pool, hot tub, 2 tennis courts, exercise room, children's programs (summer only), concierge floor. AE, DC, MC, V.*

Outdoor Activities and Sports

BICYCLING
Team Bicycle Rentals (⊠ 8465 Indianapolis Ave., ☎ 714/969–5480) rents touring and other bicycles.

TENNIS
Edison Community Center (⊠ 21377 Magnolia St., ☎ 714/960–8870) has four courts available on a first-come, first-served basis in the daytime. The **Murdy Community Center** (⊠ 7000 Norma Dr., ☎ 714/960–8895) has four courts, also available first-come, first-served during the day. Both facilities accept reservations for play after 5 PM; both charge $2 an hour.

Shopping

In search of authentic beach clothes or a new surfboard? Head to Main Street by the pier, where hard-core surf shops like **Jack's** (☎ 714/536–4516) and **Huntington Beach Surf and Sport** (☎ 714/841–4000) offer the latest styles. Or try the **Huntington Beach Mall** (⊠ Beach Blvd., off I–405, ☎ 714/897–2533).

Newport Beach

Newport Beach has two distinct personalities. It's best known for its island-dotted yacht harbor and wealthy residents (Newport is said to have the highest number of Mercedes-Benzes per capita of any city in the world). And then there's inland Newport Beach, just southwest of John Wayne airport, a business and commercial hub with a shopping center and a clutch of high-rise office buildings and hotels.

★ ⑮ **Newport Harbor,** which shelters nearly 10,000 small boats, will seduce even those who don't own a yacht or qualify as seaside high society. Exploring the charming avenues and surrounding alleys can be great fun. To see Newport Harbor from the water, take a one-hour gondola cruise operated by the Gondola Company of Newport (✉ 3404 Via Oporto, #201, ☎ 714/675–1212). It costs $60 for two.

Within Newport Harbor are eight small islands, including Balboa and Lido. The houses lining the shore may seem modest, but this is some of the most expensive real estate in the world. Several grassy areas on Lido Isle have views of Newport Harbor but, evidence of the upper-crust Orange County mind-set, each is marked "Private Community Park."

Newport Pier, which juts out into the ocean near 20th Street, serves as the centerpiece of Newport's beach community. On the pier, you're free to wander around, do some fishing, or grab a burger and shake at **Ruby's diner** (☎ 714/675–7829) at the end. Street parking is difficult here, so grab the first space you find and be prepared to walk. A stroll along Ocean Front reveals much of the town's character. On weekday mornings, head for the beach near the pier, where you're likely to encounter fishermen hawking their predawn catches, as they've done for generations. On weekends the walk is alive with kids of all ages on Rollerblades, skateboards, and bikes dodging pedestrians and whizzing past fast-food joints, swimsuit shops, and seedy bars.

⑯ Newport's best beaches are on **Balboa Peninsula.** Different sections are protected by jetties, creating many good swimming spots. The **Balboa Pavilion,** perched on the bay side of the Balboa Peninsula on Main Street (off Balboa Boulevard), was built in 1905 as a bath- and boathouse. Today it houses a restaurant and shops and is a departure point for harbor and whale-watching cruises. Adjacent to the pavilion is the three-car ferry that connects the peninsula to Balboa Island. Several blocks surrounding the pavilion contain restaurants, beachside shops, and the small **Fun Zone**—a local hangout with a Ferris wheel, video games, rides, and arcades.

⑰ The **Orange County Museum of Art** has an esteemed collection of abstract expressionist paintings and cutting-edge contemporary works by California artists. ✉ *850 San Clemente Dr.,* ☎ *714/759–1122.* ✍ *$4.* ☉ *Tues.–Sun. 11–5.*

Dining and Lodging

$$$ ✕ **Aubergine.** A husband-and-wife team runs this restaurant inside a
★ homey little cottage. He mans the kitchen and she handles the dining room. Only a few Californian touches influence the otherwise modern French menu. ✉ *508 29th St.,* ☎ *714/723–4150. AE, MC, V. Closed Sun.–Mon. No lunch.*

$$$ ✕ **Pascal.** You'll think you're in St-Tropez once you step inside this
★ bright and cheerful bistro in a shopping center. And, after one taste of Pascal Olhat's light Provençal cuisine, the best in Orange County, you'll *swear* you're in the south of France. Try the sea bass with thyme, the rack of lamb, and the lemon tart. ✉ *1000 N. Bristol St.,* ☎ *714/ 752–0107. AE, DC, V. Closed Sun. No dinner Mon.*

$$$ ✕ **The Ritz.** This is one of the most comfortable restaurants in southern California—the bar area has black leather booths, etched-glass mirrors, and polished brass trim. Don't pass up the smorgasbord appetizer, the roast Bavarian duck, or the rack of lamb from the spit. ✉ *880 Newport Center Dr.,* ☎ *714/720–1800. AE, D, DC, MC, V. No lunch weekends.*

$$ ✕ **The Cannery.** The building once was a cannery, and it has wonderful wharf-side views. The seafood entrées are good and the sandwiches at lunch are satisfying, but the location and lazy atmosphere are the real draw. ✉ *3010 Lafayette Ave.,* ☎ *714/675–5777. AE, D, DC, MC, V.*

$$ ✕ **Marrakesh.** In a casbah setting straight out of a Hope-and-Crosby road movie, diners become part of the scene—you eat with your fingers while sitting on the floor or lolling on a hassock. Chicken *b'stilla* (a traditional chicken dish served over rice), rabbit couscous, and skewered pieces of marinated lamb are the best of the Moroccan dishes. ✉ *1100 Pacific Coast Hwy.,* ☎ *714/645–8384. AE, DC, MC, V. No lunch.*

$–$$ ✕ **P. F. Chang's China Bistro.** The tasty Cal-Chinese food at this trendy spot includes Mongolian spicy beef and Chang's chicken, stir-fried in a sweet-and-spicy Szechuan sauce. Almost every table has an ocean view, but many diners are too busy people-watching to notice. Food can also be ordered at the lively bar. ✉ *Newport Fashion Island, 1145 Newport Center Dr.,* ☎ *714/759–9007. Reservations not accepted. AE, MC, V.*

$ ✕ **Crab Cooker.** If you don't mind waiting in line, this shanty serves fresh fish, grilled over mesquite, at low-low prices. The clam chowder, crusty Fisherman's bread, and coleslaw are quite good. ✉ *2200 Newport Blvd.,* ☎ *714/673–0100. Reservations not accepted. No credit cards.*

$ ✕ **El Torito Grill.** Southwestern cooking incorporating south-of-the-bor-
★ der specialties is the attraction here. The just-baked tortillas with fresh salsa and the blackened chicken with shrimp pasta are good choices. The bar serves hand-shaken margaritas and 20 brands of tequila. ✉ *Fashion Island, 951 Newport Center Dr.,* ☎ *714/640–2875. AE, D, DC, MC, V.*

$ ✕ **Hard Rock Cafe Newport Beach.** You can pick up your official T-shirt after munching a hamburger or a sandwich at the memorabilia-strewn Hard Rock. ✉ *Fashion Island, 451 Newport Center Dr.,* ☎ *714/640–8844. Reservations not accepted. AE, DC, MC, V.*

$$$$ 🏨 **Four Seasons Hotel.** Marble and antiques fill the airy lobby of this
★ 20-story hotel. The rooms, decorated with beiges, peaches, and southwestern touches, have spectacular views, private bars, and original art on the walls. Weekend golf packages are available in conjunction with the nearby Pelican Hill golf course, as well as fitness weekend packages. Kid-friendly amenities include balloons, cookies and milk, and a small game book. ✉ *690 Newport Center Dr., 92660,* ☎ *714/759–0808 or 800/332–3442,* ℻ *714/759–0568. 285 rooms. 2 restaurants, bar, pool, massage, sauna, steam room, 2 tennis courts, health club, mountain bikes, concierge, business services. AE, D, DC, MC, V.*

$$$$ 🏨 **Sutton Place Hotel.** An eye-catching ziggurat design is the trademark of this ultramodern hotel in Koll Center. Despite its modern exterior, the inside remains traditional with beige and burgundy accents. Rooms are spacious and well equipped; many have canopy beds. ✉ *4500 MacArthur Blvd., 92660,* ☎ *714/476–2001 or 800/243–4141,* ℻ *714/476–0153. 435 rooms. Restaurant, bar, in-room modem lines, minibars, refrigerators, pool, 2 tennis courts, health club, concierge, business services, airport shuttle. AE, D, DC, MC, V.*

$$$ 🏨 **Newport Beach Marriott Hotel and Tennis Club.** A large foreign clientele patronizes this hotel overlooking Newport Harbor. Arriving guests'

first view of the interior is a distinctive fountain surrounded by a plant-filled atrium. Two towers hold rooms, each with balconies or patios, that look out onto lush gardens or the Pacific. ✉ *900 Newport Center Dr., 92660,* ☎ *714/640–4000 or 800/228–9290,* FAX *714/640–5055. 570 rooms, 8 suites. 2 restaurants, bar, 2 pools, sauna, golf course, 8 tennis courts, health club, concierge, business services. AE, D, DC, MC, V.*

$$$ 🏨 **Sheraton Newport Beach.** Bamboo trees and palms decorate the lobby of this beach-style hotel. Vibrant teals, mauves, and peaches make up the color scheme. A complimentary morning paper, a buffet breakfast, and cocktail parties are offered Monday through Thursday. The hotel is convenient to John Wayne airport. ✉ *4545 MacArthur Blvd., 92660,* ☎ *714/833–0570 or 800/325-3535,* FAX *714/833–3927. 329 rooms, 4 suites. Restaurant, bar, pool, 2 tennis courts, exercise room. AE, D, DC, MC, V.*

Nightlife

The **Cannery** (✉ 3010 Lafayette Ave., ☎ 714/675–5777) is a packed seaside restaurant and bar that has karaoke and live entertainment. The house drink, a Purple Hooter, contains vodka, Chambord, and pineapple juice over ice. The **Studio Cafe** (✉ 100 Main St., Balboa Peninsula, ☎ 714/675–7760), locally famous for its potent blue drinks, has blues and jazz musicians nightly. **Tibbie's Music Hall** (✉ 4647 MacArthur Blvd., ☎ 714/252–0834), open weekends only, is a small dinner theater (you can also come only for the show).

Outdoor Activities and Sports

BOAT RENTAL

You can rent sailboats ($25 an hour) and small motorboats ($30 an hour) at **Balboa Boat Rentals** (✉ 510 E. Edgewater, ☎ 714/673–7200). You must have a driver's license, and some knowledge of boating is helpful; rented boats are not allowed out of the bay. Ocean boats are also for hire at $65 an hour.

BOAT TOURS

On the two-hour **Cannery Restaurant weekend brunch cruise** (✉ 3010 Lafayette Ave., ☎ 714/675–5777) you see Newport's harbor. Cruises, which are $31, depart at 10 AM and 1:30 PM. **Catalina Passenger Service** (✉ 400 Main St., ☎ 714/673–5245) at the Balboa Pavilion operates sightseeing tours ($6 to $8), fishing excursions ($33), and, during the winter, whale-watching cruises ($14). **Hornblower Dining Yachts** (✉ 2431 W. Coast Hwy., ☎ 714/646–0155) books 2½-hour Saturday dinner cruises with dancing for $56.95; Sunday brunch cruises are $39.45. Reservations are required.

CAMPING

Newport Dunes Resort (✉ 1131 Back Bay Dr., ☎ 714/729–3863) has RV and tent spaces, picnic facilities, changing rooms, water-sports equipment rentals, and a place to launch boats. The resort is surrounded by Newport Bay, a large preserve for ducks, geese, and other wildlife.

GOLF

Newport Beach Golf Course (✉ 3100 Irvine Ave., ☎ 714/852–8681), an 18-hole, par-59 course, is lighted for nighttime play. Greens fee: $11 to $17; hand carts ($2) only. Reservations are required one week in advance.

Pelican Hill Golf Club (✉ 22651 Pelican Hill Rd. S, ☎ 714/640–0238) has two 18-hole courses (par 70 and 71). Greens fee: $135–$215 which includes a mandatory cart.

RUNNING

The **Beach Trail** runs along the coast from Huntington Beach to Newport. Paths throughout **Newport Back Bay** wrap around a marshy area inhabited by lizards, squirrels, rabbits, and waterfowl.

SPORTFISHING

Davey's Locker (✉ Balboa Pavilion, 400 Main St., ☎ 714/673–1434) operates sportfishing trips starting at $24 and has a complete tackle shop.

SURFING

The River Jetties in northern Newport are good for beginners. The Wedge, farther south, is famous for its steep, punishing shore break.

TENNIS

Call the recreation department (☎ 714/644–3151) for information about use of the eight public courts at **Corona del Mar High School** (✉ 2101 E. Bluff Dr.). You can play on the courts at the **Newport Beach Marriott Hotel and Tennis Club** (✉ 900 Newport Center Dr., ☎ 714/640–4000) for $20 per hour.

Shopping

The outdoor **Fashion Island** complex contains upscale shops; the Bloomingdale's, Robinsons-May, Neiman-Marcus, and Macy's department stores; and some excellent restaurants. ✉ *Newport Center Dr. between Jamboree and MacArthur Blvds., off Pacific Coast Hwy.,* ☎ *714/721–2022.*

Corona del Mar

South of Newport Beach on Hwy. 1.

A small jewel on the Pacific Coast, Corona del Mar has exceptional beaches that some say resemble those in northern California. **Corona del Mar Beach** (☎ 714/644–3044), which is really made up of two beaches—Little Corona and Big Corona—is separated by a cliff. Facilities include fire pits, volleyball courts, food stands, rest rooms, and parking. Two colorful reefs (and the fact that it's off-limits to boats) make Corona del Mar a great place for snorkeling.

Crystal Cove State Park (☎ 714/494–3539), midway between Corona del Mar and Laguna, is a hidden treasure: 3½ mi of unspoiled beach with some of the best tide pooling in southern California. Here you can see starfish, crabs, and other sea life on the rocks. On the inland side of Pacific Coast Highway, the park offers 2,400 acres of backcountry, perfect for hiking, horseback riding, and mountain biking. Docents conduct nature walks on weekend mornings. Parking costs $6 per car.

The town of Corona del Mar stretches only a few blocks along Pacific Coast Highway, but some of the fanciest stores in the county line the route.

⑱ Sherman Library and Gardens, a botanical garden and library specializing in Southwest flora and fauna, provides a diversion from sun and sand. You can wander among cactus gardens, rose gardens, a wheelchair-height touch-and-smell garden, and a tropical conservatory. ✉ *2647 Pacific Coast Hwy.,* ☎ *714/673–2261.* ☞ *$3; free Mon.* ☉ *Gardens daily 10:30–4.*

Laguna Beach

★ *10 mi south of Newport Beach on Hwy. 1.*

Laguna Beach has been compared with New York City's SoHo, although its location is decidedly more picturesque. An artist colony, the town attracted the beat, hip, and far-out during the 1950s and '60s (along with what has grown to be Orange County's most visible gay community), but has always been a haven of conservative wealth. The two camps coexist in relative harmony, with Art prevailing in the congested village, and Wealth entrenched in the surrounding canyons and hills. A 1993 fire, which destroyed more than 300 homes in the hillsides surrounding Laguna Beach, miraculously left the village untouched.

A statue commemorates Eiler Larsen, Laguna's town greeter, who for years stood at the edge of town saying hello and good-bye to visitors. In recent years a man who calls himself Number One Archer has assumed the role of greeter, waving to tourists from a spot at the corner of Pacific Coast Highway and Forest Avenue.

Walk along the town's main street, Pacific Coast Highway, or along side streets, such as Forest or Ocean, and you'll pass fine-art and crafts galleries, clothing boutiques, and jewelry.

At the **Pageant of the Masters** (☎ 714/494–1147 or 800/487–3378), Laguna's most impressive event, live models and carefully orchestrated backgrounds are arranged in striking mimicry of famous paintings. The festival usually takes place in July and August.

⑲ The Laguna branch of the **Orange County Museum of Art** displays late-19th- and 20th-century works, including California impressionist and abstract art. Special exhibits change quarterly. ✉ *307 Cliff Dr.,* ☎ *714/494–6531.* 🎟 *$5.* 🕐 *Tues.–Sun. 11–5.*

Laguna Beach's **Main Beach Park,** at the end of Broadway at South Coast Highway, has sand volleyball, two half-basketball courts, children's play equipment, picnic areas, rest rooms, showers, and street parking. **Aliso County Park** (☎ 714/661–7013) in south Laguna is a recreation area with a fishing pier, a playground, fire pits, parking, food stands, and rest rooms. **Woods Cove,** off Coast Highway at Diamond Street, is especially quiet during the week. Big rock formations hide lurking crabs. As you climb the steps to leave, you can see an English-style mansion that was once the home of Bette Davis.

Dining and Lodging

$$$–$$$$ ✕ **Five Feet.** Others have mimicked this spot's innovative blend of Chinese and French cooking styles, but Five Feet remains the leader of the pack. From the delicate pot stickers and goat cheese wontons with raspberry coulis to fish in a garlic black-bean sauce or rabbit with foie gras and wild mushrooms, every dish is scrumptious. The setting is pure Laguna: exposed ceiling, open kitchen, high noise level, and brick walls adorned with works by local artists. ✉ *328 Gleneyre St.,* ☎ *714/497–4955. AE, D, DC, MC, V. No lunch Sat.–Thurs.*

$$ ✕ **Beach House.** A Laguna tradition, the Beach House has a water view from every table. Fresh fish, lobster, and steamed clams are the drawing cards. It's open for breakfast, lunch, and dinner. ✉ *619 Sleepy Hollow La.,* ☎ *714/494–9707. AE, MC, V.*

$–$$ ✕ **Ti Amo.** Laguna's newest Mediterranean restaurant, which opened in 1997, quickly became its best, justifiably acclaimed for the refinement of its setting and creativity of its main courses. Try the seared tuna with a sesame-seed crust or farfalle with smoked chicken and sun-dried tomato sauce. All the nooks and crannies are charming, candlelit, and private, but to maximize romance, request a table in the lush garden in back. ✉ *31727 S. Coast Hwy.,* ☎ *714/499–5350. AE, D, DC, MC, V. No lunch.*

$ ✕ **Tortilla Flats.** This hacienda-style restaurant specializes in first-rate chili rellenos, soft-shell tacos, and beef or chicken fajitas. There's also a wide selection of Mexican tequilas and beers. Sunday brunch is served. ⊠ *1740 S. Coast Hwy.,* ☎ *714/494–6588. AE, MC, V.*

\$\$\$\$ 🖵 **Surf and Sand Hotel.** Laguna's largest hotel is right on the beach. Rooms are decorated in soft sand colors and bleached wood and have wooden shutters and private balconies. The ocean-view restaurant and lounge on the top floor is a great place to end the evening; there's a piano bar and welcoming fireplace. ⊠ *1555 S. Coast Hwy., 92651,* ☎ *714/ 497–4477 or 800/524–8621,* ℻ *714/494–2897. 153 rooms, 4 suites. 2 restaurants, 2 bars, pool, beach, concierge. AE, D, DC, MC, V.*

\$\$\$–\$\$\$\$ 🖵 **Inn at Laguna Beach.** Set on a bluff overlooking the ocean, this
★ Mediterranean-style inn with white walls and terra-cotta tile floors provides luxurious amenities, including breakfast in bed. The rooms, many with views, are decorated in warm mauves and sea greens. The location here is ideal: It's close to Main Beach yet far enough away to be secluded. ⊠ *211 N. Coast Hwy., 92651,* ☎ *714/497–9722 or 800/ 544–4479,* ℻ *714/497–9972. 70 rooms. In-room VCRs, minibars, refrigerators, pool. AE, D, DC, MC, V.*

\$\$\$ 🖵 **Eiler's Inn.** A light-filled courtyard is the focal point of this European-
★ style bed-and-breakfast. Rooms are individually decorated with antiques. Breakfast is served outdoors, and in the afternoon there's wine and cheese. A sundeck in back has an ocean view. ⊠ *741 S. Coast Hwy., 92651,* ☎ *714/494–3004,* ℻ *714/497–2215. 12 rooms. AE, D, MC, V.*

\$\$\$ 🖵 **Hotel Laguna.** This downtown landmark, which opened in 1890, is the oldest hotel in Laguna. Lobby windows look out onto manicured gardens, and a patio restaurant overlooks the ocean and the hotel's private beach. Four rooms have canopy beds and reproduction Victorian furnishings. Other rooms are decorated with white-washed furniture and pastel bedspreads and curtains. Continental breakfast is served in bed, and there's complimentary wine and cheese in the afternoon. Rooms here don't have air-conditioning. ⊠ *425 S. Coast Hwy., 92651,* ☎ *714/494–1151 or 800/524–2927,* ℻ *714/497–2163. 63 rooms. 2 restaurants, bar. AE, D, DC, MC, V.*

\$ 🖵 **Coast Inn.** Gay men and some lesbians have been coming to the Coast Inn for more than three decades. Rooms range from standard motel type to larger ones with private decks and fireplaces. ⊠ *1401 S. Coast Hwy.,* ☎ *714/494–7588 or 800/653–2697,* ℻ *714/494–1735. 23 rooms. Restaurant, bar. AE, D, DC, MC, V.*

Nightlife

The **Boom Boom Room** (⊠ Coast Inn, 1401 S. Coast Hwy., ☎ 714/ 494–7355) is Laguna Beach's most popular gay club. The **Sandpiper** (⊠ 1183 S. Coast Hwy., ☎ 714/494–4694), a hole-in-the-wall dancing joint, attracts an eclectic crowd. Laguna's **White House** (⊠ 340 S. Coast Hwy., ☎ 714/494–8088), a chic club on the main strip, has nightly entertainment and dancing that runs the gamut from rock to Motown, reggae to pop.

Outdoor Activities and Sports

BICYCLING AND ROLLERBLADING

Rent equipment at **Rainbow Bicycles** (⊠ 485 N. Coast Hwy., ☎ 714/ 494–5806).

GOLF

Aliso Creek Golf Course (⊠ 31106 S. Coast Hwy., ☎ 714/499–1919) is a nine-hole facility with a putting green. Greens fee: \$14–\$20; carts \$8. Reservations are taken up to a week ahead.

TENNIS

Six metered courts can be found at **Laguna Beach High School.** Two courts are available at the **Irvine Bowl.** Six courts are available at **Alta**

Laguna Park on a first-come, first-served basis. **Moulton Meadows** has two lighted courts. For more information, call the **City of Laguna Beach Recreation Department** (☎ 714/497–0716).

WATER SPORTS

Because its entire beach area is a marine preserve, Laguna Beach is a good spot for snorkeling. Scuba divers head to the Marine Life Refuge area, which runs from Seal Rock to Diver's Cove. Rent surfboards and bodyboards at **Hobie Sports** (⊠ 294 Forest Ave., ☎ 714/497–3304).

Shopping

Georgeo's Art Glass and Jewelry (⊠ 269 Forest Ave., ☎ 714/497–0907) contains a large selection of etched-glass bowls, vases, and fine jewelry. **Marcus Animation Gallery** (⊠ 220 Forest Ave., ☎ 714/494–8102) displays 3-D multimedia art and animation from Disney and Warner Bros. The **Art Center Gallery** (⊠ 266 Forest Ave., ☎ 714/376–7596) exhibits the works of local artists.

Dana Point

10 mi south of Laguna Beach on Hwy. 1.

Dana Point is Orange County's newest aquatic playground, a small-boat marina tucked into a dramatic natural harbor surrounded by high bluffs. **Dana Point Harbor** was first described more than 100 years ago by its namesake Richard Henry Dana in his book *Two Years Before the Mast.* At the marina are docks for small boats, marine-oriented shops, and some restaurants.

Swim Beach inside Dana Point Harbor has a fishing pier, barbecues, food stands, parking, rest rooms, and showers. **Doheny State Park** (☎ 714/496–6171), at the south end of Dana Point, one of the best surfing spots in southern California, has an interpretive center devoted to the wildlife of the Doheny Marine Refuge, and there are food stands and shops nearby. Camping is permitted here, though there are no hookups, and there are picnic facilities and a pier for fishing.

☺ ❷ Two indoor tanks at the **Orange County Marine Institute** contain touchable sea creatures, and you can see a complete skeleton of a gray whale. Anchored near the institute is *The Pilgrim,* a full-size replica of the square-rigged vessel on which Richard Henry Dana sailed. You can tour the boat Sunday from 10 to 2:30. Weekend cruises are available on the *Sea Explorer.* You can arrange to go whale-watching from January through March or to explore regional tide pools year-round. ⊠ 24200 Dana Point Harbor Dr., ☎ 714/496–2274. 🖾 Donation requested. ⊙ Daily 10–4:30.

Dining and Lodging

$$$ ✕ **The Dining Room.** The restaurant in the Ritz-Carlton Laguna Niguel Hotel offers a prix-fixe menu of contemporary French-Mediterranean specialties. Try chef Yvon Goetz's foie gras with baby leeks in a truffle vinaigrette, followed by monkfish medallions with pearl onions or roasted duck breast. You can choose two to five courses; the price depends on the number of courses. This Dining Room is an elegant space, with subdued lighting, crystal chandeliers, original paintings on the walls, and antiques tucked into corners. ⊠ 1 Ritz-Carlton Dr., ☎ 714/240–2000. Reservations essential. Jacket required. AE, D, DC, MC, V. No lunch.

$$ ✕ **Luciana's.** This intimate Italian restaurant is a real find, especially for couples seeking a romantic evening. The small dining rooms are dressed with crisp white linens and warmed by fireplaces. The well-prepared food—linguine with clams, prawns, calamari, and green-

lip mussels in a light tomato sauce; grilled cured pork chops in a fennel-herb marinade and an apple and red-onion compote; veal medallions with haricot verts and oven-dried tomatoes—is served with care. ✉ *24312 Del Prado Ave.,* ☎ *714/661–6500. AE, DC, MC, V. No lunch.*

$ ✕ **Proud Mary's.** The best burgers and sandwiches in south Orange County are served here, and you can dine alfresco, overlooking the fishing boats and pleasure craft in Dana Point Harbor. Breakfast is available all day long. Steaks, chicken, and other American standards are served for dinner. ✉ *34689 Golden Lantern,* ☎ *714/493–5853. AE, D, MC, V. No dinner. Free parking.*

$$$$ 🏨 **Blue Lantern Inn.** Perched atop the bluffs, this white clapboard New
★ England–style B&B has harbor and ocean views. Relax by the fire that warms the intimate living area, sip coffee during a game of backgammon, or commune with the many teddy bears that grace the inn. Rooms, furnished colonial-style, have a fireplace, a soda-filled refrigerator, and a whirlpool bath. Room rates include breakfast and afternoon refreshments. The tower suite, which rises majestically from the rest of the inn, has a 180-degree ocean view. ✉ *34343 St. of the Blue Lantern, 92629,* ☎ *714/661–1304,* FAX *714/496–1483. 29 rooms. Health club, concierge. AE, DC, MC, V.*

$$$$ 🏨 **Marriott's Laguna Cliffs Resort.** Formerly known as the Dana Point Resort and reminiscent of Cape Cod establishments, this white-washed hillside hotel has a beautiful view of the Pacific. On Sunday evenings in summer, the Capistrano Valley Symphony performs on the resort's landscaped grounds. ✉ *25135 Park Lantern, 92629,* ☎ *714/661–5000 or 800/533–9748,* FAX *714/661–5358. 332 rooms, 18 suites. Restaurant, bar, 2 pools, 2 spas, basketball, croquet, health club, volleyball. AE, D, DC, MC, V.*

$$$$ 🏨 **Ritz-Carlton Laguna Niguel.** Sumptuous decor, an unrivaled setting
★ on the edge of the Pacific, and flawless service have earned the Ritz-Carlton worldwide recognition. With its colorful landscaping outside and imposing marble-columned entryway, the hotel has the feel of a Mediterranean country villa. Rooms have marble bathrooms and private balconies with ocean or pool views. Afternoon tea is served in the library. ✉ *1 Ritz-Carlton Dr., 92629,* ☎ *714/240–2000 or 800/241–3333,* FAX *714/240–0829. 332 rooms, 31 suites. 3 restaurants, lobby lounge, 2 pools, beauty salon, massage, golf privileges, 4 tennis courts, health club, concierge. AE, D, DC, MC, V.*

$$ 🏨 **Best Western Marina Inn.** The three-level Best Western is convenient to docks, restaurants, and shops. Rooms, many with balconies and harbor views, vary in size from standard to family units with kitchens and fireplaces. ✉ *24800 Dana Point Harbor Dr., 92629,* ☎ *714/496–1203 or 800/255–6843,* FAX *714/248–0360. 126 rooms, 10 suites. Pool, exercise room. AE, D, DC, MC, V.*

Outdoor Activities and Sports

RENTALS

Embarcadero Marina (✉ 34512 Embarcadero Pl., ☎ 714/496–6177) in Dana Point has powerboats and sailboats for rent near the launching ramp at Dana Point Harbor. Rental stands for surfboards, Windsurfers, small powerboats, and sailboats can be found near most of the piers. **Hobie Sports** (✉ 294 Forest Ave., ☎ 714/496–2366) rents surfboards and Boogie boards. **Dana Wharf Sportfishing** (✉ 34675 Golden Lantern St., ☎ 714/496–5794) has charters year-round and runs whale-watching excursions in winter.

San Juan Capistrano

5 mi north of Dana Point on Hwy. 74.

San Juan Capistrano is best known for its mission and for the swallows that migrate here each year from their winter haven in Argentina. The arrival of the birds on St. Joseph's Day, March 19, launches a week of festivities. After summering in the arches of the old stone church, the swallows head home on St. John's Day, October 23.

If you arrive by train, you will be dropped off across from the Mission at the San Juan Capistrano depot. With its appealing brick café and preserved Sante Fe cars, the depot retains much of the magic of early American railroads. If you're driving, park near Ortega and Camino Capistrano, the city's main streets, which are lined with colorful restaurants and boutiques.

★ ㉑ **Mission San Juan Capistrano,** founded in 1776 by Father Junípero Serra, was the major Roman Catholic outpost between Los Angeles and San Diego. The original Great Stone Church is permanently supported by scaffolding. Many of the mission's adobe buildings have been preserved to illustrate mission life, with exhibits of an olive millstone, tallow ovens, tanning vats, metalworking furnaces, and padres' living quarters. The bougainvillea-covered Serra Chapel is believed to be the oldest building in California. Mass takes place at 7 AM daily. ✉ *Camino Capistrano and Ortega Hwy.,* ☎ *714/248–2048.* ☞ *$5.* ☉ *Daily 8:30–5.*

㉒ The **San Juan Capistrano Library,** a postmodern structure erected in 1983, is near Mission San Juan Capistrano. Architect Michael Graves combined a classical design with the style of the mission to striking effect. The library's courtyard has secluded places for reading. ✉ *31495 El Camino Real,* ☎ *714/493–1752.* ☉ *Mon.–Thurs. 10–9, Fri.–Sat. 10–5.*

Dining

$–$$ ★ ✕ **L'Hirondelle.** Duckling, prepared three different ways, is the specialty at this French and Belgian restaurant where you can dine inside or out on the patio. ✉ *31631 Camino Capistrano,* ☎ *714/661–0425. AE, MC, V. Closed Mon. No lunch Tues.*

$ ✕ **El Adobe.** This early California–style eatery serves enormous portions of mildly seasoned Mexican food. Mariachi bands play Friday and Saturday nights and for Sunday brunch. ✉ *31891 Camino Capistrano,* ☎ *714/830–8620. AE, D, DC, MC, V.*

Nightlife

Coach House (✉ 33157 Camino Capistrano, ☎ 714/496–8930) presents comedy, musical, and other acts.

OFF THE BEATEN PATH — **SAN CLEMENTE** – With 20 mi of prime terrain, San Clemente, which is 10 mi south of Dana Point on Pacific Coast Highway, draws bicyclists from around the region. Camp Pendleton, the country's largest Marine Corps base, welcomes cyclists to use some of its roads—just don't be surprised to see a troop helicopter taking off right beside you. San Clemente State Beach (☎ 714/492-3156) is popular with surfers. It has ample camping facilities, RV hookups, and fire rings. San Onofre State Beach, just south of San Clemente, has some of California's best surfing. Below the bluffs here are 3½ mi of sandy beach, where you can swim, fish, and watch wildlife.

ORANGE COUNTY A TO Z

Arriving and Departing

By Bus

The **Los Angeles MTA** has limited service to Orange County. You can take Bus 460 to Anaheim from downtown; it goes to Knott's Berry Farm and Disneyland. **Greyhound** (☎ 714/999–1256) serves Anaheim and Santa Ana.

By Car

Two major freeways, I–405 (the San Diego Freeway) and I–5 (the Santa Ana Freeway), run north and south through Orange County. South of Laguna, I–405 merges into I–5 (which is called the San Diego Freeway south from this point). Avoid these freeways during rush hours (6–9 AM and 3:30–6 PM), when they can back up for miles.

By Plane

The county's main facility is **John Wayne Orange County Airport** (✉ MacArthur Blvd. and I–405, ☎ 714/252–5252) in Santa Ana. It is serviced by Alaska, America West, American, Continental, Delta, Northwest, Southwest, TWA, United, and several commuter airlines. *See* Air Travel *in* the Gold Guide for airline phone numbers.

Los Angeles International Airport is only 35 mi west of Anaheim. **Ontario International Airport,** just northwest of Riverside, is 30 mi north of Anaheim. **Long Beach Airport** is 24 mi from Anaheim. *See* Los Angeles A to Z *in* Chapter 12 for information about these airports.

BETWEEN THE AIRPORTS AND HOTELS

Airport Bus (☎ 800/772–5299), a shuttle service, carries passengers from John Wayne airport and LAX to Anaheim, and Buena Park. The fare from John Wayne to Anaheim is $10, from LAX to Anaheim $14.

Prime Time Airport Shuttle (☎ 800/262–7433) provides door-to-door service to LAX and John Wayne airports, hotels near John Wayne, and the San Pedro cruise terminal. The fare is $11 from Anaheim hotels to John Wayne and $12 from Anaheim hotels to LAX.

SuperShuttle (☎ 714/517–6600) provides 24-hour door-to-door service from all the airports to all points in Orange County. The fare to the Disneyland area is $10 per person from John Wayne, $34 from Ontario, $13 from LAX, and $33 from Long Beach Airport. Shuttle fares listed are for one person; fares for additional members of the same party are substantially reduced.

By Train

Amtrak (☎ 800/872–7245) makes several daily stops in Orange County: Fullerton, Anaheim, Santa Ana, Irvine, San Juan Capistrano, and San Clemente.

Getting Around

By Bus

The **Orange County Transportation Authority** (OCTA, ☎ 714/636–7433) will take you virtually anywhere in the county, but it will take time; OCTA buses go from Knott's Berry Farm and Disneyland to Huntington and Newport beaches. Bus 1 travels along the coast.

By Car

Highways 22, 55, and 91 head west to the ocean and east into the mountains: Take Highway 91 or Highway 22 to inland points (Buena Park, Anaheim) and take Highway 55 to Newport Beach. Highway 91 has a toll lane called the Fast Track. Pacific Coast Highway (Highway 1, also known locally as PCH) allows easy access to beach communities and is the most scenic route.

Contacts and Resources

Emergencies

Ambulance (☎ 911). **Fire** (☎ 911). **Police** (☎ 911).

Anaheim Memorial Hospital (✉ 1111 W. La Palma, ☎ 714/774–1450). **Western Medical Center** (✉ 1025 S. Anaheim Blvd., Anaheim, ☎ 714/533–6220). **Hoag Memorial Presbyterian Hospital** (✉ 301 Newport Blvd., Newport Beach, ☎ 714/645–8600). **South Coast Medical Center** (✉ 31872 Pacific Coast Hwy., Laguna Beach, ☎ 714/499–1311).

Guided Tours

GENERAL-INTEREST TOURS

Pacific Coast Gray Line Tours (☎ 714/978–8855) provides guided tours from Orange County hotels to Disneyland, Knott's Berry Farm, Universal Studios Hollywood, Six Flags Magic Mountain, and the San Diego Zoo.

Visitor Information

Anaheim–Orange County Visitor and Convention Bureau (✉ Anaheim Convention Center, 800 W. Katella Ave., 92802, ☎ 714/999–8999). **Huntington Beach Conference and Visitors Bureau** (✉ 101 Main St., Suite 2A, 92648, ☎ 714/969–3492). **Laguna Beach Visitors Bureau and Chamber of Commerce** (✉ 252 Broadway, 92651, ☎ 714/494–1018). **Newport Beach Conference and Visitors Bureau** (✉ 3300 W. Coast Hwy., 92663, ☎ 800/942–6278). **San Juan Capistrano Chamber of Commerce and Visitors Center** (✉ 31931 Camino Capistrano, Suite D, 92675, ☎ 714/493–4700). **Southern California Golf Association** (☎ 818/980–3630). **Southern California Public Links Golf Association** (☎ 714/994–4747). **Visitor Information Hot Line** (☎ 714/635–8900).

14 San Diego

To visitors, the city and county of San Diego may seem like a conglomeration of theme parks: Old Town and the Gaslamp Quarter historically oriented ones, the wharf area a maritime-heritage playground, La Jolla a genteel throwback to southern California elegance, Balboa Park a convergence of the town's cerebral and action-oriented personae. There are, of course, real theme parks—Sea World and the San Diego Zoo—but the great outdoors, in the form of forests, landscaped urban areas, and a string of sandy beaches, forms the biggest of them all.

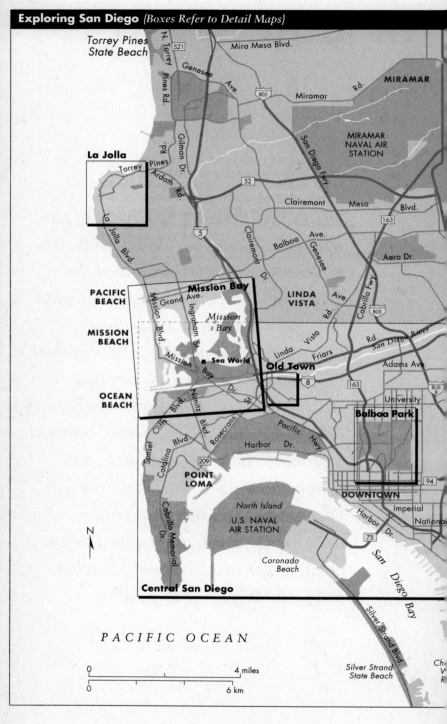

Exploring San Diego *(Boxes Refer to Detail Maps)*

Torrey Pines
State Beach

S21

N. Torrey Pines Rd.

Mira Mesa Blvd.

Genesee Ave.

MIRAMAR

805

Miramar Rd.

Miramar

La Jolla

Torrey Pines Rd.

Ardath Rd.

Gilman Dr.

52

MIRAMAR
NAVAL AIR
STATION

Clairemont Mesa Blvd.

163

5

La Jolla Blvd.

Clairemont Dr.

Balboa Ave.

Genesee Ave.

Aero Dr.

PACIFIC
BEACH

Mission Bay

Grand Ave.

Mission Blvd.

Ingraham St.

*Mission
Bay*

LINDA
VISTA

Cabrillo Fwy.

805

MISSION
BEACH

Mission Bay Dr.

Linda Vista Rd.

Friars Rd.

San Diego River

Nimitz Blvd.

■ Sea World

Old Town

Adams Ave.

8

OCEAN
BEACH

163

University Ave.

BUS
8

Sunset Cliffs Blvd.

Catalina Blvd.

Rosecrans St.

Pacific Hwy.

Balboa Park

209

Harbor Dr.

94

**POINT
LOMA**

North Island

DOWNTOWN

Imperial

Cabrillo Memorial Dr.

U.S. NAVAL
AIR STATION

Harbor Dr.

Nationa

75

N

*Coronado
Beach*

San Diego Bay

Central San Diego

Silver Strand Blvd.

PACIFIC OCEAN

0   4 miles

0   6 km

*Silver Strand
State Beach*

Ch
V
R

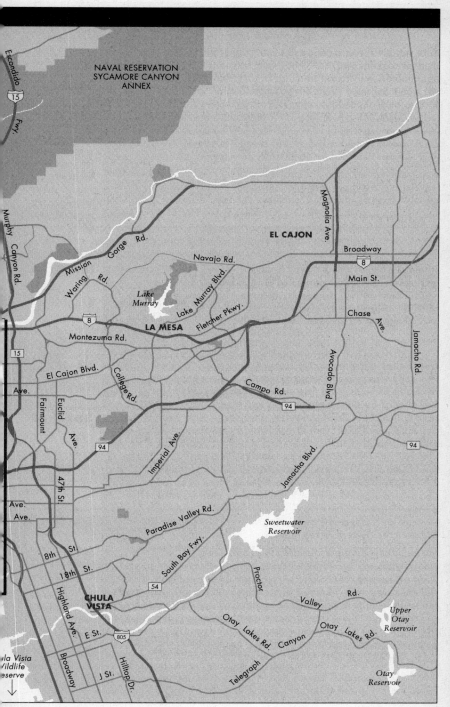

NAVAL RESERVATION
SYCAMORE CANYON
ANNEX

Escondido Fwy

15

Murphy Canyon Rd.

Mission Gorge Rd.

Waring Rd.

Navajo Rd.

EL CAJON

Magnolia Ave.

Broadway

8

Main St.

Lake Murray

Lake Murray Blvd.

Fletcher Pkwy.

Chase Ave.

8

LA MESA

Montezuma Rd.

15

El Cajon Blvd.

College Rd.

Ave.

Campo Rd.

94

Avocado Blvd.

Jamacha Rd.

Fairmount Ave.

Euclid Ave.

94

Imperial Ave.

94

Jamacha Blvd.

47th St.

Ave.

Ave.

Paradise Valley Rd.

Sweetwater Reservoir

8th St.

South Bay Fwy.

18th St.

Proctor

CHULA VISTA

54

Valley Rd.

Upper Otay Reservoir

Highland Ave.

E St.

805

Otay Lakes Rd.

Canyon

Otay Lakes Rd.

ula Vista Wildlife eserve
↓

Broadway

J St.

Hilltop Dr.

Telegraph

Otay Reservoir

SAN DIEGO COUNTY is the nation's sixth largest—larger than nearly a dozen U.S. states—with a population of more than 2.5 million. It sprawls east from the Pacific Ocean through dense urban neighborhoods to outlying suburban communities that seem to sprout on canyons and cliffs overnight. Its eastern boundaries are the Cleveland National Forest, where the pines and manzanita are covered with snow in the winter, and the Anza-Borrego Desert, where delicate pink and yellow cactus blooms herald the coming of spring. San Diegans visit these vast wildernesses for their annual doses of seasonal splendor, then return to the city, where flowers blossom year-round and the streets are dry and clean. One of the busiest international borders in the United States marks the county's southern line, where approximately 60 million people a year legally cross between Mexico's Baja California peninsula and San Diego. To the north, the marines at Camp Pendleton practice land, sea, and air maneuvers in southern California's largest coastal greenbelt, marking the demarcation zone between the congestion of Orange and Los Angeles counties and the more relaxed expansiveness of San Diego.

EXPLORING SAN DIEGO

By Edie Jarolim   San Diego is more a chain of separate communities than a cohesive city. Many of the major attractions are separated by some distance from one another. The streets are fun for getting an up-close look at how San Diegans live, but true southern Californians use the freeways, which crisscross the county in a sensible fashion. If you are going to drive around San Diego, study your maps before you hit the road. The freeways are convenient and fast most of the time, but if you miss your turnoff or get caught in commuter traffic, you'll experience a none-too-pleasurable hallmark of southern California living—freeway madness.

If you stick with public transportation, plan on taking your time. San Diego's trolley line has expanded into Old Town; a light-rail line called the *Coaster* runs from Oceanside into downtown; and the bus system covers almost all the county—but making the connections necessary to see the various sights is time consuming. With the large distances between sights, taxis can be expensive and are best used for getting around once you're in a given area.

Great Itineraries

IF YOU HAVE 3 DAYS

Head over to the San Diego Zoo in Balboa Park on the morning of your first day, and have lunch at the café in the San Diego Museum of Art or north of the park in Hillcrest. Spend the remainder of your afternoon in the park at the museums along El Prado.

Start your second day downtown at Seaport Village, and then take a ferry to Coronado. Back in San Diego after lunch, stroll north on the Embarcadero to Ash Street; if you've gotten back early enough from Coronado, you can view the Maritime Museum.

On the third morning, visit La Jolla. Have lunch here before heading back into town on I–5 to the Gaslamp Quarter.

IF YOU HAVE 5 DAYS

Follow the three-day itinerary above and begin your fourth day with a morning visit to Cabrillo National Monument. Have lunch at one of the seafood restaurants on Scott Street, and then head over to Old Town (take Rosecrans Street north to San Diego Avenue). If the daily schedule lists low tide for the afternoon, reverse the order to catch the tide pools at Cabrillo.

En route to San Diego North County on day five, stop off at Torrey Pines State Park. Then get on I–5 and head up to Del Mar for lunch, shopping, and sea views. If you have the time, head inland to the charming town of Julian (take S6 east to Escondido, then I–15 north, briefly, to Highway 78 heading east).

BALBOA PARK

Balboa Park is set on 1,400 beautifully landscaped acres. Hosting the majority of San Diego's museums and a world-famous zoo, the park serves as the cultural center of the city, as well as a recreational paradise. Many of the park's Spanish-Moorish buildings were intended to be temporary structures housing exhibits for the Panama–California International Exposition of 1915, which celebrated the opening of the Panama Canal. The Spanish theme first instituted in the early 1900s was in part carried through in new buildings designed for the California Pacific International Exposition of 1935–36.

If you're driving in via the Laurel Street Bridge, the first parking area you'll come to is off the Prado to the left, going toward Pan American Plaza; you'll see more lots as you continue down along the same road. Free trams that operate around the park provide an alternative to walking to and from your car. Trams run every 20 minutes from April to October 9:30 to 5:30, and the rest of the year 11 to 5.

Two Good Walks

Numbers in the text correspond to numbers in the margin and on the Balboa Park map.

Enter via Cabrillo Bridge through the West Gate, which depicts the Panama Canal's linkage of the Atlantic and Pacific oceans. Park just south of the **Alcazar Garden** ①. It's a short stretch north across El Prado to the landmark **California Building,** modeled on a cathedral in Mexico and home to the **San Diego Museum of Man** ②. Look up to see busts and statues of heroes of the early days of the state. Next door is the **Simon Edison Centre for the Performing Arts** ③, which adjoins the sculpture garden of the **San Diego Museum of Art** ④.

Continuing east, you'll come to the **Timken Museum of Art** ⑤, the **Botanical Building** ⑥, and the Spanish colonial-style **Casa del Prado,** where the San Diego Floral Association has its offices and a gift shop. At the end of the row is the **San Diego Natural History Museum** ⑦; you'll have to detour a block north to visit the **Spanish Village Art Center** ⑧. If you continue north, you'll come to the **carousel** ⑨, the **miniature railroad** ⑩, and, finally, the entrance to the **San Diego Zoo** ⑪.

Return to the history museum and cross Plaza de Balboa to reach the **Reuben H. Fleet Space Theater and Science Center** ⑫. You're now on the opposite side of the Prado and heading west. You'll next pass **Casa de Balboa** ⑭, home to history, model-railroad, photography, and sports museums. Next door in the newly restored **House of Hospitality** ⑮ is the **Balboa Park Visitors Center.** Just across the Plaza de Panama, the **Mingei International Museum** ⑯ resides in a recently constructed Spanish-style building that blends well with older park architecture. Your starting point, the Alcazar Garden, is just west of the Mingei.

Another option is to walk south from the Plaza de Panama, which doubles as a parking lot. Just as most of the buildings along El Prado were created for the 1915 exposition, the majority of those along this route

Balboa Park

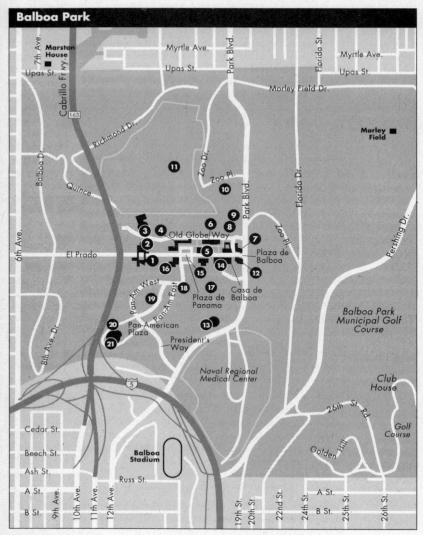

Alcazar Garden, **1**

Botanical Building, **6**

Carousel, **9**

Casa de Balboa, **14**

Centro Cultural de la Raza, **13**

House of Hospitality, **15**

House of Pacific Relations, **19**

Japanese Friendship Garden, **17**

Mingei International Museum, **16**

Miniature Railroad, **10**

Museum of Photographic Arts, **14**

Museum of San Diego History, **14**

Reuben H. Fleet Space Theater and Science Center, **12**

San Diego Aerospace Museum and International Aerospace Hall of Fame, **21**

San Diego Automotive Museum, **20**

San Diego Hall of Champions–Sports Museum, **14**

San Diego Model Railroad Museum, **14**

San Diego Museum of Art, **4**

San Diego Museum of Man, **2**

San Diego Natural History Museum, **7**

San Diego Zoo, **11**

Simon Edison Centre for the Performing Arts, **3**

Spanish Village Art Center, **8**

Spreckels Organ Pavilion, **18**

Timken Museum of Art, **5**

date to the 1935 fair, when the architecture of the Maya and native peoples of the Southwest was highlighted. The first building you'll pass is the **Japanese Friendship Garden** ⑰. Next comes the ornate, crown-like **Spreckels Organ Pavilion** ⑱. The round seating area forms the base, with the stage as its diadem. The road forks here; veer to the left to reach the **House of Pacific Relations** ⑲, a Spanish Mission–style cluster of cottages and one of the few structures on this route built for the earlier exposition. Another is the Balboa Park Club, which you'll pass next. Used for park receptions and banquets, the building resembles a mission church on the New Mexico Pueblo of Acoma; you might want to step inside to see the huge Depression-era mural. Continue on beyond the Palisades Building, which hosts the Marie Hitchcock Puppet Theater, to reach the **San Diego Automotive Museum** ⑳, appropriately housed in the building that served as the Palace of Transportation in the 1935–36 exposition.

The road loops back at the space ship–like **San Diego Aerospace Museum and International Aerospace Hall of Fame** ㉑. As you head north again, you'll notice the Starlight Bowl on your right. It sits in the flight path to Lindbergh Field; during the live musicals presented in the summer on its outdoor stage, actors freeze in their places when planes roar overhead. The Gymnasium Building—slated to become the home of the sports museum in a few years—follows. Perhaps the most impressive structure on this tour, the **Federal Building,** used for indoor sports these days, is next: Its main entrance was modeled after the Palace of Governors in the ancient Maya city of Uxmal, Mexico. You'll be back at the Spreckels Organ Pavilion after this, having walked a total of a little less than a mile.

TIMING

You'll want to devote an entire day to the zoo. Most of the park's museums are open daily from 10 to 4; during the summer, a number have extended hours. On Tuesday, the museums have free admission on a rotating basis; call the Balboa Park Visitors Center (☞ House of Hospitality, *below*) for the schedule. Free concerts take place Sunday afternoons and summer Monday evenings at the Spreckels Organ Pavilion, and the House of Pacific Relations hosts Sunday afternoon folk-dance performances.

Sights to See

❶ Alcazar Garden. The gardens surrounding the Alcazar Castle in Seville were the model for the landscaping here; you'll feel like royalty resting on the benches by the tiled fountains. The flower beds are ever-changing horticultural exhibits, with bright orange and yellow poppies blooming in the spring and deep rust and crimson chrysanthemums appearing in the fall. The garden is off El Prado, next to the Mingei International Museum and across from the Museum of Man.

❻ Botanical Building. The graceful redwood-lathed structure built for the 1915 exposition houses more than 500 types of tropical and subtropical plants. Ceiling-high tree ferns shade fragile orchids and feathery bamboo. There are benches beside miniature waterfalls for resting in the shade. The Lily Pond, filled with giant koi fish and blooming water lilies, is popular with photographers. ✉ *1550 El Prado,* ☎ *619/235–1110.* ✍ *Free.* ☼ *Fri.–Wed. 10–4.*

❾ Carousel. Riders on this antique merry-go-round stretch from their seats to grab the brass rings suspended an arm's length away and earn a free ride. ✉ *1889 Zoo Pl. (behind zoo parking lot).* ✍ *$1.25.* ☼ *Daily 11:30–5:30 during extended summer vacation; during school yr, only school holidays and weekends.*

⓮ **Casa de Balboa.** This building on El Prado's southeast corner houses four museums: the Museum of Photographic Arts, the Museum of San Diego History, the San Diego Hall of Champions–Sports Museum, and the San Diego Model Railroad Museum. *See* individual museum descriptions, *below.* ✉ *1649 El Prado.*

⓭ **Centro Cultural de la Raza.** An old water tower was converted into this center for Mexican, Native American, and Chicano arts. Attractions include a gallery with rotating exhibits and a theater, as well as a permanent collection of mural art, a fine example of which may be seen on the tower's exterior. ✉ *2004 Park Blvd.,* ☎ *619/235–6135.* 🎟 *Free.* ⏲ *Wed.–Sun. noon–5.*

⓯ **House of Hospitality.** At the refurbished home of the **Balboa Park Visitors Center** you can pick up schedules and route maps for the free trams that operate around the park. You can also purchase the Passport to Balboa Park, which affords entry to nine museums for $19; it's worthwhile if you want to visit more than a few and aren't entitled to the discounts that most give to children, senior citizens, and military personnel. The **Terrace on the Prado** (☎ 619/236–1935) restaurant's Spanish and early-California menu includes recipes from the gold-rush days; there's also a tapas bar here. ✉ *1549 El Prado,* ☎ *619/239–0512.* 🎟 *Free.* ⏲ *Daily 9–4.*

⓳ **House of Pacific Relations.** This is not really a house but a cluster of red tile–roof, stucco cottages representing more than 25 foreign countries. And the word "pacific" refers not to the ocean—most of the nations represented are European, not Asian—but to the goal of maintaining peace. The cottages, decorated with crafts and pictures, hold open houses each Sunday. ✉ *2160 Pan American Rd. W,* ☎ *619/292–8592.* 🎟 *Free.* ⏲ *Sun. 12:30–4:30; hrs may vary with season.*

⓱ **Japanese Friendship Garden.** The rocks and trees are arranged to inspire contemplation in the park's Eastern-style garden, which is still being developed. It currently includes an exhibit house where origami and flower arranging are taught, a traditional sand-and-stone garden, a picnic area with a view of the canyon below, a snack bar, and a small gift shop. ✉ *2215 Pan American Rd. E,* ☎ *619/232–2780.* 🎟 *$2.* ⏲ *Fri.–Sun. and Tues. 10–4.*

★ ⓰ **Mingei International Museum.** All ages will enjoy the colorful and creative exhibits of toys, pottery, textiles, costumes, and gadgets from around the globe at the Mingei. You'll find everything from antique American carousel horses to the latest in Japanese ceramics in the light-filled museum. ✉ *1439 El Prado,* ☎ *619/239–0003.* 🎟 *$5.* ⏲ *Tues.–Sun. 10–4.*

❿ **Miniature railroad.** Adjacent to the zoo parking lot, a pint-size 48-passenger train runs a ½-mi loop through eucalyptus groves. The engine is a small-scale version of the General Motors F-3 locomotive. ✉ *2885 Zoo Pl.,* ☎ *619/239–4748.* 🎟 *$1.25.* ⏲ *Weekends and school holidays 11:30–4:30 (daily during school summer break).*

⓮ **Museum of Photographic Arts.** World-renowned photographers such as Ansel Adams, Imogen Cunningham, Henri Cartier-Bresson, and Edward Weston are represented in the museum's collection, along with lesser-known contemporary artists. ✉ *Casa de Balboa, 1649 El Prado,* ☎ *619/239–5262.* 🎟 *$3.50.* ⏲ *Daily 10–5.*

⓮ **Museum of San Diego History.** The San Diego Historical Society maintains its research library in the Casa de Balboa's basement and organizes shows on the first floor. Permanent and rotating exhibits survey local urban history after 1850, when California became part of the United

States. ⊠ *Casa de Balboa, 1649 El Prado,* ☎ *619/232–6203.* ⊡ *$6.* ⊘ *Wed.–Sun. 10–4:30.*

★ ⑫ **Reuben H. Fleet Space Theater and Science Center.** Children and adults enjoy the Fleet center's clever interactive exhibits that teach scientific principles. The IMAX Dome Theater screens exhilarating nature and science films. The gift shop is akin to a museum, with toys and gadgets that inspire the imagination. A multimillion-dollar expansion program that will double the facility's size is scheduled for completion by May 1998. ⊠ *1875 El Prado,* ☎ *619/238–1233 or 619/232–6866 for advance tickets.* ⊡ *Science Center $2.50, or included with price of theater ticket; Space Theater tickets $6.50; planetarium show $3.* ⊘ *Mon.–Tues. 9:30–6, Wed.–Sun. 9:30–9 (hrs change seasonally; call ahead).*

㉑ **San Diego Aerospace Museum and International Aerospace Hall of Fame.** Every available inch of space in the rotunda is filled with exhibits about aviation and aerospace pioneers, including examples of enemy planes during the world wars. A collection of real and replicated aircraft fills the central courtyard. ⊠ *2001 Pan American Plaza,* ☎ *619/234–8291.* ⊡ *$6, active military personnel free.* ⊘ *Daily 10–4:30.*

⑳ **San Diego Automotive Museum.** Even if you don't know a choke from a chassis, you're bound to admire the sleek designs you'll see here. The museum maintains a core collection of vintage motorcycles and cars, ranging from an 1886 Benz to a De Lorean, as well as a series of rotating exhibits from collections around the world. ⊠ *2080 Pan American Plaza,* ☎ *619/231–2886.* ⊡ *$6.* ⊘ *Daily 10–5.*

⑭ **San Diego Hall of Champions–Sports Museum.** Celebrate local jock heroes via a vast collection of memorabilia, uniforms, paintings, photographs, and computer and video displays. An amusing bloopers film is screened at the Sports Theater. ⊠ *Casa de Balboa, 1649 El Prado,* ☎ *619/234–2544.* ⊡ *$3.* ⊘ *Daily 10–4:30.*

⑭ **San Diego Model Railroad Museum.** When the six model-train exhibits are in operation, you'll hear the sounds of chugging engines, screeching brakes, and shrill whistles. ⊠ *Casa de Balboa, 1649 El Prado,* ☎ *619/696–0199.* ⊡ *$3.* ⊘ *Tues.–Fri. 11–4, weekends 11–5.*

★ ④ **San Diego Museum of Art.** Known primarily for its Spanish Baroque and Renaissance paintings, including works by El Greco, Goya, Rubens, and Van Ruisdale, San Diego's most comprehensive art museum also has strong holdings of Southeast Asian art, Indian miniatures, and contemporary California paintings. If traveling shows from other cities come to San Diego, you can expect to see them here. An outdoor Sculpture Garden exhibits both traditional and modern pieces in a striking natural setting. The IMAGE (Interactive Multimedia Art Gallery Explorer) system allows visitors to locate the highlights of the museum's collection on a computer screen and custom-design a tour. The **Sculpture Garden Café** has drinks and a small selection of gourmet lunches. ⊠ *Casa de Balboa, 1450 El Prado,* ☎ *619/232–7931.* ⊡ *$7 Tues.–Thurs., $8 Fri.–Sun.* ⊘ *Tues.–Sun. 10–4:30.*

② **San Diego Museum of Man.** Exhibits at this highly respected anthropological museum focus on southwestern, Mexican, and South American cultures. Carved monuments from the Maya city of Quirigua in Guatemala, cast from the originals in 1914, are particularly impressive. Rotating shows might include intricate examples of beadwork from across the Americas, and demonstrations of such skills as weaving and tortilla-making are regularly held. Among the museum's more recent additions is a hands-on Children's Discovery Center. ⊠ *California Bldg., 1350 El Prado,* ☎ *619/239–2001.* ⊡ *$4.* ⊘ *Daily 10–4:30.*

➐ San Diego Natural History Museum. The museum focuses on the plants and animals of southern California and Mexico; it frequently schedules free guided nature walks on the weekends, as well as films and lectures throughout the week. An $18 million expansion program began in 1997. ✉ *1788 El Prado,* ☎ *619/232–3821.* 🎟 *$6.* ☉ *Sun.– Wed. and Fri.–Sat. 9:30–5:30, Thurs. 9:30–6:30.*

★ **⑪ San Diego Zoo.** Balboa Park's—and perhaps the city's—most famous attraction is its 100-acre zoo. Nearly 4,000 animals of 800 diverse species roam in expertly crafted habitats that spread down into, around, and above the natural canyons. The zoo's charm and fame come from its tradition of creating hospitable environments that replicate natural habitats as closely as possible: The flora and the fauna in the zoo, including many rare species, are even more costly than the animals.

Exploring the zoo fully requires the stamina of a healthy hiker, but open-air trams that run throughout the day allow visitors to see 80% of the exhibits on their 3-mi tour. The Kangaroo bus tours include the same informed and amusing narrations as the others, and you can get on and off as you like at eight different stops. The Skyfari ride, which soars 170 ft above ground, gives a good overview of the zoo's layout and, on clear days, a panorama of the park, downtown San Diego, the bay, and the ocean, far past the Coronado Bridge.

Still, the zoo is at its best when you wander the paths that climb through the huge, enclosed **Scripps Aviary,** where brightly colored tropical birds swoop between branches just inches from your face. **Gorilla Tropics,** beside the aviary, is among the zoo's latest ventures into bioclimatic zone exhibits, where animals live in enclosed environments modeled on their native habitats.

The zoo's simulated Asian rain forest, **Tiger River,** brings together 10 exhibits with more than 35 species of animals. The mist-shrouded trails winding down a canyon into Tiger River pass by fragrant jasmine, ginger lilies, and orchids, giving the visitor the feeling of descending into a South American jungle. In **Sun Bear Forest,** playful cubs constantly claw apart the trees and shrubs. At **Hippo Canyon**—a 2-acre African rain forest at the base of Tiger River—you can watch the huge but surprisingly graceful beasts frolicking underwater. Four frisky polar bears plunge into a chilly pool at a popular exhibit where Siberian reindeer, white foxes, and other Arctic creatures are separated from the predatory bears by camouflaged moats.

But these and other zoo locals are being overshadowed by the hoopla surrounding two glamorous overseas visitors: Shi Shi and Bai Yun, a pair of giant pandas on loan for 12 years from the People's Republic of China. Seeing them is certainly a not-to-be-missed experience, but if you're traveling with children, it's best not to raise their expectations too high: The pandas are kept apart because they don't get along very well, and the one you see may be sleeping—both like to snooze during the day. The pandas are here for conservation research purposes, so there's also a chance that they won't be on exhibit when you visit.

Goats and sheep at the **Children's Zoo** beg to be petted and are particularly adept at snatching bag lunches; bunnies and guinea pigs seem willing to be fondled endlessly. In the nursery windows, you can see baby lemurs and spider monkeys playing with Cabbage Patch kids, looking much like the human babies peering from strollers through the glass. The exhibits are designed in size and style for four-year-olds, but that doesn't deter children of all ages from having fun.

The **Wedgeforth Bowl,** a 3,000-seat amphitheater, holds various animal shows throughout the day. Behind-the-scenes tours, walking tours, tours in Spanish, and tours for people with hearing or vision impairments are available; inquire at the entrance. ✉ *2920 Zoo Dr.,* ☎ *619/ 234–3153.* ✆ *$15 includes zoo, Children's Zoo, and animal shows; $21 includes above, plus 35-min guided bus tour and Skyfari ride; Kangaroo bus tour $8 additional; zoo free for children under 12 in Oct. and for all on Founder's Day (Oct. 3). AE, D, MC, V.* ☉ *Fall–spring, daily 9–4 (visitors may remain until 5); summer, daily 9–9 (visitors may remain until 10); Children's Zoo and Skyfari ride close earlier.*

❸ Simon Edison Centre for the Performing Arts. Even if you're not attending a play, the complex, comprising the Cassius Carter Centre Stage, the Lowell Davies Festival Theatre, and the Old Globe Theatre, is a pleasant place to relax between museum visits. The theaters, done in a California version of Tudor style, sit between the Sculpture Garden of the San Diego Museum of Art and the California Tower. A gift shop sells theater-related wares, including posters, cards, and brightly colored puppets. ✉ *1363 Old Globe Way,* ☎ *619/239–2255 or 619/234–5623.*

❽ Spanish Village Art Center. Glassblowers, enamel workers, woodcarvers, sculptors, painters, jewelers, photographers, and other artists rent space in the 35 little red tile–roof studio-galleries that were set up for the 1935–36 exposition in the style of an ancient Spanish village. The artists give demonstrations of their work on a rotating basis, aware, no doubt, that it's fun to buy wares that you've watched being created. ✉ *1770 Village Pl.,* ☎ *619/233–9050.* ✆ *Free.* ☉ *Daily 11–4.*

⓲ Spreckels Organ Pavilion. The 2,000-seat pavilion, dedicated in 1915 by sugar magnates John D. and Adolph B. Spreckels, holds the 4,445-pipe Spreckels Organ, believed to be the largest outdoor pipe organ in the world. You can hear this impressive instrument at one of the year-round, 2 PM Sunday-afternoon concerts. ✉ *2211 Pan American Rd. E,* ☎ *619/226–0819.*

❺ Timken Museum of Art. This modern structure is made of travertine marble imported from Italy. The small museum houses a selection of minor works by major European and American artists as well as a superb collection of Russian icons. ✉ *1500 El Prado,* ☎ *619/239–5548.* ✆ *Free.* ☉ *Oct.–Aug., Tues.–Sat. 10–4:30, Sun. 1:30–4:30.*

OFF THE BEATEN PATH	**UPTOWN DISTRICT AND HILLCREST** – Northwest of Balboa Park, Hillcrest is the center for the gay community and artists of all types. University, 4th, and 5th avenues are filled with cafés, boutiques, and excellent bookstores. Like most of San Diego, Hillcrest has been undergoing redevelopment. The largest project is the Uptown District, on University Avenue at 8th Avenue. This self-contained residential-commercial center was built to resemble an inner-city neighborhood, with shops and restaurants within easy walking distance of high-priced town houses.

DOWNTOWN

Downtown's natural attributes were easily evident to its original booster, Alonzo Horton, who arrived in San Diego in 1867. Horton looked at the bay and the acres of flatland surrounded by hills and canyons and knew he had found San Diego's heart. Though Old Town, under the Spanish fort at the Presidio, had been settled for years, Horton understood that it was too far away from the water to take hold as the commercial center of San Diego. He bought 960 acres along the bay at 27½¢ per acre and gave away the land to those who would develop it or build houses. Within months, he had sold or given away 226 city blocks; settlers camped on their land in tents as their houses and businesses rose.

As downtown grew into San Diego's transportation and commercial hub, residential neighborhoods blossomed along the beaches and inland valleys. The business district gradually moved farther away from the original heart of downtown, at 5th Avenue and Market Street, past Broadway, up toward Balboa Park. Downtown's waterfront fell into disrepute during World War I, when sailors, gamblers, and prostitutes were drawn to one another and the waterfront bars.

But Alonzo Horton's modern-day followers, city leaders intent on prospering while preserving San Diego's natural beauty, have reclaimed the downtown area. Replacing old shipyards and canneries are hotel towers and waterfront parks. The San Diego Convention Center, which hosted its first events in 1990, is thriving; spurred by its success in hosting the Republican National Convention in 1996, the administrators of the 760,000-square-ft facility have plans to double its size. A few blocks inland, the hugely successful Horton Plaza shopping center led the way for the hotels, restaurants, shopping centers, and housing developments that are now rising on every square inch of available space in downtown San Diego.

There are reasonably priced ($3 to $7 per day) parking lots along Harbor Drive, Pacific Highway, and lower Broadway and Market Street. The price of many downtown parking meters is $1 per hour, with a maximum stay of three hours; unless you know for sure that your stay in the area will be short, you're better off with a lot. If you're planning to tour the Embarcadero, the lot on the Cruise Ship pier, which costs only $1 an hour with a maximum of $3 a day, is a bargain.

Two Good Walks

Numbers in the text correspond to numbers in the margin and on the Central San Diego map.

Most people do a lot of parking-lot hopping when visiting downtown, but for the energetic, two distinct areas may be explored on foot.

Those who want to stay near the water might start a walk of the **Embarcadero** ① at the foot of Ash Street on Harbor Drive, where the *Berkeley*, headquarters of the **Maritime Museum** ②, is moored. A cement pathway runs south from the *Star of India* along the waterfront to the pastel B Street Pier. Another two blocks south on Harbor Drive brings you to the foot of Broadway and the Broadway Pier, where you can catch the ferry to Coronado. Continue south past Tuna Harbor to **Seaport Village** ③. The **San Diego Convention Center** is just east of Seaport Village; north across Harbor Drive from the convention center is the **Children's Museum.** Six blocks north of Seaport Village on Kettner Boulevard is the **Transit Center** ④; you'll see the mosaic-domed Santa Fe Depot and the tracks for the Tijuana Trolley out front. Right next door is the downtown annex of the **Museum of Contemporary Art, San Diego** ⑤.

A tour of the working heart of downtown might begin at the corner of 1st Avenue and Broadway, near Spreckels Theatre, a grand old stage that presents pop concerts and touring plays these days. A block east and across the street sits the historic **U.S. Grant Hotel** ⑥. If you cross Broadway, you'll be able to enter **Horton Plaza** ⑦, San Diego's favorite retail playland. Fourth Avenue, the eastern boundary of Horton Plaza, doubles as the western boundary of the 16-block **Gaslamp Quarter** ⑧. Head south to Island Avenue and the William Heath Davis House, where you can get a touring map of the district.

TIMING

The above walks take about an hour each, though there's enough to do in downtown San Diego to keep you busy for at least two days—or three if you really like to shop. In January and February, when the gray whales migrate from the Pacific Northwest to southern Baja, it's a must to book a whale-watching excursion at the Broadway Pier. For a guided tour of the Gaslamp Quarter, visit the area on Saturday.

Sights to See

Children's Museum of San Diego. The chatter and clatter of kids at play animates this space filled with interactive, experiential environments. There's a toddler area and an art zone where children can work on group projects or their own ones to take home. ⊠ *200 W. Island Ave.,* ☎ *619/233–5437.* ≊ *$5.* ☉ *Tues.–Sun. 10–5.*

❶ **Embarcadero.** The bustle along Harbor Drive's waterfront walkway comes less these days from the activities of tuna and other fishing folk, but it remains the nautical soul of San Diego. People here still make a living from the sea: Restaurants line the piers, as do sea vessels of every variety—cruise ships, ferries, tour boats, houseboats, and naval destroyers. Many boats along the Embarcadero have been converted into floating gift shops, and others are awaiting restoration.

On the north end of the Embarcadero, at Ash Street, you'll find the Maritime Museum (☞ *below*). Just south of it, the pastel **B Street Pier** is used by ships from major cruise lines as both a port of call and a departure point. The cavernous pier building has a cruise-information center and a small, cool bar and gift shop.

Day-trippers getting ready to set sail gather at the **Broadway Pier,** also known as the excursion pier. Tickets for the harbor tours and whale-watching trips are sold here.

The navy's Eleventh Naval District has control of the next few waterfront blocks to the south—destroyers, submarines, and carriers cruise in and out, some staying for weeks at a time. **Tuna Harbor** is the former hub of one of San Diego's earliest and most successful industries, commercial tuna fishing. These days, you'll see only a few boats that continue in this trade tied up at the docks.

The **San Diego Convention Center,** on Harbor Drive between 1st and 5th avenues, was designed by Arthur Erickson; the backdrop of blue sky and sea complements the building's nautical lines. The center often holds trade shows that are open to the public, and tours of the building are available.

❽ **Gaslamp Quarter.** The 16-block National Historic District centered on 5th and 4th avenues from Broadway to Market Street contains most of San Diego's Victorian-style commercial buildings from the late 1800s. In the latter part of the 19th century, businesses thrived in this area, but at the turn of the century, downtown's commercial district moved west toward Broadway, and many of San Diego's first buildings fell into disrepair. During the early 1900s, the quarter became known as the Stingaree district. Prostitutes picked up sailors in lively area taverns, and dance halls and crime flourished here.

In 1974, history buffs, developers, architects, and artists formed the Gaslamp Quarter Council. Bent on preserving the district, they gathered funds from the government and private benefactors and began cleaning up the quarter, restoring the finest old buildings, and attracting businesses and the public back to the heart of New Town. Their efforts have paid off. Former flophouses have become choice office buildings, and the area is dotted with shops and restaurants.

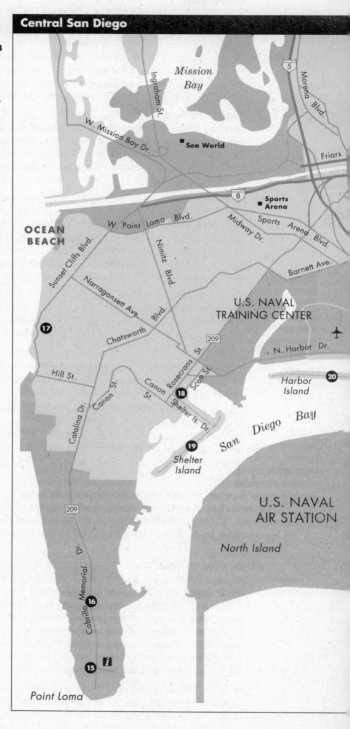

Central San Diego

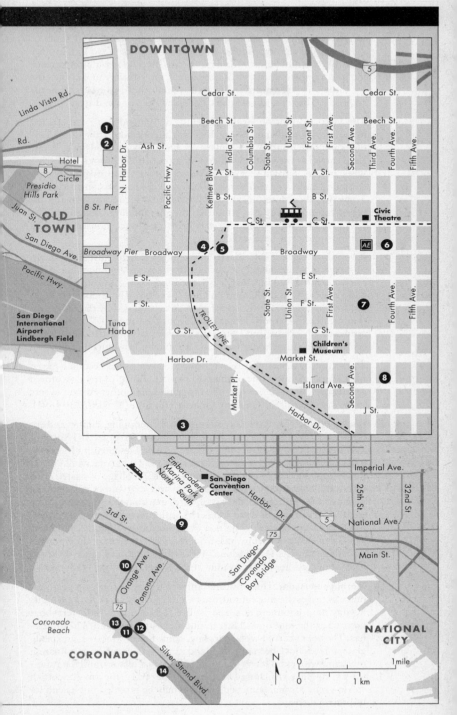

DOWNTOWN

Cedar St.
Beech St.
Ash St.
A St.
B St.
C St.
Broadway
E St.
F St.
G St.
Harbor Dr.
Island Ave.
J St.

Cedar St.
Beech St.

Civic Theatre

Linda Vista Rd.
Rd.
Hotel Circle
Presidio Hills Park
OLD TOWN
Juan St.
San Diego Ave.
Pacific Hwy.

San Diego International Airport Lindbergh Field

N. Harbor Dr.
Pacific Hwy.
B St. Pier
Broadway Pier
Tuna Harbor
Kettner Blvd.
India St.
Columbia St.
State St.
Union St.
Front St.
First Ave.
Second Ave.
Third Ave.
Fourth Ave.
Fifth Ave.

Market Pl.
TROLLEY LINE
Harbor Dr.

Children's Museum
Market St.

Second Ave.
Fourth Ave.
Fifth Ave.
First Ave.

Embarcadero Marina Park North South
San Diego Convention Center
Harbor Dr.

Imperial Ave.
25th St.
32nd St.
National Ave.
Main St.

3rd St.
Orange Ave.
Pomona Ave.
Silver Strand Blvd.
San Diego-Coronado Bay Bridge

Coronado Beach
CORONADO

NATIONAL CITY

N

0   1 mile
0   1 km

The **William Heath Davis House** (⊠ 410 Island Ave., at 4th Ave., ☎ 619/233–4692), one of the first residences in town, serves as the information center for the Gaslamp Quarter. Docents give $1 tours of the house during museum hours—weekdays from 10 to 2, Saturday from 10 to 4, and Sunday from noon to 4. Two-hour walking tours of the historic district leave from the house on Saturday at 11; the cost for these or a self-guided audio tour (phone ahead to reserve a headset) is $5. The museum also has a detailed map of the district.

The Victorian **Horton Grand Hotel** (⊠ 311 Island Ave.) was created in the mid-1980s by joining together two historic hotels, the Kahle Saddlery and the Grand Hotel, built in the boom days of the 1880s; Wyatt Earp stayed at the Kahle Saddlery—then called the Brooklyn Hotel—while he was in town speculating on real estate ventures and opening gambling halls. The two hotels were dismantled and reconstructed on a new site, about four blocks from their original locations. A small Chinese Museum serves as a tribute to the surrounding Chinatown district, a collection of modest structures that once housed Chinese laborers and their families.

If you don't have much time to spend in the quarter, just stroll down 5th Avenue, where highlights include the Backesto Building (No. 614), the Mercantile Building (No. 822), the Louis Bank of Commerce (No. 835), and the Watts-Robinson Building (No. 903). The Tudor-style Keating Building (⊠ 432 F St., at 5th Ave.) was designed by the same firm that created the famous Hotel Del Coronado. Johnny M's 801, at the corner of 4th Avenue and F Street, is a restored turn-of-the-century tavern with a 12-ft mahogany bar and a stained-glass domed ceiling.

The section of G Street between 6th and 9th avenues has become a haven for galleries; stop in one of them to pick up a map of the downtown arts district. For information about openings and other current events in the district, call the **Gaslamp Quarter Hot Line** (☎ 619/233–4691).

★ ❼ **Horton Plaza.** Downtown's centerpiece is the shopping, dining, and entertainment mall that fronts Broadway and G Street from 1st to 4th avenues and covers more than six city blocks. Designed by Jon Jerde and completed in 1985, Horton Plaza is far from what one would imagine a shopping center—or city center—to be. A collage of pastels with elaborate, colorful tile work on benches and stairways, cloth banners waving in the air, and modern sculptures marking the entrances, Horton Plaza rises in staggered levels to six floors; great views of downtown from the harbor to Balboa Park and beyond can be had here. The complex's architecture has strongly affected the rest of downtown's development. The **International Visitor Information Center,** at street level on the corner of 1st Avenue and F Street, is a good resource.

❷ **Maritime Museum.** Three restored ships that may be toured for one admission price, the museum affords a glimpse of San Diego during its heyday as a commercial seaport. The *Berkeley,* an 1898 ferryboat moored at the foot of Ash Street, doubles as the museum's headquarters. The boat's carved-wood paneling, stained-glass windows, and plate-glass mirrors have been restored, and its main deck serves as a floating museum, with exhibits on oceanography, naval history, and the America's Cup Race. Anchored next to the *Berkeley,* the small Scottish steam yacht *Medea,* launched in 1904, may be boarded but has no interpretive displays.

The most interesting of the three ships is the *Star of India,* a windjammer built in 1863. The ship's high wooden masts and white sails flapping in the wind have been a harbor landmark since 1927. The *Star of India* made 21 trips around the world in the late 1800s, when it traveled the

East Indian trade route, shuttled immigrants from England to New Zealand, and served the Alaskan salmon trade. ⊠ *1306 N. Harbor Dr.,* ☎ *619/234–9153.* ⊠ *$5.* ⊙ *Ships daily 9–8.*

❺ Museum of Contemporary Art, San Diego. The downtown annex of the city's modern art museum, which opened in 1993 while the main facility in La Jolla was undergoing renovation, has taken on its own personality. The two-story building has four small galleries that host rotating shows. It's fronted by a sculpture plaza. ⊠ *1001 Kettner Blvd.,* ☎ *619/234–1172 or 619/454–3541 for exhibition information.* ⊠ *$4; free 1st Tues. of month.* ⊙ *Tues.–Thurs. and Sat. 10–5, Fri. 10–8, Sun. noon–5.*

★ ❸ Seaport Village. Three shopping plazas reflect the architectural styles of early California, especially New England clapboard and Spanish Mission. A ¼-mi wooden boardwalk that runs along the bay and 4 mi of simulated dirt-road and cobblestone paths lead to specialty shops, snack bars, and restaurants—about 75 in all. Charles I. D. Looff crafted the hand-carved, hand-painted steeds on the **Broadway Flying Horses Carousel** for the Coney Island amusement park in 1890. The ride was moved from its next home, Salisbury Beach in Massachusetts, and faithfully restored for Seaport Village's West Plaza; tickets are $1. The Time Out entertainment center near the carousel has video games. ☎ *619/235–4014 or 619/235–4013 for events hot line.*

❹ Transit Center. The Mission Revival–style **Santa Fe Depot,** which replaced the original 1887 station on this site, serves north- and southbound Amtrak passengers. A booth at the tile-domed depot has bus schedules, maps, and tourist brochures. Formerly an easily spotted area landmark, it's now overshadowed by nearby **1 America Plaza.** At the base of this 34-story office tower, designed by architect Helmut Jahn, is a center that links the train, trolley, and city bus systems. The building's signature crescent-shape glass-and-steel canopy arches out over the trolley tracks. ⊠ *Broadway and Kettner Blvd.*

❻ U.S. Grant Hotel. Far more formal than most other hotels in San Diego, the doyenne of downtown lodgings has a marble lobby, gleaming chandeliers, white-gloved doormen, and other touches that hark back to the more gracious era when it was built (1910). Over the years, it became noted for its famous guests—U.S. presidents from Woodrow Wilson to George Bush have stayed here—but it got a different kind of press in 1969, when the old-boy's-clubby Grant's Grill became the site of a sit-in by eight local women who objected to its policy of allowing only males to enter before 3 PM. ⊠ *326 Broadway.*

CORONADO

The streets of Coronado are wide, quiet, and friendly, with lots of neighborhood parks where young families mingle with the area's many senior citizens. Grand old homes face the waterfront and the Coronado Municipal Golf Course, under the bridge at the north end of Glorietta Bay. The course is the site of the annual Fourth of July fireworks. Community celebrations and concerts take place in Spreckels Park on Orange Avenue.

Coronado is visible from downtown and Point Loma and accessible via the arching blue 2.2-mi-long San Diego–Coronado Bridge, a landmark just beyond downtown's skyline. There is a $1 toll for crossing the bridge into Coronado, but cars carrying two or more passengers may enter through the free car-pool lane.

You can board the ferry, operated by San Diego Harbor Excursion (☎ 619/234–4111; 800/442–7847 in CA), at downtown San Diego's Embarcadero from the Broadway Pier at Broadway and Harbor Drive, or from a new stop at the Convention Center; you'll arrive at the Ferry Landing Marketplace. San Diego Harbor Excursion (☎ 619/235–8294 for reservations and schedules) also offers water-taxi service from Seaport Village to Ferry Landing Marketplace, Le Meridien Resort, and the Hotel Del Coronado. The fare is $5.

Numbers in the text correspond to numbers in the margin and on the Central San Diego map.

A Good Tour

Coronado is easy to navigate without a car. When you depart the ferry, you can explore the shops at the **Ferry Landing Marketplace** ⑨ and, from there, catch the shuttle (50¢ fare) that runs down **Orange Avenue** ⑩, Coronado's main tourist drag. The **Hotel Del Coronado** ⑪ is at the end of Orange Avenue. Right across the street from the Del is the **Glorietta Bay Inn** ⑫, another of the island's outstanding early structures. A bit northwest of the Hotel Del is the **Coronado Beach Historical Museum** ⑬. If you've brought your swimsuit, you might continue on to **Silver Strand Beach State Park** ⑭.

TIMING

A leisurely stroll through Coronado takes an hour or so, more if you shop or walk along the beach. If you're a history buff, you might want to visit on Thursday or Saturday, when you can combine the tour of Coronado's historic homes that departs from the Glorietta Bay Inn at 11 AM with a visit to the Coronado Beach Historical Museum, open Wednesday through Sunday afternoons. Whenever you come, if you're not staying on the island, remember to get back to the dock in time to catch the final ferry out. The last shuttle to the Ferry Landing Marketplace leaves from the Loews Coronado Bay Resort at 5:57.

Sights to See

⑬ **Coronado Beach Historical Museum.** A restored Cape Cod–style cottage contains a museum that celebrates the island's history with photographs and displays of its formative events and major sites: the Hotel Del Coronado, including an original chamber pot from one of the rooms; Tent City, a summer resort just south of the Del developed by John Spreckels at the turn of the century; the early ferry boats; and the North Island Naval Air Station. ✉ *1126 Loma Ave.,* ☎ *619/435–7242.* ☞ *Free; donations accepted.* ☺ *Wed.–Sat. 10–4, Sun. noon–4.*

⑨ **Ferry Landing Marketplace.** The aptly named point of disembarkation for the ferry, this collection of shops is actually a new development on an old site. Its buildings resemble the gingerbread domes of the Hotel Del Coronado, long the area's main attraction. ✉ *1201 1st St. at B Ave.,* ☎ *619/435–8895.*

⑫ **Glorietta Bay Inn.** The former residence of John Spreckels, the original owner of North Island and the property on which the Hotel Del Coronado stands, is now a popular hotel. On Tuesday, Thursday, and Saturday morning at 11, it's the departure point for a 1½-hour walking tour of historical homes that includes—from the outside only—some spectacular mansions and the Meade House, where L. Frank Baum wrote *The Wizard of Oz.* ✉ *1630 Glorietta Blvd.,* ☎ *619/435–5892 or 619/435–5444 for tour information.* ☞ *$6 for historical tour.*

★ ⑪ **Hotel Del Coronado.** The island's most prominent landmark, selected as a National Historic Site, the Del, as natives call it, has a colorful history, integrally connected with that of Coronado itself. The hotel was completed in 1888. Thomas Edison himself threw the switch as the Del became the world's first electrically lighted hotel. A red carpet leads up the front stairs to the main lobby, with its grand oak pillars and ceiling, and out to the central courtyard and gazebo. To the right is the cavernous **Crown Room,** whose arched ceiling of notched sugar pine was constructed without nails. The **Grand Ballroom** overlooks the ocean and the hotel's long white beach. The patio surrounding the sky-blue swimming pool is a great place for just sitting back and imagining what the bathers looked like during the '20s, when the hotel rocked with the good times. ⊠ *1500 Orange Ave.,* ☎ *619/435–6611.* ☞ *$10 for guided tour, $5 for headsets for self-guided tour.* ☺ *1-hr guided tours (from lobby) Thurs.–Sat. at 10 and 11.*

⑩ **Orange Avenue.** It's easy to imagine you're on a street in Cape Cod when you stroll along this thoroughfare, Coronado's version of a downtown: The clapboard houses, small restaurants, and boutiques—many of them selling nautical paraphernalia—are in some ways more characteristic of New England than they are of California. But the East Coast illusion tends to dissipate as quickly as a winter fog when you catch sight of one the many citrus trees—or realize it's February and the sun is warming your face. Just off Orange Avenue is the **Coronado Visitors Bureau** (⊠ 1047 B Ave., ☎ 619/437–8788 or 800/622–8300).

⑭ **Silver Strand Beach State Park.** The stretch of sand that runs along Silver Strand Boulevard from the Hotel Del Coronado to Imperial Beach dispels the illusion that Coronado is an island. The clean beach is a perfect family gathering spot, with rest rooms and lifeguards.

En Route San Diego's Mexican-American community is centered in Barrio Logan, under the Coronado Bridge on the downtown side. **Chicano Park,** spread along National Avenue from Dewey to Crosby streets, is the barrio's recreational hub. It's worth taking a short detour to see the huge murals of Mexican history painted on the bridge supports at National Avenue and Dewey Street; they're among the best examples of folk art in the city.

HARBOR ISLAND, POINT LOMA, AND SHELTER ISLAND

Point Loma curves around the San Diego Bay west of downtown and the airport, protecting the center city from the Pacific's tides and waves. Its bayside shores front huge estates, with sailboats and yachts packed tightly in private marinas. Harbor Island and Shelter Island were constructed out of detritus from San Diego Bay.

Numbers in the text correspond to numbers in the margin and on the Central San Diego map.

A Good Tour

Take Catalina Boulevard all the way south to the tip of Point Loma to reach **Cabrillo National Monument** ⑮. Just north of the monument as you head back into the neighborhoods of Point Loma, you'll see the white headstones of **Fort Rosecrans National Cemetery** ⑯. Continue north on Catalina Boulevard to Hill Street and turn left to reach the dramatic **Sunset Cliffs** ⑰, at the western side of Point Loma near Ocean Beach. Return to Catalina Boulevard and backtrack south for a few blocks to find Canon Street, which leads toward the peninsula's eastern (bay) side. Almost at the shore, you'll see **Scott Street** ⑱, the main commercial drag of Point Loma. Scott Street is bisected by Shelter Island Drive, which leads to two areas formed of landfill, **Shelter Island** ⑲ and (via Rosecrans Street and North Harbor Drive) **Harbor Island** ⑳.

TIMING

If you're interested in seeing the tidal pools at Cabrillo National Monument, you'll need to call ahead to find out when low tide will occur. Scott Street is a good place to find yourself at lunchtime, and Sunset Cliffs Park is where you might want to be when the daylight starts to wane. This drive takes about an hour if you stop briefly at each sight.

Sights to See

★ **⑮** **Cabrillo National Monument.** This 144-acre preserve marks the site of the first European visit to San Diego, made by Portuguese explorer Juan Rodríguez Cabrillo—his real name was João Rodrigues Cabrilho, but it was later Hispanicized. Cabrillo, who had earlier gone on voyages with Hernán Cortés, came to this spot, which he called San Miguel, in 1542. Government grounds were set aside in 1913 to commemorate his discovery, and today the monument, with its rugged cliffs and shores and outstanding overlooks, is one of the most frequently visited of all National Park Service sites. The **visitor center** presents films and lectures about Cabrillo's voyage, the sea-level tidal pools, and the gray whales migrating offshore. Exploring the grounds consumes time and calories; bring a picnic and rest on a bench overlooking the sailboats headed to sea.

Interpretive stations with recorded information in six languages—including, appropriately enough, Portuguese—have been installed along the walkways that edge the cliffs. Signs explain the views and posters depict the various navy, fishing, and pleasure craft that sail into and fly over the bay.

A **statue of Cabrillo** overlooks downtown from the next windy promontory, where visitors gather to admire the panorama over the bay, from the snowcapped San Bernardino Mountains, 130 mi north, to the hills surrounding Tijuana to the south.

The moderately steep 2-mi **Bayside Trail** winds through coastal sage scrub, curving under the clifftop lookouts and bringing you ever closer to the bayfront scenery. The oil lamp of the **Old Point Loma Lighthouse** was first lit in 1855. The lighthouse is open to visitors.

The western and southern cliffs of Cabrillo National Monument are prime whale-watching territory. More accessible sea creatures can be seen in the **tidal pools** at the foot of the monument's western cliffs. Drive north from the visitor center to the first road on the left, which winds down to the coast guard station and the shore. When the tide is low, you can walk on the rocks around saltwater pools filled with starfish, crabs, anemones, octopuses, and hundreds of other sea creatures and plants. ⊠ *1800 Cabrillo Memorial Dr., ☎ 619/557–5450. ☞ $4 per car, $2 per person entering on foot or by bicycle; free for Golden Age, Golden Access, and Golden Eagle passport holders, and children under 17. ☉ Park daily 9–5:15, Old Lighthouse 9–5, Bayside Trail 9–4, tidalpool areas 9–4:30.*

⑯ **Fort Rosecrans National Cemetery.** Many of the 65,000 people laid to rest here were killed in battles that predate California's statehood. Perhaps the most impressive structure in the cemetery is the 75-ft granite obelisk called the Bennington Monument, which commemorates the 66 crew members who died from a boiler explosion and fire on board the U.S.S. *Bennington* in 1905. ☎ *619/553–2084. ☉ Weekdays 8–5, weekends 9–5, Memorial Day 8–7.*

⑳ **Harbor Island.** In 1961, a 1½-mi-long peninsula was created adjacent to San Diego International Airport out of 12 million cubic yards of sand and mud dredged from San Diego Bay. Restaurants and high-rise hotels now line the inner shores of Harbor Island. Across from the western end of Harbor Island, at the mainland's **Spanish Landing Park,** a bronze plaque marks the arrival in 1769 of a party from Spain that headed north from San Diego to conquer California.

⑱ Scott Street. Running along Point Loma's waterfront from Shelter Island to the Marine Corps Recruiting Center on Harbor Drive, this thoroughfare is lined with deep-sea fishing charters and whale-watching boats. It's a good spot from which to watch fishermen (and women) haul marlin, tuna, and puny mackerel off their boats. The fish market at **Point Loma Sea Foods** (✉ 2805 Emerson St., ☎ 619/223–1109), off Scott Street behind the Vagabond Inn, sells some of the catch straight from the boat. At the take-out counter you can buy seafood cocktails and salads, seviche, and crab and shrimp sandwiches made with freshly baked sourdough bread.

⑲ Shelter Island. Actually a peninsula, the island is the center of San Diego's yacht-building industry. A long sidewalk runs from the landscaped lawns of the **San Diego Yacht Club** (tucked down Anchorage Street off Shelter Island Drive), past boat brokerages to the hotels and marinas, which line the inner shore, facing Point Loma. Along the grass are picnic tables, fire rings, and permanent barbecue grills. The huge Friendship Bell was given to San Diegans by the people of Yokohama in 1960.

⑰ Sunset Cliffs. As their name suggests, the 60-ft-high bluffs on the western side of Point Loma just south of Ocean Beach are a perfect place to watch the sun descend over the sea. To view the tidal pools along the shore, you can descend a staircase on Sunset Cliffs Boulevard at the foot of Laredo Street.

LA JOLLA

La Jollans have long considered their village to be the Monte Carlo of California, and with good cause. Its coastline curves into natural coves backed by verdant hillsides and covered with homes worth millions. The Native Americans called the site La Hoya, meaning "the cave," referring to the grottos dotting the shoreline. The Spaniards changed the name to La Jolla, "the jewel," and its residents have cherished the name and its allusions ever since.

To reach La Jolla from I–5 if you're traveling north, take the Ardath Road exit and drive slowly down Prospect Street so you can appreciate the view. If you're heading south, get off at the La Jolla Village Drive exit, which will lead into Torrey Pines Road. Prospect Street and Girard Avenue, the village's main drags, are lined with expensive shops and office buildings.

Numbers in the text correspond to numbers in the margin and on the La Jolla map.

A Good Tour

At the intersection of La Jolla Boulevard and Nautilus Street, turn toward the sea to reach **Windansea Beach** ①, one of the best surfing spots in town. **Mount Soledad** ②, about 1½ mi east on Nautilus Street, is La Jolla's highest spot. The town's cultural center, the **Museum of Contemporary Art, San Diego** ③, is on the less trafficked southern end of Prospect. A bit farther north, at the intersection of Prospect and Girard Avenue, sits the pretty-in-pink **La Valencia Hotel** ④. The hotel looks out onto the village's great natural attraction, **La Jolla Cove** ⑤. Just past the far northern point of the cove, in front of the La Jolla Cave and Shell Shop, a trail leads down to **La Jolla Caves** ⑥. The beaches along La Jolla Shores Drive north of the caves are some of the finest in San Diego. Inland a bit is **Stephen Birch Aquarium-Museum** ⑦.

La Jolla

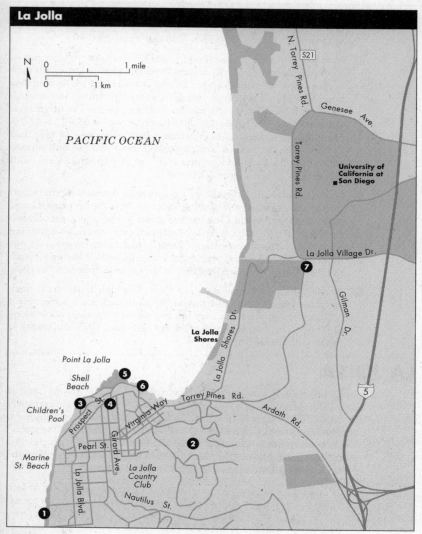

N

0 —————— 1 mile
0 —————— 1 km

PACIFIC OCEAN

N. Torrey Pines Rd.

S21

Genesee Ave.

Torrey Pines Rd.

University of
California at
San Diego

La Jolla Village Dr.

7

Gilman Dr.

La Jolla Shores Dr.

**La Jolla
Shores**

5

Point La Jolla

*Shell
Beach*

5

6

3

4

Torrey Pines Rd.

Ardath Rd.

*Children's
Pool*

Prospect St.

Virginia Way

2

Girard Ave.

Pearl St.

*Marine
St. Beach*

La Jolla
Country
Club

La Jolla Blvd.

Nautilus St.

1

La Jolla Caves, **6**
La Jolla Cove, **5**
La Valencia Hotel, **4**
Mount Soledad, **2**
Museum of
Contemporary Art,
San Diego, **3**
Stephen Birch
Aquarium-
Museum, **7**
Windansea Beach, **1**

TIMING

This tour makes for a leisurely day, though it can be driven in a couple of hours, including stops to take in the views and explore the village of La Jolla. The Museum of Contemporary Art is closed Monday.

Sights to See

6 La Jolla Caves. It's a walk of 145 sometimes slippery steps down to Sunny Jim Cave, the largest of the grottoes in La Jolla Cove; they may be entered behind the La Jolla Cave and Shell Shop. Claustrophobic types can stay behind and look at the photos of the caves in the shop, and browse a good selection of shells and coral jewelry. ⊠ *1325 Coast Blvd.,* ☎ *619/454–6080.* ⊠ *$1.50.* ☼ *Mon.–Sat. 10–5, Sun. 11–5, sometimes later in summer.*

★ **5 La Jolla Cove.** The wooded spread that looks out over a shimmering blue inlet is what first attracted everyone from the Native Americans to the glitterati to La Jolla; it remains the reason for the village's continuing cachet. You'll find it beyond where Girard Avenue deadends into Coast Boulevard, marked by towering palms that line the sidewalk. The **Children's Pool,** at the south end of the park, is aptly named for its curving beach and shallow waters, protected by a sea wall from strong currents and waves. Walk through **Ellen Browning Scripps Park,** past the groves of twisted junipers to the cliff's edge.

4 La Valencia Hotel. The art deco–style La Valencia, which has operated as a luxury hotel since 1928, has long been a gathering spot for Hollywood celebrities. The hotel's grand lobby, with floor-to-ceiling windows overlooking La Jolla Cove, is a popular wedding spot, and the Whaling Bar is still a favorite meeting place for La Jolla's power brokers. ⊠ *1132 Prospect St.,* ☎ *619/454–0771.*

2 Mount Soledad. The top of this mountain, on which there's a large white cross, is an excellent vantage point from which to get a sense of San Diego's geography: Looking down from here, you can see the coast from the county's northern border to the south far beyond downtown— barring smog and haze.

★ **3 Museum of Contemporary Art, San Diego.** The oldest section of San Diego's modern art museum was a residence designed by Irving Gill for philanthropist Ellen Browning Scripps in 1916. Robert Venturi and his colleagues at Venturi, Scott Brown and Associates updated and expanded the compound in the mid-1990s. The architects respected Gill's original geometric structure and clean, Mission-style lines while adding their own distinctive touches. The result is a striking contemporary building that looks as though it's always been here.

The artwork inside the museum gets major competition from the setting: You can look out from the top of a grand stairway onto a garden that contains rare 100-year-old California plant specimens and, beyond that, to the Pacific Ocean. The permanent collection of post-1950s art naturally has a strong representation of California artists but also includes examples of every major art movement of the past half century, plus important pieces by San Diego and Tijuana artists. ⊠ *700 Prospect St.,* ☎ *619/454–3541.* ☼ *Tues. and Thurs.–Sat. 10–5, Wed. 10–8, Sun. noon–5.* ⊠ *$4; free 1st Tues. of month.*

7 Stephen Birch Aquarium-Museum. The largest oceanographic exhibit in the United States, a program of the Scripps Institution of Oceanography, sits at the end of a signed drive leading off North Torrey Pines Road just south of La Jolla Village Drive. More than 30 huge tanks are filled with colorful saltwater fish, and a 70,000-gallon tank simulates a La Jolla kelp forest. Next to the fish themselves, the most interesting attraction is the 12-minute simulated submarine ride. ⊠ *2300 Expedition Way,* ☎ *619/534–3474.* 🖃 *$6.50, active military free, parking $3.* ⊙ *Daily 9–5.*

❶ **Windansea Beach.** Fans of pop satirist Tom Wolfe may recall *The Pump House Gang,* which pokes fun at the So-Cal surfing culture. Wolfe drew many of his barbs from observations he made at Windansea, the surfing beach just west of La Jolla Boulevard near Nautilus Street. The wave action here is said to be as good as that in Hawaii.

MISSION BAY

The 4,600-acre Mission Bay aquatic park is San Diego's monument to sports and fitness. Playgrounds and picnic areas abound on the beach and low grassy hills of the park. On weekday evenings, joggers, bikers, and skaters line the path. In the daytime, swimmers, water-skiers, fishers, and boaters—some in single-person kayaks, others in crowded powerboats—vie for space in the water. Swimmers should note signs warning about water pollution; certain areas of the bay are chronically polluted, and bathing is strongly discouraged.

Numbers in the text correspond to numbers in the margin and on the Mission Bay map.

A Good Tour

If you're coming from I–5, the **Visitor Information Center** ① is just about at the end of the Clairemont Drive–East Mission Bay Drive exit (you'll see the prominent sign). Where East Mission Bay Drive turns into Sea World Drive you can detour left to **Fiesta Island** ② or around the curve to the west for the turnoff sign for **Sea World** ③. You'll next come to Ingraham Street, the central north–south drag through the bay. If you take it north, you'll soon see Vacation Road, which leads into the focal point of this part of the bay, the waterskiing mecca of **Vacation Isle** ④. At Ingraham, Sea World Drive turns into Sunset Cliffs Boulevard and intersects with West Mission Bay Drive. Almost immediately south of where West Mission Bay Drive turns into Mission Boulevard is the resurrected **Belmont Park** ⑤.

TIMING

It would take less than an hour to drive this tour. You may not find a visit to Sea World fulfilling unless you spend at least a half day. The park is open daily, but not all its attractions operate year-round.

Sights to See

❺ **Belmont Park.** The once-abandoned amusement park between the bay and Mission Beach boardwalk is now a shopping, dining, and recreation area. Twinkling lights outline the refurbished **roller coaster**, created as the Giant Dipper in 1925. There is also an antique carousel. **The Plunge,** an indoor swimming pool, opened in 1925 as the largest— 60 by 125 ft—saltwater pool in the world. It's had fresh water since 1951. ⊠ *3146 Mission Blvd.,* ☎ *619/491–2988 or 619/642–0220 for park, 619/488–1549 for roller coaster, 619/488–3110 for pool.*

❷ **Fiesta Island.** The most undeveloped area of Mission Bay Park is popular with dog owners—it's the only place in the park where their pets can run free—as well as with jet skiers and speedboat racers. At Christmas, it provides an excellent vantage point for viewing for the bay's Parade of Lights.

❸ **Sea World.** One of the world's largest marine-life amusement parks is spread over 100 tropically landscaped bayfront acres. The traditional favorite exhibit at Sea World is the **Shamu show**, with giant killer

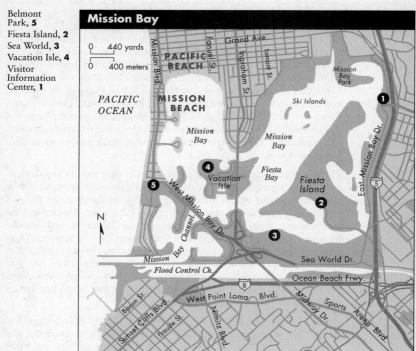

Mission Bay

whales entertaining the crowds, but performing dolphins, sea lions, and
otters at other shows also delight audiences. **Baywatch at Seaworld** features waterski stunts and beachfront antics similar to those seen on the
syndicated TV show. Other exhibits include the **Penguin Encounter,**
the **Shark Encounter,** the hands-on **California Tide Pool,** and **Mission:
Bermuda Triangle,** which replicates the thrills of a submersible dive to
the ocean bottom. Many hotels offer Sea World specials, worth seeking out as the children's fee ($22.95) is quite hefty. ⊠ *1720 South Shores
Rd., near west end of I–8,* ☎ *619/226–3815 or 619/226–3901 for
recorded information.* ⌨ *$30.95; parking $5 cars, $2 motorcycles, $7
RVs and campers; 90-min behind-the-scenes walking tour $6 additional.
D, MC, V.* ☾ *Daily 10–dusk; extended hrs during summer; call ahead
for park hrs on day of your visit.*

4 **Vacation Isle.** Ingraham Street bisects this Mission Bay island, which
provides two distinct experiences to visitors. The west side is taken up
by the Princess Resort, but you don't have to be a guest to enjoy the
hotel's lushly landscaped grounds and bayfront restaurants. The waterski clubs congregate at **Ski Beach** on the east side of the island, where
there's a parking lot as well as picnic and rest room facilities.

1 **Visitor Information Center.** In addition to being an excellent resource
for San Diego tourists, the center is also a gathering spot for runners,
walkers, and exercisers. It's the place to pick up a list of rules for playing in the water at Mission Bay Park or a self-guided tour map of the
park's environmental resources. ⊠ *2688 E. Mission Bay Dr.,* ☎ *619/
276–8200.* ☾ *Mon.–Sat. 9–5 (until 6 in summer), Sun. 9:30–4:30 (until
5:30 in summer).*

OLD TOWN

Although Old Town is often credited as being the first European settlement in southern California, the true beginnings took place overlooking Old Town atop Presidio Park, where Father Junípero Serra established the first of California's missions, San Diego de Alcalá, in 1769. In 1774, the hilltop was declared a Royal Presidio, or fortress, and the mission was moved to its current location along the San Diego River, 6 mi west of the original. Native Americans, responding to the loss of their land as the mission expanded along the riverbed, attacked and burned it in 1775. A later assault on the presidio was less successful, and their revolt was short-lived.

The pioneers living within the presidio's walls were mostly Spanish soldiers, poor Mexicans, and mestizos of Spanish and Native American ancestry, many of whom were unaccustomed to farming San Diego's arid land. They existed marginally until 1821, when Mexico gained independence from Spain, claimed its lands in California, and flew the Mexican flag over the presidio. In 1846, during the war between Mexico and the United States, a detachment of marines raised the U.S. flag over the plaza on a pole said to have been a mainmast. The flag was torn down once or twice, but by early 1848, Mexico had surrendered California, and the U.S. flag remained. In 1850, San Diego became an incorporated city, with Old Town as its center.

On San Diego Avenue, the district's main drag, art galleries and expensive gift shops are interspersed with curio shops, restaurants, and open-air stands selling inexpensive Mexican pottery, jewelry, and blankets. The Old Town Esplanade between Harney and Conde streets is best of several mall-like affairs constructed in mock Mexican-plaza style. Shops and restaurants also line Juan and Congress streets.

Numbers in the text correspond to numbers in the margin and on the Old Town San Diego map.

A Good Tour

Visit the information center at Wallace Street and San Diego Avenue in Old Town Plaza to orient yourself to the various sights in **Old Town San Diego State Historic Park** ①. Cross north on the west side of the plaza to **Bazaar del Mundo** ②, where you can shop or enjoy some nachos on the terrace of a Mexican restaurant. From the Bazaar, walk back to San Diego Avenue and head east to the **Thomas Whaley Museum** ③ and **El Campo Santo** ④ cemetery. **Heritage Park** ⑤ is perched on a hill above Juan Street, north of the museum and cemetery. Drive west (you can walk but this longish route is steep in places) on Juan Street and north on Taylor Street to Presidio Drive, which will lead you up the hill on which **Presidio Park** ⑥ and the **Junípero Serra Museum** ⑦ sit.

TIMING

Try to time your visit to coincide with the free daily tours of Old Town given at 2 PM by costumed volunteers at the Robinson-Rose House. If possible, avoid coming here on weekends—the parking lots are even fuller than usual when San Diegans are off work (this won't be a problem if you opt to take the San Diego Trolley). It takes about two hours to walk through Old Town. If you drive to Presidio Park, allot another hour to explore the grounds and museum.

Sights to See

② **Bazaar del Mundo.** North of San Diego's Old Town Plaza lies the area's unofficial center, built to represent a colonial Mexican square. The central courtyard is always in blossom, ballet Folklorico and flamenco dancers perform on weekend afternoons, and the bazaar frequently hosts

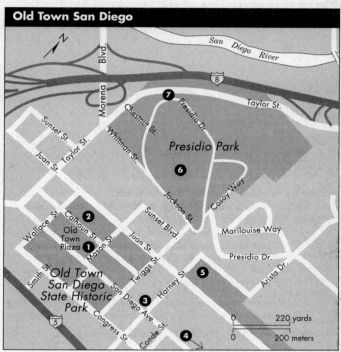

Old Town San Diego

arts-and-crafts exhibits and Mexican festivals. Colorful shops border the square. **La Panadería bakery** on the bazaar's southeast corner sells hot *churros*—long sticks of fried dough coated with cinnamon and powdered sugar. Get some and then sit out on one of the benches and enjoy the live music at the bandstand (weekends only). ⊠ *2754 Calhoun St.,* ☎ *619/296–3161.* ⊙ *Shops daily 10–9.*

④ El Campo Santo. The old adobe-walled cemetery established in 1849 was the burial place for many members of Old Town's founding families, as well as for a number of the gamblers and bandits who passed through town until 1880. Most of the markers give only approximations of where the people named on them are buried; a number of the early settlers laid to rest at El Campo Santo really reside under San Diego Avenue. ⊠ *North side of San Diego Ave. S, between Arista and Ampudia Sts.*

⑤ Heritage Park. Among the interesting former residences here is the Sherman Gilbert House, which has a widow's walk and intricate carving on its decorative trim. Bronze plaques detail the history of all six of Heritage Park's houses, some of which may seem surprisingly colorful; they are in fact accurate representations of the bright tones of the era. The climb up to the park is a little steep, but the view of the harbor is great. ⊠ *2455 Heritage Park Row (park office),* ☎ *619/694–3306.*

⑦ Junípero Serra Museum. The original Spanish presidio and California's first mission were perched atop the 160-ft hill overlooking Mission Valley; it's now the domain of a museum devoted to the history of the Spanish and Mexican periods. ⊠ *2727 Presidio Dr.,* ☎ *619/297–3258.* ⊠ *$3.* ⊙ *Tues.–Sat. 10–4:30, Sun. noon–4:30.*

★ ① Old Town San Diego State Historic Park. The six square blocks on the site of San Diego's original pueblo are the heart of Old Town. Most

of the 20 historic buildings preserved or re-created by the park clus-
ter around **Old Town Plaza,** bounded by Wallace Street on the west,
Calhoun Street on the north, Mason Street on the east, and San Diego
Avenue on the south.

The tour map available at the Robinson-Rose House gives details on all
of the historic houses on the plaza and in its vicinity; a few of the more
interesting ones are noted below. All the houses are open to visitors daily
from 10 to 5 (winter hours, which start in November, are shorter); currently none charge admission, though donations are appreciated.

The **Robinson-Rose House** (✉ 4002 Wallace St., ☎ 619/220–5422),
on the west end of Old Town Plaza, serves as the park office. This was
the original commercial center of old San Diego, housing railroad offices, law offices, and the first newspaper press. One room has been
restored and outfitted with period furnishings; park rangers distribute
information from the living room. An excellent free walking tour
leaves from here daily at 2 PM, weather permitting. From 10 to 1 every
Wednesday and the first Saturday of the month, park staff and volunteers in period costume give cooking and crafts demonstrations at
the Machado y Stewart adobe; adjacent to the Bandini House near Juan
Street, you can watch a blacksmith hammering away at his anvil, starting at 10 every Wednesday and Saturday.

On San Diego Avenue, beside the state park headquarters, **Dodson's
Corner** is a modern retailer in a mid-19th-century setting; two of the
shops in the complex, which sell everything from quilts and western
clothing to pottery and jewelry, are reconstructions of homes that
stood on the spot in 1848.

On Mason Street, at the corner of Calhoun Street, **La Casa de Bandini**
is one of the prettiest haciendas in San Diego. Built in 1829 by a Peru-
vian, Juan Bandini, the house served as Old Town's social center during
Mexican rule. Albert Seeley, a stagecoach entrepreneur, purchased the
home in 1869, built a second story, and turned it into the Cosmopolitan Hotel, a comfortable way station for travelers on the day-long trip
south from Los Angeles. These days, Casa Bandini's colorful gardens and
main-floor dining rooms house a popular Mexican restaurant.

Seeley Stable, next door to La Casa de Bandini on Calhoun Street, became San Diego's stagecoach stop in 1867 and was the transportation
hub of Old Town until near the turn of the century, when the Southern Pacific Railroad became the favored mode of travel. The stable now
houses a collection of horse-drawn vehicles and western memorabilia,
including an exhibit on the California *vaquero*, the original American
cowboy, and an array of Native American artifacts.

La Casa de Estudillo was built on Mason Street in 1827 by the commander of the San Diego Presidio, Jose Maria Estudillo. The largest
and most elaborate of the original adobe homes, it was occupied by
members of the Estudillo family until 1887. After being left to deteriorate for some time, it was purchased and restored in 1910 by sugar
magnate and developer John D. Spreckels, who advertised it in bold
lettering on the side as "Ramona's Marriage Place." (The small chapel
in the house was believed to be the setting for the wedding in Helen
Hunt Jackson's popular novel.)

The **San Diego Union Newspaper Historical Museum** (✉ Twigg St. and
San Diego Ave.) is in a New England–style wood-frame house pre-
fabricated in Maine and shipped around Cape Horn in 1851. The building has been restored to replicate the newspaper's offices of 1868, when
the first edition of the *San Diego Union* was printed.

❻ Presidio Park. The rolling hillsides of the 40-acre green space overlooking Old Town from the north end of Taylor Street are popular with pic-nickers, and many couples have taken their wedding vows on the park's long stretches of lawn, some of the greenest in San Diego. It's a nice walk to the summit from Old Town if you're in good shape and wearing the right shoes—it should take about half an hour. At the end of Mason Street, a footpath on the left leads up to the **Presidio Ruins,** where adobe walls and a bastion have been built above the foundations of the original fortress and chapel.

❸ Thomas Whaley Museum. Thomas Whaley was a New York entrepreneur who came to California during the gold rush. He wanted to provide his East Coast wife with all the comforts of home, so in 1856 he had southern California's first two-story brick structure built. The house, which served as the county courthouse and government seat during the 1870s, stands in strong contrast to the Spanish-style adobe residences that surround the nearby historic plaza and marks an early stage of San Diego's "Americanization."

Period furnishings in the living quarters include a miniature dress dummy designed to look like Mary Todd Lincoln, a sofa from Andrew Jackson's White House, and a piano that belonged to singer Jenny Lind. Among the historical artifacts in the reconstructed courtroom is one of the six life masks that exist of Abraham Lincoln. A garden out back includes rosebushes from a pre-hybrid era. The place is perhaps most famed, however, for the ghost that is said to inhabit it; this is one of the few houses authenticated by the United States Department of Commerce as being haunted. ⊠ *2482 San Diego Ave.,* ☎ *619/298–2482.* ▨ *$4.* ⊙ *Daily 10–5 (call ahead for shorter winter hours).*

DINING

By Kathryn Shevelow

In the recent past, a "good San Diego restaurant" usually resembled the bland Chamber of Commerce eatery humorist Calvin Trillin dubs "La Maison de la Casa House," but these days fine new restaurants appear on the scene with dizzying rapidity. A stroll down 5th Avenue will provide ample evidence of San Diego's love affair with Italian cuisine, echoed in other parts of the city, but the cooking of Spain and France, as well as the various cuisines of Latin America, Asia, the Middle East—and even the United States—are well represented. Of course, San Diego has numerous palaces of California cuisine, which borrows from all these culinary traditions. Another hybrid is Pacific Rim cuisine, a mélange of North American, Latin American, and Asian influences and ingredients.

In addition to downtown, other areas of San Diego share in the new sense of energy, fueled by a collective "caffeine high" acquired in the coffeehouses (some of which are listed *in* Nightlife and the Arts, *below*) springing up everywhere from the Gaslamp Quarter to the gas station on the corner. The "Uptown" neighborhood of Hillcrest reminds many people of San Francisco, partly because of its large gay population, partly because of its culinary sophistication. It's no accident that the best new restaurant to open in San Diego in recent memory, Laurel, is on the border of Hillcrest and downtown. And once sleepy La Jolla is now bursting with restaurants.

The guide that follows introduces some of San Diego's most accomplished eateries. Because many of its best practitioners are outside the areas of the city commonly visited by tourists, we've included fewer examples of Asian cooking than of other cuisines. **Phuong Trang** (⊠ 4170 Convoy St., ☎ 619/565–6750) and **Pho Hoa** (⊠ 6921 Linda Vista

Rd., ☎ 619/492–9108) are two of several excellent Vietnamese establishments. Two area Chinese restaurants are widely considered to be the best in the city: **Emerald Chinese Seafood Restaurant** (✉ 3709 Convoy St., ☎ 619/565–6888) and **Jasmine** (✉ 4609 Convoy St., ☎ 619/268–0888). San Diegans like to argue about which is better.

Coronado has recently begun to establish a reputation for fine dining, though the area still has less variety than elsewhere in San Diego. The best restaurants, which are often in hotels, tend to serve elaborate and pricey Continental cuisine. If you wish to eat well in Coronado and money is no object, your first choice should be **Marius** (☞ French cuisine, *below*). If you wish to eat elsewhere in Coronado, here are some of your best bets, listed in descending order from expensive ($$$–$$$$) to moderate ($$): **Azzura Point** (✉ Loews Coronado Bay Resort, 4000 Coronado Bay Rd., ☎ 619/424–4000), serving a mixed menu of Continental and California cuisine with an emphasis upon seafood; **Peohe's** (✉ Ferry Landing Marketplace, 1201 1st St., ☎ 619/437–4474), a lavishly decorated seafood restaurant; the **Prince of Wales Room** (✉ Hotel Del Coronado, 1500 Orange Ave., ☎ 619/435–6611, ext. 8818), which focuses on grilled food and American regional cuisine; **Chez Loma** (✉ 1132 Loma Ave., ☎ 619/435–0661), a Continental restaurant in a historic Coronado house; and **Primavera Ristorante** (✉ 932 Orange Ave., ☎ 619/435–0454), specializing in northern Italian cuisine.

Whether you are visiting San Diego for business or pleasure, there will inevitably arise times when you need fast food. Besides **KC's Tandoor** (☞ Indian cuisine, *below*), highly recommended restaurant chains with locations around the city are the **La Salsa** Mexican eateries, whose tasty tacos and burritos manage to lower the fat while heightening the flavor; **Saffron Chicken** (☞ Thai cuisine, *below*); and **Chick's** and **Koo Koo Roo,** which specialize in spit-roasted chicken with health-conscious side dishes. Although not a fast-food restaurant, **Pizza Nova** efficiently serves good designer pizzas as well as enormous salads, pasta dishes, and sandwiches.

The restaurants below are grouped first by type of cuisine, then by neighborhood. San Diego is an informal city. Of the restaurants listed, only Anthony's Star of the Sea Room requires men to wear jackets.

CATEGORY	COST*
$$$$	over $50
$$$	$30–$50
$$	$20–$30
$	under $20

*per person for a three-course meal, excluding drinks, service, and 7¼% sales tax

American

Beaches

$ ✗ **Mission Cafe and Coffeehouse.** Large and slightly shabby, this Mission Beach café contradicts its appearance by serving stylishly presented American, Latino, and "Chino-Latino" cuisine. Breakfast dishes are served throughout the day. Try the French toast—slices of homemade cinnamon bread arranged over a drizzle of blackberry puree—or the tamales with eggs and green-chili salsa. For dinner try one of the fusion dishes, such as the Pacific Rim risotto. All menu items may be made vegetarian. The café serves good beer on tap, specialty coffee drinks, and shakes and smoothies. ✉ *3795 Mission Blvd.,* ☎ *619/488–9060. AE, MC, V.*

Downtown

$$$ ✕ **Rainwater's.** Classy Rainwater's is as well known for the size of its
★   portions as for the quality of its cuisine. The menu includes meat and
     fish dishes, but this is really the place to come if you crave a perfectly
     done, thick and tender steak. All the entrées are accompanied by tasty
     side dishes such as shoestring potatoes, onion rings, and creamed corn.
     ✉ *1202 Kettner Blvd., 2nd floor,* ☎ *619/233–5757. AE, MC, V. No
     lunch weekends.*

La Jolla

$–$$ ✕ **Brockton Villa Restaurant.** This informal restaurant in a restored beach
      cottage overlooks La Jolla Cove and the ocean. Come for breakfast or
      lunch to take advantage of the fabulous daytime view, but don't over-
      look dinner, whether you're in the mood for a turkey burger or rack
      of lamb. The Brockton serves a good range of coffee drinks. You'll have
      to fight the brunch crowd on sunny weekends. ✉ *1235 Coast Blvd.,*
      ☎ *619/454–7393. AE, D, MC, V. Call ahead for dinner hrs.*

$ ✕ **Hard Rock Cafe.** The high-energy shrine to rock-and-roll and Amer-
      ican food cranks its music up to ear-shattering decibels and hangs rock
      memorabilia on every available inch of wall space. This is not a place
      to come for intimate—or audible—conversation, but the burgers are
      fine. ✉ *909 Prospect St.,* ☎ *619/454–5101. Reservations not ac-
      cepted. AE, D, DC, MC, V.*

$ ✕ **Mission Coffee Cup Cafe.** This sibling of the Mission Cafe (☞ *above*)
      serves a similar menu, but it's less funky and open only for breakfast
      and lunch. ✉ *1109 Wall St.,* ☎ *619/454–2819. AE, MC, V.*

Uptown

$$ ✕ **Montanas American Grill.** One of Hillcrest's most popular restaurants
      serves hearty California-American food in a sleek, trendy setting. Stick
      with the least complicated dishes: pastas, barbecued meats, chicken, and
      salmon, or try the venison chili accompanied by jalapeño cornbread.
      The appetizer duck cakes are tasty and rich. Wash down your barbe-
      cue with one of the microbrewery beers on tap. ✉ *1421 University Ave.,*
      ☎ *619/297–0722. AE, DC, MC, V. No lunch weekends.*

$ ✕ **Crest Cafe.** Often jammed with locals, this Hillcrest institution spe-
      cializes in good renditions of basic American café food. You can't go
      wrong with old favorites such as pancakes, burgers, onion rings, sal-
      ads, and the homemade desserts. ✉ *425 Robinson Ave.,* ☎ *619/295–
      2510. Reservations not accepted. AE, D, MC, V.*

$ ✕ **Hob Nob Hill.** This comforting restaurant is still under the same own-
      ership and management as it was when it started in 1944; with its dark
      wood booths and patterned carpets, Hob Nob Hill seems suspended
      in the '50s. But you don't need to be a nostalgia buff to appreciate the
      bargain-price American home cooking—dishes such as pot roast, fried
      chicken, and corned beef like your mother never really made. Reser-
      vations are suggested for Sunday's copious breakfasts. ✉ *2271 1st Ave.,*
      ☎ *619/239–8176. AE, D, MC, V.*

Belgian

Beaches

$$–$$$ ✕ **Belgian Lion.** Among the signature dishes here is the cassoulet, a won-
        derful rich stew of white beans, lamb, pork, sausage, and duck that
        makes you feel protected from the elements (even in San Diego, where
        there aren't that many elements). Lighter meals include braised sea scal-
        lops with leeks or poached salmon with fresh vegetables. An impres-
        sive selection of wines complements the food. ✉ *2265 Bacon St.,
        Ocean Beach,* ☎ *619/223–2700. Reservations essential. AE, D, DC,
        MC, V. No lunch. Closed Sun.–Wed.*

San Diego Dining

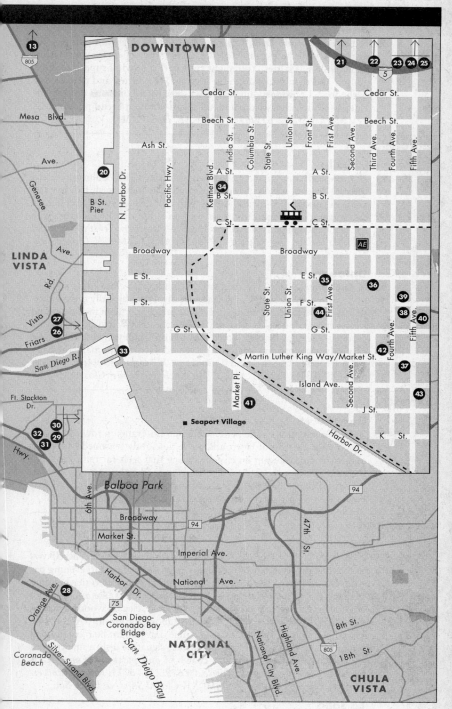

DOWNTOWN

LINDA VISTA

Mesa Blvd.

Genesee Ave.

Vista Rd.

Friars

San Diego R.

Ft. Stockton Dr.

Hwy.

Cedar St.
Beech St.
Ash St.

N. Harbor Dr.
Pacific Hwy.
Kettner Blvd.
India St.
Columbia St.
State St.
Union St.
Front St.
First Ave.
Second Ave.
Third Ave.
Fourth Ave.
Fifth Ave.

Cedar St.
Beech St.

A St.
B St.
C St.

A St.
B St.
C St.

Broadway
Broadway

E St.
F St.
G St.

State St.
Union St.
First Ave.

E St.
F St.
G St.

Martin Luther King Way/Market St.

Island Ave.

Second Ave.
Fourth Ave.
Fifth Ave.

J St.

K St.

Market Pl.

■ Seaport Village

B St. Pier

AE

Balboa Park

6th Ave.

Broadway

Market St.

Imperial Ave.

National Ave.

Harbor Dr.

94

94

47th St.

Orange Ave.

Silver Strand Blvd

San Diego Bay

San Diego-Coronado Bay Bridge

75

NATIONAL CITY

National City Blvd.

Highland Ave.

805

8th St.

18th St.

CHULA VISTA

Coronado Beach

Harbor Dr.

Cajun and Creole

Downtown

$–$$ ✕ **Bayou Bar and Grill.** Ceiling fans, dark-green wainscoting, and light-pink walls help create a New Orleans atmosphere for spicy Cajun and Creole specialties. You might start with a bowl of superb seafood gumbo and then move on to the sausage, red beans, and rice, or any of the fresh Louisiana Gulf seafood dishes. Rich Louisiana desserts include a praline cheesecake and an award-winning bread pudding. ✉ *329 Market St.,* ☎ *619/696–8747. AE, D, DC, MC, V.*

California

La Jolla

$$–$$$ ✕ **Triangles.** This bar and grill strives for variety. The "California-Continental" menu, which changes seasonally, includes fresh fish (try the ahi tuna) and grilled meats. Along with rich dishes, you'll find lighter and vegetarian preparations, as well as some dazzling salads. The small enclosed patio is pleasant at lunch. ✉ *Northern Trust Bldg., 4370 La Jolla Village Dr.,* ☎ *619/453–6650. AE, DC, MC, V. Closed Sun. No lunch Sat.*

Uptown

$$ ✕ **California Cuisine.** The menu at this minimalist-chic dining room—
★   gray carpet, white walls, and changing displays of locally created artworks—is consistently innovative. Daily selections might include grilled fresh venison and a succulent seared ahi; the tasty warm chicken salad entrée is a regular feature. You can count on whatever you order to be carefully prepared and elegantly presented. Heat lamps make the back patio a romantic year-round option. ✉ *1027 University Ave.,* ☎ *619/543–0790. AE, D, DC, MC, V. No lunch weekends. Closed Mon.*

Chinese

Downtown

$–$$ ✕ **Panda Inn.** One of the better Chinese restaurants in town, this din-
★   ing room at the top of Horton Plaza serves subtly seasoned Mandarin and Szechuan dishes in an elegant setting that feels far removed from the rush of commerce below. The fresh seafood dishes are noteworthy, as are the Peking duck, the spicy Szechuan bean curd, and the twice-cooked pork. ✉ *506 Horton Plaza,* ☎ *619/233–7800. AE, D, DC, MC, V.*

Continental

Downtown

$$–$$$ ✕ **Dobson's.** At lunchtime, local politicos and media types rub elbows
★   at the long polished bar of this highly regarded restaurant; evening patrons include many theatergoers. Although the small two-tier building is suggestive of an earlier era—the lower level looks like a men's club and the upper level has a wrought-iron balcony, elegant woodwork, and gilt cornices—there's nothing outdated about the cuisine. Among the carefully prepared entrées, which change daily, might be roasted quail with fig sauce or chicken risotto. Dobson's signature dish, a superb mussel bisque, comes topped with a crown of puff pastry. The wine list is excellent. ✉ *956 Broadway Circle,* ☎ *619/231–6771. Reservations essential on weekends. AE, DC, MC, V. Closed Sun. No lunch Sat.*

La Jolla

$$$–$$$$ ✕ **The Marine Room.** Popular young chef Bernard Guillas prepares inventive American and Continental cuisine with accents from around the world. Representative entrées include a roasted salmon in a pecan sesame-curry crust served on a couscous red-lentil cake with a blood-orange lavender sauce. The Marine Room, a La Jolla Shores institution, overlooks the ocean. ⊠ *2000 Spindrift Dr.,* ☎ *619/459–7222. AE, D, DC, MC, V.*

$$$–$$$$ ✕ **Top O' the Cove.** Although glitzier newcomers now rival this once peerless La Jolla institution, the cozy Top O' the Cove still receives high marks from San Diego diners for its romantic ocean view. Abalone and ostrich are among the unusual items on the highly regarded menu; the less adventuresome might try the filet mignon or the roasted rack of lamb. ⊠ *1216 Prospect St.,* ☎ *619/454–7779. AE, DC, MC, V.*

Deli

La Jolla

$ ✕ **SamSon's.** You can't go wrong with a lox plate for breakfast or a triple-decker sandwich or one of the soup-and-sandwich specials (especially the whitefish when it's available) for lunch. ⊠ *8861 Villa La Jolla Dr.,* ☎ *619/455–1462. AE, D, DC, MC, V.*

French

Coronado

$$$–$$$$ ✕ **Marius.** The choices at Le Meridien hotel's highly touted restaurant range from Parisian haute cuisine to country-French cooking. The food and presentation are top-notch, the service attentive and professional. The wine-tasting menu is particularly recommended. ⊠ *2000 2nd St.,* ☎ *619/435–3000. Reservations essential on weekends. AE, D, DC, MC, V. Closed Sun.–Mon. No lunch.*

La Jolla

$$–$$$ ✕ **Cindy Black's.** This quietly elegant restaurant in La Jolla's Bird Rock neighborhood serves modern interpretations of French cuisine— subtle, stylishly presented dishes, often with a Mediterranean touch. The menu changes seasonally, but possibilities include an arugula and red-pepper salad, a hearty spaghetti with white beans in a Chianti sauce, tender grilled salmon on caramelized onions, and some seductive desserts: a house soufflé and a beyond-decadent Belgian-chocolate "brownie" with homemade caramel ice cream. Reasonable prix-fixe meals are served all Sunday evening and during the early-bird hours on weeknights. ⊠ *5721 La Jolla Blvd.,* ☎ *619/456–6299. AE, D, DC, MC, V. No lunch.*

French and Mediterranean

Uptown

$$$ ✕ **Laurel.** Chef Douglas Organ's acclaimed restaurant spotlights the
★ cooking of southern France and the Mediterranean. Its culinary philosophy is straightforward: the best fresh ingredients prepared simply, but with flair. The menu changes daily, but many favorite dishes appear regularly. For starters, try the red-pepper-and-seafood soup or the lightly smoked trout served with warm potato salad. Among the entrées, roasted fish and risotto (especially when it's made with wild mushrooms) are always good. The wine list is renowned; desserts include a rich *pot au chocolat.* ⊠ *505 Laurel St., at 5th Ave.,* ☎ *619/239–2222. AE, D, DC, MC, V. No lunch weekends.*

Greek

Downtown

$ ✕ **Athens Market.** The appetizers at this cheerful Greek restaurant—
taramousalata (fish roe dip), hummus, stuffed grape leaves, and the
like—are particularly tasty. You can make a meal of an assortment.
Greek music and belly dancers add to the festive atmosphere on weekend evenings. The adjacent Victorian-style coffeehouse, under the same
ownership, is open from early morning into the evening, when many
patrons switch from coffee to drinks and cigars. ⊠ *109 W. F St.,* ☎
619/234–1955. AE, D, DC, MC, V.

Indian

Mission Valley

$ ✕ **KC's Tandoor.** True, this is a fast-food restaurant, in one of the city's
ubiquitous minimalls, but the tandoori chicken is flavorful, the nan bread
is rich and chewy, and the curries are truly impressive. Hearty appetites
will find a bargain in the all-you-can-eat buffet brunch (Mission Center location only) on Sundays. A second KC's is northeast of the University of California off I–805. ⊠ *Friars Mission Center, 5608 Mission
Center Rd.,* ☎ *619/497–0751;* ⊠ *9450 Scranton Rd.,* ☎ *619/535–
1941. MC, V.*

Italian

Beaches

$ ✕ **Tosca's.** With its fluorescent lighting and red-checkered vinyl table-
cloths, this eatery is typical of pizza restaurants everywhere. But you
are, after all, in California, which means you can opt for wheat or
semolina crusts for your individually sized pizzas or calzones; choose
toppings or fillings that include artichokes, pesto, and feta cheese; and
wash it all down with a microbrew. ⊠ *3780 Ingraham St., Pacific Beach,*
☎ *619/274–2408. No lunch weekdays. AE, D, DC, MC, V.*

Downtown

$$–$$$ ✕ **Bella Luna.** This small restaurant has developed a loyal following.
The menu includes dishes from all over Italy: For an appetizer, try the
rolled mozzarella or the stuffed eggplant. Linguine with clams, fettuccine
with salmon, and black squid-ink linguine served with a spicy seafood
sauce are among the many fine pastas; if you still have room for an
entrée, consider the rack of lamb. ⊠ *748 5th Ave.,* ☎ *619/239–3222.
Reservations essential on weekends. No lunch Sun. AE, DC, MC, V.*

$$–$$$ ✕ **Trattoria Mamma Anna.** A few examples of the owners' native Si-
★   cilian cuisine show up on the menu, such as the tasty *fagottini di
melanzane* appetizer, eggplant stuffed with bread crumbs, peppers,
pine nuts, and raisins. But the fare here ventures into the rest of Italy
as well: the ravioli *con salsa di funghi* (spinach and ricotta ravioli with
cream and mushroom sauce) is exquisite, as is the deceptively simple
fettuccine *montanari* (homemade pasta with garlic, tomatoes, and
wild mushrooms). Be forewarned: Portions are generous. If you can
get as far as the second courses, try the *pollo campagnola* (chicken breast
with vegetables and olives) or the simple grilled swordfish served with
lemon. ⊠ *644 5th Ave.,* ☎ *619/235–8144. Reservations essential on
weekends. AE, D, DC, MC, V.*

$$ ✕ **Fio's.** Glitzy young singles mingle with staid business-suit types in
this lively Gaslamp Quarter restaurant. Contemporary variations on
traditional northern Italian cuisine are served in a high-ceiling brick-

and-wood dining room overlooking the 5th Avenue street scene. The menu includes pizzas baked in the wood-fire oven and good appetizers and pastas. ⊠ *801 5th Ave.,* ☎ *619/234–3467. Reservations essential on weekends. AE, D, DC, MC, V. No lunch weekends.*

La Jolla

$$ ✕ **Piatti Ristorante.** On weekends, this trattoria is filled to overflow-
★ ing with singles and local families. A wood-burning oven turns out fla-
vorful pizzas; pastas include the *pappardelle fantasia* (wide saffron
noodles with shrimp, fresh tomatoes, and arugula) and a garlicky
spaghetti *alle vongole* (served with clams in the shell). Among the *sec-
ondi* are good versions of roast chicken and Italian sausage with po-
lenta. The weekday lunch menu includes salads and *panini* (sandwiches);
brunch is served weekends. ⊠ *2182 Avenida de la Playa,* ☎ *619/
454–1589. AE, DC, MC, V.*

Latin American

Old Town

$ ✕ **Berta's Latin American Restaurant.** The food at Berta's manages to
be tasty and health-conscious at the same time. Try the Brazilian
seafood *vatapa* (shrimp, scallops, and fish served in a sauce flavored
with ginger, coconut, and chilies) or the Peruvian *pollo a la huancaina*
(chicken with chilies and a feta-cheese sauce). The simple dining room
is small, but there's also a patio. ⊠ *3928 Twiggs St.,* ☎ *619/295–2343.
AE, MC, V.*

Mexican

Beaches

$–$$ ✕ **Palenque.** A welcome alternative to the standard Sonoran-style
★ café, this family run restaurant in Pacific Beach serves regional Mex-
ican dishes. Recommendations include the chicken with *mole,* in the
chocolate-based or green-chili version, and the mouth-watering *ca-
marones en chipotle,* large shrimp cooked in a chili-and-tequila cream
sauce (an old family recipe of the proprietor). Palenque is a bit hard
to spot from the street and service is often slow, but the food is worth
your vigilance and patience. ⊠ *1653 Garnet Ave., Pacific Beach,* ☎
619/272–7816. AE, D, DC, MC, V. No lunch Mon.

Mission Valley

$ ✕ **El Tecolote.** In addition to the usual taco-burrito fare at El Tecolote
are Mexican regional specialties—enchiladas in mole sauce, fish fillet
Ensenada style, or the Aztec layered cake (tortillas stacked with cheese,
chilies, enchilada sauce, guacamole, and sour cream). ⊠ *6110 Friars
Rd. W,* ☎ *619/295–2087. AE, D, DC, MC, V. No lunch Sun.*

Old Town

$ ✕ **Old Town Mexican Café.** You'll find all the Mexican standards here,
along with specialties such as *carnitas,* chunks of roast pork served with
fresh tortillas and condiments. The enchiladas with spicy ranchero or
green-chili sauce are delectable variations on an old theme. You can
watch the corn tortillas being handmade on the premises and pick up
a dozen to take home. The Café opens at 7 AM for breakfast. ⊠ *2489
San Diego Ave.,* ☎ *619/297–4330. AE, D, MC, V.*

Uptown

$ ✕ **Chilango's Mexico City Grill.** A tiny but cheerful storefront restau-
rant, Chilango's has one of the most interesting menus in town. The

burritos and *tortas* (sandwiches) are like no others in the city; daily specials might include enchiladas in mole *verde* (green chili sauce) and the fabulous chicken mole *poblano* (a sauce made with chilies and bittersweet chocolate). This much-loved restaurant quickly fills to overflowing, so consider coming in off-hours or ordering takeout. ⊠ *142 University Ave., ☎ 619/294–8646. Open for breakfast Fri.–Sun. No credit cards.*

$ ✕ **El Indio Shop.** The menu at El Indio is extensive; try the large burritos, the *tacquitos* (fried rolled tacos) with guacamole, or the giant quesadillas. Low on atmosphere both at the tables inside and on the patio across the street, El Indio is perfect for beach-bound takeout. There's a branch downtown, and one in Pacific Beach, too. ⊠ *3695 India St. (take I–5 to Washington St. exit), ☎ 619/299–0333; ⊠ 409 F St., ☎ 619/239–8151.*

Pacific Rim

La Jolla

$$$ ✕ **Cafe Japengo.** The cuisine here is Asian-inspired, with many North and South American touches. There's a selection of grilled, wood-roasted, and wok-fried entrées for dinner; try the shrimp and scallops with dragon noodles or the grilled swordfish with red-bean miso stew. The curry fried calamari and the Japengo pot stickers appetizers are guaranteed to wake up your mouth. You can also order very fresh sushi from your table or from a seat at the sushi bar. ⊠ *Aventine Center, 8960 University Center La., ☎ 619/450–3355. AE, D, DC, MC, V. No lunch weekends.*

Seafood

Downtown

$$$–$$$$ ✕ **Anthony's Star of the Sea Room.** The flagship of Anthony's local
★ fleet of seafood restaurants ensconces its patrons in a formal dining room whose vaguely marine decor got a much-needed facelift in 1997. The house-smoked salmon, sliced at the table, melts in the mouth; the delicious "lobster cappuccino" soup resembles coffee only in name; and the various grilled and roasted seafood entrées are splendidly prepared. A terrace scheduled for completion by fall 1997 will take greater advantage of the choice waterfront location of one of San Diego's premier seafood restaurants. ⊠ *1360 N. Harbor Dr., ☎ 619/232–7408. Jacket required. AE, D, DC, MC, V. No lunch.*

$$$ ✕ **Blue Point Coastal Cuisine.** High ceilings, gleaming woodwork, ample booths, and expansive windows give this seafood establishment an urbane air. The extensive selection of home brews and house martinis contributes to the atmosphere of East Coast sophistication. But Blue Point situates its cuisine firmly on the Pacific Rim, incorporating Asian accents and south-of-the-border flavors. Go for the appetizers and seafood entrées here—the pasta dishes are disappointing. Try the griddled oysters or crab cakes, and follow them with the grilled swordfish, the mustard catfish, or the sesame-crusted salmon with sake butter. ⊠ *565 5th Ave., ☎ 619/233–6623. AE, D, DC, MC, V. No lunch.*

$$$ ✕ **Sally's.** Order the light, greaseless crab cakes, the best in town, and bite into chunks of fresh crab. Recommended entrées include a seafood paella studded with pieces of fish and shellfish, a rich bouillabaisse, and an unusually moist and tender grilled swordfish. The three-course prix-fixe daily special at dinner is often irresistible. At the Sunday "jazz

brunch," from 11 to 3:30, you can listen to music while you enjoy an appetizer, an entrée, and unlimited champagne and orange juice for the bargain price of $16. Outdoor dining is available. ⊠ *Hyatt Regency San Diego, 1 Market Pl.,* ☎ *619/687–6080. AE, D, DC, MC, V.*

$–$$$ ✕ **The Fish Market.** Diners at this informal restaurant choose from a large variety of fresh fish, mesquite grilled and served with lemon and tartar sauce. Also good are the shellfish dishes, such as steamed clams or mussels, and the sushi. Most of what is served here has lived in the water, but even dedicated fish-avoiders may think it worth their while to trade selection for the stunning view: Enormous plate-glass windows look directly out onto the harbor. A more formal restaurant upstairs, the Top of the Market, has a distinctive menu of exquisitely prepared seafood. It's expensive but worth the splurge. ⊠ *750 N. Harbor Dr.,* ☎ *619/232–3474 for the Fish Market, 619/234–4867 for the Top of the Market. AE, D, DC, MC, V.*

La Jolla

$$$ ✕ **George's at the Cove.** At most restaurants you get either good food
★ or good views; at George's, you get both. The elegant main dining room, with a wall-length window overlooking La Jolla Cove, is renowned for its daily fresh seafood specials; the menu also includes several good chicken and meat dishes. The soups and the fresh pasta entrées are highly recommended. Desserts are uniformly excellent. For more informal dining, try the Cafe ($–$$) on the second floor. The rooftop Ocean Terrace ($–$$) has a sweeping view of the coast. Wonderful for breakfast, lunch, or brunch on a fine day, the Terrace (like the Cafe) does not take reservations, so you may have a wait. ⊠ *1250 Prospect St.,* ☎ *619/ 454–4244. Reservations essential for main dining room on weekends. AE, D, DC, MC, V.*

Old Town

$$–$$$ ✕ **Cafe Pacifica.** The airy Cafe Pacifica serves eclectic California cui-
★ sine with an emphasis on seafood. You can't go wrong with any of the fresh fish preparations. Other good bets include the pan-fried catfish, greaseless fish tacos, and superb crab cakes. The crème brûlée is worth blowing any diet for. ⊠ *2414 San Diego Ave.,* ☎ *619/291–6666. AE, D, DC, MC, V. No lunch Sat.–Mon.*

Thai

Uptown

$ ✕ **Saffron Chicken.** The specialty at this take-out restaurant is chicken spit-roasted over a wood fire and served with a choice of sauces: Try the peanut or chili. Among the accompanying side dishes, the Cambodian salad is fresh and crunchy. There's limited outdoor seating, but this is an ideal place to pick up a meal to take to Mission Bay or the beach. ⊠ *3731B India St. (from downtown, take I–5 to Washington St. exit),* ☎ *619/574–0177. Reservations not accepted. MC, V.*

$ ✕ **Taste of Thai.** Almost always packed with value-minded diners, this modest café serves up yummy Thai and vegetarian cuisine at reasonable prices. Try the seafood noodles, the red or yellow curry, and the meat or tofu with basil and hot peppers. ⊠ *527 University Ave.,* ☎ *619/291–7525. AE, MC, V.*

LODGING

Updated by
Cynthia Queen

San Diego is spread out, so the first thing to consider when selecting lodgings is location. If you plan to do a lot of sightseeing, take into account a hotel's proximity to the attractions you most want to visit. Even the most expensive areas have some reasonably priced rooms. A few bed-and-breakfast accommodations are listed below. For additional referrals, contact the **Bed & Breakfast Guild of San Diego** (☎ 619/523–1300) for in-town B&Bs and the **Bed & Breakfast Directory for San Diego** (✉ Box 3292, 92163, ☎ 619/297–3130 or 800/619–7666) for establishments in San Diego County.

CATEGORY	COST*
$$$$	over $175
$$$	$120–$175
$$	$80–$120
$	under $80

*All prices are for a double room in high (summer) season, excluding 10½% San Diego room tax

Coronado

$$$$ 🏨 **Hotel Del Coronado.** "The Del" is a social and historic landmark. The rooms and suites in the ornate 1888 building are charmingly quirky. Some have sleeping areas that seem smaller than the baths. Other rooms are downright palatial; two are even said to come with a resident ghost. The public areas are grand, if a bit dark for modern tastes. More standardized accommodations are available in the newer highrise. ✉ *1500 Orange Ave., 92118,* ☎ *619/435–6611 for hotel, 619/522–8000 or 800/468–3533 for reservations,* FAX *619/522–8262. 692 rooms. 3 restaurants, deli, in-room modem lines, room service, 2 pools, barbershop, beauty salon, outdoor hot tub, massage, sauna, steam room, 6 tennis courts, croquet, exercise room, beach, boating, bicycles, shops, video games, concierge, business services, convention center, parking (fee). AE, D, DC, MC, V.*

$$$$ 🏨 **Le Meridien San Diego at Coronado.** Flamingos greet you at the en-
★ trance to this 16-acre landscaped resort. Large rooms and suites in low-slung buildings are done in a cheerful California–country French fashion, with colorful Impressionist prints; all rooms have separate showers and tubs and come with plush robes. The spa facilities are top-notch, as is the award-winning Marius restaurant (☞ Dining, *above*), which serves innovative Provençal cuisine. ✉ *2000 2nd St., 92118,* ☎ *619/435–3000 or 800/543–4300 for central reservations,* FAX *619/435–3032. 265 rooms, 7 suites, 28 villa units. 2 restaurants, bar, in-room modem lines, room service, 3 pools, barbershop, beauty salon, 2 outdoor hot tubs, massage, sauna, spa, 6 tennis courts, aerobics, health club, beach, snorkeling, windsurfing, bicycles, pro shop, shops, children's programs, laundry service, concierge, business services, convention center, parking (fee). AE, D, DC, MC, V.*

$$$$ 🏨 **Loews Coronado Bay Resort.** You can park your boat at the 80-slip marina of this resort set on a secluded 15-acre peninsula on the Silver Strand. Rooms are formally but tastefully decorated, and all have furnished balconies with views of water—either bay, ocean, or marina. The Azzura Point restaurant, which specializes in Pacific seafood, has won numerous awards. ✉ *4000 Coronado Bay Rd., 92118,* ☎ *619/424–4000 or 800/815–6397,* FAX *619/424–4400. 403 rooms, 37 suites. 2 restaurants, bar, deli, in-room modem lines, room service, 3 pools, barbershop, beauty salon, 3 hot tubs, 5 tennis courts, health club, beach, windsurfing, boating, jet skiing, waterskiing, bicycles, pro shop, children's programs, laundry service, concierge, business services, convention center, parking (fee). AE, D, DC, MC, V.*

$$–$$$ 🏨 **Glorietta Bay Inn.** The main building of this property was built in 1908 for sugar baron John D. Spreckels, who once owned most of downtown San Diego. Rooms in this Edwardian-style mansion and in the newer motel-style buildings are attractively furnished. Tours ($6) of the island's historical buildings depart from the inn's lobby three morn-

ings a week. ⊠ *1630 Glorietta Blvd., 92118,* ☎ *619/435–3101 or 800/ 283–9383,* FAX *619/435–6182. 98 rooms. In-room modem lines, refrigerators, pool, outdoor hot tub, bicycles, coin laundry, business services, free parking. AE, D, DC, MC, V.*

Downtown

$$$$
★
🏨 **Hyatt Regency San Diego.** This high-rise adjacent to Seaport Village successfully combines Old World opulence with California airiness. Palm trees pose next to ornate tapestry couches in the light-filled lobby, and all of the British Regency–style guest rooms have views of the water. The hotel's proximity to the convention center attracts a large business trade. The "Business Plan" includes access to an area with desks and office supplies; each room on the special business floor has a fax machine. But the Regency also provides well-heeled leisure travelers a superb location and facilities. ⊠ *1 Market Pl.,* ☎ *619/232–1234 or 800/233–1234 for central reservations,* FAX *619/233–6464. 820 rooms, 55 suites and Regency Club rooms. 2 restaurants, in-room modem lines, room service, bar, lobby lounge, piano bar, pool, outdoor hot tub, sauna, steam room, 3 tennis courts, health club, boating, bicycles, shops, laundry service, business services, convention center, parking (fee). AE, D, DC, MC, V.*

$$$$
🏨 **San Diego Marriott Hotel and Marina.** This twin-towers high-rise next to the San Diego Convention Center has everything a businessperson could want, not to mention a superb view of the bay and city from the upper floors. Vacationers will appreciate the location right on the San Diego Bay boardwalk. Be aware that standard rooms are smallish. The hallways can be noisy at night. ⊠ *333 W. Harbor Dr., 92101,* ☎ *619/ 234–1500 or 800/228–9290 for central reservations,* FAX *619/234–8678. 1,299 rooms, 56 suites. 4 restaurants, bar, in-room modem lines, room service, 2 pools, barbershop, beauty salon, outdoor hot tub, sauna, 6 tennis courts, aerobics, basketball, health club, jogging, bicycles, shops, recreation room, coin laundry, concierge, business services, convention center, car rental, parking (fee). AE, D, DC, MC, V.*

$$$–$$$$
🏨 **Embassy Suites San Diego Bay.** Business travelers will find it easy to set up shop here; the hotel provides a 24-hour fax and photocopy service. Families can make good use of the in-room refrigerators, microwaves, and separate sleeping areas. A cooked-to-order breakfast and afternoon cocktails are complimentary, as are airport transfers. ⊠ *601 Pacific Hwy., 92101,* ☎ *619/239–2400 or 800/362–2779 for central reservations,* FAX *619/239–1520. 337 suites. Restaurant, bar, pool, barbershop, beauty salon, sauna, health club, shops, bicycles, coin laundry, business services, meeting rooms, airport shuttle, parking (fee). AE, D, DC, MC, V.*

$$$–$$$$
🏨 **U.S. Grant Hotel.** The crystal chandeliers and polished marble floors in the lobby of the U.S. Grant and the Queen Anne–style mahogany furnishings in the stately and spacious rooms recall a more gracious era, when such dignitaries as Charles Lindbergh and Franklin D. Roosevelt stayed here. ⊠ *326 Broadway, 92101,* ☎ *619/232–3121 or 800/237– 5029,* FAX *619/232–3626. 220 rooms, 60 suites. Restaurant, bar, café, piano bar, room service, exercise room, bicycles, concierge, business services, shops, airport shuttle, parking (fee). AE, D, DC, MC, V.*

$$$–$$$$
★
🏨 **Westgate Hotel.** A nondescript modern high-rise across from Horton Plaza hides what must be the most opulent hotel in San Diego. Rooms are individually furnished with antiques, Italian marble counters, and bath fixtures with 24-karat-gold overlays. From the ninth floor up, the views of the harbor and city are breathtaking. Afternoon high tea is served in the lobby to the accompaniment of piano music. ⊠ *1055 2nd Ave., 92101,* ☎ *619/238–1818 or 800/221–3802; 800/522–1564 in CA;* FAX *619/557–3737. 223 rooms. 2 restaurants, bar, deli, in-room*

Bahia Hotel, **20**
Balboa Park Inn, **56**
Bay Club Hotel &
Marina, **27**
Bed & Breakfast Inn at
La Jolla, **3**
Best Western Blue Sea
Lodge, **18**
Best Western Hacienda
Hotel
Old Town, **35**
Best Western Hanalei
Hotel, **38**
Best Western Inn
by the Sea, **2**
Best Western Island
Palms Hotel &
Marina, **26**
Best Western Posada
Inn, **32**
Catamaran Resort
Hotel, **16**
Colonial Inn, **5**
Crystal Pier Motel, **14**
Dana Inn &
Marina, **19**
Days Inn Hotel
Circle, **57**
Embassy Suites
San Diego Bay, **50**
Gaslamp Plaza
Suites, **51**
Glorietta Bay Inn, **42**
Heritage Park Bed &
Breakfast Inn, **23**
Holiday Inn Express, **1**
Holiday Inn on the
Bay, **46**
Horton Grand
Hotel, **47**
Hotel Del
Coronado, **43**
Humphrey's Half
Moon Inn, **28**
Hyatt Islandia, **22**
Hyatt Regency
La Jolla, **10**
Hyatt Regency
San Diego, **45**
Kona Kai Continental
Plaza Resort and
Marina, **25**
La Jolla Cove Suites, **8**
La Pensione, **53**
La Valencia, **7**
Le Meridien San Diego
at Coronado, **41**
Lodge at Torrey
Pines, **11**
Loews Coronado Bay
Resort, **44**
Mission Bay Motel, **17**
Ocean Manor
Apartment Hotel, **24**
Outrigger Motel, **30**
Pacific Shores Inn, **15**

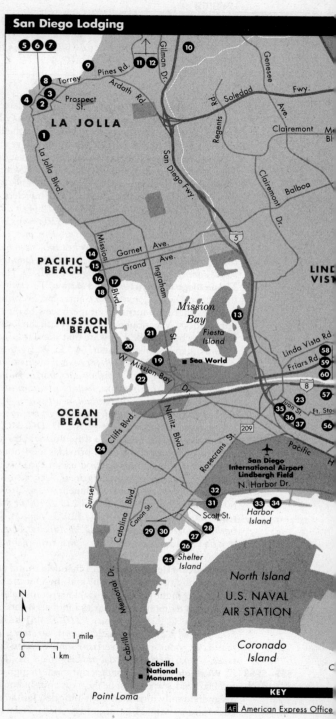

San Diego Lodging

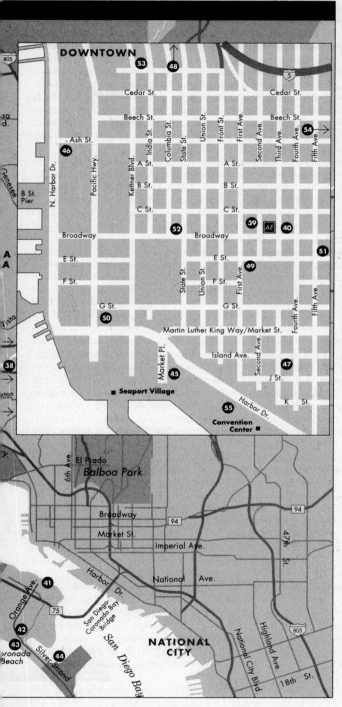

modem lines, room service, barbershop, exercise room, bicycles, concierge, business services, meeting rooms, airport shuttle, parking (fee). AE, D, DC, MC, V.

$$$–$$$$ 🏨 **Wyndham Emerald Plaza Hotel.** This property's office and conference facilities draw many business travelers. Still, the Wyndham is also fine for vacationers who want to be near downtown shopping and restaurants. Many of the upper-floor accommodations have panoramic views. ⊠ *400 W. Broadway, 92101,* ☎ *619/239–4500 or 800/996–3426,* 🆇 *619/239–4527. 416 rooms, 20 suites. 2 restaurants, bar, in-room modem lines, pool, outdoor hot tub, sauna, steam room, health club, shops, children's programs, concierge, business services, convention center, parking (fee). AE, D, DC, MC, V.*

$$$ 🏨 **Holiday Inn on the Bay.** Rooms at this Embarcadero high-rise are unsurprising but spacious and comfortable, and the views from the balconies are hard to beat. ⊠ *1355 N. Harbor Dr., 92101,* ☎ *619/232–3861 or 800/877–8920 for central reservations,* 🆇 *619/232–4924. 600 rooms, 17 suites. Restaurant, bar, in-room modem lines, pool, exercise room, shops, coin laundry, business services, meeting rooms, airport and Amtrak shuttle, parking (fee). AE, D, DC, MC, V.*

$$$ 🏨 **Westin Hotel San Diego–Horton Plaza.** Although it is fronted by a startling lighted blue obelisk, this high-rise, formerly the Doubletree, is all understated marble and brass. The spacious rooms are in pastels of coral blue and pale orange. With its prime downtown location the hotel attracts many business travelers. ⊠ *910 Broadway Circle, 92101,* ☎ *619/239–2200 or 800/528–0444 for central reservations,* 🆇 *619/239–0509. 450 rooms, 14 suites. Restaurant, lobby lounge, sports bar, in-room modem lines, room service, pool, outdoor hot tub, sauna, 2 tennis courts, health club, business services, parking (fee). AE, D, DC, MC, V.*

$$–$$$$ 🏨 **Balboa Park Inn.** Directly across the street from Balboa Park, this all-suites B&B is housed in four Spanish colonial–style 1915 residences connected by courtyards. One- and two-bedroom suites are decorated in contemporary Italian, French, Spanish, or early Californian; some have fireplaces, wet bars, whirlpool tubs, patios, and kitchens. Continental breakfast and a newspaper are delivered to guests every morning. ⊠ *3402 Park Blvd., 92103,* ☎ *619/298–0823 or 800/938–8181,* 🆇 *619/294–8070. 26 suites. AE, D, DC, MC, V.*

$$–$$$$ 🏨 **Horton Grand Hotel.** A Victorian confection in the heart of the historic Gaslamp District, the Horton Grand comprises two 1880s hotels moved brick by brick from nearby locations. Its delightfully retro rooms are furnished with period antiques, ceiling fans, and gas-burning fireplaces. The choicest rooms overlook a garden courtyard. The hotel is a charmer, but service can be erratic. ⊠ *311 Island Ave., 92101,* ☎ *619/544–1886 or 800/542–1886,* 🆇 *619/239–3823. 105 rooms, 24 suites. Restaurant, bar, business services, meeting rooms, airport shuttle, parking (fee). AE, D, DC, MC, V.*

$$–$$$ 🏨 **Gaslamp Plaza Suites.** Listed on the National Register of Historic Places, this 11-story structure just a block from Horton Plaza was built in 1913 as San Diego's first "skyscraper." Elegant public areas have old marble, brass, and mosaics. Guests can enjoy the view and a complimentary Continental breakfast on the rooftop terrace. Book ahead if you're visiting in high season. ⊠ *520 E St., 92101,* ☎ *619/232–9500 or 800/874–8770,* 🆇 *619/238–9945. 52 suites. Restaurant, bar. AE, D, DC, MC, V.*

$–$$ 🏨 **Rodeway Inn.** This property is clean, comfortable, and nicely decorated. Continental breakfast is included in the room rate. ⊠ *833 Ash St., 92101,* ☎ *619/239–2285, 800/228–2000 for central reservations; 800/522–1528 in CA;* 🆇 *619/235–6951. 45 rooms. In-room modem lines, hot tub, sauna, coin laundry, business services, meeting rooms, free parking. AE, D, DC, MC, V.*

$ ☒ **La Pensione.** Rooms at this small hotel near the Old Town trolley line are modern, with good working areas and kitchenettes. ☒ *1700 India St., 92101,* ☎ *619/236–8000 or 800/232–4683,* FAX *619/236–8088. 80 rooms. Café, kitchenettes, coin laundry, free parking. AE, D, DC, MC, V.*

$ ☒ **Super 8 Bayview.** This motel's location is less noisy than those of other low-cost establishments. The accommodations are nondescript but clean, and some have refrigerators. Room rates include Continental breakfast. ☒ *1835 Columbia St., 92101,* ☎ *619/544–0164 or 800/537–9902,* FAX *619/237–9940. 101 rooms. Pool, coin laundry, airport and Amtrak shuttle, free parking. AE, DC, MC, V.*

Harbor Island, Shelter Island, and Point Loma

$$$$ ☒ **Sheraton San Diego Hotel & Marina.** Of this property's two high-rises, the smaller, more intimate West Tower has larger rooms with separate areas suitable for business entertaining. The East Tower has the better sports facilities. Rooms throughout are California-style spiffy. Views from the upper floors of both sections are superb, but because the West Tower is closer to the water it has fine outlooks from the lower floors, too. ☒ *1380 Harbor Island Dr., 92101,* ☎ *619/291–2900 or 800/325–3535 for central reservations,* FAX *619/692–2337. 1,050 rooms. 3 bars, deli, patisserie, in-room modem lines, room service, 3 pools, wading pool, 2 outdoor hot tubs, massage, 4 tennis courts, health club, jogging, beach, boating, bicycles, pro shop, playground, airport shuttle, parking (fee). AE, D, DC, MC, V.*

$$$–$$$$ ☒ **Bay Club Hotel & Marina.** Rooms in this appealing low-rise Shelter Island property are large, light, and furnished with rattan tables and chairs and Polynesian tapestries; all have refrigerators and views of either the bay or the marina from outside terraces. A buffet breakfast and limo service to the airport or Amtrak are included in the room rate. ☒ *2131 Shelter Island Dr., 92106,* ☎ *619/224–8888 or 800/672–0800,* FAX *619/225–1604. 95 rooms, 10 suites. Restaurant, bar, room service, pool, outdoor hot tub, exercise room, bicycles, concierge, business services, meeting rooms, free parking. AE, D, DC, MC, V.*

$$$–$$$$ ☒ **Travelodge Hotel Harbor Island.** Lodgers here get the views and amenities of more expensive hotels, with such perks as in-room coffeemakers and free local phone calls. The Waterfront Cafe & Club overlooks the marina, and (Gen-Xers take note) actress/singer Florence Henderson has been known to pull her boat into a slip here and join in the karaoke evenings on Friday and Saturday nights. ☒ *1960 Harbor Island Dr., 92101,* ☎ *619/291–6700 or 800/578–7878 for central reservations,* FAX *619/293–0694. 201 rooms, 6 suites. Restaurant, bar, in-room modem lines, pool, outdoor hot tub, exercise room, jogging, shops, laundry service, meeting rooms, airport shuttle, free parking. AE, D, DC, MC, V.*

$$–$$$$ ☒ **Humphrey's Half Moon Inn.** This sprawling South Seas–style resort has grassy open areas with palm trees and tiki torches. Rooms, some with kitchens and some with harbor or marine views, have modern furnishings. The hotel hosts outdoor jazz concerts from June to October. ☒ *2303 Shelter Island Dr., 92106,* ☎ *619/224–3411 or 800/345–9995 for reservations,* FAX *619/224–3478. 128 rooms, 54 suites. Restaurant, bar, in-room modem lines, room service, pool, hot tub, putting green, croquet, Ping-Pong, boating, bicycles, airport and Amtrak shuttle, coin laundry, business services, meeting rooms, free parking. AE, D, DC, MC, V.*

$$–$$$$ ☒ **Kona Kai Continental Plaza Resort and Marina.** Though the Kona Kai name may suggest a Polynesian theme, this 11-acre property has been refurbished in a mixture of Mexican and Mediterranean styles.

The spacious and light-filled lobby, with its Maya sculptures and terra-cotta tiles, opens onto a lush esplanade that overlooks the hotel's marina. The rooms are well appointed, if a bit small, and most look out onto either the marina or San Diego Bay. ⊠ *1551 Shelter Island Dr., 92106,* ☎ *619/221–8000 or 800/566–2524,* 𝔽𝔸𝕏 *619/221–5953. 168 rooms, 38 suites. Restaurant, bar, room service, 2 pools, 2 hot tubs, 2 saunas, 2 tennis courts, jogging, health club, volleyball, beach, airport and Amtrak shuttle, free parking. AE, D, DC, MC, V.*

$$–$$$ 🏨 **Best Western Island Palms Hotel & Marina.** Standard accommodations at this waterfront inn are fairly small; if you're traveling with family or more than one friend, the two-bedroom suite with an eat-in kitchen is a good deal. ⊠ *2051 Shelter Island Dr., 92106,* ☎ *619/222–0561 or 800/922–2336,* 𝔽𝔸𝕏 *619/222–9760. 68 rooms, 29 suites. Restaurant, bar, in-room modem lines, pool, outdoor hot tub, business services, meeting rooms, free parking. AE, D, DC, MC, V.*

$–$$ 🏨 **Best Western Posada Inn.** Many of the rooms at this comfortable if plain inn have harbor views. Point Loma's seafood restaurants are within walking distance. ⊠ *5005 N. Harbor Dr., 92106,* ☎ *619/224–3254 or 800/231–3811,* 𝔽𝔸𝕏 *619/224–2186. 112 rooms. Pool, outdoor hot tub, exercise room, airport shuttle, free parking. AE, D, DC, MC, V.*

$ 🏨 **Outrigger Motel.** A short walk along the bay from the Outrigger leads to Harbor and Shelter islands. Some rooms show signs of wear (such as water stains on the bathroom wallpaper), but the operators' gradual upgrade of the premises will bring new carpeting and kitchen appliances. Pets are permitted ($25 fee). ⊠ *1370 Scott St., 92106,* ☎ *619/223–7105 or 800/232–1212,* 𝔽𝔸𝕏 *619/223–8672. 36 rooms. Kitchens, pool, laundry service, free parking. AE, D, DC, MC, V.*

$ 🏨 **Ramada Limited Point Loma.** Recent renovations make this motel nicer than its next door neighbor the Outrigger, but there are no kitchen units. The location is convenient, though on a busy street, and the rooms with bay views are quite a deal. This establishment serves complimentary Continental breakfast and has a heated pool and a bayview bar with billiards. ⊠ *1403 Rosecrans St., 92106,* ☎ *619/225–9461,* 𝔽𝔸𝕏 *619/225–1163. 86 rooms. Bar, breakfast room, pool, free parking. AE, D, DC, MC, V.*

$ 🏨 **Travelodge Point Loma.** For far less money, you'll get the same view here as at the higher-priced hotels. Of course, there are fewer amenities and the neighborhood (near the navy base) isn't as serene, but the rooms—all with coffeemakers—are adequate and clean. ⊠ *5102 N. Harbor Dr., 92106,* ☎ *619/223–8171 or 800/578–7878 for central reservations,* 𝔽𝔸𝕏 *619/222–7330. 45 rooms. Pool, free parking. AE, D, DC, MC, V.*

Hotel Circle, Mission Valley, and Old Town

$$$–$$$$ 🏨 **Doubletree Hotel San Diego Mission Valley.** Public areas at this hotel are light-filled and comfortable. Spacious rooms decorated in contemporary pastels have ample desk space and built-in modem hook-ups on every phone; complimentary coffee and irons and boards are also provided. ⊠ *7450 Hazard Center Dr., 92108,* ☎ *619/297–5466 or 800/547–8010 for central reservations,* 𝔽𝔸𝕏 *619/297–5499. 294 rooms, 6 suites. Restaurant, 2 bars, in-room modem lines, room service, 2 pools, outdoor hot tub, sauna, 2 tennis courts, shops, nightclub, business services, convention center, airport shuttle, free parking. AE, D, DC, MC, V.*

$$$–$$$$ 🏨 **San Diego Marriott Mission Valley.** This high-rise hotel is well equipped
★   for business travelers—the front desk provides 24-hour fax and photocopy services, and rooms come with desks, computer modem hook-ups, and private voice mail—but the Marriott also caters to vacationers with

comfortable rooms (with individual balconies), a friendly staff, and free transportation to the nearby malls. ⌧ *8757 Rio San Diego Dr., 92108,* ☎ *619/692–3800 or 800/228–9290 for central reservations,* FAX *619/ 692–0769. 347 rooms, 6 suites. Restaurant, sports bar, in-room modem lines, room service, pool, outdoor hot tub, sauna, tennis court, exercise room, coin laundry, business services, free parking. AE, D, DC, MC, V.*

$$$–$$$$ ⊞ **San Diego Mission Valley Hilton.** Directly fronting I–8, this property has soundproof rooms decorated in a colorful contemporary style. The stylish public areas and lush greenery in the back will make you forget this hotel's proximity to the freeway. Although geared toward business travelers—the hotel has a business center and guests are allowed complimentary use of an IBM personal computer—children stay free, and small pets are accepted ($25). ⌧ *901 Camino del Rio S, 92108,* ☎ *619/543–9000, 800/733–2332, or 800/445–8667;* FAX *619/543–9358. 342 rooms, 8 suites. Restaurant, bar, sports bar, in-room modem lines, pool, outdoor hot tub, exercise room, free parking. AE, D, DC, MC, V.*

$$–$$$$ ⊞ **Heritage Park Bed & Breakfast Inn.** The beautifully restored man-
★ sions in Old Town's Heritage Park include this romantic 1889 Queen Anne. Rooms range from smallish to ample, and most are bright and cheery. A two-bedroom suite is decorated with period antiques. Breakfast and afternoon tea are included in the room rate. ⌧ *2470 Heritage Park Row, 92110,* ☎ *619/299–6832 or 800/995–2470,* FAX *619/299– 9465. 10 rooms, 1 suite. In-room modem lines. AE, MC, V.*

$$–$$$ ⊞ **Best Western Hacienda Hotel Old Town.** Pretty and white, with balconies and Spanish-tile roofs, the Hacienda is in a quiet part of Old Town, away from the freeway and the main retail bustle. Accommodations are not large enough to earn the "suite" label the hotel gives them, but they're decorated in tasteful southwestern style and equipped with microwaves, coffeemakers, minirefrigerators, clock radios, and VCRs. ⌧ *4041 Harney St., 92110,* ☎ *619/298–4707 or 800/888– 1991,* FAX *619/298–4771. 159 rooms. Restaurant, bar, refrigerators, pool, outdoor hot tub, exercise room, concierge, free parking. AE, D, DC, MC, V.*

$$–$$$ ⊞ **Best Western Hanalei Hotel.** As its name suggests, the theme of this friendly Hotel Circle property is Hawaiian: Palm trees, waterfalls, koi ponds, and tiki torches abound. Rooms are decorated in tropical prints. Free transportation is provided to local malls and Old Town. The hotel is virtually surrounded by heavy traffic, which can make for a noisy stay. ⌧ *2270 Hotel Circle N, 92108,* ☎ *619/297–1101 or 800/ 882–0858,* FAX *619/297–6049. 416 rooms. 2 restaurants, bar, in-room modem lines, pool, hot tub, free parking. AE, D, DC, MC, V.*

$$–$$$ ⊞ **Ramada Plaza Hotel Old Town.** The hacienda-style Ramada has Spanish colonial–style fountains, courtyards, and painted tiles, and southwestern decor in the rooms. Breakfast, a cocktail reception, and transfers to the airport, bus, and Amtrak are all complimentary. Business-class rooms have modem lines and other amenities. ⌧ *2435 Jefferson St., 92110,* ☎ *619/260–8500 or 800/272–6232 for central reservations,* FAX *619/297– 2078. 152 rooms. Restaurant, pool, outdoor hot tub, exercise room, airport and Amtrak shuttle, free parking. AE, D, DC, MC, V.*

$–$$ ⊞ **Days Inn Hotel Circle.** Rooms in this large complex are par for a chain motel but have the bonus of Nintendo for the kids and irons and boards; some units also have kitchenettes. Airport, Amtrak, zoo, and Sea World shuttles are provided. ⌧ *543 Hotel Circle S, 92108,* ☎ *619/ 297–8800, 800/227–4743 on weekdays 8–4:30, 800/325–2525 for central reservations;* FAX *619/298–6029. 280 rooms. Restaurant, refrigerators, pool, hot tub, barbershop, beauty salon, coin laundry, airport and Amtrak shuttle, free parking. AE, D, DC, MC, V.*

$–$$ 🏨 **Vacation Inn.** Already an excellent value for Old Town, this cheer-
  ★   ful property further pleases its guests by throwing in such perks as garage
parking, Continental breakfast, and afternoon snacks. You'll find all
of today's conveniences—coffeemakers, microwave ovens, and refrigerators—but rustic colors and reproduction furnishings lend rooms an
old-country-inn feel. Families and tourists will appreciate the proximity
to Old Town attractions and restaurants, along with the heated pool
off the shaded courtyard. ✉ *3900 Old Town Ave.,* ☎ *619/299–7400
or 800/451–9846,* ℻ *619/299–1619. 125 rooms. In-room modem lines,
refrigerators, pool, outdoor hot tub, coin laundry, business services,
meeting rooms, airport shuttle, free parking. AE, D, DC, MC, V.*

La Jolla

$$$$ 🏨 **Sheraton Grande Torrey Pines.** The view of the Pacific from this low-
  ★   rise, high-class property atop the Torrey Pines cliffs is superb. Amenities include complimentary butler service and free town-car service to
La Jolla and Del Mar. The oversize accommodations are simple but
elegant; most have balconies or terraces. In addition to easy access to
the Torrey Pines course, guests also have privileges ($7.50) next door
at the fine health club–sports center at the Scripps Clinic. The fare at
the hotel's spiffy-chic Torreyana Grille changes with seasons. ✉ *10950
N. Torrey Pines Rd., 92037,* ☎ *619/558–1500 or 800/325–3535 for
central reservations,* ℻ *619/450–4584. 392 rooms, 17 suites. Restaurant, 2 bars, in-room modem lines, in-room safes, minibars, room service, pool, outdoor hot tub, sauna, 2 tennis courts, exercise room, putting
green, aerobics, croquet, volleyball, bicycles, concierge, business services, meeting rooms, parking (fee). AE, D, DC, MC, V.*

$$$–$$$$ 🏨 **Hyatt Regency La Jolla.** The Hyatt is in La Jolla's Golden Triangle,
  ★   about 10 minutes from the beach and the village. The postmodern de-
sign elements of the striking lobby continue in the spacious rooms, where
warm cherry-wood furnishings contrast with austere grey closets.
Fluffy down comforters and cushy chairs and couches make you feel
right at home, though, and business travelers will appreciate the end-
less array of office and in-room services. The hotel's four trendy restau-
rants include Cafe Japengo (☞ *Dining, above*). ✉ *Aventine Center, 3777
La Jolla Village Dr., 92122,* ☎ *619/552–1234 or 800/233–1234 for
central reservations,* ℻ *619/552–6066. 400 rooms, 25 suites. 4 restau-
rants, bar, pool, outdoor hot tub, beauty salon, massage, 2 tennis
courts, aerobics, basketball, health club, jogging, business services, meet-
ing rooms, parking (fee). AE, D, DC, MC, V.*

$$$–$$$$ 🏨 **La Valencia.** This pink Spanish-Mediterranean confection drew film
  ★   stars down from Hollywood in the 1930s and '40s for its setting and
views of La Jolla Cove. Many rooms have a genteel European look,
with antique pieces and richly colored rugs. The personal attention pro-
vided by the staff, as well as in-room features such as plush robes and
grand bathrooms, make the stay even more pleasurable. The hotel is
near the shops and restaurants of La Jolla Village and what is arguably
the prettiest beach in San Diego. Rates are lower if you're willing to
look out on the village. ✉ *1132 Prospect St., 92037,* ☎ *619/454–0771
or 800/451–0772,* ℻ *619/456–3921. 100 rooms. 3 restaurants, bar,
pool, outdoor hot tub, health club, shuffleboard, business services, meet-
ing rooms, parking (fee). AE, D, DC, MC, V.*

$$$–$$$$ 🏨 **Scripps Inn.** Kitchen facilities and lower weekly and monthly rates
(not available in summer) make this inn attractive to long-term guests.
All accommodations have ocean views and minirefrigerators, and two
have fireplaces. Continental breakfast (included in the room rate) is
served in the lobby each morning. ✉ *555 S. Coast Blvd.,* ☎ *619/454–
3391,* ℻ *619/456–0389. 13 rooms. AE, D, MC, V.*

$$$–$$$$ 🏨 **Sea Lodge.** This low-lying compound on La Jolla Shores beach has a Spanish flavor. Rooms, a few with kitchenettes, have rattan furniture and floral-print bedspreads; all have hair dryers, coffeemakers, irons, and wooden balconies that overlook lush landscaping and the sea. ✉ *8110 Camino del Oro, 92037,* ☎ *619/459–8271 or 800/237–5211,* FAX *619/456–9346. 128 rooms. Restaurant, bar, in-room modem lines, room service, pool, outdoor hot tub, sauna, 2 tennis courts, exercise room, Ping-Pong, beach, coin laundry, business services, meeting rooms, free parking. AE, D, DC, MC, V.*

$$–$$$$ 🏨 **Bed & Breakfast Inn at La Jolla.** Noted architect Irving Gill designed this B&B in a quiet section of La Jolla across the street from the Museum of Contemporary Art and one block from the beach. Rooms are of various sizes and styles—some are done in Laura Ashley prints, others have wicker or rattan furnishings—but all are pretty. Nice touches include complimentary full breakfast and fresh fruit, sherry, and terry robes. ✉ *7753 Draper Ave., 92037,* ☎ *619/456–2066 or 800/582–2466,* FAX *619/456–1510. 16 rooms, 15 with bath. MC, V.*

$$–$$$$ 🏨 **Colonial Inn.** A tastefully restored Victorian-era building, this is the oldest hotel in La Jolla. In keeping with the period, rooms are formal (some could use new carpets and furniture coverings). Ocean views cost more than village views. The inn is on one of La Jolla's main thoroughfares, near boutiques, restaurants, and La Jolla Cove. ✉ *910 Prospect St., 92037,* ☎ *619/454–2181 or 800/832–5525; 800/826–1278 in CA;* FAX *619/454–5679. 74 rooms. Restaurant, bar, refrigerators, pool, business services, meeting rooms, parking (fee). AE, DC, MC, V.*

$$–$$$$ 🏨 **La Jolla Cove Suites.** It may lack the charm of some of the older properties of this exclusive area, but this motel with studios and suites (some with spacious oceanfront balconies) gives its guests the same first-class views of La Jolla Cove at much lower rates. Snorkelers and divers can take advantage of lockers and outdoor showers. A Continental breakfast is served in the sunroom. The free underground lot is also a bonus in a section of town where a parking spot is a prime commodity. ✉ *1155 S. Coast Blvd., 92037,* ☎ *619/459–2621 or 800/248–2683,* FAX *619/454–3522. 96 rooms. Kitchenettes, pool, hot tub, putting green, coin laundry, business services, meeting rooms, free parking. AE, D, DC, MC, V.*

$$–$$$$
★ 🏨 **Prospect Park Inn.** One block from the beach and near some of the best shops and restaurants, this European-style inn with a delightful staff sits in a prime spot in La Jolla Village. Many rooms, some with kitchenettes, have sweeping ocean views from their balconies. A delicious Continental breakfast is included in the room rates. There is no smoking on the premises. ✉ *1110 Prospect St., 92037,* ☎ *619/454–0133 or 800/433–1609,* FAX *619/454–2056. 20 rooms, 2 suites. In-room modem lines, library, business services, free parking. AE, D, DC, MC, V.*

$$–$$$ 🏨 **Best Western Inn by the Sea.** In a quiet section of La Jolla Village, within five blocks of the beach, the five-story Inn by the Sea has all the modern amenities at reasonable rates for La Jolla. Rooms are done in pastel tones and have private balconies with views of either the sea or the village. Continental breakfast, the morning newspaper, and La Jolla phone calls are on the house. ✉ *7830 Fay Ave., 92037,* ☎ *619/459–4461 or 800/462–9732; 800/526–4545 in CA and Canada;* FAX *619/456–2578. 150 rooms. In-room modem lines, pool, outdoor hot tub, coin laundry, business services, meeting rooms, free parking. AE, D, DC, MC, V.*

$$ 🏨 **Holiday Inn Express.** Many rooms at this modest property in the southern section of La Jolla are remarkably large, with huge closets; some have kitchenettes, and three suites have separate eat-in kitchens. The decor is nothing to write home about, but this is a good value for families who want to stay in La Jolla and still have a few dollars left over for shopping and dining. Complimentary Continental breakfast is included in the room rates. ✉ *6705 La Jolla Blvd., 92037,* ☎ *619/454–7101 or 800/ 451–0358,* FAX *619/454–6957. 58 rooms, 3 suites. Pool, outdoor hot tub, billiards, coin laundry, free parking. AE, D, DC, MC, V.*

$$ 🏨 **Lodge at Torrey Pines.** On a bluff between La Jolla and Del Mar,
★   the lodge commands a view of miles and miles of coastline. The public Torrey Pines Golf Course is adjacent, and scenic Torrey Pines State Beach and nature reserve are close by; the village of La Jolla is a 10-minute drive away. Most rooms have dark wood furnishings and contemporary fabrics. One drawback: The building is old; walls between units are thin, and the plumbing can be noisy. Still, the service here is excellent and the lodge is a good value, especially for golfers. ✉ *11480 N. Torrey Pines Rd., 92037,* ☎ *619/453–4420 or 800/995–4507,* FAX *619/453–0691. 74 rooms. 2 restaurants, bar, coffee shop, lobby lounge, pool, golf privileges, free parking. AE, D, DC, MC, V.*

Mission Bay and the Beaches

$$$–$$$$ 🏨 **Catamaran Resort Hotel.** Tiki torches light the way for guests stay-
★   ing at one of the six two-story buildings or the 14-story high-rise. The room decor—dark wicker furniture and tropical prints—echoes the Polynesian theme. The popular Cannibal Bar hosts rock bands; a classical or jazz pianist tickles the ivories at the Moray Bar. Though the Catamaran is couples-oriented, children 18 or under stay free. ✉ *3999 Mission Blvd., 92109,* ☎ *619/488–1081 or 800/288–0770, 800/233–8172 in Canada;* FAX *619/488–1387 for reservations, 619/488–1619 for front desk. 320 rooms. Restaurant, bar, piano bar, pool, hot tub, exercise room, nightclub, bicycles, parking (fee). AE, D, DC, MC, V.*

$$$–$$$$ 🏨 **Crystal Pier Motel.** A landmark since the 1930s, this place is no longer the bargain it once was, nor does it have the amenities of the other properties in its price category. You're paying for character and proximity to the ocean—the blue-and-white cottages here are literally on the pier. The units sleep up to four but cost the same no matter what the occupancy. Call four to six weeks in advance for reservations. The minimum stay permitted is three nights from mid-June through mid-September, two nights the rest of the year. ✉ *4500 Ocean Blvd.,* ☎ *619/483–6983 or 800/748–5894,* FAX *619/483–6811. 29 cottages. Kitchenettes, free parking. D, MC, V.*

$$$–$$$$ 🏨 **San Diego Hilton Beach and Tennis Resort.** Trees, Japanese bridges, and ponds surround the bungalow accommodations at this deluxe resort; rooms and suites in a high-rise building have views of Mission Bay Park. Most of the well-appointed rooms have wet bars, spacious bathrooms, and patios or terraces. ✉ *1775 E. Mission Bay Dr., 92109,* ☎ *619/276–4010 or 800/445–8667 for central reservations,* FAX *619/ 275–7991. 337 rooms, 20 suites. 2 restaurants, bar, coffee shop, in-room modem lines, pool, wading pool, 2 hot tubs, 4 putting greens, 5 tennis courts, exercise room, boating, bicycles, playground, car rental, free parking. AE, D, DC, MC, V.*

$$$–$$$$ 🏨 **San Diego Princess Resort.** This 44-acre resort is so beautifully landscaped that it's been the setting for a number of movies, and it provides a wide range of recreational activities as well as access to a marina. Bright fabrics and plush carpets make for a cheery ambience; unfortunately, the walls here are motel-thin. All rooms have private patios and coffeemakers, and a number have kitchens. Of the resort's various eateries, the Barefoot Bar and Grill is the most fun; guests and visitors come here to kick off their shoes and boogie in a sand-filled, strobe-lit setting. ✉ *1404 W. Vacation Rd., 92109,* ☎ *619/274–4630 or 800/344–2626,* FAX *619/581–5929. 462 cottages. 3 restaurants, 2 bars, room service, 5 pools, outdoor hot tub, sauna, 19-hole putting* *golf course, 6 tennis courts, croquet, health club, jogging, volleyball, boating, bicycles, free parking. AE, D, DC, MC, V.*

$$$ 🔳 **Bahia Hotel.** This huge complex on a 14-acre peninsula in Mission Bay Park has furnished studios and suites with kitchens; many have wood-beam ceilings and tropical decor. Rates are reasonable for a place so well located—within walking distance of the ocean—and with so many amenities, including use of the facilities at the Catamaran Hotel. ✉ *998 W. Mission Bay Dr., 92109, ☎ 619/488–0551 or 800/288–0770; 800/233–8172 in Canada; FAX 619/488–7055 or 619/ 488–1387 for reservations. 321 rooms. Restaurant, bar, piano bar, pool, outdoor hot tub, 2 tennis courts, bicycles, rollerblading, free parking. AE, D, DC, MC, V.*

$$$ 🔳 **Best Western Blue Sea Lodge.** Many of the rooms at this Pacific Beach low-rise have balconies and ocean views; some have kitchenettes. A shopping center with restaurants and boutiques is nearby. ✉ *707 Pacific Beach Dr., 92109, ☎ 619/488–4700 or 800/258–3732, FAX 619/488–7276. 100 rooms. In-room safes, pool, hot tub. AE, D, DC, MC, V.*

$$$ 🔳 **Hyatt Islandia.** Its location in appealing Mission Bay Park is one of the many pluses of this property, which has rooms in several low-level lanai-style units, as well as marina suites and rooms in a high-rise building. Many of the modern accommodations overlook the hotel's gardens and koi fish pond; others have dramatic views of the bay area. This hotel is famous for its lavish Sunday champagne brunch. ✉ *1441 Quivira Rd., 92109, ☎ 619/224–1234 or 800/233–1234 for central reservations, FAX 619/224–0348. 346 rooms, 76 suites. 2 restaurants, in-room modem lines, pool, outdoor hot tub, exercise room, marina, boating, laundry service, meeting rooms, free parking. AE, D, DC, MC, V.*

$$–$$$ 🔳 **Dana Inn & Marina.** This hotel with an adjoining marina is a bargain. Recent renovations have improved the rooms with bright pastels, and the new lobby includes a fun aquarium. High ceilings in the second-floor rooms give a welcome sense of space, and some even have a view of the inn's marina. Many sports facilities are on the premises, and Sea World and the beach are within walking distance. ✉ *1710 W. Mission Bay Dr., 92109, ☎ 619/222–6440 or 800/445–3339, FAX 619/222–5916. 196 rooms. Restaurant, bar, room service, pool, outdoor hot tub, 2 tennis courts, Ping-Pong, shuffleboard, boating, bicycles, coin laundry, business services, free parking. AE, D, DC, MC, V.*

$$ 🔳 **Pacific Shores Inn.** Rooms at this property less than a half block from the beach are decorated in a simple contemporary style. Kitchen units with multiple beds are available at reasonable rates; your pet (under 20 lbs.) can stay for an extra $25. Continental breakfast is included in the room rate, and all rooms have minirefrigerators. ✉ *4802 Mission Blvd., 92109, ☎ 619/483–6300 or 800/826–0715, FAX 619/483– 9276. 55 rooms. Refrigerators, pool, coin laundry, free parking. AE, D, DC, MC, V.*

$–$$ 🔳 **Mission Bay Motel.** A half block from the beach and right on the local main street, this motel has modest units, some with kitchenettes. Great restaurants and nightlife are within walking distance, but you may find the area a bit noisy. ✉ *4221 Mission Blvd., 92109, ☎ 619/ 483–6440. 50 rooms. Pool, free parking. D, MC, V.*

$–$$ 🔳 **Ocean Manor Apartment Hotel.** Some folks have been returning for years to this Sunset Cliffs hotel, which rents units by the day (three-day minimum for ones with kitchens), week, or month in winter; you'll need to reserve well in advance. The comfortable studios and one- and two-bedroom suites are furnished plainly in the style of the 1950s. There is no maid service, but fresh towels are always provided. ✉ *1370 Sunset Cliffs Blvd., 92107, ☎ 619/222–7901 or 619/224– 1379 for guest calls. 25 units. Pool, Ping-Pong, shuffleboard, free parking. MC, V.*

Hostels

HI–The Metropolitan Hostel–Downtown San Diego (✉ 521 Market St., San Diego 92101, ☎ 619/525–1531 or 800/909–4776, code #43, FAX 619/338–0129).
HI–Point Loma Hostel (✉ 3790 Udall St., San Diego 92107, ☎ 619/ 223–4778).
Ocean Beach International Backpacker Hostel (✉ 4961 Newport Ave., 92107, ☎ 619/223–7873 or 800/339–7263, FAX 619/223–7881).

NIGHTLIFE AND THE ARTS

Updated by
Kate Deely

Check the daily *San Diego Union-Tribune,* the weekly *Reader,* or *San Diego* magazine's "Restaurant & Nightlife Guide" for arts and after-dark possibilities.

Nightlife

Music at local pop-music clubs ranges from easy-on-the-ears rock to alternative fare from San Diego's finest up-and-coming groups. Dance clubs and bars in the Gaslamp Quarter and at Pacific and Mission beaches tend to be the most crowded spots in the county on the weekends, but don't let that discourage you from visiting these quintessential San Diego hangouts. Authentic country-western music is also an option for those willing to go a bit farther afield. Should your tastes run to softer music, there are plenty of piano bars in which to unfrazzle and unwind. The coffeehouse culture here has become so lively that java joints, especially those along Hillcrest's Coffeehouse Row and scattered along the beach communities, have become legitimate nightlife destinations in themselves.

California law prohibits the sale of alcoholic beverages after 2 AM; last call is usually at about 1:40. You must be 21 to purchase and consume alcohol, and most places will insist on current identification. Be aware that California also has some of the most stringent drunk-driving laws in the United States; roadblocks are not an uncommon sight.

Rock, Pop, Folk, Reggae, and Blues
Belly Up Tavern (✉ 143 S. Cedros Ave., Solana Beach, ☎ 760/481–9022), an eclectic live-concert venue, hosts critically acclaimed artists who play everything from reggae, rock, new wave, Motown, and other music.
Blind Melons (✉ 710 Garnet Ave., Pacific Beach, ☎ 619/483–7844) is frequented by the local beach and college crowd. This bustling bar features rock, blues, and reggae bands every night of the week.
Bodie's (✉ 528 F St., Gaslamp Quarter, ☎ 619/236–8988) presents the best rock and blues bands in San Diego, as well as up-and-coming bands from out of town.
Brick by Brick (✉ 1130 Buenos Ave., Bay Park, near Mission Bay, ☎ 619/275–5483) is always abuzz with the music of San Diego's top alternative and experimental rock groups.
Casbah (✉ 2501 Kettner Blvd., near the airport, ☎ 619/232–4355), a small club, showcases rock, reggae, funk, and every other kind of band—except Top 40.
Livewire (✉ 2103 El Cajon Blvd., North Park, ☎ 619/291–7450), an underground twenty-something hole-in-the-wall, has plenty of character; there are usually more tattoos and pierced body parts than people.
Patrick's II (✉ 428 F St., downtown, ☎ 619/233–3077) serves up live New Orleans–style jazz, blues, and rock in an Irish setting.
Winston's Beach Club (✉ 1921 Bacon St., Ocean Beach, ☎ 619/222–6822), a bowling alley turned rock club, hosts local bands, reggae groups,

and occasionally '60s rockers bands. The crowd, mostly locals, can get rowdy.

Jazz

Croce's (✉ 802 5th Ave., Gaslamp Quarter, ☎ 619/233–4355), the intimate jazz cave of restaurateur Ingrid Croce (singer-songwriter Jim Croce's widow), books superb acoustic-jazz musicians. Next door, Croce's Top Hat puts on live R&B nightly from 9 until 2.

Elario's (✉ 7955 La Jolla Shores Dr., La Jolla, ☎ 619/459–0541), perched on the top floor of the Summer House Inn, delivers an ocean view and a lineup of internationally acclaimed jazz musicians.

Humphrey's by the Bay (✉ 2241 Shelter Island Dr., Shelter Island, ☎ 619/523–1010 for concert information), surrounded by water, is the summer stomping grounds for musical legends such as Harry Belafonte and Three Dog Night. From June to September, this dining and drinking oasis hosts the city's best outdoor jazz, folk, and light-rock concert series. The rest of the year the music moves indoors to Humphrey's Lounge.

Pal Joey's (✉ 5147 Waring Rd., Allied Gardens, near San Diego State University, ☎ 619/286–7873) is a smoky neighborhood bar with a loyal clientele that enjoys dancing Friday and Saturday nights to authentic jazz and blues with a lot of soul.

Country-Western

In Cahootz (✉ 5373 Mission Center Rd., Mission Valley, ☎ 619/291–8635), with its great sound system, large dance floor, and occasional big-name performers, is the destination of choice for cowgirls and -boys and city slickers alike.

Zoo Country (✉ 1340 Broadway, El Cajon, ☎ 619/442–9900) attracts herds of line-dancin', two-steppin' cowpersons. There is live music Friday through Sunday and a DJ seven nights a week.

Dance Clubs

Club Emerald City (✉ 945 Garnet Ave., Pacific Beach, ☎ 619/483–9920) attracts an uninhibited clientele for loud alternative dance music. This beach-town spot is unpredictable and worth a visit for the adventurous.

Green Circle Bar (✉ 827 F St., Gaslamp Quarter, ☎ 619/232–8080) is frequented by a mostly under-30 Euro-type crowd that grooves to anything from acid jazz to blues and soul. Live bands perform on Wednesday and Thursday nights.

Johnny M's (✉ 801 4th St., Gaslamp Quarter, ☎ 619/233–1131) patrons get down and boogie to '70s and '80s dance music at this huge disco. A blues room is open Wednesday, Friday, and Saturday from 10 PM to 1:30 AM.

Taxxi (✉ 1025 Prospect St., La Jolla, ☎ 619/551–5230) is for serious nightclubbers. On the busy bar and restaurant strand in La Jolla, this dance club lures Hollywood club-types who dance to disco, funk, and house music.

Bars and Nightclubs

Aero Club (✉ 3365 India St., Middletown, ☎ 619/297–7211), a neighborhood bar, has friendly bartenders and a first-rate selection of beer.

Bitter End (✉ 770 5th Ave., Gaslamp Quarter, ☎ 619/338–9300) is a sophisticated martini bar (above) and a hip dance club (below). With its variety of beverage, music, and atmosphere, this dual-level hot spot in the heart of downtown will please the most finicky of cosmopolitans.

Blue Tattoo (✉ 835 5th Ave., Gaslamp Quarter, ☎ 619/238–7191) is a popular destination for San Diego's young professionals. A strict dress code is enforced (no jeans, T-shirts, hats, sweat shirts, or tennis shoes) on Friday and Saturday nights. Entertainment varies nightly.

Club 66 (✉ 901 5th Ave., downtown, ☎ 619/234–4166), under the restaurant Dakota's, takes the old Route 66 as its inspiration, with stainless-steel decor and gas-station memorabilia. Dance to disco, high energy, and Top 40.

E Street Alley (✉ 919 4th Ave., downtown, ☎ 619/231–9200) is a treat for the senses. The Blue Room, with its scattered plush couches and pool tables, serves up live jazz on Thursday and blues the rest of the week. Club E is a smartly designed, spacious dance club with a DJ spinning Top 40 tunes. Chino's is an exquisite restaurant featuring American cuisine with a Southeast Asian flair. The club is on E Street between 4th and 5th avenues.

Hurricane's Bar and Grill (✉ 315 Ocean Front Walk, Mission Beach, ☎ 619/488–1870) has taken Mission Beach by storm. Noise from the waterfront property carries all the way to the breaking waves as talented rock bands perform nightly for a lively crowd.

Jimmy Love's (✉ 672 5th Ave., Gaslamp Quarter, ☎ 619/595–0123) combines a dance club, a sports bar, and a restaurant all into one venue. Rock and jazz bands alternate for nightly entertainment.

Moose McGillycuddy's (✉ 1165 Garnet Ave., Pacific Beach, ☎ 619/274–2323), a major pick-up–palace, is also a great place to go with friends or hang out with the locals. Fun music powers the dance floor, and the staff serves up drinks and Mexican food.

O'Hungrys (✉ 2547 San Diego Ave., Old Town, ☎ 619/298–0133) is famous for its yard-long beers and barwide sing-alongs. Be sure to drink up quickly though—this landmark saloon closes at midnight.

Pacific Beach Bar and Grill (✉ 860 Garnet Ave., Pacific Beach, ☎ 619/272–4745) has a huge outdoor patio so you can enjoy star-filled skies as you party with locals and visitors. There is plenty to see and do, from billiards and satellite sports to an interactive trivia game.

Piano Bars/Mellow

Hotel Del Coronado (✉ 1500 Orange Ave., Coronado, ☎ 619/435–6611) has piano music in its Crown Room and Palm Court. The Ocean Terrace Lounge has live bands nightly from 9 PM to 1 AM.

Top O' the Cove (✉ 1216 Prospect St., La Jolla, ☎ 619/454–7779) pianists play show tunes and standards from the '40s to the '80s at this magnificent Continental restaurant.

Westgate Hotel (✉ 1055 2nd Ave., downtown, ☎ 619/238–1818), one of the most elegant settings in San Diego, has piano music in the Plaza Bar.

Comedy and Cabaret

Comedy Isle (✉ Bahia Hotel, 998 W. Mission Bay Dr., Mission Bay, ☎ 619/488–6872) serves up the latest laughs from local and national talent.

Comedy Store (✉ 916 Pearl St., La Jolla, ☎ 619/454–9176), just like its sister establishment in Hollywood, hosts some of the best national touring and local talent.

Tidbits (✉ 3838 5th Ave., Hillcrest, ☎ 619/543–0300) showcases the best of southern California's female impersonators in hilarious nightly cabaret and comedy "tidbits," with charity benefit shows on Sunday.

Singles Bars

Barefoot Bar and Grill (✉ San Diego Princess Resort, 1404 W. Vacation Rd., ☎ 619/274–4630), a beachfront bar, attracts flocks of singles, especially on spring and summer Sunday nights. Live music and happy-hour specials fill the joint up early, making for long latecomer lines.

Dick's Last Resort (✉ 345 4th Ave., downtown, ☎ 619/231–9100) becomes crowded weekends, as fun-loving party people pile into the barnlike restaurant and bar.

Jose's (✉ 1037 Prospect St., La Jolla, ☎ 619/454–7655) is a hit with yuppies from La Jolla and other neighboring beach communities. This small but clean hole-in-the-wall's lack of space gives suave singles an excuse to get up close and personal.

Old Bonita Store & Bonita Beach Club (✉ 4014 Bonita Rd., Bonita, ☎ 619/479–3537), a South Bay hangout, has a DJ spinning retro house music.

U. S. Grant Hotel (✉ 326 Broadway, downtown, ☎ 619/232–3121) is the classiest spot in town for meeting fellow travelers while relaxing with a Scotch or a martini at the mahogany bar. The best local Latin, jazz, and blues bands alternate appearances.

Gay and Lesbian Nightlife

GAY MALE BARS

Bourbon Street (✉ 4612 Park Blvd., University Heights, ☎ 619/291–0173), resembling its New Orleans namesake with its relaxing surroundings and courtyard, is a piano bar with live entertainment nightly.

Brass Rail (✉ 3796 5th Ave., Hillcrest, ☎ 619/298–2233), the oldest gay bar in San Diego, hosts dancing nightly and go-go boys on the weekends.

Flicks (✉ 1017 University Ave., Hillcrest, ☎ 619/297–2056) plays music and comedy videos on four big screens. Drink specials and video formats vary each night.

Kickers (✉ 308 University Ave., Hillcrest, ☎ 619/491–0400) rounds up country-music cowboys to do the latest line dance.

Rich's San Diego (✉ 1051 University Ave., Hillcrest, ☎ 619/497–4588), a dance bar, has nightly male revues.

LESBIAN BARS

Club Bombay (✉ 3175 India St., Middletown, ☎ 619/296–6789) occasionally has live entertainment and always attracts a dancing crowd. It also hosts Sunday barbecues.

The Flame (✉ 3780 Park Blvd., Hillcrest, ☎ 619/295–4163), a San Diego institution, is a friendly dance club that caters to lesbians most of the week. On Tuesday, the DJ spins for the popular Boys' Night.

Coffeehouses

Brockton Villa (✉ 1235 Coast Blvd., La Jolla, ☎ 619/454–7393), a palatial café overlooking La Jolla Cove, has scrumptious desserts and coffee drinks.

Café Crema (✉ 1001 Garnet Ave., Pacific Beach, ☎ 619/273–3558) is a meeting spot for the pre- and post-bar crowd. It's easy to lose track of time here.

Euphoria (✉ 1045 University Ave., Hillcrest, ☎ 619/295–1769) has a Gen-X feel. For many people, it's a great alternative to bar-hopping.

Gelato Vero (✉ 3753 India St., Middletown, ☎ 619/295–9269) attracts a youngish crowd for desserts and coffee.

Pannikin (✉ 523 University Ave., Hillcrest, ☎ 619/295–1600) has two rooms, one relatively sedate, the other more lively.

The Study (✉ 401-A University Ave., Hillcrest, ☎ 619/296–4847) attracts those who value seclusion with cubicle-like seating areas.

Twiggs Tea and Coffee Co. (✉ 4590 Park Blvd., University Heights, ☎ 619/296–0616) has outdoor seating. The adjacent green room hosts poetry readings and music.

Zanzibar Coffee Bar and Gallery (✉ 976 Garnet Ave., Pacific Beach, ☎ 619/272–4762), a cozy, dimly lit spot along Pacific Beach's main strip, is a great place to mellow out.

The Arts

Half-price tickets to most theater, music, and dance events can be bought on the day of performance at the **Times Arts Tix** (✉ Horton Plaza, ☎ 619/497–5000). Only cash is accepted. Advance full-price tickets may also be purchased through Times Arts Tix. Visa and MasterCard holders may buy tickets for many scheduled performances through **Ticketmaster** (☎ 619/220–8497).

Dance

California Ballet Company (☎ 619/560–5676 or 619/560–6741) performs high-quality contemporary and traditional works, from story ballets to Balanchine, September to May, along with an annual *Nutcracker.*

Film

On the Omnimax screen at the **Reuben H. Fleet Space Center** (✉ Balboa Park, 1875 El Prado, ☎ 619/238–1233) you'll see science, space-documentary, observation-of-motion, and sometimes psychedelic films. **Sherwood Auditorium** (✉ 700 Prospect St., La Jolla, ☎ 619/454–2594) regularly hosts foreign and classic film series and special cinema events, including the wildly popular Festival of Animation, January to March.

Music

La Jolla Chamber Music Society (☎ 619/459–3724) presents internationally acclaimed chamber ensembles, orchestras, and soloists at Sherwood Auditorium (☞ *below*) and the Civic Theatre.

Open-Air Theatre (✉ San Diego State University, ☎ 619/594–6947) presents top-name rock, reggae, and popular artists in summer concerts under the stars.

San Diego Opera (✉ Civic Theatre, 202 C St., downtown, ☎ 619/232–7636 or 619/236–6510) draws international artists. Its season of five operas runs from January to April in the 3,000-seat Civic Theatre. **Sherwood Auditorium** (✉ 700 Prospect St., La Jolla, ☎ 619/454–2594), a 550-seat venue in the Museum of Contemporary Art, hosts classical and jazz events.

Spreckels Theatre (✉ 121 Broadway, ☎ 619/235–9500), a designated-landmark theater erected more than 80 years ago, hosts musical events—everything from Mostly Mozart to small rock concerts. Ballets and theatrical productions are also held here.

Theater

Diversionary Theatre (✉ 4545 Park Blvd., University Heights, ☎ 619/220–0097) is San Diego's premier gay and lesbian company.

Gaslamp Quarter Theatre Company (✉ Hahn Cosmopolitan Theatre, 444 4th Ave., downtown, ☎ 619/234–9583) stages comedies, dramas, mysteries, and musicals at a 250-seat venue.

La Jolla Playhouse (✉ Mandell Weiss Center for the Performing Arts, University of California at San Diego, 2910 La Jolla Village Dr., ☎ 619/550–1010) crafts exciting and innovative productions, May to November, under the artistic direction of Michael Greif.

Old Globe Theatre (✉ Simon Edison Centre for the Performing Arts, Balboa Park, 1363 Old Globe Way, ☎ 619/239–2255) is the oldest professional theater in California, performing classics, contemporary dramas, and experimental works.

San Diego Repertory Theatre (✉ Lyceum, 79 Horton Plaza, ☎ 619/235–8025), San Diego's first resident acting company, performs contemporary works year-round.

Sledgehammer Theatre (✉ 1620 6th Ave., ☎ 619/544–1484), one of San Diego's cutting-edge theaters, stages avant-garde pieces in St. Cecilia's church.

The Theater in Old Town (✉ 4040 Twiggs St., Old Town, ☎ 619/688–2494) presents punchy revues and occasional classics. Shows like *Forbidden Broadway, Ruthless, Gilligan's Island*, and *Forbidden Hollywood* have made this a popular place.

Welk Resort Theatre (✉ 8860 Lawrence Welk Dr., Escondido, ☎ 760/749–3448 or 800/932–9355) puts on polished Broadway-style productions.

OUTDOOR ACTIVITIES AND SPORTS

At least one stereotype of San Diego is true—it is an active, outdoors-oriented community. People recreate more than spectate. It's hard not to, with the variety of choices available, from boccie and ballooning to golf, surfing, sailing, and volleyball.

Beaches

San Diego's beaches are among its greatest natural attractions. In some places, the shorefront is wide and sandy; in others, it's narrow and rocky or backed by impressive sandstone cliffs. You'll find beaches awhirl with activity and deserted spots for romantic sunset walks. For a surf and weather report, call 619/221–8884. For a general beach and weather report, call 619/289–1212.

Overnight camping is not allowed on any San Diego city beaches, but there are campgrounds at some state beaches throughout the county (☎ 800/444–7275 for reservations). Lifeguards are stationed at city beaches from Sunset Cliffs up to Black's Beach in the summertime, but coverage in winter is provided by roving patrols only. Dogs are permitted on most San Diego beaches and adjacent parks on leashes between 6 PM and 9 AM; they can run unleashed anytime at Dog Beach at the north end of Ocean Beach and at Rivermouth in Del Mar. It is rarely a problem, however, to bring your pet to isolated beaches during the winter.

Pay attention to signs listing illegal activities; undercover police often patrol the beaches, carrying their ticket books in coolers. Glass is prohibited on all beaches, and fires are allowed only in fire rings or elevated barbecues. Alcoholic beverages—including beer—are completely banned on some city beaches; others allow you to partake between 8 AM and 8 PM. Check out the signs posted at the parking lots and lifeguard towers before you hit the shore with a six-pack or some wine coolers. Imbibing in beach parking lots, on boardwalks, and in landscaped areas is always illegal.

The beaches below are listed from south to north, starting just above the Mexican border. Pollution, long a problem with the beaches near Mexico, has been inching northward; check the weather page of the *San Diego Union-Tribune* for up-to-the-minute pollution reports.

South Bay

Border Field State Beach. This marshy area with wide chaparrals and wildflowers is a favorite among horse riders and hikers. The beach is usually open from 9 AM to sunset, Thursday through Sunday, in summer. However, swimming is prohibited, and the beach is often closed in winter because of sewage contamination from Tijuana. Parking is plentiful, and there are rest rooms. ✉ *Exit I–5 at Dairy Mart Rd. and head west along Monument Rd.*

Imperial Beach. In July, this classic southern California beach is the site of one of the nation's largest sand-castle competitions. The surf here is often excellent, but sewage contamination can be a problem. There are summertime lifeguards, rest rooms, parking, and nearby food vendors. ⊠ *Take Palm Ave. west from I–5 until it hits water.*

Coronado

Silver Strand State Beach. This quiet Coronado beach, named for the tiny silver seashells found in abundance near the water, is ideal for families. The water is relatively calm; lifeguards and rangers are on duty year-round, and there are places to rollerblade or ride bikes. Adundant parking is available. Sites at a campground ($12–$16 per night) for self-contained RVs are available on a first-come, first-served basis. ⊠ *From San Diego–Coronado Bay Bridge, turn left onto Orange Ave., which becomes Hwy. 75, and follow signs,* ☎ *619/435–5184.* ⌨ *Parking $4, but not always collected Labor Day–Feb.*

Coronado Beach. This beach is perfect for sunbathing or games of Frisbee and Smash Ball (played with paddles and a small ball). Parking can be difficult on the busiest days, but there are plenty of rest rooms and service facilities, as well as fire rings. ⊠ *From the bridge turn left on Orange Ave. and follow signs.*

Point Loma

Sunset Cliffs. Beneath the jagged cliffs on the west side of the Point Loma peninsula is one of the more secluded beaches in the area. It's popular with surfers and locals. At the south end of the peninsula, near Cabrillo Point, tidal pools teeming with small sea creatures are revealed at low tide. Farther north, the waves lure surfers and the lonely coves attract sunbathers. Stairs at the foot of Bermuda and Santa Cruz avenues provide beach access, as do some (treacherous at points) cliff trails. There are no facilities. A visit here is more enjoyable at low tide; check the local newspaper for tide schedules. ⊠ *Take I–8 west to Sunset Cliffs Blvd. and head south.*

San Diego

Ocean Beach. Much of this mile-long beach is a haven for volleyball players, sunbathers, and swimmers. The area around the municipal pier at the south end is a hangout for surfers and transients; the pier itself is open to the public for fishing and walking and has a restaurant at the end. You'll find food vendors and fire rings; limited parking is available. Swimmers should beware of unusually vicious rip currents here. ⊠ *Take I–8 west to Sunset Cliffs Blvd. and head south. Turn right on Santa Monica Ave.*

Mission Beach. A boardwalk paralleling the beach is popular with walkers, roller skaters, bladers, and bicyclists. Surfers, swimmers, and volleyball players congregate at the south end. Toward the north end, near the Belmont Park roller coaster, the beach narrows and the water becomes rougher. The crowds grow thicker and somewhat rougher as well. Parking can be a challenge, but there are plenty of rest rooms and restaurants in the area.

Pacific Beach/North Pacific Beach. The boardwalk turns into a sidewalk here, but there are still bike paths and picnic tables along the beachfront. Pacific Beach runs from the north end of Mission Beach to Crystal Pier. North Pacific Beach extends from the pier north. The scene here is particularly lively on weekends. There are designated surfing areas, and fire rings are available. On-street parking is your best bet, or you can try the big lot at Belmont Park near the south end. ⊠ *Exit I–5 at Garnet Ave. and head west to Mission Blvd. Turn north and look for parking.*

La Jolla

The beaches of La Jolla combine unusual beauty with good fishing, scuba diving, and surfing. On the down side, they are crowded and have limited parking facilities. Don't think about bringing your pet—dogs aren't even allowed on the sidewalks above some beaches here.

Tourmaline Surfing Park. This is one of the area's most popular beaches for surfing and sailboarding year-round. Parking here is easier than at nearby Windansea Beach. ⊠ *Take Mission Blvd. north (it turns into La Jolla Blvd.) and turn west on Tourmaline St.*

Windansea Beach. The surf at Windansea—whose habitués were lampooned in Tom Wolfe's *The Pump House Gang*—is truly world-class. ⊠ *Take Mission Blvd. north (it turns into La Jolla Blvd.) and turn west on Nautilus St.*

Marine Street Beach. This is an ideal stretch of sand for sunbathing and beach games. The water is good for surfing and bodyboarding, though you'll need to watch out for riptides. ⊠ *Accessible from Marine St., off La Jolla Blvd.*

Children's Pool. For the tykes, a circular seawall preserves this shallow lagoon. Small waves and no riptide make for a safe, if crowded, haven. The pool is popular with scuba divers who explore the offshore reef when the surf is low. It's also a good place to watch marine mammals—seals and sea lions frequent the cove. ⊠ *Follow La Jolla Blvd. north. When it forks, take the left, Coast Blvd.*

Shell Beach. Just north of the Children's Pool is a small cove, accessible by stairs, with a relatively secluded beach. The exposed rocks just off the coast have been designated a protected habitat for seals. ⊠ *Continue along Coast Blvd. north from the Children's Pool.*

La Jolla Cove. This is one of the prettiest spots in the world. A palmtree-lined park sits on top of cliffs formed by the incessant pounding of the waves. At low tide the tidal pools and cliff caves provide a destination for explorers. Divers and snorkelers can explore the underwater delights of the San Diego–La Jolla Underwater Ecological Reserve. The cove is also a favorite of rough-water swimmers for whom buoys mark distances. ⊠ *Follow Coast Blvd. north to signs, or take the La Jolla Village Dr. exit from I–5, head west to Torrey Pines Rd., turn left, and drive down hill to Girard Ave. Turn right and follow signs.*

La Jolla Shores. On summer holidays, all access routes are usually closed to one of San Diego's most popular beaches. The lures here are a wide sandy beach; fun surf for boogie-boarders, bodysurfers, and regular surfers; and a concrete boardwalk paralleling the beach. Arrive early to get a parking spot. ⊠ *From I–5 take La Jolla Village Dr. west and turn left onto La Jolla Shores Dr. Head west to Camino del Oro or Vallecitos St. Turn right and look for parking.*

Black's Beach. The late-1970s prohibition against public nudity doesn't stop nudists from frequenting this public beach, officially called Torrey Pines City Park Beach. Storms have weakened the cliffs over the past few years; they're dangerous to climb and should be avoided. Access to parts of the shore coincides with low tides. The powerful waves attract surfers, and secluded trails attract nudist nature lovers. There are no lifeguards on duty, and strong ebb tides are common: Only experienced swimmers should take the plunge. ⊠ *Take Genesee Ave. west from I–5 and follow signs to Glider Port; easier access, via a paved path, available on La Jolla Farms Rd., but parking limited to 2 hrs.*

Del Mar

Torrey Pines State Beach/State Reserve. One of San Diego's best beaches contains 1,700 acres of bluffs, bird-filled marshes, and sandy shoreline. A network of trails leads through rare pine trees to the coast below. The large parking lot is rarely full. Lifeguards are on duty weekends (weather permitting) from Easter until Memorial Day, daily from then until Labor Day, and again on weekends through September. Torrey Pines tends to get crowded during the summer, but more isolated spots under the cliffs are a short walk in either direction. ⊠ *Take the Carmel Valley Rd. exit west from I–5,* ☎ *619/755–2063.* ⊞ *Parking $4.*

Del Mar Beach. The numbered streets of Del Mar, from 15th to 29th, end at a wide beach popular with volleyball players, surfers, and sunbathers. Parking can be a problem on nice summer days, but access is relatively easy. The portions of Del Mar south of 15th Street are lined with cliffs and are rarely crowded. ⊠ *Take the Via de la Valle exit from I–5 west to Old Hwy. 101 (also known as Camino del Mar in Del Mar) and turn left.*

Participant Sports

Bicycling

On any given summer day Highway S21 from La Jolla to Oceanside looks like a freeway for cyclists. Never straying more than a quarter mile from the beach, it is easily the most popular and scenic bike route around. For more leisurely rides, Mission Bay, San Diego Harbor, and the Mission Beach boardwalk are all flat and scenic. **Bicycle Barn** in Pacific Beach (⊠ 746 Emerald St., ☎ 619/581–3665) and **Hamel's Action Sports Center** in Mission Beach (⊠ 704 Ventura Pl., ☎ 619/488–5050) are among the places that rent bikes.

Diving

At La Jolla Cove, you'll find the **San Diego–La Jolla Underwater Ecological Park.** Farther north, off the south end of Black's Beach, the rim of **Scripps Canyon** lies in about 60 ft of water. The canyon plummets to more than 900 ft in some sections. Another popular diving spot is **Sunset Cliffs** in Point Loma, where the sea life and flora are relatively close to shore. Strong rip currents make it an area best enjoyed by experienced divers.

Diving equipment and boat trips can be arranged through **San Diego Divers Supply** (⊠ 4004 Sports Arena Blvd., ☎ 619/224–3439) or the **Diving Locker** (⊠ 1020 Grand Ave., Pacific Beach, ☎ 619/272–1120; ⊠ 405 N. Highway 101, Solana Beach, ☎ 619/755–6822). For recorded diving information, contact the San Diego City Lifeguards Office (☎ 619/221–8884).

Fishing

No license is required to fish from a public pier, such as the Ocean Beach pier. A fishing license from the state **Department of Fish and Game** (⊠ 4949 Viewridge Ave., San Diego 92123, ☎ 619/467–4201), available at most bait-and-tackle stores, is required for fishing from the shoreline. Children under 15 do not need a license.

Fisherman's Landing (⊠ 2838 Garrison St., Point Loma, ☎ 619/221–8500), **H&M Landing** (⊠ 2803 Emerson St., Point Loma, ☎ 619/222–1144), and **Seaforth Boat Rental** (⊠ 1641 Quivira Rd., West Mission Bay, ☎ 619/223–1681) operate from half-day to multiday fishing excursions out of San Diego.

Fitness

The **24 Hour Fitness Centers** in the area (⊠ 5885 Rancho Mission Rd., Mission Valley, ☎ 619/281–5543; ⊠ 3675 Midway Dr., Sports Arena–

Point Loma area, ☎ 619/224–2902; ✉ 4405 La Jolla Village Dr., Golden Triangle/UTC, ☎ 619/457–3930) allow nonmembers to use the facilities for a small fee.

Golf

Most public courses in the area provide an inexpensive current list of fees and charges for all San Diego courses. The following are a few of the better places to play in the area.

Courses

Coronado Municipal Golf Course (✉ 2000 Visalia Row, Coronado, ☎ 619/435–3121) has 18 holes, a driving range, equipment rentals, and a snack bar. Views of San Diego Bay and the Coronado Bridge from the back 9 holes on this good walking course make it popular—and rather difficult to get on. Greens fee: $20–$30.

Torrey Pines Municipal Golf Course (✉ 11480 N. Torrey Pines Rd., La Jolla, ☎ 619/452–3226) has 36 holes, a driving range, and equipment rentals. Torrey Pines has views of the Pacific from every hole and is sufficiently challenging to host the Buick Invitational in February. It's not easy to get a good tee time here; out-of-towners are better off booking the instructional Golf Playing Package, which includes cart, fees, and a golf-pro escort for the first three holes. Greens fee: $45–$50.

Resorts

La Costa Resort and Spa (✉ Costa del Mar Rd., Carlsbad, ☎ 760/438–9111 or 800/854–5000) has two 18-hole PGA-rated courses, a driving range, a clubhouse, equipment rentals, an excellent golf school, and a pro shop. One of the premier golf resorts in southern California, La Costa hosts the Mercedes Championships in January. Greens fee: $130–$170.

Rancho Bernardo Inn and Country Club (✉ 17550 Bernardo Oaks Dr., Rancho Bernardo, ☎ 619/675–8470, ext. 1) has 45 holes on-site, a driving range, equipment rentals, and a restaurant. Guests can play three other golf courses at company-operated resorts: Mt. Woodson, Temecula Creek, and Twin Oaks. Ken Blanchard's Golf University of San Diego, based here, is world famous. Rancho Bernardo Inn lays out one of the best Sunday brunches in the county. Greens fee: $65–$80.

Hiking and Nature Trails

Guided hikes are conducted regularly through Los Penasquitos Canyon Preserve and the Torrey Pines State Reserve (☞ La Jolla *in* Exploring San Diego, *above*), the San Dieguito River Valley Regional Open Space (✉ 21 mi north of San Diego on I–5 to Lomas Santa Fe Dr. east 1 mi to Sun Valley Rd. north into park, ☎ 619/235–5440), and the Tijuana Estuary (☎ 619/575–3613). A list of scheduled walks appears in the Night and Day section of the Thursday *San Diego Union-Tribune*.

Jogging

From downtown, the most popular run is along the Embarcadero, which stretches around the bay. Trails snake through the canyons of Balboa Park. Mission Bay is renowned among joggers for its wide sidewalks and basically flat landscape. Trails head west around Fiesta Island from Mission Bay, providing distance as well as a scenic route. Del Mar has the finest running trails along the bluff; park your car near 15th Street and run south along the cliffs for a gorgeous view of the ocean. Some tips: Don't run in bike lanes, and check the local newspaper's tide charts before heading to the beach.

Surfing

See Beaches, *above*, for descriptions of surf conditions. Many local surf shops rent boards, including **Star Surfing Company** (☎ 619/273–

7827) in Pacific Beach and **La Jolla Surf Systems** (☎ 619/456–2777)
and **Hansen's** (☎ 760/753–6595) in Encinitas.

Swimming
The most spectacular pool in town is Belmont Park's **The Plunge** (✉ 3115 Ocean Front Walk, Mission Bay, ☎ 619/488–3110). The **Downtown YMCA** (✉ 500 W. Broadway Ave., ☎ 619/232–7451) is centrally located.

Tennis
Public facilities in San Diego include the **Balboa Tennis Club at Morley Field** (☎ 619/295–9278) in Balboa Park, which has 25 courts, 19 of which are lighted. Nonmembers can make reservations after paying a $4 fee. The **La Jolla Tennis Club** (✉ 7632 Draper Ave., ☎ 619/454–4434) has 9 free public courts near downtown La Jolla, 5 of them lighted.

Water Sports
Boats and equipment can be rented from **Seaforth Boat Rentals** (✉ 1641 Quivira Rd., near Mission Bay, ☎ 619/223–1681). Sailboats can be rented from **Harbor Sailboats** (✉ Harbor Island Dr., ☎ 619/291–9570). Windsurfing rentals and instruction are available at the **Bahia Hotel** (✉ 998 W. Mission Bay Dr., ☎ 619/488–0551) and other resorts in the Mission Bay area. **California Water Sports** (☎ 619/434–3089) has information about Jet Ski rentals and purchases.

Spectator Sports
Qualcomm Stadium (✉ 9449 Friars Rd., ☎ 619/525–8282), formerly San Diego Jack Murphy Stadium, is at the intersection of I–8 and I–805. To get to the **San Diego Sports Arena** (✉ 3500 Sports Arena Blvd., ☎ 619/224–4171), take the Rosecrans Street exit off I–5 and turn right onto Sports Arena Boulevard.

Baseball
The National League **San Diego Padres** (☎ 619/283–4494) play at Qualcomm Stadium. Tickets are usually available on game day.

Football
The **San Diego Chargers** (☎ 619/280–2111) of the National Football League fill Qualcomm Stadium.

Horse Racing
The annual summer meeting of the **Del Mar Thoroughbred Club** (☞ Del Mar *in* Side Trip to the San Diego North Coast, *below*).

Soccer
The **San Diego Sockers** (☎ 619/224–4625)—whose games can be raucous fun—compete in the Continental Indoor Soccer League from June through September at the San Diego Sports Arena (☎ 619/224–4171).

SHOPPING
Coronado
By Bobbi Zane   **Orange Avenue,** in the center of town, has six blocks of ritzy boutiques and galleries. The **Hotel Del Coronado** (✉ 1500 Orange Ave.) houses 28 exclusive specialty shops. **Coronado Holidays** (✉ Ferry Landing Marketplace, ☎ 619/435–6097) is a year-round Christmas shop.

Downtown

Horton Plaza, bordered by Broadway, 1st Avenue, G Street, and 4th Avenue, has one-of-a-kind shops, multilevel department stores, fast-food counters, classy restaurants, live theater, and cinemas. Victorian buildings and renovated warehouses in the historic **Gaslamp Quarter** along 4th and 5th avenues house art galleries, antiques, and specialty shops. **The Paladion** (✉ 777 Front St., ☎ 619/232–1685) is San Diego's answer to Rodeo Drive.

Kensington, Hillcrest, and North Park

More than 20 dealers in the **Adams Avenue** area of Kensington sell everything from postcards and kitchen utensils to cut glass and porcelain. Gay and funky **Hillcrest** is home to many gift, book, and music stores, especially in the area around 4th, 5th, and University avenues. The **Uptown District,** an open-air shopping center on University Avenue, houses several furniture, gift, and specialty shops. "Nostalgia" shops along **Park Boulevard** and **University Avenue at 30th Street** in the North Park neighborhood carry clothing, accessories, furnishings, and wigs.

La Jolla

High-end and trendy boutiques line Girard Avenue and Prospect Street. Shopping hours vary widely in La Jolla, so it's wise to call specific stores in advance. The **Green Dragon Colony** (✉ Prospect St., near Ivanhoe St.), La Jolla's historic shopping area, dates back to 1895. Perched on a bluff overlooking La Jolla Cove, the Green Dragon and adjacent **Coast Walk Plaza** contain 22 shops and three restaurants.

La Jolla Surf Systems (✉ 2132 Avenida de la Playa, ☎ 619/456–2777) carries swimsuits and other resort wear for men and women. **The Collector** (✉ 1274 Prospect St., ☎ 619/454–9763) is a world-renowned source for colored gemstones and contemporary pieces designed by international jewelers and resident goldsmiths. **La Jolla Cave and Shell Shop** (✉ 1325 Coast Blvd., ☎ 619/454–6080) stocks specimen and decorative shells, coral, and nautical gifts.

Mission Valley/Hotel Circle

The Mission Valley/Hotel Circle area, northeast of downtown near I–8 and Highway 163, has four major shopping centers: **Fashion Valley** (✉ 452 Fashion Valley), **Hazard Center** (✉ 7676 Hazard Center Dr.), **Mission Valley Center** (✉ 1640 Camino del Rio N), and **Rio Vista Shopping Center** (✉ Rio San Diego Dr., Stadium Way exit off I–8).

SIDE TRIP TO THE SAN DIEGO NORTH COAST

San Diego proper has more open space than most cities its size, but even its residents like to repair occasionally to the less-congested (though rapidly growing) North County and Anza-Borrego Desert. North County attractions continue to multiply as the 1990s draw to a close—the expected 1999 opening of a Lego theme park in Carlsbad will only increase tourism to the area, whose major stops already include San Diego Wild Animal Park, the mountain town of Julian, and miles of shoreline.

Numbers in the margin correspond to points of interest on the San Diego North County map.

Del Mar

23 mi north of downtown San Diego on I–5, 9 mi north of La Jolla on S21.

Del Mar is best known for its race track, chic shopping strip, celebrity visitors, and wide beaches. Access to Del Mar's beaches is from the streets that run east–west off Coast Boulevard. Along with its collection of shops, **Del Mar Plaza** (⊠ 15th St. at S21—a.k.a. Camino del Mar) also contains outstanding restaurants and landscaped plazas and gardens with Pacific views. Summer evening concerts take place at **Seagrove Park** (⊠ 15th St., west end), a small stretch of grass overlooking the ocean.

❶ The **Del Mar Fairgrounds** is home to the **Del Mar Thoroughbred Club** (⊠ 2260 Jimmy Durante Blvd., ☎ 619/755–1141). Crooner Bing Crosby and his Hollywood buddies—Pat O'Brien, Gary Cooper, and Oliver Hardy, among others—organized the club in the '30s. The racing season here (usually July to September, post time Wednesday to Monday at 2 PM) is one of the most fashionable in California. There is also a satellite wagering facility here. Del Mar Fairgrounds hosts more than 100 different events each year, including the San Diego County Fair. ⊠ *Head west at I–5's Via de la Valle Rd. exit,* ☎ *619/755–1161.*

☾ **Freeflight,** a small exotic-bird training facility adjacent to the Del Mar Fairgrounds, is open to the public. Visitors are allowed to handle the birds—a guaranteed child pleaser. ⊠ *2132 Jimmy Durante Blvd.,* ☎ *619/481–3148.* ☞ *$1.* ☉ *Daily 10–4.*

Dining and Lodging

$$$–$$$$ **✗ Pamplemousse Grill.** A notable newcomer to North County's fine-
★ dining scene, the "Grapefruit Grill," which is on the Del Mar–Solana Beach border, achieves the elegant simplicity of a French country inn. The grilled meats and fish are perfectly prepared. Other menu items include an excellent lamb stew, a seafood stew with lobster, some colorful salads, and good crab cakes. ⊠ *514 Via de la Valle, Solana Beach,* ☎ *619/792–9090. AE, D, DC, MC, V. Call for Mon. hrs; no lunch weekends.*

$$–$$$ **✗ Cilantros.** Seafood enchiladas, Portobello mushroom fajitas, and spit-roasted chicken with a mild chili sauce are among the subtly spiced Southwest-style dishes served at this Del Mar favorite. Less expensive tapas are another option. For a quick lunch, try the "gourmet wrapps"—rice and other ingredients wrapped in a spinach or tomato tortilla. ⊠ *3702 Via de la Valle,* ☎ *619/259–8777. AE, DC, MC, V.*

$$ **✗ Il Fornaio.** Come here for good homemade pastas and crispy pizza, served in the Italianate dining room or on the terrace. The grilled meats can be dry, but the fish and pasta dishes are generally quite good. Il Fornaio also operates a wine bar in the adjacent outdoor piazza, where oenophiles can sit under an umbrella and enjoy the ocean view. ⊠ *1555 Camino del Mar, Suite 301,* ☎ *619/755–8876. AE, DC, MC, V.*

$$ **✗ Pacifica Del Mar.** The ocean view alone would lure crowds to this
★ contemporary restaurant, which emphasizes Pacific Rim cuisine. The least-complicated dishes are generally the most successful. Try the "tacoshimi" appetizer, the barbecued king salmon, and the various stir-fries. ⊠ *1555 Camino del Mar, Suite 321,* ☎ *619/792–0476. AE, D, DC, MC, V.*

$$ **✗ Torrey Pines Cafe.** Dishes here are categorized according to size, inviting diners to mix, match, and share. The menu changes seasonally—the simplest dishes, such as the tasty osso buco, are generally the best bets. ⊠ *2334 Carmel Valley Rd.,* ☎ *619/259–5878. AE, D, DC, MC, V.*

San Diego North County

$$$–$$$$ ✕⌘ **L'Auberge Del Mar Resort and Spa.** L'Auberge is filled with dark-wood antiques, and all its spacious rooms have wet bars; many have fireplaces, full marble baths, and private balconies with garden and coastal views. The spa specializes in aromatherapy and European herbal wraps and treatments. The four-course specials served in the Dining Room between 5:30 and 6:30 PM are among the best culinary bargains in San Diego. ✉ *1540 Camino del Mar, 92014,* ☎ *619/259–1515 or 800/553–1336,* FAX *619/755–4940. 120 rooms. 2 restaurants, bar, 2 pools, outdoor hot tub, beauty salon, spa, 2 tennis courts, health club, meeting rooms. AE, D, DC, MC, V.*

$$–$$$ ⌘ **Stratford Inn.** Rooms at this inn three blocks from the ocean are large, with ample closet space and dressing areas; some have views of the water. Room rates include Continental breakfast. ✉ *710 Camino del Mar, 92014,* ☎ *619/755–1501 or 800/446–7229,* FAX *619/755–4704. 93 rooms. 2 pools. AE, D, DC, MC, V.*

Rancho Santa Fe

4 mi east of Del Mar and Solana Beach on S8 (Lomas Santa Fe Dr.), 29 mi north of downtown San Diego on I–5 to S8 east.

Groves of huge, drooping eucalyptus trees cover the hills and valleys of exclusive Rancho Santa Fe, which achieved unwanted notoriety in 1997 when members of the Heaven's Gate cult committed suicide at a mansion here. Lillian Rice, one of the first women to graduate with a degree in architecture from the University of California, designed the town, modeling it after villages in Spain. Her first structure, a 12-room house built in 1922, evolved into the Inn at Rancho Santa Fe, which became a gathering spot for celebrities such as Bette Davis, Errol Flynn, and Bing Crosby.

Dining and Lodging

$$$$ ✕ **Mille Fleurs.** The recent winner of a *Gourmet* magazine "top tables"
★ award, this gem of a French auberge has a setting that is as romantic as its contemporary French cuisine is exquisite. The menu, which changes daily, might include first courses such as rabbit in aspic or shrimp bisque with cognac and asparagus flan, followed by entrées of poached pike quenelles with saffron sauce on spinach or confit of duck with braised Belgian endive, wild-blueberry sauce, and new potatoes. ✉ *6009 Paseo Delicias,* ☎ *619/756–3085. Reservations essential. AE, DC, MC, V. No lunch weekends.*

$$$$ ✕⌘ **Rancho Valencia Resort.** One of southern California's hidden
★ treasures has luxurious accommodations in Spanish-style casitas scattered among landscaped grounds. Each suite has a private patio and wet bar. Rancho Valencia is adjacent to three well-designed golf courses and is one of the top tennis resorts in the country. The inn's first-rate restaurant has earned raves for its California cuisine. ✉ *5921 Valencia Circle, 92067,* ☎ *619/756–1123 or 800/548–3664,* FAX *619/756–0165. 43 suites. Restaurant, bar, 2 pools, 2 outdoor hot tubs, 18 tennis courts, croquet, health club, hiking, bicycles. AE, DC, MC, V.*

$$–$$$$ ✕⌘ **Inn at Rancho Santa Fe.** Understated elegance is the theme of this genteel old resort in the heart of the village. This is the sort of place where people don their "whites" and play croquet on the lawn Sunday afternoons. Most accommodations are in red-tile-roof cottages scattered about the property's parklike 20 acres. Some cottages have two bedrooms, private patios, fireplaces, and hot tubs. ✉ *5951 Linea del Cielo, 92067,* ☎ *619/756–1131 or 800/654–2928,* FAX *619/759–1604. 90 rooms. 3 dining rooms, bar, room service, pool, golf privi-*

leges, 3 tennis courts, croquet, exercise room, meeting rooms. AE, DC, M, V.

Encinitas

6 mi north of Solana Beach on S21, 7 mi west of Rancho Santa Fe on S9, 28 mi north of downtown San Diego on I–5.

Flower breeding and growing is the major industry in Encinitas. An example of the area's dedication to horticulture can be found at the ❷ **Quail Botanical Gardens,** home to thousands of different varieties of plants, especially drought-tolerant species. Individual displays include Central American, Himalayan, Australian, and African tropical gardens; a California native plant display; an old-fashioned demonstration garden; and plantings of subtropical fruit. ⊠ *230 Quail Gardens Dr.,* ☎ *760/436–3036.* ⊡ *$3.* ☉ *Daily 9–5.*

Dining

$–$$ ✕ **El Callejon.** The extensive menu at this Mexican café highlights regional dishes not available at most restaurants, such as shrimp or beef in cilantro sauce and chicken in chipotle sauce. The bar pours several dozen tequilas, making the margarita combinations virtually endless. ⊠ *Moonlight Plaza Shopping Center, 345 1st St. (Hwy. 101),* ☎ *760/ 634–2793. AE, D, MC. V.*

$ ✕ **George's.** Surfboards dangle from the ceiling and surfer memorabilia adorns a wall at this funky reminder of Encinitas's days as the quintessential North County beach town. Overstuffed omelets, good burgers, grilled sandwiches (named after local surfing beaches), and thick shakes hark back to the days before anyone had heard the word "cholesterol." You can order a salad instead of a burger, or ask for fruit rather than fries with your sandwich, but who are you kidding? ⊠ *641 1st St.,* ☎ *760/942–9549. MC, V.*

Carlsbad

6 mi from Encinitas on S21, 36 mi north of downtown San Diego on I–5.

Carlsbad owes its name and Bavarian look to John Frazier, who lured people to the area a century ago with talk of the healing powers of mineral water bubbling from a coastal well. The water was found to have the same properties as water from the German mineral wells of Karlsbad—hence the name of the new community. Remnants from this era, including the original well and a monument to Frazier, are found at the **Alt Karlsbad Haus** (⊠ 2802A Carlsbad Blvd.).

In spring, you can walk through the **Flower Fields at Carlsbad Ranch,** where the hillsides are abloom with thousands of ranunculuses from March through April. During the winter holidays, these same fields are ablaze with scarlet poinsettias from the nearby Ecke Nursery. ⊠ *Palomar Airport Rd., east of I–5,* ☎ *760/431–0352.*

Dining and Lodging

$$$$ ✕⊞ **La Costa Hotel and Spa.** Don't expect glitz and glamour at this famous resort; it's surprisingly low-key, with low-slung buildings and vaguely Southwest contemporary–style rooms. Although many guests come for La Costa's tranquil setting, the resort has one of the most comprehensive sports programs in the area. The spa is world-famous, with services ranging from massages to nutritional counseling; spa cuisine is available in three restaurants. The complex includes Pisces Delicacies of the Sea restaurant, long one of San Diego's top seafood venues. ⊠ *2100 Costa del Mar Rd., 92009,* ☎ *760/438–9111 or 800/*

854–5000, FAX 760/931–7569. 478 rooms. 5 restaurants, 2 lounges, in-room modem lines, room service, pool, beauty salon, spa, 2 18-hole golf courses, 21 tennis courts, health club, hiking, jogging, meeting rooms, car rental. AE, D, DC, MC, V.

$$–$$$ ⛆ **Best Western Beach View Lodge.** Reservations are essential at this reasonably priced Mediterranean-style low-rise near the beach. Despite the name, few rooms have a beach view. Functional rooms have light-wood or whitewashed furnishings; some have fireplaces and balconies. Room rates include complimentary Continental breakfast. The Best Western Beach Terrace Inn on the water—better views, higher prices—is under the same ownership. ⊠ 3180 Carlsbad Blvd., 92008, ☎ 760/729–1151 or 800/433–5415, FAX 760/729–1151. 41 rooms. Kitchenettes, pool, outdoor hot tub. AE, D, DC, MC, V.

Oceanside

8 mi north of Carlsbad on S21, 37 mi north of downtown San Diego on I–5.

With 900 slips, **Oceanside Harbor** (☎ 760/966–4570) is the north coast's center for fishing, sailing, and ocean-water sports. Oceanside Pier, the longest on the West Coast, has shops and restaurants.

★ ❸   **Mission San Luis Rey** was built by Franciscan friars in 1798 under the direction of Father Fermin Lasuen to help educate and convert local Native Americans. The well-preserved San Luis Rey was the 18th and largest of the California missions. The sala (parlor), a friar's bedroom, a weaving room, the kitchen, and a collection of religious art convey much about early mission life. Retreats are still held here, but a picnic area, a gift shop, and a museum (which has the most extensive collection of old Spanish vestments in the United States) are also on the grounds. Self-guided tours are available. The mission is on Highway 76, which becomes Mission Avenue inland from S21 (from the ocean, continue east on Highway 76 approximately 4 mi, past the Mission Avenue business district area and I–5). ⊠ 4050 Mission Ave., ☎ 760/757–3651. ⛻ $3. ☉ Mon.–Sat. 10–4:30, Sun. 11:30–4:30.

Lodging

$$–$$$$ ⛆ **Oceanside Marina Inn.** This motel occupies a spit of land surrounded by water on all sides. All rooms have either ocean or harbor views. Room rates include Continental breakfast. A free bus shuttles guests to the beach. ⊠ 2008 Harbor Dr. N, 92054, ☎ 760/722–1561 or 800/252–2033, FAX 760/439–9758. 64 rooms. Kitchenettes, pool, outdoor hot tub, sauna, coin laundry. AE, MC, V.

San Diego North Coast Essentials

Arriving and Departing

BY BUS

The San Diego Transit District (☎ 619/233–3004) covers the city of San Diego up to Del Mar. The **North County Transit District** (☎ 760/743–6283) serves San Diego County from Del Mar north.

BY CAR

Interstate 5, the main freeway artery connecting San Diego to Los Angeles, follows the coastline. To the west, running parallel to it, is S21 (known locally, but not signed, as Old Highway 101, and at points signed as Highway 101), which never strays too far from the ocean. Watch the signs, because the road has a different name as it passes through each community.

BY LIGHT RAIL

Coaster (Coast Express Regional Rail Service, ☎ 760/722–6283 or 800/ 262–7837) operates commuter rail service between San Diego and Oceanside with weekday-only service to San Diego, Old Town, Sorrento Valley, Solana Beach, Encinitas, Carlsbad Poinsettia Station, Carlsbad Village Station, and Oceanside.

Visitor Information

San Diego North County Convention and Visitors Bureau (✉ 720 N. Broadway, Escondido 92025, ☎ 760/745–4741).

SIDE TRIP TO INLAND NORTH COUNTY

Even though the coast is only a short drive away, the beach communities seem far removed from the quiet lakes of Escondido or the backcountry around Julian. Home to San Diego Wild Animal Park apple farms, and innumerable three-generation California families, the inland area of North County is the quiet rural sister to the rest of San Diego County.

Escondido

8 mi north of Rancho Bernardo on I–15, 31 mi northeast of downtown San Diego on I–15.

Escondido is a thriving, rapidly expanding residential and commercial city of more than 80,000 people and the center of a variety of attractions.

★ ☙ ❹ **San Diego Wild Animal Park** is an extension of the San Diego Zoo. The 2,200-acre preserve in the San Pasqual Valley is designed to protect endangered species of animals from around the world. Five exhibit areas have been carved out of the dry, dusty canyons and mesas to represent the animals' natural habitats in North Africa, South Africa, East Africa, Asian swamps, and Asian plains.

The best way to see these preserves is on the 50-minute, 5-mi Wgasa Bushline Monorail ride (included in the price of admission). More than 3,000 animals of 450 species roam or fly through the expansive grounds. Enemy species are separated from each other by deep moats, but only the tigers, lions, and cheetahs are kept in isolation. Photographers with zoom lenses can get spectacular shots of zebras, gazelles, and rhinos (a seat on the right-hand side of the monorail is best for viewing the majority of the animals).

The park is as much a botanical garden as a zoo, and botanists collect rare and endangered plants for preservation. The 5-ft-tall desert cypress found here is native to the Sahara; only 16 such trees are still in existence there. ✉ *Take I–15 north to Via Rancho Pkwy. and follow signs (6 mi),* ☎ *760/480–0100.* ☞ *$18.95, includes all shows and monorail tour; a combination pass ($28.50) grants entry, within 5 days of purchase, to both the San Diego Zoo and the San Diego Wild Animal Park; parking $3. AE, D, MC, V.* ☉ *Daily from 9 AM; closing hrs vary with season (call ahead).*

Julian

62 mi from San Diego, east on I–8 and north on Hwy. 79.

Gold was discovered in the Julian area in 1869 and quartz was unearthed a year later. Today, this mountain town retains some historic false-front buildings from its mining days. When gold and quartz became scarce, the locals turned to growing apples and pears. The pears are harvested in September, the apples in October. During the harvest season you can buy fruit, sip cider, eat apple pie, and shop for antiques and collectibles. But spring is equally enchanting (and less congested with visitors), as the hillsides explode with wildflowers, lilacs, and peonies. Artists and craftspeople have long maintained studios in the hillsides surrounding Julian; their work is frequently on display in local shops and galleries.

Dining and Lodging

$$ ✕ **Julian Grille.** The menu at this casual restaurant inside a historic home appeals to a variety of tastes, including vegetarian. Chicken dishes are popular, as are steaks and the smoked pork chops served with apple sauce. Lunch options include good burgers, whopping sandwiches, and soups. The requisite apple pies are made by the Julian Pie Co. across the street. ⊠ *2224 Main St.,* ☎ *760/765–0173. AE, MC, V. No dinner Mon.*

$–$$ ✕ **Bailey Barbecue.** The ribs, sausages, and chicken at this backwoods barbecue joint are slowly smoked over a live-oak fire and served with a tangy, not-too-sweet sauce. Everything on the menu is available for takeout. ⊠ *2307 Main St.,* ☎ *760/765–9957. MC, V. Closed Tues.–Wed.*

$$$–$$$$ ▥ **Orchard Hill Country Inn.** Perched on a hill above town, this inn with
★ a sweeping view of the surrounding countryside sets a new standard for luxury among backcountry accommodations. All rooms are decorated with antiques and handcrafted quilts. Room rates include breakfast. Dinner is available to guests on weekends, when a minimum stay of two nights is required. ⊠ *Washington St., 92036,* ☎ *760/765–1700. 22 rooms. Meeting rooms. AE, MC, V.*

$–$$ ▥ **Julian Lodge.** This B&B near the center of town is a replica of a late-19th-century Julian hotel. The rooms and public spaces are furnished with antiques; on chilly days, guests can warm themselves at the large stove in the lobby. Room rates include a buffet-style Continental breakfast. ⊠ *4th and C Sts., 92036,* ☎ *760/765–1420 or 800/ 542–1420. 23 rooms. AE, D, MC, V.*

Inland North County Essentials

Arriving and Departing

North County Transit District (☎ 760/743–6283) routes crisscross the Escondido area. For bus routes to Julian, *see* The Desert Essentials, *below.*

A loop drive beginning and ending in San Diego is a good way to explore this area. You can take the Sunrise National Scenic Byway Highway (sometimes icy in winter) from I–8 to Highway 79 and return through Cuyamaca to I–8. If you're only going to Julian, take either the Sunrise Highway or Highway 79, and return to San Diego via Highway 78 past Santa Ysabel to Ramona and Highway 67; from here, I–8 heads west to downtown.

Visitor Information

Escondido Chamber of Commerce (⊠ 720 N. Broadway, ☎ 760/745–2125). **Julian Chamber of Commerce** (⊠ 2129 Main St., 92036, ☎ 760/ 765–1857).

SIDE TRIP TO THE DESERT

Every spring, the stark desert landscape east of the Cuyamaca Mountains explodes with colorful wildflowers. The beauty of this spectacle, as well as the natural quiet and blazing climate, lures many tourists and natives each year to Anza-Borrego Desert State Park, less than a two-hour drive from central San Diego. The desert is best visited between October and May to avoid the extreme summer temperatures. Winter temperatures are comfortable, but nights (and sometimes days) are cold, so bring a warm jacket.

Anza-Borrego Desert State Park

⑤ *88 mi from downtown San Diego (to park border due west of Borrego Springs), east on I–8, north on Hwy. 67, east on S4 and Hwy. 78, north on Hwy. 79, and east on S2 and S22.*

Today, more than 600,000 acres of desert are included in the Anza-Borrego Desert State Park, making it the largest state park in the contiguous 48 states. Rangers and displays at an excellent underground **Visitor Information Center** (✉ Palm Canyon Dr., Borrego Springs, ☎ 760/767–4205) can point you in the right direction.

Many of the Anza-Borrego Desert's sites can be seen from paved roads, but some require driving on dirt roads. Rangers recommend using four-wheel-drive vehicles when traversing dirt roads. Carry the appropriate supplies: shovel and other tools, flares, blankets, and plenty of water. Canyons are susceptible to flash flooding; inquire about weather conditions before entering.

Narrows Earth Trail is a short walk off Highway 78, east of Tamarisk Grove, that reveals the many geologic processes involved in forming the canyons of the desert. At **Borrego Palm Canyon,** just a few minutes west of the visitor center, a 1½-mi trail leads to a small oasis with a waterfall and palm trees. The Borrego Palm Canyon campground is one of only two developed campgrounds with flush toilets and showers in the park. (The other is Tamarisk Grove Campground, at the intersection of Highway 78 and Yaqui Pass Road; sites at both run $15–$16.)

Geology students from all over the world visit the Fish Creek area of Anza-Borrego to explore a famous canyon known as **Split Mountain** (✉ Split Mountain Rd., south from Hwy. 78 at Ocotillo Wells), a narrow gorge with 600-ft perpendicular walls that was formed by an ancestral stream. Fossils in this area have led geologists to think that a sea covered the desert floor at one time. A 2-mi nature trail just west of Split Mountain rewards a hiker with a good view of shallow caves created by erosion. ✉ *Park headquarters: 200 Palm Canyon Dr., Borrego Springs 92004, ☎ 760/767–5311. ☞ $5. ☉ Park year-round 24 hrs; visitor center Oct.–May daily 9–5, June–Sept. weekends and holidays 9–5.*

Borrego Springs

31 mi from Julian, east on Hwy. 78 and north on S3.

If you're not interested in communing with the desert without a shower and pool nearby, Borrego Springs has several hotels and restaurants. There is little to do in this oasis besides lie or recreate in the sun.

Lodging

$$–$$$$ 🏨 **La Casa del Zorro.** Accommodations here are in comfortable one- to three-bedroom ranch-style houses complete with living rooms and kitchens; some three-bedroom suites have private pools. The elegant Continental restaurant puts on a good Sunday brunch. ✉ *3845 Yaqui Pass Rd., 92004, ☎ 760/767–5323 or 800/824–1884, ℻ 760/767–4782. 77 rooms, including 42 suites and 19 casitas. Restaurant, bar, 3 pools, outdoor hot tubs, beauty salon, 6 tennis courts, health club, bicycles, children's programs, meeting rooms. AE, D, DC, MC, V.*

$–$$$ 🖼 **Palm Canyon Resort.** One of the largest properties around Anza-Borrego Desert State Park includes a hotel (¼ mi from the visitor center), an RV park, a restaurant, and recreational facilities. More upscale rooms have wet bars, refrigerators, ceiling fans, and balconies or patios. ✉ 221 Palm Canyon Dr., 92004, 🕾 760/767–5341 or 800/242–0044, FAX 760/767–4073. 60 rooms. Restaurant, 2 pools, 2 outdoor hot tubs, coin laundry, meeting rooms. AE, D, DC, MC, V.

Salton Sea

85 mi (to park headquarters) from Borrego Springs, Hwy. 78E to Hwy. 111N.

The Salton Sea, due east of Anza-Borrego Desert State Park, was created in 1905–07, when the Colorado River flooded north through canals meant to irrigate the Imperial Valley. The water is extremely salty, even saltier than the Pacific Ocean, and it is primarily a draw for fishermen seeking corbina, croaker, and tilapia. Some boaters and swimmers also use the lake. The state runs a park, **Salton Sea State Recreation Area** (✉ Hwy. 111N, at northeast edge of Salton Sea, 🕾 760/393–3059), with sites for recreational vehicles, and primitive camping.

A hiking trail and an observation tower at the **Salton Sea National Wildlife Refuge** make it easy to spot the dozens of varieties of migratory birds that stop at the Salton Sea. ✉ Off Hwy. 86, south end of Salton Sea, 🕾 760/348–5278.

The Desert Essentials

Arriving and Departing

BY BUS
The **Northeast Rural Bus System** (NERBS, 🕾 760/767–4287) connects Julian, Borrego Springs, and many other small communities with El Cajon, 15 mi east of downtown San Diego, and the East County line of the San Diego trolley. Service is by reservation, and buses do not run on Sunday and on some holidays.

BY CAR
From downtown San Diego, take I–8 east to Highway 67 north, to Highway 78 east, to Highway 79 north, to S2 and S22 east.

Visitor Information
Anza-Borrego Desert State Park (✉ Box 299, Borrego Springs 92004, 🕾 760/767–5311). **Borrego Springs Chamber of Commerce** (✉ 622 Palm Canyon Dr., Borrego Springs 92004, 🕾 760/767–5555). **Destinet** (🕾 800/444–7275), for campsite reservations. **Wildflower hotline** (🕾 760/767–4684), during spring blooming season only.

SAN DIEGO A TO Z

Arriving and Departing

By Bus
Greyhound (🕾 619/239–8082 or 800/231–2222) operates 26 buses a day between the downtown terminal at 120 West Broadway and Los Angeles, connecting with buses to all major U.S. cities. Many buses are express or nonstop; others make stops at coastal towns en route.

By Car
Interstate 5 stretches from Canada to the Mexican border and bisects San Diego. Interstate 8 provides access from Yuma, Arizona, and

points east. Drivers coming from Nevada and the mountain regions beyond can reach San Diego on I–15.

By Plane
San Diego International Airport Lindbergh Field (☎ 619/231–2100), about a five-minute drive from downtown, is San Diego's main airport. Carriers serving the city include Alaska, America West, American, Continental, Delta, Midwest Express, Northwest, Reno Air, Southwest, TWA, United, and US Airways. *See* Air Travel *in* the Gold Guide for airline phone numbers.

BETWEEN THE AIRPORT AND DOWNTOWN
San Diego Transit (☎ 619/233–3004) Route 2 buses leave daily from 5:30 AM–1 AM. Buses depart from the front of East Terminal's US Airways section and travel along Broadway, downtown. The fare is $1.50 per person.

Cloud 9 Shuttle (☎ 619/278–8877; in San Diego, 800/974–8885) and **Public Shuttle** (☎ 619/990–8770) operate van shuttles that take you directly to your destination, often for less than a cab would cost.

If you have rented a car at the airport, you can take Harbor Drive, at the perimeter of the airport, to downtown, only about 3 mi away. The taxi fare from the airport to downtown hotels costs from $7 to $9 plus tip.

By Train
Amtrak (☎ 800/872–7245) services downtown San Diego's Santa Fe Depot (✉ 1050 Kettner Blvd., ☎ 619/239–9021) from Los Angeles. Amtrak stops in San Diego North County at Solana Beach and Oceanside.

Getting Around
By Bus
The **San Diego Transit Information Line** (☎ 619/233–3004, TTY/TDD 619/234–5005; open daily 5:30 AM–8:30 PM) can provide details on getting to and from any location.

Regional bus companies that service areas outside the city include **ATC Van Co.** (☎ 619/427–5660), for Coronado, the Silver Strand, and Imperial Beach; **Chula Vista Transit** (☎ 619/233–3004), for Bonita and Chula Vista; **National City Transit** (☎ 619/474–7505), for National City; **North County Transit District** (☎ 760/722–6283), for the area bound by the ocean, east to Escondido, north to Camp Pendleton, and south to Del Mar; and **Northeast Rural Bus System** (☎ 760/767–4287) or **Southeast Rural Bus System** (☎ 619/478–5875), for access to rural county towns.

By Car
A car is essential for San Diego's sprawling freeway system. Avoid the freeways during rush hour when possible. All the major car-rental companies are represented in San Diego. For a list, *see* Car Rentals *in* the Gold Guide.

Limousine companies operate airport shuttles and customized tours. Rates vary and are per hour, per mile, or both, with some minimums established. Companies that provide service include **Advantage Limousine Service** (☎ 619/563–1651), **La Jolla Limousines** (☎ 619/459–5891), **Limousines by Linda** (☎ 619/234–9145), and **Olde English Livery** (☎ 619/232–6533).

By Ferry
The **San Diego–Coronado Ferry** (☎ 619/234–4111) leaves from the Broadway Pier daily, every hour on the hour, from 9 AM to 9 PM Sun-

day to Thursday, until 10 PM Friday and Saturday. The fare is $2 each way and 50¢ for each bicycle.

By Taxi

Taxi fares are regulated at the airport—all companies charge the same rate (generally $1.80 for the first mile, $1.20 for each additional mile). Fares vary among companies on other routes, however, including the ride back to the airport. If you call ahead and ask for the flat rate ($7) you'll get it, otherwise you'll be charged by the mile (which works out to $9 or so).

Cab companies that serve most areas of the city are **Co-op Silver Cabs** (☎ 619/280–5555), **Coronado Cab** (☎ 619/435–6211), **La Jolla Cab** (☎ 619/453–4222), **Orange Cab** (☎ 619/291–3333), and **Yellow Cab** (☎ 619/234–6161).

Contacts and Resources

Emergencies

Ambulance (☎ 911). **Fire** (☎ 911). **Police** (☎ 911).

Major hospitals are **Mercy Hospital and Medical Center** (✉ 4077 5th Ave., ☎ 619/294–8111), **Scripps Memorial Hospital** (✉ 9888 Genesee Ave., La Jolla, ☎ 619/457–4123), **Veterans Administration Hospital** (✉ 3350 La Jolla Village Dr., La Jolla, ☎ 619/552–8585), and **UCSD Medical Center** (✉ 200 W. Arbor Dr., Hillcrest, ☎ 619/543–6222).

Hotel Doctors (☎ 619/275–2663) provides 24-hour medical service to guests at San Diego hotels. The **San Diego County Dental Society** (☎ 619/275–0244) can provide referrals Monday through Friday to those with dental emergencies. Hotel Doctors (☞ *above*) provides dental emergency referrals.

Guided Tours

ORIENTATION TOURS

Gray Line Tours (☎ 619/491–0011; 800/331–5077 outside CA) and **San Diego Mini Tours** (☎ 619/477–8687) have daily sightseeing excursions for about $25.

Old Town Trolley (☎ 619/298–8687) travels to almost every attraction and shopping area on open-air trackless trolleys. Drivers double as tour guides. You can take the full two-hour, narrated city tour or get on and off as you please at any of the nine stops. An all-day pass costs $20. The trolley, which leaves every 30 minutes, operates daily 9 to 5 in summer, 9 to 4 in winter.

Free two-hour trolley tours of the downtown redevelopment area, including the Gaslamp Quarter, are hosted by **Centre City Development Corporation Downtown Information Center** (☎ 619/235–2222). Groups of 35 passengers leave from 225 Broadway, Suite 160, downtown, the first and third Saturday of each month at 10 AM. Reservations are necessary. The tour may be canceled if there aren't enough passengers.

Two companies operate one- and two-hour harbor cruises. **San Diego Harbor Excursion** (☎ 619/234–4111) and **Hornblower Invader Cruises** (☎ 619/234–8687) boats depart from the Broadway Pier. No reservations are necessary for the $12 to $17 voyages, and both vessels have snack bars on board. **Classic Sailing Adventures** (☎ 619/224–0800) has morning and afternoon tours of the harbor and San Diego Bay and nighttime in summer cruises for $45 per person.

The Gaslamp Quarter Historical Foundation (☎ 619/233–4692) leads two-hour historical tours ($5) of the restored downtown district on Saturday at 11 AM.

Six-passenger hot-air balloons lift off from San Diego's North Country. Most flights are at sunrise or sunset and are followed by a champagne celebration. Companies with daily service, weather permitting, are **Pacific Horizon** (☎ 619/756–1790 or 800/244–1790) and **Skysurfer** (☎ 619/481–6800; 800/660–6809 in CA). Balloon flights average $130 per person.

Civic Helicopters (☎ 619/438–8424 or 800/438–4354) has helicopter tours starting at $69 per person per half hour.

On weekends, the **California State Park System** (☎ 619/220–5422) gives free walking tours of Old Town. Groups leave from 4002 Wallace Street at 2 PM daily, weather permitting. **Walkabout** (☎ 619/231–7463) conducts several different free walking tours throughout the city each week.

Gray whales migrate south to Mexico and back north from mid-December to mid-March. As many as 200 whales pass the San Diego coast each day, coming within yards of tour boats. During whale-watching season, **Classic Sailing Adventures** (☎ 619/224–0800) tailors whale-watching expeditions for up to six people. **H&M Landing** (☎ 619/222–1144) and **Seaforth Sportfishing** (☎ 619/224–3383) have daily whale-watching trips in large party boats.

Visitor Information

International Visitor Information Center (⊠ 11 Horton Plaza, at 1st Ave. and F St., ☎ 619/236–1212). **San Diego Convention & Visitors Bureau** (⊠ 401 B St., Suite 1400, 92101, ☎ 619/232–3101). **San Diego Visitor Information Center** (⊠ 2688 E. Mission Bay Dr., 92109, ☎ 619/276–8200).

15 Palm Springs

The Desert Resorts and Joshua Tree

Palm Springs and its neighbors—Palm Desert, Rancho Mirage, Indian Wells— are among the fastest-growing and wealthiest communities in the nation. The desert lures visitors and residents for the same reasons: striking scenery and the therapeutic benefits of a warm, arid climate. Resort hotel complexes contain championship golf courses, tennis stadiums, and sparkling swimming pools—lushly landscaped oases, towering palms, natural waterfalls, and hot mineral springs round out the picture.

By Bobbi Zane

THE DESERT AROUND PALM SPRINGS hasn't always been filled with luxury resorts, but various settlers over the years have recognized the region's rich natural attributes. The Agua Caliente Band of Indians discovered the hot springs in the Coachella Valley—the valley in which the entire desert-resorts area lies—and made use of their healing properties. In the last half of the 19th century, farmers established a date-growing industry at the southern end of the valley. By 1900, word had spread about the manifold health benefits of the area's dry climate, inspiring wealthy folk from the northern United States to winter under the warm desert sun.

By the time of the Great Depression, Palm Springs had caught Hollywood's eye. It was an ideal hideaway: Celebrities could slip into town, play a few sets of tennis, lounge around the pool, attend a party or two, and, unless things got out of hand, remain safely beyond the reach of gossip columnists.

Growth hit the desert in the 1970s, as developers began to construct the world-class golf courses, country clubs, and residential communities that drew not only pop celebrities but tycoons and politicians. Privacy is still the watchword, however; many communities, particularly in Rancho Mirage and Indian Wells, are walled and gate-guarded. There has been a downside to the region's growth: urban sprawl and overbuilding—of sometimes less than stellar structures.

The city of Palm Springs lost a bit of its luster as the wealthy moved on to newer, more glamorous communities—Palm Desert, Rancho Mirage, Indian Wells—during this period. But the city, once the unrivaled hub of desert society and commerce, is reinventing itself. Once exclusive Palm Canyon Drive is a lively avenue with coffeehouses, a brew pub, outdoor cafés and bars, and frequent special events. And Palm Springs is now a well-advertised destination for lesbians and gay men, with many dining and lodging spots either hospitable to or completely oriented toward same-sex travelers.

You'll still find celebrities in the desert, where streets are named for Bob Hope, Gerald Ford, Dinah Shore, and Frank Sinatra. Hollywood stars, sports personalities, politicians, and other high-profile folk can be spotted at charity events, in restaurants, or on the golf course. Sean Connery, Kevin Costner, Roseanne, Elizabeth Taylor, and Joe Pesci have all swept into town in recent years. The prospect of a brush with glamour, along with the desert's natural beauty, heightens the area's appeal for tourists.

Pleasures and Pastimes

Desert Wildlife

Visitors who want to learn about the natural history of the desert and see some spectacular scenery can explore the terrain at ground level at the Living Desert Wildlife and Botanical Park and Joshua Tree National Park or take in the full panorama at the top of the Palm Springs Aerial Tramway. Exhibits in the Palm Springs Desert Museum explain it all.

Dining

Once considered a culinary wasteland, the desert now supports many trendy if not overly adventurous restaurants—Italian and surf-and-turf cuisine still dominate the scene. Many desert restaurant menus include heart-healthy items for those who are careful about fat and cholesterol. Dining is casual.

CATEGORY	COST*
$$$$	over $50
$$$	$30–$50
$$	$20–$30
$	under $20

per person for a three-course meal, excluding drinks, service, and 7¼% tax

Golf

The Palm Springs area has more than 90 golf courses, many of which are familiar to golf fans as the sites of championship tournaments. You can tee off where the pros play at PGA West, Mission Hills North, and La Quinta, all of which have instructors ready to help you with your swing.

Lodging

You can stay in Palm Springs for as little as $40 per night or well over $1,000. Rates vary widely from summer (low) to winter (high) season. Budget lodgings are most easily found in Palm Springs proper; the city-operated visitor center (☎ 800/347–7746) represents 85 properties. Discounts are sometimes given for extended stays. Condos, apartments, and individual houses may be rented by the day, week, month, or for longer periods. Some hotels, including Marriott's Desert Springs Resort and Spa, have villas for rent.

CATEGORY	COST*
$$$$	over $175
$$$	$120–$175
$$	$80–$120
$	under $80

All prices are for a standard double room, excluding 9%–11% tax.

Nightlife and the Arts

The Fabulous Palm Springs Follies—a vaudeville-style revue starring retired professional performers—is a must-see for most visitors. Arts festivals occur on a regular basis, especially during the winter and spring. Nightlife options include a good jazz bar (Peabody's), several dance clubs, and hotel entertainment. The "Desert Guide" from *Palm Springs Life* magazine, available at most hotels and visitor information centers, has nightlife listings, as does the "Weekender" pullout in the Friday edition of the daily *Palm Desert Sun* newspaper. The gay scene is covered in the *Bottom Line* newspaper.

Outdoor Sports and Activities

With approximately 30,000 pools in the desert region, swimming (or at least hanging out poolside) is a daily ritual. Several hundred courts make playing or watching tennis a serious pursuit. More than 35 mi of bike trails crisscross the Palm Springs area; the terrain here is mostly flat. Indian Canyons, Mt. San Jacinto State Park and Wilderness, Living Desert Wildlife and Botanical Park, Joshua Tree National Park, and Big Morongo Canyon Preserve have hiking trails. Avoid outdoor activities midday during the hot season. Take precautions against the sun and wear a hat any time of the year. Always drink plenty of water to prevent dehydration.

Shopping

Shopping is a serious pursuit in the Palm Springs area, which is beginning to look like one big mall. Well more than half the respondents to a recent visitor survey ranked shopping as the "recreation" they enjoyed most. Boutiques, art galleries, and an ever-growing collection of consignment, estate-sale, and antiques shops make for diverse browsing. El Paseo in Palm Desert has upscale galleries and shops.

Exploring Palm Springs

Some visitors' idea of "exploring" Palm Springs is to navigate the distance from their hotel room to the pool or spa—this has, after all, always been a place for indulging oneself. Most social, sports, shopping, and entertainment scenes revolve around Palm Springs and Palm Desert. Cathedral City and Rancho Mirage are west of Palm Desert (and east of Palm Springs) on Highway 111. Indian Wells, La Quinta, and Indio are all east of Palm Desert on the highway. North of Palm Springs is Desert Hot Springs. As for the region's natural wonders, Joshua Tree National Park and other outdoor attractions are easily visited as day trips from any of the resort towns.

Numbers in the text correspond to numbers in the margin and on the Palm Springs Desert Resorts map.

Great Itineraries

IF YOU HAVE 1 DAY

If you've just slipped into town for a quick look-see, focus your activities around Palm Springs. Get an early-morning scenic overview by taking the **Palm Springs Aerial Tramway** ① to the top of Mt. San Jacinto. In the afternoon, head for **Palm Canyon Drive** ② in Palm Springs, have lunch alfresco at the Blue Coyote Cafe, and drop by the **Showbiz Museum** at the Plaza Theater, where you can pick up tickets for an evening performance of the **Fabulous Palm Springs Follies** (better still, make reservations ahead of your visit). In the afternoon, visit **Palm Desert,** the trendiest of the desert cities, for a walk through the canyons and hillsides of the **Living Desert Wildlife and Botanical Park** ⑨ and a preshow dinner on **El Paseo.**

IF YOU HAVE 3 DAYS

On your first day, take the **Palm Springs Aerial Tramway** ① in the morning, and have lunch on **Palm Canyon Drive** ②. Spend the afternoon browsing the Palm Canyon shops, or (unless it's the height of the summer) hiking through the **Indian Canyons** ⑥. On day two, head to **Palm Desert** and the **Living Desert Wildlife and Botanical Park** ⑨. Have lunch in Palm Desert and work it off by browsing through the entire length of the chic **El Paseo** shopping area. On the third morning, take in the **Palm Springs Desert Museum** ④, which has a first-class art gallery and a sculpture garden. In the afternoon pamper yourself by partaking of the spa regimen at the Givenchy hotel or the Spa Experience at the Spa Hotel. Then, appropriately relaxed, take in a performance of the **Fabulous Palm Springs Follies.**

IF YOU HAVE 5 DAYS

Ride the **Palm Springs Aerial Tramway** ① and cruise **Palm Canyon Drive** ② on the first day. Explore the **Living Desert** ⑨ and have lunch and shop on **El Paseo** ⑧ or visit the **Indian Canyons** ⑥. The third day, visit the **Palm Springs Desert Museum** ④, have lunch, and then spend the afternoon lounging poolside at your hotel or touring **Moorten Botanical Garden** ⑤. Spend the entire fourth day touring **Joshua Tree National Park** ⑩, starting at the West Entrance near Joshua Tree and exiting at the Cottonwood Visitor Center (come back via I–10 unless you want to poke through some of the desert towns along slower Highway 111). Following all this activity, you'll be ready for a fifth **day of total relaxation**—including a massage, aromatherapy, herbal wraps, and other regimens.

When to Tour Palm Springs

During the "season" (January through April), the desert weather is at its best, with daytime temperatures ranging between 70° and 90°F. This is the time when you're most likely to see a colorful display of wild-

Palm Springs Desert Resorts

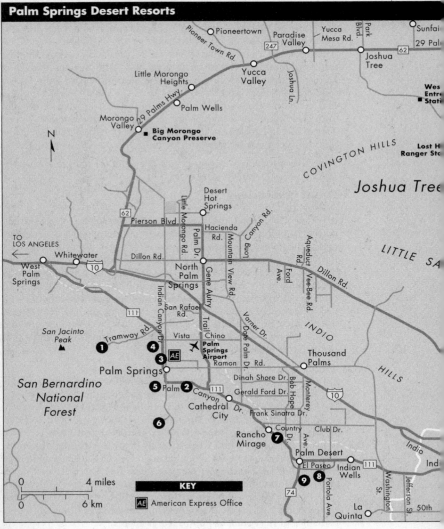

KEY

AE American Express Office

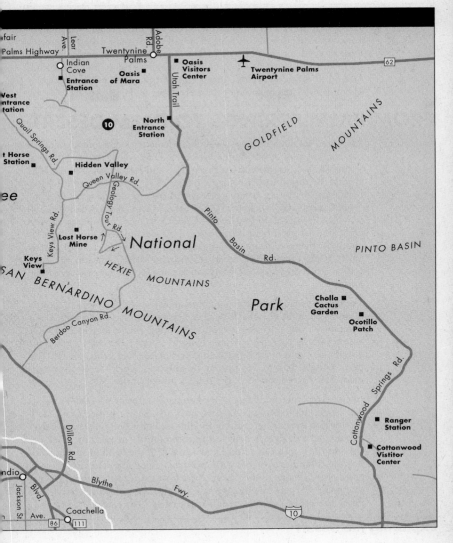

flowers and when most of the golf and tennis tournaments take place. Prices soar and accommodations can be difficult to secure without advance reservations at this time. The fall months are nearly as lovely, less crowded, and less expensive. During the summer months, daytime temperatures rise to 110°F or higher, though evenings cool to the mid-70s. Some attractions close during this period. Hotel prices frequently average 50% less in summer than in winter and early spring.

FROM PALM SPRINGS TO PALM DESERT

The Agua Caliente Band of Cahuilla Indians settled in and around the Coachella Valley about 1,000 years ago. They considered the mineral springs to be sacred, with great curative and restorative powers. The springs became a tourist attraction in 1871 when the tribe built a bathhouse on the site to serve passengers on a pioneer stage route. The Agua Caliente still own about 32,000 acres of Palm Springs desert, 6,700 of which lie within the city limits of Palm Springs. The Indians, though dedicated to preserving their historic homeland, will doubtless account for the next "boom" in the desert. Following the lead of nearby tribes, which operate profitable casinos in Indio and Cabazon, the Agua Caliente recently opened a casino in the Spa Hotel in downtown Palm Springs.

The desert became a Hollywood hideout in the 1920s, when La Quinta Hotel opened the Coachella Valley's first golf course. But it took a pair of tennis-playing celebrities to put Palm Springs on the map in the 1930s; actors Charlie Farrell and Ralph Bellamy bought 200 acres of land for $30 an acre and opened the Palm Springs Racquet Club, which soon listed Ginger Rogers, Humphrey Bogart, and Clark Gable among its members. Farrell served as the town's mayor in the '50s.

Joshua Tree, upgraded from "monument" status in the mid-1990s, is just beginning to bloom as a national park. Major projects and facilities within the park are still in the future, but it will only be a matter of time before development in the communities around the park occurs. In the meantime, nature, particularly in the form of spring wildflowers, continues to bloom with spectacular regularity. The Cottonwood Springs area is one of the desert's best for wildflower viewing. During the spring, carpets of white, yellow, purple, and red flowers stretch as far as the eye can see on the hillsides east of the freeway.

Exploring the Desert

★ ☺ ❶ A trip on the **Palm Springs Aerial Tramway** provides a stunning overview of the desert. The 2½-mi ascent brings you to an elevation of 8,516 ft in less than 20 minutes. On clear days, which are common, the view stretches 75 mi from the peak of Mt. San Gorgonio to the north to the Salton Sea in the southeast. At the top you'll find several diversions. The Mountain Station has an alpine cafeteria, cocktail lounge, apparel and gift shops, a theater screening a 22-minute film on the history of the tramway, and picnic facilities. The tram is a popular attraction; lines can be long. ⊠ *1 Tramway Rd.,* ☎ *760/325–1391.* ☎ *$17.95.* ⊙ *Tram cars depart at least every 30 mins from 10 AM weekdays and 8 AM weekends; last car up leaves at 8 PM, last one down 9:45 PM. Closed Aug. for maintenance.*

Mt. San Jacinto Wilderness State Park, accessible only by hiking or taking the Palm Springs Aerial Tramway, has 54 mi of hiking trails, and camping and picnic areas; guided wilderness mule rides are available here during snow-free months. During winter the Nordic Ski Center has cross-country ski equipment for rent. ☎ *909/659–2607 for park* *information.* ✉ *Free; permits (also free) required for day or overnight wilderness hiking.*

❷ A stroll down **Palm Canyon Drive,** which is lined with shops, includes the Palm Springs Starwalk, stars imbedded in the sidewalk (à la the Hollywood Walk of Fame) honoring celebrities. The tiny but illuminating **Showbiz Museum** (✉ 132 S. Palm Canyon Dr.) is adjacent to the Plaza Theater (✉ 128 S. Palm Canyon Dr.). On Thursday night ★ the **Village Fest** fills the section between Tahquitz Canyon Way and Baristo Road with street musicians, a farmers' market, and stalls with food, crafts, art, and antiques.

❸ Three small museums at the **Village Green Heritage Center** (✉ 221 S. Palm Canyon Dr., ☎ 760/323–8297) illustrate pioneer life in Palm Springs. There's a nominal fee for entrance to each. The adjacent **Agua Caliente Cultural Museum,** admission to which is free, is devoted to the culture and history of Cahuilla Indians.

❹ The **Palm Springs Desert Museum** is a fine facility that focuses on natural science, the visual arts, and the performing arts. The display on the natural history of the desert is itself worth a visit, and the grounds hold several striking sculpture courts. A modern-art gallery holds works by artists such as Alberto Giacometti, Henry Moore, and Helen Frankenthaler. Of interest to movie fans are the exhibits of the late actor William Holden's art collection and furniture designed and crafted by actor William Montgomery. The Annenberg Theater presents plays, concerts, lectures, operas, and other cultural events. ✉ *101 Museum Dr.,* ☎ *760/325–0189.* ✉ *$6; free 1st Fri. of month.* ☉ *Tues.–Thurs. and weekends 10–4, Fri. 10–8.*

The **Palm Springs Air Museum** showcases several dozen World War II aircraft including a B-17 Flying Fortress bomber, a P-51 Mustang, a Lockheed P-38, and a Grumman TBF Avenger. Guided tours are conducted weekends at noon and 2 PM. ✉ *745 N. Gene Autry Trail,* ☎ *760/778–6262.* ✉ *$7.50.* ☉ *Wed.–Mon. 10–5.*

❺ Four-acre **Moorten Botanical Garden** nurtures more than 3,000 plant varieties in settings that simulate their original environments. Indian artifacts and rock, crystal, and wood forms are exhibited. ✉ *1701 S. Palm Canyon Dr.,* ☎ *760/327–6555.* ✉ *$2.* ☉ *Mon.–Sat. 9–4:30, Sun. 10–4.*

❻ The **Indian Canyons** are the ancestral home of the Agua Caliente Band of Indians, who selected them for their lush oases, abundant water, and wildlife. Visitors can see remnants of this life: rock art, house pits and foundations, irrigation ditches, bedrock mortars, pictographs, and stone houses and shelters built atop high cliff walls. Three canyons are open: Palm Canyon, noted for its lush stand of Washingtonia palms; Murray, home of Peninsula bighorn sheep and a herd of wild ponies; and Andreas, where a stand of fan palms contrasts with sharp rock formations. The trading post in Palm Canyon has hiking maps, refreshments, Indian art, jewelry, and weavings. ✉ *38-500 S. Palm Canyon Dr.,* ☎ *760/325–5673.* ✉ *$5.* ☉ *Daily 8–5, summer 8–6.*

❼ Elegant resorts, fine dining, world-class golf and tennis tournaments, and celebrity residents come together in **Rancho Mirage.** The Eisenhower Medical Center, the Betty Ford Center, and numerous celebrity estates are here.

Children's Discovery Museum of the Desert, which was scheduled for a late 1997 opening, will hold instructive hands-on exhibits for kids— a miniature rock climb, a magnetic sculpture wall, make-it-and-take-it-apart projects, a rope maze, a family center, and an area for toddlers.

The admission fee and hours of operation had not been determined at press time. ✉ *71–701 Gerald Ford Dr., Rancho Mirage,* ☎ *760/321– 0602.*

❽ Some of the best desert people-watching, shopping, and dining can be found along trendy **El Paseo,** just west of Highway 111 in Palm Desert (☞ Shopping, *below*).

★ **❾** Come eyeball to eyeball with coyotes, mountain lions, cheetahs, bighorn sheep, golden eagles, warthogs, and owls at the **Living Desert Wildlife and Botanical Park.** Easy to challenging trails traverse desert gardens populated with plants of the Mojave, Colorado, and Sonoran deserts. One exhibit pinpoints the San Andreas earthquake fault across the valley. During the holidays, the park presents Wildlights, an evening light show. Shuttle service, interpretive tours, wildlife shows (daily in Tennity Amphitheater), strollers, and wheelchairs are available. An authentic African village with an open marketplace and animal exhibits is expected to open in late 1998. ✉ *47-900 Portola Ave. (follow signs west from Hwy. 111), Palm Desert,* ☎ *760/346–5694.* ▱ *$7.50.* ☾ *Oct.– mid-June, daily 9–5, mid-June–July and Sept., daily 8 AM–noon.*

The **Santa Rosa Mountains National Scenic Area Visitor Center,** operated by the Bureau of Land Management, contains exhibits illustrating the natural history of the desert and is staffed by knowledgeable volunteers. A landscaped garden displays native plants and frames a sweeping view. ✉ *51-500 Hwy. 74, Palm Desert,* ☎ *760/862–9984.* ☾ *Fri.–Mon. 9 AM–4 PM.*

Dining

CATHEDRAL CITY

$ ✕ **Red Bird Diner.** Host Gayla Morris serves '50s-style food at her diner, which is decorated with life-size murals of the decade's icons: James Dean, Ed Sullivan, and a bright-red T-Bird. Lamb is the Red Bird's specialty, but the chef also cooks country-fried steak, liver and onions, and chicken and dumplings. ✉ *35-955 Date Palm Dr.,* ☎ *760/324–7707. AE, D, DC, MC, V.*

LA QUINTA

$–$$ ✕ **La Quinta Cliffhouse.** Sweeping mountain views at sunset and the early ★ California ambience of a western movie set draw patrons to this restaurant perched halfway up a hillside. The eclectic menu roams the globe: grilled shrimp Provençale, Caesar salad with chicken, ahi tuna Szechuan style, and a chocolate macadamia-nut pie. Sunday brunch is always crowded. ✉ *78-250 Hwy. 111,* ☎ *760/360–5991. AE, MC, V.*

PALM DESERT

$$$–$$$$ ✕ **Cuistot.** Chef-owner Bernard Dervieux trained with French culi- ★ nary star Paul Bocuse, but he's taken a more worldly approach at his own restaurant, tucked into the back of an El Paseo courtyard. Signature dishes include spinach linguine with shrimp, Chinese-style duck, and rack of lamb with rosemary. ✉ *73-111 El Paseo,* ☎ *760/340– 1000. AE, DC, MC, V. Closed Mon. No lunch Sun.*

$$–$$$ ✕ **Doug Arango's.** The popular Palm Desert purveyor of nouvelle Italian cuisine occupies a postmodern space with white columns and tomato-red walls. The restaurant's housemade sausages are included in several dishes; zucchini pancakes and seafood pasta plates are among the best selections. ✉ *73-520 El Paseo,* ☎ *760/341–4120. Reservations essential. AE, D, DC, MC, V. Closed Mon. and July–mid-Sept.*

$$–$$$ ✕ **Ristorante Mamma Gina.** The Tuscan chef at this simply furnished trattoria prepares deep-fried artichokes, fettuccine with porcini mushrooms, prawns with artichokes and zucchini, robust soups, and other specialties in an open kitchen. ✉ *73-705 El Paseo,* ☎ *760/568–9898.*

Reservations essential. AE, DC, MC, V. No lunch Sun. Summer hrs vary.

$$ ✗ **Palomino Euro Bistro.** One of the desert's longtime favorites specializes in grilled and roasted entrées: spit-roasted garlic chicken, oak-fired thin-crust pizza, and oven-roasted prawns. Huge reproductions of famous French Impressionist paintings fill the walls of this active bistro. ✉ 73-101 Hwy. 111, ☎ 760/773–9091. AE, D, DC, MC, V. No lunch.

$–$$ ✗ **Café des Beaux Arts.** This desert version of a sidewalk café serves garlicky French and Italian food in a trendy setting. The Beaux Arts is very busy at lunchtime. ✉ 73-640 El Paseo, ☎ 760/346–0669. AE, MC, V. No dinner Tues.

$ ✗ **Daily Grill.** Portions are huge at this bustling deli–coffee shop that dishes up a dinner-plate-size chicken pot pie. Best buys are the blue-plate specials, which include soup or salad and turkey meat loaf, a beef-dip sandwich, or a turkey steak, plus unlimited thirst-quenching lemonade. ✉ 73-061 El Paseo, ☎ 760/779–9911. AE, MC, V.

$ ✗ **La Donne Cucina Italiana.** Families like this busy restaurant-deli and its large portions of homemade pasta, risotto, chicken, and other dishes. ✉ 72-624 El Paseo, ☎ 760/773–9441. Reservations essential. AE, D, MC, V. Closed Sun.

$ ✗ **Le Peep.** This casual coffeehouse serves breakfast and lunch. Deep-skillet entrées—down-home sausage, eggs Benedict, omelets, and frittatas—anchor the huge breakfast menu. ✉ 73-725 El Paseo, ☎ 760/773–1004. AE, D, MC, V. No dinner.

PALM SPRINGS

$$–$$$ ✗ **Blue Coyote Grill.** Diners sit under blue umbrellas and munch on burritos, tacos, fajitas (or more unusual items, such as Yucatán lamb or orange chicken) at this casual restaurant with several flower-decked patios in addition to inside dining rooms. Two busy cantinas serve up tasty margaritas to a youngish crowd. ✉ 445 N. Palm Canyon Dr., ☎ 760/327–1196. AE, DC, MC, V.

$$–$$$ ✗ **Otani Garden Restaurant.** Sushi, tempura, and teppan (grilled) specialties are served in a serene garden setting at Otani. An always fresh Sunday brunch buffet includes tempura, stir-fried entrées, salads, sushi, and desserts. ✉ 266 Avenida Caballeros, ☎ 760/327–6700. AE, DC, MC, V. No lunch Sat.

$$–$$$ ✗ **Palmie.** The humble location in the back of a shopping arcade and ★ the simple decor of Toulouse-Lautrec and other Gallic posters give nary a hint of the subtle creations prepared at this gem of a French restaurant. The two-cheese soufflé is one of several superb appetizers. Equally impressive are a duck confit and duck fillets dish served with pear slices in red wine and Palmie's signature entrée, a perfectly crafted fish stew in a thin-yet-rich butter-cream broth. ✉ Galeria Henry Frank, 276 N. Palm Canyon Dr., ☎ 760/320–3375. AE, DC, MC, V. No lunch.

$$ ✗ **Las Casuelas Original.** This tourist favorite serves great (in size and taste) margaritas and average Mexican dishes: chicken enchilada suiza, carne asada, chicken cilantro salad, and tamales in a sweetly piquant mole sauce. ✉ 368 N. Palm Canyon Dr., ☎ 760/325–3213. AE, DC, MC, V.

$ ✗ **Louise's Pantry.** A local landmark next to the Plaza Theater, this 1940s-style diner—bright yellow decor, with booths and a long counter—serves down-home cooking, such as chicken and dumplings and short ribs of beef. There's usually a line to get in. Breakfast is served all day. ✉ 124 S. Palm Canyon Dr., ☎ 760/325–5124. MC, V.

RANCHO MIRAGE

$$$$ ✗ **Morton's of Chicago.** The desert version of this national steak-house chain lures in the meat-and-potatoes crowd with its selection of prime beef and seafood, contemporary hors d'oeuvres, and traditional desserts.

Huge LeRoy Neiman serigraphs hang in the bustling dining room. The bar is quiet and clubby. ✉ *74-880 Country Club Dr.,* ☎ *760/340– 6865,* ℻ *760/340–2645. AE, DC, MC, V. No lunch.*

$$ ✕ **Bangkok V.** Dedicated spicy-food fans gather at this well-decorated
★ restaurant to savor artistically prepared traditional Thai cuisine. The spring rolls are crisp and fresh. When you order be sure to tell them how hot you want your food. ✉ *69-930 Hwy. 111,* ☎ *760/770–9508. AE, DC, MC, V. No lunch.*

$$ ✕ **Shame on the Moon.** The American and Continental entrées at this contemporary bistro include pasta, fresh seafood, and filet mignon. The service is considered the best in the desert. ✉ *69-950 Frank Sinatra Dr.,* ☎ *760/324–5515. Reservations essential. AE, MC, V. No lunch.*

Lodging

INDIAN WELLS

$$$$ 🏨 **Hyatt Grand Champions Resort.** This stark white resort on 34 acres of natural desert hosts the *Newsweek* Champions and State Farm Evert Cup professional tennis tournaments, which are played in the largest tennis stadium in the West. Suite-style rooms have balconies or terraces, sitting areas, and minibars. The most luxurious of these have courtyards with private whirlpool tubs, butler service, and fireplaces. ✉ *44-600 Indian Wells La., 92210,* ☎ *760/341–1000 or 800/233– 1234,* ℻ *760/568–2236. 336 units. 2 restaurants, coffee shop, lounge, 4 pools, wading pool, beauty salon, 2 outdoor hot tubs, massage, sauna, spa, steam room, driving range, 2 golf courses, putting green, 12 tennis courts, aerobics, health club, bicycles, pro shop, children's programs, laundry service, business services, convention center, meeting rooms. AE, D, DC, MC, V.*

$$$$ 🏨 **Renaissance Esmeralda Resort.** The centerpiece of this luxurious Mediterranean-style resort is an eight-story atrium lobby with a fountain that flows through a rivulet in the floor, into cascading pools, and outside to lakes surrounding the property. Given its size, the hotel has a surprisingly intimate ambience. Spacious guest rooms are decorated in light wood with desert-color accents; they have sitting areas, balconies, refreshment centers, two TV sets, and travertine-marble vanities in the bathrooms. One pool has a sandy beach. Golf and tennis instruction are available. ✉ *44-400 Indian Wells La., 92210,* ☎ *760/ 773–4444 or 800/552–4386,* ℻ *760/773–9250. 560 rooms. 2 restaurants, lounge, minibars, 2 pools, wading pool, 2 outdoor hot tubs, massage, sauna, steam room, driving range, 2 golf courses, putting green, 7 tennis courts, basketball, health club, volleyball, bicycles, pro shop, children's programs, coin laundry, concierge, business services, meeting rooms. AE, D, DC, MC, V.*

LA QUINTA

$$$$ 🏨 **La Quinta Resort and Club.** The desert's oldest resort, which opened
★ in 1926, is a lush green oasis. Rooms are in historic adobe casitas separated by broad expanses of lawn and in newer two-story units surrounding individual swimming pools and brilliant gardens. Fireplaces, robes, stocked refrigerators, and fruit-laden orange trees contribute to a discreet and sparely luxurious atmosphere. A premium is placed on privacy, which accounts for La Quinta's continuing popularity with Hollywood celebrities. Frank Capra, for example, lived here for many years, and it's said that Greta Garbo roamed the grounds bumming cigarettes from guests. Managed jointly with PGA West, La Quinta arranges access to some of the desert's most celebrated golf courses. John Austin, brother of Tracy, directs the Tennis Center. ✉ *49-499 Eisenhower Dr., 92253,* ☎ *760/564–4111 or 800/854–1271,* ℻ *760/564– 7656. 640 rooms, including 27 suites. 5 restaurants, bar, lounge, 25 pools, beauty salon, 38 outdoor hot tubs, 4 golf courses, 30 tennis courts,*

health club, children's programs, concierge, business services. AE, D, DC, MC, V.

PALM DESERT

$$$$ ⊞ **Marriott's Desert Springs Resort and Spa.** This sprawling business- and convention-oriented hotel has a dramatic U-shape design. The building wraps around the desert's largest private lake, into which an indoor, stair-stepped waterfall flows. Rooms have lake or mountain views, balconies, and oversize bathrooms. There are long walks from the lobby to rooms; if driving, request one close to the parking lot. ⊠ *74-855 Country Club Dr., 92260,* ☎ *760/341–2211 or 800/331–3112,* FAX *760/341–1872. 884 rooms, 51 suites. 5 restaurants, 2 lounges, snack bar, minibars, 5 pools, barbershop, beauty salon, 5 hot tubs, spa, driving range, 2 golf courses, putting green, 20 tennis courts, badminton, basketball, croquet, health club, jogging, volleyball, shops, children's programs, laundry service, business services, convention center. AE, D, DC, MC, V.*

$$–$$$ ⊞ **Tres Palmas Bed and Breakfast.** Enormous windows, high open-beam ceilings, light wood, and textured peach tile floors lend this contemporary inn near El Paseo a bright and spacious feel. The Southwest decor in common areas and guest rooms (which are functional rather than luxurious) incorporates old Navajo rugs from the innkeepers' collection. Room rates include breakfast. ⊠ *73-135 Tumbleweed La.,* ☎ *760/ 773–9858. 4 rooms. Pool, outdoor hot tub. MC, V.*

PALM SPRINGS

$$$$ ⊞ **Givenchy Hotel and Spa.** Indulgence is the word for this resort modeled after the Givenchy spa in Versailles. The ambience is totally French, from the Empire-style decor to the perfectly manicured rose gardens. Most rooms are one- or two-bedroom suites, with separate salons, some with private patios and mountain or garden views. Personalized spa services include everything from facials to marine mud wraps to aromatherapy. Restaurant menus emulate those found in Paris; spa cuisine is also offered. ⊠ *4200 E. Palm Canyon Dr., 92264,* ☎ *760/770–5000 or 800/276–5000,* FAX *760/324–6104. 98 rooms. 2 restaurants, lounge, barbershop, beauty salon, spa, golf privileges, 6 tennis courts, health club, jogging, bicycles, shops, concierge, business services, meeting rooms. AE, D, DC, MC, V.*

$$$$ ⊞ **Hyatt Regency Suites.** This hotel's six-story asymmetrical atrium lobby holds an enormous metal sculpture suspended from the ceiling. One- and two-bedroom suites have private balconies and two TVs. The suites in the back have pool and mountain views. There's free underground parking, and guests have golf privileges at Rancho Mirage Country Club and six other area courses. ⊠ *285 N. Palm Canyon Dr., 92262,* ☎ *760/322–9000 or 800/233–1234,* FAX *760/325–4027. 192 suites. 3 restaurants, lounge, pool, beauty salon, outdoor hot tub, golf privileges, exercise room, concierge, business services, meeting rooms, airport shuttle. AE, D, DC, MC, V.*

$$$$ ⊞ **Palm Springs Hilton Resort and Racquet Club.** The cool, white marble elegance of this plant-filled resort hotel just off Palm Canyon Drive makes it a popular choice. Rooms have private balconies and refrigerators. ⊠ *400 E. Tahquitz Canyon Way, 92262,* ☎ *760/320–6868 or 800/522–6900,* FAX *760/320–2126. 260 rooms. Restaurant, lounge, pool, barbershop, beauty salon, outdoor hot tub, sauna, golf privileges, 6 tennis courts, health club, pro shop, video games, children's programs, concierge, business services, convention center. AE, D, DC, MC, V.*

$$$$ ⊞ **Sundance Villas.** Two- and three-bedroom duplex homes in this complex are decorated in soft desert colors. All have full kitchens, bathrooms with huge sunken tubs, outdoor pools and hot tubs, and laundry facilities. The villas are away from most desert attractions in a secluded

residential area at the north end of Palm Springs. Rates, though high, are for up to six people. ⊠ *303 W. Cabrillo Rd., 92262,* ☎ *760/325–3888 or 800/455–3888,* ℻ *760/323–3029. 19 villas. Kitchenettes, in-room VCRs, pool, outdoor hot tub, golf privileges, tennis court, concierge, business services. AE, D, DC, MC, V.*

$$$–$$$$ 🏨 **Abbey West.** This historic property in a quiet residential neighborhood at the north end of town is a knockout, with deep-green and white decor in the art deco style of 1930s Hollywood. Large rooms have private entrances and patios, galley kitchens, and VCRs. There are several tree-shaded patios, a clothing-optional sunbathing area, and an outdoor exercise facility. Room rates at the gay-patronized Abbey include breakfast and lunch. ⊠ *772 Prescott Circle, 92262,* ☎ *760/416–2654 or 800/223–4073,* ℻ *760/322–8534. 16 rooms. Pool, outdoor hot tub. AE, D, DC, MC, V.*

$$$–$$$$ 🏨 **Harlow Hotel.** A historic resort now catering to a gay clientele, this
★   is ideal for those seeking secluded accommodations in a lush garden setting. Rooms are in hacienda-style buildings surrounding a pool; many have fireplaces, private patios, and unusually large bathrooms. Crimson bougainvillea cascades from the rooftops; date palms grow on the property, as do fruit-laden orange, tangerine, and grapefruit trees. There's a secluded clothing-optional sunbathing area. Room rates include breakfast and lunch. ⊠ *175 E. El Alameda, 92262,* ☎ *760/323–3977 or 800/223–4073,* ℻ *760/320–1218. 15 rooms. Pool, outdoor hot tub, exercise room. AE, D, DC, MC, V.*

$$$–$$$$ 🏨 **Spa Hotel and Casino.** Rooms at this hotel built over the original Agua Caliente springs are decorated in soft desert pinks and blues and light wood furniture. Not trendy or splashy, the Spa, which is owned by the Agua Caliente tribe, appeals to an older crowd that appreciates its soothing waters and downtown location. The hotel's Spa Experience is a sampling of services—sink into a tub filled with naturally hot mineral water, rest in the cool white relaxation room, swim in the outdoor mineral pool, or let the sauna warm your spirits. ⊠ *100 N. Indian Canyon Dr., 92262,* ☎ *760/778–1507 or 800/854–1279,* ℻ *760/325–3344. 230 rooms. Restaurant, lounge, pool, barbershop, beauty salon, outdoor hot tub, spa, steam room, golf and tennis privileges, bicycles, shops, casino, concierge, business services, meeting rooms. AE, D, DC, MC, V.*

$$–$$$$ 🏨 **Casa Cody.** The service is personal and gracious at this Western-style B&B just a few steps from the Palm Springs Desert Museum. Spacious studios and one- and two-bedroom suites are furnished simply. Room rates include Continental breakfast. ⊠ *175 S. Cahuilla Rd., 92262,* ☎ *760/320–9346 or 800/231–2639,* ℻ *760/325–8610. 22 units. Kitchenettes, 2 pools, outdoor hot tub. AE, D, DC, MC, V.*

$$–$$$$ 🏨 **Ingleside Inn.** The hacienda-style Ingleside attracts its share of Hollywood personalities, who appreciate the attentive good service and relative seclusion. Many rooms have antiques, fireplaces, whirlpool tubs and steam showers, stocked refrigerators, and private patios. The accommodations in the main building are dark and cool, even in summer. The adjacent Melvyn's Restaurant, which serves Continental and American dishes, is locally popular. ⊠ *200 W. Ramon Rd., 92264,* ☎ *760/325–0046 or 800/772–6655,* ℻ *760/325–0710. 30 roo᷇ ᷇s. Restaurant, bar, outdoor pool, outdoor hot tub, concierge. AE, D, DC, MC, V.*

$$–$$$$ 🏨 **La Mancha Private Pool Villas and Court Club.** Only four blocks from
★   downtown Palm Springs, this Spanish-Moroccan Hollywood-style retreat blocks out the rest of the world with plenty of panache. Opulent villas surrounded by landscaped gardens have kitchens, fireplaces, and private pools; four have private tennis courts. Convertibles for local transportation are available for rental. ⊠ *444 N. Avenida Caballeros,*

92262, ☎ 760/323–1773 or 800/647–7482, FAX 760/323–5928. 66 *villas. Restaurant, pool, putting greens, 7 tennis courts, croquet, health club, paddle tennis, bicycles, coin laundry, business services, meeting rooms, airport shuttle. AE, D, DC, MC, V.*

$$–$$$$ ⊞ **Wyndham Palm Springs.** The main appeal of this hotel is its location adjacent to the Palm Springs Convention Center. The terra-cotta Spanish-colonial building surrounds the largest swimming pool in Palm Springs. Rooms are functional rather than glitzy. Because most of the Wyndham's customers are on business, the atmosphere here is more serious than at most desert establishments. ⊠ *888 Tahquitz Canyon Way, 92262,* ☎ *760/322–6000 or 800/996–3426,* FAX *760/ 322–5551. 252 rooms, 158 suites. 2 restaurants, lounge, pool, wading pool, barbershop, beauty salon, 2 outdoor hot tubs, sauna, golf and tennis privileges, exercise room, bicycles, shops, recreation room, business services, convention center. AE, D, DC, MC, V.*

$$–$$$ ⊞ **Korakia Pensione.** This historic Moorish-style home, built in the 1920s by Scottish artist Gordon Coutts, has long been a haven for the creative set. Winston Churchill came here to paint; more recently photographer Annie Leibovitz has enjoyed the home's scenic mountain view. Inside, rooms are furnished with antiques, handmade furniture, and Oriental rugs; some have fireplaces, and most have kitchens. Innkeeper Doug Smith recently added to his complex a two-room historic house across the street. Room rates include breakfast. ⊠ *257 S. Patencio Rd., 92262,* ☎ *760/864–6411. 20 rooms. Pool, golf privileges. No credit cards.*

$$–$$$ ⊞ **Orchid Tree Inn.** Accommodations at this well-run property a block west of South Palm Canyon Drive vary from motel-style units and bungalows to a two-story town house and a detached house. Some rooms have kitchenettes, and all have contemporary furnishings. Rates include Continental breakfast. ⊠ *290 S. Belardo Rd.,* ☎ *760/325–2791 or 800/733–3435,* FAX *760/325–3855. 40 rooms. Breakfast room, 3 pools, 2 outdoor hot tubs.*

$–$$ ⊞ **Bee Charmer Inn.** This Southwest-style inn with a red-tile roof and terra-cotta tile floors caters exclusively to women. Spacious rooms surround a pool and tropical courtyard; comfortably but not lavishly decorated in soft pastel colors, they come with refrigerators and microwaves. Three rooms have wet bars, and one has a whirlpool bath. Room rates include Continental breakfast. ⊠ *1600 E. Palm Canyon Dr., 92264,* ☎ *760/778–5883. 13 rooms. Pool. AE, D, MC, V.*

$–$$ ⊞ **Hampton Inn.** This chain motel at the north end of Palm Springs occupies landscaped grounds with views of Mt. San Jacinto. Appointments are basic, but there are barbecues for guest use. Continental breakfast is included in the room rates. ⊠ *200 N. Palm Canyon Dr., 92262,* ☎ *760/320–0555 or 800/732–7755,* FAX *760/320–2261. 96 rooms. Pool, outdoor hot tub, business services, meeting rooms. AE, D, DC, MC, V.*

$–$$ ⊞ **Howard Johnson Lodge.** This typical motel-style property is popular with tour groups. Ask for special discounts. ⊠ *701 E. Palm Canyon Dr., 92264,* ☎ *760/320–2700 or 800/854–4345,* FAX *760/320–1591. 205 rooms. Pool, wading pool, outdoor hot tub, coin laundry, business services. AE, D, DC, MC, V.*

$–$$ ⊞ **Vagabond Inn.** Rooms are smallish at this centrally located motel but are clean, comfortable, and a good value. ⊠ *1699 S. Palm Canyon Dr., 92264,* ☎ *760/325–7211 or 800/522–1555,* FAX *760/322–9269. 120 rooms. Coffee shop, pool, outdoor hot tub, 2 saunas. AE, D, DC, MC, V.*

RANCHO MIRAGE

$$$$ **Marriott's Rancho Las Palmas.** The atmosphere is luxuriously laid-
★   back at this family-oriented resort on 240 landscaped acres. An early
California-Spanish theme prevails throughout the public areas and
guest accommodations. Rooms in a series of two-story buildings are
unusually large; all have sitting areas and views of colorful gardens or
well-manicured fairways and greens. ⊠ *41-000 Bob Hope Dr., 92270,*
☎ *760/568–2727 or 800/458–8786,* FAX *760/568–5845. 450 rooms.*
2 restaurants, bar, 2 snack bars, 2 pools, barbershop, beauty salon, 2
outdoor hot tubs, 27-hole golf course, putting green, 25 tennis courts,
health club, jogging, children's programs, playground, concierge, busi-
ness services, convention center. AE, D, DC, MC, V.

$$$$ **Ritz-Carlton Rancho Mirage.** This hotel is tucked into a hillside in
★   the Santa Rosa Mountains with sweeping views of the valley below.
The surroundings are elegant, with gleaming marble and brass, original artwork, plush carpeting, and remarkable comfort. All rooms are
spacious and meticulously appointed with antiques, fabric wall coverings, marble bathrooms, and often two phones and two TVs. The
service is impeccable. ⊠ *68-900 Frank Sinatra Dr., 92270,* ☎ *760/321–*
8282 or 800/241–3333, FAX *760/321–6928. 220 rooms, 19 suites. 3*
restaurants, bar, pool, barbershop, beauty salon, outdoor hot tub, spa,
golf privileges, putting green, 10 tennis courts, basketball, croquet, health
club, hiking, volleyball, pro shop, shops, children's programs, business
services, meeting rooms. AE, D, DC, MC, V.

$$$$ **Westin Mission Hills Resort.** A sprawling Moroccan-style resort on
360 acres, home to the Frank Sinatra Celebrity Golf Tournament, the
Westin is surrounded by fairways and putting greens. Rooms, in two-
story buildings that envelop patios and fountains, have soft desert colors, terra-cotta tile floors, and private patios or balconies. Paths and
creeks meander through the complex, encircling a lagoon-style swimming pool with a several-story water slide. ⊠ *71-333 Dinah Shore Dr.,*
92270, ☎ *760/328–5955 or 800/228–3000,* FAX *760/321–2955. 512*
rooms. 2 restaurants, deli, 2 lounges, 3 pools, beauty salon, 3 outdoor
hot tubs, spa, steam room, 2 18-hole golf courses, 7 tennis courts, aer-
obics, croquet, health club, shuffleboard, volleyball, recreation room,
children's programs. AE, D, DC, MC, V.

Nightlife and the Arts

BARS AND CLUBS

Cactus Corral (⊠ 155 S. Belardo Rd., Palm Springs, ☎ 760/321–
8558) attracts the country-music set with live music and dancing.

C. C. Construction Company (⊠ Smoke Tree Shopping Center, Sunrise
Way at E. Palm Canyon Dr., Palm Springs, ☎ 760/778–1234), a popular gay club, has a huge disco that is open Friday to Sunday and a
smaller dance floor open nightly.

Peabody's Jazz Studio and Coffee Bar (⊠ 134 S. Palm Canyon Dr.,
Palm Springs, ☎ 760/322–1877) attracts everyone from grannies to
grungers for live jazz and poetry readings.

Touche Nightclub and Restaurant (⊠ 42-250 Bob Hope Dr., Rancho
Mirage, ☎ 760/773–1111), which draws a thirty- to fortysomething
crowd ready to party, has live entertainment and dancing.

Zelda's (⊠ 169 N. Indian Canyon Dr., Palm Springs, ☎ 760/325–2375)
has two rooms, one featuring techno jazz and another with Top-40 dance
music and a Male Dance Revue.

CASINOS

State law restricts Indian-run casinos from providing the type of action typically seen in Las Vegas, but they do have video slot machines

that pay off with a printed chit redeemable for cash, and various versions of poker, bingo, and lottery-type games. **Casino Morongo** (✉ I–10, west of Palm Springs, ☎ 800/252-4499). **Fantasy Springs Casino** (✉ Auto Center Dr., off I–10, Indio, ☎ 760/342–5000). **Spa Casino** (✉ 140 N. Indian Canyon Dr., Palm Springs, ☎ 760/323–5865). **Spotlight 29 Casino** (✉ 46-200 Harrison St., Coachella, ☎ 760/775–5566).

FESTIVALS

The mid-January **Nortel Palm Springs International Film Festival** (☎ 760/322–2930) brings stars and more than 150 feature films from 25 countries, plus panel discussions, short films, and documentaries, to Palm Desert's McCallum Theatre and other venues. The **La Quinta Arts Festival** (☎ 760/564–1244), normally held the third weekend in March, includes some fine work and has classy entertainment and food.

THEATER

Annenberg Theater (✉ Palm Springs Desert Museum, 101 Museum Dr., ☎ 619/325–4490) hosts Broadway shows, opera, lectures, Sunday-afternoon chamber concerts, and other events.

Fabulous Palm Springs Follies (✉ Plaza Theater, 128 S. Palm Canyon Dr., ☎ 760/864–6514), the hottest ticket in the desert, presents 10 sell-out performances each week. The vaudeville-style revue stars extravagantly costumed retired (but very much in shape) showgirls, singers, and dancers. Admission is $24.50–$39.

McCallum Theatre (✉ 73-000 Fred Waring Dr., Palm Desert, ☎ 760/340–2787), the principal cultural venue in the desert, presents film, classical and popular music, opera, ballet, and theater.

Outdoor Activities and Sports

BICYCLING

Big Horn Bicycles (✉ 302 N. Palm Canyon, Palm Springs, ☎ 760/325–3367) operates tours to celebrity homes and Indian Canyons and rents bikes. **Mac's Bicycle Rental** (✉ 70-053 Hwy. 111, Rancho Mirage, ☎ 760/321–9444) will deliver mountain, three-speed, and tandem bikes to area hotels. **Palm Springs Recreation Department** (✉ 401 S. Pavilion Way, ☎ 760/323–8272) has maps of some city trails.

FAMILY FUN

Camelot Park (✉ 67-700 E. Palm Canyon Dr., Cathedral City, ☎ 760/770–7525) has miniature golf, bumper boats, batting cages, and video games.

Oasis Waterpark (✉ 1500 Gene Autry Trail, Palm Springs, ☎ 760/327–0499), open from mid-March through October (weekends only after Labor Day), has 13 water slides, a huge wave pool, an arcade, and other attractions.

FITNESS

Gold's Gym (✉ 4070 Airport Center Dr., Palm Springs, ☎ 760/322–4653; ✉ 39-605 Entrepreneur La., Palm Desert, ☎ 760/360–0565).

GOLF

Westin Mission Hills Resort Golf Club (✉ 71-501 Dinah Shore Dr., Rancho Mirage, ☎ 760/328–3198), a challenging Pete Dye–designed course, hosts major tournaments and well-known politicians and movie stars. Greens fee plus mandatory cart: $60.

PGA West (✉ 56-150 PGA Blvd., La Quinta, ☎ 760/564–7170) has two championship courses open to the public. PGA West also provides instruction and golf clinics. Greens fees plus mandatory cart: $185 (Nicklaus course) and $215 (TPC Stadium course).

Tahquitz Creek Palm Springs Golf Resort (✉ 1885 Golf Club Dr., Palm Springs, ☎ 760/328–1005) has 36 holes and a 50-space driving range. Greens fees are $40 to $50 without cart (permitted Monday to Thursday), $90 with cart (mandatory Friday to Sunday).

Tommy Jacobs' Bel-Aire Greens Country Club (✉ 1001 S. El Cielo Rd., Palm Springs, ☎ 760/322–6062) is a nine-hole executive course. Greens fee: $19 ($12 for replay).

The **Bob Hope Desert Classic** takes place January–February. **Dinah Shore LPGA Championship** is a March or April event. Palm Springs hosts more than 100 golf tournaments annually. The Palm Springs Desert Resorts Convention and Visitors Bureau **Events Hotline** (☎ 760/770–1992) lists dates and locations.

POLO

The **Eldorado Polo Club** (✉ 50-950 Madison St., Indio, ☎ 760/342–2223), known as the Winter Polo Capital of the West, is home to world-class polo events. You can pack a picnic and watch practice matches free during the week; there's a $6 per person charge on Sunday.

SPAS

Most major hotels that have spas and fitness facilities—the Givenchy and Spa hotels in Palm Springs and the Marriott Desert Springs resort in Palm Springs among them—offer day programs for nonguests as well as guests. **Futureshape Spa of El Paseo** (✉ 72–695 Hwy. 111, Palm Desert, ☎ 760/773–0032) specializes in beauty, with body wraps, massage, facials, and hair stylists. The **Palms at Palm Springs** (✉ 572 N. Indian Canyon Dr., Palm Springs, ☎ 760/325–1111, FAX 760/327–0867) has a one-day spa program that begins with a 6 AM walk. The package includes a choice of 14 classes, the use of exercise equipment, lectures, and low calorie meals. Options include massage, facials, and wraps.

TENNIS

The *Newsweek* **Champions and State Farm Evert Cup professional tennis tournaments** (☎ 760/341–2757) are held at the Hyatt Grand Champions Resort in Indian Wells for 10 days in March; they attract top-ranked players.

Demuth Park (✉ 4375 Mesquite Ave., no phone) has four lighted courts. **Palm Springs Tennis Center** (✉ 1300 Baristo Rd., ☎ 619/320–0020) has nine lighted courts—fees run $12–$14—and can make arrangements for partners to play at area hotels. **Ruth Hardy Park** (✉ Tamarisk and Caballeros, no phone) has eight lighted courts.

Shopping

SHOPPING DISTRICTS

Palm Desert's **El Paseo,** a long, Mediterranean-style avenue with fountains and courtyards, contains French and Italian fashion boutiques, shoe salons, jewelry designers, children's shops, restaurants, a new Saks Fifth Avenue branch, and nearly 30 galleries. **Palm Desert Town Center** is the largest enclosed mall in the desert, with more than 140 specialty shops, major department stores, movie theaters, an ice-skating rink, and restaurants.

Palm Canyon Drive is the main shopping destination in the city of Palm Springs. Its commercial core extends from Alejo Road on the north to Ramon Road on the south. Anchoring the center of the drive is the Desert Fashion Plaza. The Village Fest, along Palm Canyon here on Thursday nights, brings out craftspeople, antiques sellers, a farmers' market, and entertainment.

ANTIQUES AND COLLECTIBLES

Some of the items for sale in the **Heritage Gallery and Antique District,** a collection of consignment and second-hand shops centered in the 700 and 800 blocks of North Palm Canyon Drive in Palm Springs, come from the homes of celebrities and other wealthy residents.

Classic Consignment Co. (✉ 73-847 El Paseo, Palm Desert, ☎ 760/568–4948) shows full sets of Rosenthal china and Baccarat crystal, barely used contemporary glass and Lucite furnishings, accessories, fine art, and jewelry. Prices match the shop's trendy location.

Desert Estate Liquidators (✉ 803 N. Palm Canyon Dr., ☎ 760/323–2411) carries everything from overwrought bronze nudes and tacky paintings to classy furniture and jewelry.

Estate Sale Co. (✉ 4185 E. Palm Canyon Dr., Palm Springs, ☎ 760/321–7628) is the biggest consignment store in the desert, with a warehouse of furniture, fine art, china and crystal, accessories, jewelry, movie memorabilia, and exercise equipment. Prices are set to keep merchandise moving out the door.

The Village Attic (✉ 849 N. Palm Canyon Dr., ☎ 760/320–6165) specializes in '50s and '60s furniture and accessories.

DRIED FRUIT

Hadley's Fruit Orchards (✉ 48-190 Seminole Rd., Cabazon, ☎ 909/849–5255) sells dried fruit, nuts, date shakes, and wines.

Oasis Date Gardens (✉ 59-111 Hwy. 111, Thermal, ☎ 760/399–5665) sells shakes and conducts twice-a-day tours that show how dates are pollinated, grown, sorted, stored, and packed for shipping.

Shields Date Gardens (✉ 80-225 Hwy. 111, Indio, ☎ 760/347–0996) presents a continuous slide program on the history of the date and sells shakes.

FACTORY OUTLETS

Desert Hills Factory Stores (✉ 48-650 Seminole Rd., Cabazon, ☎ 909/849–6641) is an outlet center with more than 150 brand-name discount fashion shops, among them Polo, Geoffrey Beene, Giorgio Armani, Nike, and Spa Gear.

VINTAGE CLOTHING

Patsy's Clothes Closet (✉ 4121 E. Palm Canyon Dr., Palm Springs, ☎ 760/324–8825) specializes in high-fashion and designer clothing for women and men.

Side Trip to Joshua Tree National Park via Desert Hot Springs

Joshua Tree National Park in the Little San Bernardino Mountains preserves some of the desert's most interesting and beautiful scenery. For visitors it also provides a living example of the rigors of desert life. Highlights of rock formations, historic sites, and unusual plants can be seen in half a day. A more thorough exploration into the backcountry takes a day or more. There are campgrounds within the park, but no other accommodations. However, a few quaint lodgings exist in the towns along the northern edge of the park. Desert Hot Springs, Joshua Tree, and Twentynine Palms are among the towns on the northern route to the park—Gene Autry Trail north from Palm Springs to Pierson Boulevard west in Desert Hot Springs to Highway 62. If you aren't going to visit Desert Hot Springs, you can take I–10 northwest from Palm Springs to connect with Highway 62.

Desert Hot Springs
9 mi north of Palm Springs on Gene Autry Trail.

Known for its hot mineral springs, Desert Hot Springs is home to more than 40 spa resorts, ranging from tiny to large and offering a variety of exotic treatments.

LODGING

$$–$$$$ 🏨 **Two Bunch Palms Resort and Spa.** This gate-guarded resort (you must call for advance reservations) is the most exclusive and romantic resort in the desert. According to legend, gangster Al Capone built the stone-fortress watchtower. Subsequently the resort has become the spa of choice for legions of celebrities who savor the 148° mineral waters, the laid-back atmosphere, and the privacy. Massage styles include Swedish, Japanese, and Native American. The landscaped grounds contain two rock-grotto mineral pools surrounded by ancient palms, secluded picnic areas, meditation benches, and outdoor mud baths. Accommodations range from hotel-style rooms to luxury condos with separate living rooms, kitchens, private whirlpool tubs, and private patios. Room rates include a Continental breakfast. ✉ *67–425 Two Bunch Palms Trail, 92240,* ☎ *760/329–8791 or 800/472–4334,* 📠 *760/329–1874. 44 rooms and suites. Restaurant, 2 pools, 2 tennis courts, health club, hiking. AE, MC, V.*

OFF THE BEATEN PATH   **BIG MORONGO CANYON PRESERVE –** Once an Indian village and later a cattle ranch, this serene natural oasis contains a year-round stream and waterfalls that support a variety of birds and animals. One of the Mojave's largest stands of Cottonwoods and willow woodlands lines a stream favored by great horned owls and many songbirds. A shaded meadow is a fine place for a picnic, and hiking options include several choice trails. No pets are permitted. ✉ *East Dr., Morongo Valley,* ☎ *760/363-7190.* 🎫 *Free.* ⊙ *Daily 7:30 AM–sunset.*

Joshua Tree
17 mi from Desert Hot Springs, north and east on Hwy. 62.

Primarily a gateway to the national park, the town of Joshua Tree has a few fast food outlets and one lodging of note. The 🏨 **Joshua Tree Inn** (✉ 61259 29 Palms Hwy., 92252, ☎ 760/366–1188), formerly a motel, was popular with rock stars in the '70s and early '80s. It's now a sedate B&B.

Twentynine Palms
11 mi east of Joshua Tree on Hwy. 62, 56 mi from Palm Springs, northwest on I–10 and north and east on Hwy. 62.

This onetime liberty town for marines stationed at a nearby base has begun to reinvent itself for visitors to the nearby national park by installing murals depicting local history on the exterior walls of commercial buildings around town. The funky 🏨 **29 Palms Inn** (✉ 73-980 Inn Ave., 92277, ☎ 760/367–3505) on the Oasis of Mara has a popular western-theme restaurant. Another lodging option is the 🏨 **Best Western Gardens Motel** (✉ 71-487 Twentynine Palms Hwy., 92277, ☎ 760/ 367–2584).

Joshua Tree National Park
★ ⑩ *61 mi from Palm Springs, northwest on I–10, north and east on Hwy. 62 to the town of Joshua Tree; from here head southeast on Park Blvd. to the park's west entrance or continue east on Hwy. 62 to Twentynine Palms and follow signs to Utah Trail and the north entrance.*

The 794,000-acre Joshua Tree National Park contains complex, ruggedly beautiful scenery. Its mountains of jagged rock, natural cactus gardens, and lush oases shaded by tall fan palms mark the meeting place of the Mojave (high) and Colorado (low) deserts. This is prime hiking, rock-climbing and exploring country, where coyotes, desert pack rats, and exotic plants, such as the creamy white yucca, red-tipped ocotillo, and cholla cactus, reside. Extensive stands of Joshua trees give the park its name. The trees were named by early white settlers who felt their unusual forms resembled the biblical Joshua raising his arms toward heaven.

Portions of the park can be seen in a half-day excursion from desert-resort cities. A full day's driving tour would reveal highlights and allow time for a nature walk or two and stops at many of the 50 wayside exhibits, which provide insight into Joshua Tree's geology and rich vegetation. Some of the park is above 4,000 ft—it can be chilly in winter. There are no services within the park and little water; visitors are advised to carry a gallon of water per person per day.

Those planning a half-day visit to Joshua Tree National Park should enter through the West Entrance Station off Highway 62 at Joshua Tree and follow the Park Boulevard loop road to the North Entrance Station near Twentynine Palms, backtracking to the resort cities via Highway 62. The stands of Joshua trees along this route are particularly alluring in spring, when the upraised branches support creamy white blossoms. The many piles of rocks in this section are fun to explore and climb.

Those planning to spend a full day in the park can proceed through the west entrance, explore the northern loop, stop at the Oasis Visitor Center, and then take the stunning but winding desert drive southward toward the Cottonwood Springs area which in springtime has one of the desert's best displays of wildflowers. The Cottonwood Visitor Center has a small museum, picnic tables, water, and a 1-mi interpretive trail to the **Cottonwood Spring Oasis**; it gets very crowded in spring.

The **Oasis Visitor Center** (⊠ Utah Trail, ½ mi south of Hwy. 62) has an excellent selection of free and low-cost brochures, books, posters, and maps as well as several educational exhibits. Rangers are on hand to answer questions. **Oasis of Mara** (a ½-mi walk from the visitor center), inhabited first by Indians and later by prospectors and homesteaders, now provides a home for birds, small mammals, and other wildlife.

A crawl through the big boulders that block **Hidden Valley**, once a cattle rustlers' hangout, reveals a bit of the wild and woolly human history of Joshua Tree. The 1½₀-mi loop trail from Hidden Valley to **Barker Dam** goes past petroglyphs (painted over by a film crew) on the way to a dam built by early ranchers and miners; today the dam collects rainwater and is used by wildlife.

Keys View is the most dramatic overlook in Joshua Tree National Park. At elevation 5,185 ft, the view extends across the desert to Mt. San Jacinto and on clear days as far south as the Salton Sea. Sunrise and sunset are magical times, when the light throws rocks and trees into high relief before (or after) bathing the hills in brilliant shades of red, orange, and gold.

Geology Tour Road, recommended for four-wheel-drive vehicles, is a self-guided 18-mi dirt road that winds through some of the park's most fascinating landscape.

At the **Cholla Cactus Gardens,** a huge stand of the legendary "jumping cactus," a short trail interprets the wildlife and plants typical of the Colorado Desert.

If you're entering the park from the south, you'll pass the Cottonwood Visitor Center a few miles after you exit I–10 (head north) just east of the town of Mecca. The center has a small museum, picnic tables, water, rest rooms, and a 1-mi interpretative trail to the **Cottonwood Spring Oasis.**

✉ *Joshua Tree National Park, 74-485 National Park Dr., Twentynine Palms 92277, ☎ 760/367–7511. ▨ $10 per car, $5 for those who arrive by other means. ⊙ Visitor centers daily 8–4:30, park 24 hrs.*

PALM SPRINGS A TO Z

Arriving and Departing

By Bus
Greyhound (☎ 800/231–2222) provides service to the Palm Springs Depot (✉ 311 N. Indian Canyon Dr., ☎ 760/325–2053) from Los Angeles, San Diego, and elsewhere.

By Car
Palm Springs is about a two-hour drive east of Los Angeles and a three-hour drive northeast of San Diego. Highway 111 brings you right onto Palm Canyon Drive, the main thoroughfare in Palm Springs and the connecting route to other desert communities. From Los Angeles take the San Bernardino Freeway (I–10E) to Highway 111. From San Diego, I–15N connects with the Pomona Freeway (Highway 60), leading to the San Bernardino Freeway (I–10E) east. An alternative, more scenic good-weather route from San Diego begins east on I–8. Then take Highways 67, 78, and 79 north to Aguanga, where Highway 371 heads east to Highway 74 (Palms to Pines Highway), which joins Highway 111 between Palm Desert and Indian Wells. Desert exits are clearly marked: Highway 111 for Palm Springs, Monterey for Palm Desert, Washington for La Quinta. If you're coming from the Riverside area, you can also take Highway 74 east.

By Plane
Major airlines serving **Palm Springs Regional Airport** (☎ 760/323–8161) include Alaska, American/American Eagle, America West Express, Reno Air, Skywest, United/United Express, and US Airways Express. *See* Air Travel *in* the Gold Guide for airline phone numbers. Most hotels provide service to and from the airport, which is about 2 mi from downtown Palm Springs.

By Train
Amtrak (☎ 800/872–7245) passenger trains serve the Indio area, 20 mi east of Palm Springs. From Indio, Greyhound Lines bus service is available to Palm Springs.

Getting Around

By Bus
SunBus, operated by the Sunline Transit Agency (☎ 760/343–3451), serves the entire Coachella Valley from Desert Hot Springs to Mecca.

By Car
The desert-resort communities occupy a stretch of about 20 mi between I–10 in the east and Palm Canyon Drive in the west. Although some

areas such as Palm Canyon Drive in Palm Springs and El Paseo are walkable, having a car is the best way to get around.

By Taxi

Checker Cab (☎ 760/325–2868). **A Valley Cabousine** (☎ 760/340–5845).

Contacts and Resources

Car Rental

Most major car-rental companies are represented in the Palm Springs area (☞ Car Rental *in* the Gold Guide).

Emergencies

Ambulance (☎ 911). **Police** (☎ 911).

Desert Hospital (☎ 760/323–6511).

Gregory Yates, D.D.S. (☎ 760/327–8448).

Guided Tours

AERIAL TOURS

Fantasy Balloon Flights (☎ 760/398–6322) organizes trips in the Coachella Valley. **Sunrise Balloons** (☎ 800/548–9912) has balloon excursions and helicopter tours.

CELEBRITY TOURS

Palm Springs Celebrity Tours (✕ 4751 E. Palm Canyon Dr., Palm Springs, ☎ 760/770–2700) has hour-long and 2½-hour tours that cover Palm Springs area history, points of interest, and celebrity homes. Prices range from $12 to $17.

DESERT TOURS

Covered Wagon Tours (☎ 760/347–2161) takes visitors on an old-time, two-hour exploration of the desert with a cookout at the end of the journey. **Desert Adventures** (☎ 760/864–6530) takes to the wilds with Jeep tours of Indian canyons, off-road in the Santa Rosa Mountains, and into a mystery canyon. **Desert Safari Guides** (✉ Box 194, Rancho Mirage, ☎ 760/776–6087 or 888/867–2327) leads tours of various lengths through Indian Canyons and conducts nighttime full-moon desert excursions.

Vacation Rentals

Rental Connection (✉ Box 8567, Palm Springs 92263, ☎ 760/320–7336 or 800/462–7256). **Sunrise Co.** (✉ 76-300 Country Club Dr., Palm Desert 92211, ☎ 800/869–1130).

Visitor Information

Palm Springs Desert Resorts (✉ 69-930 Hwy. 111, Suite 201, Rancho Mirage 92270, ☎ 760/770–9000 or 800/967–3767; 760/770–1992 Activities Hotline). **Palm Springs Visitor Information Center** (✉ 2781 N. Palm Canyon Dr., Palm Springs 92262, ☎ 800/347–7746).

16 The Mojave Desert and Death Valley

When most people assemble their "must-see" list of California attractions, the desert isn't often among the top contenders. What with its heat and vast, sparsely populated tracts of land, the desert is no Disneyland. But that's precisely why it deserves a closer look. The natural riches here are overwhelming: rolling waves of sand dunes, black cinder cones thrusting up hundreds of feet into the air from a blistered desert floor, riotous sheets of wildflowers, bizarrely shaped Joshua trees basking in the orange glow of a sunset, and an abundant silence that is both dramatic and startling.

THE MOJAVE DESERT begins just north of the San Bernardino Mountains, along the northern edge of Los Angeles, and extends north 150 mi into the Eureka Valley and east 200 mi to the Colorado River. Death Valley lies north and east of the Mojave, jutting into Nevada near Beatty. The Mojave, with elevations ranging from 3,000 to 5,000 ft above sea level, is known as the High Desert; Death Valley, the Low Desert, with points at almost 300 ft below sea level, is the lowest spot in the United States.

By Aaron Sugarman and Dianne Aaronson

Because of the vast size of California's deserts, an area about as big as Ohio, and the frequently extreme weather, careful planning is essential for an enjoyable desert adventure. Conveniences, facilities, trails, gas stations, and supermarkets do not lurk just around the corner from many desert sights. Be sure to fill your tank before entering Death Valley—fuel is cheaper on the interstates and you'll avoid running out. Also, check your vehicle's oil and its water and tire pressure. It is advisable on the steeper grades to shut off your air-conditioning to avoid engine overheating. Different regions of the desert can be easily handled in day trips, but more extensive exploring will require overnight stays. Reliable maps are a must, as signage is limited and, in some places, nonexistent. Other important accessories include a compass, a cellular phone, extra food and water (three gallons per person per day is recommended, plus additional radiator water), sunglasses, extra clothes (for wind or cool nights), and a hat (if you're going to do any walking around in the sun). Bring along sufficient clothing to block the sun's rays. A pair of binoculars can come in handy, and don't forget your camera: You're likely to see things you've never seen before.

Pleasures and Pastimes

Camping
Because vegetation in the desert is sparse, campers are truly one with the elements, including the hot sun: Bring equipment that can handle extreme temperatures. Campgrounds are inexpensive or free; most campsites are primitive.

Dining
The Fred Harvey–operated restaurants in Death Valley range from a cafeteria to an upscale Continental restaurant. There are fast-food and chain establishments in Ridgecrest, Victorville, and Barstow. Experienced desert travelers carry an ice chest stocked with food and beverages. Replenish your food stash at the larger towns of Ridgecrest and Barstow, where you'll find a better selection and non-tourist prices.

CATEGORY	COST*
$$$$	over $50
$$$	$30–$50
$$	$20–$30
$	under $20

per person for a three-course meal, excluding drinks, service, and tax

Hiking
Hiking trails are abundant throughout the desert and meander toward sights that would be missed from the road. Plan your walks before or after the noonday sun, bring protective clothing, and be wary of tarantulas, snakes, and other potentially hazardous creatures. Paths through canyons are sometimes partially protected from the heat, so if your time is limited, save these for midday.

Lodging

Larger towns such as Barstow seem to have a motel on every corner, but there are only three in all of Death Valley, the cheapest in Stovepipe Wells Village. Those preferring quiet nights and an unfettered view of the desert sky and Mosaic Canyon will enjoy Stovepipe. Families with children may prefer the Furnace Creek end of Death Valley, with easy access to the visitor center and various sights.

CATEGORY	COST*
$$$$	over $175
$$$	$120–$175
$$	$80–$120
$	under $80

All prices are for a standard double room, excluding tax.

Exploring the Desert

The Mojave Desert is a sprawling space, but many of its visitable attractions are conveniently situated on a north–south axis along U.S. 395 and Highway 178. The Western Mojave region has Ridgecrest (on U.S. 395) as its major northern hub and Victorville (on I–15) as its southern one. If you plan to stop overnight en route to Death Valley, both Ridgecrest and Lone Pine have tourist services and accommodations, as do Barstow and Baker on I–15. The bulk of the Eastern Mojave lies between the parallel routes of I–15 and I–40. Barstow, at the junction of the two interstates, is the region's western hub. Needles, on I–40 near the Nevada border, is the eastern hub.

Numbers in the text correspond to numbers in the margin and on the Mojave Desert and Death Valley maps.

Great Itineraries

IF YOU HAVE 3 DAYS

Well-preserved Randsburg, in the **Rand Mining District** ②, is a good starting point from either San Francisco or Los Angeles. Pack a picnic lunch and drive through colorful **Red Rock Canyon State Park** ③ and take a walk among the volcanic rock formations of **Fossil Falls** ④ before moving on to ⌐ **Ridgecrest** ⑤ for a stop at the Maturango Museum, which also serves as a tourist information center. Have dinner and spend the night in Ridgecrest. The following day, see the surreal **Trona Pinnacles** ⑥, and then continue on to the ⌐ **Furnace Creek** ⑩ visitor center before catching awe-inspiring perspectives of the Death Valley region from **Artists Palette** ⑬, **Zabriskie Point** ⑭, and **Dante's View** ⑮. Return home on the third day after stopping at the **Harmony Borax Works** ⑨, where the famed 20-mule teams once toiled, and hiking through **Golden Canyon** ⑪.

IF YOU HAVE 7 DAYS

Leave from Los Angeles, driving over the **San Andreas Fault** ①, with stops at the **Rand Mining District** ②, **Red Rock Canyon** ③, and **Fossil Falls** ④ before stopping in ⌐ **Ridgecrest** ⑤ to dine and lodge. Or, from San Francisco, visit Fossil Falls and then stop briefly at the Maturango Museum in Ridgecrest before driving to Red Rock Canyon and the Rand Mining District. Take a full-day tour of the Petroglyph Canyons (spring and fall weekends only), or visit the **Bureau of Land Management Regional Wild Horse and Burro Corrals** on the way to the **Trona Pinnacles** ⑥ and ⌐ **Stovepipe Wells Village** ⑦ in Death Valley. (If you've toured Petroglyph when the days are long, you should be able to see some of the pinnacles before nightfall.) On the third morning, stroll through **Mosaic Canyon** before driving north for a full day at **Scotty's Castle** ⑧. Have lunch there or pack a picnic and eat along the roadside. Loop back toward ⊞ **Furnace Creek** ⑩ in the late afternoon. If you're in the area on a performance day, zip down to Death Valley Junction to see the 7:45 PM show at **Marta Becket's Amargosa Opera House** ⑯. Drop in at the Furnace Creek visitor center on day four, hike through **Golden Canyon** ⑪, and drive to **Badwater** ⑫, the lowest point in the Northern Hemisphere, before returning via **Artists Palette** ⑬. Visit the lookout at **Zabriskie Point** ⑭ and walk along **Dante's View** ⑮ before driving south to ⊞ **Baker** ⑰. Use Baker as your fifth-day base. Drive along Kelbaker Road to the **Kelso Dunes** ⑱ and visit the **Mitchell Caverns** in **Providence Mountains State Recreation Area** ⑲. If time permits, drive through **Afton Canyon** ⑳ before staying overnight in ⊞ **Barstow** ㉑. On day six, hike around the **Rainbow Basin National Natural Landmark** ㉒ and tour the **Calico Early Man Archeological Site** ㉔ (Wednesday through Sunday; the last tour starts at 3:30 PM). On day seven, especially if you have kids, visit **Calico Ghost Town** ㉓ before leaving the desert.

When to Tour the Mojave Desert and Death Valley

Spring and fall are the best seasons to tour the desert. Winters are generally mild, but summers can be brutal. The early morning is the best time to visit sights and avoid an excess of tourists, but museums and visitor information centers often do not open until 10 AM; some antiques shops in Randsburg are closed until noon. If you can schedule your town arrivals for late afternoon, visit the information centers just before closing hours to line up an itinerary for the next day. Plan indoor activities for midday during hot months. Keep in mind that because relatively few people visit the desert, its attractions are only open at select times: Petroglyph Canyon tours are given weekends only, the Calico Early Man Archeological Site does not offer tours Monday and Tuesday, and so on.

THE WESTERN MOJAVE

Rand Mining District and Ridgecrest

The prime Western Mojave attractions are along or near U.S. 395 or Highways 14 and 178. The key sights after the San Andreas Fault are listed clockwise, heading north and west from Randsburg, looping around eastward to the Trona Pinnacles.

❶ The infamous **San Andreas Fault** traverses the desert near Cajon Pass, a few miles south of I–15's U.S. 395 exit. If you're driving from Los Angeles, it's an apocalyptic way to start a desert trip.

Rand Mining District

❷ *137 mi northeast of Los Angeles, I–10 to I–15 to U.S. 395; 360 mi from San Francisco, I–80 to I–580 to I–5 to Hwy. 178 to Hwy. 14 to U.S. 395.*

The towns of Randsburg, Red Mountain, and Johannesburg make up the Rand Mining District. **Randsburg** is among the few authentic gold-mining communities not to have become a ghost town. It first boomed with the discovery of gold in the Rand Mountains in 1895 and, along with the neighboring settlements, grew to support the successful Yellow Aster Mine. Rich tungsten ore was discovered during World War I, and silver was found in 1919. Randsburg still has some original gold-rush buildings, plus a few antiques shops, a general store, and the city jail. *U.S. 395, 70 mi north of its intersection with I–15, 21 mi east of Hwy. 14 on Red Rock–Randsburg Rd.*

Mojave Desert

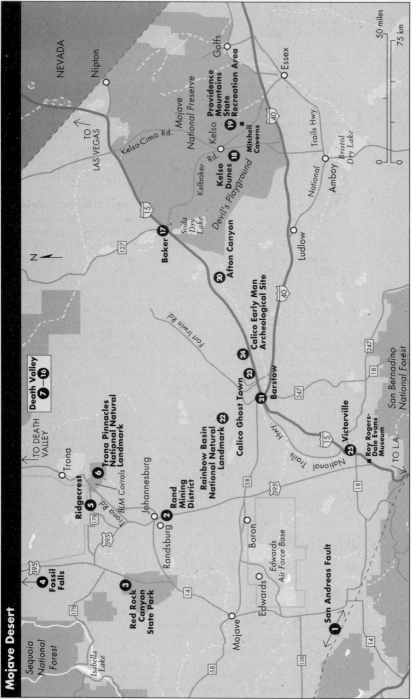

NEVADA

Nipton

TO LAS VEGAS

Mojave National Preserve

Providence Mountains State Recreation Area

Goffs

Essex

50 miles

75 km

Kelso-Cima Rd.

Kelbaker Rd.

Kelso

Kelso Rd.

19

Mitchell Caverns

18

Kelso Dunes

Devil's Playground

National Trails Hwy.

Amboy

Bristol Dry Lake

15

Soda Dry Lake

127

Baker 17

20

Afton Canyon

Ludlow

40

Calico Early Man Archeological Site

24

23

Calico Ghost Town

Fort Irwin Rd.

21 Barstow

TO DEATH VALLEY

Death Valley 7 — 16

Trona Pinnacles National Natural Landmark

6

Ridgecrest 5

Trona

Rainbow Basin National Natural Landmark 22

247

18

247

National Trails Hwy.

Victorville

25

Roy Rogers-Dale Evans Museum

TO L.A.

San Bernardino National Forest

Sequoia National Forest

Isabella Lake

178

395

Fossil Falls 4

Red Rock Canyon State Park 3

Johannesburg

BLM Corrals Rd.

Trona Rd.

Rand Mining District 2

Randsburg

58

395

14

Boron

Edwards

Edwards Air Force Base

Mojave

58

138

14

15

18

San Andreas Fault

1

N

❸ Red Rock Canyon State Park is a feast for the eyes with its layers of pink, white, red, rust, and brown rocks. Entering the park from the south, you pass through a steep-walled gorge and enter a wide bowl tinted pink by what was once hot volcanic ash. The human history of this area goes back 20,000 years to the canyon dwellers known only as the Old People. Mojave Indians roamed the land for several hundred years until gold-rush fever hit the region in the mid- to late 1800s; remains of mining operations dot the countryside. The canyon was later invaded by filmmakers and has starred in westerns. The ranger station is northwest on Abbott Drive off Highway 14. ⊠ *Hwy. 14, 17 mi west of U.S. 395 via Red Rock–Randsburg Rd.,* ☎ *805/942–0662.* ☞ *$5 (day use), $10 (camping).* ☉ *Year-round.*

En Route On the way to Fossil Falls you'll pass **Little Lake,** a good place to see migrating waterfowl in the spring and fall, including several varieties of ducks and geese and perhaps pelicans as well. The area just north of the lake is often covered with wildflowers. As you pass the lake, a red cinder cone known as Red Hill comes into view ahead of you. The hill is a small volcano that was once active and is now being mined. Approaching the falls, you cross a large volcanic field; the falls themselves drop an impressive distance along the channel cut by the Owens River through the hardened lava flows 20,000 years ago.

❹ The roughly hewn, stark black rocks of **Fossil Falls,** the direct result of volcanic eruptions in the Western Mojave area, are a study in shape and texture. ⊠ *20 mi north on U.S. 395 from Hwy. 14, then ½ mi east on Cinder Cone Rd.*

Ridgecrest

❺ *35 mi north of Randsburg, U.S. 395 to Hwy. 178.*

Ridgecrest, with stores and dining and lodging options, is a good hub for exploration of the northwestern Mojave.

The **Maturango Museum,** which also serves as a visitor information center, has pamphlets and books about the northern Mojave and Death Valley—its sights, history, flora, and fauna. Small but informative exhibits detail the natural and cultural history of the northern Mojave. ⊠ *100 E. Las Flores Ave., at China Lake Blvd., 93555,* ☎ *760/375– 6900,* ⅢX *760/375–0479.* ☞ *$2.* ☉ *Wed.–Sun. 10–5.*

★ On weekends in the spring and fall, the Maturango Museum arranges the only tours to the **Petroglyph Canyons,** among the desert's most amazing spectacles. (Call ahead; space is limited on these full-day excursions.) The two canyons, commonly called Big and Little Petroglyph, are in the Coso mountain range on the million-acre U.S. Naval Weapons Center at China Lake, which allows only limited access. Each of the canyons holds a superlative concentration of rock art, the largest of its kind in the Northern Hemisphere. Thousands of images are scratched or pecked into the shiny desert varnish—oxidized minerals—that coats the canyon's dark basaltic rocks. Some of the figures are animals and people, but others seem more abstract—it isn't clear to historians whether they're mythology of an ancient people or hunting records. Even the age of these well-preserved glyphs remains a matter of debate. ☎ *760/375–6900.* ☞ *$20, children under 10 not admitted; $40 for less regular extended trips for photographers and others who want to see sunrise and sunset in the Little Petroglyph Canyon.* ☉ *Tours Mar.– June and Sept.–1st weekend in Dec.*

....
OFF THE   **BUREAU OF LAND MANAGEMENT REGIONAL WILD HORSE AND BURRO**
BEATEN PATH   **CORRALS** – Animals gathered from public lands throughout the South-

west are fed and prepared for adoption here. Unlike at urban zoos, it's okay to feed the animals, so bring along an apple or a carrot to share with the horses (the burros are usually too wild to approach). ⊠ *Hwy. 178, 3 mi east of Ridgecrest,* ☎ *760/446–6064 to arrange tours.* ⚏ *Free.* ⊙ *Weekdays 7:30 AM–4 PM.*

❻ Trona Pinnacles National Natural Landmark is not easy to reach—the best road to the area changes with the weather and can be impassable after a rain. But it's worth the effort, especially to sci-fi buffs, who will recognize the pinnacles as *Star Trek*'s Final Frontier. These fantasy formations of calcium carbonate, known as tufa, were formed underwater along cracks in the lake bed—first as hollow tubes, then as mounds, and finally as the spires visible today. A ½-mi trail winds around this surreal landscape. Wear sturdy shoes—tufa cuts like coral. ⊠ *From the Trona–Red Mountain Rd., take Hwy. 178 east for 8 mi. Or, from its junction with U.S. 395, take Hwy. 178 for 29 mi to dirt intersection; turn southeast and go ½ mi to a fork. Continue south via right fork, cross railroad tracks, and drive onward 5 mi to pinnacles.*

Dining and Lodging

$$ ✕▦ **Heritage Inn.** This hotel has pleasantly appointed rooms, all with king- or queen-size beds. The facility is geared toward commercial travelers, but the inn's staff is equally attentive to tourists' concerns. Room rates include complimentary breakfast. A sister property nearby is an all-suites hotel. ⊠ *1050 N. Norma St.,* ☎ *760/446–6543 or 800/843–0693,* ℻ *760/446–2884. 124 rooms. Restaurant, bar, pool, hot tub, coin laundry, business services, meeting rooms. AE, D, DC, MC, V.*

⚸ **Red Rock Canyon State Park.** The park's campground is in the colorful cliff region of the southern El Paso Mountains, which present many hiking opportunities. The sites include firepits, pit toilets, and water but no hookups. ⊠ *Off Hwy. 14, 30 mi southwest of Ridgecrest,* ☎ *805/942–0662 for reservations. 50 sites.* ⚏ *$10 per evening, $1 additional for dogs.* ⊙ *Visitor center weekends.*

DEATH VALLEY

Stovepipe Wells Village and Furnace Creek

With more than 3.3 million acres, **Death Valley National Park** is the largest national park outside Alaska. Distances are deceiving here: Some sights appear in clusters, but others require extensive travel. The trip from Death Valley Junction to Scotty's Castle, for example, can take a half day. Fees of $10 per vehicle, collected at the park's entrance stations and at the Visitor Center at Furnace Creek (☞ *below*), are valid for seven days.

The topography of Death Valley is a minilesson in geology. Two hundred million years ago, seas covered the area, depositing layers of sediment and fossils. Between 35 million and 5 million years ago, faults in the earth's crust and volcanic activity pushed and folded the ground, causing mountain ranges to rise and the valley floor to drop. The valley was then filled periodically by lakes, which eroded the surrounding rocks into fantastic formations and deposited the salts that now cover the floor of the basin. Today, the area has 14 square mi of sand dunes, 200 square mi of crusty salt flats, 11,000-ft mountains, hills, and canyons of many colors. There are more than 1,000 species of plants and trees—21 of which are unique to the valley, like the yellow Panamint daisy and the blue-flowered Death Valley sage.

547

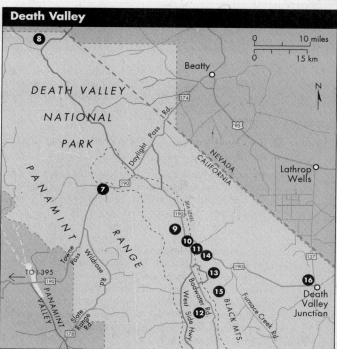

Stovepipe Wells Village

7 *102 mi northeast of Ridgecrest, Hwy. 178 to Hwy. 190.*

Stovepipe Wells Village was the first resort in Death Valley. The tiny town, which dates back to 1926, takes its name from the stovepipe that marked a nearby well. The area contains a motel, a restaurant, a grocery store, a landing strip, and campgrounds.

The polished, multicolored, partly marble walls of **Mosaic Canyon** are extremely narrow in spots. A reasonably easy ¾-mi hike yields the flavor of the area, or you can continue farther into the canyon for a few more miles. ✉ *Off Hwy. 190, on 3 mi gravel road immediately southwest of Stovepipe Wells Village.*

Dining and Lodging

$$ ✕ **Toll Road Restaurant.** This comfortable Old West–style restaurant adjoins the Badwater Saloon. Salad lovers can make a whole meal at the salad bar. ✉ *Hwy. 190, Stovepipe Wells Village,* ☎ *760/786–2604. AE, D, MC, V.*

$ ⊡ **Stovepipe Wells Village.** A landing strip for light aircraft is an unusual touch for a motel, as is a heated mineral pool, but the rest is pretty basic. The property includes a dining room (open only for breakfast and dinner) and a grocery store. ✉ *Hwy. 190, Death Valley National Park 92328,* ☎ *760/786–2387,* FAX *760/786–2389. 83 rooms. Restaurant, bar, pool. AE, D, MC, V.*

⚠ **Mahogany Flat.** The campground here has well-shaded tent spaces—plus tables and pit toilets, but no water—in a forest of juniper and piñon pine. ✉ *Off Wildrose Rd., just south of Charcoal Kilns. 10 sites.* ✉ *Free.* ☾ *Mar.–Nov.*

⚲ **Wildrose.** This canyon has tent or RV sites, none shaded, and stoves or fireplaces, tables, and pit toilets. No water is available in winter. ✉ *Off Wildrose Rd., adjacent to Wildrose Ranger Station. 39 sites.* ▨ *Free.* ☉ *Year-round.*

En Route   Visible from Highway 190 heading east past Stovepipe Wells are **sand dunes** that cover a 14-square-mi field. The sand that forms the hills is actually minute pieces of quartz and other rock.

Scotty's Castle

❽   *44 mi north of Stovepipe Wells Village; head east on Hwy. 190, then north at signs for castle.*

Scotty's Castle is an odd apparition rising out of a canyon. This $2.5 million Moorish mansion, begun in 1924 and never completed, takes its name from Walter Scott, better known as Death Valley Scotty. An ex-cowboy, prospector, and performer in Buffalo Bill's Wild West Show, Scotty always told people the castle was his, financed by gold from a secret mine. That secret mine was, in fact, a Chicago millionaire named Albert Johnson, who was advised by doctors to spend time in a warm, dry climate. The house contains works of art, imported carpets, handmade European furniture, and a tremendous pipe organ. Costumed rangers portray life at the castle in 1939. Tours are conducted frequently, but waits of up to two hours are possible. Try to arrive for the first tour of the day, which will guarantee short lines following a traffic-free drive through desert country. ☎ *760/786–2392.* ▨ *$8.* ☉ *Daily 7–6; tours 8:30–5.*

Camping

⚲ **Mesquite Springs.** There are tent or RV spaces here, some shaded, with stoves or fireplaces, tables, flush toilets, and water. ✉ *2 mi south of Scotty's Castle. 60 sites.* ▨ *$10.* ☉ *Year-round.*

Furnace Creek Area

54 mi south of Scotty's Castle, 25 mi southeast of Stovepipe Wells Village on Hwy. 190.

❾   The renowned mule teams hauled borax from the **Harmony Borax Works** to the railroad town of Mojave, 165 mi away. Those teams were a sight to behold: 20 mules hitched up to a single massive wagon, carrying a load of 10 tons of borax through burning desert. The teams plied the route between 1884 and 1907, when the railroad finally arrived in Zabriskie. The Borax Museum, 2 mi south of the borax works, houses original mining machinery and historical displays in a building that once served as a boardinghouse for miners; the adjacent structure is the original mule-team barn. ✉ *Harmony Borax Works Rd., west off Hwy. 190.*

❿   **Furnace Creek** is a bustling center of activity amid the sprawling quiet of Death Valley. Covered with tropical landscaping, it has jogging and bicycle paths, golf, tennis, horseback riding, a general store, and, rare for these parts, dining options. The Furnace Creek Ranch (☞ Dining and Lodging, *below*) operates most of the above, plus guided carriage rides and hay rides for guests and nonguests. The rides traverse trails with views of the surrounding mountains, where multicolored volcanic rock and alluvial fans form a background for date-palm trees and other vegetation.

Exhibits on the desert, trail maps, and brochures can be found at the **Visitor Center at Furnace Creek.** ✉ *Hwy. 190,* ☎ *760/786–3211.* ☉ *Daily 8–7.*

⑪ **Golden Canyon** is named for the glowing color of its walls. A mild hike into this spacious landform affords some spectacular views of yellow and orange rock. Farther up the canyon, you'll encounter a colorful formation called Red Cathedral. ⊠ *Badwater Rd., 3 mi south from Furnace Creek; turn left into parking lot.*

⑫ Reaching **Badwater,** one sees a shallow pool, containing mostly sodium chloride, saltier than the sea, lying lifeless against an expanse of desolate salt flats—a sharp contrast to the expansive canyons and elevation not too far away. Here's the legend: One of the early surveyors saw that his mule wouldn't drink from the pool and noted "badwater" on his map. Badwater is one of the lowest spots in North America—280 ft below sea level—and also one of the hottest. ⊠ *Badwater Rd., 19 mi south of Visitor Center at Furnace Creek.*

★ ⑬ The **Artists Palette** is one of the most magnificent sights in Death Valley. Artists Drive, the approach to the area, is one-way heading north off Badwater Road, so if you're visiting Badwater it's more efficient to come here on the way back. The drive winds through foothills composed of colorful sedimentary and volcanic rocks. ⊠ *8 mi north of Badwater, Badwater Rd. to Artists Dr.; 10 mi south of Furnace Creek, Hwy. 190 to Badwater Rd. to Artists Dr.*

⑭ **Zabriskie Point** is one of Death Valley National Park's most scenic spots. Not particularly high—only about 710 ft—it overlooks a striking badlands panorama with wrinkled, multicolored hills. Film buffs of a certain vintage may recognize it—or at least its name—from the film *Zabriskie Point* by the Italian director Michelangelo Antonioni. ⊠ *Hwy. 190, 5 mi south of Furnace Creek.*

OFF THE
BEATEN PATH
TWENTY MULE TEAM CANYON – The thrills in this colorful canyon are more than just natural. At times on the loop road off Highway 190, the soft rock walls reach high on both sides, making it seem like you're on an amusement-park ride. Remains of prospectors' tunnels are visible here, along with some brilliant rock formations. ⊠ *Twenty Mule Team Rd., off Hwy. 190, 1½ mi south of Zabriskie Point. Trailers not permitted.*

★ ⑮ **Dante's View** is more than 5,000 ft up in the Black Mountains. In the dry desert air, you can see most of the 110 mi the valley stretches across. The oasis of Furnace Creek is a green spot to the north. The view up and down is equally astounding: The tiny blackish patch far below is Badwater, the lowest point in the country, at 280 ft below sea level; on the western horizon is Mt. Whitney, the highest spot in the continental United States, at 14,494 ft. Those in great shape may want to try the 14-mi hike up to Telescope Peak. The view, not surprisingly, is breathtaking—as is the 3,000-ft elevation gain of the hike. ⊠ *Dante's View Rd. off Hwy. 190, 21 mi south of Zabriskie Point.*

Dining and Lodging

$$$ ✕ **Inn Dining Room.** Adobe walls, lace tablecloths, two fireplaces, and many windows with views of the Panamint Mountains make for a visual and culinary mirage at this Furnace Creek Inn restaurant. Its six-course, à la carte menu shows a Continental influence: Escargots and breast of duck are among the usual appetizers. Seasonally changing main courses might include gulf shrimp in a shallot and garlic beurre blanc or charbroiled French-cut lamb chops with minted pear; a few vegetarian entrées are usually available as well. The wine list is extensive. ⊠ *Furnace Creek Inn Resort, Hwy. 190,* ☎ *760/786–2345, ext. 150. AE, D, DC, MC, V.*

$$$$ ⊞ **Furnace Creek Inn.** This historic stone structure tumbling down the side of a hill is something of a desert oasis; the creek meanders through its beautifully landscaped gardens. The pool here is spring-fed. All the rooms have views; just fewer than half have balconies. Rates here drop in the summer. The Inn Dining Room (☞ *above*) is the best restaurant for miles. ⊠ *Hwy. 190, Box 1, Death Valley National Park 92328,* ☎ *760/786–2361,* FAX *760/786–2423. Restaurant, bar, pool, 4 tennis courts, meeting rooms. AE, DC, MC, V.*

$–$$ ⊞ **Furnace Creek Ranch.** This was originally crew headquarters for a borax company, the activities of which the on-site Borax Museum details. Four two-story buildings adjacent to the golf course have motel-type rooms that are good for families. The general store on the ranch sells supplies and gifts. ⊠ *Hwy. 190, Box 1, Death Valley National Park 92328,* ☎ *760/786–2345,* FAX *760/786–9945. 224 rooms. Restaurant, bar, coffee shop, pool, 18-hole golf course, 2 tennis courts, horseback riding, meeting rooms. AE, DC, MC, V.*

⚠ **Furnace Creek.** This campground has RV and tent sites (some shaded), tables, fireplaces, flush and pit toilets, water, and a dump station. Pay showers, a laundry, and a swimming pool are available at Furnace Creek Ranch (☞ *above*). ⊠ *Adjacent to Visitor Center at Furnace Creek,* ☎ *800/365–2267 (Destinet). 135 sites.* ▱ *$15.* ⊙ *Year-round.*

Death Valley Junction

30 mi south of Furnace Creek, 25 mi south of Zabriskie Point on Hwy. 190.

⑯ **Marta Becket's Amargosa Opera House** is an unexpected pleasure in an unlikely place. Marta Becket is an artist and dancer from New York who first saw the town of Amargosa while on tour in 1964. Three years later she came back and on impulse decided to buy a boarded-up theater amid a complex of run-down Spanish colonial buildings. Today, the population is still in single digits (cats outnumber people here), but it swells when cars, motor homes, and buses roll in to catch the show she has been presenting for more than two dozen years. To compensate for the sparse crowds her show attracted in the early days, Becket painted herself an audience, turning the walls and ceiling of the theater into a trompe l'oeil masterpiece. Now she often performs her blend of classical ballet, mime, and 19th-century melodrama to sell-out crowds. After the show, you can meet her in the adjacent art gallery, where she sells her paintings and autographs her posters and books. ⊠ *Hwy. 127,* ☎ *760/852–4441,* FAX *760/852–4138. Call ahead for reservations.* ▱ *$8. Performances Nov., Feb., Mar., and Apr., Sat. and Mon. 7:45 PM; Oct., Dec., Jan., and May (through Mother's Day weekend), Sat. only.*

THE EASTERN MOJAVE
Mojave National Preserve to Victorville

The Eastern Mojave is a sharp contrast to Death Valley, with welcome sights of vegetation and somewhat cooler temperatures. Much of this land is untended, so precautions are necessary when driving the many back roads, where towns and services are often few and far between. In many cases, cellular phones are beyond their operating range.

Baker

⑰ *84 mi south of Death Valley Junction on Hwy. 127.*

The small town of Baker lies between the East and West Mojave areas and Death Valley National Park. You can't miss the city's 134-ft thermometer, the height of which commemorates the U.S. temperature record, which was set in Death Valley on July 10, 1913. The thermometer is also a landmark for the National Park Service's **Mojave Desert Information Center** (☎ 760/733–4040). For a "hub," Baker offers only minimal provisions. There are a few lackluster grocery stores, some fast food, and several gas stations.

Dining and Lodging

$ ✕🖭 **Bun Boy Motel and Restaurant.** The no-frills Bun Boy is conveniently located at the intersection of two highways. It's small but pleasant. The large diner adjacent to the motel, one of Baker's few dining options, serves surprisingly tasty American food. ⊠ *I–15 at State Rd. 177, Box 130, Baker 92309,* ☎ *760/733–4363. 20 rooms. Restaurant. AE, D, DC, MC, V.*

Mojave National Preserve

Kelbaker Rd., south from Baker.

⑱ Although a broad range of terrain qualifies, nothing says "desert" quite like graceful, wind-blown sand dunes. And the white-sand **Kelso Dunes** are perfect, pristine desert dunes. They cover 70 square mi, often at heights of 500–600 ft, and can be reached in an easy ½-mi walk from where you leave your car. When you reach the top of one of the dunes, kick a little bit of sand down the lee side and find out why they say the sand "sings." In the town of Kelso, a Mission Revival depot dating from 1925 is one of the few of its kind still standing. ⊠ *Kelbaker Rd., 42 mi south of Baker (7 mi past town of Kelso).*

⑲ At an elevation of 4,300 ft, the visitor center at the **Providence Mountains State Recreation Area** has views of mountain peaks, dunes, buttes, rocky crags, and desert valleys. The nearby **Mitchell Caverns Natural Preserve** provides the rare opportunity to see all three types of cave formations—dripstone, flowstone, and erratics—in one place. The year-round 65°F temperature is a nice break from the heat. ⊠ *Essex Rd., 16 mi north of I–40,* ☎ *760/928–2586.* 🖃 *$6.* ☉ *Guided tours of caves conducted Sept.–June, weekdays 1:30, weekends 10, 1:30, and 3; July–Aug., weekends only. Tours gather at visitor center.*

Afton Canyon

⑳ *27 mi southwest of Baker, I–15 to Afton Canyon Rd.*

Because of its colorful, steep walls, Afton Canyon is often called the Grand Canyon of the Mojave. Afton was carved out over many thousands of years by the rushing waters of the Mojave River, which makes another of its few aboveground appearances here. And where you find water in the desert, you'll find trees, grasses, and wildlife. The canyon has been popular for a long time; Indians and later white settlers following the Mojave Trail from the Colorado River to the Pacific coast often set up camp here, near the welcome presence of water. ⊠ *Take Afton turnoff and follow dirt road about 3 mi southwest.*

Camping

⚠ **Afton Canyon Campground.** The camping here is 1,408 ft up in a wildlife area where the Mojave River surfaces. The area is surrounded by high-desert scenic cliffs and a mesquite thicket. ✉ *Afton Canyon Rd. off I–15. 22 sites.* 🏕 *$6.* ⊙ *Year-round.*

Barstow Area

㉑ *63 mi southwest of Baker on I–15.*

Barstow was established in 1886 when a subsidiary of the Atchison, Topeka, and Santa Fe Railroad began construction of a depot and hotel at this junction of its tracks and the 35th-parallel transcontinental lines. Midway between Las Vegas and Los Angeles, Barstow is home to hotel and restaurant chains and factory outlets. The **Desert Information Center** (✉ 831 Barstow Rd., ☎ 760/255–8760) has exhibits about desert ecology, wildflowers, wildlife, and other features of the desert environment. Radio information for travelers is provided at 1610 AM.

㉒ **Rainbow Basin National Natural Landmark** looks as if it could be on Mars, perhaps because so many sci-fi movies depicting the red planet have been filmed here. There is a tremendous sense of upheaval; huge slabs of red, orange, white, and green stone tilt at crazy angles like ships about to capsize. At points along the spectacularly scenic 6-mi drive, it is easy to imagine you are alone in the world, hidden among the colorful badlands that give the basin its name. Hike the many washes and you are likely to see the fossilized remains of creatures that roamed the basin 12 million to 16 million years ago: mastodons, large and small camels, rhinos, dog-bears, birds, and insects. Leave any fossils you find where they are—they are protected by federal law. ✉ *8 mi north of Barstow; take Fort Irwin Rd. 5 mi north to Fossil Bed Rd., a graded dirt road, and head west 3 mi. Call Desert Information Center in Barstow (☎ 760/255–8760) for more information.*

㉓ **Calico Ghost Town** became a wild and wealthy mining town after a rich deposit of silver was found around 1881. In 1886, after more than $85 million worth of silver, gold, and other precious metals were harvested from the multicolored "calico" hills, the price of silver fell and the town slipped into decline. Frank "Borax" Smith helped revive the town in 1889 when he started mining the unglamorous but profitable mineral borax, but that boom busted by the turn of the century. The effort to restore the area was started by Walter Knott of Knott's Berry Farm fame in 1960. Knott handed the land over to San Bernardino County in 1966, and it became a regional park. Today, the 1880s come back to life as you stroll the wooden sidewalks of Main Street, browse through several western shops, roam the tunnels of Maggie's Mine, and take a ride on the Calico–Odessa Railroad. Special festivals in March, May, October, and November add to Calico's Old West flavor. ✉ *Ghost Town Rd., 3 mi north of I–15,* ☎ *760/254–2122.* 🏕 *$6.* ⊙ *Daily 9–5.*

★ ㉔ If you're at all curious about life 200,000 years ago, the **Calico Early Man Archeological Site** is a must-see. Nearly 12,000 tools—scrapers, cutting tools, choppers, hand picks, stone saws, and the like—have been excavated from the site since 1964. Prior to finding the site, many archaeologists believed the first humans came to North America "only" 10,000 to 20,000 years ago. Dr. Louis Leakey, the noted archaeologist, was so impressed with the findings that he became the Calico Project director from 1963 to his death in 1972; his old camp is now a visitor center and museum. The earliest known Americans fashioned the artifacts buried in the walls and floors of the excavated pits. The only way in is by guided tour. Visitors are required to wear hard hats. ✉ *15 mi northeast of Barstow, I–15 to Minneola Rd. north for 3 mi,* ☎ *760/255–8760.* ⊙ *Guided tours of dig Wed.–Thurs. 1:30 and 3:30, Fri.–Sun. 9–4:30.*

Dining and Lodging

$ ✕ **Carlos & Toto's.** If your palate has tired of chain restaurants and food from your cooler, you will thoroughly enjoy this touch of Mexico. Locally famous for its fajitas, the restaurant is open seven days a week and has a Sunday buffet brunch from 9:30 AM to 2 PM. ⊠ *901 W. Main St.,* ☎ *760/256–7513. AE, D, MC, V.*

$ 🏨 **Holiday Inn.** This large facility has king- and queen-size suites in addition to comfortable standard-size rooms. It's convenient to sights, restaurants, shops, and the Desert Information Center. ⊠ *1511 E. Main St., Barstow,* ☎ *760/256–5673,* FAX *760/256–5917. 148 rooms. Restaurant, pool, hot tub, laundry service, meeting rooms. AE, D, DC, MC, V.*

⛺ **Calico Ghost Town Regional Park.** In addition to the campsites here there are cabin and bunkhouse accommodations. ⊠ *Ghost Town Rd., 3 mi north of I–15, east from Barstow,* ☎ *760/254–2122 or 800/862–2542 for reservations. 250 sites.* ▨ *$16 per night for tent camping, $20 for full RV hook-ups; 2-night minimum during festival weekends.* ⊙ *Year-round.*

Victorville

㉕ *34 mi southwest of Barstow on I–15.*

At the southwest corner of the Mojave is the quiet and sprawling town of Victorville, home of the Roy Rogers–Dale Evans Museum (☞ *below*).

Mojave Narrows Regional Park makes use of one of the few spots where the Mojave River flows aboveground. The park has 87 camping units, hot showers, secluded picnic areas, and two lakes, surrounded by cottonwoods and cattails. You'll find fishing, rowboat rentals, a bait shop, equestrian paths, and a trail for visitors with disabilities. ⊠ *18000 Yates Rd.,* ☎ *760/245–2226.* ▨ *$4 per vehicle weekdays, $5 weekends; dry camping $10 a night, camping with utilities $15 a night.* ⊙ *Daily 7:30–sunset.*

The **Roy Rogers–Dale Evans Museum** exhibits the personal and professional memorabilia of the famous stars, along with NRA testimonials and safari trophies—stuffed exotic cats and other animals "taken" by Roy and sometimes Dale. Even Trigger and Bullet have been preserved, though they apparently died of natural causes. ⊠ *15650 Seneca Rd. (take Roy Rogers Dr. exit off I–15),* ☎ *760/243–4547.* ▨ *$6.* ⊙ *Daily 9–5.*

Lodging

$ 🏨 **Best Western Green Tree Inn.** This member of the chain and its shaded lawn sit right off I–15, a few blocks from the Roy Rogers–Dale Evans Museum. Many of the rooms are suite-size and have refrigerators and microwaves, making the inn a good choice for families. The decor is no-nonsense but clean. Prime rib is a mainstay of the on-site restaurant, which prepares a weekday luncheon buffet. ⊠ *14173 Green Tree Blvd., 92392,* ☎ *760/245–3461 or 800/877–3644. 168 rooms. Restaurant, bar, coffee shop, pool, hot tub, shuffleboard, meeting rooms. AE, D, DC, MC, V.*

⛺ **Mojave Narrows Regional Park.** (☞ *above.*)

THE MOJAVE DESERT AND DEATH VALLEY A TO Z

Getting Around

By Car

The Mojave is shaped like a giant *L,* with one leg north and the other east. To travel north through the Mojave, take I–10 east out of Los Angeles to I–15 north. Just through Cajon Pass, pick up U.S. 395, which runs north through Victor Valley, Boron, the Rand Mining District, and China Lake. To travel east, continue on I–15 to Barstow. From Barstow there are two routes: I–40, which passes through the mountainous areas of San Bernardino County, whisks by the Providence mountains, and enters Arizona at Needles; or the more northerly I–15, which passes south of Calico, near Devil's Playground and the Kelso Sand Dunes, and then veers northeast toward Las Vegas.

Some travelers may wish to avoid Cajon Pass, elevation 4,250 ft. To do this, take I–210 north of Los Angeles to Highway 14 north. Head east 67 mi on Highway 58 to the town of Barstow and pick up I–15 there. Continue east on I–15 to Highway 127, a very scenic route north through the Mojave to Death Valley.

Death Valley can be entered from the southeast or the west. From the southeast, take Highway 127 north from I–15 and then link up with Highway 178, which travels west into the valley and then cuts north toward Badwater before meeting up with Highway 190 at Furnace Creek. To enter from the west, exit U.S. 395 at either Highway 190 or 178.

Much of the desert can be seen from the comfort of an air-conditioned car. Don't despair if you are without air-conditioning—just avoid the middle of the day and the middle of the summer, good advice for all desert travel. Believe everything you've ever heard about desert heat; it can be brutal. But during mornings and evenings, particularly in the spring and fall, the temperature ranges from cool and crisp to pleasantly warm and dry: perfect for hiking and driving.

Contacts and Resources

Camping

The Mojave Desert and Death Valley have about two dozen campgrounds in a variety of desert settings. For further information the following booklets are useful (*see* Visitor Information, *below,* for addresses and phone numbers): *High Desert Recreation Resource Guide,* from the Mojave Chamber of Commerce; *San Bernardino County Regional Parks,* from the Regional Parks Department; and *California Desert Camping,* from the Bureau of Land Management.

Emergencies

Ambulance (☎ 911). **Fire** (☎ 911). **Police** (☎ 911).

BLM Rangers (☎ 760/255–8700). **Community Hospital** (✉ Barstow, ☎ 760/256–1761). **San Bernardino County Sheriff** (☎ 760/256–1796 for Barstow, 760/733–4448 for Baker).

Guided Tours

Audubon Society (✉ Western Regional Office, 555 Audubon Pl., Sacramento 95825, ☎ 916/481–5332). **California Native Plant Society** (✉ 1722 J St., No. 17, Sacramento 95814, ☎ 916/447–2677). **Furnace Creek Inn** (☎ 760/786–2345, ext. 222). **Nature Conservancy** (✉ 201 Mission St., 4th floor, San Francisco 94105, ☎ 415/777–0487). **Sierra Club** (✉ 85 2nd St., San Francisco 94105, ☎ 415/977–5578).

Visitor Information

Bureau of Land Management (✉ California Desert District Office, 6221 Box Springs Blvd., Riverside 92507, ☎ 909/697–5200). **Baker Chamber of Commerce** (✉ Box 131, 92309, ☎ 760/733–4469). **Barstow Area Chamber of Commerce** (✉ 222 E. Main St., Suite 216, Barstow 92311, ☎ 760/256–8617). **California Desert Information Center** (✉ 831 Barstow Rd., Barstow 92311, ☎ 760/255–8760). **Death Valley Chamber of Commerce** (✉ Box 157, Shoshone 92384, ☎ 760/852–4524). **Mojave Chamber of Commerce** (✉ 15836 Sierra Hwy., Mojave 93591, ☎ 805/824–2481). **National Park Service** (✉ Visitor Center at Furnace Creek, 92328, ☎ 760/786–2331). **Ridgecrest Area Convention and Visitors Bureau** (✉ 100 W. California Ave., Ridgecrest 93555, ☎ 760/375–8202). **San Bernardino County Regional Parks Department** (✉ 777 E. Rialto Ave., San Bernardino 92415, ☎ 909/387–2594).

INDEX

NOTES

NOTES

NOTES

NOTES

Fodor's Travel Publications

Available at bookstores everywhere, or call 1–800–533–6478, 24 hours a day.

Gold Guides

U.S.

Alaska

Arizona

Boston

California

Cape Cod, Martha's Vineyard, Nantucket

The Carolinas & Georgia

Chicago

Colorado

Florida

Hawai'i

Las Vegas, Reno, Tahoe

Los Angeles

Maine, Vermont, New Hampshire

Maui & Lāna'i

Miami & the Keys

New England

New Orleans

New York City

Pacific North Coast

Philadelphia & the Pennsylvania Dutch Country

The Rockies

San Diego

San Francisco

Santa Fe, Taos, Albuquerque

Seattle & Vancouver

The South

U.S. & British Virgin Islands

USA

Virginia & Maryland

Walt Disney World, Universal Studios and Orlando

Washington, D.C.

Foreign

Australia

Austria

The Bahamas

Belize & Guatemala

Bermuda

Canada

Cancún, Cozumel, Yucatán Peninsula

Caribbean

China

Costa Rica

Cuba

The Czech Republic & Slovakia

Eastern & Central Europe

Europe

Florence, Tuscany & Umbria

France

Germany

Great Britain

Greece

Hong Kong

India

Ireland

Israel

Italy

Japan

London

Madrid & Barcelona

Mexico

Montréal & Québec City

Moscow, St. Petersburg, Kiev

The Netherlands, Belgium & Luxembourg

New Zealand

Norway

Nova Scotia, New Brunswick, Prince Edward Island

Paris

Portugal

Provence & the Riviera

Scandinavia

Scotland

Singapore

South Africa

South America

Southeast Asia

Spain

Sweden

Switzerland

Thailand

Toronto

Turkey

Vienna & the Danube

Special-Interest Guides

Adventures to Imagine

Alaska Ports of Call

Ballpark Vacations

Caribbean Ports of Call

The Official Guide to America's National Parks

Disney Like a Pro

Europe Ports of Call

Family Adventures

Fodor's Gay Guide to the USA

Fodor's How to Pack

Great American Learning Vacations

Great American Sports & Adventure Vacations

Great American Vacations

Great American Vacations for Travelers with Disabilities

Halliday's New Orleans Food Explorer

Healthy Escapes

Kodak Guide to Shooting Great Travel Pictures

National Parks and Seashores of the East

National Parks of the West

Nights to Imagine

Rock & Roll Traveler Great Britain and Ireland

Rock & Roll Traveler USA

Sunday in San Francisco

Walt Disney World for Adults

Weekends in New York

Wendy Perrin's Secrets Every Smart Traveler Should Know

WHEREVER YOU TRAVEL, *H*ELP IS NEVER FAR AWAY.

From planning your trip to

providing travel assistance along

the way, American Express®

Travel Service Offices are

always there to help

you do more.